Financial Accounting

AN INTEGRATED APPROACH

Fourth Edition

Financial Accounting

AN INTEGRATED APPROACH

Fourth Edition

MICHAEL GIBBINS, PhD, FCA

Winspear Professor of Professional Accounting
University of Alberta

NELSON

THOMSON LEARNING ™

Australia • Canada • Mexico • Singapore • Spain • United Kingdom • United States

NELSON

THOMSON LEARNING

Financial Accounting:
An Integrated Approach
by Michael Gibbins

Editorial Director and Publisher:
Evelyn Veitch

Acquisitions Editors:
Paul Manley and Gary Bennett

Marketing Manager:
Anthony Rezek

Developmental Editor:
Karina TenVeldhuis

Production Editor:
Natalia Denesiuk

Production Coordinator:
Hedy Sellers

Copy Editor:
Joan Rawlin

Art Director:
Angela Cluer

Interior Design:
ArtPlus Limited

Cover Design:
Peggy Rhodes

Cover Image:
Steve Cole/PhotoDisc

Compositor:
Nelson Gonzalez

Printer:
RR Donnelley

Canadian Cataloguing in Publication Data

Gibbins, Michael, 1942–
Financial accounting: an integrated approach

4th ed.
Includes bibliographical references and index.
ISBN 0-17-616845-1

1. Accounting. 2. Financial statements. I. Title.

HF5635.G5 2001   657'.48
C00-933136-0

To all students of the art of accounting

Contents

Sections 10.7 and 10.8–10.9 may be read independently of Sections 10.2–10.6.

Preface

This book presents a balanced and integrated introductory view of financial accounting. The *hows* (preparation procedures and techniques), *uses* (analysis and decisions), and the *whys* (concepts and principles that link preparation and use) are given explicit attention in all chapters. The balance among the three varies with topics, but all are present because none can stand without the other. This diagram is used periodically to emphasize the book's integrative approach and outline topic coverage.

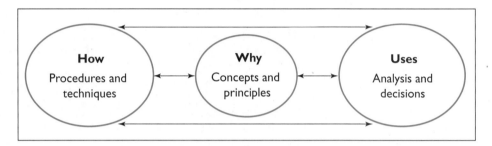

Financial accounting is presented as a utilitarian discipline, producing accounting information that is to be used, and respond, even if not always perfectly, to the needs of the people who use it and to changes in those needs over time. This presentation is aimed *both* at students who want to become managers or other users of accounting information *and* at students who want to become accountants, because intelligent use and intelligent preparation of financial accounting information require a balanced understanding.

Financial Accounting: An Integrated Approach provides a strong conceptual foundation and includes insights from accounting and related research. It also grounds the subject in the practicalities that make financial accounting a challenging discipline and accounting an interesting profession. While providing structure to the learning task to help the student gain understanding, it avoids excessive structure that might give the student the impression that financial accounting is more straightforward and less subtle than it is. The student must do the cognitive work of integrating the ideas into a personal understanding, because otherwise the understanding won't last.

This fourth edition incorporates several features aimed at improving students' knowledge and increasing flexibility in students' and instructors' use of the material. Some of these features are:

- Following the diagram above, the material has been integrated from the beginning, so that preparation and use, and linking principles are presented together or in close sequence. For example, the transactional basis of financial accounting is presented in the first chapter, along with information about users and some introductory analysis, and these are integrated into the conceptual base of accrual accounting. In later chapters, as each financial statement is presented, its purpose and principles are explained, preparation is illustrated fully, including necessary accounts and recordkeeping procedures, and its use is examined. This full integration of the material is a major change in the book from the third edition, in which preparation, use, and concepts surrounding the statements were more separated.

- The Book Overview, prior to Chapter 1, helps instructors and students plan their use of the book.

- The accounting cycle material has been brought forward from later chapters in the third edition and is now integrated into the explanation of the financial statements in Chapters 1–3. The book's considerable practical content, including demonstration of example forms (Chapter 7) and procedures (throughout) have been written to fit with the principles and uses being explained in parallel, to present the student with a broad integrative view of financial accounting.

- Because there are differing views about the best sequence for the topics in introductory financial accounting, *numerous topics have been written to be studied in alternative orders*. The book's full financial statement analysis material is presented in Chapter 10 (along with present value and "what if" analysis) but can be used any time after the financial statements have been set out in the first four chapters. These alternative potential orders are noted in the Book Overview below and are indicated in the Table of Contents and within various chapters, especially in the chapters' introductory sections.

- A number of **For Your Interest** boxes have been inserted to present interesting quirks, research findings, and managerial implications. These have been drawn partly from the research and managerial sections of the third edition, which are now integrated into the general coverage. The research and theory issues have been framed to draw attention to their practical import and implications to both preparation and use of financial statements. The book makes numerous connections to current issues such as stock market gyrations, e-commerce, international standards harmonization and other standards developments, and management's motivations in disclosing financial accounting information.

- Point-form material, graphs and charts, information about useful Web sites, and real-world examples have been used frequently. Web sites are given for all companies and organizations used as examples.

- Much of the material in the book has an informal style, directed toward easing the student into the material and generally lightening up what students feel is serious stuff. It is hoped that students and instructors will enjoy themselves, and especially that students will find financial accounting to be a lot more interesting than they might have expected. The book is written in the second person, talking directly to student readers.

- As in the third edition, numerous sidebars are presented beside text material to help students keep track of their learning, and the **How's Your Understanding?** questions at the end of each chapter section allow students to check their comprehension of the section's material. Each chapter also includes an installment of the Mato Inc. Continuing Demonstration Case, which tells the story of a small company operating at a scale students may be able to identify with. The story develops with the topics covered throughout the book and thus provides a progressive (mostly preparation-oriented) illustration of the ideas.

- Chapter 4's approach to the cash flow statement takes advantage of the "direct" method of preparing the statement now given more support by the *CICA Handbook* and presents the cash flow analysis in a more natural way as coming from receipts and disbursements, then showing how that does the same job as the traditional "indirect" method. As a result, the cash flow statement fits more appropriately with the presentation of the other financial statements than may have been the case in the past.

- The homework and discussion material has been increased and extended, especially in providing a large number of problems with fully worked-out solutions in the back of the book, plus regular homework material and cases with solutions in the separate solutions manual. The homework problems, including those with solutions in the back of the book, cover the book's topics at various levels of difficulty and with various numerical and narrative styles.

- Important terms (printed in bold in the chapter material) have been collected together into a list at the end of each chapter and all those terms have been explained further in an expanded Glossary at the end of the book.

The book's purpose is to help students develop their own understanding of financial accounting, not to deliver "the answer"—financial accounting's answers are many and varied. Examples and the homework solutions, for example, reinforce thoughtful analysis, rather than suggesting that only one answer is to be expected.

Material for instructors has been prepared to assist in course delivery. This includes an instructor's manual/exam bank, a test bank and computerized test bank, PowerPoint slides, and a solutions manual for homework and discussion problems whose solutions are not in the back of the book. Students can purchase the *Study Guide* (ISBN 0-17-616946-6) to accompany *Financial Accounting: An Integrated Approach, Fourth Edition*, through their campus bookstore. An accounting Web site has been developed with a feature site supporting *Financial Accounting: An Integrated Approach, Fourth Edition*, and links to other sites containing information of interest to accounting instructors and students. You can access this site at accounting.nelson.com.

About the Author

Michael Gibbins is the Winspear Professor of Professional Accounting and Chair of the Department of Accounting and Management Information Systems in the Alberta School of Business, University of Alberta. He was born and raised in British Columbia, where he married, earned a B.Com. from the University of British Columbia, and obtained his chartered accountancy designation in the Prince George office of what is now Deloitte & Touche. Wending his way east, he worked for the Canadian Institute of Chartered Accountants in Toronto, getting an MBA from York University and becoming a father along the way. After a trial at teaching as an assistant professor at Queen's University School of Business, he obtained his Ph.D. at Cornell University. A return to the west as assistant professor at the University of British Columbia preceded his move to Alberta.

The author's research and teaching interests lie in how people make decisions and judgments, and in the way accounting information is used in making important decisions in business and other economic spheres. A particular interest is in the professional judgment of public accountants, managers, and other professionals who cope with the pressures and risks of modern business life. He has published widely on judgment, accounting, financial disclosure, and educational subjects, is past editor of the Canadian accounting research journal *Contemporary Accounting Research*, and is active in various academic and professional bodies. He has received a number of education and teaching awards. In 1988 he was made a Fellow of both the Alberta and British Columbia Institutes of Chartered Accountants.

Balancing his professional and academic interests, the author collects beer bottles, ceramic frogs, and other art featuring frogs. He also enjoys hiking, snorkeling, cross-country skiing, and spending time in the Canadian wilderness and the Australian outback.

Acknowledgments

This book began in development work done as a project for the Centre for the Advancement of Professional Accounting Education (later called the Chartered Accountants' Centre), Faculty of Business, University of Alberta. I am grateful for the Centre's assistance.

All material originally published elsewhere is used with permission. Thanks are due to all the people and companies who gave their permission and therefore helped bring the book to life. For the large contribution their materials have made to the book, I particularly thank CAE Inc., Barcol Doors & Windows (especially Rosalie Laibida), all the companies whose financial material has been used in the book's cases and examples, and Bill Scott.

Many people helped along the way, as this book developed over several years. I am grateful to them all, and apologize to those I do not mention specifically. Special thanks are due to the students of Accounting 311 at the University of Alberta for their patience, and especially for all their ideas and criticisms, as the book developed. I am especially indebted to past coauthors of the annual "Accounting 311 Course Package," who helped me work out many of the ideas in the book: Laurie Beattie, Philip Beaulieu, Richard Chandler, Anona Lukawiecki, Christine Newton, and Duncan Sinclair. For other assistance and support, I am grateful to Loretta Amerongen, David Annand, Elaine Aultman, Peggy Barr, Andrea Berman, Allison Brooks, Dwayne Budzak, Mike Chiasson, Lane Daley, Wendy Degner, Ross Denham, Tad Drinkwater, Don Easton, Joan Finley, Jim Gaa, Stefan Gibbins, Duncan Green, Mary Hemmingsen, Karim Jamal, Dave Jobson, Jocelyn Johnston, Henry Kennedy, Janet LeBlanc, Tracey Lee, Mary Lea McAnally, Sandra Namchuk, Jim Newton, Linda Olsen, Simone Phillips, Remi Racine, Steve Salterio, Tom Scott, Lorraine Sherwood, Tanis Stamatelakis, Ken Sutley, Jerry Trites, John Waterhouse, Kathy West, and Heather Wier.

I am also grateful to the following people for their suggestions and constructive comments: Marilyn Adams (McMaster University), Robert Anderson (Brock University), H. Donald Brown (Brock University), Ray F. Carroll (Dalhousie University), Roger Collins (University College of the Cariboo), Judy Cumby (Memorial University), Maureen Fizzell (Simon Fraser University), Leo Gallant (St. Francis Xavier University), Duncan Green (University of Calgary), Charlotte Heywood (Wilfrid Laurier University), Al Hunter (University of Lethbridge), George Kanaan (Concordia University), Margaret Kelly (University of Manitoba), Terry Litovitz (University of Toronto, Scarborough Campus), Don Lockwood (University of British Columbia), Carol McKeen (Queen's University), Cameron Morrill (University of Manitoba), Richard Pedlar (Wilfrid Laurier University), Neville Ralph (Mount Allison University), Connie Reed (University of Toronto), Catherine Seguin (University of Toronto), and Nicola M. Young (St. Mary's University).

The enthusiasm and support of Peter Jackson, Jennifer Dewey, Anita Miecznikowski, Avivah Wargon, Tim Sellers, Paul Manley, Karina TenVeldhuis, and others at Nelson have been great. The late Francis Winspear supported me as the Winspear Professor and gave much other support to the University of Alberta. He has also been a fine example to me of the combination of conceptual strength and practicality that this book attempts to transmit. Finally, thanks to my parents for the example of care and thoughtfulness they set, and to my wife, Betty, and children, Stefan and Tanis, for their support over the years.

Book Overview

Welcome to an exploration of one of business's most important and, to many people, mysterious subjects: financial accounting. The goals of this book are to help you:

- understand this subject well enough to be able to use accounting reports and explain them to others;

- acquire the basics of how accounting works and how to prepare accounting reports.

Meeting these goals will benefit you whether or not you become an accountant. Nonaccountants are affected by accounting in many ways, as this book will show. For their part, accountants need to know how and why accounting reports are used, as well as how to prepare them. The going will not all be easy, but if you give it your best effort, you may be surprised at the level of sophistication you reach.

The topics are organized into four groups of chapters. As noted in the Preface, many chapter topics have been written so that they may be used in different orders, and entire chapters can be used in different orders too. Alternative sequences are mentioned below, in the chapter material, and in the Table of Contents. Here are the chapter groups.

Part 1: Introduction to Financial Accounting

1: Introduction: Linking Financial Accounting's Production and Uses

- Chapter 1 introduces the people involved in preparing and using financial accounting's reports ("financial statements") and the way financial accounting's "accrual accounting" approach measures an enterprise's performance. The chapter also introduces financial accounting's "transactional" basis and ideas about the kinds of analysis that are central to using financial statements and to accountants' value in society. This chapter is introductory but does deal with substantive content, so you will notice your understanding of financial accounting to have increased even after one chapter.

Part 2: Preparing and Using Financial Accounting's Reports

There are four chapters in this group. Together they introduce the set of financial statements and the principles and environment that influence, even determine, their nature.

2: Measuring and Evaluating Financial Position

- Chapter 2 introduces the "balance sheet," the reflection of the accounting system's accumulation of information over the life of the enterprise. The history and present nature of the "double-entry" system and its "debits and credits" are covered, as is how to interpret the resulting financial statement. The balance sheet's depiction of the enterprise's legal structure and sources of financing is reviewed. This material and that on interpreting the balance sheet are written to be read either after or before the double-entry system is described.

3: Measuring and Evaluating Financial Performance

- Chapter 3 uses the same approach to introducing the income statement, which is "accrual accounting's" fundamental measure of financial performance, and the statement of retained earnings, which connects the income statement to the balance sheet. Again, a mixture of history, present practice, preparation principles, and ways of interpreting the information demonstrates why the income statement exists and why it is important. Also again, the interpretation content may be read before or after that on the preparation of the income and retained earnings statements.

4: Measuring and Evaluating Cash Flow

- Chapter 4 introduces the cash flow statement, which is both the fourth regular financial statement and a major example of user-oriented accounting analysis.

5: Standards and Principles Surrounding the Financial Statements

- Chapter 5 completes the introduction of the financial statements by dealing with a variety of preparation and use principles and environmental forces (such as auditing, ethics, international agreements, and stock markets) acting on financial accounting. The chapter has no numbers, so also gives you a bit of time to consolidate your understanding before moving on to the greater accounting depth of the next chapters.

Part 3: Doing Financial Accounting

The four chapters in this group delve into various practices important to anyone preparing financial statements, which are also presented so that their importance to those not planning to become accountants will be apparent. Using financial statements intelligently requires some knowledge of what the accountants are trying to do in preparing them.

6: Revenue and Expense Recognition

- Chapter 6 focuses on the way accrual accounting measures income as the difference between revenues and expenses.

7: Recordkeeping and Control

- Chapter 7 outlines some reasons for financial accounting that exist separately from the financial statements but significantly influence the statements. Two main sets of reasons are examined: recordkeeping and internal control, both fundamental concerns and responsibilities of the enterprise's management.

8: Assets Accounting

9: Liabilities, Equity, and Corporate Groups

- Chapters 8 and 9 examine the accounts on the two sides of the balance sheet in more detail. Chapter 8 focuses on the left "assets" side and Chapter 9 on the right "liabilities and equity" side.

Part 4: Financial Accounting Analysis Wrap-Up

10: Financial Accounting Analysis

- Chapter 10 provides analysis relevant to preparing and using financial accounting information. Its material can be used as a wrap-up or can be studied any time after the four financial statements have been introduced (any time after Chapter 4). The chapter has three main topics, which can be used in any order: financial statement analysis (focusing on the illustrative case of CAE Inc., made familiar by various examples in earlier chapters and so brought together in this chapter), "present value" analysis of the time value of money, and "what if" or "effects" analysis used to help managers understand the effects of accounting changes or various financial and other business deals.

The book ends with solution outlines to selected (asterisked) homework problems, a glossary of terms that is crossreferenced to important chapter sections using various terms, and an index.

Introduction to Financial Accounting

PART

CHAPTER

C | Introduction: Linking Financial Accounting's Production and Uses

- Chapter 1 introduces the people involved in preparing and using financial accounting's reports ("financial statements") and the way financial accounting's "accrual accounting" approach measures an enterprise's performance. The chapter also introduces financial accounting's "transactional" basis and ideas about the kinds of analysis that are central to using financial statements and to accountants' value in society.

1 CHAPTER

Introduction: Linking Financial Accounting's Production and Uses

1.1 Chapter Overview: Use, Preparation, and Concepts

Preparation, use, and concepts are important in this first chapter.

Use. Financial accounting has value because the information it produces is used in many and varied ways. Users include managers, stockbrokers, bankers, financial analysts, and many others. Such people study accounting to learn how to use the information effectively and do their jobs better. Accountants also need to know how the information is used so they can understand the demand for their services and do their jobs better too.

Preparation. Accounting is a complex human activity. Accounting information doesn't just happen: it is produced by people. It is a human creation just as much as a skyscraper, a video, or a sweater. To be effective users of the information, people need to know something about how and why the information is prepared. Accountants' expertise is all about the how and the why.

Concepts. Users, accountants, and accounting are a connected system. The demand for useful information shapes how financial accounting information is prepared, for example, in producing annual or quarterly performance reports. How it is prepared shapes its use, for example, in financial analysis and managerial decisions. Tying it all together are the whys: the reasons it is used and prepared, and the principles that lie behind it. Many of these are quite interesting and controversial, but they are important in this book not so much for themselves as for the way they explain and connect the preparation and the uses.

The *hows* (preparation procedures and techniques), *whys* (concepts and principles), and *uses* (analysis and decisions) of financial accounting are examined throughout this book. Sometimes one of the three is emphasized for a while, but the others are never far away, because none can stand without the others. This diagram appears once in a while as a reminder of the importance of all three:

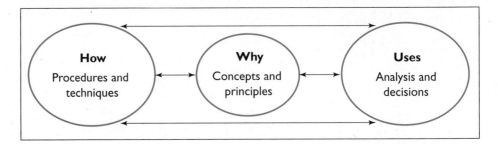

FIGURE 1.1

The Glossary of Terms at the back of the book explains terms printed in colour.

This chapter introduces you to the subject of financial accounting and illustrates some useful concepts and techniques. It outlines a way of thinking about financial accounting that will be important to your career, whether you become an accountant, or a user of accounting in business, or in other walks of life. Referring to "How" in Figure 1.1, you will be introduced to the cornerstones of the financial accounting process: the transaction, the trigger that starts the process, and accrual accounting, the broad framework beyond the transaction, within which financial accounting reports are prepared. As to "Uses," you will be introduced to two important kinds of analysis: reconciliation of numbers that do not agree, in order to find out why not, and net-of-tax analysis, useful whenever income tax affects a management decision (which is most of the time). "Why" is here too: you will see the beginnings of financial accounting's conceptual background, some reasons for using the transaction as the base of accounting, and for going beyond it into accrual accounting. Broadly, you will be introduced to the social setting of financial accounting and to some of the people involved in that setting. Attempting to serve the needs of all these people, not all of whom necessarily see things the same way, is a major reason why financial accounting is complex and requires much judgment.

Financial accounting's reports tell a financial story about the organization.

In an introductory course, learning terminology is important. To help you with that, this book has a Glossary of Terms at the back. Any term printed in colour, such as **financial accounting**, is included in the glossary. Marginal comments, such as the one on the left, highlight important ideas, and at the end of each chapter there is a list of new terms from that chapter. If you're not sure what a term means, look it up right away.

Accounting uses numbers but requires many skills beyond number-work.

Accounting is a challenging discipline that involves many capabilities: assigning numbers to represent financial phenomena, providing explanations of those numbers, analyzing and verifying others' number-work and explanations, understanding the needs of those who use accounting's reports to make decisions, engaging in oral and written communication with the many people involved in an organization's financial activities, having familiarity with computers and other electronic media, and maintaining judgment that is sound, objective, and ethical.

Much of the challenge of accounting is in figuring out which numbers to use, deciding what "story" the numbers should tell. Adding and subtracting the numbers is often the easy part. This makes accounting both easier and harder to learn than you might have thought. Accounting is rooted in the financial setting and has its own vocabulary and viewpoints, so don't expect it all to make perfect sense at the beginning. It will take a while for you to acquire the knowledge that creates an understanding of business and accounting as they really are in our world. This understanding will be based on your knowledge of both concepts and techniques, and of the viewpoints of both accountants and the users of accounting.

Accounting is an unfinished human creation, continuing to change as conditions change.

Accounting is a human artifact, an art, a work in progress. It can be viewed up close or from a distance, critically or with enthusiasm. It changes as human tastes and societies change, and, like a kaleidoscope, its shapes and colours change if you twist it a bit. Referring to a great writer, *The Economist* magazine could have been talking about accounting when it said: "... the saga is not finished. But no work of art ever is."[1] Enjoy this book's exploration of accounting; relax about the unfinished and rough bits of accounting, and be prepared to be surprised at how sophisticated your knowledge will become.

 OR YOUR INTEREST

Accounting reports contain many examples of art, humour, and sophisticated design. Chicken producer Tyson Foods structured its 1999 annual financial report around its cover, which featured a close-up of a chicken crossing the road, and remarks in the report like "Who's Chicken?" The CBC uses pictures of its newscasters, puppets, and other radio and TV characters in its financial reports. Big Rock Brewery often uses pictures of beer bottles and labels to jazz up its numbers, and frequently reports its results using pictures of beer steins. You might enjoy looking at companies' Web sites to see how they do their financial reporting. Within company sites, try searching under Investor Relations, Investing, Annual Report, and Financial. Tyson is at www.Tyson.com, CBC is at www.cbc.ca, and Big Rock is at www.bigrockbeer.com.

1.2   FINANCIAL ACCOUNTING

Financial accounting measures an enterprise's performance over time and its position (status) at a point in time, and does so in Canadian dollars, US dollars, yen, francs, or whatever currency is judged relevant to the enterprise. This measurement of **financial performance** and **financial position** is done for all sorts of enterprises: large and small businesses, governments from local to national levels, universities, charities, churches, clubs, international associations, and many others. The **financial statements**, which are financial accounting's reports, summarize the measurements of financial performance and position in standard ways thought to be useful in evaluating whether the enterprise has done well and is in good shape. These financial statements include **notes** (sometimes dozens of pages) that contain many words of explanation and interpretation in addition to the numbers.

The statements report on the economic and financial side of things and are largely for the use of people outside the enterprise, such as investors, club members, regulatory agencies, and taxation authorities.

In summary:

Financial accounting focuses on financial performance, position, and explanation.

- Financial performance means generating new resources from day-to-day operations over a period of time.

- Financial position is the enterprise's set of financial resources and obligations at a point in time.

- Financial statements are the reports describing financial performance and position.

- Notes are part of the statements, adding explanations to the numbers.

As we will see throughout the book, financial performance and position are highly related. Good performance is likely to lead to a healthy financial position: if you make money at your job, you are more likely to have money in the bank. On the other hand, a healthy financial position facilitates performance: if you have money in the bank, that helps you afford the activities that lead to good performance and avoid the risks and worries that come from being broke.

Management accounting focuses on helping managers operate the enterprise.

Another branch of accounting, management accounting, is oriented toward helping managers and others inside the enterprise, in contrast to financial accounting's more external focus. While management accounting is not examined in this book, students interested in how financial accounting measures managerial performance will find frequent references to the relationship between managers and financial accounting. In the end, all forms of accounting exist to help people, such as managers, investors, bankers, and legislators, make decisions. As Figure 1.1 in the last section portrayed, decision-making by the users of accounting's reports is important to all aspects of accounting, and is therefore examined throughout this book.

 OW'S YOUR UNDERSTANDING?

Here are two questions you should be able to answer, based on what you have just read. If you can't answer them, it would be best to reread the material.

1. What are the two main things that financial accounting measures?

2. What is the basic purpose financial accounting serves?

1.3   THE SOCIAL SETTING OF FINANCIAL ACCOUNTING

This book will show you the many ways in which financial accounting has been shaped by the development of business and society. Some of the many functions of financial accounting include the following:

- It helps stock market investors decide whether to buy, sell, or hold shares of companies.

- It helps managers run enterprises on behalf of owners, members, or citizens (in addition to the help provided by management accounting and other sources of information).

- It provides basic financial records for the purposes of day-to-day management, control, insurance, and fraud prevention.

- It is used by governments in monitoring the actions of enterprises and in assessing taxes, such as income tax and sales taxes.

We could go on for some time listing major and minor functions of financial accounting. Whole books have been written about each of the many functions! And, though this book emphasizes externally oriented financial accounting for business firms (to avoid overwhelming you with all of accounting's uses at once), don't forget that there are many other organizations that use, and are affected by, accounting. When words like "organization," "company," or "enterprise" are used, the implications often go well beyond business firms. You'll get a taste of those implications in this book and will see them more fully as your learning develops in other courses.

Accounting is active, affected by, and affecting, business and society in general.

Financial accounting for the enterprise, the centre of interest in this book, operates within, and serves, a complex social setting. It seeks to monitor and report on financial events initiated by or happening to the enterprise. These events come from and, in turn, affect the social setting, so the accounting is not passive: it tells us what is going on, but in doing so it affects our decisions and actions and, therefore, also affects what is going on.

The social setting is composed of many people. There are at least three parties directly concerned with what financial accounting says about the enterprise:

- the owners (for example, shareholders of a corporation);

- the managers, who are running the company on behalf of the owners; and

- the external auditors, who are employed by the owners to evaluate the accounting reports presented by the managers.

This book focuses mostly on the perspectives of owners, managers, and auditors.

Shareholders own portions of the corporation—shares that can be bought and sold—but the corporation is a legal entity existing separately from its shareholder owners. Auditors report on the credibility of the enterprise's financial statements, on behalf of owners and others, as we will see.

These parties have relationships among each other, as well as with financial accounting.

Owners, managers, and auditors forge many relationships, including through accounting.

- Managers, for example, may work for a company throughout their careers and, therefore, may have as much a feeling of ownership as do shareholders who may, through buying and selling shares on the stock market, be part-owners of the company for only a few months before moving on to another investment.

- In smaller companies, managers and owners may be the same people.

- The external auditors are formally appointed by the owners, for example, at the annual shareholders' meeting, but they work with the managers day-to-day and may also offer advice on tax, accounting, and other topics of practical interest to managers, separately from the knowledge they use in their role as auditors.

- But an enterprise's external auditor is not permitted to be an owner or manager of the enterprise too. This is to ensure that the auditor is financially and ethically independent and can therefore be objective about the enterprise's financial affairs. Independence and objectivity are fundamental ideas, which are encountered frequently in this book.

Many people are involved in financial accounting, but not all necessarily have common interests.

In addition to these three central parties, and often hard to distinguish from them, is a host of other groups, companies, institutions, and parties interested in, or having an influence on, the company's financial accounting. As we will see many times in this book, these parties do not share the same interest in the company's accounting and may even be in competition or conflict with each other. Most will be in the same country as the company and its management, but, increasingly, companies and other enterprises are operating internationally. So, the other groups interested in, and affecting, the company's financial accounting may be all over the planet. Let's see a little more about who all these people are.

 OR YOUR INTEREST

Accounting can actually be quite controversial. Here are just three examples. (1) IBM's shares lost billions of dollars in value in one day in November 1999 when the company was accused of mixing one-time gains it had made in with its regular operating income. The numbers were right, but it was alleged they were in the wrong place in the report. (2) Also in November 1999, conglomerate Tyco International Ltd. lost 23% of its total stock market value in two quick blows, first, on allegations that it was using "accounting gimmicks" to make itself look better than it was, and second, on rumours that the company's auditors, embarrassed by all the fuss, would resign. (3) Accounting for movies has been an art form just like the movies for a long time. Many famous movies, seen by zillions of people, haven't made any money for the people who invested in them. Said a commentator: "Some of Hollywood's greatest special effects never make it to the screen. They're found in studio accounting books."[2]

1.4   THE PEOPLE INVOLVED IN FINANCIAL ACCOUNTING

There are many participants in the art of financial accounting. The main ones are:

Users: decision makers; Preparers: decision facilitators; Auditors: credibility enhancers.

- the information **users** (the decision makers),

- the information **preparers**, who put the information together to facilitate the users' decision-making, and

- the **auditors**, who assist the users by enhancing the credibility of the information, providing a professional opinion that the information is fair and appropriate.

Users (Decision Makers)

In financial accounting, a user or decision maker is someone who makes decisions on the basis of the financial statements, on his or her own behalf, or on behalf of a company, bank, or other organization. Financial accounting is utilitarian: ultimately, the nature and contents of financial statements are functions of the demand for decision information from users. This is not to say that such people are the only ones who matter in the process, nor are they always clear about what information they need, or necessarily satisfied with what they get. User demand, however, is the fundamental reason for financial statements; therefore, understanding the demand is important.

User demand is the reason financial statements exist.

A user's main demand is for *credible periodic reporting* of an enterprise's financial position and performance.

- *Credible* means that the information in the reports (the financial statements) appears to be sufficiently trustworthy and competently prepared for it to be used to make decisions. There is a cost–benefit issue here: huge amounts of money could be spent trying to make the reports absolutely perfect, but since that money would have to come out of the enterprise's funds, spending it would make its performance and position poorer. Users, such as owners and managers, may not want that to happen, so credibility is a relative condition, not an absolute one. Accounting information has to be worth its cost.

Financial accounting supplies a demand for credible periodic information.

- *Periodic* means that users can expect reports on some regular basis (for example, yearly or quarterly). The longer the wait, the more solid the information. But waiting a long time for information is not desirable: users are willing to accept some imprecision in the information in return for periodic reports with timely, decision-relevant information.

The main groups of users are:

Owners: individual business owners, such as proprietors, partners, and other entrepreneurs; individual investors (shareholders) in shares on stock markets who can vote on company affairs; companies that invest in other companies; pension plans and other institutions that invest in companies; people with quasi-ownership interests, such as members of clubs or voters in municipalities; and so on.

Owners and potential owners are examples of users with different interests.

Potential owners: people, of the same sort as the owners listed above, who do not at present have a financial interest in the enterprise, but may be considering making an investment. Because potential owners often buy shares from present owners, for example, by trading shares on the stock market rather than investing directly, there is often a significant difference in outlook between present owners, who would like to sell their shares for as much as possible, and potential owners, who would like to pay as little as possible. Saying that accounting responds to demands from users does not mean that all the users will have the same demands!

Creditors often have a substantial interest in an enterprise and a say in its decisions.

Creditors and potential creditors: suppliers, banks, bondholders, employees, and others who have lent money to the enterprise, or who are owed funds in return for supplying something of value, or who are considering taking on such a role. Creditors do not have the legal control of the enterprise that owners have, but they often have a large say in enterprise decisions, especially if the enterprise gets into difficulty. In cases of extreme difficulty, creditors may have the right to take control of the enterprise from the owners. Sometimes the difference between creditors and owners is hard to discern because it may depend on subtle legalities about who has what rights, and some people may play both roles for a given enterprise; for example, an owner invests money in a business, but in addition may lend the business further money, becoming a creditor as well as an owner.

Managers are very interested in what financial accounting says about their performance.

Managers: those who run the enterprise on behalf of the owners. They have a great interest in the way accounting reports on their activities and results. Often, managers' salaries, bonuses, and the likelihood of staying in their jobs are directly affected by the contents of the financial statements. Especially in small businesses, the owner may also be the main manager.

Employees: nonmanagement employees and their unions or other associations. These groups are interested in the enterprise's ability to pay wages, maintain employment levels, and keep such promises as paying pensions.

Taxation authorities and other government bodies and agencies: groups that may use the financial statements to calculate taxes payable or to evaluate whether the enterprise is following various rules and agreements.

Government stock market regulators, stock exchange administrators and accounting standard-setters: groups that establish rules and regulations affecting accounting and monitor enterprises' compliance with them.

Financial and market analysts: people who study companies' performance and prepare reports for others by analyzing those companies. Analysts often make recommendations about whether to invest, lend, or do neither.

Accounting information intended for one group of users may inform others also.

Competitors: some of the people who get the financial statements may be trying to understand the enterprise's operations for the purpose of making life more difficult for the enterprise. Sometimes managers are reluctant to disclose information to shareholders, for example, because competitors can then also obtain it and act to reduce the enterprise's prospects.

Accounting researchers: people (mostly university professors, but also some based in public accounting firms and other organizations) who study accounting with the objective of understanding it and contributing to its improvement.

Miscellaneous third parties: various other people who may get access to an enterprise's financial statements and use them in various ways. Once statements have been issued, many people may make use of them. Politicians may make judgments about industry efficiency or taxation levels, for example. News reporters may write stories about employment practices. Judges and juries may evaluate enterprises' ability to pay damages in the course of lawsuits.

Financial accounting serves many users with many interests and decisions to make.

Think about all these users and decisions! It is a great challenge to develop one set of periodic financial statements for an enterprise so that they can be useful for all. Perhaps you will not be surprised that there is much controversy about whether financial statements do this well, and whether financial accounting methods serve some users or decisions better than others.

 OR YOUR INTEREST

If you plan to be an accountant, the value of studying financial accounting is clear. It may not be so clear, however, if you have other plans, such as a career in management, marketing, finance, engineering, law, human resources, or production. To provide some perspective for those of you not planning an accounting career, and to help you understand the managers you will work with if you do become an accountant or auditor, comments will be made frequently about managers and financial accounting. Financial accounting is directly relevant to managers because it reports on their performance as decision makers, as caretakers of the enterprise, as representatives of the owners, as legal officers of the enterprise, and so on. Any manager cannot help but be interested in how her or his performance is being measured and in how that performance is analyzed, projected, and evaluated. Managers' bonuses, promotions, dismissals, transfers, and other rewards and penalties are often directly based on the numbers and commentaries prepared by accountants. Every manager should have an intimate understanding of how accounting is measuring his or her performance and should be able to conduct a "reasonableness check" of the information being provided to her or him and have a comfortable understanding of the accounting implications of what is going on.

Preparers (Decision Facilitators)

Three main groups are responsible for the information in the financial statements:

Managers are both preparers and users of financial accounting information.

Managers: people responsible for running an enterprise, including issuing accounting and other information and controlling its financial affairs. The fact that managers are also users, vitally interested in the results, has created a fundamental conflict of interest for them and has led to the development of the auditing function, as will be discussed below. Managers, as a group, are often referred to as "management."

Bookkeepers and clerks: under the direction of management, those who keep the enterprise's basic records and create the data upon which financial accounting is built. Many bookkeeping and clerical functions are now performed by computers with all the benefits and frustrations those machines provide.

Professional accounting designations include CA, CGA, CMA, and CPA.

Accountants: people whose job it is to shape the financial statements by applying the principles of accounting to the enterprise's records under the direction of management. Many accountants are members of professional societies and are accredited, such as CAs (chartered accountants), CGAs (certified general accountants), CMAs (certified management accountants), and CPAs (certified public accountants, the largest group in the United States). Often, accountants and their societies also have auditing experience and interests, and sometimes auditing roles, but the task of preparing the financial statements is quite different in principle from the task of verifying those statements once they are prepared.

Auditors (Credibility Enhancers)

Professional accountants may act as accountants or auditors—very different roles.

Auditors have the job of assisting the users, by verifying that the financial statements have been prepared fairly, competently, and in a manner consistent with accepted principles. The auditing role is a very old one, arising because users demanded some assurance that managers' reports on their performance were not self-serving, biased, or downright untruthful. This book refers frequently to external auditors, who report on the financial statements on behalf of external users, but there are also internal auditors, who work within the enterprise to support the credibility of information being used by management, and other auditors (such as tax auditors, who verify taxpayers' computation of tax). While external auditors may be asked for advice in preparing the statements, especially for small companies, they must avoid responsibility for the statements because their role is to scrutinize the preparation process. They cannot credibly audit statements they have prepared! (Professional accountants often do prepare financial statements, but in doing so they are not acting as external auditors, and they make this clear in covering letters and footnotes attached to the statements.)

External auditors are expected to be objective and expert professionals.

The external auditor's role falls between those of the preparer and the user, so he or she must be acceptable to both. Such acceptability is helped if the auditor is an independent professional who will collect his or her fee whether the financial results are good or bad—or whether the managers or users are happy or unhappy. The external auditing function is considered so important that the right to perform it is usually restricted to members of recognized professional accountants' societies who have auditing expertise and experience.

Public accounting firms offer a wide range of services beyond external auditing.

External auditors may work alone, but most work with other auditors in public accounting firms. Some of these firms are very large, having thousands of partners and other senior people, tens of thousands of employees, and offices in many cities and countries. Public accounting firms offer their clients not only external auditing, but also advice on income tax, accounting, computer systems, and many other financial and business topics. In offering such other advice to enterprises that they also audit, public accountants are not supposed to get so involved that they are in effect auditing their own work, or creating any conflict-of-interest problems. Managing this requires considerable professional skill and attention to ethics and rules of professional conduct, and whether this is being done successfully is a matter of much controversy at present. In early 2000, as just one example, a report accused one of the biggest American public accounting firms of not keeping its auditors sufficiently independent of the companies they audit.[3]

People and Ethics

Ethics, mentioned above, will be raised throughout this book. Ethical issues can arise in just about any area of accounting. Here are some examples, all of them real:

Should the financial statements provide information that could damage the enterprise?

- An enterprise has been sued by a recently fired employee, who claims that the firing was based on the employee's age and so broke employment laws. The enterprise's president denies any impropriety. The enterprise's chief accountant, who personally feels the former employee's claim is justified, has suggested to the boss that the lawsuit should be mentioned in a note to the financial statements, so that users of the statements will know there is a potential for loss if the former employee wins. The president feels the chief accountant should ignore the lawsuit in preparing the financial statements to avoid embarrassment and the appearance of admitting guilt. The president fears that such an apparent admittance could be used against the enterprise in court and so could cause the enterprise to lose the lawsuit. What should the chief accountant do?

What if the auditor's responsibilities to different clients conflict?

- While doing the audit, another enterprise's external auditor learns that the enterprise may have been cheating one of its customers. The customer, who is unaware of this and quite happy with things, is another client of the auditor. The auditor, who is bound by rules of conduct designed to protect the confidentiality of information gained during the audit, knows that saying anything to anyone could result in lawsuits in all directions. Should the auditor just keep quiet about what was found?

Should managers implement an accounting method that makes them better off?

- A third enterprise's president is paid a bonus each year, calculated as a percentage of the enterprise's income. The president is considering a proposed change in an accounting method that, among other things, will raise income and increase the president's bonus. So the proposal would put money in the president's pocket. Should the president refuse to implement the accounting change, or request that the bonus calculation ignore the change, or just go ahead and enjoy the higher bonus?

These illustrative problems do not have easy answers, so none are offered at this point. They are dilemmas for the chief accountant, the auditor, and the president. This book will address ethical issues from time to time and so help you sharpen your ethical sense along with your accounting knowledge, for the two are inseparable.

 OR YOUR INTEREST

In an effort to understand and help with problems, many people conduct research into accounting issues, such as choosing appropriate accounting methods; maintaining auditor independence; stock market responses to accounting information; disputes about accounting among contending parties; exercising professional judgment about accounting; ethics of professional accountants; history of accounting methods; social issues, such as the role of women in accounting; practical solutions to computing management bonuses and other performance incentives; income tax calculation; and even the use of graphs and pictures in accounting reports. A lot of accounting research is going on and there are many accounting research journals with titles such as *Accounting, Organizations and Society*, *The Accounting Review*, *Contemporary Accounting Research*, *Journal of Accounting and Economics*, and *Journal of Accounting Research*. References to research results are made frequently in this book, wherever it helps in understanding an issue.

 OW'S YOUR UNDERSTANDING?

Here are two questions you should be able to answer, based on what you have just read. If you can't answer them, it would be best to reread the material.

1. Who is a "user" of financial reports, and why would such a person want them?

2. What is the difference between a "preparer" and an "auditor," why is the difference important, and where does company management fit into the picture?

1.5   AN EXAMPLE: GRADES

To outline how financial accounting works, let's use an analogy: the example of students going to university and getting grades for their efforts. The parallel with financial accounting isn't exact, but it will illustrate the main issues.

Students go to university to learn, among other reasons, and they get grades as a measure of their learning. Grades are not a perfect measure of learning, but they are a very important part of the process in modern universities.

Grades are used, for better or worse.

• Grades are used by the students themselves and by others, including parents and university administrators, to assess students' knowledge at various stages and to monitor their performance over time. They are also used by employers to predict future job performance, by scholarship agencies to allocate awards, and so on. Many good and bad things can happen because of a student's grades, even though the student and other people who use grades may feel that they are not necessarily the best reflection of the learning they are supposed to measure.

Grades have standard features thought to make them more useful.

- Grade reports come out at standard times of the year and in standard formats, and preparing them occupies much of professors' and administrators' time. Great effort goes into minimizing error and fraud. For example, official transcripts are prepared carefully and certified so that anyone using them can be confident that they have not been tampered with. Cheating and other tampering with the grading system can land a student in very hot water indeed.

Grades may affect students' learning choices; they don't just report on results.

- Because of the importance of grades, students may choose courses and make other choices in the expectation that these choices will mean better grades, whether or not they care much about what they are learning. Sometimes the grades, which are only supposed to reflect the learning, seem so important that they drive the system instead!

Here are some parallels between the grade example and financial accounting:

1. The student is in university to learn, but not only for that reason. Similarly, businesses and other organizations are concerned about financial position and financial performance, but not only those. Those are, however, financial accounting's focus.

2. Learning has many dimensions, and course grades represent only some of them. Financial performance and position also have many dimensions. Financial accounting keeps track of several of these dimensions, but not all. They are not perfect, but grades and financial accounting have been with us for a long time and continue to be important.

3. Individual course grades are measures of performance. A good grade point average is an indication that the student's knowledge is good and may be used to predict good performance in the future. In accounting, good financial performance is expected to accumulate to provide a healthy financial position, and a healthy financial position is expected to lead to good subsequent performance. While they are useful to have, such expectations do not always work out, either for students or enterprises.

4. Like grades and grade reports, which summarize the results of many tests, projects, and other activities, financial accounting's reports (financial statements) are summaries of a large number of individual events. In a course, the final exam may matter more than the term paper does in calculating the course grade. In accounting, too, some events may be more important than others in compiling the financial report.

5. Knowing how employers, student loan offices, graduate schools, parents, students, and others use grade transcripts helps us to understand why they are as they are. Similarly, the use of financial accounting's reports must be understood in order to appreciate the role they play. A company president may be just as anxious about how people will interpret and use an accounting report as a student is about people's reaction to a grade transcript. Career prospects, salary, and other important things may be in the minds of both president and student.

Grades and financial accounting are information systems with many parallels.

6. Grade transcripts summarize the students' performance over specific periods of time, such as the school year. Comparisons to performance in other years

are made easier by the format of the transcripts. Financial statements also appear at regular intervals (at least once a year and often on a quarterly or even monthly basis) and are prepared using a fairly standard format to increase their usefulness as a tool of comparison for different companies or the same company in different years.

7. Much trouble is taken to minimize error and fraud in both grading and the preparation of financial statements. So that people may rely on the statements, auditors verify that they are prepared in a fair manner and in accordance with accepted principles.

8. It is unfortunate, but understandable, that some students choose courses not because they will learn much but because a high grade can be easily obtained. Because financial statements are so important, some managers similarly seem to worry more about making their accounting numbers look good than about running the business properly.

 OW'S YOUR UNDERSTANDING?

Here are two questions you should be able to answer, based on what you have just read. If you can't answer them, it would be best to reread the material.

1. Why are students interested in the grades they receive for courses taken?

2. What are some parallels between students' interest in grades and people's interest in accounting reports?

1.6   FINANCIAL ACCOUNTING'S TRANSACTIONAL FILTER

Accounting is an information system, filtering and summarizing data.

Accounting is an information system to filter and summarize data. Information systems select observations from the world, collect those results into data banks, and organize and summarize the data to produce specific kinds of information. This is useful because decision makers cannot cope with masses of raw, unorganized observations, and it is economically efficient to have one system organize data into information on behalf of various users.

Information systems are choosy, designed to select and present relevant data.

An everyday example of filtering and summarizing is the daily newspaper: the editors group stories and features so that you know where to look for what you want. There's a sports section, an entertainment section, a page for letters to the editor, and so on. No newspaper contains exactly what you want, but it gets close enough to what most people want so that it can be published at a low cost compared to what it would cost you to hire reporters to get information just for you. In order to make this work, every information system has to be choosy: it has to filter all the available data and pick what is relevant to its purpose. You don't expect the newspaper, or accounting reports, to contain glossy reproductions of Rembrandt paintings suitable for framing, or to print the grades you got in your university courses: you go to other information sources for such things.

An information system such as financial accounting is inherently limited. It can report only what its sensors pick up as it seeks out data or filters data from the mass of ongoing events. No information system tells you "*the* truth," and certainly not "*the whole* truth," because it can only pass along information based on what it has been designed or permitted to gather as data.[4] Figure 1.2 represents the situation:

- The gap in the wall is the system's filter or "window on the world."

- Once a piece of raw data is admitted, recording activity takes place and it is stored in a bank of data (in accounting it is stored in manual or computerized places with names like accounts, ledgers, journals (the books), which we will learn about later).

- The data in this bank are then organized to produce usable information (in accounting: financial statements and reports).

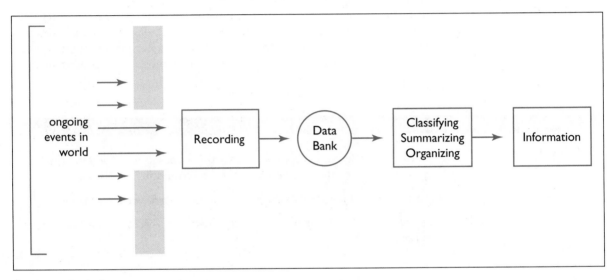

FIGURE 1.2

In accounting, we generally refer to the left part of the diagram, the data recording and some routine classifying and summarizing, as "bookkeeping." We refer to the right part, the turning of data into information for users, as "accounting" or "reporting." Financial accounting information is contained in the system's final product, the financial statements and notes.

Accounting reports are based on, and are limited by, the data collected. Therefore, if you are to understand the reports, you have to understand how accounting filters, notices, and chooses events to record into its data bank. Financial accounting's filter, its window on the world, is the transaction. *Generally*, if an event is a transaction, it is recorded into financial accounting's database; if it is not, the routine accounting system ignores the event.

The transaction is financial accounting's window on the world.

The following are examples of accounting transactions. They should be recorded routinely by the financial accounting system.

The financial accounting system should record transactions routinely.

a. The payroll department issues a cheque to pay an employee.
b. A customer pays, in cash, an account owing since last month and gets a receipt.
c. A sales clerk prepares an invoice for a customer, for the sale of goods the customer is taking with her and promises to pay for.
d. The head cashier deposits the day's receipts into the bank.
e. The stockroom receives a shipment of spare parts for the delivery trucks, along with an invoice from the parts supplier.

There is no limit to the number or kinds of transactions that human ingenuity can devise. Accounting has to deal with them, and must change as they change. Nowadays, many companies are scrambling to handle Internet transactions, those happening through Web pages and other areas of e-commerce, all of which are promising to change many accounting systems fundamentally. Transactions are partly defined by the legal and economic system. In our society, promises to pay can be enforced in the courts, so they are considered transactions, as in example (c) above. Speaking very roughly, there are two general kinds of transactions important in accounting: cash transactions, which feature the exchange of cash, and credit transactions, which feature (partially or fully) promises to exchange cash in the future.

The following are examples of events that are *not* accounting transactions and that will therefore *not* be recorded routinely, if at all, by the accounting system.

Events that are not transactions will not be recorded routinely, if at all.

   i. The president of the company breaks her leg while skiing.
  ii. The credit department manager decides that a particular customer is probably never going to pay the account the customer owes.
 iii. The main warehouse burns to the ground overnight.
 iv. A customer orders a machine to be delivered next month.
  v. Real estate reports indicate the company's land has gone up in value by 14% since last year.

Some such events may be brought into the system by special adjustments to the routine recording system that we will learn about later. Events (ii) and (iii) are examples. But many are never included in financial accounting's information system. Event (i) is an example. Other events are recorded only after something more has happened. Event (iv) is recorded by the accounting system only when the machine is delivered, and in Canadian accounting, event (v) is recorded only if the land is sold. Human ingenuity comes in here: some large or innovative companies have accounting systems that routinely record events that are not transactions that other or smaller companies ignore or leave to be done as special adjustments. Some examples of nontransactions recorded by large or innovative firms are internal transfers of goods from department to department in the company, monthly changes in the market values of investments, estimated income earned on partially completed construction contracts, and revisions in estimates for warranty payments. These may be included for various reasons, such as because other information systems in the company provide the necessary data so it can be used easily, or because management believes more finely-tuned accounting information to be useful in decision-making.

What distinguishes accounting transactions, such as those in the first list above, from the sorts of events in the second list? All of those in the second list may be important economically, but they are not routinely recorded by the accounting system. In order to qualify as a financial accounting transaction, an event must normally have *all five* of the following characteristics:

Three fundamental economic and legal characteristics

1. *Exchange:* the event must involve an exchange of goods, money, financial instruments (such as cheques or bonds), legal promises, or other items of economic value.
2. *Past:* The exchange must have *happened*, even if just seconds ago (financial accounting is essentially a historical information system).

3. *External:* the exchange must have been between the entity being accounted for and someone else, such as a customer, an owner, a supplier, an employee, a banker, or a tax collector (the exchange must have been across the entity's boundary, so to speak).

Two supplementary characteristics, needed for accounting's recordkeeping

4. *Evidence:* there must be some documentation of what has happened (on paper or electronically recorded).
5. *Dollars:* the event must be measurable in dollars or the currency unit relevant in the country where the transaction happens.

These transaction characteristics indicate the nature and value of financial accounting information.

- First, transactions are linked to the legal and economic concept of an exchange: completing a contract by giving or receiving consideration in return for the goods or services that change hands. The transactional basis of financial accounting thus has roots in the fundamental legal and economic processes by which society and business operate. It is no accident that accounting recognizes as transactions events that have a broader legal and business importance too.

- Second, they constitute a large part of the underlying rationale for the historical cost basis of accounting, which is firmly founded on the transaction. If a transaction has *happened*, it should be in the accounting system and in the financial statements. It is history. If it has not happened, it is not the same sort of legal event and will not be in the historical accounting system. We can figure out how to get some events that have not happened into accounting anyway, but they often do not fit in well and can be controversial because reasonable people often disagree about whether and how to bring them in.

- Third, the characteristics of the transaction provide the basis on which the records can be verified (audited) later as part of the process of ensuring that the accounting information is credible. Events that do not have these characteristics would be difficult to verify later, and therefore inevitably lack credibility as measures of financial performance or position.

Let's look at the events from the first list above and see that they fit the set of transaction characteristics:

	Exchange	External party	Evidence	Dollars
a.	money	employee	cheque	cheque
b.	money	customer	receipt	cash
c.	goods, promise	customer	invoice	price
d.	money	bank	deposit slip	cash
e.	goods, promise	supplier	invoice	price

The events in the second list lack several characteristics, especially that of being a past economic exchange. (Event (iv), for example, is not yet an exchange because the machine hasn't yet been delivered.)

Margin notes:

Financial accounting transaction: exchange, past, external, evidence, dollars.

Transactions are based on the legal and economic concept of exchange.

Transactions are the basis of financial accounting as a historical information system.

Transactions are documented and therefore make verifiable accounting records.

The transactional records are "adjusted" to incorporate nontransactional data.

What if an accountant is not satisfied with the set of data recorded by an accounting system and wishes to adjust that data to reflect some event, estimate, or other phenomenon he or she thinks is important in measuring financial performance or position? He or she can record the special alterations in the data bank with an "adjustment." Deciding whether to make such adjustments and determining the dollar amounts to use in them requires expertise and good judgment, since they involve events that are not external exchanges, are not accompanied by normal evidence, or are not readily measurable in dollars. Items (ii) and (iii) in the second list above are examples of events that are normally handled by adjustment entries. Item (v) is an example that is not normally adjusted for because it is too far from accounting's historical cost basis, though there are constant suggestions to alter financial accounting to bring in such information; it is acceptable to do so in some countries, such as Australia and the United Kingdom. You'll see much more about adjustments throughout the book because most people believe that the transactional base of accounting, while absolutely essential to accounting's valued objectivity, is not enough to serve users' decision-making needs.

 OW'S YOUR UNDERSTANDING?

Here are two questions you should be able to answer, based on what you have just read:

1. Why is a "transaction" important in financial accounting?

2. How do we distinguish transactions from events that are not transactions?

1.7   ACCRUAL ACCOUNTING

Financial accounting must deal with large amounts of data, not all of it clear or complete.

Financial accounting's task of producing financial statements is a complex one. For even a small business, thousands of transactions have to be recorded and their financial effects evaluated. For large corporations like Inco, McDonald's, Bank of Montreal, Wal-Mart, and Toyota, or organizations like the University of Alberta, the City of New York, the United Nations, or the Red Cross, the number of transactions runs into the millions or billions. Frequently, when the time comes to prepare the financial statements, transactions have not been completed, are in dispute, or have an otherwise unclear status.

Here are examples in which appropriate figures may be difficult to determine:

• The value of Inco's supply of nickel ore depends on the cost of digging it out, smelting and finishing it, and on international nickel prices that can vary significantly from one day to the next.

• The value of the Bank of Montreal's loans to third-world countries (that is, the money actually to be received back from those loans) depends on the health of the borrowing countries' economies, stability in international money transfer arrangements (often disrupted by wars, politics, and natural disasters), and the relative values of various countries' currencies, which, like nickel prices, can change a lot from day to day.

• The value of donations promised to the Red Cross but not yet received depends on how committed donors are to actually producing the cash, which

Important business complexities must somehow be fitted into financial statements.

can be affected by unemployment, rising prices for food and other goods the donors need, and other things beyond the Red Cross's control.

To cope with these complexities, financial accounting for most businesses and organizations uses the accrual accounting approach to financial accounting. This means that in preparing the financial statements, attempts are made to:

- include all the cash receipts and payments that have already happened,
- incorporate future cash receipts and payments that should be expected based on existing transactions,
- measure the value of incomplete transactions,
- estimate figures when exact amounts are unknown, and

Accrual accounting's objective is to provide economically meaningful information.

- generally make an economically meaningful assessment of awkward problems.

For example:

- Someone tries to estimate how much money Inco has spent on nickel ore and whether nickel prices are higher or lower than Inco's cost to produce more nickel, in order to determine whether Inco's supply of nickel is worth what it cost to produce.
- Someone studies the loan repayment record of various countries for the Bank of Montreal and estimates how much money the bank will be able to collect, in order to judge the value of the bank's uncollected loans.
- Someone advises the Red Cross on how much, if any, of the promised donations are likely to be received to help the Red Cross make its spending plans.

Accrual accounting uses estimates and judgment to produce meaningful information.

Accrual accounting has been developed because financial statements cannot be based just on the routine accounting records of what has happened. Measuring economic performance is more complex than that, and the appropriate measures can be elusive, or can depend on one's point of view. Many augmentations to the transactional record (estimates, adjustments, judgments, and verbal explanations) must be made so that the statements will be meaningful. The resulting statements, therefore, depend to a great extent on the quality and fairness of such augmentations. Managers, accountants, and auditors must use their judgment constantly.

Financial statements are meaningful and useful, and therefore not necessarily precise.

Financial accounting, because it relies on many judgments, is far more imprecise than most people, even many regular users of financial statements, realize. To help students understand the reality of modern financial accounting, much time must be spent on the real-life imprecision of preparing and using financial statements. Accrual accounting is therefore the presumed method in this book, though there will be some comparisons between it and simple cash-based accounting. Modern financial accounting starts with cash receipts and payments and then builds a very large accrual accounting process *in addition to* the cash records in order to provide the sophisticated measures of financial performance and position that today's world demands.

The chart below summarizes and gives examples of the way accrual accounting information is assembled. The foundation is cash transactions, which even the simplest accounting records include. Most accounting systems also include credit transactions, because most enterprises extend credit to customers and/or use credit from their suppliers and employees. Short-term and long-term adjustments are needed in preparing financial statements, unless the company's accounting system is sophisticated enough to have already built those in (some are, though there are always new issues to be dealt with as the world keeps changing). Finally, extensive narrative and supplementary disclosures (especially the "notes" to the financial statements) are made, sometimes using many more pages than the statements themselves do. The result is that accrual accounting is a very complex information system, and it will take the rest of this book to introduce you to it properly.

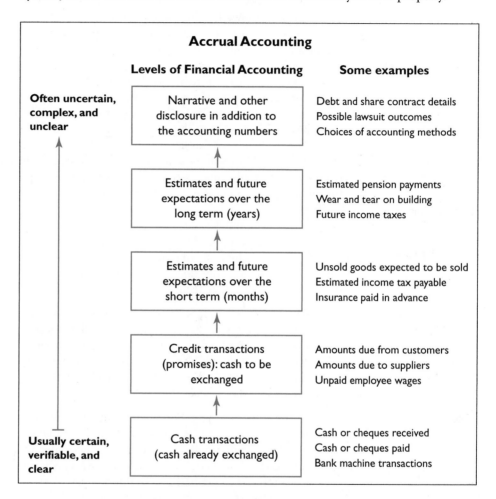

FIGURE 1.3

Here are two questions you should be able to answer based on what you have just read. If you can't answer them, it would be best to reread the material.

1. Does accrual accounting ignore cash transactions, or instead build on the record of them?

2. Why is accrual accounting thought necessary even though a record of transactions already exists?

1.8   AN EXAMPLE: SIMONE'S JEWELLERY BUSINESS

Here is an example of how accrual accounting works. The example is of a small business, one you should be able to imagine easily, but the accounting issues it raises are exactly the same as those faced by big businesses.

Simone works in an office during the day, but in the evenings and on weekends she makes silver jewellery in a studio she has set up in her basement. The jewellery is sold in local craft stores, and Simone keeps a separate bank account to deposit the cash from her sales and to pay the bills for supplies.

Financial statements must be fitted to each business's circumstances.

Accounting is a way of portraying an enterprise; put another way, a visual image may help you. Try to picture her working in her studio, driving around to craft stores to deliver her products and collect cash, and relaxing with her friends when things are going well. It is important that accounting's reports be consistent with the reality of her business, so keep the image in mind as this example develops.

Last year, 2000, was Simone's first year in business, and she received $4,350 in cash from the craft stores for sales of her jewellery and paid $1,670 in cash for silver and for other supplies and expenses. How much money did she make from her business in 2000? Well, the simple answer is that she made a cash income of $2,680 ($4,350 cash collected, minus $1,670 cash paid out). Her bank balance increased by that amount during the year. This is a simple, understandable calculation.

Cash income equals cash receipts minus cash payments for day-to-day business events.

The notion behind accrual accounting is that maybe the simple calculation is too simple, that it really does not properly measure what Simone accomplished during the year. Accrual accounting tries to take into account a number of things.

Accrual accounting: uncollected sales.

- At the end of 2000, Simone was still owed $310 for sales by one craft store because the owner had been out when she stopped by. The store paid her a few weeks later, but shouldn't that amount be counted as income for the year the sales were made? It was a credit transaction in that year, not a cash transaction. The amount was legally owed to Simone at the end of the year and she expected to collect the cash.

Accrual accounting: unused goods.

- At the end of the year, Simone had supplies and both finished and unfinished jewellery on hand that had cost $280. These were paid for during the year, but because they will be used to produce sales in the next year, shouldn't their cost be deducted next year instead? This is an example of a short-term expectation represented by the middle box of Figure 1.3: Simone expects to be able to use the supplies and sell the jewellery, and this expectation should be taken into account, because otherwise the economic value represented by the goods would not be recognized.

Accrual accounting: unpaid bills.

- At the end of the year, Simone had some unpaid bills for business expenses totalling $85. She paid those early in the next year, but aren't they really expenses for the year in which she incurred them, rather than for the year in which she paid them? She has bills for these, so they represent other credit transactions, only this time involving promises by Simone to pay her suppliers rather than by her customers to pay her.

- In making the jewellery, Simone used some equipment she had bought earlier for $1,200. The equipment is expected to last about ten years; so shouldn't the wear and tear on it during the year 2000 be counted as an expense? It is not easy to figure out how much wear and tear results from a particu-

Accrual accounting: wear and tear on equipment.

lar period, but say that she feels the year was a normal one of the ten the equipment should last. The cost of the wear and tear, therefore, is about 10% of the original cost of the equipment, or $120. (This $120 figure is what accountants call "amortization." It can be calculated in several ways, as we will see later on.) This is an example of a long-term estimate or expectation. Because it involves prediction of an uncertain future, and for other reasons we'll see, people have all sorts of disagreements about amortization.

OR YOUR INTEREST

Amortization is accounting's estimate of the consumption of economic value in a period.

Accounting is continually evolving. An example is in the terms **amortization** and **depreciation**. Both terms apply to the idea of measuring the "consumption" of the economic value of long-term resources such as equipment. Amortization is slowly supplanting depreciation as the more general term for this idea, but you will see both terms (and other terms) used in companies' financial reports and in this book.

Just using these four additional pieces of information, accrual accounting would calculate Simone's business income for the year 2000 (her first year in business) in the following way, taking into account the various estimates and incomplete transactions described:

Exhibit

Accrual accounting measures performance with revenues, expenses, and resulting income.

Simone's Jewellery Business Calculation of Accrual Income for the Year 2000	
Revenue* ($4,350 collected, plus $310 still to be received)	$4,660
Expenses ($1,670 paid, minus $280 deducted because the goods are still on hand, plus $85 unpaid, plus $120 estimated amortization)	1,595
Accrual income*based on the information provided	$3,065

Notes:
  * **Revenue** is the benefit received or expected from the sale of goods or services during the year, so it goes beyond cash received.
  ** **Expenses** are costs incurred or resources consumed during the year in order to earn the revenue, so they go beyond cash paid.
  *** **Accrual income** for the year is the difference between revenue and expenses.

Accrual income is more complete than cash income.

Accrual accounting can and does handle many more complexities than the four included above. Even with this uncomplicated example, you can see that the $3,065 accrual income is a more complete measure of Simone's business performance than is the cash income of $2,680, which is the change in cash balance alone. (By the way, accrual income is not necessarily higher than cash income—it just happens to be so in this example.)

But there are some difficulties.

Accrual income is more complicated than cash income.

- The accrual income requires extra calculation and so is more complex, as portrayed with the vertical arrow in Figure 1.3. This might confuse some people, and it leaves more room for error than the simpler calculation.

- The accrual income doesn't match the change in bank account balance any more, so Simone might be less sure of how much she can take out of the bank for her next holiday. The accrual income and cash income can always be reconciled, however. We'll see how to do this in the next section.

The more we try to accomplish with it, the more complex accrual accounting becomes.

- Accrual accounting is a bit of a "slippery slope." Once you start trying to add and subtract things in calculating income, where do you stop? For example, should there be some deduction for the cost of Simone's time in making all the jewellery? The accrual income calculation seems to imply that her time was free, yet she would probably not agree with that. (Accounting for the value of the owner's time in a small business like Simone's would make economic sense but is generally not done because it is not based on transactions, is hard to measure, and is not allowable in Canadian income tax calculations.) What about the costs of using the room in her basement for her studio and her car for deliveries? Should some calculation of such costs be made, even though it would be hard to be exact about them? What about income tax? If she has to pay income tax on what she earns from her business, should that tax also be deducted as a business expense? Or is it a personal expense that does not belong in the business's financial statements?

Let's not get mired in such complexities! For now, just remember that accrual accounting tries to provide a more thorough measurement of financial performance and other aspects of an enterprise than simple cash-based accounting. In order to do so, it incorporates more complex ideas, as well as estimates and judgments. Much of your task is to understand the complexities, estimates, and judgments so that you will be able to understand the resulting financial statements and what they say about the enterprise.

Let's look at Simone's business again. Suppose 2000 was *not* her first year in business. That means she may have had uncollected sales, unused goods on hand, and unpaid bills at the end of 1999 (beginning of 2000). Would those make any difference to the cash income calculation for 2000? No, they wouldn't—they don't involve any change in cash receipts or payments during the year. Would they make any difference to the accrual income calculation for 2000? Yes, they would. Let's see how.

To keep the example uncluttered, let's use exactly the same numbers again, but add three new items as at the end of 1999: uncollected sales of $240; unused goods costing $230, and unpaid bills of $50. Let's call this "Simone revised." What effect do these have on the accrual income calculation?

Some of the $4,350 cash received in 2000 was not for that year's activity, but rather was collecting $240 revenue that was part of the accrual income calculation in the previous year, 1999. That amount has to be subtracted from $4,350 in the 2000 accrual income calculation because it was already in 1999's accrual income and shouldn't be counted twice.

The unused goods costing $230 at the end of 1999 have to be added to the expense calculation for 2000, because they were there at the beginning of 2000 and so got used up during the year.

The unpaid bills totalling $50 at the end of 1999 were included in the cash payments in 2000 and so counted in the 2000 expenses above even though they had already been included in the 1999 expenses. So they are deducted from the 2000 expenses because they don't belong in 2000.

You may have wondered what would be the effect if some amounts left over from 1999 were still left over at the end of 2000. An amount owing by a customer in 1999 might still be owed. Well, these 1999 amounts must still be adjusted for as indicated above, because they were in the 1999 calculation and if not taken out of the 2000 calculation, would be included twice.

Using the information above, here's Simone's accrual income *if 2000 was not her first year*:

1-2

Exhibit

Simone's Jewellery Business Revised Calculation of Accrual Income for 2000	
Revenue ($4,350 collected, minus $240 from 1999, plus $310 still to be received)	$4,420
Expenses ($1,670 paid, minus $50 from 1999, plus $230 unused brought forward from 1999, minus $280 unused taken forward to 2001, plus $85 unpaid at the end of 2000, plus $120 estimated amortization for 2000)	1,775
Accrual income based on the information provided	**$2,645**

Accrual income is affected by adjustments at both the beginning and end of the year.

Cash income is still $2,680, unaffected by the new information. But accrual income is changed, *as it always is*, by noncash items existing *both* at the beginning and end of the year.

OW'S YOUR UNDERSTANDING?

Here are two questions you should be able to answer, based on what you have just read. If you can't answer them, it would be best to reread the material.

1. Your cousin, a medical student, says, "In our course on managing a medical practice, we were told that our financial reports will use accrual accounting. What does that mean?"

2. Fred started his delivery business a few years ago. This year, he collected $47,000 from his customers and paid $21,000 in expenses. At the beginning of this year, his customers owed $3,500, and he owed his suppliers $700. At the end of this year, his customers owe him $3,200; he owes his suppliers $1,450; and his truck amortization (depreciation) for the year was $4,600. Using just this information, what is this year's cash income? What is this year's accrual income? (You should get cash income $26,000 ($47,000 cash receipts minus $21,000 cash payments) and accrual income $20,350 (revenue of $47,000 − $3,500 + $3,200 = $46,700; expenses of $21,000 − $700 + $1,450 + $4,600 = $26,350; income = $46,700 − $26,350 = $20,350).)

1.9   INTRODUCTORY EXAMPLES OF ACCOUNTING ANALYSIS: RECONCILIATION AND CHANGE EFFECTS

Analysis is one of accountants' most important skills. Doing it, or at least understanding it, is central to decision-making. This book often focuses on analysis, because it is so important to accountants and users alike, and because it is generally useful, beyond any single course. In this section, two kinds of analysis will be introduced: reconciliation and what we will call change effects analysis or "what if" analysis.

Reconciliation

Reconciliation is a very useful technique in general because if you can't make two numbers reconcile when they should, that may mean there are errors in one or both of them. This idea is used in business in many ways. Here are three examples.

1. *Reconciliation of cash and accrual income.* In the previous section, when 2000 is designated as her first year in business, we calculated Simone's cash and accrual income. Here's a way to reconcile the two numbers (accountants often designate subtraction by putting brackets around the number, as in (205) below):

Cash income (day-to-day cash receipts minus payments)	$2,680
Add revenue not yet received in cash	310
Add back cost of goods paid for, but not yet sold	280
Deduct expenses not paid in cash in 2000 ($85 + $120)	(205)
Equals accrual income for her first year in business	$3,065

Accrual income and cash income can always be reconciled.

We should have more confidence in both cash and accrual income because we see that they do connect in a logical way. (Below, we'll also do a reconciliation for the second, "Simone revised" example.)

Your bank account record and the bank's record often differ.

2. *Bank reconciliation.* Here, the idea is to figure out what the bank thinks you have in your account, and what you think you have, and identify any differences. The differences usually arise because the bank has not yet deducted all the cheques you have written, since it takes time for them to work through the system, but there may be other reasons, some of which are errors by you or the bank.

Reconciliation is a method of figuring out the ways the two records may differ.

Suppose you have kept careful track of your bank deposits, cheques, and cash withdrawals from the bank machine, and your record shows that you have $534 in the bank. You get a statement from the bank showing that you have $613. Are both records right? Reconciliation will tell you. Let's get some more data. You check your cheques and withdrawals off against the bank statement and determine that two cheques are still "outstanding" (not deducted by the bank yet), one for $43 and one for $28. There are no outstanding deposits: the bank has credited you with all the deposits your own record shows. You also see on the statement that the bank has charged you $7 for some bank charges you didn't know about. And you discover that the bank has deducted someone else's cheque for $55 from your account. Finally, there is a deposit for $70 you can't remember making. From this information you can do a bank account reconciliation:

1-3

Exhibit

Bank's records		Your records	
Balance according to the bank	$613	Balance in your record	$534
Add back error made by bank	55	Deduct bank charges not recorded	(7)
Deduct cheques still outstanding	(71)	Add deposit not recorded	70
Revised balance according to bank	$597	Revised balance in your records	$597

Now you know exactly why the two amounts differ, and you can make sure that errors in both records are corrected. You also know that you can't spend the whole amount the bank's statement shows because you have written some cheques that the bank has not deducted yet, but will.

Reconciliation provides information for corrective action.

3. *Credit card reconciliation.* The idea is exactly the same as for the bank reconciliation. Suppose your Spendthrift Card statement's balance is $492 owing, and you have credit card slips totalling $688. Is the $492 correct? You take your pile of credit card slips, check them off the statement you got from Spendthrift Card, and identify the differences. You find out that you have $302 of slips whose charges have not yet appeared on the statement and that the statement includes $106 in charges for which you don't have slips.

The two balances reconcile: $492 + $302 − $106 = $688. So now you know what to check into further. You can ask the card company for evidence about the $106, or maybe look around for slips you forgot to file. You can expect the card company to bill you for the other $302 next month, which helps you predict your cash needs next month.

OR YOUR INTEREST

Use common sense when solving accounting problems.

Reconciling your bank and credit card accounts is an important procedure you should be doing to help control your financial affairs. You may feel these examples are routine, hardly worth the space they take, just common sense, but much of accounting is just common-sense techniques like these reconciliation examples. You may find you are already using accounting techniques without having labelled them as accounting! As you work through the book, use your common sense—it will often help you see how to handle problems that at first glance seem complicated.

Change Effects Analysis ("What If" Analysis)

This type of analysis depends on some accounting knowledge and a lot of common sense. Here is a taste of it. The central idea is to focus just on what changes or differs between two situations, thereby simplifying the analysis by leaving out everything that doesn't change. It is a form of marginal analysis that you may have seen used in economics.

To simplify the comparison of alternatives, focus on what differs between them.

1. *Comparison of cash versus accrual accounting.* Above, we did a reconciliation of Simone's cash and accrual accounting incomes for just the first example, where 2000 was her first year in business. Here's another way to think about that, which works equally well for both examples of Simone's business.

(Here's where accounting knowledge comes in: we know that some items are positive in their general effect on accrual income and some are negative. Those are noted below.)

1-4

Exhibit

	Simone		Simone revised	
Cash income		$2,680		$2,680
Changes over the year in:				
Uncollected revenue (positive)	($310 – $0)	310	($310 – $240)	70
Unused goods (positive)	($280 – $0)	280	($280 – $230)	50
Unpaid bills (negative)	($(85) – $0)	(85)	($(85) – $(50))	(35)
Amortization (negative)	($(120) – $0)	(120)	($(120) – $0)	(120)
Accrual income		$3,065		$2,645

This is another way to look at the reconciliation analysis above. It's also useful in answering "what if" questions, such as "What would be the effect on Simone's income if she used accrual accounting instead of cash basis accounting?" (You'll see this sort of analysis later, especially when we study the cash flow statement in Chapter 4.)

2. *Net-of-tax analysis.* Here's another example of "what if" analysis, here incorporating that factor we all love to hate: income tax. Suppose Kamble Manufacturing Inc. has annual revenue of $11,310,200 and expenses of $9,774,800. Its income tax rate is 40%. The president of the company wants to know, "What would be the effect on net income (after tax) if we revised our selling prices, which increased revenue by $230,000 per year?"

Well, we can laboriously figure out the net income now and the net income then and answer the president's question. Let's do that. For the present, if we subtract $9,774,800 expenses from $11,310,200 revenue, we get income before tax of $1,535,400. Subtracting 40% of that for income tax ($614,160) leaves present net income of $921,240. If the revenue goes up by $230,000, that will take it to $11,540,200. Deducting the expenses gets revised income before tax of $1,765,400. Deducting 40% income tax ($706,160) leaves revised net income of $1,059,240. Finally, deducting the present net income of $921,240 from $1,059,240 gives an increase of $138,000. Whew! We've answered the president's question, but worn out our pencil, and there were lots of opportunities for calculation errors.

Net-of-tax analysis focuses on what *changes* and just applies the tax to that. It then goes a bit further and notes that what we are usually interested in is what we have left after tax. If we have $100 and it is taxed at 40%, we pay $40 and are left with $60. What we are left with is $100 times (1 minus the 40% tax rate). We can apply this to the president's question. As soon as the president stops for breath, we can say, "The effect on income is $230,000 × (1 – 0.4) = $138,000." Pretty impressive, there is no worn-out pencil, little chance of calculation error, and there may be a raise for being so quick off the mark. We'll see net-of-tax analysis in various forms as the book proceeds. (This example was a simple one, which assumed that nothing else changed. For example, we assumed that to get the increased revenue the president expected, the company didn't have to spend more on advertising to persuade customers to pay higher prices.)

HOW'S YOUR UNDERSTANDING?

Here are three questions you should be able to answer, based on what you have just read. If you can't answer them, it would be best to reread the material:

1. Jeanette's accounting records show that she has $32,412 in her business bank account at June 30. The bank statement dated June 30 shows a balance of $41,985. What sorts of things might account for the difference?

2. Jeanette received a credit card statement asking her to pay $2,888. She had an envelope containing credit card slips totalling $3,226. When she checked the slips off against the statement, there were was $594 worth of slips totalling $594 left that had not yet been billed by the credit card company. She also discovered that the company had billed her for a purchase made by someone else. How much was that purchase? How much should she pay the credit card company? (The other person's purchase was $256 ($2,888 + $594 − $3,226) and she should pay $2,632 ($2,888 − $256 not hers).)

3. North Country Resorts Ltd., which pays income tax at a rate of 35%, is thinking of increasing its mosquito-control expenses by $48,300. What will that do to the company's net income? (It will decrease net income by $48,300 × (1 − 0.35) = $31,395. Note that to answer this, we don't need to know present income, revenue, mosquito-control expenses or anything else. They don't change so don't affect the answer.)

1.10 TERMS TO BE SURE YOU UNDERSTAND

The following important terms were used in this chapter. Make sure you know what they mean *in financial accounting*. If any are unclear to you, check the chapter again or refer to the Glossary of Terms at the back of the book. Most will be used many times as the book proceeds, so your understanding of them will deepen.

Accountant(s)	Credit transaction(s)	Managers
Accounting	Creditor(s)	Marginal analysis
Accounting research	Depreciation	Net income
Accrual accounting	e-commerce	Net-of-tax analysis
Accrual income	Exchange	Notes
Adjustment(s)	Expense(s)	Objectivity
Amortization	External auditor(s)	Owner(s)
Analysis	Financial accounting	Preparer(s)
Auditor(s)	Financial performance	Public accounting firms
Bookkeeping	Financial position	Reconciliation
Books	Financial statements	Revenue(s)
Cash income	Historical cost	Shareholders
Cash transaction(s)	Independence	Stock market
Change effects analysis	Information systems	Transaction(s)
Corporation	Internal auditor(s)	User(s)
Cost–benefit	Management accounting	"What if" analysis

1.11 CONTINUING DEMONSTRATION CASE

INSTALLMENT I   Toward the end of each of the chapters in this book is an installment of the "Continuing Demonstration Case." The case describes the founding and initial growth of wholesale distribution company Mato Inc. and develops as the chapters' topics develop. Each installment presents additional data and then shows the results of using that data. The main purpose is to illustrate the technical side of the chapter's topics, so that you can use it to reinforce your learning. Make whatever use of the case is helpful to you, but remember to think about the data provided each time and sketch out what you would do with it before you look at the suggested results. If you look at the results before thinking about them, the case will be less helpful to you.

This first installment provides background information about the two people who run Mato Inc. The founding of the company will be dealt with in Installment 2.

Data for Installment I

"Hi, Tomas, this is Mavis. Just calling to thank you for attending my grandfather's funeral last week. I appreciate the support. Gramps was a great person and always encouraged me to make my mark in the world. Even now he's encouraging me, because in his will he left me some money that he said was to help start my own business. Maybe in a while we could get together and talk about that."

Mavis Janer and Tomas Brot have been friends for several years, ever since their days studying business together at the university. They have often talked about going into business for themselves. Mavis majored in marketing and, since graduation, has worked for a national retailer, moving up the ladder to become a department head in one of the retailer's local stores. While she likes the company and seems to be doing well, she would really prefer to be on her own, making decisions and taking risks. She is full of ideas that cannot be implemented at her level in the retailing company and is afraid that if she stays there too long she will lose her entrepreneurial zeal.

Tomas majored in finance and has worked as a commercial loans officer for a bank since graduating. As he puts it, "After I'd seen a hundred business plans from people wanting to borrow money, I was sure I could put together a better plan for myself, if only I had the opportunity. The local economy hasn't been terribly encouraging, but I have seen lots of good ideas and know there's room for mine to succeed too."

With the catalyst of Mavis's inheritance, and being a careful pair, the two decided to get together and get started on a business plan by writing down (a) the objectives they would have for any business they might operate together, such as making money, and (b) the risks, constraints, and worries they'd want to avoid or minimize, such as losing their own money. Tomas was more interested in list (b) than Mavis was: he already saw himself playing the role of keeping her entrepreneurial enthusiasm "within bounds," as he called it. Their two lists are given below. Before looking at them, jot down some of the things you think they might have listed.

Results for Installment I

Below are the lists summarizing what Mavis and Tomas agreed on. The lists will help determine the context within which the accounting for their eventual business will operate and the uses to which the business's financial statements will be put. Financial statements and the accounting system behind them must fit the needs of the company, its owners, its managers, and other interested parties.

a. Objectives

- Be a source of personal pride and satisfaction.

- Be able to continue as an independent business indefinitely.

- Be a business both can contribute to, so both will want to be fully involved.

- Be a challenge to their skills and even be fun to be involved in.

- Provide enough cash income to support both Mavis and Tomas (moderate support now, but greater support in the future, when both expect to have families).

- Grow in value so that it will be a future source of wealth for financing a desired comfortable lifestyle and eventually selling out at retirement.

- Be a useful learning experience that will help them restart their careers if it does not work out.

b. Risks and constraints

- Disagreements or problems that will strain their friendship or make it difficult for them to continue working together in the business.

- Catastrophic financial loss (they don't want to lose what they will invest, but they especially don't want to lose even more than that).

- Environmental degradation related to the business or its products.

- A weak start by being undercapitalized (having too little money invested to give the business a good chance to succeed—a problem Tomas had often seen in his banking work).

- Loss of control because of having to raise significantly more capital than they can find themselves.

- Excessive initial business growth that may be hard to handle.

- Excessive time demands that will damage their family lives and other life quality factors.

- Physically difficult or dangerous products.

- Distant physical locations, which will mean frequent, long commutes.

- Unethical products or services (they did not define what they meant, but thought they would know something was unethical when they saw it).

(1.12) HOMEWORK AND DISCUSSION TO DEVELOP UNDERSTANDING

At the beginning of each homework section, some homework problems are marked with an asterisk (*). For each of these, there is an informal solution outline at the end of the book. These outlines are intended to facilitate self-study and additional practice: don't look at the solution for any of these without giving the problem a serious try first, because once you have seen the solution it always looks easier than it is. Please note that *a problem can have several solutions*—it is possible for your answer to differ in some details from the solution outline provided and still be a good answer, especially if you have made valid, alternative assumptions or happen to know a lot about the particular situation in the problem.

PROBLEM 1.1*
Review of some basic ideas

Answer the following questions:

1. What is the difference between an accountant and an auditor?
2. What is the difference between accrual income and cash income?
3. Are users of financial accounting information all the same in their information needs? Why or why not?

PROBLEM 1.2*
Principles of performance evaluation

Suppose you have the job of designing a general system for measuring and evaluating the performance of managers on behalf of an enterprise's owners. List the principles (characteristics) that you think such a system would need in order to be acceptable to both the owners and the managers. Which principles would you expect the owners and managers to agree on fairly easily, and which would you expect to be more controversial?

PROBLEM 1.3*
Identify transactions

Gould Inc. experienced the following events. For each, say whether or not it is an accounting transaction and why, or why not.

a. A painter repainted the reception lobby bright blue.
b. A customer, who had owed Gould money for several years, finally paid, to everyone's surprise.
c. The president decided that the company's main factory would be reorganized next month.
d. The company received shop supplies it had ordered earlier.
e. The company signed a new 5-year lease on its Windsor warehouse.
f. The company sold some land, for which it would receive 10 annual payments starting next year.
g. The company acquired a new truck for cash plus the trade-in of an old truck.
h. An employee was discovered to have stolen a large amount of cash.
i. The company received a bill from the supplier for the shop supplies in item (d).
j. The company was sued for a large amount by a customer who fell down in the parking lot.

PROBLEM 1.4*
Cash balance and accrual accounting income

Calculate (1) the cash in bank as at the end of 2001 and (2) the 2001 accrual accounting income for Dawn's Diving Trips, according to the following information:

Cash in bank as at the end of 2000	$12,430
Owing from customers as at the end of 2000 (collected in 2001)	1,000
Cash collected from customers during 2001 for 2001 trips	68,990
Owing from customers as at the end of 2001 (collected in 2002)	850
Payable to suppliers as at the end of 2000 (paid in 2001)	1,480
Cash paid to suppliers during 2001 for 2001 expenses	36,910
Payable to suppliers as at the end of 2001 (paid in 2002)	2,650
Amortization on diving equipment during 2001	3,740
Cash used by Dawn for personal purposes during 2001	28,000

PROBLEM 1.5*
Bank reconciliation

Wayne has been facing some cash flow problems; specifically, he has been having trouble keeping his bank account straight. He went to the bank to find out his balance and was told that it was $365 as of September 15. As far as he could remember, he had made a deposit of $73 that had not yet been credited by the bank and had written cheques of $145, $37, $86, and $92 that had not yet been deducted from his account by the bank.

At the same time a good, but impatient, friend is demanding repayment of a loan of $70. Does Wayne have enough money in his bank account to repay it?

PROBLEM 1.6*
Reconciliation of cash income and accrual income

Turku Services Company had cash income for its first year in business of $67,450 and accrual income of $53,270. Show how the two amounts reconcile using the following information:

a. Uncollected revenue at the end of the year was $18,730.
b. Unpaid bills for expenses at the end of the year totalled $24,880.
c. Unsold supplies on hand at the end of the year totalled $3,410.
d. Expenses for the next year, paid already, totalled $2,300.
e. Amortization on the company's equipment was $13,740 for the year.

PROBLEM 1.7*
Change effects and net-of-tax analysis

Mountain Crest Enterprises Inc. has revenue this year of $5,645,231, expenses other than income tax of $4,889,811, and an income tax rate of 30%. The president is considering a new marketing plan that is expected to add $342,500 to expenses and $645,000 to revenue.

1. Calculate the plan's expected effect on net income.
2. Show that your answer to question 1 is correct by (a) calculating the expected total revenue, total expenses other than income tax, income before tax, income tax expense, and net income, and (b) subtracting the present net income from the expected net income to show that the result is your answer in question 1.

PROBLEM 1.8*
Effects of more items on Simone's cash and accrual incomes

Suppose the following were discovered about Simone's business (section 1.8). For *each* item, show the dollar effect (if any) and the direction (up or down) that correcting the item would have on (i) Simone's cash income for her *first year in business* and (ii) Simone's accrual income for that year. Explain each of your answers briefly.

a. It was discovered that another $100 of unsold goods were on hand at the end of 2000.
b. It turned out that Simone had paid $45 more in expenses in 2000 than she thought.
c. Amortization should have been $135 for 2000, not $120.
d. Simone decided that one customer, owing $30, would never pay.
e. Included in the cash receipts was a $75 customer deposit on a future sale.

PROBLEM 1.9*
Identify accounting transactions

The following things happened to Bartlett Inc. last month. Decide if each is an accounting transaction and explain briefly why it is or isn't.

a. A customer ordered $6,000 of products, to be shipped next month.
b. Another customer paid $528 for some marketing advice from the company.
c. Bartlett's share price went up by $0.50. As there are 100,000 shares outstanding, this was a value increase of $50,000.
d. Bartlett ran an ad on TV, and promised to pay the TV station the $2,000 cost next month.
e. One of the company's employees worked overtime earning $120 that would be paid next pay period.
f. The company paid a teenager $50 to compensate for a ripped shirt suffered when the teenager tried to run away after being accused of shoplifting.
g. Bartlett received a shipment of new goods for sale, paying $1,000 cash and agreeing to pay the other $12,250 in a few days.
h. Bartlett paid the other $12,250.
i. The company made a donation to a political party of $500. (The donation turned out later to have been against the election law, to the company's embarrassment.)
j. Grand Bank made the company a $20,000 short-term loan.

PROBLEM 1.10*
Credit card bills reconciliation

Dave was in an awful tangle over his Vista credit card. He had just received a bill from Vista that was much larger than he'd expected and thought the company must have made a mistake. After he calmed down, he got out all his credit card slips and other documents. This is what he found:

Amount owing according to Vista, $1,125.

Total unpaid credit card slips in Dave's pile, $904.

Two slips that, as far as Dave could tell, Vista had not yet billed him for, $112.

A cash advance that Dave had taken against the card but had forgotten about, $200.

One charge on the Vista bill that Dave did not have a slip for and did not remember, $148.

Does Dave have it all sorted out now? What do you think would be the right amount to pay Vista?

PROBLEM 1.11
What are various people's interests in financial accounting?

Describe briefly what each of the following people would likely want to learn from the financial statements of BrandX Inc., and how each might be affected if the statements showed a good or bad financial performance or financial position.

    a. The president of the company.
    b. The company's chief accountant.
    c. The chairperson of the company's board of directors (the board evaluates the president's performance on behalf of the shareholders).
    d. The partner of auditing firm Dimbleby & Co., for whom BrandX Inc. is a client.
    e. The local manager of tax collections for Revenue Canada.
    f. John Flatstone, who owns 100 shares of BrandX Inc.
    g. Mildred Evans, who is thinking of buying some shares of the company.
    h. The local manager of Big Bank, which has made a large loan to BrandX Inc.

PROBLEM 1.12
Should management be able to choose accounting methods?

Do you think professors should have the right to use their own judgment in determining course grades, or should those grades be based on objectively set exams administered by someone other than professors? Why? Do you think companies' management should have the right to choose the accounting policies and methods by which their performance is measured? Why? How do these two cases differ, if at all?

PROBLEM 1.13
Resentment of auditor by the person audited

Student radio station CBBS is owned by the student association of the university. The student treasurer of the club that operates the station prepares an annual financial report for the executive committee of the association, and that report is audited. A local accounting firm does the audit for a minimal fee, in order to help the students out. The club treasurer was heard complaining a little the other day about the audit, first, because having one seemed to imply that the treasurer was not trusted and, second, because the audit fee had to be paid by the club, which was always short of money.

    The auditor thus has to deal with some resentment by the treasurer. Make a list of the difficulties the auditor might have because of this resentment, and any other difficulties you think might face such an auditor. (These problems are likely to be encountered by any auditor who is responsible for verifying financial statements prepared by management for use by owners and creditors.)

PROBLEM 1.14
Calculate and reconcile cash and accrual income

Leslie has a part-time business, Quick Crack-Fix, repairing small cracks and stars in car windshields using a special polymer filler that makes the damage almost invisible and stops the cracks from spreading. The repair takes only a few minutes using equipment and supplies stored in the trunk of Leslie's car. The main customers are used car lots, car rental companies, service stations, and insurance companies, but some business is done with individual customers in the driveways of their homes.

    For the current year, Leslie's business records show the following:

Collections from customers during the year	$24,354
Payments to suppliers during the year	5,431
Royalty payments to owner of Crack-Fix trademark during the year	2,435
Money taken out of the business by Leslie during the year	14,000
Amortization on business equipment and car for the year	3,200
Amounts owing by customers at the end of the previous year	1,320
Amounts owing by customers at the end of the current year	890
Amounts owing to suppliers at the end of the previous year	436
Amounts owing to suppliers at the end of the current year	638
Supplies on hand at the end of the previous year	0
Cost of supplies on hand at the end of the current year	345

Leslie's business bank account showed a balance of $1,332 at the end of the previous year.

1. Calculate the business's cash income for the current year, explaining whether you have treated the money Leslie took out of the business as a business expense (deducting it in calculating cash income for the business) or a personal withdrawal (not deducting it in calculating cash income for the business).

2. Calculate the bank account balance at the end of the current year, using your answer from part 1.

3. Calculate the business's accrual income for the current year.

4. Reconcile your answers to parts 1 and 3.

PROBLEM 1.15
Calculate accrual income and change in cash

"I just don't understand it!" Dwight Benat had received his accountant's calculation of Dwight's business income, showing an accrual income for his first year in business of $45,290. "If I made so much money, why don't I have that much in the bank? My bank account shows only $7,540 on hand!"

Dwight operates Benat Supply, which provides stationery and office supplies to business customers. He has no store, just a small rented warehouse, and only one employee. Here are the data he and his accountant used. Explain clearly to Dwight (1) how the accountant calculated the $45,290 income and (2) why there is only $7,540 on hand.

Collected from customers during the year	$143,710
Still owing from customers at the end of the year (collected next year)	15,220
Paid for products to resell and for other expenses, including wages, during the year	128,670
Owing for products and other expenses at the end of the year (paid next year)	9,040
Cost of unsold products on hand at the end of the year (all sold next year)	26,070
Amortization (depreciation) on equipment during the year	2,000
Personal withdrawals by Dwight during the year	7,500

PROBLEM 1.16
Identify whether or not events are accounting transactions

The following events happened at the Guzzle Beer Corporation. For each, indicate whether or not it is an accounting transaction for Guzzle Beer Corp. and state, in five or ten words, why.

a. A large tank containing beer mixture broke and all of the mixture spilled.
b. A major shareholder sold 50,000 shares on the stock exchange.
c. The corporation paid $60,000,000 for a Mexican brewery.
d. An invoice for next week's TV advertising arrived.
e. A pub took delivery of its weekly shipment of Guzzle Beer.

PROBLEM 1.17
Identify transactions

The following events took place on February 1, 2001. For each event, state what part(s) of the event are accounting transaction(s), and why.

a. Smith Ltd. purchased supplies to be used immediately. The purchase price of the supplies was $5,000. Only $2,000 was paid in cash on delivery. The balance is due in 30 days.
b. The company decided to rent a service vehicle for $4,800 per year. A rental contract was signed February 1, 2001, to take effect March 1, 2001. Smith Ltd. paid $400 cash to the rental company on February 1, 2001, which represented the rent for March 2001.
c. Some of Smith's repairmen were not busy on February 1. The manager had them paint the inside of a storage room. Assume the repairmen's salaries of $300 were paid in cash at the end of the day.
d. A shareholder sold her car to the company. The vehicle cost her $15,000 two years ago. An equivalent used vehicle would have been worth about $8,000 on February 1, 2001. No cash changed hands, but the shareholder expects the company to pay her for the car eventually.
e. An invoice for $5,000 was received relating to repairs and maintenance work done in December 2000. The company's year-end is December 31. This expense was not recorded in the 2000 financial statements.

PROBLEM 1.18
Identify transactions

Southward Stores Ltd. is a general merchandise retailer operating in the suburbs. During a recent month, the events listed below happened. For each event, decide if all, or part of it, is an accounting transaction and state briefly why or why not.

a. Southward borrowed $500,000 from the Great Pacific Bank (Canada). Payment is due in three years, but the loan can be called on ten days' notice if Southward fails to make any of the monthly interest payments, which begin next month.
b. Southward ordered goods for resale costing $300,000, to be delivered in 40 days, and sent a deposit of $10,000 with the order.
c. Southward renewed its lease on the store premises, signing an agreement that provides for a monthly rent increase from $21,000 to $23,000 beginning in three months.
d. Southward was charged with unfair pricing of its main line of merchandise. News of this sent the company's shares (listed on a stock exchange) down in price from $10 to $8.50 each. The company has 1,000,000 shares outstanding, all publicly traded.
e. The company paid a dividend of $0.50 per share, on each of its 1,000,000 issued shares. This news sent the company's shares up by $0.40 each on the stock exchange.

PROBLEM 1.19
Bank reconciliation

Reconcile Henry's month-end bank account balance and indicate what corrections you would make to Henry's records based on your analysis.

Month-end bank balance according to the bank's statement, $8,791.

Month-end bank balance according to Henry's records, $7,371.

Outstanding cheques (not processed by the bank yet), $1,877.

Outstanding deposit (not processed by the bank yet), $250.

Bank charges Henry had not known about, $43.

Someone else's cheque put through Henry's account by the bank, $185.

Interest on the bank balance credited to by the bank but not known to Henry, $21.

PROBLEM 1.20
Reconcile a credit card statement to the cardholder's records

Sue has just received her monthly credit card statement from MonsterCard. It says she owes $2,320. She is horrified, not having anticipated such a large amount, though she does have an envelope full of credit card slips that total a net of $1,615 (adding up all the charges and deducting some credits for goods returned to stores). Using the following information, reconcile the statement to Sue's envelope of slips and determine how much you think Sue should pay MonsterCard this month.

a. Three of Sue's slips, totalling $198, have not yet been included in the MonsterCard statement because she charged the amounts after the statement date.
b. One of the items on the statement for $555 was for a major car repair that Sue remembers having done, though she can't find the credit card slip.
c. MonsterCard charged Sue $35 to renew the card for another year and added that amount to her other charges for the month.
d. One of the items on the statement was for a $175 meal in a city Sue had never even been to.
e. Sue had returned an item costing $138 to Retail Emporium Co. three months ago, but had not yet been credited for the return on MonsterCard's statement.

PROBLEM 1.21
Effects and net-of-tax analysis

Grandiloquent Gestures Inc. is a major supplier of costumes and party supplies and will plan any affair for a customer, such as a romantic evening for popping the question, or a celebration of many years of marriage, or a congratulations party for finding employment. The company's income tax rate is 35%. The company is considering some changes in its operations. Calculate separately the effect on the company's net income of each of the following proposals.

a. The company might spend more on advertising adding $140,000 to its advertising expenses.
b. The company might raise some selling prices adding $52,000 to revenue.
c. The company might fire the chief accountant, and use a cheap computer program instead. The chief accountant is paid $75,000 per year, and the cheap computer program will cost $4,450 a year.

d.   If the company fires the chief accountant, it will incur additional losses due to shoplifting and employee theft of $15,000 per year.

e.   The company might make a $75 donation to the Poor Accountants' League.

PROBLEM 1.22
Effects and net-of-tax analysis

Authors Agency Inc. manages many best-selling authors in their relations with publishers, movie companies, TV producers, and so on. In the current year, its revenues total $15,452,200 and its expenses (not including 40% income tax) total $13,222,500. The company is negotiating with famous author Stephen Queen to take on Queen's account. This is a big deal: if Authors Agency manages Queen's account, its revenues will increase by $5,300,000 and its expenses (Queen likes limos and 5-star hotels) will increase by $4,800,000.

What is Authors Agency's net income for the current year?

What would the company's net income be if it took Queen's account on?

Show that your answer to part 2 is right. If you did part 2 the long way, do it the short way here. If you did it the short way, do it the long way here.

PROBLEM 1.23
Effects and net-of-tax analysis

Economy Chicken Inc. sells poultry to discount grocery stores, restaurants, the Army, and other customers. The company's income statement for 2000 follows:

Economy Chicken Inc. Income Statement for the Year 2000		
Revenues		$67,455,892
Expenses:		
Cost of poultry sold	$32,555,678	
Operating, selling, and administrative expenses	21,223,590	
Interest and other financial expenses	3,210,443	
Amortization	6,789,420	63,779,131
Income before income tax		$ 3,676,761
Income tax expense		1,323,634
Net income for the year		$ 2,353,127

The Army wants to renegotiate its contract with Economy Chicken, and proposes that if the company spends $2,500,000 per year more on quality control, the Army will buy $2,100,000 more in chicken from the company. If the company does not agree to this, the Army will likely take its considerable business elsewhere. Calculate the company's revised net income if the Army's proposal is accepted.

PROBLEM 1.24
(CHALLENGING)
Explain the transactional basis of financial accounting

Your boss has just returned from a breakfast meeting of her small business association. The meeting had had an accountant as speaker who explained quite a few things about how accounting worked, but made a comment your boss is unclear about. As best your boss can remember the comment, the accountant said, "Every information system has to start somewhere in getting its data. Accounting starts with business transactions, and as a result financial accounting is really a careful history of the business, not a measure of the business's current value."

Explain the accountant's comment to your boss.

**PROBLEM 1.25
(CHALLENGING)
Why is accrual
accounting valued?**

An executive of an international economic consulting firm recently said, "I find it interesting that as companies, or even countries, grow in sophistication, they tend to move from simple cash-based financial reports to accrual accounting reports." If this observation is valid, why would you suppose this movement to accrual accounting is happening?

**PROBLEM 1.26
(CHALLENGING)
Discuss ethical
problems**

Discuss the example ethical problems given at the end of section 1.4. What ethical issues do you see? What do you think the chief accountant, the auditor, and the president should do?

**PROBLEM 1.27
(CHALLENGING)
More effects of
additional items of
information on
Simone's cash and
accrual incomes**

This problem is like Problem 1.8* but involves items this chapter has not illustrated. Use your common sense to compare the items below to Simone's results in section 1.8 and the answers to Problem 1.8* and, for *each* item, show the dollar effect (if any) and the direction (up or down) that correcting the item would have on (i) Simone's cash income for her first year in business, and (ii) Simone's accrual income for that year. Explain each of your answers briefly.

  a. Simone agreed to give a customer a refund of $110 for faulty jewellery sold in 2000. The refund will be paid in 2001. The jewellery had cost Simone $67 in material, but she will not recover any of that cost because the jewellery has to be thrown away.

  b. One of the amounts Simone paid out in 2000 was $160 for some more equipment. That should not have been recorded as an expense. On the other hand, there should have been amortization of 10% on that equipment, the same as for the other equipment.

  c. Simone decided she should charge her business rent for the basement studio space, but to avoid reducing the business cash, Simone would delay paying the rent to her personal bank account for a few years. She decided the rent for 2000 should be set at $500.

**PROBLEM 1.28
(CHALLENGING)
Factors in compar-
ing companies' per-
formance**

The president of Gobble Gobble Foods Inc., which makes everything from soup to nuts out of turkey meat, is comparing Gobble Gobble's performance to that of Curdled Products Inc., which does much the same using tofu and other bean curds. The president has the following data for Curdled Products, which she saw in the Glower and Flail newspaper yesterday (note that figures inside brackets indicate a loss):

Income for 1995	$1,565,000
Income for 1996	2,432,000
Income for 1997	(985,000)
Income for 1998	123,000
Income for 1999	1,249,000
Income for 2000	2,915,000
Income for first half of 2001	873,000

Without knowing much about accounting except the introductory ideas of this chapter, use your intelligence and experience in comparing things to make a list of the factors you think the president of Gobble Gobble should take into account in comparing her company's performance to that of Curdled.

PROBLEM 1.29 (CHALLENGING) Objectives and risks in investment	Suppose you had a few thousand dollars on hand and were offered a chance to invest in a small local business. What would be the objectives you would like to see such an investment meet? What risks would you want reassurance about before committing your funds? (You can get some hints about this from the Continuing Demonstration Case.)
CASE 1 Accrual and cash income in measuring performance	Manitoba Wings is an airline services company with a plant near the Winnipeg Airport and service centres in several provinces. It provides meals, napkins and other food-related items, airplane cleaning, interior maintenance, and several other services to various airlines. The company has been fairly successful, though recessions and deregulation of air services have put significant pressure on its operations. When the company began in the late 1970s, it had a relatively weak financial position (mainly because of borrowing to get set up) and its financial performance, while satisfactory, has not enabled it to reduce its debt load very much. It seems that every time the company gets a little ahead, new equipment must be purchased or new product lines developed, and the company finds itself borrowing again.

A recent year provides a good example. The company's accrual income was $188,000 and its cash income was $241,000. (The difference was due to amortization expense of $96,000 and uncollected revenue being $43,000 higher at the end of the year than at the beginning. In the company's financial statements, the phrase "net income for the year" was used to describe the accrual income and "cash generated by operations" described the cash income.) The president had looked forward to using some of the cash to pay down debts, but late in the year the company had to buy new food-handling and -wrapping equipment for $206,000 to meet revised standards announced by its airline customers. Therefore, the company ended up only a few thousand dollars ahead in cash, not enough to make much of a dent in its debts.

The president has a regular half bi-yearly meeting with the company's external auditor to discuss accounting and auditing issues. After the above results were known, the president phoned the auditor and made the following comments: "I thought I'd ask you to think about a few things before our meeting next week. When it comes to our accounting, I think the company has too many masters and too many measures. What I mean is, first that too many people are concerned with what our financial statements say. Why can't we just prepare financial statements that meet my needs as president—why do we have to worry about all the other people outside the company? Sometimes I'm not even sure who all those other people are, since you accountants and auditors often just talk about 'users' without being too clear about what you mean. Also, I'm confused by the existence of both a 'net income' figure and a 'cash generated by operations' figure in our financial statements. Why can't we just have one or the other to measure our performance?"

The president raised issues that will be addressed frequently as this book develops your understanding. But for now, what would you say to the president?

NOTES

1. "Patrick O'Brian," *The Economist* (15 January 2000): 88.
2. Eric Auchard, "IBM Financial Reporting Criticized, Shares Drop," Reuters, 24 November 1999. "Tyco: Aggressive or Out of Line?" *Business Week* (1 November 1999): 160–65. Michael Fleeman, "Opening the Book on the Weird World of Movie Math," *The Edmonton Journal*, 13 September 1999, C4.
3. "Accounting Giant Accused of Conflict of Interest in Audits," *The Edmonton Journal*, 7 January 2000, F3.
4. Robert H. Crandall, "Information Economics and Accounting Theory," *The Accounting Review* (July 1969): 457–66. Thank you for the original ideas used in this section. Since the sixties, much work has been done in the fields of management information systems, accounting information systems, decision analysis, and the Internet to develop accounting and other systems that are properly responsive to decision-making needs.

Preparing and Using Financial Accounting's Reports

2 PART

The four chapters in this group introduce the set of financial statements and the principles and environment that influence, even determine, their nature.

- Chapter 2 introduces the "balance sheet," the reflection of the accounting system's accumulation of information over the life of the enterprise. The history and present nature of the "double-entry" system and its "debits and credits" are covered, as is how to interpret the resulting financial statement. The balance sheet's depiction of the enterprise's legal structure and sources of financing is reviewed.

- Chapter 3 uses the same approach to introducing the income statement, which

is "accrual accounting's" fundamental measure of financial performance, and the statement of retained earnings, which connects the income statement to the balance sheet.

- Chapter 4 introduces the cash flow statement, which is both the fourth regular financial statement and a major example of user-oriented accounting analysis.

- Chapter 5 completes the introduction of the financial statements by dealing with a variety of preparation and use principles and environmental forces (such as auditing, ethics, international agreements, and stock markets) acting on financial accounting.

2 CHAPTER

Measuring and Evaluating Financial Position

2.1   Chapter Overview

Chapter 1 introduced accrual accounting and its transactional base. Now we turn to four chapters that set out financial accounting's *results* and outline the *recordkeeping system* that leads to those results. This chapter focuses on measuring financial position at a particular date. Chapter 3 then looks at measuring financial performance (income) over a period of time, and Chapter 4 at measuring cash flow over that same period. Several additional topics, including auditing and narrative disclosure, are covered in Chapter 5. By the time you complete Chapter 5, you will have a basic understanding of what financial accounting's reports contain, how they are used, and how the supporting accounting system produces them. Later chapters provide a more in-depth examination of these areas.

Chapter 2: Position

Chapter 3: Income

Chapter 4: Cash Flow

Chapter 5: Additional

Later: More Depth

This chapter introduces financial accounting's oldest and most basic report, the **balance sheet**, which measures the enterprise's financial position at a particular date and is the basis for much financial analysis. This statement is sometimes called the **statement of financial position**, because the longer title describes exactly what the statement shows. (This book mostly uses the older, shorter, and more popular title. As in other areas of accounting, be prepared for variation in terminology!) The balance sheet summarizes, at a particular date, the enterprise's **financial position** as accounting measures it, in three categories:

- Resources (cash, products on hand, land, buildings, etc.), called **assets**;

- Obligations (loans owing, debts to suppliers, etc.), called **liabilities**; and

- Owners' interests (what's left after subtracting the obligations from the resources), called **equity**.

The balance sheet accounts measure financial position at a point in time.

The individual items in each of these lists are called accounts, so over the centuries the task of preparing them has been named account*ing*, and the people who do it are account*ants*. All these words come from *count*, which is where accounting began, just counting things and listing them.

The balance sheet portrays the enterprise by arranging its lists of accounts so that the assets sum to the same total as the other two lists, and setting them beside each other, something like this:

2-1

Exhibit

Assets		Liabilities and Equity	
Item a	$$	Item x	$$
Item b	$$	Item y	$$
Etc.	$$	Etc.	$$
Total	T$$	Total	T$$

Because the left total equals the right total, accountants say that they balance. Hence, the name balance sheet. The underlying accounting system maintains this balance by making sure that any changes in one side of the balance sheet are matched by changes in the other side. This requires that each change be recorded twice, so the accounting system is called double entry. The balance sheet turns out to be the accumulation of everything financial accounting has recorded about the enterprise since the day the enterprise began, so it is the fundamental cumulative accounting record and is the anchor to which all the other financial statements are tied.

Double-entry accounting produces a balanced balance sheet, anchoring the financial statements.

To outline what you will learn in this chapter, let's return to Figure 1.1 used at the beginning of Chapter 1:

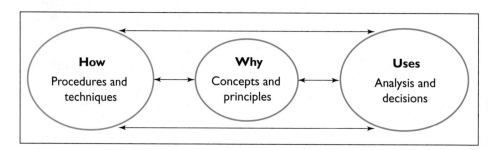

In this chapter, you will learn:

- *Procedures and techniques:* How the double-entry accounting system produces accounts, and how to assemble a balance sheet from those accounts.

- *Concepts and principles:* Why the balance sheet is important, why it is arranged as it is, and some interesting history about where it came from.

- *Analysis and decisions:* Using the balance sheet to understand how an enterprise is put together financially, and using it to do some analysis of the enterprise's financial health.

Following this book's integrative approach, the hows, whys, and uses of financial accounting are woven together into an overall portrayal. This integration is pre-

sent particularly in the first five chapters. Later in-depth chapters focus more on each of the three areas, but every chapter contains some of all three.

Corporations, which are legally incorporated companies such as Air Canada, the Bank of Montreal, Bombardier, General Motors, Microsoft, and thousands of local, national, and international businesses, produce financial statements at least annually. So do many other kinds of organizations, such as the City of Halifax, Foster Parents Plan of Canada, the Government of Canada, and your university's Student Union. (We'll focus initially on businesses, especially corporations, but other kinds of organizations will be included later in the book.) For large corporations, especially public companies (such as the five examples above) whose shares are traded on stock markets, the financial statements are included in a larger document called an annual report. An annual report typically begins with narrative material on the corporation's performance and prospects, moves on to an extensive discussion and analysis by management, and then turns to the financial statements, one of which is the balance sheet.

Because courses may cover topics in different orders, sections 2.8–2.10 can be read ahead of sections 2.4–2.7.

> A public company has an annual report that includes financial statements.

2.2   INTRODUCTION TO THE BALANCE SHEET

The balance sheet is only one of the set of financial statements, each of which is important for particular uses. But as the summary of the double-entry system, the balance sheet is financial accounting' fulcrum. It balances, containing two lists that have the same dollar total and that together describe the enterprise's financial position at a particular date.

> Assets are useful financial resources.

The first list is the enterprise's financial *resources* at that date, as measured by the financial accounting methods you will learn. These resources, called assets, include the enterprise's cash, money customers have promised to pay, goods for sale, land, buildings, equipment, and many other resources that the enterprise has accumulated and can use in the future.

The second list is the *sources*, or financing, of those resources at that date, again as measured by financial accounting methods. These financing sources include existing obligations that will have to be paid in the future, such as loans from the bank, amounts due to be paid to employees and suppliers, mortgages and other long-term borrowings, and many other debts. Some estimates of future payments are included also, even though they may not be legally owed just yet, such as promises to pay employee pensions, and estimated future income taxes based on income already earned but not yet taxed. All these legal obligations and estimates together are called liabilities. The list of sources also include amounts received from owners, which normally involve permanent financing and do not have to be repaid, plus any past accrual incomes that have not been paid out to the owners. Owners can finance an enterprise by contributing money *to* the enterprise, or by *not* taking income *out* of the enterprise, as we will see. The owners' investment is called owners' equity, or just equity. (For corporations, which are owned by shareholders, the term is usually shareholders' equity, while for unincorporated businesses the terms owner's capital or partners' capital is likely used, but all of these terms just mean owners' equity.)

> Liabilities are existing and estimated obligations; equity is the owners' investment.

Because the balance sheet balances, the total amount of **assets** must equal the total of liabilities plus equity. Arithmetically, the balance sheet equation therefore is:

Sum of Assets = Sum of Liabilities + Sum of Equity

Resources list = Sources (financing) list

This equation is fundamental to financial accounting. Accounting procedures are designed to create and maintain this equality at *all* times. For example, if you get $100 by borrowing from the bank, your balance sheet would list the $100 cash you got as a resource and the $100 obligation to repay as a liability. By maintaining this equality, financial accounting ensures that all the financing sources that go with the resources are identified, and vice versa. This balanced pair of lists is one of the main reasons for financial accounting's value as an information system, though, as we will see, keeping the lists always in balance produces some difficulties for accounting too.

Sum of A must = sum of L + sum of E.

The two lists are put side by side, or the first above the second, as in the standard style shown below.

2-2

Exhibit

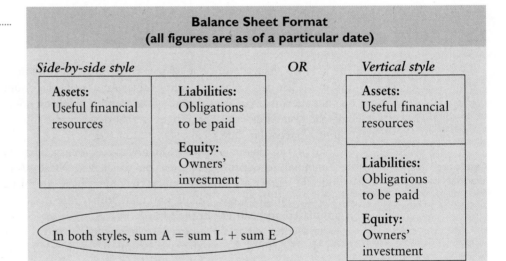

Balance Sheet Format
(all figures are as of a particular date)

Side-by-side style   OR   *Vertical style*

| Assets: Useful financial resources | Liabilities: Obligations to be paid |
| | Equity: Owners' investment |

In both styles, sum A = sum L + sum E

Vertical style:

Assets: Useful financial resources

Liabilities: Obligations to be paid

Equity: Owners' investment

Example Balance Sheet: Sound and Light Corporation

Below is a simple example balance sheet using the side-by-side style to emphasize the equality of the two lists, with assets on the left and liabilities and equity on the right. Explanations of the terms used in the balance sheet follow the example.

Exhibit

Sound and Light Corporation **Balance Sheet as at April 30, 2001** **in Thousands of Dollars**					
Assets			**Liabilities and Equity**		
Current assets:			Current liabilities:		
Cash	$ 50		Owing to the bank	$ 30	
Due from customers	75		Owing to suppliers	73	$103
Unsold products	120	$245	Noncurrent liabilities:		
Noncurrent assets:			Land mortgage owing	72	
Land (cost)	$100		Future income tax estimated	$15	87
Factory (cost)	272		Total Liabilities		$190
Accum. amort.*	(122)	250	Shareholders' equity:		
			Share capital issued	$130	
			Past income retained	175	305
TOTAL		$495	TOTAL		$495

*Accum. amort. is the total amortization on the factory recorded so far (accumulated). It is bracketed because it is negative, as will be explained below.

Let's review some features of this balance sheet:

- The title identifies the enterprise (Sound and Light Corporation), the point in time at which the balance sheet is drawn up (April 30, 2001), and the currency in which amounts are measured (thousands of dollars).

- The balance sheet balances! As of April 30, 2001, total resources of $495 thousand are exactly equalled by the total sources of these resources. It is a summary, so we cannot tell exactly which source produced which resource; for example, the $50 thousand of cash came partly from bank borrowing and partly from other sources, such as past earnings.

- The balance sheet shows several individual accounts, telling us about the company's particular financial structure. For example, the company expects to receive $75 thousand due from customers and owes $73 thousand to its suppliers (it is their customer). The land and factory are mortgaged, with $72 thousand still owing on the mortgage. The company owes $30 thousand to the bank but has chosen not to pay it all back, keeping more than that ($50 thousand) on hand as cash. (These accounts are usually aggregates of many smaller accounts; for example, there is an account for each customer who owes money to Sound and Light.)

- The $495 thousand of assets have been financed by $190 thousand ($103 + $87) of liabilities and $305 thousand of owners' investment.

The balance sheet describes the financial structure at a particular date.

Explanations of the Three Balance Sheet Categories

Assets. These are a mixture of the resources that the company needs to do business, for instance, products to sell, a building to operate from, and the resources that it has accumulated as a result of doing business, including amounts due from customers for past sales. *An asset is a resource, owned or controlled by the enter-*

Resources are assets if they are controlled and expected to bring future benefits.

prise, that is needed or available to do business in the future, and which has value because it is expected to bring benefits as it is used or sold. Sound and Light's assets include cash, amounts due from customers (accounts receivable), unsold products (inventory), land, and the factory. (The "accumulated amortization" will be explained later.)

Other "assets" of Sound and Light might include happy employees and a safe working environment, yet these do not directly appear on its balance sheet. There is a distinction between the assets that accounting recognizes and these other "assets." There are objective, standard measures for, and economic control of, the first group, but not the second group. In the first group, an inventory of machine parts is owned by the enterprise and has a dollar cost that can be verified by anyone. In the second group, a happy employee is, in theory, more productive than an unhappy employee, but it is difficult to measure with any consistency how much more productive a very happy employee is compared with an only mildly happy employee. Moreover, at least in our society, an enterprise does not own its employees! Accounting generally records assets only where there is economic control and where there can be a reasonable level of consistency in measurement techniques and results. This places limits on the scope of the financial statements.

Assets are usually separated into shorter-term ones (current assets) and longer-term ones (noncurrent assets). Current assets are those that are expected to be used, sold, or collected within the next year, and noncurrent assets therefore are expected to have benefits for more than a year into the future. Sound and Light has $245 thousand in current assets and $250 thousand in noncurrent assets.

Liabilities. These are amounts due to creditors, such as to banks and suppliers, or amounts estimated to be due later, such as future pension payments to retired employees, estimated future income taxes, or interest building up on a bank loan. *A liability is a legally existing or estimated debt or obligation of the enterprise to another party, arising from a past transaction and so representing a claim on the assets at the balance sheet date.* Not all liabilities are expected to be paid in cash; some are "paid" by providing goods or services. An example is a deposit received from a customer for goods to be shipped later. The enterprise has the money (an asset) and records a corresponding liability for the deposit, but expects to give the customer the agreed-upon goods to discharge the liability. In the meantime, the customer has a claim on the enterprise, expecting either to get the goods or the cash back if the goods are not supplied. Sound and Light's liabilities include amounts owing to the bank and owing to suppliers (accounts payable), a mortgage on its property, and estimated future income taxes.

Following the same rule as for assets, liabilities generally include only obligations with objective, standard measures. If you are in debt to a friend for $10, it appears on your balance sheet. But, if you are "in debt" to a friend for saving your life, that does not appear on your balance sheet. Requiring that the obligation has arisen from a past transaction means that a promise to pay is a liability if the enterprise has already received the benefit (for example, has received cash from the bank, or goods from a supplier, or hard work from an employee expecting a pension). An expectation to pay later is *not* a liability if the transaction bringing the benefit has not happened (for example, an agreement to borrow before the cash has been received is not a liability, nor is an order to purchase something before the goods have arrived). Because some of these expected or possible future events may result in future payments even if they do not meet the definition of a liability

Accounting's definition of an asset does not include everything that has a future benefit.

Current assets are expected to provide benefits within a year.

Noncurrent assets provide benefits further into the future.

Liabilities arose in the past and represent legal or estimated claims on the assets.

Accounting's definition of liability does not include all possible future payments.

Current liabilities are due within a year; noncurrent liabilities are due further into the future.

and so do not appear in the balance sheet, they are sometimes described in the notes to the financial statements so that the users of the financial statement are aware of them.

Like assets, liabilities are usually separated into shorter-term ones (current liabilities) and longer-term ones (noncurrent liabilities). Current liabilities are those that are due (expected to be paid or otherwise discharged) within the next year, and noncurrent liabilities therefore are due more than a year into the future. Some liabilities, such as many house mortgages, extend for years into the future but are partly paid each year, so the balance sheet would show both a current and a noncurrent portion for them. Sound and Light has $103 thousand in current liabilities and $87 thousand in noncurrent liabilities.

Equity is the owners' interest and equals the assets minus the liabilities.

Equity. This is the owners' interest in the enterprise.

That interest can come from direct contributions the owners have made, or from the accumulation of earnings that the owners have chosen not to withdraw.

The details of the owners' equity section of the balance sheet depend on the legal structure of the enterprise and its ownership arrangements, which will be examined further later in this chapter.

The balance sheet does not distinguish between assets whose sources are liabilities and assets provided by owners. Complex financial events make this impractical, so the assets represent a pool of resources provided by all sources.

The owners' interest can also be considered as a "residual" of the sum of the assets minus the obligations the enterprise has taken on (if $A = L + E$, then the equation can also be written $A - L = E$).

The owners' equity (book value) is not likely to equal the market value of the enterprise.

Because the balance sheet's equity figure equals assets minus liabilities, this residual or net concept of equity is often referred to as the book value of the whole enterprise. Book value is an arithmetically valid idea, as the equation above shows. But it may not tell us very much. For example, if Sound and Light suddenly went out of business, the owners would be unlikely to receive exactly the equity of $305 thousand, because who knows what the assets would fetch if they had to be sold off all at once, and the liabilities perhaps would be settled for something other than the expected future payments used to record them. Similarly, if the owners decided to sell the business, the price they'd get would depend on their and the buyers' views as to the future success of the business, not just on the accumulated assets and liabilities recorded in the balance sheet. Thus, it is very unlikely that the amount would equal the balance sheet equity figure. Owners' equity is based on historical transactions, and does not, except by coincidence, equal the current market value of the whole business. You can see this with many high-technology and Internet companies in recent years: they may have small equity amounts in their balance sheets, but huge stock market values (market capitalization, share price times number of shares outstanding). The stock market may be considering all sorts of "assets" not included by accounting, such as competitive strength or smart employees, and/or expecting good future performance not part of accounting's historical measures.

Share capital is the investment contributed by shareholders directly to the corporation.

Contributions from owners can come in many forms, which we will look into a little later. For a corporation like Sound and Light, the most usual contribution is share capital: people give the corporation money in exchange for shares, which are portions of ownership interest. Sound and Light owners (shareholders) have contributed $130 thousand to the corporation. For example, some owners probably contributed cash to get Sound and Light started, so they would be among the sources of the cash asset. (Many corporations' shares, also called stocks, are traded on stock markets. In such markets, shares are traded between owners. The corporations issuing the shares get money only when they issues the shares to the first owners. Therefore, trades subsequent to the initial share issue are not reflected in the corporation's share capital— these trades are transactions for the owners, but not for the corporation.)

Retained earnings are the investment that owners have made by not withdrawing income.

Past income retained, usually called retained earnings, represents past accrual income not yet given to owners. (The terms earnings, income, and profit are used pretty much interchangeably, but they all refer to accrual income, as described in Chapter 1.) As we'll see in later chapters, earning income means that there will be more assets (such as cash) and/or fewer liabilities, so income is a source of assets. Sound and Light has $175 thousand in retained earnings, which means it has $175 thousand more in assets than it would have had if those earnings had all been paid out. The owners could have withdrawn cash or other assets from the company (for instance, by declaring themselves a dividend, which is a payment of some of the retained earnings to the owners), but they have chosen instead to leave the assets in the corporation. Thus, those assets are resources of the corporation and retained earnings are their source. The corporation can use the assets to earn more income in the future.

Negative equity is a sign of serious trouble.

Since $E = A - L$, it is arithmetically possible, and unfortunately seen sometimes in real enterprises, for equity to be negative. If the assets are *less* than the liabilities, which would indicate an enterprise with more obligations than resources (not a good position to be in!), the equity, and, therefore, the enterprise's book value, will be negative. Such a situation is a sign of serious financial problems and is likely to be followed by bankruptcy or other unpleasant results.

FOR YOUR INTEREST

A deficit is negative equity, retained earnings, income, or cash flow.

Probably you are getting tired of all the terms and definitions being introduced in this section! Getting the vocabulary of accounting across is a main function of an introductory textbook, and of these early chapters in particular. The vocabulary can be important, with much confusion if it is not used clearly. Here's an example, prompted by the possibility of negative equity just mentioned. Let's look at the term "deficit." It has several meanings, all negative versions of items we usually prefer to be positive:

- Negative accrual income (a loss).

- Or negative retained earnings.

- Or negative equity.

- Or negative cash income (cash flow).

It's useful to be sure which meaning is intended when you're reading a newspaper article or watching a talking head on TV.

These different meanings of deficit relate to one another. Large or persistent negative income can overcome any past retained earnings and produce negative retained earnings (retained losses, you might say). This could be large enough to overwhelm share capital and produce negative equity: assets must have become less than liabilities. During all this trouble, the enterprise likely also had negative cash flow.

Some Preliminary Analysis of the Sound and Light Balance Sheet

From the Sound and Light balance sheet, we can answer some questions about the corporation's financial condition:

1. Is the enterprise soundly financed? Sound and Light has financed its $495 thousand in assets by borrowing $103 thousand short-term and $87 thousand long-term, and by getting $130 thousand in contributions from owners and not paying past earnings of $175 thousand out to owners. Its $495 thousand in assets are therefore financed by $190 thousand (38.4%) from creditors and $305 thousand (61.6%) from the owners. Its debt–equity ratio is $190 / $305 = 62.3% (often written 0.63:1). So, it is not much in debt, proportionately. What would you think if the creditors were owed $450 thousand, and the owners' equity was only $45 thousand? This would be a debt–equity ratio of $450 / $45 = 1,000% (10:1), a lot more risky for the creditors, because a lot more of their money than the owners' money would be at risk if the company ran into trouble.

Debt–equity ratio equals liabilities divided by equity.

2. Can the enterprise pay its bills on time? Sound and Light owes $103 thousand in the short term and has only $50 thousand in cash. Therefore, to pay its bills it will have to collect cash from its customers either by getting them to pay what they already owe or by selling them some unsold products for cash. There is likely no problem here: collections and sales, and payments to creditors, are probably going on continuously. The company has $245 thousand of current assets that it should be able to turn into cash to pay the $103 thousand of current liabilities. It is said to have $245 thousand – $103 thousand = $142 thousand in working capital and a working capital ratio (also called the current ratio) of $245 / $103, or 2.38. The working capital is positive, and the ratio indicates there is more than twice as much in current assets as current liabilities, so Sound and Light appears to be all right.

Working capital equals current assets minus current liabilities.

W/C ratio is CA/CL.

3. But you can see that if the company had a slow period of sales or collections, it could have difficulty paying its bills. But if you were concerned about the company's ability to sell unsold goods to pay its bills, you could calculate the quick ratio (also called the acid test ratio). It is like the W/C ratio but has only cash, very short-term investments that could be sold, and amounts due from customers in its numerator. For Sound and Light, the quick ratio would be ($50 thousand + $75 thousand) / $103 thousand = 1.21. The company could pay its current liabilities without having to sell unsold goods. What would you think if the company had only $10 thousand in cash and $160 thousand in unsold products? In that case, though its working capital and working capital ratio would be the same, it would likely be overstocked and cash short, and might have trouble paying bills. Now the quick ratio would be ($10 thousand + $75 thousand) / $103 thousand = 0.83. The company would have to sell some goods to meet its current liabilities. All ratios are only indicators. They require interpretation of the specific circumstances of each enterprise, so we don't know from our calculations if the company is in trouble, but a low quick ratio would be a signal to look further into the situation.

The quick ratio compares near-cash assets to current liabilities.

4. Should the owners declare themselves a dividend? If so, how large should it be? Legally, the board of directors (who manage the company on behalf of the shareholders) might be able to declare a dividend to shareholders of $175 thousand, the full amount of the retained earnings. But there is not nearly enough cash for that. Those past earnings have been reinvested in inventory of unsold products, building, equipment, and so on, and are therefore not sit-

Ability to pay dividends depends on the amount of both cash and retained earnings.

ting around in cash waiting to be paid to owners. This is true of nearly all corporations: they invest past earnings in operating assets and so do not have a lot of cash on hand. Probably a dividend of more than about $25 thousand, only one-seventh of the retained earnings, would cause Sound and Light some cash strain. What would you think if the corporation had no buildings or equipment but $300 thousand in cash instead? It would appear to be cash-rich in that case and should either invest the cash productively or pay a dividend to the owners so they can do what they like with the money.

5. What is that negative "accumulated amortization" item on the asset side of Sound and Light's balance sheet? In the example of Simone's jewellery business in section 1.8, we deducted amortization from Simone's revenue in calculating accrual income, so that there would be an expense to represent the wear and tear on her equipment. Sound and Light has done the same: in calculating its income, it has deducted amortization expense on its factory. The income that is in the retained earnings part of the equity is, therefore, smaller than it would have been without this deduction. The accumulated amount of that expense, built up over the years, is deducted from the assets in the balance sheet to show how much of the economic value of the assets is estimated to have been used up so far. Accumulated amortization is, therefore, a "negative asset" used to reduce the amounts of other assets. In this case, the factory cost $272 thousand, against which amortization of $122 thousand has accumulated, so the "net" book value of the factory is the remainder, $150 thousand. (Some balance sheets report only the net amount and give cost and accumulated amortization amounts in the notes.) Comparing the cost and the accumulated amortization tells us something about the age of the factory. The $122 thousand accumulated amortization is less than half the factory's cost, so the company estimates that less than half the economic value of the factory has been used. What would you think if the accumulated amortization was $250 thousand? The factory would be nearing the end of its estimated life.

> An amortized asset's book value is its cost minus its accumulated amortization.

F OR YOUR INTEREST

There we go again! The term "book value" can refer both to the net value of amortized assets (cost minus accumulated amortization) and to the equity of the enterprise (assets minus liabilities). As with the term "deficit," you need to know the context to know what book value means.

Three Common Balance Sheet Presentation Styles

So you see that the balance sheet provides interesting information if you know how to read it. Your skill in reading it will grow as you work with it. There are different styles of presentation of the balance sheet; all have the same information, but it is arranged differently. Three common styles, including the side-by-side and vertical formats we saw earlier, are illustrated below using the Sound and Light figures.

2-4

Exhibit

Sound and Light Corporation
Balance Sheet as at April 30, 2001
in Thousands of Dollars

Side-by-side style

Assets		Liabilities and Equity		
Current assets	$245	Current liabilities		$103
Noncurrent assets	250	Noncurrent liabilities		87
		Total liabilities		$190
		Owners' equity:		
		Contributed capital	$130	
		Retained earnings	175	305
TOTAL	$495	TOTAL		$495

Vertical style

Assets

Current assets	$245
Noncurrent assets	250
TOTAL	$495

Liabilities and Equity

Current liabilities		$103
Noncurrent liabilities		87
Total liabilities		$190
Owners' equity:		
Contributed capital	$130	
Retained earnings	175	305
TOTAL		$495

Working capital style

Net Assets

Current assets	$245
Less current liabilities	103
Working capital	$142
Noncurrent assets	250
TOTAL	$392

Financing Sources

Noncurrent liabilities		$ 87
Owners' equity:		
Contributed capital	$130	
Retained earnings	175	305
TOTAL		$392

Ⓗ OW'S YOUR UNDERSTANDING?

Here are two questions you should be able to answer, based on what you have just read.

1. The balance sheet is a summary of certain things at a point in time. What things?

2. Assemble a balance sheet for Northern Inc. from the following information and comment on the company's financial position at that point in time: Share capital, $1,000; Receivable from customers, $1,100; Payable to suppliers, $2,100; Inventory of unsold products, $1,700; Retained earnings, $2,200; Cash, $500; Equipment, $2,000. (You should get current assets $3,300; noncurrent assets $2,000; total assets $5,300; current liabilities $2,100; noncurrent liabilities $0; contributed capital $1,000; retained earnings $2,200; total liabilities and equity $5,300. Working capital is $1,200; the working capital ratio is 1.57, so, currently, it is not as strong as Sound and Light. The quick ratio is 0.76, not strong either. Liabilities of $2,100 are 39.6% of total sources, with a debt–equity ratio of 65.6%, so the company's financing is similar to Sound and Light's, though all of its liabilities are current, which is unusual. With $500 cash, it does not have enough cash to pay all of its $2,200 retained earnings to owners as dividends.)

2.3　A BRIEF HISTORY OF EARLY ACCOUNTING

Accounting has served society for thousands of years.

Here is a brief review of some accounting history. Understanding how we got to where we are helps a lot in understanding why we do the things we do now and how to do them. Financial accounting is an ancient information system indeed, with many of its ideas originating hundreds or thousands of years ago.

Like other complex human inventions, financial accounting did not just appear one day fully formed. It has developed over thousands of years and has been thoroughly intertwined with the development of civilization. A science writer, quoting a brewery owner, had this to say on the topic of accounting and beer:

Whatever the reason, [the early farmers in Mesopotamia] grew grain [and] "if you have grain, you need storehouses; if you have storehouses, you need accountants; if you have accountants, bang—you're on the road to civilization" (or the world's first audit).[1]

Accounting changes as the demands on it change, though not always smoothly.

Our focus here is on accounting, not on history. Nevertheless, the past has a bearing on accounting in that accounting evolves as business, government, and other institutions in society evolve. As the needs for information change, accounting changes to meet those needs. Accounting's evolution is not always smooth, and not always efficient; at any given time there are aspects of accounting that may not seem to fit current needs well, but over time, we can expect that accounting will, as it has in the past, meet those needs if they persist.

When commerce consisted mainly of trading among families or tribal units, information demands were not complicated. Money had not been invented, so even simple financial reports could not have been prepared. People would want to know what they had on hand and would need some sort of documentation to accompany shipments, so that they and their customers would agree on what was being traded. To meet such needs, accounting began as simple list making. Especially important would be lists of the family or tribe's resources and, later, lists

The need for verifiable records of resources and debts is very old.

of debts to traders or other families. Later still, as commercial activities became more complex, families began to employ others to run aspects of their businesses and began also to create large business units with several locations. Accounting had to become more complex too, providing records that could be used to monitor the activities of employees and businesses in far-flung locations. People found that they needed to be able to verify what employees and traders said was happening. Because of these needs, the practice of having systematic records that could be audited later was begun.

To help you understand how present-day financial accounting concepts and techniques arose, a brief history, taking us from about 4500 B.C. in Mesopotamia to the 15th century Italian Renaissance will be explored. Later, we will focus on more recent history. Keep in mind that the purpose of the review is to help you understand accounting, not to explain general history.

This history review focuses on the West; the rest of the world has interesting stories too.

Because modern accrual accounting, as practised in North America and much of the rest of the world, has its roots in the development of Western civilization, our review of accounting history is oriented to that development. The interesting stories of the development of accounting in other parts of the world, such as China, India, and Africa, are, therefore, not included. The comments below are necessarily brief. If you would like to read further, some reading suggestions on accounting history are provided at the end of the chapter.[2]

Mesopotamia to Rome: 4500 B.C. to A.D. 400

For a society to demand accounting, it must have active trade and commerce, a basic level of writing, methods of measuring and calculating, and a medium of exchange or currency.[3] The earliest known civilization with an active recordkeeping system flourished in Mesopotamia (now Iraq and Syria). Generally, a common language (such as Babylonian) existed for business, and there was also a good system of numbers and currency and of recordkeeping using clay tablets. As far as we know, ordinary merchants and general traders did not keep official records. Officials of the government and religious leaders of the temples decided what records were to be maintained for official purposes, and scribes did the recordkeeping. A scribe apprenticed for many years to master the craft of recording taxes, customs duties, temple offerings, and trade between governments and temples. Records consisted of counts and lists of grain, cattle, and other resources, and

Today's balance sheets owe much to the list making of earlier times.

of obligations arising from trade. We can still see that today: the balance sheet of any enterprise includes items like unsold products and equipment, and trade obligations such as amounts due from customers and due to suppliers. All of these balance sheet figures are summaries supported by detailed lists.

When a scribe determined that a particular record was complete and correct, the scribe's seal was pressed into a clay tablet to certify that this was so, and the tablet was baked to prevent alteration.[4] The scribe was a forerunner of today's

Some sort of audit was needed in earlier times, just as today.

accountants and auditors; today's auditor writes a report instead of attaching a seal, but the function of providing assurance is an old one. This scribe-based form of recordkeeping was used for many years, spreading across land and time to Egypt, Greece, and Rome. Media other than clay tablets, such as papyrus, were used as time passed.[5] (Do you suppose people accustomed to clay tablets resisted the introduction of papyrus, just as some people accustomed to pencil and paper now resist the introduction of computers for accounting?)

Trade and commerce grew over thousands of years, from small, family operations to very large activities involving kings, religious leaders, and various levels of government. For example, as the Greek civilization spread, and the Roman Empire grew, administrative regions were organized in conquered lands in order to simplify governing them. Local administrators or governors, who managed these regions, generally could neither read nor write. When an accounting of their management was required, an official of the central government would come out and listen to an oral report. This event was, therefore, a "hearing," and the listening official was there to "audit" (from the Latin word for "hear"). Today, the person who comes to inspect and approve the financial statements of an enterprise is called an auditor, though a lot more goes on today than just listening!

The auditor heard the local manager's story, then gave a judgment. Not so different from today!

The Dark Ages to the Renaissance: A.D. 400 to A.D. 1500

With the fall of the Roman Empire in about the 5th century A.D, both trade and associated recordkeeping became stagnant in Europe, though activities still continued in Constantinople, North Africa, the Middle East, India, China, and elsewhere. Many ideas and inventions that we now take for granted slowly seeped into Europe: algebra from Arabia, gunpowder from China, and bookkeeping from India by way of Arabia and Constantinople. In Europe, great stimulus to trade began with the period of the Crusades, around the 11th century, when kings and princes could not themselves provide the material to support their retinues of crusaders bound for the Holy Land. This was a prosperous time for the lesser nobles

The Crusades helped merchants and banks to develop in the Mediterranean area.

and private merchants who supplied the crusaders from ports such as Venice. A shift of supply and economic power from governments to the private sector began, and large merchant banks developed, such as the Medici in Florence. These banks got heavily involved in the businesses and governments they helped to finance.

Because of all these activities, a more exact system of recordkeeping was developed in order to keep track of materials supplied, cash received and spent, and especially who owed whom how much money.[6] For the traders, merchants, and bankers, the stimulus provided by the Crusades set recordkeeping off in a more organized and systematic direction. The new direction was made possible also by refinements in the use of numbers and arithmetic that had taken place in Arab countries during Europe's Dark Ages. The number system we use in accounting and in our daily lives originated from these refinements.

> **Much of the development of arithmetic needed by accounting happened in Arab countries.**

The exact way that accounting, or more precisely, the recordkeeping basis of accounting we call bookkeeping, evolved during this busy time is a subject of debate among accounting historians. A major event, however, was the publication in 1494, using the newly invented printing press, of a treatise on "double-entry" bookkeeping by Friar Luca Pacioli of Tuscany and Venice, in Renaissance Italy. In the book, he referred to the method as an established procedure that had been in use in the Medici banks of Italy and in other businesses for some time. Pacioli's book was an important contribution to the knowledge of algebra and arithmetic, and had value specifically because of its detailed description and codification of the double-entry system. It was rapidly translated into all the major European languages, and, using these translations, European scholars extended Pacioli's ideas. Major international celebrations of Pacioli's work were held in 1994, to mark 500 years since his book was published.

> **Modern bookkeeping still uses the double-entry system Pacioli described 500 years ago.**

Double-Entry Bookkeeping

Pacioli's concepts were revolutionary and sound: they form the fundamental basis of modern financial accounting, providing a method of pulling together all the lists of resources and obligations in a way that helps to prevent errors. The idea is that each trade or other commercial transaction is recorded (entered) twice, hence the double entry:

- once to recognize the resource involved in the transaction; and
- once to recognize the source or effect of that resource change.

Instead of the disconnected lists that existed before double-entry bookkeeping was invented, the lists of resources and sources were now connected to each other. Now a balance sheet of the modern kind could be prepared. Double-entry bookkeeping, which might be seen as a pretty humdrum sort of activity, turns out to have a solid conceptual basis and a long and important history.

> **Double entry is designed to ensure both aspects of transactions are recorded.**

If a dollar amount (or that in any other medium of exchange—pounds, francs, yen, marks, and so on) can be assigned to each transaction, that amount can be used to record both sides of the transaction. The two sides, and the sums of the two sides of all the transactions recorded, act as a check on each other. If errors are made, they are likely to be found because the two sides will not add up to the same amount. If they do add up, we say they "balance" (hence, the "balance sheet," shows that the two sides do add up). The recordkeeping system Pacioli described to the world is one of the most far-reaching of human inventions.

TO THE READER: The next seven sections cover the accounting methods underlying the balance sheet and give examples of real companies' balance sheets. You can start with the methods (sections 2.4–2.7) or with the examples (section 2.8, which has useful preliminary information about forms of business and financing, and the examples in 2.9 and 2.10).

2.4   RECORDING TRANSACTIONS: DOUBLE-ENTRY BOOKKEEPING

There is more than one way to see how the double-entry system works. We'll start with a balance sheet view and then focus on the transactions themselves. Both are equivalent, but perhaps one will work better for you than the other.

A Balance Sheet View of Double Entry

One way to understand double entry is to start with the balance sheet, which is the summary of all the transactions and adjustments recorded in the accounts. The balance sheet balances; that is, the dollar value of all the resources on the left is equal to the dollar value of all the sources on the right. If the balance sheet is to **balance**, then *every transaction and adjustment must also balance*, that is, their effects on the two sides of the balance sheet must be equal:

A balanced balance sheet requires a balanced double-entry recording system.

- If a resource (asset) is increased, a source (liability or equity) must be increased by the same amount, or another resource decreased by the same amount, or there must be some mixture of source increases and other resource decreases that equals the original resource's increase.

- Conversely, if a resource is decreased, a source must be decreased by the same amount, or another resource increased by the same amount, or some mixture of source decreases and other resource increases that equals the original resource's decrease.

This is just arithmetic. Double entry is a form of algebraic notation, really, in which an equation (the balance sheet equation) must be maintained.

For reasons that are now largely lost in the mists of time, increases to resources (assets), on the left side, are called debits, and increases to sources (liabilities and equity), on the right side, are called credits. Perhaps confusingly, *negatives* on the left side are also called credits, and *negatives* on the right side are also called debits. Financial accounting uses only two names to cover the four kinds of effects, which will turn out to have some advantages as we learn more about the way accounting works. Thus the balance sheet looks like this:

Left side: Resources (Assets)	Right side: Sources (Liabilities, Equity)
Positive items: debits	**Positive items: credits**
Negative items: credits	**Negative items: debits**

Debit: assets up, liabilities or equity down.

Credit: liabilities or equity up, assets down.

$$\text{Sum of resources} = \text{Sum of sources}$$
$$\text{Assets} = \text{Liabilities} + \text{Equity}$$

For now, look at two simple examples of double entry.

1. Purchasing, on credit, goods for resale:

    a. The resource (an asset) is an addition to the enterprise's unsold products.
    b. The source (a liability) is an obligation created to pay the supplier.

If the goods cost, say, $452, we have

- a *debit* of $452—an addition to the account for the resource, in this case the inventory of unsold products; and

- a *credit* of $452—an addition to the account for the source, in this case the obligation to the supplier, usually called accounts payable.

The balance sheet stays in balance due to this double entry, because both resources and sources are increased (are "up") by $452:

The debit of $452 equals the credit of $452, so the balance sheet stays in balance.

Resources	Sources
Up (debit) $452	Up (credit) $452
Assets up $452 =	Liabilities up $452 (no change in equity)

2. Borrowing money from the bank on a long-term loan:

    a. The resource (asset) is an addition to the amount of cash on hand.
    b. The source (a liability again) is that an obligation is created to repay the bank.

If the borrowed cash is, say, $1,000, we have

- an addition to the asset "cash," so total resources go up $1,000; and

- an addition to the liability "long-term bank loan," so the total sources also go up $1,000.

Again, the balance sheet stays in balance:

The debit of $1,000 equals the credit of $1,000, so the balance sheet stays in balance.

Resources	Sources
Up (debit) $1,000	Up (credit) $1,000
Assets up $1,000 =	Liabilities up $1,000 (no change in equity)

If we sum the two records, we get:

Assets up a total of $1,452 = Liabilities up a total of $1,452
                                               (no equity change)

Total debits = $1,452   Total credits = $1,452

A Transaction Recording View of Double Entry

Recording transactions keeps the balance sheet in balance, but we might also focus on the transactions themselves. In a transaction, there is an exchange, as we saw in Chapter 1. Two parties are involved, and each gives something to and gets something from the other. The genius, and that's the right word, of double-entry bookkeeping is that it records the two aspects of the exchange at once, from the point of view of the enterprise whose records are being created. We might think of it this way, just a little simplified:

Double entry recognizes an exchange as something received and something given.

    a. What has happened to the enterprise's resources (assets)?
        Assets are the enterprise's wealth, so you can think of this as the reason the enterprise engaged in the transaction: gaining some resources or, if necessary, giving some up.

b. What is the other side of the resource change?

In an exchange, a resource is only gained if something else is given: another resource, or a promise to pay later, or an investment by owners. Was the resource, say cash, gained because it was provided by a customer, or borrowed, or obtained by selling or collecting another asset, or provided by an owner? Was the resource, say cash, lost because it was given to a supplier or employee, used to reduce a debt, used to obtain another asset, or given to an owner as a dividend?

As we saw above, the system used for recording transactions uses debits and credits:

Increases in assets are debits	Increases in liabilities and/or equity are credits
Debits = Credits	
Decreases in assets are credits	Decreases in liabilities and/or equity are debits
Credits = Debits	

Double entry means that debits always equal credits.

We will focus on recording revenues and expenses in Chapter 3. For now, if you're curious, revenues increase income, and, therefore, equity via retained earnings, and so they are credits. Expenses decrease income, and, therefore, equity via retained earnings, and so they are debits.

Both parties record the transaction, both using double entry.

An interesting aspect of a transaction is that, because it is an exchange, *both parties* to the exchange would record it, each from that party's point of view. If Enterprise A gains cash for a loan from Enterprise B, Enterprise A would record an increase in cash (a debit) and in a loan liability (a credit), while Enterprise B would record a decrease in cash (a credit) and an increase in an asset for the loan receivable, to be collected (a debit).

Here are examples of some exchanges and of how both parties would record the two aspects of each. There is a tradition of recording the debits first in the double entry; that is sometimes disregarded here, so that you can see the parallels between Party A's and Party B's records.

2-5 ....

Exhibit

Party A	Party B
1. Bob borrows $1,000 cash from the bank	**The bank lends Bob $1,000 cash**
Bob's records:	The bank's records:
Debit Cash 1,000	*Credit* Cash 1,000
Credit Loan payable 1,000	*Debit* Loan receivable 1,000
To record bank loan.	To record loan to Bob.
2. Jan pays a $500 phone bill recorded earlier	**The phone company receives the $500 cash**
Jan's records:	The phone company's records:
Credit Cash 500	*Debit* Cash 500
Debit Accounts payable 500	*Credit* Accounts receivable 500
To record payment of	To record receipt of cash
phone bill.	from Jan.

These are simple examples, but they illustrate several features of the bookkeeping system. (For hundreds of years, accounting records were kept in bound books. In spite of the advent of computers, "books" are still used by many enterprises, as we will see.) Some features illustrated by the examples include:

Transactions are recorded into accounts, the basis of the financial statements.

a. Each double-entry record names one (or more) accounts that are *debited*, and one (or more) that are *credited*. Accounts contain all the transaction records and any adjustments, and therefore reflect everything recorded in the system. The Cash account, for example, lists all transactions and adjustments that have affected cash. Accounts are used directly in preparing the balance sheet and other financial statements (except the cash flow statement, as Chapter 4 will show).

For each journal entry, the sum of the debits must equal the sum of the credits.

b. The double-entry records shown in the example are called journal entries. A journal entry can list as many accounts as are needed to record the transaction, but for *each* journal entry, *the sum of the debits must equal the sum of the credits*. If not, the balance sheet equation will not be maintained (the "books" will not balance).

c. It is traditional for the debits to be listed first in each journal entry, and for the debits to be written to the left and the credits to the right. Neither of these is arithmetically necessary, but keeping a consistent style reduces mistakes and helps keep the records understandable.

d. It is customary to omit the dollar signs in writing the entries. The transaction has to be measurable in dollars, so putting in dollar signs is thought redundant.

e. It is also customary to write a short explanation below each entry, as a memorandum of what the recorded transaction was about. Again, this is not necessary but it helps to make the record understandable and assist any follow-up or error correction.

Bookkeeping involves several useful procedural details.

f. Every journal entry should also be dated and is usually numbered so that there is no doubt when the transaction was recorded. (This is not done in the examples above.) The date can have important legal and tax implications, and, of course, it is necessary to know which fiscal period a transaction belongs when financial statements are being prepared.

Both parties to the transaction record it, because it is an exchange for both.

g. There's a saying that "Every person's debit is another person's credit." You can see that in the examples in Exhibit 2.5. Bob's debit (increase) in cash goes with the bank's credit (decrease) in cash. The bank's cash has become Bob's. Conversely, Jan's cash has become the phone company's. These reflect the exchange that lies behind the accounting concept of a transaction.

The journal entry function may be performed by records specialized by type of transaction.

Enterprises with many transactions to record, which means most enterprises, do not create a separate journal entry for each transaction, but instead use specialized records for each general kind of transaction, such as a sales record, a cash receipts record, and a cheque record. A company could list only cash receipts debits in one record, and only cash sales revenue credits in another record. The books (the balance sheet) will balance only if the two records have the same totals, so keeping them separate may be a useful control to reduce error. The people maintaining the two records have to be very careful or their records will not have the same totals. (More will be said about such specialized records in a later chapter.) Also, many bookkeeping systems are computerized; many versions of accounting software exist to perform the task. These systems may or may not produce records that look like the preceding examples, but they have the same arithmetical function of keeping all the debits equal to all the credits.

A Complex Journal Entry

The examples above were rather simple. Here is an example of a more complex transaction, just so you can see how the rules set out above are maintained no matter how complex the transaction. On December 14, 2001, Sorhem Inc. acquired a factory from Johnston Ltd.

- The agreed upon price was $523,000; but since Sorhem was a little short of cash, it financed the purchase by borrowing $150,000 from the bank, and Johnston agreed to wait for some years to be paid part of the price, therefore holding a long-term mortgage on the land and building of $178,000.

- Sorhem, therefore, had to pay only $195,000 of its own cash (total payment equalling $345,000, including the borrowed cash).

- Sorhem acquired the following, at values agreed to by it and Johnston: Land, $105,000; Building, $254,000; Equipment, $87,000; Goodwill, $77,000. (Goodwill is the difference between the individual values of the group of assets and the total paid: "The whole is greater than the sum of the parts." This might represent factors valuable to Sorhem such as a good factory location, good relationships with customers.)

The following journal entry records this transaction in the accounts of Sorhem Ltd.:

2-6

Exhibit

December 14, 2001		Debits	Credits
DR Cash	(current asset)	150,000	
DR Land	(noncurrent asset)	105,000	
DR Building	(noncurrent asset)	254,000	
DR Equipment	(noncurrent asset)	87,000	
DR Goodwill	(noncurrent asset)	77,000	
CR Cash	(current asset)		345,000
CR Bank loan	(current liability)		150,000
CR Mortgage payable	(noncurrent liability)		178,000

To record the purchase of a factory from Johnston Ltd.

Quite a long journal entry!

- It meets the arithmetic requirement: the sum of the debits equals the sum of the credits ($673,000: you might like to add the two sides and see).

- It uses whatever account names make sense to record the transaction (different companies or bookkeepers could well have named the accounts differently).

- Debits are abbreviated DR, and credits as CR, as is customary.

OW'S YOUR UNDERSTANDING?

Here are two questions you should be able to answer, based on what you have just read:

1. What are the effects on the balance sheet of the following transaction? Whatzis Inc. received $20,000 cash from a shareholder in return for $5,000 in newly issued shares and promised to pay the shareholder the other $15,000 back at the end of three years. (Cash asset up $20,000; Share capital equity up $5,000; Noncurrent debt liability up $15,000. Result is total increase to assets $20,000, total increase to sources of assets $20,000.)

2. What is the journal entry to record the following transaction in which Whatzis used the cash from the shareholder? The company bought a large truck, which cost $89,000, by putting $20,000 down in cash and financing (borrowing) the rest from the truck dealer's finance company. (DR Truck asset 89,000, CR Cash asset 20,000, CR Truck loan liability 69,000. Result is net total increase to assets $69,000; total increase to sources of assets $69,000. Total debits 89,000, total credits 89,000.)

2.5   MORE ABOUT ACCOUNTS

Accounts collect all the transactions and adjustments and underlie the financial statements.

The balance sheet and further statements to be described in Chapter 3 are prepared from the underlying accounts, which have been recorded using the double-entry system so that the sum of the dollars in all the debit accounts equals the sum in all the credit accounts. But what is an account exactly? Let us use the following working definition: an account is a record of the dollar amounts comprising a particular asset, liability, equity, revenue, or expense. The net effect of these amounts is a debit or credit and is called the account's balance.

OR YOUR INTEREST

Another term used more than one way! Accountants use the word "balance" to refer to the equality of the assets, liabilities, and equity, as in "the balance sheet balances." They also use it to refer to the net sum of the debits and credits recorded in an account, as in "the cash account's balance is $xxx."

Here is an example of the "Cash in bank" account for a company:

2-7

Exhibit

| CASH IN BANK | | | | | |
Date	Description	Entry No.	Debits	Credits	Balance
Dec. 1/01	First deposit	1	10,000		10,000 DR
Dec. 2	Deposit	3	1,146		11,146 DR
Dec. 2	Cheque	7		678	10,468 DR
Dec. 2	Cheque	8		2,341	8,127 DR

The general ledger contains all the accounts and it balances (debits equal credits).

You see the idea. Each account is really just a convenient summary of the entries affecting it. In turn, the balance sheet is a summary of all the account balances. The general ledger is the complete set of all the accounts (assets, liabilities, equity accounts, revenues and expenses) that lie behind the financial statements.

Because the general ledger contains all the accounts, all of which came from balanced journal entries, it must balance (sum of debit-balance accounts equalling sum of credit-balance accounts) and it leads to a balanced balance sheet. Because errors might have been made, a standard bookkeeping procedure is to check that the ledger does balance by adding up all the debit and all the credit account balances and making sure the two totals are equal. There is always a little uncertainty that this will work, so the calculation is called a trial balance.

A trial balance is a list of all the account balances to make sure the general ledger does balance.

You might think of the ledger as a set of account pages (real pages, such as in the bound books the bookkeepers of old used, or representations in a computer system) like the one above, in which the sum of all the debit balance accounts equals the sum of all the credit balance accounts. Figure 2.2, using the same balance sheet format as is shown in Exhibit 2.2, near the beginning of section 2.2, and using the Cash in bank account from Exhibit 2.7, might be useful:

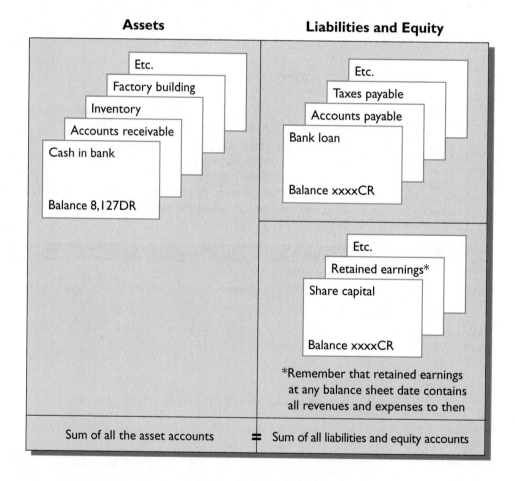

FIGURE 2.2

A T-account is a representation of a ledger account used in analysis or demonstration.

For demonstration and analysis purposes, accountants and accounting instructors often use a simplified version of an account called a "T-account," which includes only the debits and credits columns of the account, without calculating the balance after every entry. A T-account version of the above cash account example would look like this:

CASH IN BANK	
10,000	678
1,146	2,341
11,146	3,019
8,127	

Below are some examples of how account balances are calculated. Modern computerized accounting systems can produce accounts in various formats thought to be useful, but they all use the arithmetic illustrated below.

a. If the enterprise's cash began at $500 and there was a receipt of $400 and one of $750, and a payment of $300 and one of $525, the Cash asset account would show a balance of $825 (a debit because there is a positive balance in this asset account).

Cash = $500DR + $400DR + $750DR − $300CR − $525CR = $825DR

b. If share capital began at $1,000 and more shares were sold for $400 (which, let's say, caused the cash receipt above), the Share capital equity account would show a balance of $1,400 (a credit because there is a positive balance in this equity account).

Share capital = $1,000CR + $400CR = $1,400CR

c. If amounts owing to trade creditors began at $950 and a creditor was paid $300 (the first payment above), the Accounts payable liability account would show a balance of $650 (a credit because there is a positive balance in this liability account).

Accounts payable = $950CR − $300DR = $650CR

d. If a cash collection from a customer was made for $750 (the second cash receipt above), the Accounts receivable account, with a balance of say $2,000 prior to the collection, would show an amount of $750 (a credit because this reduces the accounts receivable asset, which has been transformed into cash through the collection transaction).

Accounts receivable = $2,000DR − $750CR = $1,250DR

e. If a $525 cash payment (the second cash payment above) was made on the company's bank loan, a liability account with a name like "Bank loan" would be debited with this payment. Suppose the loan had a balance of $15,000 before the payment. Then the account balance would be calculated to show the deduction of the payment.

Bank loan (part of liabilities) = $15,000CR − $525DR = $14,475CR

Balance sheet accounts continue indefinitely.

Financial statement amounts often are aggregates of several ledger account balances.

Balance sheet accounts continue indefinitely, as long as events happen that affect them.

The figures on the financial statements may be made up of various individual account balances. The financial statements are summaries, often of many accounts. For example, a company's balance sheet showed "Accounts receivable $145,290," which turns out to be the sum of four account balances in the company's detailed accounting system:

• Accounts receivable from customers	$129,300 plus
• Loans to employees	5,000 plus
• Travel advances	3,860 plus
• Due from associated company	7,130
Figure on the balance sheet	$145,290

 OW'S YOUR UNDERSTANDING?

Here are two questions you should be able to answer, based on what you have just read:

1. How do transactions and adjustments, recorded by journal entries, find their way onto the financial statements?

2. Amble Corp.'s general ledger has the following account balances at January 31: Cash 550DR; Accounts receivable 1,750DR; Inventory 2,200DR; Land 1,000DR; Factory 4,100DR; Accumulated amortization on factory 1,320CR; Bank loan 900CR; Accounts payable 1,430CR; Noncurrent debt 2,400CR; Share capital 1,000CR; Retained earnings 2,550CR. What are the sums of debits and credits from the ledger trial balance and the balance sheet totals at that date? (Sum of debits = sum of credits = 9,600; balance sheet's net total assets = total liabilities and equity = 8,280. The difference in the two totals is accumulated amortization, a credit balance account that is deducted as a negative amount on the assets side of the balance sheet.)

2.6   HOW DEBITS AND CREDITS MAKE THE ACCOUNTING SYSTEM WORK

This section offers an example of how financial accounting uses debits and credits to record events and, from those records, produce financial statements. The focus will be on the balance sheet for now. In Chapter 3, the example will be extended to cover more financial statements.

CappuMania Inc. is a small corporation that operates a coffee bar in the concourse of an office building. The company's balance sheet at the end of March 2001 is below.

CappuMania Inc.
Balance Sheet as at March 31, 2001

Assets			Liabilities and Shareholders' Equity		
Current assets:			Current liabilities:		
Cash	$ 4,000		Owing to suppliers	$ 1,200	
Inventory of unsold food	800		Sales and other taxes owing	600	
Inventory of supplies	1,900			$ 1,800	
	$ 6,700		Noncurrent liabilities:		
Noncurrent assets:			Loan to buy equipment	5,000	
Equipment cost	$ 9,000			$ 6,800	
Accumulated amortization	(1,500)		Shareholders' equity:		
	$ 7,500		Share capital contributed	$ 3,000	
			Retained earnings	4,400	
				$ 7,400	
	$14,200			$14,200	

These accounts are assets and so have *debit* balances:

- Cash, Inventory of unsold food, Inventory of supplies, and Equipment.

This account is a negative asset and so has a *credit* balance:

- Accumulated amortization.

These accounts are liabilities and equities and so have *credit* balances:

- Owing to suppliers, Sales and other taxes owing, Loan to buy equipment, Share capital contributed, and Retained earnings.

We already know the accounts are in balance because the balance sheet balances (left side total = right side total). But let's do a trial balance anyway, to demonstrate that the sum of all the debits equals the sum of all the credits (we will drop the $ signs):

Account names	Account balances	
	Debits	Credits
Cash	4,000	
Inventory of unsold food	800	
Inventory of supplies	1,900	
Equipment cost	9,000	
Accumulated amortization		1,500
Owing to suppliers		1,200
Sales and other taxes owing		600
Loan to buy equipment		5,000
Share capital contributed		3,000
Retained earnings		4,400
	15,700	15,700

The balance sheet may rearrange the ledger's accounts, but the balance is maintained.

So it balances! Accumulated amortization, a credit balance account, is deducted from the Equipment cost on the balance sheet, so the sum of the debits is not the same amount as the total of the assets side of the balance sheet, nor is the sum of the credits the same as the total of the liabilities and equity side of the balance sheet. But this sort of rearrangement of the presentation of accounts in the balance sheet still keeps the accounts in balance even though totals change, because any such rearrangement always retains the debit or credit signs.

Now let's see how the following four transactions, all happening on April 1, 2001, are recorded using accounting's double-entry method (ignoring the details of the particular computer or manual recordkeeping system):

1. CappuMania pays $500 of its taxes owing.
2. CappuMania buys $450 of more supplies, paying $100 cash and owing the rest.
3. A shareholder is given more shares in return for personally paying $1,100 on the equipment loan.
4. CappuMania buys a new coffee urn for $200 cash.

Here are the journal entries, all dated April 1, 2001:

	Debit	Credit

Transaction 1 reduces an asset and a liability.

1. *Resource effect:* Cash is reduced. Cash is a debit, so a negative effect on cash would be a credit.
   Source effect: Tax liability is reduced. A liability is a credit, so a negative effect would be a debit.
   Entry:

	Debit	Credit
DR Sales and other taxes owing (liability)	500	
CR Cash (asset)		500

   Double-entry method: There is both a DR and a CR and the two are the same. (The tradition is to list the DR(s) first in an entry, but all that really matters is that for each entry, $DR = $CR.)

Transaction 2 increases one asset, decreases another, and increases a liability.

2. *Resource effects:* Inventory is increased $450. It is an asset, so this is a debit. Cash is decreased $100, so this is a credit, as above.
   Source effect: The liability to suppliers is increased $350, so this is a credit.
   Entry:

	Debit	Credit
DR Inventory of supplies (asset)	450	
CR Cash (asset)		100
CR Owing to suppliers (liability)		350

   Double-entry method: There are both DRs and CRs and the sum of the DRs equals the sum of the CRs. (An entry can have any number of DRs and CRs as long as the sums of each are equal.)

Transaction 3 reduces a liability and increases an equity, having no effect on assets.

3. *Resource effect:* None.
   Source effects: The equipment loan, a liability, is decreased $1,100, so this is a debit. The share capital, an equity, is increased $1,100, so this is a credit.

	Debit	Credit

Entry:

DR Loan to buy equipment (liability)   1,100

  CR Share capital contributed (equity)   1,100

Double-entry method: This transaction affects only the right side of the balance sheet, but the balance sheet stays in balance because one account on the right side goes up and another goes down.

Transaction 4 increases one asset and reduces another, with no other effect.

4. *Resource effects:* Equipment, an asset, is increased $200, so this is a debit. Cash is decreased $200, which is a credit as in transactions 1 and 2.

Source effect: None.

Entry:

DR Equipment cost (asset)   200

  CR Cash (asset)   200

Double-entry method: This transaction also affects only one side of the balance sheet, this time the assets side, but again the balanced entry keeps the balance sheet in balance.

Posting means entering the journal entries in the ledger accounts.

These entries are recorded (**posted**) by adding them to or subtracting them from the previous (March 31) balances in the accounts. This is done below, using a computer spreadsheet format (in this case, *Microsoft Excel*®, but the particular spreadsheet does not matter). *Arbitrarily*, the debits are recorded as positive and the credits as negative. This does not mean debits are good and credits are bad!

2-10

Exhibit

	A	B	C	D	E	F
1		CappuMania Inc. Example, in Spreadsheet Form				
2						
3			March 31/01			April 1/01
4			Trial balance	Transactions*		Trial balance
5			Debit or credit	Debits	Credits	Debit or credit
6						
7	Cash		4000		(1) −500	3200
8					(2) −100	
9					(4) −200	
10	Inventory of unsold food		800			800
11	Inventory of supplies		1900	(2) 450		2350
12	Equipment cost		9000	(4) 200		9200
13	Accumulated amortization		−1500			−1500
14	Owing to suppliers		−1200		(2) −350	−1550
15	Sales and other taxes owing		−600	(1) 500		−100
16	Loan to buy equipment		−5000	(3) 1100		−3900
17	Share capital contributed		−3000		(3) −1100	−4100
18	Retained earnings		−4400			−4400
19						
20		Totals	0	2250	−2250	0

* The numbers in brackets have been added to the spreadsheet printout to refer to the four transactions described in the text.

You can see from the spreadsheet that the March 31 trial balance was in balance because the total of adding all the debits and subtracting all the credits is zero. The

Accounting systems have the same basic design, but vary in their formats and details.

transaction entries are in balance because the sum of the debits equals the sum of the credits. The April 1 trial balance is in balance too.

It would be unlikely that another balance sheet would be prepared just one day after the March 31 balance sheet, but to complete the example, let's see what the balance sheet, after recording the four transactions, would be.

2-11

Exhibit

CappuMania Inc. Balance Sheet as at April 1, 2001				
Assets			**Liabilities and Shareholders' Equity**	
Current assets:			Current liabilities:	
Cash	$ 3,200		Owing to suppliers	$ 1,550
Inventory of unsold food	800		Sales and other taxes owing	100
Inventory of supplies	2,350			$ 1,650
	$ 6,350		Noncurrent liabilities:	
Noncurrent assets:			Loan to buy equipment	3,900
Equipment cost	$ 9,200			$ 5,550
Accumulated amortization	(1,500)		Shareholders' equity:	
	$ 7,700		Share capital contributed	$ 4,100
			Retained earnings	4,400
				$ 8,500
	$14,050			$14,050

In summary, the CappuMania example shows how accounting works.

- First, transactions are recorded in a two-sided (double) entry in a journal.

- Next, the journal's entries are recorded (posted) in the accounts.

- Then, the ledger of accounts is checked for balancing via a trial balance.

- Last, the trial balance is used to prepare the balance sheet.

There are many choices, judgments, and details behind this, and most accounting systems have their own particular formats for entries and accounts, but now you have the basics.

(F) OR YOUR INTEREST

Recordkeeping is important for managers. To a large extent, management decision-making and evaluations of management performance depend on accounting information. Such decisions and evaluations may be constrained by the nature of the underlying data. For example, a principal characteristic of the transaction is that an exchange *has happened*. The basis of the financial accounting system, therefore, is a historical record of events. This can be awkward for managers seeking to look forward and predict future choices and events. Though accounting's historical focus improves its reliability, many managers wish financial accounting were more forward looking. Top managers often want to override the routine transactional system with special adjustments and accruals, but because such action has a manipulative flavour, it is often ineffective in convincing users, and management's frustration remains. When we make predictions for the future, we are guided by the past. Managers' predictions are guided by the historical results of financial accounting; however, managers must have a lot of other information beyond accounting to make their predictions accurate. Probably, that is as it should be: there is no reason to expect accounting to tell managers everything they need to know. If accounting does its job well, it provides managers a good base on which to add other information, so the managers can do their jobs well.

OW'S YOUR UNDERSTANDING?

Here are two questions you should be able to answer, based on what you have just read:

1. On April 1, 2001, a fifth transaction occurred. CappuMania paid $800 on its equipment loan. Write a journal entry to record this event. (DR Loan to buy equipment 800, CR Cash 800.)

2. A sixth transaction also occurred on April 1, 2001: CappuMania acquired new equipment costing $1,550 from a shareholder who was issued share capital in that amount. What would the following revised figures have been on the April 1 balance sheet after both the fifth and sixth transactions: cash, current assets, total assets, total liabilities, total equity, total liabilities, and shareholders' equity? ($2,400, $5,550, $14,800, $4,750, $10,050, $14,800.)

2.7   ARRANGING ACCOUNTS ON THE BALANCE SHEET

In the Sound and Light and CappuMania examples, there were two important aspects of arranging accounts on the balance sheet:

The balance sheet's classification of accounts into categories conveys information.

1. Accounts were organized into the balance sheet's main categories: current assets, noncurrent assets, current liabilities, noncurrent liabilities, and equity. This was done because the arrangement of accounts is meant to convey information beyond the account balances themselves. The placement of each account tells the reader of the balance sheet what kind of account it is: a short-term asset or a long-term one, a short-term liability or a long-term one, or an equity. This enables the calculation of meaningful ratios and other analyses. The balance sheet is said to be *classified*, because accounts are classified into meaningful categories. This means that the accountant preparing the balance sheet has to look into an account with a title like "bank loan," for example, and determine whether it should be included in current liabilities or noncurrent liabilities. (We'll see that the other financial statements also classify figures into categories.) Moving items around within the balance sheet (or within other financial statements) is called reclassification and is done by accountants whenever they believe it will make the financial statement more informative.

2. The accumulated amortization account, though having a credit balance, is not put on the right side of the balance sheet, but instead appears as a negative amount on the left side. As long as the accountant remembers whether an account is a debit or credit, it can be put anywhere on the balance sheet without throwing the statement out of balance. Accounting is just arithmetic, and if you think of the balance sheet equation (A = L + E) as a real algebraic equation, you can move things around from one side to the other, just as in algebra, and when you move something that is positive on one side, it becomes negative on the other side, just as in algebra. A reminder of this use of credits on the left and debits on the right is the word net often used in accounting. It tells you that something has been deducted from something else: a debit account minus a smaller credit account results in a net debit, and a credit account minus a smaller debit account produces a net credit. The assets total is the net of all the positive assets minus any negative amounts, and the liabilities and owners' equity total is the net of all the positive liabilities and equity items minus any negative amounts. Amounts can be moved around on the balance sheet to produce the most useful presentation of the information without disturbing the rule that the balance sheet must balance.

> Both debit and credit balance accounts can appear anywhere on the balance sheet.
>
> Credits on the left side are negative; debits on the right side are negative too.

Three Examples of Account Classification

(a) Current and noncurrent portions of noncurrent liabilities. Many noncurrent liabilities, such as mortgages, bonds, and debentures, require regular payments, and although most of the debt is noncurrent, not all of it is. Accountants therefore reclassify the amount to be paid on the principal of the debt within the next year into current liabilities, and show only the residual (due more than a year away) as noncurrent. (The interest to be paid in the next year is not included in this, because it is not due until the future time passes.)

(b) Bank overdrafts are another example. Suppose a company has a bank overdraft of $500, which means that its cash-in-bank asset is negative (the bank has allowed the company to remove $500 more cash from the account than there was in it, in effect, lending the company the $500). The company's other assets total $12,400. Its net assets are therefore $11,900, and this is also the total of its liabilities and owners' equity. There are at least two ways of presenting this information:

| Other assets of $12,400 minus bank overdraft of $500 | = | Liabilities and owners' equity of $11,900 |

or

| Other assets of $12,400 | = | Liabilities and owners' equity of $11,900 plus bank overdraft of $500 |

> Reclassification is used to move items around and make the balance sheet informative.

For bank overdrafts, it is customary to use the second method, to move the negative bank amount to the other side of the balance sheet. Even if the company normally has cash in the bank so that the account is normally an asset, the account is a liability at this point because the bank has, in effect, lent the company $500 and will want the money back.

(c) Some negative amounts are left as deductions, not moved to the other side to make them positive as was done with the overdraft. Accumulated amortization is an important example of a negative-balance account. It is the amount of all the amortization calculated to date on assets such as buildings and equipment. For accumulated amortization, there are at least three ways of presenting the information, all of which maintain the balance sheet equation:

- It could be shown on the right side of the balance sheet (in former times, it was, and in some countries, still is). In North America, most accountants feel that it is more informative for users to deduct it from the asset figures so that the net book value of the assets is shown. Remember that the net book value is the assets' original value (cost) minus their accumulated amortization; it tells the user how much of that original value has yet to be amortized.

- It could be separately disclosed as a deduction on the left side of the balance sheet, as it was in the Sound and Light and CappuMania balance sheets. This is very common, but if there are a lot of different kinds of assets and amortization amounts, it can make the balance sheet a little cluttered.

- It could be deducted from the assets' cost and just the net book value could be disclosed on the balance sheet, so that accumulated amortization is not mentioned on the face of the statement. In the Sound and Light example, the noncurrent assets would be listed in the following sort of way: Noncurrent assets (net) $250. CappuMania's would be Noncurrent assets (net) $7,700. This method, which is becoming quite popular, would be accompanied by a note to the financial statements listing the cost and accumulated amortization amounts separately, and so keeping the balance sheet uncluttered and allowing some additional explanations of the figures if that were thought useful.

Notes to the statements provide useful details that would clutter the statements.

This discussion illustrates an important characteristic of the balance sheet equation. It is an invention maintained by the double-entry system and thought to be useful as a conceptual tool for the measurement of financial position. It is an arithmetical result, not some sort of basic truth. The task of recording balanced journal entries to make sure that the balance sheet is in balance is really just the starting point for the fundamental accounting question of how to measure and describe financial position most appropriately.

FOR YOUR INTEREST

Accounting and finance research, like any other use of the balance sheet, is dependent on how accounts are classified. Much research is done using large databases prepared from companies' published financial statements, and those databases depend on the accounting judgments made in preparing the statements. A few years ago, a major set of national financial statements contained errors when the people putting it together did not realize that accumulated amortization was a negative asset and so added it on to the assets, rather than subtracting it. As a result, the data were seriously out of balance and all the ratios calculated from the data were wrong! Accounting researchers regularly have to scrutinize their data for such errors. To add to the research challenge, various databases classify balance sheet information slightly differently, for example, sometimes adding the current portion of noncurrent debt onto the noncurrent portion. Everyone using databases of financial information has to be aware of what the databases have done with the information.

 OW'S YOUR UNDERSTANDING?

Here are two questions you should be able to answer, based on what you have just read:

1. Why are accounts classified as they are on the balance sheet, and why are they sometimes reclassified?

2. Prepare a balance sheet for Mike's Tire Repair (owner, Mike) from the following amounts: Cash on hand, $90; Bank overdraft, $120; Due from customers, $640; Unsold goods (inventory), $210; Equipment cost, $890; Accumulated amortization on equipment, $470; Due to suppliers, $360; Owner's equity, $880. (You should show the first, third, fourth, and fifth amounts as positive assets and the sixth as a negative asset, with (net) total assets of $1,360. The second and seventh amounts are liabilities, totalling $480, and equity equals $880, so that the total of liabilities and equity is also $1,360.)

2.8   PROPRIETORSHIPS, PARTNERSHIPS, CORPORATIONS, AND FINANCING

The balance sheet is a summary of much of the organization's financing: it shows what sources of debt and equity were used to produce the list of resources (assets). Just in case you are unfamiliar with the main kinds of business organizations and their financing, this section provides a few explanations. Remember the balance sheet equation:

Assets = Liabilities + Owners' Equity

This section considers the right-hand terms, outlining how the form of the business organization determines the way owners' equity is shown on the balance sheet and how both right-hand terms indicate how the assets are financed. This short introduction will help you deal with the material in this book. While such information is explored more deeply in books or courses on corporate law and finance, many details will also necessarily come up here as we proceed. This book's glossary will also provide help in understanding terminology.

There are many important forms of organization, such as businesses organized as partnerships, corporations, or cooperatives, and nonbusiness organizations, such as clubs, charities, governments, and political parties. They cannot all be described here. Instead, we focus on the four main kinds of business organization, and their main methods of financing.

Four Kinds of Business Organization

We have seen that each balance sheet has an owners' equity section, and that for a business enterprise there are two general kinds of equity:

- *Directly* contributed equity (investments), in which owners have provided money or other assets to the enterprise; and

- *Indirectly* contributed equity (retained earnings), in which owners have allowed income earned by the enterprise to remain there, to help earn more income in the future.

Equity exists only when owners have dealt with the enterprise. Trading shares among owners, such as on a stock market, provides no equity for the enterprise, as it is not involved in such trading (no transaction).

The balance sheet's equity section reflects the legal form of the organization.

The legal meaning of being an owner depends on the way the enterprise is legally organized. The equity section of the balance sheet reflects that legal meaning, so that owners and other users will understand the status of their equity. Four main kinds of business organizations are the proprietorship, the partnership, the corporation, and the corporate group.

Proprietorship

A proprietorship, like Simone's venture in section 1.8, is a business owned by one person (the *proprietor*) and does not legally exist separately from the owner. Because the business does not exist as a separate legal entity, it is said to be *unincorporated*. If Simone just starts up a jewellery business one day, without further legal steps, the business is a proprietorship. Legally, such a business is not distinguishable from Simone's nonbusiness affairs. If she wishes, she can use the business cash to buy groceries, and if she does not pay her business bills, her creditors can claim against any nonbusiness assets she has.

A proprietorship has no legal existence separate from the owner, so direct contributions by the owner and indirect contributions by leaving income in the business are not legally distinguishable. Accordingly, the equity section of the proprietorship's balance sheet does not distinguish between the two. Both kinds of equity are simply lumped together as owner's capital. A proprietorship's balance sheet can list whatever assets and liabilities the owner considers relevant to the business (there being no separate legal entity to own any assets or owe any liabilities), and the owner's equity section of the balance sheet just says:

A proprietorship's equity ("capital") does not separate investment and retained earnings.

Owner's equity (or Proprietor's equity)
Owner's capital $XXXX

Because the proprietorship balance sheet is arbitrarily distinguished from the owner, it is usual to specify who the owner is and whether the owner's other financial affairs affect the business.

Partnership

A partnership's equity should show the capital attributable to each partner.

A partnership is also unincorporated, but it has more than one owner. Again, the owners' personal assets can generally be claimed by business creditors, so there is the same somewhat arbitrary distinction between business affairs and personal affairs. But the fact that there is more than one owner introduces some formality into the business. For example, there is (or should be) an agreement about how the earnings of the business are to be split among the partners and about how much each partner can withdraw from the business. Because stress can develop in partnerships (as with friendships), provinces, states, and countries have partnership laws that provide some structure if the partners do not do so themselves. A partnership's balance sheet may, like a proprietorship's, list whatever assets and liabilities the owners consider relevant to that business. Also, the owners' equity section, like that for a proprietorship, does not distinguish between owners' direct contributions and retained earnings. The only difference is that each owner's total capital is identified on the face of the balance sheet (or, if there are many partners, as in firms of lawyers, accountants, or engineers, in a note or separate schedule). Therefore, the partners' capital section of the partnership's balance sheet shows:

Partners' equity
Partners' capital:

Partner A	$XXXX
Partner B	XXXX
Partner C	XXXX
Total capital	$XXXX

Corporation

Financial accounting recognizes that a corporation is legally separate from its owners.

A corporation is an incorporated entity that has a legal existence of its own, separate from that of its owners. The corporation continues to exist even if the owners die or quit working, and if the business fails, owners' losses are limited to their equity in the business. Unless they have signed personal guarantees to creditors such as banks, owners will not lose personal assets if the business goes under. A corporation can own property, employ people, and otherwise conduct business just as a person can. It can even sue and be sued. You can usually tell that a business is incorporated because it will have some indication at the end of its name, like "Limited," "Ltd.," "Inc.," or other symbols that the incorporating jurisdiction (province, state, or country) specifies. A corporation's balance sheet usually calls its equity section shareholders' equity to emphasize the nature of its ownership.

Corporations can be very complex. Just a few complexities are mentioned here.

a. Forms of Share Capital

The share capital part of equity is the historical amount contributed to the corporation.

People become owners of a corporation by buying *shares* (called *stock* in the United States) that give them voting or other powers in it. When a corporation first issues a share, the money received for it is put in the corporation's bank account and the source of that asset is called share capital, which is an owners' (shareholders' or stockholders') equity item. Innovations are always being made in corporations' ownership structures. For example, some corporations are owned through "trusts" that provide tax or other advantages. If you wanted to invest in The North West Company, a Winnipeg-based retailer, or Luscar Coal, an Edmonton-based coal mining company, you would buy shares in the trusts, which own the companies.

Canadian companies usually have no-par shares, which mean they can issue their shares for whatever amount seems appropriate. Par value (or stated value) shares, rare in Canada, but used elsewhere, have a legal minimum issue price, the par or otherwise stated value. Such a minimum share price was used in the past to prevent corporations from abusing present shareholders by selling newly issued shares cheaply, but other protections exist nowadays, so corporations now tend to have no-par shares.

There are several classes of shares, including:

- Common shares or *ordinary* shares. Owners of these vote; they are the corporation's basic (*residual*) owners, the ones who decide who shall be on the board of directors that manages the corporation for the owners and declares dividends to owners.

- Preferred shares or other special shares. Owners of these usually do not vote unless there is a problem, but in return they have rights such as receiving a fixed dividend each year or converting their preferred shares to common shares.

- Class A, Class B, and other such categorizations. Whether these are more like common shares or preferred shares depends on the specific rights they carry. Many corporations use these arbitrary terms because the complexity of rights often prevents a simple categorization into common or preferred.

The balance sheet or notes disclose any special classes of shares or rights.

The face of the balance sheet or, more usually, a note, will list all the kinds of shares the corporation is authorized to issue, specify any special rights, and show the amount of share capital obtained on the original issuance of each kind of share. The cash or other consideration received for such share capital is the property of the corporation: except in specific circumstances, the shareholders have no right to get it back.

b. Retained Earnings

The balance sheet discloses the accumulated amount of retained earnings.

Earnings of a corporation belong to the corporation, not to its owners. The shareholders can receive the earnings only if the board of directors declares a dividend. The balance sheet shows the amount of any retained earnings (past earnings minus past dividends) as a separate owners' equity item.

c. Other Items in Shareholders' Equity

Shareholders' equity can contain some peculiar items, because business affairs are much more complex than just two categories, share capital and retained earnings. Because of this, American companies and some others have a whole schedule of shareholders' (stockholders') equity. Here are three you are likely to see:

- *Capital in excess of par (or stated) value.* If the company's shares have a stated issue price or par value, and shares are issued for more than that, the difference is put into a special equity account with a name like "contributed surplus" or "capital in excess of stated value."

- *Treasury shares.* In some legal jurisdictions, companies whose shares are publicly traded on stock markets are allowed to buy some of their own shares. Treasury shares could have been listed with the company's assets, as an investment in itself, but that is thought to be double counting because the shares' value is represented by the other assets already. Instead, the cost of such shares is deducted from the owners' equity to produce a net equity figure, the equity of real owners, other than the corporation itself.

- *Accumulated foreign currency translation adjustment.* This mouthful of an item is a bit of an embarrassment. It arises from changes in the relative values of currencies. For example, if a company has assets in a foreign branch,

A corporation's equity may contain items other than share capital and retained earnings.

purchased in the foreign currency, their values on the balance sheet will change if they are converted to Canadian dollars at current dollar exchange rates, which are different than the rates existing when they were acquired. The conversion to Canadian dollars, necessary in preparing the balance sheet, can therefore produce a change in the assets' values. Nothing except the exchange rate has changed, so the effects of the exchange rate change are put into an equity account called foreign currency translation adjustment, so that the balance sheet will balance (double entry means that changing the assets' values requires changing something else too). This account, which can be positive or negative, accumulates all the adjustments needed over time to prepare Canadian dollar balance sheets. It is included in equity largely because there doesn't seem to be anywhere else to put it. In future years, this adjustment may be part of the calculation of income and so form part of retained earnings, but for now, it just sort of sits there in equity.

d. Format of a Corporation's Shareholders' Equity Section

Thus, in addition to its lists of assets and liabilities, a corporation's balance sheet has an owners' equity section showing various legal details to assist present owners and potential future owners:

2-12

Exhibit

Shareholders' (or stockholders') equity	
Share capital:	
Authorized shares (narrative, normally in the notes)	
Issued capital received:	
Class A shares (for example)	$XXXX
Class B shares (for example)	XXXX
Capital in excess of stated value (if any)	XXXX
Total issued capital	$XXXX
Retained earnings	XXXX
Foreign currency translation adjustment (+ or −)	(XXXX)
	$XXXX
Less treasury shares, at cost	(XXXX)
Net total shareholders' equity	$XXXX

Corporate Groups

Many companies we are familiar with, such as General Motors, Bombardier, Bank of Nova Scotia, Sears, and Pepsico, are not single corporations, but rather they are groups of many, often hundreds, of corporations. The balance sheet of such a corporate group attempts to represent what that group looks like as a "consolidated" *economic* entity, and so looks a lot like that of a single corporation, though it is an aggregation of many legally separate corporations. Doing this aggregation requires complex accounting techniques that are mostly beyond the scope of this book (except for brief coverage in section 9.7). For now, there are some points worth keeping in mind about a consolidated balance sheet of a corporate group:

- Look for the word "consolidated" at the top of the balance sheet and the other financial statements. That may be your main clue that you are dealing with a corporate group.

- The shareholders' equity section represents the equity of the primary (or parent) corporation in the group. The whole balance sheet is done from the point of view of the parent corporation and its owners, the group's controlling owners.

- Sometimes some of the other corporations in the group (called subsidiaries) are partly owned by other people or corporations outside the parent corporation. Such other partial owners are called minority or noncontrolling interests, and their equity in the subsidiary corporation is shown as a liability on the consolidated balance sheet, not as part of equity. You can think of this minority interest liability as representing the obligation of the parent company to the minority owners.

A corporate group has a consolidated balance sheet, likely with minority interest and goodwill.

- Frequently, the parent company pays more for the equity (assets minus liabilities) of another corporation than the individual assets minus liabilities appear to be worth. The parent might do this because it values some factors not on the subsidiary's balance sheet, such as skilled employees or management, brand reputation, innovative marketing strategies, or expected savings or synergies to be realized when the two corporations combine some of their efforts. The whole of the subsidiary, you might say, is worth more than the sum of its parts. In such a case, and depending on the particular accounting method used, the difference between what the parent corporation paid and the sum of the subsidiary's assets and liabilities added into the balance sheet, adjusting for such things as minority interest, is called consolidated goodwill (or just goodwill) and is shown on the consolidated balance sheet in the noncurrent assets section.

The balance sheet of a corporate group therefore looks something like this (goodwill and minority interest appear only if the group's financial arrangements make them appropriate):

2-13

Exhibit

Corporate Group, Inc.	
Consolidated Balance Sheet as at (Date)	
ASSETS	**LIABILITIES AND SHAREHOLDERS' EQUITY**

Current assets:
    Cash, receivables, inventories,
    etc.
Noncurrent assets:
    Land, buildings, etc., less
    amortization
    Consolidated goodwill, less
    amortization
	Current liabilities:
	    Bank loans, payables, etc.
	
	Noncurrent liabilities:
	    Mortgages, bonds, future income
	    tax, etc.
	    Minority (noncontrolling) interest
	Shareholders' equity:
	    Share capital *(parent company only)*
	    Retained earnings *(parent company only)*

Summary of the Kinds of Business Organizations

Exhibit 2.14 shows a summary of the four kinds of business organizations.

Exhibit

Summary of Kinds of Business Organizations			
Kind	**Legality**	**Owner(s)**	**Equity accounts**
Proprietorship	Not separate from owner	One proprietor	Capital and retained earnings are combined
Partnership	Partly separate from owners	Several or many partners	Capital and retained earnings are combined, but each partner's total is calculated
Corporation	Separate from owners	Usually several or many shareholders	Legal share capital is disclosed separately from retained earnings
Corporate Group	Consists of legally separate corporations	Usually several or many shareholders	Legal share capital of parent corporation is disclosed separately from retained earnings

Business Financing

The balance sheet's left side lists the assets; the right side lists the sources of the assets. Here is a list of the main sources (more information about them is in later chapters):

Current Liabilities (due within a year):

- Loans from banks due on demand or otherwise potentially payable sooner rather than later.

- Financing provided by suppliers and other trade creditors by allowing the enterprise to charge its purchases and pay for them later.

- Wages earned by but not yet paid to employees, and taxes withheld from them that are to be turned over to the taxation authorities.

- Estimates of amounts owing for things such as power, interest charges, legal costs, and other debts building up but not yet actually billed to the enterprise.

- Income taxes and other taxes owed by the enterprise.

- Dividends owed by the enterprise (if it is a corporation), declared by the board of directors, but not yet paid to the shareholders.

- Short-term portions of longer-term debts, such as the principal payments due over the next year on long-term mortgages.

Noncurrent Liabilities (debts due more than a year in the future):

- Mortgages, bonded debt (bonds are certificates of debt issued by the enterprise that include detailed legal requirements), debentures (similar to bonds), equipment-purchase agreements, and other debts extending over several years.

- Certain long-term liabilities, such as special loans from owners in addition to their share capital, long-term tax estimates, and estimated liabilities for pensions to be paid to employees when they retire (in excess of money already put aside [funded] for such pensions).

Owners' Equity:

- For a proprietorship: owner's capital (contributed capital and income not withdrawn by proprietor).

- For a partnership: owners' capital (contributed capital and income not withdrawn by partners).

- For a corporation: share capital received for each kind of share plus retained earnings (plus some other items if legal or accounting complexities require them).

Financial Instruments:

Financial instruments may or may not be included in the balance sheet. The term describes the set of contracts, debts, shares, and other arrangements a corporation uses to conduct its business, and to protect itself against changes in prices of important supplies or in important foreign currencies. Double-entry accounting does not incorporate much of the information about these instruments and related activities like hedging (betting both ways on price changes), so the notes to the financial statements are increasingly used to summarize the company's activities, risks, and current position with regard to these. Many of the promises and other arrangements needed to run a business do not meet the accounting definition of assets or liabilities and so are often referred to as off-balance-sheet financing.

FOR YOUR INTEREST

When making financial decisions, managers, investors, and bankers frequently want to know what the assets, liabilities, and equity are worth today, not what they were valued at when they were recorded in a transaction that might have happened years ago. Much research has been done on alternative bases of accounting, for example, current value accounting, which would show assets and liabilities at current market values, not values determined by historical transactions. From the sixties to the early eighties, authors such as E.O. Edwards, P.W. Bell, R.J. Chambers, and R.R. Sterling explored how to improve financial accounting by getting closer to such current values. Considerable theoretical and other research was done into how to do current value accounting, and there have been some experiments with current values in countries, or times, when inflation was high. In Canada in the mid-1980s, for example, companies were encouraged to try it out in addition to their regular financial statements.

But the research and experimentation have demonstrated fairly conclusively that non-transactional current value accounting is an idea whose time has not yet come. It becomes more attractive in times of high inflation, when historical transaction values tend to differ greatly from current values, but inflation has not been very high for some years. More seriously, people can agree on what a transaction is, but they have a lot of trouble agreeing on what current value to use, because current values are unavoidably hypothetical, being based on judgments of what values might be rather than actual events. You don't really know what your car is worth until you sell it. Most accounting researchers have concluded that the historical transaction basis of financial accounting is going to be with us for the foreseeable future.

OW'S YOUR UNDERSTANDING?

Here are two questions you should be able to answer, based on what you have just read:

1. The owners of Blotz Consulting Partnership wonder if they should incorporate their business as Blotz Consulting Inc. What difference would this make to the owners' equity section of the business's balance sheet?

2. What are some common examples of current and noncurrent liabilities, and how do the two types differ?

2.9   A CLOSER LOOK AT BALANCE SHEET CONTENT

The previous sections should have prepared you to understand a real company's balance sheet. The balance sheet of Canadian corporation CAE Inc. in Exhibit 2.15 is taken from the company's Web site www.cae.com. CAE is a high-technology company, a major product being flight simulators, something like large, sophisticated video games for training pilots. Here is how CAE introduced itself in its 2000 annual report, which contained the balance sheet and other financial statements:

CAE at a Glance

Business Profile

CAE is the world's premier provider of simulation and control technologies for training and optimisation solutions in Aerospace, Defence and Forestry.

Business Units

Commercial Simulation and Training

CAE's Commercial Simulation and Training business is the world leader in the design and production of commercial flight simulators and visual systems. CAE is making a major, disciplined move into the pilot training market to fuel growth. Together with the pursuit of simulator maintenance and support activities, specific emphasis will be placed on the establishment of independent training centres and alliances with major airlines and other flight training companies.

Military Simulation and Controls

In the military simulation and training industry, CAE is the premier designer and manufacturer of military flight and land-based simulation and training systems. In the marine controls industry, CAE is the world leader in the supply of control systems for marine applications.

Forestry Systems

CAE's Forestry Systems business is the world leader in providing advanced technology solutions to enable customers to increase the recovery of fibre and the value of their wood products. In the wood products industry, CAE combines proprietary software, sensors and control systems with advanced mechanical designs to provide leading-edge sawmill optimisation and wood processing solutions for the hardwood, softwood and engineered wood industries. In the pulp and paper industry, CAE provides advanced screening solutions worldwide.[7]

Among the things you may notice as you review CAE's balance sheet are:

1. It is *comparative*: it contains figures at two dates (2000 and 1999) to help the users recognize changes. It is standard practice for the more recent figures to be to the left, closer to the words describing those figures.
2. To avoid clutter, the figures are shown in millions of dollars, not exact amounts to the cent. For example, the company had over $163 million in cash at the end of 2000.
3. References are made to various notes. It is not possible to explain every important item on the face of the balance sheet, so extensive explanatory notes are appended to most balance sheets, and the other financial statements. (CAE's notes are *not* provided here: many raise issues we have not yet covered.)

CAE's balance sheet is comparative, consolidated, and heavily footnoted.

4. The balance sheet is described as *consolidated*, which tells us that CAE is a corporate group, not a single corporation.
5. The balance sheet date is March 31. Though December 31 is the most popular accounting year-end ("fiscal" year-end), many companies choose other dates.
6. The balance sheet has been signed by two members of the board of directors to show that the board approves it and to indicate the board's responsibility for it.

Exhibit

CAE Inc.
Consolidated Balance Sheets

As at March 31
(amounts in millions of dollars)

	2000	1999
Assets		
Current assets:		
Cash	$ 163.5	$ 25.6
Short-term investment	71.1	—
Accounts receivable	325.3	266.2
Inventories (note 3)	108.1	121.6
Prepaid expenses	14.5	14.9
Income taxes recoverable	28.6	26.8
	711.1	455.1
Net assets of discontinued operations (note 2)	105.2	147.6
Property, plant and equipment (note 4)	214.8	243.7
Goodwill	144.1	162.5
Other assets (note 5)	49.0	56.3
	$1,224.2	$1,065.2
Liabilities and Shareholders' Equity		
Current liabilities:		
Accounts payable and accrued liabilities	$ 306.7	$ 201.4
Deposits on contracts	219.2	141.1
Long-term debt within one year	0.9	0.9
	526.8	343.4
Long-term debt (note 6)	270.7	296.2
Deferred liabilities	40.6	75.5
Deferred income taxes	6.8	11.8
	844.9	726.9
Shareholders' equity:		
Capital stock (note 8):	122.1	154.2
Retained earnings	272.1	194.2
Currency translation adjustments	(14.9)	(10.1)
	379.3	338.3
	$1,224.2	$1,065.2

(Indicated notes are not included in this book.)

Approved by the Board:

D. H. Burney
Director

L. R. Wilson
Director

Here are some comments about CAE's assets, liabilities, and equity accounts.

Assets: An asset is a resource that an individual, an enterprise, or a country owns or controls and that is expected to provide future benefit.

Some of CAE's assets are cash, accounts receivable (money due from customers), inventories (raw materials, supplies, partly completed products and finished but unsold products), prepaid expenses (expenses paid in advance), property and plant (land, buildings, machinery and equipment), and consolidated goodwill.

The property and plant and goodwill figures are net of cost minus accumulated amortization: in Note 4, CAE tells us that the accumulated amortization on property and plant was $161.8 million at March 31, 2000. Adding that to the $214.8 million net book value on the balance sheet indicates that those assets cost CAE $376.6 million. We can deduce that those assets are 43% amortized ($161.8/376.6). The company does not tell us anywhere what the accumulated amortization on goodwill is, but we know that the goodwill figure is also net of cost minus accumulated amortization.

CAE's recorded assets totalled $1.2242 billion at March 31, 2000.

CAE is also expecting to get over $28 million in income taxes back. (You may have received a tax refund for overpaid income tax—corporations can be in this happy position too.) Finally, CAE has separated the assets of parts of the business it intends to sell off: at the end of 2000, these amounted to $105.2 million. Note 2 tells us that these include property, equipment, goodwill, and current assets (minus some current liabilities). They are gathered together and classified separately on the balance sheet so that they will not be confused with the assets that CAE intends to use to earn income in the future.

Liabilities: A liability is a presently existing commitment to transfer an individual's, enterprise's, or country's resources to others in the future. Liabilities can be legally owed debts, but they also can be estimates of future payments based on past agreements. As examples of the first group, CAE has accounts payable to its suppliers and long-term debt. As examples of the second group, CAE has $6.8 million of estimated future income tax ("deferred income taxes") and $40.6 million of other unspecified long-term liabilities. CAE shows no minority interest liability because the company has bought 100% of every subsidiary company, leaving no minority owners still involved. The company also has received $219.2 million from customers as deposits on contracts, which are liabilities until the company completes the contracts. CAE does not expect to have to return that money, but might have to if the work for some reason is not completed, and, in any case, the company has not yet earned the money, so the amount is shown as a liability. The balance sheet is showing us something about how the company does business.

CAE's liability financing totalled $844.9 million at March 31, 2000.

Working capital: What is CAE's current financial strength? We can calculate the company's working capital at March 31, 2000 ($711.1 – $526.8 = $184.3) and (1999 = $111.7), and its working capital ratio for 2000 ($711.1/$526.8 = 1.35) and (1999 = 1.33). The company's working capital and working capital ratio both increased from 1999 to 2000. The proportion of working capital made up of unsold inventories has declined since 1999. All in all, the company is in a good current position, apparently able to pay its current liabilities as required, and with sizeable cash and short-term investments should some accounts payable have to be paid before enough accounts receivable have been collected.

CAE's working capital and working capital ratio have increased from 1999 to 2000.

The company's current position may be viewed as even stronger than the working capital calculation implies. Customer deposits totalled $219.2 million at the end of 2000. Assuming that these deposits will not have to be repaid but will be kept by CAE when the contracts are completed, you could recalculate working capital and the working capital ratio, leaving those deposits out of the current liabilities. This is an example of a general rule of using ratios: you should consider altering standard ratios to take into account what you know about a company's particular circumstances.

Owners' equity: The third term in the balance sheet equation is owners' equity, the residual ownership interest in the enterprise. CAE has $122 million of contributed share capital ("capital stock"), all of which is in common shares because, as Note 8 explains, the company has not issued any of the preferred shares it is authorized to issue. Total share capital has declined from 1999 because the company bought back some of its own shares during the year. Instead of keeping these shares as treasury shares, the company just cancelled them, reducing its share capital.

CAE's equity financing totalled $379.3 million at March 31, 2000.

The company has also earned income and has not paid enough dividends to distribute all of the assets representing that income to shareholders, so it had retained earnings of $272.1 million at the end of 2000, more than its share capital. That is more than the company's cash on hand, because accrual income includes more than cash income, and because cash also is raised and spent by borrowing, investing in noncurrent assets, etc. The "Currency translation adjustment" had a negative balance of nearly $15 million at the end of 2000. Because of CAE's extensive foreign operations, this adjustment (which involves all the asset and liability accounts, with the net effect shown in equity) is quite large.

CAE is financed more by creditors than by owners (shareholders).

Debt versus equity financing: We can see from the balance sheet what proportion of the assets are financed by liabilities versus equity, creditors versus owners. The assets totalled $1.224 billion at the end of 1999: $844.9 million of that was financed by debt and $379.3 million by equity. The debt–equity ratio was thus 2.22 ($844.9/$379.3) at the end of 2000 (2.15 at the end of 1998). So creditors have provided more money to the company than owners have, and the proportion provided by creditors has increased a little since 1999.

(F) OR YOUR INTEREST

Why do managers care about their companies' balance sheets? The basic reason is that many outsiders do, including owners, creditors, tax authorities, and unions. Read any issue of a business newspaper or magazine, and you will see opinions like the following expressed:

- "T Inc. has a weak financial structure. Management must solve this problem before risk-shy investors can be expected to take an interest in the company."

- "H Ltd. has large cash reserves, so one can only guess that management is looking to buy another company to add to H's consolidated group."

- "The prices for corporate bonds have responded poorly to recent changes in interest rates because too many corporate balance sheets show too much debt."

- "In the current turbulent business climate, managers must pay more attention to financing short-term assets with something other than bank borrowing."

The balance sheet reports what the organization's financial position (assets, liabilities, and owners' equity) is at a point in time. It shows the assets that management has chosen to acquire for the organization, and how management has decided to finance those assets. Therefore, it provides a useful picture of the state of the company and is used by many outsiders to evaluate the quality of management's decisions on obtaining, deploying, and financing assets. For better or worse, it is the summary of all the information recognized by accounting and is, to many people, the basic scorecard of management's stewardship of the company. That's why the balance sheet is usually signed by members of the board of directors, the uppermost level of management, responsible to the owners and creditors.

The balance sheet is a measure of assets, liabilities, and owners' equity at a certain date: it is a snapshot of the organization, listing its stock of resources, obligations, and ownership interest at that date. One deficiency with the balance sheet is that it is a static snapshot, not a video: it does not tell us how the organization arrived at the position of having a particular set of assets or liabilities. For that information, we need to look at the other parts of the financial statements, which we will do in Chapters 3 and 4.

 OW'S YOUR UNDERSTANDING?

Here are two questions you should be able to answer, based on what you have just read:

1. What sort of assets does CAE have for conducting its business?

2. If CAE issued additional common shares for $150 million cash right after midnight March 31, 2000, what would be its (a) working capital, (b) current ratio, and (c) debt–equity ratio? ((a) $334.3, which equals $711.1 + $150 − $526.8; (b) 1.63, which equals ($711.1 + $150) / $526.8; (c) 1.60, which equals $844.9 / ($379.3 + $150).)

2.10   A LOOK AT A BANK'S BALANCE SHEET

To emphasize that each company's balance sheet reflects the kind of business the company does and the way the company is organized, here is the October 31, 1999, balance sheet of the Toronto-Dominion Bank (see the bank's Web page at www.tdbank.ca). You'll see that there are some recognizable accounts, but in general the balance sheet is much different from CAE's. (As in the CAE example, the financial statement notes are *not* provided—the TD's notes are very long and complex, because there is much about the bank's financing and use of financial instruments that must be explained, so they are not included either.)

The Toronto-Dominion Bank
Consolidated Balance Sheets

As at October 31 *(millions of dollars)*	1999	1998
Assets		
Cash resources:		
Cash, deposits with Bank of Canada and		
non-interest-bearing deposits with other banks	$ 1,464	$ 1,379
Interest-bearing deposits with other banks	4,762	1,700
	6,226	3,079
Securities purchased under resale agreements	25,708	12,291
Securities (Note 2)		
Investment	18,029	12,512
Trading	51,064	37,207
	69,093	49,719
Loans (net of allowance for credit losses) (Note 3)		
Residential mortgages	31,483	32,255
Consumer instalment and other personal	20,443	15,160
Business and government	35,559	37,511
	87,485	84,926
Other		
Customers' liability under acceptances	9,040	9,948
Land, buildings and equipment (Note 4)	1,738	1,666
Other assets	15,127	20,202
	25,905	31,816
Total assets	$214,417	$181,831
Liabilities and Shareholders' Equity		
Deposits (Note 6)		
Personal	$ 52,774	$ 47,693
Banks	30,901	17,063
Business and government	56,711	55,921
	140,386	120,677
Other		
Acceptances	9,040	9,948
Obligations related to securities sold short	15,044	13,034
Obligations related to securities sold under repurchase		
agreements	19,241	8,421
Other liabilities (Note 7)	15,621	17,612
	58,946	49,015
Subordinated notes (Note 8)	3,217	3,606
Non-controlling interest in subsidiary	335	—
SHAREHOLDERS' EQUITY		
Capital stock (Note 9)		
Preferred	833	845
Common	2,006	1,301
Retained earnings	8,694	6,387
	11,533	8,533
Total liabilities and shareholders' equity	$214,417	$181,831

A. Charles Baillie   William T. Brock
Chairman and   *Deputy Chairman*
Chief Executive Officer

Each balance sheet is a picture of that particular organization's financial character.

The bank's balance sheet is just an example of how accounting adjusts to the kind of organization being accounted for. Many other kinds of organization have balance sheets that are quite different from the standard sort of format we saw for CAE, such as governments, charities, and insurance companies. Here are some brief comments about the bank example:

- The numbers are huge: at October 31, 1999, TD Bank had assets exceeding $214 *billion*.

- The bank doesn't use the current and noncurrent categorizations for assets and liabilities. Using an arbitrary one-year definition for such categorization is not thought to make sense for a bank's assets or liabilities, because monies flow in and out under all sorts of frequently complex arrangements.

- The bank has perhaps surprisingly little cash. If we all wanted the money in our accounts at the same time, the bank wouldn't have it. You can see that personal deposits alone (under liabilities) of $52.7 billion far exceed the bank's cash.

- The money people have in the bank is recorded as a liability (the bank owes the money to the depositors) and the money people owe for loans by the bank is an asset. You can see how the bank does its business: at October 31, 1999, it had deposits from customers of $140 billion, had lent out $87 billion and invested $69 billion.

- The TD is a corporate group. It has a small noncontrolling interest (minority interest) liability, $335 million, and included in its $15.127 billion of other assets is a small amount of goodwill.

- The bank sets its shareholders' equity section out the same way as most companies. Given the size of the bank's assets and liabilities, its equity is quite small.

- You may conclude, rightly, from all this that you cannot use standard ratios like the working capital, debt–equity, or quick ratios to analyze banks. The information for such ratios is either not provided or the ratio would not be meaningful in the ordinary way. An example is the debt–equity ratio. The TD's ratio at the end of 1999, using the standard formula, would be 17.6 (($140,386 + $58,946 + $3,217 + $335) / $11,533). This is a huge ratio, and for an ordinary company would spell big trouble, but for the bank it just reflects the way banks operate. They take in money and lend it out or invest it, and to do so do not need capital from owners so much as from depositors (the bank's creditors). On the other hand, banks can be precarious financially—you can see that if there were a "run" on the bank, everyone wanting their deposited money at once, the bank would have difficulty. The depositors are taking a much bigger risk, relatively, than are the bank's shareholders.

2.11 TERMS TO BE SURE YOU UNDERSTAND

A great many terms were introduced in this chapter. As suggested in section 1.10, make sure you know what they mean *in accounting*. If any are unclear to you, check the chapter again or refer to the Glossary of Terms at the back of the book. Many of the terms will be used repeatedly as the book proceeds, so your understanding of them will deepen. Some particularly important terms introduced in Chapter 1 are included again here as a helpful reminder.

Account(s)	Debts	Overdrafts
Accounts payable	Deficit	Owner's capital
Accounts receivable	Dividend(s)	Owners' equity
Accumulated amortization	Double entry	Pacioli
Acid test ratio	Earnings	Par value
Annual report	Equity	Parent
Asset(s)	Exchange	Partners' capital
Balance	Financial instruments	Partnership
Balance sheet	Financial position	Post(ed)
Balance sheet equation	Foreign currency translation	Preferred shares
Board of directors	adjustment	Profit
Bond(s)	General ledger	Proprietorship
Book value (asset)	Goodwill	Public companies
Book value (equity)	Income	Quick ratio
Bookkeeping	Inventory(ies)	Receivable
Common shares	Journal entry(ies)	Reclassification
Company(ies)	Liability(ies)	Retained earnings
Consolidated	Loss	Share capital
Consolidated goodwill	Market capitalization	Shareholders' equity
Corporate group	Market value	Shares
Corporation(s)	Minority interest liability	Stated value
Creditors	Minority interest(s)	Statement of financial
Credits	Mortgage(s)	position
Current assets	Net	Stock markets
Current liabilities	Noncontrolling interest(s)	Stocks
Current ratio	Noncurrent assets	Subsidiary(ies)
Current value accounting	Noncurrent liabilities	Treasury shares
Debenture(s)	No-par	Trial balance
Debits	Note(s)	Working capital
Debt–equity ratio	Off-balance-sheet	Working capital ratio

2.12 CONTINUING DEMONSTRATION CASE

INSTALLMENT 2

Data for Installment 2

In Installment 1, Mavis Janer and Tomas Brot were thinking about starting a business together and began working on a business plan by listing their objectives in having a business and the risks and constraints they were concerned about. If you have forgotten about those, you might look back to the "Results for Installment 1" in section 1.11 to see the lists.

After much investigation and debate, Mavis and Tomas came up with a proposal for a business. They had observed a large growth in boutique-style retail stores, usually managed by families, in their region of the country, but felt such stores were not well supported either by supplies of attractive merchandise or marketing ideas. They saw a niche they could fill by setting up a regional wholesale distribution company that would provide the boutique retailers with better access to national and international suppliers of goods, and would help in both fitting their product lines to local markets and marketing the products well.

There were other such wholesale distributors in North America, but the local region seemed not well serviced by them, and Mavis and Tomas felt they had some ideas the other distributors had not thought of. The field would be very competitive, but they saw considerable opportunity for growth as baby boomers reached middle age and increased the demand for boutique retailers, and as international trade opened more opportunities for supplying interesting products at attractive prices.

Mato Inc.'s Financial Starting Point

Many things had to be done before the business could start. Here are some of the actions Mavis and Tomas took.

- They decided to incorporate a company, to provide a financing focus and some limited liability for themselves. They decided to call it Mato Inc., after the first two initials of their first names, and because it sounded vaguely exotic and international.

- They had to raise initial capital. Tomas felt they needed about $125,000 in share capital and substantial additional bank financing to support the inventory the company would carry. They planned to use modern techniques to minimize inventory levels, but, still, inventory would be a significant asset in the business as they foresaw it. After some analysis and discussion with relatives and friends, they assembled the following capital: Mavis would buy 40% of the issued voting shares with $50,000 cash from her inheritance, and Tomas would buy 24% of the shares. He did not have the $30,000 cash to make the purchase, but he would contribute his car to the business, at an agreed value of $10,000, and $20,000 in cash from his savings. Five friends and relatives agreed to contribute $45,000 cash for the remaining 36% of the shares. In addition, Tomas's father agreed to lend the business $15,000. He wanted to be a creditor of the new company; he did not want shares because he was worried about his health and wanted to be able to get the money back if he needed it.

- The company needed a management structure. It was decided that the board of directors would consist of Mavis (as chairperson), Tomas, and a representative of the five relatives and friends. Mavis would be president, and Tomas would be vice-president. Basically, Mavis was to look after business development and marketing, and Tomas would see to financing and day-to-day operations.

- They found a vacant warehouse building that could be rented at an attractive rate and was located both centrally in the region they wanted to serve and reasonably close to their homes. The building would require some renovation to meet their needs, but otherwise they could move right in and get going.

- Tomas put together a business plan and approached several banks and other financial institutions for support. On the strength of his and Mavis's background and of having their business plan and the above investments already arranged, he was able to secure the support he required: basically, a line of credit (a preapproved borrowing limit) under which the company would have approved credit of up to $80,000 now, and further credit based on inventories and accounts receivable once operations got underway. Mavis and Tomas had to personally guarantee the line of credit to the company and pledge their shares in the company as collateral on any loan.

On March 1, 2000, the new business was established. On that day:

- The company was officially incorporated, having only one class of no-par shares;

- The company received its first bill (a fee of $1,100 to be paid to the lawyer handling the incorporation);

- The various investors paid their cash;

- A five-year lease was signed for the warehouse space;

- Tomas signed his car over to the company; and

- Mavis left her job to become the new company's only full-time employee at a monthly salary of $2,500.

Tomas would stay in his bank job for a while, and Mavis would spend most of this initial period making contacts with suppliers and retailers, supervising renovations, and doing other tasks necessary to get the business started. They felt it would be better if Tomas kept his paying job at the bank, instead of quitting and increasing the demands on the new company's cash. Until he left his bank job, Tomas would keep track of the time he put in on the company and be paid later at the same rate as Mavis, prorated over 200 hours per month, which was the number of hours per month Mavis expected to put in while getting the business started.

Results for Installment 2

Journal entries

These entries record the March 1, 2000 transactions:

- No entry for the company incorporation. Not an accounting transaction.

- DR Incorporation costs asset   1,100

    CR Accounts payable   1,100

    To record the lawyer's bill for incorporating the company.

- DR Cash   130,000

    CR Loan payable   15,000

    CR Share capital   115,000

    To record the initial investments in the company.

- No entry for the lease signing. Not an accounting transaction.

- DR Car asset   10,000

    CR Share capital   10,000

    To record signing Tomas's car over to the company for its agreed value in shares.

• No entry for Mavis's becoming the company's employee. Not an accounting transaction.

Company's initial balance sheet

1. Mavis and Tomas prepared two balance sheets, one with details of everyone's contributions and a second in a more standard format. The first one is shown below:

Mato Inc.
Balance Sheet Details as at March 1, 2000

Assets		Sources of Assets	
Cash:		Due to lawyer	$ 1,100
From Mavis	$ 50,000	Investments:	
From Tomas	20,000	Mavis's shares	50,000
From other		Tomas's shares	30,000
shareholders	45,000	Other shareholders	45,000
From Tomas's father	15,000	Tomas's father	15,000
Car	10,000		
Incorporation costs	1,100		
TOTAL	$141,100	TOTAL	$141,100

2. The second starting balance sheet is shown below. In it, Mavis and Tomas classified the loan from Tomas's father as a current liability because he had said he might want it back any time. The cost to the company of Tomas's car was the agreed value, as discussed above. The incorporation costs were shown as an asset because Tomas and Mavis felt there was a future benefit resulting from the incorporation of the company. However, they were not entirely sure about that because it was hard to say what the benefit actually was or for how long it would have value.

Mato Inc.
Formal Balance Sheet as at March 1, 2000

Assets		Liabilities and Shareholders' Equity	
Current assets:		Current liabilities:	
Cash	$130,000	Accounts payable	$ 1,100
Noncurrent assets:		Loan payable	15,000
Automobile (at cost)	10,000	Shareholders' equity:	
Incorporation costs	1,100	Share capital	125,000
TOTAL	$141,100	TOTAL	$141,100

2.13 HOMEWORK AND DISCUSSION TO DEVELOP UNDERSTANDING

PROBLEM 2.1*
Prepare a simple balance sheet, calculate working capital

Bluebird Bakery, a partnership that rents its bakery premises, had the following account balances at July 31, 2001. Prepare a balance sheet for the partnership by placing each account in the appropriate location in the balance sheet. From the balance sheet, calculate the partnership's working capital and working capital ratio.

Bakery equipment cost	$129,153	J. Bird partner's capital	$52,921
Demand loan from bank	14,500	Accumulated amortization	43,996
Supplies inventory cost	13,220	Cash on hand	895
Owing to suppliers	11,240	Owing by customers	3,823
B. Blue partner's capital	27,425	Cash in bank	4,992
Wages owing to employees	2,246	Unsold baked goods cost	245

PROBLEM 2.2*
Prepare separate and then combined balance sheets for a couple

Janet and Sam, who were engaged to be married, each made lists of their financial resources and the claims on these resources on Friday, June 15, 2001. Here are their lists:

Janet's list:	
Cash in chequing account	$ 500
Stereo	2,000
Damage deposit on hall (for wedding)	300
Sam's list:	
Cash in chequing account	$1,000
Student loan	2,100
Furniture	500
Prepaid rent on hall (for wedding)	400

1. Prepare a June 15, 2001, balance sheet for Janet using her list.
2. Prepare a June 15, 2001, balance sheet for Sam using his list.
3. On Saturday, June 16, 2001, Janet and Sam were married. Their wedding presents included:

Cash	$2,000
Household gifts	1,500
Parents' payment toward Sam's loan	2,100

The couple paid $1,000 immediately for the band that played at their wedding. There were no damages to the hall during the reception. After the party, they took a honeymoon weekend (lasting until Tuesday evening) and charged all their expenses on Janet's credit card, which they knew would be due at the end of July 2001. The honeymoon cost $600.

Prepare a balance sheet for the couple as at Wednesday, June 20, 2001. Be sure to include all the financial information given above.

PROBLEM 2.3*
Examples of balance sheet categories

1. Define each of the following and choose an example of each from the CAE balance sheet in section 2.9 of this chapter (or from the balance sheet of any company familiar or interesting to you).

   a. current asset
   b. noncurrent asset
   c. current liability
   d. noncurrent liability
   e. owners' equity item

2. Do you think the examples you selected will always be classified in the same way by all enterprises? Why or why not? Give examples if possible.

PROBLEM 2.4*
Personal balance sheet and debt–equity ratio

1. List your own personal resources and obligations and try to fit them into accounting's standard balance sheet format in which the resources are listed on one side and debts and claims against the resources are listed on the other, keeping in mind that total resources must balance total debts plus residual equity. In doing this, think about:

   • which of your resources and obligations would or would not be reported on the balance sheet;

   • what would likely be disclosed about each;

   • which are short-term or long-term; and

   • which are easy or difficult to value numerically.

   (If you have completed a credit application or student loan application, the things you reported there might be a good starting point.)

2. What decision-making information might your list of resources and obligations provide?
3. Calculate your personal debt–equity ratio (total liabilities divided by total equity). Are you soundly financed?

PROBLEM 2.5*
Journal entries for simple transactions

The events listed below all took place on December 15, 2001. Provide the journal entry necessary to record each event in the accounts of Company A on that date. If no entry is required, indicate that and give reasons. If you feel an assumption is necessary, state it.

   a. A new general manager is hired at an annual salary of $60,000.
   b. Company A receives a bill for $200 from a newspaper for an advertisement to be run on December 31, 2001. Payment is not due for 60 days.
   c. A bond is purchased by Company A for $2,000 cash. The bond will have a maturity value of $2,500 in three years because interest will accumulate.
   d. A landscaper agrees to improve land owned by Company A. The agreed price for the work is $700.
   e. An order for $900 of merchandise is received from a customer along with a cash deposit of $300.
   f. A $600 insurance premium for coverage over the period from December 15, 2001, to December 14, 2002, is paid in cash.

PROBLEM 2.6*
Journal entry for a business acquisition

Big Ideas Inc. decided to buy parts of the business of a competitor, which was cutting back operations. For a price of $4,200,000 (a $1,000,000 down payment and the rest in four equal annual installments plus interest at 12% per annum), Big Ideas got inventory it valued at $280,000, land it valued at $1,500,000, a retail store building it valued at $1,800,000, furniture and equipment it valued at $470,000, and some dealership rights it valued at $40,000. Big Ideas also agreed to pay a bank loan of $130,000 secured by the inventory.

Write a journal entry to record Big Ideas Inc.'s purchase.

PROBLEM 2.7*
Prepare simple balance sheet, notes, what-if analysis

Clambake Kate's Inc. is a Maritime eatery specializing in shellfish and soups. The premises are rented and all sales are for cash, so the company has only a few balance sheet accounts. The accounts as at May 31, 2001, are as follows.

Food supplies cost	$ 2,100	Payable to suppliers	$ 5,300
Equipment cost	64,900	Long-term loan	25,000
Other supplies cost	4,500	Wages payable	900
Cash in bank	2,200	Share capital issued	10,000
Accumulated amortization	27,400	Retained earnings	5,100

1. Prepare a balance sheet for Clambake Kate's Inc. as at May 31, 2001. Include any notes to the balance sheet that you think might be useful.
2. Comment on the company's financial position as shown by your balance sheet.
3. Suppose, when you were reviewing the company's accounts after preparing the balance sheet, you found an error in the records. The company had paid a supplier $2,900, but that payment had inadvertently not been deducted from the company's bank account record nor from its record of accounts payable to suppliers. You decided to record that payment. What changes therefore resulted in the balance sheet you prepared in part 1 and in your comments in part 2?

PROBLEM 2.8*
Prepare a balance sheet from simple transactions

South Shore Manufacturing Ltd. had this balance sheet on July 31, 2001:

South Shore Manufacturing Ltd. Balance Sheet as at July 31, 2001				
Assets			**Liabilities and Owners' Equity**	
Current assets:			Current liabilities:	
Cash	$ 24,388		Bank indebtedness	$ 53,000
Accounts receivable	89,267		Accounts payable	78,442
Inventories, cost	111,436		Taxes payable	12,665
Expenses paid in			Current part of	
advance	7,321		mortgage	18,322
	$232,412			$162,429
Noncurrent assets:			Noncurrent liabilities:	
Land, cost	$ 78,200		Mortgage, less current	$213,734
Factory, cost	584,211		Pension liability	67,674
	$662,411		Loan from shareholder	100,000
Accum. amortization	(198,368)			$381,408
	$464,043		Shareholders' equity:	
			Share capital issued	$ 55,000
			Retained earnings	97,618
				$152,618
	$696,455			$696,455

On August 1, 2001, South Shore Manufacturing experienced the following transactions:

1. $10,000 of the shareholder's loan was repaid.
2. A customer paid one of the accounts receivable, $11,240.
3. Additional inventory costing $5,320 was purchased on credit.
4. The company issued new shares for $22,000 cash.
5. The proceeds of the share issue were used to reduce the bank loan.
6. More land costing $52,000 was purchased for $12,000 cash plus a new long-term mortgage for the rest.
7. More factory equipment costing $31,900 was purchased on credit, with $13,900 due in six months and the rest due in 24 months.

Prepare a new balance sheet for the company as of August 1, 2001, after taking these transactions into account. You can do this directly by just reasoning out the effect of each transaction on the balance sheet accounts, or using journal entries with a computer spreadsheet, or with a set of accounts written on paper.

PROBLEM 2.9*
Explain some accounting terms without accounting jargon

Explain each of the following terms in words a nonaccountant might understand (that is, with a minimum of accounting jargon):

1. transaction
2. balance
3. debit

4. to debit something
5. account
6. general ledger
7. trial balance

PROBLEM 2.10*
Record and post entries, do trial balance and balance sheet

Cynthia has just started a proprietorship she calls Beach Ready. She will have a six-bed tanning salon and will sell various lotions, beachwear, and other summery stuff. To get the business started, she contributed $15,000 from her savings plus a sound system for playing music in the tanning booths. She values the system at $1,500.

She bought the needed tanning beds, a computer to keep track of customers' tanning minutes and other equipment for $21,200, paying $9,200 down and agreeing to pay the rest in 24 monthly installments of $500 plus interest at 10%. After checking out several possible locations, she signed a 2-year lease for space in a neighbourhood mall, costing $1,100 rent per month. Then she fixed up and painted the store at a cost of $1,600 cash. (This created an asset that you might call "leasehold improvements" because she owns the improvements although not the property she improved.) The last thing she did before the grand opening was to stock up on lotions, beachwear, and other things to sell. All that inventory cost $17,100. She paid the suppliers an initial $2,300 and promised to pay the rest within 60 days.

1. Prepare journal entries for the transactions indicated above.
2. Create a general ledger, by hand, or using a computer spreadsheet, and post your entries to it.
3. Prepare a trial balance to show that your ledger is in balance.
4. From your trial balance, prepare a properly classified balance sheet for Beach Ready.
5. Calculate the proprietorship's working capital and debt–equity ratios from your balance sheet.

PROBLEM 2.11*
Classified balance sheet

Identify what is wrong with the following balance sheet and prepare a properly classified balance sheet instead.

Assets		Liabilities and Shareholders' Equity	
Inventory	$ 28,000	Bank loan	$ 20,000
Cash on hand	6,000	Accumulated amortization	36,400
Bank account	(7,100)	Mortgage due in 5 years	41,500
Account payable overpaid	200	Income tax refund expected	(1,800)
Treasury shares	1,500	Share capital	40,000
Currency translation adjustment	(600)	Goodwill (net of amortization)	(14,000)
Property and plant	83,000	Minority interest	2,200
Accounts receivable	31,200	Accounts payable	20,900
Deficit	4,100	Estimated interest due	1,100
	$146,300		$146,300

PROBLEM 2.12*
Forms of business organization

Match each term on the left with the most fitting description on the right.

a. Owner's capital
b. Minority interest
c. Retained earnings
d. Consolidated equity
e. Owners' capital
f. Common shares
g. Par value shares

1. Partnership equity
2. Directly contributed equity
3. The corporation invests in itself
4. Can't be issued for less than the stated amount
5. Indirectly contributed equity
6. Proprietorship equity
7. Investment cost exceeds details of what was acquired

h. Consolidated goodwill
i. Capital in excess of par
j. Treasury shares

8. Parent corporation owners' interest
9. Interest of owners outside the parent company
10. Shares were issued for more than the stated amount

PROBLEM 2.13
Users and uses of the balance sheet

Consider any company you are familiar with or interested in and make a list of all the people who might be interested in its balance sheet. Make your list using the headings:

<u>Person (decision maker)</u>   and   <u>Use (decision to be made)</u>

Try to think about the "use" issue broadly: your list could easily be a long one. You might make it even more broad by including people you think might like to use the balance sheet but whose needs are not served by it as you understand it, or who do not have timely access to it.

PROBLEM 2.14
Double-entry transactional records: strength and weakness

In a flight of accounting passion, Professor Lump exclaimed, "The double-entry transactional recording system is financial accounting's greatest strength and its greatest weakness!" Lump went on to explain this odd comment. Write down what the professor probably said in explanation.

PROBLEM 2.15
A real company's resources, sources, and debt–equity ratio

Using the Toronto-Dominion Bank balance sheet in section 2.10 (or that of any other company) as an example, answer the following questions:

1. What resources does the company have?
2. How are those resources financed?

PROBLEM 2.16
Prepare and comment on a simple initial balance sheet

John Graham decided to set up a business as a downtown courier, calling his business QuickJohn Courier. Before he could operate his courier service, there were a few things he needed: a bicycle, a bike lock, a delivery bag, and a good pair of running shoes. He had $200 in savings, but quickly realized that he would need more funds to purchase all of the required items. John asked his Aunt Elizabeth for a loan of $200 and promised that he would pay her back as soon as he could. She said yes.

John purchased a bike for $500, placing $275 down and promising to pay the rest later. He then bought a bike lock for $15, a pair of shoes for $60, and a delivery bag for $25, paying cash for all these items. He began his business on April 15, 2001.

John asked a friend to prepare an initial balance sheet for the new business. The friend had a couple of questions to ask first:

"John, when do you have to repay your Aunt Elizabeth?"

"She never said. But my intention is to pay her back by the end of 2002. I'm sure she would complain if I took longer than that. She wants the money for a big birthday party that year."

"How about the amount you owe on the bicycle: when is that due?"

"The store wants the money right away. I told them I would have to raise the funds by sales in my business, so they said they wanted me to pay just as soon as I could. They made me sign a form saying they could take back the bike and the other stuff if I don't pay."

With this information, prepare the initial balance sheet for QuickJohn Courier as at April 15, 2001, including any notes you think might be useful, and comment on the business's financial condition.

PROBLEM 2.17
Identify transactions and write journal entries for them

The following events happened today at Billowy Balloons, Inc., a sightseeing and advertising company featuring large hot-air balloons. For each event listed below, state whether or not it is an accounting transaction for Billowy and why. If it is an accounting transaction, write a journal entry to record it.

a. The president, despondent over poor sales performance, jumped out of a balloon from 1,000 feet up. The president's salary was $75,000 per year.
b. The president's widow immediately sued the company for $500,000, stating that job-related stress caused him to jump.
c. The company agreed with the barn owner that after the funeral it would pay $10,000 to repair the barn roof that the president had fallen through.
d. Learning about the president's action, shareholder Jumpy John sold his shares, which had cost him $20,000, to Happy Harry for $18,000.
e. Learning about the president's action and concerned about its possible effects on the company's share price, the board of directors declared a dividend of $25,000 to be paid in two weeks as a shareholder morale booster. (A dividend is removed from retained earnings when it is declared, because at that point it becomes a liability to the shareholders until paid.)

PROBLEM 2.18
Purpose and origin of balance sheet

You have been working at a summer job as a clerk in a small store. The new owner of the store comes over to you waving the balance sheet for the store saying, "You're studying accounting, I hear. Can you explain to me what my balance sheet is supposed to be telling me and why it is designed to have two sides? Where did such a way of measuring a business come from, anyway?" Give your reply.

PROBLEM 2.19
Balance sheet information and a nonaccounting career

Write a paragraph in which you identify a nonaccounting career you or someone you know may pursue and explain the interest in balance sheet information that this career might imply. If you really cannot see any relationship between that career and anything reported in a balance sheet, explain why not.

PROBLEM 2.20
Explain balance sheet ideas to a business executive

You are the executive assistant to Stephane Solden, a particularly hard-driving and successful owner of a chain of restaurants. Not long ago, Solden and you were flying to another city and the in-flight movie was so bad the two of you ended up talking about all sorts of things. One subject was Solden's impatience with accountants and accounting, which, probably because the annual audit of the company's accounts was then taking place, seemed particularly strong. How would you respond to the following questions from Solden?

1. The main thing that sticks in my mind about the balance sheet is that the thing balances! Who cares? Why should it matter?
2. My auditor keeps wanting to talk to me about what the balance sheet says about the company's finances and how I've managed them. But I always look to the future—why should I care about the balance sheet when it's just history?
3. Last year, I had a really good idea about the balance sheet. You know, I consider our restaurant managers to be the most important asset the company has. I was going to have the managers added to the balance sheet as assets, so it would show all our assets. But the accountants and auditors didn't seem interested in my idea. Why not?
4. Someone told me once that the balance sheet is a photograph of the business at a particular instant in time, and that you have to be careful because some accountant might have touched up the photo, airbrushed away the warts. What did they mean? Isn't the balance sheet an exact list of all the company's assets and liabilities?

PROBLEM 2.21
Prepare a balance sheet from accounts

Blue Moon Love Products Ltd. manufactures and sells various aids to middle-aged romantics, including special flower bouquets, French "beer for lovers," seductive apparel, and recipes for aphrodisiac cookies. Here are the company's balance sheet accounts as at June 30, 2001, in alphabetical order.

Blue Moon Love Products Inc.
Balance Sheet Accounts as at June 30, 2001

Accumulated amortization	$ 63,700	Owing from customers	$ 6,200
Bank account balance	14,300	Owing to suppliers	21,900
Bank loan	21,200	Retained earnings	47,500
Building	102,100	Share capital issued	25,000
Cash on hand	2,500	Short-term part of mortgage	8,000
Employees' tax not yet remitted	600	Unpaid employee wages	1,800
Fixtures and equipment	37,900	Unsold finished products	29,600
Land	48,000	Unused office supplies	1,400
Long-term part of mortgage owing	71,000	Unused product raw materials	18,700

1. Prepare the company's June 30, 2001, balance sheet from the above accounts.
2. Comment briefly on the company's financial condition as shown by the balance sheet.

PROBLEM 2.22
Identify items as asset, liability, or owners' equity

State whether or not, and why, each of the following items is likely to be an asset, liability, or equity account (perhaps more than one category in some cases) recorded in the balance sheet of the company indicated:

Company	Item
1. Walt Disney Co.	List of subscribers to *Discover* magazine
2. Interpacific Forest Products Ltd.	Funds collected from employees, to be repaid to them after retirement as pensions
3. Wal-Mart	Wal-Mart's satisfied customers
4. Branko Inc.	A lawsuit against the company by a plumber who alleges that Branko failed to pay for work done on the company's premises
5. Canada Safeway Ltd.	Land that Safeway has agreed to sell to a real estate developer once it has been surveyed
6. Wal-Mart	Wal-Mart's dissatisfied customers
7. Dow-Jones Inc.	The *Wall Street Journal*'s skilled group of editors and reporters
8. Imperial Oil Ltd.	Oil discovered on Imperial's property, but still underground and likely to stay there for many years
9. Edmonton Eskimos Football Club	Players under contract to the team
10. The Brick Warehouse	Deposits received from customers of The Brick for furniture not yet delivered to them
11. Torstar Corp.	Profits earned by the *Toronto Star*, but not yet paid out to the owners as dividends
12. Sears Inc.	A fleet of delivery trucks leased by Sears from several truck-leasing firms
13. Downtown Buick Sales Ltd.	A car Downtown Buick leases to real estate salesperson Don Wharton
14. Redpath Industries Ltd.	Funds owing to Redpath by a customer who recently declared bankruptcy
15. Keg Restaurants Ltd.	The phrase "The Keg" and the round logo, both registered trademarks
16. Loblaws	The parking lots surrounding the company's stores
17. Grand Centre Ltd.	A guarantee Grand Centre has made on a bank loan owed by an associated company
18. National Bioengineering Ltd.	A newly developed chemical that shows promise in curing adolescent blemishes once and for all, but that has to be approved by the government

PROBLEM 2.23
Prepare a balance sheet from transactions

Fed up with her dead-end career with a big company, Tanya decided to start her own business manufacturing and selling fresh pasta and a line of associated sauces, and selling cookware and other equipment to go with the food. It took her several weeks to get set up, before she made a single sale.

Record (using journal entries and paper accounts or a computer spreadsheet) the transactions below for PastaPastaPasta Inc., which happened in the preparatory weeks, and prepare the company's balance sheet at the end of the preparatory time.

1. Tanya put personal savings of $45,000 into a new bank account opened in the company's name. She decided that $35,000 of that would go for shares of the company and the rest would be a loan she hoped the company could pay back in a few years.
2. Tanya also provided her large set of recipes and her minivan, to be owned by the new company. She thought the recipes would be worth about $500 and the minivan about $7,500. She was in no hurry to be paid for these items, but thought they should be included in the company's assets.
3. A group of friends and relatives gave her company $25,000 in cash, in return for shares.
4. The company rented space in a small strip mall and paid $2,000 as rent in advance.
5. Another friend, who had no cash but wanted to help, agreed to do some renovations and repainting in the new space, in return for some shares in the company. Tanya and the friend agreed that the work done would have cost $4,500 if she had paid someone else to do it.
6. The company bought a large amount of food processing and storage equipment for $63,250, paying $28,000 in cash and agreeing to pay the rest in five equal annual installments, beginning in six months.
7. Pasta-making supplies costing $4,720 and cookware for resale costing $3,910 were purchased for $1,000 in cash, with the remainder to be paid in 60 days.
8. The company got a $20,000 line of credit from the bank and actually borrowed $2,500 of that, repayable on demand. Tanya had to sign a personal guarantee for anything borrowed under the line of credit.
9. The company paid a lawyer $1,800 for costs of incorporation.

PROBLEM 2.24
Record transactions

The following events happened to Green Stuff Restaurant Inc. For each event that is an accounting transaction:

1. Write a journal entry to record the transaction in Green Stuff's accounts, and
2. Write a journal entry to record the transaction in the accounts of the *other party* to the exchange.

   a. Green Stuff paid a $1,200 bill from its lawyer. A month earlier, the bill had been recorded as owing.
   b. Green Stuff borrowed $5,000 from the Northernmost Bank.
   c. Green Stuff collected $200 from a customer who had owed the money for several months.
   d. Green Stuff was sued for $50,000 by a customer who was scalded when a teapot broke.
   e. The four owners of Green Stuff invested $10,000 cash each in newly issued no-par-value preference shares.

f. Green Stuff took $25,000 of the cash from (e) and invested it temporarily in a 3-month GIC (guaranteed investment certificate) at Southernmost Bank.

g. One of the owners of Green Stuff bought out another by paying that owner $75,000 for her common shares and $10,000 for her preferred shares.

h. A customer who had run short of cash offered to pay his six-month-old bill of $450 by giving Green Stuff a painting that had cost the customer that amount. The painting would look good in the restaurant entrance, so Green Stuff agreed to the customer's offer.

i. The holder of a $70,000 mortgage on Green Stuff's property agreed to convert the mortgage to no-par-value preferred shares in that amount.

j. Green Stuff ordered supplies costing $2,150, to be received next week and paid for within 30 days.

PROBLEM 2.25
Answer questions about balance sheet figures

Answer the question in each case below. No other statements besides the balance sheet are involved or necessary to solve each case.

a. A Ltd.'s property and plant are 40% amortized. The accumulated amortization is $520,000. What is the cost of the property and plant?

b. B Ltd.'s working capital ratio has fallen from 2.20 last year to 1.60 this year. Its current assets went up over that time from $4,290,000 to $5,304,000. What was the dollar change in current liabilities?

c. C Ltd. has the following balance sheet amounts. Current assets $215,300; Share capital $200,000; Noncurrent liabilities $421,300; Noncurrent assets $512,110; Current liabilities $189,230. What is missing and how much is it?

d. D Ltd. has decided to borrow some cash but does not want its debt–equity ratio to go above 2. According to the balance sheet, the company has assets of $6,245,000 and liabilities of $4,116,000. How much can the company borrow?

e. E Ltd.'s debt–equity ratio has been rising even though its working capital ratio has been rising too. There has been little change in current assets or in equity, so what has been happening to cause this change in ratios?

f. F Ltd. has decided to make a major change in its financial structure by persuading some holders of its bonded debt to exchange their bonds for shares. The company's share capital is now $15,000,000 and its retained earnings (the only other item in equity) equal $32,000,000. The intention is to get the company's debt–equity ratio down from 2.1 to 1.4. How many dollars of bonds must be exchanged for shares to meet this goal?

PROBLEM 2.26
Identify the other side of a transaction

Below is a series of changes in balance sheet accounts. For each, identify the one (or more) kinds of transaction that would have prompted such a change *assuming that only other balance sheet accounts are affected*. For each kind of transaction, specify the other balance sheet account(s) likely affected, and in what direction it or they would change. No other financial statements or non-balance-sheet accounts are involved in any of the items below.

a. Accounts receivable go down.

b. Share capital goes up.

c. Accounts payable go up.

d. Treasury stock goes up.

e. Goodwill goes up.

f. Prepaid expenses go up.

g. Mortgage noncurrent liability goes up.

h. Mortgage noncurrent liability goes down.

i. Inventory goes up.

j. Net book value of property and plant goes up.

PROBLEM 2.27
The importance of the bookkeeping system to a manager

Fergie, president of Fergie's Foodstuffs, has received some bad news. The company's long-time accounting clerk has quit to become a beet farmer, and Fergie has to do something about the accounting, fast. Two options seem most attractive. One would be to hire another accounting clerk to take over. The other would be to hire an external bookkeeping service to do the work. Fergie hadn't really realized before that the company's bookkeeping costs money, because the former clerk had been part of the company's salary cost for years, but the costs became pretty clear when Fergie reviewed what the company would have to pay for either option—thousands of dollars a year.

Fergie is wondering whether the bookkeeping is worth what it costs. To help Fergie, explain why bookkeeping is important to a manager, including what the nature of the bookkeeping system means to the information a manager and others receive about the business.

PROBLEM 2.28
Users and financial statements vs. detailed data

Financial statements are highly summarized documents representing thousands of transactions. Financial newspapers and commentators produce information about companies that is even more summarized. Why would users accept, or even prefer, summarized information to detailed data? How important is it for the user to understand the procedures and assumptions behind such summarizations?

PROBLEM 2.29
(CHALLENGING)
Record transactions in CAE accounts

Assume that the following events happened to CAE Inc. on April 1, 2000, the day after the company's fiscal year-end.

a. CAE paid the current portion of its long-term debt, in cash.

b. CAE received all but $5 million of its expected income tax recovery.

c. CAE issued no-par-value common shares for $5.2 million in cash to a group of senior managers.

d. CAE bought the factory of a small technology company for $10 million in cash plus newly issued CAE common shares valued at $14 million.

e. CAE signed a contract for new flight simulators to cost $11 million when delivered in 2001, and received a deposit of $2 million from the customer.

f. CAE refinanced $52 million of its long-term debt exchanging present notes carrying 7.5% interest for new notes carrying 7.9% interest, but which are due several years further into the future.

g. CAE bought a patent on a new processing technology for $1.2 million cash.

h. CAE owed $3 million to a supplier company that also happened to be a customer owing $7 million to CAE. The two companies agreed to offset the money CAE owed against the larger amount the customer owed.

1. Record in journal entry form, in millions of dollars, any events that are accounting transactions, using the account titles in CAE's balance sheet (section 2.9) as much as you can. Specify any appropriate additional accounts where necessary. (Only balance sheet accounts are needed to record all transactions below.)

2. Post your entries to CAE's accounts and do a trial balance after your entries to show that the balance sheet is still in balance.

**PROBLEM 2.30
(CHALLENGING)
General versus user-specific balance sheets**

Write a paragraph giving your considered views on the following question: Can a single balance sheet ever satisfy all the users of a company's financial statements, or should there be different balance sheets prepared to meet the differing needs of users?

**PROBLEM 2.31
(CHALLENGING)
Pacioli's double entry**

Luca Pacioli's book on mathematics and double-entry bookkeeping was a huge best-seller across Europe 400 to 500 years ago. It was translated into many languages, including English. Merchants and other business people took to double entry with great enthusiasm and it quickly became the standard method wherever Europeans did business (such as in the Americas).

Why do you think double-entry bookkeeping was (and is) so popular?

**PROBLEM 2.32
(CHALLENGING)
Balance sheets without dollars**

In the high mountains of Whimsia, two shepherds, Doug and Bob, sit arguing about their relative positions in life, an argument that has been going on for years. Doug says that he has 400 sheep, while Bob has only 360 sheep; therefore, Doug is much better off. Bob, on the other hand, argues that he has 30 acres of land, while Doug has only 20 acres. But Doug's land was inherited, while Bob traded 35 sheep for 20 acres of land ten years ago and this year gave 40 sheep for 10 acres of land. Bob also makes the observation that, of Doug's sheep, 35 belong to another man and he merely keeps them. Doug counters that he has a large one-room cabin that he built himself and claims to have been offered 3 acres of land for it. Besides these things, he has a plough, which was a gift from a friend and is worth a couple of goats; 2 carts, which were given him in trade for a poor acre of land; and an ox, acquired in return for 5 sheep.

Bob goes on to say that his wife has orders for 5 coats to be made of homespun wool and that she will receive 25 goats for them. His wife has 10 goats already, 3 of which were received in exchange for 1 sheep just last year. She also has an ox for which she traded 3 sheep and a cart, which had cost her 2 sheep. Bob's two-room cabin, though smaller than Doug's, should bring him 2 choice acres of land in a trade. Doug is reminded by Bob that he owes Ted, another shepherd, 3 sheep for bringing him his lunch each day last year.

Who is better off? State any assumptions you make. Try to develop a common numerical representation of the shepherds' situations to support your evaluation.[8]

**PROBLEM 2.33
(CHALLENGING)
Accountants, ethics, and balance sheets**

Managers of businesses and other organizations are very concerned about how the balance sheet reflects their management of the enterprise. This is very natural, and generally appropriate too, because such concern is likely to lead managers to want to do a good job of managing. But it can also lead to a temptation to alter the information in a manager's favour. The possibility of such a temptation is part of the reason auditors are employed to examine financial statements, including the balance sheet. This temptation can also produce ethical problems for professional accountants employed by the enterprise. On the one hand, such an accountant is bound by the ethical rules of the profession to see that proper accounting methods are followed in preparing the company's balance sheet, which would imply that the information should not be altered in management's favour. On the other hand, such an accountant works for senior management and is likely bound by the contract of employment to put the enterprise's interests first. What does such an accountant (for example, the chief accountant responsible for preparing the enterprise's financial statements) do if senior management (for example, the president) wants to alter the balance sheet to make things look better and makes a good case that such an action will help the enterprise get bank loans and other assistance it needs?

Discuss this situation from the point of view of both the president and the chief accountant.

PROBLEM 2.34 (CHALLENGING) Assemble a balance sheet from information fragments

You are a corporate spy trying to find out about the financial situation of Extreme Web Inc., a high-technology firm that is privately owned and does not release its balance sheet publicly. After considerable effort, you manage to be in a nightclub near a group of Extreme Web senior managers who are having too much to drink and have gotten into a discussion of financial matters. From all the confused talk, not all of which is necessarily relevant, but is recorded below, see if you can assemble the company's present balance sheet.

- "You guys are lucky, you don't have to work on our new financial plan. It's awful work, because the president wants to get our debt–equity ratio down from 2 to maybe only, gee this is great beer, half of that, and I don't think it can be done. More Buffalo wings?"

- "You think I'm lucky? I'm the person who has to collect the money from the customers that the sales department digs up from under rocks, or something. Our receivables are twice our payables, and everyone thinks it's my fault. Ya, I'll have some wings! Didya know that the payables are only one-third of our current debt, but our receivables are about 90% of our current assets? My hide is on the line if I can't get the cash in. The bank says we can't have any more money than the $9 million it's already advanced us, and that it is pushing us to pay back soon. How will we do that?"

- "You two are always complaining. Get out of my calamari! Sure our working capital is the pits, but we have great people and great technology. Put that all together and we're gonna play in the big leagues yet! I bought some shares on the employee plan because I've got confidence that they'll be worth a lot more than the $10 each I paid. Some day we'll go public, and the value of the company will skyrocket. The president has good ideas and was smart to make 80% of the company's assets equipment rather than relying on those customers, who I agree are slow to pay."

- "Yes, but it'll be a big risk for investors. I bought some shares too, but only spent what I could afford to lose, because the company has yet to make money, and with a deficit about a quarter the size of our share capital, we aren't gonna look too great. Hey, who's that over there taking notes? Any of you guys know? Let's get out of here before we say too much!"

CASE 2A
Financial reporting on the Internet

This book mentions the Web pages for many companies. Increasingly, corporations and other organizations are putting out detailed information about themselves on the Internet. But how good is that information? Is it easy to find in the company's Web material? is it up to date? is it displayed usefully? Can it be downloaded easily?[9] This is a case you can construct for yourself, and discuss in class either by comparing various companies or by comparing various people's reactions to the same company.

So pick a company that interests you or that is assigned by your instructor and go to its Web site and see what is there regarding the company's balance sheet and related data. If you don't know the company's Web address, just type the company name into your search engine and you'll likely get to it easily. Once you get to the company's Web page, start your examination and consider questions such as those below, which could be addressed in a report or in a class discussion:

- How attractive and user-friendly is the initial Web page? Does it concentrate on marketing the company's products, providing general information, telling you about recent news media attention to the company, or other purposes?

- How easy is it to find the company's financial information, if it is there at all? (Many Web pages direct you to Investor Information or some such area for financial information, others specify the financial reports directly, others make it quite hard to find.)

- How much does the company tell you about itself to help you put the financial information in context? Can you easily relate the background to the financial stuff, or do you have to jump all over the Web site to find it all?

- How useful do you find the balance sheet to be? Is it up to date? Is it analyzed or commented upon by the company? Is it related to recent events affecting the company? Or, is it just plunked on the Web as is? (You could look for a "Management Discussion" and "Analysis" section if the balance sheet is just included in the company's current annual report, posted as is on the Web.)

- Is the balance sheet and supporting material easy to download and/or print? Would it be readily available for insertion in an analysis of the company?

CASE 2B
Government of Canada's balance sheet

Discuss the article below about changes in the Government of Canada's accounting, which would produce a balance sheet more like that of corporations like CAE. The Government's traditional accounting deducted expenditures on noncurrent assets from income, therefore in effect deducting these assets from the Government's version of retained earning and turning that into a very large negative, a deficit, with the Government's debt being hundreds of billions of dollars greater than its assets. In your discussion, you might address questions such as these: Do you think it is a good idea for the government to make its accounting more "business-like"? What do you think of the concern that politicians might think the government is better off than it is, if the unrecognized assets were added to the balance sheet? You might be able to find the Government's balance sheet by going to its Web site (www.gc.ca), or the Department of Finance's site (www.fin.gc.ca).

Accounting overhaul could net Ottawa $50B

Auditor-general warns windfall "changes nothing"

BY KATHRYN MAY

OTTAWA • Canada's $580-billion accumulated deficit will magically shrink by at least 10% in 2001 in what is considered to be the biggest overhaul of the nation's record-keeping since Confederation.

With the stroke of a pen, the federal government could find itself with an extra $50-billion worth of assets on its books.

Over the next two years, federal departments and agencies will be introducing accrual accounting, which means for the first time in history the government will put a value on all its fixed assets. Early indications are that value could reach $50-billion.

But Denis Desautels, the Auditor-General, who has long pressed the government to adopt accrual accounting, warns that the sudden appearance of $50-billion worth of assets on the balance sheet won't change Canada's financial position. The country's debt would still rest at $639-billion.

"It changes nothing to the financial position of Canada and no one should draw the conclusion that we are suddenly richer so we should spend more or reduce taxes," Mr. Desautels said. "This does nothing to reduce the debt we are carrying."

Similarly, John Williams, the Reform MP, who chairs the Commons public accounts committee, said these newly recorded assets can't be considered a windfall to justify increased spending by politicians or bureaucrats.

"This isn't an extra $50-billion to go shopping with. These are assets bought and paid for in the past. It's like finding another car in the garage—you don't go out on a spending spree unless you sell that car."

The shift to more business-oriented accounting practices is intended to revolutionize the way departments manage their affairs. Departments have been accused of poor fiscal management, largely because they had little idea of costs or assets.

It will also reconcile the books, which have overstated the government deficit, accumulated year after year since Confederation.

The government's assets are now officially worth nothing. They have never been recorded on the books and everything purchased or built over the years has been expensed—and piled on the deficit—the year the deals were sealed.

For example, a new $100-million building is purchased or built. Currently, that $100-million cost is charged as an expense the year the facility is purchased.

Under accrual accounting, that same building, which is expected to last 40 years, would be recorded as a $100-million asset and depreciated by $2.5 million a year over its 40-year life.

During the next two years, everything worth more than $10,000 will be counted, whether bought yesterday or 50 years ago, as long as the item is still used. Tanks, airplanes, laboratories, embassies, land, office buildings, ships, vehicles, harbours, computer equipment, telephone systems and the list goes on.

The only exceptions are national and historical treasures, such as museums and their collections, archives and national parks, for which there are no market comparisons and will never be sold.

All assets will be valued at their historical cost or original price. Some, however, will not be counted because they were built or bought so long ago that their book value has disappeared.

Mr. Desautels has argued for years that the capitalization of assets was critical to departments' "management discipline" and their "accountability to Parliament." For example, the manager of a government laboratory never had to consider the cost of the space the lab occupied or the equipment it used when determining the price-tag of its programs.

Mr. Desautels argues these figures become more critical with the government's push to recover more of its costs from user fees. Without a handle on costs, it would be impossible for the government to determine and justify the fees it charges.

"Canada is now coming into the 20th century as we are leaving it," said Mr. Williams. "But finally the true cost of delivering programs to Canadians will be brought out.

"If an office in Calgary is operating 40% more efficiently than one in Halifax, we can . . . find out what's wrong. We can't do that today so we just pay the bill."

Mr. Desautels also says one of the consequences of existing accounting policies is that many of Canada's assets were neglected and left to "rust out" over the past decade of fiscal restraint. A department, faced with a $100-million bill to replace worn-out equipment, would often delay the purchase or try some cheap repairs rather than foot the bill for new material and increase the deficit. In a 1994 audit, Mr. Desautels found the government delayed repairs on many of its buildings for so long that some were unsalvageable and others required billions of dollars to fix. He concluded the move to accrual accounting would eliminate this short-sighted "bias against capital expenditures and take advantage of long-term investments of capital investments."

For 35 years, the government has been warned of the consequences of its archaic accounting practices by two royal commissions and a series of auditor-general reports. The government finally took steps to convert to accrual accounting 10 years ago, but efforts died out until Paul Martin, the Finance Minister, made it a priority in the 1998 budget, as part of the Liberal's massive program review. Canada now joins the United Kingdom, Australia, New Zealand and the United States as part of a global push to accrual accounting.

But Mr. Desautels admits there are pitfalls to such a radical change in accounting policy.

After a decade of deficit-cutting, he worries politicians and bureaucrats may suddenly go on a spending spree because capital costs can not be spread over years and no longer appear as the drain on the books.

Such "adverse behaviour" would "weaken the resolve for fiscal restraint" and pile up more debt.

But both Mr. Desautels and Mr. Williams say accrual accounting won't work unless Parliament changes the way it approves the budgets of departments every year. Traditionally, Parliament allocates funds for capital assets the year they are bought or built, which will be completely out of synch with departments' plans to capitalize those assets.

"If that isn't harmonized, Parliament will be simply buying a pig in a poke," said Mr. Williams.

Southam News

Reprinted from *National Post*, 20 July 1999, by Kathryn May.

NOTES

1. Judith Stone, "Big Brewhaha of 1800 B.C.," *Discover* (January 1991): 14. (The words quoted in the excerpt are those of Fritz Maytag, owner of the Anchor Brewing Company of San Francisco.)

2. Information about the history of accounting and business is published in many places. A variety of professional and academic journals have shown an interest in such material, and there is a journal devoted specifically to it: the *Accounting Historians Journal*. See also the references below and at the end of Chapter 3.

3. George J. Coustourous, *Accounting in the Golden Age of Greece: A Response to Socioeconomic Changes* (Champaign: Center for International Education and Research in Accounting, U. of Illinois, 1979).

4. Orville R. Keister, "The Mechanics of Mesopotamian Record-Keeping," in *Contemporary Studies in the Evolution of Accounting Thought*, ed. Michael Chatfield (Belmont: Dickenson Publishing Company, 1968), 12–20.

5. O. ten Have, *The History of Accounting* (Palo Alto: Bay Books, 1976), 27–30.

6. Ibid., 30–46.

7. CAE, "CAE at a Glance," CAE 2000 Annual Report. On-line, World Wide Web, cited 8 July 2000, available from http://www.cae.com.

8. Adapted from *Accounting Education: Problems and Prospects* (Sarasota: American Accounting Association, 1974).

9. For an article that raises numerous issues about Web-based financial reporting, see Hollis Ashbaugh, Karla M. Johnstone, and Terry D. Warfield, "Corporate Reporting on the Internet," *Accounting Horizons* 13(3), September 1999, 241–57.

3 CHAPTER

Measuring and Evaluating Financial Performance

3.1   Chapter Overview

The balance sheet provides important information about the enterprise's financial structure and strength, but its description of the enterprise's financial position is not the only story to be told. Its picture is static: it tells us what the position is. Most managers, owners, and creditors also want to know how well the enterprise is performing and how it got to where it is. Comparing the balance sheets at two different times would show some changes but would not really explain why they happened. To provide that explanation, three additional financial statements have been developed. In this chapter, you will learn about the most important one, the **income statement**, which measures **accrual income**. When people talk about **financial performance**, they usually mean the income statement and its summary information **net income** and **earnings per share**. These are often considered the heart of modern financial reporting, as we will see.

The income statement measures accrual income over a period of time.

You will also learn about a statement used to connect the income statement to the balance sheet, called the **statement of retained earnings**. In Chapter 4, you will learn about the third additional financial statement, which focuses on cash inflows and outflows. It is examined separately because it analyzes the company from a different perspective than the income statement does.

The statement of retained earnings links the income statement to the balance sheet.

Balance sheet, income, and retained earnings statements are a connected system.

The income and retained earnings statements both cover a period of time, whereas the balance sheet is at a point in time. You could say that the two statements in this chapter cover the time between two balance sheets, often called the beginning and ending balance sheets. Suppose a company's fiscal year-end is December 31. Then we would have a progression in which the ending balance sheet flows not only from the beginning one directly but also from the explanation of what happened during the year provided in the income and retained earnings statements:

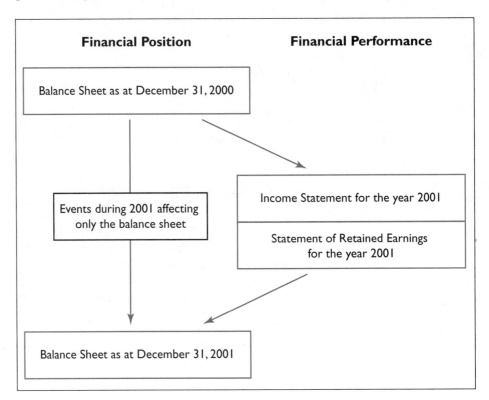

FIGURE 3.1

Referring to Figure 1.1 used at the beginning of Chapters 1 and 2, you will learn in this chapter:

- *Procedures and techniques:* How the double-entry accounting system produces accrual-based income and retained earnings accounts, how to assemble the income and retained earnings statements from those accounts, and how the retained earnings statement connects the income statement and the balance sheet.

- *Concepts and principles:* Why the income statement is important, why it is arranged as it is, what net income and earnings per share mean, and some interesting history about where the income statement came from.

- *Analysis and decisions:* Using the income statement to understand how an enterprise does its business, and using it to do some analysis of the enterprise's financial performance.

Because courses may cover topics in different orders, sections 3.4–3.7 have been written to be studied in any order.

3.2   INTRODUCTION TO THE INCOME AND RETAINED EARNINGS STATEMENTS

Financial accounting describes much more about a business than the financial position set out in the balance sheet. Another important matter is the business's financial performance. A business exists over a period of time. If the owners and managers are successful, it may prosper for a long time. The Hudson's Bay Company (now "The Bay") is such a business: incorporated in 1670, it is more than 300 years old! Suppose a measure of the company's financial performance were desired for comparison to other companies, for assessing income tax, for help in deciding how much to sell the company for, or for many other reasons we will come to. How could such performance be measured?

Well, we might measure the company's financial performance by closing it down, selling off all its assets, paying off all its liabilities, and seeing how much is left for the owners. Good performance would be indicated if the money left for the owners plus the amounts they withdrew over the years was greater than the amount they put in when they founded the company, perhaps adjusted for inflation over that time and for the owners' costs of raising the money they put in. But killing the business to measure how well it has been doing is a little drastic! Waiting until it dies of natural causes seems hardly a better solution: the Hudson's Bay Company has outlasted many generations of owners and managers, and the Ford Motor Company has outlasted a number of Ford family members. It would be more useful to measure performance over selected shorter periods of time: annually, quarterly (every three months), or on a monthly basis. People could then make their decisions about investing in the company or getting out, and hiring managers or firing them, when they wanted to do so.

The Income Statement

The income statement measures performance as net accrual income.

This is where the income statement comes in. This statement uses accrual accounting to measure financial performance over a period of time, usually a year, three months, or one month, coming up with the "bottom line" net income for the period, its accrual income, calculated as revenues minus expenses. Remember the income statement for Simone's jewellery business in section 1.8 of Chapter 1:

Exhibit

Revenue ($4,350 collected plus $310 still to be received)	$4,660
Expenses ($1,670 paid minus $280 deducted because the goods are still on hand plus $85 unpaid plus $120 estimated amortization)	1,595
Accrual income based on the information provided	$3,065

This simple income statement illustrates the form of all business income statements as they are done in North America and much of the rest of the world:

Net Accrual Income for the period
= Revenue(s) – Expenses for the period

Net income means accrual income after deducting income tax expense.

Simone's income statement shows no income tax on her income. Her business is a proprietorship, and any income tax is her personal responsibility, so proprietorships' income statements normally do not include income tax. The income statements of corporations, which are responsible for their own income taxes, do have income tax deducted as one of the expenses. The phrase "net" income is usually used to refer to the amount of accrual income left after the income tax. (By the way, income tax in Canada and most other countries is based on accrual income, not the cash income we saw for Simone's business in section 1.8 and will see again in Chapter 4.)

Exhibit 3.2 summarizes the usual format for the income statement, showing the separation of income tax expense from the other expenses. Most income statements have much more detail than this!

3-2

Exhibit

Income Statement Format (all figures are for a particular period of time)	
Revenue(s)	$XXXX
Less expenses other than income tax	XXXX
Income before income tax	$XXXX
Less income tax expense	XXXX
Net income for the period (accrual income)	$XXXX

Revenues and Expenses

Net income is the difference between revenues and expenses. So, what are these two performance measures?

Revenues are increases in the company's wealth arising from the provision of services or sales of goods to customers. Wealth increases because customers:

- pay cash;

- promise to pay cash (such promises are accounts receivable); or

- more rarely, pay with other forms of wealth, such as by providing other assets to the company or forgiving debts owed by the company.

Revenues are increases in wealth arising from providing goods or services to customers.

So, if, *in return for services or goods*, a customer paid $1,000 in cash, another customer promised to pay $1,000 later, another gave the company $1,000 in equipment, or another forgave a $1,000 debt the company had owed the customer, these would each be called a revenue of $1,000.

Expenses are the opposite of revenues. They are *decreases in the company's wealth that are incurred in order to earn revenues.* Wealth decreases because operating costs have to be borne; customers have to be given the goods they have paid for; long-term assets wear out as they are used to earn revenue; and liabilities may be incurred as part of the process.

Expenses are decreases in wealth incurred in order to earn revenues.

So, if, *as part of its attempt to earn revenues*, the company paid $600 in rent, or the goods bought by a customer cost the company $600 to provide, or the building depreciated by $600, or the company promised to pay an employee $600 in wages later on, each of these would be called an expense of $600.

Cost of goods sold expense is the cost to the enterprise of the goods given up to generate the revenue.

A major expense category that sometimes causes confusion is the cost of goods sold (COGS) expense. In the examples above, if the goods bought by the customer cost the company $600 to provide, then $600 is the *cost* of the goods sold that earned revenue of $1,000. The revenue is what the customer agrees to pay; the cost of goods sold is what it costs the enterprise to provide those goods. So a transaction with a customer who is buying goods has two aspects: (1) the enterprise is better off because of the revenue gained, and (2) the enterprise is worse off because of the cost of the goods that the customer takes away. When the enterprise buys the goods for sale, they begin on the balance sheet in the asset account "inventory of unsold goods," and when they are sold, their cost is transferred from the asset account to the expense account "cost of goods sold." This is done as a separate accounting activity from recording the revenue, because it is a separate economic event. Whether the enterprise makes money on the deal depends on whether the revenue gained is greater than the cost of goods sold (plus any other expenses incurred to make the sale, such as sales commissions and shipping costs).

A net loss is negative net income, resulting when expenses exceed revenues.

Both revenues and expenses are measured following the concepts of accrual accounting; therefore, they represent increases or decreases in wealth, whether or not cash receipts or payments occur at the same time. As net income is the difference between revenues and expenses, it represents the net *inflow of wealth* to the company during the period. The reporting of net income means that the company has become wealthier during the period. If net income is negative, that is, if revenues are less than expenses, it is instead called net loss and represents a net *outflow of wealth*. In this case, the company has become less wealthy.

FOR YOUR INTEREST

Terminology again. As mentioned in section 2.2, sometimes a net loss is called a deficit. This is especially the case when people are referring to a government, which, if its annual revenues are less than its annual expenditures, is said to be incurring a deficit. This meaning of deficit is not the same as negative retained earnings: negative earnings may eventually lead to negative retained earnings for a business corporation, but government accounting does not record retained earnings, usually just showing the difference between assets and liabilities as a residual figure, much like a proprietorship's equity. Here, the people governed are the proprietor(s)! In another difference with business accounting, governments have typically grouped their expenses together with the amounts spent on new assets together under the heading of "expenditures," which in accounting is just another word for "payments."

Transactions with owners are kept off the income statement.

Expenses include all the costs of earning the revenues, including income and other taxes, but they do *not* include payment of returns to owners (withdrawals by proprietors or partners, or dividends to shareholders of corporations). The income statement measures wealth changes resulting from customer-oriented activity, not transactions with owners. (Though, of course, sometimes people wear more than one "hat": owning shares in Coca-Cola doesn't stop you from buying a Coke when you're thirsty and so being both an owner and a customer of the company.) Payments or promises of payment of returns to owners (such as when a corporation's board of directors *declares*, or promises, a dividend) are considered to be distributions of net income to owners. The undistributed remainder is kept in the company as retained earnings.

The Retained Earnings Statement

The statement of retained earnings shows what has been done with the period's income. Retained earnings is the sum of past net incomes or earnings, measured since the company began, minus dividends declared (even if not yet paid) to owners since the beginning. The statement of retained earnings updates the balance sheet's retained earnings figure (in owners' equity) from the end of the preceding period (year, quarter, month, or whatever), which is also the beginning of the present period, to the end of the present period and so shows why the balance sheet's figure has changed from the last period:

Retained earnings on the balance sheet at end of period	=	Retained earnings at beginning of period + net income (or − net loss) for the period − dividends declared during the period

The retained earnings statement explains changes in the balance sheet's retained earnings.

The statement of retained earnings, therefore, shows that the net income for the period is part of the retained earnings at the end of the period, by showing that the income is part of the *change* in retained earnings *over the period covered by the income statement*. The usual format of the retained earnings statement is:

3-3

Exhibit

Start with retained earnings, beginning of period (that is, end of previous period)	$ XXXX
Add net income for the period	XXXX
Deduct dividends declared during the period	(XXXX)
Add or subtract miscellaneous adjustments	XXXX
Equals retained earnings, end of period	$ XXXX

Retained earnings can be explained in layers, period by period since the beginning.

You might be interested to know that you can, *if you have the past records*, go back year by year, figuring out how much income was added to retained earnings each year and how much in dividends was deducted. You could go all the way back to the first day of the company, when there had not yet been any income and therefore not yet any retained earnings. Retained earnings are therefore like an onion: you can keep peeling away each year's layer until you have peeled everything away and are back to zero. You can similarly peel away each year's transactions in every balance sheet account; for example, you can trace all the changes in cash back to the very beginning. For this reason, the balance sheet can be said to reflect everything that has ever been recorded in the accounts: it is the accumulation of everything that happened from when the company began until now. Accounting really is a historical information system!

Declared dividends reduce retained earnings, becoming liabilities of the corporation until paid.

In a corporation, the board of directors is the senior level of management, operating the company on behalf of the owners. When the board declares a dividend, the amount is deducted from retained earnings at that time. At that point, the corporation has a liability to the owners, which it pays off by sending the owners the promised cash, or, in some cases, something called stock dividends, by sending the owners more shares of the company. Dividends, like other transactions with owners, are kept off the income statement so that income can be measured *before* including them. If they are owed dividends, the owners are also creditors for the dividends payable.

Connecting the Income Statement to the Balance Sheet

The balance sheet shows all assets, liabilities, and owners' equity accounts *as at a point in time*. Usually the balance sheet is *comparative*, showing the accounts at both the beginning of the income statement's period (that is, the end of the previous period) and at the end of the income statement's period, and therefore showing both the beginning retained earnings and the ending retained earnings. This progression was depicted in Figure 3.1 in section 3.1. It can also be depicted as follows (shortening retained earnings to RE):

Beginning Assets   = Beginning Liabilities + Beginning Equity (including RE)

Ending Assets   = Ending Liabilities   + Ending Equity (including RE)

Change in Assets = Change in Liabilities + Change in Equity (including RE)

Suppose a corporation had assets of $1,200 at the beginning of a year and $1,450 at the end, and liabilities of $750 at the beginning and $900 at the end. We can deduce that its equity was $450 at the beginning and $550 at the end. These data produce the following calculation of the changes in the balance sheet categories:

Beginning:	$1,200 Assets	=	$750 Liabilities + $450 Equity
End:	$1,450 Assets	=	$900 Liabilities + $550 Equity
Changes:	$ 250 Assets	=	$150 Liabilities + $100 Equity

Where did the change in equity come from? Upon investigation, we find out that the company issued more share capital of $40, earned income of $185, and declared a dividend of $125. Thus:

Share capital change:		
Equity increase due to issued share capital		$ 40
Retained earnings change:		
Equity increase due to income	$185	
Equity decrease due to declaration of dividend	(125)	60
Change in equity between balance sheets		$100

Explaining the retained earnings change articulates the income statement and balance sheet.

We know what the income was, but not what the company did to earn it. This is what the income statement is for: describing the revenues and expenses that produced the $185 income. But once we have that, it is useful to know how that factors into the balance sheet. The beginning and ending balance sheets define the financial position before and after the period over which the income statement measures performance. The net income is part of the change in retained earnings, which, in turn, is part of the change in the balance sheet over that period. The statement of retained earnings therefore "knits" the income statement and the balance sheet together by showing that the net income is part of the change in the balance sheet over the period. (Accountants refer to this knitting together as the articulation of the income statement and the balance sheet.) Income is part of the change in retained earnings for the period, therefore:

Income is part of the equity component of the balance sheet equation.

Make sure you understand how this works:

- A *revenue* increases wealth, so it either increases assets or decreases liabilities, and therefore increases equity.

- An *expense* decreases wealth, so it either decreases assets or increases liabilities, and therefore decreases equity.

- Positive net income has the overall effect of increasing assets and/or decreasing liabilities, and therefore increases equity (increases due to revenues exceed decreases due to expenses).

- A net loss, which is negative net income, does the opposite, decreasing equity (decreases due to expenses exceed increases due to revenues).

Income increases wealth, so it also increases owners' equity through retained earnings.

Later in this chapter, the double-entry debits and credits involved in this are explained. For now, focus on understanding the idea that income is part of equity through retained earnings.

FOR YOUR INTEREST

People sometimes think that the whole balance of retained earnings is available to pay dividends. Legally that may be true, but, practically, it is very unlikely to be true, because income comes from changes in all the forms of wealth on the balance sheet. A company that has made good incomes and used the money earned to invest in new plant and equipment, for example, would have to sell the plant and equipment if it were to pay out all the retained earnings as dividends. Also, since income is based on accrual accounting, it is represented by changes in noncash accounts like accounts receivable (uncollected revenues) and accounts payable (unpaid expenses), so the income in retained earnings is not all cash, and the company might have to clear up all its receivables and payables to get the cash to pay a big dividend. The owners may not even want a dividend: many companies that pay small or no dividends have excellent share prices on the stock market, because shareholders believe that the companies will grow and prosper if the money that could have been paid as dividends is instead retained by the company and used to make profitable business investments.

A Further Example of Income Statement and Balance Sheet Articulation

Bratwurst Inc. had the following balance sheet at the end of 2000 (beginning of 2001): Assets, $5,000; Liabilities, $3,000; Equity, $2,000.

- The beginning equity figure was made up of the owners' invested share capital of $500 plus $1,500 retained earnings accumulated to the end of 2000. (That $1,500 was therefore the sum of all the net incomes the company had ever had up to the end of 2000, minus all the dividends ever declared to owners up to that point.)

- During 2001, the company had revenues of $11,000 and expenses of $10,000, and declared dividends to owners of $300.

- At the end of 2001, the company had assets of $5,900, liabilities of $3,200, and equity of $2,700, made up of the owners' invested share capital of $500 plus retained earnings of $2,200.

Exhibit 3.4 shows the three financial statements reporting all this. Note that all these statements are simplified for this example: companies report much more detail than this, but for this example the detail might confuse the main articulation point.

Bratwurst Inc.
Income Statement for 2001

Revenues	$11,000
Expenses (including income tax)	10,000
Net income for 2001	$ 1,000

Bratwurst Inc.
Statement of Retained Earnings for 2001

Retained earnings, beginning of 2001 (end of 2000)	$1,500
Add net income for 2001 (from income statement)	1,000
	$2,500
Deduct dividends declared during 2001	300
Retained earnings, end of 2001 (transfer to balance sheet)	$2,200

Bratwurst Inc.
Balance Sheets at Beginning and End of 2001

Assets	End	Begin	Liabilities and Equity	End	Begin
Assets	$5,900	$5,000	Liabilities	$3,200	$3,000
			Shareholders' equity:		
			Share capital	500	500
			Retained earnings*	2,200	1,500
Total	$5,900	$5,000	Total	$5,900	$5,000

*Balance sheet retained earnings figures are transferred from retained earnings statement.

You can see from this example that

- the income statement's bottom line is transferred to the statement of retained earnings, and

- the retained earnings statement's bottom line is transferred to the balance sheet,

- showing that the three statements tie together (articulate) through retained earnings.

The Bratwurst example shows that the income and retained earnings statements could be said to be detailed explanations of the change in the balance sheet retained earnings figure. The balance sheet could instead have had the following format under the retained earnings part of owners' equity:

Exhibit

Retained earnings:

Beginning balance	$ 1,500
Add revenues	11,000
	$12,500
Deduct expenses	10,000
	$ 2,500
Deduct dividends declared	300
Ending balance	$ 2,200

The information is there, but the balance sheet would be rather cluttered, and there would hardly be room to provide details about the various revenues, expenses, and dividends. Also, the concept of income as a measure of performance would be obscured. Therefore, the income and retained earnings statements were developed to provide the detailed performance measure demanded by users of the information without complicating the balance sheet.

OW'S YOUR UNDERSTANDING?

Here are two questions you should be able to answer, based on what you have just read:

1. In financial accounting, what is a revenue and what is an expense?

2. Suppose Bratwurst Inc.'s accounting records showed the following for the next year, 2002: Revenues earned, $14,200; Cash collected from customers, $13,800; Expenses incurred, $12,900; Expenses paid in cash, $11,200; Dividends declared, $600; and Dividends paid in cash, $500. Can you show that Bratwurst's retained earnings as at the end of 2002 was $2,900, by calculating 2002 net income and incorporating other information we have about Bratwurst? (Begin RE = $2,200. Net income = $14,200 − $12,900 = $1,300. End RE = $2,200 + $1,300 − $600 dividends declared = $2,900.)

3.3   FINANCIAL PERFORMANCE AND THE DEVELOPMENT OF STOCK MARKETS

England and the United Kingdom: From 1500 to the Early 1800s

Good stewardship of the owners' enterprise by management has been important for centuries.

Prior to Pacioli, English recordkeeping had much in common with Roman methods used hundreds of years earlier. "Stewards" were employed to manage the properties of the English aristocracy, much as local governors had been in Roman-held areas. In 1300, Oxford University offered an accounting course: Roman recordkeeping for stewards![1] The concept of stewardship, of a person managing something on behalf of someone else, is still an important aspect of accounting. It is often said, for example, that an enterprise's financial statements demonstrate the quality of management's stewardship of the enterprise on behalf of its owners.

Financial accounting worldwide has grown from roots in the United Kingdom.

In the several hundred years since Pacioli's treatise, accounting developed to suit the social and business circumstances of each country. France, for example, had a strong, centralized government and developed a national accounting system written by a central board of administrators. On the other hand, England (which with its neighbours became the United Kingdom) had less government involvement in commerce and trade and a smaller civil service and relied more heavily on the initiatives of the private sector and the courts.[2] The financial accounting system now used in the United Kingdom, Canada, the United States, and many other countries relies heavily on the precedents set in England during this period. The

FIGURE 3.2   During the Reformation, European merchants and bankers established companies that were early versions of modern business corporations. One such merchant is the subject of this 1630 engraving by Rembrandt. The merchant's scale and ledger book demonstrate his reliance on organization, documentation, and qualification. Careful attention to these facilitates his control of capital (bags of money or gold) and trade goods (casks and chest). Reproduced by permission of The Bettmann Archive.

English approach used Pacioli's double entry for the recordkeeping and built the financial statements' reporting system on that. Americans, Canadians, and others have elaborated that further. Financial accounting in continental Europe developed on a somewhat different path. Russia, China, Japan, and many other countries took different financial accounting paths too. However, the British-American approach is still gaining popularity worldwide; for example, China adopted it for much of its financial reporting in the early 1990s. Efforts are being made worldwide to "harmonize" financial accounting to assist international trade, and the sort of financial accounting set out in this book seems likely to become the international standard. International issues will be outlined further in a later chapter.

Until the mid-1600s accounting and recordkeeping (bookkeeping) were largely synonymous. Records were a private matter for the attention of the lord, merchant, or banker. But then a significant development occurred: the advent of companies that sold stocks (shares of ownership) to private citizens. These citizens could not all crowd into the company's office to inspect the records, even if they could understand them. This produced a demand for some form of reporting to the shareholders, for financial statements that could be relied on as accurate summaries of the records. There was a demand that the balance sheet be more detailed in its description of the owners' equity and the changes in it than had been necessary before there had been such dispersed ownership. There was even some demand for regulation of such reports: for example, in 1657 Oliver Cromwell, as regent of England, required the East India Company to publish its balance sheet.[3] Accounting was on its way to developing the standards of calculation and disclosure that are very important in modern accounting and that distinguish accounting from the underlying recordkeeping. Progress in this direction was not rapid, but it picked up steam with the arrival of the Industrial Revolution.

However, there were some interesting events in the interval. In 1670, a famous company was formed, namely, The Governor and Company of Adventurers of England Trading into Hudson's Bay. The Hudson's Bay Company, or "The Bay," as it now calls itself in its advertisements, has played a very significant economic role over the centuries, and is still an important part of Canadian business. Many of the records kept by its far-flung employees still exist and provide detailed pictures of business and society over the years.[4] In 1720, the spectacular collapse of the South Seas Company prompted the first known written audit, conducted in order to determine the assets of the company.[5] The developing Industrial Revolution of the late 1700s and early 1800s helped to fuel the emerging commercial sector of Britain, and accounting practices became an important part of the system. In 1825, the British Parliament eased hundred-year-old prohibitions on trading shares in companies, and the modern era of stock markets and publicly owned companies began in earnest. A few years later, Parliament required annual audits of the balance sheets of such companies.[6] Accounting and auditing continued to develop in response to the changing needs of the society of which they were a part.

> **External financial reporting began to be important as the Industrial Revolution proceeded.**

Developments in the 19th Century[7]

> **Accounting was challenged by the rise of large, long-lived industrial companies.**

Up to the early 19th century most business enterprises were formed for specific ventures, were financed by a few wealthy owners, and were disbanded when the ventures were completed. The sharing of profits among the owners of the enterprise or venture took place at the end, when all of the assets were sold, the liabilities were paid off, and the net amount remaining was distributed among the owners. When, as industrialization increased, large industrial plants began replac-

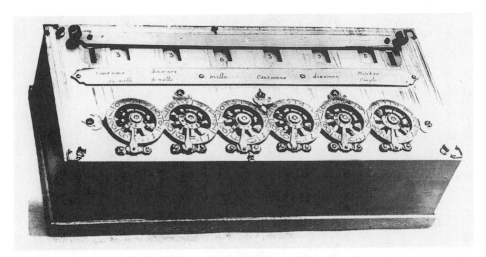

FIGURE 3.3

An invaluable accounting tool, the first successful European mechanical calculator was invented by Blaise Pascal in 1642 and soon became an international marvel. Pascal was already known as a scientist and mathematician when he invented the adding machine at the age of 19. Among many other things, Pascal is also known as the inventor of the barometer. Reproduced by permission of The Bettmann Archive.

ing short-term ventures as the major form of business enterprise, the traditional method of financing and profit sharing was no longer acceptable. The large cost of constructing and maintaining these more capital-intensive enterprises was often more than a few owners could afford, and the long life of the assets made it unsatisfactory to wait for the winding up of the enterprise to share profits.

Various pieces of legislation regarding companies were introduced in Britain in the 1830s, 1840s, and 1850s. This legislation allowed incorporated companies, also called **corporations**, to sell shares in **stock markets** (which, because the initial issuing of shares provides capital, that is to say, equity funds for the companies, are also called **capital markets**). The legislation also provided a major feature of corporations: liability of the corporation's owners to the corporation's creditors was, and still is, limited to the amount of the owners' equity in the corporation. The justification for the limited liability feature was that individual investors could not always be aware of the actions of the directors they elected or the managers who were in turn engaged by the directors. Therefore, investors should not be liable for any more than the amount of money they invested in the enterprise. But of course no investors would want to lose even that, so as capital markets developed, the demand for information about the corporations involved grew.

Corporations used capital markets, so they had to tell the markets about themselves.

Limited liability of its owners and an existence separate from its owners largely define the corporation. Modern laws and business practices complicate the operation of capital markets and can reduce the protection of limited liability, but the idea that a corporation is a "legal person," able to act on its own and survive changes in owners, is still central to business and to much of the rest of our lives. In financial accounting, the focus is on the economic entity that is exchanging physical and financial goods and promises with other entities, but since laws began to define what corporations are (and sometimes what proprietorships, partnerships, and corporate groups are, too), accounting also must reflect the legal nature of economic exchanges and the structure of the organization.

Accounting focuses on the economic entity but must also reflect legal issues.

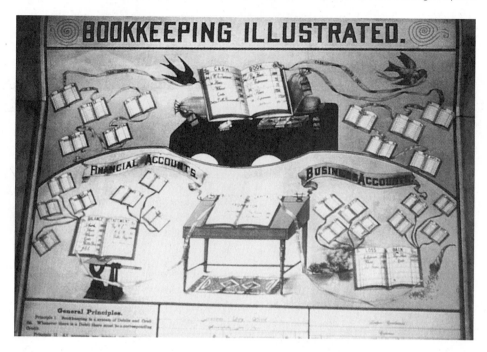

FIGURE 3.4   A portion of an antique bookkeeping poster. The linking ribbons in the illustration suggest the relationship between financial accounts and business decisions. Courtesy of Ursus Books and Prints Ltd., New York.

An important legal issue is sharing profits. The problem of how to ensure fair calculation and sharing of ownership interests led legislators to require that a corporation present its balance sheet annually to its shareholders and that an auditor be present to report to the shareholders on the validity of that financial statement. Legislation also required that any annual payments to shareholders should not come out of the sale of, or by decreasing the value of, a corporation's long-term capital assets. Such payments should be made out of monies earned yearly from these assets after all yearly debts are paid. We can think of "monies earned yearly" as revenues, and "yearly debts" as expenses, so this meant, roughly, that payments to shareholders should come out of yearly income. This is close to the dividend requirement placed on most corporations today (dividends can normally only be paid out of net income). Corporations began to compute income in statements or schedules separate from the balance sheet, so that they could demonstrate that they had performed well enough to permit the distribution of dividends or the issuing of more shares.

As businesses grew in size and complexity, the demand for information on financial performance increased. The static picture presented by the balance sheet was not good enough for the emerging stock markets, for the increasingly large group of nonowner professional managers, or for governments that wished to evaluate (and tax!) businesses' performance (to mention just a few of the groups interested in evaluating performance). The income statement came into its own as a central part of financial reporting in the last hundred years, and its measurement of financial performance is central to economic activity and performance evaluation in most of the world.

The income calculation is important in determining availability of dividends.

The income statement is a response to demand for performance measurement.

In responding to these demands for better performance information, accountants were limited by a lack of accounting theories or conventions to illustrate and define how to prepare balance sheets and income statements. There was no nationally organized association of accountants in Britain until the end of the 19th century (although the Accountants' Society of Edinburgh received a royal charter in 1854, an event that led to the term "chartered accountant"). Financial accounting methods developed situation by situation, with no overall plan or concepts throughout this period. Some model financial statements and examples from legislation were being used, and income statements were becoming established, but it was becoming necessary to establish a rational basis, that is, principles, for preparing financial statements and for extending the principles to new settings, as business and commercial activity continued to increase. Toward the end of the 19th century, several British court cases had established that accountants and auditors had to decide what were proper and fair financial statements, and could not expect courts and legislatures to decide for them. A prominent accountant, Ernest Cooper, voiced his concern in 1894: "... the already sufficient responsibilities and anxieties of an Auditor will be extended beyond those known of any trade or profession."[8] Accounting was on its way to formulating the professional rights, responsibilities, and criteria for competence, as had the already-established professions of law, engineering, and medicine. We'll see more later on about how this has worked out in modern times.

> **In the 19th century, financial accounting lacked a general conceptual structure.**

 OW'S YOUR UNDERSTANDING?

Here are two questions you should be able to answer, based on what you have just read:

1. Why has financial accounting become more and more sophisticated over the centuries?

2. What sort of information demands prompted the development of the income statement?

TO THE READER: The next four sections have the following content:

- Section 3.4 has an example of a real company's income and retained earnings statements;

- Section 3.5 focuses on the way these statements are formatted to provide useful information;

- Section 3.6 shows how double-entry accrual accounting produces the accounts behind the two statements, especially revenues and expenses; and

- Section 3.7 has a second double-entry accrual accounting example to help establish your intuition about how the two statements work and fit with the balance sheet.

The four sections can be read in any order. You can start with the statements and finish with the accounting entries, or vice versa.

3.4 A CLOSER LOOK AT INCOME AND RETAINED EARNINGS STATEMENTS' CONTENT

In Chapter 2, we looked at CAE's balance sheet. To continue that example, Exhibit 3.6 shows the company's 2000 income statement (statement of earnings) and statement of retained earnings. Like the balance sheet, both statements are comparative to 1999 and are consolidated because CAE is a group of corporations.

3-6

Exhibit

CAE Inc. **Consolidated Statements of Earnings**		
Years Ended March 31 (amounts in millions except per share amounts)	2000	1999
Revenue		
Commercial Simulation and Training	$480.2	$352.8
Military Simulation and Controls	384.9	355.7
Forestry Systems	299.2	197.4
	$1,164.3	$905.9
Operating earnings		
Commercial Simulation and Training	$82.3	$55.9
Military Simulation and Controls	15.4	25.2
Forestry systems	43.8	32.8
Earnings from continuing operations before interest and income taxes	141.5	113.9
Interest expense, net	10.0	9.6
Earnings from continuing operations before income taxes	131.5	104.3
Income taxes (note 9)	40.8	30.6
Earnings from continuing operations	90.7	73.7
Results of discontinued operations (note 2)	7.8	3.6
Net earnings	$98.5	$77.3
Earnings per share from continuing operations	$0.83	$0.66
Net earnings per share	$0.90	$0.70
Average number of shares outstanding	109.5	111.1

(Indicated notes are not included in this book.)

Consolidated Statements of Retained Earnings

Years Ended March 31 (amounts in millions of dollars)	2000	1999
Retained earnings at beginning of year	$194.2	$134.7
Net earnings	98.5	77.3
Dividends	(20.6)	(17.8)
Retained earnings at end of year	$272.1	$194.2

Among the things you may notice as you review the two statements are:

1. The statements cover periods of time (years ending March 31), not a point in time as the balance sheet does. Like the balance sheet, they are shown in millions of dollars.
2. As for balance sheets, explanatory notes are referred to and appended. The notes are not attached here, as they are not necessary to this chapter.
3. The upper part of the income statement generally contains the ordinary revenues, along with the ordinary expenses incurred to earn those revenues. Below those can be various special items, as section 3.5 explains. CAE has one of those: "results of discontinued operations," and so has both earnings from continuing operations ($90.7 million in 2000) and net income (earnings of $98.5 million in 2000). The income taxes shown on the income statement ($40.8 million in 2000) apply just to the continuing operations. The discontinued operations income ($7.8 million in 2000) appears below the income tax expense line, so it has already had its own income tax deducted.
4. The net income ("net earnings") from the income statement is carried down to the statement of retained earnings, as in our Bratwurst Inc. example earlier.

CAE's retained earnings statement connects its income statement to its balance sheet.

5. The statement of retained earnings starts with the beginning balance (note the ending balance for 1999 is the same as the beginning one for 2000), adds the $98.5 million net income, deducts $20.6 million of dividends declared, and ends with $272.1 million. If you refer back to the CAE balance sheet in section 2.9, you'll see that its retained earnings figure is the same as the ending ones in the statement of retained earnings. CAE has *articulated* its income statements and balance sheets through the retained earnings statements.

Let's look at some of the income and retained earnings statements' content.

- Revenue, which is increases in wealth due to transactions with customers, has increased from 1999's $905.9 million to 2000's $1,164.3 million. (Both these figures are for continuing operations only. Any revenues from discontinued operations are part of the calculation of discontinued operations results further down on the income statement.) This is a 28.5% increase, which is a little more than the 23% increase in income from continuing operations ($73.7 million in 1999, $90.7 million in 2000).

- Understanding what happened to produce the increased income is hampered by CAE's decision not to disclose its cost of goods sold and other expenses. (These were disclosed on the income statement in prior years.) All we have is the operating earnings from the three lines of business. From those, we can construct the following table of year 2000 expenses and returns from each line of business, all in millions of dollars (you might try doing so for 1999 too, to check your understanding):

Line of Business	Revenue Disclosed	Operating Earnings	Expenses Deduced	Expenses as a % of Revenue
Commercial Simulation etc.	$480.2	$82.3	$397.9	82.9%
Military Simulation etc.	384.9	15.4	369.5	96.0%
Forestry Systems	299.2	43.8	255.4	85.4%
Continuing before interest, tax	1,164.3	141.5	1,022.8	87.8%

From this, we can see that the lines of business are not equally profitable. Military Simulation is the least profitable, with expenses equalling 96% of revenue, while Commercial Simulation is the most profitable, with expenses equalling 82.9% of revenue. But we have no information about how these results arose. It is possible that CAE does not want its competitors to know such details. The annual report's "Management Discussion and Analysis" section discusses some reasons for the results but does not give any further figures. This is an example of a company's making choices about its accounting presentation and disclosure—and a reminder that there is choice in many areas of accounting, so when you are using financial statements, you have to be prepared for the effects of such choices.

Rearranging CAE's figures allow some analysis, but not gross margin analysis.

- CAE's lack of disclosure of expenses means that we do not know a major expense most companies have: cost of goods sold. This is the cost to the company of the products sold to customers. Without knowing that, we cannot calculate the company's gross margin (revenue minus cost of good sold) or the gross margin ratio, which is an important standard ratio. This ratio tells us what the company's average markup on cost is, what the average margin for profit the company adds to its costs when billing its customers. You can see that a company might not want to disclose this, because both customers and competitors might use it to pressure the company to reduce its prices. Whatever the reason, the lack of disclosure of cost of goods sold and other expenses makes the income statement less useful.

- The company's borrowing cost, interest expense related to continuing operations, went up from $9.6 million in 1999 to $10 million in 2000, a negligible increase. It is not a big enough expense to affect net income much. The company's main interest-bearing debt is long-term debt. Going back to the balance sheets in section 2.9, we see that long-term debt (including current portion, which carries interest just as does the long-term portion) was $297.1 million at the end of 1999 and $271.6 million at the end of 2000, a decrease. The decrease in debt combined with the increase in interest expense implies that the average interest rate the company incurred on its debt increased from 1999 to 2000.

- The company's income tax rate can be estimated from the income statement. In 1999, the income tax expense was $40.8 million on continuing income before tax of $131.5 million, or 31%. In 1999, $30.6 million was 29% of $104.3 million income before tax, a slight increase in the average tax rate. With this, we can do the sort of net-of-tax analysis illustrated in Chapter 1. For example, if in 2000, the company increased its price on a product by $1,000 without having an increase in other expenses, the net income would go up by $690 ($1,000 × (1 − 0.31)) because the increased income would attract 31% increased income tax.

Net-of-tax analysis can be done using CAE's income tax expense figure.

- Below the net income (net earnings) figure is a ratio that is very important for public companies because financial analysts and investors use it to compare companies' performance. This is earnings per share (EPS), which is net income divided by the average number of common (voting) shares outstanding. CAE reports EPS and tells us the average number of shares outstanding, so we can see how EPS was calculated. This per-share information is useful because it removes the company's size from the income figure and allows earnings to be compared to the particular number of shares the investor happens to own. If you know that CAE made $98.5 million in income in 2000, that is hard to relate to your own investment, say 1,000 shares, but if you know it was 90 cents a share, you can say that your investment earned $900 in 2000 and you can compare that to the share price to see if CAE is earning a comparable return for the price to that of other companies. Because it has both continuing and discontinued operations, CAE reports EPS on both earnings numbers: 83 cents on continuing operations in 2000, 90 cents overall, so 7 cents on discontinued operations.

- The statement of retained earnings shows dividends declared of $20.6 million in 2000, which is 20.9% of the $98.5 million net income, close to the 23% of net income declared as dividends in 1999. CAE keeps most of its earnings for internal uses, presumably to generate further growth in income, but does pay just under a quarter of the earnings out to shareholders as dividends.

(H) OW'S YOUR UNDERSTANDING?

Here are two questions you should be able to answer, based on what you have just read (the second question adds a bit of "what if" effects analysis you should be able to reason through):

1. How did CAE's performance in earning income in 2000 compare to that in 1999?

2. Suppose CAE discovered that a $1 million credit sale had not been recorded in 2000 but should have been. It wasn't recorded until April 2000, which was in the 2001 financial year. The cost of the goods sold had been properly included in the 2000 expenses; it is just that the revenue was recorded in the wrong year. What would recording this sale properly in 2000 do to: (a) the 2000 continuing income before income tax, (b) the 2000 net income, (c) the working capital at the end of 2000, (d) the retained earnings at the end of 2000, and (e) the revenue for 2001. ((a) Continuing income before tax for 2000 would go up by $1 million due to adding the revenue in. (b) Net income would go up by $690,000, because 31% income tax would have to be deducted. (c) Working capital at the end of 2000 would go up $1 million as this amount would be added to accounts receivable. (d) Retained earnings at the end of 2000 would go up by $690,000, the increase in net income. (e) Revenue for 2001 would go down by $1 million as the sale was removed from the 2001 year and added to the 2000 year.)

3.5   FORMAT OF INCOME AND RETAINED EARNINGS STATEMENTS

This section elaborates the format ideas introduced in section 3.2. Like the balance sheet, the income and retained earnings statements are designed to provide information not only through their contents but also through the classification of their contents. There are just a few principles behind the income and retained earnings statements' classification of accounts:

- The income statement begins with the more ordinary, regular revenues and expenses, and separates those from significant (material) nonordinary accounts that are shown further down on the statement. As noted in section

3.4, disclosure of cost of goods sold expense makes the income statement more useful, but whether to do so is the company's choice.

- There may be some ordinary items that are unusual in size and so may be disclosed separately, but even these unusual items should be kept closer to the ordinary revenues and expenses and separated from the nonordinary ones.

- To signal the company's general ability to earn income, most income statements report a subtotal at this point, called Income before income tax, or Continuing income before income tax. Section 3.4 shows that CAE's 2000 income statement did this.

- Income tax expense, which includes amounts payable currently and amounts estimated to be payable in the future based on current-year events (called future or deferred tax), is deducted next. Including both current and future tax is called interperiod tax allocation (across time periods) because income tax estimated to be paid in the future as a consequence of present-period events should be included in this year's expense when those events are measured in this year's income. The total income tax expense should be calculated on the income before any nonordinary accounts and then the income after this tax should be reported, so that the reader of the financial statements can see what the company's ordinary, continuing income after income tax is. This figure is thought useful for making predictions about the future as well as evaluating past performance. Many companies call this after-tax figure income from continuing operations. In section 3.4, CAE's 2000 income from continuing operations is shown as $90.7 million.

Income from continuing operations is an important after-tax measure of performance.

- Then, the nonordinary items are added or deducted. Because income tax has already been deducted on continuing operations, each of these items should have its own income tax effects shown with it, to avoid mixing those effects in with the income tax on continuing operations. This means that income tax is allocated to each item that is below the continuing operations line. This is called intraperiod tax allocation (limited to one period), to separate it from the interperiod (across periods) tax allocation represented by the future/deferred income tax calculation mentioned above. Each intraperiod income tax amount may be currently payable, a future estimate, or some of each. It is common to disclose both the gross effect and the income tax effect of any of these nonordinary items. CAE disclosed this tax detail in a note to the year 2000 statements.

Intraperiod tax allocation assigns each nonordinary item its own income tax effects.

- The two main nonordinary items shown at the bottom of the income statement, both shown after their own income tax effects, are discontinued operations and extraordinary items. Discontinued operations are divisions or lines of business that were shut down and/or put up for sale during the year. Because such operations will not be part of the company in the future, separating them from the regular continuing operations should help in predicting future performance because they can be left out of such a prediction. CAE had such discontinued operations results in 2000. Extraordinary items are truly large and outside the company's control, such as a sudden expropriation of property by a government. Extraordinary items are seldom seen on income statements, but in these days of corporate restructuring and reorganization, discontinued operations have been quite often disclosed. CAE had no extraordinary items in 2000.

Net income is after any separately shown extraordinary or discontinued operations items.

- The income statement's "bottom line" is the net income, which is the income from continuing operations plus or minus any discontinued operations or extraordinary items.

- Earnings per share, which is income divided by average the number of voting shares outstanding during the year, is usually shown both before and after extraordinary and discontinued items, to help people judge the effect of these nonrecurring items on likely future income. Section 3.4 shows that CAE did this. (The nonrecurring items affect this year but should not affect future years.)

The retained earnings statement can also have its own nonordinary items.

- Net income is transferred to the statement of retained earnings. Before that is done, however, retained earnings are adjusted for the effects of three main kinds of nonordinary items, all net of any of their own income tax effects. The first is the correction of errors in prior years' incomes discovered this year. The second is the effects on past years' results of accounting policy changes adopted this year. The third is transactions with shareholders, such as costs of redeeming shares that are kept off the income statement following the rule that income is measured by relationships with customers, employees, suppliers, and others, but not with shareholders. CAE didn't have any of these items in 2000.

Exhibit 3.7 illustrates the effect of the above principles on the format of the two statements. The principles are quite well established and most companies follow them in general, but each company has its own specific interpretations and wordings, so you have to be prepared to see many variations in applying the principles, and even exceptions to them.

FOR YOUR INTEREST

Determining income is one of the most important tasks of accounting. To many people, it is *the* most important. Income and its revenue and expense components are financial accounting's main measures of an enterprise's economic performance over a period of time. The way of measuring income developed by accountants over the centuries, and now pretty well defined by various accepted accounting standards and methods, is not easy to connect to economic theory about performance. There is certainly a relationship, but it is both complex and subtle. For example, accounting treats debt-holders differently from equity-holders: interest on debts is deducted as an expense in calculating income, but dividends to owners are not. Dividends are treated as distributions of income, in the statement of retained earnings. Yet both groups have invested in the company, and they both are concerned about its ability to give them the return they expect. In economics and finance, evaluations of performance, risk, and returns to investors depend on a host of factors (such as economy-wide interest rates, inflation, and overall stock market movements) that are difficult to tie to accounting's measurement of an individual company's performance. Accrual accounting's measurement of economic performance is not universally accepted, and though the accounting measure of income does correlate with such economic indicators as stock prices, it is not at all the same. We'll see more about this later.

Exhibit 3-7

Illustrative Format of Income and Retained Earnings Statements

Income Statement for the Period

Revenue		$XXXX
Operating expenses (COGS may be separately disclosed)		XXXX
Operating income		$XXXX
Nonoperating items		
Ordinary items (interest, asset sale gains		
and losses, etc.)	$XXXX	
Any unusual items separately disclosed	XXXX	XXXX
Continuing income before income tax		$XXXX
Income tax expense (current and future		
deferred portions)		XXXX
Income from continuing operations		$XXXX
Any discontinued operations, net of income tax	$XXXX	
Any extraordinary items, net of income tax	XXXX	XXXX
Net income for the year		$XXXX

Retained Earnings Statement for the Period

Retained earnings as reported at the end of the	
prior period	$XXXX
Any adjustments to beginning balance for error	
corrections or accounting policy changes,	
net of income tax	XXXX
Revised beginning retained earnings	$XXXX
Add net income (or deduct net loss) from	
income statement	XXXX
Add or deduct any adjustments from transactions	
with shareholders, net of income tax	XXXX
Deduct dividends declared during the period	XXXX
Ending retained earnings (to balance sheet)	$XXXX

(H)OW'S YOUR UNDERSTANDING?

Here are two questions you should be able to answer, based on what you have just read:

1. Why are nonordinary items on the income and retained earnings statements shown net of their own income tax effects?

2. Laura Inc. has the following figures for this year: revenue $432,000, operating expenses $375,000, interest expense $11,000, unusual gain on sale of land $22,000, income tax expense $17,000, loss on discontinued operations $50,000, income tax recovery on the discontinued operations $12,000, beginning retained earnings $142,000, correction of error that overstated a prior year's income calculation $5,000, costs of a share redemption $8,000, dividends declared $10,000. What are the income from continuing operations, the net income, and ending retained earnings? ($51,000, $13,000, $132,000)

3.6   DEBITS AND CREDITS, REVENUES AND EXPENSES

In sections 2.4–2.6, we saw how entries and accounts were used to record events as transactions in the double-entry accounting system. The CappuMania Inc. example there was limited to balance sheet accounts. Let's expand the example to bring in income statement accounts and to "close" (transfer) those to retained earnings, so that the articulation of the income statement and balance sheet accounts may be illustrated. Section 3.7 has another example more focused on an intuitive understanding of the process—you can read that section before this one if you wish.

We'll continue the CappuMania example from section 2.6. As a reminder, here is the company's April 1, 2001, balance sheet from the end of section 2.6:

3-8

Exhibit

CappuMania Inc.				
Balance Sheet as at April 1, 2000				
Assets		**Liabilities and Shareholders' Equity**		
Current assets:		Current liabilities:		
Cash	$ 3,200	Owing to suppliers		$ 1,550
Inventory of unsold food	800	Sales and other taxes owing		100
Inventory of supplies	2,350			$ 1,650
	$ 6,350	Noncurrent liabilities:		
Noncurrent assets:		Loan to buy equipment		3,900
Equipment cost	$ 9,200			$ 5,550
Accumulated amortization	(1,500)	Shareholders' equity:		
	$ 7,700	Share capital contributed		$ 4,100
		Retained earnings		4,400
				$ 8,500
	$14,050			$14,050

Now let's add a year's business activities to that starting point. It's the year ended March 31, 2002, which will be referred to as the year 2002 below. Here is a list of ten items, a mixture of routine transactions and year-end adjustments so that you can see they are all recorded by the same technique of balanced journal entries. A full set of entries will follow.

1. Revenue for 2002 was $89,740. The coffee bar does mostly cash business, so of this, $85,250 was in cash and the rest was on credit.
2. General expenses for 2002, not including amortization or income tax, totalled $67,230. Most of the expenses for coffee supplies and so on were on credit, so of this, only $2,120 was in cash.
3. At the end of the year (March 31, 2002), it turned out that unsold food on hand cost $550 and supplies on hand cost $1,740. Therefore, the Food inventory account has to be reduced by $250 ($800 – $550) and the Supplies inventory account has to be reduced by $610 ($2,350 – $1,740). Using up these inventories is part of the cost of earning revenue, so these reductions will be included in the company's general expenses.
4. Amortization expense for the year 2002 was $2,380.

5. The company's income tax expense for 2002 was estimated at $4,460. (It is estimated because until the income tax authorities issue a formal assessment of tax, the company does not know for sure what its tax will be for the year.)
6. The company's board of directors declared a dividend of $1,000.
7. Collections of the revenue on credit totalled $3,330 during the year.
8. Payments to suppliers for expenses on credit totalled $59,420 during the year.
9. The company paid $3,000 toward its income tax during the year.
10. Only $800 of the dividend had been paid by the end of the year.

Now we can do entries to record these activities. To help you understand the entries, here are two important points:

- Because income is a part of retained earnings, which is an equity account and therefore a credit account on the balance sheet, anything that helps income is a credit. Revenue is therefore a credit balance account.

- Conversely, anything that hurts income, reduces retained earnings and equity, is therefore a debit. An expense is therefore a debit balance account. When dividends are declared, they are deducted from retained earnings; therefore, such deductions are debits because they reduce equity.

Revenues represent increases in equity and are therefore credits.

Expenses represent decreases in equity and are therefore debits.

This produces the following table of double-entry accounting's debits and credits (you already know this, but the table may help in making sure you understand the entries):

3-9
Exhibit

Debits	Credits
Increases in assets	Decreases in assets
Decreases in liabilities	Increases in liabilities
Decreases in equity:	Increases in equity:
Dividends declared	Contributed capital
Expenses	Revenues

Here are the entries for the ten items given above. Some entries break the usual rule of putting the debits first, leading with the part of the entry that may be most readily seen from the information above. The important thing is that each entry balances:

3-10

Exhibit

1. **Revenue**

	CR Revenue (equity increased)		89,740
DR	Cash (assets increased)	85,250	
DR	Accounts receivable (assets increased)	4,490	

2. **General expenses**

DR	General expenses (equity decreased)	67,230	
	CR Cash (assets decreased)		2,120
	CR Accounts payable (liabilities increased)		65,110

3. **Using up of inventories**

	CR Inventory of unsold food (assets decreased)		250
DR	General expenses (equity decreased)	250	
	CR Inventory of supplies (assets decreased)		610
DR	General expenses (equity decreased)	610	

4. **Amortization of equipment**

DR	Amortization expense (equity decreased)	2,380	
	CR Accumulated amortization (assets decreased)		2,380

5. **Estimated income tax expense**

DR	Income tax expense (equity decreased)	4,460	
	CR Sales and other taxes owing (liabilities increased)		4,460

6. **Dividend declared**

DR	Retained earnings (equity decreased)	1,000	
	CR Dividend payable (liabilities increased)		1,000

7. **Collections of accounts receivable**

DR	Cash (assets increased)	3,330	
	CR Accounts receivable (assets decreased)		3,330

8. **Payments of accounts payable**

	CR Cash (assets decreased)		59,420
DR	Accounts payable (liabilities decreased)	59,420	

9. **Payments toward income tax**

	CR Cash (assets decreased)		3,000
DR	Sales and other taxes owing (liabilities decreased)	3,000	

10. **Payment toward dividend**

	CR Cash (assets decreased)		800
DR	Dividend payable (liabilities decreased)	800	

A spreadsheet can act as an alternative format for the general ledger and its accounts.

We can post these ten entries to the company's accounts, using the spreadsheet basis we used in section 2.6. The resulting spreadsheet is shown in Exhibit 3.11. Note that the April 1, 2001 figures, which are what we ended with in section 2.6, are now in the first column, the starting figures. (We could have continued by adding our new columns (now columns D, E, and F) as columns G, H, and I to the right of the ending column F in section 2.6, but that would have produced a cluttered example.) Some new accounts (such as accounts receivable and revenue) are needed to record the entries: the titles of these are shown in italics. *The spreadsheet represents CappuMania's general ledger. Each line (or multiple lines, for Cash) of the spreadsheet is a record of the entries to the account named in that line, so each line stands for one of the ledger accounts described in section 2.5. Accounting systems may have different formats, but they all do the same thing!*

3-11

Exhibit

	A	B	C	D	E	F
1		CappuMania Inc. Example, in Spreadsheet Form (Continued)				
2						
3			April 1/01	Events and	Events and	March 31/02
4			Trial balance	Transactions*	Transactions*	Trial balance
5			Debit or credit	Debits	Credits	Debit or credit
6						
7	Cash		3200	(1) 85250	(2) −2120	26440
8				(7) 3330	(8) −59420	
9					(9) −3000	
10					(10) −800	
11	Accounts receivable		0	(1) 4490	(7) −3330	1160
12	Inventory of unsold food		800		(3) −250	550
13	Inventory of supplies		2350		(3) −610	1740
14	Equipment cost		9200			9200
15	Accumulated amortization		−1500		(4) −2380	−3880
16	Accounts payable		−1550	(8) 59420	(2) −65110	−7240
17	Sales and other taxes owing		−100	(9) 3000	(5) −4460	−1560
18	Dividend payable		0	(10) 800	(6) −1000	−200
19	Loan to buy equipment		−3900			−3900
20	Share capital contributed		−4100			−4100
21	Retained earnings		−4400	(6) 1000		−3400
22	Revenue		0		(1) −89740	−89740
23	General expenses		0	(2) 67230		68090
24				(3) 250		
25				(3) 610		
26	Amortization expense		0	(4) 2380		2380
27	Income tax expense		0	(5) 4460		4460
28						
29		Totals	0	232220	−232220	0
30						
31						
32						
33						
34						
35						

* The numbers in brackets have been added to the spreadsheet printout to refer to the 10 events and transactions described in the text.

You can see that everything is still in balance. The sums of the debits and credits in the ten entries are $232,220, and the March 31, 2002, accounts add up to zero (remember that, *arbitrarily*, debits are shown as positive amounts and credits as negative ones). The ledger's trial balance is represented by the March 31, 2002, column. The spreadsheet can be instructed to automatically sum rows and columns as you post journal entries, so that you can see immediately if you have done something arithmetically wrong.

The spreadsheet acts as the trial balance as well as the ledger.

To highlight the calculation of income from the expanded set of accounts, a second version of the spreadsheet is shown in Exhibit 3.12. It is the same as the spreadsheet we just saw, except that the balance sheet accounts and the income statement accounts are now separately subtotalled. You will see that income (the difference between the revenue and expense accounts) equals $14,810. It is a credit, which is what equity is. You will also note that without the income statement accounts, the balance sheet accounts are out of balance by the same $14,810. We will do something about that shortly.

The income statement accounts are part of the ledger and so are needed to balance it.

3-12

Exhibit

	A	B	C	D	E	F
38		CappuMania Inc. Example, in Spreadsheet Form (Continued)				
39		(With subtotals to show income calculation)				
40						
41			April 1./01	Events and	Events and	March 31./02
42			Trial balance	Transactions	Transactions	Trial balance
43			Debit or credit	Debits	Credits	Debit or credit
44						
45	Cash		3200	85250	−2120	26440
46				3330	−59420	
47					−3000	
48					−800	
49	Accounts receivable		0	4490	−3330	1160
50	Inventory of unsold food		800		−250	550
51	Inventory of supplies		2350		−610	1740
52	Equipment cost		9200			9200
53	Accumulated amortization		−1500		−2380	−3880
54	Accounts payable		−1550	59420	−65110	−7240
55	Sales and other taxes owing		−100	3000	−4460	−1560
56	Dividend payable		0	800	−1000	−200
57	Loan to buy equipment		−3900			−3900
58	Share capital contributed		−4100			−4100
59	Retained earnings		−4400	1000		−3400
60	**Balance sheet subtotals**		0	157290	−142480	14810
61	Revenue		0		−89740	−89740
62	General expenses		0	67230		68090
63				250		
64				610		
65	Amortization expense		0	2380		2380
66	Income tax expense		0	4460		4460
67	**Inc. stmnt. subtotals**		0	74930	−89740	−14810
68						
69		Totals	0	232220	−232220	0

Exhibit 3.13 shows the company's income statement for 2002, taken from the spreadsheet's March 31, 2002, balances for the income statement accounts.

3-13

Exhibit

CappuMania Inc. Income Statement for the Year Ended March 31, 2002		
Revenue		$89,740
Expenses:		
General	$68,090	
Amortization	2,380	70,470
Income before income tax		$19,270
Estimated income tax expense		4,460
Net income for the year		$14,810

Transferring revenues and expenses to retained earnings keeps the ledger in balance.

Before going on to the statement of retained earnings and the balance sheet, let's see how accountants close the revenue and expense accounts. The idea here is to transfer balances from those accounts to retained earnings, so that the income is transferred to retained earnings and the revenue and expense accounts are reset at zero and can then be used to record revenue and expenses for the next year (2000). The closing entry also illustrates how amounts can be moved around from account to account, to group accounts together, or otherwise rearrange balances in a desired way.

To close the revenue and expense accounts, each account with a credit balance is debited by that amount, and each account with a debit balance is credited by that amount. This brings all those accounts to zero:

DR Revenue	89,740	
CR General expenses		68,090
CR Amortization expense		2,380
CR Income tax expense		4,460
CR Retained earnings (the net income)		14,810

(Computerized accounting systems don't usually require a specific closing entry, because the computer can just reset the revenue and expense accounts to zero and adjust retained earnings automatically. But in principle, the above is what is happening.)

This entry is posted to the accounts in the spreadsheet in Exhibit 3.14, showing the closing amounts in bold italics. You will see that all the revenue and expense accounts have a zero balance now, and retained earnings now has a balance of $18,210. The March 31, 2002, balance sheet figures are now in balance, as you can see from the balance sheet subtotals line.

3-14

Exhibit

	A	B	C	D	E	F
70		CappuMania Inc. Example, in Spreadsheet Form (Continued)				
71		(With transfer ("closing") of income to retained earnings)				
72						
73			April 1/01	Events and	Events and	March 31/02
74			Trial balance	Transactions	Transactions	Trial balance
75			Debit or credit	Debits	Credits	Debit or credit
76						
77	Cash		3200	85250	−2120	26440
78				3330	−59420	
79					−3000	
80					−800	
81	Accounts receivable		0	4490	−3330	1160
82	Inventory of unsold food		800		−250	550
83	Inventory of supplies		2350		−610	1740
84	Equipment cost		9200			9200
85	Accumulated amortization		−1500		−2380	−3880
86	Accounts payable		−1550	59420	−65110	−7240
87	Sales and other taxes owing		−100	3000	−4460	−1560
88	Dividend payable		0	800	−1000	−200
89	Loan to buy equipment		−3900			−3900
90	Share capital contributed		−4100			−4100
91	Retained earnings		−4400	1000	*−14810*	−18210
92	**Balance sheet subtotals**		0	157290	−157290	0
93	Revenue		0	*89740*	−89740	0
94	General expenses		0	67230	*−68090*	0
95				250		
96				610		
97	Amortization expense		0	2380	*−2380*	0
98	Income tax expense		0	4460	*−4460*	0
99	**Inc. stmnt. subtotals**		0	164670	−164670	0
100						
101		Totals	0	321960	−321960	0

Now we can prepare the other two financial statements.

3-15
Exhibit

CappuMania Inc.
Statement of Retained Earnings
for the Year Ended March 31, 2002

Retained earnings, beginning of year	$ 4,400
Add net income for the year, per income statement	14,810
	$19,210
Deduct dividend declared during the year	1,000
Retained earnings, end of year	$18,210

3-16
Exhibit

CappuMania Inc.
Balance Sheet as at March 31, 2002

Assets			Liabilities and Shareholders' Equity	
Current assets:			**Current liabilities:**	
Cash	$26,440		Accounts payable	$ 7,240
Accounts receivable	1,160		Sales and other taxes owing	1,560
Inventory of unsold food	550		Dividend payable	200
Inventory of supplies	1,740			$ 9,000
	$29,890		**Noncurrent liabilities:**	
Noncurrent assets:			Loan to buy equipment	3,900
Equipment cost	$ 9,200			$12,900
Accumulated			**Shareholders' equity:**	
amortization	(3,880)		Share capital contributed	$ 4,100
	$ 5,320		Retained earnings	18,210
				$22,310
	$35,210			$35,210

Well, there you have it! This example has illustrated how accounting accumulates information about revenue and expense activities through journal entries posted to accounts, and how the financial statements are prepared from the accounts. The three financial statements fit together (*articulate*) because they are all based on the double-entry accounting system:

- A set of accounts is created, which is in balance (sum of all the debit account balances = sum of all the credit account balances).

- From these accounts are produced:
  - ▸ the income statement, the "bottom line" net income of which is transferred to
  - ▸ the statement of retained earnings, the "bottom line" ending retained earnings of which is transferred to
  - ▸ the balance sheet, which summarizes all the accounts.

Activities affecting income therefore affect the balance sheet through the double-entry system. Looking back at the entries above, for example:

- Entry 1 increased the balance sheet's assets and increased revenue on the income statement (thereby also increasing income, which is transferred to retained earnings, therefore increasing equity, which keeps the balance sheet in balance).

Journal entries that affect income must also affect the balance sheet by the same amount.

- Entry 2 decreased the balance sheet's assets and increased its liabilities and increased expenses on the income statement (thereby also decreasing income, therefore decreasing equity, which keeps the balance sheet in balance).

We will see this sort of relationship among the financial statements many times. It is fundamental to accrual accounting and to one of the most important uses of financial statements: analyzing the financial statements in order to evaluate financial performance and financial position.

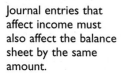

OW'S YOUR UNDERSTANDING?

Here are two questions you should be able to answer, based on what you have just read:

1. At the end of 2000, Hinton Hats Ltd. had retained earnings of $29,490. During 2001, it had revenue of $112,350, general expenses of $91,170, amortization expense of $6,210, and income tax expense of $3,420. Dividends of $5,000 were declared during 2001. At the end of 2001, the company's accounts were closed in preparation for 2002. After closing, what were the balances in the following accounts: Revenue, General expenses, Amortization expense, Income tax expense, and Retained earnings? (You should get $0, $0, $0, $0, and $36,040.)

2. The company's first event in 2002 was to pay $1,200 cash for the rent on its store for the first month of 2002. What did this event do to: assets, liabilities, income for 2002, retained earnings, equity? (You should get: down $1,200, no effect, down $1,200, down $1,200, down $1,200.)

3.7   ANOTHER PREPARATION ILLUSTRATION

Accounting's process should make intuitive sense to you, so this example uses intuition.

Having a solid understanding of how the financial statements reflect, through the accounts, the activities of the enterprise is very important to your understanding of accounting. Therefore, this section presents another example of preparation of financial statements, using a more intuitive approach than the previous section (but showing journal entries too).

The income and retained earnings statements report on performance over a period of time. As was shown in the diagram in section 3.1, there is one balance sheet at the beginning of that period, and another at the end. A sequence that will help you keep things straight is, therefore:

1. **Balance sheet at the beginning of the period, then**
2. **Income statement for the period, then**
3. **Retained earnings statement for the period, then**
4. **Balance sheet at the end of the period**

The financial statements are constructed to tell an integrated (articulated) story.

The Flashy Fashions example given below will further illustrate several things, among them:

- How the income and retained earnings statements are prepared from the accounts;

- How the accrual basis of calculating net income works;

- How the accounts themselves reflect business events; and

- How the above sequence connects (articulates) the beginning and ending balance sheets to the other two statements.

Flashy Fashions Inc. is a small company in a coastal town. It rents its premises and its sales are all on credit (customers do not pay cash when they get the goods, but rather pay later, when billed, so a sale produces an account receivable until the cash is paid). It has only three expenses: cost of goods sold, rent, and income tax. Cost of goods sold, often abbreviated as COGS, is what the company pays to acquire and prepare for sale the goods that customers buy. It is an expense the company incurs in order to get sales revenue.

At the end of its previous fiscal year, September 30, 1997, Flashy's balance sheet was as shown in Exhibit 3.17.

3-17

Exhibit

Flashy Fashions Inc. Balance Sheet as at September 30, 2000			
Assets		**Liabilities and Equity**	
Current assets:		Current liabilities:	
Cash	$ 800	Purchases payable	$ 600
Accounts receivable	400	Rent payable	300
Inventory	900	Shareholders' equity:	
		Share capital	500
		Retained earnings	700
	$2,100		$2,100

During the year ended September 30, 2001, the following information was recorded in the company's accounts:

3-18

Exhibit

Events	Journal entries		
1. Revenue from credit sales, $10,000	Dr Accounts receivable Cr Revenue from credit sales	10,000	10,000
2. Collections from customers, $9,600	Dr Cash Cr Accounts receivable	9,600	9,600
3. Purchases of inventory for sale, $6,100	Dr Inventory Cr Purchases payable	6,100	6,100
4. Payments to suppliers, $6,300	Dr Purchases payable Cr Cash	6,300	6,300
5. Cost of goods sold, $6,400	Dr Cost of goods sold expense Cr Inventory	6,400	6,400
6. Rent charged by the landlord, $2,400	Dr Rent expense Cr Rent payable	2,400	2,400
7. Rent paid to the landlord, $2,900	Dr Rent payable Cr Cash	2,900	2,900
8. Income tax payable for the year, $350	Dr Income tax expense Cr Income tax payable	350	350
9. Cash dividends declared, $450	Dr Dividends declared Cr Dividends payable	450	450
10. Dividends paid, $450	Dr Dividends payable Cr Cash	450	450

After recording these ten items, the company's accounts showed the following balances:

3-19

Exhibit

	Debits	Credits
Cash ($800 + $9,600 − $6,300 − $2,900 − $450)	$ 750	
Accounts receivable ($400 + $10,000 − $9,600)	800	
Inventory ($900 + $6,100 − $6,400)	600	
Purchases payable ($600 + $6,100 − $6,300)		$ 400
Dividends payable ($450 − $450)		0
Rent payable ($300 + $2,400 − $2,900)	200	
Income tax payable (owing for this year)		350
Share capital (no change)		500
Retained earnings (not changed yet by closing)		700
Dividends declared	450	
Revenue from credit sales		10,000
Cost of goods sold expense	6,400	
Rent expense	2,400	
Income tax expense	350	
	$11,950	$11,950

All the account changes should make intuitive sense.

Before we prepare financial statements, let's be sure you understand what happened in the accounts between 2000 and 2001.

a. Cash went up because of collections and down because of payments to suppliers, the landlord, and the shareholders (dividends).

b. Accounts receivable went up because of credit sales revenue and down because of collections.

c. Inventory went up because of purchases and down because the cost of goods sold was transferred to an expense account to recognize the value given up when the customers took the goods away.

d. Purchases payable went up because of purchases and down because of payments to suppliers.

e. Dividends payable went up when the dividends were declared and down when they were paid.

f. Rent payable went up because of bills from the landlord and down because of payments to the landlord. During the year, the landlord was paid more than had been billed, so rent payable reversed its sign: it's now a debit (prepaid rent). (Many accounts can be debits or credits, depending on temporary circumstances like overpaying. Even cash can be a credit: if you write too many cheques you can end up with an overdraft, in which case you have negative cash because you owe the bank instead of having money in the bank.)

g. Income tax payable went up from zero because the company owes tax on its income for this year (it did not owe any at the end of last year).

h. A new account, Dividends declared, was used to hold the dividend declared during the year. It will be transferred to retained earnings, so it is not really necessary—retained earnings could have been debited directly. However, if the company declares dividends regularly, having a separate account for them helps in keeping track and in preparing the retained earnings statement.

i. Revenue and expense accounts have only this year's revenues and expenses. Previous years' ones were transferred to retained earnings at the end of each year.

Now let's prepare the accrual basis financial statements for 2001 using the sequence given at the beginning of this section (the September 30, 2000, balance sheet was already presented above). First is the income statement, shown in Exhibit 3.20.

3-20
Exhibit

Flashy Fashions Inc. Income Statement for the Year Ended September 30, 2001		
Revenue		$10,000
Operating expenses:		
Cost of goods sold	$ 6,400	
Rent	2,400	8,800
Income before income tax		$ 1,200
Income tax expense		350
Net income for the year		$ 850

The accrual basis income statement depends on economic events, not cash flows.

So, the accrual income (net income) is $850. This is not the change in cash but is rather a measure of economic events, not all of which are settled in cash during the year. Events summarized on the income statement are:

- Customers promised to pay $10,000. That is the accrual basis revenue, not whatever was collected ($9,600).

- Customers took goods that had cost Flashy $6,400. That is the accrual basis COGS expense, not whatever was purchased ($6,100).

- Rent of $2,400 was billed. That is the accrual basis expense, not whatever was paid to the landlord ($2,900).

Accrual income requires more complete accounting than keeping track of cash does.

- Income tax of $350 is due on the income. That is the accrual basis expense, even though no tax has yet been paid for the year.

The accrual income brings in more phenomena than the cash change does. To emphasize the nature of accrual income, we can reconcile the accrual income to the change in cash as follows:

3-21
Exhibit

Accrual income, according to the income statement		$850
Increase in accounts receivable (revenue not yet collected)	$(400)	
Decrease in unsold inventory (releasing tied-up cash)	300	
Decrease in unpaid purchases (this took more cash)	(200)	
Change from rent payable to prepaid rent (took more cash)	(500)	
Increase in income tax payable (an expense not paid in cash)	350	(450)
Cash income		$ 400
Dividends paid		(450)
Decrease in cash over the year (began at $800, ended at $750)		$ (50)

Dividends are not shown on the income statement. These are considered a distribution of income, not an expense of producing the income. Dividends are on the statement of retained earnings, shown in Exhibit 3.22.

3-22
Exhibit

Flashy Fashions Inc. **Statement of Retained Earnings** **for the Year Ended September 30, 2001**	
Beginning balance (September 30, 2000)	$ 700
Add net income for the year, from the income statement	850
	$1,550
Deduct dividends declared	(450)
Ending balance (September 30, 2001)	$1,100

The retained earnings statement serves as a transition from the income statement to the balance sheet. We can see this in two ways. First, we can close the income statement accounts and dividends to retained earnings by debiting income accounts with credit balances and crediting income accounts (and dividends) with debit balances:

Dr Revenue	10,000	
Cr Cost of goods sold expense		6,400
Cr Rent expense		2,400
Cr Income tax expense		350
Cr Retained earnings (the net income)		850
Dr Retained earnings (dividends declared)	450	
Cr Dividends declared		450

Second, we can prepare the post-closing trial balance to check the ledger's balance:

3-23

Exhibit

Post-closing List of Accounts (Trial Balance)

	Debits	Credits
Cash	$ 750	
Accounts receivable	800	
Inventory	600	
Purchases payable		$ 400
Rent payable (now prepaid rent)	200	
Income tax payable		350
Share capital		500
Retained earnings ($700 + $10,000 − $6,400 − $2,400 − $350 − $450)		1,100
	$2,350	$2,350

After closing, only balance sheet accounts have balances; income statement ones are zero.

Retained earnings contains all past incomes, minus past dividends declared.

The accounts still balance, but now retained earnings contains all the information in the income and retained earnings statements. It is an accumulation of all the incomes (revenues minus expenses) minus all the dividends declared since the company began.

Now, we can combine the September 30, 2000, balance sheet we started with and the post-closing trial balance above to prepare comparative balance sheets at the ends of 2000 and 2001 (Exhibit 3.24).

Flashy Fashions Inc. **Balance Sheet as at September 30, 2001** **(with Comparative Figures for September 30, 2000)**		
	2001	2000
Assets		
Current assets:		
Cash	$ 750	$ 800
Accounts receivable	800	400
Inventory	600	900
Prepaid rent	200	–
	$2,350	$2,100
Liabilities and Equity		
Current liabilities:		
Purchases payable	$ 400	$ 600
Rent payable	–	300
Income tax payable	350	0
	$ 750	$ 900
Shareholders' equity:		
Share capital	$ 500	$ 500
Retained earnings	1,100	700
	$1,600	$1,200
	$2,350	$2,100

The income statement and balance sheet are joined via double-entry accrual accounting.

The 2001 balance sheet account balances consist of the 2000 balances, plus or minus cash transactions, and plus or minus revenues and expenses. (For example, 2001 accounts receivable equal the 2000 balance plus 2001 revenue from credit sales minus 2001 cash collections.) This demonstrates again an essential feature of accrual accounting and the balanced double-entry system: the calculation of income implies the calculation of balance sheet values, and vice versa. The income statement and the balance sheet are intimately and necessarily related: one always implies the other. Whenever income is affected (via a change to a revenue or expense account), the balance sheet is affected by the same amount. This point is one of the most important in understanding financial accounting, and we will encounter it frequently.

OW'S YOUR UNDERSTANDING?

Here are two questions you should be able to answer, based on what you have just read:

1. Garf Ltd. had accounts receivable at the beginning of the year of $5,290. During the year, it had revenue from sales on credit of $39,620 and collected $41,080 from its customers. What balance did the company's Accounts receivable account show at the end of the year? ($3,830)

2. Garf Ltd.'s net income for this year was $2,940, and it declared $900 in dividends to its shareholders during the year. Retained earnings were $7,410 at the beginning of the year. What are retained earnings at the end of the year, after closing? ($9,450)

3.8   ACCRUAL ACCOUNTING ADJUSTMENTS

The transactional records provide the foundation of the financial accounting system. In order to implement accrual accounting, such records usually require adjustments. Three main kinds of adjustments are needed:

Adjustments may be needed to correct errors.

a. Correction of errors discovered in the transactional record.

Adjustments are needed for accruals that the accounting system doesn't do routinely.

b. Implementation of routine accruals, such as revenues earned but not yet collected, expenses incurred but not yet paid, cash received from customers prior to the related revenues having been earned, and amortization of assets. The degree to which accrual adjustments are needed in any accounting system depends on the sophistication of the system: sophisticated accounting systems may go beyond the transactional records and routinely include many adjustments that for simpler systems are made at year-end in a special set of journal entries. Most companies keep track of sales and purchases on credit: such uncollected revenue and unpaid purchases are accruals, but they are transaction-based and are frequent so they are routinely recorded. Many large companies have monthly accruals for interest expenses and other expenses as they build up, and monthly allowances for amortization of assets. Many small companies don't bother with these nontransactional items until annual financial statements are needed.

Adjustments implement other choices and estimates necessary for the financial statements.

c. Recognition of nonroutine events or estimates needed to bring the financial statements into line with what management (or the auditors) believe is the economic and business substance of the enterprise's performance and position. Examples here could include reducing the balance sheet figure for ("writing down") assets whose economic value has been impaired due to changes in market value or poor management, changing the way warranties are accounted for as a result of lawsuits about product quality, and re-estimating income tax liability on the basis of recently announced tax law revisions.

Accrual accounting adjustments follow the same double-entry format as do the transactional records:

- Some account or accounts must be debited; and

- Some account or accounts must be credited; and

- The sum of the debits must equal the sum of the credits.

Accountants call such adjustments adjusting journal entries. They are just the same as any other journal entries, except that they do not involve cash (except to correct errors). Their purpose is to augment the transaction-based (especially cash-based) figures, to add to the story told by the transactional records. *They implement accrual accounting.*

The objective of accrual accounting is to improve the measurement of financial performance and position. However, because different choices can be made about what accounts need to be adjusted and by how much, accrual accounting can be a mechanism for manipulating results and producing misleading reports. Anyone can write an adjusting journal entry to alter the financial statements' figures; what is important is whether such an adjustment is *proper* (or whether an adjustment *not* made *should* have been). Therefore, the auditors give particular attention to the kinds of accrual adjustments a company makes or should make, and most of the criticism of financial reporting is directed at subjective accrual adjustments, made using judgment and perhaps lacking strong documentation, rather than at the more objective, verifiable transactional records. In spite of the subjectivity and criticism, most accountants believe the accrual accounting basis to be superior to the cash basis, because it provides a more complete record that is also more representative of economic performance than the cash basis. Not everyone agrees with this; in particular, modern finance theory puts more emphasis on cash flow than on accrual accounting's income measure. Chapter 10 has more on this.

An Example: The Northern Star Theatre Company

This example begins with the recording transactions and then shows the adjustments necessary to go from the records to the financial statements. To help you see how adjustments are built on the foundation of transactional records, *this example uses simple accounting records so that numerous adjustments will be necessary.* More sophisticated companies have accounting systems that go beyond transactions and make some adjustments routine.

Step 1: The Company and Its Initial Transactions

A group of aspiring actors from a small town decided to form a theatre company to perform in Canada's various "fringe" and other summer festivals. Here are events that happened to Northern Star Theatre Company in its first production, presented at a major Fringe Theatre Festival in 2001:

1. The theatre company (really, an informal partnership) was formed November 5, 2000, and a bank account was arranged for in the partnership's name. Six actors each agreed to put $500 into the company, but not until the money was needed.
2. The company applied in December 2000 for a place in the August 2001 Fringe, paying a fee of $400. Each actor paid $75 of the agreed amount to provide the money for the fee.
3. The Fringe notified the company in January 2001 that it had been accepted and allocated seven performances.
4. The company would have to pay a royalty to the play's author after the performances. The details were agreed with the author in March 2001.

5. Rehearsals began in March, and costumes and other props costing $470 were purchased. To pay for those items, each of the actors paid $100 more of the agreed amount, except one, Fred, who was broke at the time but promised to pay soon.

6. In early August, one of the actors, Elaine, drove to the city to see the performance venue and settle some staging details. The trip cost $290 in gas and other expenses, all of which the company reimbursed after collecting another $100 from each member of the company except Fred, who was still broke in July.

7. In mid-August, the six actors drove to the city, a few days ahead of their performance date. They stayed with friends and spent the time constructing a set for the play and gathering up other props. The set and props cost $610 in materials to construct, all of which was promised to be paid as soon as the play was over. The cost of the car gas and motels along the way was $190, and the members who had paid for such expenses were also promised repayment after the play was over.

8. The play opened to a moderately enthusiastic audience. The Fringe collected $960 ($8 × 120 seats) and turned $897 over to the company that day after deducting $63 in sales tax. The money was deposited in the company's bank account using a city branch of the bank.

Each enterprise's accounting system should meet its needs and sophistication.

We'll now work through how these simple events are recorded (if at all) and accumulated in a very simple accounting system. Note that though this system is much simpler than large companies would have, it probably is all this partnership of actors needs at this stage in its existence. It is important to match the accounting system to the needed level of sophistication.

Step 2: Recording the Transactions in a Journal

A general journal to record the transactions above is shown in Exhibit 3.25 below. Exact dates would be necessary in practice, but only the months were given above and they are used below. (Journals and ledgers are recorded to the penny, but we will ignore cents here.)

3-25

Exhibit

		Northern Star Theatre Company **General Journal**		
No.	Date	Description	Debits	Credits
1.	Nov. 2000	No transaction so no entry		
2a.	Dec. 2000	Cash (Bank)	450	
		Partners' capital		450
		Initial contributions by partners: 6 × $75, per bank records.		
2b.	Dec. 2000	Performance fees expense	400	
		Cash (Bank)		400
		Fee paid to Fringe to apply for a performance venue in 1998.		

(continued)

3-25

**Exhibit
(continued)**

No.	Date	Description	Debits	Credits
3.	Jan. 2001	No transaction so no entry		
4.	Mar. 2001	No transaction so no entry		
5a.	Mar. 2001	Cash (Bank)	500	
		Partners' capital		500
		Further contributions by five partners: 5 × $100. (No contribution from Fred.)		
5b.	Mar. 2001	Costumes and props expense	470	
		Cash (Bank)		470
		Costumes and props purchased, per suppliers' bills.		
6a.	Jul. 2001	Cash (Bank)	500	
		Partners' capital		500
		Further contributions by five partners: 5 × $100. (No contribution from Fred.)		
6b.	Jul. 2001	Travel expense	290	
		Cash (Bank)		290
		Reimbursement to Elaine for her trip to the city to check out the venue.		
7a.	Aug. 2001	Travel expense	190	
		Accounts payable		190
		Recording the liability to those partners who spent money getting the group to the city for the Fringe.		
7b.	Aug. 2001	Costumes and props expense	610	
		Accounts payable		610
		Recording the liability to various people for sets and props constructed in the city.		
8.	Aug. 2001	Cash (Bank)	897	
		Performance revenue		897
		Gate receipts for the first night.		

Step 3: Posting (Summarizing) Journal Entries in General Ledger

The recorded transactions, posted to general ledger accounts, are shown in Exhibit 3.26. The accounts are listed in the order in which they arose in the entries, not necessarily in balance sheet or income statement order.

Exhibit

Northern Star Theatre Company
General Ledger

Cash (Bank)

Date	Entry	Debit	Credit	Balance
Dec. 00	2a	450		450 DR
Dec. 00	2b		400	50 DR
Mar. 01	5a	500		550 DR
Mar. 01	5b		470	80 DR
Jul. 01	6a	500		580 DR
Jul. 01	6b		290	290 DR
Aug. 01	8	897		1,187 DR

Partners' Capital

Date	Entry	Debit	Credit	Balance
Dec. 00	2a		450	450 CR
Mar. 01	5a		500	950 CR
Jul. 01	6a		500	1,450 CR

Performance Fees Expense

Date	Entry	Debit	Credit	Balance
Dec. 00	2b	400		400 DR

Costumes and Props Expense

Date	Entry	Debit	Credit	Balance
Mar. 01	5b	470		470 DR
Aug. 01	7b	610		1,080 DR

Travel Expense

Date	Entry	Debit	Credit	Balance
Jul. 01	6b	290		290 DR
Aug. 01	7a	190		480 DR

Accounts Payable

Date	Entry	Debit	Credit	Balance
Aug. 01	7a		190	190 CR
Aug. 01	7b		610	800 CR

Performance Revenue

Date	Entry	Debit	Credit	Balance
Aug. 01	8		897	897 CR

Step 4: Trial Balance to See if Ledger Balances

Now, as we can see from Exhibit 3.27, the ledger balances! This is an unadjusted trial balance, because the accounts do not yet include the adjustments necessary for financial statements.

3-27

Exhibit

Northern Star Theatre Company General Ledger Unadjusted Trial Balance, mid-August 2001		
Account	Debit	Credit
Cash (Bank)	1,187	
Partners' capital		1,450
Performance fees expense	400	
Costumes and props expense	1,080	
Travel expense	480	
Accounts payable		800
Performance revenue		897
TOTALS	3,147	3,147

The group of actors agreed that a set of financial statements would be a good idea, as soon as the Fringe production was over. A date of August 26, 2001, was selected for the financial statements. Before the play's production ended, however, there were only three more cash transactions (continuing the numbering started above):

9. A local printing shop was paid $320 for printing programs and brochures describing the theatre company, to be handed out as people entered the venue to see the play and to be used generally to promote the play. These were available and used the first night, but were not paid for until two days later.
10. Of the amounts owing for props and set materials, $525 were paid.
11. The play was a moderate success. The audience was small after an initial bad review, but more people came to later performances. Total revenue for the remaining performances was $4,840. The group was not invited to perform at any of the "after the Fringe" events, so August 26 turned out to be as good a date as any for partnership financial statements.

Step 5: Accruals and Adjustments

Several matters required decisions and adjustments in order to prepare the August 26 financial statements. Continuing the above numbering sequence, these were:

12. The play's writer was owed her royalty, which had been agreed to at $450.
13. Additional travel expenses for getting back to the actors' hometown, to be reimbursed to various members of the group, totalled $215.
14. Costumes and props had cost $1,080. The group estimated that costumes and props costing about $420 were not reusable, but that the rest were reusable and would last on average about five engagements, including the just-finished Fringe as one of the five. The actors agreed to keep going, and therefore agreed that the costumes and props could be accounted for on a going concern basis, that is, assuming there would continue to be a theatre company

and therefore that the usable costumes and props had some future value. As the items had been included in Costumes and Props expense, their cost would have to be "capitalized": removed from expense and included with the assets.

15. There were some programs and brochures left over. The programs were pretty well useless, but the brochures describing the company could be used to seek future engagements and generally advertise. Brochures costing about $80 were thought still to be useful. (This adjustment works the same way as #14's capitalization.)

16. After talking to the bank, one of the actors estimated that, to August 26, about $20 in interest would have been earned by the money in the bank account. This wasn't much, but everyone wanted to see an accurate set of financial statements, so this was deemed material (significant) enough to be included.

17. The actors agreed that they would share any income or loss equally. The one who was broke said that rather than pay any cash in, he would transfer to the other members, out of his share of the income, the $200 he had not paid in, to settle his obligation. (This is an example of an adjustment that does not affect income but that is necessary to the balance sheet's classification of information.

Exhibit 3.28 shows the journal entries to *record* the three additional cash transactions and to *adjust* the accounts to recognize the effects of the additional information.

Recording and adjusting journal entries looks the same; only their objectives differ.

3-28

Exhibit

No.	Date	Description	Debits	Credits
		Northern Star Theatre Company **General Journal**		
9.	Aug. 01	Programs and brochures expense Cash (Bank) Programs and brochures to be handed out at performances.	320	320
10.	Aug. 01	Accounts payable Cash (Bank) Paying some of what is owed for materials for set and props.	525	525
11.	Aug. 01	Cash (Bank) Performance revenue Gate receipts for the remaining performances.	4,840	4,840
12.	Aug. 01	Royalties expense Accounts payable Royalty owed to author.	450	450
13.	Aug. 01	Travel expense Accounts payable Expenses for getting back to home town.	215	215

(continued)

**Exhibit
(continued)**

No.	Date	Description	Debits	Credits
14a.	Aug. 01	Costumes and props asset Costumes and props expense Capitalizing the cost of the costumes and props having future value.	660	660

14b.	Aug. 01	Amortization expense
		Accumulated amortization
		Amortization of costumes and props
		  assets: 1/5 of cost for the 2001
		  Fringe engagement.
			132	132

15.	Aug. 01	Brochures inventory Programs and brochures expense Recognizing the inventory of usable brochures still on hand, at cost.	80	80
16.	Aug. 01	Interest receivable Interest revenue Estimated interest earned by the bank account to August 26, 2001.	20	20

17.	Aug. 01	Partners' capital (Fred)
		Partners' capital (Others)
		Transfer from Fred to the other
		  partners to make up for the $200 in
		  cash not paid in by Fred as originally
		  agreed. *(This last entry has no effect
		  on the summary figures in the
		  financial statements, but is written to
		  recognize an economic event
		  important to the partners, Fred's
		  agreement to settle his obligation by
		  transferring some of his capital to the
		  other partners. The entry's effects are
		  on the details of partners' balances
		  within the capital account, not on the
		  account's total. The exact form of the
		  entry depends on the partners'
		  decision about how to rearrange their
		  capital accounts.)*
			200	200

Step 6: Posting the Remaining Transactions and the Accrual Adjustments

These entries have to be posted, just as the earlier transactional ones were. Do that on your own for practice, starting with the account balances in the trial balance in Exhibit 3.27, and see if you agree with the August 26 trial balance in Exhibit 3.29.

Step 7: Another Trial Balance

Exhibit 3.29 shows the adjusted trial balance at August 26, 2001, using the original accounts from Step 4 and additional accounts from Step 5. Accounts are now in financial statement order.

3-29
Exhibit

Northern Star Theatre Company		
General Ledger Adjusted Trial Balance, August 26, 2001		
Account	Debit	Credit
Cash (Bank)	5,182	
Interest receivable	20	
Brochures inventory	80	
Costumes and props	660	
Accumulated amortization		132
Accounts payable		940
Partners' capital		1,450
Performance revenue		5,737
Amortization expense	132	
Costumes and props expense	420	
Performance fees expense	400	
Programs and brochures expense	240	
Royalties expense	450	
Travel expense	695	
Interest revenue		20
TOTALS	8,279	8,279

If you have trouble getting any of these account balances, here are the calculations for some, beginning with the mid-August trial balance from Exhibit 3.27:

Cash = $1,187 − $320 − $525 + $4,840 = $5,182
Accounts payable = $800 − $525 + $450 + $215 = $940
Performance revenue = $897 + $4,840 = $5,737
Costumes and props expense = $1,080 − $660 = $420
Travel expense = $480 + $215 = $695

Revenue and expense accounts are usually closed only at the end of the year.

The financial statements to be drawn up at August 26 are "interim" ones: they are not year-end statements, so the accounts for the year are not closed at this point. *If they were closed on August 26*, the closing entry would be:

DR Performance revenue	5,737	
CR Amortization expense		132
CR Costumes and props expense		420
CR Performance fees expense		400
CR Programs and brochures expense		240
CR Royalties expense		450
CR Travel expense		695
DR Interest revenue	20	
CR Partners' capital		3,420

So far in the year, the partnership has an income of $3,420. In the details of the partners' capital, the $3,420 would be allocated to the partners under the agreement among the six actors, so each would be allocated one sixth, $570. To August 26, none of the partners has withdrawn any share of the income, so the partnership is like a corporation that has not declared any dividends from retained earnings. The financial statements in Exhibits 3.30, 3.31, and 3.32 reflect this. (Note that the fourth member of the usual set of financial statements, the cash flow statement, is not included below because it is not covered until Chapter 4 of this book.)

Step 8: The August 26 Financial Statements

3-30
Exhibit

Northern Star Theatre Company Income Statement for the Period November 5, 2000, to August 26, 2001		
Performance revenue		$5,737
Expenses:		
Amortization of costumes and props	$132	
Costumes and props not reusable	420	
Performance fees	400	
Programs and brochures	240	
Royalties	450	
Travel	695	2,337
Operating income		$3,400
Other income (bank interest)		20
Partnership income for the period (*Note 1*)		$3,420

3-31
Exhibit

Northern Star Theatre Company Statement of Partners' Capital for the Period November 5, 2000, to August 26, 2001	
Beginning capital	$ 0
Capital contributed during the period	1,450
Income for the period, per income statement	3,420
Withdrawals during the period	0
Capital at end of the period (*Note 2*)	$4,870

3-32

Exhibit

Northern Star Theatre Company
Balance Sheet at August 26, 2001

Assets

Current assets:

Cash in bank	$5,182	
Bank interest receivable	20	
Inventory of brochures	80	$5,282

Noncurrent assets:

Costumes and props, at cost	$ 660	
Less accumulated amortization	132	528
TOTAL		$5,810

Liabilities and Capital

Current liabilities:

Accounts payable	$ 940
Partners' capital (*Note 2*)	4,870
TOTAL	$5,810

Northern Star Theatre Company
Notes to the August 26, 2001, Financial Statements

1. The company is an unincorporated partnership of six actors who share incomes and losses equally. No provisions have been made in the financial statements for salaries to the partners or for such personal expenses as income taxes.

2. At August 26, 2001, the six partners' capital accounts are:

	Part. A	Part. B	Part. C	Part. D	Part. E	Part. F	Total
Contributed	$275	$275	$275	$275	$275	$ 75	$1,450
Transfer	40	40	40	40	40	(200)	0
Income	570	570	570	570	570	570	$3,420
Capital	$885	$885	$885	$885	$885	$445	$4,870

Here are two questions you should be able to answer, based on what you have just read:

1. Why are adjusting journal entries necessary?

2. Write adjusting journal entries for the following, decided upon by the partners of Northern Star Theatre Company after they reviewed the financial statements above, and explain what the effect of each is on income for the period since the company began. (1) An unrecorded and unpaid bill for $131 in travel expenses should have been included; (2) The inventory of brochures should have been set at $180, not $80. (The first item: DR Travel expenses 131, CR Accounts payable 131. Income down $131. The second item: DR Inventory of brochures 100, CR Programs and brochures expense 100. Income up $100.)

3.9   A FURTHER EXAMPLE OF ACCRUAL ACCOUNTING ADJUSTMENTS

Just to make sure you understand how accrual accounting adjustments work, here is another example. Pelforth Retail Inc. had the preliminary trial balance shown in Exhibit 3.33 after the completion of the year's routine recordkeeping. Accountants often refer to such a preliminary trial balance, which requires some adjustments at the year-end, as the unadjusted trial balance. Because not all accounts yet have the appropriate balances, the revenue and expense accounts have not yet been closed to retained earnings.

An unadjusted trial balance is based on the routine transactional records.

3-33

Exhibit

Preliminary Year-End Trial Balance for Pelforth Retail Inc.	Debits	Credits
Cash	23,000	
Accounts receivable	78,000	
Inventories	216,000	
Prepaid expenses	6,000	
Land	80,000	
Building	240,000	
Furniture and fixtures	110,000	
Accumulated amortization		180,000
Investment in Reddy Ware Corp.	60,000	
Bank loan		70,000
Accounts payable		112,000
Mortgage payable		150,000
Share capital		75,000
Retained earnings (prior to closing)		193,000
Revenue		620,000
Cost of goods sold expense	409,000	
Operating expenses	114,000	
Amortization expense	35,000	
Interest expense	18,000	
Income tax expense	11,000	
	1,400,000	1,400,000

The following items are not yet incorporated in the preliminary trial balance:

Adjustments are used to bring nonroutine, nontransactional information into the accounts.

a. The prepaid expenses have not been adjusted since last year. The appropriate amount of prepaid expenses at the end of this year is $4,000.

b. The investment in Reddy Ware Corp. looks like a loser. Management believes it should be written down to $25,000, its current market value.

c. $2,000 in mortgage and bank loan interest should be accrued, based on the accountant's estimate of unpaid interest at the end of the year.

d. Management believes additional revenue of $15,000 should be recognized as earned, based on some special contracts with customers.

e. The cost of goods sold to go with that additional revenue is $7,000, so that amount should be removed from inventory.

f. Management believes that an accrual for warranty expense should be made, because some of the products sold this year were unusually badly made. The likely warranty costs to be incurred in the future based on this year's sales are estimated at $3,000. All the warranty costs are expected to be incurred within the next year.

g. An old customer died while on a back country ski trip, and the management believes the company will not ever collect the $1,000 the customer owed at the end of the year.

Adjustments have the same form as any other journal entries.

h. Because all of the above change the company's income before income tax from the preliminary amount of $44,000 ($620,000 − ($409,000 + $114,000 + $35,000 + $18,000)) down to only $9,000, the estimated income tax expense should be $3,000, not the $11,000 paid already. The company should expect a refund of the difference within a few months.

Let's write adjusting journal entries to implement the decisions and calculations above:

3-34

Exhibit

a. DR   Operating expenses   2,000
        CR   Prepaid expenses   2,000
   To reduce prepaid expenses from $6,000 to $4,000.

b. DR   Loss on investment (an expense)   35,000
        CR   Investment in Reddy Ware   35,000
   To reduce the investment down to market of $25,000.

c. DR   Interest expense   2,000
        CR   Accrued interest liability   2,000
   To record estimated accrued mortgage and bank interest.

d. DR   Accounts receivable   15,000
        CR   Revenue   15,000
   To recognize revenue earned on special contracts.

e. DR   Cost of goods sold expense   7,000
        CR   Inventories   7,000
   To recognize the COGS for entry (d).

(continued)

3-34

Exhibit
(continued)

f. DR	Warranty expense (or Operating expenses)	3,000	
	CR　Warranty liability		3,000

To record estimated warranty expense arising this year.

g. DR	Bad debts expense	1,000	
	CR　Accounts receivable		1,000

To write off a receivable that will never be collected.

h. DR	Income tax receivable	8,000	
	CR　Income tax expense		8,000

To reduce tax expense and record estimated refund.

An adjusted trial balance provides a more complete portrayal than an unadjusted one.

Posting all these adjustments to the general ledger results in the adjusted trial balance shown in Exhibit 3.35. Note that it has accounts that the preliminary trial balance did not. Accrual accounting adjustments typically make the accounts more complex and more complete in their portrayal of the enterprise, because accrual accounting is intended to incorporate more information than the routine accounting system usually does.

3-35

Exhibit

Adjusted Year-End Trial Balance for Pelforth Retail Inc.

	Debits	Credits
Cash	23,000	
Accounts receivable	92,000	
Income tax refund receivable	8,000	
Inventories	209,000	
Prepaid expenses	4,000	
Land	80,000	
Building	240,000	
Furniture and fixtures	110,000	
Accumulated amortization		180,000
Investment in Reddy Ware Corp.	25,000	
Bank loan		70,000
Accounts payable		112,000
Accrued interest		2,000
Estimated warranty liability		3,000
Mortgage payable		150,000
Share capital		75,000
Retained earnings (prior to closing)		193,000
Revenue		635,000
Cost of goods sold expense	416,000	
Operating expenses	116,000	
Amortization expense	35,000	
Bad debts expense	1,000	
Warranty expense	3,000	
Interest expense	20,000	
Loss on investment	35,000	
Income tax expense	3,000	
	1,420,000	1,420,000

Now the company's financial statements can be prepared from the adjusted trial balance. Doing that is left to you as an exercise. You should get total current assets of $336,000, net noncurrent assets of $275,000, total current liabilities of $187,000, noncurrent liability of $150,000, shareholders' equity of $274,000 (including retained earnings after closing of $199,000), and net income of $6,000.

HOW'S YOUR UNDERSTANDING?

Here are two questions you should be able to answer, based on what you have just read:

1. Brazza Ltd. management wishes to record $12,000 revenue that it believes has been earned on a contract it has with a customer. No revenue for the contract has yet been collected from the customer or previously recorded. What journal entry would accomplish management's wish? (DR Accounts receivable 12,000; CR Revenue 12,000)

2. Brazza Ltd. management also wishes to record an additional adjustment. This year, the company began to offer a warranty with its products. Therefore, it incurs an expense for future estimated warranty service costs each time it makes a sale. Management estimates that for the sales recorded so far this year, the warranty costs will be $3,200. What journal entry would record the estimated expense and liability incurred so far? (DR Warranty expense 3,200; CR Liability for estimated warranty costs 3,200)

3.10   MANAGERS, INVESTORS, AND MANAGING EARNINGS

The income statement is a major spotlight on management's performance.

Managers' own incomes, promotions, careers, pensions, and reputations depend on other people's decisions that, in turn, rest to some extent on information in the financial statements, particularly the income statement, and especially where capital markets, such as stock markets, are involved. Managers of large, publicly traded companies are under constant pressure because of the spotlight on earnings (net income or profit) and its components. Business and social observers often comment that this spotlight is too intense, that there is more to managerial performance than the income statement shows, and that the income statement is doubtful as a measure because it reflects the limitations of accrual-based, double-entry accounting. Nevertheless, the spotlight is there.

An indication of the importance placed on the bottom line can be found in the financial section of almost any newspaper, in the regular announcements of corporations' annual and/or quarterly earnings. Exhibit 3.36 shows three such announcements from a set of about 25 reported by the *Globe and Mail* on a single day, February 4, 2000.

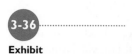

3-36

Exhibit

Corporate Earnings

CAE Inc.
(CAE-TSE)

3 months to December 31		Year ago
Revenue	34,861,000	235,455,000
Net profit	37,555,000	23,032,000
Net profit share	0.34	0.21
Avg. shares	110,226,000	110,972,000
9 months to December 31		Year ago
Revenue	841,210,000	649,150,000
Net profit	74,939,000	53,518,000
Net profit / share	0.68	0.48
Cash flow	82,771,000	61,563,000
Avg. shares	110,226,000	110,972,000

Year ago cash flow figures have been restated. The net income for the quarter and nine months ended Dec. 1999 included earnings from discontinued operations of $11.8 million or $0.11 per share and $8.7 million or $0.08 per share, respectively. Earnings from discontinued operations in the year-ago quarter and nine months were $2.2 million or $0.02 per share and $1.9 million or $0.01 per share, respectively.

Canadian Tire Corp.
(CTR.A–TSE)

3 months to January 01		Year ago
Revenue	1,285,865,000	1,137,092,000
Net profit	12,971,000	44,016,000
Net profit / share	0.16	0.56
Cash flow	n/a	n/a
Cash flow / share	1.24	0.95
Avg. shares	77,21,000	79,793,000
Year to January 01		Year ago
Revenue	4,728,259,000	4,347,283,000
Net profit	145,929,000	166,980,000
Net profit / share	1.89	2.09
Cash flow	n/a	n/a
Cash flow /share	3.95	3.26
Avg. shares	77,211,000	79,793,000

Manitoba Telecom Services Inc.
(MBT–TSE)

3 months to December 31		Year ago
Revenue	181,900,000	179, 400,000
Net profit	20,500,000	24,000,000
Net profit / share	0.30	0.34
Cash flow	105,700,000	96,300,000
Avg. shares	67,700,000	70,000,000
Year to December 31		Year ago
Revenue	722,100,000	696,900,000
Net profit	93,900,000	95,400,000
Net profit /share	1.34	1.36
Cash flow	315,800,000	292,000,000
Avg. shares	69,900,000	70,000,000

Certain year ago figures are reclassified. The net income for the year ended Dec. 1998 included a gain on sale of an investment of $4.1 million or $0.06 per share.

Earnings announcements provide important summary information.

These announcements, which are prepared by the companies but formatted by the newspaper, focus on income statement information, including earnings per share. (The newspaper does not use the word income, preferring "net profit.") Cash flow information is also included if available—more about this in Chapter 4. Some narrative comments are added if thought helpful. The CAE announcement updates the data from the 1999 income statement (the 1999 CAE figures are in section 3.4), showing earnings for the 9 months to December 31, 1999, to be 68 cents per share, almost equal to the 70 cents per share for the full year ended March 31, 1999, and most of the 90 cents per share CAE would eventually report for the year ended March 31, 2000 (section 3.4). CAE had effects of discontinuing operations in late 1999, and as indicated in the format specified in section 3.5, those effects are separately specified: 11 cents of the 68 cents per share earnings were from such discontinued operations.

Stock market prices and earnings tend to be correlated.

Stock market traders pay particular attention to the factors that produce good, or poor, earnings. Stock market prices and earnings are positively correlated: when earnings go up, share prices tend to be going up too, because investors want to buy the shares; and when earnings go down, share prices tend also to be going down, because investors want to sell them. During the year, investors learn about various good or poor management decisions, based on news reports, financial analysts' reports and other sources, and form expectations about what earnings will be. There is much accounting research to show that the stock market's share price for a company's shares tends to change when the original good or poor news comes out, and then if the earnings announcement is a positive or negative surprise, they change again. The earnings per share are up for CAE, nearly unchanged for Manitoba Telecom, and down for Canadian Tire. The announcement is news, and therefore affects share prices, only if it varies from expectations. In general, stock market prices and earnings, as announced from time to time, tend to end up moving in the same direction and so are correlated.

Managers of public companies are very aware of their companies' financial statements.

We can conclude that the performance factors measured by accrual accounting are similar to the factors share buyers and sellers are assessing when they decide to try to buy or sell a corporation's shares. Managers of corporations with traded shares are therefore keenly aware of accounting's income measurement, because accounting is tracking factors investors are concerned about, and if the investors do not learn about these factors from other sources, they will certainly learn about them from the income statement and other financial statements. Managers of many companies, especially (but not only) larger corporations, go to great lengths to explain their performance to investors and to people on whom investors rely, such as stock market analysts and business journalists.

FOR YOUR INTEREST

It is harder to tell if the income statement is as important for managers of smaller or private companies, the shares of which are not traded and about which there is less news in general, but there is no reason to think the importance is not comparable. Managers and owner-managers of smaller companies are at least as concerned as managers of larger companies are about management bonuses, income tax, and other effects of the figures in the income statement, and the kind of changes in confidence that change stock market prices are likely to be present for smaller companies too.

Because of income's importance to managers, they may wish to "manage" the results. Considerable accounting research has been done on earnings management, and what it does to share prices, managers' career prospects, and the validity of accrual accounting information. Here are two examples of earnings management.

Income Smoothing

Accrual income generally is smoother than cash income.

Many companies' senior managers choose accounting methods that have the effect of making their reported accounting income look smoother over time than it might otherwise be. "Smooth" here means that income goes up and down less than it might, so that if you plotted a company's income over time, the year-to-year variations would be smaller than they would otherwise be. There is not necessarily any "blame" to managers here, because accrual accounting generally produces a smoother measure of income than cash income does anyway. The cash receipts and payments behind cash income depend on all sorts of factors beyond the economic performance accrual accounting tries to track. For example, making an estimate of future warranty costs and using that to adjust warranty expense each year will usually produce a smoother expense (and so income) than just letting cash payments be the warranty expense, but doing so is also prudent accounting, because those future costs are really a liability that is incurred now, when the products are sold. So a manager who is smoothing income may partly be just being a good accountant!

When managers do make deliberate accounting choices that produce a smoother income, such choices are not necessarily motivated by a wish to mislead—there may be income tax and other good reasons for such choices—but the idea behind income smoothing is that managers would prefer the smoother trend of earnings shown in column B below to the trend in column A, even though the total income over the five years is the same and both columns show an increasing trend.

	A (original)	B (smoother)
Income for 1998	$ 1,800,000	$ 4,150,000
Income for 1999	6,570,000	4,310,000
Income for 2000	2,650,000	4,570,000
Income for 2001	8,230,000	4,820,000
Income for 2002	3,620,000	5,020,000
Sum over the 5 years	$22,870,000	$22,870,000

These data are presented in graph form in Figure 3.5 The main reason for wanting to show a smoother trend in earnings seems to be that the smoother trend makes it appear that management has a firm hold on the company, that it is competent and in control of events. The less smooth trend implies more risk, more variation. So if managers are held accountable to owners for keeping risk down, they may prefer the smoother trend.[9]

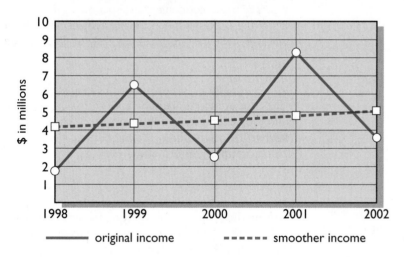

FIGURE 3.5

——— original income   - - - - - - smoother income

The Big Bath

"Counter-smoothing" accounting choices have also been studied by accounting researchers. An example is the so-called Big Bath, in which a company having a bad year (poor earnings or even a loss) chooses accounting methods that make the

Accrual accounting may also be used to make income less smooth, as in the Big Bath.

results look even *worse*. Managers apparently think that they are going to be in trouble anyway, and so decide that they won't be in much worse trouble if they make the results even worse by writing off doubtful assets, recognizing future costs as expenses now, or otherwise cleaning up the accounting records. A new president may also want to blame the previous president for past trouble, and so want to clear the accounts of some assets (by charging them off as expenses) that the previous president thought were valuable but the new president thinks are not. This produces a terrible year as far as the accounting numbers go, but increases the chances that in future years, accounting results will be better than would happen without the Bath. An example is writing off the cost of an investment in a factory that the company no longer wishes to operate, rather than keeping the cost on the balance sheet and amortizing it in the future. This leaves less cost to be amortized in the future, and so should mean that future incomes will be higher than they would be otherwise because of lower future amortization expenses.

3.11 TERMS TO BE SURE YOU UNDERSTAND

This chapter introduced more terms and emphasized some already in earlier chapters. If you don't understand any of these, check the chapter again or refer to the Glossary of Terms at the end of the book.

Accounts receivable	Dividend	Inventory
Accrual basis	Earnings	Markup
Accrual income	Earnings management	Material
Adjusted trial balance	Earnings per share	Net income
Adjusting journal entries	Economic entity	Net loss
Adjustments	EPS	Net-of-tax analysis
Articulation	Expenditure(s)	Post(ed)
Big Bath	Expense(s)	Post-closing trial balance
Board of directors	Extraordinary items	Revenue(s)
Capital markets	Financial performance	Statement of retained
Capitalize(d)	General journal	earnings
Classification	General ledger	Stewardship
Close	Gross margin	Stock dividend
Closing entry	Income from continuing	Stock markets
COGS	operations	Trial balance
Corporation(s)	Income smoothing	Unadjusted trial balance
Cost of goods sold	Income statement	Unusual items
Deficit	Interperiod tax allocation	
Discontinued operations	Intraperiod tax allocation	

3.12 CONTINUING DEMONSTRATION CASE

INSTALLMENT 3

Data for Installment 3

Mato Inc.'s First Six Months

During the first six months of the company's existence, life was hectic for Mavis and Tomas. The main pressure was to get set up and get goods out to retailers in time for the heavy selling season from July to December. Mavis regretted several times not having started earlier, because it took much more time to make arrangements with suppliers and retailers and get goods delivered than she had expected. The first six months did generate some revenues, but the period was largely one of building.

Some important events in the six months to August 31, 2000, took place.

- The warehouse space was occupied in early March, and the renovations ("leasehold improvements," consisting of partitions, shelving, and other fixtures) were completed in early June, a month later than had been desired.

- A computer was bought to handle the company's accounting, purchases, sales, inventory, and customer relations records, plus software packages suitable to these tasks.

- Tomas quit his bank job and began to work full-time for the company in July, after having devoted most of his evenings and weekends to the company since March.

- Mavis travelled both around the region, to talk to retail boutique owners and line up orders, and out of the region to meet with suppliers. The company ran up large phone bills in connection with all the business development activity, but that had been anticipated in the business plan.

- Finding that they did not have enough cash to keep operating, Tomas and Mavis arranged for a demand bank loan. This money was primarily used to finance the needed level of inventory.

- In mid-August, an employee was hired to maintain all the records and help Mavis organize her activities.

Results for Installment 3

Journal entries to record the first six months' events follow, in summarized form.

1. Dr Leasehold improvements asset	63,964	
Dr Equipment and furniture asset	29,740	
Dr Computer equipment asset	14,900	
Dr Software asset	4,800	
Cr Accounts payable		113,404
Noncurrent assets acquired during the six months.		
2. Dr Inventory	101,816	
Cr Accounts payable		101,816
Inventory purchased during the six months.		
3. Dr Accounts receivable	42,674	
Cr Revenues		42,674
Revenues for the six months.		
4. Dr Cost of goods sold expense	28,202	
Cr Inventory		28,202
Cost of goods sold for the six months.		

5. Dr. Salary expense – Mavis	15,000	
Dr Salary expense – Tomas	9,280	
Dr Salary expense – Other	1,200	
Dr Travel expense	8,726	
Dr Telephone expense	2,461	
Dr Rent expense	12,000	
Dr Utilities expense	1,629	
Dr Office and general expenses	3,444	
Cr Accounts payable		53,740

Remaining expenses for the six months.

6. Dr Cash	23,951	
Cr Accounts receivable		23,951

Collections from customers for the six months.

7. Dr Cash	75,000	
Cr Bank loan		75,000

Demand bank loan obtained.

8. Dr Accounts payable	224,444	
Cr Cash		224,444

Cash payments for the six months.

There was also one large adjusting journal entry. Tomas recorded amortization on the physical and nonphysical assets, improvements to leased premises, and computer software as follows: car, leasehold improvements, computer, and software: 1/2 year × 20% of cost; other equipment and furniture: 1/4 year × 10% of cost.

9. Dr Amortization expense—auto	1,000	
Cr Accumulated amortization—auto		1,000
Dr Amortization expense—leasehold improvements	6,396	
Cr Accumulated amortization—leasehold improvements		6,396
Dr Amortization expense—equipment	744	
Cr Accumulated amortization—equipment		744
Dr Amortization expense—computer	1,490	
Cr Accumulated amortization—computer		1,490
Dr Amortization expense—software	480	
Cr Accumulated amortization—software		480

Amortization recorded for the six months.

Posting these entries to the accounts and incorporating the beginning balance sheet figures from Installment 2 (section 2.12) produce the following adjusted trial balance at August 31, 2000. (If you are not sure where any of these amounts come from, just take any account, start with the March 1 balance, and add/subtract the entries above that affect the account.)

Debit balance accounts		Credit balance accounts	
Cash	$ 4,507	Bank loan	$ 75,000
Accounts receivable	18,723	Accounts payable	45,616
Inventory	73,614	Loan payable	15,000
Automobile	10,000	Share capital	125,000
Leasehold improvements	63,964	Revenues	42,674
Equipment and furniture	29,740	Accum. amort. — auto.	1,000
Computer	14,900	Accum. amort. —	
		leasehold imp.	6,396
Software	4,800	Accum. amort. — equip.	744
Incorporation costs	1,100	Accum. amort. — computer	1,490
Cost of goods sold expense	28,202	Accum. amort. — software	480
Salary — Mavis	15,000		
Salary — Tomas	9,280		
Salary — other	1,200		
Travel expense	8,726		
Telephone expense	2,461		
Rent expense	12,000		
Utilities expense	1,629		
Office and general expenses	3,444		
Amort. expense — auto.	1,000		
Amort. expense — leasehold			
imp.	6,396		
Amort. expense — equipment	744		
Amort. expense — computer	1,490		
Amort. expense — software	480		
	$313,400		$313,400

From that trial balance, Tomas prepared the following financial statements for the new company.

Mato Inc. Statement of Loss and Deficit for the Six Months Ended August 31, 2000		
Revenues		$42,674
Cost of goods sold		28,202
Gross profit		$14,472
Operating expenses:		
Salaries	$25,480	
Travel	8,726	
Telephone	2,461	
Rent	12,000	
Utilities	1,629	
Office and general	3,444	
Amortization	10,110	63,850
Net loss for the six months (no tax)		$49,378
Deficit as at August 31, 2000		$49,378

Mato Inc.
Balance Sheets as at August 31 and March 1, 2000

Assets			Liabilities and Shareholders' Equity		
	August	**March**		**August**	**March**
Current assets:			Current liabilities:		
Cash	$ 4,507	$130,000	Bank loan	$ 75,000	$ 0
Receivables	$ 18,723	0	Payables	45,616	1,100
Inventory	73,614	0	Loan payable	15,000	15,000
	$ 96,844	$130,000		$135,616	$ 16,100
Noncurrent assets:			Shareholders' equity:		
Equip. cost	$ 54,640	$ 10,000	Share capital	$125,000	$125,000
Equip. acc. amort.	(3,234)	0	Deficit	(49,378)	0
Leasehold (net)*	57,568	0		$ 75,622	$125,000
Software (net)**	4,320	0			
Incorp. costs	1,100	1,100			
	$114,394	$ 11,100			
TOTAL	$211,238	$141,100	TOTAL	$211,238	$141,100

* Net book value of leasehold improvements = $63,964 cost − $6,396 accumulated amortization.
** Net book value of software = $4,800 − $480 accumulated amortization.

3.13 HOMEWORK AND DISCUSSION TO DEVELOP UNDERSTANDING

PROBLEM 3.1*
Define terms

Define the following terms in your own words:

- Revenue
- Expense
- Net income
- Dividend
- Retained earnings
- Owners' equity

PROBLEM 3.2*
Basic balance sheet, income, and retained earnings ideas.

Labott's Bottlery Ltd. had the following recent balance sheet:

Labott's Bottlery Ltd.
Balance Sheet as at September 30, 2001

Cash	$1,642	Mortgage	$1,000
Inventory	1,480	Share capital	3,000
Land	2,100	Retained earnings	1,222
	$5,222		$5,222

1. Why is "land" on the balance sheet, and what does it represent?
2. On October 5, 2001, the company borrowed $2,410 from the bank and used the money immediately to buy more land. What was the total dollar figure of the company's assets after this point?
3. Why did the company not just use the $3,000 share capital to buy more land instead of borrowing from the bank?
4. Explain how "retained earnings" comes to be on the balance sheet and what it represents.
5. For the year ended September 30, 2001, the company's revenues were $10,116, and its expenses (including income tax) were $9,881. What was its net income for the year?
6. During the year ended September 30, 2001, the company declared dividends of $120. Considering this and part 5, what was the balance in retained earnings at the *beginning* of that year (October 1, 2000)?
7. If the expenses for the year to September 30, 2001, were $11,600 instead of the figure in part 5, and the company did not declare any dividends, what would the retained earnings be at September 30, 2001?
8. The answer to part 7 is a negative number, which would be a deficit. Would you think such a deficit should be shown with the assets on the left side of the company's balance sheet, so that it becomes a positive number, rather than showing it as a negative number deducted from equity on the right side of the balance sheet? Why or why not?

PROBLEM 3.3*
Prepare a simple set of financial statements from accounts.

Following are account balances of Arctic Limo Services Ltd. Prepare a 2001 income statement, a 2001 statement of retained earnings, and comparative 2000 and 2001 balance sheets. (Note that the 2001 income and dividends have not yet been closed to retained earnings.) State any assumptions you feel are necessary.

	September 30, 2001	September 30, 2000
Accumulated amortization	$ 30,000	$20,000
Cash on hand	2,000	4,000
Dividends declared	80,000	
Due from Lucky Eddie		1,000
Due to Amalgamated Loansharks		10,000
Income tax expense	35,000	
Limousines amortization expense	10,000	
Limousines cost	90,000	60,000
Long-term limousine financing	50,000	30,000
Other expenses	70,000	
Retained earnings	4,000	4,000
Revenue	300,000	
Share capital	1,000	1,000
Wages expense	100,000	
Wages payable	2,000	

PROBLEM 3.4*
Explain terms in nontechnical language

Explain the following in nontechnical language that a person who has not read this book would understand:

1. What is net income as it is meant in financial accounting?
2. Why is net income part of owners' equity?
3. If net income is part of owners' equity, why is it necessary to have a separate income statement? Why not just report net income on the balance sheet?
4. Why are dividends to shareholders not considered to be an expense in calculating net income?

PROBLEM 3.5*
Prepare financial statements from accounts

A list of accounts for Geewhiz Productions at November 30, 2001, is shown below, in no particular order.

Salaries expense	$ 71,000	Dividends declared	$ 11,000
Income tax payable	2,800	Accumulated amortization	94,000
Land	63,000	Cash in bank	18,000
Employee benefits expense	13,100	Income tax expense	6,900
Tax deductions payable	5,400	Credit sales revenue	346,200
Accounts receivable	16,400	Inventory on hand	68,000
Cash sales revenue	21,600	Prepaid insurance asset	2,400
Dividends payable	5,500	Beginning retained earnings	92,800
Amortization expense	26,700	Accounts payable	41,000
Cost of goods sold expense	161,600	Interest income	1,700
Insurance expense	11,200	Building	243,000
Share capital	200,000	Trucks and equipment	182,500
Office expenses	31,100	Salaries payable	4,100
Mortgage payable	114,000	Miscellaneous expenses	8,200
Bank loan owing	21,800	Interest expense	16,800

1. Decide which ones are income statement accounts.
2. Calculate net income based on your answer to part 1.
3. Calculate ending retained earnings based on your answer to part 2.
4. Prepare the following financial statements, demonstrating that your answers to parts 2 and 3 are correct:
   a. Income statement for the year ended November 30, 2001.
   b. Statement of retained earnings for the year ended on that date.
   c. Balance sheet at November 30, 2001.
5. Comment briefly on what the financial statements show about the company's performance for the year 2001 and financial position at November 30, 2001.

PROBLEM 3.6*
Derive accounting numbers

Fill in the blanks in the following schedule of financial accounting numbers for Vekeng Corporation. Start with 1998 and work forward from there.

	1998	1999	2000	2001
Revenue for the year	$ 38,000	_____	$ 61,000	$ 65,000
Expenses for the year (except income tax)	_____	42,000	50,000	_____
Income before income tax for the year	9,000	7,000	_____	4,000
Income tax expense for the year	2,000	_____	_____	1,000
Net income for the year	_____	5,500	8,000	_____
Retained earnings, beginning of the year	_____	_____	_____	_____
Dividends declared during the year	3,000	_____	4,500	0
Retained earnings, end of year	25,000	_____	33,000	_____
Other owners' equity, end of year	35,000	38,000	38,000	_____
Liabilities, end of year	_____	85,000	111,000	105,000
Assets, end of year	140,000	152,500	_____	189,000

PROBLEM 3.7*
Journal entries and statements for a small new business

Graham Cline, a second-year university student, was tired of low-paying, temporary summer work. He decided to go into business by setting up a company, Graham Cline Inc., to sell hot dogs in city parks over the summer.

The company commenced operations on January 1, 2001, and completed its first year of operations on December 31, 2001. During the year, the following events occurred:

a. On January 1, 2001, the company issued 100 shares to Graham at $1 each. In addition, Graham's father lent the company $5,000. The loan has no repayment terms and is not interest bearing.

b. On January 1, 2001, Graham Cline Inc. negotiated a contract with a local butcher shop to store its supplies in a refrigerated locker. Looking to the future, the company signed a two-year agreement that would expire December 31, 2002. The agreement called for payments of $120 on January 1, 2001 (which was made), and $130 to be made on January 1, 2002.

c. On June 1, 2001, Graham Cline Inc. purchased food for the summer for cash, consisting of 500 dozen buns at $1 per dozen and 500 dozen wieners at $3 per dozen.

d. On June 1, 2001, Graham Cline Inc. purchased two portable hot dog stands from a retiring vendor for $300 each. The company agreed to pay the former owner $100 at the purchase date, and the balance plus interest at 10% per year on December 31, 2001. The company also incurred an expense of $60 for fixing up the hot dog stands. The economic value of the stands will be "used up" by the end of the first summer and, therefore, costs related to them are all expenses for 2001.

e. During the year, sales for Graham Cline Inc. totalled $7,000.

f. The company hired another student to run one of the hot dog stands. The student was paid $800 per month for the three months she worked for the company (June through August).

Other information, not yet recorded in the accounts, is as follows:

g. The inventory at December 31, 2001, consisted of:

Buns   10 dozen
Wieners   10 dozen

h. The company's income tax rate is 20%. It paid its taxes owing on December 31, 2001.

i. All contractual commitments of the company have been satisfied up to December 31, 2001.

j. On December 31, 2001, the company declared and paid a dividend of $5 per share.

1. Prepare journal entries to record the foregoing events in the records of Graham Cline Inc. for the year ended December 31, 2001.

2. Prepare a balance sheet as at December 31, 2001, and statements of income and retained earnings for the year ended December 31, 2001.

3. Has Graham been successful at his venture? Would you recommend that he continue his operations next summer? Consider qualitative aspects as well as the financial statements you prepared.

PROBLEM 3.8*
Prepare financial statements from transactions

At the end of last year, Fergama Productions Inc., a company in the movie industry, had the following balance sheet accounts (in no particular order):

Cash	23,415	Share capital	20,000
Accounts payable	37,778	Office equipment cost	24,486
Accumulated amortization	11,134	Accounts receivable	89,455
Retained earnings	51,434	Inventory of supplies	10,240
Long-term loan payable	15,000	Taxes payable	12,250

During this year, the company's activities resulted in the following:

a. Revenue, all on credit, totalled $216,459.

b. Production expenses totalled $156,320, $11,287 of which was paid in cash and the rest charged on credit.

c. Amortization on the office equipment came to $2,680 for the year. (This produces an expense, which is a debit, and an increase in the accumulated amortization balance sheet account, which is a credit.)

d. The company bought, on credit, new supplies costing $8,657 and used up supplies costing $12,984 during the year.

e. Income tax expense for the year was estimated to be $12,319.

f. The board of directors declared a dividend of $25,000.

g. Collections from customers totalled $235,260.

h. Payments to suppliers totalled $172,276.

i. Payments of taxes totalled $18,400.

j. A $5,000 payment was made on the long-term loan.

k. The dividend was paid in cash to shareholders.

1. To get you started, prepare a balance sheet for Fergama Productions Inc. as at the end of the last year.

2. Record the activities for this year using journal entries and post those entries to accounts (using paper or a computer spreadsheet).

3. Prepare a trial balance of your accounts to show that they are in balance (if you are using a computer spreadsheet, it should do this for you).
4. From those accounts, prepare the following financial statements:
   - Income statement for this year.
   - Statement of retained earnings for this year.
   - Balance sheet at the end of this year (it would be useful to prepare a comparative balance sheet for this year and last year together).
5. Comment on what the three financial statements show about the company's performance for this year and financial position at the end of this year. Would you say the company is better off than it was last year?

PROBLEM 3.9*
Explain and write entries for changes in account balances

The following changes were observed in Boddin Inc.'s accounts. For each of the ten items, say in a few words what would have caused the changes and write a journal entry to account for them. Here is an example: Cash up $5,000, Bank loan up $5,000. Cause would have been that the company borrowed $5,000 from the bank. Journal entry: DR Cash 5,000, CR Bank loan 5,000.

1. Accounts payable up $573, Repairs expense up $573.
2. Revenue up $1,520, Cash up $200, Accounts receivable up $1,320.
3. Share capital up $2,000, Cash up $2,000.
4. Retained earnings down $500, Cash down $500.
5. Accounts receivable down $244, Cash up $244.
6. Mortgage payable down $1,000, Cash down $1,000.
7. Inventory up $2,320, Accounts payable up $2,320.
8. Inventory down $400, Cost of goods sold expense up $400.
9. Building up $25,000, Cash down $5,000, Mortgage payable up $20,000.
10. Revenue down $249,320 (to zero), Retained earnings up $249,320.

PROBLEM 3.10*
Prepare statements of income and retained earnings

Prepare properly classified statements of income and retained earnings from the following items listed in alphabetical order. Not all items are relevant to the solution.

Beginning retained earnings	1,693,740
Cost of goods sold	2,345,670
Cost of redeeming shares during year	18,200
Deferred revenue liability	110,000
Dividends declared during year	85,000
Error correction (prior year's expense too high)	3,300
Extraordinary gain	40,000
Gain on sale of building	25,000
Goodwill	120,000
Income tax expense	213,420
Interest expense	139,200
Interest income	14,030
Investment in marketable securities	210,000
Loss on discontinued operations	200,000
Operating expenses	1,123,580
Revenue	4,200,650

PROBLEM 3.11*
Prepare adjusting journal entries if necessary

The accountant for Super Office Supplies Inc. (SOS) is reviewing the year-end unadjusted trial balance and considering the following items of information. For each item, decide if an adjustment to the accounts is necessary; if it is, write a journal entry to make the adjustment.

  a. A shipment of inventory that arrived late in the last day of the year was not recorded. The shipment cost $11,240 and was paid for routinely about three weeks later.
  b. The accountant estimated that bank loan interest of $330 had built up between the last payment of interest to the bank and the end of the year.
  c. In the last few days of the year, the company's share price on the Toronto Stock Exchange had fallen about $0.20 per share. The company has 500,000 shares outstanding.
  d. There had been an error in calculating amortization expense during the year. To correct the error, additional expense of $14,500 would need to be recorded.
  e. A customer owing $2,100 went bankrupt on the last day of the year and SOS cannot expect to collect any of the money it expected.
  f. A review of the warranty liability indicated that the liability should be increased by $780.
  g. At a Board of Directors meeting on the last day of the year, the company's president and other senior executives were awarded raises totalling $11,100 annually, to begin the next day.
  h. The company had bought 12 months' building insurance two months before the end of the year, at a cost of $2,400, and debited the cost to insurance expense.
  i. One of the cash receipts credited to sales revenue turned out to be a deposit of $400 made by a customer on an order that will be filled a week after the end of the year.
  j. The accountant determined that a major sales order had been filled on the last day of the year, even though it was not recorded until three days later. The order was for $7,200, and the goods supplied had cost SOS $3,300. The customer paid two weeks later.

PROBLEM 3.12*
Identify common business transactions

Below are two lists. The left-hand list describes *half* of a common business transaction, and the right-hand list identifies various kinds of business transactions. Match the list on the left to that on the right.

  a. Accounts payable go down
  b. Accounts receivable go down
  c. Accounts receivable go up
  d. Employee tax deducted goes down
  e. Factory asset goes up
  f. Goodwill goes up
  g. Inventory goes down
  h. Inventory goes up
  i. Retained earnings go down
  j. Sales tax due goes up

  1. Acquisition of a noncurrent asset
  2. Another business acquired
  3. Collections from customers
  4. Cost of goods sold
  5. Dividend declared
  6. Goods purchased
  7. Payment of tax to the government
  8. Payment to creditors
  9. Revenue earned
  10. Tax collected for the government

PROBLEM 3.13*
Identify and describe common adjustments

The list below describes *one side* each of common accrual accounting adjustments. Describe what the purpose of the adjustment is and state what the other side of the entry is. State any assumptions you feel are necessary.

    a.　CR Accumulated amortization
    b.　CR Accrued interest liability
    c.　DR Noncurrent assets
    d.　DR Prepaid insurance asset
    e.　CR Warranty liability
    f.　CR Dividends payable
    g.　CR Income tax payable
    h.　CR Customer deposits liability
    i.　DR Supplies inventory
    j.　CR Bonuses payable

PROBLEM 3.14*
Record and post adjusting journal entries, close accounts

Here are the unadjusted accounts for Tucker Northern Inc. at the end of its first year in business:

Cash	25,600	Employee deductions due	2,500
Accounts receivable	88,200	Sales taxes due	3,220
Inventory	116,900	Mortgage debt	185,780
Land	100,000	Share capital	275,000
Buildings and equipment	236,100	Revenue	349,600
Accounts payable	74,900	Cost of goods sold	142,500
		Operating Expenses	181,700

The company has determined that the year-end adjustments listed below are required.

    a.　An uncollectible account receivable of $2,400 should be written off to expense.
    b.　Amortization of $13,000 should be recorded.
    c.　Additional revenue of $11,200 has been earned and should be recorded.
    d.　The COGS to go with the revenue in (c) is $4,600.
    e.　Accrued interest on the mortgage at the end of the year is $900.
    f.　A bonus of $5,000 was awarded to the president by the board of directors.
    g.　Income tax for the year is estimated to be $2,700. No tax has been paid yet.

1.　Record these in journal entry form.
2.　Post them to the accounts (creating new accounts if you need them).
3.　Prepare a balanced adjusted trial balance.
4.　Close the revenue and expense accounts to retained earnings.
5.　Calculate the following: net income, working capital, shareholders' equity.

**PROBLEM 3.15
Identify items as
revenues or
expenses**

State whether or not, and why, each of the following items is likely to be a revenue or expense for this year of the company indicated:

Company	Item
1. Noranda Inc.	Cost of advertising for new employees
2. Canadian Utilities Ltd.	Collection of old accounts from customers who had skipped town and were tracked down by a collection agency
3. Royal Bank of Canada	Cost of renovating its main Winnipeg branch
4. Zellers	Increased value of the land under Zellers department stores
5. Wendy's Restaurants	Food sold to customers who paid with their Visa cards
6. Pacific Furniture Mart	Money paid by customers in advance on special furniture orders
7. The Bay	A lawsuit by a customer who fell down the escalator and was injured
8. Northern Gold Mines Ltd.	Cost of issuing new shares to raise funds for exploration
9. XXX Escort Agency	Bribes paid to try to avoid having employees arrested for prostitution
10. Grand Centre Ltd.	Income taxes paid in France
11. Advanced Management Ltd.	Special good-performance bonuses promised this year but not to be paid until next year
12. Advanced Management Ltd.	Special dividends to owners, all of whom are also employees
13. Sears Inc.	Decreased value of the land under some of its inner-city locations
14. Procter & Gamble Inc.	Cost of scientific research aimed at developing new products
15. General Motors Inc.	Estimated amount of money needed to provide pensions to this year's employees when they retire
16. Hattie's Handbags Ltd.	Goods lost to shoplifting
17. Hattie's Handbags Ltd.	Salary of floor-walker who tries to catch shoplifters
18. PCL Construction Ltd.	Contract payments to be received over the next five years for construction work on a large bridge project

PROBLEM 3.16
Discuss comments on importance of accounting information

Accounting is important to the extent that people rely on accounting information in making decisions that are important to them. Below are various comments on the importance of accounting information. Discuss briefly why each comment may be valid or invalid.

1. The arithmetically balanced balance sheet is important in creating trust in the information.
2. The income statement's segregation of activities into revenues and expenses is important to interpreting net income (revenue minus expenses).
3. The statement of retained earnings is important in indicating to shareholders how much cash is available for paying dividends.
4. Effort by some top managers to smooth accounting income or to otherwise alter the way accounting measures performance is evidence of its importance.
5. The definitions of assets, liabilities, equity, revenues, and expenses underlying financial statements are important to the way the statements measure financial performance and position.
6. Understanding how accrual accounting reflects economic activities is important to interpreting the financial statements.

PROBLEM 3.17
Identify transactions and write journal entries for them

The following events took place on February 1, 2001. For each event, give the journal entry (if any) that should be made to record the transaction in the account of Smith Ltd. Indicate clearly where in the financial statements you think the accounts involved belong. State any assumptions you feel are necessary.

a. The company purchased supplies to be used immediately. The purchase price of the supplies was $5,000. Only $2,000 was paid in cash, on delivery. The balance was due in 30 days.
b. The company decided to rent a service vehicle for $4,800 per year. A rental contract was signed February 1, 2001, to take effect March 1, 2001. Smith Ltd. paid $400 cash to the rental company on February 1, 2001, which represented the rent for March 2001.
c. Some of Smith's repairmen were not busy on February 1. The manager had them paint the inside of a storage room. Assume the repairmen's salaries of $300 were paid in cash at the end of the day.
d. A shareholder sold her car to the company. The vehicle cost her $15,000 two years ago. An equivalent used vehicle would have been worth about $8,000 on February 1, 2001. No cash changed hands, but the shareholder expects the company to pay her for the car eventually.
e. An invoice for $5,000 was received, relating to repairs and maintenance work done in December 2000. The company's year-end is December 31. This expense was not recorded in the 2000 financial statements.

PROBLEM 3.18
Identify transactions and write journal entries for them

Southward Stores Ltd. is a general merchandise retailer operating in the suburbs. During a recent month, the events listed below happened. For each event, decide if it is an accounting transaction. If it is an accounting transaction, state briefly why and record it in journal entry form. Indicate where in the financial statements you wish each account to appear. If it is not an accounting transaction, state briefly why it is not.

a. Southward borrowed $500,000 from the Great Pacific Bank (Canada). Payment is due in three years, but the loan can be called on ten days' notice if Southward fails to make any of the monthly interest payments, which begin next month.

b. The retailer ordered inventory for resale costing $300,000, to be delivered in 40 days, and sent a deposit of $10,000 with the order.

c. The company renewed its lease on the store premises, signing an agreement, which provides that, beginning in three months, the monthly rent would rise from $21,000 to $23,000.

d. Southward was charged with unfair pricing of its main line of merchandise. News of this sent the company's shares (listed on a stock exchange) down in price from $10 to $8.50 each. The company has 1,000,000 shares outstanding, all publicly traded.

e. The company declared a dividend of $0.50 per share, to be paid in one week, on each of its 1,000,000 outstanding shares. This news sent the company's shares up by $0.40 each on the stock exchange.

PROBLEM 3.19
Comment on income smoothing and management's motivation in measuring income

Gordon Inc. has had the following net incomes for the past several years:

1994	$2,500,000
1995	3,600,000
1996	4,700,000
1997	3,200,000
1998	5,100,000
1999	4,600,000
2000	5,500,000

The company is now finishing its accounting for 2001. Some items have yet to be settled, but it is possible that the net income for 2001 could be any of three figures: $6,400,000, $5,400,000, or $4,100,000.

1. Which of the three possible 2001 net income figures would be the "smoothest" given the company's past income pattern. Why?

2. The difference between the highest and lowest net income possibilities for 2001 is in how to account for a major contract. If its revenue and expenses are included in 2001, the highest 2001 figure results; if it is postponed to 2002, the lowest 2001 figure results. It has been proposed that a portion of the contract could be included in 2001; if that were done, the middle 2001 figure, $5,400,000, results. Arguments have been advanced for all three possibilities. What support do you think might have been advanced for each?

3. Do you think a company should choose its accounting according to the net income that results, or should the company just use the most appropriate accounting, and let the net income be whatever it therefore is? Why?

PROBLEM 3.20
Questions about accounting asked by a businessperson

Jeanette is an electrical engineer and has been working for a large company in its technical electronics area for several years. She has decided to go into business for herself, offering electronics design and general consulting to other companies. To prepare for this venture, she has raised the necessary capital and has been reading books on business management and talking to business people about running a business. She learns that you are taking a financial accounting course and says,

"Maybe you can help me understand some of the peculiarities of accounting!" You protest that you have just started your course, but she asks you to try to answer her questions anyway. Provide brief answers without using jargon to the following questions she has asked you:

1. Everyone says they will be interested to see if my company can make a profit. How will the accountants measure my profit? I know it's done on the income statement, but I really don't understand what that statement includes or doesn't include.
2. One reason I can see for wanting a good profit is that it will put money in the bank. But someone told me that accrual accounting doesn't depend on money in the bank for its measure of profit. What does that mean?
3. One of the books I've read says that a company's accounting will use the double-entry system and said that that means the balance sheets and income statements all fit together. How does that work?
4. One person told me to keep my company's accounting income low to save income tax. Another person said to keep it high to attract other investors and soothe creditors. Why is there any choice? I thought that financial accounting just reported the facts!

PROBLEM 3.21
Write adjusting journal entries

Write an adjusting journal entry, if required, for each of the following items, which have been encountered during preparation of Ajax Sales Inc.'s January 31, 2001, financial statements.

1. A pile of sales invoices totalling $3,124 has yet to be recorded.
2. A customer had paid a deposit of $500 on a special order, which has not yet arrived. The deposit was included in the sales amount for the day it was paid.
3. The company has a $123,000 bank loan owing. Interest at 8% was last paid 23 days before the end of the year.
4. The year-end inventory count showed that goods costing $87,943 were on hand. The inventory account (perpetual system) showed a balance of $89,221 on the same day.
5. At the end of January, the account for advances to employees for travel expenses had a balance of $3,200. Expense accounts received after that date showed that employees had spent $1,823 of this by the end of January.
6. The credit manager decided to write off, to expense, some hopeless accounts receivable totalling $320.
7. After a study of the company's employee pensions, it was decided that an additional $38,940 should be accrued for pensions earned during the year. This amount would be paid to the pension fund trustee in March 2001.
8. A court case involving another company showed that one of the company's patents was worthless, so management decided to write the patent off. It was on the accounts at a cost of $74,500 and there was accumulated amortization of $42,100 against it.
9. A search of cheque payments during February turned up $5,430 of payments that related to expenses incurred before the end of January.
10. The board of directors declared a $150,000 dividend January 25, to be paid in mid-February 2001.

PROBLEM 3.22
Do adjusting journal entries

The accountant for Chewie Crusts Ltd., a bakery specializing in pizza crusts for the fast-food trade, is working on the year-end accounting for the company. For each item below, decide what (if anything) needs to be done and prepare any journal entry needed to implement your decision. Use whatever account titles you like, but be clear where on the statements the accounts would be located and write clear explanations for your entries. This is the company's first year of existence.

1. The company paid $1,120 for cleaning and office supplies, all of which have been expensed. The accountant discovered that another $114 is owing but not recorded and that supplies costing $382 are still on hand and usable at the end of the year.
2. The company's sales are all on credit because its customers are restaurants, stores, and institutions, such as hospitals. All cash collections have been recorded as sales revenue. The accountant added up the customers' bills still not collected and got a total of $11,621.
3. All purchases of flour and other raw materials have been expensed, and there is no significant inventory of finished products at the end of the year because each night's production is shipped in the morning to ensure maximum freshness. However, usable raw materials costing $6,210 are on hand at the end of the year.
4. Purchases of small tools and parts (still on hand) totalling $238 were charged to expenses during the year.
5. The accountant found an unpaid invoice for $900 for advertising services on behalf of the company. The advertising campaign had been planned and advertising contracts signed before the year-end, but the campaign took place just after the year-end.
6. The president of the company directed that $2,316 originally included in repairs and maintenance expense be capitalized to recognize the creation of valuable equipment and fixtures. This is unusual for the company, but the repairs were so good that the useful life of the assets involved had been extended by several years more than originally expected.
7. All payments on the company's building mortgage had been made on time. Since the last payment, $187 of mortgage interest (the accountant's estimate) had accumulated, but the next regular payment was not due for ten days.
8. The company's board of directors declared a dividend of $14,000 to shareholders. The board meeting to declare the dividend was held three days before the year-end, but the dividend was explicitly not to be paid until two months after the year-end.
9. The general manager's employment contract specifies that at the end of the third month of each year, she is to be paid a bonus of 8% of the company's pre-tax and pre-bonus income. The accountant calculated the first year's pre-tax income, after all accruals and adjustments, to be $38,226.

PROBLEM 3.23
Explain and write entries for changes in account balances

Here are more account changes that occurred to Boddin Inc. (see Problem 3.9* for others, including an example). For each of the ten items, say in a few words what would have caused the changes and write a journal entry to account for them.

1. Accounts payable down $3,220, Cash down $3,220.
2. Income tax expense up $5,900, Cash down $5,000, Income tax payable up $900.

3. Travel advances receivable up $200, Cash down $200.
4. Travel advances receivable down $200, Cash up $11, Travel expenses up $189.
5. Cash up $350, Customer deposits liability up $350.
6. Auditing expense up $3,000, Accounts payable up $2,400.
7. Equipment up $5,200, Share capital up $5,200.
8. Share capital down $1,000, Cash down $1,000.
9. Cash up $1,200, Accounts receivable up $3,300, Revenue up $4,500, Inventory down $2,750, Cost of goods sold expense up $2,750.
10. Cost of goods sold expense down $147,670 (to zero), Retained earnings down $147,670.

PROBLEM 3.24
Reconstruct journal entries from T-accounts

Sanderson Electronics is a new retail store that sells mainly small parts, such as switches, circuit boards, and wire. Sanderson's ledger accounts are shown below in T-account form, with entries made for the first month of business.

Cash		Accounts Receivable		Prepaid Supplies	
(a) 30,000	(c) 1,200	(e) 900	(g) 650	(i) 300	
(f) 1,300	(h) 1,000	(f) 1,400			
(g) 650	(j) 560				

Equipment		Inventory		Accounts Payable	
(c) 3,600		(b) 5,000	(e) 540	(h) 1,000	(b) 5,000
			(f) 1,620		(d) 700

Notes Payable		Common Shares		Sales Revenue	
(j) 500	(c) 2,400		(a) 30,000		(e) 900
					(f) 2,700

Supplies Expense		Interest Expense		Cost of Goods Sold	
(d) 700	(i) 300	(j) 60		(e) 540	
				(f) 1,620	

For each of the transactions from (a) to (j), write the general journal entry that was used to post the accounts, including an explanation of the entry.

PROBLEM 3.25
Prepare month-end financial statements from accounts

Matilda Jamison runs a successful second-hand clothing shop, Waltzing Matilda's Boutique Ltd. She buys quality new and used clothes from several sources and then sells them at reasonable prices. To establish her business, Matilda invested $1,500 of her savings and her mother contributed $500. Both received shares in the company in return for their investment, so the company's share capital is $2,000. The company also took out a $3,000 bank loan.

Matilda rents retail space in a shopping mall on a monthly basis at $200 per month. She pays rent in advance for a six-month period (in other words, $1,200 twice a year) on January 1 and July 1 of every year. The company owns the display units, racks, shelving, and hangers she uses in her business, which cost $2,400 in total. She expects these items to last for five years and has, therefore, amortized them by $480 per year ($2,400/5 years = $480 per year). The resulting accumulated amortization is included on the balance sheet. The insurance policy is an annual policy purchased January 1 for $1,200.

Matilda pays her employees for work done from the 1st to the 15th of each month, on or about the 20th of each month. As a result, half of the wages earned by employees during the month have been paid (that earned from the 1st to the 15th of the month) and the remaining half is still payable. The company's income tax rate is 20%. Matilda transfers (closes) her revenues and expenses to retained earnings monthly, so revenue and expense accounts contain only one month's data at a time.

From the account balances at the end of April 2001 shown below, prepare income and retained earnings statements for Waltzing Matilda's Boutique Ltd. for the month of April 2001 and a balance sheet as at April 30, 2001. Notes to the statements are not necessary.

	Resources	Sources
Balance sheet accounts as at April 30, 2001:		
Cash	$ 780	
Accounts receivable	1,300	
Inventory of unsold goods	10,000	
Office supplies on hand	500	
Prepaid insurance	800	
Prepaid rent	400	
Shelving/hangers/display units	2,400	
Accumulated amortization	(1,120)	
Bank loan		$ 3,000
Accounts payable		2,800
Wages payable		500
Taxes payable		1,200
Share capital		2,000
Retained earnings March 31, 2001		4,360
Income Statement accounts for April 2001:		
Revenue		7,000
Cost of goods sold		(3,500)
Wages		(1,000)
Insurance		(100)
Rent		(200)
Janitor and miscellaneous		(580)
Office supplies used		(50)
Interest		(30)
Amortization		(40)
Income tax		(300)
	$15,060	$15,060

PROBLEM 3.26
Income and retained earnings format with special items

The accounts for Prentice Retail Ltd. for last year included the following (in alphabetical order):

Correction of error in previous year's income	CR	$ 2,430
Cost of disposing of an unneeded division	DR	62,340
Dividends declared	DR	87,000
Income tax expense	DR	121,315
Income tax saved by disposing of division	CR	23,895
Loss on expropriation of land by municipality	DR	14,210
Miscellaneous revenue from investments	CR	23,570
Operating expenses	DR	1,689,260
Retained earnings, beginning of year	CR	354,290
Revenue from sales	CR	2,111,480

Prepare an income statement and statement of retained earnings for the company for last year, in as good a form as you can with the information provided.

PROBLEM 3.27
Prepare financial statements from transactions

Frothingslosh Beverages Inc. began business this year with $100,000 in cash provided by the owner, Froth, in return for $35,000 in share capital and the company's promise to repay the rest in five years. The company rents its premises and equipment, so it has no noncurrent assets. Below are the transactions that occurred in the company during this first year. Record the transactions as journal entries, post them to general ledger accounts (by hand or using a computer spreadsheet), and then prepare an income statement and statement of retained earnings for the year, and balance sheet at the end of the year.
Transactions for the year:

a. The company had bought inventory costing $298,420 by the end of the year and had paid for all but $43,960 of it.
b. Employees earned $122,080 in wages during the year. Of this, $90,300 had been paid to employees, $18,340 in tax and other deductions had been remitted to the government, and at the end of the year, $11,520 was still owing to employees and $1,920 in deductions was still owing to the government.
c. Customers bought products for $495,610 during the year, paying $300,890 in cash and charging the rest on credit. Of the amount on credit, all but $22,540 had been collected by the end of the year.
d. The goods bought by customers had cost the company $249,880. In addition, $4,210 of inventory had mysteriously disappeared during the year, probably shoplifted.
e. Other business expenses for the year totalled $68,830, all but $2,310 paid in cash.
f. The year's income tax expense was estimated as $12,650, but because the company is a new one, none of this has to be paid until next year.
g. At the end of the year, the company declared a dividend of $10,000 to be paid early next year, and invested $50,000 of cash in a short-term investment certificate at the bank.

PROBLEM 3.28
Write a closing
entry

Write an entry to close the accounts of Frothingslosh Beverages (Problem 3.28) at the end of the year and present the post-closing account balances for the company showing that they are in balance as the next year begins.

PROBLEM 3.29
Correct a set of
financial statements

WideAway Manufacturing Ltd. hired a new accountant without checking the person's qualifications out too thoroughly. The accountant worked away diligently on the financial statements for 2000, but was unable to remember where everything was supposed to go, and could not get the balance sheet to balance even though the computer showed that the underlying accounts were all correct, so the balance sheet certainly should have balanced!

The accountant's financial statements are below. Redo them in correct form. (If you do, the balance sheet will balance.)

WideAway Manufacturing Ltd.
Balance Sheet as at December 31, 2000

Assets		Liabilities and Equity	
Current assets:		Current liabilities:	
Cash	$ 52,000	Bank loan	$ 35,000
Inventory	116,000	Accounts payable	98,000
Cost of goods sold	538,000	Income tax expense	41,000
Share capital	150,000	Current portion of mortgage	22,000
Current assets	$856,000	Amortization expense	74,000
Noncurrent assets:		Current liabilities	$270,000
Factory	$612,000	Noncurrent liabilities:	
Mortgage (minus current)	(242,000)	Other noncurrent liabilities	$ 16,000
Net noncurrent assets	$370,000	Shareholders' equity:	
		Land	$100,000
		Retained earnings (below)	656,000
		Equity	$756,000
TOTAL	$1,226,000	TOTAL	$1,042,000

WideAway Manufacturing Ltd.
Statement of Income and Retained Earnings
for the Year Ended December 31, 2000

Revenues:		
Revenue	$949,000	
Add accounts receivable	117,000	$1,066,000
Expenses:		
Operating expenses	$229,000	
Accumulated amortization	236,000	
Prepaid expenses	21,000	
Current portion of mortgage	22,000	
Dividend declared	20,000	528,000
Income before income tax		$538,000
Income taxes payable		27,000
Net income for the year		$511,000
Retained earnings — beginning of year		145,000
Retained earnings — end of year		$656,000

PROBLEM 3.30
Show that the finan-cial statements articulate as figures change

Answer each of the following questions. Each one begins with the information given and derived by you for previous ones.

1. Wanderlee Inc. began in business with cash of $100,000 and share capital of $100,000. In its first year, it showed a net income of $13,000 but declared no dividends. At the end of that year, it had liabilities of $42,000, all current. What did the company's assets total at the end of that first year?
2. If those assets were 60% noncurrent, what was the company's working cap-ital at the end of its first year?
3. As the company began its second year, it made a big sale for $40,000, all on credit (the customer would pay in a month). The cost of goods sold to the cus-tomer, which had been in inventory, equalled $18,000. Ignoring income tax and assuming the income from the sale was added to retained earnings, what were the new amounts after the sale for current assets, total assets, equity, and total of liabilities and equity?
4. Observing the result of the big sale, the president said, "Our income from this very pleasant event is reflected in both our assets and our equity." Use your answer to part 3 to show why the president was right.

PROBLEM 3.31
Prepare income statement from transactions plus adjustments

(This problem follows from Problem 2.23, PastaPastaPasta Inc. You should review that problem before doing this one, but it is not necessary to have answered that problem in detail before attempting this one.)

Below are events that happened to Tanya's new company during its first six months of operation. From these events, prepare an income statement for the first six months. Preparing journal entries for these events will assist you in keeping the numbers straight.

(If you did Problem 2.23, you could also go on to record the events and prepare a balance sheet at the end of the six months.)

1. Customers took away pasta, sauces, cookware, etc. for which they promised to pay $87,340. By the end of the six months, Tanya had collected $78,670 of this, had taken back $420 of defective merchandise (which she had to just throw away), and had given up on collecting $510 so that amount has to be transferred to expense. She expected the $7,740 remainder to be collected within a month or two.

2. Tanya purchased $32,990 of food and pasta-making supplies, and $19,320 of cookware for resale. By the end of the six months, she had paid the suppliers $47,550 toward these purchases and those owing at the end of the preparatory time described in Problem 2.23.

3. The pasta and sauces taken by customers cost Tanya $31,840 to make, so at the end of the six months, $5,870 of food and pasta-making supplies were still on hand. The cookware and other equipment taken by customers cost Tanya $9,110 to buy, so at the end of the six months, $14,120 of goods for resale were still on hand.

4. Tanya estimated the following for the six months: amortization on equipment, $3,950; amortization of improvements to rented space, $450; amortization of minivan, $750. She was not sure what to do about the recipes, because they had shown themselves to be very valuable, or the incorporation costs, because the company should last many years. She thought perhaps each could be amortized at 10% of cost per year.

5. The company paid $8,000 in rent during the six months. The landlord was charging $2,000 per month and was concerned that, while at the beginning of the period the company had paid $2,000 in advance, it had fallen behind by $2,000 by the end. Tanya promised to pay the rent more promptly in the future.

6. The company paid the first $7,050 installment on the equipment liability, plus $1,410 interest on the total debt at 8% per annum. The second installment would be due in another year.

7. The $2,500 bank loan was paid off, including $80 in interest.

8. In consultation with the other owners, Tanya set her monthly salary at $2,100. She took only $8,000 of that in cash. The company paid $950 more to Revenue Canada as income tax deductions and still owed $190 for such deductions. Tanya decided to take the remaining $3,460 in a few months, when she wanted to go on a holiday.

9. Other expenses for the six months came to $6,440, all but $760 having been paid by the end of the period.

10. Tanya's accountant said that the company did not yet owe any income tax, but that there would likely be a small tax liability by the end of the year. The accountant estimated that about $1,500 would be owed for the first six months' income.

11. Everyone agreed that no dividends to owners should be declared yet, but the hope was that about $3,000 of the first six months' income would eventually be paid as dividends.

**PROBLEM 3.32
(CHALLENGING)
Analyze some finan-
cial statement rela-
tionships**

Answer each of the following *unrelated* questions. State any assumptions you feel
you need to make.

1. A Ltd. has assets of $45,000, liabilities of $32,000, and a deficit of $7,000.
   How much have its shareholders contributed as share capital?
2. B Ltd. has current assets of $234,000, total assets of $459,000, and equity of
   $100,000. The company wants to reorganize its liabilities so that its working
   capital ratio is 2:1. If it does, what will its *noncurrent* liabilities be?
3. The board of directors of C Ltd. wishes to declare a $75,000 dividend. The
   company's retained earnings equal $257,000, and the company has $41,000
   in the bank, a $20,000 bank loan, and $55,000 in accounts receivable. The
   bank will lend only $10,000 more, so the credit manager is told to collect
   some cash quickly from customers, *if necessary*. How much cash does the
   credit manager have to collect, if any?
4. D Ltd. has revenue of $783,000 and net income of $21,000 after income tax
   expense of $17,000. What do its other expenses total?
5. For this year, E Ltd. has net income of $43,000 and declared a dividend of
   $11,000. The company's beginning retained earnings totalled $217,000. At
   the end of the year, the company had current assets of $387,000, noncurrent
   assets of $414,000, current liabilities of $205,000, and share capital of
   $181,000. The company decides to issue new long-term bonds for cash in
   order to raise its working capital to $250,000. If it does so, what will the total
   noncurrent liabilities be?
6. F Ltd. has revenue of $540,000 and income before income tax of $59,400,
   which equals 11% of $540,000. After income tax of 40% on the $59,400, the
   company's net income is $35,640. The president is unhappy with this net income
   and wants to raise it to $60,000. Assuming that income tax stays at 40% and
   that expenses other than income tax rise proportionately with revenue, what will
   the revenue have to be to meet the president's net income target?

**PROBLEM 3.33
(CHALLENGING)
Do entries plus
statements from
accounts and events**

To diversify his activities, hockey player Knuckles Gronsky opened a boutique for
children's sportswear. He incorporated a company under the name Gronsky's
Great Things Ltd., and the boutique opened for business on September 1, 2000.

Account balances and other information for the year ended August 31, 2001,
for Gronsky's company follow.

Cash	$ 2,600
Accounts receivable	3,500
Inventory of clothing (after fire)	30,000
Sales revenue	240,000
Wage and salary expense	27,500
Rent paid in advance	2,000
Furniture and fixtures	15,500
Accumulated amortization	3,000
Income tax expense	7,000
Loan payable	8,000
Accounts payable	23,000
Investment in Number One Ltd.	10,000
Inventory sold (Cost of goods sold)	100,000

Supplies purchased	14,500
Rent expense	24,000
Capital from shareholder	15,000
Amortization expense	3,000
Costs associated with incorporation	1,900
Interest paid on loan	500
General operating expenses	5,000
Dividends payable	2,000
Dividends declared	4,000
Loss due to storage room fire	40,000

The following information will explain some of the preceding items:

a. On August 20, 2001, someone started a fire in the storage room and burnt $40,000 worth of inventory. There will be no insurance claim on this loss.

b. The loan is payable in yearly payments of $2,000 plus interest. Payments are to be made on August 31 each year over the next four years. The payment and interest for August 31, 2001, are already reflected in the preceding balances.

c. The investment is shares in Number One Ltd., a private company. Gronsky has no intention of selling the shares in the immediate future.

d. On August 30, 2001, the board of directors declared dividends of $4,000, $2,000 of which were paid on August 31, 2001, and the remaining $2,000 of which were to be paid September 12, 2001.

Four other events may need to be incorporated:

e. The supplies are included in expenses immediately when purchased. At August 31, 2001, supplies were counted and $9,000 remained on hand. The count has not been reflected in the above account balances.

f. On August 31, 2001, a customer brought back unused clothing the customer had paid $450 for. The customer was given a credit note, which could be used to buy clothes any time in the next year. The clothes, which had cost the company $225, were returned to inventory as they had not even been unwrapped from their packages. The above account balances do not reflect this event.

g. Late in the day on August 31, Gronsky received an offer of $18,000 for the shares in Number One Ltd. Gronsky still didn't want to sell, though the shares were obviously worth more than had been paid for them.

h. An income tax advisor estimated that the income tax expense for the year should have been $6,250, so the company should be able to get a refund of overpaid tax.

1. Write a journal entry for any of the items (e) to (h) that require an entry.
2. Prepare an income statement for 2001 for Gronsky's Great Things Ltd.
3. Prepare a statement of retained earnings for the same year.
4. Prepare the company's balance sheet as at August 31, 2001.

**PROBLEM 3.34
(CHALLENGING)
Explain and write
entries for incompletely described
changes in account
balances**

BranBolter Inc. had the following changes in some of its accounts. Most changes are not completely described, so you will have to think about the rest of what happened. For each item, state in a few words what probably caused the changes and write a journal entry to account for them, consistent with your explanation. (For a simple example, see the beginning of Problem 3.9*.)

1. Inventory down $387, Inventory shortage expense up $387.
2. Retained earnings down $5,000, Cash down $2,000.
3. Investment in Bozo Mining Inc. down $40,000 (to zero), Cash up $5,000.
4. Long-term debt down $10,000, Share capital up $10,000.
5. Inventory up $3,290, Cash down $748.
6. Bonuses payable up $5,200.
7. Lawsuit loss expense up $40,200, Legal fees expense up $11,340.
8. Demand bank loan up $32,000.
9. Accounts receivable up $24,000, Inventory up $36,000, Factory assets up $100,000, Goodwill up $40,000.
10. Expenses down $743,210 (to zero), Revenues down $730,670 (to zero).

**PROBLEM 3.35
(CHALLENGING)
Entries and statements for a used car
business**

You've decided to take a job as a part-time accountant, working for a friend of yours, John Rogers, who operates a used car lot called Honest John's Used Cars Ltd. John's records consist primarily of a cheque book and a bank deposit book. He uses a cheque to pay for every purchase and always describes the purchase on the cheque stub, which remains in the cheque book. He also describes each deposit on the duplicate deposit slip, which he keeps.

John likes having things simple. He rents a small lot with a furnished sales office for $1,000 per month (including utilities). He carries no parts and provides no service on cars. His company's share capital is $50, so most of the owner's investment is retained earnings. The company has no employees except him (he gets a monthly salary of $3,000). At January 31, 2001, he had a $20,000 operating loan that carried interest at 12% (1% per month) and was payable on demand. All interest had been paid up to January 31, 2001. His inventory of unsold cars (all of which the company paid cash for) at January 31, 2001, was as follows:

Unsold Cars on Hand — January 31, 2001	Purchase Price
1996 Ford	$ 4,500
1995 Volkswagen	4,000
1994 Oldsmobile	5,000
1996 Camaro	7,500
1995 Mazda	4,800
1997 Toyota	6,200
	$32,000

John has assured you that all cash and cheques received in February 2001 were deposited in the bank. His receipts and disbursements for that month were as follows:

Cheques written during February (from cheque stubs)

Cheque #	Date	Description (Paid to, etc.)	Amount
51	Feb. 1/01	XL Property Management — Rent for February and March 2001	$ 2,000
52	Feb. 4/01	XL Property Management — Alterations to sales office	4,000
53	Feb. 10/01	Jack Yee — Purchase of 1997 Chrysler, paid in full	6,500
54	Feb. 15/01	John Rogers — Salary for February 2001	3,000
55	Feb. 22/01	Skyline Auto Auctions — Purchase of 3 cars (1994 Lincoln — $8,500; 1998 Nissan — $6,000; 1996 Honda — $4,500)	19,000
56	Feb. 28/01	Royal Bank — Payment of February interest in full	200
		Total Cash Disbursements	$34,700

Cash and cheques received in February (from duplicate bank deposit slips)

	Date	Description (Received from, etc.)	Amount
	Feb. 6/01	Tim Boychuk — Sale of Camaro, paid in full	$10,000
	Feb. 12/01	Bob Scott — Sale of Oldsmobile, paid in full	7,400
	Feb. 19/01	Downtown Dodge Used Cars — Sale of Mazda and Ford, paid in full	10,300
	Feb. 28/01	Additional operating loan from bank	5,000
		Total Cash Receipts	$32,700

John has informed you that no other cars were purchased or sold during February and that no amounts are owed by, or to him at January 31 or February 28, 2001. You also learned that the balance in his bank account on January 31, 2001, was $6,800. *Ignore sales taxes throughout this problem.*

1. Prepare a balance sheet for Honest John's Used Cars Ltd. as at January 31, 2001. (Deduce the retained earnings from the other account balances.)
2. Record the February 2001 transactions in journal entry form.
3. Post these transactions to the general ledger of Honest John's Used Cars Ltd.
4. Prepare a balance sheet as at February 28, 2001, and statements of income and retained earnings for the company for the one-month period ended February 28, 2001.
5. Make up a list of unsold cars at February 28, 2001, and their purchase prices. The total of these amounts should agree with the inventory account in your general ledger and balance sheet as at February 28, 2001.

6. Compare the company's net income for the month of February with the change in the bank account balance between January 31, 2001, and February 28, 2001. Reconcile them to show why they are different.

7. What are some advantages of John's having monthly financial statements? (In the past, John has prepared one set of statements each year for income tax purposes.)

PROBLEM 3.36 (CHALLENGING)
General or user-specific income statements

Write a paragraph giving your considered views on the following question:

Do the accrual basis and the standard content and format of the income statement provide useful information to all people who are interested in companies' financial performance, or should there be different kinds of income statements prepared to suit the needs of different kinds of users?

PROBLEM 3.37 (CHALLENGING)
Income calculation without dollars

A year has elapsed since you solved the argument between Bob and Doug, the shepherds (Problem 2.32). After studying your solution, Doug and Bob grudgingly accepted your opinion as to their relative wealths at the end of last year. The passage of time has not diminished their penchant for argument, however. Now they are arguing about who had the largest income for the year just ended.

Doug points out that the number of sheep that he personally owns at year-end exceeds his personal holdings at the beginning of the year by 80, whereas Bob's increase was only 20. Bob replies that his increase would have been 60, had he not traded 40 sheep during the year for 10 acres of additional land. Besides, he points out, he exchanged 18 sheep during the year for food and clothing items, whereas Doug exchanged only 7 for such purposes. The food and clothing have been pretty much used up by the end of the year.

Bob is happy because his wife made 5 coats during the year (fulfilling the orders she had at the beginning of the year) and received 25 goats for them. She managed to obtain orders for another 5 coats (again for 25 goats)—orders on which she has not yet begun to work. Doug points out that he took to making his own lunches this year; therefore, he does not owe Ted anything now. Doug was very unhappy one day last year when he discovered that his ox had died of a mysterious illness. Both men are thankful, however, that none of the other animals died or was lost.

Except for the matters reported above, each man's holdings at the end of the current year are the same as his holdings at the end of last year. Provide advice to the two men as to who had the higher income for the year.[10]

PROBLEM 3.38 (CHALLENGING)
Income smoothing and ethics

1. Section 3.10 referred to income smoothing as a way of manipulating a company's net income in order to create a desired impression of management's capability and performance. Other kinds of income manipulation by management have also been alleged. Do you think it is ethical for management to manipulate the figures by which its performance is measured? Why or why not?

2. The usual answer to part 1 is that such behaviour is unethical. Can you think of any circumstances under which such manipulation of income would be ethical? Putting it another way, are there any people, other than management, whose interests would be served by such behaviour?

**CASE 3A
Reporting
Nonrecurring
charges in the
income statement**

Read the following article, "Never Say Never" and discuss the problem of how companies report their real, or not-so-real "recurring charges." These are the sorts of things that are supposed to be shown separately in the income statement as explained in section 3.5. The article raises the issue of management's using such items to manipulate earnings, recalling some of the points in section 3.10. Discuss how serious the problem may be, and what solutions to it there might be, including whether companies should be allowed to make the kinds of accounting choices that seem to be at the centre of the problem. (By the way, the article uses the word "reserve" in a couple of ways: one to mean creating a deduction from loans or accounts receivable, and an expense to match, to recognize likely noncollection of such receivables, and one to mean creating a long-term liability for costs expected to be spent in the future. Both result in more expenses and less income in the current period.)

Never Say Never

The use of "nonrecurring charges" in financial reports can manipulate corporate earnings. Perhaps that's why management reaches for this tool so often

By J. Douglas Hanna

Powerful incentives act upon management as it exercises its judgment, particularly when the judgment can trigger a stock market response that will, in turn, affect the corporation in numerous ways. Of course, it's management's job to manage earnings; but from an investor's perspective not all of the methods used to achieve this goal are equally desirable. For example, management can either increase productivity or it can strategically manipulate accounting choices to affect earnings. The latter method need not come with any associated changes in productivity.

Canadian accounting standards require firms to report, separately, in the income statement "transactions or events that are not expected to occur frequently over several years, or do not typify normal business activities of the entity."[1] In the United States, Accounting Principles Board Opinion 30, "Reporting the results of operations," requires similar disclosure. Nonrecurring items do not qualify to be accounted for as either extraordinary items or as discontinued opera-

tions, and are accounted for "above the line" by default, as a component of earnings from continuing operations.

The US Securities and Exchange Commission (SEC) has expressed concern that the increasing frequency with which firms report large nonrecurring charges is impairing the quality of earnings. In a speech given at New York University in September 1998, Arthur Levitt, SEC chair, observed, "In the zeal to satisfy consensus earnings estimates and project a smooth earnings path, wishful thinking may be winning the day over faithful representation. As a result, I fear that we are witnessing an erosion in the quality of earnings, and, therefore, the quality of financial reporting."[2]

Levitt identified five accounting "gimmicks" that he believes are being used to manage earnings. Three of the five gimmicks involve nonrecurring charges; the other two involve revenue recognition and the application of materiality.

The term "quality of earnings" has been used to mean different things, but for the purposes of this examination it can be defined as the usefulness of reported earnings for predicting the future earnings of a firm. While a close relationship exists between the *current* and *expected* future earnings of a firm with high earnings quality, little or no relationship exists between these measures for a firm with low earnings qual-

ity. When nonrecurring charges are included in income, the quality of earnings is lowered because the relationship between current and expected future earnings is weakened.

Because management determines the amount and timing of the nonrecurring charges it reports, it has an opportunity for strategic earnings management. As Katherine Schipper has noted, managers might undertake strategic earnings management to convey inside knowledge of the firm and its future prospects (resulting in higher quality earnings), or to convey intentionally misleading information (low quality earnings).[3] Although management can use judgment to either improve or impair the representational faithfulness of financial statements, the SEC and market analysts seem suspicious of the increasing frequency with which firms are reporting large nonrecurring charges.

John Elliott and I found that nonrecurring charges are overwhelmingly "income-decreasing"—which suggests such suspicions may be justified.[4] There is no reason to expect that nonrecurring events should be primarily income-decreasing. Nonetheless, the events that management chooses to report as nonrecurring do exhibit this tendency.

The literature on contracting cites several incentives for strategic earnings management.[5] To the extent that contracts are drawn on accounting numbers, overstating earnings may, for example, avoid the violation of debt covenants. An additional incentive relates to management compensation. Disappointing the stock market by reporting earnings that are lower than analysts' forecasts can affect stock price. Management's perception that its compensation depends on short-term stock prices provides it with a strong incentive to meet earnings expectations. In the extreme, disappointing earnings results may cause shareholders to replace management.

When it comes to strategically timing expense recognition, one of the devices available to management is the "big bath." A big bath affects the timing of expense recognition but not the amount. For example, if managers expect poor earnings for a number of years, and if they receive a bonus based on earnings, then they may be able to increase their bonuses by recognizing a large amount of expenses in one year and smaller amounts in the other (usually later) years. Moving later years' expenses to the current year makes the already bad year look worse, but improves the reported earnings and, perhaps, the bonuses of later years. The practice of making an already bad result even worse has become known as "taking a bath."

John Elliott and Wayne Shaw examined a sample of firms that reported large nonrecurring charges and found evidence that the big-bath strategy partially explains the reason for doing so.[6] Firms reporting large nonrecurring charges tend to be performing poorly even before the financial impact of the charge is considered. John Strong and John Meyer find a strong correlation between changes in upper management and big baths.[7] The new management can "clear the decks" in a book-value sense by attributing the need for the write-down to prior management, thereby improving reported earnings results under the new administration. Firms usually report big baths as nonrecurring charges against income.

While the big-bath story has intuitive appeal, the more general phenomenon of reporting nonrecurring charges can involve not only timing issues, but also whether an expense is ever recognized in the earnings numbers used to

evaluate management. This strategy requires multiple definitions of earnings. When managers have the ability to shift expenses between time periods or to classify expenses so that they appear in different places on the income statement, they can create a variety of predictable effects.

A truly nonrecurring event provides no information about future periods' earnings. A decision-maker who wants to forecast future results properly ignores such an event. Financial analysts, who are in the business of predicting future earnings, issue forecasts of earnings *before* nonrecurring charges, or "core" earnings (GAAP earnings from continuing operations excluding the after-tax impact of nonrecurring charges). Naturally, management tries to meet or beat the analysts' forecasts. The use of nonrecurring charges may help them achieve that goal.

Bonus plans are also frequently based on core earnings; as such, they appear to protect management from the adverse implications of nonrecurring charges. In other words, both corporate performance evaluation and managerial bonuses are based on reported core earnings—not on income from continuing operations or net income. Patricia Dechow, Mark Huson and Richard Sloan find that, over average, managers' bonuses appear to be determined on a "pre-nonrecurring charges" basis.[8] Further, Jennifer and Kenneth Gaver suggest that managers are not only protected from nonrecurring loses but are rewarded for nonrecurring gains.[9]

It makes sense, then, that firms should want to report nonrecurring charges whenever possible. Bonus plans ignore them in setting compensation, and analysts ignore them in evaluating core earnings performance. Little wonder that managers are tempted to treat ordinary expenses as nonrecurring. Even better, why not put "extra" expense into the nonrecurring charge (since management doesn't care how big the charge is) and create some sort of reserve that can be drawn down in later periods? For example, upon the acquisition of a financial institution, management could report a nonrecurring loss for anticipated additional bad

debts and overstate the firm's loan loss reserves. When those reserves eventually prove to be unnecessary, they will be reversed into earnings. Often, firms include such reversals or draw-downs in core earnings. In this example, management might reverse the overstated amount of loan loss reserves by reducing future bad debt expense, thereby increasing future periods' core earnings. Thus, nonrecurring charges become a low-cost vehicle to manage core earnings—the earnings number that management really cares about.

For users of financial information who try to predict future earnings, there are no quick fixes to address the additional complexity added by reported nonrecurring charges. Accurate separation of the recurring (core) and nonrecurring components of earnings allows a more intuitive use of the earnings information in valuing a firm. Core earnings might be capitalized in some fashion, and the nonrecurring component of earnings might be analyzed and included in the valuation estimate in some situation-specific manner. Capitalizing core earnings while considering nonrecurring earnings to be single events suggests that the value of an additional dollar of core earnings is greater than the value of an additional dollar of nonrecurring gain.

A problem arises, however, when nonrecurring charges have implications for *core* earnings in future periods. Firms might use nonrecurring charges to write off assets they would otherwise depreciate in later periods, thereby bolstering core earnings in those periods. To do so strategically requires that management have some discretion in determining the amount of nonrecurring charge. Some transactions involve more judgment than do others, thus allowing more room for manipulation.

Jennifer Francis, Linda Vincent and I examined whether market participants who interpret nonrecurring charges appreciate the potential for managerial discretion.[10] We found a significant *negative* stock price reaction to announcements of nonrecurring inventory write-downs. This result is consistent with inventory values being easily verified and the reported write-down primarily conveying bad news. However, we also observed a *positive* stock price reaction to announcements of goodwill write-downs. This is not consistent with the announcements conveying only bad news about declines in asset values. In apparent recognition of the subjective nature of goodwill, the market looks beyond the change in book value and attributes some alternative—and possibly strategic—meaning to the announcement. John Elliott and Wayne Shaw discuss the possible reasons for a "good news" interpretation of write-offs. They argue that if analysts interpret nonrecurring charges as a signal that management is going to address some problem within a particular firm, then the announcement of the charge may communicate good news for the firm's future performance.

Nonrecurring charges could have other implications for future period earnings if management reports such charges on a regular basis. Users might begin to suspect that not all significant events are reflected in core earnings. John Elliott and I examined firms that report sequences of nonrecurring charges and found that the market responds to both the recurring and nonrecurring components of earnings, but to different extents. On average, the market reacts more to an additional dollar of recurring earnings than it does to an additional dollar of nonrecurring charges. We also found that firms reporting nonrecurring charges tend to report more nonrecurring charges in future periods. That is, nonrecurring charges become part of the corporate accounting culture. Firms that regularly report nonrecurring charges have a reduced market response to an additional dollar of *core* earnings than do firms that do not regularly report nonrecurring charges. To appreciate this last result, we need to consider the alternative responses available to rational investors.

First, investors could ignore any nonrecurring charges and focus exclusively on core earnings. Eventually, these investors will understand that the firm regularly disposes of expenses through nonrecurring charges. John Elliott and I found that more than 20% of firms listed on the major US exchanges reported large nonrecurring charges in 1993. For firms that regu-

larly report nonrecurring charges, core earnings tend to overstate corporate performance. Also, if a firm uses nonrecurring charges to create reserves to absorb future expenses, investors may observe trends in core earnings that are actually the result of strategic manipulation—rather than the result of changes in the firm's underlying economic performance.

Alternatively, investors might include the nonrecurring charge in the current period's earnings and focus on the GAAP-defined earnings from continuing operations. This alternative penalizes the current period too much, especially if the charge contains items that would otherwise have been recognized in later fiscal periods.

As an example, consider a strategic write-down of depreciable assets. The firm could write off a $500 asset that continues in use. The firm would otherwise depreciate the asset over the next five years at $100 a year. If investors ignore the write-down in evaluating the current year, they effectively allow the firm to increase core earnings by $100 of avoided depreciation. If investors include the entire write-down in the current period, they penalize the firm's performance too much because $400 of the charge properly belongs to other fiscal periods. Current reporting standards do not require management to disclose the fiscal periods from which it is "shifting" expenses. As a result, investors do not have the ability to simply add back the entire charge and deduct the "normal" amount. In the period of the write-off, investors see the $500 explicitly, but they cannot see that the firm would otherwise depreciate this amount over five years. Thus, while the initial amount of nonrecurring charge is relatively transparent, the implications of that charge for surrounding fiscal periods' earnings are more opaque.

Or, if management were to use a nonrecurring charge to create "extra" reserves (increasing a reserve for restructuring activities, for example, where those activities are not explicitly identified), the knowledge of when the reserves might increase future earnings would generally be unknown. In either case, investors require a number that does not appear in the financial state-

ments. The desired performance estimate is a number somewhere between core earnings and operating earnings, and a subjective assessment of performance is necessary. As a result of the greater uncertainty regarding corporate performance, rational investors might conclude that they face more "information risk" and attach a higher discount rate to the firm's earnings or cash flow streams. This increased discount rate could explain the reduced market response to an additional dollar of core earnings that John Elliott and I documented.

Most users of financial information are aware of the opportunities for earnings management and act accordingly. However, management's determination of goodwill value—or the charge to be recorded in association with an anticipated restructuring transaction—is inherently subjective. Little evidence exists to allow objective verification. The fact that these measurements are subjective offers opportunities for financial analysts to add value through their expert interpretation of reported nonrecurring charges.

The increasing frequency of reported nonrecurring charges makes it difficult for users to infer trends in economic performance from the observed trends in reported earnings. A natural result is the increasing use of other sources of information in valuation estimates. Dan Collins, Ed Maydew and Ira Weiss examine the changing relevance of earnings and book values for the purpose of explaining firm value.[11] They find that the "value-relevance" of net income has decline and attribute at least part of this decline to the increasing frequency and magnitude of nonrecurring items. They do not examine the value-relevance of core earnings. However, if a company's management has recently started using nonrecurring items to strategically manipulate core earnings, it's probable that the value-relevance of these numbers will also change.

The problems created by nonrecurring charges have no simple solutions. If standard-setters do away with the ability to classify these items separately, then firms will likely use other media to communicate the same information. IBM, a firm that analysts have criticized for reporting too many nonrecurring charges, recently announced that it was going to stop the practice and include those items with other operating expenses.[12] The company added, however, that it would also report the amount of nonrecurring charges that were not separately disclosed in the income statement in a press release.

Problems associated with nonrecurring items are analogous to problems previously experienced with the reporting of extraordinary items. Stricter rules, especially in Canada, have reduced management's ability to manipulate income from continuing operations (by classifying negative charges as extraordinary items, while similar positive items remain above the line). Making the "below the line" rules stricter implies that many unusual or infrequent items remain in operating income by default. Analysts and other users of financial information do not simply accept the classification of items as reported on the income statement, and they continue to make adjustments to obtain an estimate of core earnings. Management recognizes this; instead of strategically using extraordinary items, it has simply moved its attention above the line and is now using nonrecurring charges.

Recent efforts in Canada and the United States[13] to lessen the problems caused by the disclosure of nonrecurring items do not appear to have succeeded; witness Arthur Levitt's recent speech. Stricter rules governing the types of expenses that may be classified as nonrecurring might lessen the problem, or they might move it to another category of expense in the income statement, or they might move such disclosures outside of the financial statement altogether (as in IBM's proposed press release disclosures). It's unlikely that new rules will stop the flow of such information.

Instead of attempting to reduce the flow of information about nonrecurring charges, the accounting profession might consider expanding it. Analysts want to react when they perceive that firms are reporting nonrecurring charges too frequently. The problem is

that an appropriate response is difficult to ascertain. If firms were required to disclose when expenses would have been recognized (had they not been included in a nonrecurring charge), then analysts would be able to calculate "without charge" earnings numbers. This would provide information about multiple fiscal periods—not just the period in which the nonrecurring charge was reported. Perhaps firms could also provide more information about the components of nonrecurring charges, thereby allowing analysts to perform a more in-depth analysis before determining their response. However the issue is addressed, nonrecurring charges will no doubt continue to be one of the primary reasons that financial analysis is more of an art than it is a science.

J. Douglas Hanna, MAcc, PhD, CA, is an associate professor of accounting at the University of Chicago's Graduate School of Business.

Technical Editor: John Friedlan, PhD, CA, Schulich School of Business, York University, North York, Ontario.

NOTES

1. *CICA Handbook*, Canadian Institute of Chartered Accountants, Section 1520.03 (1).

2. A. Levitt, "The 'numbers game,'" Text of a speech at the NYU Center for Law and Business, September 28, 1998.

3. K. Schipper, "Commentary on earnings management," *Accounting Horizons*, December 1989, pp. 91–102.

4. J. Elliott and D. Hanna, "Repeated accounting write-offs and the information content of earnings," *Journal of Accounting Research*, Supplement 1996, pp. 135–155.

5. R. Watts and J. Zimmerman, *Positive Accounting Theory*, Prentice-Hall, 1986; and P. Healy, "The effect of bonus schemes on accounting decisions," *Journal of Accounting and Economics*, April 1985, pp. 85–107.

6. J. Elliott and W. Shaw, "Write-offs as accounting procedures to manage perceptions," *Journal of Accounting Research*, Supplement 1988, pp. 91–119.

7. J. Strong and J. Meyer, "Asset writedowns: managerial incentives and security returns," *Journal of Finance*, July 1987, pp. 643–663.

8. P. Dechow, M. Huson and R. Sloan, "The effect of restructuring charges on executives' cash compensation," *The Accounting Review*, January 1994, pp. 138–156.

9. J. and K. Gaver, "The relation between nonrecurring accounting transactions and CEO cash compensation," *The Accounting Review*, April 1998, pp. 235–253.

10. J. Francis, D. Hanna and L. Vincent, "Causes and effects of discretionary asset write-offs," *Journal of Accounting Research*, Supplement 1996, pp. 117–134.

11. D. Collins, E. Maydew and I. Weiss, "Changes in the value-relevance of earnings and book values over the past 40 years," *Journal of Accounting and Economics*, December 1997, pp. 39–67.

12. B. Ziegler, "IBM's method of accounting for cutbacks bucks trend of taking repeated charges," *The Wall Street Journal*, March 6, 1996, p. C1.

13. Emerging Issues Committee Abstract 60, "Liability recognition for costs to exit an activity," Canadian Institute of Chartered Accountants, 1994; Emerging Issues Task Force Abstract 94–3, "Liability recognition for certain employee termination benefits and other costs to exit an activity." Financial Accounting Standards Board, 1995; and Financial Accounting Standard 121, "Accounting for the impairment of long-lived assets and for long-lived assets to be disposed of," Financial Accounting Standards Board, 1995.

Reprinted from *CA Magazine* (pp. 35–39), August 1999, by J. Douglas Hanna.

CASE 3B
Dramatic examples of earnings manipulation

The following article, "Earnings Hocus-Pocus," alleges that companies "jazz up their earnings" partly in response to perceived pressure from stock market investors for good performance. This was a 1998 article, but the problems continue, with new corporate offenders turning up regularly. Discuss the article and suggest what might be done about the problem, and how much "blame" you might assign to managers, accountants, stock market regulators, investors, and other players in the game.

Earnings Hocus-Pocus
How companies come up with the numbers they want

When America Online's management put together its quarterly financials early this summer, it was with some measure of pride, says new Chief Financial Officer J. Michael Kelly. Indeed, the results were remarkable. AOL would be posting a 900% rise in operating profits, to $57 million. At 23¢ per share, earnings would handily beat Wall Street's estimate of 19¢.

The excitement didn't last long. Soon, the Securities & Exchange Commission's officials began peppering the company with inquiries. Their beef, according to AOL: the company's plans to use a controversial accounting technique to instantly write off much of the value of two companies it had just purchased. By taking a charge for "in-process R&D" under way at the companies, AOL figured it could write off fully $20 million of the $29 million it was paying for NetChannel, an Internet television company, and a "substantial portion" of the $287 million it would pay for Mirabilis, a developer of real-time chat software.

The SEC appears to have found the size of the charges troubling, however, and by Aug. 4, the date of AOL's fourth-quarter earnings release, the issue hadn't been resolved. So Kelly did something rarely seen in Corporate America: He announced quarterly results that didn't go to the bottom line. There was simply no way to calculate net income without the SEC's blessing on the charges. "We had such phenomenal operating results," says Kelly. "To hold that back for an unfinished accounting matter didn't seem

appropriate." Investors didn't take the matter so lightly. In two days, they dumped 23 million shares, sending the stock down 5%.

AOL ought to have known better. After all, it's not the first time the company's accounting practices have been questioned. In 1996, after dubious investors challenged its policy of writing off marketing expenses over two years, AOL restated its numbers in a move that erased all its previous profits overnight. But a company that once might have been dismissed as a rogue is now just one face in a troubled crowd. Across Corporate America, a wave of concern is rising about the quality of corporate earnings—and the tactics companies are using to calculate them.

Headlines this summer have been dominated by spectacular cases involving allegations of outright accounting lies: Cendant Corp. accused some former executives of fraudulently inflating income before charges by $500 million over three years, in large part by booking fictitious revenues. Livent Inc. allegedly kept two sets of books to mask extravagant expenses.

But forget about fraud for now. Regulators and investors are starting to focus on a far broader problem: companies bolstering their performance by using every legal accounting game in the book. They appear to be exploiting opportunities to jazz up their earnings like never before—all without stepping outside the loose confines of generally accepted accounting principles (GAAP).

That has led to a slew of spectacular collapses of companies caught playing fast and loose with their numbers.

Investors in such onetime highfliers as Green Tree Financial, Waste Management, and Sunbeam have seen years of seemingly solid earnings vanish overnight. The culprit: overly rosy or misleading information about sales or expenses sometimes buried deep within their financial statements.

"BIG BATH." And that's only one part of the problem. SEC officials are also worried about the abuse of huge, virtually unrestricted "big-bath" write-offs. Indeed, write-offs such as Motorola's recent $1.98 billion restructuring charge have become all too common. Even that is small change compared with the multibillion-dollar charges taken by high-tech acquirers such as Compaq Computer Corp. and WorldCom Inc. to write off "in-process" research when they close a deal. Meanwhile, others have taken so many "extraordinary" charges year in and year out that the only truly out of the ordinary is a year without write-offs.

Of course, companies have always taken write-offs and restructuring charges. But nervous regulators and investors fear that such huge multiyear write-offs are increasingly distorting corporate earnings—so much so, in fact, that some question whether the underlying meaning of profit numbers and their value as a true reflection of corporate performance is getting trampled.

To understand why, remember what the earnings number is supposed to represent: an accurate snapshot of how well a company's operations performed in a given year. And one of the basic principles of accounting is that both revenues and costs should be matched to the year in which they occur. Otherwise, managers have too much leeway to massage the numbers, and "annual" performance becomes meaningless.

But the aim of many of today's giant write-offs is to frontload expenses. Charge off three years of expenses all at once, and by definition future earnings will be better. It's akin to making three years of mortgage payments at once, then claiming your income has grown.

Fueling the trend is the fact that stock traders tend to ignore big "one-time" charges, focusing instead on prospects. So even if the total dollars spent are the same, companies have a far greater incentive to take one large charge rather than stretch expenses out as money actually spent. Indeed, the market's reaction encourages executives to make charges as big as possible. And that's got investors and the SEC worried that companies are burying all sorts of normal operating expenses into their restructuring charges. "Somebody woke up to the fact that if you take something as a restructuring charge, investors will forgive you immediately," says Robert S. Miller, the nonexecutive chairman brought in to clean up Waste Management. "We've almost lost the notion of what are earnings and what are one-time charges."

Why are so many questions about the quality of earnings arising now? For one, there's a mismatch between today's deal-oriented, high-tech economy and a decades-old accounting system in which only "real" assets such as bricks and mortar can be easily valued. Throw in an eight-year bull market in which earnings growth came to be the only measure many investors looked at, and add the pressure those market forces have created on managers to make the numbers look as good as possible. If anyone had set out to invent a system in which the means, motives, and methods to encourage companies to stretch earnings all came together perfectly, they couldn't have done a better job.

But with the economy slowing and Wall Street jittery, concerns are growing that companies desperate to keep up earnings and stock prices will practice even more aggressive accounting.

Warns J. Michael Cook, chairman and CEO of Deloite & Touche: "As economic pressures get tougher over the next 3 to 12 months, I worry whether the system will measure up."

MORE DISCLOSURE? He's not the only one. On Sept. 28, SEC chief Arthur Levitt will give a speech at New York University outlining plans to improve the accuracy of earnings. "We have become concerned that the quality of financial reporting is eroding," Levitt says. In recent weeks, the SEC's new chief accountant, Lynn Turner, has met with officials of Big Five accounting firms, Wall Street analysts, and CFOs to discuss concerns. "If the basic accounting foundation ever loses credibility with investors," Turner says, "then the whole [investing] process would fall apart."

The SEC won't say what steps it plans, but it may require more disclosure about restructuring reserves and the valuation of R&D write-offs. It's also concerned about how companies account for mergers. Talks on mergers and restructuring charges are also under way at the Financial Accounting Standards Board (FASB), an industry body chartered by the SEC that created and updates GAAP. But any FASB-driven changes could take years to iron out.

Of course, not every accounting charge reflects management efforts to fool investors. In many cases, the charges reflect real operating problems. Some experts argue, too, that in some ways the earnings picture is actually clearer today. Gabrielle Napolitano, an accounting analyst and portfolio strategist at Goldman, Sachs & Co., points out that low inflation has improved accounting for inventory and depreciation expenses.

Still, what's troubling is that massive charge-offs have been wiping out earnings at a time when the economy is booming. According to earnings-watcher First Call Corp., the number of companies taking restructuring charges jumped from 96 in 1995 to 230 last year. And despite a then seven-year-old expansion, companies in the Standard & Poor's 500-stock index wrote off $7.04 a share in earnings in 1997, topping the previous high of $6.61 in

1993, when Corporate America was struggling to dig out from the lingering effect of a recession. Fueled by merger-related charges, the S&P companies wrote off fully 17.7% of their earnings last year—more than triple the 5.6% Napolitano predicted at the year's start.

That's why the manner in which companies handle big write-offs is far from an arcane accounting debate. They can significantly alter the earnings picture investors see. Consider the case of Lucent Technologies Inc. As part of the process of Lucent's spin-off from AT&T in a 1996 public offering, the company took a big-bath charge in which it set up a $2.8 billion reserve to cover restructuring costs. To come up with that figure, the company in late 1995 estimated how much the restructuring would cost over several years. Lucent's reserve was to cover severance for 20,000 employees and the cost of exiting businesses such as AT&T's Phone Center Stores.

So far, so good—and there's where the first benefit comes in. By writing off several years worth of costs all at once rather than taking them each year as the money is spent, Lucent eliminated future costs from its books. It's a common practice—and one that automatically improves earnings down the line.

The gains didn't end there. As it turned out, Lucent put aside far more than was needed to cover the restructuring expenses—and the excess reserves have since helped the company smooth out what might otherwise have been much choppier earnings. One reason for the excess: The booming economy helped lower Lucent's costs as former employees quickly found new work. So Lucent converted some of its restructuring reserve back into income. Over three years, it took $382 million from reserves and added it back to pretax income. Thus, even as the reserve cut expenses, Lucent's income got a big boost, too.

Lucent has also benefitted from an accounting technique that's becoming wildly popular among high-tech companies—while drawing increased scrutiny from the SEC. As Lucent bought companies over the past two years, it wrote off $2.3 billion of in-process research and development. That figure—Lucent's estimate of the future value of R&D at the companies it bought—has allowed Lucent to avoid $2.3 billion in "goodwill." That's an accounting term for the premium paid for a business or asset above the value recorded on its books, which would normally have to be written off as an expense over many years.

Now, it's worth emphasizing that everything Lucent has done has been found to be in accordance with GAAP by its auditors, Pricewaterhouse-Coopers. The SEC has not challenged one of these moves. The company's filings and press releases clearly disclose exactly what it is doing. Indeed, every decision was made under the "Letter and intent of the law," says controller James S. Lusk. "I don't believe in accounting cocaine." And Wall Street certainly likes the results: Lucent's shares have outperformed the S&P by 255% since its IPO.

But the question remains: What if Lucent hadn't taken a one-time charge but spread restructuring costs over the years it took to clean up? And what if the R&D had been written off over 10 years, a typical period?

The answer, according to Jack T. Ciesielski, a well-known accounting expert and money manager, is that Lucent's books would have reflected a much less smooth but possibly more accurate picture of management's ability to drive growth. Using the numbers Lucent reported in its SEC filings, Ciesielski first eliminated the effects of the restructuring reserve. Instead, he treated the expenses as normal costs in the years they occurred. Then, he eliminated the income created by the reserve reversals and calculated what goodwill would have been without the R&D write-offs. Along the way, he assumed all acquisitions came at the start of the year, and he used the corporate tax rate Lucent paid each year.

How do his figures compare with Lucent's operating income—net profits excluding special charges—the number that investors most closely watch? He calculated that in 1996, Lucent would have lost $49 million rather than its $1.05 billion operating earnings gain. Earnings last year, he figures, would have been a modest $1.11 billion, well below Lucent's $1.51 billion. And for the first three quarters of fiscal 1998,

Lucent would have made $1.51 billion, $229 million less that the $1.74 billion it reported. "The reason managers love these [moves] is that they buy them time," says Ciesielski, publisher of *The Analyst's Accounting Observer*. "You wouldn't have a stock trading at the multiple Lucent is if they hadn't had this time to work all this out."

Lucent declined to comment on Ciesielski's analysis, saying through a spokesman: "To speculate or hypothesize about 'what if' scenarios when we adhered to strict accounting standards is simply not meaningful or productive."

So how can there be such disagreement over how to crunch the numbers? One culprit is an accounting system that many find obtuse and out of touch with an economy that is increasingly driven by technology and deal-making. The gray areas in GAAP are plentiful, and its terminology can be ill-defined. What constitutes a legitimate "one-time" charge, and how does it differ from the normal operating costs of doing business every quarter? GAAP offers few clues. Some vital intangible assets, such as the brainpower of a team of microchip designers, aren't measured at all. Other intangibles, such as patents, are valued by appraisal—a type of educated guess that is far from foolproof. Concludes Lawrence Revsine, a prominent accounting professor at Northwestern's J. L. Kellogg Graduate School of Management: "Accounting stinks."

One of the best illustrations of the mismatch between yesterday's accounting system and today's economy is seen in the exploding use of those R&D write-offs. Virtually unknown a decade ago, they have soared since IBM successfully used the technique to write off much of the cost of its 1995 acquisition of software maker Lotus Development. Today, such charges can reach billions of dollars.

To see why they're so popular, check out the payoff in WorldCom's $37 billion purchase of MCI Communications Corp. WorldCom estimates that MCI had R&D worth $6 billion to $7 billion under way but not yet ready for commercial application. Since WorldCom may never see any benefit from that R&D—conceivably, it could all come to naught—account-

ing rules allow WorldCom to write it all off at once.

Does that mean MCI was really only worth $31 billion? Not necessarily The real significance of that number lies elsewhere. Normally, any premium paid over "book value" would be called goodwill, which WorldCom would have to depreciate. Since that would cut into expenses for years, acquirers generally want to keep goodwill to a minimum.

Now here's where things get good. Since every dollar WorldCom can assign to in-process R&D is one less it has to call goodwill, it has every incentive to make the charge as big as possible. And acquirers have enormous leeway in valuing R&D. That's what really has the SEC worked up. It fears that companies are overstating these charges. Moreover, as with all front-loaded charges, writing-off all R&D costs today will likely give future earnings a boost. When WorldCom actually turns some of that R&D into salable products, its earnings will look far juicier than they would have otherwise.

Gary Brandt, WorldCom's chief of investor relations, defends the treatment. But he conceded that if the charge were considered goodwill, WorldCom earnings would be cut by a minimum of $100 million a year, or 5¢ per 1.9 billion shares outstanding. If the SEC doesn't challenge the charge that it isn't reduced by WorldCom, it will be the largest in-process R&D write-off ever.

But the potential to inflate research costs isn't the SEC's only worry concerning write-offs. Some of these charges can also provide cover for ongoing operating costs that should be booked as they occur. McDonald's Corp. got its hand slapped for just such a move in August. The hamburger vendor elected to take all at once a $190 million charge for the cost of ditching old grills and ovens and installing new ones. But the SEC disagreed that these charges were a one-time extraordinary cost. After all, if upgrading kitchen equipment isn't a normal cost of doing business for a restaurant chain, what is?

HOOKED. After discussions with the SEC, McDonald's decided to take the expenses as they are incurred. The company says it was not attempting to boost earnings by taking the one-time charge. Still, the shift will chop $25 million to $35 million a quarter from earnings through late 1999, estimates Merrill Lynch & Co. analyst Peter Oakes.

If companies get away with them, big charges can become addictive. Kellogg, AT&T, and General Motors have all taken a remarkable number of restructuring write-offs this decade—leading critics to question how "extraordinary" they are. For a clear picture of the benefits a company can derive from repeated write-offs, look no further than Eastman Kodak Co. Since 1991, Kodak has taken six extraordinary write-offs totaling $4.5 billion. That's more than all of its net profits for the past nine years.

Kodak has been in a major transition period, exiting five major business lines as sales have dropped 25% since the write-offs began. Still, critics point out that Kodak managed to report operating earnings throughout that period—but the repeated need for such extraordinary charges implies that those operating figures may have been of little value. "Charges after charges after charges—that says Kodak overreported earnings," says David W. Tice, publisher of *Behind the Numbers* and manager of the Prudent Bear Fund, which invests in undervalued stocks. Kodak declined to comment.

Meanwhile, the SEC is also taking a close look at another corporate addiction: merger mania. Some $1.2 trillion worth of deals have been announced already this year—greater than in all of 1997—and as many as one-third would not have been done without the in-process R&D charge or a technique known as pooling-of-interest accounting, says Stephen S. Smith, a managing director at investment bank Broadview Associates. Pooling lets companies combine their assets at book value, eliminating goodwill. Miller estimates that when USA Waste Services Inc. and Waste Management used pooling to combine in March in a $16 billion deal, they added $3 billion to $4 billion to earnings over the next several decades.

It isn't supposed to be easy to qualify for a pooling; companies must meet 12 tough criteria. Still, the incentive is so strong that pooling deals jumped from just 11 in 1990 to 364 so far this year, according to Securities Data Co. That's a problem, critics say, because the result can be to hide the premium one company is paying for another. "The real concern is that the acquiring company overpaid," says Bear, Stearns & Co. accounting analyst Pat McConnell. "If they overpaid and management was stupid, that's important."

If many of the problems stem from ambiguities in GAAP, however, only so much blame can go to the system. After all, accounting's rules have been loose for years. What's pushing more managers through the loopholes today is the rise of momentum investing. For many on Wall Street, the only number that counts is the quarterly growth of earnings per share. One measure of the intensified interest: For years, First Call compiled daily lists during weeks when companies issue earnings, of which companies made, missed, or beat analysts' estimates. Now, First Call updates those lists two or three times a day. It even puts out lists during what's now called "pre-announcement season."

Meanwhile, many ignore the fundamentals behind the numbers. "There aren't enough skeptical investors," says the manager of a $4 billion mutual fund. "When investors punish companies for missing their quarterly earnings, it sends a message that they don't care how they get there."

KILLING FIELD. That shift in market psychology has vastly increased the pressure for managers to meet earnings projections. And those that don't make the numbers generally get killed. "The penalties for missing your earnings are intense," says T.J. Rodgers, president and CEO of Cypress Semiconductor Corp. "If you miss one or two quarters, you can see your net worth and market cap cut in half. . . . It's harder to retain people if their stock options aren't worth anything. . . . Lots of CEOs have succumbed to that pressure." Indeed, the resulting pain is intensely personal, since more than half of CEO pay comes from stock options.

That market pressure can lead to disastrous accounting tricks such as those at Sunbeam, Waste Management, and Cendant. New management at the latter two have since conceded that the desire to meet Wall Street expectations seems to have been a huge driver of the problems, and analysts think it played a big role in Sunbeam's downfall as well.

The good times have also served to take investor's eyes off the ball. During the eight-year-long bull market, many took a "don't ask, don't tell" approach. As long as earnings were up, why look too closely at how management pulled it off? But those days are over. "There's a phenomenon in up markets that most analysts don't pay too much attention to accounting," says Gerald I. White of New York investment firm Grace & White Inc. "In bad markets, these problems come home to roost, and that's when people pay attention."

Those are exactly the sorts of issues that the stock market is starting to sort out. One result is that investors may put companies under more pressure to show that they have a solid foundation under their earnings. But the SEC seems more concerned there will be a rush in the other direction, toward more accounting smoke and mirrors. And some investment pros are arguing for a return to more fundamentals-driven stock picking. White argues that the current trend confirms his view that searching out companies with conservative accounting is best. Other investors are turning to other measures of corporate performance, such as Economic Value Added—net operating profit after taxes in excess of the cost of capital. That tool is used at Goldman Sachs and Credit Suisse First Boston.

The argument for those numbers is that they are harder to manipulate. But they are still not foolproof. Any company intent on jazzing up the numbers is probably going to figure out a way to obscure its true performance. "Increasingly, this culture is one of getting away with what you can," says investor Gary L. Pilgrim, founder of Pilgrim Baxter & Associates. "What we need is more integrity"—integrity in managers and integrity in their numbers.

By Nanette Byrnes in New York and Richard A. Melcher in Chicago, with Debra Sparks in New York

Reprinted from *Business Week* (pp. 134–42), 5 October 1998, by Nanette Byrnes, Richard A. Melcher, with Debra Sparks.

NOTES

1. Michael Chatfield, "English Medieval Bookkeeping: Exchequer and Manor," in *Contemporary Studies in the Evolution of Accounting Thought*, ed. Michael Chatfield (Belmont: Dickenson Publishing Company, 1968), 36.

2. O. ten Have, *The History of Accounting* (Palo Alto: Bay Books, 1976), 56–74.

3. Ibid., 67.

4. Peter C. Newman, *Company of Adventurers* (Markham: Viking/Penguin Books, 1985), xii.

5. C.J. Hasson, "The South Sea Bubble and M. Shell," in *Contemporary Studies in the Evolution of Accounting Thought*, ed. Michael Chatfield (Belmont: Dickenson Publishing Company, 1968), 86–94.

6. Ross M. Skinner, *Accounting Standards in Evolution* (Toronto: Holt, Rinehart and Winston, 1987), 15–16.

7. Some of the ideas in this part were developed with reference to Skinner's *Accounting Standards in Evolution*.

8. Ibid., 23.

9. For more on income smoothing, see Joshua Ronen and Simcha Sadan, *Smoothing Income Numbers: Objectives, Means, and Implications* (Reading: Addison-Wesley, 1981). Smoothing and other apparent manipulations of income figures has often been the subject of articles in business magazines such as *Forbes*, *Fortune*, and *Business Week*. For critical and very readable commentaries on income manipulation, see a series of articles and books by Abraham Briloff, including *Unaccountable Accounting* (New York: Harper & Row, 1972).

10. Adapted from *Accounting Education: Problems and Prospects* (Sarasota: American Accounting Association, 1974).

4 CHAPTER

Measuring and Evaluating Cash Flow

4.1   Chapter Overview

Financial reporting goes beyond the three financial statements introduced in Chapters 2 and 3.

Chapters 2 and 3 introduced the three financial statements that are based on the accounts. These provide measures of financial position and performance that are considered central by most users and preparers of financial accounting information. But important as the balance sheet, income statement, and statement of retained earnings are, they do not contain everything that is useful to know about an enterprise's financial performance and position. This chapter and Chapter 5 focus on the supplementary material provided with most financial statements, material that has become very important in its own right.

The cash flow statement is a standard part of the set of financial statements.

Back in Chapter 1, the difference between cash income and accrual income was illustrated. Chapters 2 and 3 emphasized accrual accounting, especially as to its broad economic view of income, going beyond current cash receipts and payments to include items like accounts receivable, amortization, cost of goods sold, accounts payable, future income taxes, and future pensions. To many people, however, the enterprise's ability to generate cash to pay its bills and dividends is just as important as its ability to generate accrual income. The accounting system contains cash information too, and so to help understand the enterprise's performance, a financial statement has been developed to describe what has been going on with the company's cash during the year. The statement is called the cash flow statement or statement of changes in financial position (SCFP). You will see both titles, so this chapter will use both. This statement is now a standard part of the set of financial statements for virtually every kind of enterprise.

The cash flow statement is a kind of financial analysis.

The cash flow statement is prepared from the information in the accounting records, but it does not come from the accounts directly. Instead of coming from a section of the general ledger or trial balance as the three statements in Chapters 2 and 3 do, this statement is prepared by analyzing the other statements. Thus, this whole chapter focuses on a kind of financial statement analysis beyond the ratios and comparisons in the earlier chapters, but like the reconciliation analysis introduced in section 1.9.

To outline what you will learn in this chapter, let's return to the diagram used at the beginning of Chapter 1:

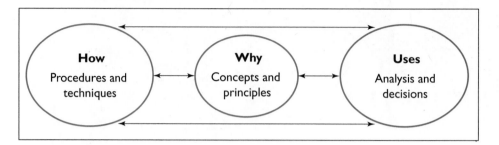

In this chapter you will learn:

- *Procedures and techniques:* How to assemble the cash flow statement and make sure it reconciles to the other financial statements.

- *Concepts and principles:* Why the cash flow statement is important, why it is arranged as it is, and what information demands it satisfies.

- *Analysis and decisions:* In addition to how the cash flow analysis works, using it to understand how the enterprise has performed in managing its cash and how to do some analysis of that performance.

This chapter completes your introduction to the set of financial statements. Chapter 5 considers the notes, auditor's report, and other material surrounding the four standard statements, and begins a deeper examination of the accounting principles behind them. Later chapters continue that deeper examination, and the book ends with another full chapter on financial statement analysis.

4.2   THE PURPOSE OF CASH FLOW ANALYSIS

Managing cash flow is a central part of managing an enterprise.

Performance in generating additional wealth for the enterprise, as measured by the accrual accounting-based income statement, is very important to managers, investors, tax authorities, and many others. But the world is a complex place, and there is more to performance than generating accrual income. An additional important aspect of performance is managing the inflow and outflow of cash so that the enterprise has enough cash to pay its bills, finance its growth, and keep its borrowing under control. We all have to worry about cash flow, about how much cash is available, and where needed additional cash will come from. Businesses are no different, spending much effort on their cash management.

No business enterprise can survive without cash. Nor can other organizations, such as governments, as we have seen in recent years with governments struggling to raise enough cash from taxes and other charges to meet their financial and social obligations. Employees, suppliers, and tax authorities must be paid, loans must be repaid, and assets must be kept up to date. Many new and established firms have had positive net income figures, yet they have still run out of cash and gone bankrupt. Thus it is important for present and potential investors and creditors to have information about a firm's cash inflows and outflows and its resulting cash position. Can the firm meet all its debts and other obligations whenever

Liquidity: cash to cover immediate needs.

Solvency: ability to met obligations when due.

they become due, an ability commonly referred to as solvency, and does it have enough cash and short-term assets now to cover its immediate debts and other obligations, a condition commonly called liquidity? Enterprises can get into difficulty by not managing their cash properly. On the other hand, some enterprises seem to have rather a lot of cash, raising questions about why they are so well off and what is being done with the cash. Keeping a large supply of cash lying around idle is no way to earn a return for owners: the cash should be put to work by making investments, improving the buildings and equipment, attracting new customers, or paying off interest-bearing debt.

Accrual income does not necessarily provide cash to be spent.

The cash situation can be obscured somewhat by accrual accounting. Let's take an extreme example. Suppose a company has revenue of $1,000 but it is all on credit, and none of the customers have paid yet. In order to generate the revenue, the company has expenses of $700, and they all have to be paid soon. The accrual income will be the revenue minus the expenses, or $300. Looks good: a 30% return on revenue. But the company is in trouble: it has no cash to pay its expenses; instead, it has $1,000 of accounts receivable, which cannot be used to pay expenses unless the customers pay or some other way is found to get cash for the receivables. The company is likely to want to borrow money from a bank or other lender to provide it the needed cash. How much should it borrow? Should it hound the customers for payment? Should it beg its creditors for more time to pay the $700 in expenses? How will it be able to afford a planned new machine to keep its product quality competitive? All of these questions are about the management of cash, and they are not easy to answer by examining the accrual accounting income statement, retained earnings statement, and balance sheet.

To assist with such questions, the fourth major financial statement has been developed. The cash flow statement (statement of changes in financial position or SCFP) provides information about a firm's generation and use of cash and highly liquid short-term assets, and, therefore, assists in evaluating the firm's financial viability.

In the example of Simone's jewellery business in section 1.8 of Chapter 1, it was shown that accrual income is not the same as cash income, because some revenues and expenses do not involve an inflow or outflow of cash in the present period. The example of uncollected revenue has already been mentioned. Amortization is another example: the cash flow happened when the asset was acquired, so the amortization expense does not involve any current cash flow.

Even cash income does not cover all inflows and outflows of cash.

Even cash income is not a complete measure of what has happened to cash. It refers to operating results, from transactions with customers, suppliers, and employees. Certain inflows of cash (such as those resulting from getting a bank loan or issuing shares) or outflows of cash (such as dividends or a purchase of land) are not part of the day-to-day process of generating revenue and incurring expenses, so they would not be covered even by a cash income measure. They reflect management decisions beyond generation of income in the current period.

The purpose of the analysis of cash flow is, therefore, twofold:

The cash flow statement reports cash income, calling it cash from operations.

1. To produce a measure of performance based on day-to-day cash flow, cash generated by ordinary business activities, instead of accrual accounting's net income performance measure. This cash measure, which we have called cash income and which the cash flow statement calls cash from operations, *does not imply that accrual income is invalid*; rather, it provides a different perspective on performance and so enhances the information for users.

2. To incorporate other nonoperating cash inflows and outflows, such as from investing in new assets, selling off old ones, borrowing or repaying debts, obtaining new capital from owners, or paying dividends to the owners. By including these nonoperating cash flows, the cash flow statement can provide a complete description of how the firm's cash was managed during the period. It can tell the full story of why the firm has more, or less, cash at the end of the period than it had at the beginning.

The cash flow statement also reports nonoperating cash flows from financing and investing activities.

With this information, the user can evaluate management's strategy for managing cash and make a better judgment of the company's liquidity, solvency, risk, and opportunities than could be made just from the balance sheet, income statement, and statement of retained earnings.

 OR YOUR INTEREST

Things keep changing. The cash flow statement is a relatively recent addition to the set of financial statements, becoming a standard part in only the last few decades. During that time, it has undergone several changes in name, format, and content, the latest changes effective in 1999. This book is based on the 1999 version, but you should be alert for other titles left over from the past. Other terms and titles you may encounter are Statement of Changes in Financial Position (SCFP), **statement of source and application of cash**, and **funds statement**.

 OW'S YOUR UNDERSTANDING?

Here are two questions you should be able to answer, based on what you've just read:

1. What does cash flow have to do with liquidity and solvency?

2. What else is there to cash flow beyond the cash income we saw in Simone's jewellery business in Chapter 1?

4.3   THE CASH FLOW STATEMENT

The cash flow statement, like the other statements, has a standard format. It is useful to know, because variations from that format may be a signal of special circumstances or problems.

Exhibit

4-1

Cash Flow Statement Standard Format

Operating activities:
Cash generated by operations from day-to-day cash receipts and payments related to the activities that generate income.

Investing activities:
Cash used to invest in additional noncurrent assets, including investments in other companies, minus any cash proceeds obtained by disposing of such assets.

Financing activities:
Cash obtained from borrowing and from issuing share capital, minus borrowing repaid or shares redeemed.

Any cash transactions in retained earnings (that is, not included in calculating net income) are also included here, especially dividends and share issue costs.

Change in cash (and equivalents) for the period:
Net sum of the above three categories.

Cash (and equivalents) at the beginning of the period:
Brought forward from last period's cash flow statement and balance sheet.

Cash (and equivalents) at the end of the period:
Equals what is shown on the balance sheet at the end of the period.

Some important features of this format are:

1. The cash flow statement covers the same period as the income statement.
2. Cash includes some equivalents: very liquid near-cash assets that can be turned into cash without any risk of loss, such as demand bank deposits and certificates with a maturity of three months or less.
3. In some cases, cash may include temporary negative bank balances (overdrafts) if they are just a result of cash management activity and the bank balances regularly vary from positive to negative.
4. If there is anything unusual about the enterprise's definition of cash (and equivalents), or any other category of the statement, that should be explained in the notes to the financial statements. You may even see a little reconciliation at the bottom of the cash flow statement.
5. The cash flow statement follows some rules to ensure that its focus stays on cash. For example, if a dividend has been declared but not all paid, only the paid part is included in the cash flow statement's financing activities section. Another example is that if there is an account payable for a noncurrent asset, the investing activities figure shows only the amount paid so far.

All parts of the cash flow statement focus on what happened to cash during the period.

6. Following from point 5, any asset acquisitions, borrowing, or share issues that are done without cash, such as acquiring land in return for shares, are excluded from the cash flow statement. (This is a change in 1999: previously, such noncash transactions were included *as if* they had involved cash.)
7. Any of the numbers in the cash flow statement can be positive or negative, according to what happened during the period. For example, a really bad year can result in cash from operations being negative, in which case it might be

Operating, investing,
and financing cash
flows can all be either
positive or negative.

described as cash used in operations! As another example, a company under-going significant restructuring could have more cash coming in from selling off assets than going out to buy more, so its investing section could be a pos-itive cash inflow instead of the usual cash outflow.

8. Deriving the cash flow from day-to-day operations is one of the main reasons for having the cash flow analysis. The cash from operations figure takes away accrual accounting's many adjustments, which are very important in measur-ing income but obscure the cash effects. To emphasize this, most cash flow statements begin with the net income figure from the income statement and then explicitly remove the effects of changes in accounts receivable, accounts payable, amortization, and other accruals. This is called the indirect method of deriving cash from operations, as distinct from the direct method of just listing operating cash receipts and deducting operating cash payments (also called disbursements).

The last point requires further comment, because accountants are being encour-aged to change from the traditional indirect method to the direct method of cal-culating cash from operations. Figure 4.1 compares the two methods, *both of which end up with the same figure for cash from operations.*

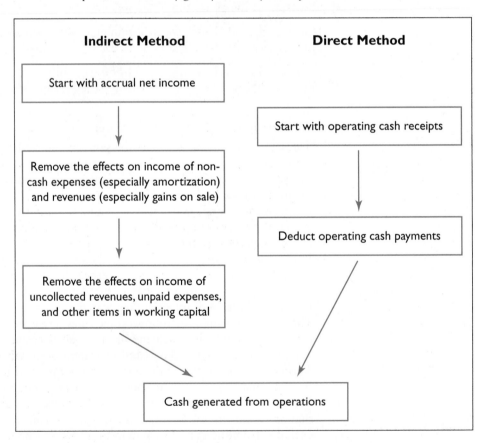

Indirect Method

Start with accrual net income

Remove the effects on income of non-cash expenses (especially amortization) and revenues (especially gains on sale)

Remove the effects on income of uncollected revenues, unpaid expenses, and other items in working capital

Direct Method

Start with operating cash receipts

Deduct operating cash payments

Cash generated from operations

FIGURE 4.1

Cash flow analysis is a good way to cement your understanding of what the finan-cial statements contain and to sharpen your analytical skills. This chapter starts with the simpler direct method of preparing the cash flow statement, then turns to the indirect method, both because most accountants use it (it is more traditional and more usual in financial statements), and because it allows some practice in reworking the financial statements for analysis. The chapter ends with some more complex and realistic examples.

HOW'S YOUR UNDERSTANDING?

Here are two questions you should be able to answer, based on what you have just read:

1. What are the summary categories of cash flow used in the cash flow statement?

2. Dubroy Inc. defines its cash and equivalents to include the following (this year's and last year's figures shown in that order for each): cash ($13,000; $4,000), demand deposit in MegaBank ($25,000; $50,000), and occasional bank overdraft ($7,000; $3,000). What is the net total change in cash that the cash flow statement for this year will explain? (Cash and equivalents at the beginning = $4,000 + $50,000 − $3,000 = $51,000. At the end they = $13,000 + $25,000 − $7,000 = $31,000. So the change in cash is negative $20,000.)

4.4   CASH FLOW ANALYSIS USING RECEIPTS AND PAYMENTS

The direct method classifies information from the Cash Ledger account and supporting detailed cash receipts and payments records into the cash flow statement categories shown at the beginning of section 4.3. It's probably the way you'd expect cash flow analysis to be done, so let's begin with it. An example will show you how this works.

The following information is summarized from Roebuck Industries Inc.'s cash records for this year:

4-2

Exhibit

Cash on hand at the beginning of the year		$ 813,430
Cash receipts for the year:		
Cash sales	$ 73,320	
Collections from customers for credit sales	17,894,530	
Proceeds from sale of land	1,200,000	
Proceeds from issue of new bonded debt	5,300,000	
Proceeds from issue of new shares	840,000	25,307,850
		$26,121,280
Cash payments (disbursements) for the year:		
Expenses paid in cash	$ 49,210	
Payments to suppliers and employees	$14,992,860	
Income tax paid	765,500	
Paid to acquire new noncurrent assets	6,733,310	
Repayments on noncurrent debt	3,112,300	
Costs of new share issue	21,340	
Dividends paid	400,000	26,074,520
Cash on hand at the end of the year		$ 46,760

Preparing the cash flow statement from this information is straightforward—just put the figures above into the appropriate statement categories. Note that there is no mention of accrual income, in fact there is no way to tell what it is. The cash flow statement follows some principles also used in the income and retained earnings statements. Two of these are:

- Segregate operating cash flows (those related to day-to-day income-generating activities) from the more intermittent nonoperating cash flows for investing and financing; and

- Identify cash flows related to the statement of retained earnings and put them into the financing category (for example, share issue costs and dividends paid).

The cash flow statement's categories match the separation between income and other transactions.

Here is the resulting statement.

4-3

Exhibit

ROEBUCK INDUSTRIES INC.

Cash Flow Statement for This Year (Direct Method)

Operating activities:	
Operating cash receipts ($73,320 + $17,894,530)	$17,967,850
Operating cash payments	
($49,210 + $14,992,860 + $765,500)	(15,807,570)
Cash obtained from operations	$ 2,160,280
Investing activities:	
Acquisitions of new noncurrent assets	$ (6,733,310)
Proceeds from sale of land	1,200,000
Cash used for investing	$ (5,533,310)
Financing activities:	
Proceeds from issue of new bonded debt	$ 5,300,000
Repayments on noncurrent debt	(3,112,300)
Proceeds from issue of new shares	840,000
Costs of new share issue	(21,340)
Dividends paid	(400,000)
Cash obtained from financing	$ 2,606,360
Change in cash for the year	$ (766,670)
Cash at the beginning of the year	813,430
Cash at the end of the year	$ 46,760

The cash flow statement's analysis is quite informative.

This analysis shows that Roebuck's cash went down almost to zero during the year, because the company spent more cash acquiring new assets than it raised through operations and financing. Though by far the largest inflows and outflows of cash were from day-to-day operations, the net contribution of operations to the company's cash supply was smaller than the net contribution through financing activities. Some details are interesting. The company raised about a sixth of the cash needed for the new assets by selling some land. The financing was primarily debt this year, not shares, so the company is further in debt than it was (we can see that the debt–equity ratio will have gone up this year, though we don't know by how much without having the balance sheet). In paying for new assets and paying dividends, the company almost exhausted its cash. While this may have left it in a more risky position in regard to paying its bills, it is not necessarily an unwise thing to have done, because having a lot of cash sitting around earns the company little (maybe just a little bank interest), and the money may have been quite productively spent on new assets or paying off noncurrent debt.

These points illustrate two important features of cash flow analysis:

- It gives insight into the company's strategy for managing its financial affairs, and at the very least suggests a list of questions that could be followed up in more detail. For example, did the company sell the land because it was short of cash, or was it offered a price that was too good to pass up?

The cash flow analysis indicates strategies, especially in combination with the other statements.

- For maximum usefulness, it should be combined with other information about the company, especially the information in the other financial statements. For example, what is the company's debt load, and did the increase this year put it in a difficult position? (The balance sheet can help with that question.) Or, what proportion of income is the company paying out as dividends? (The income and retained earnings statements help with that question.)

HOW'S YOUR UNDERSTANDING?

Here are two questions you should be able to answer, based on what you have just read:

1. How can you best draw insights from the cash flow statement's analysis?

2. Suppose on the last day of this year, Roebuck experienced the following three cash transactions in addition to those already included above. What would be the resulting figures for operations, investing, financing, and change in cash for the year? (1) A customer who had been very slow in paying came in and paid an old account receivable of $50,000. (2) The company got additional bank loan financing of $120,000. (3) The company issued new shares valued at $75,000 in exchange for a small plot of land it wanted for expansion of its factory. (The first item is an operating receipt, increasing cash from operations by $50,000. The second is a financing inflow, increasing cash from financing by $120,000. The third does not involve any cash and so would not be reflected in the cash flow statement. Results: Cash from operations now $2,210,280, cash for investing unchanged at $(5,533,310), cash from financing now $2,726,360, change in cash now $(596,670).)

4.5   CASH FLOW ANALYSIS USING ADJUSTED ACCRUAL INCOME AND BALANCE SHEET CHANGES

The direct method illustrated in section 4.4 just requires information from the cash records. But in fact the cash flow statement has traditionally been prepared, and presented, in quite a different way, by analyzing changes in the balance sheet and combining that analysis with information from the income and retained earnings statements. This is done for many reasons, including tradition, but also because, in practice, digging out the details of cash receipts and payments over a whole year

The indirect method has been used in preparing most companies' cash flow statements.

Because of double entry, changes in cash must be explained by changes in all other accounts.

The indirect method determines changes in all noncash balance sheet accounts, eliminating those not involving cash.

can be a large task, especially if there are several or many cash and bank accounts, as is true for most medium to large companies. The indirect method is explained in this section, because without understanding it, you will be mystified by the format of the cash from operations section of most published cash flow statements. The analysis also will help polish your analytical skill and knowledge of the other statements, as well as your insight about what cash flow analysis depicts.

The indirect method relies on a basic property of double-entry accounting. Since cash is one of the accounts that make up a balanced balance sheet, any change in cash must be *exactly* reflected in one or more *other* balance sheet accounts. So we can analyze cash changes by looking instead at *changes in all the other accounts in the balance sheet*: those changes will tell us what the company did with its cash.

The indirect method uses this basic approach: construct the cash flow statement by placing all balance sheet account changes in the appropriate categories of the cash flow statement after adjusting for (eliminating) all noncash components of those account changes. This method can handle great complexity, and accountants have procedures to ensure that no changes are forgotten in the analysis, but such complexities and procedures are beyond the scope of this book. The schedule below shows how the indirect method works for the categories of the cash flow statement. Brief additional explanations follow the schedule, then the Roebuck Industries example is redone using the indirect method.

Exhibit

Categorization of the Changes in Noncash Balance Sheet Accounts

Operating activities:
>   Start with net income or if different, income from continuing operations for this period (part of the retained earnings change)

>   Adjustments to eliminate noncash components of income:
>> Remove revenues and expenses (usually nonoperating) that are entirely noncash: gains and losses, write-downs and write-offs of investments and noncurrent assets in general

>> Remove revenues and expenses that relate to noncurrent past or future cash flows: amortization (asset cost paid in the past), and future costs to be paid (future income taxes, warranties, pension costs, etc.)

>> Remove the effects on accrual income of working capital account changes: accounts receivable, inventories, prepaid expenses, accounts payable, estimated accrued liabilities, etc., and investments whose trading is part of operations

Investing activities:
>   Additions to plant and equipment and intangible and other assets, minus any amounts not yet (or ever) paid in cash and so still showing as payable

>   Proceeds from disposal of plant and equipment and intangible and other assets (account changes due to elimination of cost and accumulated amortization of disposed assets are ignored because they are not cash items)

4-4

Exhibit
(continued)

> Additions to and proceeds of disposal of mainly noncurrent
>   investments
>
> **Financing activities:**
>   Changes in current and noncurrent debt financing, minus any parts
>   not involving cash (such as exchanges for shares or noncash
>   assets)
>   Changes in share capital, minus any parts not involving cash (such as
>   exchanges for debt or noncash assets)
>   Changes in retained earnings *other than* net income for this period:
>   dividends, share issue costs, etc., minus any parts not paid in cash
>   (e.g. stock dividends or dividends payable)

Comments on some items above will be useful, then we will look at an example of how the indirect method works.

Changes in equity and liabilities relate positively to changes in cash. Changes in assets relate negatively to changes in cash: up together, down together.

Asset changes negatively relate to cash changes: assets up so cash down, assets down so cash up.

Income positively relates to cash changes: up together, down together.

The indirect cash from operations calculation starts with net income and removes all the accruals that differ it from cash income.

1. Changes in liabilities and equity have the same sign as changes in cash, whereas changes in noncash assets have the opposite sign. This should be intuitively sensible: borrowing money, for example, increases the debt liability and the cash, and paying the debt back reduces both. Issuing shares also increases cash, and dividends both reduce equity and reduce cash when they are paid. On the other hand, paying cash for a new asset increases the asset but decreases cash, and reducing an asset (say by selling land or collecting accounts receivable) increases cash. Increasing noncash assets implies using cash to do so, and decreasing noncash assets implies getting cash for them.

2. Though accrual income does not necessarily increase cash right now, on average, earning income will increase cash. Again, the intuition should be clear. Earning income helps cash. If you find this a bit subtle, think of the opposite: surely it would not make sense to expect cash to go *down* when income goes up, or cash to go up when the company incurs a loss.

3. Given the starting point of net income, the adjustments A, B, and C to it in the operating activites part of Exhibit 4.4 just *remove* from income all the things that were done to create accrual income instead of cash income. These are the same sorts of adjustments we saw in section 1.8 when reconciling Simone's Jewellery accrual and cash incomes. Therefore, items that *increased* accrual income are *deducted* in these adjustments, such as gains on sale, increases in accounts receivable (uncollected revenue), and increases in inventory (unused goods). Conversely, items that *decreased* accrual income are *added* in these adjustments, such as amortization expense, asset write-downs and write-offs, and increases in accounts payable and accrued estimated liabilities.

4. The last point is a bit tricky, but actually is useful because it relates to how the stock market reacts to financial information. If a company makes a gain on the sale of a noncurrent asset, it does so because it received cash (or a promise of cash) exceeding the book value of the asset, that is, exceeding the net value of the asset's cost minus its accumulated amortization. A loss on sale happens if the cash is less than book value. Such an asset sale is recorded this way:

> Dr Cash (the proceeds)
>> Cr Asset cost (to remove the cost from the accounts)
>
> Dr Accumulated amortization (to remove the accumulated amortization from the accounts)
>
> Dr Loss or sale, or Cr Gain on sale (the difference between proceeds and book value)

Here's the tricky part. The gain or loss on sale, which is in the income statement and so is part of accrual net income, is *not* what we want on the cash flow statement, because it is not the cash part, it is just the *difference* between the cash and the book value. So the gain or loss has to be removed from the net income and the cash proceeds inserted instead, but in the *investing activities* section as it is not a result of day-to-day operations. A gain helped income, so it must be deducted from net income in the operating activities section to remove it. A loss reduced income, so it must be added back to net income to remove it. (The removal of the asset cost and the accumulated amortization is ignored in the cash flow analysis because neither is a cash item.) If a noncurrent asset, such as a factory or an investment in another company, is written down or written off because it is felt to have less or no value, the entry above has no "proceeds" amount, because there is no cash. So the whole amount of the write-down or write-off, which is in income, must be added back to net income in the operating activities section. This can drastically affect the difference between net income and cash from operations, because such write-downs and write-offs may be quite large (remember the Big Bath from Chapter 3, for example). If it is large, cash from operations might be quite positive even if accrual income was low or negative because of the write-down or write-off. Perhaps because of the lack of cash effect, the stock market often seems to ignore large write-offs, write-downs, or losses on disposal, not penalizing companies which report them on their income statements.

The indirect method's appeal may begin to appear to you from these points. By identifying the changes in noncash accounts (assets, liabilities, and equity), the analysis identifies where the company's cash came from and what the company did with the cash. This can all be done without having to go through the cash account(s) and write down what each transaction seemed to be for. Since the indirect method analyzes changes in the balance sheet (the statement of financial position), it analyzes changes in financial position and so the cash flow statement is frequently titled Statement of Changes in Financial Position (SCFP).

An Indirect Method Example: Roebuck Industries Again

Financial information about Roebuck Industries Inc., which we saw in the previous section about the direct method, is in Exhibit 4.5. As the indirect method is based on balance sheet *changes*, those are shown in Exhibit 4.5 (each change just equals this year's account balance minus last year's), plus the income statement (which is given more completely because several items in it are useful for the analysis) and the retained earnings *changes* from the retained earnings statement. All the changes must have some connection with cash flow—a purely noncash transaction such as issuing shares in return for land (Dr Land, Cr Share capital) is ignored, so assume any such purely noncash changes have been eliminated from the information in Exhibit 4.5.

4-5

Exhibit

ROEBUCK INDUSTRIES INC.
Balance Sheet Changes
(This Year Minus Last Year)

ASSETS

Current assets:

Cash down	$ (766,670)
Accounts receivable up	2,875,870
Inventory down	(1,225,770)

Noncurrent assets:

Asset cost up*	6,328,310
Accum. amortization up	(3,794,630)
TOTAL CHANGES	$ 3,417,110

LIABILITIES AND EQUITY

Current liabilities:

Accounts payable down	$(1,359,410)
Dividend payable up	100,000
Equipment payable** up	220,000

Noncurrent liabilities:

Bonded debt up	5,300,000
Other debt down	(3,112,300)

Equity:

Share capital up	840,000
Retained earnings up	1,428,820
TOTAL CHANGES	$ 3,417,110

* Cost change = $6,953,310 new assets minus $625,000
   cost of land sold.
** Owing on new assets acquired.

ROEBUCK INDUSTRIES INC.
Income Statement for the Year

Revenue	$20,843,720
Expenses:	
COGS, etc.	$14,390,490
Amortization	3,794,630
	$18,185,120
Operating income	$ 2,658,600
Gain on land sold*	575,000
Income before tax	$ 3,233,600
Income tax expense	1,283,440
Net income	$ 1,950,160

* Gain = $1,200,000 proceeds minus $625,000 land cost.

ROEBUCK INDUSTRIES INC.
Retained Earnings Changes for the Year

Add net income	$1,950,160
Deduct dividends declared*	(500,000)
Deduct costs of share issue	(21,340)
NET CHANGE	$1,428,820

* $100,000 owing at year-end.

Generating the cash flow statement from these changes requires putting the changes in the appropriate categories of the cash flow statement and eliminating any noncash items, as explained earlier in this section. The result is a cash flow statement that has exactly the same category totals as the example in section 4.4, and differs from that statement only in the way cash from operations is derived. (The statement in Exhibit 4.6 includes various explanations to help you follow what is going on—these would not usually be shown on a statement because accountants assume the reader of the statement has some understanding of how the statement is assembled. Also, in this example we do not have the figures for beginning and ending cash for the bottom of the statement, but those would be included normally because the accountant has access to the actual balance sheets, not just the changes used in this example.)

ROEBUCK INDUSTRIES INC.

Cash Flow Statement for This Year (Indirect Method)

Operating activities:

Net income for the year	$ 1,950,160
Deduct noncash revenue to eliminate it: gain on land sale	(575,000)
Add back noncash expense to eliminate it: amortization	3,794,630
Deduct increase in accounts receivable to eliminate its effect	(2,875,870)
Add back reduction in inventory to eliminate its effect	1,225,770
Deduct decrease in accounts payable to eliminate its effect	(1,359,410)
Cash obtained from operations	$ 2,160,280

Investing activities:

Acquisitions of new noncurrent assets ($6,953,310 – $220,000)	$(6,733,310)
Proceeds from sale of land	1,200,000
Cash used for investing	$(5,533,310)

Financing activities:

Proceeds from issue of new bonded debt	$ 5,300,000
Repayments on noncurrent debt	(3,112,300)
Proceeds from issue of new shares	840,000
Costs of new share issue	(21,340)
Dividends paid ($500,000 – $100,000)	(400,000)
Cash obtained from financing	$ 2,606,360
Change in cash for the year	$ (766,670)

Take a few moments and go through the balance sheet changes for Roebuck Industries. You'll see that every change is somewhere on the cash flow statement:

- The change in cash is the cash flow statement's "bottom line."

- Decreases in noncash assets and increases in liabilities and equity are all positive in their effects on cash. The opposites, increases in noncash assets and decreases in liabilities and equity, are all negative in their effects.

- The change in retained earnings has three components: net income, share issue costs, and dividends. They are all on the cash flow statement. Income is combined with several other changes to get cash from operations. Dividends are combined with the change in dividends payable to get dividends paid.

- The change in noncurrent assets cost is there too. The cost of new assets ($6,953,310 according to the footnote) is combined with the change in equipment payable to get the cash spent on new assets, $6,733,310. The cost of the old land removed is also represented, because that $625,000 is replaced on the cash flow statement by two amounts: the positive $1,200,000 cash proceeds and the negative $575,000 gain deduction, which net to $625,000.

Every balance sheet change is appropriately represented on the cash flow statement.

- The $3,794,630 change in accumulated amortization, which looks as though it increases cash on the cash flow statement, does not really do that; it is there in operating activities to *cancel out* the effect on income of having deducted the noncash amortization expense in calculating the net income.

The indirect method statement is not much different from the direct version, except in the operations section, but that section does highlight some issues not obvious from the direct version. One is the difference between accrual accounting income and cash income (cash from operations): accrual income is slightly lower here, but in many cases is quite different. Another is the effect of changes in working capital accounts. Roebuck has tied up $2,875,870 of additional cash by letting the accounts receivable grow, and has used another $1,359,410 by paying off more accounts payable. On the other hand, there is $1,225,770 less cash tied up in inventory.

 OW'S YOUR UNDERSTANDING?

Here are two questions you should be able to answer, based on what you have just read:

1. What are the kinds of adjustments the indirect method makes to net income, and why are they done?

2. Suppose Roebuck Industries Inc. experienced the following transactions on the last day of this year, in addition to those already included above. What would be the resulting figures for operations, investing, financing, and change in cash for the year? (1) The company bought more inventory on credit for $60,000. (2) The company issued more shares for $130,000 cash. (3) The company paid off its equipment loan, causing a temporary bank overdraft. (The first item reduces both the inventory decrease and the accounts payable decrease by the same amount, having no net effect on cash from operations, which is appropriate because there was no cash involved. The second item raises the proceeds from new shares by $130,000 and reduces the negative cash change by the same amount. The third item eliminates the equipment loan change and so increases cash paid for new assets by $220,000 to $6,953,310. The second and third items together cause a net reduction in cash of $90,000, changing the total cash change to negative $856,670. If we go back to Roebuck's cash account information in section 4.4, we can see that cash on hand at the end of the year is now negative ($46,760 − $90,000 = $(43,240)) because of the temporary bank overdraft, included in the cash and equivalents calculation.)

4.6   A SECOND ADJUSTED INCOME AND BALANCE SHEET CHANGES CASH FLOW EXAMPLE

Just to be sure you have the basic idea of using balance sheet changes and net income adjustments to analyze cash flow, let's do a second example. Below are the balance sheet changes for Simplistic Enterprises Ltd., and then the cash flow statement derived from them. The cash flow statement includes some comments to help you see what each cash flow item stands for.

4-7

Exhibit

Simplistic Enterprises Ltd.
Balance Sheets for 2001 and 2000,
with Changes Calculated

	2001	2000	Change
Assets			
Current assets:			
Cash	$150	$130	$20
Accounts receivable	200	160	40
Noncurrent assets:			
Building cost	500	420	80
Accumulated amortization*	(180)	(130)	(50)
	$670	$580	$90
Liabilities and Equity			
Current liabilities:			
Temporary bank overdraft	$ 10	$ 25	$(15)
Accounts payable	110	65	45
Noncurrent liabilities:			
Mortgage debt	140	175	(35)
Future income tax	100	90	10
Equity:			
Share capital issued	100	85	15
Retained earnings**	210	140	70
	$670	$580	$90

* The change in accumulated amortization is due to $50 in amortization expense deducted in determining 2001 accrual income.

** According to the statement of retained earnings, the change in retained earnings is due to the 2001 net income of $95 having been added to the 2000 balance, minus dividends paid of $25.

4-8

Exhibit

**Simplistic Enterprises Ltd.
Statement of Changes in Financial Position
(with additional comments)
for the Year 2001**

Operations

Net income for the year (accrual net income as shown in the income statement and part of the change in retained earnings on the balance sheet)	$ 95
Add back amortization expense (the change in accumulated amortization: this expense reduced accrual income but did not reduce cash income so adding it back helps to calculate cash income)	50
Add back future income tax expense (the change in the liability: as for amortization, this expense did not reduce cash income so adding it back also helps to calculate cash income)	10
Deduct the change in accounts receivable (the receivables are higher, so some of the 2001 income is from revenue that has not been collected, so cash income was lower because of the cash that has not yet come in)	(40)
Add change in accounts payable (the higher payables mean that some of the expenses deducted from 2001 income have not yet been paid, saving cash for now and meaning cash income was higher because of that)	45
Cash generated from operations (cash income)	$160

Investing

Increased investment in the building (increasing a noncurrent asset would have taken cash, so this has a negative effect in the SCFP)	$ (80)

Financing

Decrease in mortgage debt (reducing the mortgage would have taken cash)	$ (35)
Increase in share capital (this would have brought cash)	15
Dividends paid during the year (part of the change in retained earnings)	$ (25)
Net cash used in financing	$ (45)

Net total change in cash and cash equivalents for the year	$ 35
Cash and equivalents, beginning of the year	105
Cash and equivalents, end of the year	$140
Cash and equivalents consist of:	
Cash	$150
Minus temporary bank overdraft	(10)
Cash and equivalents	$140

The cash flow statement is an insightful analysis. Just by rearranging the balance sheet changes between two dates (2000 and 2001), we have produced several pieces of information:

- Simplistic increased its cash and equivalents by $35 during the year: cash went up by $20 and the temporary bank overdraft went down by $15.

- This increase was entirely due to day-to-day operations because investing and financing activities both reduced cash.

- Cash from operations ($160) was nearly twice the accrual net income ($95) because the net income was reduced by noncash expenses for amortization and future income taxes. It is normal for cash from operations to exceed net income because of such expenses.

- Cash from operations would have been even higher had Simplistic collected more of its accounts receivable. On the other hand, the company hung onto some cash by not paying some accounts payable.

- The company spent $80 on its building during the year, which was more than the $50 amortization expense. This is evidence that the company is keeping its building up to date, not just letting its value decline through use.

- The company raised some cash by issuing shares ($15), but that was more than offset by the $35 needed to make payments on the mortgage principal during the year and the $25 in dividends paid.

The cash flow analysis shows us why the company's net income of $95 did not produce an equal increase in cash. Many more things were going on involving cash.

 OW'S YOUR UNDERSTANDING?

Here are two questions you should be able to answer, based on what you have just read:

1. What does the cash flow statement's analysis show beyond the performance portrayed in the income statement?

2. Horizon Inc. has the following results and balance sheet changes from last year to this year. Calculate the three categories of the cash flow statement and determine the total change in cash and equivalents for the year. Net income for the year, $23,950; dividends declared and paid, $9,250; amortization expense, $16,900; future income tax expense, $2,200; increase in cost of noncurrent assets, $57,260; increase in accounts receivable, $1,205; increase in accounts payable, $4,320; increase in mortgage debt, $10,000; increase in share capital, $15,000. (Cash from operations = $23,950 + $16,900 + $2,200 − $1,205 + $4,320 = $46,165. Cash used in investing = $57,260. Cash from financing = $25,000 − $9,250 = $15,750. Net total change in cash = $46,165 − $57,260 + $15,750 = $4,655 increase.)

4.7   INTERPRETING A COMPANY'S CASH FLOW STATEMENT

In Chapters 2 and 3, we saw the comparative balance sheets, income statements, and statements of retained earnings of CAE Inc. Now let's see what the company's cash flow statement has to tell us (see Exhibit 4.9, which includes Note 10 on noncash working capital changes, but not other notes).

CAE Inc.
Consolidated Statements of Cash Flow

Years ended March 31 (amounts in millions of dollars)	2000	1999 (note 1)
Operating activities		
Earnings from continuing operations	$ 90.7	$ 73.7
Adjustments to reconcile net earnings to cash flows from operating activities:		
Amortization	33.7	28.6
Deferred income taxes	(7.6)	(1.6)
Other	(0.3)	(2.0)
Decrease (increase) in non-cash working capital (note 10)	133.5	(70.3)
Cash provided by continuing operating activities	250.0	28.4
Investing activities		
Proceeds on disposition of business unit (note 2)	52.5	–
Acquisitions (note 15)	–	(111.5)
Short-term investments	(71.1)	–
Capital expenditures	(30.9)	(76.3)
Proceeds from sale and leaseback of assets	35.5	–
Other	(11.4)	(4.1)
Net cash used in continuing investing activities	(25.4)	(191.9)
Financing activities		
Proceeds from (repayments of) long-term debt borrowings	(5.5)	8.7
Dividends paid, net of stock dividends	(20.4)	(17.6)
Purchase of capital stock	(36.3)	–
Other	0.2	(3.5)
Net cash used in continuing financing activities	(62.0)	(12.4)
Net cash used in discontinued operations (note 2)	(21.6)	(8.9)
Effect of foreign exchange rate changes on cash	(3.1)	7.6
Net increase (decrease) in cash	137.9	(177.2)
Cash at beginning of year	25.6	202.8
Cash at end of year	$163.5	$25.6

(See note 10 below. Other indicated notes are not included in this book.)

Note 10 Supplementary Cash Flow Information
        Cash provided from (used for) non-cash working capital:

	2000	1999
Accounts receivable	$ (54.6)	$ 8.7
Inventories	9.3	(28.4)
Prepaid expenses	0.3	(9.4)
Income taxes recoverable	10.9	(10.6)
Accounts payable and accrued liabilities	88.4	(70.7)
Deposits on contracts	79.2	40.1
	$133.5	$(70.3)
Net cash paid during the year for		
Income taxes	$ 0.5	$ 16.8
Interest	$ 13.1	$ 12.7

This is a consolidated statement, as were CAE's other statements. Therefore, it describes the cash flows of the group of companies making up CAE. For CAE, cash is uncomplicated, being defined as just the cash asset, which you can verify by looking back at the balance sheet in section 2.9. An immediately striking piece of information is that CAE's change in cash went from negative $177.2 million in 1999 to positive $137.9 million in 2000, a positive swing of over $300 million. What caused this?

The first major factor behind this swing in cash is in Operating activities. In 1999, cash from operations was $28.4 million, whereas in 2000, it rose to $250 million. Income (continuing operations—see the income statement in section 3.4) rose less than $20 million, so that doesn't explain the great change in cash. The big difference is in the noncash working capital changes adjustment, which was negative $70.3 million in its effect on cash in 1999, but positive $133.5 million in 2000, accounting for over $200 million of the cash improvement. Note 10 gives us some details. Nearly every working capital account changed significantly. On the negative side, accounts receivable went up by $54.6 million in 2000, postponing the receipt of that much cash from customers who owed CAE money. But the company more than made up for that with its great increase in accounts payable: those had gone down $70.7 million in 1999 but instead went up by $88.4 million in 2000, a change of nearly $160 million. As there is not usually interest to pay on accounts payable, this represents a major, and cheap, form of financing for CAE in 2000.

The cash analysis indicates that much was going on in CAE's noncash working capital accounts.

The company also reduced the cash tied up in every other current asset account: inventories were reduced $9.3 million, prepaid expenses were down a bit, $0.3 million, and the income taxes recoverable were reduced (collected) $10.9 million. As another offset to the increase in accounts receivable, the company's cash benefited from having $79.2 million more in customer deposits than in 1999, which itself had shown a $40.1 million increase over 1998. Probably the accounts receivable and customer deposits are related: the same customer who ordered more flight simulators and made a deposit on them would probably not be chased too hard to pay up for simulators already shipped.

The cash flow statement includes information based on detailed data not in the other statements.

If you look back at the balance sheet in section 2.9, you'll see that these year 2000 changes in noncash working capital accounts don't seem to match the changes you'd calculate from the balance sheet directly. For example, the change in accounts receivable in the balance sheet is $325.3 – $266.2 million = $59.1 million up, not the $54.6 million up that Note 10 reports. All the other changes in Note 10 also differ somewhat from those you'd calculate from the balance sheet accounts. What is going on? CAE seems to have classified some changes in Note 10 differently than in the balance sheet, probably due to offsets between accounts receivable and payable or customer deposits, or perhaps leftovers from the company's big acquisition drive in 1999 (when $111.5 million was spent on acquisitions of other companies, including their accounts receivable, inventories, etc., now added into the consolidated accounts we see). If you go to the balance sheet and add up all the changes it shows in the six accounts listed in Note 10, you get a net total change of $135.6 million, which is pretty close to the $133.5 million in Note 10. This is an important point about cash flow statements: they use detailed account information not available from just reading the balance sheet and so usually cannot be reproduced exactly from balance sheet account changes without having that detailed information. The cash flow statement therefore adds some information not available from just looking at balance sheet changes.

Like the other statements, the cash flow statement separates continuing and discontinued operations.

Another kind of added information comes from the attempt to separate continuing from discontinued operations in the income statement, which we saw in section 3.4. If you are going to separate the income statement items, it also makes sense to separate the balance sheet accounts for business units being discontinued. The balance sheet in section 2.9 shows that there were net discontinued operations assets of $105.2 million at the end of 2000, and $147.6 million at the end of 1999. Note 2 (not included in this book) tells us that some of these assets were current assets, and that in calculating the net assets, some current liabilities were deducted. Since these items are separated on the income statement and balance sheet, it makes sense to separate them on the cash flow statement too, and so you see near the bottom of the cash flow statement a line "Net cash used in discontinued operations," $(21.6) million. This is a reminder that cash from operations is cash from *continuing* operations.

The investing activities section shows several significant management decisions.

Looking at the investing activities section of the cash flow statement, the company's investing activities cost $25.4 million cash in 2000, a big decline from the $192.9 million used in 1999. The company made no acquisitions of other companies in 2000, after buying a lot in 1999, reduced its capital expenditures on property and plant from the 1999 level, and sold off some assets that it then leased back (trading a cash inflow now for greater outflows in the future for lease payments). The discontinuing of operations appears again, the investing section of the statement showing that $52.5 million were brought in from selling off a business unit. Short-term investments are an interesting investing activity. These were increased from zero at the end of 1999 to $71.1 million at the end of 2000. While this took cash, these investments are pretty close to being cash (they're shown right after cash on the balance sheet), and so represent a pool of near-cash assets that is almost 50% of the strictly cash assets. These investments would have been included in cash had they had maturities less than three months, so we can deduce that these have maturities between three and twelve months: enough to qualify as current assets but not enough to qualify as cash.

The financing activities section also reports significant management decisions.

Turning to financing activities, we see that, as in 1999, financing activities cost CAE cash in 2000, rather than bringing it more cash as you might expect financing to do. The two main items here were paying dividends and buying back shares. Not a major financing story here, though we might wonder why the company thought buying its own shares was a good use of its cash. (Having fewer shares outstanding means that earnings per share will be higher for the same level of net income, and companies have been known to buy back some of their shares so that EPS will rise. More positively, the company may have felt that during a temporary stock market downturn, buying its own shares would be a good investment!)

Cash flow analysis provides insight into business strategy as well as plain cash management.

The cash flow analysis has therefore revealed several important things about CAE and its business strategy that were not so apparent from the balance sheets and income statements. If we'd wanted to work at those statements, we could have derived some of the information (not all, as some was included in account balance changes that we could not see readily from the other statements). But the cash flow statement saves us the trouble, as long as we know how to read it. We have learned, among other things:

- CAE raised millions of dollars in cash in 2000, but spent only about half of it, so that cash increased during the year. This is a contrast with 1999, when the company raised little cash and spent a lot.

- In contrast with 1999, CAE had a large inflow of cash from continuing operations. This was largely due to letting accounts payable increase greatly in 2000, whereas in 1999 cash was used to get the accounts payable down. (Accounts payable had increased a lot in 1998, similar to the 2000 result.)

- The company did not need any new noncurrent or equity financing in 2000 (or in 1998), meeting its cash needs mostly from operations. The only non-operating sources of cash were from selling off a business unit and selling some assets that were then leased back.

- The company showed rather a cyclical pattern in its cash flows. Not apparent from this year's cash flow statement, cash built up in 1998 (from letting accounts payable rise), then, as this cash flow statement does show, in 1999 the cash was spent largely on acquisitions and getting accounts payable down again. In 2000, cash built up again, with accounts payable increases playing a major role again, and there were no acquisitions. Instead, the little spending of cash was for some capital expenditures, paying dividends and buying back CAE's own shares.

- Understanding the company's cash situation requires careful reading of the cash flow statement, because one of the uses of cash was to make large short-term investments. These are close to being cash, so they can be seen as a way to get a little interest income on excess cash. Adding those $71.1 million in investments to the year-end cash of $163.5 indicates that the company's liquid assets are nearly $235 million at the end of 2000, a substantial amount and higher than at the end of 1998, prior to 1999's acquisitions. Might the company be building up a cash hoard for more acquisitions in 2001, or will the cash be used more prosaically to reduce accounts payable?

- CAE's spending on property and plant indicates that assets are being kept up to date. Capital expenditures in 2000 were about the same as amortization expense, after having been much larger than amortization expense in 1999, so 2000 was a leaner year for keeping assets up to date than 1999 was.

- The company's transactions with shareholders included maintaining dividends and buying back some shares, to reduce its share capital.

- Cash from operations (cash income) was much greater than accrual net income in 2000, largely because of increases in accounts payable. This was the reverse of the situation in 1999, when accrual income was greater than cash income. The company's accrual income is much less variable than its widely varying cash income.

HOW'S YOUR UNDERSTANDING?

Here are two questions you should be able to answer, based on what you have just read:

1. CAE did not rely on external financing in 2000. How can we tell this?

2. Which figures on the cash flow statement would you compare to get an indication of whether a company appears to be renewing its noncurrent assets as they lose their value through use?

4.8   CASH FLOW AND THE MANAGER

Cash flow and income are related, but not the same, especially in the short run.

Managers are responsible not only for earning income for the company, but also for managing cash so that bills can be paid on time, excess borrowing and interest costs can be avoided, and the company's liquidity and solvency can be generally protected. Effectively employing available cash so that it does not remain idle, earning nothing, is also important. Cash flow and income are generally positively correlated (good performance tends to move them both up, and poor performance tends to move them both down), and over a long enough time (years), they are almost the same. But in the short run their relationship can be complex, as these two examples illustrate:

Long-run profitability may depend on the short-run cash situation.

1. A few years ago, Quebec increased gasoline taxes to a higher rate than that in Ontario. This caused immediate problems for Quebec gas stations near the Ontario border: driving a few kilometres to buy gas in Ontario made a big difference in the price, unless a Quebec gas station owner decided to "swallow" the difference in tax. A CBC reporter interviewed a Quebec owner and asked, "What are the implications of this for your long-run profitability?" The owner said, "Unless I can get some cash in the short run, there isn't going to be a long run!"

Sometimes new businesses with growing income have cash problems.

2. A problem new businesses can have is to grow too fast. Often the product demand and the entrepreneurial enthusiasm are high: the business was founded in the hope that people would want the product or service, and it is exciting to everyone when they do! The income statements of such businesses often show high profits (net incomes), but the cash flow statement and the balance sheet may tell a different story. In the enthusiasm of making sales and satisfying customers, inventory levels often get too high (making sure there is something for everyone on hand) and collections from customers often lag (receivables get too high as the entrepreneur concentrates on the pleasures of selling rather than the nuisance of collecting). The accrual income-based cash flow analysis deducts the increases in inventories and receivables from accrual-basis net income, and may show that operating cash flows are small or even negative. When this happens, you do not need a cash flow statement to know you are in trouble: your bank balance tells you that! But the cash flow statement reports the whole story to others, so that they can see what you have accomplished in obtaining and using cash in your operating, financing, and investing activities. You then have to be prepared to explain such activities to users of the financial statements.

The cash flow statement provides a measure of managerial performance in managing cash, so smart managers must be aware of how their efforts are reflected in it, just as they are aware of the income statement and balance sheet measures of performance and position.

F OR YOUR INTEREST

Stock market prices do seem to respond to cash flow information in addition to income.

There has been increasing research on the value of the cash flow statement, mostly in connection with public companies' share price changes (buy-and-sell decisions by investors). Most research, so far, defines cash flow simply as net income plus amortization (depreciation) expense. Such research usually finds that share prices do respond a little to the added information. While most of the share price response is to the earnings (accrual net income) figure, some response to the cash flow information has also been found.[1]

4.9   REVISITING CASH BASIS VS. ACCRUAL BASIS ACCOUNTING

This section returns to ideas first encountered in the Simone's Jewellery example in section 1.8 and referred to since: the comparison of cash basis and accrual basis accounting. It aims to consolidate your knowledge of cash flow analysis, and should also help your understanding of how accrual accounting works by augmenting records of cash receipts and disbursements. Income tax is ignored, to avoid cluttering up the example.

Information for Goblin Consulting Ltd. for this year is:

Exhibit

Cash in bank, end of last year		$ 2,800
Cash receipts:		
Collections on last year's revenue	$ 1,600	
Collections on this year's revenue	75,200	
Deposit received on next year's revenue	1,000	
Long-term debt issued	6,000	
Sale of old equipment (proceeds)	500	$84,300
		$87,100
Cash disbursements:		
Payment of last year's expenses	$ 900	
Payment of this year's expenses	61,300	
Advance payment on next year's expenses	2,200	
Payments on long-term debt	3,000	
Purchase of new equipment	14,000	81,400
Cash in bank, end of this year		$ 5,700
Increase in cash during the year ($5,700 − $2,800)		$ 2,900
Additional information:		
Equipment amortization for this year	$ 3,100	
Uncollected revenue at the end of this year	2,500	
Unpaid expenses at the end of this year	1,700	
Book value of old equipment at date of sale	300	
Gain on sale of equipment (proceeds		
− book value = $500 − $300)	200	

If we did a cash basis income statement for this year, we would get something like this:

Operating receipts ($1,600 + $75,200 + $1,000)	$77,800
Operating expenditures ($900 + $61,300 + $2,200)	64,400
Cash income for this year	$13,400

There are also:

- Nonoperating receipts of $6,500 ($6,000 debt + $500 proceeds); and

- Nonoperating expenditures of $17,000 ($3,000 debt payments + $14,000 new equipment).

If we added and subtracted those from $13,400, we'd get the total increase in cash during the year of $2,900:

Cash income	$13,400
Nonoperating receipts	6,500
Less nonoperating expenditures	(17,000)
Increase in cash during the year	$ 2,900

In contrast, the accrual basis income statement for this year would look like this, recognizing this year's earned revenues and incurred expenses:

Revenue ($75,200 cash sales + $2,500 uncollected)		$77,700
Expenses:		
General ($61,300 paid + $1,700 unpaid)	$63,000	
Amortization (specified above)	3,100	66,100
Operating income		$11,600
Gain on sale of equipment (calculated above)		200
Income for this year		$11,800

Because both cash flow and accrual figures are important, we want people to be able to understand how they are related to each other, and how they differ. That is what the cash flow statement is for. Here's what that statement for this year would look like:

Operations:		
Income for the year (accrual basis)		$11,800
Add back noncash expense (amortization)		3,100
Deduct back gain on sale (cash is in "proceeds" below)		(200)
		$14,700
Changes in noncash working capital accounts:		
Accounts receivable (up $2,500 – $1,600)	$ (900)	
Prepaid expenses ($2,200 now, none last year)	(2,200)	
Deferred revenue ($1,000 now, none last year)	1,000	
Accounts payable (up $1,700 – $900)	800	(1,300)
Cash from operations		$13,400
Investing:		
Purchases of new equipment	$(14,000)	
Proceeds from equipment sale	500	$(13,500)
Financing:		
Issue of long-term debt	$ 6,000	
Repayment of long-term debt	(3,000)	3,000
Increase in cash for this year		$ 2,900
Cash at beginning of this year		2,800
Cash at end of this year		$ 5,700

You can see that the cash flow statement's $13,400 "cash from operations" figure (which is derived from the $11,800 accrual basis income) is what you'd have as your cash income had you done the income statement on the cash basis. This was also demonstrated with the diagram at the end of section 4.3 and the two ways of doing the Roebuck Industries cash flow statements in sections 4.4 and 4.5. The cash flow statement **reconciles** the two ways of calculating income. The statement also provides the rest of the information (investing and financing) to allow you to see the total effects on cash for the year.

Therefore, with the accrual basis income statement plus the cash flow statement, you get the broader economic measure of performance that accrual accounting provides, as well as cash flow information with which to evaluate the company's cash management. The set of financial statements provides an integrated, mutually reinforcing package of information.

OW'S YOUR UNDERSTANDING?

Here are two questions you should be able to answer, based on what you have just read:

1. The owner of Frenzied Productions Inc. was looking at the company's income statement and said, "I understand this statement was prepared using accrual accounting. What does accrual accounting try to do, and why isn't it good enough just to report my company's cash receipts and disbursements?" Briefly answer the owner's question.

2. In 2001, Frenzied collected $53,430 from customers for sales made in 2000 and $421,780 for sales made in 2001. In 2002, it collected $46,710 from customers for sales made in 2001. At that point, all 2000 and 2001 sales had been collected. What were the operating cash receipts for 2001 and the accrual accounting revenue for 2001? ($475,210; $468,490)

4.10 TERMS TO BE SURE YOU UNDERSTAND

Again, here are important terms introduced or emphasized in this chapter. Make sure you know what they mean *in accounting*. If any are unclear to you, check the chapter again or refer to the Glossary of Terms at the back of the book. As was the case for the terms in Chapters 1, 2, and 3, many of these will be used repeatedly as the book proceeds, so your understanding of them will deepen.

Accrual income
Cash and equivalents
Cash flow statement
Cash from operations
Cash income
Cash payments
Cash receipts
Change in cash
Direct method of cash flow analysis
Disbursements
Financing activities

Funds statement
Indirect method of cash flow analysis
Investing activities
Liquidity
Nonoperating cash flows
Operating activities
Reconcile(s)
SCFP
Solvency
Statement of changes in financial position
Statement of source and application of cash

4.11 CONTINUING DEMONSTRATION CASE

INSTALLMENT 4

Data for Installment 4

In order to prepare for the board of directors' meeting, Tomas thought it would be a good idea to be able to explain what had happened to the company's cash during the first six months. As a reference, here is the comparative balance sheet we saw in Installment 3:

Mato Inc.
Balance Sheets as at August 31 and March 1, 2000

Assets	August	March	Liabilities and Shareholders' Equity	August	March
Current assets:			Current liabilities:		
Cash	$ 4,507	$130,000	Bank loan	$ 75,000	$ 0
Receivables	$ 18,723	0	Payables	45,616	1,100
Inventory	73,614	0	Loan payable	15,000	15,000
	$ 96,844	$130,000		$135,616	$ 16,100
Noncurrent assets:			Shareholders' equity:		
Equip. cost	$ 54,640	$ 10,000	Share capital	$125,000	$125,000
Equip. acc. amort.	(3,234)	0	Deficit	(49,378)	0
Leasehold (net)*	57,568	0		$ 75,622	$125,000
Software (net)**	4,320	0			
Incorp. costs	1,100	1,100			
	$114,394	$ 11,100			
TOTAL	$211,238	$141,100	TOTAL	$211,238	$141,100

* Net book value of leasehold improvements = $63,964 cost − $6,396 accumulated amortization.
** Net book value of software = $4,800 − $480 accumulated amortization.

Tomas decided that for his cash analysis, he would define cash and equivalents as just cash, because the demand bank loan was a source of financing the company would likely rely on for some time, and was not like a temporary bank overdraft. He began his analysis by identifying the changes in financial position since March 1, which resulted in the analysis below.

Changes in Financial Position between March 1 and August 31, 2000

Changes in Assets		Changes in Liabilities and Equity	
Cash	$(125,493)	Bank loan	$75,000
Receivables	18,723	Payables	44,516
Inventory	73,614	Loan payable	0
Equipment cost*	44,640	Share capital	0
Accum. amort.**	(3,234)	Deficit	(49,378)
Leasehold cost	63,964		
Accum. amort.**	(6,396)		
Software cost	4,800		
Accum. amort.**	(480)		
Incorp. costs	0		
	$ 70,138		$70,138

 * Computer, $14,900; other equipment and furniture, $29,740.
** The changes in accumulated amortization were all due entirely to amortization expenses recorded for the period.

Results for Installment 4

Tomas then wrote down all the categories of the cash flow statement and filled in the appropriate figures, producing the statement shown below. *(The statement is shown in more detail than might be done in practice, so that you can trace every figure from the balance sheet change analysis above to the cash flow statement. Make sure you do this, to improve your understanding of the derivation and interpretation of the cash flow statement.)*

Mato Inc. Cash Flow Statement for the Six Months Ended August 31, 2000		
Operations:		
Net loss for the six months		$(49,378)
Add back amortization for the period		
($3,234 + $6,396 + $480)		10,110
		$(39,268)
Changes in noncash working capital accounts:		
Increase in accounts receivable	$(18,723)	
Increase in inventory	(73,614)	
Increase in accounts payable	44,516	(47,821)
Cash *used* in operations		$(87,089)
Investing activities:		
Equipment, computer, and furniture acquired	$(44,640)	
Leasehold improvements made	(63,964)	
Software acquired	(4,800)	(113,404)
Financing activities		
Bank loan obtained		75,000
Decrease in cash during the six months		$125,493
Cash on hand, March 1, 2000		130,000
Cash on hand		$ 4,507

The cash flow statement shows that the dramatic decline in cash has two causes.

- First, day-to-day operations produced a cash loss of $87,089. This was a combination of expenses exceeding revenues and the buildup of current assets, especially inventory. The increase in accounts payable helped to finance this, but even after, in essence, borrowing from suppliers, the company still fell far behind in its cash flow.

- Second, noncurrent asset acquisitions cost $113,404 in cash.

Without the bank loan, cash would have been negative $70,493. The company clearly has to get on top of its cash problems quickly.

4.12 HOMEWORK AND DISCUSSION TO DEVELOP UNDERSTANDING

PROBLEM 4.1*
Questions about cash flow statement and cash management

Answer the following questions briefly:

1. Why is managing cash flow important?
2. Can a company have a good net income and little cash generated from operations in the same year? If it can, how does this happen?
3. Why is cash generated from operations usually larger than net income?
4. What is "cash and equivalents"?

PROBLEM 4.2*
Cash flow basics plus some "what if" questions

1. What does the cash flow information in the cash flow statement tell you that you cannot get directly, if at all, from the income statement and balance sheet?
2. Beta Company's cash flow statement showed the following figures: Cash generated from operations, $127,976; Cash used in investing activities, $238,040; and Cash obtained in financing activities, $107,000. What was the net change in the company's cash for the year?
3. Indicate the effect on Beta Company's cash flow statement of each of the following events, if they had occurred during the year:
   a. What if a new truck was purchased at a cost of $38,950?
   b. What if $20,000 were borrowed long-term to help pay for the truck?
   c. What if collections of accounts receivable had been $6,000 less than actually happened?
   d. What if the company had paid an additional dividend of $15,000?
   e. What if the company borrowed $25,000 from the bank as a demand loan?
   f. What if the company had decided to record an additional $5,000 in amortization expense for the year?

PROBLEM 4.3*
Comment on a company's cash management

Axiomatic Inc.'s cash flow statement for last year is shown below. Make as many observations as you can about how the company managed its cash during the year.

Axiomatic Inc.
Cash Flow Statement for Last Year

Operations:		
Net income for the year		$ 94,900
Add back noncash expenses:		
Amortization expense	$216,800	
Deferred income tax expense	14,200	
Pension expense	38,900	269,900
Noncash working capital changes:		
Increase in accounts receivable	$(143,900)	
Increase in inventories	(71,600)	
Increase in accounts payable	87,000	(128,500)
Cash generated by operations		$236,300
Investing activities:		
Additions to noncurrent assets	$(429,100)	
Proceeds on disposal of noncurrent assets	27,700	(401,400)
Financing activities:		
Short-term bank loan	$ 30,000	
Additions to noncurrent debt	343,200	
Repayments of noncurrent debt	(316,000)	
Share capital issued	200,000	
Dividends paid during the year	(40,000)	217,200
Increase in cash for the year		$ 52,100
Cash, beginning of year		(93,500)
Cash, end of year		$ (41,400)

PROBLEM 4.4*
Cash flow analysis from account information

Prepare a cash flow statement from the following cash account information, which is in alphabetical order.

Bank loan obtained	60,000	Employee wages and salaries	
Cash expenses	8,920	paid	223,610
Cash sales	31,610	Income tax paid	14,920
Cash, beginning of year	68,920	Land purchased for cash	81,000
Cash, end of year	93,620	Payments to suppliers	513,600
Collections on accounts		Proceeds from sale of old	
receivable	797,640	truck	7,000
Common shares issued	140,000	Repayments on mortgage	80,500
Cost of redeeming preferred		Truck purchased	
shares	25,000	($5,000 still owing)	49,000
Dividends paid ($20,000			
declared)	15,000		

PROBLEM 4.5*
Correct a badly pre-
pared cash flow
statement

Fred talked his way into a job with Aragon Ltd., convincing the company's boss that he had enough accounting knowledge to do the company's accounting. All went well for a while: Fred managed to get the year's accounting done and came up with an appropriate balance sheet, income statement, and statement of retained earnings. But he just hasn't been able to get the cash flow statement to work out. He has calculated all the balance sheet changes correctly, but it just doesn't work out right. In response to a loud "Help!" you go over to Fred's desk to see if you can do anything. You find Fred's draft cash flow statement below, and you are able to determine that all his numbers are taken correctly from the other statements, so all that is needed is to rearrange Fred's draft and get everything in the right direction, and it should all work out.

Using Fred's draft, prepare a cash flow statement for Aragon Ltd. in proper format.

Aragon Ltd.
Draft Cash Flow Statement

Operations:		
Net income for the year		$216,350
Cash on hand		48,340
Less amortization for the year	$(218,890)	
Add deferred income tax expense	21,210	(197,680)
Working capital changes:		
Cash and equivalents	$ 62,070	
Increase in accounts receivable	(223,120)	
Decrease in inventory	80,200	
Decrease in accounts payable	91,970	
Increase in current income tax payable	(6,530)	4,590
Cash from operations		$ 71,600
Investing:		
Additions to noncurrent assets	$(393,980)	
Proceeds from sales of noncurrent assets	(11,260)	(405,240)
Financing:		
New noncurrent debt	$(250,500)	
Repayments of noncurrent debt	78,800	
Dividends paid	75,000	
Share capital issued	120,000	126,700
Change in cash for the year		$(206,940)

PROBLEM 4.6*
Prepare a cash flow
statement from bal-
ance sheet changes

Lambic Beverages Inc. makes special high-powered beers, some fermented in the bottle, and nonalcoholic sparkling drinks. Below are the company's balance sheets for the end of this year and last year, and some information about income and dividends during this year. From this information, prepare a cash flow statement for this year and comment on what it tells you. While you're at it, calculate the company's working capital ratio and debt–equity ratio for both years and comment on those, in relation to the cash flow analysis.

Lambic Beverages Inc. **Comparative Balance Sheets for This Year and Last Year**						
Assets			**Liabilities and Equity**			
	This Year	Last Year			This Year	Last Year
Current assets:			Current Liabilities:			
Cash	$ 560	$ 1,120	Bank loan		$ 400	$ 1,500
Accounts receivable	3,210	2,060	Accounts payable		7,240	6,220
Inventory	4,440	4,910	Income tax payable		0	330
	$ 8,210	$ 8,090			$ 7,640	$ 8,050
Noncurrent assets:			Noncurrent liabilities:			
Property and plant	$26,670	$24,820	Long-term debt		$12,740	$13,280
Accumulated amort.	(7,760)	(5,130)	Future income tax		1,320	1,070
	$18,910	$19,690			$14,060	$14,350
			Shareholders' equity:			
			Share capital		$ 1,500	$ 1,200
			Retained earnings		3,920	4,180
					$ 5,420	$ 5,380
	$27,120	$27,780			$27,120	$27,780

Other information:

- The company had a net loss of $210 for this year. Not expecting that, the company paid a $50 dividend early in the year.
- Amortization expense for the year was $2,630 and future income tax expense was $250.

PROBLEM 4.7*
Prepare a cash flow analysis from a narrative

You're having lunch with a family friend, the president of a local company you wouldn't mind working for some day. She starts to complain about the company's cash problems, and you decide to impress her by doing an analysis of those problems. So as she talks, you scribble the figures she mentions down on your napkin, with a plan to organize those into an analysis.

Here's what she said. Use the information to prepare a rough cash flow statement and then use that to provide helpful comments to her.

"You students often complain about being short of cash. The problem can affect companies too. Look at my company. Last year, we had $50,000 in the bank, a good solid position, and we didn't owe the bank anything. Now, we have only $5,000 and we owe the bank $90,000 in short-term loans, and I worry about how to pay the loans. It is hard to understand how we got into this difficulty. Part of it was because we had to finance a big expansion in our factory—that cost $600,000, and we only got $30,000 back from selling off some old equipment. The bank was sticky about lending money for the expansion, but we were able to increase our mortgage by $250,000, and we got another $100,000 from issuing some more shares. It was too bad we had the cash problems this year, because we had a good income, $100,000, and only paid out $40,000 of that in dividends. Our accountant said we brought in more cash than that, said it had to do with the $200,000 amortization, but I didn't really catch what that meant, because I know that amortization doesn't actually involve any cash. I do know that we have had increasing difficulty collecting from our customers, because some of them seem to have cash problems as well, so our accounts receivable are up $150,000 from last year. And the accountant said that our inventories were getting a bit high, being up $25,000 from last year. It's been frustrating—we earn income but don't seem to have cash!"

PROBLEM 4.8* **Prepare a cash flow statement for Northern Star Theatre**	Near the end of section 3.8, the balance sheet for Northern Star Theatre Company was presented, along with the income statement and statement of partners' capital for the first months of the partnership's existence. Use that information to prepare a cash flow statement for the partnership for the period to August 26, 2001.

PROBLEM 4.9*
Effects on cash flow statement of unpaid dividends and building disposal

1. You have just prepared a cash flow statement for Frogmorton Corp., and it works out to the correct change in cash and equivalents. You then discover that included in the current liabilities is an account for dividends payable that you had not realized was there. Explain why the cash from operations and financing figures on your cash flow statement are incorrect and why the total change in cash is correct in spite of your error.
2. You are struggling with the cash flow statement for Magdalen Inc. You know that the net total change in noncurrent assets over the year is an increase of $459,200 and that amortization expense for the year was $236,100. You then learn that during the year, the company sold a building for $200,000. The building had cost $840,000 and there was accumulated amortization on it of $650,000 at the date of sale.
   a. Calculate the apparent amount spent on acquisitions of noncurrent assets during the year.
   b. Calculate the gain or loss on the sale of the building.
   c. Specify the adjustments to income in the operations section of the cash flow statement arising from noncurrent assets.
   d. Specify the figures in the investing activities section of the cash flow statement.

PROBLEM 4.10*
Prove to given cash flow figures

The following summarized data are from Grantham Inc.'s financial statements. (CEA = cash and equivalent assets; OCA = other current assets; NCA = noncurrent assets; CEL = cash equivalent liabilities (temporary bank overdraft); OCL = other current liabilities; NCL = noncurrent liabilities; CAP = share capital; RET = retained earnings; REV = revenue; EXP = general expenses; INT = interest expense; NRE = nonoperating revenues and expenses; TAX = income tax expense; SEI = special and extraordinary items; INC = net income)

Assets			Liabilities & Equity			Income		
	1999	1998		1999	1998		1999	
CEA	$ 2,000	$ 1,000	CEL	$ 2,000	$ 3,000	REV	$125,000	
OCA	9,000	8,000	OCL	4,000	2,000	EXP	(84,000)	(amort.
								= $5,000)
NCA	37,000	32,000	NCL	17,000	18,000	INT	(2,000)	
			CAP	12,000	10,000	NRE	4,000**	
			RET*	13,000	8,000	TAX	(19,000)	(future
								= $3,000)
						SEI	(13,000)***	
	$48,000	$41,000		$48,000	$41,000	INC	$ 11,000	

*   Dividend of $6,000 was declared and paid in 1999.
** $4,000 nonoperating income is a gain on an NCA sale: proceeds $7,000 minus $3,000 book value.
*** $(13,000) special item = $21,000 write-off minus $8,000 future tax reduction.

Show that the following are correct for the 1999 cash flow statement (SCFP):

a. Cash generated from operations $29,000

b. Cash obtained from financing activities   0

c. Cash disbursed for investing activities (net)   (27,000)

d. Increase in cash and equivalents $ 2,000

PROBLEM 4.11*
Prepare the cash flow statement from complete balance sheet

Here are the balance sheet changes between 2000 and 2001 for Tamarack Systems Inc.

Tamarack Systems Inc. Balance Sheets for 2000 and 2001, with Changes Calculated			
	2001	2000	Change
Assets			
Current assets:			
Cash	$ 16,064	$ 12,440	$ 3,624
Temporary investments	0	65,000	(65,000)
Accounts receivable	220,668	143,962	76,706
Inventories	176,962	187,777	(10,815)
Prepaid expenses	9,004	14,321	(5,317)
Total current assets	$422,698	$423,500	$ (802)
Noncurrent assets:			
Land cost	$ 82,500	$ 75,000	$ 7,500
Building cost	600,898	420,984	179,914
Accumulated amortization	(243,224)	(173,320)	(69,904)
Net total noncurrent assets	$440,174	$322,664	$117,510
Totals	$862,872	$746,164	$116,708
Liabilities and Equity			
Current liabilities:			
Bank loan	$ 64,900	$ 43,200	$ 21,700
Accounts payable	199,853	163,866	35,987
Income taxes payable	17,228	16,090	1,138
Dividends payable	0	6,000	(6,000)
Current portion of bonds payable	22,000	20,000	2,000
Total current liabilities	$303,981	$249,156	$ 54,825
Noncurrent liabilities:			
Bonds payable	$213,000	$235,000	$ (22,000)
Provision for warranty costs	8,925	11,850	(2,925)
Future income tax	43,439	38,923	4,516
Total noncurrent liabilities	$265,364	$285,773	$ (20,409)
Equity:			
Share capital issued	$150,000	$100,000	$ 50,000
Retained earnings	143,527	111,235	32,292
Total equity	$293,527	$211,235	$ 82,292
Totals	$862,872	$746,164	$116,708

Further information:

1. The change in retained earnings is composed of net income $56,292 minus dividends declared of $24,000.

2. Land that had cost $35,000 was written off to expense as being worthless.
3. Payments to customers for warranty claims during 2001 equalled $7,000.
4. Land costing $5,000 was obtained in exchange for shares issued.
5. During 2001, a garage was sold for $25,000 cash. The cost of the garage was $100,000, and its accumulated amortization at the date of sale was $70,000.

From this information, prepare a cash flow statement for Tamarack for 2001 and comment on what the statement shows about the company's cash management.

PROBLEM 4.12*
Effects analysis questions on Tamarack Systems

These two questions are based on the Tamarack Systems information in Problem 4.11*. You can do some analysis without having done that problem, but the specific answers are based on having done the cash flow statement required in that problem.

1. What would have changed on Tamarack's 2001 cash flow statement if the cash received for the garage sale had been $40,000 instead of $25,000?
2. What would have changed on the cash flow statement if the accumulated amortization on the garage had been $82,000 instead of $70,000? (Ignore part 1.)

PROBLEM 4.13
Explain what the cash flow statement tells about a company

Explain to your uncle (who has never studied accounting) what the cash flow statement tells him about a company in which he owns shares.

PROBLEM 4.14
Prepare and interpret basic cash flow analysis from balance sheet changes

Another student has been having an awful time trying to prepare a cash flow statement for Greenplace Restaurants Inc. for the 2001 fiscal year. You go over to help and find the disorganized list of balance sheet changes below. About all that can be said for it is that it does balance, so the student has managed to identify all the changes from 2000.

1. Take the list below and prepare a cash flow statement for Greenplace for 2001.
2. Explain what your statement reveals about the company's 2001 cash management.

List of Balance Sheet Changes for Greenplace Restaurants Inc. for Fiscal Year 2001

	Direction	A↑, L↓, E↓	A↓, L↑, E↑
Trade payables	Up		$ 54,240
Accumulated amortization	Up		67,300
Cash in bank	Up	$ 4,328	
Receivables	Down		34,984
Bank loan	Up		35,400
Inventories	Up	53,202	
Net income	Positive		87,345
Dividends declared and paid	Positive	30,000	
Prepaid expenses	Up	12,540	
Buildings, equipment	Up	295,631	
Mortgage payable	Up		65,000
Taxes payable	Down	13,568	
Share capital	Up		50,000
Term deposits (30 days)	Down		15,000
Sums of changes		$409,269	$409,269

PROBLEM 4.15
Prepare and interpret a basic cash flow analysis from financial statements

1. Prepare a cash flow statement from the following financial statements of Fuzzy Wuzzy Wines Ltd.
2. Comment on what your statement tells you about the company's cash management during the year ended August 31, 2001. If you were a shareholder in Fuzzy Wuzzy, would you be happy with management's performance?

Balance Sheets as at August 31, 2001 and 2000

Assets	2001	2000	Liabilities and Equity	2001	2000
Current assets:			Current Liabilities:		
Cash	$ 80	$ 175	Bank loan	$ 140	$ 100
Short-term investment	0	150	Payables	$ 425	$ 200
Receivables	520	350		$ 565	$ 300
Inventories	340	250	Noncurrent liabilities:		
	$ 940	$ 925	Long-term loans	225	400
				$ 790	$ 700
Noncurrent assets:					
Factory cost	$1,450	$ 925	Shareholders' equity:		
Accum. amort.	(475)	(350)	Share capital	$ 700	$ 500
	$ 975	$ 575	Retained earnings	425	300
				$1,125	$ 800
	$1,915	$1,500		$1,915	$1,500

Fuzzy Wuzzy Wines Ltd.
Statement of Income and Retained Earnings
for the Year Ended August 31, 2001

Revenue		$3,000
Expenses:		
Amortization	$ 210	
Building write-off*	45	
General	2,320	2,575
Income before income tax		$ 425
Income tax expense		190
Net income for the year		$ 235
Retained earnings—beginning of year		300
Dividends declared and paid		(110)
Retained earnings—end of year		$ 425

* Building written off cost $130 and had accumulated amortization of $85.

PROBLEM 4.16
Interpret a simple cash flow statement and answer "what if" questions

A high-school friend of yours, Natasha Wheeler, is currently in second-year fine arts and, in addition to many other talents, happens to have an entrepreneurial flair. For the last two summers, she has operated a bicycle rental business near a local park. Last year (2000), even though the business was just getting started, she made enough money to get herself through the school year. Encouraged by this initial success, she bought several more bikes this year (2001) and constructed a movable shed out of which she operated her business and serviced the bikes.

Business was even better this summer, but Natasha is confused. While her business income was much up from last year, there is no cash for her to withdraw. She does not know how she will pay her university expenses this year.

Knowing that you are taking an accounting course, she comes to you for help. She realizes that you cannot lend her any money, but maybe you can explain what is going on with her business. (Ignore income tax throughout.)

1. Using the cash flow statement below, explain to Natasha how it is possible that the income statement can show a profit, while there is no cash for her to withdraw from the business. Explain to her where all the cash went.

2. In order to be able to pay herself a dividend, Natasha proposes to have her business borrow another $5,000 from her parents, who will not expect her to repay the money in the near future, and another $2,000 from the bank, which is looking very carefully at Natasha's cash position (*and* at her very salable bicycles) and expecting to be repaid as soon as possible. Ignoring any dividend she might pay, what effect will these two events have on the statement of changes in financial position?

3. Is it a good idea to borrow to pay a dividend? Does Natasha have any other alternatives?

Wheeler's Bicycle Rental Ltd. Cash Flow Statement for the Year Ended August 31, 2001 with Comparative Figures for 2000		
	2001	2000
Operations:		
Net income	$ 9,000	$ 5,500
Add back amortization expense	3,000	1,000
Cash from operations	$12,000	$ 6,500
Investing:		
Purchases of bikes	(15,000)	(5,000)
Purchase of shed	(5,000)	—
Financing:		
Bank loan	7,000	—
Loan from parents	—	3,000
Share capital issued	—	2,000
Dividend paid	—	(5,500)
(Decrease) or increase in cash	$ (1,000)	$ 1,000
Cash balance—beginning of year	1,000	0
Cash balance—end of year	$ 0	$ 1,000

PROBLEM 4.17
Prepare a cash flow statement from cash receipts, disbursements, and other information

Below in alphabetical order is information about Chantal Inc. Prepare a cash flow statement in good form.

Accumulated amortization on equipment that was sold	12,000
Advance payment on next year's expenses	8,920
Amortization for this year	46,912
Cash in bank, end of last year	63,419
Collections of this year's revenue	385,650
Collections on last year's revenue	22,795
Cost of equipment that was sold	16,000
Deposit received on next year's revenue	6,099
Noncurrent debt issued	75,000
Payment of this year's expenses (including income tax)	296,966
Payment on last year's expenses	1,890
Proceeds on sale of equipment	2,400
Purchase of new equipment	182,420
Repayment of noncurrent debt	30,000
Uncollected revenue at the end of this year	31,240
Unpaid expenses at the end of this year	29,352

PROBLEM 4.18
Prepare a cash flow statement from account balances

Below are Wharton Industries Ltd.'s balance sheet accounts in alphabetical order, for the two years 2001 and 2000. Use them to prepare the company's cash flow statement for 2001. The changes in accumulated amortization, deferred (future) income tax liability, and pension liability are all due entirely to the related expenses for 2001. No noncurrent assets were sold during the year. One other piece of information will be useful: the company declared and paid a dividend of $9,000 in 2001.

	2001	2000
Accounts payable	189,500	194,400
Accounts receivable	188,900	186,700
Accumulated amortization	214,200	192,000
Bank loan, due 2006	143,000	0
Building cost	368,400	301,300
Cash in bank	27,300	23,200
Cash on hand	1,100	1,500
Current income tax liability	2,200	3,100
Equipment cost	261,400	164,600
Deferred (future) income tax liability	26,200	24,500
Bank loan	63,200	84,100
Inventory	224,500	218,600
Land	90,000	70,000
Long-term investment	35,000	5,000
Mortgage, due 2010	388,800	395,400
Pension liability	22,100	18,600
Prepaid insurance	300	1,400
Retained earnings	27,700	23,200
Share capital	120,000	55,000
Temporary investment	0	18,000

PROBLEM 4.19
Cash flow analysis with large write-off and other adjustments

Here are the summarized 2001 and 2000 balance sheets for Saint John Enterprises Inc., showing the changes calculated by subtracting 2000 from 2001. Using them and the additional information below, prepare the SCFP for 2001.

	2001	2000	Changes
Cash equivalent assets	$ 17,400	$ 14,300	$ 3,100
Other current assets	164,100	123,500	40,600
Noncurrent assets, net	319,800	286,200	33,600
	$501,300	$424,000	$77,300
Cash equivalent liabilities	$ 11,200	$ 9,100	$ 2,100
Other current liabilities	117,900	90,600	27,300
Noncurrent liabilities	174,800	175,300	(500)
Share capital	80,000	60,000	20,000
Retained earnings	117,400	89,000	28,400
	$501,300	$424,000	$77,300

Additional information:

- The 2001 net income was $38,400. This was after recording a large noncurrent asset write-off of $112,000, which the company had thought necessary because an investment had gone bad during the year.

- Dividends declared during the year were $10,000.

- $1,500 of the dividends were still unpaid at the end of 2001 (there had been none unpaid at the end of 2000).

- There was an expense in 2001 for future income tax, recorded by increasing the noncurrent income tax liability by $8,800.

- The cash equivalent liabilities were temporary bank overdrafts. Some of the noncurrent liabilities were paid off during the year.

- During the year, the company sold for $8,400 a truck that cost $25,000 and had accumulated amortization of $17,300. There was thus a gain on sale of $700 (proceeds of $8,400 − book value of $7,700 ($25,000 − $17,300)).

- Amortization expense for the year, shown on the income statement and added to the accumulated amortization account on the balance sheet was $37,700.

- Acquisitions of noncurrent assets came to $191,000 for the year.

PROBLEM 4.20
Prepare cash flow statement with several accrual adjustments and comment on it

Using the following comparative balance sheets and additional information for Prairie Products Inc., prepare a cash flow statement for the year ended November 30, 2001. State any assumptions you find necessary. Comment on what your statement shows about the company's cash management for 2001.

Prairie Products Inc.
Balance Sheet at November 30, 2001
with 2000 Figures for Comparison
(in thousands of dollars)

Assets			Liabilities and Equity		
	2001	2000		2001	2000
Current assets			*Current liabilities*		
Cash	$ 31	$ 38	Bank loan	$ 25	$ 30
Marketable securities	100	200	Accounts payable	195	284
Accounts receivable	281	315	Taxes payable	34	20
Inventories	321	239	Dividends payable	20	30
Prepaid expenses	12	18		$ 274	$ 364
	$ 745	$ 810	*Noncurrent liabilities*		
Noncurrent assets			Mortgage payable	$ 240	$ 280
Land cost	$ 182	$ 70	Bonds payable	200	0
Buildings cost	761	493	Future income tax	138	111
Equipment cost	643	510	Warranty liability	126	118
	$1,586	$1,073		$ 704	$ 509
Accum. amortization	631	569	*Shareholders' equity*		
	$ 955	$ 504	Share capital	$ 600	$ 450
Investments, cost	365	438	Retained earnings	487	429
	$1,320	$ 942		$1,087	$ 879
TOTAL	$2,065	$1,752	TOTAL	$2,065	$1,752

Additional information for 2001 (all figures are in thousands of dollars):

 a. Net income was $98 and dividends of $40 were declared.

 b. A building was sold for $42 that had cost $110 and had accumulated amortization of $56.

 c. Amortization expense for the year was $118.

 d. One of the noncurrent investments, which had cost $73, was sold for $102.

 e. The change in future income tax liability was entirely due to the future (deferred) portion of income tax expense.

 f. The change in warranty liability was composed of warranty expense of $23 minus payouts on warranties of $15.

PROBLEM 4.21
Prepare a cash flow statement from information that is not all relevant

Prepare a cash flow statement from the following information for this year, presented in alphabetical order. Some of the information may not be relevant. (Hint: use the direct method.)

Account receivable written off*	1,200	Inventory purchased on credit	310,990
Amortization expense for the year	111,120	Investment written down**	33,000
		New bonded debt issued	386,000
Bank overdraft, beginning of year	0	New equipment purchased	483,620
		Old bonded debt repaid	311,000
Cash at the end of the year	36,020	Payments on accounts payable	693,860
Collections on accounts receivable	787,480	Proceeds of building sold***	240,000
Customer deposits received	40,000	Shares issued for cash	75,000
Dividends declared	80,000	Shares issued in return for land	145,000
Dividends payable, beginning of year	0	Temporary bank overdraft, end of year	14,610
Dividends payable, end of year	20,000		

 * The account receivable was deemed uncollectible and was written off directly to expense.
 ** The investment was written down from its $50,000 cost to its market value of $17,000.
 *** The building sold had cost $410,000 and had accumulated amortization of $200,000.

PROBLEM 4.22
Cash versus accrual income and cash from operations

From the following information:

 1. Calculate cash income for the year.

 2. Calculate accrual net income for the year.

 3. Explain why they are different by showing cash from operations as calculated by the indirect method.

 4. Calculate cash from operations by the direct method.

Collections:	On last year's revenue	46,665	Cash proceeds on new shares issued		210,000
	On this year's revenue	848,911	Cost of issuing new shares		4,622
	On next year's revenue	20,000	Amortization expense for the year		114,618
Payments:	On last year's expenses	78,640	Uncollected revenue:	Beginning of year	53,116
	On this year's expenses	649,925		End of year	73,007
	On next year's expenses	14,610	Unpaid expenses:	Beginning of year	78,640
Sale of land for cash (cost $80,000)		135,000		End of year	115,304
Paid to purchase new noncurrent assets		441,486	Cash:	Beginning of year	13,023
Still owing on those noncurrent assets		61,000		End of year	84,316

PROBLEM 4.23
Effects on income and cash of big accounting changes

When the new president of Comblay Inc. took office, he decided that the previous president had made some poor business decisions and that "the balance sheet needs to be cleaned up." Accordingly the following accounting changes were implemented at the president's instruction:

- Uncollectible accounts receivable of $538,000 were written off directly to expense.

- Long-term investments costing $15,600,000 were written down to their estimated market value of $3,000,000.

- An investment in a foreign country, costing $5,200,000 was written off altogether.

- Liability for future warranty payments was increased by $230,000 additional expense.

- Income tax savings of $3,810,000 were expected from all this.

Before the new president took office, net income for the year was $620,000 and cash from operations was negative $371,100.

1. Calculate the revised net income for the year.
2. Calculate the revised cash from operations for the year.
3. A commentator criticized the new president for implementing a "Big Bath." What are your views about the propriety of the president's actions?

PROBLEM 4.24
Cash flow for Gronsky's Great Things Ltd.

If you did Problem 3.35 on Gronsky's Great Things Ltd., you will have prepared income and retained earnings statements and an ending balance sheet for the company. Use that information to prepare a 2001 cash flow statement for the company. Assume the company began the year with $15,000 cash, obtained in return for share capital issued to Gronsky.

PROBLEM 4.25
(CHALLENGING)
Use a cash flow statement to derive an ending balance sheet

Give your knowledge of the financial statement relationships a workout by deriving the balance sheet of TGIF Industries Ltd. at the end of 2001 from the two statements given below (the balance sheet at the end of 2000 and the cash flow statement for 2001). When you have done that, prepare some comments on what the company's cash management strategy seemed to be for 2001, and whether that left the company financially stronger or weaker at the end of 2001 than at the end of 2000.

TGIF Industries Ltd.
Balance Sheet at December 31, 2001
(in thousands of dollars)

Assets		Liabilities and Equity	
Current assets		*Current liabilities*	
Cash on hand	$ 19	Demand bank loan	$ 2,205
Cash in bank	238	Other bank indebtedness	840
Accounts receivable	2,868	Accounts payable, accruals	1,948
Inventories	2,916	Income, other taxes payable	213
Prepaid expenses	184		$ 5,206
	$ 6,225		
		Noncurrent liabilities	
Noncurrent assets		Mortgage payable	$ 516
Land cost	$ 416	Loans from shareholders	600
Automotive equipment cost	892	Other long-term loans	318
Buildings cost	2,411	Deferred (future) income tax	248
Equipment cost	1,020	Estimated pension liability	163
	$ 4,739		$ 1,845
Accumulated amortization	863	*Shareholders' equity*	
	$ 3,876	Share capital	$ 1,000
Investments, cost	740	Retained earnings	2,790
	$ 4,616		$ 3,790
TOTAL	$10,841	TOTAL	$10,841

TGIF Industries Ltd.
Cash Flow Statement for the Year Ended December 31, 2001
(in thousands of dollars)

Operations:		
Net income for the year		$ 614
Add expenses (deduct revenues) not		
involving cash:		
Amortization expense	$ 291	
Loss on sale of investments	85	
Deferred (future) income tax expense	68	
Estimated pension expense	53	
Gain on sale of land	(210)	
Gain on sale of building	(38)	249
Add (deduct) effects of changes in noncash		
working capital:		
Accounts receivable	$1,134	
Inventories	647	
Prepaid expenses	37	
Accounts payable, accruals	(587)	
Income, other taxes payable	(14)	1,217
Cash generated by operations		$2,080
Investing activities:		
Investment in term deposits	$ 100	
Proceeds from sales of long-term assets:		
Investments (cost $560)	475	
Land (cost $80)	290	
Building (cost $890)	514	
Cost of acquisitions of long-term assets:		
New building	(1,670)	
New equipment	(643)	(1,134)
Financing activities:		
Decrease in demand bank loan	$(1,137)	
Decrease in other bank indebtedness	(360)	
Payments on mortgage	(103)	
Additional loans from shareholders	250	
Debenture debt issued	300	
Payments of other long-term loans	(74)	
Payments of employee pensions	(43)	
Share capital issued	250	
Dividends paid ($100 declared)	(40)	(957)
Decrease in cash (cash on hand up $6, cash in		
bank down $17)		$ (11)

**PROBLEM 4.26
(CHALLENGING)
Why pay attention
to the cash flow
statement?**

A senior financial executive for a large public company remarked to a stock market analyst: "I don't know why you people worry so much about what is in our cash flow statement. Managing cash flow is our responsibility as managers; it involves paying close attention to cash on a daily basis. Why don't you pay attention to our income performance and just forget about cash flow? We'll look after that!"

Respond to the executive's comments. You do not have to agree or disagree entirely.

**PROBLEM 4.27
(CHALLENGING)
Why not just have
cash-basis
accounting?**

A business commentator made the following remark during a discussion of the financial performance of a large, but struggling, company: "These accountants are something to behold! They spend lots of money to create complicated financial statements, especially income statements, that use what they call 'accrual' accounting, and come up with an income number they expect us to take seriously. Then they spend a whole lot more money creating cash flow statements, which are just as complicated as the other statements, and that take away all the accruals and supposedly return us to the cash income number we would have had anyway, if they hadn't bothered with accrual accounting in the first place! Nice work! You get paid to create a dubious income measure and then more money to uncreate it. What kind of idiots do they take the business community for? Why don't they just give us the cash income and leave it at that? We can understand that, and it would make a simple income statement and no need for a cash flow statement to just cancel out the income number, as we have now."

If you were an accountant involved in the discussion and everyone turned to you to hear what you would say in response to the commentator, what would you say?

**PROBLEM 4.28
(CHALLENGING)
"What if" questions
involving cash flow**

By making certain business decisions or choosing the location of items in their financial statements, companies may be able to alter the "story" the cash flow statement tells. For each action or choice below, explain what effect (if any) would result in the cash flow statement for the present year (including cash and equivalents at the bottom) if the action or choice happened.

1. Company A arranges with the bank to let it have a temporary bank overdraft of $100,000 as a way of getting some immediately needed financing.
2. Company B decides to classify $50,000 of its accounts receivable as long-term assets instead of current assets.
3. Company C decides to buy land for $500,000, arranging for 100% long-term debt financing instead of by issuing new share capital.
4. Company D decides to increase its amortization expense for this year by $75,000.
5. Company E decides to declare a $40,000 dividend to shareholders payable immediately in cash.
6. Company F decides to donate $25,000 to the Poor Accountants' League (the donation will be included with business expenses).

**PROBLEM 4.29
(CHALLENGING)
Interpret trends in
cash management**

Apex Accessories Inc. makes, imports, and sells various goods for the fashion trade, including costume jewellery, belts and other leather goods, hats, and many kinds of apparel. The business is both seasonal and unstable, with products coming and going as fashions and availability from foreign suppliers change. During a "business issues" TV program about the fashion industry, some of Apex's financial results were displayed in an on-screen table, while a narrator gushed about the marvellous management the company had. Here is that table:

Year	Year-end total assets	Year-end total bank borrowing	Net income for the year	Year's cash flow from operations
1992	$24,400,000	$ 8,300,000	$2,100,000	$3,200,000
1993	29,100,000	9,600,000	2,400,000	3,900,000
1994	28,500,000	8,900,000	2,300,000	3,200,000
1995	34,700,000	10,300,000	2,600,000	2,500,000
1996	37,800,000	12,000,000	2,800,000	2,200,000
1997	35,400,000	14,100,000	3,000,000	1,800,000
1998	37,000,000	14,200,000	3,100,000	3,800,000
1999	39,600,000	15,200,000	3,300,000	3,400,000
2000	43,000,000	16,400,000	3,200,000	2,800,000
2001	45,700,000	18,500,000	3,400,000	1,900,000

1. Which column of figures do you suppose the narrator was referring to when gushing about the "marvellous management"?
2. Provide as many comments as you can about the company's results. Do you think the management is marvellous?
3. For this particular company (which is listed on a stock exchange), would you expect market traders to respond much to the cash flow information once they know the net income figures? Put another way, do you think the cash flow information has any added value to the net income information?

**PROBLEM 4.30
(CHALLENGING)
Ethics of cash flow
manipulation**

There is an interesting ethical issue behind the very reason the cash flow statement is thought by some people to have advantages over the income statement. The reason is that people are often mistrustful of the income statement because they feel its accrual accounting methods can be used to manipulate net income as a measure of performance, and they think that the cash flow figures are more "real." For example, a company might claim large revenues, not yet collected, that make its income higher (and because the revenues are not collected, the accounts receivable are also higher), but if the cash has not been collected, the increase in accounts receivable will be deducted from net income on the cash flow statement, and the lack of "real" cash inflow will be apparent because cash from operations will be lower than would be expected from the income number. Thus, it is thought, the cash flow statement's cash from operations figure is more believable than net income and, if it is too different from net income, will unmask manipulations of the net income.

The ethical issue is that it is possible to manipulate the cash flow figures too. For example, a company might accelerate or delay receivables collections in order to change the cash flow figures, whether or not the net income is also being manipulated. There may be a difference from manipulating net income because changing cash flow figures requires real actions, affecting customers or suppliers or employees, so there are real consequences, such as irritating customers or having to offer inducements for early payment. Nevertheless, it can be done.

It seems that most people would feel that altering the accruals just to make net income better (or worse, or smoother) is ethically questionable, even if it is understandable because of the way management is evaluated and rewarded. But is altering the cash flow ethically questionable? Is there an ethical problem if management decides to put pressure on customers to accelerate collections and improve the company's cash position? Sounds like good management, not like manipulation.

Suggest two or three ways, not included above, by which operating, investing, or financing cash flows could be altered from their normal levels. For each, discuss whether, or under what conditions, you would think there is an ethical problem in such alteration.

PROBLEM 4.31 (CHALLENGING) Prepare a full set of statements, including cash flow

Grandin Ltd. manufactures a single product and has revenue from related service activities. The company had been growing slowly but steadily until this year (2001), when revenue, especially from services, increased substantially.

The company's bookkeeper was part way through preparing the 2001 financial statements (with 2000 for comparison) and asked you for help in completing them. When you went to the company's offices you got the information below. Assume these figures are correct.

Account Name	2001	2000
Accounts payable	$ 12,300	$ 8,900
Accounts receivable	44,200	21,300
Accumulated amortization	36,000	32,000
Administrative expenses	14,600	11,900
Bank loan — current	29,000	19,000
Cash	4,700	5,400
Cost of goods sold	103,190	71,650
Current income tax expense	5,200	3,000
Future income tax expense	250	500
Future income tax liability	4,350	4,100
Amortization	4,000	5,800
Dividends paid	4,000	6,000
Equipment	87,000	87,000
Equipment financing	20,000	24,000
Income taxes payable	2,200	1,000
Interest expense	4,800	3,900
Inventory	42,500	37,000
Packaging and shipping expense	8,100	7,500
Prepaid expenses	2,100	800
Retained earnings — beginning	37,500	33,300
Revenue — product sales	163,290	116,250
Revenue — service	73,700	32,600
Service wage expense	69,500	28,200
Share capital	25,000	25,000
Utilities expense	9,200	6,200

1. Prepare a comparative balance sheet, income statement, and statement of retained earnings for 2001 and 2000.
2. Prepare a cash flow statement for 2001 (you do not have the information to do comparative figures for 2000).

CASE 4A
Discuss issues related to cash flow analysis

The three financial statements included in Chapters 2 and 3 are all based on accrual accounting, which generates a net income figure and related balance sheet accounts that attempt to measure the enterprise's economic performance. In this chapter, the cash flow statement was used to report the enterprise's results as if accrual accounting had not been used, focusing instead on cash flow. Discuss the following questions, using as an example CAE (see its statements in sections 2.9, 3.4, and 4.7) or any company whose statements you can obtain from the company Web page or the library. (For current information about CAE, go to www.cae.com.)

1. Does the cash flow statement really help the person who is trying to understand the enterprise's performance, or is it just another complicated accounting statement that is mysterious to nonaccountants? Which parts of it are most understandable, which parts are least understandable?
2. Is it a good idea to indicate, by preparing the cash flow statement, that knowing about an enterprise's income performance is not enough? What does the presence of the cash flow statement say about the value of the income measure? Conversely, what does the presence of the broader income measure say about the value of the more narrowly defined cash flow measure?
3. For CAE (or any other company you select), is the story told by the cash flow statement consistent with, or supportive of, the story told by the income statement? Would you expect good performance in one to imply good performance in the other, long-term or short-term? What kinds of differences in the stories the two statements tell would you expect to be significant enough for readers of the statement to react (such as by buying or selling shares of the company and so changing its share price)?
4. Are there events you would like to see reflected, or separately disclosed, in the cash flow statement that are not? Are there things in the cash flow statement you think are unnecessary? (For example, do you think people need the reconciliation with accrual income in the cash from operations section, or would it be satisfactory to just state what cash from operations is without all the reconciling items?)
5. What sorts of clues about the enterprise's business and financial strategies can you get from the cash flow statement? Are there other issues the statement can raise questions about, even if it alone cannot answer them?

CASE 4B
Examine the CBC's financial statements

The Canadian Broadcasting Corporation (CBC) is wholly owned by the Government of Canada (the proprietor of the CBC). About 60% of the CBC's revenue is operating grants from the Government, and most of the rest is advertising revenue. The Government also provides general advances to ensure that the CBC has sufficient working capital to operate properly and funds for the CBC to use to purchase capital assets (equipment, etc.).

Even though it has only one owner and its balance sheet is prepared as that of a proprietorship, the CBC is a corporation and owns property, signs contracts, and employs people. It also has a number of "capital leases" (primarily to do with its recently completed broadcasting centre in Toronto). Such leases do not give the CBC legal ownership of the property, but they are so close to doing so that they are accounted for as if they were owned property, by including the economic value of the leased assets in noncurrent assets and including the future payment obligations in a capital lease liability. The CBC uses conventional business accounting for its assets, liabilities, revenues, and expenses, and on that basis derives, for example, a "net operating loss" for the year. However, the government operating funding is then shown so that the government can see the result after this funding. This gives the CBC two "income" numbers: the "net operating loss" and something called the "net results of operations for the year."

These differences between government funding and business operations also affect the cash flow statement. For example, the government's capital funding is amortized onto the income statement (the "Statement of Operations") as an increase in income, but as that positive amortization is not equal to the actual cash obtained each year, both numbers end up on the cash flow statement, one in the operations section and one in the financing section.

Well, citizens of Canada have a financial and cultural stake in the CBC. Below are the company's 1999 comparative statements: Statement of Operations and Proprietor's Equity, Balance Sheet, and Statement of Cash Flow, plus a few notes to the financial statements. Based on this information and your own knowledge of the CBC and of radio and television in general:

1. What do the financial statements tell you about the way the CBC does its business and how it is financed? Pay particular attention to the cash flow statement here.
2. How are the CBC's financial statements similar to or different from those of ordinary business corporations? Are those differences helpful in understanding the CBC?
3. How fully do you think the balance sheet and income statement represent the CBC's real value to the country and the risks the corporation faces?

Statement of Operations and Proprietor's Equity

for the years ended March 31	1999	1998
Revenue	*(thousands of dollars)*	
Advertising and program sales	329,735	383,306
Specialty services (Note 4)	90,471	87,383
Miscellaneous	63,859	54,603
	484,065	525,292
Expense		
Television and radio service costs	1,074,176	1,065,009
Specialty services (Note 4)	92,285	86,096
Transmission, distribution and collection	60,136	64,107
Radio Canada International	14,729	15,264
Payments to private stations	12,519	12,295
Corporate Management	16,204	15,073
Amortization of capital assets	161,205	135,379
Downsizing program	—	18,336
Total expense before taxes	1,431,254	1,411,559
Net operating loss before government funding and taxes	(947,189)	(886,267)
Government Funding		
Parliamentary appropriation for operating expenditures	759,481	759,654
Frozen allotment to offset the 95/96 repayable advance (Note 3)	—	(56,669)
Net funding for operating expenditures	759,481	759,654
Funding reserved for Radio Canada International (Note 4)	15,525	15,360
Amortization of deferred capital funding (Note 7)	160,763	135,120
Net results of operations before taxes	(11,420)	(32,802)
Provision for income and large corporations taxes (Note 5)	2,745	2,708
Net results of operations for the year	(14,165)	(35,510)
Proprietor's equity, beginning of year	(65,434)	(33,510)
Working Capital Funding (Note 3)	4,000	4,000
Proprietor's equity, end of year	(75,599)	(65,434)

The accompanying notes form an integral part of the financial statements.

Balance Sheet

as at March 31

	1999	1998
	(thousands of dollars)	
Assets		*(Restated)*
Current		
Cash and short-term investments	73,772	38,624
Accounts receivable	122,530	183,826
Program inventory	113,183	87,964
Prepaid expenses	22,665	35,094
	332,150	345,508
Capital assets (Note 6)	1,115,209	1,142,146
Deferred charges	27,154	25,499
	1,474,513	1,513,103
Liabilities		
Current		
Accounts payable and accrued liabilities	234,244	236,796
Accrued vacation pay	38,958	38,078
Obligations under capital leases (Note 10)	4,133	3,850
	277,335	278,724
Long-term		
Employee termination benefits	77,644	69,932
Deferred pension liability (Note 9)	89,785	97,639
Obligations under capital leases (Note 10)	381,260	385,345
Deferred capital funding (Note 7)	724,088	746,897
	1,272,777	1,299,813
Proprietor's Equity		
Proprietor's equity (Note 3)	(75,599)	(65,434)
Commitments and contingencies (Notes 11 and 12)		
	1,474,513	1,513,103

The accompanying notes form an integral part of the financial statements.

Approved on behalf of the Board of Directors:

Director   Director

Statement of Cash Flow

for the years ended March 31

	1999	1998
	(thousands of dollars)	
		(Restated)
Operating Activities		
Net results of operations for the year	(14,165)	(35,510)
Gain on disposal of capital assets	(1,469)	(100)
Items not involving cash:		
Amortization of capital assets	161,205	135,379
Amortization of deferred charges	8,581	5,390
Employee termination liability and		
vacation pay	8,592	2,098
Deferred pension contribution	(7,854)	(109)
Amortization of deferred capital funding	(160,763)	(135,120)
Net change in working capital balances excluding		
cash and short-term investments (Note 14)	48,648	(125,043)
	42,775	(153,015)
Financing Activities		
Parliamentary appropriations (Note 3):		
Capital funding	132,954	90,140
Working capital funding	4,000	4,000
Government funding for capital purchases for RCI	5,000	—
Proceeds on disposal of capital assets		
financing from other organizations	2,104	1,287
	144,058	95,427
Investing Activities		
Acquisition of capital assets	(137,597)	(93,613)
Capital portion of lease payments	(3,802)	(10,889)
Deferred charges	(10,286)	(15,423)
	(151,685)	(119,925)
Increase (decrease) in cash and short-term		
investments	35,148	(177,513)
Cash and short-term investments, beginning of year	38,624	216,137
Cash and short-term investments, end of year	73,772	38,624

The accompanying notes form an integral part of the financial statements.

Notes to the Financial Statements

3. Parliamentary Appropriations

Parliamentary appropriations approved and the amounts received by the Corporation during the year are as follows:

a. Parliamentary Appropriations Approved and Received

	1999	1998
	(thousands of dollars)	
Approved appropriations for:		
Operating Funding		
• Annual Funding	745,531	769,014
• Funding for downsizing & other costs	92,401	—
• Transfer to capital funding [1]	(36,485)	—
• Frozen allotment to be reprofiled through Capital to the 1999–2000 fiscal year	(41,966)	—
• Funding for RCI (Note 4)	—	(9,360)
	759,481	759,654
• Frozen allotment to offset the 1995–1996 repayable advance including imputed interest thereon [2]	—	(56,669)
Capital Funding (Note 7)	94,469	105,740
• Additional funding – Supplementary Estimates B	2,000	—
• Add transfer from operating funding [1]	36,485	—
• Less transfer to 1998–1999 fiscal year [1]	—	15,600
	132,954	90,140
• Capital funding received from the government for RCI	5,000	—
	137,954	90,14
Working Capital Funding	4,000	4,000

[1] In the event that significant changes in current year requirements occur, amounts are transferred from one vote to another or reprofiled from one fiscal year to the next through Appropriation Acts tabled in the House of Commons.
[2] In 1995/96, the Corporation received a $50 million repayable advance to be recovered in future years through reduced funding levels.

b. Reconciliation of Net Results of Operations to Government Funding Basis

The Corporation receives a significant portion of its funding through Parliamentary appropriations, which is based primarily on cash flow requirements. Items recognized in the Statement of Operations and Proprietor's Equity in one year may be funded through Parliamentary appropriations in different years. Accordingly, the Corporation has different net results of operations for the year on a government funding basis than on a generally accepted accounting principles basis. These differences are outlined below:

	1999	1998
	(thousands of dollars)	
Net results of operations for the year	(14,165)	(35,510)
Items expensed but funded in other years	322	30,429
Net results of operations on a government funding basis	(13,843)	(5,081)
Government funding surplus (deficit), beginning of the year	29,444	34,525
Government funding surplus (deficit), end of the year	15,601	29,444

c. Net Results for Capital

The Corporation's capital asset purchases are also financed through a Parliamentary appropriation. Certain items recognized as additions to assets in one year may be funded through Parliamentary appropriations in different years. Once again, the Corporation has different net results of operations for the year on a government funding basis than on a generally accepted accounting principles basis. These differences are outlined below:

	1999	1998
	(thousands of dollars)	
Parliamentary appropriations and transfers	132,954	90,140
Government funding for RCI	5,000	—
Parliamentary appropriations and government funding	137,954	90,140
Proceeds on disposal of capital assets' financing from other organizations	2,104	1,287
Total capital funding for the year	140,058	91,427
Acquisition of capital assets	(137,597)	(93,613)
Capital funding surplus (deficit) for the year	2,461	(2,186)
Year over year change in proportionate share of consolidation assets	375	(170)
Net results for capital for the year, government funding basis	2,836	(2,356)
Government funding surplus (deficit), beginning of the year	1,890	4,246
Government funding surplus (deficit), end of the year	4,726	1,890

6. Capital Assets

	Cost	Accumulated Amortization	Net Book Value 1999	1998
			(thousands of dollars)	
Land	35,501	—	35,501	35,515
Buildings	369,923	202,525	167,398	166,991
Technical equipment	1,071,144	719,441	351,703	428,966
Furnishings, office equipment and computers	81,519	56,258	25,261	22,687
Automotive	35,465	24,063	11,402	11,654
Leasehold improvements	3,738	2,745	993	1,620
Property under capital leases	511,636	92,057	419,579	434,960
Uncompleted capital projects	103,372	—	103,372	39,753
	2,212,298	1,097,089	1,115,209	1,142,146

Effective April 1, 1998 the Corporation changed its estimated useful life for technical equipment, other than transmitters and towers, from ten years to five years. The effect of this change was to increase the amortization of capital assets expense on the Statement of Operations and Proprietor's Equity by $44.8 million for the 1998–99 fiscal year.

Current year amortization expense of $15.4 million (1998 – $15.3 million) relating to property under capital lease is included in the amortization of capital assets on the Statement of Operations and Proprietor's Equity.

7. Deferred Capital Funding

	1999	1998
	(thousands of dollars)	
Balance, beginning of year	746,897	791,877
Government funding for capital expenditures (Note 3)	137,954	90,140
Amortization of deferred capital funding	(160,763)	(135,120)
Balance, end of year	724,088	746,897

10.   Obligations Under Capital Leases

a. Capital leases consist mainly of premises occupied by CBC in Toronto.
Future minimum lease payments and obligations are as follows:

(thousands of dollars)

2000	33,039
2001	33,039
2002	33,039
2003	33,039
2004	33,039
Thereafter to 2027	776,410
Total future minimum payments	941,605
Deduct imputed interest (7.53%) and executory costs	556,263
Obligation under capital lease	385,342
Less current portion	4,133
Long term portion	381,209

CBC owns the land on which the Toronto Broadcasting Centre is located. Interest relating to the Broadcasting Centre lease, which is included in current year expenditures, is $29.2 million. At the end of the lease, CBC will own the building.

b. Other
As at March 31, 1999, the Corporation's obligation relating to a Joint Venture capital lease amounted to $51,000.

14.   Net Change in Non-Cash Working Capital Balances

	1999	1998
	(thousands of dollars)	
Cash provided by (used for):		
Accounts receivable	61,296	(74,140)
Program inventory*	(22,525)	8,553
Prepaid expenses	12,429	(13,733)
Deferred income taxes	—	20,523
Accounts payable and accrued liabilities	(2,552)	(66,246)
	48,648	(125,043)

*Excluding $2,694 million in amortization of capital assets.

NOTES

1. For more information on the "cash flow" research results, see W.H. Beaver, *Financial Reporting: An Accounting Revolution*, 2nd ed. (Englewood Cliffs: Prentice-Hall, 1989), 116; or P.A. Griffin, ed., *Usefulness to Investors and Creditors of Information Provided by Financial Reporting*, 2nd ed. (Stamford: Financial Accounting Standards Board, 1987), 144–45. Accounting research journals such as *The Accounting Review, Contemporary Accounting Research, Journal of Accounting and Economics*, and *Journal of Accounting Research* occasionally have articles examining cash flow or comparing cash flow to accrual net income.

5 CHAPTER

Standards and Principles Surrounding the Financial Statements

5.1 Chapter Overview

GAAP are a system of principles and standards that govern financial accounting.

Doing accounting and using accounting require concepts as well as numbers.

You have now seen the four financial statements forming the standard set that is the main product of financial accounting. To round out your understanding of the statements, this chapter introduces you to the system of **accounting standards** and principles that govern the way the financial statement figures are calculated and presented, including **generally accepted accounting principles (GAAP)**, the **external audit**, notes and other supplementary information, and some related ideas about professional ethics and the capital markets' use of accounting information.

This chapter has no numbers. (Perhaps the break from numbers will help the previous material settle into your understanding!) Instead, this chapter focuses on the large system of standards and principles that govern the way accountants assemble the numbers. We have seen that accrual accounting, and even transaction recording, require judgment and managerial decisions—now we will delve into the concepts that guide the accountants and the accounting. Doing accounting and making good use of accounting information both require a solid conceptual understanding, in addition to being able to work with the numbers. This chapter is a foundation for succeeding chapters that get into the specifics of doing accounting and making accounting choices and which use the principles from this chapter continuously.

Using the learning categories summarized at the beginning of each chapter, this is what you will learn in this chapter:

- *Procedures and techniques:* How to incorporate standards and principles into choosing accounting numbers and surrounding information.

- *Concepts and principles:* Why financial accounting has the standards and principles it has, where these came from, and how they relate to decisions by capital markets and managers.

- *Analysis and decisions:* How principles and standards affect the interpretation of accounting information, and how to watch for differences between Canadian and other countries' standards.

5.2   ACCOUNTING PRINCIPLES AND THEIR USE IN PRODUCING ACCOUNTING INFORMATION

Practising accountants use accounting principles to guide their actions.

How do accountants decide what accounting is needed and then put their decisions into practice? This section outlines the conceptual background that guides accountants. Doing accounting well takes expert knowledge, considerable experience, and continuous attention to new problems and solutions. Concepts and principles are very important in accounting because they form a logical structure that practising accountants use every day to consider problems, make or recommend decisions, and explain solutions.

Three general groups of highly related ideas lie behind the chart shown in Figure 5.1, which concerns the accounting for a company, corporate group, or other accounting entity:

1. *Decision criteria:* how to meet the needs of those who use and pay for the accounting.
2. *Generally accepted accounting principles:* financial accounting's conceptual structure.
3. *Preparation steps:* how decisions are put into practice for that entity.

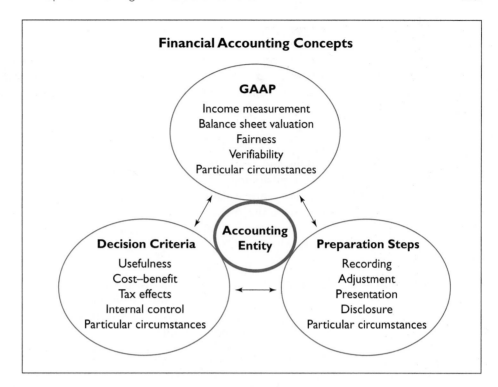

FIGURE 5.1

These three groups of ideas are in constant flux, both with each other and with the changing nature of the business and professional environment. The double-headed arrows indicate this flux, and the lack of a beginning or end to the chart indicates that the accountant might start just about anywhere and work back and forth through the various issues in doing the job of making accounting work. The flux also depends on the particular accounting entity, the enterprise for which the accounting is being done. The neighbourhood cappuccino bar is just as appropriate an entity to be accounted for as are the groups of hundreds of corporations making up IBM or the Royal Bank of Canada, but decision criteria would imply different accounting needs for the cappuccino bar entity, so GAAP would be applied differently in doing the preparation steps.

> All the accounting revolves around the accounting entity that is its focus.

Here's an outline of the ideas within each group. You'll get to know them all more deeply as you use them in learning about how to do accounting in the rest of the book.

Decision criteria: These criteria refer to serving the needs of shareholders, managers, creditors, and others who use accounting information. The five sets of ideas in this group are:

> Accounting information fundamentally should be useful, in numerous ways.

- *Usefulness:* Fundamental reasons for having financial accounting, including relevance (decision usefulness), materiality (size of impact on user's decisions or interests), and some ways in which accounting can be useful, including timeliness (getting the information in time to use it in making a decision), value in *prediction*, value in calculating various parties' *shares of results* (such as dividends and management bonuses), value in evaluating the *performance*, *accountability*, and *stewardship* of management.

- *Cost–benefit:* Like anything else, accounting should be worth its cost, so the usefulness criteria have to be balanced against costs, including the cost of *doing* accounting, plus, possibly, the costly *consequences* of accounting. Costly consequences might include lawsuits and other legal problems as well as competitive, political, or social difficulties. Releasing information to benefit some users, such as shareholders, can be costly if, for example, competitors also get the information and use it to compete better.

- *Tax effects:* In our society, income and other taxes are significant considerations and accounting information is used in assessing many taxes, so every enterprise subject to tax (on itself or its owners) must consider the tax effects of accounting methods, which can make or break accounting decisions, or even be the real reasons for such decisions. This book mentions tax frequently and has later sections on some specific tax issues in accounting, including the GST and income tax.

- *Internal control:* Managers are responsible for running the enterprise on behalf of owners, and accounting is a major part of the information used in managing and controlling the operations and assets of the enterprise, so, like tax, internal control considerations often lie behind accounting decisions. Chapter 7 has more on internal control.

- *Particular circumstances:* Every entity for which accounting is done has its own circumstances (depending on its industry, the way it does business, its financial situation, its legal situation, and its managers' information preferences), so decision criteria have to be interpreted in the light of those circumstances.

Generally accepted accounting principles: These principles form the conceptual structure of financial accounting and have been developed over the years to represent both the decision criteria above and broader social and professional criteria of appropriateness. The five sets of ideas in this group are:

> GAAP are a set of practical concepts intended to ensure the information is useful and fair.

- *Income measurement:* Measuring income is fundamental to financial accounting and solutions are judged according to the central concepts of recognition and matching of revenues and expenses. Revenues and expenses should be *recognized* (entered into the accounts) only when they have been earned or incurred, and they should *match* each other so that the net income, which is revenues minus expenses, is meaningful. Chapter 6 explores these income measurement ideas in more depth.

- *Balance sheet valuation:* Valuing assets, liabilities, and equity is just as fundamental as measuring income is, so solutions are judged according to the cost principle and conservatism, the two main valuation concepts. Accounting is still largely a historical cost-based information system (assets, liabilities, and equity all being shown mostly at values arising up to, but not past, the balance sheet date). Being *conservative* (prudent and cautious) about the values used in cases where historical values are not appropriate (such as when an asset's value has declined below its cost) is considered important to avoiding optimistically misleading figures. Chapters 8 and 9 focus on accounting principles behind the balance sheet numbers.

- *Fairness:* Several principles are involved in meeting the objective that financial accounting information should depict the enterprise fairly. One is *objec-*

tivity: the information should be *neutral* (not favouring any of the users) and "*representationally faithful*," telling the story according to what really has happened and not being influenced by the interests of any party(ies), who might wish things had been different. Another is the *continuity* or *going concern* principle, the idea that the user of the information should be entitled to assume that the enterprise will continue in business unless the user is informed otherwise, and so that using principles such as cost or matching is appropriate (a liquidation basis, for example, would be appropriate if the enterprise is not a going concern). The information should also be *reliable*, accurately compiled, and free of intentional or inadvertent error. Users can be expected to want to compare the enterprise to others and to its own past history; the information should be *comparable* to others and *consistent* over time. All of these principles seek to ensure that the information is valid and not misleading. You will hear much about the principles in this paragraph, so here is a list of the main ones again: fairness, objectivity, neutrality, going concern, reliability, comparability, and consistency.

- *Verifiability:* If accounting information is to meet the standards indicated above, anyone should be able to go back and see, or check, how the information was put together and evaluate its appropriateness. This means that there should be documents and other evidence behind the accounting information so that it can always be verified. Verifiability leads to a need for documents to back up accounting records, as well as to careful records that the external auditor can check. Section 5.8 has more about auditing.

- *Particular circumstances:* Just as for the decision criteria, the above principles have to be interpreted, and sometimes rethought in accordance with the entity's circumstances. What is fair for one company may not be fair for another whose financing, management, ownership interests, or prospects are different.

Accounting's preparation steps also are aimed at making the information useful.

Preparation steps: Accounting involves a series of procedures for producing the information users get. These procedures are usually, though not always, done in the order below, and accountants may decide at a later stage that an earlier stage needs to be rethought. There is more about the preparation steps in Chapter 7.

- *Recording:* This is when the business and economic events are turned into accounting data using the double-entry system of recording transactions. We saw this step in Chapters 1 and 2 particularly.

- *Adjustment:* At this stage, recorded data are changed or augmented to comply with additional information or to meet any of the criteria in the two groups above. It is the stage when the accountant is acting consciously as an interpreter of the business world. Adjustments were part of Chapter 3's coverage of accrual income.

- *Presentation:* Here the recorded and adjusted data are organized, formatted, and fitted with captions to produce the financial statements and other reports the users get. In doing this work, the accountant has to ensure that all the information combines into an appropriate overall depiction of the enterprise, remembering, for example, that decisions about income measurement affect balance sheet valuation and vice versa because of the ways that the financial statements *articulate*. Financial statement presentation and articulation were emphasized in Chapters 2, 3, and 4.

- *Disclosure:* Doing the numbers appropriately is not enough. The accountant also has to decide whether to group numbers together or disclose them separately, and how to supplement the numbers with notes and other narrative, tabular, or graphic disclosure. There is more about disclosure in this chapter.

- *Particular circumstances:* As in the other two groups of ideas, each entity's circumstances affect what is actually done. No two enterprises have quite the same accounting systems and problems, so the procedures followed by accountants from enterprise to enterprise are not quite the same.

HOW'S YOUR UNDERSTANDING?

Here are two questions you should be able to answer, based on what you have just read:

1. Why is the accounting entity important to the way accounting is done?

2. What is the purpose of financial accounting's GAAP conceptual structure?

5.3   AN EXAMPLE OF THE APPLICATION OF ACCOUNTING PRINCIPLES TO A COMPANY

Well, let's bring all this down to earth. Let's see how we might think about the concepts behind financial accounting by relating them to the company whose financial statements were studied in Chapters 2, 3, and 4: CAE Inc. Back in section 2.9, we learned that CAE has three main lines of business:

Commercial Simulation and Training: commercial flight simulators and visual systems like fancy video games, complete with training centres and alliances with airlines for pilot training.

Military Simulation and Controls: similar simulators and related systems for military use, extending to land-based simulation and training, and more extensions to marine controls.

Forestry Systems: technological services to the wood products and pulp and paper industries, including software, sensors, and mechanical control systems.

In section 3.4, we learned about how the lines of business and CAE overall performed in earning income, and in section 4.7 we saw that the company generated large cash flows from operations in 2000. If in the material below you need to refresh your memory about CAE's operations and performance, please review sections 2.9, 3.4, and 4.7. For current information about CAE, consult the company's Web site, www.cae.com.

Information Use Scenarios

CAE is an ambitious technologically oriented company. Let's think now about some of the users of the company's financial statements:

Scenario 1: The board has to evaluate how the CEO is doing in managing the company.

1. The company's board of directors manages the company on behalf of the shareholders. One function of the board that involves the financial statements is hiring and evaluating the performance of the company's top operating management, especially the president and chief executive officer (CEO). Suppose you are a member of CAE's board and are preparing for a discussion of the CEO's performance at the next board meeting. CAE's financial statements have been provided to the board prior to the meeting, and will be a major input to this evaluation.

Scenario 2: A financial analyst has to decide whether to recommend the company's shares.

2. The company's shares are listed (that is, can be bought and sold) on the Toronto Stock Exchange (trading symbol CAE: you could look in today's financial newspaper under the TSE stock price listings and see how CAE is doing). Suppose you are a financial analyst for a Canadian investment dealer and are preparing a report projecting future earnings and making recommendations about whether the company's shares are worthwhile to buy, or to keep if already held, or instead should be sold. You have the company's financial statements and will use them as support to your report.

Scenario 3: A bank lending officer has to review the company's borrowing status.

3. CAE has several millions of dollars in bank borrowing (part of its long-term debt) and has lines of credit (pre-authorized borrowing capability) for millions of dollars more. Suppose you are a commercial lending officer for a bank, conducting a regular review of the company's borrowing status. You must consider the quality of the company's financial performance and assets (some of which have been assigned as security on bank loans and, therefore, could be seized if the company didn't pay its loans back on schedule). Financial performance is important because good net income usually goes with generation of cash to pay loans, and a good past record suggests that the company is likely to be able to earn income and generate cash in the future. You have requested recent financial statements to use in your review.

Scenario 4: A supplier has to decide whether to sign a contract with the company.

4. CAE depends on a large number of suppliers to obtain raw materials and components of the products and services it sells. The company operates worldwide, and with its commitment to meet the needs of its own customers, has to be on good terms with all sorts of suppliers. Suppose you are the sales manager of an electronic components manufacturer and are considering signing a long-term supply contract with CAE. You want to sign the contract because your company would like the business, but you have to be satisfied that your shipments will be paid for and that CAE is well run, as your reputation will be tied to CAE's to some extent. More positively, you hope that if you do a good job, you will have an opportunity to grow with CAE. Most of the information you need has been received already, but you have obtained recent CAE financial statements and are reviewing them as you make your final decisions about the contract.

These scenarios have been chosen to add to your insight into the use of financial accounting information. They are not complete. *In all cases*, the financial statements would be only *part* of the set of information used in the decision-making. Also, as we saw in earlier sections, there are many other uses of financial statements, some of which might make different demands on the quality of the information than are discussed here.

Demands on the Quality of Financial Accounting Information

Let's think about what the users in these scenarios might reasonably expect of the financial statements. You'll see that important accounting concepts and principles, included in section 5.2 above, arise. Those are described in italics below.

1. The financial statements should not be deliberately misleading. The bank loans officer would want to feel confident that the statements were not prepared in such a way as to make the company appear to be a better lending risk than it is. The board of directors similarly would want the statements to provide an objective portrayal of the CEO's performance in running the company.

   This is the criterion of fairness. It is so important that the auditors' report (see section 5.8) refers to it explicitly. The auditors state their opinion that the financial statements "present fairly" the company's financial position and results. There is much flexibility and judgment involved in financial accounting, so the auditors cannot say that the statements are "correct," but they can testify to their fairness.

   As described in section 5.2, a very important fairness-related criterion for choosing accrual accounting methods is matching: revenues and expenses should be determined using compatible methods so that the net income (which is revenues minus expenses) makes sense. Matching is central to many accounting methods, including those for income tax, inventory, and cost of goods sold, amortization, pensions, and warranties. Much of the income measurement content of Chapter 6 has to do with matching.

2. Preparing financial statements, like any other activity, costs money and takes time. Most people would be satisfied if the statements were fair as to the *important* things and would not mind a few minor errors in them, especially if preventing small errors cost the company money (reducing the company's income and cash flow) or delayed the release of the statements. The supplier sales manager would not want to wait for the statements while CAE's accountants tried to get every tiny detail in the statements just right, nor would any other user who had to make a decision soon.

   This is the criterion of materiality (significance). Financial statements are supposed to be materially fair, so that users can be confident that the statements do not contain major errors. Materiality is also explicitly mentioned in the auditor's report: the auditors say that the statements present fairly, "in all material respects," or words to that effect. Just what is or is not material is a matter of judgment and has been the subject of considerable research and study by accountants and auditors. It is generally felt that an item, error, or disclosure is material if it would change someone's decision. Usually, people judge materiality by considering the size of a possible error compared to the net income or the total assets. For example, an accountant or auditor might judge that an error over 5% of net income or 1% of total assets is material and a smaller one is not. But, as you might expect, the materiality judgment depends on any particular uses of the information that are expected, and on whether the error seems to be a unique random problem or part of a repeated pattern of mistakes, or even fraud.

3. The criteria of fairness and materiality imply some standard against which an accounting method or number can be judged. The financial analyst would

---

The four example users all want the information they use to be fair.

Anyone evaluating performance would expect revenues and expenses to be matched.

Users are unlikely to be concerned about insignificant errors in the information.

like to know that CAE's financial statements were materially fair, *given* accepted current methods. In the income statement, for example, sales revenue should mean what a knowledgeable analyst or other user would expect for such a company. As a second example, CAE is actually a group of companies, so its financial statements are consolidated, and it would be reasonable to expect that the company's method of calculating consolidated figures is proper, in accordance with accepted practices for consolidation.

GAAP represent the quality standard against which the financial statements are held.

This is where GAAP come in. To assure the users that accepted methods have been followed, the auditor's report also says that the auditors' opinion is that the statements have been prepared "in accordance with generally accepted accounting principles." This does not necessarily mean that any one particular method has been followed: GAAP often include several acceptable methods, depending on the circumstances. Therefore, following GAAP means that the company's accounting methods and the resulting figures are appropriate to its circumstances. Remember the repeated references to the entity's particular circumstances in the previous section (5.2).

4. If accounting information is to tell people about the economic forces affecting the company and the business arrangements the company has made to deal with those forces, it should connect to such important underlying phenomena. A financial statement that is fair would also thus agree with these phenomena, and the auditors should be able to trace the accounting back to the phenomena to verify that the accounting does agree. The board of directors should be able to assume that the company's figure for sales revenue is supported by sales invoices, cash records, shipping records, and other evidence of actual sales.

All users want their financial statements to be reliable and verifiable.

This is the criterion of reliability. The financial statements should report the economic substance of events happening to the company; the numbers should be verifiable back to evidence of such events, and the numbers should measure the events neutrally, neither overstating nor understating their impact. (Verifiability involves being able to reconstruct the accounting numbers by checking evidence, identifying assumptions and estimates, and redoing calculations.)

Conservative accounting avoids overstating the good news in financial statements

Most accountants, and those who set the standards for companies to follow, believe that it is prudent to be cautious when estimating uncertain amounts, such as future collections and the value of unsold inventory. This leads to another criterion, conservatism. This often controversial criterion states that under uncertainty, assets, revenues, and income should not be overstated and liabilities, expenses, and losses should not be understated. Conservatism should involve being careful, not deliberately biasing important numbers, but just where prudence ends and bias begins is a matter of judgment.

5. The previous criteria indicate that the financial statements necessarily reflect judgment on the part of the preparers. Also, the figures in the statements are summaries of many accounts: for example, "accounts receivable" and "long-term debt" may include dozens or thousands of different customers or creditors. The bank loan officer may want to know what sort of long-term debts the company has, so that those may be evaluated against the bank borrowing by the company. The bank would not want other creditors to interfere with the company's ability to pay the bank back. The financial analyst may want

to know if the company has made commitments to issue more shares (such as in a plan to motivate senior management by issuing shares to them cheaply if they perform well), because issuing those might reduce the equity of anyone buying the shares now.

This raises the principle of disclosure. The financial statements include a large number of notes and account descriptions intended to make it clear to the reader which important accounting methods have been followed (especially if those methods are not what might be expected) and to provide supplementary information on debts, share capital, commitments, lawsuits, and other things thought to be helpful, or necessary, in understanding the statements. Disclosure beyond the accounting figures is increasingly extensive: many pages of notes often accompany the set of statements, and companies disclose additional information to taxation authorities, to securities regulators (such as the Ontario Securities Commission and the U.S. Securities and Exchange Commission), and to important other parties who have a reason to get the information (such as the bank loan officer and the financial analyst). Several aspects of disclosure are explored later in this chapter.

> **Extensive disclosure beyond the numbers is helpful in many situations.**

6. The banker and the financial analyst are also involved with other companies. They would like to be able to compare CAE's financial statements to those of similar companies, such as other technology and engineering companies. It may be difficult to be sure that a company is performing well or badly in an absolute sense, but it can always be compared to others, as long as the financial statements have been prepared in a comparable way.

    You will not be surprised that this principle is called comparability. It will be important when we review techniques for financial statement analysis in Chapter 10.

> **Most users want to be able to compare the company validly to others.**

7. The banker, the analyst, and the board of directors' members will also want to study the trend in financial performance and position over time. Is the net income improving over time, or deteriorating? How about liquidity? Or the ratio of debt–equity financing? It is important to know if significant events have happened to make comparisons over time difficult or even impossible. It is also important to know if the company has changed its accounting methods over time, because such changes may affect the comparability of the accounting figures from year to year.

    Keeping the same accounting methods over time is called consistency. It is usually presumed that if the company is following GAAP, that includes using consistent methods or else telling the reader of the statements what the effects of changes in accounting methods are (if they are material).

> **Comparisons over time are facilitated by consistency in accounting.**

These "information use scenarios" should help you see that accounting principles and concepts are central to the practice of accounting. They have a big influence on the numbers you actually see in financial statements, because companies generally try to follow them in ways suitable for each company. But sometimes following one principle seems to violate another.

Tradeoffs among Accounting Principles

> **The various concepts within GAAP do not always fit together well.**

If you think about the criteria and principles mentioned above, you may see that they do not always fit together well. Here are five examples:

- Conservatism is often argued to be a bias that interferes with fairness.

- If a company's circumstances are unusual, conforming rigorously to GAAP as followed by other companies may mean that the company's financial statements are not a fair portrayal of that particular company.

- If some other companies with which a company is likely to be compared (such as others in its industry) change their accounting methods, the company has to decide whether to change its methods too for the sake of comparability, even though that means inconsistency in its own figures over time.

- Similarly, when a new or revised accounting standard is announced, following the new standard (that is, conforming with GAAP as they now exist) will mean inconsistency over time for all companies that did not previously use the approved new method.

- Some people argue that it does not matter a great deal if a company's revenues and expenses are not properly matched, as long as the problem and information to adjust to other accounting methods are disclosed. The idea is that users of the company's financial statements can adjust the results to improve the match, if they do not like what the company did. (Doing such an adjustment is not always easy, however, even if all the information is available—some examples of making adjustments to reflect different accounting methods are given in later chapters.)

People's information needs and interests vary and conflict, and so do GAAP concepts.

You might feel that GAAP are not very well constructed if such problems can happen. People have certainly criticized GAAP for being inadequate and inconsistent. Many studies have been done to try to remove problems, including a multi-million-dollar study for the Financial Accounting Standards Board in the United States, called the "Conceptual Framework Project." That project was launched in the mid-1970s and was largely abandoned 10 years later. It appears that one framework, one way of thinking about financial statements, cannot deal with *all* the conflicting interests and priorities of the many users, preparers, and auditors. The inherent struggle and competition among people in our economic system tend to rule out single solutions, no matter how internally logical they may be, and the result is the rather imperfect but also flexible set of principles that make up GAAP. You might say there is something for everyone in GAAP, but not everything for anyone!

Here is an example of a tradeoff that simply cannot be avoided:

- It would seem sensible that the more reliable the accounting information is, the better. You get more reliable information by being very careful about how you prepare it, checking it carefully, having the auditors come in and verify it, maybe even waiting until some major uncertainties are resolved, so you do not have to guess about them.

- It also seems sensible that decision makers need information relevant to their decisions when they are making the decisions. This means that information should be timely: people should not have to wait for the information they need. Decision relevance and timeliness are two concepts behind GAAP mentioned in the previous section of this chapter.

Let's take the example of a company trying to report on its liability for pensions to employees. It has thousands of employees who will retire at various times over the next 40 years, if they do not quit, die, or get fired first. The pensions paid will depend on how much the employees earn before they retire, and that is not known yet for most of them—the younger ones' earnings are all in the future, and who knows what the future holds? The pensions also depend on how long the employees live after they retire and on whether they will have surviving spouses to be supported as long as they live. The company is trying to put aside enough money to cover all these pensions and will earn interest on the money saved for this purpose, so the amount of money required now also depends on how much interest will be earned on it over the years before the employees retire.

How is that for a mass of uncertainty? Any number you come up with for the pension liability will be based on all sorts of estimates of unknown future events. So to get a liability figure that is at all reliable, you really have to wait 20 or 30 years until most of the employees have retired. You can always expect to get reliability by just waiting a while, even years, to see how things turn out. But waiting 20 or 30 years will hardly provide timely information, relevant to decisions like those being made by the board of directors, investment analyst, banker, and supplier mentioned above. Such decisions require the best information we can come up with now, even if it is necessarily based on estimates and assumptions.

Therefore, there is almost never a solution that produces both the most reliable and timeliest, relevant accounting information. As time passes, reliability rises and timely relevance falls, so we have to try to find some mid-point where there is enough of both, but not as much as we would like of either! Figure 5.2 illustrates this relevance–reliability tradeoff.

A relevant figure may be unreliable, but waiting to make it reliable may make it irrelevant.

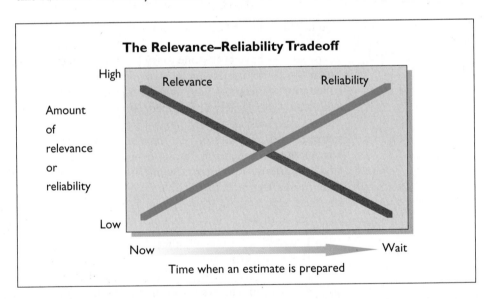

FIGURE 5.2

Here are two questions you should be able to answer, based on what you have just read:

1. You have just opened the annual report of CAE Inc. and found that the auditor's report says that it is the auditor's opinion that the financial statements have been prepared in accordance with generally accepted accounting principles. What concepts of information value would the auditor have assumed as part of GAAP?

2. Can accounting numbers, such as those in CAE's financial statements, be relevant, reliable, fair, and conservative all at once?

5.4   FINANCIAL ACCOUNTING STANDARDS AND THEIR DEVELOPMENT

We left the review of historical developments relevant to financial accounting in section 3.3, with the development of stock markets and the income statement. Chapter 4 added the last financial statement, the relatively recent cash flow statement. The main development in the just-ended 20th century is the great growth in official accounting standards. This section traces their growth and present nature.[1]

The OSC and the TSE are very important in Canadian financial accounting, but so is the SEC.

Canadian accounting practice has its main roots in Britain, but in the last hundred years it began to develop more independently from that in Britain, but also coming under the stronger influence of events in the United States and internationally. Canada's federal system of government, different from the more centralized one in Britain, meant that legislation affecting accounting and professional accounting associations in Canada had strong provincial as well as national influences. As an example, in the early part of this century, Ontario led the rest of the country in introducing legislation that affected accounting methods. Today, the Ontario Securities Commission (OSC: www.osc.gov.on.ca) is the most important regulator of capital markets in Canada and therefore has great influence on the accounting used by corporations whose shares are traded on stock exchanges (especially the Toronto Stock Exchange, or TSE, the country's largest: www.tse.com). There is no national securities commission in Canada, while in the United States, the national Securities and Exchange Commission (SEC: www.sec.gov) plays an even more dominant regulatory role there than does the Ontario Securities Commission in Canada, and because of the influence of the United States on much of Canada's business practice, as in the rest of Canadian life, the SEC is also an important influence on Canadian accounting.

Income tax and U.S. investment have been significant to the development of Canadian accounting.

By 1920, legislation in Canada had established mandatory reporting of the financial position of incorporated companies (corporations) and had begun to set requirements for the contents of the income statement. The income statement became important both because income tax legislation passed in 1917 established rules for calculating revenues and expenses, and because the growing amount of equity investment in Canadian industry called for better performance measures and for more financial disclosure in general. Another reason for the income statement's growing prominence was the increased investment in Canadian industry by investors from the United States, which created a demand, similar to that in the United States, for disclosure of how net incomes, and therefore the dividends declared on the basis of the incomes, were calculated.

Capital market regulators pay close and increasing attention to financial accounting.

Though these pressures for more disclosure existed, the general prosperity in North America during the 1920s prevented serious concern about companies' financial disclosure. The 1929 stock market crash and ensuing Great Depression permanently changed this. From the 1930s onward, accounting practices, like many aspects of companies' financial and productive operations, attracted great, and often critical, attention from legislators and the public. The U.S. SEC was established in the mid-1930s, and securities commissions were also established in some of Canada's provinces, such as the OSC in Ontario. Their impact on business and financial accounting has steadily increased in the period since the Second World War.

Regulation of Financial Accounting: Accounting Standards

Professional associations of accountants began to develop more rigorous accounting standards and auditing standards for their members to follow, and legislation began to require companies to adhere to these standards. In Canada, the Dominion Association of Chartered Accountants (now called the Canadian Institute of Chartered Accountants or the CICA) presented briefs to Parliament on accounting issues, issued bulletins making suggestions on financial accounting and auditing standards, and in the late 1960s began to issue official standards in the *CICA Handbook*.[2] *CICA Handbook* standards are given considerable authority by company legislation and securities commissions' regulations and will be referred to frequently in this book. Having a detailed set of accounting standards with legal authority is quite a recent phenomenon in Canada, as it is in many parts of the world, but this is growing rapidly worldwide.

The *CICA Handbook* is the main source of financial accounting standards in Canada.

The *CICA Handbook* is a looseleaf package hundreds of pages long (quite a handful!) that is continuously updated to reflect the standard-setters' judgments about how to deal with ever-changing circumstances. The public can get information about accounting standards through the CICA's Web site www.cica.ca and subscribers to the *CICA Handbook* receive it on-line through that site. Many professional accountants receive it as part of their professional membership. The *Handbook* consists of various discussions of accounting (and auditing) topics, accompanied by "Recommendations" on what to do in those cases that the standard-setters have resolved. The *Handbook* recognizes that its recommendations cannot cover everything and that there may even be circumstances where following them would be misleading. Therefore, accountants and auditors must exercise their professional judgment about each accounting issue: they cannot just ignore the *Handbook*, but neither can they just follow it if it does not apply appropriately to the issue. The overriding criterion is that the financial statements should present the company's financial affairs *fairly*. Fairness is a fundamental criterion in financial accounting; we will see it again shortly.

The *CICA Handbook*'s recommendations are intended to produce fair financial reporting.

In the United States, the American Institute of Accountants (now called the American Institute of Certified Public Accountants or the AICPA: www.aicpa.org) also began to issue pronouncements on financial accounting and auditing. The AICPA still issues auditing standards, but in the early 1970s its financial accounting standard-setting body, the Accounting Principles Board, was replaced by a new body set up to be independent of the AICPA: the Financial Accounting Standards Board (FASB: www.fasb.org). (This is unlike the situation in Canada, where the *CICA Handbook* standards are set by the Accounting Standards Board, a committee of the CICA. At this book's writing, information about the CICA's accounting standards could be found under "Standards and Guidance" at www.cica.ca.) The U.S. SEC generally supports the FASB's position as financial accounting standard-setter for the United States, which gives the FASB great influence in accounting throughout much of the world, including Canada. As in many countries, there has been quite a proliferation of accounting standards in the United States, with well over 100 separate FASB standards (many of those very long and complex) and many SEC pronouncements issued over the last 20 or so years.

The FASB is the main source of financial accounting standards in the United States.

There are many other voices in the setting of financial accounting standards and in the development of financial accounting. There is, for example, legislation requiring particular accounting methods for some sensitive companies, such as banks and trust companies. Standard-setting activities are also sometimes carried out by other associations, and courts often establish precedents in accounting issues as in other areas. There is much activity at the international level, such as that of the International Federation of Accountants (IFAC: www.ifac.org), and the International Accounting Standards Committee (IASC: www.iasc.org.uk), which,

Financial accounting standards arise from sources other than the CICA and FASB.

founded in 1973, has published a large number of international financial accounting standards. These standards have so far been less binding than such national standards as those issued by the CICA or the FASB, but there is great interest in harmonizing standards so that investors, managers, and other interested parties will be able to rely on the content and quality of financial statements no matter where in the world the statements originate.

FOR YOUR INTEREST

Managers may be interested in accounting standards for several reasons. On the positive side, standards should:

1. Make reporting managers' performance clearer;

2. Make for easier comparisons with other companies;

3. Reduce the costs of accounting (each company would not have to work through and invent accounting methods on its own);

4. Increase the company's credibility to important users of financial statements in general; and

5. Help to evaluate the conceptual and numerical effects of accounting choices and business decisions managers may have to make.

On the negative side:

1. Standards may specify general methods that do not work well for, or even mismeasure, some specific companies or situations.

2. Not all managers may wish to be measured clearly or have their company's performance easily comparable to that of other companies.

3. Some complex standards may be quite costly to follow for some companies.

4. New standards may cause difficulty for loan agreements, bonus plans, or other arrangements that depend on accounting information and that were agreed to prior to the implementation of the new standards.

With reasons like these, it should be no surprise that the top managers of many companies take accounting standards very seriously. Many companies seek to influence accounting standards through lobbying standard-setters (such as CICA or FASB), securities commissions, other government agencies, and doing studies of the effects of proposed standards.

Financial accounting continuously affects, and is affected by, society's economic activity.

The 20th century saw great growth in business and commercial activity, in stock markets and other capital markets, in international trade, in governments, in the sophistication of managers and investors, and in the communication links among them all. At any hour of the day, there is a major stock market open somewhere, with investors from all over the world trading on it. Business activity is truly a 24-hour-a-day, 365-day-a-year affair, with information about business activities flowing throughout the world via electronic, paper, and other media. Financial accounting is being continually shaped by all this activity. The basic double-entry model of financial accounting has endured for hundreds of years, but the way that model is applied and the supplementary information associated with it have developed far beyond Pacioli's description. Financial accounting's measures of financial position and performance are central to national and international economies and political structures, and financial accounting and its standards themselves are economically and politically powerful institutions in society.

Financial accounting is continuously evolving as the nation and the world evolve. This is not to say that every change is for the better, any more than it is in other human endeavours, but rather to emphasize that financial accounting is an organic, evolving discipline: the best prediction we can make about future balance sheets, income statements, and cash flow statements is that they will not be exactly the same in the future as they are now. This book attempts to develop in you an understanding of how financial accounting got to where it is and what the pressures on it are. This understanding will help you to keep in mind that financial accounting is not cast in stone and will equip you to deal with the changes that are sure to come. If you want to keep up with what is going on, accounting associations have active Web sites containing information about changing business practices, accounting developments, and professional activities. Here are some to try (some were already mentioned in the discussion above):

Both preparers and users of financial accounting should keep up with ongoing change.

- Canadian Institute of Chartered Accountants: www.cica.ca

- CGA-Canada: www.cga-canada.org

- Society of Management Accountants of Canada: www.cma-canada.org

- American Institute of Certified Public Accountants: www.aicpa.org

- Financial Accounting Standards Board (U.S.): www.fasb.org

- Institute of Chartered Accountants in England and Wales: www.icaew.co.uk

- International Accounting Standards Committee: www.iasc.org.uk

Financial accounting concepts are based on good practice as well as theory.

Financial accounting has a surprisingly large set of concepts and principles to guide accountants in preparing financial statements, auditors in verifying them, and users in interpreting them. A very large amount has been written about the conceptual and theoretical side of accounting, and as we have seen, several groups are involved in setting financial accounting standards and otherwise regulating accounting information. All this material occupies many metres of library and office shelves and much space in computer databases and Web sites. These concepts have been deduced by accountants, researchers, and standard-setters from logic and observation of good practices, and they are used to guide everyone who prepares, audits, uses, or studies financial accounting. The *CICA Handbook*, for example, accompanies its standards with much conceptual material, including a whole section devoted to financial accounting concepts.

GAAP, including authoritative standards, always leave room for professional judgment.

GAAP are the rules, standards, and usual practices that companies are expected to follow in preparing their financial statements. They are a combination of the **authoritative standards** issued by accounting standard-setters (such as the CICA in Canada, the FASB in the United States, the IASC internationally) and the accepted ways of doing accounting that are not included in such standards. Year by year, the set of authoritative standards grows, as does the larger set of generally accepted accounting principles that includes those standards and other accepted practices. However, the world continues to increase in complexity, so neither the standards nor GAAP are ever extensive enough to include everything. Economic complexity seems likely to keep increasing, so it is likely that there will always be a gap between the demand for good financial accounting and the authoritative and generally accepted responses to the demand. Perhaps that is just as well: accounting rules that tried to cover everything would be enormously complex themselves and might even get in the way of useful economic change. The existence of a gap between what is authoritative or merely acceptable practice and the demand for good accounting means that accounting professionals will continue to play an important role for society by exercising their judgment and expertise to solve financial accounting problems.

Figure 5.3 depicts the great growth in authoritative standards and other parts of GAAP as the world's business and accounting complexities continue to grow.

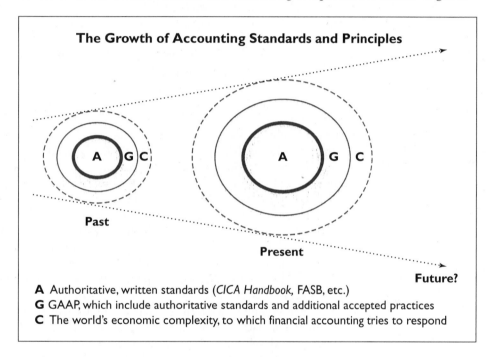

The Growth of Accounting Standards and Principles

A Authoritative, written standards (*CICA Handbook,* FASB, etc.)
G GAAP, which include authoritative standards and additional accepted practices
C The world's economic complexity, to which financial accounting tries to respond

FIGURE 5.3

(H)OW'S YOUR UNDERSTANDING?

Here are two questions you should be able to answer, based on what you have just read:

1. Why do we have accounting standards and who issues them?

2. Are these authoritative accounting standards all there is to GAAP?

5.5   INTERNATIONAL AND NONBUSINESS ACCOUNTING STANDARDS

This section is a reminder that there is much more to financial accounting than implied by this book's focus on Canadian business corporations. International accounting standards were mentioned in the previous section: let's begin with them.

International Accounting Standards

As in business and economics generally, international issues are coming increasingly to the fore in financial accounting. So far, the standards of national bodies are still most important in each country (the CICA in Canada, the FASB in the U.S., etc.), but as was noted earlier, there has been an International Accounting Standards Committee since 1973 and it issues standards too. The IASC's members include nearly 120 professional accounting bodies in nearly 90 countries, and it has issued more than 30 individual standards. These standards cover about the same areas as the Canadian and U.S. standards: the goal is to develop common standards that could be used by companies operating in several countries, and eventually that all countries could use within their own borders. The term for this is harmonization, meaning that accounting standards would be alike from country to country so that international trade, stock markets, transfers of funds, and other international business could be assisted, or at least not impeded. As it is, each country's accounting standards are often quite different from those of other countries. Horror stories of companies showing huge incomes according to one country's rules and huge losses, in the same year, according to another country's rules are embarrassing to the accounting profession and awkward for regulators such as the SEC and OSC to deal with.

> International harmonization of accounting standards is a goal supported by many people.

There is a great amount of enthusiasm for international standards harmonization among the accounting professions in Western countries, though such countries do not want their own standards "watered down" to the level of less-developed countries. The less-developed countries are not necessarily keen to adopt the complex Western accrual accounting methods, especially since such countries may lack the legal, professional, and financial structures that have influenced the development of Western accounting over several hundred years. Governments in many countries see financial accounting as very important to their national economic and business goals, and do not support accounting methods seen as impeding or not promoting such goals. And many governments do not take the "hands off" attitude to accounting standards that has been the usual case in Canada, the U.S., the U.K., and similar countries. Some governments have passed laws that set strict requirements for financial accounting in accordance with national priorities and culture.

> Internationally harmonized accounting standards may not be to the liking of all countries.

> International standards harmonization will probably increase, in spite of many difficulties.

An illustration of the challenge to international standards is the attempt to make even the Canadian, U.S., and Mexican accounting systems similar, given that the three countries have signed the North American Free Trade Agreement (NAFTA). A recent study, *Financial Reporting in North America*, tackles the three countries' financial accounting and finds a great many differences.[3] Canadian companies wishing to do business in the U.S. already must pay close attention to U.S. standards, but even between Canada and the U.S., there were accounting differences. The study included Mexico in the comparison with the U.S. and found 32 categories of differences among a sample of surveyed companies, including differences in such major areas as the content of the cash flow statement, the way deferred (future) income tax expense is calculated, and the way shareholders' equity is reported.[4] Some of these differences have been addressed since the study came out, but it will take a while to iron out all of them. It may be optimistic to think they can ever all be removed, given that the three countries are different in important legal and business ways that affect accounting. It will take a great deal longer to accomplish the harmonization goal among the more than 100 countries (at last count) that belong to IASC! At this writing, the International Accounting Standards Committee is being reorganized to improve its ability to develop international standards that will be acceptable in both developed and less-developed countries, but it is too soon yet to say if the reorganization will persuade countries like Canada and the U.S. to adopt IASC standards instead of their own CICA and FASB standards. In spite of the difficulties, there seems to be considerable momentum toward strong and common international standards, accepted in all major countries, so it seems a good bet to say they will exist some day.

An Example: Disclosures of Changes in Equity

FASB standards in the U.S. require more attention to changes in shareholders' equity than is typical under CICA standards in Canada. As a result, U.S. companies do not have just a Statement of Retained Earnings, but rather roll that statement, along with explanations of changes in all the other equity accounts, together into a Statement of Stockholders' Equity. Here is a 1999 example, taken from the Web site of U.S. company Emerson Electric Co. (www.emersonelectric.com).

5-1

Exhibit

Consolidated Statements of Stockholders' Equity
Emerson Electric Co. and Subsidiaries

Years ended September 30
(Dollars in millions except share amounts)

	1999	1998	1997
Common stock	$ 238.3	238.3	238.3
Additional paid-in capital			
Beginning balance	27.9	3.3	12.3
Stock plans	(3.5)	(43.4)	(2.8)
Treasury stock issued for acquisitions and other	(.5)	68.0	(6.2)
Ending balance	23.9	27.9	3.3
Retained earnings			
Beginning balance	7,056.5	6,348.9	5,707.7
Net earnings	1,313.6	1,228.6	1,121.9
Cash dividends (per share: 1999, $1.30; 1998, $2.18; 1997, $1.08)	(566.4)	(521.0)	(480.7)
Ending balance	7,803.7	7,056.5	6,348.9
Accumulated other nonstockholder changes in equity			
Beginning balance	(236.2)	(205.9)	(29.2)
Translation adjustments	(35.4)	(30.3)	(176.7)
Ending balance	(271.6)	(236.2)	(205.9)
Treasury stock			
Beginning balance	(1,283.2)	(963.9)	(575.7)
Acquired	(361.2)	(498.4)	(427.2)
Issued under stock plans	27.9	108.5	18.3
Issued for acquisition and other	2.7	70.6	20.7
Ending balance	(1,613.8)	(1,283.2)	(963.9)
Total stockholders' equity	$6,180.5	5,803.3	5,420.7
Nonstockholder changes in equity (Net earnings and Translation adjustments)	$1,278.2	1,198.3	945.2

Is the U.S. standard for more disclosure about equity changes preferable to the Canadian practice?

There is more information than we've seen in Canadian examples. Each equity account is shown, just as the retained earnings changes were in the examples in Chapter 3, and a summary line even separates the total changes from those directly involving stockholders (shareholders). If accounting standards were harmonized even just between these two countries, would you want the more-informative U.S. version, or prefer to stay with just the retained earnings changes reported in Canada? The principle of disclosure would suggest that the more information the better, and so support the U.S. version. On the other hand, some people feel that adding information to already-complex financial statements would not help all the users who already struggle with trying to understand them. (Because of the U.S.'s importance in Canada, quite a few Canadian companies use the U.S. disclosure, which more than satisfies Canadian standards.)

 OR YOUR INTEREST

There can even be lack of harmonization within one country! In Canada, as in other countries, there has been a controversy over whether the financial accounting appropriate for large traded corporations like Emerson and CAE is also appropriate for small businesses. Such accounting is expensive and may be overly complex for reporting on simpler enterprises. In 1999, a CICA study group came down on both sides of the issue, recommending that small business enterprises ("SBEs") follow GAAP to ensure that their financial statements are credible to bankers and taxation authorities, but that where the financial reporting needs of SBEs are clearly different than those of larger public corporations, different accounting standards be developed for them.[5] The controversy will doubtless continue.

Governments

This book emphasizes business organizations because they provide quite enough complexity for an introductory study of financial statements! But there are many other kinds of organizations that produce financial statements, and because these organizations are often structured as they are for particular reasons, their accounting must adapt to their legal, organizational, and financial peculiarities. Two common nonbusiness organizations are governments and not-for-profit organizations.

Governments represent people but do not have owners, nor are they created to earn income or retain earnings. Therefore, government financial statements differ from those of business in many ways, including:

- No owners' equity section (usually just a "fund balance" that indicates assets minus liabilities).

- No income statement (instead, a statement of revenues and expenditures, using only partial accruals, for short-term receivables and payables, and related to authorized budgets and other rules set by legislatures).

- No or little reporting of long-term assets or their amortization (traditionally this is because income measurement is not a goal and so amortization of assets acquired in the past was thought less relevant than reporting current expenditures on long-term assets)—though more and more governments are now moving toward asset accounting and amortization, as mentioned in Case 2B about the Federal Government.

- Lack of provision for long-term obligations such as civil servant and tax-payer pension plans (the cost of which governments appear to expect to meet out of future tax revenues).

Financial accounting for governments reflects governments' differing circumstances.

- Lack of consolidation, because various special funds require separate accounting and legislator scrutiny (here too, there is some movement toward aggregating various government operations in financial reporting).

Government accounting is changing in Canada to incorporate more of the accrual accounting features that financial accounting for businesses has. However, because governments are the makers of the laws, a private organization's set of standards (such as the *CICA Handbook*) can have only a persuasive effect, not an authoritative one. It is likely that over the next decade or so, many government financial balance sheets will come to resemble business ones; however, the business concept of "net income" is probably too different from the objectives of government to make it likely we'll see a governmental income statement along business lines.

Not-for-Profit Organizations

Financial accounting for not-for-profit organizations is becoming more business-like.

An enormous range of organizations, including private clubs, charities, such as the Red Cross, sports teams, universities, political parties, research units, the Girl Guides, churches, and unions, are classified as not-for-profit (or nonprofit) organizations. The members of such organizations do not own them as do owners of businesses and do not have a right to a share of any equity (assets minus liabilities). Members of such organizations are not usually as oriented to making income, as are business owners, because most such organizations are created to perform a specific service or other function. Some of the accounting methods used by these organizations are similar to those of governments, but many such organizations, especially those close to being businesses, use fairly complete accrual accounting, including amortization.

Not-for-profit organizations often have special funds, such as capital funds raised from donation appeals, government grants, and bequests made in people's wills. Keeping various designated funds separate and accounting for operations separately from other activities (like fund-raising) requires accounting methods that can be more complex than those used by private businesses. Amortization and other accrual accounting procedures can also be more complex. The trend, encouraged by the *CICA Handbook*, is to bring the accounting for such organizations as much as possible under the same GAAP structure as that applying to businesses, without removing such important features as keeping designated funds separate and without obscuring the fair reporting of nonprofit activities by reporting them as if they were intended to generate profit.

 H OW'S YOUR UNDERSTANDING?

Here are two questions you should be able to answer, based on what you have just read:

1. What might lead the financial statements of governments and not-for-profit organizations to differ from those of businesses?

2. What might make international harmonization of accounting standards difficult?

5.6 THE ANNUAL REPORT AND THE SET OF FINANCIAL STATEMENTS

Financial reporting is important for many organizations. All incorporated companies, and most other legally constituted organizations, are required to prepare a set of financial statements at least annually, explaining their financial performance and position. Public companies, which are those whose shares are traded on a stock exchange or in more informal "over-the-counter" markets, usually also issue some interim or quarterly financial information, especially on the subject of earnings. Proprietorships, partnerships, and closely owned "private" corporations prepare annual financial statements, at their bankers' request or for inclusion with personal or corporate income tax returns, even if there are no other reasons for doing so. Such enterprises usually do not go to the lengths of disclosure and explanation that public companies do, or prepare annual reports, as the set of financial statements and notes are sufficient.

The standard set of financial statements has four statements plus notes.

In Canada, the standard set of financial statements has five components:

1. Balance sheet (statement of financial position).
2. Income statement.
3. Statement of retained earnings.
4. Cash flow statement (SCFP).
5. Notes to the financial statements (more on these in section 5.7).

The external auditor's report covers all five components of the set of statements.

A sixth item accompanies the financial statements and notes: the auditor's report on the fairness of the set. The contents of the statements and its notes are the responsibility of management, and the auditor's report consists of the auditor's opinion about those statements and notes. You should be skeptical of financial statements that have not been audited or those whose audit report is not attached. Letters or reports providing less than the audit assurance are often attached to financial statements; you should read any such assurances carefully because they usually are very careful about what level of assurance they do—and don't—provide. (More about the auditor's report is in section 5.8.)

Public companies and many other organizations include their set of financial statements in a much larger annual report. This report usually contains (in approximately the following order):

1. Summary data on the company's performance for the year, usually in a graphical or other easy-to-read form, and comparisons going back five or ten years;
2. A letter to the shareholders from the company's chief executive officer, who is usually its president or chairperson of the board of directors;
3. Information about the company's history, strategies, plans, products, locations, employees, and other matters to help the reader understand the company and put the rest of the annual report in context;
4. An often extensive "management discussion and analysis," including a description of the economic, financial, and other factors behind the company's business, usually broken down by its main products or departments;
5. A short section explaining that the financial statements and the general internal control of the business are the responsibility of management;

The annual report contains much in addition to the four financial statements and notes.

6. The set of financial statements, with extensive notes, and the auditor's report;
7. Various details about the company's legal status, names of its directors and officers, and other information the company thinks is important.

The following comment is from an article about the annual report:

> Although recent years have ushered in many changes in corporate financial reporting
> ... the annual report remains the centrepiece of the whole reporting process.... The
> world of financial reporting is changing. Recognition of users' needs has expanded
> such reporting far beyond the financial statements.[6]

Many people besides the company's accountants and the external auditors are
involved in preparing the annual report. The top managers set its tone, and advertising and public relations staff design its presentation, often using photos and
attractive graphs. Overall, the annual report can be quite a fancy document, and
75 or more pages long! Here are some comments about annual reports:

> At one time, annual reports were little more than a collection of financial numbers in
> a stapled booklet. Today, they've become full-blown magazine efforts, with ... as
> much information and pizzazz as they can pack between two covers ... [reflecting] the
> image the firm wants to project.[7]

> People want more, more, more [information]. But some things don't change, such as
> the need for honest, candid interpretation of company performance presented in such
> a way the average person can understand it.[8]

> Unlike academic report cards, the students whose work is assessed in these glossy cat-
> alogues get to grade their own work.... So enjoy the pretty pictures. But don't believe
> everything you read.[9]

> Annual reports—the yearly report card, photo album, and corporate promo in one.
> Some trumpet the successes of the 12 months past, real or not. Others just trumpet.[10]

In this book, much reference has been made to the financial statements contained
in CAE Inc.'s year 2000 annual report. At this writing, the company's Web page
(www.cae.com) has the full annual report available for reading, printing, or downloading under the headings Investors and then Financial Reports. You might be
interested to know that the CICA and the *National Post* newspaper sponsor a
yearly Annual Reports Awards competition. This has been going on since 1951,
and the overall winner in 1999 was CAE Inc.! Other award-winners were Mark's
Work Wearhouse Ltd., Bank of Montreal, and Nortel Networks.[11]

Annual reports, news, and other current information are on companies' Web pages.

Most companies, and many other organizations, have active Web sites. Your
Web search engine can usually find the home page you want if you just type in the
company or organization name. Please give accessing a company you're interested
in a try, and when companies are mentioned in this book, try their Web pages for
current information. With the advent of the Web, some companies have questioned the necessity of printing an expensive glossy annual report and have put
more information on their Web pages. Such Web pages also often have quarterly
reports and other "interim" news. Data services available through libraries and
commercial services like business newspapers have thousands of annual reports
available for electronic access and downloading. Look for investor relations or
shareholders' information sections in the companies' Web pages.

Here are two questions you should be able to answer, based on what you have just read:

1. What kinds of information would you expect to see in the annual report of a large public company like IBM, Bank of Nova Scotia, McDonald's, or Loblaws?

2. What parts of the annual report are normally included in the assurance provided by the external auditor's report?

5.7   NOTES AND OTHER SUPPLEMENTARY INFORMATION

The financial statement notes are an integral part of the set of statements.

Because the four standard financial statements are not enough to transmit all the information required by users of the statements, a variety of supplementary narrative and tabular data are appended to the statements. This is true whether or not the company prepares a full annual report with even more data, as described above. Accepted accounting practices provide that, at a minimum, certain added pieces are sufficiently important that they are considered an integral part of the statements and are covered by the auditor's report. Here are outlines of the kinds of information typically covered by the notes and supplementary disclosures.

1. Normally Required and Covered by the Auditor's Report

   a. A description of the company's significant accounting policies, understanding of which is necessary in interpreting the statements' figures (usually the first note following the statements).

   b. Backup details on any statement figures needing further explanation, typically the amortization figures, long-term debts, share capital, pension liability, and any accounts unusually calculated or very significant for the particular company.

   c. Information on some things not included in the figures, such as "contingent" (potentially possible) liabilities, purchase commitments, lawsuits, relationships with associated companies or persons, and significant "subsequent" events since the official balance sheet date (for example, a major fire).

   d. Analysis of revenues and contributions to income of any significant product-line or geographical "segments" of the company's business (for example, contribution of a lumber product line vs. a food line, or operations in Canada vs. the United States).

2. Also Fairly Standard, Especially for Larger Companies

   a. Comparative income and balance sheet figures going back at least five years, often ten. If a company changes any important accounting policy, it has to go back and change such trend analyses to keep past figures comparable.

   b. An explanation of the different responsibilities of management and the external auditors for the financial information and of management's responsibility to maintain control over the company's assets.

c. The "management discussion and analysis" of the decisions and results for the year, often several pages long, has become an important source of the background behind the numbers and notes in the financial statements. Look for the "**MD&A**" whenever you are trying to understand a company's performance and prospects.

3. Still Largely Voluntary

a. Graphs and other pictorial supplements.
b. Details of employment contracts, product specifications, business policies, donations, business objectives, and other such details.
c. Lists of subsidiary and associated companies, senior managers, office addresses and the home Web page.
d. Reports on pollution control, excellent employees, customer relations, human resource management, trade with unpopular countries, and other socially sensitive information.

 OW'S YOUR UNDERSTANDING?

Here are two questions you should be able to answer, based on what you have just read:

1. What kinds of footnoted information are covered by the auditor's report?

2. What is the MD&A?

5.8   THE EXTERNAL AUDITOR'S REPORT

The external auditor provides a professional opinion on the financial statements' fairness.

Several references to the external auditor (who normally is actually a firm of auditors) have been made already. The external auditor is a professional accountant, engaged to provide assurance about the fairness of the financial statements. Assurance refers to adding credibility to the financial statements by doing an expert examination of them and so adding the auditor's reputation to the statements. Fairness refers to lack of significant error, conformance with accepted accounting standards, and consistency. The auditor's report is normally a routine statement by the auditor, saying that in the auditor's opinion, the financial statements are fair. Such a routine report is often referred to as a clean opinion because it is not cluttered by problems or special circumstances. But if it is not routine, the auditor is trying to tell the users something important. The auditor may report a qualified opinion, indicating that the auditor has some concern about the statements; in extreme cases, the report may even say that the financial statements are not fair, or that the auditor cannot say one way or the other. These result from some very serious objection by the auditor to the contents of the statements or to restrictions on the auditor's ability to do a good job. Always check to see if the financial statements you are using have been audited, and if so, what the auditor's report says.

Financial statements are not necessarily audited fully—or even at all.

Often, smaller companies have something less than a full audit done on their financial statements. An example is a "review," in which a professional accountant has scrutinized the financial statements and conducted some more limited verification intended to catch major problems. In such a case, instead of an auditor's report, there will be a letter from the accountant or accounting firm stating that somewhat less has been done: read such a letter *carefully* so that you know how much assurance the accountants are offering. Even less review is provided by a "compilation," in which the professional accountant has assembled the financial statements from information provided by the enterprise and takes no responsibility at all for the validity of that information. You may well see financial statements that are entirely unaudited, accompanied by no professional assurance of any kind. Your reliance on such statements depends entirely on your reliance on the people who prepared the statements.

What does an external auditor or auditing firm do? *External auditing* refers to the evaluation of an organization's financial statements by an auditor who is supposed to be unconnected with, and so independent of, the management of the organization. The role of the external auditor has two fundamental parts:

- To have an independent, unbiased, and professional perspective; and

- To render a competent opinion on the fairness of the financial statements according to accepted accounting and auditing standards.

Many companies, governments, and other organizations also have *internal auditors*. Such auditors work within the organization and help management operate the organization. Their work is not dealt with in this book.

External auditors are almost always members of professional associations.

Let's begin with independence and professionalism. Auditors are members of professional associations, such as the Canadian Institute of Chartered Accountants and the corresponding provincial institutes (CAs), and, in the United States, the American Institute of Certified Public Accountants and corresponding state societies (CPAs). Other professional accounting associations also have auditing components, such as the Certified General Accountants' Association of Canada (CGA-Canada) and provincial associations (CGAs) and the Society of Management Accountants of Canada and provincial societies (CMAs). Laws usually restrict the right to be an external auditor, especially of public companies and other large enterprises, to members of specified professional associations. But there is no restriction on who can act as an accountant to prepare the financial statements.

A fundamental objective of these professional associations is to protect society by ensuring the professionalism and independence of the external auditors who belong to them. Protecting society should be consistent with protecting the association's members' professional reputations. To this end, there are complex rules of professional ethics that prohibit the external auditor from having a financial interest, directly and in most indirect ways as well, in the client companies or other organizations being audited. These rules and similar ones related to other relationships between the auditor and the client are intended to ensure that the auditor has no personal interest in whether the financial statements report one kind of performance or another. In other words, the auditor should be an unbiased, professionally skeptical reviewer of the financial statements and not someone who wants the result to turn out one way or another. Another term for this desirable state is objectivity. Here's what the rules of professional conduct say CAs in Alberta must do on any professional engagement, including an audit. CAs are told that they must be:

> ... free of any influence, interest or relationship which, in respect of the engagement impairs the member's professional judgment or objectivity or which, in the view of a reasonable observer, would impair the member's [the CA's] professional judgment or objectivity.[12]

Professional ethics require the external auditor to be independent and skeptical.

CGAs, CMAs, and American CPAs have similar independence rules of conduct to follow when doing audits and other professional engagements. Such rules do not yet exist in every country.

Maintaining this independence and objectivity is not easy, because the auditors are business entrepreneurs themselves and their clients pay them for doing the audit. The idea is that independence is maintained because the auditor is appointed by, and reports to, the shareholders, not management. Since the financial statements are reports on management's stewardship performance, the auditor is presumed to be working for the shareholders in verifying management's reports. In practice, however, external auditors must have a close working relationship with client management.

Also, managers are in a strong position to recommend a change in auditor if the relationship is not to their liking. Maintaining independence under these circumstances is difficult and is complicated further by the fact that auditing (public accounting) firms offer tax, consulting, and many other nonauditing services, the revenue for which may exceed the fee for doing the audit. It is also complicated by the fact that if users of financial statements suffer losses, they can, and often do, sue the auditor, so the auditor must be very careful not to be compromised by the relationship with management.

FOR YOUR INTEREST

External auditor independence is a continuously controversial issue. Articles abound with titles like "Who Can You Trust? Auditors, analysts and earnings reports are supposed to help you. Too often they don't,"[13] "Ethics Be Damned, Let's Merge"[14] (talking about mergers between big accounting/auditing firms and law firms, intended to provide broader services to clients), and "Certified Public Accomplice"[15] (criticizing U.S. CPAs who offer services like selling life insurance on which they may earn higher fees than as auditors). As the big professional firms get bigger and more global, they are often as big as many of their clients, with complicated business arrangements. Capital market regulators and the accounting professions are frequently embroiled in independence problems, especially when particular embarrassing examples occur. In an article titled "Where are the Accountants? Why auditors end up missing so many danger signs," this comment was made:

> It all seems so straightforward … the role accountants are supposed to play in keeping the financial system honest. The problem is, it doesn't seem to happen as often as it should. As one apparently prosperous company after another saw earnings crumble in the wake of an accounting scandal over the past year, the auditors— at least in their public statements—often acted as surprised as investors to see years of reported profits go up in smoke. None of the major [accounting] firms has emerged unscathed.[16]

The auditor's report is a professional opinion—not a guarantee—that the financial statements are fair.

The second part of the auditor's role is to render a competent opinion on the financial statements. In some of the above problems, there may have been more of a problem with competence than objectivity! The auditor's report is an opinion, not a guarantee, nor does it say that the company has performed well or badly. It simply says that the performance and the position have been measured and presented in a generally accepted and unbiased way. Given the complexity of accounting, auditing, and business in general, the auditor's opinion is fundamentally a professional judgment. The auditor must be competent but, in addition, must weigh all sorts of factors in determining whether the overall result is fair. Concerned about the quality of their judgment, auditing firms in North America have sponsored a great deal of research into the professional judgment of auditors.

The auditor focuses on detecting any material problems.

An external auditor tends to focus on issues that could have a significant effect on the financial statements (the "materiality" or significance criterion), because most people consider it uneconomical to have the auditor concern herself or himself with the many small errors and irregularities that may crop up during the year. Auditors plan their work so that they have a reasonable likelihood of detecting material misstatements and errors. This criterion has been claimed by auditors to apply to fraud and misrepresentation by management or employees, and so only those instances of fraud that are large enough to materially affect the overall financial information should be caught by the external auditors. For a large company, one with a net income of $100,000,000 or more, that would have to be a very large case of fraud indeed—in the millions of dollars. In practice, however, many client companies wish their external auditors to assist them in protecting and controlling cash and other assets subject to theft or misappropriation, so the auditors often spend significantly more time verifying cash and other such assets than would be warranted by the size of such assets in the financial statements.

Here is the external auditor's report on the CAE Inc. year 2000 financial statements that have been examined earlier in this book:

5-2

Exhibit

Auditors' Report to the Shareholders of CAE Inc.

CAE Inc.

We have audited the Consolidated Balance Sheets of CAE Inc. as at March 31, 2000 and 1999, and the Consolidated Statements of Earnings, Retained Earnings and Cash Flow for the years then ended. These financial statements are the responsibility of the Corporation's management. Our responsibility is to express an opinion on these financial statements based on our audits.

We conducted our audits in accordance with Canadian generally accepted auditing standards. Those standards require that we plan and perform an audit to obtain reasonable assurance as to whether the financial statements are free of material misstatement. An audit includes examining, on a test basis, evidence supporting the amounts and disclosures in the financial statements. An audit also includes assessing the accounting principles used and significant estimates made by management, as well as evaluating the overall financial statement presentation.

In our opinion, these consolidated financial statements present fairly, in all material respects, the financial position of the Corporation as at March 31, 1999, and the results of its operations and cash flows for the years then ended in accordance with Canadian generally accepted accounting principles.

PricewaterhouseCoopers LLP

Chartered Accountants   Toronto, Canada
                                         April 27, 2000

The form and content of the auditor's report changes every few years, as auditors rethink how best to communicate with the users of financial statements. Because the auditors are formally reporting to the owners of the company, not to management, the report is usually specifically addressed to the owners (the shareholders). The CAE auditor's report uses the current standard format, which has three paragraphs:

The external auditor's report usually has three standard paragraphs for its findings.

1. The first identifies the company and the set of statements and their date and states that they are the responsibility of management and that the auditors' responsibility is to express an opinion on them.
2. The second paragraph outlines what the auditors did to enable them to express an opinion, stating in particular that they followed generally accepted auditing standards (GAAS) in assessing the accounting principles and estimates used by management.
3. The third paragraph states what the auditors' opinion is concerning the fairness of, and adherence to, generally accepted accounting principles of the statements (or, if there are problems, the lack thereof).

You should expect to find most auditor's reports to be worded pretty well the same. This sounds boring, but there is a purpose: any nonstandard wording is likely a warning to anyone planning to use the financial statements in decision-making. For example, the first paragraph should cover all the statements you plan to use, prepared as of the date you expect. The second paragraph should say that the auditors followed GAAS in doing their work, that they did what professional auditors believe was appropriate. Any problems here, or restrictions on the evidence the auditor was able to examine, will be noted by the auditor and could be significant to the users of the statements. The third paragraph should say that the auditor's opinion is that the statements are fair, in accordance with GAAP. As mentioned earlier, there are three main exceptions to this *clean* opinion: a *qualified* opinion, when the auditor is generally satisfied except for a specified problem in doing the work or a specified departure from GAAP in the statements; an *adverse* opinion, when the auditor says that her or his opinion is that the financial statements are *not* presented fairly in accordance with GAAP; and *denial* of an opinion, when the auditors are unable to express an opinion either way because of a limitation in the work the auditors were able to do.

(H)OW'S YOUR UNDERSTANDING?

Here are two questions you should be able to answer, based on what you have just read:

1. The external auditor's report on a company's financial statements refers to "generally accepted auditing standards." Why is the auditor referring to GAAS?

2. The president of a small company recently said, "We need to have an external auditor for our financial statements so we can guarantee their accuracy to our bank." Will that be the result if an auditor is appointed?

5.9   THE NATURE OF A PROFESSION AND PROFESSIONAL ETHICS

Professionals and professional ethics are important in financial accounting.

Ethics came up in the above discussion of the auditor's report. But ethics involve more people than the auditors. Evolving systems of standards, such as GAAP and GAAS, work reasonably well partly because professionals, who are both expert and ethical, are involved. Ethical behaviour comes from personal standards plus various written codes of ethical conduct, all of which we might group together as professional ethics. Those who may be tempted not to be ethical know that severe penalties (including fines, penalties assessed by professional associations, and even imprisonment) can result from unethical behaviour.

Professional accountants are bound by standards of competence and ethics.

For many people today, there is strong concern about being professional. There are, however, certain occupations that have established status as the professions. In today's world, some groups that have this status are physicians, lawyers, engineers, architects, and professional accountants. Part of the reason these groups stand out is that entry into each of them requires a post-secondary education, including training and examination by practitioners, and members are bound by a code of conduct or professional ethics. Members of each professional group usually enjoy a monopoly in their particular area of expertise. Associations of architects, physicians, engineers, lawyers, and other members of legally recognized professions can all prevent people from calling themselves members of their particular professions and practising in that capacity. Such groups have to convince the public (as represented by governments, for example) that they have expertise and appropriate codes of ethical conduct, but also that entrance to their area of expertise should be regulated for the public good. In Canada, CAs, CGAs, and CMAs, and in the U.S., CPAs, all have entrance examinations, codes of ethical conduct, and other professional trappings. The same is true for professional accountants in many countries.

Professional accountants have a legally protected status and responsibilities to go with it.

Uncertified accountants do not enjoy the same powers or privileges that members of the above professions do. You, your friend, or anyone can all call yourselves "accountants." There are no restrictions preventing you or anyone else from advertising in the paper, yellow pages, or any other publication to attract clients. However, if you want to call yourself a CA, CGA, or CMA, you must meet various requirements, for these titles are professional designations protected by law, as are other professional designations. For professional accountants, there are both powers and restrictions (for example, advertising must meet certain standards of content and decorum). The rights that a particular profession enjoys come in return for promises made about the quality and ethics of its members' work. If a professional accountant has not lived up to the standards of conduct held by the profession, he or she can be reprimanded or expelled by the profession and/or sued in court. Anyone can be sued, of course, but professionals are usually held to a higher standard of performance than are nonprofessionals.

All told, being in a profession has many advantages (including service to society, monopoly over an area of work, collegial support, social prestige, and good pay), but one must remember that in return there is the social responsibility of discharging one's duties competently and in accordance with the profession's code of ethics. Professional codes of ethics involve not only behaving in a professional manner (for example, with integrity and objectivity), but also maintaining the level of expertise required in order to perform skillfully. This involves following procedures (often as set out in documents like the *CICA Handbook*) and exercising informed judgment that will, or should, ensure that high standards of work and performance are met.

Professional
accountants may
encounter many
ethical dilemmas.

Here are examples of ethical problems that may be faced by professional accountants. What would you, as a member of society or as someone who may rely on accounting information or auditors' reports, think would be appropriate ethical behaviour in each case?

- Mary works for a public accounting firm and is part of the team doing the external audit of Westward Industries Inc. Staff at Westward are all very friendly, and Mary is offered the chance to buy one of the company's high-quality sound systems for only half the usual price. Should she accept the deal?

- Karim is also on the Westward external audit team. He is a member of a bowling league. During a game, he hears a member of another team boast of cheating Westward systematically by overbilling on printing invoices. Should he tell Westward?

- Joan and Henry fall in love and decide to marry. Both are professional accountants: Joan is the chief accountant of Westward, responsible for preparing all the company's financial statements, and Henry is a partner of the public accounting firm and is in charge of the external audit of the company. Should Henry turn the audit over to another partner, or perhaps even ask the accounting firm to resign as auditor (because as a partner, he shares in the firm's income from all audits)?

- Michel is another member of the Westward external audit team. During some audit tests, he discovers that Westward engaged in some business activities that appear to be illegal. Breaking that particular law can bring large fines and even jail terms. Should Michel go to the police?

- Erin works for the same public accounting firm. During the audit of Basic Electronics Ltd., she discovers that an employee of Basic is overcharging Westward by applying too high a markup to services contracted with Westward. Documents indicate that Basic's management is aware of this and is happy to be getting away with it, because it has a material effect on Basic's income. Should she tell the management of Basic that she knows what they are doing? Should she tell Henry, the partner responsible for the Westward audit? Should she tell Westward?

- Giorgio is a partner of the same public accounting firm. For years, his father has owned a few shares of Westward, among a whole portfolio of shares of many companies. His father has just died and willed all the shares to Giorgio. Should he sell the Westward shares?

Ethical rules help in
these dilemmas, but
professional judgment
is also required.

Well, we could go on for some time. One of the more interesting and challenging aspects of being a professional is dealing with such ethical issues. Some of the examples above do not have clear answers, but here are some ideas:[17]

- The external auditors are supposed to be independent scrutineers of their clients' financial affairs. Mary should probably not accept the deal, unless it is available to anyone who turns up at a retail store, because accepting it would undermine her independence. Being friendly with clients is fine, but auditors also have to maintain some distance from clients to protect their independence and integrity.

- Karim should tell Westward what he heard and suggest they look into their printing costs. When doing their work, auditors acquire much confidential information about their clients and must be very careful about how they use it. In this case, the information was not acquired under circumstances of confidentiality. He may find himself in court over the issue, however, so he may need to seek legal advice before speaking to Westward.

- Henry needs to take some action to remove himself from the job of auditing his wife's work, to protect both her and his integrity. The public accounting firm probably has rules about such relationships, which likely involve transferring the job to another partner and keeping Henry entirely ignorant of the work on the Westward audit. The firm might have to resign the audit (this would likely be expected in the United States, for example); Westward might even ask the firm to do so to protect the credibility of its audited financial statements.

- Michel's situation is very complex. There is a mixture of confidentially acquired information and a duty to society. Much more has to be known before any advice could be offered to Michel. At the very least, Michel and the public accounting firm would have to get legal advice immediately. The board of directors of most large companies has an **audit committee** (usually composed of directors who are not also officers or employees of the company) to give the auditors a way to bring criticisms of management to the board's attention. Michel's firm would likely raise this with Westward's audit committee.

- Erin's is another very complex situation. Erin is responsible for protecting the confidentiality of her client, Basic, and would be in trouble if she told another company what she learned on the audit. But her firm is responsible to both clients. Again, she and the firm would need immediate legal advice.

- Most public accounting firms have rules prohibiting members of the firm from having an interest in any clients audited by the firm. Giorgio would probably have to sell his shares of Westward.

(H)OW'S YOUR UNDERSTANDING?

Here are two questions you should be able to answer, based on what you have just read:

1. Why do professional accountants have to abide by codes of ethics, and what difference might that make to the users of their services?

2. What ethical issues do you see in the following situation? During the audit of Westward Industries Inc., Sonya discovered that an accounting clerk, needing money for a child's operation, had temporarily taken some cash collected from customers. The clerk had returned the money a short time later, before anyone had known it was missing, and was otherwise a very competent and valued employee. The company's controls over cash have since been tightened, and it is unlikely that the clerk would be able to repeat the theft. Sonya is the only person, other than the clerk, who knows about the theft.

5.10 CAPITAL MARKETS

Frequent references have been made to stock markets and their investors/traders, and the importance such markets have for financial accounting, both directly and through the influence of regulators such as the OSC in Canada and the SEC in the U.S. This section provides some background on capital markets (which include stock markets) and their connection with financial accounting. Nearly everyone is affected by how these markets work, through pension plans, retirement savings plans, and individual investments, and they have provided a powerful impetus to research in economics, finance, and accounting.[18]

Stock Markets and Other Markets for Financial Capital

As business corporations developed, ownership rights in them were sold more and more broadly. The owners (shareholders) began to invest in several businesses at once and to buy and sell their shares from and to each other. To facilitate such buying and selling ("trading") of shares among these investors, stock markets organized as stock exchanges developed. Today there are many such exchanges, including the major international ones in New York, London, Tokyo, Paris, and Toronto, as well as specialized or regional exchanges. There are also "over-the-counter" markets and other alternatives to the major exchanges. Brokers, investment banks, market analysts, and others conduct, assist in, and advise on trading.

> Stock markets facilitate the exchange of shares by investors.

Trading goes on in more than just shares of companies. There is also trading of rights (using terms such as "warrant" or "options") to buy or sell shares in the future, to convert from one kind of share to another, to receive dividends, and to perform a wide variety of other future actions. New rights and financial instruments to convey such rights are being invented and traded all the time. Special markets have been developed for some of these, such as an options exchange in Chicago, but many are traded on regular stock exchanges. Corporate and government bonds are also traded, and there is such a variety of financial instruments that the distinction between ownership shares, creditorship bonds, and other rights and instruments is often blurred. For example, some bonds carry the right to be converted into shares at the option of the holder.

> Many bonds and other kinds of financial instruments are also traded on exchanges.

Many exchanges and over-the-counter markets use computerized trading systems for the listed companies whose shares and other securities (the usual general name for all these shares, bonds, and other financial instruments) trade on the exchanges and other markets, and, increasingly, investors can buy or sell securities pretty well 24 hours a day somewhere in the world. Taken together, all these exchanges, markets, and buying and selling activities are usually called capital markets. They include both share (stock) trading and trading of all the other securities that corporations and governments use to finance their assets.

> All kinds of securities and exchanges make up the world's capital markets.

These markets operate quite separately from the companies and other organizations that initially issue the securities.

> Capital markets follow their own paths, separate from the issuers of securities.

- For example, when a company (a corporation) decides to issue some bonds or shares, these securities are offered to the market(s), and the company receives the proceeds of the initial sale of them (less commissions to brokers and others involved). After that, however, the company ceases to be a direct participant. Investors buy the securities from each other and sell them to each other with no participation from the company.

- Investors may even act in the face of opposition from the company. For example, an investor may try to get enough shares together to get voting control of the company (a "takeover"). There is always a risk for so-called public companies (companies whose shares members of the public are able to buy or sell from each other without permission of the companies) that the markets will behave in ways the companies do not like.

- There are other examples of investors acting in ways not desired by the company. One is that the company may announce a new management team that it expects will improve the company's performance, only to see the price of its shares fall because the people buying and selling the shares do not like the new team and more people want to sell their shares than want to buy them, producing a fall in the share price.

- The markets often create new securities out of the ones the company initially issued and then trade those. For example, a share may carry the right to buy another share in the future. That right may be bought and sold separately on the market, so that you could own the share without any such right, or the right without any such share. You might even be able to buy an "option" consisting of a bet as to whether the share price will rise or fall in the next month or year, or buy a bet as to the overall price of the market's shares in the future. (Overall price measures, such as the Dow Jones Average or the Toronto Stock Exchange Index, are closely watched by many people. At this writing, for example, the Web sites of the CBC (www.cbc.ca), the *National Post* (www.nationalpost.com), the *Globe and Mail* (www.globeandmail.com), and many other organizations report these averages and other stock market information daily.)

Security Trading and Security Prices

Capital markets work about the same as any market. People trade (buy and sell) what they own for something else, usually money or a promise of it.

- There are people who own securities, such as shares of CAE Inc., Bombardier, IBM, or any other public company. Some of these people will be willing to sell their shares, if the price is right. If no one was willing to sell at any price, there would be no trading!

- There are people who don't own the securities, but who are willing to buy them from the above people, if the price is right. If no one was willing to buy at any price, there would be no trading! Let's call the first group the "sellers" and the second group the "buyers." Suppose we had the following list of possible prices of CAE shares (hypothetical, but in the range of CAE's recent trading prices on the Toronto Stock Exchange):

Price	Sellers' Willingness to Sell	Buyers' Willingness to Buy
$18	Everyone would sell	No one would buy
$14	Most would sell	A few would buy
$10	Half would sell	Half would buy
$ 6	Some would sell	Most would buy
$ 2	None would sell	All would buy

Securities' prices on capital markets are set by supply and demand forces, like any market.

You'll recognize from this list of prices that we have a supply curve and a demand curve. Capital market prices are set by the interaction between those wanting to sell and those wanting to buy. At a price of $18, there'd be lots of shares for sale but no buyers; at a price of $2, there'd be lots of buyers but no sellers. Each day's market price for the shares is set by the balance between people willing to buy and people willing to sell:

- If there are more sellers than buyers, the price will fall, roughly down to the level at which there is an equal number of buyers and sellers (or at least, shares demanded and shares for sale); and

- If there are more buyers than sellers, the price will rise, roughly up to the level at which there is an equal number of sellers and buyers (or shares for sale and shares demanded).

In the above example, we'd expect the buyers and sellers to agree to trade (buy and sell) at a price around $10. So if we looked up CAE's shares in the newspaper's listing of TSE prices, we'd expect to see today's price to be about $10. But the daily price is set by the pressures of supply and demand, so it will vary depending on how many buyers and sellers make offers to buy or sell, and, therefore, it will vary around $10 as those pressures vary.

Role of Information in a Capital Market

Why would the pressures of supply and demand vary? Broadly speaking, there are three kinds of reasons that are of interest in understanding the role financial accounting information plays:

Part of the capital market's supply and demand is not particularly related to information.

1. *Noninformation-based trading.* The circumstances of some buyers and sellers may require them to sell, or even buy, almost regardless of anything to do with the particular company whose shares are being traded. An owner of some shares may die and the estate may have to sell the shares in order to distribute the money to the beneficiaries of the owner's will. Or an "institutional" investor, such as a pension plan, may need some cash to pay pensions or other payments. Or a person may win a lottery and buy shares in a mutual fund (an investment consisting of a sample of shares of many companies), so that the mutual fund in turn has to buy some shares. Therefore, some trading is likely to be occurring continuously for reasons of raising or spending available cash. Such trading is referred to as "liquidity trading."

Part of the capital market's supply and demand is related to general information.

2. *General information-based trading.* Companies whose shares are traded are part of a general economic system, and some general events may change people's views on the wisdom of investing in anything and so cause changes in all or most shares traded on an exchange. The share price of companies such as CAE may therefore change along with the rest. Examples of such general events are changes in national interest rates, announcements of trends such as inflation or consumer confidence, wars, illness, or death of important people, and elections that change the party in power. If the Canadian federal government announced a new special tax on corporations' incomes, we might expect pretty well every company's share price to fall, including CAE's, because investors would see this as hurting every company's future incomes and, therefore, the returns investors would get from owning shares in any company. Market-wide price changes coming from the economic system are often called "systematic" effects. It is not clear theoretically why general informa-

tion generates trades, because if all companies are affected, why bother to trade? Some of the trades may happen because investors think some companies will be hurt or helped more than others, and some investors may be getting out of that market altogether, such as by selling their shares and buying gold or real estate.

Much of the capital market's supply and demand relates to security-specific information.

3. *Specific information-based trading.* Information specifically about CAE's future prospects may also cause changes in the willingness of people to buy or sell its shares. For example, if the company announces that it is going to buy another company, some people may like that idea (and, wanting to buy, increase the demand for shares) and other people may dislike the idea (and, wanting to sell, increase the supply of shares). If most people think buying the other company is a good idea, the share price will rise; if most people think it is a bad idea, the share price will fall. This phenomenon, in which share prices reflect people's evaluation of the impact or meaning of an event on the wisdom of holding a company's shares, is very important to understanding share prices and accounting's information role. We can say that the stock market "prices" the information, in that the change in the trading price of the shares (up, down, or not at all) is a measure of the value of the information to the market. We might say that *decision-relevant information* is *material* to the market if knowing about it changes, or would change, a security's market price or, perhaps, would prompt trading (buying and selling) even if the net effect on price were zero.

A great amount of analysis and research in accounting, finance, and economics uses this third role of information to measure the apparent value of all sorts of company-specific and security-specific information, such as the company's annual announcement of its net income ("earnings announcement"), announcements of changes in management, and news about other events initiated by or affecting the company. (Using change in capital market prices as a measure of information value requires some faith in the market system, and confidence in the market's ability to respond appropriately to information.)

Return and Risk

The return from holding a security is part current cash flow and part price change.

The return you earn by owning a security such as a CAE share is the sum of:

- the cash you get (from dividends or interest payments), and
- the change (hopefully an increase) in the market price of the security.

So you get a cash return plus a holding gain or "capital gain" (or loss).

Price change risk may be systematic (general) or unsystematic (security-specific).

If the security you own varies in market price, that variation is, according to capital market theory, a measure of the *risk* from owning the security, since price could go up or down. Risk is calculated as the variance or standard deviation of the prices around the average price, or trend in average price, of that security. A risky security, therefore, is one whose price varies all over the place. As described above, a security's price may vary because the whole stock market or bond market is going up or down, or because of information specific to that security, or to the company issuing the security. So, analytically, the price change risk is separated into:

- *systematic risk*: the portion of the security's variation that relates to or correlates with variation in the overall market; and

• *unsystematic risk*: the security's own residual variation not related to the market. "Beta" (a term coming from the mathematical model used to relate a firm's returns to those of the market overall) is a measure of the security's relationship to overall market variations. Securities can be classified according to this relationship: a *low-beta* security's prices vary *less* than overall market prices do, while a *high-beta* security's prices vary *more* than the market.

Accounting
information has
modest value in
predicting prices and
price change risk.

A natural question at this point might be, "Does accounting information (especially income or cash flow) help to predict security prices and, therefore, risks and returns?" Market prices are pretty hard to predict, period. Therefore, accounting information isn't much help, but neither is anything else. However, accounting information can be helpful indirectly. When important events that do affect security prices are also represented in the accounting information (perhaps later on, since accounting reports come out only quarterly or annually), then the accounting information will indirectly be predictive too. It depends on how well accounting does represent the original event: it seems that if phenomena reported in the accounting information have a clear economic meaning (such as when they represent an impact on cash or risk), they do have some incremental predictive value.

Accounting
information does
relate to actual price
changes that happen.

After the fact, however, it is clear that accounting information (especially earnings) does correlate highly with market prices. The longer the accounting–price relationship is measured, ordinarily the better it is: accounting earnings, for example, usually correlate better with stock prices over several years than over a few months. Accounting does relate to whatever affects markets, though calling the shots in advance is hard!

Aggregates

A portfolio of
investments has less
unsystematic risk than
individual securities
have.

Securities markets involve aggregate behaviour. To reduce risk, investors will invest in a group of securities, termed a *portfolio*. By choosing securities with differing risks, the investor can assemble a portfolio with whatever overall risk the investor wishes. Generally, a portfolio is less risky than any individual security because, by adding together a group of securities with different unsystematic risks, the unique variations in each partially cancel out. When one's price goes up, another's may go down. Thus, a portfolio is a way of "diversifying away" the unsystematic risk.

Portfolio thinking has become pervasive in the investment community. Most research on the impact of accounting information presumes that investors have portfolios of securities, and when companies are accounting for their *own* investments (marketable securities and pension funds, for example), they increasingly make the same presumption.

Market Informational Efficiency

An efficient capital
market revises its
prices properly and
quickly for any
information.

Efficiency of information use means that markets respond so quickly and smoothly to information that, once the information becomes public, its effects are immediately reflected in prices through the trading of securities. People who think the information implies that they should buy, do so, from people who think they should sell. This fast response means that if the market is efficient, you can't use publicly available information (such as public financial statements everyone can read) to "beat" the market; by the time you have the information and can act, the market will already have reacted to the information and produced a new trading price that reflects the information. You, as an individual trader, don't have the power to do much about the price that the overall sum of buys and sells has produced, so, unless you can trade on your information before anyone else knows it, you will find that the price already reflects the information. If everyone gets an accounting report at the same time, probably only those traders nimble enough to act immediately will be able to take advantage of any news in the report.

An efficient capital market responds to information it does not expect.

Capital markets operate on information, but they do so in light of expectations already formed, in accordance with what was already known. Therefore, the markets tend to respond to new information only if it is *unexpected*. The argument can be made that for an efficient capital market, only the unexpected portion of earnings (or of any other such item or announcement) is information to the market. The market will not respond much to financial results that are exactly as everyone expected. There always is some response, though, because of liquidity trading and because various market traders have different expectations and beliefs—these differences make the markets work!

Capital market efficiency is a hypothesis, not a fact, but is supported by research.

Research indicates that some markets (for example, the New York Stock Exchange) are quite efficient with respect to publicly available information, but many people doubt these findings. The research is by no means conclusive, and the behaviour of many markets is not well understood. Because informational efficiency is a difficult phenomenon to demonstrate conclusively, it is often called a hypothesis about how markets work: the **efficient market hypothesis**.

Fair trading requires a fair distribution of information.

Securities commissions and other market regulators are responsible for ensuring that securities trading is as fair as possible. One problem securities commissions worry about is so-called asymmetric information: some market traders know more than others do about a security and, therefore, potentially can take advantage of the more ignorant traders. If you know that bad things are ahead, you sell to people who don't know that the price will fall when everyone learns about the bad things, or if you know that good things are ahead, you buy from people who don't know their shares are worth more than they think. A major role of financial accounting is to reduce information asymmetries by producing information that informs everyone.

Insiders may know more than other traders, so their trading is scrutinized by regulators.

An example of the effects of asymmetric information is that people on the "inside" of the company might use their private knowledge to take advantage of other investors. Such insiders can buy or sell before other investors learn about something and, therefore, before the market can reach a new price based on the information. If you were a senior executive of CAE, and you knew that tomorrow the company would release an unexpectedly poor earnings report that will cause the share price to fall, you could sell out today to share buyers who are ignorant of what you know. Securities commissions require that any significant information be released quickly and to everyone at once, and they keep an eye on "insider trading."

Accounting standards that require companies to release significant information as soon as it is known, along with other efforts to remove information asymmetries, probably assist the markets to behave fairly in that prices will be set by buyers and sellers all equally knowledgeable about the company. However, even if someone less knowledgeable is being unfairly taken advantage of, the market will still be efficient in that its prices will still reflect whatever the various people know.

Corporate disclosure is a continuous process, of which financial accounting is only a part.

Financial statements are one of the ways that companies provide information about themselves to outsiders. Capital markets certainly pay attention to financial accounting information, but in a world in which many people buy and sell bonds, shares, and options several times a day, quarterly or annual financial statements are only helpful infrequently. **Disclosure** is a continuous and varied process. Much of the information in the financial statements leaks out over the year, in press releases, announcements, and official information filings with securities commissions or stock exchanges. For example, the audit of a company's December 31 financial statements may be completed in February and the financial statements printed and issued in April, but throughout the prior year there will have been announcements about important events, of quarterly per-share-earnings figures and, as early as January (before the audit has been completed), the final earnings per share for the year. Not surprisingly, accounting research shows that stock price changes generally happen before the official earnings reports are released, and this is more likely to happen for larger firms, about which there tends to be more information available between accounting reports. An efficient capital market may be able to make sense out of narrative disclosure, such as a management discussion, even if its implications are not built into the accounting numbers, so such disclosure has become almost as important as the numbers for many companies.

Immediate disclosure helps to keep capital markets fair.

There is, therefore, a continual flow of financial statement-related and other significant information from public companies to capital markets. The general idea is that information should be released as soon as it is known, so that general market traders are not disadvantaged compared to insiders. This helps to keep the system fair for all, but also it assists the market's pricing system to reflect informed evaluations of companies' prospects, so that the market prices are consistent with society's overall interest in appropriate allocation of economic resources.

OW'S YOUR UNDERSTANDING?

Here are two questions you should be able to answer, based on what you have just read:

1. Why might a particular piece of accounting information, such as an announcement of the year's earnings per share, often not have much impact on share prices?

2. If a capital market is described as being "efficient," what does that imply about the usefulness of financial accounting information and narrative disclosure in that market?

5.11 CONTRACTS AND FINANCIAL ACCOUNTING INFORMATION

Financial accounting has many roles besides providing information to capital markets.

Reporting to capital markets is not all that financial accounting is good for, or that managers worry about. There are many other roles financial accounting plays that are important to managers and other parties. Financial accounting information is used in resource-allocation decisions made by governments, in assessing income taxes, in negotiations with and by labour unions, and perhaps also in enhancing or attacking the political power of certain groups (such as the corporate sector) in society.

This section has some ideas about the contractual relationships among people involved in a business, and about a consequent role of accounting information in how such contracts work. There has been much research on contracts, as on capital markets, so this section only summarizes what is known.[19] The area goes by several other names, with differences that aren't important to this discussion, including "agency theory," "principal–agent theory," and "positive accounting theory."

Contracts are formal or informal, in which one party agrees to act on another's behalf.

In a contract, people agree to do things on each other's behalf and to be compensated for doing so properly. For example, managers, auditors, lawyers, or physicians are entrusted with acting on behalf of one or more other people (the owners, creditors, defendants, or patients). Contracts may be formally written ones (such as legally binding "indentures" providing protection to bondholders), less formal employment contracts or supplier agreements, or informal arrangements such as a handshake between partners. The person who is to do something and be compensated is often called the agent, and the person who wants it done is the principal. Many contracts involve both parties doing things for the other, and in any case, it is usually assumed that a valid contract requires that both parties entered into it freely, because both expect to benefit.

The parties to a contract generally will not have the same interests.

There is a fundamental characteristic of contracts among self-interested participants: *the people are unlikely to have the same interests.* Conflict of interests is not viewed as being bad, but rather as being the natural state of affairs. For example, if the agent is to provide effort on behalf of the principal, it would be natural for the agent to want to work less hard than the principal wishes. For the agent, effort is costly and might therefore be minimized, whereas the principal would want the agent's effort to be maximized.

Managers are stewards with their own interests, running the company for the owners.

In the contract setting, accounting has a major role in reporting on what the agent did on behalf of the principal. This is the stewardship role of accounting information (in monitoring the past stewardship of the agent, such as company managers, on behalf of the principal, such as the owners or shareholders), as distinct from the future-oriented, decision-making role of such information in capital markets. Now the focus is on how the managers behave, rather than on how the capital market, consisting of shareholders and potential shareholders, behaves. You can think of the information produced by financial accounting as resulting from the wish by the various parties to provide incentives and controls over each other's behaviour, especially agents' behaviour. This wish exists because agents are assumed to want to act in their own interests and, in the absence of appropriate incentives and controls, their interests are assumed not necessarily to coincide with those of their principals.

Accounting information is appropriate if it helps in the contractual relationship.

From this point of view, accounting information is a part of the contract and should serve the monitoring and other needs of the contracting parties. Principals and agents specify what they need and accounting serves that, so accounting is useful, and not in any sense "right" or "wrong." If conditions change between various parties, accounting (and auditing) will change to meet the new conditions. Principals and agents will demand whatever information they require to manage the contractual relationship between them, and information, therefore, can be judged only in terms of that specific relationship. Is it what they need, or isn't it?

Owners and managers may have different views about how to pay the managers.

Here is an example. Suppose the shareholders of Lakewood Inc. wanted management to work hard to maximize the price of Lakewood's shares, which are traded on a stock exchange. The higher the price, the better the return to the owners from owning the shares and the higher their wealth. The owners might, through their representatives on Lakewood's board of directors, propose a management contract that specifies that the top managers get no salary, but instead get 20% of the change in the company's share price over each year. The top managers might well reply that this is too risky for them because all sorts of things might affect share price, including things they have no control over such as wars, recessions, or other unexpected problems. The share price could go up, but it might as likely go down. The managers may then propose that they should be paid a flat salary of $200,000 each, regardless of changes in share price, believing that the owners should take the risks. This isn't what the owners want, because they are concerned that the managers will not be sufficiently conscientious if they are guaranteed a salary regardless of performance.

The managerial compensation is negotiated between owners and managers.

Therefore, the two parties negotiate. Finally, a contract is agreed upon. Suppose it says that the managers will get $150,000 each plus performance bonuses of 5% of the annual net income and 3% of the increase in share price, with no penalty for negative income or negative change in share price, but with no bonuses then either. (The owners, interested in maximizing the share price, and the managers, feeling that they have more control over net income than share price, would in this case have agreed to include both factors in the bonus calculation.) Management compensation contracts are often very complex and a subcommittee of the board of directors may be created specifically to design and monitor such contracts. Securities commissions increasingly require public companies to disclose the nature of such contracts and the compensation that results from them, especially for the chief executive officer and other senior managers. Management compensation contracts in which pay depends on performance and that pay off in shares, or options to buy shares cheaply, in addition to cash have become very common in recent years.

Both parties to the contract are interested in relevant accounting information.

The result is that the managers, as agents for the owners (the principals), have agreed to work for the owners, and the owners have agreed to employ the managers. Both parties entered into the contract for their own reasons, and both are satisfied with it (or they would not have agreed). Now the owners can use financial accounting information to monitor the managers' performance and to calculate their bonuses based on net income. Both parties, because of their contract, are interested in the accounting information; neither would be satisfied without accounting. They may specify in their contract that GAAP be used to calculate net income, for the sake of convenience or because they prefer it that way. They also may specify other ways of calculating net income that they think are to their mutual advantage.

GAAP play a role in measuring managers' performance on behalf of owners.

If many companies have these sorts of bonus arrangements or other incentive contracts in which financial accounting information plays a role, there can be strong pressures on the development of GAAP or official accounting standards in directions that improve the effectiveness of such contracts. These pressures are likely to be in similar directions to those of, say, capital markets, because the owners are trading their shares on such markets. They will not be exactly the same, though, because the managers have to agree to the contracts too and may not want, for example, to bear as much risk as the capital market might like them to.

Auditors evaluate the managers' accounting information on behalf of owners.

There is also a clear role for auditors in the smooth functioning of contracts. If the managers are responsible for the accounting information and are being paid on the basis of it, the owners (who are perhaps some distance from the company's offices and in any case would not want to have to show up to ask questions about accounting) may not be inclined to trust the managers' figures and would prefer having an outside auditor evaluate them. Adding credibility to management's information is the oldest reason for auditing, and still central to it.

Some contracts may be very specific about accounting information.

There are many kinds of formal and informal contracts, with many parties other than managers (such as suppliers, associated companies, foreign business partners, and governments) that may use financial accounting information. The parties to such contracts will necessarily have an interest in the financial statements, in GAAP, in auditing, and in the other aspects of financial accounting. They will, therefore, act as part of the system of information demand and use that shapes accounting. Some of the contracts that are likely to be of interest from a financial accounting point of view include management compensation contracts, as illustrated above, labour contracts, contracts with suppliers and/or customers, and financial contracts such as those drawn up for issuance of bonds, other debt, or equity. One reason for written contracts is the conflict of interests mentioned earlier. For example, bondholders receive a claim on the company, or its assets, that has a higher legal priority than the shareholders' residual claim. A contract, such as a "bond indenture," is written specifying the exact rights of the bondholders. The indenture might say that if the company's working capital falls below a certain level, the bondholders have the right to demand early payment or some other penalty. This doesn't remove the conflict of interests, but clarifying the situation makes everyone's assessments of the company's performance and prospects more informed.

OW'S YOUR UNDERSTANDING?

Here are two questions you should be able to answer, based on what you have just read:

1. What is the "contractual" view of the value of financial accounting information?

2. Green Inc. has a set of management bonus contracts for its senior executives, specifying that their pay will be based partly on how well the company performs. Brown Inc., however, just pays its managers a flat salary. What differences would you expect in the attitudes of the two groups of managers to their company's financial statements?

5.12 TERMS TO BE SURE YOU UNDERSTAND

Here is this chapter's list of terms introduced or emphasized. Many will reappear in later chapters, so make sure you know what they mean *in accounting*, and if any are unclear to you, check the chapter again, or refer to the Glossary of Terms at the back of the book.

Accounting entity	Clean opinion
Accounting standards	CMA
Accounting Standards Board	Comparability
Agent	Compilation
Annual report	Conservatism
Assurance	Consistency
Audit committee	Contracts
Auditor's report	Cost–benefit
Authoritative standards	Cost principle
Board of directors	CPA
CA	Disclosure
Capital markets	Efficiency (of information)
CGA	Efficient market hypothesis
CICA Handbook	External audit

External auditor
Fairness
FASB
Financial Accounting Standards Board
Financial instruments
Financial reporting
GAAP
GAAS
Generally accepted accounting principles
Generally accepted auditing standards
Going concern
Harmonization
Historical cost
IASC
Independence
International Accounting Standards
   Committee
Investors
Letter to the shareholders
Listed
Management discussion and analysis
Matching
Materiality
MD&A

Neutrality
Objectivity
Ontario Securities Commission
OSC
Principal
Professional ethics
Professionalism
Public companies
Qualified opinion
Recognition
Relevance
Reliability
Review
SEC
Securities
Securities and Exchange Commission
Stewardship
Stock exchanges
Stock markets
Timeliness
Toronto Stock Exchange
TSE
Verifiability

5.13 CONTINUING DEMONSTRATION CASE

INSTALLMENT 5

Data for Installment 5

The preparation of the standard set of financial statements for Mato Inc. to August 31, 2000, has been illustrated. We left Mavis Janer and Tomàs Brot preparing for the board of directors' meeting and thinking about how to get their company out of trouble. As they reviewed their financial statements, Mavis and Tomas had some questions about their accounting. They are not accountants, remember, and are anxious to get on with running the business. Here, then, are some of their questions:

1. Should they hire an accountant to "do their books" so they will not be responsible for that job?
2. Do their financial statements have to follow the *CICA Handbook*'s standards?
3. What things, if any, in the financial statements will require policy decisions by them as the owners/managers?
4. Should their company appoint an external auditor?

Results for Installment 5

1. Hiring an accountant is really a matter of preference and money. If they do not want to do the job and feel strongly enough about it to want to pay someone else, and can afford to do so, they should go ahead. Their new employee may be able to do what is needed, with the help of the software they already have. However, this does not absolve them of their ultimate managerial responsibility for the accounting and financial statements.

2. No, their statements do not *have* to follow the *CICA Handbook*. The *Handbook* is a guide, not law. However, their company is incorporated and the statute under which it is incorporated will require that annual financial statements be prepared following accepted principles. The statute may even state or imply that the *Handbook* is the source of what is acceptable. Also, groups of people such as their bankers, the other investors, prospective purchasers of their business, income tax authorities, and external auditors will object to their financial statements if they diverge much from the guidelines in the *Handbook*.

3. From the financial statements in Installments 3 and 4, some possible financial accounting issues are:

- Amortization seems to be calculated in a simple way. While this is not a bad thing, the simple calculations may not provide figures that are useful in evaluating the performance of this particular business.

- Inventory is getting large. If the customers are boutique retailers who are likely to be sensitive to seasonal and other changes in demand, the company may have to deal with obsolete or out-of-style inventory items and may need an accounting policy for valuing such items (reducing their value to some estimate of market value).

- The balance sheet does not say much about the company's authorized and issued share capital, such as the number of shares or rights of shareholders. A note to the statements giving this information would be a good idea (and expected by GAAP).

- The company may have made commitments to purchase various items, such as those intended for the Christmas season. Users of the financial statements might like to know about any such commitments.

- The company is operating in leased premises and has spent a large amount of money to improve those premises. Users of the financial statements may find some information about the lease useful, especially its term and any renewal privileges.

- Users of the financial statements might like more information about the loan made by Tomas's father, such as confirmation of the fact that it is repayable on demand, as it appears to be (and so may be more like the bank loan than it now seems) and what interest is payable on the loan, if any.

- The income statement shows no interest expense at all, yet there is a significant bank loan. There appears either to be an error or an unrecorded liability. (Or perhaps interest has been paid and is included in the office and general expenses.)

- It is likely that the bank can seize the inventory and accounts receivable to collect on its loan: this and other security on the bank loan should be disclosed.

- It is common to disclose salaries paid to directors and officers (in other words, those of Mavis and Tomas) separately from other salaries.

4. There is probably little need to have their financial statements audited at this point. Auditing does cost money! However, they will have to satisfy the income tax authorities, their banker, and the other investors as to the credibility of their financial statements, so they should keep careful records and look into hiring an outside accountant to at least review the financial statements and report that no substantial errors appear to have been made. (There are several levels of external help, including simple advice, a more substantial review, and even a full audit.)

5.14 HOMEWORK AND DISCUSSION TO DEVELOP UNDERSTANDING

PROBLEM 5.1*
Connections among the financial statements

Why should the set of financial statements that is included in the annual report be interpreted as a set? Putting it another way, does the income statement tell you anything about the balance sheet; does the balance sheet tell you anything about the cash flow statement, etc.?

PROBLEM 5.2*
Reasons for and difficulty of auditor independence

Auditors play an important role in the financial reporting system, and their independence from their clients is an essential feature of this system.

1. Why is such independence considered necessary?
2. Why is it difficult to maintain?

PROBLEM 5.3*
What is important in the annual report's financial information

A busy businessperson said, "I've made some investments in Canadian companies, so I receive their annual reports. The reports are many pages long—I don't have time to read all that. Tell me what is important in the annual report's financial information and what I should pay attention to."
   Give your answer.

PROBLEM 5.4*
Explain why various organizations are accounting entities.

Explain briefly why each of the following is an "accounting entity," for which financial statements may be prepared.

1. Simone's jewellery business in Chapter 1.
2. The Toronto-Dominion Bank in Chapter 2.
3. The group of corporations making up the oil company Exxon.
4. The University of Lethbridge.
5. Continuing Case company Mato Inc.
6. The large accounting partnership firm Ernst & Young.
7. The City of Moose Jaw.
8. International fast-food giant McDonald's Corporation.

PROBLEM 5.5*
Suggest nonbusiness characteristics of some organizations

The organizations below all have some characteristics that lead their financial accounting to be different from that of ordinary business enterprises. Identify one or two such characteristics for each:

1. The Government of Canada.

2. Large retailer YourStore that is being operated by a bankruptcy trustee while it is being wound up and its useful assets are being sold off.
3. Any student club in your university.
4. Sick Children's Hospital.
5. Banff National Park.

PROBLEM 5.6*
Identify some accounting concepts and principles

Identify the accounting concepts or principles that relate to each of the following sentences and explain what effect the concepts or principles have on financial statements:

1. Users of financial statements should be able to believe that the numbers represent real events.
2. Financial statements should avoid undue optimism about the future.
3. It is hard to say absolutely that a company is performing well or badly, but you can evaluate its relative performance.
4. Financial accounting should be helpful both in understanding the past and looking ahead to the future.
5. The content of financial statements should not depend on who prepares them.

PROBLEM 5.7*
Capital markets, contracts, and accounting

1. Briefly describe two important connections between accounting information and capital market behaviour.
2. Briefly describe two important connections between accounting information and the behaviour of parties who have business or employment contracts with other parties. .

PROBLEM 5.8*
Settle an argument about financial accounting's purpose

Two students are arguing. One says that financial accounting exists in order to provide information to outsiders (for example, capital markets) for assessing company performance. The other says that it exists in order to provide a monitoring and control system over managers who are running the company as the agents of the owners. Settle the argument.

PROBLEM 5.9*
Accounting concepts and economic agents

1. Explain why each of the following concepts is important in financial reporting to markets and other economic agents who rely on such reporting:
   a. Economic entity assumption.
   b. Historical cost basis of accounting.
   c. Fairness.
   d. Generally accepted accounting principles.
   e. Professional ethics of the accountants and/or auditors involved in producing financial statements.
2. How have each of these concepts been incorporated into the financial statements of a large public company you know about? Give specific examples.
3. Now apply these ideas to a small private company, such as a local nonchain pizza joint, automotive repair company, or clothing store. Are these concepts still relevant? Why?

PROBLEM 5.10*
Is disclosure enough if GAAP are not followed?

Section 1500, paragraph .06 of the *CICA Handbook* recommends:

"Where the accounting treatment or statement presentation does not follow the recommendations in this Handbook, the practice used should be explained in notes to the financial statements with an indication of the reason why the recommendation concerned was not followed."[20]

Does paragraph .06 mean that a company is free to use whatever accounting treatment or statement presentation it likes, as long as the notes to the financial statements explain the situation? Why or why not?

PROBLEM 5.11*
Explain the origin and present importance of some terms

Explain where the following terms came from in the history of business and accounting and indicate what importance each might still have now in the new millennium's financial accounting:

1. Stewardship
2. Securities regulation
3. Authoritative accounting standards
4. Harmonization
5. Independence
6. Disclosure

PROBLEM 5.12*
Explain the relevance–reliability tradeoff

Nonna is a financial analyst, responsible for making recommendations to clients of her employer, investment broker MEB Securities, about which companies would make good investments. She studies the characteristics of each company's shares and other securities and is particularly careful to understand what each company's balance sheet, income statement, and other financial statements indicate about the company's performance and prospects. She has been concerned lately about the reliability of some of the numbers in financial statements, particularly estimates of future consequences of past transactions, such as accounts receivable for uncollected revenues and long-term pension liabilities. While she believes that knowing about such things is important to her analyses, she feels that some of these important numbers have low reliability and thus are less useful to her than they would be if she could believe in them more.

Explain to Nonna why financial accounting numbers may be reported even if they are not entirely reliable.

PROBLEM 5.13*
Describe the role of accounting professionals in financial accounting

Why is it important that professional accountants are involved in financial accounting? Answer by outlining the characteristics of professionalism that you think have an impact on the nature of the financial accounting information.

PROBLEM 5.14
Purpose, value, and limitations of the auditor's report

1. What purpose is served by the external auditor of a corporation?
2. Review the auditor's report included with the financial statements of any company you like. What is the report telling you?
3. To an investor, what value has been added to the financial statements by the auditor's report? Why?
4. Suggest some limitations on the value of the auditor's report that an investor should be aware of.

PROBLEM 5.15
Which GAAP principles apply and how are they applied?

You happen to be walking past your boss's office and you hear her exclaim, "These generally accepted accounting principles give me a headache! How can I figure out which ones apply to my business and decide how to apply them?" Wanting to impress your boss, you rush into her office and blurt out some answers to the questions. What do you say?

PROBLEM 5.16
Measurement, valuation, and articulation of balance sheet and income statement

"When an accountant is preparing a balance sheet and income statement, the principles behind balance sheet valuation and income measurement affect each other because the two statements articulate through double-entry accounting."

Explain what this statement means by reference to the set of generally accepted accounting principles described in section 5.2.

PROBLEM 5.17
Is having no GAAP worse than the present GAAP complexity?

Write a paragraph or two discussing the following topic: "The only thing worse than the large and complex set of practices, standards, and theories that make up GAAP would be if there were no such thing as GAAP."

PROBLEM 5.18
Apply financial accounting principles to a company

In section 5.3, some accounting principles were applied to the use of CAE's financial statements. Using another company, indicate why and how the following principles might be important to an investor who is using the company's financial statements to help in deciding whether to buy the company's shares. (If you have trouble thinking of a company, you could use the one that makes or sells your favourite car, beverage, cereal, designer clothes, takeout food, entertainment products, or home products.)

1. Fairness
2. Materiality
3. Comparability
4. Consistency
5. Going concern
6. Conservatism
7. Timeliness
8. Disclosure

PROBLEM 5.19
Discuss an ethical issue: independence versus expertise

It is generally expected that external auditors should be independent of their clients, so that they will be objective and neutral in considering the fairness of the financial statements. It is also expected that the external auditors should be expert and knowledgeable about their clients, so that their work will be done with necessary competence.

Suppose you have been appointed as the external auditor of the widely owned public company Jaffer Inc., which will be one of several clients you have. Jaffer has been struggling in recent years, and senior management has been criticized in the media. The audit of Jaffer will bring you an annual audit fee of about $25,000. Soon after your appointment, the president of Jaffer takes you out to a nice restaurant and offers you a consulting contract with the company. The contract would bring an annual fee of $100,000, and would be in force as long as you were auditor. In return for the fee, you would advise the president about business and financial strategies—you can see that you would really be a personal advisor to the president. However, doing the consulting would make you much more knowledgeable about the company, and you could doubtless put that knowledge to use in doing your audit work.

The president asks you to think about the consulting offer. Discuss the factors favouring and opposing your doing the consulting and indicate whether you think you should accept the contract.

PROBLEM 5.20 **Are international accounting standards a good idea?**	There is always a tension between making accounting the same for every enterprise and allowing flexibility. The more sameness, the less each enterprise can present itself on the basis of its own particular characteristics. Not every enterprise will fit into the same mould. But if each enterprise can choose its own accounting, comparability is lost and users of financial statements have to learn anew each enterprise's accounting methods. The opportunity for misleading information may be increased. If these points are put on the global stage, and "country" is substituted for "enterprise" above, we have the same problem but on a large scale. Does it make sense for every country to use the same accounting methods? Some differences among countries go very deep, affecting the legal rules under which enterprises operate, affecting what is considered good and poor managerial performance, and even affecting what the objectives of accounting and business are taken to be. Do you think it makes sense to try for international accounting standards? Would such standards have to be so general that they would have less real impact on enterprises than more specific national standards? Would they be unwieldy and slow to change as global conditions change? Can they be the basis for regulation of capital markets, for the administration of various contracts, and for the objective assessment of performance? Discuss the question of whether international accounting standards are desirable, and if they are, how detailed or specific they should be.
PROBLEM 5.21 **Authoritative standards, capital markets, and contracts**	Many of the accounting methods we study in this book are based on authoritative standards (*CICA Handbook*, FASB *Statements*, and so on) that attempt to specify how companies' financial accounting should be done. Such standards don't cover everything: companies must still make many choices when they are preparing their financial statements. Why are there authoritative standards for companies to follow? Why don't they cover everything? Should we have more or less of them? Put your answer in the context of this chapter's ideas about auditing, capital markets, and contractual uses of information.
PROBLEM 5.22 **Usefulness of accounting concepts and principles**	Harold is a hard-driving, impatient business executive. You work for him and can feel the grey hair sprouting on your head from all the pressure. One day, he returns from a lunch meeting with his accountant and says, "That accountant told me that there are accounting concepts and principles that tell me important things about why my financial statements are useful, why they are worth all the money they cost to produce and audit. I'm not convinced."

Choose any five of the concepts and principles in sections 5.2 and 5.3 and explain to Harold why those five are useful. Make your explanations brief and to the point: Harold hates long-winded answers!

PROBLEM 5.23
Can one criterion of materiality suit different users?

The president of a public corporation recently commented:

Our auditor says that our financial statements present fairly our financial position and the results of our operations. I challenged her as to how she determined such fairness. She replied that fairness means that the financial statements are not misstated in amounts that would be considered material, that is, significant.

I believe that there is some confusion with this materiality concept, since different users of our financial statements may have different ideas as to what is material. For example, bankers, institutional investors, small investors, and tax assessors all have different perceptions of materiality.

Discuss the issues raised by the president.

PROBLEM 5.24
Answer accounting questions from the treasurer of a club

Roy has just been elected treasurer of Club Ped, a bicycle-touring club, and has been handed the club's accounting records by the previous treasurer. The club accounts for its revenue on the accrual basis, but records expenditures from cash, not accrual expenses. Roy has taken a course in business accounting, but feels his accounting skills are quite modest and he is nervous about the accounting he will be responsible for as treasurer. Answer the following questions Roy has asked you:

1. "Will I have to follow GAAP in doing the club's financial statements?"
2. "The club has not had an income statement, but has had a 'statement of revenue and expenditure' that shows how much revenue excess (or deficit) is left over each year. Why is there no income statement as a business would have?"
3. "The club members are concerned about several things—like the number of members we have, the sources of grants we've received, and the success of various bicycle tours we've taken. Can I include these sorts of things in the financial statements?"
4. "Do we have to have the financial statements audited?"

PROBLEM 5.25
Should nonbusiness organizations use business accounting approaches?

There is debate over the extent to which nonbusiness organizations should use the accrual accounting approach that is the basis for business accounting. Questions have been raised over such topics as:

• Whether amortization, which is used to help measure business income by accounting for the economic consumption of assets, makes sense for public assets like roads, parks, and waterways;

• Whether it makes sense to think of nonbusiness organizations as having anything like the "accrual net income" that is the measure of business performance;

• Whether a balance sheet that, in business, balances owners' equity against assets and liabilities, makes sense for an organization that has no owners, but instead has members, voters, or citizens;

• Whether the whole idea of using accrual accounting in nonbusiness organizations represents a mind-set about economic efficiency, performance, and "the bottom line" that is inappropriate to organizations that may not exist for the economic reasons that businesses do.

Choose any one of the following organizations and list factors favouring, and opposing, the use of accrual accounting methods for that organization's accounting:

a. The Government of Canada.
b. The University of Toronto.
c. Any church, mosque, synagogue, or temple in your community.
d. Any club you belong to or know about.
e. Parks Canada.

PROBLEM 5.26
Discuss some statements about professional ethics

The following comments about professional accountants have been made. Discuss each, indicating how valid you think each is.

1. "Professional ethics is rather an empty phrase when applied to accountants, because accounting is a technical task that has right or wrong answers, not ethical dilemmas."
2. "When accountants claim to be using professional judgment, they are just avoiding committing themselves to the right answer, or maybe showing their lack of competence in solving the problems they face."
3. "CAs, CGAs, and CMAs are not really professionals because they are required to serve their clients or employers and do not have a responsibility to the public, as real professionals like physicians and lawyers do."
4. "Ethical people have a strong sense of morals and a conscience. While accountants may well have these, when the professional associations write down ethical rules, they undermine accountants' ethical sense by turning them into rule-followers."

PROBLEM 5.27
(CHALLENGING)
Reasons for and value of accounting standards

During a speech to a business club, an accounting professor, who was describing the benefits of business competition, remarked:

"Over the last 200 years, there has been a large increase in the regulation of financial accounting by professional associations and government agencies. This has led to a large political component in the setting of financial accounting standards: accounting thus has to respond to the concerns of the time, rather than being objective and stable. This sort of thing is part of what has made measuring each company's financial performance quite complicated and expensive. In my opinion, financial accounting costs a company more than it is worth to the company."

Exercise your knowledge of the world, as well as of accounting, by answering the following questions briefly. There are not any definitive answers to these questions, but the issues are important.

1. Why do you think society appears to desire that financial accounting be regulated—that there be standards a company has to follow in its financial accounting?
2. Is it possible that a company's financial accounting may cost more than that company feels it is worth, but be worthwhile doing anyway?
3. Should accounting standards be set as part of society's political processes, or should such standards be stable and uninfluenced by changes in society?

4. If the professor is right in saying that financial accounting and its standards are complicated and expensive, why do they not prevent such questionable phenomena as income smoothing and the Big Bath?

PROBLEM 5.28 (CHALLENGING) Should small businesses have different GAAP?

Several people or groups, such as the CICA study group mentioned in section 5.5, have addressed the question of whether small business enterprises should have their own set of GAAP rather than be required to comply with all the recommendations presently in the *CICA Handbook*. The writers reason that many current accounting principles seem to be geared to large businesses and that small ones should not be asked to implement recommendations that are irrelevant or that do not justify their costs through greater benefits.[21]

1. Give arguments for having one set of GAAP for all sizes of businesses.
2. Now argue for small businesses having their own set of GAAP.

PROBLEM 5.29 (CHALLENGING) Is accounting neutral?

A speaker at a recent conference stated:

Many groups, including governments, financial institutions, investors, and corporations in various industries, argue that their interests are affected by present and proposed accounting pronouncements. The sometimes contradictory interests of these groups are recognized by the accounting profession. However, accounting is neutral and is not influenced by the self-interest of any one group.[22]

Discuss the above quotation.

PROBLEM 5.30 (CHALLENGING) What if top managers disagree with GAAP?

Should top managers be held responsible for their companies' accounting if authoritative standards prescribe accounting methods they disagree with? Why or why not?

PROBLEM 5.31 (CHALLENGING) Threats to an auditor's independence

Pat is the partner on the audit of Hardwood Emporium Ltd. Comment on whether or not, and why, each of the following may be a threat to Pat's independence.

1. Pat and the chief financial officer of Hardwood Emporium play golf together every few weeks.
2. During the audit, Pat notices that the company has a serious problem with its computer system. Pat's accounting firm is then hired by Hardwood Emporium to do a major redesign of the system, for a large fee.
3. As part of the completion of the audit, Pat works with the company to determine its likely income tax liability for the year, including helping to prepare the company's income tax returns. Pat bills the company for the tax advice separately from the audit fee.
4. Pat's former assistant on the Hardwood Emporium audit is hired by the company as the chief financial accountant, responsible for preparing all the company's financial statements.
5. Pat is asked to submit a bid on the next year's Hardwood Emporium audit fee, in competition with several other accounting firms. Pat decides to submit a very low bid because the income from tax and consulting services would make up for the lower audit revenue.

PROBLEM 5.32 (CHALLENGING) Purpose and consequences of accounting standards

Quite often, proposed or even published authoritative accounting standards are controversial. An example is changing the way some forms of share capital are distinguished from debt, such as in considering whether shares that have a limited life, and are scheduled therefore for redemption on a specific date, should really be considered to be debt rather than equity. This may be an apparently sensible, even innocuous, idea, but implementing it changes a corporation's debt–equity ratio for the worse and may change the way the owners of such shares (or is it debt?) view their relationship with the corporation. When such a controversy arises, the idea of accounting standards as objective, neutral ways of doing accounting "best" is raised by defenders of the standards. Opponents argue that standards should not complicate or spoil sensible business arrangements, but merely ensure that such arrangements are reported clearly so that users of financial statements can make their own judgments about what matters. Standard-setting committees get caught in the middle, trying to find a way to have standards that matter (that is, that do change the way financial accounting is done, at least for some enterprises), but that do not put unnecessary burdens on enterprises, their owners, their accountants, or other parties.

Should accounting standards impose solutions on enterprises, or instead should they just be guidance to the "best practice" that enterprises can use or not use?

PROBLEM 5.33 (CHALLENGING) Auditors and forecast information

Recently, there has been pressure to expand the role of auditors because investors and other groups are demanding more forward-looking information. If these demands are met, auditors may be expected to review the plans and forecasts of a company that will be reporting to the public, and to determine the fairness of such forward-looking financial statements.

Discuss the implications of this expanded role for auditors, using such concepts as fairness, independence, information value, comparability, relevance, reliability, objectivity, efficient capital markets, contracts, and any other concepts that you feel are important.

PROBLEM 5.34 (CHALLENGING) Capital markets and auditors

1. On October 31, 2000, analysts predicted that the earnings per share of Laurel Oakes Corp. would equal $4.80 for the year ended December 31, 2000. Actual results were announced on February 27, 2001. Earnings per share for 2000 came to $3.95. Consider the three dates noted above (October 31, 2000, December 31, 2000, and February 27, 2001). At which of these dates would you expect to see share prices react to earnings information? Why? Can you predict the direction in which share prices would react on any of these dates? If yes, explain why, if no, explain why not.

2. Explain the importance of the audit function in the context of a large company where the ownership (composed of a large number of private investors) and the management are separated. Who are the auditors primarily responsible to? Who hires them? Do they have any responsibility for the kinds of market responses discussed in Part 1? What would the market's investors expect of the auditors? Do your answers indicate anything inconsistent in the auditor's role as an independent party?

**PROBLEM 5.35
(CHALLENGING)
Should NAFTA
countries use the
same accounting?**

Canada, Mexico, and the U.S. are all signatories to the North American Free Trade Agreement (NAFTA). Other countries are likely to join NAFTA as full or partial members. Do you think all members of NAFTA should use the same financial accounting principles and financial statement formats? Why, or why not?

**PROBLEM 5.36
(CHALLENGING)
Does considering
ethics add to under-
standing accoun-
tants and financial
statements?**

Discuss the following comment, made by a businessperson after hearing a speech on professional ethics in accounting.

Professional ethics in accounting has always seemed a doubtful subject to me, because I don't see that there is much to it beyond good business sense. Being independent, for example, means that the external auditor offers a better service because the auditor's opinion on the financial statements means more than if the auditor was not independent. It doesn't require an ethical sense to see that. In general, we all try to be ethical in what we do, and an ethical accountant will command a higher pay than an unethical one as a consequence. So an accountant will do the right thing because it is good business, it makes the accountant better off to do that. Please don't take this as cynicism: I genuinely wonder what talking about ethics really adds to the understanding of what accountants should do and what their financial statements should be like.

**CASE 5A
Interpret a non-
Canadian financial
report**

Below are the July 31, 1999, interim financial statements for United Kingdom company Kingfisher plc (www.kingfisher.co.uk). These include the usual financial statements (but in U.K. format), notes, and, because the statements were not audited, a letter from a firm of chartered accountants saying what they did to review the statements.

Read the material and discuss the company's results. The statements are not in the usual Canadian format and use somewhat different terminology, but your accounting knowledge, and some questioning and discussion, should lead you to figure out what they are telling you. (DIY, by the way, is the company's home improvements stores division. VAT is a tax something like the GST.) In your discussion, consider issues such as:

• How informative is the United Kingdom format in comparison to the Canadian one?

• Having examined the Kingfisher statements, do you think international harmonization would be a good idea, or would not be very necessary?

• What assurance do you get from the accountants' letter?

• Do you see any differences in the application of the sorts of accounting principles outlined in sections 5.2 and 5.3 in the Kingfisher case?

• How useful to capital markets do you think interim reporting like this example would be?

Consolidated profit and loss acount (unaudited)

For the half year ended 31 July 1999

£ millions	Notes	Half year ended 31 July 1999	Half year ended 1 August 1998	Year ended 30 January 1999
Turnover – continuing operations				
Retail	1	**4,844.3**	3,008.4	7,354.4
Property		**35.1**	19.6	41.1
Financial services		**32.1**	32.5	62.3
		4,910.5	3,060.5	7,457.8
Operating profit – continuing operations				
DIY		**174.2**	86.1	191.1
Electrical		**51.3**	46.6	173.4
General Merchandise		**26.4**	29.7	186.1
Property		**37.7**	30.7	69.1
Exceptional item-other operating (expense) income	2	**(3.7)**	44.7	44.7
Other operating costs		**(21.3)**	(11.6)	(27.3)
Operating profit		**264.6**	226.2	637.1
Exceptional items				
(Loss) / profit on dispsoal of properties—continuing operations		**(0.6)**	(1.0)	2.1
Profit on ordinary activities before interest		**264.0**	225.2	639.2
Interest		**(14.3)**	1.1	(9.9)
Profit on ordinary activities before tax		**249.7**	226.3	629.3
Taxation on ordinary activities		**(76.2)**	(67.0)	(183.5)
Profit on ordinary activities after tax		**173.5**	159.3	445.8
Minority interests		**(45.2)**	(0.3)	(8.9)
Profit attributable to the members of Kingfisher plc		**128.3**	159.0	436.9
Dividends on equity shares	3	**(54.6)**	(50.8)	(175.3)
Retained profit for the period		**73.7**	108.2	261.6
Earnings per share (pence)	4			
– basic		**9.5**	11.8	32.3
– diluted		**8.9**	11.6	31.7
– basic before exceptional items		**9.8**	9.5	29.9
– diluted before exceptional items		**9.2**	9.3	29.3

Consolidated balance sheet (unaudited)

As at 31 July 1999

£ millions	Notes	31 July 1999	1 August 1998	30 January 1999
Fixed assets				
Intangible assets		**389.8**	58.4	267.3
Tangible assets		**3,143.1**	1,933.7	2,885.4
Investments		**63.5**	71.9	66.4
		3,596.4	2,064.0	3,219.1
Current assets				
Development work in progress		**54.3**	76.3	69.0
Stocks		**1,614.6**	970.9	1,465.4
Debtors		**737.5**	568.6	752.9
Securitised consumer receivables	303.2		189.7	321.0
Less: non-recourse secured notes	(238.3)	**64.9**	(147.3) 42.4	(247.4) 73.6
Investments		**347.6**	278.8	311.7
Cash at bank and in hand		**336.2**	80.8	241.2
		3,155.1	2,017.8	2,913.8
Creditors				
Amounts falling due within one year		**(3,082.2)**	(1,759.1)	(2,726.0)
Net current assets		**72.9**	258.7	187.8
Total assets less current liabilities		**3,669.3**	2,322.7	3,406.9
Creditors				
Amounts falling due after more than one year		**(921.1)**	(409.1)	(768.8)
Provisions for liabilities and charges		**(20.7)**	(14.5)	(21.8)
		2,727.5	1,899.1	2,616.3
Called up share capital	9	**170.5**	169.4	170.0
Reserves		**2,147.4**	1,729.4	2,080.6
Equity shareholders/ funds		**2,317.9**	1,898.8	2,250.6
Equity minority interests		**409.6**	0.3	365.7
		2,727.5	1,899.1	2,616.3

Approved by the Board
Sir Geoffrey Mulcahy, *Director*
Philip Rowley, *Director*
13 September 1999

Summary consolidated cash flow statement (unaudited)

For the half year ended 31 July 1999

£ millions	Notes	Half year ended 31 July 1999	Half year ended 1 August 1998	Year ended 30 January 1999
Net cash inflow from operating activities	5	327.6	113.9	698.3
Returns on investment and servicing of finance				
Net interest (paid) / received		(6.8)	1.1	(13.3)
Taxation				
Net tax paid		(34.3)	(17.8)	(169.2)
Capital expenditure and financial investment				
Net purchase of tangible fixed assets		(309.5)	(143.6)	(378.6)
Net purchase of fixed asset investments		(0.9)	(13.9)	(14.4)
Net cash outflow from capital expenditure and financial investment		(310.4)	(157.5)	(393.0)
Acquisitions and disposals				
Purchase of subsidiaries and business undertakings		(146.3)	(48.6)	(430.6)
Payments for additions to joint ventures/associated undertakings		(4.6)	—	(3.8)
Net cash outflow from acquisitions and disposals		(150.9)	(48.6)	(434.4)
Equity dividends paid		(99.0)	(106.0)	(153.8)
Management of liquid resources				
Net movement in short-term deposits		(56.0)	0.6	22.3
Net purchase of short-term investments		(37.0)	(23.1)	(43.1)
Net cash outflow from management of liquid resources		(93.0)	(22.5)	(20.8)
Financing				
Issue of ordinary share capital		15.8	5.9	13.6
Capital element of finance lease rental payments		(3.7)	(1.5)	(6.4)
Net increase of loans		329.7	227.9	433.2
Net cash inflow from financing		341.8	232.3	440.4
Decrease in cash	6	(25.0)	(5.1)	(45.8)

Notes to the interim financial statements

1. Retail sales from continuing operations

£ millions	Half year ended 31 July 1999	Half year ended 1 August 1998	Year ended 30 January 1999
Kingfisher	**4,844.3**	3,008.4	7,354.4
DIY	**2,310.3**	959.9	2,055.4
B&Q	**1,186.1**	995.9	1,908.4
Castorama	**1,124.2**	–	147.0
Electrical	**1,311.7**	874.0	2,458.1
Darty	**500.1**	472.6	1,123.8
Comet	**380.1**	344.5	862.4
Wegert	**213.7**	–	253.0
BUT	**137.5**	–	80.3
Other	**80.3**	56.9	138.6
General Merchandise	**1,222.3**	1,138.5	2,840.9
Woolworths	**702.3**	676.2	1,763.2
Superdrug	**394.7**	366.7	798.6
Other	**125.3**	95.6	279.1

2. The exceptional other operating expense represents the costs incurred during the period on the attempted merger with ASDA Group pic. For the half year ended 1 August 1998 the exceptional other operating income represents the release of an accrual for VAT on outstanding credit balances as at 28 February 1997 following the withdrawal of the Standard Method of Gross Takings by HM Customs & Excise. Following the Court of Appeal ruling on 17 February 1998 in a case involving Littlewoods Home Shopping Ltd., the accrual was no longer required.

3. An interim dividend of 400p amounting to £54.6 million (1998: 3.75p, £50.8 million) will be paid on 19 November 1999 to shareholders on the Register on 1 October 1999. A scrip dividend will be offered and forms of election will be sent to shareholders on 12 October 1999.

4. The calculation of basic earnings per share is based on the profit on ordinary activities, after taxation and minority interests, of £128.3 million (1998: £159.0 million) and the weighted average number of shares in issue during the period of 1,354.4 million (1998: 1,350.6 million). The diluted earnings per share is based on the diluted profit on ordinary activities, after taxation and minority interests, of £124.6 million (1998: £159.0 million) and the diluted weighted average number of share in issue during the period of 1,393.8 million (1998: 1,373.1 million).

5. Reconciliation of cashflow from operating activities

£ millions	Half year ended 31 July 1999	Half year ended 1 August 1998	Year ended 30 January 1999
Operating profit	**264.6**	226.2	637.1
Depreciation	**87.3**	63.8	141.0
	351.9	290.0	778.1
Decrease/(increase) in development work in progress	**15.5**	(25.0)	(15.8)
Increase in stock	**(155.6)**	(61.6)	(94.3)
Decrease in debtors	**5.2**	35.5	66.1
Increase/(decrease) in creditors	**109.6**	(125.8)	(46.0)
Share of associates profits	**(2.1)**	(2.2)	(4.6)
Loss on disposal of fixed assets	**3.1**	3.0	14.8
Net cash inflow from operating activities	**327.6**	113.9	698.3

6. Reconciliation of net borrowings

£ millions	Half year ended 31 July 1999	Half year ended 1 August 1998	Year ended 30 January 1999
Net debt at start of period	**(693.4)**	(203.5)	(203.5)
Decrease in cash	**(25.0)**	(5.1)	(45.8)
Acquisitions	**–**	–	(41.0)
Net movement in short-term deposits	**56.0**	(0.6)	(22.3)
Net purchase of short-term investments	**37.0**	23.1	43.1
Change in market value of investments	**(0.4)**	1.0	(0.5)
Net increase of loans	**(329.7)**	(227.9)	(433.2)
Foreign exchange effects	**12.7**	(1.7)	9.8
Net debt at end of period	**(942.8)**	(414.7)	(693.4)

On 25 May 1999, the Group established a Euro 2.5 billion Euro-Medium Term Note Programme.

7. The interim financial statements have been prepared on the basis of the accounting policies set out in the Group's financial statements for the year ended 30 January 1999. The taxation charge is calculated by applying the best estimate of the annual tax rate to the profit for the period.

8. Acquisition of Screwfix Direct Limited

On 26 July 1999, B&Q plc, a 57.6% subsidiary of the Group, acquired the entire share capital of Screwfix Direct Limited, a mail order and e-commerce retailer of building, plumbing and electrical products, for £84.5 million including expenses. Provisional goodwill, calculated on the closing acquisition balance sheet, of £81.9 million has been capitalized and is being amortized in accordance with Group policy. In its last financial year ended 31 January 1999 Screwfix Direct Limited and its subsidiaries made a profit of £2.2 million.

Acquisition of Dickens Limited

On 22 April 1999, B&Q plc, a 57.6% subsidiary of the Group, acquired the entire share capital of Dickens Limited, a DIY retailer in the North East of England, at a provisional cost of £40.3 million including expenses. Provisional goodwill arising on the acquisition of £18.3 million has been capitalized and is being amortized in accordance with Group policy. In its last financial year ended 31 January 1999 Dickens Limited made a loss after tax of £1.1 million.

Acquisition of Wegert Grosslabor GmbH

On 12 April 1999, the Group acquired the entire share capital of Wegert Grosslabor GmbH, a German photographic processing company, at a cost of £12.4 million including expenses. Provisional goodwill arising on the acquisition of £11.3 million has been capitalized and is being amortized in accordance with Group policy. In its last financial year ended 31 December 1998 Wegert Grosslabor GmbH under local accounting rules made a profit of £0.7 million.

Other acquisitions

Effective 30 June 1999, Promarkt Holding KG, a 60% subsidiary of the Group, completed the acquisition of proMarkt GmbH & Co. KG Audio Video Elektro Foto, a German electrical retailer, for £6.6 million including expenses. The provisional goodwill arising on the acquisition of £3.0 million has been capitalized and is being amortized in accordance with Group policy. On 10 March 1999, the Group subscribed for a 55% interest in a new subsidiary, Tangens GmbH, a German mobile phone service provider, for £4.8 million, of which £3.1 million has been paid to date. Also, during the period the Group subscribed for a 40% interest in LibertySurf S.A., a pan-European internet service provider, for a consideration of £7.4 million, of which £4.6 million has been paid to date. This is included as an associate within investments.

9. On 2 July 1998, following approval on 27 May 1998, the authorized ordinary shares of 25p each in the capital of the company were divided into 2 ordinary shares of 12.5p each.

10. The results for the year to 30 January 1999 are based on full audited accounts which were filed with the Registrar of Companies and on which the auditors made a report under section 235 of the Companies Act 1985 which does not contain a statement under sections 237(2) or (3) of the Companies Act 1985 and is unqualified.

11. Copies of the results will be sent to shareholders during the week commencing 20 September 1999 and additional copies will be available from the Company Secretary, Kingfisher plc, North West House, 119 Marylebone Road, London NW1 5PX.

12. The Group has continued to charge the costs of year 2000 compliance work to the profit and loss account as they are incurred. During the last 6 months the remaining work on the internal computer systems has continued together with work on supply chain and embedded systems. Testing procedures on all systems are scheduled to be completed early in the

second half of the year. Work on other areas of the year 2000 programmes, including monitoring other organizations we are dependent on and the formulation of contingency plans, is being completed to timetable and will continue through to the end of the year. Deadlines for completing all aspects of the work are linked to the business cycle which differs by company. Costs of £6.7 million were charted in the first half of the year, bringing the total to date to £21.2 million. This is forecast to increase to £30.6 million by the year end. These charges represent incremental, external costs only and do not include costs incurred in the course of normal systems enhancement programmes.

Independent review report to Kingfisher plc

We have been instructed by the Company to review the financial information set out on pages 14 to 16 and the notes 1 to 11 thereto, and we have read the other information contained in the interim report for any apparent misstatements or material inconsistencies with the financial information.

Directors' responsibilities
The interim report, including the financial information contained therein, is the responsibility of, and has been approved by, the directors. The Listing Rules of the London Stock Exchange require that the accounting policies and presentation applied to the interim figures should be consistent with those applied in preparing the preceding annual accounts except where any changes, and the reasons for them, are disclosed.

Review work performed
We conducted our review in accordance with guidance contained in Bulletin 1999 / 4 issued by the Auditing Practices Board. A review consists principally of making enquiries of group management and applying analytical procedures to the financial information and underlying financial data, and based thereon, assessing whether the accounting policies and presentation have been consistently applied unless otherwise disclosed. A review excludes audit procedures such as tests of controls and verification of assets, liabilities and transactions. It is substantially less in scope than an audit performed in accordance with Auditing Standards and therefore provides a lower level of assurance than an audit. Accordingly we do not express an audit opinion on the financial information.

Review conclusion
On the basis of our review we are not aware of any material modifications that should be made to the financial information as presented for the six moths ended 31 July 1999.

PricewaterhouseCoopers
Chartered Accountants
London
13 September 1999

CASE 5B
Should GAAP be tightened up?

Over coffee one morning, some accountants were discussing a newspaper editorial criticizing GAAP. Here is the editorial.

IT'S TIME TO NARROW THE GAAP GAP

Financial reporting in Canada is just not good enough. There is too much deliberate, legally sanctioned, holier-than-thou confusion. It's pleasantly called the GAAP gap.

The Ontario Securities Commission is scrutinizing one side of the reporting issue — getting the company to put out the "facts." And hopefully, public companies will soon become liable for continually good disclosure.

But good reporting also embraces the way in which the so-called "facts" are colored, or spun, on the way out of the company's mouth. And that's the notorious GAAP gap.

GAAP stands for Generally Accepted Accounting Principles. Every public company must report according to GAAP, by law.

Well, GAAP is too elastic. Like a child's balloon, a company can make its earnings or assets grow bigger or smaller under GAAP, provided its accountants blow or suck hard enough.

In other words, public companies can adopt a careful, conservative approach to financial reporting or one that's freewheeling. It's up to them.

Well, this won't do. The accounting profession and the regulators must narrow the GAAP gap, so that investors can understand what's going on in companies into which they put their precious savings.

Here are some examples of companies riding horses through the GAAP gap. In all cases, the company's accounting falls within GAAP's legal limits.

A trust company conglomerate reports a $16-million profit, which could also be interpreted as a $12-million loss.

A holding company suddenly reclassifies some short-term investments as long term, raising a morass of valuation and liquidity issues.

A beverage company capitalizes some of its expenses, controversially. This practice maximizes assets and profits at the same time.

Some companies account for subsidiaries by cost accounting, which does not recognize the subsidiaries' losses, when they could use equity accounting, which does.

Another company has used slower depreciation schedules than the rest of its industry without explaining why. And so it goes on.

When confronted with these cases, the accounting profession argues, loftily, that GAAP must be elastic enough to allow for the reporting of unusual situations.

Well, some regulators paint a darker picture. Too many company accountants have become rule oriented, they say. When challenged about a loose presentation, the accountant often replies: "Show me where it says I can't do that?"

Well, if the accountants are becoming rule-oriented, give them tighter rules, within GAAP. That's the answer.

Investors are too often led into confusion through the GAAP gap. It must be narrowed.

Source: "It's Time to Narrow the GAAP Gap," *Financial Post*, January 29–31, 1994, S1.

Here are some comments the accountants made. What do you think?

"Those journalists are always after accountants and auditors. Don't they realize that we are professionals and exercise our judgment carefully, so that there were undoubtedly circumstances that made the editorial's examples sensible to the accountants and auditors involved? Even if they were not sensible, they are only a few examples—what about some examples of all the times the accountants and auditors did the right thing? Not newsworthy, I guess."

"Don't be too hard on the media. They're an important part of the workings of GAAP—after all, we find out that way if what we do really is generally accepted! Remember some of the media attention that led to improvements in accounting? Like the trouble over pooling of interests consolidation, and poor accounting by governments and nonprofit organizations?"

"You know, the editorial does make me wonder just what advantage GAAP provide society. I remember an editorial somewhere after a plane crash, where the claim was that air regulations weren't strong enough to prevent crashes, and the counter-claim was that anytime you take off in an aluminum tube that is heavier than air, you're taking a chance and sooner or later someone will crash, regulations or not. Investing in businesses and managing them is at least as risky as flying, and people shouldn't expect GAAP to remove that risk. People need to become familiar with accounting principles and with the companies they invest in, so they can tell if something is amiss."

"I'll bet you could make an argument that having flexible GAAP to permit companies to tell their financial stories to the public in ways that fit those companies is cheaper for society in the long run than trying to control every accounting number with detailed rules. The rules would cost so much in accounting time, computers, and paper to administer that the cost of a few bad apples in the accounting barrel would be small in comparison."

"The editorial makes a good point about the dark side of the rules. If you have detailed rules, the accountants and auditors just turn into rule-followers rather than professionals. You could extend that argument to say that GAAP are already too detailed."

"That's not what the editorial means. It is saying that accountants view rules as constraints, preventing them from doing things, not as guides to appropriate behaviour. It says that the accountants seem to think that unless a rule exists, they can do anything, so I think it means that the accountants don't exercise professional judgment at all."

CASE 5C
Discuss ethics of an accounting manager's behaviour

Discuss the ethical issues involved in the situation described below.

Leslie was chief accountant for a municipality. The job included responsibility for the municipality's computer systems, which are mostly used for financial records such as tax billings and collections, budgets, operating expenditures, payrolls, and services such as parks and swimming pools, but also are used by the police, fire department, welfare office, and other municipal operations. Recent budget pressures and technological developments have created some information system challenges, so the municipal Council set up a task force to respond to the challenges and put Leslie in charge. The task force was specifically directed to find ways to save money that the municipality desperately needed elsewhere, in particular for services to several kinds of disadvantaged citizens.

Leslie was recently fired by Council for "insubordination and incompetence" resulting from the task force's work. Two problems were especially irritating to Council.

1. The task force developed an integrated computer system for recording and responding to emergency calls. The system would connect the emergency response system to tax records and other information about citizens, to dis-

courage abuse and ensure that the municipality billed people for all services provided. Considerable financial benefit to the municipality would result, but at the cost of delays in responding to emergency calls and substantially reduced privacy for callers. Leslie was concerned about these costs, because delays could cost lives and loss of privacy might discourage needy people from calling. However, a meeting of the task force with the Finance Committee of Council, chaired by the mayor, resulted in instructions to Leslie to disregard those concerns because the efficiencies gained would allow other needy people to be helped with the funds saved. Leslie was not satisfied with this, feeling that the impact on emergency response was too high a price to pay, and as the person responsible for computer systems and head of the task force, wrote a confidential memo to the mayor stating that the Finance Committee's instructions were inappropriate and giving careful reasons. Someone leaked the memo to the local media, with sensational results that were quite embarrassing to Council.

2. As Council investigated the first problem, a second one came to light. Earlier in the task force's work, a list of abuses of municipal resources and services had been developed, so that the new system could be designed to reduce or eliminate them. The list included such things as people avoiding property taxes on home improvements, plowing and cleaning streets of important citizens first, people making multiple welfare claims, municipal employees taking unauthorized holiday leaves, sending several ambulances to one emergency call because of duplications in recording calls, senior citizens receiving more than authorized discounts on recreation fees, and gifts by some contractors to municipal employees who send business their way. In the interests of task force efficiency, because not everything could be solved at once, Leslie had shortened the list and asked the task force to focus only on the remaining abuses. Leslie had thought a lot about which abuses to keep on the list and had eliminated several that potentially involved large dollars but seemed to Leslie to be socially acceptable, like the seniors' discounts. Council members questioned Leslie's judgment on these issues and criticized Leslie for presuming to make the eliminations in the first place.

NOTES

1. Some of the ideas in section 5.4 were developed with reference to George Murphy, "Corporate Reporting Practices in Canada: 1900–1970," *Working Paper Series*, Vol. 1 (The Academy of Accounting Historians, 1979).

2. For a description of accounting standard-setting in Canada in the 130 years from 1864 to 1992, see G. Baylin, L. MacDonald, and Alan J. Richardson, "Accounting Standard-Setting in Canada, 1864–1992: A Theoretical Analysis of Structural Evolution," *Journal of International Accounting & Taxation*, 5 no. 1(1996): 113–31.

3. *Financial Reporting in North America*, A Joint Study Undertaken by: Canadian Institute of Chartered Accountants, Instituto Mexicano de Contadores Publicos, AC, and Financial Accounting Standards Board of the United States, FASB (and available from the three national bodies), 1995.

4. *Financial Reporting in North America*, 119.

5. A. Lavigne, "Standards with a Differential," *CA Magazine* (October 1999): 49–50.

6. G.D. Trites, "Read It in the Annual Report," *CA Magazine* (December 1990): 45–48.

7. B. Gates, "Reports Deliver Message with Style and Pizzazz," *Financial Post* (27 November 1990): 17.

8. S. Noakes (quoting P. Creighton), "Reports Gain New Prominence," *Financial Post* (2 December 1993): 16.

9. D. Olive, "Watch Out for Glossy Truths," *National Post* (10 April 1999): B10.

10. G.M. Kang, "It's Corporate America's Spring Hornblowing Festival," *Business Week* (12 April 1993): 31.

11. Annual report contest winners were announced in *The Canadian Accountant*, a CICA newsletter, 5 no. 2 (Winter 2000): 3.

12. Quoted by D. Vansen, in "Objectivity…," *Monthly Statement* (Alberta: Institute of Chartered Accountants of Alberta, March 1999): 8.

13. S. Bartlett, "Who Can You Trust?" *Business Week* (5 October 1998): 133.

14. J.E. Garten, "Ethics be Damned, Let's Merge," *Business Week* (30 August 1999): 26.

15. J. Novack, "Certified Public Accomplice," *Forbes* (15 November1999): 282–83.

16. R. Melcher, "Where are the Accountants?" *Business Week* (5 October 1998): 144, 146.

17. For ideas on how to deal with such ethical dilemmas, see L.J. Brooks, *Professional Ethics for Accountants* (West Publishing, 1995), or L.A. Ponemon and D.R.L. Gabhart, *Ethical Reasoning in Accounting and Auditing* (Vancouver: CGA-Canada Research Foundation, 1993).

18. For good summaries of accounting implications of capital market concepts and research, see W.R. Scott, *Financial Accounting Theory* (Scarborough: Prentice-Hall Canada, 1997), especially Chapters 3, 4, and 5; C.M.C. Lee, "Measuring Wealth," *CA Magazine* (April 1996): 32–37; G. Foster, *Financial Statement Analysis*, 2nd ed. (Englewood Cliffs: Prentice-Hall, 1986), especially Chapters 9 and 11; R. L. Watts and J.L. Zimmerman, *Positive Accounting Theory* (Englewood Cliffs: Prentice-Hall, 1986), especially Chapters 2 and 3; W.H. Beaver, *Financial Reporting: An Accounting Revolution*, 2nd ed. (Englewood Cliffs: Prentice-Hall, 1989); or T.R. Dyckman and D. Morse, *Efficient Capital Markets and Accounting: A Critical Analysis*, 2nd ed. (Englewood Cliffs: Prentice-Hall, 1986).

19. For more ideas about contracts and their relationship to accounting, see R.L. Watts and J.L. Zimmerman, *Positive Accounting Theory* (Englewood Cliffs: Prentice-Hall, 1986), Chapters 8 and 9; J.E. Butterworth, M. Gibbins, and R.D. King, "The Structure of Accounting Theory: Some Basic Conceptual and Methodological Issues," in *Research to Support Standard Setting in Financial Accounting: A Canadian Perspective*, ed. S.J. Basu and A. Milburn (Toronto: The Clarkson Gordon Foundation, 1982): 9–17, especially. This article was reprinted in *Modern Accounting Research: History, Survey, and Guide*, ed. R. Mattessich (Vancouver: Canadian Certified General Accountants' Research Foundation, 1984), 209–50.

20. *CICA Handbook* (Toronto: Canadian Institute of Chartered Accountants, 31 December 1999). Reprinted by permission of The Canadian Institute of Chartered Accountants, Toronto, Canada.

21. Adapted from the 1979 National CA Uniform Final (Qualifying) Examination. By permission of the Canadian Institute of Chartered Accountants, Toronto, Canada.

22. Adapted from the 1984 National CA Uniform Final (Qualifying) Examination. By permission of the Canadian Institute of Chartered Accountants, Toronto, Canada.

Doing Financial Accounting

3
PART

The four chapters in this group delve into various practices important to anyone preparing financial statements, which are also presented so that their importance to those not planning to become accountants will be apparent.

- Chapter 6 focuses on the way accrual accounting measures income as the difference between revenues and expenses.

- Chapter 7 outlines recordkeeping and internal control considerations that exist separately from the financial statements but significantly influence the statements.

- Chapters 8 and 9 examine the accounts on the two sides of the balance sheet in more detail. Chapter 8 focuses on the left "assets" side and Chapter 9 on the right "liabilities and equity" side.

6 CHAPTER

Revenue and Expense Recognition

6.1 Chapter Overview

This chapter begins four chapters on *doing* financial accounting by focusing on how accrual accounting's measures of revenue and expense are constructed and matched to provide the measure of income. It is all based on double-entry accounting and on the concepts of revenue and expense, and the ways of adjusting accounts that were introduced in Chapter 3. With the conceptual and technical background provided by the first five chapters, this whole chapter is devoted to revenue and expense recognition, because accrual accounting is at the heart of financial accounting and is absolutely essential to understanding the income statement. Also, in many ways, the balance sheet is a "residual" of the measurement of revenues, expenses, and income, so this chapter extends your understanding of the balance sheet as well. Later chapters examine various parts of the balance sheet in more depth, using this chapter's explanation of accrual accounting.

Accrual accounting is all about choosing *when* to recognize phenomena in the accounts.

The key to accrual accounting is that it frees financial accounting from having to follow cash transactions only. With accrual accounting, revenues, expenses, assets, and liabilities can be recorded (recognized, as accountants say) before or after cash transactions happen. This can be done by the familiar method of debiting something and crediting something. The big question is *when* to recognize these income statement and balance sheet amounts by recording them in the accounts. For example, if revenue can be recorded at another time than when cash changes hands, such as by debiting accounts receivable and crediting revenue before the customer pays, when is it appropriate to do that? What evidence, principles, or assumptions support recognition before the cash changes hands, or after?

Here is the familiar diagram of this book's learning objectives. In this chapter, there is a full mixture of all three components.

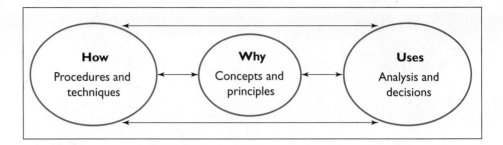

This is what you will learn in this chapter:

- *Procedures and techniques:* How to tell when to recognize revenues in the accounts, and how to match the recognition of expenses to those revenues. You will see how to use financial accounting's supply of journal entries to create whatever measures of revenues and expenses are appropriate, whenever the time is right.

- *Concepts and principles:* What the conceptual structure of accrual accounting is, how it is based on the principles in Chapter 5, why matching of revenues and expenses is fundamental to the whole process, and what kinds of accounting policies companies have for measuring revenues and expenses.

- *Analysis and decisions:* How to understand and evaluate companies' accounting policies for revenues and expenses, and how to estimate the effects of alternative policies.

6.2 WHAT IS ACCRUAL ACCOUNTING?

Accrual accounting involves estimates, judgments, and subjectivity.

Accrual accounting is the dominant form of financial accounting in the world today. It exists because cash flow information is simply not complete enough to assess financial performance or financial position. Keeping track of cash flow is crucial for business success, but it is not enough. We have to go beyond cash flow to assess economic performance more broadly and to assess noncash resources and obligations. We do this even though it forces us to make estimates, judgments, and other accounting choices that, in turn, make the results less precise than we would wish, and more subjective than transaction-based cash flow figures.

As a reminder of the ideas about accrual accounting introduced in Chapters 1 and 3, let's imagine the following conversation between a student and a relative who is also a professional accountant:

Accountant: Well, you spent the summer working at High-Class Boutique. How did you do?

Student: I had a great time. Met some great people, learned a lot about retailing, and so decided to major in marketing.

Accountant: No, I meant how did you do financially?

Student: Let's see. I received $6,460 over the four months. I have $4,530 left in the bank; so, I guess I must have spent $1,930. Gee, $4,530 doesn't make me rich after a summer's work! But the Boutique still owes me for my last week of work.

Accountant: What did you spend the $1,930 on?

Student: I blew some of the money on burgers and evening entertainment, and on that trip to the lake. But also, I bought clothes for the fall term, and I have the answering machine, and the fancy calculator I got so that I might be able to pass accounting.

Accountant: Don't forget you have to pay your Uncle Al back the money he lent you in May. That's in your bank account too, so it looks as if you spent more than $1,930. You promised to pay him, plus interest, at the end of the summer. And then there's your university tuition for next year. And didn't you say once that you owed a friend something for gas for that trip to the lake?

Student: I don't think we should count the tuition because it doesn't really apply until I register. Although I guess that *is* why I was working. Now I'm not sure if I had a good summer or not!

Accrual accounting incorporates many phenomena besides the period's cash flows.

This example illustrates many of the issues accrual accounting tries to deal with, including:

1. The more you think about it, the more complex measuring performance and position seems to be, and the less satisfactory cash by itself seems to be as a measure.
2. Some of what is earned may not yet have been received in cash (payment for the last week of work).
3. Similarly, some costs incurred may not yet have been paid (the gas for the lake trip).
4. Some cash payments result in resources still having economic value at the end of the period (the answering machine, the calculator, and maybe the clothes).
5. Some cash receipts result in obligations still outstanding at the end of the period (Uncle Al's loan).
6. The longer-term resources may have deteriorated during the period (not all the clothes purchased during the summer will still be valuable because fashions change, and the answering machine and calculator are now used items).
7. Obligations may build up during the period (the interest on Uncle Al's loan).
8. There is often doubt about whether some things should be included in measuring performance for a given period or position at a given point in time (the university tuition).

Accrual accounting aims for relevance without losing too much reliability.

Think of accrual accounting as an attempt to measure economic performance and financial position in a more complete way than just using cash. There is always a tradeoff here: the closer to cash, the more precise the measure is, but also the more limited and less informative it is. The more accountants try to make the financial statements economically relevant, the more they must include estimates and other sources of imprecision or error. Referring back to the relevance–reliability tradeoff diagram in section 5.3, *accrual accounting aims for more relevance but the price paid is less reliability.* To minimize the damage to reliability, there are many rules and standards surrounding accrual accounting, as we saw already in Chapter 5, and considerable evidence is normally required to back up the accrual figures. Companies are expected to choose sensible policies for doing their accrual accounting, and to stay with those policies over the years unless there is good reason for changing them.

 OW'S YOUR UNDERSTANDING?

Here are two questions you should be able to answer, based on what you have just read:

1. If accrual accounting produces less precise figures than just using cash transactions would, why is accrual accounting used?

2. Here's a review of earlier material. In its first year, new company Affleck Inc. collected cash from its customers of $85,000, paid cash bills of $74,000, and bought a truck for $50,000, borrowing $40,000 from the bank in order to do that and so ending the year with $1,000 in the bank. If at the end of the year, the company had uncollected revenues of $13,000 and unpaid expenses of $4,000, and $5,000 of the truck's value was thought to have been used (amortization), what was the company's accrual income for the year? ($15,000: the accrual income measure incorporates some noncash or not-yet-cash figures (the uncollected revenues, unpaid expenses, and amortization), and does not incorporate some cash figures (the truck purchase, and the bank loan). So: $85,000 − $74,000 + $13,000 − $4,000 − $5,000 = $15,000.)

6.3   CONCEPTUAL FOUNDATION OF ACCRUAL ACCOUNTING

Accrual accounting recognizes economic phenomena whether or not realized in cash.

Accrual accounting is based on the idea that events, estimates, and judgments important to the measurement of financial performance and position should be recognized by entries in the accounts (and therefore reflected in the financial statements), whether or not they have yet, or already, been realized by cash received or paid out. To slightly oversimplify, we might say that *the objective is to recognize economic flows in addition to cash flows*. The result affects income, through the revenue and expense figures, but also affects the balance sheet, through accounts like accounts receivable and accounts payable that are used to create the appropriate revenues and expenses. The income statement and balance sheet articulate through accrual accounting.

Let's build the accrual accounting approach from some basics. These four cornerstones have come up already in this book, but we'll give them brief definitions again and build from there:

- Revenues are *inflows* of economic resources from customers. We might say that earning revenues is the reason a company is in business.

- Expenses are *outflows* of economic resources to employees, suppliers, taxation authorities, and others, resulting from business activities to generate revenue and serve customers. We might say that incurring expenses is the cost of earning revenues.

- Net income is the *difference* between revenues and expenses over a period of time, such as a month, a quarter, or a year. We might say that net income is the measure of success in generating more revenues than it costs to generate those revenues.

Matching revenues and expenses is supposed to produce a logical net income measure.	• **Matching** is the *logic* of income measurement, ensuring that revenues and expenses are measured comparably, so that deducting the expenses from the revenues to calculate net income produces a meaningful result. We might say that matching ties accrual accounting together into a coherent system.

Note some features of these cornerstones:

Revenues and expenses are economic concepts extending beyond transactions.	• Revenues and expenses refer to inflows and outflows of economic resources. These flows may be represented by the kinds of events recognized by the transactional recordkeeping system, but they may also involve nontransactional phenomena. In particular, they may involve phenomena that arise *before* or *after* cash changes hands, as well as at the time of the cash flow.
Properly measured revenues and expenses should lead to proper net income.	• Net income depends on how revenues and expenses are measured, and is not well defined separately from revenues and expenses. Accountants don't, or shouldn't, choose the income number first and force the calculation of revenues and expenses to result in that income. Instead, they measure revenues and expenses as properly as they can. Net income then is just the difference between these revenues and expenses.
Many criteria besides matching help ensure that revenues, expenses, and income are proper.	• Matching involves trying to line up measures of economic inflows with those of economic outflows. It is logical, but not the only logic one could imagine applying. For example, if revenues are overestimated and then expenses are overestimated to match, the net income figure may be about right because the overestimations roughly cancel out, but the figures for revenues and expenses will be misleading, as will any balance sheet accounts related to them, such as accounts receivable and accounts payable. If the method of recognizing revenue is poor, it hardly makes sense to argue for a poor expense recognition method for the sake of matching. So, many other criteria enter into revenue and expense recognition and income measurement to fine-tune the system and ensure that the matched measures are sensible. Examples of such criteria are fairness, comparability, consistency, conservatism, and other concepts in Chapter 5, plus various detailed methods for determining how much revenue has been earned and how much expense has been incurred, which we will see.

A Conceptual System for Accrual Income Measurement

Accrual accounting includes cash flows plus both earlier and later economic phenomena.	Accrual accounting's purpose is to extend the measurement of financial performance and position by recognizing phenomena prior to and subsequent to cash flows, as well as at the point of cash flows, making accrual accounting more complete than just using transactions, especially just cash transactions. (In sophisticated companies, many of the routine noncash parts of accrual accounting, such as recognizing uncollected revenue as accounts receivable, are handled with transactional records, but those are still based on the principles explained in this chapter.) Let's work through how this is done, focusing on revenues and expenses for the time being. Exhibit 6.1 summarizes accrual revenue and expense recognition and shows how that fits with the cash flows that are also happening. It is important to remember that accrual accounting *does not ignore cash flows*; it just permits revenues and expenses to be recognized *earlier* or *later* than the related cash receipts and payments. Cash flow is still part of the picture.

Summary of Accrual Accounting Revenue and Expense Recognition

	Revenues	Expenses

(1) Start with cash transactions	DR Cash
	    CR Revenues
		DR Expenses
		    CR Cash

(2) Stretch the time out so that revenues and expenses are recognized *before* the cash transactions

	Revenues	Expenses

(a) Recognition	DR Accounts receivable
	    CR Revenues
		DR Expenses
		    CR Accounts payable#

(b) Cash transactions	DR Cash
	    CR Accounts receivable
		DR Accounts payable#
		    CR Cash

Note that the sums of entries 2(a) and 2(b) equal entries (1). The accounts receivable and payable accounts are temporary accounts used to allow *earlier* recognition of revenues and expenses and are eliminated when the cash flows.

(3) Stretch the time out the other way so that revenues and expenses are recognized *after* the cash transactions

	Revenues	Expenses

(a) Cash transactions	DR Cash
	    CR Deferred revenue**
		DR Assets*
		    CR Cash

(b) Recognition	DR Deferred revenue**
	    CR Revenues
		DR Expenses
		    CR Assets*

Note that the sums of entries 3(a) and 3(b) equal entries (1). The assets* and deferred revenue** accounts are temporary accounts used to allow *later* recognition of revenues and expenses and are eliminated by that recognition.

\# Other liabilities than accounts payable may be involved, such as accrued interest, income tax payable, warranty liability, pension liability, and deferred income tax.

* Example asset accounts that might be debited at the cash transaction stage include inventories, prepaid insurance, and factory. These are eliminated (over time) by entries that credit such accounts and debit cost of goods sold, insurance expense, and amortization expense.

** Deferred revenue is a temporary liability account used to record cash received before the revenue has been earned, such as with customer deposits.

Accrual accounting is all about *timing* of revenue and expense recognition.

Parts (2) and (3) of Exhibit 6.1 can be rearranged to show the four possible revenue and expense recognition scenarios *other than* just recognizing revenues and expenses when the cash flow happens (which was Part (1) of Exhibit 6.1). Exhibit 6.2 does this, showing how accrual accounting implements different *timing* than that of the cash flows through eight general kinds of journal entries that allow revenue and expense recognition to happen before or after the cash transactions. In this exhibit, the "current accounting period" is the one in which the accounting is now being done—the "past" period has already finished and the "next" period has not started. "Period" can be any period over which income is being measured: a year, a quarter, a month, or whatever. The arrows indicate accounts used to allow the revenue or expense recognition to diverge from the cash flow; as noted in Exhibit 6.1, these accounts are temporary in concept, and eventually are eliminated by later cash flow or later recognition.

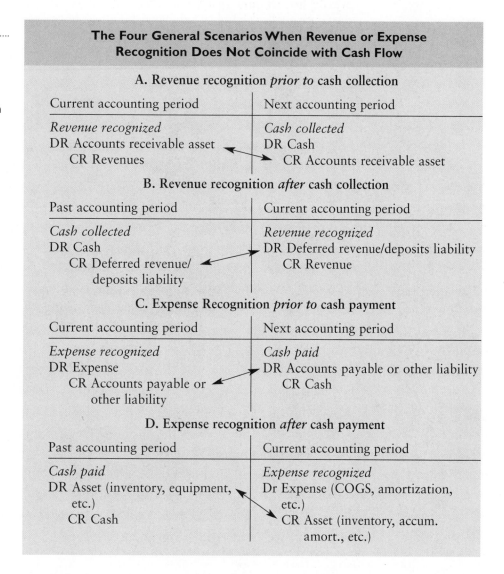

The Four General Scenarios When Revenue or Expense Recognition Does Not Coincide with Cash Flow

A. Revenue recognition *prior to* cash collection

Current accounting period	Next accounting period

Revenue recognized
 DR Accounts receivable asset
    CR Revenues
	Cash collected
	 DR Cash
	    CR Accounts receivable asset

B. Revenue recognition *after* cash collection

Past accounting period	Current accounting period

Cash collected
 DR Cash
    CR Deferred revenue/
    deposits liability
	Revenue recognized
	 DR Deferred revenue/deposits liability
	    CR Revenue

C. Expense Recognition *prior to* cash payment

Current accounting period	Next accounting period

Expense recognized
 DR Expense
    CR Accounts payable or
    other liability
	Cash paid
	 DR Accounts payable or other liability
	    CR Cash

D. Expense recognition *after* cash payment

Past accounting period	Current accounting period

Cash paid
 DR Asset (inventory, equipment,
    etc.)
    CR Cash
	Expense recognized
	 Dr Expense (COGS, amortization,
	    etc.)
	    CR Asset (inventory, accum.
	    amort., etc.)

Here in Exhibit 6.3 are some examples to help you see how the accrual accounting system works. We'll use types of entries you've already seen in earlier chapters. The example entries involve manufacturer Northern Gear Ltd. Now you should be able to see how the records and adjustments you already know how to do aggregate into an overall structure that makes accrual accounting a system.

As you know, Canada has a system of GST and provincial sales taxes in most provinces. To make the examples more realistic, some such taxes are also included in the example entries: the basic idea is that when tax is charged to customers, it has to be paid to the government and so is a liability, and when tax is incurred on the company's purchases, it can be claimed back from the government and so reduces the liability. Companies also must deduct income taxes and other deductions from employees' pay, so the examples include that too. In Chapter 7, more time will be devoted to how these practical tax considerations work. These complications are included just to illustrate that accrual accounting adapts to whatever the business and legal requirements are, and so can become quite complex. But the conceptual structure in Exhibits 6.1 and 6.2 underlies whatever complex procedures an enterprise uses.

Exhibit

Recognition prior to cash flow

Revenue

Northern Gear made a sale on credit	DR	Accounts receivable	2,464	
	CR	Revenue		2,200
	CR	Sales taxes due		264

Expense

Employees worked for wages paid later	DR	Wages expense	1,860	
	CR	Deductions due		340
	CR	Wages payable		1,520
Interest was due on a bank loan	DR	Interest expense	240	
	CR	Interest payable		240
Legal advice was obtained, plus GST	DR	Legal advice expense	500	
	DR	Sales taxes due	35	
	CR	Accounts payable		535

Cash flows related to prior recognition

Collection

A customer made a payment on account	DR	Cash	1,100	
	CR	Accounts receivable		1,100

Payment

The company paid a supplier	DR	Accounts payable	775	
	CR	Cash		775
The company remitted employee deductions	DR	Deductions due	825	
	CR	Cash		825

Cash revenues and expenses

Cash revenue

A customer made a minor purchase	DR	Cash	90	
	CR	Sales taxes due		10
	CR	Revenue		80

Cash expense

Northern Gear made a donation to charity	DR Donations expense	100	
	CR Cash		100
The company bought supplies, plus GST	DR Supplies expense	210	
	DR Sales taxes due	15	
	CR Cash		225

Cash flows related to later recognition

Collection

A customer paid for an order in advance	DR Cash	784	
	CR Deferred revenue		784

Payment

Northern Gear bought new machinery	DR Machinery asset	5,200	
	CR Cash		5,200
The company bought inventory, plus GST	DR Inventory asset	2,300	
	DR Sales taxes due	161	
	CR Cash		2,461
The company paid for insurance in advance	DR Prepaid insurance asset	840	
	CR Cash		840

Recognition after cash flow

Revenue

The customer's prepaid order was shipped	DR Deferred revenue	784	
	CR Sales taxes due		84
	CR Revenue		700

Expense

Cost of goods sold on a week's sales	DR COGS expense	23,611	
	CR Inventory asset		23,611
Amortization for a year	DR Amort. expense	41,500	
	CR Accum. amort.		41,500
Insurance used during a month	DR Insurance expense	70	
	CR Prepaid insurance		70

Accrual accounting is a flexible system that can handle many phenomena.

These entries don't cover quite everything accrual accounting can do, and you might be able to think of events that combine some of the above entries. An example is buying inventory on credit. That is a debit to Inventory and a credit not to Cash, but to Accounts payable. This entry allows both recognition of the expense later *and* payment of the cash later. Buying machinery or other noncurrent assets on credit would work the same way. Accrual accounting is quite flexible and can

handle all sorts of events and adjustments. All you need to do is figure out what
to debit and what to credit.

OR YOUR INTEREST

Does accrual accounting matter? Here are some comments about research results:
"Accrual accounting can be viewed as one potentially cost-effective compromise
between merely reporting cash flows and a more ambitious system of fuller disclosure."[1] ("Fuller disclosure" might include reporting all the company's transactions and
other events and just letting the user of the information construct his/her own version of income, assets, etc., in whatever way that person thought appropriate. You can
think of accounting principles as decisions on behalf of presumed users of what they
would like to know, so there is always, at least conceptually, the possibility of not making such a decision and just reporting everything.) "There is a significant, positive correlation between (share) price changes and earnings changes."[2] "Price changes appear
to be more highly correlated with earnings changes than with changes in 'cash flow'."[3]
"The research provides clear evidence that investors and creditors can use accounting information to predict many phenomena of interest."[4] (So the principles, entries,
and other efforts by accountants do make a difference. A good thing for accountants!)

OW'S YOUR UNDERSTANDING?

Here are two questions you should be able to answer, based on what you have just
read:

1. How do accrual accounting entries work to separate the earning of revenue from
   the receipt of cash? Is it always necessary to separate them, or can they happen
   at the same time?

2. In what way can it be said that amortization expense and cost of goods sold
   expense are examples of the same thing?

6.4   ACCOUNTING POLICY CHOICES

There are complications, but we have seen that the general pattern behind accrual
accounting's revenue and expense recognition system is:

- *Recognition of revenue prior to cash collection:* Create an asset, usually
  called accounts receivable, to hold the economic value gained through the
  revenue until the cash is collected.

- *Recognition of revenue after cash collection:* Create a liability, usually called
  customer deposits or deferred revenue, to hold the cash value until the revenue has been earned.

- *Recognition of expense prior to cash payment:* Create a liability account,
  such as accounts payable, wages payable, pension liability, or future income

tax liability, to hold the economic value lost through the expense until the cash is paid.

- *Recognition of expense after cash payment:* Create an asset account, such as inventory or buildings and equipment, to hold the economic value until it is consumed, when it is then transferred to an expense such as cost of goods sold or amortization expense.

Accrual accounting uses a variety of accounts to represent noncash economic values.

Since accrual accounting is a system, decisions about when and how to record the various recognition and other entries described above and in the previous section should not be made in an unorganized way. Instead, the enterprise should make accounting policy choices about how its accrual accounting is to be conducted.

What Is an Accounting Policy?

Management needs to provide direction about how the accounting is to be done.

Imagine the following scenario: the bookkeeper for MegaMega Stores Inc. has to decide whether or not each sales invoice should be recorded as revenue (credit revenue, debit cash, or accounts receivable) and so, each time, phones the president and asks whether that invoice should be recorded. Pretty silly, eh? What the company needs to do is decide, *in advance and in general*, what sort of transaction constitutes a sale that is to be recorded as revenue. Then this decision can be communicated to the bookkeeper, who can apply the criteria to each invoice and so decide what to record without phoning the president. The president can run the company instead of talking to the bookkeeper every few minutes.

An accounting policy is a decision made in advance about how, when, and whether to record or recognize something. Typically, companies make policy choices in many areas. The following are only a few examples:

- When and how to recognize revenue.

- How to compute amortization on plant and equipment assets.

- How to value inventories and calculate cost of goods sold.

- How to value receivables, including how to estimate the effects of bad debts.

- Which expenditures on noncurrent assets should be added to the asset accounts and which should be included with expenses such as repairs and maintenance.

Accounting policies apply to everything in the financial statements.

Many choices are needed in assembling meaningful financial statements. When you choose the location of an account in the financial statements (such as putting it in current liabilities rather than noncurrent liabilities), you are making an accounting policy choice!

Accounting policy choices are very important to the interpretation and analysis of the financial statements. Without knowing how the statements were assembled, it is difficult to use them intelligently. For this reason, the first of the notes following the financial statements is usually a summary of the company's significant accounting policies. These are the topics covered in CAE's year 2000 Significant Accounting Policies note: [5]

- Consolidation method
- Revenue recognition
- Definition of cash and short-term investments
- How inventories are valued
- Plant and equipment values
- Amortization methods
- Foreign currency translation

- Financial instruments
- Goodwill valuation
- Future income taxes
- Other income tax issues
- Pensions and similar benefits
- Earnings per share calculation
- The basis of accounting estimates

Other notes to CAE's statements provide further details on important policies. Companies do not overwhelm the reader with descriptions about every accounting policy: those that are obvious or that follow standard rules that an informed reader (which is what you are becoming!) should know about are usually not described. For example, the definitions of current assets and current liabilities are well known and would be mentioned only if something unusual was being done.

Why Is There a Choice?

Accrual accounting forces the preparers of financial statements to make choices, whether they like it or not.

Accrual accounting requires that accounting policy choices be made.

1. The basis of accrual accounting is to augment the transactional records to produce a more complete economic picture of the enterprise's performance and position. How to do this is a matter of judgment and of criteria such as fairness and matching. Accrual accounting therefore *necessitates* choices about accounting figures, notes, and methods.
2. Even the basic transactional records of accounting require decisions about what is a transaction, which accounts to use, and how and when transactions are to be recorded.
3. In Canada, the United States, Britain, Australia, New Zealand, and many other countries, governments and professional accounting standard-setters (such as the CICA and the FASB) have been reluctant to try to specify all solutions and require all enterprises to follow them. Such authorities appear to believe that choices in accounting are appropriate to fit the accounting to each enterprise's circumstances, and perhaps inevitable in our free enterprise economic system. Stock market participants, financial analysts, and others who rely on financial statements are expected to attain sufficient knowledge of accounting and the enterprise to make informed decisions, just as they would when buying the enterprise's products or having other interactions with the enterprise.

Not all countries give as much policy choice to companies as Canada does.

   Authorities in many countries (such as China, France, Germany, and Japan) specify accounting methods more strictly than in Canada. In such countries, the material covered in this chapter would put more emphasis on how to implement the approved accounting methods and less on how to choose among a variety of acceptable methods.
4. Because the complete financial statements include the titles and classifications of figures and the footnotes and other narrative disclosures, there is fre-

Recording something in the accounts, having a narrative disclosure, or both, is a choice.

quently a decision to be made as to whether to adjust the figures for something or to disclose it in the narrative material instead, or give it a special title, or even all of these. For example, if the company has been sued by a disgruntled customer, should that be recorded as a liability? If recorded, should it be separately listed in the balance sheet? Should it instead just be disclosed in the notes, or perhaps in a note even if it is recorded?

General Criteria for Accounting Policy Choices

When deciding how to account for revenues, inventories, amortization, and other matters (*including* what to say in footnote disclosures), companies have to consider the following kinds of criteria and work out how they apply to the specific policy choice situation. These criteria were examined in depth in sections 5.2 and 5.3.

The principles in Chapter 5 are essential to making accounting policy choices.

1. Fairness (objectivity, lack of bias, correspondence with economic substance).
2. Matching (fitting revenue recognition to the economic process, fitting expense recognition to the economic process and to the revenue).
3. Consistency over time.
4. Comparability to other companies (especially in the same industry).
5. Conformance with authoritative standards and less formal aspects of GAAP.
6. Materiality to (significance to decisions of) known or presumed users of the information.
7. Conservatism (taking anticipated losses into account before the transaction happens, but not taking anticipated gains into account until the transaction happens).

In addition, various criteria specific to the particular accounting policy choice issue must be considered. Examples are the cost of implementing the policy, tax effects, internal control considerations, and other business implications and consequences. These criteria will be indicated as topics are covered in this and later chapters.

How Much Freedom of Choice Is There?

Accounting policy choices are constrained by authoritative standards and broader GAAP.

Accounting policy choices are made within the standards set out by the *CICA Handbook*, the FASB, and other standard-setters and regulators as described in Chapter 5. While companies ordinarily do not *have* to follow these standards, or the less-formal parts of GAAP, they can get into considerable trouble if they do not. Stock markets may refuse to list their shares. Taxation authorities may refuse to accept their financial statements as evidence of income for tax purposes. Shareholders and creditors may sue for alleged misrepresentation. Embarrassing newspaper articles may be written about them. So many policy choices are highly constrained, and are expected to be made with reference to standard criteria. There are some areas of accounting that are new or controversial enough that there is no or little guidance from standard-setters, and then the company is a little more free to make its own policy decisions.

Even when there is an authoritative standard or a clear tradition, the necessity of fitting the accounting policy to the particular circumstances of the enterprise necessitates, in turn, the exercise of professional judgment by the preparers and auditors of the information. As the *CICA Handbook*'s Introduction to Accounting Recommendations says:

Standards cannot cover everything, so people still have to use their heads.

No rule of general application can be phrased to suit all circumstances or combination of circumstances that may arise, nor is there any substitute for the exercise of professional judgment in the determination of what constitutes fair presentation or good practice in a particular case.[6]

OR YOUR INTEREST

Does accounting policy choice provide a way for company management to alter the picture presented in the financial statements—to present the story they want to tell rather than the "truth"? The short answer is yes. The whole idea of accrual accounting is to permit a company to choose how its performance and position are to be depicted. There is a fine line between choosing the accounting policies that suit the company's circumstances and therefore produce fair reporting, and choosing policies that tell a desired story that may not be fair. *The vast majority of companies and their managers are scrupulous about their accounting* and consider producing fair financial statements to be both ethical and good business practice. But we do learn of companies that have stepped over the line and "doctored" their accounts to make themselves look better or to hide some embarrassing result. Some types of doctoring are:

- What accountants and the business press often call **aggressive accounting**: seeking out

    ▶ accounting methods and policy choices that serve management's objectives for growth,

    ▶ financing, bonuses, or other purposes that seem to violate fairness or conservatism.

- The examples of income manipulation in Chapter 3: the **Big Bath** and income smoothing.

Manipulation dangers can be overrated. Few managers are crooked in their accounting: most are honest and anxious that their accounting be fair and truthful. Most believe that good financial reporting is important to the company's reputation and ability to borrow, raise share capital, and generally do business. Most consider good financial reporting to be part of good business and professional ethics. However, the danger of manipulation is always there, so accountants, auditors, and users who rely on financial statements for their decisions must be vigilant.

A Few Technical Points

Accounting policy choices generally do not affect cash and cash flow.

1. *Cash flow.* Generally, accounting policy choice does not affect cash flow. Policy choices are made by accrual accounting entries, which are intended to go beyond cash and so seldom affect cash directly. There may be indirect or eventual effects, especially through income tax. But, at the instant an accounting policy choice is implemented, there is no cash or cash flow effect except in the rare case where a cash account is involved. The cash flow statement is useful partly because its analysis helps to identify accounting policy choices that may have taken the income a little too far from cash flow.

Accounting policy choices that affect income must also affect the balance sheet.

2. *Dual effects of changes.* Because the financial statements are fundamentally connected through double-entry accounting, most accounting policy changes affect both the balance sheet and the income statement. *They must affect both if they are to affect net income.* This is financial statement articulation. Here are some examples:

Balance Sheet Accounts	Main Income Statement Accounts
Temporary investments	Nonoperating revenue or expense
Accounts receivable	Revenue, bad debts expense
Inventories	Cost of goods sold expense
Prepaid and accrued expenses	Various expense accounts
Property and plant assets	Amortization expense
Intangible and leased assets	Amortization expense
Liabilities	Various expense accounts
Equity	None*

* Transactions with owners, such as share capital issues and redemptions and dividends, are ordinarily not considered part of the measurement of income. However, there are some technicalities in which this may be violated—this book will not cover such technicalities.

Classification and disclosure choices are part of accounting policy choice.

3. *Classification and disclosure.* There are accounting policy choices in two areas, besides the example of Equity accounts above, that do not affect income:

- Classification policies (decisions about where within the balance sheet or where within the income statement to show accounts) do not affect income because they do not involve both the balance sheet and income statement, as do recognition policies, but instead affect only one statement or the other.

- Disclosure policies relate to what is said about the figures in the words used in the statements and in the notes to the statements. Changes in accounting policies are also disclosed, including a description of the change and a calculation of the effect the change has had on the financial statements. Many changes have to be given retroactive effect; for example, if the revenue recognition method is changed, past years' financial statements have to be recalculated to show them on the new basis. Therefore, if a company has changed its accounting policy in some area, the prior years' figures in this year's annual report may not be the same as the ones you would have seen in last year's annual report.

(H)OW'S YOUR UNDERSTANDING?

Here are two questions you should be able to answer, based on what you have just read:

1. Sue Wong, an experienced investor, reacted in frustration on having difficulty comparing the financial statements of two companies she was considering investing in, because the companies had made different choices about accounting for some items. Why do enterprises make choices, and why might they be different choices?

2. The president of Burning Issues Ltd., a political polling firm, is concerned about how to account for large expenditures on developing mailing and phone lists. The question is whether these expenditures should be included in the assets of the firm or deducted as expenses. What criteria should the president use in deciding how to account for the expenditures?

6.5   THE FISCAL PERIOD

Measuring financial performance and position requires defined fiscal periods.

Financial statements all have a time dimension. Balance sheets are prepared as at specific points in time, and the other three statements cover specified periods of time. Business and other economic activities go on continuously, so if the financial statements are to be at, or begin and end at, particular dates, financial accounting must somehow find a way to separate all those activities into fiscal periods. Accrual accounting is the method, because it is designed to incorporate economic phenomena that happen before or after the cash transactions. But how does accrual accounting separate the records and adjustments into periods?

Here's an example of the problem. Quantum Inc. earns its revenue through a series of projects, done one at a time. Cash receipts for revenues happen once or twice during each project, and cash payments for expenses happen about a month after expenses are incurred.

Accrual accounting must cut continuous business activities into fiscal periods.

To calculate net income for, say, 2001 using accrual accounting, we can use the various categories of entries set out in section 6.3. We can recognize revenues and expenses before or after cash inflows and outflows. But how much of these apply to 2001 rather than to other years? We need to find a way to "cut off" the accounting records of what are continuous activities, so that 2001 can be separated from 2000 and 2002. The 2001 net income is a measure of the economic value added by the projects *during that year*. By the matching criterion, that measure is produced by calculating the increase in resources (revenues) minus the decrease in resources (expenses), determined using comparable methods so that their difference is a meaningful income figure.

Here are Quantum's projects affecting 2001:

Exhibit

	Revenues	Expenses
Project #39		
Work began on the project		Nov. 00
Some cash received from the customer	Dec. 00	
Disbursements for expenses began		Dec. 00
Work completed on the project		Feb. 01
Disbursements for expenses ended		Mar. 01
Remaining cash received from the customer	Apr. 01	
Project #40		
Work began on the project		Mar. 01
Disbursements for expenses began		Apr. 01
All cash received from the customer	Sep. 01	
Work completed on the project		Oct. 01
Disbursements for expenses ended		Nov. 01
Project #41		
Some cash received from the customer	Nov. 01	
Work began on the project		Nov. 01
Disbursements for expenses began		Dec. 01
Work completed on the project		Mar. 02
Disbursements for expenses ended		Apr. 02
Remaining cash received from the customer	Apr. 02	

Let's try to do this project by project.

- Project 40 is easiest. All the revenue was earned and collected in 2001. All the expenses were incurred and paid in 2001. The cash basis works fine here.

- Project 39 is more awkward. There were two cash inflows, Dec. 2000 and Apr. 2001. If the Dec. 2000 inflow was less than the amount of revenue earned by the end of the year, then there should be a Dec. 31, 2000, *account receivable* created for the rest of the revenue earned but not collected. However, if the Dec. 2000 inflow was *greater* than the amount of revenue earned by the end of the year, then there should be a Dec. 31, 2000, *deferred revenue liability* created for the unearned portion. For the expenses, there are two problems. First, the expenses incurred in December would not be paid until January, so a Dec. 31, 2000, account payable should be created for those. Second, the amount of expenses recognized in 2000 should match the revenue recognized for 2000, so that their difference, net income, is meaningful.

- Project 41 has the same sort of awkwardness as 39, except it has to be cut off properly at the end of 2001.

- So 2001 revenues, expenses, and resulting net income will be a combination of the part of Project 39's revenues and expenses *not* recognized in 2000, all of Project 40's revenues and expenses, and the part of Project 41's revenues and expenses recognized in 2001. You can see that *both* the cutoff at the end of 2000 and the one at the end of 2001 have to be appropriate if the 2001 revenues, expenses, and net income are to be fair. Because of this, the 2001 results involve estimates on Projects 39 and 41 that also affect the fairness of the results for 2000 and 2002. The revenues and expenses for those projects have to be properly *allocated* among the years they involve, and the results for all those years will be affected by the quality of the allocations.

Making effective cutoffs for revenues and expenses is a major task for accrual accounting. Much effort is put into determining whether revenues are placed in the appropriate years, whether there are bills outstanding for expenses that should be taken into account, whether inventories of goods and supplies are actually on hand, and so on. Generally, the larger and less frequent an enterprise's revenue and expense transactions are, the harder it is to do this, and for enterprises that have many short and simple transactions, the easier it gets. But even there it can be difficult if there are thousands of transactions in process across a year-end.

When should the fiscal (accounting) year begin and end? Companies have an initial choice, but once they make it, reasons of habit and legal and tax rules usually force them to stay with that choice indefinitely. They may select a fiscal year-end that is a relatively quiet time, so that there aren't many unfinished transactions in process and the revenue and expense cutoffs can be made more cleanly. However, in practice, most companies select December 31 as their fiscal year-end. *Financial Reporting in Canada 1999* reported that 71% of the 200 companies it surveyed chose December 31, with every other month-end being chosen by some companies, and March and August being the most common noncalendar year-end.[7] Sometimes a date other than a month-end is used. Though history, tradition, and income tax reasons make December 31 the majority choice, the large minority choosing other fiscal periods has many reasons for other dates, including a better fit with the company's "natural" business year (some food companies choose dates just before or after the harvest season, and some retailers prefer dates other than December 31 because they like to avoid the hectic Christmas season), but choosing other dates may just be traditional too. "Regardless of the reasons for odd fiscal years, this much is certain for many firms. The business calendar quickly becomes engraved in stone. Procter & Gamble, for example, closes its books at the end of June. No one remembers why. Is a change likely? Not on your life."[8]

HOW'S YOUR UNDERSTANDING?

Here are two questions you should be able to answer, based on what you have just read:

1. Why is the fiscal period an important issue in financial accounting?

2. Sheaf Farm Products Ltd. is considering changing its accounting policy for revenue recognition, to match the revenue better to expenses. It is now 2001. The policy being considered would increase revenue in 2001 by $53,200. Accounts receivable at the end of 2000 would increase by $38,900 and at the end of 2001 would increase by $92,100, the difference being the $53,200 revenue effect in 2001. If the policy change were made, how much revenue would be moved from 2001 to 2000, and how much from 2002 to 2001? ($38,900, $92,100)

6.6   REVENUE RECOGNITION

Accuracy versus Decision Relevance

Income for the life of the enterprise can be determined from cash flows, without accruals.

It can be said that income over the life of an enterprise is easy to determine. At the end of the enterprise's life, all expenses have resulted in cash outflows and all the revenue earned has resulted in cash inflows. There is no need for accrual accounting, or for estimates of any kind; the results are known with certainty. Income over the life of the enterprise is simply the sum of the cash on hand at the end plus any cash withdrawn by the owners over the enterprise's life (such as dividends), minus any cash contributed by the owners over that time (such as share capital).

Decision-making cannot wait until the firm's life ends, so we have accrual accounting.

Decision makers want information about performance earlier than at the end of the enterprise's life. It is difficult, though, to cut the essentially continuous operations of a company into discrete time periods. Income determined before the end of the company's life, so that it is relevant for evaluating the enterprise's performance over shorter decision periods, is unavoidably subject to estimates and judgments because the whole story is never known until the end.

This takes us back to the ever-present tradeoff between reliability and relevance in income measurement, illustrated in section 5.3 as relevance versus reliability of estimates. If revenues and expenses are recognized earlier, so that they are more relevant for decision-making, then they will not be as reliable (accurately measured) as they would be if recognition were delayed until later, when outcomes of the various economic activities are better known. Because the tradeoff is very important to accrual accounting, Figure 6.1 illustrates it again, now relating it to *when* phenomena are recognized in the accounts.

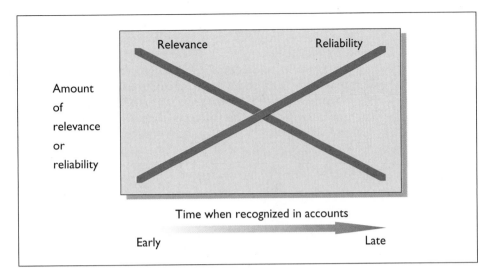

FIGURE 6.1

Critical Event Simplification

If we are to describe the firm's operations for a given period by calculating the income for that period, we must define a means by which to measure the amount of income that can be attributed to that period. We accomplish this by:

- Defining how much revenue can be *recognized* in that period; and then

- *Matching* to that revenue the expenses which were incurred to generate the revenue.

Income is the result of revenue recognition matched by expense recognition.

Income, the value added by the activities of the firm, is just the *difference* between the recognized revenue and the recognized expenses. Revenue recognition is important because, by the matching criterion, expense recognition and therefore income measurement should correspond with the revenue. This can get rather messy in practice, as you might imagine. For example, some expenses, often called period expenses, are only indirectly related to revenue, being incurred as time passes (interest is an example). Others, often called discretionary expenses, arise more haphazardly or as other business decisions are made by management (such as donations, research and development, or maintenance). But for simplicity, let's assume that revenue recognition is the primary driver of income measurement.

What are the revenues, or the expenses, for a period? From an economic and business point of view, income is earned by a wide variety of actions taken by the enterprise. There is a whole sequence of activities intended to help generate income, which therefore generate revenue and incur expenses, including, for example:

1. Organizing the firm in the first place
2. Building the factory
3. Buying or making inventory
4. Advertising
5. Selling
6. Delivering to a customer
7. Billing
8. Collecting cash
9. Providing warranty service

How should we recognize revenue when there is such a series of activities as those listed above? Recognizing it a bit at a time as each activity is carried out would approximate the economic process underlying the business. This would be relevant, all right, but by the same token it would be very subjective and imprecise, because it is difficult to say what each activity actually adds. How do you tell, when the company is just being organized, what revenue that form of organization will help to generate, for example? It would also be expensive to implement, with armies of accountants scurrying about measuring the small value change generated by each of the various activities and writing masses of journal entries to recognize each value change. The upward-sloping solid line in Figure 6.2 illustrates the presumed increase in value generated by the sort of activities listed above.

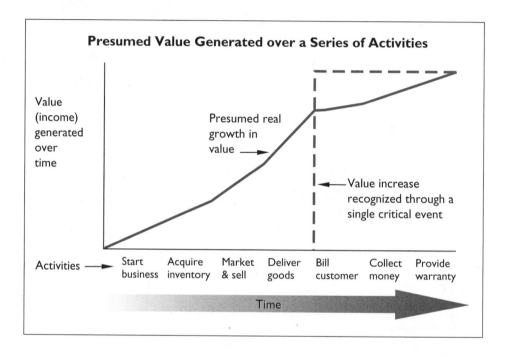

Presumed Value Generated over a Series of Activities

Value (income) generated over time

Presumed real growth in value →

Value increase recognized through a single critical event

Activities → Start business | Acquire inventory | Market & sell | Deliver goods | Bill customer | Collect money | Provide warranty

Time

FIGURE 6.2

Recognizing revenue at a single critical event is practical but theoretically awkward.

Instead, for greater objectivity and verifiability and less accounting cost, accountants usually choose *one* activity in the sequence of value-producing activities above as the critical event in the revenue generation sequence that can be readily documented, and recognize all of the revenue at that point. This is a simplification, because clearly some revenue could have been recognized when earlier activities were carried out, and probably some should be recognized when later activities take place. In theory, revenue is under-recognized prior to that point and over-recognized after it. Figure 6.2 also illustrates this. The critical event is designated by the vertical dotted line at the end of the delivery activity. Income earned prior to this event is not recognized by the accounting system, so the value produced by the activities to the left of it is not recognized until, all at once, 100% of the value is recognized. Until the rest of the activities are completed, the result (to the right of the dotted line) is over-recognition of the value because there are still things to be done.

Revenue recognition records the asset (or liability reduction) obtained for the revenue.

To recognize the earning of revenue when the critical event has taken place, we make a recognition entry like this:

DR Accounts receivable or
    Cash or
    Deferred revenue liability   XXXX
CR Revenue   XXXX

Delivery of goods or services is the most common critical event for recognizing revenue.

For some companies, such as those building big projects like power stations or pipelines, or project-based companies such as Quantum Inc. in section 6.5, it is worthwhile and fair to estimate revenue at several points along the way. That means chopping the amount of revenue up into pieces and recording *each* piece with an entry like the one above, instead of all at once. We'll see examples of how to recognize revenue and therefore income in smaller steps that more closely fit the continuously increasing value. However, most companies use the practical simplification of the critical event. *The most common critical event used is the point of completing delivery of the goods or services to the customer.*

Criteria for Revenue Recognition

Revenue recognition, then, becomes the first step in determining income for the period. The revenue recognition criteria discussed below have been formulated for the purpose of making sure that revenue will be recognized only when there is objective evidence that revenue has indeed been earned. This is an attempt to ensure that the result is reliable. The following four criteria must normally *all* be met in order that revenue may be recognized. For most enterprises, the activity nearest to fitting these criteria is chosen as the critical event, and for most of them that is delivery. However, as we'll see, there are exceptions (as usual!).

These four criteria must normally all be met before revenue is recognized.

1. All or substantially all of the goods or services to be provided to customers have been provided or performed (the "delivery" criterion mentioned above).
2. Most of the costs to generate the revenue have been incurred, and those remaining can be measured with reasonable accuracy.
3. The amount of the revenue can be reasonably measured in dollar terms (for example, if some customers are likely to return goods for a refund, such returns can be reasonably estimated).
4. Cash, a promise of cash (a receivable), or another asset that can be measured with reasonable precision, has been received.

Although the above criteria seem fairly clear, there are still many judgments to be made about when the criteria are met. For instance, how should the "delivery" criterion be defined? Is it when 100% of the services have been performed? 90%? 80%? People must use their heads and exercise good judgment.

(H)OW'S YOUR UNDERSTANDING?

Here are two questions you should be able to answer, based on what you have just read:

1. Why is the "critical event" a simplification and why is it used anyway?

2. Suppose Friendly Construction earned $1,000,000 revenue from a building contract, progressively, as follows: 10% when the contract was signed, 20% when the foundation was finished, 40% when the building exterior was finished, 20% when the interior was finished, and 10% after the owner had moved in and final adjustments and corrections were made. The company's expenses on the contract were $850,000, incurred according to the same progression as the revenue. If delivery were used as the critical event, how much revenue, expense, and net income would be recognized at that point, and how much would really have been

earned/incurred then? (100% of revenue, expense, and income would be recognized: $1,000,000; $850,000; $150,000. Assuming delivery was when the owner moved in, only 90% of all the above would really have been earned/incurred: $900,000 revenue earned, $765,000 expenses incurred, $135,000 income earned. Using a single critical event would have understated income until that event and then overstated it.)

6.7   REVENUE RECOGNITION METHODS

Look again at the journal entry to recognize revenue shown just above the revenue recognition criteria in section 6.6. With this entry in mind, let's take a closer look at five commonly used methods of revenue recognition.

1. At Delivery (Point of Sale or Shipment)

Point of delivery usually meets the revenue recognition criteria given in section 6.6.

For most retail, service, and manufacturing businesses, revenue is recognized when the product or service is sold. "Sold" is usually defined as being when the goods or services have been delivered, or at least shipped to the purchaser, when legal title passes to the purchaser. It's a single critical event.

- At that point substantially all of the service has been performed, terms and price have been set, and cash has either been received, or is reasonably certain to be received.

- Even though there is some risk involved in extending credit, this can usually be adequately estimated and adjusted for by creating an allowance for doubtful accounts receivable and a corresponding bad debts expense. More about this is in Chapter 7.

- Another risk at the point of sale is the possibility of returns and the likely service obligation under the warranties for the product or service sold. These can usually be adequately estimated and recognized as an expense of the business and matched against the revenue of that period.

Delivery (point of sale) is so common a revenue recognition method that most companies do not mention in their financial statements that they are using it. You are expected to assume it is the one being used if you are not told otherwise. In accordance with this, you should be told if one of the other methods below is being used. (CAE makes sure we know. In its year 2000 annual report, CAE reports that other than for long-term contracts (more about those below), it recognizes revenues and related cost of goods sold at the time the product is shipped or the services are provided.[9])

2. During Production

Recognizing revenue only once for multi-period projects distorts income in all periods.

Sometimes the earnings process extends well beyond one fiscal period, as is the case in building construction, road building, shipbuilding, and other lengthy processes. In such situations, if a company waited until the point of delivery to recognize revenue, it might report no revenue for one or more years, and then, when the project was complete, would report all the revenue. This would distort the performance picture for the duration of the project: some years with no revenue, then one year with huge revenue, even though the company was working faithfully on the contract all along. The "How's Your Understanding?" item above illustrated this.

In the case of construction and similar operations, there are not likely many projects going on at once (few, anyway, in comparison to the number of hamburgers making up a burger bar's revenue), and these projects include enough documentation that the value added can usually be estimated and verified. Therefore, in an attempt to provide users with relevant information and reflect the economics of what is happening, revenue may be recognized during production. (With matching, this also means recognizing expenses and therefore income during production.) A typical description of this is the following from the 1992 annual report of United Dominion Industries: "For financial statement purposes, income on construction projects is recognized on the percentage-of-completion basis. Provisions for anticipated losses on uncompleted contracts are made in the period in which such losses are first determinable."[10] This early-recognition approach is applied in a conservative way: if a project looks as if it will make money (project revenues greater than expenses), a portion of that income is recognized in the period in which the portion seems to have been earned, but if a project looks as if it will lose money (project revenues less than expenses), the whole anticipated loss is recognized right away.

> **Recognizing revenue during production is fair if applied conservatively.**

> **Recognizing revenue during production requires a great deal of judgment.**

Percentage of completion, mentioned by United Dominion Industries above, and also used by CAE for its long-term contracts, is the most common method of recognizing revenue during production. This method entails determining what proportion of the project has been completed during the year and recognizing that proportion of total expected revenue, expenses (costs), and, therefore, income, as was done in the "How's Your Understanding?" item above. Often, this is done by measuring the proportion of expected total costs incurred during the period. In order to recognize revenue in this manner, total costs must be reasonably determinable, the contract price (total revenue) must be reasonably certain, and there must be reasonable assurance of payment. The frequent use of the word "reasonable" here shows that a lot of judgment is required in using this method!

Let's assume Greenway Construction had a large, three-year project with total revenue of $4,000,000 and total costs of $3,400,000. (Prior to expense recognition, project costs are charged to an inventory account for costs of construction in process. Like other inventories, this account holds costs until they are matched to revenues.) Total income for the project over the three years was therefore $600,000. The project was 20% completed at the end of the first year, 65% completed at the end of the second year, and 100% completed at the end of the third year. Ignoring complications that arise when revenues and costs do not work out as expected, here are journal entries to implement percentage of completion revenue (*and matched expense*) recognition during production. (All amounts are in thousands of dollars.)

	Year 1		Year 2		Year 3	
Percentage of contract done in the year	20%		45%		35%	
Revenue recognition:						
DR Accounts receivable	800		1,800		1,400	
CR Revenue		800		1,800		1,400
Percentage earned each year.						
Expense recognition:						
DR Cost of goods sold expense	680		1,530		1,190	
CR Construction in process inventory		680		1,530		1,190
Percentage matched to revenue.						
Resulting income each year	$120		$270		$210	

Percentage of completion spreads revenues and income out over several fiscal periods.

You can see the *timing* effect of accrual accounting here. The annual entries have the effect of *spreading the $600,000 project income out over the three years*: 20% to the first year, 45% to the second, 35% to the third.

3. Completion of Production

This method defers all revenue and income until the end of the process.

In the percentage of completion method, revenue is recognized as the work proceeds. But it is also possible to wait until the work is all done and recognize the revenue then. Waiting until the end is like the point-of-sale method, except if the work takes a long time, perhaps several accounting periods, then it is *very conservative* because no revenue would be recognized for a long time, then all of it at once. The distortion mentioned above would be implemented deliberately, because it is believed that no revenue or income can be said to be earned until everything is done, even if that takes a long time. It would be like not getting any grades for your years of courses until the last day of the last class, when you'd get all the grades at once and find out if your four years had been a success or a failure. In the Greenway Construction example above, if revenue and the associated expenses were recognized on the completion of production, the project income would be:

- $0 in Year 1;
- $0 in Year 2; and
- $600,000 in Year 3.

This method differs greatly from the more economically appropriate first method.

Compared to the percentage of completion method, income would be:

- $120,000 *lower* in Year 1;
- $270,000 *lower* in Year 2; and
- $390,000 *higher* in Year 3.

So if Greenway wanted to know "what if" it changed to the completion of production (or **completed contract**) method, there's the answer, ignoring income tax.

If there is no customer yet, even the completed contract method is likely inappropriate.

If there is no customer yet, but the production is done, is that a legitimate time to recognize revenue? That is appropriate only under very limited circumstances, such as when there are ready or guaranteed markets for the product, stable prices, and minimal marketing costs. It would not be appropriate for a construction company building houses in standard styles and selling them later. Revenue recognition should wait until the sale happens, so that the criteria listed in section 6.6 are met. Historically, revenue from gold mines was recognized at the point of completion of production; producers could expect to sell all they produced since there was a world price for gold and Western governments provided a ready market. This is no longer the case for all gold mines, and today almost the only time revenue is recognized at time of completion when there is no customer yet is in agricultural concerns that produce within government quotas.

4. When Cash Is Received

Waiting for the cash to recognize revenue is an exception, not the rule.

If there is serious doubt as to the collectibility of cash from a revenue-generating transaction, revenue recognition is delayed until the collection has taken place. This does not mean that revenue recognition is delayed every time a business extends credit to a customer. In the vast majority of cases, revenue is recognized before the cash is received. Most businesses have accounts receivable, which are recognized but uncollected revenue. Revenue recognition is only delayed when the risk is great and the amount collectible cannot be reasonably determined, or is not sufficiently predictable. Delay is proper until the revenue recognition criteria have been met.

Particular business circumstances may require cash basis revenue recognition.

An example of waiting for the cash is in the case of certain real estate transactions that are speculative in nature and/or for which the collection of cash is contingent upon some future condition (such as the purchasers of a shopping mall successfully leasing a certain percentage of the space). Another example of revenue recognition at time of collection is the "Installment sales" method. When the majority of the revenue will come in over a long series of Installments, and there is substantial uncertainty that a given customer will actually make all the payments, the revenue is recognized in stages as the cash comes in. The Installment sales method has some complexities, but in principle it is just a way of recognizing revenue on a cash received basis. A final example is that many businesses do not extend credit to their customers, but deal only on a cash basis. Fast-food restaurants, coffee shops, some movie theatres, and numerous other "cash only" businesses recognize revenue on a cash basis because that is the only basis they have. (By the way, if customers pay with credit cards, those payments are normally treated as cash. If there is any receivable, it is a bulk one with the credit card company related to delays in processing the credit card slips, not resulting from extending credit to individual customers.)

5. At Some Point after Cash Has Been Received

Circumstances may require delaying revenue recognition past when cash is received.

Revenue recognition methods 1, 2, and 3 use accrual accounting, while method 4 essentially uses the cash basis for recognizing revenue. It is also possible to defer recognition for some time *after* the cash has been collected. Even though cash has been received, all revenue may not be recognized immediately because of some circumstance, such as a guaranteed deposit refund policy or a policy of "satisfaction guaranteed or money back."

A current liability account (Deferred revenue) is credited when the cash is collected:

DR Cash

CR Deferred revenue or Deposits received liability

Revenue will be recognized at a point in the future, normally after the refund time has expired or the required after-delivery service has been performed:

DR Deferred revenue or Deposits received liability

CR Revenue

(We saw this pair of entries in the conceptual discussion in section 6.3.)

Customer deposits are not revenue until the goods or services are delivered.

Deferring revenue recognition to a point after cash has been received is standard practice if, for some reason, a customer has paid in advance. Examples are magazine subscriptions or fitness club memberships, which are prepayments by the customers for service to be received later. This is a very conservative method, but that is really not the reason it is used. It is used because until the services or goods have been delivered, the revenue and therefore the income have not yet been *earned*. The revenue recognition criteria have not been met. Fairness requires waiting until they have been met.

HOW'S YOUR UNDERSTANDING?

Here are two questions you should be able to answer, based on what you have just read:

1. What circumstances make each of the five revenue recognition methods appropriate?

2. During the year, Smokey Inc. completed and billed projects having total revenue of $150,000, one of which had a $10,000 "return if not satisfied" promise. At the end of the year, one more project with a revenue of $14,000 was complete but it had not been billed because the client had not yet taken possession of the goods. At the end of the year, further projects with eventual revenue of $45,000 were 60% complete. Cash of $132,000 had been collected on the billed projects, $10,000 on the completed but undelivered project, and $20,000 on the incomplete ones. What would be the revenue for the year on each of the five methods in this section? (1. $150,000; 2. $191,000 ($150,000 + $14,000 + .60 x $45,000); 3. $164,000 ($150,000 + $14,000); 4. $162,000 ($132,000 + $10,000 + $20,000) or just a conservative $132,000; 5. $140,000 ($150,000 − $10,000). Quite a variety of revenue figures, and more combinations of the given data could be imagined!)

6.8   EXPENSE RECOGNITION AND MATCHING

Usually, expenses incurred in a period are assumed to match revenues for that period.

According to the "matching" criterion, expense recognition should be timed to match the revenue recognition method. The basic idea is that expense accounts should be debited in parallel to the crediting of revenue accounts. In practice, this is done quite routinely for most expenses. When expenses such as wages, interest, heat, property taxes, or advertising are incurred, they are recognized as expenses on the assumption that they were incurred to help earn revenues in the same period. Sometimes this assumption is a bit strained; for example, advertising may stimulate revenue over more than the current period, but the subjectivity of estimating multi-period effects and the simplicity of just expensing such costs when incurred lead most companies to just expense them, matching them to current revenues.

A franchisee buys the right to use the franchiser's brand, etc., under specified conditions.

There are cases, however, when the accounting has to be more refined. We saw expense matching to the revenue recognized during production in the Greenway Construction example above. Just to help you see the potential accrual accounting offers for fine-tuning revenue and expense recognition, here's another example, from the growing field of franchising.

WonderBurgers Ltd. is a franchiser, which means it sells the right to sell its products in particular geographic areas. For example, a franchisee might pay $25,000 for the right to set up a WonderBurgers fast-food restaurant in Sudbury, and no one else would be able to use the WonderBurgers brand name and other features, such as its recipes, in Sudbury.

Revenue from selling franchises is recognized over time, like construction revenue.

Let's suppose that the management of WonderBurgers estimates that it takes three years for a franchise to become viable and knows that during that time it will have to provide a lot of help. Suppose the sort of schedule of cash flows and economic activity that WonderBurgers has experienced for a typical $25,000 franchise fee is much like the one shown below. The "percent-of-fee-earned" amounts could have been determined by how much revenue was collected or how much support cost was spent, but because of the kinds of effort the company and its franchisees go through in getting a franchise going, management has worked out a general policy of recognizing 40% of the revenue in the first year of a franchise and 30% in each of the next two years. (It's a lot like the percentage of completion method we saw above, which is no accident. Franchise accounting is a form of the percentage of completion method.)

6-6

Exhibit

Year	Cash Paid by Franchisee	Cash Cost to Help Franchisee	Percent of Fee Earned
1	$15,000	$4,000	40%
2	5,000	3,000	30%
3	5,000	1,000	30%
	$25,000	$8,000	100%

Using management's estimates of percent of fee earned as the basis of revenue recognition, the revenue recognized from the typical franchise sale would be:

- Year 1, $10,000 (40%); and

- Years 2 and 3, $7,500 each (30% each).

Expenses related to the franchise are recognized so as to match the revenue.

According to the matching criterion, the expense of helping the franchisee should be recognized on the same schedule, so the expense recognized would be:

- Year 1, $3,200 (40%); and

- Years 2 and 3, $2,400 each (30% each).

Expense matching produces income that follows the same pattern as revenue.

This matching process means that the income from the contract follows the same pattern. The total expected income is $17,000 ($25,000 minus $8,000), and the matching process produces an income pattern of:

- Year 1, $6,800 (40% of $17,000, which is $10,000 revenue recognized minus $3,200 expense recognized); and

- Years 2 and 3, $5,100 (30% of $17,000 each, which is $7,500 revenue minus $2,400 expense).

The resulting income schedule and differences between accrual basis and cash basis income are below.

6-7

Exhibit

	Accrual Basis Income			Cash Basis Income		
	(a)	(b)	(c)	(d)	(e)	(f)
Year	Revenue	Expense	Income	Received	Spent	Income
1	$10,000	$3,200	$ 6,800	$15,000	$4,000	$11,000
2	7,500	2,400	5,100	5,000	3,000	2,000
3	7,500	2,400	5,100	5,000	1,000	4,000
	$25,000	$8,000	$17,000	$25,000	$8,000	$17,000

	Difference		
Year	(a)–(d)	(b)–(e)	(c)–(f)
1	$(5,000)	$ (800)	$(4,200)
2	2,500	(600)	3,100
3	2,500	1,400	1,100
	0	0	0

The accrual and cash bases eventually produce the same total income, by different routes.

You can see the point again about accrual accounting being a matter of *timing*. Both the accrual and the cash basis get to the same point, $17,000 income over the three years, but they take different routes to get there. In Year 1, the accrual income is $4,200 less than the net cash inflow of $11,000, but in Years 2 and 3, the accrual income is greater than the net cash inflows. The cash flow statement's Operations section reconciles accrual income to cash flow.

All methods of managing the accounts, so that the accrual income can be different from the cash flow, involve creating balance sheet accounts to hold the differences until they disappear. Accounts for doing this have names like accounts receivable, inventory, contract work in process, deferred revenue liability, and accounts payable. The details of their workings are often complicated, and each company has its own system.

F OR YOUR INTEREST

Accrual accounting's purpose is to move beyond cash flows toward a broader economic concept of earnings and financial position. From a manager's point of view, this has several implications:

- As a more inclusive way of measuring performance and position, accrual accounting reflects more of what a manager is trying to do than cash flow can. This should make accrual accounting attractive to managers who want to be evaluated fairly and who are interested in comparing their companies to others.

- Financial accounting reports the results of actions, not the reasons for them (except by implication). Managers may therefore feel that the accounting statements are incomplete because they miss the "why" behind the revenues, expenses, assets, and liabilities.

- To many people, earnings should be defined as changes in the market value of the company. Managers may be compensated using market-value mechanisms like bonuses and stock options. The evidence-based accounting procedures for revenue recognition, expense recognition, and matching them to measure income may not relate very well to managers' efforts to increase the market value of their companies.

- Accrual accounting's procedures require evidence to support entries and conservatism in estimating the effects of future events (provide for expected losses, but not for expected gains until they occur). To managers seeking an even-handed evaluation of their performance, accounting may seem overly skeptical about the future and downwardly biased in its measures. Managers may wish that accrual accounting recognized their optimism about the future more than it does.

- The criteria as to when and how to recognize revenues and expenses are inescapably judgmental and, therefore, to many managers' tastes, are both arbitrary and subjective. Many managers find accrual accounting too loose and flexible and would prefer less estimation and subjectivity.

Managers should take financial accounting seriously so that they can know when the accounting measures seem appropriate and when they do not. Accrual accounting has many advantages and is very widely used, but managers should not accept it uncritically.

OW'S YOUR UNDERSTANDING?

Here are two questions you should be able to answer, based on what you have just read:

1. Why is matching revenues and expenses important?

2. Suppose everything was the same in the WonderBurgers example except that the percentages of fees earned and expenses incurred over the three years were 20%, 40%, and 40%. Calculate the following: accrual income for Years 1, 2, 3, and total; difference from cash basis income for Years 1, 2, 3, and total. ($3,400, $6,800, $6,800, $17,000; $(7,600), $4,800, $2,800, $0.)

6.9   PREPAID AND ACCRUED EXPENSES

Prepaid and accrued expenses serve to line expense recognition up with the fiscal period.

This section is about a very common use of accrual accounting: to line up expenses such as insurance, interest, rent, and property taxes with the fiscal period to which they apply, whether or not they were paid for before, during, or after that period. The ideas in this section apply most usually to current assets and liabilities, adjusting for fairly short-term differences between the expense and the cash payment, but they can also apply to longer-term deferred assets and liability accruals.

Prepaid and accrued expenses result from two factors (which we saw in the conceptual discussion in sections 6.2 and 6.3):

1. Matching expense recognition to the fiscal period over which the expense is incurred (and during which revenue is recognized); and
2. Cash flow for paying the expense not coinciding with the expense recognition.

Only two journal entries are needed to implement the two factors:

1. *Expense recognition:* An annual or more usually monthly adjustment to the accounts to create an expense account and recognize that *either* a prepaid asset has been consumed *or* that an accrued liability has been incurred:

   > Dr Some expense account
   >> Cr Some balance sheet account (prepaid expense or accrued liability)

2. *Cash payment:* Recorded whenever the payment is made for the expense:

   > Dr The balance sheet account (prepaid expense or accrued liability)
   >> Cr Cash

Prepaid expenses arise when expenses are paid prior to the period to which the expenses apply.

Prepaid expenses are assets that arise because an expenditure has been made, but there is still value extending into the future. They are usually classified as current assets because the future value usually continues only into the next year. But sometimes the value extends beyond a year, and the company may then appropriately show a noncurrent prepaid expense or "deferred charge" if it is a significant enough amount to warrant such classification. Prepaid expenses arise whenever the payment schedule for an expense is ahead of the company's fiscal period, such as for annual insurance premiums when the policy's ending date is past the fiscal year-end, or property taxes that are based on the municipality's tax assessment schedule and cover a period past the company's fiscal period.

Prepaid expense assets have value in reducing future cash payouts.

Prepaid expenses are not assets in the same way as are receivables (to be collected in cash) or inventories (to be sold for cash). They arise from accrual accounting, in cases where the expense recognition follows the cash flow. As was indicated earlier in this chapter, this is conceptually the same reason inventories and factory assets are on the balance sheet: something of value exists and therefore its cost should not yet be deducted as an expense. Here, the value is in the fact that, having spent the money already, the company will not have to spend it in the next period. They have an economic value because future resources will not have to be expended.

The purest case of a prepaid expense arises where entry #1 above always *follows* entry #2: payment is always in advance. Here is a diagram, *where the horizontal arrow is fiscal periods and the vertical axis has prepaid expense asset above the arrow and accrued liability below it.* The cash payments are made at times X, Y, and Z, and *after* each of those times, the prepaid expense is transferred to expense by entries like #1 over the period to which it applies. In this pure prepaid case, there is no accrued liability.

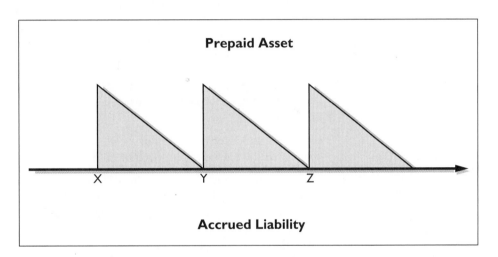

FIGURE 6.3

Accrued. expenses are liabilities, usually current, that arise from exactly the same timing difference as do prepaid expenses, but in their case the cash flow happens *after* the economic value has been obtained. An example is accruing interest that is building up on a bank loan. Another is paying for an audit only after the work has been done for the present fiscal year.

The purest case of an accrued expense arises where entry #1 above always *precedes* entry #2: payment is always afterwards ("in arrears"). Here is the diagram again, where the horizontal arrow is still fiscal periods, with prepaid expense asset above it and accrued liability below it. The cash payments are still made at times X, Y, and Z, and *prior to* each of those times, the expense is created by building up the accrual to expense over the period to which it applies. In this pure accrual case there is no prepaid expense.

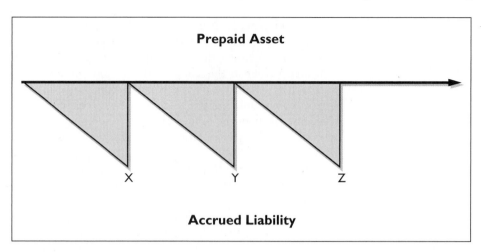

FIGURE 6.4

A mixed case is also common, in which sometimes the cash paid is prior to the incurrence of the expense, and sometimes follows it. Suppose a company has a June 30 fiscal year-end and pays property taxes to the local municipality. Property taxes apply to the calendar year:

- Prepaid property taxes at the fiscal year-end of June 30 arise if property taxes for the whole of the calendar year are paid in June, before the end of the fiscal year.

- Accrued property taxes at the fiscal year-end of June 30 arise if property taxes for the calendar year are not paid until July, after the fiscal year-end.

Here is an illustration of the mixed case. The cash payment times X, Y, and Z are now not regular: X and Y are made before the whole expense has been incurred, and then there is a long delay before Z is made. The balance sheet account varies from being an accrued liability to being a prepaid expense. A single balance sheet account could be used, and it could be put in the current assets if its balance is a debit, and in the current liabilities if its balance is a credit. (This happens with other accounts, too. If an account payable is overpaid, it would have a debit balance and would be included with the accounts receivable, on the assumption the overpayment would be refunded or used to purchase more goods. Conversely, if an account receivable is overpaid by the customer, it would have a credit balance and would be shown with the accounts payable, on the same assumption.)

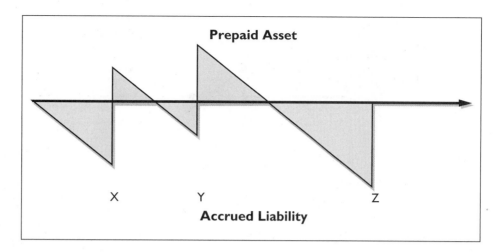

Prepaid Asset

X   Y   Z

Accrued Liability

FIGURE 6.5

Depending on payment timing, an expense may be either accrued or prepaid.

Therefore, *accrued (unpaid) expenses and prepaid expenses are just opposite sides of the same coin*, reflecting a mismatch between the cash payment and the expense (use of the economic value). They arise as accrual accounting tries to arrange the expenses to reflect economic use rather than cash flow. They are assets or liabilities depending on how the cash flow and the expense recognition happen to mismatch, so you often see similar kinds of items as prepaid expense assets and as accrued expense liabilities, or even as an asset one year and a liability the next. Common examples include insurance, property taxes, sales commissions, interest, licences, and current income taxes (payable if owing, or refundable if overpaid).

Here is an example. Day and Night Inc. has ten local corner stores that are part of a national chain. Each year, it pays a franchise fee to the chain for use of the chain's logo and other rights during the calendar year. No matter when the fee is paid, its economic value applies to the calendar year. The company's fiscal year-end is September 30, however, so it is measuring expenses over the period October 1 to September 30, not the calendar year to which the payments apply. This is the kind of mismatch of periods that gives rise to prepaid and accrued expenses. *The expense is allocated to fiscal periods regardless of when it is paid.*

Illustration 1: The fee is paid on August 31 every year.

The diagram of this case shows the payment made at A (end of August) each year. This pays off an accrued expense that had been building up since the beginning of the year and creates a prepaid expense for the rest of the year. By S (end of September), there is still some prepaid expense, and by D (end of December) there is neither a prepaid expense nor an accrued liability. The expense for any fiscal year is a combination of the consumption of the three-month prepaid existing at the end of September last year, the eight-month January to August accrual for this year, and one month's consumption of the prepaid existing at the end of August this year.

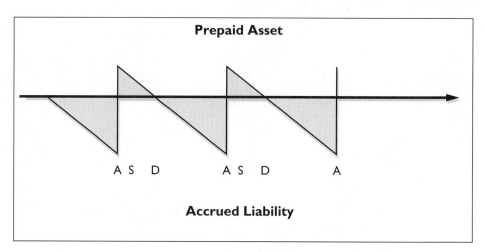

FIGURE 6.6

Illustration 2: The fee is paid on November 30 every year.
The diagram of this case shows the payment made at N (end of November) each year. This pays off an accrued expense that had been building up since the beginning of the year and creates a prepaid expense for only one month. By S (end of September), there is an accrued expense, and by D (end of December) there is neither a prepaid expense nor an accrued liability. The expense for any fiscal year is a combination of the consumption of the one-month prepaid existing at the end of November last year, and the eleven-month January to November accrual for this year.

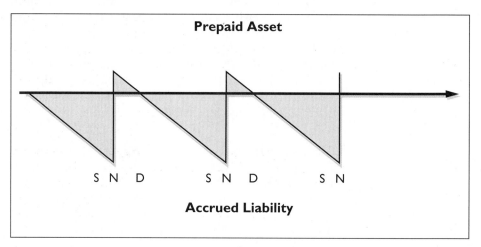

FIGURE 6.7

The expense is independent of payment timing; together expense and payment make an asset or liability.

Accrual accounting has used a prepaid expense asset in the first case and an accrued expense liability in the second case to produce the same calculation of expense: 3/12 of last year's fee (the October to December part) plus 9/12 of this year's (the January to September part). *The happenstance of the payment date does not affect the expense, but it does affect the balance sheet.* The balance sheet's asset or liability accounts arise as a consequence of accrual accounting's method of measuring expenses (and therefore income) properly, in combination with the timing of the payment of the fee. For such prepaid and accrued accounts, we could say that the balance sheet values are just residuals of the particular combination of expense incurrence and cash payment and don't have any deeper meaning.

OW'S YOUR UNDERSTANDING?

Here are two questions you should be able to answer, based on what you have just read:

1. Why might the balance sheet account related to a particular expense be a prepaid expense asset at the end of one year and an accrued expense liability at the end of another year?

2. Mah Stores Inc. pays its insurance premium in advance every year on September 30 for the year beginning that date. This year, the premium (paid last September) was $5,280 and next year it is estimated to be $5,400. If the company's fiscal year-end is July 31, what is the prepaid insurance asset or accrued insurance liability at this July 31? If the company failed to pay its premium for next year until November 1, what would be the prepaid insurance asset or accrued insurance liability on its quarterly balance sheet at October 31? (Asset, $880 (2/12 × $5,280); Liability $450 (1/12 × $5,400).)

6.10 TERMS TO BE SURE YOU UNDERSTAND

Here is this chapter's list of terms introduced or emphasized. Make sure you know what they mean *in accounting*, and if any are unclear to you, check the chapter again or refer to the Glossary of Terms at the back of the book.

Accounting policy
Accounting policy choices
Accrual accounting
Accrued expenses
Aggressive accounting
Articulate
Articulation
Authoritative standards
Big Bath
Cash received basis
Classification
Comparability
Completed contract
Conservatism
Conservative
Consistency
Critical event
Cutoff
Delivery (point of sale)
Disclosure
Discretionary expenses

Expense recognition
Expenses
Fairness
Fiscal periods
Franchising
GAAP
Income
Income smoothing
Matching
Materiality
Net income
Percentage of completion
Period expenses
Prepaid expenses
Realized
Recognition
Recognized
Revenue recognition
Revenues
Significant accounting policies

6.11 CONTINUING DEMONSTRATION CASE

INSTALLMENT 6

Data for Installment 6

The Continuing Case is intended to give you a little extra practice, mostly on preparation of accounting information. It has been a while since sets of journal entries were illustrated, so this Installment presents the entries for the second six months of Mato's operation. You can see that the ideas behind accrual accounting, especially cutting the business's activities into fiscal periods, are present in the standard entries to record revenues and expenses. Later Installments will deal with the company's accounting policy choices and analysis of its first year's financial statements.

Here again is the August 31, 2000, general ledger trial balance produced in Installment 3 and used to produce the financial statements for the first six months of the company's existence.

Debit balance accounts		Credit balance accounts	
Cash	$ 4,507	Bank loan	$ 75,000
Accounts receivable	18,723	Accounts payable	45,616
Inventory	73,614	Loan payable	15,000
Automobile	10,000	Share capital	125,000
Leasehold improvements	63,964	Revenues	42,674
Equipment and furniture	29,740	Accum. amort. — auto.	1,000
Computer	14,900	Accum. amort. —	
		leasehold imp.	6,396
Software	4,800	Accum. amort. — equip.	744
Incorporation costs	1,100	Accum. amort. — computer	1,490
Cost of goods sold expense	28,202	Accum. amort. — software	480
Salary — Mavis	15,000		
Salary — Tomas	9,280		
Salary — other	1,200		
Travel expense	8,726		
Telephone expense	2,461		
Rent expense	12,000		
Utilities expense	1,629		
Office and general expenses	3,444		
Amort. expense — auto.	1,000		
Amort. expense — leasehold			
imp.	6,396		
Amort. expense — equipment	744		
Amort. expense — computer	1,490		
Amort. expense — software	480		
	$313,400		$313,400

Alarmed by the company's loss for the six months ($49,378 per Installment 3) and negative cash generation (decrease in cash of $125,493 per Installment 4), Mavis and Tomas took strong action over the next six months. They put extra effort into sales, pressed the boutiques for collection as much as they could without damaging their new relationships with these customers, reduced inventory levels, and generally tried to run "a lean shop," as Tomas put it.

Here are events for the six months ended February 28, 2001, grouped and identified for later reference:

a. Revenue for the six months totalled $184,982, all on credit. (It will turn out later that they had been collecting and paying GST during this time—that will be dealt with in a later Installment, to avoid complicating this one.)

b. Collections from customers during the six months were $189,996.

c. Purchases for the six months were $71,004, all on credit.

d. Payments to suppliers during the six months came to $81,276. (To conserve cash, the company continued to rely on the patience of its suppliers more than Tomas liked. But doing so did save interest expense, because the suppliers did not charge interest while the bank did!)

e. Cost of goods sold for the six months was $110,565.

f. An inventory count on February 28, 2001, revealed inventory on hand costing $33,612. (This allowed Tomas to deduce that there had been a shortage in inventory, because there was a little less on hand than expected based on the cost of what had been sold. There was inventory of $73,614 on hand at the end of August, $71,004 more was purchased, and the cost of goods sold was $110,565. $73,614 + $71,004 − $110,565 = $34,053 which should have been on hand. The count showed $33,612 so there was a shortage of $441.)

g. Tomas decided to combine the three salary expense accounts into one, effective September 1, 2000.

h. Salaries for the six months to February 28, 2001, totalled $42,000. The company had paid all of this, except that it owed the government $2,284 in income tax and other deductions, and the employees $2,358 in net salaries at the end of February.

i. Various operating expenses for the six months were: travel, $1,376; phone, $1,553; rent, $12,000; utilities, $1,956; office and general expenses, $2,489. All of these were paid by February 28, except for $1,312.

j. The company bought further necessary equipment at a cost of $2,650 cash on November 3, 2000.

k. The company's bank loan rose and fell during the period. A total of $32,000 in further borrowing was incurred, and $59,500 was repaid.

l. Bank loan interest of $4,814 was paid during the six months (including a portion for the period prior to August 31, 2000, that had not been included in the accounts to that date).

m. Unfortunately (personally and financially), Tomas's father's health had deteriorated over the autumn and so he requested that his loan be repaid. The company did that on December 15, 2000, including interest of $1,425.

The employee (mentioned in an earlier Installment) had been hired in August and looked after the bookkeeping for the company. The above events were made up of hundreds of individual transactions recorded by the employee, but they are summarized by the journal entries that follow. *See if you can do them before you look at the results!*

Results for Installment 6

Journal entries for the period September 1, 2000, to February 28, 2001, follow, corresponding with the events listed previously. To save clutter, they are not accompanied by explanations or DR and CR indications, other than in the placement of the figures (the debits to the left). Since they are summary entries, their dates are also omitted.

a.	Accounts receivable	184,982	
	Revenue		184,982
b.	Cash	189,996	
	Accounts receivable		189,996
c.	Inventory	71,004	
	Accounts payable		71,004
d.	Accounts payable	81,276	
	Cash		81,276
e.	Cost of goods sold expense	110,565	
	Inventory		110,565
f.	Inventory shortage expense	441	
	Inventory		441
	($73,614 + $71,004 − $110,565 − $33,612)		
g.	Salaries Expense	25,480	
	Salary — Mavis		15,000
	Salary — Tomas		9,280
	Salary — Other		1,200
h.	Salaries expense	42,000	
	Deductions payable		2,284
	Salaries payable		2,358
	Cash (deduced)		37,358
i.	Travel expense	1,376	
	Phone expense	1,553	
	Rent expense	12,000	
	Utilities expense	1,956	
	Office and general expense	2,489	
	Accounts payable		1,312
	Cash (deduced)		18,062
j.	Equipment and furniture	2,650	
	Cash		2,650
k.	Cash	32,000	
	Bank loan		32,000
	Bank loan	59,500	
	Cash		59,500
l.	Interest expense	4,814	
	Cash		4,814
m.	Loan payable	15,000	
	Interest expense	1,425	
	Cash		16,425

Posting these journal entries results in the following general ledger account balances at February 28, 2001 (arranged in balance sheet order, as is usually, but certainly not always, done in a trial balance). Credits are shown in brackets.

Account	Balance Aug. 31/00	Transactions for period to February 28, 2001	Balance Feb. 28/01
Cash	4,507	189,996 (81,276) (37,358) (18,062) (2,650) 32,000 (59,500) (4,814) (16,425)	6,418
Accounts receivable	18,723	184,982 (189,996)	13,709
Inventory	73,614	71,004 (110,565) (441)	33,612
Automobile	10,000	0	10,000
Accum. amort. — auto	(1,000)	0	(1,000)
Leasehold improvements	63,964	0	63,964
Accum. amort. — leasehold imp.	(6,396)	0	(6,396)
Equipment and furniture	29,740	2,650	32,390
Accum. amort. — equip.	(744)	0	(744)
Computer	14,900	0	14,900
Accum. amort. — computer	(1,490)	0	(1,490)
Software	4,800	0	4,800
Accum. amort. — software	(480)	0	(480)
Incorporation cost	1,100	0	1,100
Bank loan	(75,000)	(32,000) 59,500	(47,500)
Accounts payable	(45,616)	(71,004) 81,276 (1,312)	(36,656)
Deductions payable	0	(2,284)	(2,284)
Salaries payable	0	(2,358)	(2,358)
Loan payable	(15,000)	15,000	0
Share capital	(125,000)	0	(125,000)
Revenue	(42,674)	(184,982)	(227,656)
Cost of goods sold expense	28,202	110,565	138,767
Salary — Mavis	15,000	(15,000)	0
Salary — Tomas	9,280	(9,280)	0
Salary — other	1,200	(1,200)	0
Salaries expense	0	25,480 42,000	67,480
Travel expense	8,726	1,376	10,102
Phone expense	2,461	1,553	4,014
Rent expense	12,000	12,000	24,000
Utilities expense	1,629	1,956	3,585
Office and general expense	3,444	2,489	5,933
Interest expense	0	4,814 1,425	6,239
Inventory shortage expense	0	441	441
Amortization expense — auto.	1,000	0	1,000
Amortization expense — leasehold	6,396	0	6,396
Amortization expense — equipment	744	0	744
Amortization expense — computer	1,490	0	1,490
Amortization expense — software	480	0	480
Net Sums	0	0	0

6.12 HOMEWORK AND DISCUSSION TO DEVELOP UNDERSTANDING

PROBLEM 6.1*
Explain how revenues and expenses differ from cash flows

1. Explain the difference between a revenue and a cash receipt.
2. Give examples of items that are revenue of a given period but not receipts of that period, items that are receipts but not revenue, and items that are both revenue and receipts.
3. Explain the difference between an expense and a cash disbursement (payment).
4. Give examples of items that are expenses of a given period but not disbursements of that period, items that are disbursements but not expenses, and items that are both expenses and disbursements.

PROBLEM 6.2*
Match accrual accounting terms

Match the terms on the left with the most appropriate phrases on the right.

1. Accounts receivable
2. Inventory
3. Cash
4. Prepaid expense
5. Deferred revenue
6. Pension liability
7. Future tax liability
8. Accrued expense liability
9. Income tax payable
10. Amortization

a. Consumption of long-term assets
b. Revenue recognized after collection
c. An estimate of what the government wants soon
d. Goods waiting to be expensed
e. Revenue recognized before collection
f. Usually unaffected by accounting policy choice
g. Expense paid before being consumed
h. An estimate of what the government wants much later
i. Promises to employees expensed already
j. Expense paid after economic value has been obtained

PROBLEM 6.3*
Calculate accrual net income from various accounts

Pottery Galore Ltd. has just finished its 2001 fiscal year. From the following data, calculate net income or loss for 2001:

Collections from customers during 2001	$174,320
Accounts receivable, end of 2000	11,380
Accounts receivable, end of 2001	9,440
Bad debts (written off to expense directly from accounts receivable in 2001)	520
Payments to suppliers and employees during 2001	145,690
Accounts and wages payable, end of 2000	12,770
Accounts and wages payable, end of 2001	15,510
Inventory of unsold goods, end of 2000	21,340
Inventory of unsold goods, end of 2001	24,650
Bank loan, end of 2001	12,000
(The loan was taken out a month before the end of 2001 at an interest rate of 8%. No interest has yet been paid.)	
Income tax payable, end of 2001 (none end of 2000)	2,340
Income tax paid during 2001	3,400
Future income tax liability, end of 2001 (none end of 2000)	1,230

PROBLEM 6.4*
Answer two questions about revenues and expenses

1. Why is revenue recognition not always so simple as just debiting accounts receivable and crediting revenue at the point of sale?
2. In 2001, Flimsy Construction Ltd. has recognized 38% of the total expected revenue from a contract to build a garage onto Professor Blotz's house. The total contract price is $43,000 and Flimsy expects its costs for the contract to be $29,500. Costs so far have been in line with expectations. How much contract expense should Flimsy recognize for 2001 and what would be the resulting contract income for 2001?

PROBLEM 6.5*
Discuss the conflict between flexible and standard accounting

As you have seen, there is a general conflict between two financial reporting objectives. The first objective is to fit the accounting to each company's circumstances so that the resulting reports are relevant to understanding or evaluating that company. The second is to make accounting consistent from company to company so that intercompany comparisons may be facilitated and the overall credibility of the information maintained.

Give your views on how important this conflict is and how (if at all) it should be dealt with.

PROBLEM 6.6*
Revenues, expenses, and income for a construction contract

Rockheads Inc. is a construction contractor specializing in roads and other large constructions of earthworks, rocks, and concrete. Here is information about one of its multi-year contracts, Job 48.

Total revenue agreed in the contract: $5,200,000
Rockheads' estimate of its total costs over the life of the contract:
   $4,300,000
Year 1: Spent $900,000, billed $1,300,000, collected $1,000,000
Year 2: Spent $1,990,000, billed $1,800,000, collected $2,030,000
Year 3: Spent $1,410,000, billed $2,100,000, collected $2,170,000

Calculate the revenue, expense, and income from Job 48 for *each year* and for the *whole contract* on each of the following bases:

   a. Completed contract basis.
   b. Percentage completion basis (using proportion of cost spent as the measure of percentage completed and rounding percentages to the nearest whole percent).
   c. Cash received basis (hint: match expense recognition to the proportion of total cash received each year).

PROBLEM 6.7*
Prepaid and accrued expenses

For each of these examples, calculate whether the company had a prepaid asset or an accrued liability at the end of 2000, what the amount of that was, and what the related expense for 2000 was.

1. Westridge Manufacturing Inc. has significant costs for worker training. These costs are sometimes paid in advance and sometimes after they have been incurred. At the beginning of 2000, the company had paid $123,775 in advance. During 2000, the company incurred training costs of $840,370 and paid $714,555. In addition, the company suffered injury costs totalling $127,530 in spite of the training.

2. Athabasca Eco-Tours pays for some of the costs of its tours in advance, some during the tours, and some later, after the tours have occurred. At the beginning of 2000, the company owed $57,890 on prior tours. During 2000, the company incurred $658,280 in tour costs and paid $717,430.

PROBLEM 6.8*
Revenue recognition policy for a fashion house

Molloy House Inc. makes and sells high-priced made-to-order clothing. All sales are one-time-only designs, made to the buyer's specifications after much consultation and demonstrations of fabrics and styles. Prices average over $10,000 for a dress and more than that for gowns, suits, and other larger items. Sales volumes are not high, but profit margins are: gross margin is usually over 60% and net income is usually over 20% of sales. Customers are promised absolute satisfaction, and about 10% of sales are returned or need costly adjustment. Customers pay about 25% of the price before work begins and are billed for the rest upon delivery, which is normally some weeks or months later. Most customers pay within a month or two of delivery, but some long-time customers are slower than that. Occasionally, due to death or bankruptcy, the remaining 75% is never paid—this happens in about one in 50 sales.

    a. Specify the revenue recognition policy that you would recommend Molloy House use and explain why that policy is appropriate.

    b. Most deliveries are made during three periods: the spring (coming out balls, graduations, and horse races), the summer (weddings), and the fall (opera and charity balls), but the company's staff are busy all year filling orders, which are often made far in advance and so allow the company to maintain fairly steady production. All fabric and other materials and supplies are purchased only as each order requires them; the company has no significant general inventory.

       (i) An unfilled order is both an asset and a liability for Molloy House. Explain why this is true.

      (ii) When would be a good date for the company's fiscal year-end? Why?

PROBLEM 6.9*
Discuss some terms

Discuss what each of the following terms has to do with income measurement and related balance sheet valuation:

    a. Aggressive accounting
    b. Articulation
    c. Deferred revenue
    d. Matching
    e. Period expenses
    f. Conservatism

PROBLEM 6.10*
Calculate prepaid and accrued expense

A local company pays its property taxes on a rather erratic basis. Here is a schedule of its property tax bills and payments over the last few years:

   • Was billed in April 1999 for the calendar 1999 taxes of $4,500.

   • Paid those taxes September 20, 1999.

   • Was billed in April 2000 for the calendar 2000 taxes of $4,800.

- Paid those taxes November 30, 2000.

- Was billed in April 2001 for the calendar 2001 taxes of $5,100.

- Paid those taxes August 15, 2001.

Calculate the prepaid or accrued property taxes and the property tax expense *for the fiscal years 2000 and 2001*, if the company had *each* of the following fiscal year-ends:

   a. April 30
   b. June 30
   c. September 30
   d. December 31

PROBLEM 6.11*
Recommend revenue recognition policies

What revenue recognition policy would you recommend for each of the following companies? Why?

   a. Harry's Hamburgers, an all-night fast-food joint on the highway.
   b. EngSoft, a designer and installer of high-priced, custom-fitted software for engineering and other high-tech companies.
   c. Nevada Gold, a miner of gold in northern Nevada.
   d. Fast Furniture, a seller of cheap furniture, which has the slogan "buy now and pay nothing until a year from now."
   e. Goldenrod Construction, which does building contracts with governments and large corporations.
   f. Handsome Homes, which builds homes in the new part of town and hires agents to sell the homes upon completion.

PROBLEM 6.12*
Adjusting journal entries

It is the end of International Fabrics Inc.'s fiscal year. You are working on the company's financial statements, and have discovered the items listed below. For each item:

1. State whether or not the item requires that an adjustment be made in the company's accounts according to the principles of accrual accounting; and
2. If the answer to part 1 is yes, write a journal entry to adjust the company's accounts.
   a. Sales of $3,200 made on account just before the end of the fiscal year were not recorded until the beginning of the next year.
   b. The cost of goods sold for those sales, totalling $1,900, has not yet been recognized.
   c. During the year, deposits of $5,300 were made by customers on special orders and were credited to the deposit liability account. Deposits of $1,400 are still being held, but all the other special orders have been completed and the customers have paid the rest of the price for those orders (those payments are included in sales revenue).
   d. Maintenance expenses seemed rather high, and on investigation it turned out that an addition to the company's store, constructed over a period of several months at a cost of $62,320, had been included in the maintenance expenses.

e. Just before the year-end, the company was sued by a customer whose expensive curtains lost their colour as soon as they were exposed to sunlight. The lawsuit was for $4,300 to replace the curtains and $50,000 in pain and suffering damages. Legal advice indicates that the curtains should be replaced (which would cost the company about what it is being sued for) but that the customer will not succeed with the pain and suffering damages.

f. The company's auditors sent a bill for $2,350 for the year's audit work.

g. Effective just before the year-end, the company agreed to buy an automobile from a major shareholder for $17,220.

h. At the beginning of the year, the company had paid $2,000 for the exclusive right to distribute in Canada fabrics made by Silk Dreams Inc. of Pennsylvania. The exclusive distributorship is for a period of four years.

PROBLEM 6.13*
Explain some accrual accounting topics

Explain to a businessperson who is not an accountant and is impatient with jargon what each of the following topics has to do with accrual accounting, what impact it has on companies' financial statements, and how important it is in understanding the financial statements.

a. Recognizing revenue when it has been earned.

b. Using the balance sheet to hold the "residual" effects of income measurement.

c. Matching expense recognition to the fiscal period in which the expense was incurred.

PROBLEM 6.14
Whose role should it be to choose accounting policies?

Should management have the responsibility and authority to choose companies' accounting policies, or should that role be someone else's (for example, the government's, the auditor's, an independent board's)? If you think it should be management's role, why? If you think it should be someone else's role, whose? Why?

PROBLEM 6.15
Can the auditor prevent unfair accounting policies?

A commentator on the accounting scene remarked, "Management makes its accounting choices to serve its own interests, and there's no way the poor lonely auditor can hold the fort of fairness when you consider how vague and judgmental accrual accounting's criteria for accounting policy choices are."

What are your views on the commentator's remarks?

PROBLEM 6.16
Issues about the significant accounting policies note

1. What is the purpose of the significant accounting policies note that usually is the first note to a company's financial statements?

2. How should a company decide what to include in that note?

3. A business commentator suggested that, when a company uses an accounting policy that is unusual, its significant accounting policies note should include a calculation of the effect on income of using that policy as compared to the more usual practice. What do you think of that idea?

PROBLEM 6.17
Comment on various remarks about accounting policies

Comment briefly on the following remarks by a businessperson:

1. "No one cares what our accounting policy choices are because they have no effect on the price of the company's shares."
2. "Our accounting policies are mainly a signal about the kind of company we are (conservatively managed, careful to follow authoritative rules) and so they are fairly consistent overall."
3. "Once we have established proper accounting policies, all those notes at the end of the financial statements are really an irrelevant nuisance."

PROBLEM 6.18
Discuss the basis of accrual accounting

Discuss the following:

1. Speaking positively, it might be said that accrual accounting improves on the cash flow information. Speaking negatively, it might be said that accrual accounting messes up the picture by introducing noncash flow factors. Whether or not you like the result they achieve, how do accrual accounting entries work to alter the cash flow story?
2. Why can it be said that timing is at the centre of accrual accounting?

PROBLEM 6.19
Explain why accrual accounting diverges from cash flow

Respond, in point form, to the following complaint by a businessperson:

"I find modern financial accounting really annoying. The basis of financial strength is the availability and use of real resources, like cash and machinery, yet accrual accounting produces an income measure that is deliberately different from the cash return earned by the business. Why is this so? Why should accrual accounting diverge from the measurement of cash flow?"

PROBLEM 6.20
Examine some accrual accounting phenomena

1. On December 31, the end of the accounting period of Ultra Corp, the company accountant is about to make some adjustments. Describe a set of circumstances where, in making the typical year-end adjustments:
   a. An expense is debited and a liability is credited.
   b. An expense is debited and an asset contra account is credited.
   c. An asset is debited and revenue is credited.
   d. A liability is debited and revenue is credited.
2. A business executive remarked, "Accountants use a dual standard for measuring assets. Some are on the balance sheet because they have real future economic value. Others are there only because they're left over from the income measurement process … sort of expenses waiting to be deducted. Similarly with liabilities: some are really owed but some are just leftovers of the accrual accounting process for measuring income."

   Discuss the remark, citing examples of assets and liabilities that might fit the executive's four categories.

PROBLEM 6.21
Managers and accrual accounting

Now that you are a famous businessperson, you are frequently asked to make after-dinner speeches on business topics. Without thinking about it too much, you agreed to make a speech on accrual accounting to a class of graduating business students. Now you have to think of something to say, and you have decided to title your talk, "Why managers like me like accrual accounting and why we worry about it." List the topics you plan to talk about under this heading.

PROBLEM 6.22
Calculation of accrual income from cash records

Mike Stammer is a private investigator. He keeps his accounting records on a cash basis and has produced the following income statement, *as he calls it.*

Mike Stammer Income Statement for the Year Ended June 30, 2001	
Fees collected in cash	$85,000
Less cash expenses	34,600
Net income	$50,400

An examination of Mike's records shows these balances at the beginning and end of fiscal 2001:

	July 1, 2000	June 30, 2001
Fees receivable	$10,350	$ 3,900
Client deposits on continuing investigations	—	1,200
Accrued expenses	3,490	5,250
Prepaid expenses	1,700	2,500

1. a. What amount of the fees Mike collected in fiscal 2001 were received for investigations he actually completed in fiscal 2000?
   b. What amount of the fees received in 2001 will he earn in 2002?
   c. How much in fees did he earn in 2001, but not collect?
2. a. What amount of the expenses Mike paid in fiscal 2001 should be matched with his efforts in fiscal 2000 or 2002?
   b. What amount of expenses paid in previous years should be matched with revenues Mike earned in 2001?
3. Use your answers to Parts 1 and 2 to prepare an accrual basis income statement for Mike Stammer for the year ended June 30, 2001.
4. Add or subtract whichever adjustments to the cash income statement are necessary to reconcile Mike's $50,400 "income" to your figure.
5. Compare the two income statements. Why might Mike Stammer (or others using his financial information) prefer to use the cash basis of accounting? Why might he (or others) prefer the accrual basis?

PROBLEM 6.23
Likely revenue recognition policies for various cases

When is a sale a sale? When does the accounting system recognize revenue as having been earned? Indicate what you think would be the revenue recognition policy in each of the following cases. Remember to think of whether the general criteria for revenue recognition have been met, the concept of a "critical event" for revenues recognized all at once, and the proportionate recognition that is available for revenue earned over several accounting periods.

   a. The Coogee Bay Coffee Café, an informal joint near the beach.
   b. Alcatraz Development Inc.'s housing subdivisions in eastern cities.

    c. Atco Gas's sales of natural gas to businesses and residences.

    d. *Maclean's* magazine subscription sales.

    e. The Stratford Festival's ticket sales.

    f. The Big Warehouse's Installment sales of appliances and furniture.

    g. BV Resources Inc.'s revenue from drilling oil wells on others' property.

    h. Imperial Oil's revenue from oil production on its own land.

    i. Potter Henny Glover's revenue from sales of pottery on consignment through local craft shops.

    j. CBC-TV's revenues from advertising on sports programs.

    k. Fibreglass Canada's revenues from sales of manufactured products.

    l. Computer Wizard Shop's sales of software.

    m. Sears Canada's revenue from clothing sales (some people pay cash, some charge on their Sears cards, some charge on other credit cards, and some return their purchases after deciding they don't like them).

    n. Your university or college's revenue from student tuition fees.

    o. The Canadian Red Cross's revenues from donations.

    p. Western Greenhouses Inc.'s revenues from contract landscaping work for homeowners.

PROBLEM 6.24
Choose suitable revenue recognition policies

In each of the following independent cases below, indicate when you think the company in question should recognize revenue. Support your decision with reference to the generally accepted criteria for revenue recognition.

    a. Alaska Gold Co. mines and refines gold. The company waits to sell the gold until it feels the market price is favourable. The company can, if it wishes, sell its entire inventory of gold at any time at the prevailing market price.

    b. Crazy Freddie sells cheap, ugly furniture on the Installment plan. His customers take delivery of the furniture after making a down payment. In the course of the past year, Crazy Freddie has had to repossess over 50% of the furniture that he sold, due to customers defaulting on payments.

    c. Tom and Mark's Construction Co. undertakes long-term construction contracts. The company only accepts contracts that will pay a fixed fee. Costs can be estimated with reasonable accuracy, and there has never been a problem collecting from customers.

    d. Cecily Cedric Co. is a toy manufacturer, producing toys that are shipped to various retail customers upon receipt of their purchase order. Sales are billed after shipment. The company estimates that approximately 2% of credit sales prove to be uncollectible.

PROBLEM 6.25
Recommend revenue and expense recognition policy

Gary Slapstick Promotions Inc. (G.S.P.I.) acquired the rights to use the names of a number of hockey players on life-sized stuffed dolls it purchases from a toy manufacturer. The dolls are marketed through mail order advertisements in the TV-listings inserts of large newspapers. When an order is received (with a money order, cheque, or credit card number), G.S.P.I. contacts the toy manufacturer. The toy manufacturer is responsible for manufacturing and shipping the doll to the lucky boy or girl. G.S.P.I. is notified at the time of shipment. The customer has the option of returning the doll within two weeks of the day it is received. G.S.P.I. pays the toy manufacturer within 30 days after delivery. Response to the dolls this

Christmas has been overwhelming. In fact, the toy manufacturer is working extra shifts to try to keep up with the demand.

1. Identify three points in time that G.S.P.I. could recognize revenue on the dolls. Which would you recommend? Why?
2. Identify two different points in time that the toy manufacturer could recognize revenue on the dolls.
3. Discuss how G.S.P.I. should account for its payments to hockey players for the right to use their names. (Assume that each player is paid a lump sum initially and a royalty on each doll sold that uses his name.)

PROBLEM 6.26 **Builder's revenues,** **expenses, and assets**	A builder formed a construction company in September. After several months' effort, the company completed a residence at a total cost of $70,000 and advertised it for sale. By December 31, the company had received three offers: one of $78,000 cash; another of $83,000, to be paid in monthly Installments over 20 years plus 10% annual interest; and another of $50,000 cash plus a residential lot worth $31,000. The builder decided to wait for a higher offer, which he seemed certain to get. 1. What was the amount of the construction company's revenue for the year? 2. How much were its expenses? 3. In what form, if any, were its assets on December 31? 4. Taking each offer separately, assume the offers were accepted and calculate the amount of revenue and expense for the four-month period ended December 31 in each case. Assume that for each situation the sale closed December 26.
PROBLEM 6.27 **Accounting for a** **health club**	Carrot Club is a local health club, with exercise machines, a health food bar, and other features. The club offers a membership package of $400 for 100 visits. The package has to be paid for $100 down plus $100 per month over the next three months. A few new members fail to pay the $300 they owe. The company uses accrual accounting, and therefore its financial statements have accounts receivable for unpaid memberships and deferred revenue liability for members' unused visits. • At the end of the 2000 fiscal year, members' unused visits totalled 85,000. At that date, members owed $22,000. • During the 2001 fiscal year, the club sold 1,200 new memberships and experienced 140,000 visits by members. Bad debts of $1,400 were written off against the accounts receivable. • At the end of the 2001 fiscal year, the club estimated that $1,500 of the $17,500 members' accounts owing then were doubtful. 1. Ignoring the possibility that some members may never use visits they've paid for, calculate: a. Revenue for the 2001 fiscal year. b. Deferred revenue liability for unused visits, as at the end of the 2001 fiscal year. 2. The company's auditor suggested that the financial statements should take into account the fact that some paid-up members move, lose interest, or oth-

erwise end up never using all the visits they have paid for. If the company adopted this accounting policy, indicate the effect (up, down, or no effect) on each of the following, and say why you chose the answer you did.

a. Accounts receivable at the end of 2001.

b. Revenue for 2001.

PROBLEM 6.28
Franchise revenue amounts and policies

Pickin Chicken Inc. (PC) and Country Delight Ltd. (CD) both sell franchises for their chicken restaurants. The purchaser of the franchise (the franchisee) receives the right to use PC's and CD's products and benefit from national training and advertising programs for ten years. The buyers agree to pay $50,000 for a franchise. Of this amount, $20,000 is paid upon signing the agreement and the remainder is payable in five equal annual Installments of $6,000 each.

Pickin Chicken recognizes all franchise revenue when franchise agreements are signed. Country Delight recognizes franchise revenue as cash is received. In 1999 the companies each sold eight franchises. In 2000 they each sold five. In 2001 and 2002 neither company sold a franchise.

1. Determine the amount of franchise revenue recognized by each company in 1999, 2000, 2001, and 2002.
2. Do you think that revenue should be recognized when the franchise agreement is signed, when cash is received, or over the life of the franchise agreement? Why? Fully support your answer.

PROBLEM 6.29
Construction accounting

Rimrock Construction Ltd. has several contracts to construct buildings:

Contract No.	Expected Revenue	Expected Expense	Expected Income	Percentage Completed	
				End of 2000	End of 2001
48	$1,000,000	$ 800,000	$200,000	70%	100%
49	1,500,000	1,300,000	200,000	10%	80%
50	860,000	710,000	150,000	0%	100%
51	2,430,000	1,950,000	480,000	0%	90%
52	1,600,000	1,320,000	280,000	0%	20%

1. Assuming all revenues, collections, expenses, and payments are as expected, calculate income before income tax for 2001:
   a. Using the competed contracts basis to recognize contract revenues and expenses.
   b. Using the percentage of completion basis to recognize contract revenues and expenses.
2. Which of these two bases is the more conservative? Why?
3. No revenue has yet been collected on Contract #50, but all expenses related to it have been paid. It has been learned that Contract #50 has run into legal trouble. Rimrock now expects to receive only $100,000 of the expected revenue. Write the journal entry, if any is needed, to recognize this information. (Assume the completed contract basis if necessary.)

**PROBLEM 6.30
(CHALLENGING)
Conversion from
cash to accrual basis**

Temporary Help Ltd. is a company offering specialized personal services (for example, secretarial assistance, delivery of advertising, errands, shopping for gifts). The company's accounts have been kept on a cash basis, but its banker has asked that the accounting be changed to the accrual basis. Income for 2001 on the cash basis was $147,000. Using the following figures (note the order of the years), calculate the company's 2001 income on the accrual basis.

	Assets		Liabilities	
	2001	2000	2001	2000
Cash basis:				
Current	$ 98,000	$ 56,000	$35,000	$35,000
Noncurrent	—	—	—	—
Accrual basis:				
Current	182,000	112,000	70,000	49,000
Noncurrent	21,000	28,000	14,000	—

**PROBLEM 6.31
(CHALLENGING)
Questions on audi-
tors, judgment, and
accounting policies**

Write a paragraph on each of the following topics, using the perspective on accounting policy choice and methods provided in this chapter:

1. Why the auditor's report refers to whether the company's financial statements have been prepared in accordance with GAAP.
2. Why professional judgment is needed in preparing financial statements.
3. Whether it is justifiable to use an aggressive revenue recognition policy (recognizing revenue early in the production-sale-collection cycle process).

**PROBLEM 6.32
(CHALLENGING)
Accounting versus
economic view of
revenue**

An economist might argue that revenue is created or earned continuously by a wide variety of the firm's activities (such as production, sales, delivery), yet the accountant in a typical case selects only one of these steps (the "critical event") to signal the time at which all revenues are to be recognized.

a. Assuming that the economist's view is correct, under what circumstances would the accountant's method lead to an undistorted measure of periodic income? In other words, under what conditions will the opinion that income is continuously earned agree with income as determined by accountants?
b. What are the obstacles to the practical implementation of the economist's view as the basis for accounting income determination?

**PROBLEM 6.33
(CHALLENGING)
Explain accrual
concepts to a
businessperson**

A businessperson you know has just received the financial statements of a company in which that person owns shares. Answer the following questions asked by the person. Try to answer without jargon and use examples that will make your answers clear.

1. I've been told that these accrual accounting numbers are "mainly a matter of timing." What does that mean?

2. I see the company has a note in its financial statements describing its "revenue recognition" method. Why would I want to know that?

3. I know from my business experience that sometimes you collect cash sooner or later than you expect. Customers may have cash, or not, for all sorts of reasons that have nothing to do with you. I understand that accrual accounting takes this into account so that it doesn't matter when cash is collected; you get the same revenue figure anyway. Is this true?

4. I understand that accountants try to be sure that revenues and expenses "match" each other so that the income you get by subtracting expenses from revenues makes sense. Seems quite appropriate. But what effect, if any, does this matching procedure have on the balance sheet figures?

PROBLEM 6.34 (CHALLENGING) Is accrual accounting a tool of management?

A professor said recently that accrual accounting was invented because managers wanted something they could manipulate to their own purposes more than was possible with transaction-based, cash-based data. Accrual accounting, the professor continued, is a tool of management and has driven accounting away from the goal of producing information that is representative of any real phenomena and toward fanciful reports largely devoid of real meaning.

1. What do you think of the professor's views? Are there any better reasons for accrual accounting?

2. The professor said that academics and practitioners tend to differ in their responses to his views. What do you think the differences would be?

3. If the professor is right, what does that say about the dictum that management bears the responsibility for providing financial information about an enterprise?

PROBLEM 6.35 (CHALLENGING) Contract cash flow and income calculations

The Swazy Construction Company has secured a contract with the Alberta government for the construction of 15 km of highway at a contract price of $100,000 a kilometre. Payments for each kilometre of highway are to be made according to the following schedule:

- 40% at the time the concrete is poured

- 50% when all work on that kilometre is completed

- 10% when all 15 km of highway have been completed, inspected, and approved

At the end of the first period of operation, 5 km of highway have been entirely completed and approved, concrete has been poured on a second stretch of 5 km, and preliminary grading has been done on the third 5-km stretch.

The job was originally estimated to cost $80,000 a kilometre. Costs to date have coincided with these original estimates and have totalled the following amounts: on the completed stretch, $80,000 a kilometre; on the second stretch, $65,000 a kilometre; and on the third stretch, $10,000 a kilometre. It is estimated that each unfinished stretch will be completed at the costs originally estimated.

1. How much should the Alberta government have paid Swazy during or at the end of the first period of operation under the terms of the contract? Show computations.

2. How much income would you report for this period? Show your calculations and justify your method.

PROBLEM 6.36 (CHALLENGING) Accounting methods for a frequent buyer program

Bert, the owner of Bert's Books, has been struggling with the competition from big bookstore chains and has decided to offer customers a reward points plan to encourage repeat business. The plan is free, and if a customer joins, every dollar spent on a book earns the customer 10 cents toward future books. This is not a discount on future purchases, but has to be used to obtain books just on points. For example, if a customer wants to get a $20.00 book on points, she would have to have spent $200.00 before then. If she has only spent, say, $150.00, she cannot use the points accumulated so far to get a discount on the book but must wait until she has spent another $50.00, and then she will get the book free.

1. *Ignoring the possibility that some customers may never redeem their points,* describe the accounting policy you would recommend the company use for this new points plan. Your policy should be the one you think is conceptually sound—don't worry here about the practical implications of your policy, such as keeping track of needed information. Answer in two parts:
    a. How would you account for points earned by customers before they redeem any free books?
    b. How would you account for the redemption of points for free books?
2. Bert observed that some customers will never redeem their points. Explain how, if at all, you would modify the policy you recommended above in accounting for this factor.
3. The bookstore's auditor observed that both conservatism and matching are important to the policy choice. Explain why both are important in this case.

PROBLEM 6.37 (CHALLENGING) Income on various revenue recognition bases

The Latanae Company produces a single product at a cost of $6 each, all of which is paid in cash when the unit is produced. Selling expenses of $3 a unit are paid at the time of shipment. The sale price is $10 a unit; all sales are on account. No customer defaults are expected, and no costs are incurred at the time of collection.

During 2000, the company produced 100,000 units, shipped 76,000 units, and collected $600,000 from customers. During 2001, it produced 80,000 units, shipped 90,000 units, and collected $950,000 from customers.

1. Ignoring income tax for now, determine the amount of income that would be reported for each of these two years:
    a. If revenue and expense are recognized at the time of production.
    b. If revenue and expense are recognized at the time of shipment.
    c. If revenue and expense are recognized at the time of collection.
2. Would the asset total shown on the December 31, 2001, balance sheet be affected by the choice among the three recognition bases used in part 1? What would be the amount of any such difference?
3. Redo part 1, assuming that the company's income tax rate is 30%.

PROBLEM 6.38 (CHALLENGING) Revenue and expense recognition for a franchiser

The Pie Place, Inc. (TPP) was started in 2000 to franchise a chain of fast-food outlets that would sell only pies: meat, mince, pecan, sugar, and the like. A specialty was to be "pi-pie," a recipe made from various roots (ginger, ginseng, etc.) and invented by Janet Randolph, the founder and owner of TPP.

Janet has divided each major city into population sectors of about 200,000 each and plans to sell one franchise per sector. For smaller cities, franchises will cover rural areas as well. The franchises will be good for ten years, renewable for at least two more ten-year periods, and will sell for $20,000 each. Each franchisee must pay TPP $5,000 down in cash, pay the remainder in three equal annual installments (with no interest charges), and agree to buy various ingredients from TPP. In return, TPP will provide expert advice (Janet's), recipes, help with locating and constructing the food outlet, management training, and some national advertising. (Most advertising costs will be charged back to the franchises on a pro rata basis.)

Here are data for TPP's first year, ended August 31, 2001:

Franchise agreements signed	28
Down payments received	26
Fast-food outlets opened	18
Franchise-related costs	$230,000
Other general expenses	$55,000

One of the franchises has already gone out of business (having paid only the initial $5,000), two others of those that have opened do not look as if they are going to make it, and one of the unopened franchises looks as if it will never get going.

1. List as many methods as you can think of for recognizing revenue from franchise sales.
2. Rank those methods from least conservative to most conservative.
3. List as many methods as you can think of for recognizing expenses from franchise-related costs.
4. Match each expense recognition method to the revenue recognition method that seems most appropriate.
5. Compare the income before tax for 2001 that would be produced by two or three of the more reasonable matched methods of recognizing revenue and expense.
6. Choose a matched method that you think would be most appropriate for TPP.
7. Draft an "accounting policy" footnote describing your chosen revenue/expense recognition method for TPP's August 31, 2001, financial statements.

PROBLEM 6.39 (CHALLENGING) Real company's revenue, expense recognition

Using the financial statements, MD&A, and other information of any company you are interested in (such as from the company's Web page), write a comprehensive review of the company's revenue and expense recognition policies. Cover such points as:

a. What the nature of the company's business is and how it earns its revenue and incurs its expenses.
b. What the company's financial statements and notes disclose about its important revenue and expense recognition policies.
c. Based on (a) and (b) and on your own thinking about the company, the appropriateness of the company's revenue and expense policies and what questions or concerns you have about them.
d. What the company's cash flow statement (SCFP) tells you about how close the company's accrual net income is to cash income.

**PROBLEM 6.40
(CHALLENGING)
Comment on a
newspaper article
critical of
accounting**

Below is a newspaper article critical of managing earnings through aggressive accounting.[11] The article does not talk about revenue and expense recognition directly, but implies it through the techniques it mentions:

- The Big Bath, which we have seen before, which depresses current income by moving expenses forward from the future in order to make the future income higher.

- Immediately writing off part of the costs of acquiring another company, rather than keeping them on the balance sheet and amortizing them against future income.

- Paying managers with stock options; giving them cheap shares instead of cash and thereby not showing the real cost of employing them, because instead of an expense that reduces income, there is just a lower amount of share capital in the equity section of the balance sheet.

- Capitalizing research and development costs as assets to be amortized instead of deducting them as expenses now, which has the opposite effect to those of the first two income management methods.

Comment on the issues raised in the article. Some of these are: Do you think the problems are particularly serious in high-tech companies that rely on R&D, give big incentives to creative people, and sell ideas more than goods? Would it solve anything to have Canadian companies follow American practices more closely, even though there are problems in the United States too? Is it possible for a company to use aggressive accounting practices and still be conservative?

Tech firms' accounting methods assailed

Aggressive practices boost earnings, but may not be sustainable in long term: report

SIMON TUCK
Technology Reporter, Ottawa

Some of Canada's largest technology companies are boosting their earnings through the use of aggressive accounting practices, according to a report from Merrill Lynch Canada Inc.

The report warns that earnings created by the aggressive methods, which are far more widespread in the United States, are not sustainable in the long term. That would be especially perilous for the companies if the economy weakens and investors become more skittish.

"In these times of turbulent markets," the report says, "we feel this may

be the time to take a more critical look at earnings quality issues in the sector."

The report says Canadian technology heavyweights Northern Telecom Ltd., Newbridge Networks Corp., JDS Fitel Inc., ATI Technologies Inc. and Mitel Corp. were the companies reviewed and "almost all could see a reduction to their reported and estimated [earnings] after adjusting for some accounting practices."

The report is careful to point out that the accounting practices are not illegal, or even inappropriate. But it does state that such methods are "a red flag worth monitoring."

However, many analysts and investors are ignoring the red flag, said Tom Astle, senior technology analyst at Toronto-based Merrill Lynch Canada. "Technology companies have discovered that Wall Street and Bay Street tend to ignore writeoffs."

The report points out four areas of concern:

- "Big-bath accounting" that loads writeoffs onto quarters where a company would record a loss in any case. That increases expenses in one quarter, but boosts income in future quarters, creating the impression of a brightening financial picture.

- Writing off "research and development in process" from acquisitions. That also has the effect of transferring costs from future quarters to the current one, and boosting earnings in subsequent periods.
- Unrecorded costs for employee stock options. The report says that such options have a value that should be recorded as an expense at the time of issue, but rarely is.
- Recording expenditures on research and development as assets that are then subject to amortization, rather than as expenses. This pracitce increases profit in the short term, but reduces it in subsequent quarters as the asset is amortized. Such expenditures should be recorded as expenses as they occur, the report says.

Tim Saunders, Mitel's vice-president and corporate controller, said the report addresses an important and timely issue, but he said his Kanata, Ont.-based firm uses conservative accounting practices.

Marc René de Cotret, a spokesman for Nepean, Ont.-based JDS Fitel, said his company uses "very clean" accounting methods. "We have very, very conservative accounting practices."

ATI's accounting practices are also conservative, said spokeswoman Jo-Anne Chang, adding that Canadian high-tech firms are not as aggressive as their U.S. counterparts.

Northern Telecom, of Brampton, Ont., and Newbridge, of Kanata, Ont., did not comment. However, the report itself states that all the firms are operating within the law and within generally accepted accounting principles.

But the report says that just obeying the rules does not provide an entirely clear picture for investors. "Simply complying with generally accepted accounting principles in either Canada or the United States does not guarantee earnings quality."

The silver lining for Canada's technology industry is the report's even heavier criticism of the accounting practices of U.S. firms.

The report suggests that Canadian companies begin following accepted American accounting practices "so that we can compare apples to apples."

Reprinted from *The Globe and Mail*, 29 March 1999, by Simon Tuck.

PROBLEM 6.41 (CHALLENGING) Comprehensive revenue and expense issues

CompCom Inc. is engaged in developing a computerized scheduling, shipping, maintenance, and operations system for the North American trucking industry, which has been "loosened up" by deregulation.

CompCom has spent the last five years conducting systems development work and this year (ended November 30, 2001) sold its first systems. Initial funding of $2,500,000 came from the founder, who invested $1,250,000 for shares and $1,250,000 in the form of a loan. In the past, the company was not very concerned about accounting issues and financial statements, but now it is seeking external financing and is required to prepare financial statements to obtain this financing.

It is now December 19, 2001. The president is very concerned about how the company's results for the year ended November 30, 2001, will appear to investors. She understands that GAAP allow choices to be made regarding accounting policies and is interested in the choices available for the following two issues:

- Costs totalling $2,500,000 have been incurred evenly over the last five years in developing systems. Of these costs, $1,000,000 relate to failed efforts on a system that was found this year to be unmarketable. The rest of the costs are attributable to the development of a system that is currently being sold. The company expects to be able to sell the system for five years before it becomes technologically obsolete, becoming more obsolete (therefore, harder to market) as the five years progress. Right now, the company anticipates selling the system as follows:

Fiscal year ended Nov. 30, 2001   2 systems already sold
Fiscal year ended Nov. 30, 2002   4 systems expected to be sold
Fiscal year ended Nov. 30, 2003   3 systems expected to be sold
Fiscal year ended Nov. 30, 2004   2 systems expected to be sold
Fiscal year ended Nov. 30, 2005   1 system expected to be sold

- Sales commenced in the last half of 2001. Each sales contract is priced to provide a $250,000 margin over estimated contract costs. Sales arise as follows: a contract is negotiated covering the services to be provided; a nonreturnable deposit of 10% of the negotiated price is required before work commences; as work continues, regular billings are made at specific stages of completion of the system. To November 30, 2001, the following sales have occurred:

Sold to	Total Contract Price	Deposit	Contract Billings So Far	Cash rec'd Including Deposit	Completed So Far	Cash Paid for Costs So Far
Co. A	$2,000,000	$200,000	$750,000	$600,000	40%	$500,000
Co. B	2,250,000	225,000	Nil	225,000	Nil	Nil
	$4,250,000	$425,000	$750,000	$825,000		$500,000

Prior to making any accounting decisions involved in the above issues, the company's account balances at November 30, 2001, are:

	Debit	Credit
Cash	$ 325,000	
Contract costs paid	500,000	
Contract receipts		$ 825,000
Development costs	2,500,000	
Share capital		1,250,000
Shareholder loan		1,250,000
	$3,325,000	$3,325,000

The following additional information is relevant:

- a. Of the costs to date, $500,000 has been paid in cash and an additional $200,000 has been incurred but not paid. The only cash inflow this year has been from contract deposits and billings.
- b. The company is still in the development stage and is not required to pay income tax for 2001 or prior years.
- c. The founding shareholder's loan is interest-free and due on demand, but the shareholder has signed a letter confirming that he will not withdraw the funds over the course of the next year.

Given all of the above information, answer the following:

1. Suggest two different methods of recognizing revenue from sales of the systems. (No calculations are needed—just describe the methods.)

2. Choose a revenue recognition method for CompCom and state why you prefer it.

3. Based on the method you chose in part 2, calculate the company's revenue and contract cost expense for the year ended November 30, 2001.

4. The president wants to capitalize the development costs. How much would you recommend be capitalized, and why?

5. Explain to the president why amortization of any such development cost asset is necessary.

6. Choose a method of amortizing the development cost asset that makes sense to you and calculate the amortization expense for 2001 and the accumulated amortization at November 30, 2001.

7. Based on your answers to the previous parts, prepare an income statement and statement of retained earnings for 2001 and a balance sheet as at November 30, 2001, with appropriate notes.

8. If you're not exhausted, also prepare a statement of changes in financial position for 2001.

CASE 6A
A variety of revenue and expense recognition problems in real companies

Much of this book has involved large companies in the public eye. But income measurement is important in all kinds of enterprises. Discuss the accounting methods, ethics, and business practices in the following examples, *all real companies* with their identities disguised. In each example, try to figure out which accounts in the income statement and balance sheet are involved so that you can say what the effects are on the financial statements.

1. Great Chicken was founded to sell fast-food franchises using the name of a well-known entertainer. Quite a few retired couples and other hopeful people signed up to buy franchises, usually putting up their savings and promising to pay the rest out of the profits of their franchise. Great Chicken recorded the total value of each franchise as revenue on the day the deal was signed. The company had no expenses to speak of at the beginning (except advertising and promotion), so its income statement showed high profits, which encouraged more people to sign up for franchises, which produced more profits. The company's profit growth was huge. But then it became apparent that the franchisees had not chosen good locations, didn't know much about running a chicken shop, couldn't cook and serve the food properly, and so couldn't pay their promised franchise payments. It also became apparent that Great Chicken really didn't know how to help them. To the despair of everyone, the whole operation, franchiser and franchisees, went out of business.

2. Intensive Research Inc., located next to a major university, raised funding to develop some drugs for treating serious illnesses. During several years of research and development, the company had very small revenues (interest and some research grants and fees for consulting to other companies) and very large R&D expenses. The president believed it would be inappropriate accounting to match the high R&D to zero revenues yet from the drugs, and bad for the company's image to have losses all this time, so the company capitalized R&D (removed it from expense and put it on the balance sheet as a long-term asset). Enough was capitalized each year to bring the company's net income to just above zero.

3. Central Community Association rented out its hall on weekends for weddings and other functions. The money earned by these rentals was a major part of

the association's funding, largely paying the salary of the association's manager. However, a fair number of renters managed to disappear from town or otherwise avoid paying, so the association instituted a policy of payment in advance. In the first year of this policy, the association showed a large increase in income, because rental reservations often well into future months had been included in the revenue. An argument broke out at the association's regular board of directors meeting when an accountant suggested that each function's reservation revenue be deferred until the function had been held. It turned out that the association's manager, flush with cash, had spent a lot more on repairs and cleaning than usual, and if the revenue was deferred, the association would show a loss for the year, contrary to its by-laws. The manager argued that the deferral of revenue was unnecessary because after the first year of the new policy, things would pretty much even out, revenues coming in at about the same rate as expenses, and so the policy of requiring payment in advance brought in effect a permanent gain for the association.

4. The president of Morgan Lumber always kept the results of the annual inventory count secret. Even the company's chief accountant was not told how much inventory was on hand until a preliminary income figure had been determined for the year. Then the president would consult the records of the inventory count and provide a year-end inventory cost figure, from which the chief accountant deduced the cost of goods sold (beginning inventory plus purchases minus ending inventory equals the cost of what must have been sold). Each year, the final income turned out to be just about what the president wanted, in line with indications given to the bank and with installments paid on the company's income tax.

5. Western Business Bank had a large portfolio of loans receivable, all secured by property mortgages. Some of these loans were not being repaid very well, or at all, but the bank did not worry about this much as long as the market values of the mortgaged properties exceeded the loans amounts. So each month, the bank added interest on the loans to interest revenue and to the loans receivable, which therefore continued to rise because many were not being repaid by borrowers. Therefore, the bank's reported assets and revenue (and income) grew even if the borrowers were not keeping up their payments. The bank reasoned that it could always seize the mortgaged properties, sell them, and recover its money. Then, to everyone's horror, the real estate market collapsed, driving market values of mortgaged properties down below the accumulated "loans plus accrued interest" receivables. The bank went out of business soon after, leaving many shareholders and depositors without their money.

6. Brilliant Software had a small but innovative set of software to be sold in the educational market. Having made promises to investors that the company would succeed, the president was disappointed at the great competition the company faced and resultant slow sales. The company's sales force was therefore issued with "sales call reports" that looked just like sales invoices. When a salesperson made a call, the report was filled in with the number of software packages the potential customer had expressed an interest in, though not actually agreeing to buy. These reports came back to head office, where signatures were forged onto them to turn them into sales orders, which were then booked as revenue. To complete the process, the software had to be shipped, but to where? The so-called customer had not actually ordered it. So

Brilliant Software quietly rented a warehouse in an obscure part of town, and "shipped" the software there. Somehow no one seemed to question the consequent growth in accounts receivable, and the "shipped" software gathered dust in the warehouse until the whole mess was uncovered.[12]

CASE 6B
A crackdown on earnings management?

Below are excerpts from the article "The Crackdown Is Here," about planned increased action by the SEC in the United States against companies that "manage" their earnings.[13] The excerpts focus on revenue recognition, but mention some other earnings management methods, such as the following:

- A "cookie jar reserve" works by overestimating expenses and liabilities or underestimating revenues and accounts receivable in a good year, thereby lowering income and making it easier to reverse these "errors" in a future year in order to boost income then. So it's an income-smoothing device.

- Recording "phantom" revenue or under-recording expenses overstates income this year. If repeated, especially in larger and larger amounts each year, this produces a higher income trend. Eventually the misrepresentation gets so large it can't be sustained, and the scheme collapses. Companies that report suddenly having to adjust past-reported earnings downwards may be suspected of engaging in this.

Read the article excerpts and then discuss such questions as these:

1. Do accounting standards for revenue and expense recognition need to be stronger?
2. Do penalties for improper earnings management need to be harsher?
3. Is this sort of problem just a consequence of accrual accounting in the real world that has to be lived with?
4. Do a few bad apples mean the whole box is bad, or are these sorts of problems just part of the price of a "free enterprise" economic and financial reporting system?
5. Is the problem more an ethical one than an accounting one?
6. Should top managers be paid on the basis of their performance if they have some control over the performance measures?

The Crackdown Is Here

Someplace right now, in the layers of a Fortune 500 company, an employee—probably high up and probably helped by people who work for him—is perpetrating an accounting fraud. Down the road that crime will come to light and cost the company's shareholders hundreds of millions of dollars.

Typically, the employee will not have set out to be dishonest, only to dodge a few rules. His fraud, small at first, will build, because the exit he thought just around the corner never appears. In time, some subordinate may say, "Whoa!" But he won't muster the courage to blow the whistle, and the fraud will go on.

Until it's uncovered. The company's stock will drop then, by a big percent. Class-action lawyers will leap. The Securities and Exchange Commission will file unpleasant enforcement actions, levy fines, and leave the bad guys looking for another line of work. Eventually someone may go to jail.

And the fundamental reason, very often, will be that the company or one of it divisions was "managing earnings"—trying to meet Wall Street expectations or those of the boss, trying also to pretend that the course of business is smooth and predictable when in reality it is not.

Jail? This is not a spot that CEOs and other high-placed executives see themselves checking into, for any reason. *Jail for managing earnings?* Many corporate chiefs would find that preposterous, having come to believe that "making their numbers" is just what executives do. Okay, so the pressure might lead some of them to do dumb (but legal) things—like making off-price deals at the end of a quarter that simply steal from full-priced business down the road. Who cares? Others might even be driven to make hash of the rules that publicly owned companies are required to abide by, Generally Accepted Accounting Principles, known as GAAP. Sure, that might mean crossing a legal line, but so what?

Well, the "so what" is Arthur Levitt, chairman of the SEC and the grand enforcer when it comes to GAAP. Last year, with his attorneys and accountants digging into Bankers Trust and Cendant and W.R. Grace and Livent and Oxford Health Plans and Sunbeam and Waste Management—and who knows what other big companies the SEC isn't talking about—Levitt finally reached the gag point. He simply declared war on bad financial reporting.

One U.S. Attorney in tune with the SEC's tough new line is Mary Jo White, of New York's Southern District. White has brought a string of accounting-fraud actions and says she still has "a lot" in the pipeline. Her district has two bigtime criminal cases even now—Livent and Bankers Trust, both stemming from managed earnings. However, as White points out, "On the criminal side, we don't use that polite a term; we call it accounting fraud or 'cooking the books.'" White has also prosecuted smaller cases that she prizes for their deterrence value. Object lessons don't work in most areas of the law, she says, but "significant jail time" for a white-collar executive is apt to give others of his ilk severe shakes.

What qualifies as significant? In March, Donald Ferrarini, the 71-year-old former CEO of a New York insurance brokerage, Underwriters Financial Group (UFG), got 12 years. (He is appealing.) Ferrarini had cooked the most basic recipes in the book: He overstated revenues and understated expenses, a combo that magically converted UFG from a loser into a money-maker. The scam, uncovered in 1995, cost shareholders, policyholders, and premium finance companies close to $30 million.

A case alleging still another horrific fraud could soon come out of Newark. There, in what one knowledgeable person describes as "conference rooms jammed with lawyers," the office of the U.S. Attorney for New Jersey is boring in on the celebrated case of Cendant. Or, put more precisely, what's under the microscope are the flagrant accounting violations (of which more later) at CUC International, which merged with HFWS Inc. in 1997 to form Cendant. The subsequent news of chicanery at CUC clobbered Cendant's stock by more than $14 billion in a single day.

For its part, the SEC has a "formal investigation" in progress on Cendant—that's its term for "you're in trouble"—and the same thing going on at Sunbeam and Waste Management and, down the line in size, Mercury Finance and telecommunications company Telxon. These all are companies that in recent times made major restatements of earnings, usually the first sign of serious accounting problems. Another restater is Oxford Health Plans, which is the subject of a lesser SEC investigation called an "informal inquiry." The big question about Oxford is whether its books got out of control simply because of the well-publicized chaos in its computer systems or because of irregularities as well.

Never fear that the SEC will run out of accounting cases to examine and perhaps move in on, because seldom does a month pass that those ugly words "restatement of earnings" do not fasten themselves to a new company. Joining the crowd recently from the FORTUNE 1,000 were drugstore chain Rite Aid, holding company MCN Energy Group, and drug wholesaler McKesson HBOC.

Like any good general, Arthur Levitt has a strategy for going after this enemy called managed earnings. In his September speech, in fact, he unveiled a list of five accounting problems that would get the unremitting attention of the SEC. They were "big bath" restructuring charges, acquisition accounting, "cookie-jar reserves," the abuse of "materiality," and revenue recognition.

Of these, that last item—the wrongful booking of sales—seems the closest to outright fraud. GAAP includes some firm rules for recognizing revenue, and most don't leave a lot of room for playing around. That hasn't stopped the bad guys. A recent study done for the Committee of Sponsoring Organizations of the Treadway Commission (called COSO), which is supported by various accounting and financial bodies, studies 200 alleged frauds carried out by publicly owned companies in the 11 years ended in 1997. Roughly 50% had a revenue-recognition component. Many of the cases involved small companies, which for that matter pack the list when it comes to fraud of any kind.

Even so, some of the biggest accounting scandals of the past few years (and now McKesson's to boot) have also featured revenue-recognition schemes. Executives at Sensormatic held the books open at the end of quarters so that they could get enough sales in the door to meet their earnings targets. Richard Rubin, former CEO of apparel company Donnkenny, is awaiting sentence for creating false invoices that he used to book sales. And Al Dunlap, who was fired as CEO of Sunbeam by its board, is alleged to have carried out (among other things) a "bill and hold" scam. In other words, Sunbeam recorded the sale of goods but simply held them in its own warehouse, a forbidden combo unless a customer has taken bona fide ownership of the goods and requested they be stored. (Dunlap, says his lawyer, relied on Arthur Andersen's assurances that Sunbeam was conforming to GAAP.) Walter Schuetze, chief accountant of the SEC's Division of Enforcement, sees in these scandals a simple theme: "When it comes to cooking the books, revenue recognition is the recipe of choice."

The SEC is right now busy drawing a line in the sand about materiality. In the past it has sometimes permitted managements to get by with irregularities in their financial reports just as long as the deliberate misstatements could be classed, often by some ad hoc mathematical logic, as immaterial. But it is now preparing to say—in a staff bulletin soon to appear—that intentional errors made for the purpose of managing earnings just won't be tolerated.

In the W.R. Grace case, moreover, it went after intentional errors made several years back. It seems that in the early 1990s a division of that company, National Medical Care (NMC), made more in profits than it had expected. So NMC, according to SEC, deliberately underreported its earnings (thereby creating an "irregularity"), stuffing the excess into a cookie-jar reserve that in time got to be $60 million in size. Then in 1993, when profits needed a sugar fix, NMC started feeding the reserve into earnings (thereby compounding the irregularities). Meanwhile, Grace's auditors, Price Waterhouse, went along with these contortions on the grounds that they weren't material.

The SEC, launching its case, objected to the entire goings-on. By June it had exacted cease-and-desist consents from two Pricewaterhouse Coopers partners and from Grace itself, which agreed as well to set up a $1 million educational fund to further awareness of GAAP. The commission has also filed cease-and-desist proceedings against seven former Grace officers (among them CEO J.P. Bolduc), of whom three get special attention. These three, who include Grace's former chief financial officer, Brian Smith, are licensed CPAs whom the SEC views as having engaged in "inappropriate professional conduct." So the commission wants an administrative judge to bar them from practicing before the SEC. That means they could not play any part in preparing the financial statements of publicly owned companies or any other SEC registrant.

Smith's lawyer, Wallace Timmeny, once an SEC staffer himself and now at Dechert Price & Rhoads, plans to lean on the materiality argument in defending his client. But he also argues in essence that it would be bitterly unfair for Smith and a couple of other unlucky parishioners to get excommunicated for sins rampant in the rest of the congregation. "If you think what my client did constitutes fraud," he protested to the SEC before the charges came, "then every company in the FORTUNE 500 is engaged in fraud."

The Grace case is important to Levitt's initiative because it sends such a strong message to other companies, some of which should be thinking, "There but for the god of Grace go I." In an entirely different way, the Cendant case demands attention because it displays such gross behavior. The misdeeds are fully documented as well, in a remarkable and unsparing 146-page report done for the audit committee of Cendant's board by the law firm of Wilkie Farr & Gallagher and auditors imported for the project, Arthur Andersen. Here are some of the report's findings:

- In the three years 1995-97, CUC's operating income before taxes was improperly inflated by $500 million, which was more than one-third of its reported pretax income for those years.
- Though may of the improprieties occurred in CUC's biggest subsidiary, Comp-U-Card, they reached to 16 others as well. No fewer than 20 employees participated in the wrongdoing.
- Several CUC employees who were interviewed said they understood that the purpose of inflating earnings was to meet "analysts' expectations."
- In the first three quarters of each of the infected years, CUC put out unaudited financial statements that headquarters deliberately falsified, mostly by "adjusting" Comp-U-Card's revenues upward and its expenses downward. These favorable "adjustments" grew: They were $31 million in 1995, $87 million in 1976, and $176 million in 1997.
- At the end of each year, before its outside auditors, Ernst & Young, came in to make their annual review, CUC undid those improprieties (which would almost certainly have been discovered in the audit process) and instead created the earnings it needed mainly by plucking them from cookie-jar reserves.

Reprinted from *Fortune* (pp. 75–92), 2 August 1999, by Carol J. Loomis.

NOTES

1. W.H. Beaver, *Financial Reporting: An Accounting Revolution*, 2nd ed. (Englewood Cliffs: Prentice-Hall, 1989), 8.
2. Ibid., 105.
3. Ibid., 105.
4. P.A. Griffin, ed., *Usefulness to Investors and Creditors of Information Provided by Financial Reporting*, 2nd ed. (Stamford: Financial Accounting Standards Board, 1987), 14.
5. CAE accounting policy topics, 2000 Annual Report, 31–32.
6. Canadian Institute of Chartered Accountants, "Introduction to Accounting Recommendations," in *CICA Handbook* (Toronto: Canadian Institute of Chartered Accountants, 31 December 1999), 6.
7. C. Byrd, I. Chen, and H. Chapman, *Financial Reporting in Canada, 1999* (Toronto: Canadian Institute of Chartered Accountants, 1999), 2.
8. Christopher Power, "Let's Get Fiscal," *Forbes* (30 April 1984): 103.
9. CAE, 2000 Annual Report, 31.
10. United Dominion Industries, "Notes to Consolidated Financial Statements," 1992 Annual Report.
11. S. Tuck, "Tech Firms' Accounting Methods Assailed," *The Globe and Mail* (29 March 1999): B1, B9.
12. Based on the article "Anatomy of a Fraud," by M. Maremont, *Business Week* (16 September 1996): 90–92, 94.
13. C.J. Loomis, "The Crackdown Is Here," *Fortune* (2 August 1999): 75–92.

7 CHAPTER

Recordkeeping and Control

7.1   Chapter Overview

Financial accounting and its records are important for control and management beyond financial statements.

This chapter's goal is to show you that financial accounting has more purposes than just preparing financial statements and reporting to outside users of the statements. It is also very useful to managers in running the enterprise, in fulfilling their responsibilities as stewards of the enterprise's resources, and generally keeping the enterprise under control. This chapter focuses on some aspects of internal accounting that are closely related to the financial reporting system earlier chapters have described, and that can have some impact on the financial reporting. These aspects include the importance of good recordkeeping, the nature of internal control of the enterprise, and control of several specific resources and obligations. This chapter provides a link to management accounting, which develops these topics much further.

This is what you will learn in this chapter:

- *Procedures and techniques:* How the accounting system uses documents to support its records, and how to establish good internal control in cash, accounts receivable, GST and sales taxes collected, employee payroll deductions, and inventory.

- *Concepts and principles:* Management's responsibility to be in control of the enterprise and principles of good internal control.

- *Analysis and decisions:* How to decide whether controls are worthwhile in specific areas and even a little about the risk of fraud.

7.2   ACCOUNTING'S "BOOKS" AND RECORDS

The Importance of Good Records

Records provide essential knowledge for managers and people evaluating managers.

Complete and accurate records are important: they provide the observations behind the accounting information and the history of the enterprise. Without knowing what has happened, investors and managers cannot make plans for the future, evaluate alternatives properly, or learn from past actions. In today's complex business environment, especially since enterprises have become very large, the number of business events is much too great for anyone to keep track of without having accurate records (written or, these days, computerized records). Records provide the basis for extrapolations into the future, information for evaluating and rewarding performance, and a basis for internal control over the existence and quality of an enterprise's assets. Internal control, furthermore, not only provides systematic protection from theft and loss, but also documentation for legal and insurance purposes. Recordkeeping, however, does cost money, and therefore records should be worth their cost. How complex and sophisticated to make one's records is a business decision, as are such decisions as how to price or market one's product.

These are fundamental points about records:

Without good records, the enterprise's managers are flying blind.

- Records are the basis of accounting information, as we have seen beginning with the transactional base of financial accounting in Chapter 1. Therefore, the better the records, the better the accounting.

- Records also provide essential evidence of what people do, request, and promise. They are the backbone of managing what happens in and to the enterprise and therefore are fundamental to managers. Without good records, managers are flying blind.

- Many outside parties, like auditors, bankers, and tax authorities, want to scrutinize records that support the enterprise's claims about the income it has earned, the sales it has made, the bills it has paid, the tax it has collected for the government, or owes on its own income, and so on. Records are so important to income tax, for example, that the law requires enterprises (and individuals) to keep records and allows the taxation authorities to make their own judgments about tax liability in the event good records haven't been kept.

- And, last but not least, it is very expensive to catch and correct errors, prepare proper financial statements, or any other reports, or uncover fraud, if good records have not been kept. Without good records, enterprises can get into spectacular messes! Here are some real examples:

  ▸ A big American life insurance company called Equity Funding suffered multi-million-dollar losses because its records of issuing life insurance were so unreliable that some fraud artists induced it to pay out vast sums for insurance policies that did not exist.

  ▸ A charitable organization in Western Canada let its records get into such terrible shape that it could not even figure out what cash and bank balances it should have. While there did not seem to be any fraud, the charity had to go through the embarrassment and expense of trying to reconstruct events that had happened years earlier, and ended up having to have its Board of Directors pass a special motion to declare that the charity had to give up trying to sort out the mess and would deem its bank and cash balances to be whatever the current best guesses were.

▶ A fired employee took a magnet to the electronic records of a large whole-sale company, destroying its records of what its customers owed it. The company was forced to rely on the honesty of its customers to pay what they thought they owed.

▶ A large Canadian university implemented a faulty computerized record-keeping system. By the end of the first year of the new system, the university's departments had no information about how much of their budgets had been spent or how much could be carried over from year to year, and the university's internal financial statements were a tangle, with amounts being added to and subtracted from accounts seemingly at random. Armies of clerks had to be employed to try to connect the documents the university had to the information the computers were producing.

Summary of Financial Accounting's Procedures

Financial accounting information should be prepared through a well-defined set of procedures.

The general steps that should be followed in coming up with a set of audited financial statements, outlined in previous chapters, but repeated here as reminders, are:

1. Record transactions as individual journal entries or in specialized records for various routine transactions, such as cash receipts or cheques written.
2. Summarize the transactions by posting them to accounts.
3. Choose accounting methods and policies to be followed consistently in reporting performance and position.
4. In accordance with those methods and policies, make end-of-period accruals, corrections, and other adjustments.
5. Prepare the balance sheet, income statement, and retained earnings statement from the accounts.
6. Prepare the cash flow statement from the other three statements and additional information about changes in noncurrent assets and liabilities and owners' equity.
7. Prepare the accounting policy notes and other footnote disclosures, and add comparative figures for last year.
8. Have the full set of statements and notes audited (usually, the auditing process begins earlier, before the year-end and before the statements have been prepared).
9. Append the auditor's report to the set of statements and notes and have the balance sheet signed as approved by the board of directors.
10. Release the statements, notes, and auditor's report as a set.
11. Somewhere after step 5, close the income, dividends, and retained earnings adjustments accounts to retained earnings to make all those accounts' balances zero in preparation for next year's step 1 (the balance sheet accounts continue into the next year and so are not closed). Computerized accounting systems usually do this step automatically.

The Underlying Accounting System

All of these procedures require evidence. We've seen some examples already, such as in the evidence needed of an exchange for a transaction to be recorded and of delivery for revenue to be recognized. To help you see the role that the underlying accounting system and the evidence supporting it play in producing the account information we've been using in the text, this section shows you examples of how the evidence is assembled, and what some of it looks like. This will also prepare you for the internal control topic later in the chapter, because internal control both depends on and contributes to the enterprise's recordkeeping system.

a. Source Documents and the Transactional Cycle: A Real Example

Accounting recordkeeping depends upon sets of source documents to show that transactions have occurred. Such documents are kept so that the accounting records can be checked and verified to correct errors, permit auditing, be used in case of dispute, and support income tax claims and other legal actions. The transactions themselves reflect various events in operating the business. Examples below were supplied by an Edmonton company, Barcol Doors & Windows Ltd., which is a manufacturer and supplier of doors and windows to the building, retail, and home trade.[1] Keep in mind that these are examples only: every company has its own system and documents, and many of the "books" people refer to are actually electronic records in computer systems.

At Barcol, a work order agreed to by the customer starts the recordkeeping process.

1. Barcol sells products made from components and raw material that it buys from other companies. The first step is to determine what the customer wants and get the customer's agreement to the product and costs. This is done via a work order, which is Barcol's record of what it is to make and what will be charged for it. This is not an accounting transaction, as there has been no exchange yet, but it is important evidence in case the customer and Barcol disagree later on what the customer wanted and how much would be paid. See Figure 7.1 for Barcol's work order form. It is dated and prenumbered, and has spaces for details like the agreed terms of payment.

BARCOL
DOORS & WINDOWS
"Serving Albertans Since 1952"

CONDITIONAL SALES CONTRACT

WORK ORDER
G 08384

☐ **HEAD OFFICE**
14820 - YELLOWHEAD TRAIL
EDMONTON, ALBERTA T5L 3C5
TELEPHONE (780) 452-7140
FAX (780) 451-0724

☐ **SOUTHSIDE BRANCH**
2854 CALGARY TRAIL S.
EDMONTON, ALBERTA T6J 6V7
TELEPHONE (780) 440-3667
FAX (780) 463-6061

☐ **FORT SASKATCHEWAN**
8732 - 112 STREET
FORT SASKATCHEWAN, AB T8L 2S7
TELEPHONE (780) 998-9759
FAX (780) 998-9760

Date ____________ 19____

How did you Hear of BARCOL?
Yellow Pages ☐ **Referral** ☐ **Coupon** ☐ **Other** ☐

BILL TO:
POSTAL CODE
CUSTOMER No.

LOCATION:
JOB #
CUSTOMER P.O. #

ORDERED BY: ____________
SEE: ____________

BUSINESS PHONE ____________ CELL PHONE ____________
RESIDENCE PHONE ____________

QTY. ORDERED	QTY. SHIPPED	SIZE	DESCRIPTION	AMOUNT	TOTAL

SUB TOTAL	
G.S.T. #R100395565	
TOTAL	
DEPOSIT	
BALANCE DUE ►	

____
BARCOL Representative

X ____________
Customer Signature
By placing my signature on this Conditional Sales Contract, I understand and agree that it is subject to the terms and conditions on the reverse side

____
Loaded by

Materials received in good order as requested by X ____________
Customer Signature

TERMS: COD ☐ NET 30 ☐ CASH ☐ CHEQUE ☐ MC ☐ AMEX ☐ VISA ☐

DATE COMPLETED: ____________

CARD NUMBER: ____________ EXPIRY DATE: ____________

—FOR OFFICE USE ONLY—

DATE	INSTALLER	INSTALLATION/TRAVEL TIME	P.O. No.	SUPPLIER	DATE	REC'D			
							32		
							33		

PT. 1 (WHITE) - H.O. PT. 2 (YELLOW) - CUSTOMER PT. 3 (PINK) - OFFICE PT. 4 (GREEN) - REQUISITION PT. 5 (YELLOW) - CUSTOMER

FIGURE 7.1

Barcol uses purchase orders and expects that others will use them too.

2. Ordering any raw material not on hand but needed to complete the work order is the next step. Like the work order stage, ordering raw materials is not an accounting transaction, so orders are not recorded in the accounts. However, documenting and keeping track of orders is very important to Barcol, so it uses "**purchase order**" forms for this. Figure 7.2 provides an example. You'll see that it is dated and prenumbered, so that it may be followed up in case of problems, and the items ordered are listed in detail so they can be checked against what actually arrives from the supplier. If you look back at Figure 7.1, you'll see that near the top it has a space for the "Customer P.O.#" so Barcol is expecting its customers (those that are other businesses, at least) to use purchase orders too.

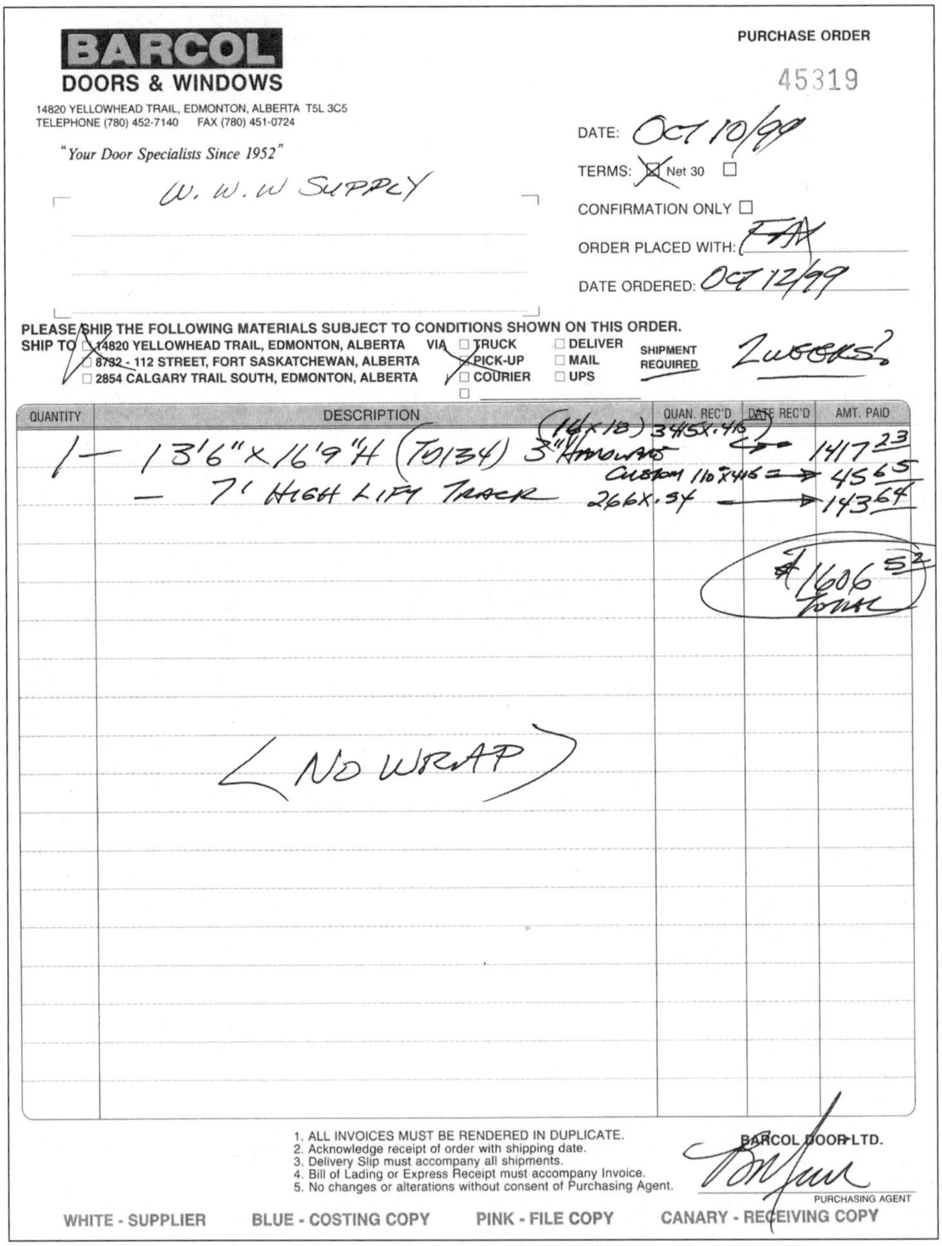

BARCOL DOORS & WINDOWS

14820 YELLOWHEAD TRAIL, EDMONTON, ALBERTA T5L 3C5
TELEPHONE (780) 452-7140 FAX (780) 451-0724

"*Your Door Specialists Since 1952*"

W. W. W SUPPLY

PURCHASE ORDER

45319

DATE: OCT 10/99

TERMS: ☒ Net 30 ☐

CONFIRMATION ONLY ☐

ORDER PLACED WITH: FAX

DATE ORDERED: OCT 12/99

PLEASE SHIP THE FOLLOWING MATERIALS SUBJECT TO CONDITIONS SHOWN ON THIS ORDER.

SHIP TO ☒ 14820 YELLOWHEAD TRAIL, EDMONTON, ALBERTA
☐ 8732 - 112 STREET, FORT SASKATCHEWAN, ALBERTA
☐ 2854 CALGARY TRAIL SOUTH, EDMONTON, ALBERTA

VIA ☐ TRUCK ☒ PICK-UP ☐ COURIER ☐ DELIVER ☐ MAIL ☐ UPS

SHIPMENT REQUIRED: 2 WEEKS?

QUANTITY	DESCRIPTION	QUAN. REC'D	DATE REC'D	AMT. PAID
1	13'6"x16'9"H (T0134) 3" HARDWARE (14x18) 345X.41			1417.23
	CUSTOM 110X.415			45.65
	— 7' HIGH LIFT TRACK 266X.54			143.64
				$1606.52 TOTAL
	<NO WRAP>			

1. ALL INVOICES MUST BE RENDERED IN DUPLICATE.
2. Acknowledge receipt of order with shipping date.
3. Delivery Slip must accompany all shipments.
4. Bill of Lading or Express Receipt must accompany Invoice.
5. No changes or alterations without consent of Purchasing Agent.

BARCOL DOOR LTD.
PURCHASING AGENT

WHITE - SUPPLIER BLUE - COSTING COPY PINK - FILE COPY CANARY - RECEIVING COPY

FIGURE 7.2

When Barcol accepts a delivery, the packing slip is evidence of an accounting transaction.

3. When ordered items arrive, they are checked against purchase orders and the supplier's packing slips, to ensure the order is correct. A copy of a **packing slip** from one of Barcol's suppliers is shown in Figure 7.3. It has no financial details but is evidence that the transaction happened in case there is any disagreement when the supplier bills Barcol or when the customer wonders how the work is going on the product ordered. This document, prepared by Barcol's supplier, is headed Sales Order because it is the supplier's version of the same sort of evidence Barcol wanted when it prepared the purchase order in Figure 7.2. The packing slip even quotes Barcol's purchase order number: you can see what a complete, cross-referenced set of records Barcol, its customers, and its suppliers are creating.

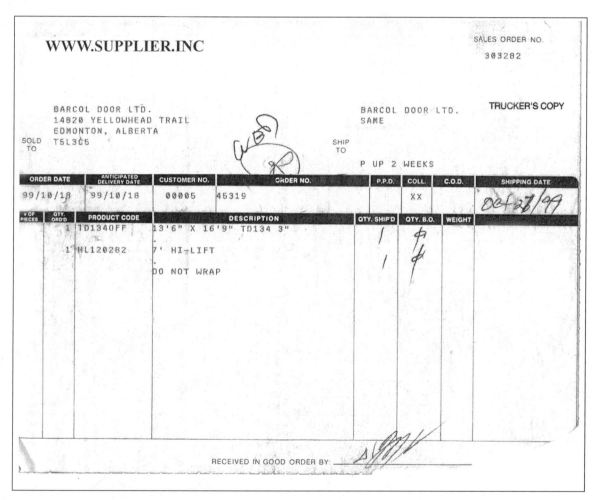

FIGURE 7.3

A sales invoice is Barcol's formal evidence that a revenue transaction has happened.

4. Selling the products is what Barcol is in business to do. When the product is complete and delivered to the customer, a sales invoice is prepared, specifying various useful details as in the example in Figure 7.4, which is the invoice for the goods involved in the previous three figures. A copy of this invoice supports the sale transaction recorded as DR Accounts receivable and CR Sales revenue. You can see there is $294.56 GST on the total, so the invoice also supports a debit to Accounts receivable and a credit to GST payable for the tax, which is not part of Barcol's revenue, but instead is collected on behalf of the government. (We'll see more about accounting for sales taxes like GST later in this chapter.)

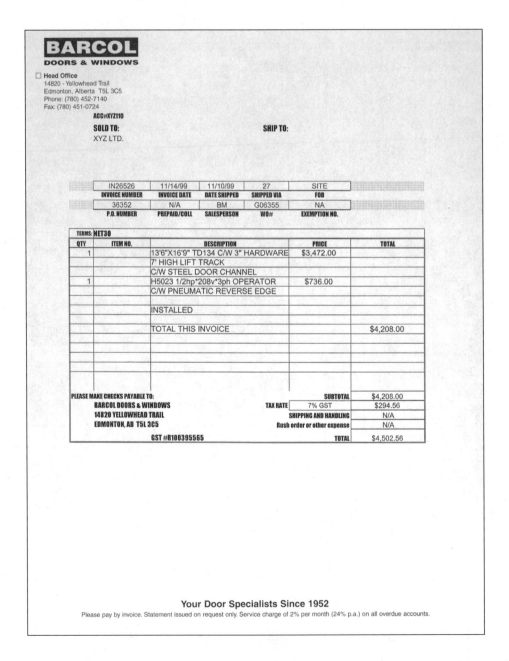

FIGURE 7.4

Barcol keeps track of its purchases and payables as well as its sales, and ties those to cheques written to suppliers.

5. Barcol's suppliers also send invoices to it for payment of the raw materials it has ordered. At the top of Figure 7.5 is an example of the accounts payable record Barcol creates from these invoices (which it has checked back to its purchase orders, Figure 7.2, and suppliers' packing slips, Figure 7.3). Barcol uses this record to explain to the supplier which invoices it is paying. The top of Figure 7.5 has room to list several invoices. Only one is given in this example, which also says that cheque #6777 is to pay for the invoice total of $130.54. With this record, both Barcol and the supplier can readily track down any missing or disputed shipments or invoices. The cheque is attached to this record when Barcol pays the amount indicated.

VENDOR: WWW110	www.supplier.ltd				CHEQUE NO. 6777	Nov/7/2000
OUR REF. NO.	YOUR INV. NO.	INVOICE DATE	INVOICE AMOUNT	AMOUNT PAID	DISCOUNT TAKEN	NET CHEQUE AMOUNT
	37630	10/20/00	130.54		0.00	130.54
			130.54		0.00	130.54

Please Detach Before Cashing

BARCOL
DOORS & WINDOWS
Your Door Specialists Since 1952   14820 YELLOWHEAD TRAIL N.W.
EDMONTON, ALBERTA T5L 3C5

CANADIAN IMPERIAL BANK OF COMMERCE   006777

CHEQUE NO.	CHEQUE DATE
6777	Nov/7/2000

One Hundred Thirty and 54/100******

CHEQUE AMOUNT
***130.54

PAY
TO THE
ORDER
OF   www.supplier.ltd

PER _____

PER _____

FIGURE 7.5

6. Collecting from customers is the last event in Barcol's revenue generation cycle. Three kinds of collection are illustrated here.

Cash receipts complete the cycle: order, purchase, payment, sale, collection.

a. Figure 7.6 shows a list of cash received from customers that is being deposited. This is from Barcol's cash receipts records, which support the cash records and the credits Barcol posts to reduce customers' accounts receivable for the payments they have made. Details are given of the customers, for tracing to cash sales or accounts receivable records, and the form even specifies that all the cash is in Canadian dollars. Barcol prepares the same sort of list for cheques received from customers (not illustrated).

Date: Monday, October 02, 2000   2:17PM   **Barcol Doors and Windows**   Page 1
A/R Bank Deposit Slips (ARDPST01)

From Batch No.   [2700] To [2700]

Customer Number	Payer	Check/Remittance Number		Amount
Bank ID: 1	Account: 1110		Date: 9/29/00	
Batch Number: 2,700	Deposit Slip Number: 2,118		Currency: CAD	
3				
KEL025	MR. A	000002700-0000001		3,156.50
LEC104	MR. B	000002700-0000002		124.92
DUT040	MS. C	000002700-0000003		234.06
FOR046	CASH SALE	000002700-0000004		132.95
BIR038	MR. D	000002700-0000005		48.10
COU090	MS. E	000002700-0000006		102.19
HAY024	CASH SALE	000002700-0000007		487.43
KUN099	CASH SALE	000002700-0000008		396.97
PAR007	F LTD	000002700-0000009		1,169.51
LIE040	G LTD	000002700-0000010		839.95
CLA112	MS. H	000002700-0000011		1,075.35
CAR0064	MR. I	000002700-0000012		1,245.48
MAC0013	MR. J	000002700-0000013		390.55
ARM037	MR. K	000002700-0000014		860.28
ALY099	CASH SALE	000002700-0000015		1,850.39
MAC017	M LTD	000002700-0000016		377.22
ALL070	A LTD	000002700-0000017		1,000.00
INV111	B INGO LTD	000002700-00018		2,068.31
		3 Total:		15,560.16

Date: Monday, October 02, 2000   2:17PM   **Barcol Doors and Windows**   Page 2
A/R Bank Deposit Slips (ARDPST01)

	Cash	
_____	X 1	_____
_____	X 2	_____
_____	X 5	_____
_____	X 10	_____
_____	X 20	_____
_____	X 50	_____
_____	X 100	_____
_____	Coins	_____
	Total 3	15,560.16
	Total Deposit	15,560.16

FIGURE 7.6

b. These days, Barcol, like many businesses, relies on credit cards for customers' payments on many sales. When a customer pays by credit card, the credit card slip is deposited into the bank just like cash or a cheque (the credit card company bills Barcol for its fee monthly). Figure 7.7 shows a little form that Barcol's credit card computer record prints out to go with all the credit card slips: you'll see that Barcol would be depositing slips from three different credit card companies. You'll also notice the "Inst paymnt" amount, small on that day. That is the record of "Interac" direct-withdrawal payments by customers.

```
         BARCOL OVERDOOR 1980 LTD
           14820 YELLOWHEAD TRAIL
              EDMONTON      AB
     STORE  991364      TERM A0991364
          *** END OF DAY REPORT ***
     BATCH 002 SHIFT 001 DAY 189 EMPL=
     SEPT/29/00 15:42
             * * * * * * * * *
     DAILY SUMMARY
                       SHIFT    ACCUM. TOTAL
     INST PAYMNT   $1,352.38     $1,352.38
     VISA         $15,560.16    $15,560.16
     M/C           $6,641.08     $6,641.08
     AMEX          $1,599.16     $1,599.16
     TOTAL        $25,152.78    $25,152.78
             * * * * * * * * *
     HOST REPORT
     DAY IN BALANCE
     ACCOUNT CREDITED           $25,152.78
```

FIGURE 7.7

c. More electronic, some customers pay Barcol by just notifying their and its banks to transfer the money to pay, without bothering with cheques or credit cards. This sort of electronic funds transfer (EFT) is becoming more common at Barcol, especially by large regular customers. Figure 7.8 is the form a customer faxed to Barcol to tell it that a transfer had been made.

```
                              XYZ INC


                         REMITTANCE ADVICE
                      Date: 28 SEP 2000


  BARCOL DOORS & WINDOWS LTD
  14820 - YELLOWEAD TRAIL
  EDMONTON, AB   T5L 3C5
  Attention To: Accounts Receivable
  Fax: 7804510724




  This statement is to notify you of an electronic deposit that will
  be made to your bank account for the following transaction(s).

  Transaction number   : 144443
  Deposit date         : 02-OCT-00
  Supplier number      : 65313


  Invoice    Invoice
  Date       Number             Description            Discount     Amount
  ---------  ------------------- ------------------------ --------  -----------
  31-AUG-00  IN40351                                                   763.00

                                                          Total:      763.00
```

FIGURE 7.8

Barcol's cash receipts have little actual cash in them in today's world of electronic and plastic payments.

Without keeping track of EFTs, credit card payments, and Interac payments, Barcol would have little idea of what its bank balances should be, because these three forms of customer payment are much more important for Barcol now than cash and cheques combined.

Barcol uses other kinds of documents also. It has more electronic transfers, for example, to pay all employees by direct deposit into their bank accounts. There are many kinds of documents used by various companies. Each company adapts documents to its own needs, especially to provide legal evidence and support accounting transactions records. You can count on two things about any company, government, sports club, or other organization: (1) it will have various documents to back up its accounting system, and (2) those documents will be suited to that organization and so might not be quite like any other organization's.

b. Books of Original Entry

Specialized paper or electronic journals are used to record routine repetitive transactions.

Based on source documents, accounting transactions are recorded. Because this is when the business event first is recorded by the accounting system, these basic transactional records are often called "books of original entry." These records specify the accounts to which transactions are to be debited or credited. Typically, transactions of a similar nature are grouped together and separate, specialized records are used to record frequent routine transactions. Some examples of specialized records are:

- A sales journal, listing all sales in sales invoice order;

- A cash receipts journal, listing payments received from customers (Barcol's collections lists are forms of this); and

- A cheque register or cash disbursement journal, recording all cheques issued, in cheque number order. Companies usually have separate cheque registers (and bank accounts) for major areas, such as payment of accounts payable, general payroll, executive payroll, and dividend payments. Records for cash disbursements using EFT or other automatic payment systems are generated automatically by the system.

The general journal is used for adjustments and less routine transactions.

Each company will also have a "general journal," used mainly to originate journal entries for transactions that are not provided for in specialized journals, and for accruals and adjustments of any kind. No adjustments are just written into the ledger accounts: all must originate with journal entries in the general journal. Journal entries, like the rest of accounting's records, must be organized and kept on hand for later reference, and they must be supported by documents or calculations of some kind so that they may be verified later (or even just plain understood after the original reasons for the entries have faded from people's memory).

c. Ledgers

Ledgers are books (or computer records) having a separate page or account code for each individual account referred to in the books of original entry. Each area or page contains a summary of all the transactions relating to that particular account and therefore "posted" to it. (Remember the set of accounts in page format illustrated in Section 2.5.)

The general ledger includes all the accounts behind the financial statements.

General ledger—the collection of all the asset, liability, equity, revenue, and expense accounts, summarizing the entire operations of the business. The general ledger is the central record of the financial accounting system and is the basis on which the balance sheet, retained earnings statement, and income statement are prepared. The ledger may be a "book" or it may be space on a computer disk. Many companies now keep their records on the computer and print out information only as they require it. As we saw in earlier chapters, a "trial balance" of all the general ledger accounts and their balances is prepared periodically (such as at the end of each month) in order to demonstrate that the ledger is in balance, that the sum of its debit-balance accounts equals the sum of its credit-balance accounts. (A listing of just the account names without balances, useful in designing or redesigning the accounting system and relating it to the financial statements' format, is called a "chart of accounts.")

Subsidiary ledgers list details backing up general accounts such as accounts receivable.

Specialized (or subsidiary) ledgers—accounts receivable and accounts payable ledgers are two examples of specialized ledgers. For instance, if a company extends credit to its customers, it may want to keep a separate ledger account for each customer. These ledgers are balanced by making sure that their accounts add up to the same amount as is shown in the relevant general ledger account (for example, the accounts receivable "control" account in the general ledger, which is the account used to prepare the financial statements, should have the same balance as the list of customers' individual accounts). A subsidiary ledger does not "balance" by having its debits equal its credits, but rather by having its sum equal the amount in the primary account in the general ledger. Making sure this is true is an important way of ensuring that individual customer accounts receivable, for example, are correct. Subsidiary ledgers, therefore, are part of the internal control system; their details are not in the financial statements, but they support the validity of the main "control" account that does appear in the financial statements. (More about control accounts is in section 7.7.)

d. Electronic Commerce

With the advent of sophisticated interconnected computer systems, especially via the Web, many business transactions are now being conducted entirely electronically. Electronic commerce (e-commerce) is quite a challenge to financial accounting, and to internal control, because its essence is the absence of the painstaking "paper trail" that has traditionally supported accounting records. Many people, not just accountants, think some sort of credible trail, even if not in paper, needs to be continued in some form, but how? Enterprises still need good records for all the reasons outlined at the beginning of this section, but clearly the form of those records is changing dramatically. These days, Barcol sees little cash and not as many cheques as it used to from customers, with most payments, even by other businesses, being made by credit card or electronically. It doesn't pay its own employees by cash or cheque, just depositing their pay directly into their personal bank accounts.

E-commerce has other interesting implications for accounting. One is that there needs to be some compatibility between computer systems if the accounting systems on both sides of a transaction are to recognize it properly, and some trust in the electronic media to make the system work. The Web is developing interfaces that provide the compatibility, and credibility mechanisms with names like "encryption" and "Web Trust" are beginning to appear. A second implication is that there can be a lot of "in-transit" activities, because physical transfers (shipments, deliveries, etc.) are usually slower than the electronic system. If you order a book from an on-line retailer, you, the retailer, and your credit card company will have all the electronic records completed long before the book shows up. The tendency of records to be speedier, and separated from the physical movements, means that in-transit items can be a challenge to control and reconcile.

A third implication for accounting is that the parties to e-commerce can be bound together quite closely, with the ability to make enquiries into each other's computer systems to find out order specifications, progress on production of goods, and other things to smooth the business relationship. This means that not only must the financial statements be right, but the underlying records must be good too, so that business partners' enquiries are answered reliably. Some external parties, like banks, tax authorities, or securities regulators, may want to go straight to the underlying records without waiting for financial statements. There's a bit of a paradox here: e-commerce both operates without paper *and* demands a good trail of evidence.

Financial reporting itself is going on-line and becoming continuous rather than waiting for ritual quarterly or annual reporting dates: numerous references to companies' Web pages have been made in this book, and many versions of on-line and even interactive financial reporting are being developed.[2] E-commerce and electronic financial reporting are likely to change accounting and financial reporting dramatically in future years. Maybe in the future, books like this will be on-line to match the on-line accounting they will then be describing!

Barcol's receipts and payments are becoming more and more electronic.

E-commerce binds companies together, in both accounting and their underlying records.

E-commerce and the Web are part of big changes coming in accounting and financial reporting.

HOW'S YOUR UNDERSTANDING?

Here are two questions you should be able to answer, based on what you have just read:

1. Why are good records and careful documentation important to an organization, with and without e-commerce?

2. What are each of the following documents and records for? Purchase order. Sales invoice. Cash receipts journal. Cash disbursements journal. General journal. General ledger. Accounts receivable subsidiary ledger.

7.3   INTERNAL CONTROL

Financial accounting has several important uses.

We have so far identified several different uses for financial accounting information, including:

a. Evaluation of management's performance, for the purpose of deciding whether to reward or punish managers;

b. Prediction of future performance, for the purpose of deciding whether to invest in or lend to the company (Chapter 10 will emphasize this);

c. Division of the company's returns (incomes) into portions for various parties: management bonuses, income taxes, dividends to owners, and so on; and

The rest of this chapter focuses on another important use:

d. Maintenance of internal control over assets and such day-to-day activities as making sales, collecting cash, and incurring expenses.

Accounting records are important for control as well as for preparing financial statements.

An appropriate recordkeeping system for any organization is one that can be used to keep track of resources, thus discouraging misappropriation of the organization's property or inefficient use of resources and helping management safeguard assets. Yet, it should not be overly cumbersome or bureaucratic. Records also help management meet its responsibility to run the enterprise effectively, and generally to control what is going on. Such internal control is not only a matter of recordkeeping: physical protection, insurance, and proper supervision of employees are also important to internal control. The Barcol Doors & Windows documents in section 7.2 were part of the company's internal control system; they were numbered and dated, and contained several details that could be used to follow up if problems arose.

This is a brief introduction to an interesting area of management responsibility that accountants and auditors consider part of their area of expertise. The *CICA Handbook* (paragraph 5200.05) provides the following definition for internal control:

Internal control comprises the plan of organization and all the co-ordinate systems established by the management of an enterprise to assist in achieving management's objective of ensuring, as far as practical, the orderly and efficient conduct of its business, including the safeguarding of assets, the reliability of accounting records and the timely preparation of reliable financial information.[3]

Main Components of Internal Control

As the *CICA Handbook* excerpt above points out, internal control is the responsibility of management. Here are some ways that management can establish proper control over the enterprise's affairs:

Control: Manage competently.

1. *Run the enterprise competently.* Looking after the enterprise's assets and making sure various activities, including recordkeeping, are done well is just part of being a good manager. A well-run enterprise has a climate of efficiency and records that crosscheck each other, as well as competent managers who are likely to realize quickly when something is going wrong. Having a good internal control system contributes to the profitability and efficiency that good managers seek.

Control: Have good records.

2. *Maintain effective records.* Having a comprehensive, connected set of records, as was illustrated for Barcol Doors & Windows, provides an early warning system and helps to motivate good performance by everyone, because the records provide routine monitoring and act as the basis for hourly pay, performance appraisals, bonuses, and other parts of the motivation system. Records also provide an audit trail of events that can be traced back to identify the causes of problems. An effective recordkeeping system goes well beyond accounting transactions (we saw the example of Barcol's purchase order system), but accounting records are likely to be at the heart of it. Many modern organizations have integrated their accounting and other records into a decision-oriented management information system that can be used to support a wide range of management decisions and evaluations.

Control: Use the records and learn from them.

3. *Use the records to act and learn.* It is an unfortunate fact of life in many organizations that many records seem to be maintained just for the sake of doing that. We all have chafed at bureaucratic form filling and having to prepare multiple copies of things for no apparent good reason. If management allows records to grow of their own accord, money is wasted, and perhaps equally important, people in the organization learn that the records don't matter, that mistakes and worse will not be acted upon or corrected. This can seriously undermine the control aspect of recordkeeping, and is likely to produce records that are useless for managers to learn from events, because the records either have too many errors or have become irrelevant to the organization's current needs.

Control: Segregate duties.

4. *Keep recordkeeping separate from asset handling.* An effective way of providing security over assets like cash, accounts receivable, and inventories is to have records showing how much of each asset is supposed to be on hand at any time. But if the person who handles assets (say, cash) also keeps the records, then errors or fraud can be hidden by altering the records. Accountants call separation of recordkeeping from handling assets "segregation of duties." One person collects the cash, and another person maintains the cash records. So if one or the other makes a mistake, a difference will arise between the count of cash on hand and what the record shows should be on hand. This difference then can be investigated and the cause corrected. Segregation of duties can also be used within the recordkeeping system: for example, one person can maintain the general ledger, with the total accounts receivable account, and another can maintain the accounts receivable subsidiary ledger, with the detailed list of customer accounts. It is hard for smaller enterprises with few employees to spread the jobs around enough to

segregate all the important tasks, but it should be done as much as is sensible. If segregation of duties doesn't exist, the boss needs to keep a close eye on important assets, such as cash and inventories.

Control: Treat employees well.

5. *Adequately pay and motivate employees.* A more positive side of internal control is to pay and reward people for their efforts on behalf of the enterprise, so that they try to do a good job and are not tempted to subvert recordkeeping and other control systems. Disgruntled employees may not care if things go wrong or may even take some pleasure when the enterprise suffers losses. As you can imagine, the control provided by segregation of duties is destroyed if the people involved "collude" (work together) to cover up errors or fraud, and while such actions can never be wholly prevented, their probability is reduced if people feel good about the enterprise and feel they are fairly treated.

Control: Carry insurance.

6. *Carry insurance on assets.* Like anything else, internal control has to be worth its cost. It is probably worth the cost to have a careful control system for the main part of the enterprise's activities (for example, buying and selling goods), but there will be some unusual circumstances that are not anticipated or for which setting up elaborate controls doesn't seem worthwhile. Some events, such as earthquakes or fires, may be entirely or mostly beyond management's control. So it makes sense to protect the owners' investment by carrying insurance for some events against which internal control systems cannot provide adequate protection. There is a side benefit of insurance: insurance companies tend to want to know a lot about how the enterprise is protecting and managing its assets, and satisfying the insurance company about this can result in improvements in controls.

Control: Physically protect assets.

7. *Physically protect sensitive assets.* This control method is rather obvious, but it's easy to overlook too. Sensitive assets, such as cash, inventories, and tools, should be behind lock and key, kept in particular storage areas, or otherwise protected from unauthorized or casual access. Many enterprises are sloppy about access to their inventories in particular, and sometimes protection is a good idea for assets you might not think of. For example, many manufacturers produce scrap as a byproduct, and the scrap can be very valuable. One Canadian manufacturer put its scrap in the backyard and found out later that thousands of dollars worth had been lifted over the back fence and sold on the scrap market.

Effective internal control is common-sense management.

There is much more to internal control. Designing effective control systems requires an understanding of management's objectives, a sensitivity to the cost–benefit balance needed between tight but costly controls and loose but cheap controls, knowledge of computer systems and other recordkeeping methods, and considerable insight into the subtleties of human motivation and behaviour. It also requires some common sense: complete protection is not possible, and tying the enterprise up in red tape in order to try to get complete protection is not what a good internal control system does.

HOW'S YOUR UNDERSTANDING?

Here are two questions you should be able to answer, based on what you have just read:

1. What should a good internal control system do?

2. What are some components of an internal control system?

7.4   TOP MANAGEMENT'S RESPONSIBILITY FOR INTERNAL CONTROL

Section 7.3 stated that management is responsible for internal control. Here is what top management of CAE Inc. said about their responsibility in the company's year 2000 annual report:

7-1

Exhibit

CAE Inc.

Management is responsible for the integrity and objectivity of the information contained in this annual report and for the consistency between the financial statements and other financial and operating data contained elsewhere in the report. The accompanying financial statements have been prepared by management in accordance with accounting principles generally accepted in Canada, using policies and procedures established by management, and reflect the Corporation's financial position, results of operations and cash flow.

Management has established and maintains a system of internal control which is designed to provide reasonable assurance that assets are safeguarded from loss or unauthorized use and that financial information is reliable and accurate. The Corporation also maintains an internal audit function that evaluates and formally reports to management and the Audit Committee on the adequacy and effectiveness of internal controls.

The financial statements have been examined by external auditors appointed by the shareholders. Their examination provides an independent view as to management's discharge of its responsibilities insofar as they relate to the fairness of reported operating results and financial condition. They obtain an understanding of the Corporation's accounting systems and procedures and conduct such tests and related procedures as they deem necessary to arrive at an opinion on the fairness of the financial statement.

Ultimate responsibility to the shareholders for the financial statements rests with the Board of Directors. An Audit Committee is appointed by the Board to review the financial statements in detail and to report to the Directors prior to such statements being approved for publication. The Audit Committee meets regularly with management, the internal auditors and the external auditors to discuss their evaluation of internal accounting controls, audit results and the quality of financial reporting. The external auditors have free access to the Audit Committee, without management's presence, to discuss the results of their audit.

D. H. Burney

D. H. Burney
President and
Chief Executive Officer

Paul G. Renaud

P. G. Renaud
Vice President, Finance,
Chief Financial Officer, and Secretary

Top management sets the internal control tone for the whole company.

CAE's top managers are taking responsibility for the whole financial reporting system in this statement, including internal control. Even the auditors' access to the Board of Directors, which is part of the board's control at the very top of the company, is mentioned. Control really means that top management knows what is going on around the company, knows what is going on inside the company, and manages the company well in whatever climate of change or turbulence management finds itself. At the best, this means prudent management at the top, setting the tone for the whole company and leading to informed and appropriate actions throughout.

Good internal control is just good management.

For most companies, this works pretty well. But there are many dramatic examples of what happens to companies whose management is not in control: banks fail because of over-lending to questionable borrowers—one big bank failed because a security trader was able to bet the bank's assets on a currency exchange and lost; sports stadiums and government buildings cost far more than expected because of loss of control over construction processes; big retail chains lose control over their buying and marketing and so lose their customer base; fast-food chains build more outlets than there are stomachs to fill; and many growing companies let their receivables and inventories get too large as they try to serve all possible customers. These are examples of bad management, not just bad control, because in essence, management and control are the same thing. As we turn now to specific control areas, the overriding role of top management in running the business properly should be kept in mind.

(H)OW'S YOUR UNDERSTANDING?

Here are two questions you should be able to answer, based on what you have just read:

1. Why is internal control a top management responsibility?

2. Where does CAE say the ultimate responsibility for the financial statements lies?

7.5 INTERNAL CONTROL OF CASH

Cash is the asset usually most susceptible to theft because of its liquid and generally anonymous nature.

A real case: Mike, a junior auditor in a northern town, was assigned to do a surprise count of the cash on hand at a local clothing store. The cash counted was short as compared to what was expected, based on the auditors' projections of cash from sales and bank deposit records. The store's accounting clerk accused Mike of stealing the cash himself while counting it, and so he had to call the police from the store and insist that they search him and so demonstrate that he had not stolen it. It turned out that the accounting clerk had been stealing cash and covering up the thefts by changing the sales records—a classic case of poor internal control through lack of segregation of duties, because the clerk had access to both the cash and the records of the cash. The theft was discovered only because Mike's surprise cash count referred to sales records that the clerk had not yet altered to cover up the shortage. The clerk was fired, and promised to make restitution, though it was difficult to tell how much had been taken because sales records had been altered for several years. The owner of the store was quite critical of the auditors for "not preventing the loss," but the auditors showed that they had indeed warned the owner, who had said that it would be too expensive to employ someone else to keep the sales records or control the cash.

The general principles in section 7.3 apply to the specific cash control situation.

For cash sales, one of the most common controls is to have locked-in sales registers or other carefully controlled records. Registers (such as those you would see at any supermarket) usually print a consecutive number on the locked-in tape for each transaction. The access key is kept by a single person, perhaps a supervisor, who balances cash to sale records. The proceeds that should have been received will be recorded on the tape. The person who keeps the key should count the cash with the cashier, compare it to the sales proceeds, and check that the tape numbers are consecutive from one person's shift to that of the next person. If this sort of system is to work, there has to be no collusion between the people controlling the cash and checking the records—often collusion is difficult to prevent, so having yet another person provide overall monitoring of the process is a good idea. And as we saw in the Barcol case, there are many forms of "cash" needing control attention besides currency and cheques, including "Interac" direct payments to the company, credit cards, and electronic funds transfers.

> A real case: A large company established a "petty cash" fund in its front office to be used to pay for small purchases, such as office supplies and courier charges. The receptionist was given a fund of $1,000 in cash, and when most of that was spent, submitted all the receipts in an envelope and was reimbursed for the cash spent to bring the petty cash fund back up to $1,000. The internal control therefore was that, at any time, the receptionist should have cash on hand plus receipts for payments totalling $1,000. What the company did not know was that the receptionist was involved with the delivery driver from the store from which the company got most of its office supplies, and nearly all invoices from that company paid through petty cash were inflated. The company paid far more than it should have for the supplies, but no one knew because the people who got the supplies did not see the invoices, which were kept by the receptionist as evidence of cash payouts. The people who reimbursed the receptionist had not seen the office supplies and so did not know the invoices were inflated. The thefts and the collusion between the receptionist and driver were discovered long after the two had moved to another city: someone noticed that office supplies costs were lower than they used to be! The company has no good idea of how much was stolen, but it probably exceeded $10,000 over the years.

Prenumbering documents is an example of a control technique that helps to catch errors.

Another way to control cash from sales is to have multi-copied, prenumbered sales invoices, as Barcol Doors & Windows has. The invoice copies are then removed by one person: for cash sales, the amounts are crosschecked to cash records, and for credit sales, the amounts are crosschecked to accounts receivable records. Any gaps in the invoices' numerical continuity are investigated. For this control to work, supervisors must ensure that an invoice is prepared for each sales transaction. An additional control is to regularly check inventory and compare it with the sales records. This should prevent, or at least detect, someone selling inventory and pocketing the cash.

Take, for example, the Mayfield Pro Shop, which accumulated $10,000 in sales at the end of a month according to the invoice copies in the locked box. If the inventory at the start of the month was worth $25,000 and at the end of the month was worth $14,000 (based on the retail price of the goods), the shop should have sold $11,000 worth of goods. The $1,000 difference could be due to one of the following:

1. Someone could have kept $1,000 worth of cash from sales and not written any invoices for those sales.
2. Someone could have shoplifted $1,000 worth of goods.
3. The inventory could be inaccurate, or other errors could have occurred.

Combining cash and inventory controls is useful for both assets.

Point 3 is a reminder that there are usually other reasons for shortfalls besides theft, but keeping track of cash and inventory together is one method of highlighting the possibilities and investigating them.

These examples of cash-control problems are presented to illustrate that accounting records are important beyond their use in preparing financial statements. The examples are not intended to suggest that employees or customers are crooks, but to show that management must be prudent in meeting its responsibility of good stewardship in taking care of the owners' assets. Part of that responsibility lies in not putting employees or others in such poorly controlled situations that they are tempted to steal, and paying people with responsibility for cash well enough that they do not start thinking of themselves as underpaid and therefore deserving of more money from the company!

A real case: An armoured truck company had developed a good business picking up cash from supermarkets and other stores and delivering it to banks. The company trusted its employees and had never had problems. Usually the trucks were staffed by two people, a driver and a second person who rode in the back. The two had to sign various forms and, in a sense, they kept an eye on each other so no one got tempted: there was often a million dollars or more in unmarked, untraceable cash in the truck. Sometimes, though, one of the two people was sick, or on vacation, or called away on some errand for the company, and there would be just one person to drive the truck and collect the money. On one day like that, there was a particularly large amount of money in the truck, and the driver, apparently on impulse, just took it and departed for foreign parts!

Before leaving the subject of cash control, a major additional control warrants mention. Cash on hand is important, but as we saw with Barcol, most of the company's cash is likely to be in, or going in and out of, its bank accounts. It is central to cash control to prepare a formal **bank reconciliation** frequently, at least monthly. This example of reconciliation was outlined in Chapter 1, section 1.9. Keeping close track of bank accounts is important not only to prevent (or at least catch) errors and fraud, but also to ensure that managers have accurate accounting information when they are making decisions. A company that is not sure how much cash it has in the bank is likely to be poorly managed, and because errors and other problems are always possible, regular bank reconciliation is essential.

Here are two questions you should be able to answer, based on what you have just read:

1. John is in charge of a $200 petty cash fund. When he counted his cash today, he had $45.95 on hand, and decided that he should replenish the fund. He therefore requested a cheque to "cash" from the company, submitting receipts in support of the request. What amount did he request, and what was the total of the receipts he included with his request? ($154.05 is the answer to both questions.)

2. The Mayfield Pro Shop began this month with cash of $1,200 and inventory (priced at retail) of $26,700. The shop had sales of $9,500 this month, received more inventory having a retail price of $7,800, and had $2,300 cash on hand at the end of the month. How much cash did the shop deposit this month and how much inventory, at retail prices, should there have been on hand at the end of the month? ($8,400, which = $1,200 + $9,500 − $2,300; $25,000, which = $26,700 + $7,800 − $9,500. You can see the integration of cash and inventory control because the $9,500 sales appear in both calculations.)

7.6   CONTROL OF SALES TAXES COLLECTED AND EMPLOYEE DEDUCTIONS TO BE REMITTED

Accrual accounting has been described so far as a method of going beyond cash flow to produce a more comprehensive measure of income and valuation of balance sheet accounts. But by going beyond cash, accrual accounting also creates records that are very important from an internal control point of view. Here are three general examples:

Accrual accounting provides very useful noncash control accounts.

- The journal entry "DR Accounts receivable, CR Revenue" recognizes revenue that has been earned but not yet collected in cash. While it does that, it also creates the accounts receivable account, which then becomes a record of what customers owe the enterprise. This account, which is often called the accounts receivable control account, is supported by a subsidiary ledger or list of what individual customers owe, and is a very important part of the control system. It should be difficult to forget about a customer or to forget to give a customer credit for paying, because the control account should reflect everything customers have promised to pay, minus everything they have paid, at any date.

- The journal entries (a) "DR Inventory, CR Accounts payable or Cash" and (b) "DR Cost of goods sold expense, CR Inventory" also produce a control account for inventories, telling us what should be on hand at any date. We saw a retail-priced example of this in the Mayfield Pro Shop in the previous section; more explanation about the use of the accounting records for inventory control will be given in section 7.8.

- The journal entry "DR Expense or Inventory, CR Accounts payable" produces a control account for accounts payable, showing what is owed to suppliers at any date.

This section examines a very important use of accounting records for keeping track of some important current liabilities other than the accounts payable in the last example above. This use is in keeping track of *money the enterprise owes on behalf of others*. Two examples that occur in practically every business and most other organizations as well are:

Collecting sales taxes creates a liability to the government(s).

a. Collecting sales taxes from customers on behalf of the government. The taxes are not the enterprise's money—it is acting as a tax collector on behalf of the government and so is required to turn it over to the government. When you buy something in a store and the store adds provincial sales tax (PST), the federal goods and services tax (GST), or the blended PST-GST combination used in some provinces (harmonized sales tax, or HST, which works essentially the same way as the GST, from an accounting viewpoint), this is your contribution to the government and the store is just a channel to get it from you to the government.

Making deductions from employees' pay creates liabilities to various outside parties.

b. Deducting income tax, pension contributions, union dues, medical insurance fees, and many other possible deductions from employees' pay. You've probably experienced these employee deductions: you think you have earned, say $250, but your paycheque is, say, only $180 because of all the deductions. Here again, the enterprise, the employer, is acting as a channel to get your income tax and other contributions to the government, the union, the medical insurer, or wherever it is to go.

Let's examine each of these examples, so you can see how the accounting records create control totals, and how each example incorporates its particular economic and legal circumstances.

Collecting Sales Taxes

The simplest example here is the collection of PST. When a sale, say $100, is made and, say, 6% PST is added, the following journal entry records the transaction:

```
DR Cash or Accounts receivable              106
    CR Revenue                                      100
    CR PST due (a current liability account)          6
```

Legally, the customer must pay $106, now or later, but only $100 is the seller's revenue. The $6 is owed to the government. You can see that the "PST due" account can be used to accumulate all the PST collected on all the applicable sales. When the PST due is paid to the government, the liability account is reduced:

```
DR PST due                                  xx
    CR Cash                                          xx
```

PST due account's balance shows whatever has been collected but not yet remitted.

At any date, the PST due account shows what has been collected but not yet remitted. It is therefore a control account for the seller's obligation to the government. It shows the way the seller has been a channel for the government's money, because it goes up when sales subject to PST are made, and down when the money is sent to the government.

GST (and HST) provide a more complicated example, because the seller is normally able to deduct any GST the seller pays on its own purchases and expenses from the amount to be sent on to the government. Therefore the GST due to the government is only the difference between GST collected and GST paid. Suppose we have the following: a $1,000 sale (having a COGS of $735), and a $400 purchase, both subject to 7% GST:

```
DR Cash or Accounts receivable              1,070
    CR Revenue                                      1,000
    CR GST due                                          70
DR Cost of goods sold expense                 735
    CR Inventory                                       735
DR Inventory                                  400
DR GST due                                     28
    CR Cash or Accounts payable                     428
```

Now the seller owes only $42 in net GST, as shown by the GST due control account. When it is remitted to the government, the GST due liability is debited and cash/bank is credited. (It is possible for the GST due account to be a debit (an asset) if the company makes particularly large purchases and has small sales in a given period, but this would be rare.) The inventory control account and COGS expense are maintained at the goods' cost without GST, because GST is controlled in a separate account.

GST due account's balance is the net of GST collected and paid, minus remittances.

The journal entries for PST and GST can be combined, to show the total tax in a province that has both taxes, and the HST's blended PST/GST. The point of the example is to show you how the accrual accounting system produces useful control accounts for the PST, GST, or whatever, due to the government. The control accounts can be as sophisticated as the tax law requires (many complications have been left out of these examples).

Deducting from Employees

Accounting has to keep track of deductions plus any fringe benefits.

Employee deductions have some complications that the accounting system has to handle. One is that each deduction normally has to be sent to a different place: for example, income tax deducted goes to the government, union dues deducted go to the union, United Way donations go to the United Way. A second complication is that the employer often has to pay "fringe benefits" in *addition* to the amount deducted from the employee. Pensions, Canada Pension, employment insurance, and many kinds of medical and other insurance are examples. Therefore, the wages the employee earns are not the only expense the employer incurs. The accounting system can handle these without difficulty, using control accounts for all.

Suppose an employee earns $1,100 and the following deductions are made: income tax $200, employment insurance $40, union dues $50, medical coverage $65. Therefore, the employee will receive only a net "take-home pay" of $745. In addition, the employer has to pay some fringe benefits: employment insurance $45, workers' compensation insurance $15, medical coverage $67. So, to the employer, the total cost of having the employee for the period is $1,100 plus benefits, or $1,227. Let's see how the accounting records would show all this (in the two entries below or one combined entry):

```
DR Wages expense                                          1,100
    CR Income tax deductions due liability                       200
    CR Employment insurance due liability                         40
    CR Union dues due liability                                   50
    CR Medical premiums due liability                            65
    CR Wages payable liability                                   745
DR Fringe benefits expense (or include in Wages expense)   127
    CR Employment insurance due liability                        45
    CR Workers' compensation insurance due liability             15
    CR Medical premiums due liability                            67
```

All the accounts credited in the example are control accounts for payments to be made.

The control accounts show how much is due to be remitted: $200 income tax, $85 employment insurance ($40 + $45), $50 union dues, $132 medical premiums ($65 + $67), and $15 workers' compensation insurance. As in the sales taxes examples, these control accounts' balances show how much has been deducted and/or due as fringe benefits owing by the employer, minus the amounts remitted to the appropriate bodies. It is the company's legal responsibility to remit these to the outside parties involved. The wages payable account is also a control account, showing how much is to be paid to the employee. Its balance is therefore the sum of the net take-home pays the employees have earned, minus amounts paid to the employees.

OW'S YOUR UNDERSTANDING?

Here are two questions you should be able to answer, based on what you have just read:

1. Last month, Apex Retailing had cash sales of $18,000 and collected PST of $1,080 and GST of $1,260 on those sales. In addition, Apex paid GST of $680 on its own cash purchases of $9,700. How would the sales and purchases be recorded, and how much PST and GST were owing for the month? (DR Cash 20,340, CR Revenue 18,000, CR PST due 1,080, CR GST due 1,260. DR Inventory 9,700, DR GST due 680, CR Cash 10,380. PST due = $1,080; GST due = $580.)

2. In the same month, Apex employees earned wages of $9,000, from which various deductions totalling $2,200 were made. Apex was responsible for fringe benefits of $2,400 on these wages. What were: the total expense of having the employees for the month, the employees' take-home pay, and the total remittances due for the month? ($11,400; $6,800; $4,600)

7.7   CONTROL ACCOUNTS AND CONTRA ACCOUNTS

Just about every balance sheet account can be considered to be a control account. Cash is a record of the cash that should be there if counted. Accounts receivable is the sum of all the individual customers' accounts. Inventory is the amount that should be found if the company lists or counts all the unsold goods physically on hand. GST due is the net amount of GST collected on all sales minus GST paid on all purchases and any remittances to the government. The number of shares outstanding should be traceable to the share capital account. (The particular owners may change, due, for example, to trading on the stock market, but the company should always know how many shares it has issued and what it originally received for them.) Even the property, plant, and equipment asset accounts are controls, as all the assets whose costs are included should be physically present.

The value of all these balance sheet accounts as control accounts is that the amounts in them should be supported by or reconcilable to detailed lists or subsidiary ledgers, or some such background data. What do we do, then, when we want to make a change in a balance sheet account without changing the underlying records and lists? Here are some examples of when we might want to change the balance sheet account and why at the same time we might be reluctant to do it:

- There has been an overall decline in the market value of the inventory, so for conservatism we want to reduce the inventory asset account on the balance sheet but do not want to change the inventory control account because it should correspond to the sum of the costs of all the goods on hand.

- We have become worried that we might not collect all the accounts receivable, so for conservatism and proper income measurement, we want to recognize that we have probably suffered some "bad debts" expense, but do not want to change the accounts receivable control account because it should correspond to the list of all customers' accounts and we are not yet giving up on collecting any so the control feature is still useful.

- The property and plant assets are being used up economically, so we want to record amortization expense as part of our income measurement, but we do not want to change the asset cost account balances because their costs are not changing, but rather their economic values are being used.

Can financial statement adjustments be made without interfering with internal control?

In all these examples, the financial statement objectives of proper balance sheet valuation and income measurement seem to conflict with maintaining the accounts for control purposes.

What to do? Well, accrual accounting is very flexible. A perhaps peculiar kind of account called a contra account has been invented to allow us to recognize expenses and value changes without changing the control account. It is useful both for income measurement and to preserve the internal control aspects of the accounts, and so bridges between accounting's role in internal control and in financial statement preparation.

Contra accounts solve the apparent conflict between financial statements and control.

Contra accounts have balances that are in the *opposite direction* to that of the control account with which they are associated: for example, contra asset accounts have credit balances that are "contra" the assets' debit balances. They are used for managing accruals, usually for expenses, separately from the asset, liability, or equity accounts to which they relate, and therefore they keep the accruals from being mixed into those accounts. *Contra accounts only have meaning in conjunction with the control accounts to which they are matched.* We'll see below how this works.

Contra accounts are used to avoid making expense adjustments to control accounts.

Here we will focus only on the two most common uses of contra accounts: accumulating amortization (depreciation) and allowing for doubtful accounts receivable. Virtually all enterprises have both. These accounts illustrate how the accounting system can meet one objective (expense recognition) and *avoid* compromising another objective (control) by creating accounts that recognize expenses but do not change the control accounts related to those expenses (asset costs and accounts receivable).

Accumulated Amortization (Depreciation)

Amortization is a general word that includes depreciation.

The accumulated amortization contra accounts are used to accumulate amortization on fixed assets, such as buildings and equipment. The terminology is changing here: until recently, such amortization was called "depreciation" and the word "amortization" was used for intangible assets, such as goodwill, leasehold improvements, and patents. Many companies still use the word depreciation, and call the contra account "accumulated depreciation."

In the case of amortization, a contra account is created when the periodic expense for using the asset is recognized. For example, the annual amortization charge of $100,000 on a building would be recognized this way:

DR Amortization expense	100,000	
CR Accumulated amortization		100,000

The amortization expense entry's credit is to the contra account, not the asset account.

The debit is an expense account in the income statement. The credit is a contra asset account. The credit side of the journal entry could have been to the asset account "Building." Instead the contra account is used, so that by leaving the asset cost account alone, the balance sheet presents the acquisition cost of the asset along with the accumulated amount of expense that has previously been recognized. Showing both of these items allows users to make a rough guess as to how long the asset has been in service. It also allows the asset cost account to be a control account supported by a list of the assets owned and their costs, which can be checked periodically by making sure that all the assets owned are indeed still on hand.

The accumulated amortization contra is the sum of amortization expenses over time.

Remember that accumulated amortization on the balance sheet is the *amount of amortization accumulated over the life of the asset to date*, whereas the amount of amortization charged *this year* (to match the revenues the asset consumption is presumed to have helped generate) can be determined from the amortization expense account in the income statement and added back to income on the cash flow statement.

Let's look at a simple example involving the dog pound's purchase of a new truck to catch strays. If the truck cost $50,000 and an annual amortization expense of $8,000 was determined, the annual journal entry to recognize amortization would be:

DR Amortization expense	8,000	
CR Accumulated amortization		8,000

Net book value is the cost minus the contra accumulated amortization.

On the balance sheet, the asset account for the truck's cost would continue to show a balance of $50,000, but each year the accumulated amortization contra asset account would increase by $8,000. Deducting accumulated amortization from the long-term asset account leaves a figure known as the net book value. So, we would have:

	Cost	Accumulated Amortization Contra	Net Book Value
Date of purchase	$50,000	$ 0	$50,000
End of first year	50,000	8,000	42,000
End of second year	50,000	16,000	34,000

In a disposal, both the asset cost and its accumulated amortization are removed.

If the truck were sold at any time, the cost would be removed from the ledger, but so would the contra account. The contra is meaningful only in comparison to the cost, and when the truck is gone neither account is needed any more. Suppose the truck was sold for $37,000 at the end of the second year. Then we would have the following entry:

DR Cash (the proceeds)	37,000	
CR Truck asset (*removing the cost*)		50,000
DR Truck accumulated amortization (*removing the contra*)	16,000	
CR Gain on sale of truck (on the income statement)		3,000

The gain on sale is just the difference between the proceeds and the net book value at the date of sale, as was explained in section 4.5, cash flow analysis.

A gain or loss on sale is the difference between proceeds and net book value.

- If the proceeds had been $29,000 instead, the debit to cash would have been $29,000, and there would have been a $5,000 debit to loss on sale (perhaps included with an account such as "other expenses" in the income statement). The loss is the difference between the $29,000 proceeds and the $34,000 net book value.

A write-off can be thought of as a disposal without proceeds.

- Let's suppose that at the end of the second year the truck was used to pick up a particularly ornery bunch of dogs, and they turned out to have a highly contagious disease. The truck had to be junked, and the insurance company refused to pay anything because such a risk was not contemplated when the insurance was written. Now we have what accountants call a "write-off": a disposal without proceeds. The journal entry would still credit cost for $50,000 and debit the contra for $16,000, and there would now be a $34,000 debit to a loss on disposal or write-off account (probably still included in a line such as "other expenses" on the income statement, unless it was considered material (significant) enough to warrant being shown separately). The whole net book value is said to have been written off.

Gains, losses, and write-offs are all just variations on the same theme:

▸ Proceeds greater than 0 and greater than net book value: Gain on sale.

▸ Proceeds greater than 0 and equal to net book value: No gain or loss.

▸ Proceeds greater than 0 and less than net book value: Loss on sale.

▸ Proceeds equal 0 and so less than net book value: Write-off.

Accumulated amortization for intangible assets may be deducted from the asset cost.

When **intangible assets** (noncurrent, nonphysical assets, such as goodwill, patents, franchise rights, and capitalized costs such as development costs or incorporation costs) are amortized, the accumulated amortization is often just deducted from the asset cost on the balance sheet, not shown separately (or disclosed in a footnote) as it is for physical assets' accumulated amortization. If there is not seen to be an internal control reason for keeping the cost and accumulated amortization accounts separate, the amortization entry may just debit expense and credit the asset account. If there are internal control reasons (keeping track of asset costs), there may well be an accumulated amortization account in the ledger, which is deducted from the asset cost account when the balance sheet is being prepared. Gains, losses, and write-offs on such assets are calculated the same as for the physical assets.

Enterprises may have hundreds of ledger accounts, kept separate for internal control purposes, which are aggregated into the relatively few figures on the balance sheet. Accumulated amortization is a contra account that is typically kept separate in the ledger and disclosed on the balance sheet. We now turn to an example account that is typically kept separate in the ledger but *not* disclosed on the balance sheet.

Doubtful Accounts Receivable

Now, let's look at the other most common use of contra accounts, the allowance for doubtful accounts. When a company sells to a customer on account, there will always be some risk that the customer will fail to pay. Therefore, a portion of the

The credit side of the bad debts expense entry is to the allowance contra account.

sales on account will be doubtful, and that portion should be deducted from revenue on the income statement in the period of sale to match the bad debts expense (resulting from the probable failure to collect) to the revenue recognized that period. Let's assume that a company determines, by past experience or current evidence of customers' troubles, that about $500 of sales on account will likely not be paid. The journal entry to recognize the expense is:

DR Bad debts expense   500
    CR Allowance for doubtful accounts   500

Having an allowance contra account leaves the accounts receivable control account alone.

The credit in this entry is again to a contra asset account, just as it was for amortization. (That account was in the noncurrent assets section of the balance sheet, while this one is in the current assets section.) The reason for not deducting the amount directly from the accounts receivable asset is to maintain the asset account as a control: even after the usual collection time has passed, the company may still try to collect on the accounts and therefore doesn't want to alter the accounts receivable amount. The list of individual accounts should have the same total as that of the accounts receivable account for control reasons, and so the account should not be changed just because collection is doubtful.

The expense and contra are created when collection is doubtful, while there is still hope.

We might say that when the bad debts expense and the allowance account are created, this is the "worry stage": there is doubt about collectibility of some accounts, and that doubt is recorded as an expense because it is thought that some economic value has been lost, but the company has not yet given up on trying to collect all the accounts.

The allowance and the bad debts expense are seldom disclosed in the financial statements.

The main difference between this situation and that of amortization is that only the net amount of the accounts receivable less the allowance for doubtful accounts is usually disclosed on the balance sheet. This contra account is deemed to be less useful for readers of the balance sheet than the accumulated amortization contra account, and perhaps more sensitive if disclosed. Also, the income statement always discloses the amortization expense but seldom discloses the bad debts expense, which is just included with other expenses somewhere.

At the write-off point, doubt about collection has been replaced by lack of hope.

Eventually, after pursuing a nonpaying customer for months, a company may decide to *write the account off*, to give up keeping the account in the list of customer accounts and the accounts receivable control account. The hope of collecting is now being abandoned, and it is thought not necessary to keep the receivable in the list of accounts whose collection is being pursued and whose total equals the balance in the accounts receivable control account.

Another journal entry is needed because the expense recognition entry above did not touch the accounts receivable control account, and now we *do* want to change that account. Suppose the bad account in question equals $100 (it was one of the risky ones contemplated when the allowance was created above), then the write-off entry is:

DR Allowance for doubtful accounts   100
    CR Accounts receivable   100

Writing off a bad debt reduced the receivable and the allowance without affecting income.

This entry eliminates the account from the books of the company completely, but you'll notice that it does not affect expenses (or, therefore, income): that effect was created when the allowance and expense were recorded earlier. The power to write off an account is usually quite tightly controlled and great care is taken to keep track of payments received. The reason should be fairly obvious: if you write an account off it is no longer on the books anywhere, and then, if the deadbeat customer pays, the person who receives the money could simply keep it and no one else in the company would know.

You'll note that this write-off is handled differently from the noncurrent asset write-offs described above. The reason is that the allowance for doubtful accounts is considered to apply to the whole list of accounts receivable, in aggregate. We don't necessarily know *which* specific accounts receivable were allowed for: for example, the $500 allowance for doubtful accounts was probably based on an average experience, such as that, say, 15% of accounts over 40 days old will not be collected. We don't need to know exactly which accounts are doubtful in order to make such an allowance for the aggregate risk being taken. There was a contra accumulated amortization for each building or truck, but there is no particular contra for each account receivable, so both the account receivable asset and an equal amount of the allowance for doubtful accounts contra are just eliminated in the above bad debt write-off. It's like assuming that the written-off receivable had been 100% allowed for.

Bad debt write-offs can throw the system off if they are large enough. For example, in the above case, what if a customer account for $800 had to be written off? That's more than there is in the allowance! There are methods for adjusting the allowance to take such problems into account, but this book will not include them beyond a brief comment in the Jellyroll Sweets example at the end of this section.

It is possible to operate the accounting without an allowance for doubtful accounts. As has been mentioned briefly in earlier chapters, bad accounts can be written off directly to accounts receivable, by the so-called direct write-off method. This is used when a company has few accounts receivable or when a large account not contemplated in the allowance suddenly goes bad. Suppose an account totalling $1,500 is to be written off directly. Then the entry would be:

DR Bad debts expense	1,500	
CR Accounts receivable		1,500

This is equivalent to allowing for it first and then writing it off, using the "worry stage" and "write-off" entries shown earlier:

DR Bad debts expense	1,500	
CR Allowance for doubtful accounts		1,500
DR Allowance for doubtful accounts	1,500	
CR Accounts receivable		1,500

As this example shows, the allowance can be seen as a temporary holding account for amounts the company worries about, to be cancelled out if the account is ever written off. But during the holding period, an expense has been recognized and the asset value on the balance sheet has been reduced. Using an allowance is thought usually preferable to direct write-off, not only because of the internal control advantages the contra account provides, but also because the allowance provides for a way to have an expense *before* the company gives up on collection, and so is generally more conservative in its effects on the balance sheet and income statement.

Here is a final example of the use and effect of an allowance for doubtful accounts contra.

• Jellyroll Sweets Inc. sells confections to retail stores. At the end of 2000, it had accounts receivable of $53,000 and an allowance for doubtful accounts of $3,100. *Therefore, the estimated collectible amount of the accounts receivable was $49,900 at the end of 2000.*

At the end of the year, write-offs and necessary further allowance are determined.

- During 2001, the company had credit sales of $432,800 and collected $417,400 from customers. Therefore, at the end of 2001, the accounts receivable stood at $68,400 ($53,000 + $432,800 − $417,400).

- At that point, the sales manager went through the list of accounts receivable and determined that accounts totalling $1,200 were hopeless and should be written off, and furthermore that an aggregate allowance at the end of 2001 of $4,200 was required.

Here are journal entries to accomplish what is needed.
   Write off the bad ones:

DR Allowance for doubtful accounts	1,200	
CR Accounts receivable		1,200

Allow for the doubtful ones:

DR Bad debts expense	2,300	
CR Allowance for doubtful accounts		2,300

(Balance in allowance = $3,100 − $1,200 = $1,900
Allowance needed at the end of 2001   = $4,200

Additional allowance = $4,200 − $1,900 = $2,300)

Year-end adjustments take into account any prior allowances and write-offs.

The allowance and write-off entries could be done in the other order, but in this case, the sales manager was thinking of really old receivables, from last year, to write off, and newer ones to allow for. The order of entries does not matter as long as the final balances are adjusted to be the same, so the calculation for the allowance entry takes into account any preceding or planned write-off. If the entries were done in the opposite order, the calculation of the allowance entry would start with $3,100 and subtract that from ($4,200 + $1,200 = $5,400) to provide for the planned write-off. The entry would still be for $2,300 more bad debts expense and then the write-off would reduce the allowance from $5,400 to the desired $4,200.

No matter what order the entries were made in, the accounts receivable balance is now $67,200 ($68,400 − $1,200) and the contra balance is $4,200.

- Therefore, the estimated collectible value of the accounts receivable (the net balance sheet value) is $63,000 at the end of 2001 ($67,200 − $4,200).

- Bad debts expense for 2001 is $2,300.

A write-off against the allowance has no effect on the net receivable amount in the balance sheet.

- The write-off of the hopeless ones cleaned them out of the list of receivables, but did not affect either income or the net balance sheet value. You can see this by redoing the calculation of the allowance and expense entry with no write-off of the hopeless ones:

  ▶ If none had been written off, the allowance balance would still be the $3,100 from last year.

  ▶ But now the allowance needed would be $4,200 for the doubtful ones and $1,200 for the hopeless ones (still in the receivables), totalling $5,400.

  ▶ Subtracting the $3,100 from that total leaves $2,300, so the second journal entry and therefore the bad debts expense would be the same.

▸ Now the accounts receivable would be $68,400, and the allowance would be $5,400. So, the estimated collectible amount of the accounts receivable (the net balance sheet value) would still be $63,000.

(H)OW'S YOUR UNDERSTANDING?

Here are two questions you should be able to answer, based on what you have just read:

1. Argyll had a building that cost $438,000. At the beginning of the year, the accumulated amortization on the building was $233,000. The building was sold for $190,000 late in the year, after a further amortization expense of $34,000 was recorded. What were the journal entries to record (1) the amortization expense and (2) the disposal? ((1) DR Amortization expense 34,000, CR Accumulated amortization 34,000. (2) DR Cash (proceeds) 190,000, CR Building cost 438,000, DR Accumulated amortization 267,000, CR Gain on sale 19,000. The gain on sale is the proceeds of $190,000 minus the book value of $171,000 ($438,000 − $267,000).)

2. Argyll also has accounts receivable. At the end of the year, the total in the accounts receivable control account is $321,000 and the balance in the allowance for doubtful accounts is $22,000 (after recording bad debts expense for the year of $11,000). Upon examination of the accounts, management decides that $5,000 of the accounts is hopeless and should be written off, and that the allowance should be increased by $7,000 after that. What are bad debts expense for the year, accounts receivable control account balance at the end of the year, allowance for doubtful accounts at the end of the year, and estimated collectible amount at the end of the year? ($18,000; $316,000; $24,000; $292,000)

7.8   INVENTORY CONTROL

This chapter has emphasized the importance of keeping records to provide information to both internal and external users. Many of the records kept have to do with the control of inventory. Inventory control is an important issue for management because a high percentage of working capital may be tied up in inventory. Inventory may be perishable or become obsolete if held too long, and, due to the physical attributes of some types of inventory, there may be a great potential for theft.

Inventory control is separate from reporting inventory in the financial statements.

Several different inventory control systems may be used, depending on the nature of the inventory and the objectives of management. The methods explained below are the three most commonly used by businesses. Each provides a different amount of information at a different cost. It is important to note that the choice of inventory control system is a recordkeeping choice as opposed to a reporting choice: management is simply deciding how to record the inventory. How inventory is reported in the financial statements will be dealt with in Chapter 8.

The Perpetual Accounting Control Method

When an order of inventory items is received, the quantity received is added to the quantity recorded as being already on hand. When items are sold, they are deducted from the recorded quantity. Therefore, the perpetual method shows how many items are supposed to be on hand at any time:

- Take the quantity on hand at the beginning of the period.

- Add the quantity purchased during the period.

- Deduct the quantity sold during the period.

- Equals the quantity that should be on hand at the end of the period.

The perpetual control method's records show how much inventory should be on hand.

The name perpetual inventory control comes from the idea that the accounting system has a continuously updated figure for the amount that should be on hand. If a physical count of the inventory fails to show that quantity, the company knows that something has been lost or stolen, or that there has been an error in the records. Just as for cash, bank accounts, accounts receivable, and GST due, the records provide accounting control in addition to any physical protection. The accounting records tell the company what to expect to be on hand.

If the cost of items is included in the count along with the quantity, the perpetual record can be used to estimate the total cost of inventory at any time, without having to bother counting and pricing everything.

> **Beginning inventory cost (support with physical count if desired)**
> **+ Cost of purchases of inventory (records)**
> **− Cost of inventory sold (records)**
> **= Ending inventory cost (support with physical count if desired)**

In the perpetual method, COGS is known and is removed from inventory when there is a sale.

The perpetual control method has been assumed in most of the examples so far in the text, because purchases have been recorded as debits to inventory asset and cost of goods sold has been credited to the asset and debited to COGS expense.

The perpetual method provides additional management information. Suppose that after the above calculation, the expected ending inventory cost was $100,000, but a count to support that showed only $96,500 of inventory on hand. Management would know there had been a $3,500 shortage or other error, and could intensify controls over inventory if that was thought to be cost-effective. If it cost $10,000 to improve the controls, management might well conclude that losing $3,500 was the cheaper option. The inventory asset account would be adjusted to the count by an adjusting entry to CR Inventory $3,500 and DR Inventory shortage expense. The accounts would then show the expense being incurred by the imperfect controls. (If there were *more* inventory on hand than expected, there could instead be an inventory overage account, a credit balance so a sort of negative expense, though this would probably indicate an error somewhere as it is unlikely any thieves were breaking in and adding inventory!) The overage/shortage expense account would probably be included with COGS in the income statement, as management would usually consider this information to be an internal matter, and it would not likely, we hope, be large enough to be material in its effect on COGS.

The Retail Accounting Control Method

This is like the perpetual method, except that records are based on selling prices of goods rather than just quantities or costs. In the retail inventory control method, a department or branch is charged with the total selling value (sales price times quantity) of all items for sale delivered to it. Revenue from sales is then deducted from this total value as the items are sold. This ties inventory control to cash control, as in the Mayfield Pro Shop example in section 7.5. At any point in time, the department or branch should have inventory, plus cash from sales made since the last revenue report, plus records of sales on credit or via credit cards, equal to the current total retail value:

- Start with the retail price of all goods received by the department (on hand at the beginning of the period plus received during the period).

- Deduct the department's sales (connected to cash, cheque, electronic funds transfer, and credit card control procedures).

- Difference equals inventory that should be on hand, priced at retail.

The retail method is like the perpetual method, but using selling prices instead of costs.

If a physical count, with items priced at retail, fails to show the expected total retail value, the company knows that some items have been lost or stolen, or that there has been an error in the records. An adjustment for the shortage or overage can be made in the same way as for the perpetual method. Total cost of the inventory can be estimated at any time by deducting the average markup from the current total retail value. The retail method is, however, a little complicated in practice because of the need to keep track of markdowns, returned goods, special sale prices, and other price adjustments if the method is to work accurately.

The Periodic Count Method

When goods are bought, they are put on the shelf or in the storeroom, and when they are sold or used, they are taken off the shelf or out of the storeroom. With the above two control systems, records are kept of these movements, to provide expected quantities or values on hand. But if complete records of such inventory changes are not kept, the enterprise does not have records to indicate what should be on hand. The only way to tell what is on hand is to go and count it. Because this sort of counting tends to be done only periodically, when an inventory figure is needed for financial statements or insurance purposes, this *lack* of accounting control is called the "periodic inventory" method. While there may be other features of internal control present, such as physical protection and insurance, it lacks the parallel recordkeeping that gives the above two methods their value. There is no way to reconcile counts to records in order to discover errors as in the other two methods because records created for this purpose do not exist, but it is simple and cheap to operate because no continuing records are kept. Recordkeeping does cost money!

The periodic count method lacks records to show how much inventory should be on hand.

The periodic system works this way:

Beginning inventory (count), priced usually at cost
(or retail minus markup)
+ Purchases (records) at cost
– Ending inventory (count), priced at cost
= Cost of inventory sold (deduced)

In the periodic count method, COGS is deduced: inventory not on hand is assumed sold.

The cost of inventory apparently sold is *deduced* (rather than known from records). It might not all have been actually sold. Some could have been lost, stolen, evaporated, etc. So under the periodic method, cost of goods sold expense (cost of counted beginning inventory + cost of purchases – cost of counted ending inventory) includes all these other possibilities. They cannot be separated because the necessary records were not kept. This is not a flaw, it is just that management did not believe the extra recordkeeping was worth the money it would cost. The adjustment to a separate account for inventory shortage or overage, shown for the perpetual method above, cannot be made, because the deduced COGS includes the "real" COGS plus/minus any shortage/overage.

Cost and Benefit of Controls

The greater the value of inventory control, the more likely the perpetual method is used.

The perpetual method can be costly in terms of recordkeeping. (So can the similar retail method, though probably sales records have to be kept anyway, so the extra cost of the inventory control may not be large.) Management must pay someone to record, sort, and compile the information. What type of business uses a perpetual system? The local car dealership is a good example of one. Cars are expensive—therefore a large investment must be made if a good supply is to be on hand for customers to choose from. The high value of cars and the need to keep track for licence and insurance purposes means that serial numbers and other identification information is easily available and usually recorded in various places. Automobiles have a high risk of becoming obsolete because consumer preferences change, and the cost of theft is high even if only one car is stolen. Because of the relatively small quantity of cars sold by most dealerships, recordkeeping costs are not high.

Perpetual records should be reconciled with physical counts: the more valuable the items, the more frequent the reconciliation.

Whenever an accounting control system is used, there must be regular reconciliation between the accounting records and any other evidence available. The idea of reconciliation as a useful technique was introduced in section 1.9 and the value of bank reconciliation in particular was pointed out in section 7.5. There is no real value to accounting control unless the resulting records are compared to other evidence, such as physical counts for inventories. But valuable though reconciliation is, it does cost time and money to do. Most businesses reconcile sensitive items, such as bank accounts, cash on hand, and high-value inventories, very frequently, but leave other items, such as building assets and low-value inventories, to less frequent reconciliations, often based on just a sample of items.

Inventory Control Journal Entries: Bransworth Ltd.

Bransworth Ltd. uses a perpetual accounting control system for its inventory. It has the following data for a recent period:

Beginning accounts receivable	$ 40,000	Beginning inventory	$ 23,000
Purchases during period (all cash)	114,000	Sales (all credit)	150,000
Cash collected in period	115,000	Ending inventory count	28,000

The company's markup is 50% on cost (that is, selling price is 150% of cost, so the company can calculate COGS from sales revenue). Just to make it easier, we'll assume all sales, purchases, and collections were in single transactions. Here are summary journal entries for the company's system:

7-2

Exhibit

a. Purchases	DR Inventory asset	114,000	
	CR Cash		114,000
	Purchases during the period.		
b. Sales	DR Accounts receivable	150,000	
	CR Sales revenue		150,000
	Sales on credit during the period.		
c. Cost of goods sold	DR Cost of goods sold expense	100,000	
	CR Inventory asset		100,000
	COGS expense: $150,000 revenue minus 50% markup on cost.		
d. Count adjustment	DR Inventory shortage expense	9,000	
	CR Inventory asset		9,000
	Shortage: record indicates inventory should be $23,000 + $114,000 − $100,000 = $37,000, but only $28,000 is on hand.		
e. Collections	DR Cash	115,000	
	CR Accounts receivable		115,000
	Customer collections during the period.		

Let's review two accounts here, to ensure you see how the accounting figures help with the control:

7-3

Exhibit

The inventory account:	Beginning cost balance	$ 23,000
	Purchases	114,000
	Cost of goods sold	(100,000)
	Expected balance on hand	37,000
	Adjustment for loss*	(9,000)
	Revised ending cost balance	$ 28,000

*Because the count showed less than expected on hand.

7-4

Exhibit

The accounts receivable account:	Beginning	$ 40,000
	Sales	150,000
	Collections	(115,000)
	Ending balance	$ 75,000

There is accounts receivable control here. The company can check with the customers or otherwise verify that this amount really is a collectible asset. Cash control follows from this, too. The collections figure from the accounts receivable account is part of the deposits to cash, so it becomes part of the record-based control system for cash.

For comparison, let's see how the entries above would change if Bransworth used the periodic system, *without* accounting control. Using the same journal entry references as above, we'd have:

a. Purchases   DR Purchases expense
                      (or similar account name)   114,000
                  CR Cash   114,000

b. Sales   Same entry as for perpetual
                 method

c. COGS   No entry: the company does
                 not record COGS when sales
                 are made

d. Count adjustment   DR Beginning inventory expense   23,000
                          CR Inventory asset   23,000
                      Transferring beginning inventory
                        to expense.
                      DR Inventory asset   28,000
                          CR Ending inventory "expense"   28,000
                      Recording ending inventory by
                        removing its cost from expense
                        (that is, from Purchases +
                        Beginning inventory).

e. Collections   Same entry as for perpetual method

The cost of goods sold must be deduced, as the net sum of the three expense accounts above: Beginning inventory $23,000 + Purchases $114,000 − Ending inventory $28,000 = COGS $109,000. This is the same as the perpetual method's total of COGS $100,000 + Shortage expense $9,000. So there is no effect on the net income of choosing between the two control methods, because each contains an adjustment to the actual amount counted at the end of the year. There is no effect on the balance sheet either, because both adjusted to the same $28,000 ending amount. The differences between the methods are in their control and management information.

HOW'S YOUR UNDERSTANDING?

Here are two questions you should be able to answer, based on what you have just read:

1. What is the role of recordkeeping in internal control?

2. Granot Inc. uses the perpetual inventory method. At the beginning of the month, inventory costing $145,890 was on hand. Purchases for the month totalled $267,540 and cost of goods recorded as sold totalled $258,310. At the end of the month, a count showed inventory costing $152,730 to be on hand. What, if anything, was the inventory shortage for the month? ($2,390)

7.9   A PROCEDURAL REVIEW

By this time, you should be "thinking double-entry": aware that when one account is affected, another must be too. This is fundamental to accrual accounting, and to internal control provided by the double-entry accounting records. Consider the following examples:

7-5

Exhibit

a. *Revenue cycle*

    Recognition: DR Accounts receivable
                              CR Revenue

    Collection: DR Cash
                              CR Accounts receivable

b. *Doubtful account cycle*

    Allowance: DR Bad debts expense
                              CR Allowance for doubtful accounts

    Write-off: DR Allowance for doubtful accounts
                              CR Accounts receivable

c. *Purchases cycle (perpetual method)*

    Purchase: DR Inventory
                              CR Accounts payable

    Payment: DR Accounts payable
                              CR Cash

    Recognition: DR Cost of goods sold expense
                              CR Inventory

d. *Capitalization/amortization/disposal cycle*

    Acquisition: DR Noncurrent asset
                              CR Cash or liability account

    or Capitalization: DR Noncurrent asset
                              CR Expense

    Amortization with a contra account:
                              DR Amortization expense
                              CR Accumulated amortization contra

    or Amortization without a contra account:
                              DR Amortization expense
                              CR Noncurrent asset account

    Disposal: DR Cash (proceeds)
                              CR Noncurrent asset (cost)
                              DR Accumulated amortization contra
                              CR Gain or DR loss on sale

    Write-down or write-off   CR Noncurrent asset (cost)
                              DR Accumulated amortization
                              DR Write-down or write-off loss

HOW'S YOUR UNDERSTANDING?

Here are two questions you should be able to answer, based on what you have just read:

1. The term "write-off" is used with reference to both long-term assets and accounts receivable. What does the term mean in those cases and how does it differ between the two?

2. Flimsy's accounts receivable at the end of 2001 totalled $78,490. The allowance for doubtful accounts had been $2,310, but it was decided that this would be increased by $1,560 and then that $1,100 in hopeless accounts would be written off. What were the net collectible value of the receivables as shown on the balance sheet at the end of 2001 and the bad debts expense for 2001? ($74,620; $1,560)

7.10 TERMS TO BE SURE YOU UNDERSTAND

Here is this chapter's list of terms introduced or emphasized. Make sure you know what they mean *in accounting*, and if any are unclear to you, check the chapter again or refer to the Glossary of Terms at the back of the book.

Accounting control
Accumulated amortization
Allowance for doubtful accounts
Amortization
Amortization expense
Bad debts expense
Bank reconciliation
Books of original entry
Capitalized costs
Cash disbursements journal
Cash receipts journal
Chart of accounts
Cheque
COGS expense
Contra account
Control account
Direct write-off
E-commerce
EFT
Electronic commerce
Electronic funds transfer
Employee deductions
General journal
General ledger

GST
HST
Intangible assets
Internal control
Management information system
Net book value
Packing slip
Periodic inventory method
Perpetual inventory control
Petty cash
PST
Purchase order
Reconciliation
Retail inventory control
Sales invoice
Sales journal
Sales taxes
Segregation of duties
Source documents
Specialized ledgers
Subsidiary ledgers
Work order
Write-off (bad debts)
Write-off (noncurrent assets)

7.11 CONTINUING DEMONSTRATION CASE

INSTALLMENT 7

Data for Installment 7

After recording the transactions to February 28, 2001, in Installment 6, the trial balance of Mato Inc.'s general ledger was (credits are bracketed):

Cash	6,418	Share capital	(125,000)
Accounts receivable	13,709	Revenue	(227,656)
Inventory	33,612	Cost of goods sold expense	138,767
Automobile	10,000	Salary — Mavis	0
Accumulated amortization — auto.	(1,000)	Salary — Tomas	0
Leasehold improvements	63,964	Salary — other	0
Accumulated amortization — leasehold	(6,396)	Salaries expense	67,480
Equipment and furniture	32,390	Travel expense	10,102
Accumulated amortization — equipment	(744)	Phone expense	4,014
Computer	14,900	Rent expense	24,000
Accumulated amortization — computer	(1,490)	Utilities expense	3,585
Software	4,800	Office and general expense	5,933
Accumulated amortization — software	(480)	Interest expense	6,239
Incorporation cost	1,100	Inventory shortage expense	441
Bank loan	(47,500)	Amortization expense — auto.	1,000
Accounts payable	(36,656)	Amortization expense — leasehold	6,396
Deductions payable	(2,284)	Amortization expense — equipment	744
Salaries payable	(2,358)	Amortization expense — computer	1,490
Loan payable	0	Amortization expense — software	480

It was time to prepare the financial statements for the year ended February 28, 2001. Before that could be done, the following adjustments had to be made:

a. Based on the amortization calculations made during the first six months, the amounts for the second six months would be:
   • Car, leasehold improvements, computer, and software: 1/2 year × 20% of cost.
   • Equipment and furniture: 1/2 year × 10% of cost.
   The expenses for the second six months would therefore be: car, $1,000; leasehold improvements, $6,396; computer, $1,490; software, $480; equipment and furniture, $1,620.

b. Estimated unpaid bank loan interest to February 28 was $230.

c. Unfortunately, some of the boutique customers had run into financial difficulty. One customer who owed $894 had gone bankrupt and other accounts totalling $1,542 were doubtful.

d. Tomas had been getting some accounting assistance from a local public accountant. No bill had yet been received for this help, but Tomas estimated that the company owed about $280 at the end of February.

e. It turned out that included in the revenue figure was a deposit of $500 made by a customer on a special order from Africa that had not yet arrived.

f. Included in the office and general expenses was an insurance policy costing $1,050, good for two years from March 1, 2000.

g. Mavis and Tomas decided that they should pay the company back about $200 for Mavis and $425 for Tomas for personal use of the company automobile. Automobile expenses were included in the travel expense account.

h. Mavis was concerned that the accounts receivable list "didn't look right," as she put it. Upon checking, she discovered that shipments totalling $2,231 in revenue had been made in late January and early February, but had not yet been billed. The cost of the goods shipped had been correctly removed from the inventory account and charged to cost of goods sold.

i. Tomas decided that the sales taxes due to the government, which had been included in accounts payable, should be put in a separate account. The amount due at February 28 was $1,843. Beginning March 1, this account would be used for all GST and PST collected and remitted.

Results for Installment 7

Adjusting journal entries at February 28, 2001, to take the above information into account:

a. Amortization expense — auto.	1,000	
Accumulated amortization — auto.		1,000
Amortization expense — leasehold	6,396	
Accumulated amortization — leasehold		6,396
Amortization expense — computer	1,490	
Accumulated amortization — computer		1,490
Amortization expense — software	480	
Accumulated amortization — software		480
Amortization expense — equipment and furniture	1,620	
Accumulated amortization — equipment and furniture		1,620
b. Interest expense	230	
Accounts payable		230
c. Bad debts expense	2,436	
Allowance for doubtful accounts		2,436
($894 + $1,542 = $2,436)		
Allowance for doubtful accounts	894	
Accounts receivable		894
d. Office and general expenses	280	
Accounts payable		280
e. Revenue	500	
Customer deposits liability		500

(continued)

f. Prepaid insurance	525	
Office and general expense		525
($1,050 over two years = $525 per year)		
g. Accounts receivable	625	
Travel expense		625
($200 + $425 = $625)		
h. Accounts receivable	2,231	
Revenue		2,231
i. Accounts payable	1,843	
Sales taxes due		1,843

After posting the adjusting journal entries to the trial balance given at the beginning of this installment, the following adjusted February 28, 2001, account balances were produced (credits are bracketed as usual):

Cash	6,418		Customer deposits liability	(500)
Accounts receivable	15,671		Share capital	(125,000)
Allowance for doubtful			Revenue	(229,387)
accounts	(1,542)		Cost of goods sold expense	138,767
Inventory	33,612		Bad debts expense	2,436
Prepaid insurance	525		Salary — Mavis	0
Automobile	10,000		Salary — Tomas	0
Accumulated amortization			Salary — other	0
— auto.	(2,000)		Salaries expense	67,480
Leasehold improvements	63,964		Travel expense	9,477
Accumulated amortization			Phone expense	4,014
— leasehold	(12,792)		Rent expense	24,000
Equipment and furniture	32,390		Utilities expense	3,585
Accumulated amortization			Office and general expense	5,688
— equipment	(2,364)		Interest expense	6,469
Computer	14,900		Inventory shortage expense	441
Accumulated amortization			Amortization expense — auto.	2,000
— computer	(2,980)		Amortization expense	
Software	4,800		— leasehold	12,792
Accumulated amortization			Amortization expense	
— software	(960)		— equipment	2,364
Incorporation cost	1,100		Amortization expense	
Bank loan	(47,500)		— computer	2,980
Accounts payable	(35,323)		Amortization expense	
Sales taxes due	(1,843)		— software	960
Deductions payable	(2,284)			(71,434)
Salaries payable	(2,358)			
Loan payable	0			
	71,434			

That's enough for now! We'll do some more work with these balances, including preparing financial statements, in later installments.

7.12 HOMEWORK AND DISCUSSION TO DEVELOP UNDERSTANDING

PROBLEM 7.1*
Explain components of internal control

Ingram Inc. has the following features in its internal control system. Explain why each is a useful component of the company's controls:

a. One person looks after the accounts receivable records and another person is in charge of receiving and depositing cash.
b. The receptionist has a petty cash fund.
c. The company uses the retail inventory method.
d. The company keeps its inventory in a locked warehouse.
e. Each month, the bookkeeper reconciles the balances in the liability accounts for various employee deductions to payroll and payment records.

PROBLEM 7.2*
Answer questions about doubtful accounts receivable

Dragon Designs Ltd. had the following general ledger accounts for last year, using the T-account format. All the company's sales are on credit, to retail stores across the country. The first amount in each account is the balance at the beginning of the year; the last amount, under the solid line, is the balance at the end of the year. Other amounts are transactions and adjustments during the year.

Accounts Receivable		Allow. for Doubt. Accts.		Bad Debts Expense	
244,620			11,914	0	
1,693,784					
	1,599,005				
			9,117	9,117	
	8,293	8,293			
331,106			12,738	9,117	

Answer these questions:

1. What was the company's revenue for the year?
2. How much was collected on account of revenue for the year?
3. How much of the uncollected revenue did the company give up on during the year?
4. What was the expense the company incurred from taking the risk of extending credit to customers during the year?
5. On average, how much did the company lose on each dollar of sales? (Answer this two ways: by looking at the bad debts expense, and at the bad debts written off. What are the values of each way from management's point of view?)
6. What was the estimated collectible value of the accounts receivable at the end of the year?
7. What was the estimated collectible value of the accounts receivable *prior* to the year-end write-off of uncollectible accounts?

PROBLEM 7.3*
Explain accounting terms in plain English

Your aunt, a prominent businessperson, learns you are studying accounting and, one evening, asks you to explain the following terms to her. Your aunt is smart and successful and, maybe for that reason, is impatient with jargon, so she wants the answers to be short, to the point, and in jargon-free English.

    a. Adjustments
    b. Contra accounts
    c. Internal control
    d. Control accounts
    e. Books of original entry
    f. Write-off of uncollectible accounts
    g. Accounting control

PROBLEM 7.4*
Answer questions about factory assets and amortization

Aaron Manufacturing Inc. had the following general ledger accounts for last year, using the T-account format. The first amount in each account is the balance at the beginning of the year; the last amount, under the solid line, is the balance at the end of the year. Other amounts are transactions and adjustments during the year.

Factory Assets		Accumulated Amortization		Amortization Expense	
5,497,888			1,977,321	0	
1,032,568					
	843,992	411,883			
			793,220	793,220	
	89,245	59,200			
5,597,219			2,299,458	793,220	

Answer these questions:

1. What was the portion of the factory assets estimated to have been consumed economically in earning revenue during the year?
2. How much was spent acquiring additional factory assets during the year?
3. The assets that cost $843,992 brought $350,000 in proceeds. Did their sale result in a gain or a loss on disposal? Write the journal entry that would have recorded the sale.
4. The assets that cost $89,245 were retired and written off, bringing no proceeds. Write the journal entry that would have recorded the write-off.
5. What was the net book value of the factory assets at the end of the year?

PROBLEM 7.5*
Record sales taxes and employee deductions

Montane Tours Inc. provides guiding services in high alpine areas and operates Mountain Crest souvenir shops in some resort towns. Two groups of transactions the company recently had are described below. The payments indicated were for the amounts due before the transactions, because such remittances follow the transactions creating the amounts due.

    a. The company earned sales revenue of $72,000, on which it charged PST of $4,320 and GST of $5,040. Customers paid $69,030 of the total during the month, and the company expected to collect the rest within 60 days. The company paid the provincial government $3,900 on account of PST and the federal government $3,100 on account of GST. GST paid was lower because the company incurred $1,840 GST on its own $26,286 purchases.

b. Employees earned $39,250 in wages, from which the company deducted income tax of $11,180 and other deductions of $4,990. The company incurred fringe benefit costs of $6,315 on those wages. During the month, the company remitted $12,668 to the government on account of income taxes and remitted $11,894 to various government bodies, pension trustees, and other organizations on account of other deductions and fringe benefits.

Record the transactions described.

PROBLEM 7.6*
Describe accounting's documents and books of original entry

The financial statements are prepared from account balances from the general ledger. Behind these balances, however, are numerous documents and books of original entry. Describe the main kinds of documents used to support financial accounting and the books of original entry that are prepared from those documents.

PROBLEM 7.7*
Periodic and perpetual inventory control calculations

You are the senior accountant for a shoe wholesaler that uses the periodic inventory method. You have determined the following information from your company's records, which you assume are correct:

a. Inventory of $246,720 was on hand at the start of the year.
b. Purchases for the year totalled $1,690,000. Of this, $1,412,000 was purchased on account; that is, accounts payable were credited for this amount at the time of the purchase.
c. The ending balance in accounts payable was $47,500 higher than the opening balance.
d. A year-end inventory count revealed inventory of $324,800.

1. Calculate cost of goods sold according to the periodic inventory method.
2. Assume now that your company uses the perpetual method of inventory control, and that your records show that $1,548,325 of inventory (at cost) was sold during the year. What is the adjustment needed to correct the records, given the inventory count in item (d) above? What might the need for this adjustment indicate about company operations?
3. If the perpetual method generally provides more control over inventory for management, why don't all companies use it?

PROBLEM 7.8*
Match terms to descriptions

Match each term on the left with the most appropriate phrase on the right.

1. Allowance for doubtful accounts
2. Intangible assets
3. Chart of accounts
4. Periodic inventory method

5. Segregation of duties
6. Bad debt write-off
7. Source documents
8. Books of original entry

9. Control account

10. Retail inventory method

a. Says what should be there
b. Not a control method
c. Look them up to verify
d. Provides an expense without changing the asset
e. Based on selling prices
f. Don't let anyone do too much
g. Trial balance with no numbers
h. A contra account is not usually used for these
i. The basis for amounts posted to ledgers
j. Doesn't change the financial statements

PROBLEM 7.9*
Identify violated components of internal control

In each of the following cases, what component of good internal control is being violated (if any)? (See section 7.3 if you can't remember the components.)

a. Tough Inc. pays all its employees minimum wages and does not have pleasant working conditions.
b. Fred is a very conscientious employee and does such a good job that he does pretty much all of Whisp Ltd.'s office tasks.
c. Garand Inc. has a sophisticated internal control system that prints out various reports on discrepancies, which company management gets the accounting clerks to investigate and resolve.
d. John runs a small warehousing business. He's proud of saving money on accounting. For example, he doesn't keep track of purchases and shipments of goods because he can "look at the shelves and see if everything is all right."
e. Wildwood Restaurant is proud of its "family approach" to its employees, taking great care to make them feel important and trusted. Everyone has a key to the restaurant and several employees can often be found there in off hours, helping to clean and prepare for the next day.
f. Hadlee Corp's founder, getting on in years, has turned the president's job over to his playboy son, who is quite interested in horse racing and turns up at the office only occasionally.

PROBLEM 7.10*
Calculate income effects of various phenomena

Calculate any effect on income of each of the following independent cases.

a. A building cost $250,000. Accumulated amortization on it was $240,000. Building sold for $28,000.
b. An account receivable was $7,800. There was an allowance of $5,000 on it. Collection abandoned.
c. Goodwill cost $800,000, amortized down to book value $350,000. Remainder written off.
d. Inventory control account showed $2,850,000. Inventory count showed $2,698,000.

e. A machine cost $37,000. Accumulated amortization on it was $29,000. Machine written off.

f. Inventory purchased for $180,000 on credit. GST of 7% added on.

g. Building cost $250,000. Accumulated amortization on it was $240,000. Sold for $6,000.

h. Development expenses total $700,000. Half of these were capitalized.

i. Employees earned $110,000 plus $19,000 fringe benefits. Deductions from employees were $34,000.

j. An account receivable was $14,000. Payment of $12,000 received by electronic funds transfer.

PROBLEM 7.11* **Write journal entries to adjust accounts**	Write a journal entry, if any is needed, to adjust the accounts for each of the following independent items. State any assumptions you find necessary.

a. The allowance for doubtful accounts was $2,800 too low.

b. Amortization of $7,200 was needed on a truck.

c. GST of $420 was paid on the purchase of inventory and debited to the Inventory asset account.

d. Employee tax deductions of $39,650 were remitted to the government and debited to Wages expense.

e. It was decided to give up trying to collect an old account receivable of $235.

f. A machine with a cost of $72,600 and book value of $19,700 was sold for $14,200.

g. Upon comparing the inventory count to the perpetual records, a shortage of $4,620 was discovered.

h. An employee stole $35,000 cash that customers had paid on their accounts receivable. Insurance will cover $10,000 of the loss.

i. A storage shed that cost $89,000 and had accumulated amortization of $63,000 blew over in a storm and had to be scrapped.

j. Accounts receivable were studied and it was determined that the net collectible value was $787,000. The accounts receivable control account showed $813,000 and the allowance stood at $26,000.

PROBLEM 7.12* **Outline how internal controls mutually reinforce each other**	Outline how, in accounting for routine purchase and sale transactions, double-entry accounting can provide control accounts for cash, accounts receivable, inventories, accounts payable, and GST that interrelate and mutually reinforce each other.

PROBLEM 7.13 **Explain the value of recordkeeping to a businessperson**	At a recent Student Accounting Club wine and cheese party, local business people mixed with students. One small business entrepreneur was heard to say, "All that financial accounting information you students learn about is not relevant to me. I just started up my business. I only have five employees: four people in the shop building the product and one person in shipping/receiving. I'm out on calls, drumming up business, so I have my finger on the real pulse of the firm—that's sales. My brother pays the bills and does up the payroll every two weeks. Once in a while I write cheques too. It's all simple and smooth, so why add a lot of

time-consuming, costly recordkeeping to it all? All those books and financial statements are fine for the big public companies. I can do without the complications." Prepare an appropriate response to the businessperson.

PROBLEM 7.14
Necessary source documents and purpose of trial balance

1. Make a list of the source documents you expect would be needed to back up the transactional records in an accounting system and describe in ten words or so why each document would be useful.
2. Why does the bookkeeper (or the computer system) produce a trial balance of the general ledger regularly?

PROBLEM 7.15
Recordkeeping differences in large versus small businesses

Identify some differences you might expect to find between the transaction filters and accounting books and records of a large corporation and those of a corner store run by one person. What effects might those differences have on the company's accounting policies?

PROBLEM 7.16
Evaluate statements about accounting and recordkeeping

State whether or not you agree with each of the statements below and, in a few words, tell why.

   a. GST due is not a real liability of the company because it is just the government's money.
   b. Internal control is the responsibility of the accountants in an organization.
   c. If an event satisfies all four of the transaction criteria, you can be sure it will be recorded by the entity's accounting system.
   d. E-commerce transactions between the company and its customers are not accounting transactions in the company's records because no cash is ever involved.
   e. The perpetual method of accounting for inventory provides better internal control than the periodic method.
   f. A properly designed system of internal control over cash should prevent employee theft of cash.

PROBLEM 7.17
Explain nature and purpose of internal control to a manager

A friend, Janet, has accepted a job as president of a local company. During a meeting you attended, an accountant mentioned to Janet that she would be responsible for internal control of the company. When the accountant left the room, Janet turned to you and asked, "What is internal control, and why should I care about it?" Answer Janet's question, using clear language without technical jargon.

PROBLEM 7.18
Accounting documentation in e-commerce

Big electronic bookseller Orinoco.com operates only on the Web. It takes orders and collects payments via credit card numbers supplied by customers on its high-security Web page. Orders are transmitted automatically to book warehouser Hardback Inc., which ships the books to the customers and receives payment from Orinoco.com electronically as each book is shipped. Orinoco.com makes its money by charging just a little more to customers' credit cards than Hardback Inc.'s charges to it.

   One day, you go to Orinoco.com's Web page, order the new thriller *Tuesday's Girl*, type in your credit card number, and your book arrives in the mail less than a week later. Outline the source documents and "books of original entry" that this e-commerce transaction would probably generate for all four parties involved: you, Orinoco.com, Hardback Inc., and your credit card company.

PROBLEM 7.19
Top management responsibility for internal control

The proud owner of Beedle Inc., a successful high-tech company, is very good at hiring and motivating excellent people to develop and sell products. Delegation is the key, says the owner: "Hire good people and get out of their way!" As part of this philosophy, the owner hired the best accountants available and turned over to them all accounting, control, and finance functions. The owner concentrates on strategy and business planning, and the company has grown steadily for several years.

Explain to the owner what top management responsibilities are being neglected here. Given that the company is so successful, does such neglect really matter?

PROBLEM 7.20
Identify missing features of internal control

Read the following description of a sports club and indicate what features of good internal control seem to be missing. Are any of those offset by strength in other features?

The club earns revenue from members' fees, and from selling tickets to its games and advertising in its programs. Advertising receipts are mainly by cheque; other receipts are primarily cash, with an increasing percentage by credit card. Most expenditures are in cash, except for equipment, facility rentals, and the three employees' pay, all done by cheques. One employee does some coaching, schedules games, and coordinates players and officials. The second employee (who is married to the first) looks after equipment, prepares rental facilities for games, makes travel arrangements, and does various miscellaneous jobs. The third employee looks after cash, payroll, and accounting. The club's board of directors meets monthly and always has monthly (or annual) financial reports to scrutinize. All three employees are members of the board and other board members rely on them.

The club has a rented office/storeroom, where all employees work most of the time and where all the club's equipment and various supplies are stored. Cash, cheques, and credit card slips are deposited into the bank every two weeks, and payment cheques are issued as needed. Cash expenses are paid out of cash collected from members' fees and ticket sales, so often there is not enough cash to bother depositing. Sometimes there is not enough cash to pay cash expenses, in which case the third employee, who is authorized to sign all cheques, just writes a cheque to "cash" and cashes it at the nearby bank where the club's bank account is maintained. The board of directors discusses all major trips, equipment purchases, and other large expenditures in advance, and gives general approvals (or denials) to the employees to then look after the details.

PROBLEM 7.21
Calculate financial statement effects of various events

For each item below, give the dollar amount and direction of the effects on current assets, noncurrrent assets, and net income (ignoring income tax).

a. A Ltd. writes off $2,500 of previously allowed-for accounts receivable.

b. B Ltd., which has a perpetual inventory system, counts its year-end inventory and determines its cost to be $739,600. The inventory control account has a balance of $746,400.

c. C Ltd. sells for $179,000 cash a building that cost $690,000 and has accumulated amortization of $438,000.

d. D Ltd. is surprised by the bankruptcy of a major customer and has to record a direct accounts receivable write-off of $149,000.

e. E Ltd. writes off an old building that cost $420,000 and has accumulated amortization of $420,000.

f. F Ltd. discovers a fraud by an employee. The loss is $58,000 in cash, $30,000 of which will be covered by the company's insurance.

g. G Ltd. buys a shipment of inventory, paying $60,000 cash plus 7% GST. The company has considerable GST due, collected on its own sales.

PROBLEM 7.22
Answer questions about control topics

Answer the following questions briefly in nontechnical language.

1. Why is an accumulated amortization contra account standard practice for physical noncurrent assets but not for intangible noncurrent assets?

2. Why is using an allowance for doubtful accounts considered preferable to just writing bad debts directly off to expense?

3. Since the perpetual inventory approach provides better internal control than the periodic method, what are the advantages of the periodic method that prompts many companies, especially smaller ones, to use it for all their inventories and even large companies to use it for supplies inventories?

4. Why does the purchase of goods for resale result in the reduction of GST liability?

5. The chief accountant for a company that has a lot of short-term investments suggests setting up a contra account for market value declines in such investments. Such a contra account, which some companies use, has not been mentioned in the chapter: using the chapter's content, give some likely reasons why it would be proposed.

PROBLEM 7.23
Calculate bad debt allowance and expense

Windhook Technologies Ltd. has been having difficulty collecting its accounts receivable. For the year 2001, the company made provisions for bad debts of $43,000, bringing the balance in the allowance for doubtful accounts to $71,000. At the end of 2001, accounts receivable equalled $415,000. When the year-end audit was being done, it was decided that a further $54,000 of accounts receivable were doubtful and that $36,000 of accounts receivable previously deemed doubtful should be written off altogether.

Calculate the following:

a. Bad debts expense for 2001.

b. Allowance for doubtful accounts at the end of 2001.

c. Estimated collectible value of accounts receivable at the end of 2001.

PROBLEM 7.24
Calculations for perpetual versus period inventory

Razzmatazz Ltd. uses a perpetual inventory control system. The following data are available:

Inventory on hand at beginning of year (100,000 units at $5 cost each)	$ 500,000
Purchases for the year (850,000 units at $5 cost each)	$4,250,000
Sales for the year (865,000 units at $11 price each)	$9,515,000
Inventory on hand at end of the year (70,000 units at $5 cost each)	$ 350,000

1. Calculate the cost of goods sold expense for the year, based on the company's perpetual inventory system.
2. If the company had been using the periodic inventory method, what would the cost of goods sold expense for the year have been?
3. A perpetual system costs money to operate. Is it likely to be worthwhile for Razzmatazz?

PROBLEM 7.25
Do calculations and journal entries regarding doubtful accounts receivable

Note: Parts 1 and 2 of this question can be done independently.

A company has the following list of accounts receivable and notes by the credit manager about each.

Mr. A	$700	"slow but will pay"
Ms. B	250	"a new account—no worries"
Ms. C	650	"better allow for half"
Mr. D	420	"skipped town—we'll never see our money"
Mr. E	910	"has disputed $120 of this for more than a year"
Ms. F	175	"pays promptly"
Mr. G	520	"looks like we'll get all but $100"
Mr. H	790	"our best customer"

The company's allowance for doubtful accounts stands at $240 before considering any of the above information, and is unchanged from last year.

1. Calculate:
   a. The balance in the accounts receivable control account before any adjustments.
   b. The required doubtful accounts allowance before any write-offs.
   c. Bad debts expense for this year.
   d. Amount of any bad debts written off this year.
   e. Net collectible value of accounts receivable.

2. Write journal entries to adjust the accounts for the information given prior to Part 1.

PROBLEM 7.26
Answer questions about contra accounts and write-offs

A partial list of Boomber Inc.'s asset and income statement accounts is below.

Accounts receivable control account	$6,479,322
Allowance for doubtful accounts	87,233
Investment in Magnifico Manufacturing Inc. (cost)	1,200,000
Equipment and furniture (cost)	7,999,356
Accumulated amortization on equipment and furniture	2,865,401
Bad debts expense	43,297
Amortization expense on equipment and furniture	788,554

1. What did it cost Boomber this year to extend credit to customers who are unlikely to pay?
2. What did it cost Boomber this year to use equipment and furniture in its revenue-generating business activities?
3. What is the (a) net collectible value of the accounts receivable and (b) net book value of the equipment and furniture?
4. After seeing the above figures, Boomber's chief accountant decided that $53,522 of worthless accounts receivable should be written off. What effect would doing this have on: (a) accounts receivable, (b) allowance for doubtful accounts, (c) bad debts expense, and (d) net collectible value of accounts receivable?
5. The chief accountant also decided that some of the furniture had no use in the business any more and should be written off. No proceeds were expected on selling the furniture; instead, it would be donated to a local charity. The furniture had cost $42,500 and had accumulated amortization of $39,200. What effect would this decision have on (a) the cost of equipment and furniture, (b) accumulated amortization on equipment and furniture, (c) net book value of equipment and furniture, and (d) income for the year?
6. The chief accountant, while she was at it, suggested that 80% of the investment in Magnifico be written off. Magnifico was in serious financial trouble and it looked as if Boomber would be unable to sell it for much more than 20% of cost. What effect would this decision have on (a) total assets of Boomber, and (b) income for the year?

PROBLEM 7.27
Answer questions about sales taxes and employee deductions

A partial list of Impromptu Entertainments Ltd.'s accounts is below.

Sales taxes payable	$2,330
Employee tax deductions due	3,640
Other employee deductions and fringe benefits due	2,880
Wages payable	9,450
Revenue	243,530
Wages expense	120,360
Fringe benefits expense	31,420

1. The company has no expense account for sales taxes, though it does have expense accounts for corporate income tax and property taxes on its building. Why is that?

2. The company also has no expense account for employees' income taxes, even though it has to pay such taxes to the government. Why is that?

3. Over a period of time, will the amounts debited to wages expense equal the amounts credited to wages payable? Why or why not?

4. After the above balances were determined, the company made a sale of $10,000 and charged 7% GST and 8% PST on that sale. Which of the above accounts were affected by the sale, in what direction(s), and by how much?

5. Also after the above balances were determined, the company paid its accountant $1,000, on which it paid GST of 7%. Which of the above accounts were affected by the payment, in what direction(s), and by how much?

6. The company accountant wanted to write cheques to the provincial and federal governments for all PST and GST due. Taking into account items 4 and 5, how much would the cheques total?

7. Again, after the above balances were determined, some employees turned in extra time sheets, showing they had overtime totalling $575. The company incurred $120 in holiday pay, pension contributions, and other fringe benefits to this, and deducted $140 in income tax and $93 in other deductions. Which of the above accounts were affected by all this, in what direction(s), and by how much?

PROBLEM 7.28
Calculations and entries for various control account transactions

Parts 2 and 3 may be done independently of Part 1, and vice versa.

You have the following information for Blue Mountain Products Inc.:

- Balances beginning of year: Cash $238,500; Accounts receivable $611,820; Inventory $703,110; Prepaid expenses $87,670; Accounts payable $419,740; GST due $31,130.

- Transactions for the year: Sales on credit $3,914,160 plus GST $273,990; Collections $4,409,940; Purchases (all on credit) $2,004,140 plus GST $140,290; Payments to suppliers $2,102,680; GST remitted $141,700.

- The company's selling prices are determined by adding 100% to its cost for products.

- All the prepaid expenses were consumed during the year, and a further $14,220 were incurred but unpaid by the end of the year.

- The company operates a perpetual inventory system. At the end of the year, the inventory count showed inventory costing $737,280 to be on hand.

1. Based just on the above data, calculate the year-end balance in:
   a. Cash control account
   b. Accounts receivable control account
   c. Inventory control account
   d. Prepaid expenses
   e. Accounts payable control account
   f. GST due control account

2. Write journal entries to record all the transactions and other relevant information.

3. Assume the company used the periodic inventory method instead. Identify which entries from Part 2 are different and write the periodic method entries.

PROBLEM 7.29
Write entries to
adjust accounts for
various items

Write a journal entry, if any is needed, to adjust the accounts for each of the following independent items.

  a. $23,500 amortization of goodwill is needed.
  b. The development costs assets stands at $190,000, before considering $360,000 more spent this year and charged to expense. It is decided to capitalize half of this year's expense and then amortize the resulting asset evenly over five years.
  c. A truck with a book value of $34,750 and accumulated amortization of $66,600 is sold for $40,000, to be paid by the purchaser in 30 days.
  d. A building that cost $800,000 and has accumulated amortization of $250,000 has increased in value on the real estate market, going up from $600,000 last year to $675,000.
  e. Another building, costing $200,000 and having accumulated amortization of $20,000, is sold for $210,000 cash.
  f. An employee stole inventory costing the company $18,000 and hid the theft by altering the company's perpetual inventory record. Caught red-handed, the employee has promised to repay the company within 60 days if no legal action is taken by the company. The company agrees.
  g. Fringe benefits costing $87,920 are paid to various outside parties and the total is debited to Wages expense.
  h. GST of $18,210 added on to purchases by suppliers is deducted from the $52,790 GST added to sales by the company, and the net $34,580 is remitted to the government.
  i. Land costing $236,640 that has become swampy and unusable is written off.
  j. A large customer that the company was worried about went bankrupt. The $68,200 account receivable had been half allowed-for already because the company had believed it would collect half. Now the bankruptcy trustee advises that creditors of the bankrupt company will receive only 10% of the amounts owing.

PROBLEM 7.30
(CHALLENGING)
Discuss some issues
in contra accounts
and sales taxes

1. Most companies net the contra account for accounts receivable (allowance for doubtful accounts) against the accounts receivable balance in their balance sheet and so show only the net collectible value of the receivables. On the other hand, it is standard practice under GAAP to report the contra account for factory assets (accumulated amortization) separately on the balance sheet, or in a note, so that the reader can see the cost of the assets, the amortization accumulated, and the net book value of the assets. The contra accounts for other noncurrent assets, such as amortization on patents or goodwill, are usually not disclosed, so the reader of the financial statements can see only the net book value, much as for accounts receivable. Do these differences strike you as awkward, or unnecessary? Can you make a case for either disclosing all contra accounts or none of them?

2. It is usual to argue that since sales taxes, such as PST and GST, are collected on behalf of the government with no discretion by the company collecting them, they are not expenses of the company. The company is acting as a tax collector and just transferring the money from customers to governments. But the customers likely consider the sales taxes to be part of the cost of buying the goods or services, and if the company reduces the price of what it sells,

the customers are glad to see the taxes go down too. In fact, if the company didn't even charge the tax explicitly but just sent a portion of its revenue in to the government as the tax (such as in a "no GST sale" where the customer pays say $10.00, the company's revenue is only 100/107 of that, or $9.35, and the tax is 7% of $9.35, or $0.65), the customers would be even happier. Can you make a case for such sales taxes being considered as expenses of the company, which would be shown on the income statement?

PROBLEM 7.31 (CHALLENGING) Identify cash control problems

Many companies put a great amount of effort into controlling their cash, both that on hand and in banks, often more than for any other asset.

1. Why do you think such great effort is required to control cash?
2. List the control problems you'd expect in each of the following cases. To answer, try to visualize how the cash would probably flow into and out of the company and its bank accounts:

   a. Cash collected at the sales counter of the local fast-food outlet.
   b. Wages being paid to construction employees working on a large highway project.
   c. Donations to the Heart Fund being collected by door-to-door volunteer canvassers.
   d. Money deposited into parking meters owned by your municipality.
   e. Cash provided to the receptionist at the main entrance of a large company, to be used to pay for deliveries, buy emergency supplies, and other such minor things.

PROBLEM 7.32 (CHALLENGING) Is internal control viewed too negatively in this chapter?

In this chapter's coverage of internal control, bad debts, inventory shortages, and management's responsibilities, numerous parties were identified as playing a role in a company's internal control and/or in frauds and losses the company might experience. It could be argued that all this has represented an overly negative view of how enterprises operate and how people interact.

For the parties listed below, describe both positive and negative contributions the parties might be expected to make to an enterprise's internal control and the prevention or incurrence of losses. You might not be able to think of both pluses and minuses for every party, but if not, try to make a good description of whichever side you can think of.

   a. Top management
   b. The board of directors and its audit committee
   c. The external auditors
   d. Employees
   e. Customers
   f. Suppliers

PROBLEM 7.33 (CHALLENGING) List factors for evaluating whether to improve internal control

You work for Sydney Industries Ltd. The president has been reading other companies' annual reports and has become concerned that the company's internal controls may not be adequate. On the other hand, the president does not want to spend the company's money unnecessarily.

List the factors you would suggest the president consider in evaluating whether better internal controls would be worthwhile.

**PROBLEM 7.34
(CHALLENGING)
Correct accounts for
errors by book-
keeper**

The bookkeeper for Granite Cookies Inc. was recently appointed to that position after years as chief cookie taster. The president is not interested in accounting and thinks it is not important, so the cookie taster got the job in spite of having little accounting knowledge. Below are some items about the company and the journal entries the bookkeeper made in relation to those items. For each item, complete or correct what the bookkeeper has done.

a. The company issued some shares and sold them to employees. The book-keeper debited cash and credited revenue $100,000.

b. The company bought a truck at a price of $58,000, paying $15,000 down and financing the rest over 5 years with a bank. The bookkeeper debited truck asset and credited cash $15,000.

c. The bookkeeper recorded amortization expense for the year of $16,200, which included 10% amortization on the truck, in accordance with company policy. The amortization was debited to amortization expense and credited to accumulated amortization.

d. The company sold a cookie cutter machine it no longer needed for $200. The machine had cost $2,100 and had accumulated amortization of $1,660. The bookkeeper decided that $200 should be credited to cash and did that, but did not complete the entry, throwing the general ledger out of balance. Knowing the ledger should be in balance, the bookkeeper added an account to the ledger called "imbalance expense" and put $200 in it so everything would balance.

e. During the year, the company deducted $78,200 in income taxes from employees' pay and remitted it all to the government. When the taxes were remitted to the government, the bookkeeper debited income tax expense and credited cash. The company's wages payable account showed a rather large balance at the end of the year because employees had been paid only the net amounts.

f. At the end of the year, the company's perpetual inventory asset account showed a balance of $6,400. The bookkeeper thought that was a little high, because the company pretty well sold its cookies as it made them—there's little market for old cookies! Sure enough, when the cookie inventory was counted on that day, it had a cost of only $3,700. The rest appeared to have been eaten by employees, rats, customers, or whatever. The bookkeeper had no idea whether any entry should be made and so didn't do one.

g. At the end of the year, the company owed $120 in unpaid interest on its bank loan. The bookkeeper debited interest expense and credited interest payable for $120.

h. Granite sold some of its cookies on credit to coffee shops. It had never had any bad debts or had to make any allowance for them. But at the end of this year, two coffee shop customers were in financial trouble. One had been closed down by the health department and had gone out of business, owing Granite $320. The other had become very slow in paying since a national coffee chain had opened next door, and the bookkeeper doubted the $405 it owed would be paid. The bookkeeper recorded all this by debiting bad debts expense and crediting accounts receivable $85 ($405 – $320).

i. A customer, making a big order for cookies to be delivered later, came in and gave the company a $200 deposit on the last day of the year. This was included in the cash revenue for the day.

j. On the last day of the year, the company declared a dividend of $5,000 to be paid 20 days later. The bookkeeper debited dividends expense and credited retained earnings $5,000.

k. Net income for the year worked out to $44,320, as the bookkeeper calculated it. This amount was credited to retained earnings and debited to cash.

PROBLEM 7.35 (CHALLENGING)
Analysis of effects of decisions on net accounts receivable

Gallumphing Gourmet Inc. sells imported fancy kitchenware to retailers. Lately, the company has been having increasing problems collecting its receivables and has been forced to consider increasing its allowance for doubtful accounts. Accounts receivable at the end of last year were $784,000 and at the end of this year are $1,132,000. The allowance for doubtful accounts was $34,000 at the end of last year and has not been revised yet for this year's experience. Instead, the company has just written off some accounts receivable directly to bad debts expense; the expense therefore shows a balance of $29,000 of these write-offs for this year. The company is considering three different actions to take its current poorer collection experience into account:

a. Directly writing off additional apparently hopeless accounts totalling $43,500.

b. Adjusting the allowance for doubtful accounts to $78,000 to include the accounts in (a) and some doubtful accounts, but not giving up on the hopeless ones just yet.

c. Combining (a) and (b) by increasing the allowance to include all the hopeless and doubtful ones and then writing off the hopeless ones.

Analyze the three possible actions, calculating for each what the revised balances are in (1) accounts receivable, (2) allowance for doubtful accounts, and (3) bad debts expense, and showing what the effect of each is on (4) net collectible value of the accounts receivable, (5) working capital, and (6) income for the year.

PROBLEM 7.36 (CHALLENGING)
Write a paragraph each on various topics

Write a paragraph on each of the following topics. Feel free to go beyond this chapter's specific content to add your own experiences or views.

a. The relationship between corporate managers' responsibility for internal control and their responsibility to earn income for the shareholders.

b. The value of financial accounting's double-entry system in assisting with internal control.

c. The importance of documents to the credibility of financial accounting information.

d. The relationship between the way the enterprise records transactions and the kinds of adjustments required to meet the objectives of accrual accounting.

e. The role of the enterprise's accounting system in meeting its legal obligation to collect taxes on behalf of governments.

PROBLEM 7.37 (CHALLENGING)
Identify and determine effect on net income of a group of adjustments

The accountant for Discher Industries Inc. made a number of year-end adjustments to the accounts. Here are the company's balance sheet accounts before and after the adjustments. Identify what adjustment was probably behind each account change and specify its effect on net income for the year.

	Unadjusted	Adjusted
Cash	17,500	17,500
Accounts receivable	84,900	82,600
Allowance for doubtful accounts	6,400	7,200
Inventory	110,600	109,200
Prepaid expenses	4,200	9,000
Land	35,000	35,000
Factory	248,200	245,200
Accumulated amortization	103,700	100,900
Investments	75,000	55,000
Bank loan	74,000	74,000
Accounts payable	81,600	83,200
Accrued liabilities	2,100	3,400
Wages and deductions payable	13,400	13,400
Sales taxes due	2,800	2,800
Income taxes payable	600	9,200
Mortgage payable	74,000	74,000
Deferred income tax liability	32,100	34,300
Warranty liability	22,000	18,200
Share capital	100,000	100,000
Retained earnings	8,300	32,900

CASE 7A
Discuss control issues, especially the role of top management

Discuss the article "Control vs. Controls" below, especially the role of top management and corporate governance such as the board of directors in creating good internal control.

Control vs. controls

A corporation will reap the benefits when it discloses information that tells shareholders and stakeholders that it is in control

BY PETER JACKSON AND VIVIENNE LIVICK-CHAN

The frenetic pace of change currently affecting organizations in all sectors was aptly described in the 1999 edition of The Financial Post 500: "Business by its nature is dynamic, so change has always been a constant. The rate of change right now seems so rapid, the opportunities and the risks so enormous, that if there were a wheel of fortune governing it all, it would be spinning almost off its axle."

A wheel spinning off its axle is a good metaphor for a system that is out of control, as illustrated by some recent celebrated corporate brouhahas. Uneasy that this might happen to them, stakeholders are asking for information that will assure them that their particular organization is "in control."

In recent years, the accounting bodies, the financial marketplace and government regulators have tried to provide investors and stakeholders with adequate information to make informed decisions. One area that has attracted particular attention, and in which CAs can assist their employers and clients, is improving the quality of corporate governance and control. A look at developments in three jurisdictions—Canada, the UK and US—is helpful.

To date, disclosures in these three countries have focussed on controls rather than on control. The distinction is critical.

Internal controls ensure processes operate as designed and enhance the organization's ability to mitigate risks. As management guru Peter Drucker has pointed out, controls deal with events of the past while control deals with expectations about the future.

Control is the focus of work carried out by the CICA's Criteria of Control (CoCo). Control comprises all elements of an organization—including its resources, systems, processes, culture, structure and tasks—that, taken together, support people in the achievement of the organization's objectives. Control is effective if it provides reasonable assurance that the organization will achieve its objectives reliably.

In the UK, the Cadbury Report led in 1993 to changes in London Stock Exchange listing requirements that obliged directors to publish in the annual report disclosures relating to corporate governance, including "the effectiveness of the company's system of internal control."

This requirement was interpreted narrowly as designating internal financial controls. Nonetheless, it provoked controversy, as directors worried about how to judge effectiveness and about their legal liability if they stated controls were effective and something subsequently went wrong. Auditors were also concerned about their legal liability resulting from association with the directors' disclosures. Consequently, in most companies, directors did not make a statement about the effectiveness of controls but instead have acknowledged their responsibility for effective internal controls. The distinction is subtle but apparently addressed concerns.

In January 1998, the Hampel committee report supported what companies were actually doing by recommending that making a statement about effectiveness of controls be dropped from the listing requirements. However, it also expanded the directors' role by advising that they "maintain and review controls relating to all relevant control objectives, and not merely financial controls." In April 1999, the Institute of Chartered Accountants in England and Wales released for comment a draft of Internal Control: Guidance for Directors of Listed Companies Incorporated in the United Kingdom. This draft continues to focus on detailed control procedures and not the broader concept of control that CoCo has developed.

In the US, attention has focussed on controls over financial reporting. In March 1999, the Committee of Sponsoring Organizations of the Treadway Commission (COSO) published "Fraudulent Financial Reporting: 1987–1997." One objective of the study was to improve the corporate financial reporting environment in the US. Referring to the COSO mission, "to improve the quality of financial reporting through internal controls, governance and ethics," chair John Flaherty concludes that this study "validates the need for continued focus on all three areas" and that the study "will provide a platform for those responsible for financial reporting to improve their effectiveness ... The importance of the organization's control environment cannot be overstated."

Despite the efforts of companies, which have a vested interest in increasing their share value, and the regulatory bodies, which wish to ensure a stable economic environment, Ernst & Young stated in its 1998 survey, "Fraud—The Unmanaged Risk": "In our 1996 survey, almost 60% of respondents admitted that changes in their control systems and procedures had lagged behind changes in the growth of their organization. In the current survey, only a third felt that this was true." Even though this represents a marked improvement, there are still 33% of respondents who are concerned.

The following, from the General Electric Company's 1998 annual report (board of directors report), is an example of current US disclosure (italics ours): "The audit committee, which consists entirely of outside directors, held four meetings. It reviewed the activities and independence of GE's independent auditors and the activities of GE's internal audit staff. It also reviewed the company's financial reporting process, *internal financial controls* and compliance with key GE policies and applicable laws."

As this example indicates, external reporting in the US is limited to reporting on internal financial controls.

The picture in Canada is different. In 1994, the Dey Committee on Corporate Governance published its recommendations to improve the manner in which Canadian corporations are governed. The Toronto and Montreal stock exchanges then issued Guidelines for Effective Corporate Governance that required disclosure for all listed companies incorporated in Canada. Among other things, boards of directors are required to acknowledge their responsibility for ensuring the integrity of the corporation's internal control and management information systems and for identifying the principal risks of the corporation's business and ensuring implementation of appropriate systems to manage those risks.

In 1999, under the direction of the Toronto Stock Exchange (TSE), and the Institute of Corporate Directors, a study entitled "Report on Corporate Governance, 1999—Five Years to the Dey," produced a governance scorecard for corporate Canada. Of the 635 responses received from TSE-listed companies, 76% reported that they followed the guidelines related to internal controls and management information systems.

The following example of Canadian current "expanded disclosure" comes from a description of board, management and executive committee responsibilities in Imasco's 1998 annual report: "Fundamental to the board's efficacy is the establishment by management of control systems which can assist the board in the effective discharge of its responsibilities. A balance must be achieved so that the controls adopted provide the board with reasonable assurances without being unnecessarily bureaucratic or costly. The confidence of the board in management's ability and integrity is the paramount control mechanism." The statement on control systems addresses the TSE requirement to review the integrity of the corporation's internal control and management information systems.

Admittedly, the path to disclosure of a board's assessment of the effectiveness of control is not straightforward. The UK experience with board disclosure of effectiveness of financial controls (much narrower in scope) shows that. That is one reason why the CICA's Criteria of Control Board has focussed first on developing guidance on how to provide information relevant to the effectiveness of control to the board of directors. Guidance on Assessing Control describes a 10-step process for developing a report to the board that includes: information about the objectives and the management of the related risks that form the focus of the assessment; the process followed in gathering information; a conclusion about the effectiveness of control; information about the control elements that deserve particular attention and monitoring; and the actions being taken to address the issued identified.

Receiving such information will allow boards to experiment with disclosing information about whether the organization is "in control." For example, they might disclose their view on the matter or simply say that they have received and reviewed a management assessment. It is reasonable to expect that organizations who make this kind of disclosure will benefit from an increased stakeholder confidence and trust.

In the meantime, our challenge as CAs is to facilitate an assessment, based on the new CICA publication Guidance on Assessing Control, for our employers or for our clients that will provide valuable information for the board and stakeholders on a prospective, rather than a historical, basis. Guylaine Saucier, in her article "Tough questions" (CAmagazine, June / July 1999, p. 39), points out that simply having good governance is not enough; it's also "making sure that your employees, your lenders, your shareholders and your insurers know how you're running the organization to ensure its resilience."

Peter Jackson, CA, is director of the CICA's Criteria of Control and CAmagazine's Technical Editor for Control.

Vivienne Livick-Chan, FCA, is a principal in the CICA's CoCo department.

Reprinted from *CA Magazine* (pp. 51–52), October 1999, by Peter Jackson and Vivienne Livick-Chan.

CASE 7B
Discuss electronic on-line financial reporting

Discuss the article "Democratizing Disclosure" below. Consider the impact of disaggregated and on-line reporting on financial reporting, accounting standards, recordkeeping, and internal control.

Democratizing disclosure

A new CICA study on electronic on-line financial reporting finds that increased involvement by users carries implications for accounting standards.

By Gerald Trites

Increasing use of the World Wide Web for reporting purposes is challenging the very nature of financial reporting—its boundaries, its frameworks and even its fundamental role in society.

In 1997, the CICA commissioned a research study to examine the issues that the profession needed to consider in relation to technology's impact on financial and business reporting. The study was intended to provide an overview of the extent to which the web is being used for financial reporting in North America. It included a review of literature and current practice, and a survey of 370 companies, drawn from the approximately 10,000 companies listed on the New York Stock Exchange, NASDAQ and the Toronto Stock Exchange. The results indicate a high and increasing use of the World Wide Web for presenting financial data.

Use of the web is having a considerable impact on the information that is disclosed. For example, the web can provide information in multimedia format using sound, voice and video. Videos are already being used to present financial information, and some executives believe their use will increase, and that there is a high probability that web sites will be used for live broadcast of events such as annual meetings and analyst meetings. If this happens, the impact on the disclosure process could be considerable.

The CICA study discusses—based on user, preparer and regulator expectations—the potential impact of electronic on-line reporting on the content, timing and format of financial information, including general purpose financial statements and interim financial information. It was decided to leave audit considerations for another study, which was published earlier this year.

The study also discusses the types of business reporting (both financial and non-financial) that might be provided on-line on a continuous basis through-

out the year. Finally, the study outlines the implications of electronic on-line reporting for accounting standards.

One of the issues the study considers is boundaries of information. When information is presented on the web, it can be difficult for users to locate the boundaries of the financial information they read in electronic form. The reason for this is the use of hyperlinks that can take the user to other web pages or servers. When users click on hyperlinks, they may be looking at information that is not part of the formal financial information or, conversely, they may not see all the information that is required for a fair presentation. The linked information they do see may not be reliable. It also may not be in accordance with generally accepted accounting principles (GAAP) or it may not have been audited.

The issue of boundaries might be addressed by developing new standards of presentation—for example, situations in which hyperlinks would be allowed and the kind of information that could legitimately be linked to the financial statements. In addition, "electronic signposts" warning users that they are leaving formal financial information can be installed so that users activating certain hyperlinks would encounter them. Finally, background colour and distinctive boundaries can be used to identify a particular type of document, such as an annual report, to assist users in determining when they have left the report.

Another issue examined by the study is user-designed reporting models. Because of the ease of putting information on the web and the capacity of users to ask for information, financial information presented on-line is more likely to be presented in an unstructured or disaggregated format than has traditionally been the case with printed reports. Although it is unlikely that investors would be given access to raw data or databases, there is a likelihood of customization of sites, perhaps based

on user profiles or preferences. For example, a shareholder would get access to a shareholder configuration of the site and a customer would gain access to a customer configuration, reflecting their different interests. Analysts and others will quickly find ways to import the data into models that they build for their own purposes—in fact, some are already doing this.

Intelligent software agents are now used to search for information on the Internet and it is expected they will be integrated into a range of applications and information services over the next few years, including models for retrieval and analysis of information. The use of intelligent software agents in the corporate reporting process has the potential to provide a means by which users can search for relevant information within the extensive volumes of corporate data available to them.

The importance of models to enable users to make use of raw accounting data means that preparers, users and standard-setters should give more attention to the formulation of the user models—including the use of software agents—as distinct from generalized forms of financial statements.

The study also considers the convergence of management and financial reporting. Traditionally, management has made more information available to itself than to outside stakeholders and this is likely to continue. It is, however, probable that the web will blur the distinction between financial information used by management and information made available to the public. If an approach similar to that used for internal reporting were to be used for reporting to external stakeholders, it would focus on critical success factors and key performance indicators. A good deal of work is taking place in accounting research in the area of performance reporting. The new CICA Canadian Performance Reporting Initiative is timely in this regard, and can go a long way toward resolving the issues that relate to framework and structure.

The study also finds that the web is democratizing the disclosure process. The use of technology in financial and business reporting is leading to greater interactivity between preparers and users through various means: chat groups, customization of web sites, the opportunity to publish frequently asked questions on web sites and the use of e-mail for obtaining information. Many corporations already use the web for these purposes.

The idea of interactive reporting has been referred to as corporate dialogue. Companies participating in a corporate dialogue must set policies as to how they will participate, how they will control the information disclosed and how they will respond to requests for information. Standard-setters also need to recognize the increased interactivity of financial and business reporting.

All of this suggests the need for a new reporting model. There are major forces shaping the new world of business reporting to external stakeholders. The old concept of periodicity is changing to a more flexible concept of continuous reporting on a basis of closer to real-time reporting, and whereas the traditional model was static and unilateral, the new model will be dynamic and interactive. A move toward using more complex technology on a real-time basis affects reliability. There is also an increasing realization that users are becoming more involved in the design of reports by drawing down data and creating their own reports. Reporting is moving beyond financial measures to include non-financial measures. Balanced scorecard, value reporting and the AICPA's Special Committee on Financial Reporting model (the Jenkins model) are all variations on this shift. Finally, there is a move toward measurement of value creation—a more comprehensive concept than income measurement—to supplant traditional financial reporting. There is also a trend toward increased integration of internal reporting concepts with those of external reporting.

Many of the responsibilities and choices involved in designing financial reports will shift from the preparers to the users, and the reporting model has to be redesigned to recognize this.

First, the model must be broadened from a financial reporting to a business reporting model. This is consistent with the Jenkins model, the integrated reporting model and the need for value reporting. It also enables the model to incorporate the bits of disaggregated information that the users will demand.

Several changes should be made to the various statements on the basic concepts of financial reporting that have been issued (such as CICA Handbook—Accounting Section 1000, "Financial Statement Concepts"), including the addition of a new element that might be called "interactivity." This recognizes the new role of the user in the design of business reports and it gives a greater recognition to the ongoing nature of the reporting required.

The various statements of financial reporting concepts also need revision to reflect the addition of a new qualitative characteristic: responsiveness. Responsiveness means that business information that is directly relevant to the need of the moment must be released in time to have an efficient impact on the decisions that must be made. Accordingly, responsiveness embodies both relevance and timeliness.

It seems clear that standardized GAAP financial statements will probably remain an important part of financial reporting in the foreseeable future; there is simply too much of an investment in, and reliance on, them by the user community for it to be otherwise. However, it is also clear that they will become a relatively less significant factor as customized reporting becomes more important. The study concludes that this must be recognized in the standard-setting process.

To improve the reliability of the information that companies put on the web, and knowing that people will reply on the web site, companies should incorporate their sites in their governance procedures. This would include adding web site disclosures to the responsibilities of the board of directors and the audit committee. The board should consider setting up a special web-site subcommittee to report to it on web-site activities and security. In addition, the internal auditor should include the web site in the scope of the internal audit.

Finally, in the new reporting environment, the emphasis on periodicity must shift to there being a more continuous stream of information. It would be appropriate for the Accounting Standards Board to be proactive in developing the framework and standards under which this process should evolve.

Gerald Trites, CISA, FCA, is Associate Professor of Accounting and Management Information Systems at St. Francis Xavier University in Antigonish, Nova Scotia. He is principal author of the new CICA study "The Impact of Technology on Financial and Business Reporting."

Technical Editor: Deryck Williams, CMC, CA, PKF Hill, Toronto

Reprinted from *CA Magazine* (pp. 47–48), October 1999, by Gerald Trites.

NOTES

1. Thanks to Rosalie J. Laibida, the accountant at Barcol Doors & Windows Ltd., for providing the examples of the company's documents and permission to use them.

2. See a recent CICA research study, *The Impact of Technology on Financial and Business Reporting,* described in G. Trites, "Democratizing Disclosure," *CA Magazine* (October 1999): 47–48.

3. *CICA Handbook* (Toronto: Canadian Institute of Chartered Accountants, 31 December 1999): Paragraph 5200.05. Reprinted by permission of The Canadian Institute of Chartered Accountants, Toronto, Canada.

8 CHAPTER

Assets Accounting

8.1 Chapter Overview

Accounting policy choices affecting the balance sheet usually also affect income, but not cash flow.

This chapter and the next are about the balance sheet accounts. The focus is on **accounting policy choices** for the balance sheet, and we continue to centre attention on such choices introduced in coverage of revenue and expense recognition in Chapter 6, and part of the coverage of internal control in Chapter 7. Knowing about the choices behind the balance sheet is important in understanding the balance sheet's figures and disclosures about them in the notes, but also is important in understanding the income statement, because balance sheet accounting usually affects the income statement too, through double-entry accrual accounting and the **articulation** of the two statements. Here's an example. There are several methods of calculating amortization on the enterprise's assets. The company's choice among those methods affects amortization expense on the income statement and so net income, and therefore equity on the balance sheet, as well as accumulated amortization and therefore net book value of assets on the balance sheet. Analyzing financial statements and the effects of management decisions, covered in Chapter 10, depends on a good understanding of the balance sheet numbers and their effects on income. (Most accounting policy choices don't affect cash and therefore don't change the net cash flow for the year, though they may rearrange some of the details within the cash flow statement.)

Asset accounting involves many choices and some controversy.

Most of the income effects arise from the asset accounting choices in this chapter. Asset accounting involves choices about whether or not to capitalize expenses (take them off the income statement and put them on the balance sheet as assets), how to amortize assets, how much cost to include in the inventory asset (and so not include in COGS expense), how to handle changes in assets' market values, and other choices that affect the meaning of the balance sheet numbers and the nature of the net income figure. You might be surprised at how many choices there are and how controversial some can be.

Here again is the diagram of this book's learning objectives.

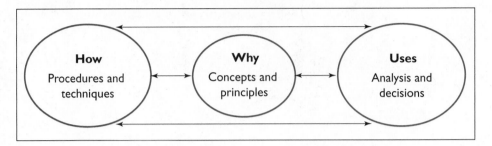

This is what you will learn in this chapter:

- *Procedures and techniques:* What methods are available to account for various assets, how those methods work and how to make any necessary adjustments for them in the accounts.

- *Concepts and principles:* What principles lie behind the various accounting alternatives and how those principles are used to make and justify choices among alternatives.

- *Analysis and decisions:* How to estimate the effects of asset accounting choices on the balance sheet and on income, and how to evaluate choices among them.

Many of this chapter's topics have been introduced in earlier chapters, so this chapter builds on earlier material and ties up a few loose ends.

8.2   BALANCE SHEET VALUATION

When we look at a balance sheet, what do the numbers, the numeric values assigned to assets (and liabilities and equity), mean? The **asset valuation** (or, more generally, **balance sheet valuation**) question is both complex and controversial. You may intuitively think that the assets should be valued at what they are worth, but what does that mean? There are five basic methods often suggested for valuing assets and liabilities:

Five main methods have been proposed for valuing assets and liabilities.

- Historical cost

- Price-level-adjusted historical cost

- Current or market value

- Value in use

- Liquidation value

No one valuation method is best for everything.

Because the financial statements articulate through double-entry accrual accounting, asset valuation usually also affects income measurement, so choosing a valuation method implies a decision about income measurement too. As you read the description below of each valuation and therefore measurement method, think about which one you believe is appropriate, and in which circumstances. There is much variety and judgment within generally accepted accounting principles, so no one method, even the main one (historical cost), is best in all circumstances. You will see versions of some methods in most financial statements: for example, the market value methods are used in the "lower of cost or market" valuation of current assets.

Historical cost valuation may produce too much of an emphasis on the past.

Balance sheet valuation is often controversial, partly because of a concern that the values should be useful in people's decision-making and a suspicion that historical cost values are not as useful as those that look more to the future. Historical cost, coming from the transactional base of financial accounting, does not reveal the changes in market conditions which can help in predicting the future, and decision makers who believe this is a problem may not think that accrual accounting adjustments go far enough to overcome the problem. Would you drive your car looking only in the rearview mirror to see where you have been and not look out the front window to see where you are going? Let's see the perspective the five balance sheet valuation methods bring to the task of choosing the numbers for the balance sheet.

Historical Cost

The general historical cost basis is interpreted specifically for each balance sheet account.

Historical cost, otherwise known as acquisition cost, values assets at the amounts of the payments made or promised to acquire the assets, and values liabilities at the amounts of any associated promises. These amounts usually come from transactional evidence, such as invoices, receipts, or contracts. Equity amounts come from past share issues and incomes retained. While we normally think of "cost" as applying to assets, the transaction-based values that cost produces for assets are also produced for liabilities and equity, hence the whole balance sheet can be described as a "historical cost" statement. Here is a brief summary of what historical cost is normally interpreted to mean for various balance sheet accounts, with the chapter sections that provide more details:

Cash	Cash and bank balances produced by prior cash transactions (section 8.4)
Accounts receivable	Already recognized, but uncollected revenue (sections 6.6, 8.5)
Inventories	Cost of making the goods available for sale (sections 8.3, 8.6)
Prepaid expenses	Costs paid but not yet transferred to expenses (section 6.9)
Investments	Cost incurred when each investment was acquired (sections 8.4, 9.6)
Property and plant	Cost to make the assets suitable for their intended use (section 8.3)
Intangible assets	Cost incurred when each asset was acquired or produced (section 8.11)
Accounts payable	Already recognized, but unpaid expenses and purchases (section 9.2)
Accrued liabilities	Estimated expenses already recognized but not yet paid (sections 6.9, 9.2)
Debt	Legal promises to pay specified in past borrowing transactions (sections 9.2, 9.3)

Share capital   Cash or other value received when each share was
                       originally issued (section 9.4)

Retained earnings   Past incomes earned minus past dividends declared
                       (section 3.2)

Historical cost valuation is the usual method under GAAP.

The ability to document the cost (see "verifiability" in sections 5.2 and 5.3) is a major reason historical cost is the usual valuation method for most assets and liabilities. Another principal reason is that an enterprise will rarely purchase assets or make promises for more than the enterprise believes them to be worth. If you believe that an asset will provide you with $10,000 worth of productive capacity, you will not rationally pay or promise more than $10,000 for it. Under this method, an asset valued at historical cost is valued at its expected lowest (or most conservative) value of future benefits at the date of acquisition. In most cases, GAAP imply the use of historical costs, unless some other valuation basis is more appropriate and is specifically disclosed in the financial statements (section 1500 of the *CICA Handbook* recommends such disclosure unless the basis is "self-evident").

Some additional points in connection with this method are worth noting.

Historical cost reflects value at the date of acquisition.

- *At the date of acquisition of an asset*, historical cost = market value = value in use, in most cases. Rational people would pay only what the asset is worth to them if used in their business and such value in use should tend to determine the market value of the asset, as various people consider how useful the asset would be to them.

Historical cost does not reflect value changes since acquisition.

- Much of the criticism of historical cost has to do with what happens after the date of asset acquisition. Suppose a piece of land was purchased 10 years ago for $50,000. Is the land worth $200,000 or $100 today on the market, or if used in the business? The historical cost does not seem as relevant as more current information to managers' decisions about whether to replace assets and investors' evaluations of management's performance.

Historical cost is not good enough if market value or value in use is seriously impaired.

- GAAP deem historical cost to be an inadequate valuation if an asset's market value or usefulness to the enterprise has been seriously impaired. Largely because of conservatism, unproductive assets should be "written down" or "written off," and the "lower of cost or market" rule is used in valuing inventories and some other current assets. We will see more about these later in the chapter.

Many assets are really unexpired costs, to be deducted from income as expenses.

- Accrual accounting's income measurement produces some asset accounts that are not particularly meaningful as *values* in that they don't represent a real asset so much as they do the residual effect of trying to get the income number right. Prepaid expenses and net book value of assets being amortized are examples of "costs waiting to be deducted from revenue in the future" or "unexpired costs." Using amortization to allocate the cost of an asset as an expense deducted from income may get a good income measure, but does not necessarily produce a meaningful balance sheet figure for the asset being amortized.

The historical cost basis may not handle intangible and high-tech assets well.

- Some items that could be assets and do have value to the enterprise, and even a market value, do not appear on the balance sheet because they do not have a clear historical cost. Such economic assets as skilled employees, innovative use of technology, or clever business methods are usually not on the balance sheet, yet are apparently used by the stock market and others in valuing the whole business. In this time of high-tech, dot-com, and Internet developments, many people feel that the historical cost basis, at least as it is currently interpreted using GAAP, seriously misrepresents the real economic assets of many companies and the income derived from them. Terms such as "economic value added, "measuring value added," "balanced scorecard," "nonfinancial performance measurement," and "strategic performance measurement" are just some that are used in discussions of how to improve or replace historical cost and GAAP. More on this controversy is in section 8.11 on "intangible" assets.

- Concerns over how assets are valued using historical cost have led people to suggest alternative methods for valuing assets and liabilities on the balance sheet. Some of the more popular alternatives are below.

Price-Level-Adjusted Historical Cost

Adjusting historical costs for inflation is an old but so far unsuccessful idea.

Price-level-adjusted historical cost adjusts for changes in the value or purchasing power of the dollar (the measuring unit), rather than for changes in the values of particular assets. The historical cost values of the assets and liabilities are adjusted for changes in the value of the dollar (using economy-wide indices such as the Consumer Price Index) since the assets were acquired or liabilities were incurred. Though this is a venerable idea, first proposed early in this century, and has been used by some companies (for example, the Philips electronics company in the Netherlands) and by some countries that had high inflation (Brazil for one), it has not found much favour in North America. One reason for its lack of popularity is that if historical cost is unsatisfactory compared to current values, adjusting the cost for inflation still leaves it unsatisfactory, only now less understandable.

Current or Market Value

Current value accounting is a good theoretical idea but its time has not yet come.

Current or market value accounting would record the individual assets and liabilities at their current particular market value. It focuses on the individual values of the balance sheet items, not on changes in the dollar itself, as price-level-adjusted accounting does. It assumes that value is market-determined and that income should be measured using changes in market values over time. The argument is that if, for example, your house's market worth is greater today than yesterday, you have made money on it today, even if you have not sold it. If its market worth is less, you have lost money on it, even if you have not sold it. This method has been the subject of much writing and experimentation in the United States and Canada and has some theoretical attraction in economics and finance, but it does not seem likely to replace historical cost as the most popular method for most assets.

Market value accounting is increasingly being used for financial assets of some companies.

Recently, there has been some impetus to market value accounting for assets that really do have a ready market, so-called financial assets, such as traded shares, bonds, and some kinds of loans and other financial instruments. It is becoming part of GAAP, especially in the United States, and especially for banks and other financial companies, to report the market values of such assets, and to use "mark-to-market" accounting to record the gains and losses on market value changes in the income statement.

Current value accounting can use either input or output values, or a mixture of the two:

a. Input market value, or entry value, refers to the amount it would cost to bring the asset into the company if it were not now in, usually measured by estimating "replacement cost" to purchase it again or "reproduction cost" to make it again. The same idea holds for the hypothetical reborrowing of liabilities.

b. Output market value, or exit value, is the amount an asset is worth if sold now (in other words, its "net realizable value") or the amount that a liability could be paid off at now, usually measured by quoted prices, appraisals, and similar estimates.

Both these versions of market value are already used in one specific area of accounting: the requirement that current assets, especially inventories, be shown at the lower of cost or market. Section 8.6 will show how this works.

Versions of market value are used in lower of cost or market calculations.

Value in Use

This approach considers that value flows from the way the company will use the asset to generate future cash flows (cash generated from revenues net of expenses). **Value in use** is usually estimated by calculating the net "present value" of future cash inflows generated by the asset, or cash outflows it will make unnecessary. (**Present value** is the future cash flows minus lost future interest implied by waiting for the cash. For example, suppose you are getting $1.00 in a year. If you had money now, you would be able to earn 10% on it, but by waiting a year, you give up that interest. The present value of the $1.00 is the amount prior to the lost interest, the amount that would build up to $1.00 in a year at 10%. That would be 91 cents. In a year, 91 cents at 10% would earn 9 cents interest, bringing the total to the $1.00 you will get in a year. The present value (91 cents) is thus always smaller than the future cash payment ($1.00), which is said to be "discounted" to a lower amount to remove the effects of future interest. (More on this is in section 10.7.) For example, a machine might be valued according to the products that it will make and that will be sold: the cash flow it will bring in, discounted back to the present. Modern theories of finance and management accounting presume that value in use, measured by discounting future cash flows to get net present value, is an appropriate method for managerial decisions about asset acquisition and financing, and many people presume it underlies market values, but the approach has been little used in producing financial accounting numbers. One exception is **capital leases**, which are included in section 8.11.

Value in use is more important in managers' decision-making than in financial accounting.

Liquidation Value

Liquidation value is like output market value, but used on a "going out of business, sell it for what you can" basis. It is the value that the company's assets would bring upon being sold and that liabilities would be paid off for, if the whole company went out of business. It is used when the company is not felt to be a **going concern**, that is, if its continued viability cannot be assumed. Therefore, the reader of financial statements prepared on the historical cost basis should be entitled to presume that the company in question is a going concern. This presumption is an important part of financial accounting, but every year it turns out to be wrong for some companies that unexpectedly fail. Such bad outcomes remind us that good judgment is required in selecting the balance sheet valuation basis, as with other aspects of financial accounting. A judgment that a company is a going concern and so should use historical cost accounting will turn out to have been wrong if the company fails. On the other hand, a judgment that it is not a going concern might be self-fulfilling: it might panic creditors and investors, and spark a failure no one wants.

Use of liquidation value indicates a company in trouble, not a going concern.

An Example: Current Market Value as an Alternative to Historical Cost

Let's look at a realistic and relevant example. Canada has many companies that specialize in acquiring and developing real estate for office buildings, shopping centres, industrial plants, housing developments, and many other uses. As you probably know, real estate values are highly variable, with frequent booms and busts. Consider two real estate development companies operating in the Toronto market. Let's call them Oxbridge and Bramview:

The two companies are the same except for the cost paid for the similar parcels of land.

- Oxbridge has undeveloped land, bought during a downturn in the Toronto real estate market, that cost $5,000,000 and has an estimated current market (output) value of $8,000,000. The company's net income has been about $700,000 per year in the last few years.

- Bramview also has undeveloped land, comparable to Oxbridge's except bought during an overheated period of the Toronto market at a cost of $11,000,000. Its estimated current market value is also $8,000,000, and the company's net income has also been about $700,000 per year.

The two pieces of land are about the same, but the companies' historical-cost-based balance sheets certainly do not look the same:

- Oxbridge: Undeveloped land, at cost $5,000,000

- Bramview: Undeveloped land, at cost $11,000,000

Should income be related to current economic or market value rather than historical cost?

Also, Oxbridge will show a higher ratio of net income to total assets, indicating apparently stronger performance than Bramview, because its total assets will be lower than Bramview's. Now, we could argue that this is as it should be, that Bramview has not really done as well because too much was paid for the land, in hindsight. But another argument is that since the two pieces of land are comparable economic assets, net income should be related to the economic value (e.g., market value) of the assets, not to costs that depend on historical happenstance rather than currently relevant economic conditions.

Let's consider the idea of changing both companies' balance sheet valuations for the land to current market value. Using the concepts from earlier in this book, what might be some pros and cons of this idea?

Pros:

- More relevant valuation for users in assessing company's value.

- More useful in comparing companies with similar economic assets.

- Fairer way of relating performance (income) to the economic value that managers are managing on behalf of owners.

- More timely data than the "obsolete" cost figures.

- Not costly to implement (unless real estate appraisers have to be paid).

- Understandable to users who know something about real estate.

Cons:

- Less reliable numbers because based on estimated selling value of land that has not been sold.

- Less consistent balance sheet values because real estate values tend to vary a great deal over time.

- Not transaction-based and therefore not verifiable.

- Not conservative in the long run because land values have tended to rise over time, especially as measured in dollars subject to inflation.

- Not a generally accepted procedure, so users accustomed to GAAP would have to adjust their performance evaluation methods and rewrite contracts, such as for lending agreements and management compensation, that depend on financial statement information.

- No effect on cash flow directly or through income tax because the land has not been sold, so there might be doubt that moving the financial statement numbers around in the absence of real economic effects would be very helpful to anyone.

Well, you can probably add more pros and cons. We don't know the significance (materiality) of the land valuation issue to the companies' financial statements or the income tax and other consequences of changing the accounting numbers. But you should see that the accounting concepts are useful in figuring out what would be the appropriate accounting procedure to use.

How might changing to market values be implemented in the accounts? Here are some possibilities (all ignoring income tax considerations):

Possibility 1: Adjust land to market value and put the difference into income.

1. Any difference between current market value and the value on the companies' balance sheets (cost, so far) could be just included in the current year's net income:

   - Oxbridge's land asset would be debited $3,000,000 to bring it up to the $8,000,000 market value, and the credit would go to an income statement account like "Other revenue," raising the current year's income by more than 400% to $3,700,000;

   - Bramview's land asset would be credited $3,000,000 to bring it down to the $8,000,000 market value, and the debit would go to an income statement account like "Other expense," changing the current year's income to a loss of $2,300,000 (more than three times the current income).

Possibility 2: Adjust land to market value and put the difference into retained earnings.

2. The difference could be put directly into retained earnings. Oxbridge's retained earnings would rise $3,000,000, and Bramview's would fall $3,000,000. Oxbridge would appear more able to pay a dividend; Bramview would appear less able. As would also happen with method (1), this could paradoxically hurt Oxbridge more than Bramview, because the accounting change could produce pressure from shareholders for increased dividends, even though there is no additional cash to pay such dividends.

Possibility 3: Adjust land to market value and put the difference in a special equity account.

3. The difference could be put into owners' equity but not into retained earnings, by creating a new equity account called something like "Unrealized changes in asset valuations." This would increase Oxbridge's equity by $3,000,000 with a new credit balance account, but would decrease Bramview's equity by $3,000,000 with a new debit balance account. Since it would not be part of retained earnings, the new account might not affect the owners' demand for dividends, thus avoiding the implication that the valua-

tion change is similar to the kinds of events behind the revenues and expenses that form net income and retained earnings. (Some methods of implementing current value and price-level-adjusted accounting that have been developed, and adopted by a few companies and countries, have used such an "Unrealized gains and/or losses" account.)

Possibility 4: Adjust land to market value only if market value is lower than cost.

4. Perhaps the principle of conservatism should be invoked, whereby one of the above methods (most likely the first) would be followed only when the market value is less than the present balance sheet value. In this case, only Bramview would adjust its figures, because its cost is higher than current market value. The other side of the adjustment would probably go to income as in the first possibility but could also go to retained earnings or a special equity account. Though the companies' accounting would still show different figures for the same sort of land, using "lower of cost or market" would be conservative, so users could rely on the balance sheet values not being overstated relative to current conditions. This might be done particularly if a decline in market value indicated a serious impairment in the land's value. GAAP already require such a write-down if there is a permanent or long-term impairment in an asset's value.

Possibility 5: Don't adjust the accounts; just disclose the information.

5. Perhaps the historical cost numbers should not be changed, but each company could disclose the current market value of the land on its balance sheet or in a note:

   • Oxbridge: Undeveloped land (current market value estimated at $8,000,000), at cost $5,000,000.

   • Bramview: Undeveloped land (current market value estimated at $8,000,000), at cost $11,000,000.

   This method provides users with information about the market values, but does not presume what they mean, as the other methods do. Users probably can make intelligent use of information as long as they know about it (that is, if it is disclosed). With full information and "what if" analytical skill, they can adjust the financial statements to reflect the information in whatever way they consider relevant to their needs, using any of the above adjustment methods they thought appropriate.

Because any change from historical cost in the absence of actually selling the land would not affect cash flow (no proceeds) and, we will assume, would not affect income tax either, there is no net effect on the cash flow statement. Cash from operations would not be affected, nor would any of the other cash flow categories. Net income at the top of the cash flow statement might change, but the change would be cancelled out by adding back any reduction of income, or subtracting any gain, because such gains or losses would be noncash items.

OW'S YOUR UNDERSTANDING?

Here are two questions you should be able to answer, based on what you have just read:

1. The owner of Staely Industries Inc. is grumbling about the limitations of historical cost accounting for valuing the company's assets and liabilities. Tell the owner what other valuation or measurement methods can be used and what each does that the historical cost basis does not do.

2. Greyhurst Land Development Inc. has large landholdings. The company's president said recently that historical cost valuation for the company's land is correct according to GAAP, but is nevertheless inappropriate for the company. Is this possible?

8.3   THE COST OF AN ASSET: THE BASIC COMPONENTS

There's more to "cost" than meets the eye!

The previous section referred to historical cost, and cost is an important part of much of the rest of this chapter. Before going further, let's tie down what financial accounting actually means by the word **cost**, particularly for tangible assets such as inventories and fixed assets. (As was indicated at the beginning of section 8.2, other balance sheet accounts are examined later in this chapter and Chapter 9.) As in other areas of accrual accounting, conceptual and practical considerations make cost a little more complex than might be thought. The principles about assigning costs to assets are important in recognizing expenses and valuing assets, because a debit added to expense reduces present income, while the same debit added to an asset increases assets now and reduces future income via amortization, cost of goods sold, or other expenses arising from consumption of assets. How then is it determined whether to assign a debit, say for an expenditure on a building, to the building asset or to repairs expense?

Many costs may be incurred on an asset besides the simple invoice cost.

On the surface, figuring out the cost of an asset looks simple. You buy a truck for $25,000 and value the truck on the balance sheet at $25,000. However, there is often more to the cost of an asset than just the simple invoice cost or direct cost. You might pay to have your company name painted on the truck. Is that part of the truck asset, or advertising expense? What about the tires, which will wear out a lot sooner than the rest of the truck and will be replaced several times over the truck's useful life? As another example, when you purchase a big computerized manufacturing machine, it may cost you $500,000 for the actual machine. But, in order to use the machine, certain other things must be added, such as temperature control, a raised floor for wiring, and a fire protection system. Therefore, a section of the factory must be renovated to meet these specifications. Is all that part of the cost of the machine? What about the cost of training people to use the machine?

Cost includes all the costs to get the asset ready for using it as the enterprise intends.

Such installation or preparation costs are a good example of expenditures that are a component of the asset's cost. Overall, the **cost** of an asset includes all those costs *required to make it suitable for its intended purpose, particularly those costs incurred prior to putting the asset into service*. For inventories, putting the asset into service mainly means selling it or using it in the business, because inventory is not held for long. Getting the cost of inventories parallels the way it is done for longer-lived assets like buildings and equipment, but there are more complexities for the longer-lived assets. Some mentions will be made about inventories in this section, especially in the table at the end of the section, but most of the focus is on longer-lived assets.

For longer-lived assets, costs are accumulated and added to the asset's overall cost until the asset is put into service. After that, its cost is amortized against the revenue the asset helps to earn. In the years following acquisition, the question of whether the asset cost should be changed will crop up again when repairs must be made. When a major repair or apparent improvement in the asset is done, the question is whether the asset's productivity or efficiency has been improved, or its useful life extended. If so, there has been a **betterment** of the asset and the cost of that should be **capitalized** (added to the cost of the asset). If not, the cost should just be charged to expense, such as to an account called repairs and maintenance expense. Expenditures that might be betterments are often expensed anyway, because they may just serve to maintain the asset on its expected pattern of declining value through use, rather than unambiguously making the asset better than expected.

These ideas are summarized in Figure 8.1. The solid line rising up on the left is the accumulation of expenditures until, at the point the asset is put into service, the asset's cost has been established. After that, net book value goes down as the asset is amortized. A betterment exists and is recorded by adding an expenditure to the asset's original cost if, and only if, the expenditure adds to the asset's economic value or extends its life (the latter is illustrated in the figure, showing the new amortization line above and extending to the right of the old one).

> **Asset cost includes expenditures to make it ready for service or better it later.**

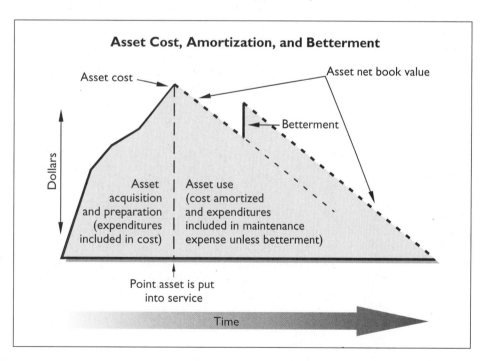

FIGURE 8.1

What exactly *are* the costs that are necessary "to make an asset suitable for its intended use"? That can sometimes be difficult to determine. For example, suppose an enterprise constructs a specialized new manufacturing machine, using some of its regular employees and resources. The cost of an asset that the

It can be difficult to decide whether some expenditures really added value to the asset.

enterprise constructs for itself, rather than buying finished, will obviously include the cost of raw materials and direct labour needed to make it. But should the salaries of supervisors, who would have been paid anyway, be included? Capitalizing such costs involves a debit to the asset account and a credit to the expense account, reducing the latter and therefore increasing current income. How about interest on monies borrowed to finance the project? Did the enterprise borrow because by paying earlier it could get a better price for materials, so that the interest really is related to the cost of the asset? Or was the enterprise just short of money, so that the interest is more a cost of a weak financial position rather than of the asset itself? It is a matter of judgment and depends on the situation. Because of conservatism, most enterprises do not include interest on borrowed funds in the cost of assets, but some do, such as electric utilities, which borrow money over the several years it takes to construct power plants. Interest would only be included if incurred prior to putting the asset into service, not after. Supervision salaries during construction probably would only be included if the supervisors clearly helped produce a good asset and could not be doing other things for the enterprise at the same time. The problems of deciding whether to capitalize costs like supervision are part of a larger issue, mentioned in section 8.2 and examined in section 8.11, of how and whether to capitalize internal costs on intangible assets like goodwill and research and development.

The choice of whether to capitalize or expense certain costs can be significant to the financial statements.

Deciding what to include in an asset's cost, which is to say whether to capitalize or expense a given cost, can make quite a difference to the enterprise's balance sheet and income statement. Suppose Gondola Inc. has spent $100,000 this year on supervisors' salaries in connection with setting up a new mountain gondola ride in the Rockies. If that cost is just deducted from revenue as an expense this year, it will reduce income and income tax expense. But if the cost is added to the gondola ride asset instead, total assets will be higher, and this year's income and income tax expense will be higher too. Over the next several years, incomes and income tax expenses will be lower because of higher amortization on the higher asset cost. So, aside from accounting appropriately and fairly for the asset, the decision about how to handle the supervisors' salaries will affect income, assets, and income tax expenses this year and in several future years. Thus, a *capitalization* entry is opposite an *amortization* entry: capitalizing reduces the expense and increases the asset, while amortizing does the opposite.

Inventory costing requires similar judgments and policies about indirect costs.

The capitalizing versus expensing choice can arise with just about any asset. Inventory is an example. Purchased inventory can be straightforward. It is basically the invoice cost plus transportation, storage, and handling costs. Manufactured inventory, on the other hand, requires some decisions. As with other assets constructed by the enterprise, the cost of raw materials and direct labour are usually included. But what about overhead? Overhead costs are those that are indirectly related to the production process, such as accountants' and supervisors' salaries, and building operating costs, including electricity, rent, depreciation, and insurance. Most manufacturing companies include some or all of such costs when they are calculating the cost of unsold manufactured goods.

Accounting policies are used for asset costs just as for other areas of accounting.

Enterprises often have accounting policies for how to determine whether expenditures, such as supervision and interest, are included in assets' costs. These policies are designed to ensure consistency in calculating cost, to fit the accounting to the enterprise's particular circumstances, and to meet other criteria, such as conservatism. They meet the same needs and follow the same rules as any policy choice (see sections 6.4 and 5.2). For example, suppose a company spends money improving leased space. Should those costs be included in a "leasehold improvements" asset or just deducted as expenses? The enterprise will make the choice according to GAAP principles such as fairness, conservatism, and matching, plus such other criteria as income tax rules, cost of gathering necessary data, and materiality.

In summary, the components of the cost of an asset include all those acquisition and preparation costs that are judged to be required to make it suitable for the purpose intended, whether it be making a computer usable in the information-gathering process or bringing inventory into salable condition. Some common components of the cost of an asset are listed in Exhibit 8.1.

8-1

Exhibit

Common Components of Asset Cost

a. **Inventory**
   - Raw materials costs;
   - Labour costs;
   - Storage costs;
   - Handling costs prior to sale;
   - Indirect overhead costs of production, such as heat, power, and supervisors' salaries.

b. **Land**
   - Purchase price, including real estate agent commissions;
   - Costs of obtaining clear title, such as legal fees and title searches;
   - Costs of clearing, removing unwanted structures, draining, and landscaping.

c. **Building (purchased)**
   - Purchase price;
   - Renovation or upgrading costs to make it suitable for the intended use;
   - Initial painting and decoration.

d. **Building (self-constructed)**
   - Materials costs;
   - Labour costs;
   - Excavating, surveying, engineering, and design costs;
   - Insurance while constructing the building;
   - Perhaps some overhead costs and even financing costs incurred during construction.

e. **Purchased Equipment**
   - Purchase price, including taxes;
   - Transportation costs;
   - Installation costs;
   - Testing costs;
   - Overhauls that extend equipment's life or increase its value (betterments).

f. **Leasehold Improvements on Rented Property**
   - Materials costs, labour costs, and other costs to construct the improvements;
   - Initial painting and decoration of the rented premises.

HOW'S YOUR UNDERSTANDING?

Here are two questions you should be able to answer, based on what you have just read:

1. Magnus Fabricators Ltd. has constructed a new factory building, using company employees and equipment for most of the work. The company's accountant said, "Various costs must be capitalized to produce an appropriate balance sheet figure for the building's cost." What did the accountant mean and what sorts of costs were likely meant?

2. How does a company determine when to stop adding expenditures to the cost of a new building and instead to add those expenditures to repairs and maintenance expense?

8.4   CASH AND TEMPORARY INVESTMENTS

As explained in Chapter 4, cash and very near-cash assets are generally considered to be "cash and equivalents," and changes in them are the focus of the cash flow statement's analysis of cash flows. This section describes some financial accounting principles that affect accounting for cash and so affect what the balance sheet and cash flow statement report.

Cash and Very Near-Cash Assets

The main principle in accounting for cash and very near-cash assets grouped with cash on the balance sheet is that what is called "cash" should really be available for immediate use, such as paying bills. So the following are included in Cash:

Cash includes all varieties of unrestricted cash on hand and in banks, anywhere in the world.

- Cash on hand, including petty cash and undeposited cash receipts and credit card slips, in any of the company's offices worldwide.

- Cash in savings and chequing accounts in the company's bank or banks, worldwide, as long as its use is unrestricted.

- "Cash in transit" that is on its way from other banks or countries (if there are complexities in such transit items, as there might be with some e-commerce and international businesses, the company will have to judge whether these are really not available for use at balance sheet date and so should be included in accounts receivable).

Cash does not include any amounts not available for immediate use.

The following are not included in Cash on the balance sheet:

- Bad cheques received from customers and refused by their banks, and therefore not really cash, but instead accounts receivable (doubtful ones), because the customers have to be chased down for the money.

- Cash that is not available for immediate use, such as a trust account holding a deposit on a planned land purchase, or a term deposit or investment certificate that cannot be cashed until a particular date (this would be a "temporary investment").

- Cash subject to other countries' exchange or currency controls that limit its availability for immediate use.

Some details to note:

Cash includes the ledger account balance, if positive, converted to Canadian dollars.

- The Cash amount on the balance sheet is the balance according to the ledger account(s), not the balance given in the bank's statement of the account(s). As was shown way back in the demonstration of bank account reconciliation in section 1.9, this means that items that have not yet cleared through the bank, but are in process of doing so, are included in calculating Cash. The main examples of such items are outstanding deposits and outstanding cheques, which have left the company and are just working their way through the banking system.

- This means, as pointed out also in section 7.5, that bank reconciliation is an essential practice in accounting for cash. The company must be sure that the cash records are correct, with errors identified and dealt with, so that the figures in the balance sheet (and cash flow statement) are proper.

- A bank overdraft, which is a credit (negative) balance in the ledger record for the bank account, happens when the company has written more cheques than there is money in the bank, according to the ledger. This credit balance is really a bank loan, and so is **reclassified** to current liabilities and shown together with the official bank loans, and is not subtracted from other positive cash or bank balances or shown as a negative asset. (As was noted in Chapter 4, a temporary overdraft may be deducted from cash to get a net cash figure for the cash flow statement.)

- Cash in foreign banks or currencies has to be converted to the currency being used as the basis of the financial statements (Canadian dollars for most Canadian companies). This requires reference to foreign exchange rates as of the balance sheet dates and can be a little complicated for currencies that are not readily exchangeable for Canadian dollars or that are rising or falling rapidly.

Temporary Investments

a. Temporary Investments and Marketable Securities

Temporary investments are used to provide a better return than bank deposits do.

Having plain cash on hand earns no interest, and bank account balances usually pay little interest, so enterprises use **temporary investments** primarily to put extra cash to work. Such investments include stocks, bonds, commercial paper (such as notes issued by financial companies), government bonds and treasury bills, and investment certificates and term deposits in banks. Guaranteed investment certificates (GICs) are a common form of the last kind.

Temporary investments are valued on the balance sheet at lower of cost or market.

Because there is no intention to hold such investments for long or to try to influence the operations or policies of the organizations that issued the securities, such investments are included in current assets. Like other current assets, these investments are valued at the **lower of cost or market** (market is measured as current market (net realizable) value, what the investments would receive if sold in an ordinary, nonpanicked way). The reader of the balance sheet should be able to assume that the value shown is not higher than what would be obtained by selling the investments. Dividends and interest from such investments are usually also included in nonoperating revenues. If the investments are **marketable securities** having a quoted market value, such as shares in public companies, that value is usually disclosed if it is different from the amount at which they are valued on the balance sheet.

You are expected to assume GAAP are being followed if you are not specifically told.

Because cash and temporary investments are often considered by management to be part of the enterprise's overall supply of cash, the two may be reported together on the balance sheet, especially if temporary investments are cashable, very short-term, or not large in comparison to cash. *Financial Reporting in Canada 1999* reports that 90% of the 200 companies it surveyed in 1996–1998 reported a cash asset, and that the most common titles for this asset were: Cash and short-term investments, Cash, and Cash and cash equivalents.[1] Many of these companies, a total of 40% of the surveyed companies, also reported bank overdrafts.[2] Seventy-five percent of the companies reported temporary investments, the vast majority just including them with cash in the balance sheet. Most of these companies did not say how they valued temporary investments, but some said that market approximated cost or that lower of cost or market was used.[3] Such lack of disclosure is an example of an assumption that the reader of the financial statements should be sufficiently knowledgeable about financial accounting principles to know what basis is used if it is not specified. Developing your knowledge about **GAAP** is one of this book's main objectives.

b. Example of Effects of Accounting Method

Wildrose Inc. has temporary investments costing $520,000. Suppose the investments' market values slipped to $484,000 on the balance sheet date. What would happen to income if the company followed the lower of cost or market rule? Suppose instead that the investments' market values went up to $585,000 on the balance sheet date. How much better off would the company appear to be if it could avoid accounting conservatism and report the investments at market value instead of lower of cost or market?

A write-down reduces income but does not affect cash flow unless the investment is considered part of cash.

In the first case, the company should write the investments down to $484,000, because current assets are assumed to be liquid and conservatively valued. The difference, $36,000, would be included as an expense (probably a nonoperating one) and the write-down would reduce income tax expense if the write-down were a tax-deductible expense. Net income would go down by $36,000, minus any tax saving. The working capital would be reduced by the write-down, also minus any reduction in income tax payable. Cash flow would not be affected as no cash is involved, unless (as used to be the case and still may be for some companies) the investments are considered part of cash—in that case, cash from operations would go down too.

If information is disclosed, you can estimate the effects of alternate accounting policies.

In the second case, the company's current assets would be $65,000 higher, and net income and working capital would be higher by that amount less any likely income tax on the increase in value. If the company cannot show the investments at market value, because writing assets up above cost is generally not permitted in Canada, management may still get the message across by disclosing the market value, which the *CICA Handbook* recommends. Then readers of the financial statements can do the above sort of effects analysis if they wish.

HOW'S YOUR UNDERSTANDING?

Here are two questions you should be able to answer, based on what you have just read:

1. What is the difference between cash and temporary investments, and why might they be grouped together on the balance sheet even if different?

2. Xie Inc. bought some shares on the stock market at a cost of $230,000 to employ some excess cash temporarily. At the balance sheet date, these shares had a current market value of $210,000. At what value would they be shown on the balance sheet, what effect would this have on income, what is the rule you followed to answer the previous questions, and why does this rule exist? ($210,000; income reduced by $20,000 before any income tax effect; lower of cost or market rule; reasons include assumed liquidity of current assets and conservatism)

8.5   ACCOUNTS RECEIVABLE

Trade Accounts Receivable

Trade accounts receivable are recognized, but uncollected revenue.

Most accounts receivable are *recognized but uncollected revenue*, created by the accrual accounting entry: DR Accounts receivable, CR Revenue. Such receivables arise from the company's day-to-day business or "trading" activities and so are often called trade receivables. They are included in current assets because they're usually expected to be collected within one year. Any interest charged to slow payers is added to the balance by an entry like this: DR Accounts receivable, CR Interest revenue (nonoperating revenue).

Valuation of Accounts Receivable

Receivables are reduced by an allowance contra if their collectible value has fallen.

GAAP's lower of cost or market rule requires that current assets which are to be turned into cash soon must be reduced in value if it does not appear they will fetch the expected cash. With receivables, there's often collection uncertainty, and many enterprises experience difficulties in collection, especially as time passes after the sale. So, if the collectible amount is now expected to be lower than originally anticipated, the receivable must be reduced to an estimated collectible amount. The method for doing this by subtracting an allowance for doubtful accounts contra account from the accounts receivable control account was described in section 7.7.

How to determine the required allowance is an accounting policy decision too. A traditional method, "aging" of the receivables to determine which ones are getting old and therefore more doubtful or even hopeless, is used by most companies. But as there may be a very large number of receivables (think of how many the Master Card, Visa, or American Express credit card operations must have!), the aging analysis is often done using samples or using analysis that identifies the most doubtful ones, such as analysis of customers' payment patterns to identify customers who have run into trouble paying. Another method is to determine the allowance by a study of the typical bad debt losses incurred according to sales volume. You might, for example, determine that 0.5% of credit sales are not collected and base the allowance on that estimate. This method is good for estimating bad debt expenses for management's scrutiny of credit policies during the year, but usually some version of the aging method is used at the balance sheet date because it focuses on the asset valuation at that point.

What you see on the balance sheet is usually just the net estimated collectible value.

The estimated collectible amount is the net of accounts receivable minus the allowance, so the allowance functions to adjust the net value down to the lower of cost (original sale value) and market (current estimated collectible amount). On the balance sheet, accounts receivable are valued at this net amount; most companies do not disclose either the original value or the allowance, just the net. They probably don't want competitors to know what proportion of their accounts receivable are in trouble! *Financial Reporting in Canada 1999* indicates that less than 20% of the 200 companies surveyed even disclosed that there was an allowance. Again, the reader is to assume that if GAAP are followed, an allowance must have been made if necessary. When the existence of an allowance was disclosed, its amount was given also.[4]

Other Receivables

Other receivables are separated from trade receivables if important.

If large, nontrade receivables are shown separately from trade receivables. But if not, they are usually just lumped in with the trade receivables. *Financial Reporting in Canada 1999* reports that, in 1998, the most recent year surveyed, 85 of the 200 companies indicated that they had more than one type of receivables and disclosed the amount of each type, 114 just gave one figure for receivables, and one did not report any receivables.[5]

There are two main kinds of other receivables.

- The first kind is **notes receivable**. These usually arise from revenue transactions and are supported by a signed contract between buyer and seller that specifies a payment schedule, an interest rate, and often other legal details. Such notes are often used for large and/or long-term receivables, such as sales of automobiles, houses, or appliances, and loans by banks and finance companies. Notes are shown at **present value** (only interest that has built up so far is included in the asset, not future interest). An "allowance for doubtful notes" is used if necessary.

- The second kind is loans to employees, officers, shareholders, and associated companies, tax refunds the company is waiting for, expense advances not yet accounted for by employees, and other receivables not arising from revenue transactions. They are accounted for and valued much as normal trade receivables and notes receivable are, but because some may arise from peculiar circumstances, companies often disclose the reasons for them and explain other circumstances about them.

 OW'S YOUR UNDERSTANDING?

Here are two questions you should be able to answer, based on what you have just read:

1. What does the balance sheet's net figure for accounts receivable represent?

2. Are you likely to see separate disclosure of the allowance contra or nontrade receivables? Why or why not?

8.6   INVENTORY VALUATION AND COST OF GOODS SOLD

Inventories, like other current assets, are valued at lower of cost or market.

Inventory accounting, like accounting for other current assets, follows the lower of cost or market rule. It starts with the historical cost of the inventory. But, because inventory is expected to be turned into cash (sold), or otherwise consumed within the next year, it is a current asset, and because it is a current asset, GAAP require that any impairment in the asset's value be recognized in the period when the impairment occurred, not leaving that until later when the asset is sold or used.

Inventory accounting affects both balance sheet values and income (via COGS).

This section explains how to determine cost. The following section, 8.7, explains how to determine market and calculate the lower of the two. Inventory accounting affects both the balance sheet (inventory valuation) and the expense recognized for the use of inventory (cost of goods sold expense, COGS). Inventories include raw materials, work still in process and not yet ready for sale, finished or purchased goods held for sale, and supplies held for use within the business. *Financial Reporting in Canada 1999* indicates that 180 of its 200 surveyed companies reported having inventories and about a third each reported: all inventories in one figure, some inventory categories separately, or all inventory categories separately.[6]

Inventory Cost Flow Assumptions

Total cost is just the sum of quantity times unit cost for all items of inventory.

- We can get the quantity by counting the items, estimating the quantity, or using records (remember inventory control in section 7.8).

- We know that unit cost includes the invoiced cost plus inward shipping, preparation, and so on (section 8.3).

- Finding total cost, therefore, seems easy: just identify each item in inventory, trace it back to the purchase records, figure out its cost, and add all the costs together.

Attaching cost to actual items of inventory is likely difficult and costly, even impossible.

But is it so easy? Imagine the trouble you'd have keeping track of the invoiced cost, shipping, and other cost components for every item in a hardware store's inventory, or the impossibility of keeping track of individual barrels of oil in an oil refinery. Even if it were possible to do it somehow, the value of the resulting "precise" costing would be unlikely to be worth the trouble and cost to do it.

Few companies use actual cost for their inventories.

In practice, the actual cost of inventory items is tracked only for high-value items (houses, automobiles, airplanes, expensive jewellery) that can be identified by serial numbers and other methods. As the cost of keeping records decreases due to computerization, more items can be tracked this way. Still, serial numbers or other ways to identify specific inventory items are needed. According to *Financial Reporting in Canada 1999*, only about 8 of the 200 companies in its survey said they used actual, or "specific identification," cost for any inventories, and they used it only for some inventories, using assumed cost flow methods for other inventories.[7]

Inventory costing usually assumes how inventories and costs flow through the business.

For most inventories, because it is not worthwhile or even possible to keep track of the cost of individual items in inventory, most companies figure out their balance sheet inventory cost and cost of goods sold expense by *assuming* some flow of inventory items and their costs through the business. Management can't know or doesn't want to have to know exactly which ones are on hand, or which have been sold, so assumptions are used.

Assumptions about inventory cost flow lead to calculations of inventory and COGS amounts. The more information used in those calculations, the more precise, the closer to "actual" cost, the result is. Usually more information is available about more important or more valuable inventories, and if the company has a perpetual inventory control system, that provides more information than a simpler periodic system does. The examples below use whatever information is available, or else ignore some of it to simplify the conceptual points about comparing the methods. Later in this section, the assumptions' relative effects on the balance sheet inventory asset and the income statement's COGS expense are summarized.

We'll start with a simple example of how **assumed cost flow** works. The example involves inventory purchased for resale (such as a retailer would purchase), but the ideas work just as well for inventory manufactured by a company: in that case, cost of *purchases* is replaced by cost of *goods manufactured*. The example is in Figure 8.2. There were 120 units on hand at the beginning and 210 were purchased, so 330 units were *available for sale* during the period. After selling 180 units, 150 units remained on hand at the end of the period. The *cost of goods available for sale* equals the cost of the beginning inventory plus the cost of those purchased (or manufactured). So we have $120 \times \$2 = \$240$, plus $100 \times \$3 = \$300$, plus $110 \times \$4 = \$440$, for a total cost of goods *available* of $980.

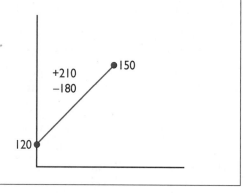

FIGURE 8.2

The period's available inventory cost is allocated between inventory asset and COGS.

The inventory costing problem is how to *allocate* the $980 between the income statement for the period (cost of goods sold expense) and the balance sheet at the end of the period (ending inventory asset). The former (expense) is directed at the **income measurement** for the period, and the latter at the **asset valuation** at the end of the period. Because the financial statements *articulate*, the former and the latter are contending "pieces of the pie": the more money allocated to the former, the less to the latter, and vice versa. *Their sum always equals the available cost, in this case, $980.*

The chart in Figure 8.3 depicts the situation.

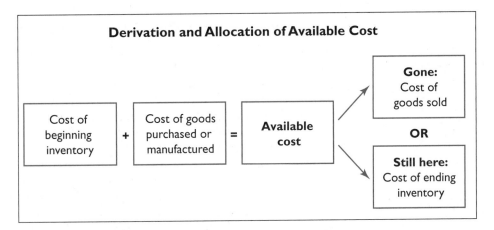

FIGURE 8.3

Exhibit 8.2 shows three different assumptions that may underlie decisions about how to do that allocation. *In each case, the sum of the ending balance sheet asset valuation and the cost of goods sold expense is $980.* The different cost flow assumptions just allocate this available cost differently between the balance sheet valuation and the income statement expense. The two boxes on the right in Figure 8.3 change in opposite directions, because their sum is unchanged.

Exhibit

	Ending Inventory Asset	Cost of Goods Sold Expense
1. **"First in, first out" assumption** — FIFO assumes that the first items acquired are the first ones sold, and, therefore, that any ending inventory on hand consists of the most recently acquired units (recent costs on balance sheet, older costs in COGS expense).	$(110 \times \$4) + (40 \times \$3) = \$560$	$\$980 - \$560 = \$420$ $([120 \times \$2] + [60 \times \$3] = \$420)$
2. **Weighted annual average assumption** — AVGE assumes ending inventory and COGS are composed of a mixture of old and new units.	Average unit cost = $\$980/330 = \$2.97$ (rounded) $150 \times \$2.97 = \$445$	$\$980 - \$445 = \$535$ $(180 \times \$2.97 = \$535)$
3. **"Last in, first out" assumption** — LIFO assumes the opposite of FIFO, saying that any inventory on hand consists of the oldest units (older costs on balance sheet, recent costs in COGS expense).	$(120 \times \$2) + (30 \times \$3) = \$330$	$\$980 - \$330 = \$650$ $([110 \times \$4] + [70 \times \$3] = \$650)$

More about Inventory Cost Flow Assumptions

The choice of inventory method matters only if purchase or manufacturing costs change.

The above example introduced three cost flow assumptions, FIFO, AVGE, and LIFO. These three assumptions are a traditional part of GAAP. If costs of purchases or manufacturing don't change much, then there won't be much difference between the inventory costs and COGS produced by the assumptions. In recent years, inflation in most Western countries has been low, so the different methods do not currently matter much to the reported income and assets of most companies, but most companies will still tell you what method is being used, because each company may experience cost price changes that matter for it. It's therefore useful to know how the assumptions work; also, inflation may return some day.

Let's examine these assumptions further. Remember that, because each assumption *allocates* the available inventory cost between the inventory asset and the cost of goods sold expense differently, the choice of assumption has an effect on *both* the balance sheet and the income statement. The significance of the effect depends on how much purchase (or manufacturing) costs per unit rise or fall during the period. Companies don't have to use a cost flow assumption that matches the physical way inventory is managed, though it makes sense if there is such a match, so choosing inventory accounting policy usually takes physical flow into consideration.

FIFO is a convenient, popular, sensible inventory flow assumption.

FIFO assigns the more recent purchase costs to the balance sheet inventory asset account, and, therefore, older costs to the COGS expense account. FIFO means "first in, first out," but it might help you to think of it also as "last in, still here" because the method uses the costs of the most recently acquired items to get the balance sheet cost.

- FIFO is used because it is convenient and produces inventory asset values that are close to current costs, which seems to many people to be appropriate for a current asset.

- It is convenient because all you really need to do is keep your purchase invoices and, when you know how many units are on hand, just go through recent invoices to find the costs. For example, suppose there are 620 boxes of chocolates on hand at Dec. 31, and recent purchase invoices showed the following costs: Dec. 29, 260 boxes at $3.20; Dec. 14, 310 boxes at $3.35; Dec. 1, 210 boxes at $3; and so on. The FIFO cost is found by starting with the most recent purchase and going back in time until all the ones on hand are accounted for (working on assumption, since we do not really know when any particular box was purchased). The reasoning is this:

Amount on hand:	620 boxes	
Most recent purchase	<u>260</u> boxes: invoice cost = $3.20 × 260	= $ 832.00
Leaves (from prior purchases)	360 boxes	
Next most recent purchase	<u>310</u> boxes: invoice cost = $3.35 × 310	= 1,038.50
Leaves (from prior purchase)	50 boxes: invoice cost = $3.00 × 50	= <u>150.00</u>
Total FIFO cost		= <u>$2,020.50</u>

You don't need complicated records, just a pile of invoices. It doesn't matter what the internal control method is, because it doesn't provide any further necessary information: all you need to know is the quantity on hand at the balance sheet date, whether determined by count or by perpetual records.

- Using FIFO, COGS can be determined just by subtracting the ending inventory determined from the purchase invoices (or manufacturing cost records) from the available cost. You can reason COGS out separately, and that will be demonstrated below, but one of the advantages of the FIFO method is that you don't have to bother.

- *Financial Reporting in Canada 1999* indicates that in 1998, 49 of the 141 companies that disclosed their cost determination method used FIFO alone, and another 23 companies that used more than one method used FIFO.[8] This is 51% of the 141 companies that disclosed, so FIFO is a popular method.

- FIFO is considered appropriate for a current asset by many people because it is the most reasonable method of physically moving inventory, especially inventory that is perishable or subject to changes in style or features, such as groceries, clothing, and other retail products. Picture a shelf in a grocery store: FIFO assumes that new stock is placed behind older stock on the shelf, so that the inventory keeps moving forward on the shelf. That way older items sell first and do not just collect dust and mould at the back of the shelf. It's the way we hope perishable inventory would actually be managed!

AVGE is sensible and popular for bulk products and raw materials.

AVGE assigns the available cost equally to the inventory asset and to cost of goods sold expense. In the example in Figure 8.2 and Exhibit 8.2 above, both inventory asset and cost of goods sold used the same $2.97 average cost per unit.

- Average cost is used largely for inventories that are a mixture of recent and older purchases and that are not particularly perishable, such as lumber, metals, oil, gas, and other bulk products and raw materials. The AVGE assumption that the inventory items are all mixed together makes sense for such inventories.

- The AVGE method is not just an average of the prices paid for the inventory items. Rather, the average is calculated by *weighting* the prices by the amount of inventory acquired at each price. Therefore, a small batch of items affects the average less than a large batch. The word "weighted" is sometimes used with the word "average" to emphasize this approach.

- The average calculation is affected by the amount of information available about inventory changes during the period. The most common average method is called "moving weighted average": using it, the average cost of the inventory on hand is recalculated every time there is a purchase (or an additional batch manufactured). The average thus moves up and down as cost prices change, and the average at the balance sheet date is whatever the most recent moving average was. The balance sheet date is nothing special, just another date in the continuing sequence of inventory changes. Calculating a moving average is very tedious when done by hand, but a computer-based perpetual inventory system can do it easily, so moving average is more likely for important or computer-controlled inventories. Let's take the following scenario:

Prior to any purchase, we have H1 units on hand at a unit cost of C.

Purchase (or manufacturing) batch 1 costs P1 per unit, and there are N1 units.

Some units are then sold, leaving H2 units on hand.

Purchase (or manufacturing) batch 2 costs P2 per unit, and there are N2 units.

And so on.

H1 units on hand	+	N1 units acq-uired	=	H1 + N1 units on hand	−	Some units sold	=	H2 units on hand	+	N2 units acq-uired	...
Unit Cost C		Unit Cost P1		Average Cost A1		Unit Cost A1		Unit Cost A1		Unit Cost P2	

Using the above example, a moving weighted average is calculated like this:

- The first moving average assumes the H1 units on hand and the N1 units added are mixed together, so their average cost is $[(C \times H1) + (P1 \times N1)] / (H1 + N1)$.

- This average, called A1 above, is used for the cost of any items on hand or COGS of any sold after that, prior to the next purchase or manufacturing batch.

- Prior to the next purchase or manufacturing batch, there are H2 units on hand.

- Second moving average is $[(A1 \times H2) + (P2 \times N2)] / (H2 + N2)$, call it A2.

- Average A2 is used for inventory on hand or COGS, until the next purchase.

- And so on.

Financial Reporting in Canada 1999 says that in 1998 the (weighted) average cost method was the most popular among its 200 companies, with 59 companies using it alone and 26 using it in combination with other methods. The total of 85 is 60% of the 141 companies disclosing their inventory costing method.[9] This popularity reflects the Canadian economy's emphasis on natural resources, such as gas, oil, lumber, and coal: companies in these sectors are very likely to use average cost.

LIFO is not a sensible flow assumption, but it saves tax in the United States (although not in Canada).

LIFO is, on the face of it, a strange valuation method. It assumes that the *newer* items are sold first and, therefore, that the *older* are the ones left on hand. In the extreme, this would imply that the grocery store's first loaves of bread are still at the back of the shelf, years later. LIFO means "last in, first out," but you could also think of it as "first in, still here" as a reminder of its odd assumption.

- LIFO is used for one very practical reason: in the United States, it is an allowable method for income tax purposes. In a period of rising purchase costs (inflation), which is pretty much constantly the case even though at a reduced rate in recent years, it produces a higher cost of goods sold expense and a lower inventory asset value than do FIFO or AVGE. Therefore, LIFO also produces lower income and lower income tax, *if* it can be used for tax purposes.

- In Canada, LIFO is *not* an allowable method for income tax purposes, so a Canadian company using it for the financial statements would have to compute inventory values all over again using one of the other methods when doing its income tax return.

- *Financial Reporting in Canada 1999* indicates that, in 1998, only 6 Canadian companies (out of the 200 surveyed) used LIFO, three using it for all inventories and three using it for only some inventories.[10] (It would make sense to use it for inventories held by U.S. subsidiaries of Canadian companies, or if a U.S. parent company used it and required it of a Canadian subsidiary.)

- It can be argued that LIFO matches revenues with expenses better than the other two methods do. For example, if a company changes its selling prices as its purchase costs change, its revenues reflect recent price changes and it then seems appropriate to deduct the more recent purchase costs as cost of goods sold expense against the revenues. The trouble is that LIFO produces inventory asset values that are based on older purchase costs and this seems awkward for valuing a current asset.

- It would be nice to use current purchase prices for cost of goods sold expense and for the balance sheet inventory value. But that can't be done if we stick to the double-entry historical cost accounting basis: the books wouldn't balance because some of the units would have been purchased at older costs and those costs would be in the accounts, too, in the inventory asset or expense accounts.

- LIFO calculations are affected by the amount of information available. Like AVGE, there is a more tedious calculation when there is more information, as a perpetual control method provides. This tedious calculation results in "layers" of costs that are attributable to various stages of the LIFO calculation. If you read about "LIFO layers," that is what is being referred to. This book will not get into these details because of LIFO's low popularity and lack of tax acceptability in Canada. However, one thing to be aware of is that if inventory quantities fall, old costs in the LIFO inventory are transferred into COGS, and this can produce a sudden decline in COGS and increase in income.

Effects Analysis and Comparative Summary

Below, an example ("Meeix") reviews how to calculate inventory costs and COGS using five methods:

1. FIFO.
2. A simple annual weighted AVGE, which does not require information about inventory movements during the year, used here to illustrate how the average works before showing the moving average.

3. Moving weighted AVGE, the better AVGE method if information is available about inventory movements during the year.
4. A simple periodic LIFO, which also does not require information about inventory movements during the period, used to emphasize the LIFO assumption before showing the perpetual LIFO.
5. Perpetual LIFO, the better LIFO method if information is available about inventory movements during the year.

The following summarizes the Meeix example's results. Without necessarily following all the calculations below, you should be able to understand the effects on the financial statements of choosing among the inventory cost methods, *assuming* that in all cases cost is lower than market value for the ending inventory asset and so making market value irrelevant in the lower of cost or market inventory valuation.

8-3

Exhibit

Cost Method	Ending Inventory Asset	Cost of Goods Sold Expense	Total Cost Available
FIFO	$6,300	$5,500	$11,800
AVGE — Annual	5,408	6,392	11,800
— Moving	5,957	5,843	11,800
LIFO — Periodic	4,500	7,300	11,800
— Perpetual	5,600	6,200	11,800

This example illustrates a result that is common when using these methods. In a period of rising purchase prices (as here) or rising manufacturing costs:

- FIFO tends to have the highest inventory asset value and lowest cost of goods sold expense (and therefore highest net income).

- LIFO tends to have the lowest inventory asset value and highest COGS (and therefore lowest net income).

- AVGE tends to be between the other two in asset values, COGS, and net income.

The three methods' effects on assets and income are predictable if prices rise or fall.

The size of the effects depends on turnover and patterns of price and quantity changes.

If purchase prices are falling, the positions of FIFO and LIFO reverse, with FIFO tending to have the lowest net income and LIFO the highest. AVGE tends again to be between the other two.

The differences among the methods are larger the more purchase cost prices rise (or fall) during the period. The differences tend to be smaller when inventory turnover is high, because price changes occurring during the time inventory is held are smaller and the size of the inventory asset relative to cost of goods sold expense is smaller. If a perpetual LIFO or moving average method is being used, the differences can also be in unexpected directions, depending on coincidental increases or decreases in inventory levels. The LIFO perpetual ending inventory for Meeix is higher than the annual average ending inventory because a large amount of the beginning inventory was sold, so the LIFO perpetual method used this information, but the annual average did not. The relationships among the methods also can stray from the typical pattern if purchase price changes and inventory quantities are moving in opposite directions (for example, if inventory levels are falling, but prices are rising, or vice versa).

An Example: Meeix Inc.

This example is used to back up the general conclusions above. Keep the conclusions in mind as you review how the methods' assumptions change the allocation of available cost between the ending inventory asset and the COGS expense. Don't get lost in the calculations.

Among the products Meeix Inc. purchases and sells is Gloop. It began last year with 1,000 units of Gloop on hand at a cost of $4 each, and during the year its purchase and sales records showed:

8-4

Exhibit

Date	Units Purchased	Units Sold	Units on Hand	Purchase Price
Jan. 1			1,000	$4
Feb. 15		350	650	
Mar. 20	600		1,250	$5
Apr. 30		750	500	
Sept. 12	800		1,300	$6
Dec. 11		200	1,100	
	1,400	1,300		

It is always useful to know what available cost has to be allocated.

Let's start with available cost. *Regardless of the cost flow assumption to be used*, we know that the beginning inventory cost is $4,000 and that purchases costing $7,800 (600 × $5 + 800 × $6) were made. Available cost, therefore, is the sum of beginning inventory and purchases, which sum is $11,800. Consequently, as long as the historical cost basis of accounting is used, any inventory cost allocation method must produce $11,800 as the sum of the ending inventory asset and cost of goods sold expense, as was depicted in Exhibit 8.3.

Given the available cost, you only need COGS expense to deduce the asset or vice versa.

This gives us a way to check our calculations. If we calculate cost of goods sold expense and ending inventory asset cost separately, they must add up to $11,800. As a short cut, we can calculate *either* the expense or the asset value and deduce the other by deducting it from $11,800. This is easier than doing it twice, but the calculations below will include both the expense and the asset so that you can see how it all works.

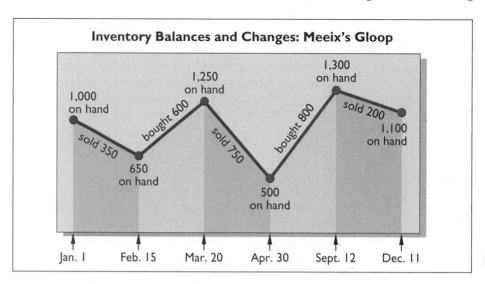

FIGURE 8.4

The chart in Figure 8.4 shows how the quantities of Gloop changed during the year. Before trying any of the methods' calculations, keep in mind how the methods' cost flow assumptions would treat the ending inventory's 1,100 units:

- FIFO:
  1,100 = 800 most recently bought + 300 of those bought Mar. 20.

- AVGE:
  Annual weighted: the 1,100 are a proportionate mixture of those on hand at the beginning and those bought Mar. 20 and Sept. 12.
  Moving weighted: the first average is the 1,250 on hand at Mar. 20, a proportionate mixture of those on hand at beginning plus those bought Mar. 20; the second average, the 1,300 on hand Sept. 12, is a proportionate mixture of the first average (on hand Apr. 30) and those bought Sept. 12.

- LIFO:
  Periodic: the 1,100 must be the 1,000 on hand at beginning plus 100 next oldest, those bought Mar. 20 (no account taken of changes in inventory balances during the period).
  Perpetual: during the year, the inventory hit a minimum of 500, so that's all of the beginning items that could still be on hand at the end, therefore 1,100 = 500 from beginning plus 600 bought in the first purchase after that, Sept. 12 (the only purchase since then).

Based on the patterns shown in Figure 8.4 and the above summary of each method's assumption about the ending inventory quantity, here are the calculations for ending inventory cost and cost of goods sold.

a. **FIFO**
    Ending inventory cost: (800 × $6) + (remaining 300 × $5) $ 6,300
    Cost of goods sold expense:
        (1,000 × $4) + (remaining 300 × $5)   5,500

    $11,800

b. **AVGE**
    b.1 *Annual weighted average*
        Average cost = $11,800 / (1,000 + 600 + 800) = $4.917 (rounded)
        Ending inventory cost: 1,100 × $4.917 $ 5,408
        Cost of goods sold expense: 1,300 × $4.917   6,392

        $11,800

    b.2 *Moving weighted average*
        The average works the same way as the above weighted
        average, but it is recalculated after each purchase, weighted
        in accordance with the inventory on hand at that point.
        Weighted average after first purchase
            = ([650 × $4] + [600 × $5]) / (650 + 600) = $4.48
        Weighted average after second purchase
            = ([500 × $4.48] + [800 × $6]) / (500 + 800) = $5.415
        Ending inventory cost (using average at that point):
            1,100 × $5.415 $ 5,957
        Cost of goods sold expense (using the average immediately
            preceding each sale):
            (350 × $4) + (750 × $4.48) + (200 × $5.415)   5,843

        $11,800

c. **LIFO**
    c.1 *Periodic basis*
        Ending inventory cost: (1,000 × $4) + (remaining 100 × $5) $ 4,500
        Cost of goods sold expense: (800 × $6) + (remaining 500 × $5)   7,300

        $11,800

    c.2 *Perpetual basis*
        The perpetual records allow us to determine whether it is
        reasonable to assume that all the original 1,000 units are
        still on hand. In this example it is not, because at one point
        the inventory was down to 500 units, so that "layer" of
        cost has been partly used up. The calculation reflects the
        "cost layer" information available from the records.
        Ending inventory cost: (500 × $4) + (remaining 600
            bought since × $6) $ 5,600
        Cost of goods sold expense: (350 × $4) + (600 × $5
            [layer all gone]) + (further 150 from the original
            layer × $4) + (200 from the most recent layer × $6)   6,200

        $11,800

OW'S YOUR UNDERSTANDING?

Here are two questions you should be able to answer, based on what you have just read:

1. Beyond the general criteria for accounting policy choice, such as fairness, how does a company decide which method to use in determining the cost of inventory?

2. Meeix Inc. also stocks a pet food called Dog's Breakfast. Last year, there were 200 crates of Dog's Breakfast on hand at the beginning of the year, and 1,500 crates were purchased and 1,450 crates were sold during the year. The crates on hand at the beginning cost $400 each. There were three purchases: early in the year, 500 crates costing $404 each were purchased; then 600 crates costing $390 each; and near the end of the year, 400 crates costing $384.50 each were purchased. What would be the cost of the inventory at the end of the year and the cost of goods sold expense under (a) FIFO? (b) simple annual AVGE? and (c) periodic LIFO? ((a) $96,125; $573,675; (b) $98,500; $571,300; (c) $100,200; $569,600.)

8.7   LOWER OF COST OR MARKET AND OTHER COSTING METHODS

Inventory Market Value for Lower of Cost or Market Rule

There are two common perspectives on this rule:

Replacement cost makes sense for the market value of inventory to be used, not sold.

- For inventory that is not to be sold, but rather to be used up (for example, manufacturing raw materials, factory supplies, and office supplies), the *input* market value or *replacement cost* seems most relevant. Replacement cost is determined by obtaining prices from suppliers and making other estimates of what it would cost to replace the items on hand. The focus is on items whose supply prices are falling because, remember, we're concerned only with cases in which market (replacement cost) is *lower* than the cost originally paid, or assumed to have been paid, for the items.

Net realizable value makes sense for the market value of inventory that is to be sold.

- For inventory that is to be sold, the *output* market value or *net realizable value* seems most relevant. Net realizable value is determined by taking selling prices and deducting any costs to complete the items (such as putting them in a box) or selling them. Again, the focus is on items whose net realizable value is below cost, so we're concerned about items whose selling prices are falling or that have been damaged, or have become obsolete, or out of style so that we can't sell them for what we thought we could.

Lower of Cost or Market

Basically, to calculate the lower of cost or market value, we just take the cost of the items and compare those costs to the market values and use the *lower* as the balance sheet inventory value. Here is an example:

Example of Lower of Cost or Market Calculation

Inventory Item	Quantity	Total Cost	Total Market	L of C or M
Part #493-A	500 units	$ 2,000	$ 2,600	$ 2,000 (C)
Part #499	60 kg	432	420	420 (M)
Product #239	1,000 units	60,000	75,000	60,000 (C)
Product #240	200 units	3,000	700	700 (M)
Etc.				
TOTALS (let's say)		$643,290	$858,400	$629,680

The inventory figure shown on the balance sheet is either:

a. the sum of the final column ($629,680), which is the sum of the lower of cost or market calculated on each individual item; or

b. the total cost ($643,290), on the assumption that since total market ($858,400) exceeds total cost, no adjustment down to market is needed.

Lower of cost or market comparison may be done by item (conservative) or overall.

Alternative (a) is more conservative, but (b) is likely to be used if there is no evidence of a serious problem overall with the inventory.

Using the conservative method (a) for illustration, the lower values for some (Part #499, Product #240, and apparently others) bring the sum of the lower values ($629,680) to less than the total cost ($643,290) by $13,610. If we were being conservative, we'd record a loss of $13,610, debiting a Loss expense account and crediting Inventory asset, assuming the perpetual control method. (Instead of crediting Inventory directly, an "Allowance for reduction in inventory" account, like the Allowance for doubtful accounts receivable, could be used.) But the loss account would be unlikely to be disclosed separately from COGS on the income statement, because as long as it is not large (material), it is a normal sort of thing and the reader should assume any company has some such minor losses. After all, if the items had been sold during the year, such as in a clearance sale, the reduced revenue would have been part of revenue and the cost would have been in COGS, so the "loss" would have been buried in the overall revenue minus the COGS part of the income calculation.

If any reduction from cost to market is necessary, it becomes an expense for the period.

In practice, companies usually focus mainly on items whose values are likely to be impaired (as might be identified during the physical count), rather than calculating market value for everything. Also, often the kind of inventory suggests both a cost flow assumption and a market value method. For example:

- Raw materials are often shown at the lower of average cost and replacement cost, while

- Goods for sale are usually shown at the lower of FIFO cost and net realizable value.

Often, choices of cost and market methods go together.

Thus we tend to see the cost and market methods going together (average with replacement, FIFO with net realizable value), though there are many exceptions. According to its year 2000 Significant Accounting Policies note, CAE uses lower of average cost and net realizable value for its inventories.[11] The retail method of costing inventory (commented on briefly below) is an amalgamation of costs and selling prices, so it, too, is an example of costs and market values going together.

Canadian financial accounting standards are not explicit about "lower of cost or cost or market" calculations. They are left to the professional judgment of

The inventory cost and market methods are both accounting policy choices.

individual accountants and auditors. In the United States there are a number of rules and regulations, including the "floor–ceiling" rule (in which market equals replacement cost as long as that does not exceed a pair of floor and ceiling values calculated from selling price), which provide more specific guidance. The complexities of these rules and guidelines are best left to other books. But what you should know for now is that figuring out lower of cost or market for inventories requires management to make accounting policy decisions about cost, about market, *and* about comparing them. *Financial Reporting in Canada 1999* reports that in 1998, 90 companies of the 161 that disclosed their market value method used a version of net realizable value only, and just 7 used only replacement cost. But of the 60 reporting using more than one method, 57 used net realizable value and 52 used replacement cost. Interestingly, two apparently conservative companies used the lower of replacement cost and net realizable value to get the market value that was then used in the lower of cost or market calculation!

 OR YOUR INTEREST

Terminology again! Here's a tiny item. This book uses the phrase "lower of cost or market," but the more common phrase is "lower of cost and market." *Financial Reporting in Canada 1999* reports that in its sample, 141 companies used "and" and only 19 used "or" in 1998.[12]

The Retail Inventory and Other Methods

In section 7.8 on inventory control, the retail inventory method was mentioned as a way of combining retail inventory prices with cash and other controls. The method can also be used to estimate inventory costs. *Financial Reporting in Canada 1999* does not mention the retail method, but an earlier edition reported that in 1994, 12 companies (out of the 300 then surveyed) used the retail method.[13] The survey was of large companies; the retail method is probably much more common among smaller companies. The retail method, which, as you might expect, is most applicable for retailers' inventories, combines purchase costs and selling prices into a single calculation. An inventory figure is first determined by valuing items at retail prices (section 7.8) and then cost is estimated by deducting estimated markups from the retail value. As section 7.8 notes, the method is simple in concept but complicated in practice.

A few other inventory costing methods are used. *Financial Reporting in Canada 1995* said that in 1994, 16 companies reported methods other than the ones described here.[14] By 1998, *Financial Reporting in Canada* reported that only 5 of its 200 companies used something other than FIFO, AVGE, or LIFO.[15] One of these, "standard costing" for manufactured inventories, uses estimated costs based on standard production costs and volumes.

OW'S YOUR UNDERSTANDING?

Here are two questions you should be able to answer, based on what you have just read:

1. In using lower of cost or market, how does a company determine "market"?

2. Lytle Inc. has three items in inventory: A (cost $5,200, market $7,000), B (cost $6,100, market $5,700), and C (cost $11,400, market $16,600). Calculate (i) lower of cost or market, (ii) the balance sheet inventory value, and (iii) any loss incurred. For all these, do two calculations and indicate which is the more conservative. (Total cost = $22,700; total market = $29,300; individually, lower of cost or market = $5,200 + $5,700 + $11,400 = $22,300. Answers: First calculation: (i) $22,700, (ii) $22,700, (iii) no loss. Second calculation: (i) $22,300, (ii) $22,300, (iii) $400 loss. The second is more conservative.)

8.8   AMORTIZATION OF ASSETS AND AMORTIZATION EXPENSE

Amortization allocates to expense the cost of all tangible assets except land.

Fixed assets (so-called tangible assets, including land, buildings, equipment, furniture, vehicles, computers, etc.) have value because the company intends to receive economic benefits from using them in the future. However, with the exception of land, no fixed assets have an unlimited useful life, so all must eventually be retired from service. Amortization is the process of allocating the cost over years of benefit, and the annual deduction from revenue is amortization expense. According to GAAP, all fixed assets except land are amortized.

Amortization is based on a prediction of the future and so is inevitably inexact.

Amortization, no matter how carefully calculated, is never exact. It involves a prediction of economic use and useful life, and such a prediction can easily be wrong. If assets are grouped together for computing amortization, the errors can be reduced because some assets for which the prediction overshoots may be offset by others for which it undershoots. Any amortization amount is fundamentally arbitrary; for that reason, most companies prefer fairly simple calculations rather than complex guesses! Correcting for errors in amortization estimates is considered so routine that such error corrections are not disclosed separately in the income statement, but are just included with amortization expense.

OR YOUR INTEREST

As was noted in section 1.8, the terminology for amortization is changing. You'll see the terms "amortization," "depreciation," and "depletion" in newspapers, financial statements, databases, and elsewhere. Historically, *depreciation* has been used for physical assets, such as buildings and equipment; *depletion* has been used for "wasting assets," such as timber sales or ore bodies; and *amortization* has been used for various miscellaneous and intangible assets. The usage is changing: since 1990, the *CICA Handbook* has used **amortization** as the only term, and this book uses that term most of the time. **Depreciation** and **depletion** may eventually disappear from Canadian financial statements. But they may not: they are deeply entrenched terms, especially depreciation.

Why Allocate the Cost?

Amortization allocates the cost of a long-lived asset to expense over the asset's useful life.

Amortization is a technique for *measuring income* by matching an allocation of the asset's cost to the revenue it is presumed to help earn. Assets are resources of the enterprise, used in order to generate revenue for the owners and, ultimately, a return on their investment. One of the objectives of accrual accounting is to attempt to match expenses with the revenue earned, as we saw in Chapter 6. In the case of long-lived assets, the cost will benefit many periods in which revenue is earned. When purchasing a fixed asset such as a building or equipment, the rational purchaser will at least have an approximate idea of how much benefit the asset will provide. For example, when buying a piece of equipment to slice bread, the baker must have a reasonable idea of how many loaves it will slice, before it wears out or a better slicer becomes available. If the baker can estimate how many loaves it will slice, the baker can then deduct the cost of the machine from revenue a part at a time, over the number of years it will take to bake that many loaves of bread. If the whole asset cost were deducted from income in the period in which it was acquired, that would make that period's income relatively low, and subsequent periods' incomes relatively high. Amortization spreads the cost out over all the periods that share in the using up of the asset's economic value. Therefore, accounting amortization is a cost allocation system, used to measure income: *it is not a system to track value changes in the assets or to measure the current or market value of those assets in the balance sheet.*

Amortization's cost allocation is based on what is expected to happen in the future.

- Suppose the bread slicer mentioned above cost $5,000 and will have no value to the business after eight years. Amortization of $5,000 over eight years (for example, $625 of amortization expense each year) shows that using up the slicer's economic value over those years costs the baker something. The baker has a $5,000 economic asset now, but in eight years will have no economic asset, even if the slicer still exists physically.

Amortization allocates cost to expense, it does not track changes in market value.

- Over the years, the cost and resale value of bread slicers may keep changing due to inflation, market conditions, or technological change. The baker may be able to resell the slicer for only $3,000 after one year, so perhaps the market value used up in that year is $2,000, but if the amortization method specifies $625 per year, that is what is used in the accounts and financial statements. The balance sheet shows the net of the asset's original cost minus accumulated amortization: it does *not* mean the asset's current or market value is that net "book value" amount. In the above example, after one year the balance sheet shows the bread slicer at $4,375 ($5,000 cost less $625), not at $3,000 or any other measure of current value. Knowing what is happening to market values may be very important. If so, the manager has to look elsewhere than financial accounting for the information.

Why Not Amortize Land?

Land is not amortized because its value is not considered to be consumed as it is used.

The basic answer is that land's economic value is not considered to decline through use. Land is considered immune to physical or economic decline. As a machine is used in a production process, it wears out, like the soles of your shoes as you walk. But such wear and tear, and other natural processes, such as wind, rain, rust, fatigue, and corrosion, are not thought to affect the economic value of land, nor are nonphysical causes of economic amortization. A machine can become obsolete with the advent of newer and faster machines, economic conditions in an area can result in the closure of a plant that has many productive years left but cannot be profitable any more, and the whims of fashion can cause retail merchants to change display racks every two years when they were built to last for 10. But land continues on.

However, land can collapse, turn to swamp or otherwise lose its value, so if evidence of a loss of land value *does* appear, the land's cost can be reduced to a revised value, but that is a special case and is a write-down or write-off "loss" rather than amortization.

When Does the Cost Allocation (Amortization Expense) Begin?

The cost determined for the asset is amortized after the asset goes into service.

Amortization is meant to provide an expense to match the economic benefit obtained from the use of the asset. Therefore, when the asset is put to use and the benefit begins to be realized, amortization expense should begin. The general pattern is to capitalize costs incurred on the asset prior to putting it into service, and then, when the asset is put into service, to amortize those costs.

This pattern is illustrated in the chart in Figure 8.5, which is similar to Figure 8.1 used in section 8.3 to explain the components of asset cost. *The line sloping downward from cost need not be a straight one, as we will see.*

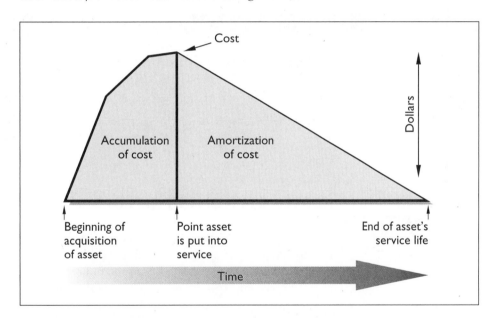

FIGURE 8.5

Amortization, Income Tax, and Cash Flow

Amortization in the accounts is irrelevant for income tax purposes in Canada.

In Canada, amortization calculated in the accounts is irrelevant for income tax purposes because the federal and provincial income tax laws requires companies (and individuals) to follow their rules, not GAAP, in computing taxable income. A company can use whatever GAAP amortization method it likes in its financial statements, but whatever that is, it is still irrelevant for income tax purposes.

Amortization has no effect on cash or cash flow.

The amortization entry (Dr Amortization expense, Cr Accumulated amortization) has no cash component, so amortization has no cash effect. The fact that amortization appears on the cash flow statement using the traditional indirect method (section 4.5) often misleads people: because it is added to income, so it seems to be a source of cash. But amortization and adjustments in it to correct errors in estimation have no effect on cash one way or the other. Amortization is added back to income at the beginning of the cash flow statement to remove its effect from accrual accounting income and so to help convert that income to cash income.

Amortization Is a Useful Part of Historical Cost Accounting

Amortization is a useful but inexact allocation of asset cost to expense, to match revenue.

Amortization does not match actual market value changes in assets, it has no cash effect, it is an estimate only, and it has no income tax effect! What good is it? That's a question often asked, and the answer goes back to the matching criterion and historical cost basis of accrual accounting. We know that some economic value is being used up as a depreciable asset is used in earning revenue. Since we are limited to using cost in measuring that value, we end up with a way of spreading the cost out over the useful life to match the presumed consumption of that cost to the benefits (revenue) gained from the use. If we didn't have the historical cost basis or matching, we probably wouldn't need amortization as it is conventionally calculated. But, since we do have them, we have it!

 OW'S YOUR UNDERSTANDING?

Here are two questions you should be able to answer, based on what you have just read:

1. What is amortization of long-lived assets supposed to accomplish?

2. Why is the basis of amortization used by financial accounting controversial, misunderstood, and/or limited in its usefulness?

8.9   GAINS AND LOSSES ON NONCURRENT ASSET DISPOSALS AND WRITE-OFFS

Gains, losses, and write-offs have been covered already, particularly in section 7.7 on contra accounts and section 4.5 on the indirect method of cash flow analysis. This section is a short summary to relate these items to what amortization is and does.

Gains and losses on noncurrent asset sales are separated from revenues and expenses.

When a noncurrent asset is sold, the sale could be handled as ordinary revenues are: the proceeds could be added to revenue and the asset's book value (cost minus accumulated amortization) could be added to the cost of goods sold. But this would mix usually infrequent noncurrent asset sales with day-to-day revenues, obscuring both and allowing one to offset the other, confusing the income statement's measure of performance.

A gain or loss results when the book value of an asset is not equal to the proceeds obtained for it. The gain or loss is just the difference between the proceeds and the book value (cost minus accumulated amortization, if any), resulting in the following entry, described in section 7.7:

A gain or loss is just the difference between proceeds and book value.

> DR Cash or nontrade receivables (proceeds)   XXXX
>   CR Cost of the noncurrent asset   XXXX
> DR Accumulated amortization to date on that asset XXXX
> DR Loss or CR Gain on sale   XXXX or XXXX

Here is an example: Company X has a truck that cost $84,000. The accumulated amortization at the date of sale is $46,000. Therefore, book value is $38,000 at the date of sale. If the company:

    a. sells it for $52,000, there is a gain on sale of $14,000 ($52,000 – $38,000);
    b. sells it for $30,000, there is a loss on sale of $8,000 ($38,000 – $30,000);
    c. throws it away, there is a loss on disposal of $38,000 ($38,000 – $0).

Gains and losses are corrections to the estimates involved in amortization.

The previous section mentioned that amortization is never exact, and so corrections in amortization estimates are routine. This goes for gains and losses on sale, too. You can think of gains and losses as *amortization corrections*. They're pretty well inevitable, given the inexactitude of estimates of useful life and eventual proceeds:

- If the company knew in advance what the proceeds would be and when the sale would happen, it could have amortized the asset down exactly to the proceeds amount by that date, and by the calculations above, there would be no gain or loss.

- If the proceeds are less than book value, there is a loss: in effect, more amortization is needed and that's what the loss really is. (Therefore, the loss is added back to income on the cash flow statement, just as amortization is.)

- If the proceeds are more than book value, there is a gain: in effect, too much amortization was taken and the gain is really just that excess (which caused the lower book value) being recognized. (Therefore, the gain is deducted from income on the cash flow statement; it's just negative amortization.)

These ideas are depicted in Figure 8.6.

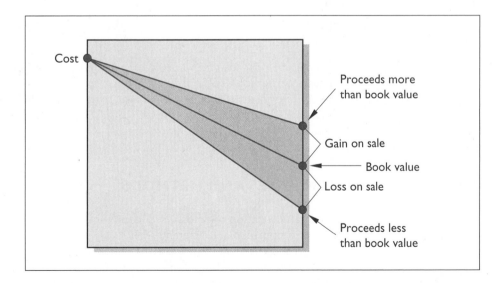

FIGURE 8.6

Many assets are amortized as a group. In such a case, there is usually no gain or loss recognized on the sale of one of the group, because its individual book value is not known. The gain or loss is in effect buried in accumulated amortization by the following journal entry (which is the same as the one above but with no gain or loss):

DR Cash or nontrade receivables (proceeds)   XXXX
        CR Cost of the noncurrent asset   XXXX
DR Accumulated amortization (cost minus proceeds)   XXXX

> A gain or loss cannot be recorded if the asset's book value is not known.

This entry wouldn't work very well if proceeds exceeded cost, but we'll leave that complication out. Burying any gain or loss in accumulated amortization assumes that such gains or losses average out to zero over time. If they do not, the accumulated amortization will get out of line over time. Dealing with this is a subject for more advanced accounting courses.

> Write-offs and write-downs are recorded as asset disposals without proceeds.

The above ideas also work for three other situations, referred to earlier in this text: sales of nonamortized noncurrent assets (investments or land, for example) and write-offs or write-downs of noncurrent assets, whether already amortized or not:

- In the first situation, the gain or loss on sale is just the difference between cost and proceeds because there is no accumulated amortization.

- In the second situation, the asset is being removed from the balance sheet, or being reduced in size, without any cash proceeds, as when the truck above was thrown away in example (c). The write-off amount is just cost, or book value if there is accumulated amortization, because there is no "proceeds" line in the journal entry.

- The write-down amount similarly involves no proceeds.

(H)OW'S YOUR UNDERSTANDING?

Here are two questions you should be able to answer, based on what you have just read:

1. In what way is a gain or loss on a noncurrent asset disposal just an amortization adjustment?

2. A company disposed of a whole factory that cost $12,500,000 and had accumulated amortization of $8,700,000. What was the gain or loss on disposal (or loss on write-off) under each of the following cases: proceeds $4,500,000; proceeds $2,400,000, proceeds zero (write-off)? ($700,000 gain; $1,400,000 loss; write-off loss $3,800,000, which is the book value)

8.10   AMORTIZATION BASES AND METHODS

> Amortization expense should match the asset's presumed contribution to revenue.

Several amortization methods are commonly used today. Different methods attempt to approximate different economic use patterns of the assets over their lives. In each case, the purpose is to *match* the amortization expense for each period to the presumed economic benefit obtained during that period, often in a simple way, since amortization is an estimate rather than an exact measure of value changes. That presumed economic benefit should be reflected in the revenue for the period, so amortization expense therefore should match with revenue.

As amortization accumulates, the book value of the asset falls.

As noted in section 7.7 on contra accounts, the accumulated amortization account is a balance sheet offset account to the asset cost account. Over time, it accumulates the total of the amortization expense recorded over the years. *As this accumulation rises, book value falls.* This falling book value is depicted in the figures in sections 8.3, 8.7, and 8.8. The decline in book value is important to understanding the methods and diagrams in this section.

Amortization methods follow four general assumptions about assets' economic benefits.

There are four basic assumptions about how an asset brings economic benefit, and a kind of amortization (cost allocation) for each (the third one, included for completeness, is rarely seen):

Assumption about Benefit	Kind of Cost Allocation
1. *Evenly over the asset's life* The asset is assumed to be equally valuable in earning income in each year of its useful life.	*Straight-line* Expense is the same each year of the useful life.
2. *Falling over the asset's life* The asset's value in its early years is assumed to be greater than that in its later years.	*Accelerated, declining balance* Expense is larger in the earlier years than in the later years.
3. *Rising over the asset's life* Opposite to assumption 2 above.	*Decelerated* Opposite to accelerated.
4. *Variable over the asset's life* The asset's value in earning income varies according to how much production is achieved each year.	*Units of production, depletion* Expense depends on each year's volume of production.

Amortization expense is a cost allocation representing the asset's economic use.

These four general kinds are compared graphically in Figure 8.7. Each has a different amortization expense per period, *the expense being designed to represent the estimated value of the asset in generating revenue per period*, and a different pattern of book value. Book value equals cost minus accumulated amortization, so, because cost is constant, the book value pattern comes from the accumulation of the amortization.

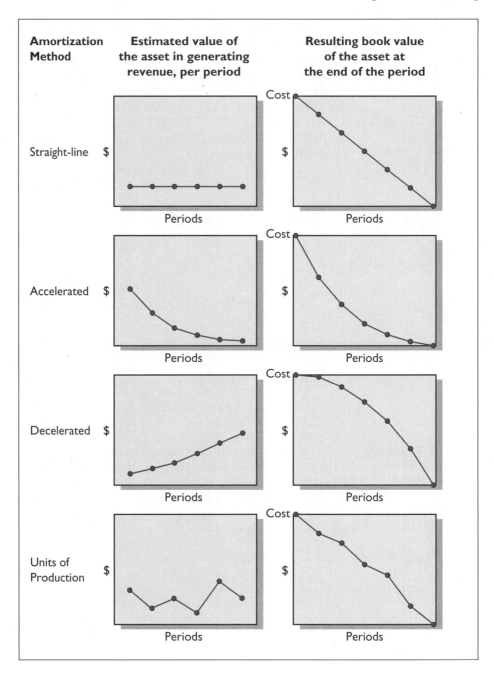

FIGURE 8.7

Terminology. You may be wondering where the names "accelerated" and "decelerated" amortization come from. They are from comparisons with straight-line amortization.

- Accelerated amortization is accelerated (higher expense) in comparison with straight-line amortization in the early years of the asset's life (compare the accelerated expense pattern with the straight-line one in the left-hand diagrams in Figure 8.7).

- Decelerated amortization has a smaller expense than straight-line amortization in the early years of the asset's life (compare the decelerated expense pattern with the straight-line one in Figure 8.7).

The reason for the name "units of production" is explained later.

I. Straight-Line Amortization

Straight-line amortization is simple and popular.

Straight-line amortization, depicted in the top panel of Figure 8.7, is the simplest and most widely used of all the amortization methods. *Financial Reporting in Canada 1999* reports that in 1998, 197 of the 200 surveyed companies disclosed their amortization, depletion, or depreciation method. Of those, 89 used only straight-line and 90 more used it for some assets, a total of 177 of the companies.[16] It is nearly always used for amortization of intangible assets (see section 8.11).

Only three things are needed for straight-line: cost, estimated useful life, and salvage.

Three pieces of information are necessary in order to compute straight-line amortization.

a. Cost of the asset—the total cost to be amortized over time (the amount capitalized to the date the asset is put into service).
b. Estimated useful life of the asset—the number of periods the asset is expected to benefit the enterprise.
c. Estimated "salvage value"—the amount expected to be recovered via the sale of the asset at the end of its useful life, that is, the expected future proceeds from disposing of the asset. (This amount is likely to be only an educated guess and is often assumed to be zero for computing amortization over long periods of time.)

The formula for straight-line amortization is:

$$\text{Amortization for one period} = \frac{\text{Cost minus estimated salvage value}}{\text{Estimated useful life (no. of periods)}}$$

Using the above formula, you can calculate annual amortization on a delivery truck used by a local business this way:

- Cost of the truck = $5,000

- Estimated useful life = 5 years

- Estimated salvage value after 5 years = $1,000

$$\text{From this, the amortization for one year} = \frac{\$5,000 - \$1,000}{5}$$
$$= \$800$$

At the end of the first year, the net book value of the truck will be:

Cost − Total amortization to date = $5,000 − $800 = $4,200

Amortization expense for each of the five years will be $800, reducing the book value by $800 per year. As shown in Figure 8.7 above, the constant expense produces a linear increase in accumulated amortization and so a linear decline in book value.

A common practice for many enterprises is to assume the salvage value of the asset to be negligible or zero, which then enables amortization to be expressed in terms of percentages instead of years. For example, a company might use straight-line amortization expressed as 20% of historical cost, rather than as a term of five years. In the above example, 20% straight-line would be an annual amortization of $1,000.

2. Accelerated Amortization

Some assets contribute most of their benefit to the enterprise in the early parts of their lives. For example, a new computer may benefit the company greatly when it is first purchased, but due to quickly changing technology and changing needs as the company grows, this same computer may be relegated to less important tasks within a few years of its purchase, as better computers are acquired. Therefore, even though the computer will continue to benefit the company, most of its economic value has been consumed near the beginning of its life.

In Canada, the most common method of calculating accelerated amortization is the declining balance method, also called diminishing balance. *Financial Reporting in Canada 1999* says that 37 of the 200 companies reported using declining balance amortization in 1998, always in combination with other methods (nearly always straight-line), as none used it alone.[17] CAE is one of these: its 1999 Significant Accounting Policies note says that both declining balance and straight-line methods are used for its property, plant, and equipment.[18] "Capital cost allowance," the form of amortization required to be used for income tax purposes (to come in section 9.3), is also usually calculated using a declining balance procedure.

The method normally ignores salvage value. Therefore, the information needed is:

a. Cost of the asset.
b. Amortization rate: the *percentage of the book value* (cost minus amortization to date) of the asset that is to be amortized in the period.
c. Total amortization recorded since the acquisition of the asset (accumulated amortization).

Note the essential difference with straight-line: in declining balance, the rate is not applied to the cost, as it was in straight-line, but rather to the book value. Book value declines over time, and so does the amortization expense using this method, hence the name declining balance.

The formula for declining balance amortization is:

Amortization for one period   = (Cost − Accumulated amortization) × Rate
= Remaining book value of the asset × Rate

Let's use the declining balance method to compute amortization for the five-year life of the same truck we had above. With this method, the amortization rate is established such that over the asset's life, the cost will be fully depreciated. Doing this exactly requires complex algebra, so approximate rates are usually used. For

Margin notes

Under straight-line, annual expense is constant, and book value declines linearly.

Straight-line is made even easier by reducing to a simple rate, if salvage is assumed zero.

Some assets contribute more in the early years of their useful life than later.

Declining balance accelerated amortization is the second-most popular.

Only three things are needed for declining balance: cost, rate, and any prior accumulated amortization.

Doubling the straight-line rate works as an approximation for the declining balance rate.

example, the amortization expense for "double declining balance" (a particular type of declining balance) uses double the straight-line rate. Double declining balance works reasonably well for assets with an expected life in the ten-year range, but not for shorter lives. Canadian capital cost allowance rates used in computing taxable income were originally based on double declining balance estimates.

Since the truck is not in the ten-year useful life range, double declining balance is not really suitable (double the straight-line rate would be 40%), so we will use 25% instead to approximate the economic consumption pattern.

- Cost = $5,000

- Amortization to date = $0 (we're at the beginning)

- Amortization rate = 25%

8-6

Exhibit

Year 1
Amortization for the year	= ($5,000 − $0) × 25%
	= $1,250
Total amortization to date	= $1,250
Remaining book value	= $3,750

Year 2
Amortization for the year	= ($5,000 − $1,250) × 25%
	= $937.50
Total amortization to date	= $2,187.50
Remaining book value	= $2,812.50

Note amortization expense gets smaller with each year.

Year 3
Amortization for the year	= ($5,000 − $2,187.50) × 25%
	= $703.13
Total amortization to date	= $2,890.63
Remaining book value	= $2,109.37

Year 4
Amortization for the year	= ($5,000 − $2,890.63) × 25%
	= $527.34
Total amortization to date	= $3,417.97
Remaining book value	= $1,582.03

Year 5
Amortization for the year	= ($5,000 − $3,417.97) × 25%
	= $395.51
Total amortization to date	= $3,813.48
Remaining book value	= $1,186.52

Although in this example the remaining book value of the truck at the end of five years is fairly close to the expected salvage value of the truck, declining balance amortization does not normally take salvage value into account. Consequently, the book value at the end of five years would be the same whether or not the company expected to recover any of the cost of the truck.

Because the annual amortization declines, the book value goes down in a curve.

The second panel of the chart in Figure 8.7 shows the kind of patterns of amortization expense and book value we calculated for the truck. The expense and book value lines are curves instead of straight lines. Will there be any difference in net income using one method instead of the other? Yes. Will there be any difference in the cash position of the company using declining balance rather than straight-line? No.

In the United States, a method of calculating accelerated amortization called "sum of the years' digits" is often used. This is a method of calculating accelerated amortization more exactly than by declining balance that was common before the advent of calculators and computers. Now sum-of-the-years'-digits amortization is less common. It is rare in Canada (*Financial Reporting in Canada 1999* does not even mention it), so in this book it is illustrated only in an endnote.[19]

3. Units-of-Production Amortization and Depletion

Either straight-line or declining balance may be too simple if annual asset usage varies.

The economic consumption of some assets may not necessarily be a function of time, but rather of use. For example, it may make more sense to say that the delivery truck is expected to last so many kilometres rather than so many years. The consumption of natural resources ("wasting assets") is also often accounted for using "depletion," a units-of-production amortization approach, because the value to the enterprise of a stand of timber, or an oil well, is tied to the number of trees remaining to be felled or the amount of oil left to be recovered. If the economic value of the asset is related to the annual usage or the physical removal of an asset, the annual economic contribution will depend on volume of usage or removal and will not necessarily be a regular amount each year, as it is with straight-line and declining balance.

Needed for units-of-production amortization: cost, salvage, total usage, this year's usage.

To compute amortization or depletion per unit of usage, the following information is needed:

a. Cost of the asset.
b. Estimated salvage value.
c. Estimated number of units to be produced during life of asset—the estimated number of board feet of lumber in the timber stand, or the estimated number of kilometres that the delivery truck will travel, or other production measures.
d. The number of units produced in the year for which the amortization is to be calculated.

The formula for computing units-of-production amortization is:

$$\text{Amortization or depletion for one unit of use or production (for example, a kilometre)} = \frac{\text{Cost} - \text{Estimated salvage value}}{\text{Estimated no. of units of use or production during life}}$$

Using the delivery truck as an example one more time, amortization of the truck over its expected useful life might be calculated this way:

• Cost = $5,000

• Estimated salvage value = $1,000

• Estimated no. of km to be driven = 200,000

$$\text{Amortization rate} = \frac{\$5,000 - \$1,000}{200,000 \text{ km}}$$

$$= \$0.02 \text{ amortization per km}$$

From this, the annual amortization can be computed:

Year 1

Suppose the truck is driven 20,000 km during the year. The amortization expense for the year will be: $0.02 × 20,000 = $400.

Year 2

If the truck is driven 80,000 km during the second year, the amortization expense for the year will be: $0.02 × 80,000 = $1,600.

Year 3

Let's say the truck is driven 65,000 km during the year. Then the amortization charge for the year will be: $0.02 × 65,000 = $1,300.

Year 4

Let's suppose the truck is driven 50,000 km during the year. We can't just base the amortization expense on the 50,000, however, because this would take the total usage over the 200,000 km used above in setting the rate. The units-of-production method has the problem that the total usage is unlikely to coincide with the original estimate, and so the usage rate ($0.02 here) is unlikely to be exactly accurate. This may be harder to get right than it is to get the total useful life right in the straight-line method, but any amortization method is unlikely to be exactly right, as noted earlier. In this case, the fourth year's amortization expense is just the remaining $700 (cost $5,000 minus $1,000 salvage and the previous years' amortizations, $400 + $1,600 + $1,300), which is less than $0.02 × 50,000 km.

Year 5

In the earlier examples, the truck was expected to last 5 years. If it is still being driven in Year 5, and if salvage value is still expected to be $1,000, there will be no amortization in the fifth year, further evidence that the original 200,000 km estimate was incorrect. This could be fixed by going back and recalculating prior years' amortizations, but in practice the error would likely not be fixed because it is normal whenever estimates of the future are used to calculate amortization and other expenses such as income taxes, warranties, and pensions. Such errors just make any year's amortization expense less accurate than it might theoretically be.

The annual units-of-production amortization varies with usage of the asset.

The bottom panel in Figure 8.7 illustrates units-of-production amortization. It is the only method that can result in the annual amortization expense going up and down from period to period. *Financial Reporting in Canada 1999* says that, in 1998, five of the 200 companies reported using only units-of-production amortization, and two more used it in combination with other methods.[20]

Depletion is often subtracted from the asset, not accumulated in a contra account.

Depletion of a wasting asset and units-of-production amortization of a fixed asset are computed in the same manner, but depletion refers to the physical consumption of an asset, rather than just the economic consumption. For the timber stand mentioned earlier, salvage value may be the value of the land after all the timber has been cut. Instead of accumulating depletion in a contra account, the asset itself may be reduced by the amount of the depletion for the period. In this case, the journal entry would debit depletion expense and credit the timber stand asset, rather than crediting accumulated amortization. The asset account would then show the remaining book value at the present time, not the original cost.

4. Decelerated Amortization

If the asset's economic value is expected to decline more slowly in earlier years and more quickly in later years, a form of decelerated amortization (the *opposite* of accelerated amortization) may be used. Under decelerated amortization, amortization expense per period *rises* over the duration of the asset's life. The third panel of the chart in Figure 8.7 illustrates this method. Such an approach is rarely used, because for most assets it does not seem to follow reasonable economic assumptions. Some companies in the real estate industry use it because if the real estate, for example, an apartment or office building, is financed by borrowing, the interest expense from the borrowing falls each year as the debt is repaid, and having amortization expense rise leaves the sum of interest and amortization more or less constant. This is thought to match revenue from leasing or renting the property, which is likely to be fairly stable over time. People who do not like this method argue that smoothing reported income should not be a reason for choosing an amortization method, but the arguments for it have persuaded some companies, so it does exist even though it is not "generally accepted" for most companies. *Financial Reporting in Canada 1999* indicates that only three companies in 1998 reported using a form of decelerated amortization, called the "sinking fund" method, and six more used it in combination with straight-line amortization for other assets.[21] The calculations for this method are complex and so will not be illustrated here.

Amortization Effects

The amortization policy choice's main effect is on income.

What differences does the choice of amortization method make to the financial statements? This accounting policy choice has its main effect on income. Use of an accelerated method like declining balance increases amortization in the early years of assets' lives, relative to the amortization produced by straight-line amortization. Therefore, income will be lower in the early years if accelerated amortization is used, and higher in the later years when the accelerated amortization falls below straight-line. A numerical example shows this. Suppose we have a machine with a cost of $10,000 and an expected useful life of 10 years, with $1,000 expected salvage value. Straight-line amortization would be $900 per year (10% of $10,000 – $1,000). Declining balance amortization, using the double declining balance (DDB) approximation, would be 20% of book value each year (salvage ignored). The following table results.

Exhibit 8-7

	10% Straight-line Amortization		20% DDB Amortization	
Year	Beginning Book Value	Amortization Expense	Beginning Book Value	Amortization Expense
1	$10,000	$ 900	$10,000	$2,000
2	9,100	900	8,000	1,600
3	8,200	900	6,400	1,280
4	7,300	900	5,120	1,024
5	6,400	900	4,096	819
6	5,500	900	3,277	655
7	4,600	900	2,622	524
8	3,700	900	2,098	420
9	2,800	900	1,678	336
10	1,900	900	1,342	268
11	1,000		1,074	
Ten-year totals		$9,000		$8,926

Example Comparison of Straight-line and Accelerated Amortization

Using the above example and the charts in Figure 8.7, straight-line and accelerated amortization may be compared:

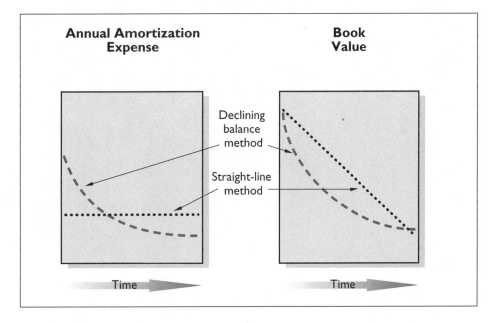

FIGURE 8.8

The specific effects depend on the details of each case, but the example shows the comparative pattern. Both methods produce about the same amortization over 10 years ($9,000 versus $8,926) and about the same book value at the end of that time ($1,000 versus $1,074), but their patterns are different. The accelerated amortization has a higher expense (and therefore a lower income) for the first four years, and a lower expense (and therefore a higher income) for the last six years.

Compared to straight-line, accelerated amortization results in the book value falling more steeply in the early years and less steeply in the later years.

No general comparison with units-of-production amortization can be made, because by design it varies with production or usage levels. But like the other two methods, it does have to amortize the same amount over time (except that declining balance ignores salvage), so the various methods all get to the same fully amortized point eventually. The choice of amortization method is therefore essentially a choice about the *timing* of the amortization expense: mostly in earlier years (accelerated), even over the years (straight-line), or variable (units-of-production). Because income (via amortization expense) and noncurrent assets (book value) are affected, the choice of amortization policy does affect the ratios of income to assets and to equity, which, as we will see in Chapter 10, are used to judge the company's income performance relative to its size.

(H)OW'S YOUR UNDERSTANDING?

Here are two questions you should be able to answer, based on what you have just read:

1. Explain to the president of Cold Lake Manufacturing Inc., which opened for business at the beginning of this year, what amortization expense is supposed to accomplish and the criteria you would recommend the company use in choosing the most appropriate method.

2. Cold Lake management is trying to decide on its accounting policy for amortization. A manager did a rough calculation and determined that if the company used each method properly, the results for the present year would be: straight-line amortization, $238,400 expense; accelerated amortization, $389,600 expense; units-of-production, $189,200 expense. What would be the following effects if the company chose either of the other two in comparison to straight-line: dollar effect on income before income tax for the present year; dollar effect on cash flow for the present year; dollar effect on current income tax payable for the present year; directional effect on income in future years? (Accelerated: income before tax reduced by $151,200; no effects on cash flow or income tax payable; will eventually show increased income as the accelerated expense declines below the straight-line. Units-of-production: income before tax increased by $49,200; no effects on cash flow or income tax payable; will eventually show lower income because it and straight-line will amortize the same book value and it has amortized less this year so has some catching up to do.)

8.11   OTHER ASSETS, INTANGIBLES, AND CAPITAL LEASES

Most of the discussion of noncurrent assets so far has involved "fixed" assets such as land, buildings, and equipment. There are other noncurrent assets on many companies' balance sheets, however:

- "Deferred charges" and other kinds of miscellaneous noncurrent assets.

- "Intangible" assets, which have economic value but lack the same "tangible" physical existence that the fixed assets have.

> • Some leased land, buildings, and equipment, which although not owned
> appear on the balance sheet anyway.

Deferred Charges

Section 6.9 examined prepaid and accrued expenses. Prepaid expenses are expenses for future periods paid already but kept on the balance sheet as assets, to be deducted from future revenue. Most of these are short-term, and thus are included in current assets. But sometimes payments made in the current or past years are thought to provide benefit for years into the future. Such noncurrent assets may be specifically identified, for example "organization costs" or "deferred financing costs," or may be just included in a general noncurrent asset called something like "deferred charges" or "other assets." Sometimes tax credits not expected to be obtained for some time and other kinds of long-term receivables are included. If these are significant assets, they are usually explained in the notes to the financial statements, because they can arise from a great variety of circumstances that may be particular to the enterprise.

Intangible Assets

Intangible assets are long-term assets that do not have a visible physical existence, as do land, buildings, or equipment. Intangible assets include:

- Patents, copyrights, trademarks, and other such legal property.

- Franchises, distributorships, and other such rights to sell someone else's products in a certain geographical area (McDonald's Restaurants, Speedy Muffler, Arthur Murray Dance Studios, and Canadian Tire are examples in which the local operator has paid for the right to use the name and sell the products).

- Product development expenditures (e.g., product-testing costs or computer software development costs) that are capitalized so they can be expensed at the time they earn revenue in the future, thus being noncurrent prepaid expenses, recorded to satisfy the matching principle.

- Purchased goodwill (arising when more is paid for a group of assets, such as a whole business, than the assets seem to be worth individually), as we saw in the Sorhem example at the end of section 2.4. Goodwill arises mainly when one company purchases another and the two are combined into a corporate group with consolidated financial statements. Consolidation is in section 9.7, but the nature of the resulting goodwill is reviewed in this section.

According to *Financial Reporting in Canada 1999*, 120 of the 200 surveyed companies reported intangible assets in 1998: 105 reported goodwill (mainly on consolidation) and 55 reported other intangible assets (broadcast rights, publishing rights, trademarks, patents, licenses, customer lists, noncompetition agreements, franchises, and purchased research and development).[22]

What Are Intangible Assets Worth?

Because such assets are intangible, their existence and value may be doubtful. Generally, the more clearly identifiable and documented the assets are (especially via external evidence such as contracts and legal documents), the less difficulty they pose. However, even for clearly owned assets such as patents and franchises, there may be considerable doubt about their future economic value. For example, what is a Wendy's franchise worth? It depends on ever-changing consumer tastes, on whether a competitor does or doesn't open across the street, and on many other business and economic factors.

Capitalizing internal development expenditures is controversial and largely not allowed.

For assets lacking clear external documentation, such as product development expenditures, there is often a real question as to whether they belong on the balance sheet at all. Capitalizing expenditures on such items may appear to create better matching and is usually seen to be proper by those making such expenditures, but this depends on whether they will ever return future value. Will the great new product sell? Will it produce revenues greater than costs? If the expenditure is capitalized, when would amortization of the asset begin and over what period? Answering such questions require difficult judgments, and many people have concluded that such assets should not appear, because these people favour conservatism in accounting, are afraid of manipulation, or just feel that recognizing such assets is not fair or appropriate. Expenditures on such things would therefore be expensed immediately and not capitalized. For these sorts of reasons, accounting standards require that general research and development expenditures be expensed as they are made, *not* capitalized as intangible assets.

F OR YOUR INTEREST

Accounting for intangibles is an active area of accounting research, partly due to the rise of Internet and other high-tech companies whose assets, as traditionally measured by financial accounting, don't seem to represent the companies' economic value very well. It is argued that financial accounting has been better developed to measure "old economy" companies such as manufacturers and raw materials processors, and that much of what makes the "new economy" companies attractive is left out. Managers who wish to present a positive image of their companies are perhaps overly constrained by GAAP, because they cannot include as assets "human capital," innovative production processes, various kinds of business networking arrangements, e-commerce techniques, and many other things that seem clearly to have economic value. In early 2000, the market capitalization (total number of shares times the current share price) of software company Oracle exceeded the sum of the market capitalizations of all the "big three" automakers, and Yahoo!'s exceeded that of Procter & Gamble,[23] yet Oracle's and Yahoo!'s balance sheets do not reveal the apparent intangible assets, business smarts, excellent people, or whatever makes them so popular. A particular issue is the accounting for research and development expenditures (**R&D**). A recent Canadian study indicates that investors and financial analysts do want some disclosure about R&D and that in response to that, companies which do R&D are more likely to disclose information about it when they are also listed in U.S. stock exchanges, are seeking capital, or are reported on by several analysts.[24] GAAP's conservative expensing and not capitalizing R&D is most strongly required in the U.S. There is some research evidence that stock market prices behave as if this is a mismatching of revenues and expenses and therefore produces a misspecification of income.[25] However, in spite of the research to date, no movement toward capitalizing is likely any time soon: standard-setters and auditors mistrust estimates of the value of internally generated intangibles.

Purchased Goodwill

Goodwill is total price minus values of assets and liabilities, for whatever reason.

Goodwill is a special case, though no less controversial. Goodwill means that the "whole" of a business purchased is worth more than the sum of the "parts" as represented by the individual assets and liabilities. More was paid for the business than you'd expect from knowing the values of assets and liabilities. The price of a business is set in the market place, and there is no reason it should tie to the accounting assets and liabilities, but still the existence of a gap between the whole and the sum of the parts raises the question of just why the gap exists. Is it because of loyal customers, good managers, good locations, reduced competition, synergy with the purchasing company, or any of many other reasons? Each of these reasons might indicate a different meaning for the goodwill asset.

From an accounting point of view, goodwill arises, in a way, because of the necessity to keep the accounts in balance. Here is an example like the Sorhem one in section 2.4: Great Inc. buys all the business assets of Small Ltd. for $800,000 cash. The best estimate of the fair market values of those assets are: receivables, $60,000; inventories, $110,000; land, $100,000; building, $260,000; equipment, $130,000; total, $660,000. No liabilities are assumed by Great.

Great would record the purchase as follows:

DR Accounts receivable	60,000	
DR Inventories	110,000	
DR Land	100,000	
DR Buildings	260,000	
DR Equipment	130,000	
CR Cash		800,000

We can calculate purchased goodwill more easily than we can evaluate or amortize it.

No problem. Except that the entry doesn't balance! So a new account called Goodwill is created and debited with $140,000, which is the $800,000, cost of the whole, minus $660,000, the sum of the fair values of the parts. This keeps the books in balance and creates a new account, the value and meaning of which are unclear. If goodwill represents unrecorded assets, what are they? If it represents a good location, good managers, or synergy with the operations of Great, what are these things really worth? How much future value do they have? How long will this value last? Does goodwill, at least sometimes, indicate that the purchaser made a bad deal and just paid too much? (By the way, in the reverse situation, if the cost of the whole is less than the sum of the parts, no "badwill" is recorded. Instead, the amounts assigned to the parts are reduced so that they add up to the cost of the whole.)

Cost of Intangibles

The purchase cost of intangible assets is determined in the same way as for tangible assets.

Goodwill's cost is determined as illustrated above. For other intangible assets, cost is determined in the same way as that of any other asset: purchase cost plus other expenditures made prior to putting the asset into service (getting economic benefits from it). There may be substantial ambiguity about the cost of internally developed assets, such as product development expenditures, because it may be difficult to determine exactly what was spent to develop the asset, separately from normal expenses. This is the same problem we saw in section 8.3 for determining the cost of assets in general. Adding this to the general uncertainty about the value of intangible assets means that many companies decline to recognize (capitalize) such assets. Internally developed goodwill is *never* capitalized (for example, expenditures on office parties that create happy employees are expensed, not capitalized).

Amortization of Intangibles

Intangible assets are amortized over their useful lives, just like fixed assets. Determining legal useful life may be fairly straightforward for assets supported by contracts or other documents (for example, contracts such as franchises normally have a specified term, and patents are good for a specific number of years), but whether this is also the economic useful life is harder to say. For other assets, such as incorporation costs or goodwill, useful life is anyone's guess. Canadian standards specify a maximum useful life of 40 years for goodwill, surely an optimistic estimate! Some standard-setters would like to see this amortization period reduced.

Intangible assets are amortized to income over estimated useful life, using straight-line.

Because of all this ambiguity, intangibles are amortized simply, using the straight-line basis over the estimated useful life, and are usually estimated reasonably conservatively. The asset account itself is usually credited with the amortization, rather than bothering with a contra account for accumulated amortization, because such an asset is more like a prepaid expense (in which the book value represents future expense deductions) than like a tangible asset whose original cost may be usefully kept separate for control reasons.

Capital Leases

Capital leases are an example of accrual accounting's inclusion of economic phenomena.

Some leased assets are included on the balance sheet because the company is deemed to have enough of the rights and obligations of ownership, the assets are significant to the company's economic performance, and leaving them off the balance sheet is thought to misrepresent the company's economic position. This is an example of accrual accounting's moving well beyond just recording transactions: there is no *legal* exchange of leased assets, but it is thought that there has been an *economic* exchange of them. Financial accounting treats capital lease assets essentially as if there were owned fixed assets instead of leased assets.

A capital lease's initial asset and liability amounts both equal the present value of future payments.

Such capital leases are included on the balance sheet (often just mixed in with owned fixed assets) as follows:

- The "cost" is the present value of the future lease payments, using an appropriate interest rate usually deduced from the lease agreement to remove the future interest from the total payments and calculate the present value. (See section 10.7 or the discussion of present value under Value in Use in section 8.2: the present value is the future cash flows but with any future interest removed.)

- At the same time, the present value of those payments is recorded as a liability.

- So the journal entry to put capital leases on the balance sheet is:

DR Capital lease asset	XXXX	
CR Capital lease obligations liability		XXXX

Once in the accounts, capital leases are treated just as tangible assets and debts are.

- After that:
  - ▶ The leased asset is amortized, just as the owned assets are, following a policy that is consistent with that used for any similar owned assets but also taking into account the terms of the lease.

▶ The liability is reduced as payments are made on the lease. Each payment is divided into deduced principal and interest portions, so that only the principal portion is deducted from the liability and the rest is considered interest expense. This maintains the liability at the present value of the remaining lease payments.

▶ The expenses for using the leased asset, therefore, are amortization and interest. Such amounts are usually combined with other amortization and interest expenses because the intent is to represent the economic situation fairly.

▶ Various particulars of significant capital leases are usually disclosed in the notes to the financial statements, so that the readers of the statements may judge the effects of such capitalization. Such separate disclosure is usual for the lease obligations liability, the terms of the lease, and related amortization and interest expenses. *Financial Reporting in Canada 1999* reports that in 1998, 67 of the 200 surveyed companies disclosed that they had capital lease assets, but 25 of those only disclosed the existence of such assets, without reporting the amount included in the assets. Perhaps the companies felt that the corresponding lease liability was more informative, because 72 companies separately disclosed the lease liability and 55 gave details of the lease obligations.[26]

Operating leases are not capitalized, so result only in rent expense, not assets or liabilities.

If the lease does *not* result in an economic equivalence of ownership (for example, if it is really a rental situation where the owner continues to pay property tax, do the repairs and maintenance, and generally control the asset), the lease is termed an "operating lease." For such leases, there is no asset or lease obligation liability recognized, and the lease payments are just expensed as rent expense. If the operating lease is significant to the company, some of its particulars may be disclosed in the notes to the financial statements. *Financial Reporting in Canada 1999* indicates that in 1998, 140 of the 200 companies disclosed that they had operating leases: 78 of these had operating leases only, and 62 of the 67 which disclosed capital leases also said they had operating leases. Eight more said they had leases, but not which kind. The *CICA Handbook* recommends that the next five years' lease payments be disclosed, whether the lease is operating (so no liability recorded) or capital (liability recorded at present value, which is less than the payments to be made). Of the 140 disclosing capital leases, 135 specified the lease payments for each of the next 5 years. Of the 72 disclosing capital lease obligations, 43 specified the payments for each of the next 5 years, a smaller proportion.[27] It is clear from all this that capital and operating leases are significant parts of the ways companies assemble economic assets for their use.

FOR YOUR INTEREST

This chapter has focused on companies' accounting policy choices for assets. Research shows that stock market prices correlate with accounting income as measured by accrual accounting, and that extends to the results of accounting policy choices that affect income, and perhaps even potential choices such as for R&D. Policy choices that have direct cash consequences (such as through higher or lower future tax assessments) are more likely to prompt a stock market response than are choices without direct cash consequences. Inventory accounting choices (usually FIFO vs. LIFO, studied with U.S. companies) do make a difference to stock prices, probably due to the income tax savings the LIFO choice provides in the United States. Amortization policy choices have little effect on stock prices, probably because there is no tax or cash flow effect. Indirect cash consequences may also exist and provoke a response. For example, if an accounting policy, such as to capitalize leases, changes the debt–equity ratio, the company's risk might appear different enough to affect interest rates on its debts and so change future interest payments.

HOW'S YOUR UNDERSTANDING?

Here are two questions you should be able to answer, based on what you have just read:

1. What are the main similarities and differences between tangible fixed assets and (a) intangible assets and (b) capital leases?

2. A company discloses the following in its financial statements and notes: licences and patents, goodwill, capital leases, and operating leases. What expense accounts would you expect to exist, related to these items? (Licences and patents: amortization expense; Goodwill: amortization expense; Capital leases: amortization expense for the lease asset and interest expense for the lease liability; Operating leases: rent expense.)

8.12 TERMS TO BE SURE YOU UNDERSTAND

Here is this chapter's list of terms introduced or emphasized. Make sure you know what they mean *in accounting*, and if any are unclear to you, check the chapter again or refer to the Glossary of Terms at the back of the book.

Accelerated amortization	Asset valuation
Accounting policies	Assumed cost flow
Accounting policy choices	Available cost
Accounts receivable	AVGE
Amortization	Balance sheet valuation
Amortization expense	Betterment
Amortize(d)	Capital lease(s)
Articulation	Capitalize(d)

Cash	LIFO
COGS	Liquidation value
Conservatism	Losses
Cost	Lower of cost or market
Cost allocation	Market value
Cost of goods sold expense	Marketable securities
Current value	Matching
Decelerated amortization	Moving weighted average
Declining balance	Net realizable value
Deferred charges	Notes receivable
Depletion	Operating lease
Depreciation	Other assets
Diminishing balance	Output market value
FIFO	Overhead costs
Financial assets	Present value
First-in, first-out	Price-level-adjusted historical cost
Fixed assets	R&D
GAAP	Reclassified
Gains	Replacement cost
Going concern	Retail inventory
Goodwill	Specific identification
Historical cost	Straight-line amortization
Income measurement	Tangible assets
Input market value	Temporary investments
Intangible assets	Trade receivables
Inventory	Units-of-production amortization
Inventory valuation	Value in use
Last-in, first-out	Write-offs

8.13 CONTINUING DEMONSTRATION CASE

INSTALLMENT 8

Data for Installment 8

In Installment 6, the February 28, 2001, adjusted trial balance was produced. Before preparing financial statements, Mavis and Tomas went through the accounts and decided on the accounting policies that should be used in the statements. To help you think about what policies might be needed, here again is the trial balance from Installment 7.

Cash	6,418	Customer deposits liability	(500)
Accounts receivable	15,671	Share capital	(125,000)
Allowance for doubtful accounts	(1,542)	Revenue	(229,387)
Inventory	33,612	Cost of goods sold expense	138,767
Prepaid insurance	525	Bad debts expense	2,436
Automobile	10,000	Salary — Mavis	0
Accumulated amortization — auto	(2,000)	Salary — Tomas	0
Leasehold improvements	63,964	Salary — other	0
Accumulated amortization —			
leasehold	(12,792)	Salaries expense	67,480
Equipment and furniture	32,390	Travel expense	9,477
Accumulated amortization —			
equipment	(2,364)	Phone expense	4,014
Computer	14,900	Rent expense	24,000
Accumulated amortization —			
computer	(2,980)	Utilities expense	3,585
Software	4,800	Office and general expense	5,688
Accumulated amortization — software	(960)	Interest expense	6,469
Incorporation cost	1,100	Inventory shortage expense	441
Bank loan	(47,500)	Amortization expense — auto	2,000
Accounts payable	(35,323)	Amortization expense — leasehold	12,792
Sales taxes due	(1,843)	Amortization expense — equipment	2,364
Deductions payable	(2,284)	Amortization expense — computer	2,980
Salaries payable	(2,358)	Amortization expense — software	960
Loan payable	0		
	71,434		(71,434)

Results for Installment 8

Here are the resulting accounting policies for Mato Inc. Some policies relate to liabilities, some details of which are covered in Chapter 9. They are included here for completeness and so that the full financial statements may be presented in Installment 9.

- Cash and equivalents were defined to be cash only. The demand bank loan was to be treated as financing (as it was in the 6-month statements in Installment 4).

- The allowance for doubtful accounts would not be disclosed in the balance sheet or notes.

- Inventory would be valued at the lower of FIFO cost or net realizable value.

- The title "Prepaid expense" would be used to group together prepaid insurance and any other prepaid expenses that might arise in the future.

- The automobile, equipment, furniture, and computer would be shown in one account called "Equipment," valued at cost (total $57,290 at the end of February).

- Accumulated amortization would be shown for those three accounts together (total $7,344 at the end of February).

- The leasehold improvements and software would be shown at net book value (cost minus accumulated amortization), with neither cost nor accumulated amortization disclosed.

- Mavis and Tomas were not too sure what to do with the incorporation cost. They decided to leave the account on the balance sheet as a noncurrent asset and not to amortize it because they could see no relationship between it and the company's 2001 revenue and so thought it did not belong as an expense.

- Accounts payable, sales taxes payable, and deductions due would be aggregated on the balance sheet under the title "Payables" (total $41,808 at February 28).

- The customer deposits account would be titled "Deferred revenue" and would include any such revenue deferrals that arose in the future.

- Share capital details would be described in a note, not on the face of the balance sheet.

- Revenue would be recognized on a critical event basis, that event being delivery of goods to customers. Mavis and Tomas reviewed the revenue cut off and decided that this basis had been properly used in 2001. They also decided that this basis was what readers of the financial statements would expect and so it did not have to be disclosed.

- Mavis and Tomas also reviewed the expenses, especially cost of goods sold, to ensure that the expenses cut off had produced a proper matching of expenses to revenue.

- It was decided to disclose cost of goods sold and all the other expenses separately, so that the reader could get a full picture of the company's operations.

- Amortization expense would be a slight exception to the above, because instead of disclosing each kind of amortization separately, just a single total amortization expense would be disclosed ($21,096).

- Policy for calculating amortization expense would be straight-line, with the rates Tomas had used: car, leasehold improvements, computer and software, 20% of cost per year; equipment and furniture, 10% of cost per year.

The resulting financial statements are presented in Installment 9.

8.14 HOMEWORK AND DISCUSSION TO DEVELOP UNDERSTANDING

PROBLEM 8.1*
Decide what items are cash or temporary investments

Decide which, if any, of the following items would likely be included in (1) cash or (2) temporary investments on the balance sheet of a large company. Explain briefly.

    a. Money on deposit in a bank in Brazil, deposited by the company's Brazilian branch.
    b. A 90-day guaranteed investment certificate with the company's main bank.
    c. Money in transit between the company's banks in Germany and Spain.
    d. Receptionists' petty cash funds in the company's various offices worldwide.
    e. Three NSF ("not sufficient funds") bad cheques bounced by the customers' banks.
    f. An investment in 90% of the shares of a company that supplies raw materials.
    g. A deposit recorded on the last day of the year but credited by the bank three days later.
    h. Money on deposit in an Indonesian bank as a guarantee of performance for a contract.
    i. An investment in 0.5% of the shares of a publicly traded company.
    j. An overdraft in the bank account maintained by the branch in Calgary.

PROBLEM 8.2*
Calculate gains, losses, write-offs, and write-downs

Determine the amount that is added to or subtracted from income, and indicate what the direction of the effect on income is for each of the following items.

    a. A truck costing $45,000 and having accumulated amortization of $18,000 is sold for $16,000 cash.
    b. An investment of $100,000 in another company turns out to have been a bad idea. It looks as if the investment can be sold for only $15,000.
    c. An old building that cost $78,000 and has accumulated amortization of $78,000 is given to the fire department to burn down for practice.
    d. Land that cost $50,000 is sold for 10 payments of $10,000 each, to be received over the next 10 years. The interest included in those payments will equal $27,000.
    e. A machine that is part of a group of assets that are amortized as a group is sold. The machine cost $3,000 eight years ago and $500 is received for it.
    f. A division is sold as a business because the company is going to get out of that line of business. The division will bring $340,000 in cash proceeds, and has assets costing $670,000, accumulated amortization of $240,000, and liabilities of $120,000.

PROBLEM 8.3*
Consider asset valuation methods

Historical cost is the usual method of valuing assets on the balance sheet, following from the transactional basis of financial accounting. Identify the other valuation methods that have been used or proposed and indicate reasons for and against their use as alternatives to historical cost.

PROBLEM 8.4*
Calculate lower of cost or market on inventory items

Classy Products Inc. has the following items in its inventory. Calculate the inventory value that would be reported according to GAAP, using (1) the most conservative method and (2) an acceptable less conservative method.

Inventory item	Quantity	Cost per unit	Market per unit
Blue bombies	6,000 units	$13.50	$25.00
Red rockies	2,000 units	11.90	7.00
Yellow yallies	10,000 units	13.00	15.00
Tangerine tackies	4,000 units	24.00	5.00
Gold glammies	5,000 units	6.50	8.20

PROBLEM 8.5*
Indicate policy change effects

Indicate the probable direction of the effect of each of the following possible accounting policy changes on the account given:

Policy Change	Effect on?
a. Capitalize R&D expenses	Assets
b. Recognize accounts receivable sooner	Revenue
c. Capitalize some repairs expenses	Net income
d. Change from moving AVGE to FIFO for inventories	Net income
e. Change to straight-line from declining balance for factory	Assets
f. Recognize doubtful accounts sooner	Net income
g. Write off spoiled inventories	Operating income

PROBLEM 8.6*
Determine the cost of an asset

Advanced Shopping Inc. has bought some land on which it intends to build a shopping centre. Calculate the cost of the land given the following information, stating any assumptions you need to make.

a. Advanced has agreed to pay the previous owner $50,000 per year for 10 years for the land title. These payments include interest totalling $150,000 over the 10 years.

b. Advanced paid a real estate broker $20,000 for conducting negotiations with the previous owner.

c. An engineering firm was paid $9,500 for a series of tests on the land to ensure that it was not environmentally contaminated and that it had a good rock base on which to build the shopping centre.

d. Advanced paid $4,000 to have several large signs made and erected on the site, announcing that the new centre would open in 18 months.

e. The site was bulldozed to get rid of the previous owner's drive-in theatre and then levelled and filled, at a cost of $35,200. Sale of scrap from the theatre brought in $1,500 cash.

f. A neighbour who did not want to live next door to a shopping centre threatened a lawsuit. Advanced settled the suit out of court for $25,000 and agreed to buy the neighbour's property too, for $110,000. That property would be held for the time being and probably sold later on, after the shopping centre had increased its value.

g. An architect was paid $66,700 for initial plans and drawings of the shopping centre, necessary to get a building permit from the municipality.

h. The president and several other senior managers of Advanced spent a total of 47 days' time on the land purchase deal, including some visits to the site. Allocating their salaries to that activity would produce an amount of $43,200. The site visits cost $7,200 in travel costs (Advanced's head office is in another city).

PROBLEM 8.7*
Explain the effects of changing from non-GAAP to GAAP

The president of a small local company has been advised by a newly hired accountant that the company's balance sheet valuation methods are not quite appropriate. One example is that the company has been valuing inventories at cost, whereas GAAP normally require that the lower of cost or market be used for such a current asset. Explain as carefully as you can what would be the effect on the company's balance sheet, income statement, and cash flow statement if the accounting for inventory were changed to the GAAP basis.

PROBLEM 8.8*
Analyze various possible inventory costing policies

Yang Inc. has been in business for three years. The company manages its inventories well, so that there are no significant inventories for which cost is less than market value. For the past three years, here are the company's inventory asset and COGS expense computed under each of three methods:

	2002	2001	2000
a. FIFO — ending inventory	$112,000	$148,000	$115,000
— COGS expense	636,000	867,000	585,000
b. AVGE — ending inventory	108,000	126,000	106,000
— COGS expense	618,000	880,000	594,000
c. LIFO — ending inventory	104,000	118,000	92,000
— COGS expense	614,000	874,000	608,000
Purchases in each year	600,000	900,000	700,000

1. Determine the inventory cost policy that would produce the highest and lowest income in each year and calculate the effect on income (before income tax) of choosing the former over the latter.
2. Given the variation of results you observed in part 1, how should a company choose its inventory cost policy?

PROBLEM 8.9*
Amortization calculations, entries, and effects

At the beginning of 2000, Garrison Inc. acquired machinery costing $100,000 and having a useful life of 10 years. The company amortized this machinery during 2000 and 2001 using the straight-line method. During 2002, it decided to change to the declining balance method of amortization for the machinery.

1. Calculate the amortization expense Garrison has recognized for 2000 and 2001, and write a journal entry to record either year's amount.
2. Calculate the amortization expense Garrison would have recorded had it been using the declining balance method for 2000 and 2001.
3. Calculate the effects of changing from straight-line to declining balance on the following (ignoring income tax):
   a. The balance sheet at the end of 2000.
   b. The income statement for 2001.
   c. The balance sheet at the end of 2001.
   d. The cash flow statement for 2001.

PROBLEM 8.10*
Effects analysis:
expensing versus
capitalizing, plus tax

The controller of Squiffle, Inc., is having a disagreement with senior management about a company accounting policy. Help out by analyzing the two cases below, both of which involve income tax. The tax effect can be reasoned out without knowing anything about income tax other than the information given.

Squiffle, in business for only a year, has capitalized $67,000 in development costs. The controller argues that such costs should be expensed instead. Assume this accounting policy affects current income tax liability only and that the company's income tax rate is 30%. What would the controller's proposal do to:

    a. the current year's net income,
    b. the current year's cash flow,
    c. working capital at the end of the current year?

PROBLEM 8.11*
Calculate inventory
costs under various
assumptions

Product FX was purchased and sold on the following basis during the year. Calculate the ending inventory and cost of goods sold expense for Product FX under each of the following: FIFO, annual weighted average, and periodic LIFO. (If you wish, go on to moving weighted average and perpetual LIFO too—the solutions for them are included with the other three.)

Beginning inventory: 200 units costing $4.20 each. Sales to March 3: 120 units for $10.00 each. Purchase March 4: 340 units for $5.10 each. Sales to August 14: 400 units for $11.00 each. Purchase August 15: 250 units for $4.00 each. Sales to December 10: 110 units for $10.50 each. Purchase December 11: 130 units for $4.50 each. Sales to the end of the year: 20 units for $10.00 each.

PROBLEM 8.12*
Answer questions
about intangible
assets

A businessperson has asked you the following questions. Answer each as clearly as you can.

    a. Why do GAAP frown on capitalizing the goodwill we generate through having good management and hiring and motivating excellent employees?
    b. Anyway, what could it hurt to capitalize such goodwill? The balance sheet would show more assets, but otherwise there'd be no effect on anything, would there?
    c. Our auditors have said that we are violating GAAP by not showing as an asset the lease we have signed on our main factory building. How can that be? Wouldn't we violate some pretty basic principles if we put something we don't even own on our balance sheet?
    d. We've been lucky enough to sign a franchise agreement with our major supplier, so now we can be the unique source of that supplier's goods in the local market. I understand that we do account for this franchise agreement. How do we do that, and why is it done differently than the goodwill I already asked you about?

PROBLEM 8.13*
Answer various
questions about
asset accounting

Answer this mixture of narrative and numerical questions about Thuringia Inc.'s accounting.

    1. Earlier in the current year, the company had sold an old building for $115,000. The building had cost $820,000 and had accumulated amortization of $762,000 at the date of sale. All that had been recorded for the sale

so far was to debit cash $115,000 and credit sales revenue $115,000. Record a journal entry to correct the accounts.

2. Thuringia Inc. has been experiencing steadily rising prices for the products it purchases for resale. In this circumstance, would the moving average basis of accounting for its inventory give higher or lower net income than the FIFO basis would?

3. The company's policy is to use replacement cost for determining the market value of its inventory of goods for resale. Replacement cost is greater than cost, which in turn is greater than net realizable value. Is the company's policy appropriate?

4. The company's accounts receivable total $785,200 and there is an allowance for doubtful accounts of $46,000. A major customer who had always paid on time and now owes $231,000 suddenly goes bankrupt, and Thuringia cannot expect to recover any of the money owing to it. The president wants to just write the whole loss off, but the vice president of sales wants to "use up the allowance for doubtful accounts first." Which approach would you recommend? Why? What difference would it make?

5. An error was found in the records for December. A $14,350 sale on credit, not actually made until early in January, which is in the next fiscal year, was recorded in December. The $9,120 cost of goods sold had also been mistakenly removed from inventory because the company's perpetual inventory control system was tied to its sales recording system. Record a journal entry as of the end December to correct the accounts.

6. An analysis of the temporary investments account (total cost $525,000) showed that the total market value of the investments was $515,000 at the end of the fiscal year. Investment market values had never been below cost before. Is there a problem?

7. To avoid all the complexities of FIFO, AVGE, or LIFO, perhaps Thuringia should just account for the actual cost of its inventories. Why might actual cost not be a solution for the company?

PROBLEM 8.14*
Is asset accounting inconsistent, and does that matter?

A financial analyst said that GAAP for assets are inconsistent, with some assets valued at the lower of cost or market, some at cost minus accumulated amortization, and some just at cost. Explain why the same valuation basis is not used for all assets, and comment on whether or not the apparent inconsistency harms the usefulness of financial statements.

PROBLEM 8.15*
Answer questions about accounts receivable

Answer the following questions about accounts receivable.

1. In what way can it be said that accounts receivable follow the "lower of cost or market" rule used for other current assets?

2. Banks disclose their allowances for doubtful loans and their losses on bad loans. Why do you think they do, and why don't most other companies?

3. A company has some receivables that are not due for payment for about four years. The president wants to just include those with the regular receivables. What else might be done, and what difference would it make if your proposal were followed?

4. Another company has sold some products on sale contracts that provide for interest to be paid. For example, one contract is for $15,000 plus $1,100

interest. The sale was recorded by debiting accounts receivable and crediting sales revenue for $16,100. What is wrong with that, and how would you fix it? In your solution, how would the interest be accounted for?

5. Why would it make sense to disclose trade receivables separately from receivables like income tax refunds and employee loans?

PROBLEM 8.16
Answer questions about asset valuation

1. What are some reasons that valuation methods other than historical cost have not replaced it in general use?

2. Greystone Inc.'s president is considering revaluing the company's land on its balance sheet to reflect current real estate market values that are much lower than the cost of the land. What might such a revaluation do to the company's assets, owners' equity, and net income?

PROBLEM 8.17
Answer questions about intangible assets accounting

1. Ransome Biometrics Inc. is negotiating to buy the assets and hire the employees and management of Frog Hollow Research Inc. At the moment, the deal looks like this: Ransome will pay $2,100,000 in cash and issue new shares with an agreed value of $12,000,000 to the owners of Frog Hollow, in exchange for the following assets (agreed values in brackets): accounts receivable ($200,000), inventory ($650,000), high-technology equipment ($2,210,000), and patents ($3,650,000). Explain how the acquisition would be accounted for in Ransome's books.

2. The president of Ransome is not happy with the accounting you've outlined in part 1, saying that no value has been assigned to the high-quality Frog Hollow personnel who will become part of Ransome's business. "The whole reason for the deal was to take advantage of Frog Hollow's excellent R&D record and use its people's expertise to help in Ransome's operations, but the accounting does not recognize that at all," said the president. Explain to the president whether the accounting does or does not recognize the value of the Frog Hollow people.

3. "Perhaps," mused the president, "we could assign an explicit value to the Frog Hollow people in the acquisition deal. They were the main reason for the deal, so at least half of the acquisition price should be assigned to them. That would be an asset on Ransome's balance sheet that I would be happy to defend." If the president's idea were accepted, what difference would that make to the company's balance sheet? Would that difference matter? Would it be acceptable under GAAP?

PROBLEM 8.18
Basic questions about temporary investments

1. Many companies have temporary investments on their balance sheets. How do these investments differ from:
   a. cash,
   b. long-term investments in associated companies?

2. Suggest why, in spite of 1(a), such investments might be included in cash and equivalents for purposes of deriving the cash flow statement's information.

3. Why are such investments valued at the lower of cost or market?

PROBLEM 8.19
Determine asset costs from various possible components

Determine the costs of land and building that would appear on the balance sheet of Smith Co. Ltd., based on the following information:

Purchase price of plant site	$ 175,000
Building materials (includes $10,000 in materials wasted due to worker inexperience)	700,000
Machinery installation charges	40,000
Grading and draining plant site	20,000
Labour costs of construction (Smith Co. used its own workers to build the plant rather than laying them off because business was slack. However, the labour to build the plant cost $40,000 more than outside contractors would have charged, due to inside workers' inexperience and inefficiency.)	500,000
Machinery purchase cost	1,000,000
Machinery delivery charges	10,000
Parking lot grading and paving	60,000
Replacement of building windows shot out by vandals before production start-up	7,000
Architect's fees	40,000

PROBLEM 8.20
Conceptual components of asset cost

The new accountant for Mactaggart Industries is wondering how to calculate the cost of a new machine the company just installed. Explain briefly whether or not you think each of the following items should be part of the machine's cost, and why:

a. The invoice price of the machine.
b. Sales tax paid on the machine.
c. Shipping charges to get the machine to the company's factory.
d. The cost of the factory manager's trip to the machine manufacturer's plant to choose the machine.
e. The cost of painting the machine light green, as other machines in the factory are painted.
f. Estimated revenue lost because the machine arrived late.
g. The cost of substandard products made while the factory personnel were learning how to operate the machine (all thrown away so as not to damage the company's reputation for quality products).
h. Interest cost on the bank loan used to finance the machine's purchase.
i. The cost of moving three other machines in the factory to make room for the new one.

PROBLEM 8.21
Record noncurrent asset transactions and adjustments

Below are several information items about the first year in business of manufacturer Borzian Inc.

a. Borzian purchased a factory from another company on the first day of the year. The total price was $4,500,000, which was allocated $1,000,000 to land, $2,300,000 to the building, and $1,200,000 to equipment in the factory. To finance the purchase, Borzian obtained a 7% mortgage loan of $2,500,000 (first payment of $250,000 plus interest was due on the first day of the next year), issued shares valued at $500,000, and paid $1,500,000 cash.

b. To convert the factory to the uses Borzian needed, $400,000 was immediately spent on the building and $800,000 on equipment. This was all paid in cash, some of it raised from selling equipment acquired in the original purchase, but not needed by Borzian. That equipment had been allocated a cost of $450,000, and Borzian sold it for $469,000.

c. Amortization for the year was calculated to be $135,000 on the building (5% per year) and $155,000 on the equipment (10% per year).

d. Right at the end of the year, equipment that had cost $70,000 was sold for $45,000 cash. This money was to be used to help make the first mortgage payment.

1. For each item, write a journal entry or entries to record any transaction or adjustment that is indicated.
2. What was the net book value of the factory at the end of the year?
3. What impact on income for the year did the four items have?

PROBLEM 8.22
Answer questions about asset accounting

1. Grafton Inc. has a variety of accounts receivable. They are listed below. Indicate how you would report them on the company's balance sheet, and what numbers the balance sheet would show as a result of your decisions.

a. Customer accounts receivable, $5,230,400.
b. Income tax refund due (expected within about six months), $1,100,000.
c. Loans to employees to buy houses (repayment not required unless an employee leaves the company or is fired; otherwise, each employee's loan will be forgiven over 10 years), $673,000.
d. Long-term income tax credit expected to be realized in about five years, $32,000.
e. Allowance for doubtful customer accounts, $232,100.

2. Starre Ltd. has a very conservative amortization policy, using higher amortization rates than most companies use. This year, the company sold a surplus building and showed a gain on sale. The president wants the gain on sale included in the calculation of her bonus pay for the year. Specify one argument for including the gain in her bonus calculation and one against doing that.

3. A business commentator said that Starre Ltd. should be praised for the conservative amortization policy "because of the income tax savings that result and the higher cash flow apparent from the large amortization added to income on the cash flow statement." Briefly evaluate the commentator's two points.

4. At a meeting of Starre Ltd.'s board of directors, the chief financial officer explained that the amortization policy was straight-line, a common policy, but the rate used was high. For example, machinery and equipment was amortized at 12 1/2 % per year with no salvage value. The directors discussed the policy at length. Give one argument for the company's policy and one against it.

5. For some years, Dobin Inc. has had a policy of recognizing an intangible asset, "development costs." The asset has been created by crediting operating expenses for some costs thought to benefit future years. The resulting asset

has been amortized by 50% per year, so any capitalized costs have been deferred for only two years into the future. At the end of 2000, the asset equalled $240,000. During 2001, $120,000 were amortized and $130,000 more were capitalized from 2001 operating expenses. It has been decided to discontinue this policy, effective at the *beginning* of 2001. The asset balance at the end of 2000 is to be put into a special "unusual expenses" account for 2001. It is now the end of 2001, and financial statements for 2001 are being prepared. Record a journal entry as at the end of 2001 to accomplish the policy change.

PROBLEM 8.23
Effects of asset accounting change to market from cost

Beauport Inc. owns several parcels of land in the Montreal area. The area has been subject to wide swings in real estate values, and Beauport's president is doubtful that the historical cost basis is appropriate for accounting for the company's land and buildings. Give short but careful answers to the following questions asked by the president:

1. If we changed to market values for the real estate instead of cost, would that make our balance sheet look better, or worse?
2. Similarly for income, would using market value instead of cost make us look more profitable, or less?
3. Does it matter what we do, as long as we disclose both cost and market value somewhere in our financial statements?

PROBLEM 8.24
Conceptual questions about LIFO and its effects

An accountant observed that: "In the United States, unlike in Canada, the LIFO inventory costing method is acceptable for tax purposes. For this reason, more companies use the LIFO inventory costing method in the United States than in Canada, especially in times of rising prices."

1. Explain the above quotation.
2. Suppose you were a shareholder in a company that switched its inventory costing method from FIFO to LIFO and, as a result, its reported net income dropped $2 million. What would be your reaction? Would your reaction depend on whether the company is a U.S. one or a Canadian one? Explain.

PROBLEM 8.25
LIFO, FIFO, and, AVGE inventory cost calculations

The following purchases of inventory were made by Anvil Corp. in April.

Date	Number of Units Purchased	Per Unit Amount	Total Cost
April 2	100	$5	$ 500
April 15	200	6	1,200
April 23	50	7	350
	350		

Sales of inventory during April were:

Date	Number of Units Sold
April 6	70
April 13	120
April 18	200
	390

Anvil's inventory on April 1 consisted of 150 units valued at $4 cost each.

1. Calculate cost of goods sold for April, using periodic LIFO, FIFO, and annual weighted average inventory cost flow assumptions.
2. Calculate ending inventory values as at April 30 under each of the three methods above.
3. Suppose the market price for these units was only $5 per unit at April 30, and the lower of cost or market valuation is applied to each unit individually. Redo part 2 above.
4. (Optional) Redo parts 1, 2, and 3, assuming Anvil uses a perpetual inventory control system and therefore would calculate LIFO using the perpetual records and AVGE using the weighted moving average.

PROBLEM 8.26
Inventory cost and market calculations

Winedark Sea Ltd. sells prints of romantic paintings. The prints are done on expensive paper and are quite costly. Pricing the prints to sell is hard because the popularity of a print is difficult to predict. If prints don't sell well, they are disposed of in bulk for use in hotels and motels.

Here are data on two prints:

	Print X		Print Y	
	Units	Cost per Unit	Units	Cost per Unit
Inventory, January 1, 2001	4	$340	11	$500
Purchases during 2001:				
During summer	10	350	25	480
During fall	15	330	30	510
Sales during 2001	23		38	

1. Calculate the following:
   a. Inventory cost, December 31, 2001, for Print X, FIFO basis.
   b. Cost of goods sold, 2001, for Print Y, AVGE basis.

2. Print Y hasn't sold since September. No one seems to like it any more. An out-of-town hotel has offered $100 each for all that Winedark has left, if Winedark will pay the $10 per print shipping cost. What amount would you suggest be used for the inventory of Print Y on the December 31, 2001, balance sheet? Why?

PROBLEM 8.27
Inventory cost and effects calculations

You work for a large local company as inventory manager. The company uses FIFO in accounting for inventory. In June, the company began to stock a new product, Painto. The June inventory record for Painto was:

Date	Purchase Price	Units Purchased	Units Sold	Units on Hand
June 1	$10	1,250		1,250
10	$11	1,000		2,250
12			250	2,000
17	$12	500		2,500
23			2,000	500
27	$13	1,500		2,000
30			800	1,200

1. Calculate, using FIFO:
   a. The cost of the June 30 inventory of Painto.
   b. The cost of goods sold for Painto for June.
2. Calculate, using LIFO (either perpetual or periodic):
   a. The cost of the June 30 inventory of Painto.
   b. The cost of goods sold for Painto for June.
3. Based on your calculations in parts 1 and 2, and ignoring income tax, what would be the effect of changing from FIFO to LIFO on the company's
   a. income before income tax for June,
   b. balance sheet at the end of June?

**PROBLEM 8.28
Various amortiza-
tion questions and
calculations**

1. Your friend Z has just completed the first year of operating a one-truck delivery company. Z explains to you that, because of careful care of the truck, the price the truck would fetch on the used truck market is not much different from the price paid for the truck a year ago. As a result, says Z, no amortization expense on the truck is needed for accounting purposes this year. Next year, Z believes the truck's value will drop a noticeable amount, but this is not a problem because the cash obtained from deducting tax amortization (capital cost allowance) and so saving income tax will compensate for the decline in market value over the year.

   Explain to Z what the accounting concept of amortization is and how Z's thinking is in error with respect to that concept.

2. Another friend is just starting a yard grooming service and has purchased a group of new lawnmowers for $20,000. The friend expects the mowers to last five years and to have negligible resale value at that point. The friend's business plan projects cutting 5,000 lawns over the five years, with per-year projections of 500, 1,000, 1,200, 1,800, and 500 lawns over the five years.

   a. Calculate the accumulated amortization balance at the end of the second year on each of the following amortization bases:
      i. Straight-line.
      ii. Declining balance (25% rate).
      iii. Units-of-production.
   b. Based on your calculations, which amortization basis would produce the highest retained earnings at the end of the second year?
   c. Your friend has never heard of the units-of-production basis. Explain why companies use it and comment on whether it would make sense for your friend's business.
   d. If the 25% declining balance method is used, accumulated amortization will be $15,254 at the end of the fifth year. Suppose that on the first day of the sixth year, all the lawnmowers are sold as junk for $100 cash in total. Ignoring income taxes:
      i. Calculate the loss on sale that would be recorded that day.
      ii. Suppose your friend objects to recording the loss on sale, pointing out that $100 more was received for the lawnmowers than had been expected five years earlier, and claims that, in any case, income for the sixth year should not be reduced by the loss when it happened on the first day on the year. Reply to your friend.

PROBLEM 8.29
Amortization calcu-
lations, entries,
effects, and choice

SD Corporation acquired machinery at the beginning of 2000, having a cost of $100,000 and an anticipated useful life of 10 years. It amortized this machinery for 2000 and 2001 using the straight-line method. Early in 2002, it decided to change to the declining balance method of amortization.

1. Prepare the journal entry to record amortization expense for 2001 using the straight-line method.
2. Prepare the journal entry to record amortization expense for 2001 using the declining balance method at a rate of 20%.
3. Show the effects of changing from straight-line to the 20% declining balance method on the 2001 income statement, the 2001 cash flow statement, and the balance sheet at the end of 2001. Ignore income tax.
4. In what circumstances is the use of declining balance amortization more appropriate than use of the straight-line method?

PROBLEM 8.30
Amortization and
gain/loss calculations
and effects

Fred's Freighthauling Ltd. has a small fleet of delivery trucks. Each one is amortized on the declining balance method (rate 20%; half that in the year of acquisition and in the year of disposal) with no salvage value. Truck 4 was purchased July 1, 1998, for $46,000 and sold three years later, on June 30, 2001, for $15,000. The company's fiscal year-end is December 31.

1. What was the total amortization on Truck 4 to the date of its disposal?
2. Based on your answer to part 1, write a journal entry to record the disposal of Truck 4.
3. Redo parts 1 and 2, assuming the company uses straight-line amortization at 15% per year and an estimated salvage value of $6,000.
4. Calculate the difference in effects between the two amortization methods on the company's 2001 income statement and cash flow statement. Ignore income tax effects.
5. What implications (if any) would the use of different amortization methods by the company have for potential creditors or investors?
6. The use of different amortization methods could affect financial performance comparability between fiscal years of a particular company, and between different companies for the same fiscal year. How are these differences moderated?

PROBLEM 8.31
Calculate any good-
will on a business
purchase

Foofaraw Ltd. paid $200,000 for land, buildings, inventories, and accounts payable of another business that will become a branch. The assets (after deducting the accounts payable of $50,000) had an aggregate fair market value of $187,000.

1. What (if anything) is the resulting asset on Foofaraw's balance sheet?
2. If Foofaraw had paid $185,000, what would be your answer to part 1?

PROBLEM 8.32
Questions about
intangibles and
capital leases

Answer the following questions briefly:

1. Why is capitalizing costs, such as intangible assets, a reasonable idea?
2. Why is it not such a good idea?
3. Explain clearly why and how capitalizing the costs of a development project as a "deferred costs" asset affects the income statement and the balance sheet.

4. Explain why capitalizing such costs does not have any direct effect on the cash flow statement's cash from operations figure.

5. Suggest some indirect effects on cash flow that such a capitalization policy may have.

6. If an asset is leased, it is not owned. Accounting standards require creating a balance sheet asset account for some leased assets. How can that be justified?

7. If a lease is treated as a capital lease rather than an operating lease, what effects does that have on the balance sheet, income statement, and cash flow statement?

PROBLEM 8.33
Answer questions about amortization and inventory costing

1. According to its financial statement notes, Egret Electric uses straight-line amortization, at various useful lives from 8 years to 40 years. Some competitors use accelerated double declining balance amortization, and Egret is considering changing to that method for the company's *more recently acquired assets*. (Older assets would be left on the straight-line method because they are getting close to being fully amortized in any case.) The change would be made beginning in the 2001 fiscal year.
   a. If this policy change were made, what would happen to 2001 net income (up, down, or no effect), and why?
   b. If this policy change were made, what would happen to total assets at the end of 2001 (up, down, or no effect), and why?

2. Also according to its notes, Egret uses a mixture of average cost and FIFO for its inventories. Consider the product Switching Panel 404-C. At the end of 2000, there were 4,000 panels in inventory at a cost of $89.00 each. During the 2001 fiscal year, 18,000 panels were manufactured at a cost of $93.00 each, and 17,000 were sold for a selling price of $160.00 each. Calculate the inventory cost at the end of 2001 on (a) Annual average cost basis, and (b) FIFO basis.

3. Net realizable value of the panels at the end of 2001 was $160.00 each. What adjustment, if any, would be made because of this in preparing the 2001 financial statements? Why?

PROBLEM 8.34
Answer questions about inventory costing and amortization

1. Ander Oil Exploration uses a mixture of average cost and FIFO for its inventories. The company, which faces steadily rising purchase costs and inventory levels, is considering changing its policy to use average cost for all inventories. The policy change would be implemented beginning in the 2000 fiscal year.
   a. If this policy change were made, what would happen to *2001* net income (up, down, or no effect), and why?
   b. If this policy change were made, what would happen to *2001* cash from operations (up, down, or no effect), and why?

2. Ander uses the units of production method for its amortization, based on production calculations made by its engineers. One of its oil production properties cost $9 million and was acquired October 1, 1997. Its useful life was then estimated at 20 years, with a salvage value of $1 million. Oil production from the property was estimated at 5 million barrels over that useful life. In 2001, 280,000 barrels of oil were produced from the property, bringing the total produced by the end of 2001 to 890,000 barrels. For that property, calculate:

a. amortization expense for the year ended September 30, 2001.

b. accumulated amortization as at September 30, 2001.

3. Assume Ander used accelerated, double declining balance amortization for the property in part 2. Calculate the amortization expense for the year ended September 30, *1999,* for that property, using that accelerated method.

PROBLEM 8.35
Accounting for goodwill

Octuplex Inc. acquired the shares of another company for $5,450,000 cash. At the date of the acquisition, the fair values of the other company's assets totalled $8,916,000 and the fair values of its liabilities totalled $3,705,000.

1. Calculate goodwill arising from the acquisition, if any.
2. Why is any such goodwill considered to be an asset of Octuplex Inc.?
3. The president of Octuplex Inc. was perplexed by accounting rules, saying: "I don't understand why, if goodwill is an asset, our advertising is not. Advertising is essential to the future profitability of our company, and seems to me more relevant to assessing our company performance than goodwill is." Explain to the president why advertising is generally not considered to be an asset.

PROBLEM 8.36
(CHALLENGING)
Questions on accounting values and income

Pull together your knowledge of how accounting numbers are derived and answer each of the following briefly:

1. Explain why balance sheet valuation and income measurement are linked.
2. Briefly discuss two of the limitations of historical cost balance sheet valuation.
3. During times of rising prices, will the following tend to be overstated or understated? Why?
   a. Assets
   b. Net income
   c. Return on equity (This is just net income divided by equity, so think about what might happen to the numerator and the denominator.)

PROBLEM 8.37
(CHALLENGING)
Oil production balance sheet and income

The Lindleigh Company is in the business of oil production. On January 1, 1995, the company paid $1,000,000 for the lease of an area near MacDonald Lake. The lease area was known to contain 5,000,000 barrels of oil in the form of tar sands.

During the five years to December 31, 2000, the company spent $5,000,000 on exploratory work in assessing the extent of the deposits, perfecting the extraction technique, and building access roads.

1. Assuming that the company commenced with a capital stock of $3,000,000 and has borrowed $3,000,000 since then, and that the transactions specified are the only ones in which the company has engaged, present a balance sheet for the Lindleigh Company as at December 31, 2000.
2. During 2001, 500,000 barrels of oil were produced. Production costs incurred during the period were $1,000,000. At the end of the period, 100,000 barrels of refined oil remained in storage, and 400,000 barrels had been sold at a price of $4 per barrel. The company owed income tax of 35% on pre-tax income.
   a. Assuming that selling expenses were $200,000, prepare an income

statement for the Lindleigh Company for 2001. Show your cost of goods sold computation.

b. How would the Assets portion of the balance sheet appear as at December 31, 2001?

PROBLEM 8.38 (CHALLENGING)
Identify possible asset valuation methods

Sports Forever Inc. has recently agreed to purchase a local arena at a price of $1,000,000. The realtor had listed the property at $1,150,000, but Mark Johnson, SFI's president, managed to talk the present owner, Shattered Dreams Limited, down to the lower price by promising full payment in cash. Mark has seen the city's property tax assessment of the arena, which revealed that the arena's total assessed value was $800,000, allocated 70% to land and 30% to the building.

Mark is also aware that the arena has firm contracts (regardless of change in ownership of the arena) for the next 20 years with both a popular football team and a highly successful local hockey team. Net total cash flows from the two contracts are expected to be approximately $250,000 per year over the full term of the contracts. This is rather convenient, since the remaining expected life of the arena is projected by a professional estimator to be 20 years.

Upon consultation with a contractor, Mark learned that the cost to replace the arena in its original condition is currently $1,500,000. The president of Shattered Dreams Limited felt that the price offered by Mark was more than appropriate, since the net book value of the building on his company's books is only $300,000. Sports Forever Inc. can borrow or invest at an interest rate of 10%.

1. Identify all possible valuations of the arena for which sufficient information has been supplied. Where calculations are required, show your work. (Present value calculations are not required, but indicate the kind of calculation that would be needed.)

2. List the potential users of each valuation and describe how they would use the information.

PROBLEM 8.39 (CHALLENGING)
Issues in accounting for tangible and intangible assets

For some years, the world economy, particularly in the more developed countries, has been undergoing what some people believe is a fundamental realignment from the "old economy" manufacturing and natural resource industries to the "new economy" high-technology, communications, service, and Internet activities. This has caused some problems for financial accounting. One is that the economic values of the intangible assets thought to give "new economy" companies their overall value are not explicitly represented in the companies' balance sheets. A second problem is that the tangible assets of the "old economy" companies may be overvalued in their balance sheets if those assets are not attractive for earning income as the economy shifts. A third problem is that the values of companies on stock markets may be less related to financial accounting's income measure, because "new economy" companies that make little income are popular in the stock market whereas "old economy" companies that are earning solid income are not popular in the stock market.

Discuss the issues raised above. What sort of changes in financial accounting might address the problems? Do you think financial accounting requires a significant overhaul? Why, or why not?

**PROBLEM 8.40
(CHALLENGING)
Asset prices, poli-
cies, effects, and
entries**

Advanced Markets Ltd., a retailer, began business on November 1, 2000. The company's balance sheets then, and at October 31, 2001, were (in thousands of dollars):

	Oct. 31, 2001	Nov. 1, 2000		Oct. 31, 2001	Nov. 1, 2000
Cash	$ 26	$100	Accounts payable	$194	$180
Accts. receivable	334	300	Share capital	500	500
Allow.					
doubt. accts.	(30)	(20)	Retained earnings	76	—
Inventory					
(FIFO)	354	240			
Fixtures	40	—			
Accum. amortization	(8)	—			
Goodwill (net)	54	60			
	$770	$680		$770	$680

The company had receivables, payables, and inventories from the beginning because it was formed to take over the business of another company whose owner had decided to retire to a warmer climate. The company's premises and equipment were all rented, so the company had no fixed assets when it began. The company need not pay any income tax this year.

1. From the information given, calculate the purchase price of the business Advanced Markets purchased November 1, 2000.
2. Net income for the company's first year, to October 31, 2001, was $76 (thousand). Calculate cash generated by operations for that year (in thousands).
3. If the company changed to average cost for its inventory, the October 31, 2001, inventory asset would be $316 (thousand). If it did so, what would the following be?
   a. Retained earnings, October 31, 2001.
   b. Cash generated by operations (based on your answer to part 2).
4. The company buys its inventories in large lots. Its purchases and sales last year were:

November 1, 2000, beginning	8,000 units @ $30 = $240 (thousand)
Sales before next purchase	6,000 units
February 15, 2001, purchase	7,000 units @ $36 = $252 (thousand)
Sales before next purchase	4,000 units
July 31, 2001, purchase	7,500 units @ $40 = $300 (thousand)
Sales before October 31, 2001	3,500 units

   a. What would the company's October 31, 2001, inventory cost be on the periodic LIFO basis?
   b. What would the 2001 cost of goods sold be on the LIFO basis?
   c. Redo parts (a) and (b) using the perpetual LIFO basis. Why are there differences in the figures?
5. On December 31, 2001, in the company's second year of operation, several unneeded counters and tables were sold for $15 thousand cash. At that date,

those assets (which had cost $18 thousand) had a book value of $12 thousand.

a. Write a journal entry to record the sale.

b. Explain why this sale affects the calculation of cash from operations in the company's cash flow statement for its second year of operation.

PROBLEM 8.41 (CHALLENGING) Accounting calculations, effects, entries

Harriett has been making quilts, aprons, pillows, scarves, and other such items for years. Recently, she took the plunge and opened a shop to sell her products and those of other local craftspeople. Her husband, who is more interested in sports than accounting, keeps her books and prepared the draft financial statements that follow.

Draft Financial Statements for Harriett's Handmades Ltd.
Balance Sheet as at December 31, 2001

Assets			Liabilities and Owners' Equity		
Current:			Current:		
Inventory	$ 43,000		Owing to bank	$ 18,000	
Owing from customers	2,140		Owing to suppliers	21,000	
Cash	4,600		Income tax owing	3,200	
		$ 49,740			$ 42,200
Noncurrent:			Store mortgage	110,000	
Store	$187,000		Owners' equity:		
Amortization so far	3,740		Shares issued	68,000	
		$183,260	Income so far	12,800	
		$233,000			$233,000

Income Statement
for the Year Ended December 31, 2001

Sales		$152,000
Cost of goods sold:		
Purchases	$118,000	
Less inventory left over	43,000	75,000
Margin		$ 77,000
Expenses:		
Store operations	$ 22,000	
Wages	24,000	
Interest	15,000	61,000
Income before tax		$ 16,000
Estimated income tax owing		$ 3,200
Income for the year		$ 12,800

1. The company's "store" assets cost the following: fixtures and shelving, $19,000; cash register and other equipment, $14,000; building, $114,000; land, $40,000; total, $187,000. Harriett's husband computed amortization at 2% of the total and included the resulting $3,740 in store operations expenses.
   a. Evaluate Harriett's husband's amortization accounting policy.
   b. Propose a more suitable amortization accounting policy, indicating any assumptions you need in order to do that.
   c. Calculate amortization for 2001, based on your proposed policy, and write a journal entry to adjust the accounts to reflect your calculation.

2. Most of the company's inventory and the cost of goods sold are recorded at actual cost because each item is tagged with the name of the person who made it plus an identification number. However, the store also sells a line of fancy wrapping paper. Purchases and sales of that paper were as follows:

Initial purchase	200 packages @ $1.20	$ 240
Sales to April 24	160 packages	
Purchase April 25	300 packages @ $1.30	390
Sales to August 15	310 packages	
Purchase August 16	500 packages @ $1.40	700
Sales December 31	450 packages	
		$1,330

Harriett's husband, working from an old accounting text, came up with the following figures for the wrapping paper:

Unit cost:	$1,330 / 1,000 = $1.33
Cost of goods sold:	920 × $1.33 = $1,224
Ending inventory:	80 × $1.33 = $106

   a. What inventory costing method was Harriett's husband using?
   b. Is that an acceptable method for the wrapping paper? Why?
   c. Using the *perpetual LIFO* method, calculate ending inventory and cost of goods sold for the wrapping paper.

3. Harriett is thinking of capitalizing $2,000 of the year's wage expenses (spent early in 2001 to build shelving) and including that in the cost of fixtures and shelving.
   a. What does it mean to "capitalize" such expenses?
   b. What would be the effect on 2001 income (ignoring income tax) if Harriett decided to capitalize the wages?

4. When Harriett reviewed the draft financial statements, she discovered the following:

   • Net realizable value of the inventory totalled $41,600.

   • One customer account totalling $150 was uncollectible, and three others totalling $280, were doubtful.

   • Cash on hand was overstated by $1,000 because her husband had recorded a $1,000 bank loan twice.

   • A $210 bill for operating expenses not incurred until January 2002 was included in accounts payable.

    • The current portion of the store mortgage was $4,200.

    Taking these items and assuming implementation of your amortization policy (part 1 above) and Harriett's wage capitalization plan (part 3), calculate the revised income before income tax for 2001.

5. Harriett's husband estimated income taxes payable by just multiplying the income before tax by 20%. In fact, when all the above information was taken into account, the income tax payable for 2001 was $2,100. (We'll ignore any future income tax.)
   a. Write a journal entry to adjust the estimated income tax recorded by the husband to reflect the above information.
   b. Taking into account (a) above and parts 1, 2, and 4, calculate the following as at December 31, 2001:
      i.   Retained earnings.
      ii. Total assets.

PROBLEM 8.42 (CHALLENGING) Accounting policies, effects, and entries

Refer to the Grandin Ltd. trial balances for 2001 and 2000 in Problem 4.31 and the financial statements you originally prepared. Assume that upon further inquiry, you have discovered the following information:

• At the very end of 2001, some equipment that had cost $4,500 11 years earlier was sold for $1,800. The bookkeeper had debited the sale proceeds to cash and credited service revenue.

• The company's amortization policy for its equipment is straight-line, with an estimated useful life of 15 years and no salvage value. No amortization is recorded in the year of sale. Amortization on the remaining assets has been recorded in the accounts.

• No other equipment was bought or sold during 2001.

• The company uses the average inventory costing policy. There were 2,000 units on hand at the end of 2000 (costing $18.50 each), and during 2001 there were the following purchases, in this order: 800 at $19, 1,200 at $16.20, 2,000 at $17.50, 1,500 at $19.20, and 500 at $20.50. Sales for 2001 were recorded at 5,666 units. On the average cost basis, 2001 cost of goods sold for 5,666 units was $103,190 and inventory at the end of 2001 was $42,500. (Weighted average cost was $18.21; the two figures above are rounded.)

• The company has decided to change its inventory costing policy to FIFO (which will be less than net realizable value, as is cost on the average basis). The change will be implemented for 2001, but the inventory cost per unit at the end of 2000 ($18.50) will not be changed. The bookkeeper has no idea how to implement the accounting policy change.

• Grandin's applicable tax rate is 25%. All income tax adjustments will be paid or refunded currently.

1. Prepare adjusting journal entries to correct the company's records.
2. Calculate the effect of the above entries on:
   a. Net income for 2001.
   b. 2001 beginning retained earnings.
   c. 2001 ending retained earnings.

3. Prepare a corrected balance sheet, statement of income, and statement of retained earnings for 2001.

4. Comment on the company's performance for 2001 and its position at year-end.

CASE 8A
Financial accounting in the new economy

An American investment broker recently said, "The quality of earnings in the United States is moot at the moment. Earnings no longer matter. A company that shows a profit is penalized in the U.S. stock market nowadays."[28] *Business Week* raised a similar issue in the article below, "What's an Old-Line CEO to Do?" Read the article and think about the asset accounting topics raised especially in sections 8.2 and 8.11, and then discuss the following issues, which are quite interrelated:

1. Financial accounting measures performance essentially by recording historical transactions and using those to determine both profit (income) and the asset base that is being used to earn the income. Accrual accounting makes adjustments to that transactional base, but financial accounting is still fundamentally a historical system. Assets are valued largely in historical costs and income is measured by procedures that lock it tightly to the way assets are valued (such as through inventory accounting, amortization, capitalization of expenses when allowed, allowances for doubtful accounts, and recording historically purchased intangibles such as goodwill). A CEO who is trying to do a good job is evaluated by numbers generated by financial accounting. In which ways may accounting's way of valuing assets and measuring income be harmful to a CEO trying to compete and manage the company well?

2. Financial accounting has developed over hundreds of years. Is its way of recognizing and valuing assets and measuring associated income suitable for the apparent transformation of the economy that seems to be happening? What is it doing right, and what seems in need of fixing?

3. Accrual accounting can do just about anything to the accounting numbers. Just debit something and credit something else. Can the standard double-entry model just be adjusted to take new kinds of assets and economic values into account?

4. Maybe the stock markets are just out of kilter. Maybe big corrections in stock prices are coming (or may have happened by the time you read this!). Is it financial accounting's fault if the market is not paying attention to companies' fundamental earning power and financial strength? Could it be that accounting serves a useful role by contributing its measures and values and at least causing people to ask questions about how to understand companies that do not look good by accounting measures as well as about companies that do look good by those measures but are not popular on the stock market?

What's an Old-Line CEO to Do?

Net-crazed investors sneer, no matter how sturdy the performance

Imagine you're the chief executive of an Old Economy company. You've posted 12 straight years of increased earnings, capped by a 15% rise in 1999. You've engineered a transforming deal that helped double your managed assets, to $50.4 billion. Yet investors are fleeing, driving your company's stock price down 35% in the past year. "It's frustrating," grouses Albert R. Gamper Jr., who is in exactly that predicament. "In the good old-fashioned American system, if you delivered consistent earnings, you were supposed to get recognition from the stock market," says Gamper, the CEO of financial-services company CIT Group Inc. "Yet I look at my Telerate screen and I see our stock in the red, going down every day. That is a real distraction."

A modern-day corporate sob story? You bet, and one that has resonance with increasing numbers of CEOs whose Old Economy stocks are laboring in what has become a stealth bear market. Even the Dow Jones' 320-point gain on Mar. 15—its biggest rally in 17 months—did little to narrow the disparity. The unprecedented flight of capital into high-tech and Internet companies is placing enormous investor pressure on old-line CEOs. They're spinning off divisions, buying back stock, and following the lead of General Electric Co. Chairman John F. Welch Jr. in attempting to make the Internet central to their business models. IBM Chairman Louis V. Gerstner Jr. believes the pressure has become so intense that "many CEOs have an air of desperation about them."

Yet these moves are virtually to no avail. It's almost as if the stock market, in its infatuation with Net stocks, suffers from attention-deficit disorder. While Old Economy titans Coca-Cola and Bank of America have each lost more than $50 billion in market value since May 1 of last year, tech superstars Cisco soared by $293.3 billion and Oracle by $198.1 billion. The top 10 gainers—all tech luminaries—saw their market caps gain a phenomenal $1.5 trillion in that time. The top 10 losers—old corporate favorites—lost an equally unbelievable $284.3 billion. "High-technology and dot-com companies are getting much bigger sums of money much sooner in their economic life cycles than any other companies in history," says Darrell K. Rigby, a partner at consultants Bain & Co. "Investors are looking for big gains, not solid returns."

The angst over the value split is being felt by a generation of chief executives raised to deliver "shareholder value" to investors. Many are turning in the financial results that ordinarily would lift their stock price, not to mention the value of their stock options. Instead, they have found themselves yesterday's news, ignored by investors seeking extraordinary returns. That's made for plenty of unhappy CEOs among Corporate America's oldest and best-known brand names. "They're envious because they want the valuations the technology companies have, angry because they're working hard and not getting a lot of credit, and fearful because they can now be cheaply bought by some of the dot-coms in their industries," says James A. Champy, chairman of Perot Systems Corp.'s consulting practice.

Many Old Economy execs are straining to understand—and fit into—a world in which the market capitalization of software maker Oracle Corp. now exceeds the combined value of the Big Three carmakers, and that of Yahoo! Inc. eclipses that of Proctor & Gamble Co. Is the consumer-goods powerhouse, which lost 81% of its market value after a Mar. 7 earnings warning, really worth $36 billion less because its annual profits will be 5% short of earlier forecasts? Perhaps not, but the loss marks the split between the hot and the cold, a drop "symbolic of the growing divergence between Old and New economies," says Edward E. Yardeni, chief global economist for Deutsche Bank Securities Inc.

The stock market's bifurcation may have further consequences. Many stable, mainline companies with underwater stock options already have found themselves vulnerable to talent raids by New Economy outfits. Instead of options, boards are being forced to offer more cash and restricted stock—both of which affect the bottom line. Execs also are starting to demand that now worthless options be repriced to give them some value, but if directors comply, they could face a shareholder revolt.

More important, though, lower valuations could make the companies vulnerable to takeovers. "If these New Economy companies nibble around the edges, they could make some great acquisitions with their high-valued stocks," says Lawrence M. Schloss, chairman of Donaldson, Lufkin & Jenrette Inc.'s merchant-bank unit. He notes that Amazon.com Inc. could use its stock to buy, rather than build, warehouses. Or it could buy an air-freight company to deliver its products to customers. In the aftermath of the proposed America On-line-Time Warner merger, such a deal isn't far-fetched. Amazon's $22.4 billion market value dwarfs that of FedEx Corp., whose market cap fell more than $7 billion in the past year, to $9.3 billion. Never mind that Amazon has yet to post a profit, or that its $1.6 billion in sales is less than 10% of FedEx's revenues.

The value split could also usher in an era of leveraged buyouts not seen since the 1980s. "Buyout firms are knocking on the doors of companies again," says Schloss. "CEOs are getting tired of being undervalued even though they're putting up good numbers. Their boards are frustrated as well."

Making matters worse, even when old-line companies seem to "get-it," they often fail to gain much recognition from the Street. Consider Eastman

Chemical Co., the former spin-off of film giant Kodak. Last year, Eastman became the first chemical maker to introduce e-commerce sales in the U.S. and Canada and will rack up more than $100 million in online revenues this year. It has forged strategic partnerships with seven Internet startups. Yet its shares are down 25% over the past year. "Most of the chemical analysts who follow us don't get it, and none of them has seen a real impact on the bottom line from our e-commerce ventures," says CEO Earnest W. Deavenport Jr. His advice? "You have to be diligent in telling your story, and you have to believe that long term, the stock market is rational."

At CIT Group, Gamper agrees. "You have to recognize that there are some fundamental changes taking place in how business is being conducted. You can't miss that opportunity. And the upside is terrific." But if you're old-line, will anyone notice?

By John A. Byrne, with Debra Sparks, in New York.

Reprinted from *Business Week* (pp. 38–39), March 27, 2000, by John A. Byrne, with Debra Sparks.

**CASE 8B
Managing, measuring, and reporting on intellectual capital**

This chapter has raised some issues about how financial accounting deals with intangible assets, such as the value of employees and management. Another way to look at such intangible assets issues is to think about how their value arises and how to manage them, and then to connect those matters to the financial accounting and to the value perceived by shareholders. Read the article "Managing the Brain Trust" below and discuss its points about managing intellectual capital and how its points connect to the asset valuation and income measurement topics in this chapter.

Managing the Brain Trust
Managing, measuring and reporting on intellectual capital is becoming recognized as an important management strategy

Intellectual capital is a relatively new and enigmatic management concept that attempts to describe the mostly intangible assets of the firm. It is often considered as that mysterious value that lies between the book value and market value of an organization.

In a recent study, Margaret Blair of the Brookings Institute in Washington shows that this "missing value" has grown from about 38% in 1982 to 62% in 1995. In health care, for example, the difference between book value and estimated market value suggests that intangibles comprise 75% of the value of these companies.

Intellectual capital is a wide variety of things: intellectual property is the value of a patent or copyright; intellectual assets such as database or R&D;

human capital such as the savvy of a CEO like Bill Gates or Jack Welch of GE; or customer capital which is the value of brand loyalty or licensing agreements.

From a measurement perspective, intellectual capital has traditionally been hidden away under "goodwill" and other intangibles. This is changing. With growing pressures from shareholders for transparency, and more complete information on the potential for profitable growth, managing, measuring and reporting on intellectual capital is becoming recognized as an important management strategy. Here's how these organizations manage their intellectual capital and what its impact is on long-term shareholder value.

Putting frameworks to work

Knowledge management at Clarica (formerly The Mutual Group), Waterloo, ON

Functioning within the knowledge economy requires an understanding of how the ground rules of business have changed. Since the traditional accounting structures are geared to tangible assets, many managers are not equipped to manage within the new knowledge economy.

According to Waterloo-based Hubert Saint-Onge, senior vice-president of Clarica and one of the leading practitioners in intellectual capital management, "Because accounting is the present picture of past performance, it's like managing through a rear view mirror. As you get into the knowledge economy, customer preferences and human and structural capital have changed faster than the management systems and frameworks that are available to monitor and measure them."

Saint-Onge explains how the company's ability to compete relies on how well they can turn organizational and human resource skills into tacit knowledge, and then into customer value. This requires a new model of management since, as Saint-Onge points out, "Strategies and management practices that existed in the industrial era have lost relevance or validity in the knowledge era."

Clarica recognizes this and is in the process of developing a knowledge management system that allows them to grow, manage, measure and report the "knowledge assets" of the organization.

Managing knowledge requires higher levels of abstraction than managing traditional tangible assets. More specifically it is based on the notion that:

1. Value creation comes from people;
2. Ideas are the source of competitiveness; and
3. Corporate growth is organic and derived from skills transfer.

Clarica's "Knowledge Capital Framework" was developed with this in mind. It builds a logistical pathway between the creation, dissemination and utilization of knowledge, to the creation of customer and shareholder value. It delineates the total capital of the firm into three components: tangible assets, financial capital and intangible assets. Knowledge capital refers to the intangible assets of the firm and is comprised of three elements: human capital, structural capital and customer capital.

Evaluation and measurement The definition of accounting is to detect, monitor and measure the value creation pathways of the organization. Those pathways in large part become the pathways of the intangible assets. The financial capital of the firm is inextricably linked to customer capital and the measurement tool for tracking this relationship at Clarica is in its early development. This first requires an understanding of customer capital over time and knowing what the key factors are that will affect it. To date, the financial frameworks at Clarica are independent of the knowledge framework, though eventually they hope to tie the two together through systems modelling.

While there are no financial models linking the knowledge capital of their sector and in their customer's business;

Clarica to its bottom line, a recent due diligence exercise has demonstrated the economic link between the corporate strategy (based upon a clear knowledge framework and the supporting knowledge infrastructure) and the creation of shareholder value.

In 1998 Clarica purchased the Canadian operations of Metropolitan Life for $1.2 billion. The due diligence was conducted in less than six weeks through the use of a widely utilized knowledge base. About 125 people, working on 25 teams, built the integration plans for the acquisition, justified the price, and in the process, put themselves ahead of the competition.

With growing pressures from shareholders for transparency, and more complete information on the potential for profitable growth, managing, measuring and reporting on intellectual capital is becoming recognized as an important management strategy.

Knowledge sharing The knowledge strategy of the organization recognizes the differences between knowledge storage, or the codifying of the knowledge of the organization, and knowledge as practice, which is real time interaction between people within the same domain of work. The exchange of information between individuals in real time is called "productive inquiries" which is an interactive sharing of knowledge in support of achieving common objectives.

Clarica's training strategy reflects this "knowledge sharing" focus in that formal courses are no longer the primary means of education. According to Saint-Onge, knowledge sharing eliminates the need for most formal corporate training and, "This is a prerequisite to developing the type of organic culture Clarica was striving for."

Information technology Clarica has established knowledge networks that contain the whole knowledge base of the organization. The IT infrastructure has seamless technology that makes the knowledge of the entire organization accessible to every individual while the data architecture allows for easy navi-

---

Special delivery

Jo-Anne Raynes, vice president, Knowledge Based Business Group, Canadian Imperial Bank of Commerce (CIBC), says when a company's primary assets are intangible, they have an even greater challenge than organizations whose core assets are hard, recognizable and easily transformed into product. For companies who rely heavily on intellectual property for future growth, they must excel in these areas:

- They must fundamentally understand their market niche and know what their customers want or need;

- They have strong relationships with key clients;

- They know their strength vis-à-vis the competition and understand current and future trends in technology for their sector and in their customer's business;

- They bring their understanding of technology trends into their thinking as they develop product, and consequently, they move both within and beyond the marketplace;

- There is a strong partnership between their key technology people and the business management team;

- The organization is typically flat, flexible, non-bureaucratic and work is carried out in teams;

- Management takes a team-based approach and is characterized by strong leadership;

- There is free-flowing information between groups;

- Employees are properly motivated through appropriate compensation schemes.

gation in a time effective manner. The knowledge architecture is built upon communities of practices and centres of competencies and the "knowledge depot" is at the centre of the architecture, crystallizing information.

Modelled after the concept of the corporate "village," Clarica has built what they call Metropolis. This IT village is divided into community centres where, via the Internet and Intranet, employees (or "members") can access "member services," (formerly known as human resources).

Banking on intellectual capital

The Knowledge Based Business Group at CIBC, Toronto, ON

It is now widely accepted that the wealth generating capabilities of organizations depends on their stock of intangible assets of "knowledge assets" as opposed to more traditional hard assets. Jo-Anne Raynes, vice president, Knowledge Based Business Group, Canadian Imperial Bank of Commerce (CIBC), says, "One of the central components of a company's knowledge assets is its ability to continuously innovate—to develop innovative products, services and processes."

CIBC recognized the importance of the hidden value of intellectual capital in Canadian industry and in so doing, has become one of the first banks in the world to devote an entire lending division to businesses whose primary assets are knowledge and innovation.

About four years ago senior level management at the CIBC began to consider the bank's role in the emergence of the knowledge-based economy of Canada. They came to the conclusion that they needed to address the banking needs of companies whose asset base was primarily comprised of intangible assets (such as their innovation capabilities, knowledge or organizational know-how; human resources; flexibility and intellectual property).

An intellectual capital management framework was developed to help the Knowledge Based Business Group understand and evaluate the new customer group on a qualitative basis. According to Raynes, "The knowledge framework allowed us to develop a new set of practices, new business models that would help us understand these

risks, and new value models that would provide a view to non-traditional sources of value."

Intellectual capital is segmented into human capital, organizational capital and customer capital. It is assessed on the basis of the actual knowledge base of the company (human resource and management expertise), how it was created, and the leverage the company has in the marketplace.

A large component in the assessment process of the Knowledge Based Business Group is determining where the organizational shortfalls may currently lie, where they occurred in the past, and what additional skills may be needed to facilitate future growth.

One of the key considerations in the "bank-ability" of a small or medium sized high-tech company would be their ability to recognize who their main contributors were from the standpoint of innovation. Learning about the level of expertise that is present in a company and how it is being applied creates an understanding of the ability of the company to continue to innovate.

Frequently, the drivers of the innovation and creativeness would stem from a small group of individuals who are tied directly to the creation of the company's products. A primary factor in determining the long term growth potential of a company is the ability of their compensation programs, profit sharing, share purchase plans and other mechanisms to:

- Attract appropriate human resources to the company;
- Maintain these individuals over the long term and;
- Motivate them to participate in future growth.

If a deficiency is found, the Knowledge Based Business Group will provide recommendations for alternative compensation structures and give advice on how to improve their capabilities to become more attractive to banking and venture capital.

Mining for hidden gold

The LivingLab at Bruncor, Halifax, NS

Bruncor is the parent company of NBTel, New Brunswick's long-standing telecommunications carrier, now part of the newly-formed Aliant, with Island Tel, MTT and NewTel. Bruncor's prod-

uct liens are divided into core business and near core businesses.

Core businesses are their traditional local and long distance telephony services and account for the most revenue and number of workers. Near-core businesses are those companies, activities and investments that surround the original investment such as phone centres, software development, (Connectivity and New North Media) multimedia and e-commerce (NBTel Interactive) and video (ImagicTV).

Gerald Pond, president of Bruncor and executive vice-president of Aliant says, "The typical situation in most companies is that while focusing on core competencies, they neglect to mould their intellectual capital and intellectual assets into future revenue streams. Much of what intellectual capital management sets out to do is to determine where these assets lie, to process or mine them into improved efficiency, cost recovery or revenue generation. Mining the intellectual capital of Bruncor begins with recognizing how innovative we can be and understanding what the value of that is to our current and future customers."

For the past several years the global restructuring of industry combined with market deregulation has created a telecom environment where big strategic alliances are being created between the world's largest communications providers, (both telephony and cable) equipment manufacturers, entertainment and other content providers, banks, software developers and other related multi-media companies. The emerging industry structure has created boundless opportunities for Bruncor.

Pond says, "Those large telecom alliances are going to need new products, services and processes to add on to their big distribution systems, which will allow them to do big things better. That's where we come in."

Bruncor has partnered with several companies in Canada and the US to develop and sell non-traditional products and services in the multimedia arena. They are now examining the concept of "the innovation process as product" and are exploring unique ways to best market their innovative know-how, customer information and data mining tools, intellectual property and other forms of knowledge capital.

Pond explains, "Our type of innovation, and the model we're using with customers, partners, and prototypes is a unique model. We call it the LivingLab and we've trademarked it. We have a LivingLab product management group and their job is to sell ideas, innovations, and experience. We deal with the whole innovative process as well as the specific marketable innovations that come out of it. It's turning the Lab into a product."

The LivingLab at Bruncor has become world renown for innovative telecom market research, testing and product development. Hundreds of visitors come each year from all over the world to learn its method of management, innovation and underlying philosophies.

Conceptually, the LivingLab is a think tank, a consulting and market research company, and as the name implies a realtime laboratory. As such, it produces, applies, packages, and sells knowledge.

One of the central components of a company's knowledge assets is its ability to continuously innovate

Currently, the major customers of the Lab are NBTel/Bruncor divisions and operational groups, New North Media, Export Consulting Group, Telco Service Providers and technology partners, vendors and suppliers such as Nortel. Each major client purchases some mix of the products and services of the lab. Each product and service is customized, yet the knowledge gained through the research process can be leveraged across customers or market segments.

The separate revenue streams of the LivingLab can be identified, measured, and managed by customer, product, service or activity as any other separate business entity. Thinking about the lab as a knowledge generator stimulates new ideas for generating revenue beyond the core to include, for example: publishing, training and education, public sector management and virtually anything that involves producing, processing, packaging, disseminating and applying the knowledge and information the lab generates. Under this framework, the growth potential for the lab is exponential. The intellectual capital of the lab is leveraged across processes, possibilities, and clients, and ideally, nothing is left on the cutting room floor.

Fad or trend? While intellectual capital management is still in its infancy, there is a growing recognition in Canadian companies like CIBC, Clarica and Bruncor, that their current and future growth hinges critically on managing the intangible assets of the firm. Assets such as human capital, customer loyalty and information are becoming increasingly important in an economy where shareholder value is tied to corporate knowledge, innovation and ultimately, bringing innovation to market.

The business community is becoming critically aware that they must "mind the gap" between market and book value, a gap that has continued to spread over the past 20 years. A closer look at what this missing value is, and how organizations should measure, manage and report it to shareholders continues to be a topic of ongoing research.

For more information on intellectual capital management, review The Management of Intellectual Capital: The issues and the practice, Issues Paper 16, CMA Canada, 1998.

Ramona Dzinkowski is principal of RND Research Group in Toronto.

Reprinted from *CMA Management*, 15 October 1999, by Ramona Dzinkowski.

NOTES

1. C. Byrd, I. Chen, and H. Chapman, *Financial Reporting in Canada 1999* (Toronto: Canadian Institute of Chartered Accountants, 1999), 208.
2. Ibid., 208.
3. Ibid., 208.
4. bid., 216.
5. Ibid., 215.
6. Ibid., 229.
7. Ibid., 231.
8. Ibid., 231.
9. Ibid., 231.
10. Ibid., 231.
11. CAE, 2000 Annual Report, 31.
12. Ibid., 230.
13. C. Byrd, 101.
14. Ibid., 107.
15. C. Byrd, 231.
16. Ibid., 269.
17. Ibid., 269.
18. CAE, 1999 Annual Report, 59.
19. *Illustration of sum-of-the-year's-digits amortization.* The variables needed to compute amortization using this method are:
    a. Cost.
    b. Estimated salvage value.
    c. Estimated life of the asset—calculated in years.
    d. The sum of the years—for example, for a three-year life: Sum = 1 + 2 + 3 = 6.
    e. Number of years of life remaining.

The formula for computing sum-of-the-years'-digits amortization is:

Amortization for the year = (C – S) × (N / SYD)

Where: Cost (C) and salvage (S) are as usually defined;
N = number of useful years remaining, and
SYD = sum of years' digits.

Let's look again at the delivery truck and compute the annual amortization:

Cost = $5,000; salvage value = $1,000; years of life = 5;
   sum of the years = 5 + 4 + 3 + 2 + 1 = 15

Amortization for year 1
   = ($5,000 – $1,000) × (5 / 15) = $1,333.33
Amortization for year 2
   = ($5,000 – $1,000) × (4 / 15) =   1,066.67
Amortization for year 3
   = ($5,000 – $1,000) × (3 / 15) =   800.00
Amortization for year 4
   = ($5,000 – $1,000) × (2 / 15) =   533.33
Amortization for year 5
   = ($5,000 – $1,000) × (1 / 15) =   266.67
                                              $4,000.00

20. C. Byrd, 269.
21. Ibid., 269.
22. Ibid., 271, 273.
23.. *Business Week* (27 March 2000): 39.
24. See two Canadian studies: G.M. Entwistle, "Exploring the R&D Disclosure Environment," *Accounting Horizons*, 13 no. 4 (December 1999): 323–41, and C.A. Carnaghan, *Factors Influencing Managerial Decisions about Intangible Asset Disclosures: The Role of Accountability Theory and Impression Management*, PhD dissertation, U. of Alberta 1999.
25. For evidence on the effects of stock market prices' response to conservative expensing and not capitalizing research and development, see B. Lev and T. Sougiannis, "The Capitalization, Amortization and Value-Relevance of R&D," *Journal of Accounting and Economics* 21 (1996): 107–38.
26. C. Byrd, 287–88.
27. Ibid., 286–88.
28. M. Fridson, managing director of Merrill Lynch New York, quoted by R. Turchansky in "Stock Markets No Place for Sane Decisions, Analysts Say," *The Edmonton Journal*, 21 January 2000, F2.

9

CHAPTER

Liabilities, Equity, and Corporate Groups

9.1   Chapter Overview

This chapter focuses on understanding the right hand side of a typical corporate balance sheet.

Chapter 8 was about the "left hand side" of the balance sheet (assets). This chapter is about the "right hand side" (liabilities and equity). Most sections in this chapter are not detailed for two reasons: we have encountered many of the issues already when considering asset and income accounting, and the accounting practices for many liabilities and equity items are very complex, beyond what this introductory book can sensibly cover. Therefore, the objective of this chapter is to set out some important principles about liability and equity accounting and provide a general understanding of some topics that are covered more fully in advanced accounting courses. The goal is to equip you to understand what you see on a typical corporate balance sheet and its accompanying notes, so that you will know the principles of how accounting is done for the right side of the balance sheet. There is additional information about the right side in Chapter 2's coverage of noncorporate forms of business: partnerships and proprietorships.

Consolidated balance sheets of corporate groups are also part of this chapter.

The right hand side of the balance sheet is where much of the complexity of modern financial arrangements has to be worked out. One complex arrangement is corporate groups created by growth of a single company into a group or by business combinations: acquisition of one company by another, and mergers of companies. Accounting for corporate groups has a significant impact on income measurement and on the asset side of the balance sheet too; however, the topic is covered in this chapter because it raises important issues that are specific to the right hand side. It is an example of an accounting method that is very complex in practice but has principles that are understandable without the practical complexities. It is also part of the goal of understanding a corporate balance sheet, because, as we saw in Chapter 2, most are consolidated, portraying corporate groups.

This is what you will learn in this chapter:

- *Procedures and techniques:* Basic methods of accounting for current and noncurrent liabilities, including such noncurrent accruals as future income taxes, pensions and warranties, and for the major categories of owners' equity.

- *Concepts and principles:* The principles behind accounting for accrued liabilities, debts, equity capital, and corporate groups, and for the extensive footnote disclosure that is typical for such items.

- *Analysis and decisions:* How to estimate the general effects of important accounting methods on the balance sheet and on income.

As was true for the asset accounting in Chapter 8, many of this chapter's topics have been introduced in earlier chapters, so this chapter builds on earlier material and ties up a few loose ends.

9.2   CURRENT LIABILITIES

Many accounting principles apply to both current and noncurrent liabilities.

In much of liability accounting, the principal difference between current and noncurrent liabilities is just their timing. A bank loan due in five months is shown as a current liability, and one due in five years is a noncurrent liability. Their due dates may be the primary feature that distinguishes them. Similarly, an accrual for an expense that is expected to be paid in five months is a current liability, and one that is expected to be paid in five years is a noncurrent liability. Both are accruals used for income measurement; they may also differ primarily in timing. Because noncurrent liabilities tend to be harder to estimate as the future is farther away, there may be more practical complexities for noncurrent liabilities than for current ones. Therefore, this section will examine some accounting principles for liabilities, current and noncurrent, and will point out some particular current liability issues. Noncurrent liability issues are picked up again in section 9.3.

Getting current liabilities right is important in measuring income and working capital.

Getting the current liabilities right is important for several reasons. The total current liabilities are part of the calculation of **working capital** and the working capital ratio, very important in assessing an enterprise's financial strength. Many of the current liability accounts are accruals of expenses, so getting income measured properly requires getting the accruals right. Conservatism supports all legitimate liabilities, especially any due in the short-run or any whose recording would increase expenses (or reduce revenue) and thus avoid overstating income. Conservatism also supports transferring any short-term part of noncurrent debts into the current category, so that the short-term demands on cash to meet those debts are recognized.

FOR YOUR INTEREST

When auditors are examining the accounts, they pay particular attention to ensuring that no current liabilities have been left out of the balance sheet. They ask banks to provide written confirmation of loans, they review payments in the next period to see if any are for liabilities and corresponding expenses that should have been recorded in the current period, and they check accruals for unpaid wages, income taxes, interest, and other expenses. Sometimes extensive searches are made for evidence of unrecorded liabilities, especially when there have been other indications of accounting errors or manipulations. A scam was uncovered when an auditor found that a client company, trying to get its income down to save tax, had recorded expenses in the current year that were not actually incurred until the next year. The supplier of the supplies and services involved had assisted with the scam by obligingly dating invoices weeks earlier than they should have been.

Liabilities are part of the balance sheet, but also affect income, mainly through expenses.

As is true of assets, liabilities are significant both for their effect on balance sheet valuation and their connection to income measurement. Their principal effect on income measurement is through their association with expenses. Expenses arise from consuming the economic value of assets, such as inventory or fixed assets, but also from incurring liabilities. Such liability incurrence arises from expense recognition *prior to* the cash flow, such as accounts payable, income tax payable, pension liability, and warranty liability, topics mentioned in earlier chapters and examined in this chapter. Liabilities are sometimes associated with revenues too, such as via the deferred revenue liability for revenue collected before it is earned, but their main importance to income measurement is through expenses.

This section summarizes some important things you should know about accounting policies for liabilities, as to their valuation on the balance sheet and their connection to income measurement. Only some parts will be new to you, but you should find the summary useful.

Legal Debts

Debts are shown at the historical value that arose when the debt was incurred.

Bank loans, trade accounts payable, wages payable, Canada Pension Plan, employees' income tax deducted from their pay and due to governments, other employee deductions and fringe benefits due, sales taxes collected and due to governments, bonded debt, mortgages, asset purchase contracts, and other legal debts are recorded when incurred and are reported at the amounts incurred (minus anything paid so far). Here are just a few details:

- Historical cost accounting applies here too. The amounts shown are those that arose when the debt was incurred. This is normally the same amount as will actually be paid, but sometimes it is not. (An example of where it is not, bonds issued at a discount or premium, is included in section 9.3.)

- There is no recognition of nonhistorical interpretations of the debt, even if the economic meaning of the debt would increase because of such recognition. Three things therefore that are *not* recognized are:

▶ Interest that will have to be paid but has not yet accrued (for example, if a debt is due in two years, only the interest to date is added, not the interest for the next two years).

▶ Inflation (even though being in debt during a period of inflation is a good idea because you pay back with dollars worth less than those you borrowed).

▶ Market value changes in public debt (for example, if interest rates have risen so much that a bond issued for $1,000, but now paying an unattractive interest rate is now selling on the bond market for only $780, the debt liability is not revalued on the balance sheet to reflect the lower market value).

Debts do not include future interest, inflation, or market value changes.

• Unless there is evidence to the contrary, the company is assumed to be a going concern and, therefore, debts are shown at the amounts that would normally be paid, and are expected to be paid, not at some other liquidation value that might be negotiated with creditors if the company got into serious financial trouble.

Liabilities' valuation assumes that the enterprise is a going concern and will pay.

• For important debts, some of the legal details are disclosed (usually by footnote). The main details here are the interest rate on the debt (especially for noncurrent debt), any assets or other securities given, repayment terms, and any special conditions such as being convertible to equity.

Footnotes usually contain details of important debts, especially noncurrent ones.

Current Portion of Noncurrent Debts

In one way, current and noncurrent debts are just two parts of the same debt. In order to determine current liabilities properly, and conservatively, GAAP require that if there is a noncurrent debt on which some payment is to be made within the next year, that payment be included in current liabilities. So a single debt is split into two parts: current and noncurrent. This does not affect the legal debt in the slightest: it is just done for accounting purposes.

The current part of noncurrent debt is only the principal portion of next year's payments.

There's a twist here you should watch for, consistent with the principle noted above of not recognizing future interest. In accordance with the above points, it's only the *principal* portion payable in the next year that's called current. Suppose, for example, that Jocelyn owes $71,000 on her mortgage and during the next year must make 12 monthly payments of $1,000, including interest. If the interest will amount to $6,400 over the next year, her balance sheet will show a current liability of $5,600 ($12,000 – $6,400) and a noncurrent liability of $65,400 ($71,000 – $5,600). The $6,400 that will be next year's interest is ignored at this point because it has not yet accrued. Her total debt is $71,000 ($5,600 + $65,400), not $77,400 or $83,000.

Short-Term Accruals and Other Current Liabilities

Short-term accruals are for income measurement and are usually not controversial.

Accrued interest, estimated after-sale service costs, estimated income tax payable, and other such estimated but not yet legally payable short-term liabilities are accounted for by debiting an expense account and crediting a current liability. Although they are not yet actual debts, they are reported in the same way as the legal debts. These accruals are not controversial for current liabilities, but can be controversial if they are noncurrent, as section 9.3 will show. Such accruals are a product of the matching process behind income measurement, and they are usually done very carefully, because if they are not, an imprecise "cutoff" of the expenses involved would make both the current year's and next year's income wrong.

Current liabilities also include various miscellaneous credit balance accounts.

Current liabilities also include other credit-balance accounts.

- One, already mentioned above, is deferred revenue or customer deposits, which represent revenue collected before it has been earned. This is not necessarily a legal debt, but it is viewed as an economic one, in that the enterprise has not yet earned the money. In a business sense, it is also a debt, because it would be a poor business practice to collect money in advance from customers and refuse to either do the agreed revenue-earning work or return the money.

- Another credit balance account, which was described in section 6.9, is the negative version of prepaid expense: an account that may usually be a prepaid expense but sometimes ends up as a credit instead, because the expense is incurred but for some reason is not paid in advance.

- Similar to this is a third kind of credit balance account, an asset that has gone negative due to an event that is not typical of the asset. Two common examples are a bank overdraft (overspent bank balance) and a credit balance in accounts receivable resulting from a customer overpaying the account. This last is like a customer deposit but usually results from inadvertent overpayment or a billing error. (The enterprise may overpay an account payable for the same reasons: if so, the debit balance in accounts payable should be transferred to accounts receivable.) Reclassification of accounts between current liabilities and current assets is important only if the amounts involved are material to the total of either category.

Ⓗ OW'S YOUR UNDERSTANDING?

Here are two questions you should be able to answer, based on what you have just read:

1. Current liabilities arise for several reasons. What are they?

2. Why is it important to get the current liabilities measured properly?

9.3 NONCURRENT LIABILITIES

Long-Term Debts

Noncurrent debt is usually secured in some way, and the security and other details are disclosed.

Debts that are due more than a year into the future are included in noncurrent liabilities, minus any part due within the next year and included in current liabilities. Most noncurrent liabilities are supported by specific agreements about repayment terms between the enterprise and its lenders. These usually involve some security to protect the lender. There are several common kinds of security, which can exist in various combinations with each other. One is a mortgage held by the lender on the enterprise's property or equipment so that the lender can claim title to those assets if the enterprise does not make the agreed payments on time. A second kind of security is a debenture, which is a more general kind of right by the lender to take some degree of control over the enterprise if necessary. A third kind is an indenture, which is a set of specifications that the enterprise must meet otherwise the lender can demand payment or take other action. Such specifications may be that the enterprise maintain a particular level of working capital, or a particular working capital ratio, or meet other conditions defined on the financial statements. (Such indentures may tempt management to choose accounting policies designed to help the financial statements meet the agreed specifications.) A fourth kind of security, often used by banks with smaller company borrowers, is to ask the owners of the company to provide personal guarantees in case the enterprise's assets are not sufficient to repay the debt if trouble comes. GAAP require some disclosure of important security on long-term debts, plus repayment terms and some other details, so the financial statement notes about long-term debts can be extensive. Some long-term debts, such as loans from shareholders, may be unsecured and have an unspecified due date, which will also be disclosed if informative.

Conditional sales contracts and capital leases are common kinds of noncurrent liabilities.

A common kind of noncurrent debt is an agreement to pay for an asset over a period of time. For land or buildings, such an agreement is usually a mortgage. But equipment and vehicles may also be acquired with such agreements, or by a particular kind called a conditional sale contract, under which the title does not pass to the enterprise until it has met all the payments. These are usually not large in comparison to other noncurrent liabilities, so there may not be much disclosure about them. Another way of acquiring economic assets, explained in section 8.11, is via capital leases. The liability for such leases, once recorded by the process described in section 8.11, is included in noncurrent (and current) liabilities just as if it was a regular debt, because the accounting principle is that they are economic debts.

Discounts or Premiums on Noncurrent Debts

Discounts and premiums result from differences between bonds' interest rates and market rates.

Sometimes noncurrent debt is issued at a discount or a premium. This is easiest to explain with bonded debt. A bond is an instrument like a share that usually can be traded among investors, but instead of carrying ownership rights, carries a portion of a mortgage, indenture agreement, or other security and has a limited term before it must be repaid and has the right to interest in the meantime. Suppose the enterprise decides to borrow using a bond issue composed of $1,000 bonds carrying 7% interest. When the bond issue is all ready, interest rates in the market for such bonds may have risen a bit, say to 8%. Lenders would not want a 7% bond. So the enterprise sells the bonds at a discount, a lower price such that the amount the lender pays will earn 8%. The lender gives the company less than $1,000 for each bond, and that lower amount is such that the $70 interest (7% of $1,000) represents the 8% the lender wants. If the interest rates have fallen, say to 6%, the lender will be willing to pay *more* than $1,000 for each bond, such that the $70 interest represents the 6% return the lender wants. So the enterprise gets a premium for the bonds, more than $1,000 each. (This explanation is a little simplified; the present value calculations behind bond prices are included in section 10.7.)

Here is an illustration: an issue of 10,000 $1,000 bonds, thus having a total legal debt of $10,000,000, which sold for a total of either $8,760,000 (a discount) or $11,180,000 (a premium). (The selling prices can be said to be the appropriate price for that bond at prevailing market interest rates, so in the first case, the bond pays interest at a rate below market rates, and in the second case, pays at a rate above market rates.) At the date of issue of the bonds, the proceeds and discount or premium are recorded this way:

Discount		Premium	
Dr Cash (proceeds) 8,760,000		Dr Cash (proceeds) 11,180,000	
Cr Bonded debt	10,000,000	Cr Bonded debt	10,000,000
Dr Bond discount 1,240,000		Cr Bond premium	1,180,000

The discount or premium is included with the legal debt on the balance sheet.

The bonded debt account is a liability. But so is the discount or premium. The premium or discount account works as a contra account, to change the balance sheet valuation of the liability without changing the legal debt account. (The premium is a credit balance account, so it is not opposite in sign as contra accounts like the allowance for doubtful accounts and accumulated amortization are.) The legal debt is what has to be repaid; the discount or premium is just an adjustment to get the proceeds to what will bring the bond market the return it requires. So on the day of issue, the enterprise's balance sheet would show a liability called bonded debt, at the amount of $8,760,000 (in the case of the discount: $10,000,000 − $1,240,000), or $11,180,000 (in the case of the premium: $10,000,000 + $1,180,000). Thus the reported liability meets the historical cost criterion: it is what was received for the bonds.

Amortizing a bond discount or premium makes the interest expense approximate the market rate.

But the amount of the proceeds is not what will eventually be repaid to the lenders. That is $10,000,000 in both cases. So the discount or premium is *amortized* over the period until the bonds are due. It therefore shrinks away until on the due date it is zero and the $10,000,000 is correctly shown as the debt on that date. The period's amortization amount is included with interest expense reported on the income statement. The discount is a debit, so amortizing it adds to the interest expense, making the reported expense higher than the $70 cash interest paid per bond. This makes sense, as the reason for the discount is that the bond market demanded a rate higher than 7%, and by selling the bonds at a discount, the enterprise provided that. The real interest cost is higher than $70. In the case of a premium, the amortization reduces the reported interest expense, which again makes sense because the bond market was happy with a rate lower than 7% and by selling the bonds at a premium, the enterprise provided that. Thus the reported interest expense approximates the market rate demanded when the bonds were sold. (If you already understand the concept of present value (section 10.7), you will see that what is happening is that the bonded debt, adjusted by the unamortized discount or premium, is being shown on the balance sheet at the present value of the bond, calculated at the market interest rate in effect when the bond was issued.) Just like amortization on assets, amortization of discount or premium is a noncash expense debit or credit that has to be adjusted for in the Operations section of the cash flow statement. Methods for calculating amortization of a discount or premium are in more advanced accounting books.

Long-Term Accruals

Long-term accruals are often imprecise, but are thought relevant anyway.

These are in principle just longer-term versions of the short-term accruals. Like the current liability accruals, they are created by debiting an expense account. But, since there will not be a payment for a long time, the credit is to a noncurrent liability. Many of these are approximate estimates, depending on many assumptions: they are recorded in order to account for the future consequences of arrangements made to help earn income today, and so their main purpose is income measurement rather than balance sheet valuation. Referring to the relevance–reliability tradeoff, imprecise estimates of future payments are thought relevant to users of the financial statements even if they are not entirely reliable.

Long-term accruals are shown at the present value of estimated future payments.

There is no debt now and it's often anyone's guess as to exactly when a debt will arise and precisely how much it will be. If feasible, such accruals are based on the present value of future estimated cash flows because of the principle, mentioned in section 9.2, of not recognizing future interest in the balance sheet liability figure. Using present value is more feasible for accruals based on contractual arrangements, such as pension liabilities, than those based on estimates of more discretionary cash flows, such as product warranties. (Present value is the total amount of future payments minus any interest included in them, because that interest accrues in the future and so is not a liability yet. The present value is thought to represent the "principal" value of the liability, likening it to a mortgage the total payments of which exceed the present principal because the future payments will include interest. More about present value is in section 10.7.)

Three examples of long-term accruals, often called provisions, are:

a. *Warranty liability:* the estimated future cost of providing warranty service for products already sold (revenue already recognized). In the period in which a product is sold, an expense is recognized to match to the revenue by the expense recognition entry DR Warranty expense, CR Warranty liability. When a warranty cost is incurred, the liability is reduced by the payment entry DR Warranty liability, CR Cash, or if a replacement product is provided, DR Warranty liability, CR Inventory. If, as is likely, some of the warranty cost will be paid within the next year, that amount is included in current liabilities.

 OR YOUR INTEREST

Here is an example of the difficulty of making a long-term accrual. Like the hippie music the radio stations play for the baby boomers, it's an oldie but goodie. In the 1960s, General Motors produced a little rear-engined car called the Corvair. It was popular and seemed trouble-free. There were Corvair clubs of devotees. It was all very sweet. GM did not have to have a very large warranty provision for the Corvair. But then Ralph Nader's famous book *Unsafe at Any Speed* came out, criticizing the Corvair as well as other cars. People returned to their car dealers in droves, complaining about their Corvairs. It was no longer so sweet. Suddenly, GM had to increase its warranty provision, current, and noncurrent, because of the cost of fixing real or imagined problems. Its warranty expense estimates had been fine under previous conditions, but were suddenly made wrong by the unanticipated event of Nader's book. It's an example of the unavoidable fact that accrual accounting estimates of the future, no matter how carefully made, can easily turn out later to have been wrong.

b. *Pension liability:* the estimated future cost of providing pensions for work already done by employees, minus cash paid to a pension trustee to be invested to fund the eventual pensions. For example, if an employee has worked five years and is already entitled to some part of a pension 30 years from now based on that work, the estimated present value of that pension entitlement is recorded as a liability. Cash paid to the trustee is deducted from the liability. You can see the problems in trying to estimate such a liability when you think of all the things that can change in those 30 years and that must be thought about in making the estimate: the employee might die first, be fired, or quit; interest rates (used in the present value calculation) will doubtless vary; the pension plan itself might change, even retroactively; laws governing such plans may change; and so on. When the employee earns a pension entitlement, that is presumed to be an expense of the period in which it is earned and is recorded by the expense recognition entry DR Pension expense, CR Pension liability. When a payment is made to a trustee or directly to a retired employee, the payment is recorded by DR Pension liability, CR Cash. Pension liabilities continually need adjustment as conditions and assumptions change, and those adjustments are just included in wages or other expense of the period of the adjustment, because they are a routine consequence of accrual accounting, just as adjustments to asset amortization, allowance for doubtful accounts, and other estimates are routinely made.

According to *Financial Reporting in Canada 1999,* 141 of its 200 surveyed companies reported having some sort of pension plan in 1998. The plans were usually mentioned in the Significant Accounting Policies note. Many of these companies had paid enough into the plans that they had no significant pension liability, but at least 26 companies did have such a liability, calling it by a great variety of names.[1]

c. *Post-employment benefits other than pensions:* since FASB pronouncements on these in the late 1980s, they are accounted for in the same sort of way as are pension obligations, and with the same sort of difficulties. With Canada's greater state support of medical costs, these obligations are usually not as large for Canadian companies as they are for companies in the United States, where the obligations can be billions of dollars. (In its 1999 annual report, for example, IBM reported a noncurrent liability of $7.4 billion![2]) The expense recognition and payment entries follow the same pattern as for pensions. According to *Financial Reporting in Canada 1999,* 73 of the 200 companies disclosed that they had accounting policies for post-retirement benefit plans in 1998.[3]

Future Income Taxes

Accounting for future income taxes is one of the most challenging topics in financial accounting. Part of the challenge results from the complexity of income tax law, and part from great disagreements about how future income tax should be accounted for, if at all. After many years of debate, the *CICA Handbook* was revised in 1997 to provide a fundamentally different way of accounting for future income taxes than had been done up till then. (Fundamentally different from the Canadian method, but more like the U.S. and IASC methods.) The new method was recommended for implementation beginning in 2000 (though enterprises were free to adopt it earlier than that: *Financial Reporting in Canada 1999* reports that in 1998, 37 of the 200 companies had done so, 141 still used the previous method, and 22 had no future income tax balances[4]). To emphasize the change in method, the name of the method and of the accounts involved was changed from deferred income tax to future income taxes. This section will outline the principles behind the newly adopted method, but you will probably see the former method and terminology still referred to for a few years yet. The focus here is on the accounting principles: you don't have to be a tax expert to understand them!

Here's the problem. Because income tax law differs in many ways from financial accounting principles, there are differences between the income tax expense

Pension liability is a good example of a complicated but still imprecise estimate.

The method of accounting for future income taxes has recently changed in Canada.

The income tax
accounting problem
arises because of
temporary differences
between accounting
and the tax law.

you'd get from the accounting income and other accounting numbers, and the income tax payable to the government for the year. Suppose, for example, that the following temporary difference exists. Accounting income before income tax is $500,000. But taxable income (income determined to be subject to income tax according to the tax law) for the year is only $300,000 because the enterprise can deduct amortization for income tax purposes (called capital cost allowance) on an accelerated basis whereas the amortization in the accounts is straight-line. As we saw in section 8.10, the two amortization methods eventually get to the same book value (salvage value, or zero), but there is *temporarily* a difference. Suppose the company's income tax rate is 35%. Then the income tax based on the accounting income would be $175,000 ($500,000 × 35%), but the income tax payable for the year, based on taxable income, would be only $105,000 ($300,000 × 35%). Which number should be the income tax expense in the income statement: $175,000, or $105,000, or even something else?

The matching
principle requires that
income tax accounting
follow the rest of the
accounting.

The simplest solution would be just to use the income tax actually payable, $105,000, as the expense for the year. Just DR Income tax expense and CR Income tax payable. Then pay the tax. Easy. Many people in business would not expect otherwise. But accrual accounting doesn't let us off the hook so easily. There is a big problem: the income tax expense would then depend on an amortization method other than the one in the accounts. The expense would not match the way other expenses are accounted for in the financial statements (amortization in this example, but many others in the reality of complex modern income taxation). This violation of the matching principle has caused accounting standard-setters to specify that in the case of temporary differences like this, *the tax expense should match the rest of the accounting*, so the entry should be to DR Income tax expense $175,000 and CR Income tax payable $105,000. A new liability, Future income taxes, is credited with the difference that arises from the temporary amortization difference, $70,000. (This amount is ($500,000 − $300,000) × 35%, so it is the tax rate applied to the temporary difference between the calculation based on accounting and that based on the tax law.)

It wouldn't work to
just use the income
tax payable as the
income tax expense.

Well, one might say, why not just use the tax amortization, capital cost allowance, in the accounts rather than the straight-line method, so that no temporary difference arises and there is then no need for the future income tax liability? Simple, too, and appealing to business people who don't want to spend a lot of money on accounting. But too simple, unfortunately. There are many differences between accounting principles and income tax law, and so unless we are prepared to scrap GAAP and just account for everything exactly the same as the tax law, we're stuck with some differences. It would be appealing to just use the tax law for accounting, but that is not thought appropriate. The tax law is written for all sorts of economic, political, and other reasons besides measuring financial performance and position, so it would make a poor basis for accounting.

Accounting standards
for income tax have
developed over many
years across many
countries.

For example, the government may say that machinery bought between July and October of year 20XX can be amortized for tax purposes faster than regular machinery, and then in September announce that the deadline has been extended to December. Or that machinery located in an economically depressed part of the country should get a faster tax amortization than the same machinery located somewhere else. This is all quite reasonable for the government to do. But should companies keep changing their accounting every time the government makes such a decision, and should the same machinery, with the same useful economic life, be amortized differently just because it is located in a different province? You might argue, yes, sure, the machinery is a different economic asset because it is in a different place or was bought in December rather than January. But after much study of the implications, involving many countries (with widely varying tax systems), over many years, accounting standard-setters have concluded that it would be inappropriate for financial accounting's income tax numbers and all the related numbers such as amortization to ignore GAAP and be based on arbitrary tax law variations.

The result is that income tax expense and liabilities are handled this way, following a principle called interperiod tax allocation, which adjusts for temporary differences between accounting and the tax law and so locates the income tax expense in the appropriate accounting period even if it is not paid then:

Current income tax payable
    DR Income tax expense—current portion   XXXX
        CR Income tax payable   XXXX
Adjustment for future income tax
    DR or CR Income tax expense—future portion   XXXX or XXXX

    CR or DR Future income tax liability (or asset) XXXX or XXXX

The adjustment for future income taxes is an accrual accounting adjustment.

In the terminology of earlier chapters, you could think of the first entry as the "cash basis" because it contains the amount of tax to be paid in cash for the year, and the second entry as the adjustment to the accrual basis, augmenting the first and creating an accrual measure that is the sum of current and future tax portions. The adjustment can go in either direction, adding to or reducing the expense based on the current portion, depending on a vast array of income tax and accounting complications best left to more advanced accounting courses. The current income tax expense can also be a credit, and instead of a credit to a payable, there can be a debit to income tax receivable or refundable, if the company has a negative income for income tax purposes.

In the example above, we would have these entries:

Current income tax payable
    DR Income tax expense—current portion   105,000
        CR Income tax payable   105,000
Adjustment for future income taxes
    DR Income tax expense—future portion   70,000
        CR Future income tax liability (or asset)   70,000

Total income tax expense is the sum of the current and future portions.

The future income tax adjustment is based on an analysis of the balance sheet accounts.

The total income tax expense, $175,000, thus equals what we'd expect if we matched the income tax to the accounting income of $500,000, which is the goal of income tax accounting.

How are the adjustment for future income taxes and its associated future income tax liability(ies) or asset(s) calculated? By vastly complicated methods! It is in this calculation that the big change in income tax accounting has been made. Previously, using the so-called deferral method, the calculation was based on historical temporary differences between accounting methods and income tax law, with no or few revisions for changes in tax rates and other factors. The objective was to get the best match between the income statement's other figures and the income tax expense (sum of current and future (called deferred) portions), in the year the income was being measured. But now the way of doing this, called the liability method even though it involves assets as well as liabilities, is to go through every balance sheet account and make the adjustment as the aggregate of all the income tax implications of every such account as it exists at the end of the year. Thus the second part of the income tax expense, the accrual or future income tax portion, is not based on matching to the rest of the income statement items, but rather is based on *matching to the present status of balance sheet accounts*. Doing this is a very detailed task.

Priority is given to getting the balance sheet's income tax assets and liabilities right.

The income statement and balance sheet do articulate, so in many cases the adjustment ends up not too different from what it would have been under the deferral method, but the big change in principle is to give the nod to the balance sheet over the income statement in deriving the adjustment. This is thought to produce more meaningful balance sheet income tax assets and liabilities, even if the adjustment might not always fit the rest of the income statement well. It's an example of the constraint of double entry mentioned also in discussing asset valuation in section 8.2: it would be nice to adjust the income statement in a way that fits it best, and adjust the balance sheet in a way that fits it best, but if the two do not agree, we have to choose one so that the adjustment entry balances. The future income tax approach, using the liability method, gives priority to the balance sheet.

Most future income balance sheet accounts are liabilities rather than assets, largely because of accelerated capital cost allowance.

The approach is called the liability method, and the great preponderance of balance sheets show a noncurrent future income tax liability rather than an asset, because the income tax law provides incentives such as faster amortization (capital cost allowance) on assets to spur economic activity and encourage reinvestment in assets, tax credits for factory location in depressed areas, and so on. The capital cost allowance versus book amortization difference is the single largest cause of the future income tax liability. Capital cost allowance is an accelerated amortization method, in some cases very accelerated, so enterprises get immediate tax savings via capital cost allowance being larger in early years than book amortization (straight-line being the most common method for the books). Most of the tax savings due to a temporarily higher capital cost allowance will have to be repaid in the future when the capital cost allowance declines (remember the comparison of accelerated and straight-line in section 8.10). That expected future repayment is the future tax liability. For this reason and for conservatism (which leads to more caution in recording future income tax assets than liabilities), future income tax liabilities are more common and larger than assets, and because the tax incentives usually last over many years, the future income tax liabilities are usually noncurrent rather than current.

Future income tax adjustments use effective tax rates and follow intraperiod tax allocation rules.

Income tax accounting uses whatever income tax rates apply in the various provinces or countries the enterprise operates. By dividing the total income tax expense, which is the combination of the current and future portions of the income tax expense, by the accounting income, the enterprise's effective income tax rate can be calculated. For example, if the current portion of the expense is $311,000 and the future portion, which can be positive or negative, is $(73,000), the total expense is $238,000. If the accounting income is $680,000, then the effective income tax rate is 35% ($238,000 / $680,000). Enterprises are supposed to explain why their effective rate differs from the official "statutory" rate if the difference is significant. Some reasons include having nontaxable revenues (dividend income, for example, is not taxed in Canada if received from another corporation that already paid income tax in Canada), having expenses that are not tax deductible (there are quite a few of these, including portions of entertainment expenses, some political contributions, and some kinds of financing expenses), or taking advantage of special industry provisions such as tax credits for oil and gas exploration. In section 3.5, intraperiod tax allocation was mentioned: income tax expense is supposed to go with the relevant income statement or retained earnings statement items, such as extraordinary adjustments or discontinued operations. Various and changing income tax rates and intraperiod tax allocation, which all affect the future income tax adjustments, make income tax accounting even more complex!

 OW'S YOUR UNDERSTANDING?

Here are two questions you should be able to answer, based on what you have just read:

1. List the main kinds of noncurrent liabilities you'd expect to see in a typical balance sheet and describe how each kind is valued (how the number representing it is determined).

2. Last year, Kite Ltd. owed $32,118 in income tax, but if you applied its effective tax rate to its income statement's "income before income tax," you'd get $43,786. If you examined the differences between accounting and income tax law for its assets and liabilities, you'd get an estimated future income tax liability of $28,976 at the end of this year (it was $18,415 at the end of last year). What would be the current portion of income tax expense for this year, the future portion, the total income tax expense, and the year-end future income tax liability? ($32,118, $10,561 (that is, $28,976 − $18,415), $42,679 (that is, $32,118 + $10,561), $28,976. The $43,786 figure is irrelevant. It might be the most appropriate total income tax expense to get the income statement right (and so was used in the deferred method), but under the liability method, preference is given to the $10,561 adjustment derived from the balance sheet, which produces the total expense of $42,679 instead.)

9.4   EQUITY.

This section reviews topics in accounting for equity of unincorporated businesses and corporations. Some of these have been mentioned earlier in the book, and complexities are left for other books. Referring back to the equity descriptions in section 2.8 may be helpful if your memory of the various forms of business and kinds of equity is hazy. Section 9.5 outlines ideas about complex financial structures and sections 9.6 and 9.7 are about corporate groups—all of these have some implications to equity accounting.

Unincorporated Businesses

Unincorporated businesses, sole proprietorships or partnerships, are not legal persons separate from their owners, as corporations are. But the accounting principle stated in Chapters 2 and 3 of separating the company's dealings with customers and suppliers (from which it earns income) from its dealings with owners is still followed. The result is the following set of accounting practices for unincorporated businesses. Because of double-entry accounting and the articulation of the income statement and balance sheet, practices for assets, liabilities, revenues, and expenses affect equity too, directly or indirectly.

Unincorporated businesses have generally similar assets and liabilities to those of corporations.

- Except for specific variations, most of which are given below, the accounting for assets, liabilities, revenues, and expenses is the same as for corporations, and so is the same as has been explained in earlier chapters. Unincorporated businesses still have accounts receivable, inventories, amortization, debts, short and long-term accruals, and other business trappings. Accounting for assets and most liabilities is virtually unaffected by the form of business.

- Five main liability differences do exist, some of which affect the accounting for equity too.

  (1) Unincorporated businesses (and "private" corporations too) cannot issue debt to the public, so you will not see bonded debt on the balance sheet.
  (2) Any sort of secured debt is really a debt of the owner, so it is a little arbitrary as to whether something like a mortgage is included in the balance sheet—usually it is included if the mortgaged asset is included on the other side of the balance sheet, but there should be a note about the legal circumstances.
  (3) Because the business and the owner are not really separable, generally there is no such thing as an owner's loan to the business corresponding to a shareholder's loan. Any investment by the owner (or owners, in the case of a partnership) is just included in equity.

Any investment or withdrawals by the owner(s) are included in equity.

  (4) Similarly, the business cannot declare a dividend, so there is no such thing as dividends payable. The owner(s) may feel that some payment should be made by the business, but until that payment is made, there has been no economic transaction. Any payments to the owner(s) are just deducted from equity when made.
  (5) Consistent with all this, and with income tax law, the business is not subject to income tax. Income tax is a personal obligation of the owner(s). Therefore there is no income tax expense on the income statement and no income tax payable or future income tax liability on the balance sheet. If the business does pay income tax on behalf of the owner, that is just deducted from equity when made, because it is really just a withdrawal of cash by the owner(s), as is true whenever the business happens to pay a personal bill for the owner.

An unincorporated business's income statement can be hard to compare to a corporation's.

- Two important expenses you'd see in a corporation are missing from the unincorporated business's income statement. There is no income tax expense and there is no expense for the owner's (or owners') wages or salaries. Any payments for income tax or to owners are deducted from equity, not shown as business expenses. The lack of an income tax expense in particular means that the income number is usually just called income, not *net* income. The lack of both of these expenses, coupled with the occasionally arbitrary classification of assets like buildings and cars, and expenses like travel and entertainment, as being part of the business or part of the owner's (owners') personal affairs, can make it difficult to compare the profitability of an unincorporated business to that of a corporation.

Unincorporated businesses lump all the equity items together into a single capital figure.

- The unincorporated business's balance sheet has a simple equity section: usually shown as just one figure called capital and calculated as beginning capital + new investment by owner(s) + income for the year (or minus loss) − withdrawals by owner(s) = ending capital. There may be a statement of owner's (or owners') capital changes, something like the statement of retained earnings except including all the equity changes listed above, and for a partnership there is usually a statement or analysis of the partners' individual capital accounts, as was illustrated in section 2.8.

- Footnotes, financial statement titles, and account names are usually used to explain the business's relationship to the owner(s) and to cover issues such as those outlined above.

Incorporated Businesses

> A corporation's balance sheet is accompanied by considerable legal detail about equity.

For an incorporated company (a **corporation** or limited company), there are several mainly legal requirements that influence the accounting:

- Dividends must ordinarily be paid out of accumulated income only and not out of invested capital. Therefore, shareholders' equity is divided into invested capital (share capital) and retained earnings, and only the latter is available for dividends.

- Share capital shows the dollar amounts, for each class of shares, contributed by shareholders over the years to buy shares directly from the company, including identifying any amounts paid in excess of par values (which may be called **contributed surplus** or some other name indicating it's an extra). These amounts are all *historical* figures.

- Various legal details about classes of shares and their rights and restrictions are disclosed separately, on the balance sheet and/or in a note.

- Retained earnings shows the accumulated income minus dividends declared since the company's incorporation. Restrictions on dividends may be disclosed. Declared dividends are liabilities of the corporation until paid.

Some other items should be mentioned here:

> Shareholders of a corporation may be creditors too.

1. Shareholders may lend the company money, for example, by advancing money that the shareholders want to have repaid rather than investing in permanent share capital. In a small private corporation, the owner-manager may lend by not withdrawing all the salary that has been recorded as an expense, perhaps because the company is short of money. Such a loan from shareholder(s) is shown under liabilities, not owners' equity, because the shareholder is acting as a creditor rather than an owner (though the distinction may strike you as rather slight).

> Treasury shares not cancelled are shown at cost as a reduction in shareholders' equity.

2. The company may (in some jurisdictions) buy a few of its own shares, as CAE did in 2000. Such shares represent an interest in the assets and do not have voting rights. Therefore, such shares are either cancelled (reducing share capital, which is what CAE did) or else called **treasury shares** and deducted from the rest of owners' equity at the cost paid for them, at least until the shares are resold or cancelled (see section 2.8).

> The foreign currency translation adjustment is in equity for lack of another place to put it.

3. Also in section 2.8, an awkward equity account, **accumulated foreign currency translation adjustment**, was explained. It's a consequence of adjusting all the other balance sheet and income statement accounts for transactions in foreign currencies, assets purchased with foreign currencies and liabilities owed in foreign currencies. It is possible that in the future the equity account will be eliminated by instead putting these adjustments into the income

statement. For now, however, this account is a feature of the equity sections of most companies with operations in other countries.

4. Two phenomena that cause a little fun in accounting for corporate equity are share splits and stock dividends. A split is when the corporation's shares are divided into twice or three times as many shares, so that their smaller value may be easier for investors to purchase. (If some venerable companies, such as IBM, had not repeatedly split their shares over the years, each one would cost thousands or hundreds of thousands of dollars on the market.) A stock dividend is when the board of directors decides to issue some new shares (a small percentage of those already outstanding) to the shareholders instead of paying a cash dividend. Note two points about these. (1) They are really just different versions of the same thing. A 2 for 1 share (stock) split means that if you owned 100 shares, you now own 200. A 10% stock dividend means that if you owned 100 shares, you now own 110. (2) If the stock markets are efficient, splits and stock dividends should not affect share values: the value of split shares should fall by 50% so that the two new ones equal the value of the one old one, and the value of shares after a 10% stock dividend should also fall so that 110% of the new shares are worth what 100% of the old shares were. But the stock markets do not always react this way. Because a split makes the shares a little easier to own, the value of split shares may fall a little less than 50%, and the value of shares after a stock dividend may be a little higher than just dividing the old value over the new number of shares.

The traditional accounting practices for these phenomena depend on a judgment that may be difficult to defend given modern stock market pricing. That judgment is that share splits provide no benefit to shareholders, but that stock dividends do. So if a corporation splits its shares, there is no accounting entry. The share records and the notes to the financial statements are just changed to show the new number of shares. On the other hand, a stock dividend is allocated a value: in the case of a 10% stock dividend, an entry is made to DR Retained earnings and CR Share capital to recognize a deemed increase in the book value of share capital. Calculating the amount and distinguishing between a small split and a big stock dividend are explained in more advanced accounting books.

Nonbusiness Organizations

As described in section 5.5, nonbusiness organizations such as governments, clubs, and churches typically have different accounting for equity because they don't have owners, share capital, dividends, and other business trappings. When you are using the financial statements of such an organization, pay particular attention to what kind of organization it is and to the way that is represented in the balance sheet equity section, because there is enormous variation that flows from tradition as well as legal particulars of each organization. Generally, nonbusiness organizations have equity sections that are simpler than that of corporations. Often they show just a single figure calculated as total assets minus total liabilities. But there can be complexities too, such as the legal necessity to keep track of the sources of funds and keep various kinds of funds separate (for example, operating funds versus funds donated to the organization for specific purposes), so these can lead to occasionally complex accounting for equity and related assets and liabilities. There is a whole branch of accounting called fund accounting developed to deal with these complexities: its basic goal is to separate the organization into segments that are accounted for separately in accordance with each segment's legal or financial situation, which, therefore, have separate equity accounting, and which frequently have accounts receivable from, accounts payable to, and even investments in each other.

HOW'S YOUR UNDERSTANDING?

Here are two questions you should be able to answer, based on what you have just read:

1. What are typical differences between an unincorporated business's equity and other balance sheet accounting and that of a corporation?

2. What are shareholder loans, share splits, and stock dividends, and what impact do they have on a corporation's balance sheet equity section?

9.5   COMPLEX FINANCIAL STRUCTURES

Modern ways of organizing and financing businesses, particularly corporations, have created liabilities and equities that are difficult to fit into the double-entry GAAP model of financial accounting, and that are sometimes difficult to assign as liabilities or equity even if they are recorded. As you are probably tired of reading, accounting for these matters is complicated and so is dealt with in advanced accounting books, so this section just describes some of the items to watch out for when reading a corporate balance sheet.

Financing That Is a Mixture of Equity and Debt

Some shares and bonds may be convertible or have other characteristics that are a mixture of equity and debt.

We have already seen that a company may mix its assets and equity up a little by buying its own shares. Such shares, if not cancelled as CAE did, are treasury shares and are deducted from, not treated as, investment assets. Other financing may mix equity and debt. Sometimes a corporation will issue convertible shares or bonds. According to certain rules, and usually at the choice of the holder of the share or bond, such a security can be converted to another kind. A preferred share may be convertible to common shares, or a bond may be convertible to common shares. Sometimes a share is redeemable, so that the company has the right to buy it back from the holder, or the holder has the right to sell it back to the company, making it a little like debt rather than the permanent capital shares normally are. Or term preferred shares may "come due" at a given date, making them also a little like debt. These sorts of securities blur the balance sheet's line between liabilities and equity. If a preferred share is more like a debt than an equity, because for example it is redeemable at the option of the holder, GAAP are beginning to require that it be included as a liability, not an equity, and dividends paid on such shares would be interest expense on the income statement, not dividends on the retained earnings statement. The standard model of financial accounting is clearly creaking under the strain of such "hybrid" securities. Some information about such securities is included in the notes, so that the reader of the financial statements can evaluate their present or potential impact on the figures. *Financial Reporting in Canada 1999* reports that in 1998, 77 of the 200 companies surveyed reported having preferred shares, 50 indicating redemption provisions and 36 indicating conversion provisions.[5]

Commitments

Warrants, stock options, and other commitments to issue more shares are disclosed.

Often, a corporation will make a commitment to issue further shares under certain conditions. Convertible bonds or preferred shares, mentioned above, are such a commitment. There are other types of commitment. A typical example is warrants, which are issued with shares and give the holder the right to buy more shares at a specified price. Another is stock options, which are often awarded to senior managers as a part of their compensation, and again give the holder the right to buy shares at a specified price expected to be attractive to the executive so that the stock option motivates the executive to try to increase the corporation's share price on the stock market because a higher share price makes the stock option more valuable. Any of these commitments that have any likelihood of being honoured are disclosed in the notes, and if issuing the potential shares could reduce the earnings per share, the potentially lower "diluted" EPS is reported. According to *Financial Reporting in Canada 1999*, 189 of the 200 surveyed companies reported commitments to issue shares in 1998, 164 of these giving details of number of shares, issue prices, and expiry dates of the commitments.[6]

Off-Balance-Sheet Financing and Contractual Obligations

New financial arrangements are being invented all the time, and the impacts they make on the balance sheet, or might make depending on the company's accounting policies, are likely to be a factor in their acceptability and popularity. Five examples of financing that may or may not be well reported in the balance sheet and/or in the notes to the financial statements include:

- Ordinary "operating" rental and leasing contracts (capital leases *are* included in the liabilities, as we saw in section 8.11);

- The sale of rights to collect accounts receivable so as to speed up the cash inflow in return for taking on potential obligations to the party buying those rights;

- Making long-term purchase commitments to get favourable terms;

- Making commitments for abnormal expenditures, such as large commitments for fixed assets; and

- Using subsidiary or associated companies to borrow money so that the commitments do not show up on the parent company's balance sheet.

Enterprises may make financial commitments that are not recorded as liabilities.

There may be a concern among users of financial statements that sometimes such sources of financing may be sought in order to avoid recording liabilities and so weakening the balance sheet. As these obligations are not included in the financial statement figures, they can only be learned about by reading the notes. GAAP require that significant contractual obligations be disclosed, and *Financial Reporting in Canada 1999* indicates that in 1998, 84 of the 200 surveyed companies provided disclosures of contractual obligations in addition to operating leases and commitments to issue shares.[7]

Financial Instruments

Financial instruments include financial assets and liabilities, whether or not recognized in the accounts.

These were mentioned briefly in section 2.8. The phrase financial instruments refers to the company's set of financial assets and liabilities. It also covers various commitments and arrangements, such as agreements to purchase currencies in advance to "hedge" against the risk of unfavourable currency fluctuations or "swap" contracts in which, for example, an outside bank agrees to pay the interest on some of the enterprise's variable-interest-rate debt if the rate varies beyond some agreed range. In its December 1999 annual report, for example, Suncor Energy Inc. included the following in its note about financial instruments:

- Cash and cash equivalents, accounts receivable, some investments, and "substantially all current liabilities and long-term borrowings."

- "Derivative financial instruments" including "revenue hedges" arranged as contracts for currency swaps "to protect future Canadian dollar earnings" and "interest rate hedges" arranged as interest rate swap contracts "when there is an opportunity to lower the cost of borrowed funds."

- Estimates of the current fair (market) value of all the company's long-term borrowings and various derivative swap contracts, including risks being taken on the latter.[8]

Existence and fair values of financial instruments are generally disclosed, but the accounts are not adjusted.

There is literally no end to the kinds of financial instruments that exist, and innovations in instruments happen practically daily. Accounting standard-setters have wrestled for several years with the problem of whether and how to represent these instruments in the financial statements. Recently, GAAP have required that such instruments be disclosed in the notes. Many people think they should be built into the financial statement numbers in some way, for example "marking to market" by recording financial instruments at market value rather than cost, but there is not yet agreement about that. Estimating fair values where applicable, as Suncor did, provides information to users of the financial statements who may wish to make their own adjustments to the financial statements. *Financial Reporting in Canada 1999* reports that in 1998, 195 of the 200 surveyed companies provided information about financial instruments in the Significant Accounting Policies note, in one of the detailed notes, or both.[9]

The amount of detail to provide about financial instruments is a matter of judgment. Suncor's 1999 note was very detailed and over two pages long! In its Significant Accounting Policies note, CAE said that "the carrying values of financial instruments approximate fair value except where indicated."[10] Management did not feel that the fair values of its cash, accounts receivable, and short and long-term debts were much different from the balance sheet values because such accounts are not mentioned further in the context of financial instruments, but some other items are described. Here is Note 7 to CAE's 2000 financial statements:

Financial Instruments

The Corporation has estimated the fair values of its financial instruments as at March 31, 2000 using quoted market values where available and other information.

At March 31, 2000, the Corporation had outstanding forward contracts to hedge its foreign currency cash flows into Canadian dollars. These forward exchange contracts have maturity dates up to December 2004. The fair value of these contracts if marked to market at March 31, 2000 would result in a gain of $2.5 million. This would be equally offset by future losses of foreign denominated cash flows over the remaining terms of the contracts.

Effective June 9, 1997, the Corporation entered into interest rate swap agreements with two different financial institutions for a total nominal value of $68 million whereby in the first instance the Corporation will receive a fixed interest rate of 7.2% semi-annually for 8 years and in the second instance the Corporation will receive a fixed interest rate of 7.7% semi-annually for 15 years. In both cases, the Corporation will pay quarterly variable interest established at bankers acceptance rates, plus a premium.

Pursuant to the requirements of its long-term project financing, on October 16, 1997, the Corporation's subsidiary entered into an interest rate swap agreement with two financial institutions for a maximum total nominal value of £12.7 million whereby the subsidiary will receive payments of floating rate interest and will pay a fixed interest rate of 6.8% semi-annually for 13 years.

Receipts and payments under interest rate swap agreements have been accounted for as adjustments to interest expense on long-term debt.

The fair value of the interest rate swap agreements if marked to market at March 31, 2000, would result in a gain of $5.8 million.[11]

(H)OW'S YOUR UNDERSTANDING?

Here are two questions you should be able to answer, based on what you have just read:

1. Why do redeemable or convertible securities issued by a corporation cause some difficulties for the traditional balance sheet format?

2. What are financial instruments, and what would it mean to mark them to market?

9.6   CORPORATE GROUPS: INTERCORPORATE INVESTMENTS

Many businesses are really groups of corporations.

Modern businesses, especially large ones, are often groups of separately incorporated companies. Such corporate groups were discussed in section 2.8. This and the next section expand on that discussion, describing consolidated financial statements for corporate groups but also some other accounting issues involved in such groups. Accounting for corporate groups is a complicated part of financial accounting and is covered in detail in the financial accounting standards of the CICA and FASB. This book introduces you to the main principles behind it and shows you how to apply the principles to do some basic calculations.

Kinds of Intercorporate Investments

Corporations invest in other corporations in many ways. Six common ways of such investment are summarized in Exhibit 9.1 and will be examined in this and the next section.

Nature and Intent of the Investment	Place on the Investing Company's Balance Sheet	Accounting Method
1. Temporary use of cash	Marketable securities	Lower of cost or market
2. Long-term passive	Noncurrent assets	Cost investment
3. Long-term active	Noncurrent assets	Equity basis investment
4. Joint venture	Noncurrent assets	Equity basis
5. Acquisition	Combined balance sheets	Purchase method consolidation
6. Merger	Combined balance sheets	Pooling of interests consolidation

Figure 9.1 illustrates a corporate group, with Corporation A at its financial centre. This section will review how to account for A's investment in corporations B, D, and H, none of which A controls, and the next section will cover accounting for A's investment in C, E, F, and G, all of which A controls.

Illustration of a Corporate Group

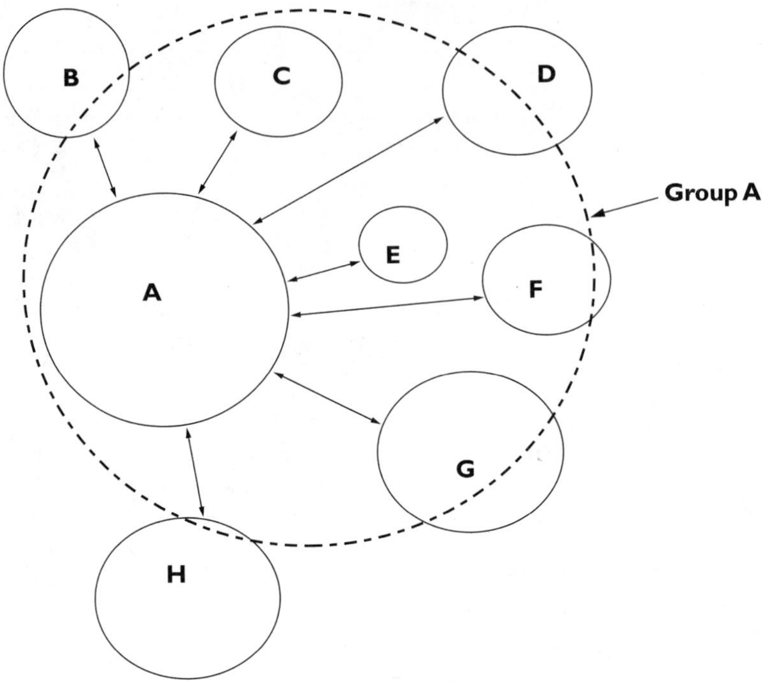

Corporation A is the main company in Group A, an economic entity greater than A
   by itself and encompassing the separate corporate legal entities.
A owns all of the voting shares of C and E: they are entirely part of Group A and
   so are combined with A in A's consolidated financial statements.
A owns more than 50% of the voting shares of F and G, so they are consolidated
   too, but some accounting has to be made for the parts of them A does not own.
A does not control D but has significant influence over it, so it will be accounted
   for as a long-term active investment (equity basis).
A has no significant portion of the voting shares of B or H, so they will be
   accounted for as passive investments, either short-term or long-term depending
   on A's intent.
Joint ventures and mergers are not illustrated here.

FIGURE 9.1

Temporary
investments are the
most short-term and
passive intercorporate
investments.

1. Temporary Investments

Temporary investments were covered in section 8.4. If these investments are other corporations' shares or other securities having a quoted market value, they are called marketable securities. These are the most short-term and passive intercorporate investments. Because there is no intention to hold such investments for long or to try to influence the operations or policies of the corporations that issued the securities, such investments are included in the current assets of the investing corporation and valued at the lower of cost or market. Dividends or interest received from such investments are usually also included in the investing corporation's non-operating revenues.

2. Long-Term Passive Investment

In a passive investment, the investor does not exercise significant influence over the investee.

The accounting for long-term intercorporate investments depends on the *intention* behind and *control* involved in the investing corporation's (*investor's*) ownership of the investment. These factors relate to the proportion of the issuing corporation's (*investee's*) voting shares held. If the proportion is low (the *CICA Handbook*, section 3050, suggests less than 20% as a guideline), the investing company is usually presumed *not* to be interested in exercising, or able to exercise, *significant influence* on the issuing organization. This is illustrated in Figure 9.1 as A's investment in B and H.

The cost basis is used for long-term passive investments.

For long-term passive investments, the accounting, called the **cost basis**, is simple:

- The investment asset is valued at cost and is shown among the noncurrent assets. (The lower of cost or market value rule is not considered relevant because there is no intention to sell the investment.)

- Revenue from the investment (interest if bonds, dividends if shares) is included with nonoperating other revenue when it is received, the same as for temporary investments.

3. Long-Term Active Investment

Significant Influence but Not Control

The equity basis is used when the investor exercises significant influence over the investee.

The investing corporation is said to exercise significant influence if it has more than the 20% voting interest suggested above but not voting control (not more than 50%). This is illustrated in Figure 9.1 as A's investment in D. In this case, the equity basis of accounting is used. Under this basis, the investing corporation includes in its income statement *and* balance sheet its share of earnings by the investee company, because it has influenced that company's performance.

Under the equity basis:

- The investor's investment asset is still valued initially at cost, as it was for passive investments using the cost basis.

The equity basis is accrual accounting, the investor's share of the investee's income is accrued.

- As the *investee* corporation earns income (or incurs losses), the investor's asset is increased for the *investor* corporation's share of that income (or decreased for its share of losses) and that share is included in the investor's income. This is an accrual of income the investor is entitled to. The investor is taking credit for its share of the investee's income (increase in retained earnings). Nonoperating "other" revenue is credited with this share and the investment asset account is debited, so that asset account is treated like an account receivable for the accrued income.

When the investor receives a dividend from the investee, that is collection of accrued income.

- When the investee pays a dividend, the investor receives some of the accrued income as its share of the dividend, so the dividend received is deducted from the investor's investment asset account, just as collection of an account receivable would be deducted from the account receivable asset. The dividend is not called income by the investor because the income has already been accrued; instead, the dividend is deducted from the investment asset because it is considered a return of some of the money invested.

- There are some other more complicated features of equity basis accounting we will not get into.

Financial Reporting in Canada 1999 reports that in 1998, 127 of the 200 companies surveyed had long-term investments other than joint ventures (mentioned at the end of this section). Of these, 27 used the cost basis, 30 used the equity basis, 50 used both, and 20 did not say what basis they used.[12]

A Cost and Equity Basis Example

This is a summary of how the two methods work (ignoring complexities):

9-2

Exhibit

	Cost basis	Equity basis
Initial carrying value of the investor's intercorporate investment asset	Original cost	Original cost
Investor's share of income earned by investee	Nothing done	Add to asset and to other revenue
Investor's share of dividend paid by investee	Add to cash and to other revenue	Add to cash and deduct from investment asset
Resulting balance sheet value of the investor's intercorporate investment asset	Just original cost	Original cost plus accrued income share minus share of dividends paid

Here is an example. Grand Ltd. acquired investments in two other corporations on January 1, 2001. These acquisitions are (a) and (b) in the list below; events (c) to (e) also took place in 2001.

a. 60,000 shares (15% of the voting interest) in AA Ltd. were purchased for $1,800,000 cash. Because this was to be a fairly passive long-term investment, Grand would account for it using the *cost basis*.

b. 145,000 shares (29% of the voting interest) in BB Ltd. were purchased for $4,640,000 cash. Since Grand intended to participate in the management of BB Ltd., Grand would account for it using the *equity basis*.

c. On June 30, both investees announced their earnings per share for the first six months of 2001: $2 per share for AA Ltd. and $2.10 per share for BB Ltd.

d. On December 10, both investees paid dividends to shareholders: $1.50 per share for AA Ltd. and $1.60 per share for BB Ltd.

e. On December 31, both investees announced their earnings per share for 2001: $3.40 per share ($1.40 additional since June 30) for AA Ltd. and $3.90 per share ($1.80 additional since June 30) for BB Ltd.

The effects of items (a) to (e) on the financial statements of Grand Ltd. at the end of 2001 are:

Investment in AA Ltd. (Cost Basis)

a. Long-term investment asset starts out at the purchase price of $1,800,000 (cash reduced by same amount).

b. (Concerns only BB Ltd.)

c. Earnings announcement is ignored for accounting purposes in the cost basis.

    d. Cash received and dividend revenue are recorded for $90,000 (60,000 shares × $1.50).

    e. Earnings announcement is ignored for accounting purposes in the cost basis.

Cost basis: no change in asset; dividend added to revenue when received. Using the cost basis, Grand Ltd.'s financial statements as of December 31, 2001, will therefore include for AA Ltd.:

Investment in AA Ltd. (noncurrent asset)	$1,800,000
Dividend revenue (in other revenue)	$ 90,000

Investment in BB Ltd. (Equity Basis)

    a. (Concerns only AA Ltd.)

    b. Long-term investment asset starts out at the purchase price of $4,640,000, the same as if the cost basis were used.

    c. Upon earnings announcement, both investment revenue and investment asset are increased by $304,500 (145,000 shares × $2.10), Grand's share of BB's income.

    d. Cash is increased by, and investment asset is reduced by, $232,000 (145,000 shares × $1.60): the dividend received is therefore deemed to be a return to Grand Ltd. of some of its investment.

    e. Upon earnings announcement, both investment revenue and investment asset are increased by $261,000 (145,000 shares × $1.80), Grand's share of BB's income.

Equity basis: asset and revenue increased for income share; asset decreased upon dividend. Using the equity basis, Grand Ltd.'s financial statements as of December 31, 2001, will therefore include for BB Ltd.:

Investment in BB Ltd. (noncurrent asset)	$4,973,500
($4,640,000 + $304,500 − $232,000 + $261,000)	
Investment revenue (in other revenue)	$ 565,500
($304,500 + $261,000)	

4. Joint Venture

A joint venture is a partnership between the investing corporation and other investors, usually formed to conduct exploration (such as in the oil and gas industry), develop new products, or pool resources in some other way. It is common in international business. Here, the investing corporation does not have control, but it does have significant influence on the joint venture because of the partnership arrangement and the business arrangements among the joint venture and the partner investors.

Joint ventures are accounted for in the investing company's financial statements using "proportionate consolidation," in which the investing company's proportionate shares of the venture's assets and liabilities (say, 50% if the venture is 50% owned) are combined with the investing company's assets and liabilities. We will not examine this method in this book.

H OW'S YOUR UNDERSTANDING?

Here are two questions you should be able to answer, based on what you have just read:

1. If Gretel Ltd. buys a noncontrolling number of shares of Hansel Inc. for $460,000, what are the criteria by which management of Gretel should decide if the investment is to be accounted for on the cost basis or the equity basis?

2. During the year, Gretel receives a $45,000 dividend from Hansel. At the end of the year, Hansel reports a net income. If Gretel's proportion of the Hansel voting shares is applied to Hansel's net income, the resulting figure is $78,500. What income from its investment in Hansel will Gretel report if it is using the cost basis? The equity basis? What is the "Investment in Hansel" asset on Gretel's books at the end of the year on the cost basis? The equity basis? ($45,000; $78,500; $460,000; $493,500)

9.7   CORPORATE GROUPS: CONSOLIDATION

This section considers the remaining two kinds of investment summarized in Exhibit 9.1, both methods of combining the financial statements of a group of corporations into one set of consolidated financial statements representing the group.

5. Acquisition by One Corporation of Another

Purchase Method Consolidation

Consolidation represents the corporate group as one economic entity.

Frequently, one corporation acquires more than 50% of the voting shares of another, becoming the majority owner of the other. This was illustrated in Figure 9.1 as A's investment in C, E, F, and G. This is done for many reasons, including to operate the two companies jointly and gain the benefits of such coordination. As long as voting control is held, the investing company can gain many benefits without having to own all the shares of the other, though it may well do so. Financial accounting uses a technique called consolidation to present the two companies as one economic entity, almost as if they were one company. As noted in Figure 9.1, the economic entity is greater than any of the individual legal entities represented by the corporations in the group.

Purchase method consolidation is used when one corporation acquires control of another.

The controlling company (the "parent") and the controlled company (the subsidiary) are not equal, because the parent is in control, so Canadian GAAP prescribe the purchase method of accounting for this business combination. A merger, where both companies really do join and there is no acquisition of one by the other, is dealt with later in this section. In Canada, acquisitions are very common and mergers are very rare, so if you see a set of consolidated financial statements, the purchase method is almost certain to be the accounting method used.

Consolidation portrays separate corporations as if they were a single entity.

Consolidation is imaginary: there is no legal, consolidated entity. Rather, it is legally a group of separate companies with connected ownership. The idea is to present the group of companies *as if* it were a single entity. This method is thought to represent the economic and business circumstances more faithfully than would reporting separate statements for all the legally separate companies and leaving the user to try to add them together.

Consolidation uses a simple idea: to prepare the financial statements of a group of companies, put the balance sheets, income statements, and other statements for all the companies side by side and, mostly, add them up. The consolidated balance sheet's cash figure would be the sum of all of the companies' cash figures, the consolidated income statement's cost of goods sold expense figure would be the sum of their cost of goods sold figures, and so on. To apply this simple idea to the complexities of modern businesses, a quite complicated set of GAAP for consolidation has arisen. In this book, the complexities will be left out in favour of a focus on three main issues in consolidation accounting:

- What to do if the parent company owns less than 100% of the subsidiary's voting shares (Corporations F and G in Figure 9.1).

- Determining the asset and liability values that are to be added together.

- Determining any "goodwill" arising from the acquisition price paid by the parent.

Three Basic Concepts in Purchase Method Consolidation

Noncontrolling (minority) interest liability is the part of the entity the parent does not own.

1. *Noncontrolling (minority) interest.* This arises if the parent owns less than 100% of the subsidiary and equals the percentage of the voting shares *not owned* by the parent times the subsidiary's shareholders' equity at the date of acquisition, adjusted for changes since that date. For example, if P Inc. bought 75% of the voting shares of S Ltd. on January 3, 2001, when S Ltd.'s shareholders' equity equalled $300,000, then the noncontrolling interest, which many consolidated financial statements refer to as the minority interest, would equal 25% of that, or $75,000. This amount is shown as a liability on the consolidated balance sheet. The liability represents the part of the joint consolidated entity's equity *not* owned by the parent company's shareholders. *It represents someone else's equity in the group, so it is not included with the consolidated equity.* It is not a debt of the consolidated entity, because it need not be paid—you could think of it as an acknowledgment that the consolidated entity has an obligation to the minority owners of S Ltd., who did *not* sell their shares to P Inc. So the noncontrolling interest is another of the accounts that blurs the distinction between liabilities and equity.

Minority's share decreases consolidated income and increases liability.

Over time, the noncontrolling interest liability is accounted for similarly to the way the investment asset was in the equity method above. The liability is increased (*and consolidated net income is decreased*) each year by the minority owners' share of the subsidiary's net income, and it is decreased (and consolidated cash is decreased) whenever the minority owners receive a dividend. So if the parent company succeeds in getting the subsidiary to earn income, some of that income is credited to the minority owners, and when the minority owners are paid a dividend, the liability is reduced just as any liability would be.

Consolidation starts by adding together all the parent's and subsidiary's accounts.

2. *Balance sheet asset and liability values.* The idea of consolidation is just to add the accounts together: the parent's accounts receivable are added to the subsidiary's accounts receivable, the land is added to the land, the accounts payable are added to the accounts payable, the revenue is added to the revenue, the income tax expense is added to the income tax expense, and so on. But two changes to the parent's and subsidiary's balance sheets are made before that is done.

The first change is that any *intercompany balances are ignored*. If S Ltd. owes P Inc. $40,000, for example, that would be on S Ltd.'s balance sheet as an account payable and on P Inc.'s balance sheet as an account receivable. If the consolidated balance sheet is to represent the two companies as if they were one entity, then this $40,000 amount is an internal matter to that entity: it is not owed to or receivable from anyone outside the entity, so it is not like the other accounts payable and accounts receivable. Therefore, it is just left out of the consolidated figures. (Intercompany sales and expenses, such as management fees, are also left out of the income statement, and any profit made by one company in dealing with the other is left out as well. Eliminating these can be complex.)

At acquisition, consolidated shareholders' equity equals just the parent's equity.

. The account for the parent company's investment in the subsidiary is also an intercompany account, so it too is *ignored* in the consolidation. Another intercompany amount left out is the parent's share of the subsidiary's shareholders' equity. It is what the parent bought, so it is included in the parent's investment account and therefore is not part of the consolidated equity external to the consolidated entity. The part of the subsidiary's equity *not* bought is transferred to the noncontrolling interest liability (as noted above), so the result is that *none* of the subsidiary's equity at the date of acquisition is included in consolidated equity. *Consolidated equity at date of acquisition equals just the parent's equity alone.* The parent purchased shares of the subsidiary, and via its voting interest, it controls the assets and liabilities of the subsidiary. The subsidiary's assets and liabilities are therefore included in the consolidated balance sheet, and to avoid double counting, the intercompany accounts for parent's investment and subsidiary's equity are eliminated.

At the acquisition date, the subsidiary's assets and liabilities are revalued only for the parent's share.

The second change is to recognize that the parent company may have had a different value in mind for various of the subsidiary's assets and liabilities when it acquired the subsidiary from the amounts shown for those on the subsidiary's balance sheet. Because a transaction did happen (the parent bought shares of the subsidiary), the historical cost basis of accounting requires that any revised values at that date be taken into account. These are called the fair values at that date: they can be viewed as the cost to the parent of the subsidiary's net assets, and there was a transaction to give them validity (the purchase of the subsidiary's shares). However, because the minority owners did not sell, there was not a transaction for their share of the subsidiary's assets and liabilities, so *the minority's share is not taken into account in revaluing the subsidiary's assets and liabilities to fair values.* We know what the parent paid for what it got; we do not know what might have been paid for what it did *not* buy (the minority's share). Therefore, at the date of acquisition, each of the subsidiary's assets and liabilities is added into the consolidated figures using the following formula:

Amount used in consolidation calculation	=	Book value in subsidiary's balance sheet	+	Parent's share of subsidiary	×	(Fair value − subsidiary's book value)

For example, if the subsidiary's land was on its balance sheet at a value (presumably cost) of $120,000, but the parent's evaluation indicated its fair value was $180,000 and the parent bought 85% of the subsidiary, that land would be included in the consolidated figures at a value of $171,000 [$120,000 + 0.85 ($180,000 − $120,000)]. The last term is the adjustment to reflect the parent's cost for the 85% interest it acquired, maintaining the historical cost basis for the consolidated financial statements. Therefore, the consolidated figures do not *fully* revalue the subsidiary's assets and liabilities: the minority owners' share of such revaluation is left out because they did not sell. (Any revaluations of assets and liabilities that are done may affect future consolidated income; for example, if the subsidiary's buildings and equipment are increased in value in the consolidation, then the consolidated amortization expense will have to be increased too, in order to take that into account. This is another complication we will not take any further!)

Consolidated goodwill equals parent's investment cost minus partially revalued subsidiary.

3. *Goodwill arising on consolidation.* What if P Inc. paid more for the shares of S Ltd. than the sum of the fair values of S Ltd.'s assets minus its liabilities? This indicates that P Inc. is buying something else *not* on S Ltd.'s balance sheet, something in addition to all the individual parts of S Ltd. This something is called goodwill, or goodwill arising on consolidation. As explained in section 8.11, it might represent good managers, a good location, faithful customers, economies of scale with the parent, reduced competition, or other factors the parent company took into account in agreeing to a price for the subsidiary's shares:

Consolidated goodwill asset	=	Cost of parent's investment − Parent's portion of (fair values of subsidiary's assets − fair values of its liabilities)

For example, if Very Big Inc. paid $1,200,000 for 80% of the voting shares of Not So Big Ltd., and at that date Very Big evaluated Not So Big's assets to be worth $4,300,000 and its liabilities to be $3,000,000, then consolidated goodwill at the date of acquisition would be $160,000 [$1,200,000 − 0.80 ($4,300,000 − $3,000,000)].

Goodwill is shown among the noncurrent assets on the consolidated balance sheet, and it is amortized over time by charges against consolidated income (goodwill amortization expense).

Goodwill appears only if it is an asset (a positive difference between cost and fair values).

Two wrinkles regarding goodwill might as well be mentioned. First, if the difference is negative (investment cost is less than the parent's portion of the net sum of the fair values), you might expect this to be called "badwill" and to be shown on the consolidated balance sheet too. But under GAAP, it is assumed that there was something wrong with the subsidiary's assets for this to happen, so the fair values are reduced in the consolidation calculation until the parent's portion exactly equals the purchase price. The result is that goodwill (or badwill) is zero. Second, if the subsidiary already had goodwill, that is wrapped into the new goodwill figure and not carried forward separately.

To summarize, the consolidated balance sheet at date of acquisition includes:

- The parent company's balance sheet figures;

- The subsidiary's assets and liabilities, revalued to reflect the parent's portion of any increases and decreases to fair values;

- Any noncontrolling (minority) interest in the subsidiary's equity;

- Any consolidated goodwill.

The consolidated balance sheet does *not* include:

- The parent's account for investment in subsidiary;
- The subsidiary's shareholders' equity;
- Any other intercompany asset and liability accounts.

An Example of Consolidation at Date of Acquisition
ABC Company purchased 80% of XYZ Company's voting shares for $500,000. We have the following information for XYZ as at the date of acquisition (no intercompany receivables or payables existed at that date):

9-3

Exhibit

XYZ Data	Book Values	Fair Values
Cash	$ 45,000	$ 45,000
Accounts receivable	75,000	60,000
Inventory	100,000	120,000
Property and equipment (net)	200,000	300,000
	$420,000	$525,000
Accounts payable	$ 90,000	95,000
Common shares	50,000	
Retained earnings	280,000	
	$420,000	
Sum of fair values of net assets		$430,000

   a. *Goodwill arising on consolidation.* ABC paid $500,000 for 80% of $430,000 (the identifiable fair values):

Purchase price	$500,000
Minus acquired fair value (80% × $430,000)	344,000
Goodwill	$156,000

   b. *Noncontrolling interest.* ABC purchased only 80% of XYZ. Therefore, the other 20% is the owners' equity of the noncontrolling owners. It is 20% of the book value of XYZ's owners' equity at the date of acquisition, or 20% × ($50,000 + $280,000) = $66,000.

   c. *Consolidated figures for ABC* are shown in Exhibit 9.4.

9-4

Exhibit

	Balance Sheet Book Values as at Date of Acquisition		Adjust 80% of FV–BV* of XYZ	Include Goodwill and Non-controlling Interest	Consolidated Balance Sheet
	ABC	XYZ			
Cash	$ 175,000	$ 45,000	$ 0		$ 220,000
Receivables	425,000	75,000	(12,000)		488,000
Inventory	660,000	100,000	16,000		776,000
Investment in XYZ	500,000	—		Ignore	—
Property & equipment	1,700,000	200,000	80,000		1,980,000
Consolidated goodwill	—	—		$156,000	156,000
	$3,460,000	$420,000			$3,620,000
Payables	$ 730,000	$ 90,000	$ 4,000		$ 824,000
Long-term debt	850,000	0	0		850,000
Consolidated noncontrolling interest	—	—		$ 66,000	66,000
Common shares	100,000	50,000		ABC only	100,000
Retained earnings	1,780,000	280,000		ABC only	1,780,000
	$3,460,000	$420,000			$3,620,000

* FV – BV = Item's fair value – Its value on XYZ's balance sheet.

A Comment on Consolidated Net Income after Acquisition

In the purchase method, consolidated net income is reduced by extra amortization, etc.

Consolidated net income is the sum of the incomes earned since acquisition, with adjustments to remove intercompany balances and any subsidiary's noncontrolling owners' interest in the income earned by the subsidiary and to reflect amortization of goodwill, among other things. The calculation is as follows:

Start with the sum of the parent's and the subsidiaries' incomes $ XXXX

Subtract:

a. Any profits earned by any of the companies on intercompany sales.   (XXXX)

b. Any income from the subsidiaries already included in the parent's or other subsidiaries' accounts through use of the equity method of accounting on the companies' individual financial statements (these are intercompany amounts too).   (XXXX)

c. Any extra amortization and other expenses resulting from adjusting subsidiaries' assets and liabilities to fair values in the consolidation.   (XXXX)

d. Any noncontrolling owners' share of the net income earned by the subsidiary of which they remain part owners (roughly equal to the noncontrolling ownership percentage multiplied by the subsidiary's net income).   (XXXX)

e. Amortization of any goodwill arising on consolidation.   (XXXX)

The result is consolidated net income $ XXXX

You can see that consolidated net income is less than the sum of the individual companies' net incomes, perhaps substantially less if goodwill is large or there are significant minority interests.

6. Merger

Pooling of interests consolidation for a merger just sums companies' accounts as they are.

When there is a real merger of two similarly sized corporations, in which neither can be said to be buying the other, the pooling of interests method of consolidation has been used for many years. Such a merger can be recognized by an exchange of shares (rather than by one company paying cash for the shares of the other), by the continuance of the management of both companies, and by other evidence that the two companies are continuing in a joint enterprise. In a pooling of interests, the consolidated financial statements are prepared simply by adding the accounts together. Assets equal the sum of the balance sheet assets of the two companies, as do liabilities, and equity is the sum of the equities. There is no revaluation of any of the balance sheet accounts, and the special consolidation accounts, "noncontrolling (minority) interest" and "goodwill," do not arise. The lack of these accounts is attractive to some business people, because the reductions to consolidated income associated with them that were indicated above are avoided.

In Canada, the conditions under which GAAP prescribe the pooling of interests method very rarely occur. The method was abused during a big merger boom in the late 1960s and early 1970s, and Canadian financial accounting standards have since been written to restrict its use and normally require the purchase method. Pooling of interests has been popular in the United States, but the CICA and FASB standard-setters are working on a proposal to largely ban pooling of interests accounting in both Canada and the United States.

HOW'S YOUR UNDERSTANDING?

Here are two questions you should be able to answer, based on what you have just read:

1. On January 1, 2001, Supersix Inc. bought 75% of the voting shares of Weaknees Ltd. for $231,000 cash. At that date, Weaknees's balance sheet showed assets of $784,000 and liabilities of $697,000. Supersix assessed the fair values of Weaknees's assets to be $800,000 and its liabilities to be $690,000 at acquisition date. Why do noncontrolling (minority) interest and goodwill appear on Supersix's consolidated balance sheet, and what were the figures for those items at acquisition date? ($21,750; $148,500)

2. At the same date, Supersix's balance sheet showed assets of $56,782,000 and liabilities of $45,329,000. What would be the consolidated equity of Supersix after consolidating Weaknees? ($11,453,000)

9.8 TERMS TO BE SURE YOU UNDERSTAND

Here is this chapter's list of terms introduced or emphasized. Make sure you know what they mean *in accounting*, and if any are unclear to you, check the chapter again or refer to the Glossary of Terms at the back of the book.

Accounting policies
Accumulated foreign currency translation
   adjustment
Bond
Bonded debt
Business combinations
Capital
Capital cost allowance
Capital leases
Conditional sale contract
Consolidated
Consolidated financial statements
Consolidation
Contributed surplus
Convertible
Corporate groups
Corporation
Cost basis
Debenture
Deferral method
Deferred income tax
Discount on bonds
Economic entity
Effective income tax rate
Equity
Equity basis
Fair values

Financial instruments
Fund accounting
Future income taxes
Going concern
Goodwill
Goodwill arising on consolidation
Historical cost
Indenture
Interperiod tax allocation
Intraperiod tax allocation
Joint venture
Liabilities
Liability method
Loans from shareholders
Marketable securities
Matching principle
Merger
Minority interest
Mortgage
Noncontrolling interest
Notes
Parent
Partnership(s)
Personal guarantees
Pooling of interests method
Premium on bonds
Present value

Proprietorship(s)	Subsidiary
Provisions	Taxable income
Purchase method	Temporary difference(s)
Redeemable	Temporary investments
Security	Term preferred shares
Share splits	Treasury shares
Significant influence	Warrants
Stock dividends	Working capital
Stock options	

9.9 CONTINUING DEMONSTRATION CASE

INSTALLMENT 9

In this Installment, we'll prepare the complete first year's financial statements and notes for the company. The statements will be analyzed in Installment 10, so make sure you are clear about how they are assembled below.

Data for Installment 9

In Installment 7, the February 28, 2001, adjusted trial balance of Mato Inc. was prepared, and in Installment 8, the company chose its accounting policies. The data are therefore the trial balance and the policies. Refer back to those Installments if you are unsure about any results below.

Results for Installment 9

With some accounting help, Tomas prepared the set of financial statements and notes for the company's first year.

Mato Inc. Statement of Income and Deficit for the Year Ended February 28, 2001		
Revenue		$229,387
Cost of goods sold		138,767
Gross profit		$ 90,620
Operating expenses:		
Bad debts	$ 2,436	
Salaries	67,480	
Travel	9,477	
Telephone	4,014	
Rent	24,000	
Utilities	3,585	
Office and general	5,688	
Inventory shortage	441	
Interest	6,469	
Amortization	21,096	144,686
Net loss for the year (no tax)		$ (54,066)
Retained earnings, March 1, 2000		0
Deficit as at February 28, 2001		$ (54,066)

Mato Inc.
Balance Sheets
at February 28, 2001, and March 1, 2000

Assets			Liabilities and Equity		
	2001	2000		2001	2000
Current assets:			Current liabilities:		
Cash	$ 6,418	$130,000	Bank loan	$ 47,500	$ 0
Receivables (net)	14,129	0	Payables	$ 41,808	1,100
Inventory	33,612	0	Loan payable	0	15,000
Prepaid expense	525	0	Deferred revenue	500	0
	$ 54,684	$130,000		$ 89,808	$ 16,100
Noncurrent assets:			Shareholders' equity:		
Equipment cost	$ 57,290	$ 10,000	Share capital	$125,000	$125,000
Accum. amort.	(7,344)	0	Deficit	(54,066)	0
Leasehold (net)	51,172	0		$ 70,934	$125,000
Software (net)	3,840	0			
Incorp. cost	1,100	1,100			
	$106,058	$ 11,100			
TOTAL	$160,742	$141,100	TOTAL	$160,742	$141,100

Mato Inc.
Cash Flow Statement
For the Year Ended February 28, 2001

Operations:		
Net loss for the year		$ (54,066)
Add back amortization for the year		21,096
Changes in noncash working capital accounts:		
Increase in accounts receivable	$ (14,129)	
Increase in inventory	(33,612)	
Increase in prepaid expenses	(525)	
Increase in accounts payable	40,708	
Increase in deferred revenue	500	(7,058)
Cash used in operations		$ (40,028)
Investing activities:		
Equipment, leasehold improvements, and software acquired		(116,054)
Financing activities:		
Bank borrowing	$ 47,500	
Repayment of loan	(15,000)	32,500
Decrease in cash during the year		$(123,582)
Cash on hand, March 1, 2000		130,000
Cash on hand, February 28, 2001		$ 6,418

Mato Inc.
Notes to the Financial Statements as at February 28, 2001

1. Significant accounting policies:
   a. Inventory is valued at the lower of cost, determined by the first-in, first-out method, and net realizable value.
   b. Noncurrent assets are recorded at cost. Amortization is calculated on a straight-line basis of 20% of cost per annum on automotive equipment, leasehold improvements, and computer equipment and software, and at 10% of cost per annum on other equipment and furniture.
2. The bank loan is secured by receivables, inventories, a general charge on the company's assets, and by the personal guarantees of the shareholders.
3. The company's authorized capital is 1,000,000 shares without par value. At the beginning of the year, 12,500 shares were issued for $10 cash each.
4. No provision for income taxes has been made in the financial statements because the current loss will result in an income tax recovery only if there are future taxable incomes against which that loss may be deducted.
5. Salaries of directors and officers of the company were $54,280 for the year.
6. The company has commitments to purchase goods that will cost $23,430 on delivery, which is expected by April 30, 2001.

Discussion of the Results

The results for the year were still negative: a loss of $54,066 and a decrease in cash of $123,582. However, there was quite an improvement compared with the first six months:

- The loss for the first six months (Installment 3) had been $49,378, so the additional loss for the second six months was relatively small at only $4,688.

- The cash decrease for the first six months (Installment 4) was $125,493, so there was an addition to cash of $1,911 during the second six months.

- The working capital at the end of August (Installment 3) was negative at $38,772 ($96,844 − $135,616) and by February 28, 2001, was still negative at $35,124 ($54,684 − $89,808), but a little less negative.

Further analysis of the results will be conducted in Installment 10. However, Mavis and Tomas wonder if the financial statements have made their company's performance appear worse than necessary and if some other choice of accounting policies might make things look more optimistic.

Mavis and Tomas's concern regarding changing their accounting policies to make things look rosier is understandable. They have worked hard to make their company succeed, but the first year's results are not positive. If they had paid themselves no salaries for their year's work, the company would have shown a tiny income ($54,280 salaries per note 5 above minus the $54,066 loss would equal $214 income before income tax). But that would have been misleading because it would fail to measure the value added by their efforts—not to mention that they would have starved! Would it make sense to try to find accounting policies that would improve the picture? The answer is no, for the following reasons:

1. Such manipulation would be ethically questionable and perhaps even dangerous, if it obscured the company's real problems and reduced the pressure on Mavis and Tomas to improve Mato's performance. They may feel disappointed, but the thing to do is to try harder to manage the company well, not "shoot the messenger" by trying to change the financial accounting "message."

2. Such a change would not likely help in dealing with the parties who are going to be most concerned about the company. The bank already has the company's assets pretty well tied up as security on its loan and is going to be interested in the company's ability to generate cash to repay the loan, as well as in its long-term viability. The bank is undoubtedly very concerned about the company and will be on the lookout for desperate actions, so optimistic reporting is unlikely to fool them—or, for that matter, suppliers, other investors, and the company's employee.

3. The cash flow statement would show the same cash flow figures regardless of accounting policy changes, so users of the financial statements who know how to read the cash flow statement would see through such changes, and might even become suspicious if the income diverged too much from the cash flow from operations.

4. For this company, there is really not much that could be manipulated even if it were ethical and successful. Receivables are not large, nor is there any obvious reason for the company to recognize revenue sooner than it does without violating GAAP. Inventories are also not large, and, since FIFO is already being used, there is likely to be little room for raising inventory value to increase income. Amortization could be slowed down, but such a move would make little difference to income. Even cutting amortization in half would reduce the year's loss by less than 20%.

9.10 HOMEWORK AND DISCUSSION TO DEVELOP UNDERSTANDING

PROBLEM 9.1*
Questions about the right-hand side of the balance sheet

Answer the following questions briefly:

1. What is the difference between liabilities and equity?
2. What is the difference, if any, between liabilities and debts?
3. Suggest two examples each of short-term and long-term accruals that require difficult estimates and indicate what the difficulty is in each case.
4. Should companies avoid long-term accruals because they are likely to be inaccurate and therefore misleading, and just pay in cash costs such as warranties and pensions as they arise?

PROBLEM 9.2*
Explain some features of accounting for equity

Answer each of the following questions briefly:

1. Why does an unincorporated business have only a single equity account, Capital?
2. What does it matter that a bond or preferred share may be convertible to a common share?
3. Why is a stock split ignored in accounting whereas a stock dividend is traditionally recorded (debit retained earnings, credit share capital)?

4. Why is there so much disclosure of the legal details of shares and other equity accounts?

5. Why does it matter if a class of shares has a minimum issue price or par value?

PROBLEM 9.3*
Bond discount or premium calculations

In each case below, (1) calculate the amount of any discount or premium on issue of the bonds, (2) record the issue of the bonds, and (3) state whether interest expense over the life of the bonds will be higher, lower, or the same as the cash interest paid on the bond each year.

a. A Ltd. issued 10,000 $100 bonds and received $97.50 cash each.

b. B Ltd. planned to issue 10,000 $100 bonds, but found that the planned interest rate of 7% was lower than market rates and so received $915,000 for them.

c. C Ltd. issued 10,000 $100 bonds for a premium of 5% on legal value.

PROBLEM 9.4*
Questions about long-term accruals

1. Balmer Inc. started the year with a pension liability of $32,000. During the year, employees earned pension entitlements with a present value of $114,600 and the company paid $123,000 to the pension trustee. State the amount of the pension expense for the year and the pension liability at the end of the year.

2. Balmer Inc. also has a warranty plan. Estimated warranty liability was $50,000 at the beginning of the year, and based on the company's sales for the year, warranty service costing $78,500 in wages and other costs, plus $62,000 in replacement products, were expected to have to be provided eventually. Actual expenditures for the year were $84,000 in wages and other costs and $78,000 in replacement products. Calculate warranty expense for the year and estimated warranty liability at the end of the year.

3. Write one or more journal entries to record Balmer Inc.'s warranty experience for the year.

4. For part 2, what would be your answers if Balmer Inc. accounted for warranties on the cash basis instead of the accrual basis?

5. Suppose Balmer Inc. had a real disaster with a product during the next year. For that product only, wages and other service costs totalled $150,000 and replacement products costing $210,000 had to be provided. Comment on what this disaster might do to the company's warranty accounting. Focus on the accounting issues—no numbers are needed.

PROBLEM 9.5*
Do current and non-current liability calculations

In each case below, calculate (1) current liability at the end of this year; (2) non-current liability at the end of this year; and (3) interest expense for the *next* year.

a. John Ltd.'s factory mortgage of $842,500 requires payments of $11,200 each month. During the next year, the interest part of the payments will equal $61,232.

b. Frieda Inc.'s land mortgage of $232,200 requires payments of $60,000 over the next year. By the end of next year, the principal due on the mortgage will have gone down to $189,400.

c. Graham Ltd.'s $87,436 property mortgage requires monthly payments of $1,500 plus interest. During the next year, payments will total $25,674.

PROBLEM 9.6*
Match liability, equity, and business combinations terms

Match each phrase on the left with the most appropriate phrase on the right.

1. Has no effect on equity at acquisition date
2. Liability arises only on consolidation
3. Left out of the income statement
4. A name that encompasses debts and some assets
5. Financing that isn't a liability or an equity
6. Accrues a share of a noncontrolled company's income
7. An expense based on analysis of balance sheet accounts
8. A promise to meet specified financial conditions
9. A usually informal kind of debt
10. Trying to give something for nothing

a. Income tax-future portion

b. Loan from shareholders
c. Stock dividend
d. Purchase method consolidation

e. Equity method

f. Proprietor's income tax

g. Minority interest

h. Financial instruments

i. Off-balance-sheet
j. Indenture

PROBLEM 9.7*
Would marking CAE's financial instruments to market matter?

In section 9.5, CAE's note about financial instruments was quoted. Based on that note and the introduction to it, would you say that there would be a significant effect on CAE's financial statements if the company's financial instruments were marked to market? Why or why not?

PROBLEM 9.8*
Explain some things about income tax allocation

Explain the following:

1. Why is it thought necessary to have a future portion of income tax expense and future income tax liability?
2. How does the resulting income tax allocation method fit accrual accounting?
3. Why is the calculation method of the future portion of the income tax expense sometimes described as not matching revenue very well?

PROBLEM 9.9*
Calculate income tax expense and future tax liability

At the end of 2001, Henrik Inc. had future income tax liability of $329,612 and retained earnings of $3,949,286. For 2002, the company's income statement showed income before tax of $648,960. There was only one temporary difference between the accounting and income tax calculations for 2002: capital cost allowance (CCA) exceeded book amortization expense by $343,502. There was also $29,650 of non-taxable revenue, so the company's taxable income was $275,808 for 2002. The company's income tax rate for 2002 was 32% and is expected to remain at that rate indefinitely. The company paid no dividends in 2002.

1. Calculate the following:
   a. Current portion of income tax expense for 2002.
   b. Future portion of income tax expense for 2002.
   c. Net income for 2002.
   d. Future income tax liability at the end of 2002.
   e. Retained earnings at the end of 2002.

2. Suppose the tax law changed a little in 2002, so that expected income tax rates in the future were now expected to vary from 32%, and the estimated future income tax liability at the end of 2002 is now $420,500. Recalculate the five numbers asked for in part 1.

PROBLEM 9.10*
Answer questions about intercorporate investments

Answer the following questions asked by a business executive upon reading a set of consolidated financial statements.

1. "I notice the consolidated balance sheet mentions a liability called 'noncontrolling interest.' What is that? When and to whom does it have to be paid?"
2. "Now that I think of it, what does it mean to say that financial statements are 'consolidated'?"
3. "Why does goodwill appear on the consolidated balance sheet even if there is none on the balance sheets of the individual corporations involved?"
4. "I understand that if I added together the net incomes of the corporations in the consolidated group, I wouldn't get the consolidated net income. Why not?"
5. "How do the accountants decide whether to consolidate an investment into the parent company's financial statements versus just showing the investment as an asset on the parent's balance sheet?"

PROBLEM 9.11*
Cost versus equity basis for nonconsolidated investment

China Sports Ltd. purchased 40% of the voting shares of Brassy Ltd. at the beginning of this year for $4,100,000. During the year, Brassy earned net income of $600,000 and paid dividends of $250,000. China Sports, which has been accounting for its investment in Brassy on the cost basis, has income of $800,000 for this year. If the equity basis were used instead, what would China Sports Ltd.'s income be?

PROBLEM 9.12*
Basic consolidation calculations and balance sheet

Seeking to expand its markets, Big Ltd. recently purchased 80% of the voting shares of Piddling Ltd. for $10,800,000. At the date of the acquisition, Piddling had assets of $14,600,000, liabilities of $8,200,000, and equity of $6,400,000. By the best estimate Big could make at the date of acquisition, the fair market value of Piddling's assets was $16,100,000 and that of its liabilities was $8,300,000.

1. Calculate the goodwill on consolidation as of the acquisition date.
2. Calculate the noncontrolling (minority) interest as of the acquisition date.
3. Complete the consolidated balance sheet figures below.

Account	Big Ltd.	Piddling Ltd.	Consolidated
General assets	$105,000,000	$14,600,000	$
Investment in Piddling	10,800,000		
Goodwill			
General liabilities	83,700,000	8,200,000	
Noncontrolling interest			
Equity	32,100,000	6,400,000	

PROBLEM 9.13*
Match intercorporate investment terms with their purposes

Match the list of terms in the left column with the purposes in the right column, written in deliberately brief and simple terms.

a. Consolidated
b. Cost basis
c. Economic entity
d. Equity basis
e. Fair values
f. Goodwill
g. Minority interest
h. Pooling of interests
i. Purchase method
j. Significant influence

1. A buyer and a seller
2. Accounted for as one
3. Don't count it until we get it
4. Just add the companies together
5. Parent and subsidiaries together
6. Take credit for influence
7. The extra we paid
8. We have a say but not control
9. What we didn't buy
10. Worth of individual parts

PROBLEM 9.14
Answer questions about liabilities

Respond to the question asked in each comment below.

1. "Warranties are honoured as part of good business practice: keep your customers happy. Whether to honour a claim and how much cost to incur are managerial judgments that depend on how good the customer is, what the reputation effects are, etc. Therefore, warranties are discretionary period expenses like donations. There is no accrual for future donations, so why is there an accrual for future warranty costs?"
2. "Employees take their pensions when they retire, years into the future. Whether there is any pension depends on whether the employee keeps working for the company, and how long the employee lives after retirement. Therefore pension costs can only be realistically determined when they are being paid in the future. Why shouldn't they be expensed then, rather than now?"
3. "After thinking about warranties and pensions, I have a proposal. Let's take accrual accounting to the next step and accrue all future expenses we can reasonably predict now. I mentioned donations already. We could add repairs and maintenance, interest, income taxes, and executive bonuses, to mention just a few."

PROBLEM 9.15
Calculate various liability and expense amounts

In each of the following cases, calculate the year-end liability and any associated expense for the year.

1. Bach Inc. has collected fees from orchestras for performance of various symphonies to which it has the rights. During the year, it collected fees of $125,000, but by the end of the year, the orchestras had performed symphonies corresponding to only $87,000 of the fees. The rest were to be performed next year.
2. Beethoven Ltd. started the year owing $112,000 to its pension plan trustee. During the year, its employees earned pensions having an estimated present value of $433,200, and the company paid the trustee $455,720.
3. Redo part 2 changing only one number: change the present value of pensions earned to $333,200. Where would the liability figure you got appear on the balance sheet?
4. Mozart Inc. has a warranty plan for the musical instruments it manufactures. The company's prices are high and its quality is good, but musicians are a

choosy lot, so the company has a substantial warranty cost, which its management feels is worthwhile to keep its reputation and repeat business up. At the beginning of the year, the estimated warranty liability was $177,740. During the year, the company incurred warranty costs of $129,430, $89,940 of that in cash and the rest in replacement instruments. This was close to the $140,000 expected on the basis of the year's sales.

5. Suppose Mozart Inc. had an unexpected problem with a new model of tuba and recalled all the tubas sold for free repairs, costing the company $75,000 in total. Knowing this, would this change either of your answers to part 4?

PROBLEM 9.16
Calculate or record various liability and expense amounts

1. Tweedsmuir Land Ltd. has substantial mortgage debt. The debt was $13,499,276 at the beginning of this year. Mortgage payments of $3,888,541 were made during the year and the mortgage balance was $10,851,299 at the end of the year. No new borrowing was made this year. Next year, the payments required total $4,105,640 and if there is no new borrowing the mortgage balance will be $7,742,879 at the end of next year. Calculate (a) Interest expense for this year; (b) Current portion of the mortgage liability at the end of this year; and (c) Noncurrent mortgage liability at the end of this year.

2. Yoho Portals Inc. issued $1,000 first-mortgage bonds having a total face value of $40,000,000 and carrying a 7.2% interest rate. They were not well received by the bond market, so Yoho received only $37,659,420 for them. (a) Record the bond issue, and (b) calculate the balance sheet liability for the bonds as of the issue date.

3. Regarding part 2, will Yoho's interest expenses for the bonds be more or less than 7.2% times the face value ($2,880,000)? Why?

PROBLEM 9.17
Answer questions about bond discounts and premiums

The president of Redstone Inc. has just been discussing a planned new bond issue with financial advisors and has come to you with some resulting accounting questions. Answer each.

1. "We are thinking of setting the interest rate on the bonds a little above current market rates to make them more attractive. I'm told this will produce a balance sheet liability higher than the face value of the bonds. How does this happen?"

2. "Your answer to my first question is troubling. How can it make sense to show a liability higher than the amount we will have to pay when the bonds come due? What will we do with the difference then?"

3. "So I guess the amount of interest expense on the bonds, as calculated by the accountants, will be less than the actual amount of interest paid each year. That will be nice, because the reduction will improve earnings and carry through to our cash flow statement, right?"

PROBLEM 9.18
Calculate various liability and expense amounts

Calculate the unknown figure in each of the following unrelated cases.

1. Current portion of long-term debt = $670,000. Payments due next year = $1,540,000. Total debt = $8,554,000. How much interest is to be paid next year?

2. Net bonded debt liability on the balance sheet = $23,230,890. Interest to be paid next year = $1,920,000. Discount amortization will be $67,000. What will the interest expense be for next year? What will be the net bonded debt liability on the balance sheet at the end of next year?

3. Pension liability at the beginning of the year = $899,900. Payments to the pension trustee during the year = $3,589,210. Liability at the end of the year = $234,568. What was the estimated present value of the pensions earned during the year? What was the pension expense for the year?

4. Warranty costs are accounted for on the cash basis, and this year the warranty expense = $134,500. An analysis of the sales and warranty patterns indicates that estimated warranty obligations were $45,620 at the beginning of the year and $78,300 at the end. If accrual accounting were used for warranties, what would the warranty expense be for this year? What difference would it make to income before income tax?

PROBLEM 9.19
Answer various questions about equity accounting

Answer each of the following questions briefly.

1. Give some examples of distinctions made in financial accounting between equity accounts and other balance sheet accounts that are in some way problematic. For each, what is the problem?

2. Given the increasing number of hybrid and generally complex financial instruments and financing methods, should financial accounting drop the debt–equity distinction on the right side of the balance sheet?

3. The business's economic earning power, assets, and liabilities are presumably what matters to external users of financial accounting information. Why then are there various rules about accounting for equity that depend on the form of the business organization (e.g., whether it is incorporated or not)?

4. The equity section of the balance sheet is recorded at historical amounts, not at the current market value of the equity, what the company could be sold for today. Given that, what aspects, if any, of the way equity is accounted for provide useful information to the owners of the equity?

PROBLEM 9.20
Calculations of partnership equity

Bagogi Partners is a firm of architects, whose partners are Barbara, Gordon, and Gilles. The partnership agreement specifies that the first two partners get 30% each of the firm's income and the third partner gets 40%. During the most recent year, the firm earned $450,000 before any withdrawals by partners. At the end of the year, the firm's liabilities totalled $332,650. At the beginning of the year, Barbara's capital account was $89,300; Gordon's was $23,900; and Gilles's was $183,200. Withdrawals for the year were: Barbara, $143,600; Gordon, $150,100; and Gilles, $81,000.

1. Calculate the partners' capital accounts as at the end of the year.

2. Present the partnership's summarized balance sheet as at the end of the year.

3. Suppose Gordon had withdrawn $175,000 instead during the most recent year. Would you think the partnership's balance sheet would or should be different from the one you presented in part 2? Why, or why not? This has not been covered in the chapter, but you should be able to consider the question on the basis of your knowledge of asset and equity accounting.

PROBLEM 9.21
Temporary differences in income tax accounting

Explain what "temporary differences" are and why the future income tax liability (or asset) depends on them but not on permanent differences between accounting and income tax calculations such as nontaxable revenues or nondeductible expenses.

PROBLEM 9.22
Calculate net income and future income tax liability

Mars Bears Ltd. has a stable income before income tax on its income statement: $120,000 each year. Its income tax rate is also stable: 36%. It has one asset costing $350,000 that it amortizes at $35,000 per year. The capital cost allowance deductible on that asset is 10% in the first year and 20% in each year thereafter, the rate being applied to the unamortized cost (CCA is a declining balance method). Calculate the following for *each* of the first three years of the company's existence:

  a. CCA deductible.
  b. Taxable income (add book amortization back to income and deduct CCA instead).
  c. Current portion of income tax expense.
  d. Future portion of income tax expense.
  e. Total income tax expense.
  f. Net income for the year.
  g. Future income tax liability at the end of the year.

PROBLEM 9.23
Explain the purpose and nature of income tax allocation

George picked up the financial statements of a company he owns shares in and noticed the following two accounts, which he didn't understand:

Future portion of income tax expense	$19,749,200
Future income tax liability	$86,293,500

Explain to George the purpose of income tax allocation accounting and what the two figures he didn't understand mean.

PROBLEM 9.24
Journal entry for income tax payable and future tax

For 2001, Great World Air Inc. had income before income tax of $23,960 (in thousands of dollars). Taxable income for 2001 was $21,407 thousand, and an analysis of balance sheet accounts indicated that temporary differences between accounting and tax rules of $3,367 thousand arose in 2001. The company's income tax rate for 2001 was 36% and that is expected to be the rate for the future.

  1. Write a journal entry to record the company's 2001 income tax expense. Show your calculations.
  2. Based on your answer to part 1, what was the company's net income for 2001?

PROBLEM 9.25
Calculate net income, future income tax liability, and other amounts

You have the following information about Gazoo Entertainments Ltd.:

Year	Income before Income Tax	Income Tax Expense Current	Income Tax Expense Deferred	DIT Liability at Beginning of Year
2000	$413,250	$102,280	$51,670	$143,970
2001	543,780	130,420	45,910	?
2002	219,540	47,780	27,890	?
2003	(51,650)	(28,080)	9,340	?
2004	43,210	26,760	(5,320)	?

Answer the following:

    a. What is the net income in 2001, 2003, and 2004?
    b. What is the future liability at the end of 2004?
    c. What is the total income tax expense for 2003?
    d. In 2003, how could there be both a negative current income tax expense and positive future income tax expense?
    e. Assuming Gazoo's future income tax arises from differences between book amortization and CCA, is amortization greater than CCA in 2000? In 2002? In 2004?
    f. What was the company's effective income tax rate in 2002? In 2003?

PROBLEM 9.26
Answer questions about income tax accounts

Answer each of the following questions:

1. Before income tax allocation accounting was introduced, the income tax expense on companies' income statements just equalled the income tax payable on each year's taxable income. For a company with new factory assets, would net income have been larger or smaller without income tax allocation? Explain.
2. Following from part 1, would net income have been larger or smaller without income tax allocation for a company with old factory assets? Explain.
3. Companies do not *have* to claim capital cost allowance deductions in calculating their taxable income if they choose not to. Thus, there are circumstances in which the full CCA available is not claimed. If a company chooses not to claim the full CCA available, what will that do to (i) current portion of income tax expense, (ii) future portion of income tax expense, (iii) total income tax expense?
4. What are the effects of each of the following on (i) current income tax expense, (ii) future income tax expense, (iii) total income tax expense?
    a. A company incurs and pays a large repair expense.
    b. A company buys a large new machine for its factory.
    c. A company buys a large shipment of inventory to be sold next year.
    d. A company receives a large nontaxable dividend from another company.
    e. A company declares and pays a dividend to its shareholders.
    f. A company makes a large sale to a good customer.

**PROBLEM 9.27
Calculate income
tax expense and
future tax liability**

At the end of 2001, Plasticorp Ltd. had future income tax liability of $2,417,983 and retained earnings of $21,788,654. For 2002, the company's income statement showed income before tax of $1,890,004 and amortization expense of $3,745,672. Inspection of the company's income tax records showed that in 2002, $75,950 of its revenue was not subject to income tax, $43,211 of its expenses were not tax deductible, and its capital cost allowance was $3,457,889, so its taxable income was $2,145,048. The company's income tax rate for 2002 was 35% and is expected to remain at that rate indefinitely. The company declared and paid a $500,000 dividend in 2002.

1. Calculate the following:
   a. Current portion of income tax expense for 2002.
   b. Future portion of income tax expense for 2002 (the difference between book amortization and CCA was the only temporary difference in 2002).
   c. Net income for 2002.
   d. Future income tax liability at the end of 2002.
   e. Retained earnings at the end of 2002.
2. Suppose expectations of future income taxes to be paid changed a little in 2002, so that the estimated future income tax liability at the end of 2002 is now $2,340,540. Recalculate the five numbers asked for in part 1.

**PROBLEM 9.28
Outline a talk on
consolidated finan-
cial statements**

You have been asked to give a talk to a group of individual investors on the subject of "What to look for in consolidated financial statements and how to understand what you see." Briefly outline the main points in your talk.

**PROBLEM 9.29
Equity and cost
bases of accounting
for an investment**

Baxter Investments Inc. owns 23% of the voting shares of Bluebird Hotel Ltd. It bought them last year for $1,500,000, and, since then, Bluebird has reported net income of $400,000 and declared dividends totalling $160,000. Baxter accounts for its investment in Bluebird on the equity basis.

1. Give the figures for:
   a. The revenue Baxter will have recognized from its investment since acquisition.
   b. The present balance in the company's balance sheet account for investment in Bluebird Hotel Ltd.
2. Give the same figures requested in part 1 if Baxter accounted for its investment on the cost basis.

**PROBLEM 9.30
Equity basis of
accounting versus
consolidation**

Accounting for intercorporate investments is subject to GAAP. Apply your knowledge of GAAP to the following situation.

International Newspapers Ltd. owns 45% of the voting shares of Nomad Printers Ltd. It acquired the shares several years ago for $10,000,000. Nomad lost money for some years after acquisition but has recently begun to be profitable: since International acquired its shares, Nomad has had losses totalling $790,000 and incomes totalling $940,000, for a total net income since acquisition of $150,000. Last year, Nomad paid its first dividend, $100,000.

1. International accounts for its investment in Nomad on the equity basis. What does this mean?

2. What is the present figure for investment in Nomad on the balance sheet of International?
3. What difference would it make to the balance sheet of International if the Nomad investment were consolidated instead?
4. Suppose that International had bought 65% of the Nomad voting shares for its $10,000,000 and that at that date the following values existed for Nomad: book value of assets, $18,000,000; sum of fair values of assets, $19,000,000; book value of liabilities, $7,000,000; sum of fair values of liabilities, $10,000,000. Calculate the goodwill that would have been shown on the consolidated balance sheet of International if the Nomad investment had been consolidated at that date.

PROBLEM 9.31
Basic consolidated figures

Fat Furniture has decided to purchase 65% of Banana Appliances Ltd. for $43,000,000 in cash. The two companies' balance sheets as at the acquisition date are (in millions of dollars):

Assets			Liabilities and Equity		
	Fat	**Banana**		**Fat**	**Banana**
Cash equivalent assets	$112	$10	Cash equivalent liabilities	$ 28	$ 0
Other current assets	304	45	Other current liabilities	260	10
Noncurrent assets (net)	432	25	Noncurrent liabilities	272	15
			Share capital	160	15
			Ret. earnings	128	40
	$848	$80		$848	$80

Fat Furniture has evaluated all of Banana's assets and liabilities as having fair value equal to book value except for its noncurrent assets, which Fat Furniture believes have a fair value of $33 million.

1. Calculate the consolidated goodwill that would appear on the consolidated balance sheet at acquisition date.
2. Calculate the following consolidated figures as at acquisition date:
   a. Consolidated total assets.
   b. Consolidated owners' equity.
   c. Consolidated total liabilities.

PROBLEM 9.32
Goodwill amount and reasons; later consolidated income

White Knight Acquisitions Ltd. recently purchased a 70% interest in Premier Publications, a small magazine wholesaler. Premier's balance sheet on the date of acquisition appears below.

Assets		Liabilities and Equity	
Cash	$ 10,000	Liabilities	$102,000
Accounts receivable (net)	55,000	Owners' equity	108,000
Inventory	70,000		
Fixed assets (net)	75,000		
	$210,000		$210,000

Premier's receivables have an adequate provision for doubtful accounts. Inventories are carried at cost and current replacement value is about $70,000. Land with a book value of $20,000 has a market value of $29,000. In the purchase agreement, White Knight assumed all of Premier's liabilities. Before the sale was final, the then owners of Premier were allowed to withdraw all cash from the company as a dividend.

1. If White Knight paid $104,000 (in addition to the $102,000 to pay the liabilities) for its interest in Premier Publications, what was the amount of purchased goodwill? (Hint: all White Knight got for its money were receivables, inventories, and fixed assets.)
2. Why would White Knight have been willing to pay this amount for goodwill?
3. Assume that in the year following the acquisition, Premier made a net income of $14,000. Therefore, decide whether the following statement is true or false and tell why: To record Premier's earnings, the consolidated retained earnings of White Knight Acquisitions will be increased by $14,000.

PROBLEM 9.33
Answer conceptual questions on consolidation

Chromium Furniture Ltd. wishes to expand operations by acquiring other furniture manufacturers and associated businesses. In relation to this, the president is curious about accounting methods for groups of companies. Answer briefly the following four questions the president has asked:

1. "Why does a subsidiary have to be consolidated with the parent's accounts?"
2. "Why doesn't consolidating a newly acquired subsidiary affect consolidated retained earnings? (After all, the subsidiary has retained earnings too.)"
3. "Since it is the sum of more than one company, won't a consolidated balance sheet present a stronger financial picture than the parent's unconsolidated balance sheet does?"
4. "What does 'Goodwill on consolidation' on the consolidated balance sheet mean?"

PROBLEM 9.34
(CHALLENGING)
Effects of pension accounting on the future

Here's a problem. Suppose companies in general did not accrue enough pension liabilities to account fully for their obligations to employees, warranty liabilities to account for their obligations to customers, etc. There are persistent worries about this in these times of aging baby boomers and less complacent consumers. A commentator said, "The real costs of company obligations are not being recognized in balance sheets and so cash is being taken out of the hands of future generations of employees and consumers."

Explain how the alleged failure to accrue enough for obligations like pensions and warranties could take cash out of the hands of future generations.

**PROBLEM 9.35
(CHALLENGING)
Accounting for executive stock options**

Stock options offered to executives by their companies are not accounted for under GAAP until the executives exercise them, and then only as new share capital. This is what happens. The company promises the executive say 100,000 shares at a price of $5.00. The current share price is $4.00. The company hopes that the executive will work hard to help get the share price up. The executive's compensation does not have as much cash salary as it might have, because the executive and the company consider the stock option to be part of the pay the executive will eventually earn. Suppose the executive does exercise the options some years later when the share price is $12.00. The only record in the company's financial statements is the issue of new shares for a total share capital inflow of $500,000, even though the executive has received shares worth $1,200,000, paying $500,000 and so getting a benefit of $700,000. There is no compensation expense recorded, either for $1,200,000 or $700,000, yet clearly the executive and the company knew about it all.

There have been suggestions that this lack of accounting for the compensation included in stock options seriously understates companies' expenses and overstates their income. Why not, say critics, debit compensation expense and credit share capital for the amount of value given to the executive?

Discuss this issue. Do you think accounting practices for stock options should be changed, and if so, how would you change them?

**PROBLEM 9.36
(CHALLENGING)
Prepare a full set of statements under GAAP**

Macro Ltd. services personal computers. Don Debit, the company's accountant, has compiled the following list of balances in the company's accounts at January 31, 2002, the fiscal year-end.

Macro Ltd. List of Account Balances, January 31, 2002	
Accounts payable	$ 40,000
Accounts receivable	48,000
Accumulated depreciation — building	6,000
Bank loan	100,000
Building	86,000
Cash	30,000
Depreciation on building for the year	6,000
Dividends declared	20,000
Dividends payable	5,000
General expenses	170,000
Investments	16,000
Income tax expense	3,000
Interest on bank loan for the year	12,000
Land	50,000
Service fee revenues	213,000
Share capital	15,000
Shareholders' loan	60,000
Repair supplies used during year	38,000
Retained earnings	25,000
Gain on sale of plant and equipment	15,000

Here is additional information about some of these figures:

1. Accounts payable will be paid in February 2002 except for $5,000, which will be paid February 1, 2003.
2. Accounts receivable will be collected in February or March 2002.
3. The bank loan is payable in yearly payments of $20,000, which are to be made December 31 of each year for the next five years. Interest on the loan has been paid up to January 31, 2002.
4. A dividend of $20,000 was declared on January 31, 2002, and $15,000 was paid to the shareholders on the same day. The balance will be paid on December 31, 2002.
5. "Investments" were purchased just before the year-end and consist of the following:

8% term deposits, due in April 2002	$ 4,000
Investment in shares of ABC Ltd.	12,000
	$16,000

   The shares of ABC Ltd. are not publicly traded, so there is no ready market for them. Macro Ltd. owns 3% of ABC Ltd.'s shares.
6. The shareholders' loan is due on demand, but no repayment is expected to be made in the upcoming year. This loan is unsecured.
7. The land and building are recorded at estimated market value, based on an appraisal done on January 2, 2002. The land had cost $40,000; the building had cost $96,000.
8. The bank loan is secured by a first mortgage on the land and building.
9. Of the cash, $5,000 is held in trust, as part of a recent sales agreement with a customer.
10. "General expenses" includes $50,000 of a bad debt expense due to the bankruptcy of a major customer during the year.
11. "Income tax expense" includes $1,000 of tax related to the sale of plant and equipment during the year, future tax of $4,000, and a claim for a tax refund of $2,000. The refund claim is included in accounts receivable.
12. "Service fee revenues" includes $20,000 of revenue that should have been recorded in the prior year.
13. It turns out that retained earnings includes a future income tax liability of $6,000 ($2,000 from the beginning of the year and $4,000 from item 11 above). Don didn't know where to put it so he just included it in retained earnings.

Prepare a properly classified balance sheet, income statement, and statement of retained earnings from the above information for the year ended January 31, 2002, as well as any notes to the financial statements that you feel are necessary to satisfy user needs and disclosure requirements under GAAP. If it is helpful, assume a prospective creditor such as a bank will use the financial statements.

**PROBLEM 9.37
(CHALLENGING)
Adequacy of GAAP
for financial
instruments**

This chapter has had several topics in which controversy exists over the way GAAP do or do not deal with modern financial activities. There is the problem of financing that is not clearly either debt or equity. There is the attempt to make estimates of future income tax payments, which may be made only in the distant future. There is the problem of pooling of interests merger accounting possibly providing inappropriate measures and managerial incentives for merger activity. A major ongoing problem is in accounting for financial instruments. Or perhaps it would be better to say "lack of accounting for financial instruments" because while GAAP require considerable disclosure about such instruments, there is little progress on accounting for them by building them, and associated gains and losses, into the financial accounting numbers. Is disclosure enough? Should "mark to market" accounting be required, so that the accounts reflect the kinds of calculations that financial managers make when making hedging, interest rate swap, and other financial arrangements?

Discuss the question of whether financial accounting is now too far removed from the way modern financial arrangements are made, and if so, what might be done about it. Would it be reasonable to change the accounting every time an innovative financial instrument was developed? Or is the problem deeper, involving a fundamental problem with financial accounting's historical cost base that is most apparent when financial instruments and financial arrangements are, in general, considered?

PROBLEM 9.38 (CHALLENGING) Goodwill and consolidated net income

Northern Supermarkets Inc. is increasing the vertical integration of its operations by buying out suppliers. On July 1, 2001, Northern purchased 70% of the common shares of Green Acres Farms, an Alabama supplier of asparagus, celery, and other produce. Green Acres is itself a bit of a conglomerate because it has extensive landholdings in Atlanta and Dallas, and owns dairies in Wisconsin and Ontario.

On July 1, 2001, Green Acres's balance sheet showed a net book value of $112,800,000. The aggregate net fair value of individual assets and liabilities was $161,000,000 as at that date. Northern paid $154,000,000 ($25,000,000 cash, the rest newly issued shares of Northern) for its investment in Green Acres.

It is now March 31, 2002, the end of Northern's fiscal year. For Northern, it has been a good year. Green Acres has also done well, reporting a net income of $33,000,000 during the nine months ended March 31, 2002, and declaring $15,000,000 in dividends during that period. On a nonconsolidated basis, Northern's investment in Green Acres stood at $166,600,000 at March 31, 2002, and its net income for the year was $74,200,000.

1. What accounting method is Northern using for its investment in Green Acres? How can you tell?
2. Two figures that may appear on the consolidated balance sheet of Northern and Green Acres are "Goodwill arising on consolidation" and "Minority interest liability." Why are the fair values of Green Acres's individual assets relevant for calculating the former but not the latter?
3. Calculate consolidated net income for the year ended March 31, 2002, as well as you can with the data provided.

PROBLEM 9.39 (CHALLENGING) Accounting effects of a business acquisition

Suppose that, to spread its business risk, a major brewing company decides to buy into the retail furniture business by acquiring a controlling interest in a national chain that sells furniture, appliances, and related goods at discount prices. Changing its usual policy of 100% ownership, the brewer acquires a 60% voting interest. On January 1, 2002, the brewer pays $54,000,000 cash for 60% of the chain's voting shares. At that date, the chain's balance sheet shows:

Cash	$ 2,000,000	Demand bank loan	$14,000,000
Other current assets	53,000,000	Other current liab.	26,000,000
Noncurrent assets	38,000,000	Noncurrent liab.	20,000,000
Less accum. amort.	(6,000,000)	Shareholders' equity	27,000,000
	$87,000,000		$87,000,000

The brewer's evaluation is that the fair values at January 1, 2002, are the same as the book value for all of the chain's assets and liabilities except land; it is on the chain's books at a cost of $4,000,000, but the brewer's evaluation is that its fair value is $7,000,000 at January 1, 2002.

The furniture chain is expected to report a substantial net income for the four months, January 1, 2002, to April 30, 2002 (the brewer's year-end), so the brewery managers are pleased with their decision to get into the furniture retailing business.

1. The brewer owns more than 50% of the furniture chain, so it should be consolidated with the brewer's other companies in preparing financial statements. But the chain is quite different from the brewer's other activities, so would it make sense to add apples in with oranges? Comment on this question.

2. Calculate the consolidated goodwill (if any) arising as at January 1, 2002, from the purchase of the furniture chain.

3. Evaluate each of the following items, stating assumptions or reasons if you wish. If the furniture chain were consolidated with the brewer as of January 1, 2002, what would happen on *that date* to:

	Would Go Up	Would Go Down	No Effect	Not Possible to Tell
a. Consolidated total assets				
b. Consolidated shareholders' equity				
c. Consolidated net income since May 1, 2001				

4. Looking ahead to the consolidated income for the year ended April 30, 2002, will the furniture chain's expected substantial net income contribute significantly to the brewer's consolidated net income? Comment on this question.

PROBLEM 9.40 (CHALLENGING) Accounting for merger versus acquisition

Winnipeg Merchandisers Ltd. and Red River Stores Ltd. are considering some form of business combination. Three alternatives are being studied: a full merger, accomplished by an exchange of shares; purchase of all the voting shares of Red River by Winnipeg; and purchase of 75% of the voting shares of Red River by Winnipeg. Management of the two companies wants to know what the combined company's consolidated balance sheet would look like, based on their present financial information. (The final figures will depend on the actual date of the combination.) Here are the two companies' balance sheets as at a recent date:

	Winnipeg Book Values	Red River Book Values	Red River Fair Values
Assets			
Current assets	$1,124,645	$1,005,789	$1,104,311
Noncurrent assets	3,678,872	2,890,003	3,040,722
Liabilities and Equity			
Current liabilities	1,076,554	879,321	899,321
Shareholders' equity	3,726,963	3,016,471	

If there is a merger, a new company, Winnipeg–Red River, will issue one share in itself in return for each share in either Winnipeg or Red River. If Winnipeg purchases all of Red River's voting shares, it is willing to pay $3,400,000, which it will finance by borrowing against the values of its and Red River's assets. If Winnipeg purchases only 75% of the voting shares, it is willing to pay only $2,400,000, because the remaining block of 25% would be held by a single person who might interfere with Winnipeg's plans for the combined company. If there is a merger, that person plans to sell all shares owned and move to another city.

1. Present the consolidated balance sheet under each of the three combinations being considered:
   a. Full merger.
   b. 100% purchase of Red River by Winnipeg.
   c. 75% purchase of Red River by Winnipeg.
2. Write a brief report to the managements of the two companies, explaining carefully, and avoiding accounting jargon:
   a. Specifically, what are the differences in the consolidated balance sheets under the three combinations and why do those differences exist; and
   b. Which of the three balance sheets, in your opinion, would be the strongest.

**CASE 9A
Are GAAP too complex for small businesses?**

The article "Standards with a Differential" below suggests that accounting standards (and by implication the GAAP to which they are central) are becoming so voluminous and complex that they are not serving the needs of smaller businesses (called Small Business Enterprises, SBEs, in the article). Discuss the article's points with particular attention to the accounting principles outlined in this chapter, plus any other examples of complexity you may wish to include, such as those for inventories, amortization, or intangible assets in Chapter 9. Have GAAP become too complex? If so, is that true for every business, or just for SBEs? If true for SBEs, should there be differential accounting standards for them, or would using different accounting principles according to the size of the company make financial accounting even more difficult for nonaccountants to comprehend and use?

Standards with a differential

Small businesses and their stakeholders really do have unique reporting needs, according to a new CICA report

By Andrée Lavigne

The recent adoption of complex accounting standards (particularly those found in Section 3860 of the *CICA Handbook—Accounting*, "Financial instruments—disclosure and presentation") brought the issue of financial reporting by small business enterprises (SBEs) back into the spotlight. Rather than address the issue on a piecemeal basis, the CICA Accounting Standards Board (AcSB) commissioned a research project to examine how the financial information needs of providers of capital to SBEs might be more effectively met, and the degree to which reporting in accordance with generally accepted accounting principles (GAAP) could be modified to meet those needs. The Study Group on Financial Reporting by Small Business Enterprises, chaired by Marc Patadis, FCA, former chair of CICA, was established to undertake this project.

For financial reporting purposes, the study group defined SBEs as "entities other than public enterprises, cooperative organizations, pension plans and financial institutions." After reviewing the available literature, communicating with standard-setting bodies that had recently studied this issue and instituting a consultation process involving users of SBE financial reports and practitioners, the study group made a number of recommendations for the AcSB to consider. These are included in the recently published CICA research report, *Financial Reporting by Small Business Enterprises*.

Users of SBE financial statements are normally few in number, consisting mainly of bankers, owner / managers, tax authorities and, in certain instances, venture capital providers. SBEs prepare GAAP financial statements primarily to meet their bankers' needs. And although these needs have changed in recent years, financial statements still play a major role in bankers' decisions concerning large loans where the entity's cash flows will provide for repayment. According to the practitioners consulted by the study group, some of the information required under GAAP is clearly of little relevance to SBEs.

One defining characteristic of SBEs is that they are generally not active on financial markets. What's more, users of SBE financial statements can usually obtain additional information if they wish. As a result, the information needs of such users are less significant than those of financial market investors and their advisers with respect to an entity's ability to provide a return on investment or stewardship responsibility.

Differential reporting within GAAP

The study group assessed the merits and deficiencies of the following approaches for SBE financial reporting:
- A different set of GAAP for SBEs
- Financial statements prepared in accordance with an appropriate basis of accounting other than GAAP to meet the needs of identified intended users
- General-purpose financial statements prepared in accordance with a basis of accounting other than GAAP—for example, the cash basis or tax basis of accounting
- A new type of financial report focussing more on management decisions
- A single set of GAAP with "differential" rules for SBEs

The findings of the consultation process demonstrate that a separate set of accounting standards for SBEs is not desirable. In fact, of all the options examined by the study group, only one was acceptable to the SBE financial reporting stakeholders consulted: the adoption of "differential" reporting within GAAP. In short, stakeholders believe SBE financial statements must be prepared in accordance with a set of standards governing all Canadian enterprises—that is, GAAP—in order to ensure the comparability and credibility of SBE financial statements. During the consultation process, however, stakeholders also indicated that these standards should be sufficiently flexible to ensure that SBEs are not subjected to requirements that do not meet the needs of their financial statement users.

In the study group's opinion, some accounting standards are intended primarily to meet the needs of public enterprises; with the harmonization of accounting standards, this tendency could intensify in the future. The financial reporting needs of SBEs should therefore be differentiated from those of other enterprises. The study group recommends that a "differential" accounting principle be established within GAAP. According to this principle, accounting standards governing SBEs should differ from accounting standards applicable to other enterprises when they do not meet SBE financial reporting needs or when the cost of applying the standards would outweigh their potential benefits. Normally, these differences should pertain only to disclosure and presentation standards. It is not impossible, however, that some future recognition or measurement standards will not meet the needs of SBEs or the cost / benefit effectiveness test. The advisability of establishing differential recognition or measurement standards will have to be examined in each case.

The study group also recommends that Section 1000, "Financial statement concepts," recognize that information needs and cost / benefit effectiveness may differ if the reporting entity is an SBE. The group hopes such recognition will help the AcSB (1) consider these differences when developing accounting standards and (2) establish differential standards whenever accounting standards do not meet SBE financial reporting needs.

Specific accounting standards

Having specified the nature and scope of the SBE financial reporting problem, the study group then focussed on *Handbook* accounting recommendations that cause serious problems for SBEs. The various parties who were consulted, especially practitioners, indicated that Section 3860, "Financial instruments—disclosure and presentation," was their primary concern. Some of the requirements under this standard do not seem to take into account the characteristics of SBE ownership or the substance of SBE financial instruments. The study group also believes that some information required under this standard is unlikely to have an effect on the decisions of SBE financial statement users. As a result, the group recommends that the requirements relating to the classification of a financial instrument as a liability or as an equity should not apply to SBEs.

The study group recommends that, except for their derivative financial instruments, SBEs should not be required to make disclosures about the fair value of financial instruments, about financial assets carried at an amount in excess of fair value, or about interest rate risk. Other information—such as the respecting the terms and conditions of recognized and unrecognized financial instruments, offsetting a financial asset and a financial liability, and credit risk—is useful and should continue to be disclosed in SBE financial statements. Moreover, SBEs should disclose appropriate information concerning the recognized and unrecognized derivative financial instruments they use.

The study group also proposes recommendations to simplify SBE disclosure requirements for discontinued operations, share capital, the relationship between transacting parties in a related-party transaction context, long-term debt with covenant violations and goodwill.

Some standards are not only problematic for SBEs; as the study group noted, they seem to cause problems for all enterprises. The group therefore recommends clarifying the scope of standards for measurement uncertainty and impaired loans and reviewing the conditions for determining the substance of leases. For standards on related-party transactions, the study group proposes that no independent evidence be required to support the exchange amount when a transaction results in unrelated parties acquiring or relinquishing control over the item transferred or service benefit provided.

The parties consulted noted that accounting standards are becoming increasingly complex and voluminous. The study group recommends that implementation guides for SBEs be prepared under the ACSB's supervision to help these enterprises understand and apply complex new accounting standards (such as those for income taxes and employees' future benefits).

Standard-setting process

The study group was asked to suggest a process the AcSB could institute to ensure that the views of SBEs are voiced, recognized and appropriately addressed. It recommends establishing a consultative committee that would report to the AcSB and provide it with timely advice on SBE financial reporting needs and on the impact that proposed accounting standards would have on these enterprises.

In addition, the study group believes that some of the members of the AcSB will need to have extensive experience with SBEs if the board as a whole is to understand their financial reporting needs. The study group also believes the proposed Accounting Standards Oversight Council should include members capable of representing SBE financial reporting needs.

Andrée Lavigne, CA, is a principal in the CICA's Research Studies department.

Technical Editor: Robert T. Rutherford, FCA, Vice-president, Studies & Standards, CICA

Reprinted from *CA Magazine* (pp. 49–50), October 1999, by Andrée Lavigne.

CASE 9B
Discuss the role of accounting standards in affecting business operations

Two articles below, "U.S. firms have to adapt to big accounting change" and "New accounting rules would make mergers a little less attractive," describe proposed changes in accounting for corporate groups that would require the "purchase method" be used for business combinations and pretty much eliminate the "pooling of interests" method. The standards changes outlined in the articles are also being considered in Canada, though in this country standards have been much less permissive regarding "pooling of interests" accounting so the "problem" is not as large, and it would not take as much change in standards to deal with it.

Without getting into the specifics of the methods, the articles raise some interesting issues, including:

- Financial accounting is supposed to report on results. Is it appropriate to change the accounting if that changes the way businesses operate, so that accounting becomes part of the results, instead of being an objective measure?

- On the other hand, if "permissive" accounting has prompted businesses to merge in order to make their accounting numbers look better, isn't accounting already part of the problem, and shouldn't it be fixed?

- This book has frequently drawn attention to managerial motivations for or against various accounting methods, so is the merger accounting situation any surprise? Can or should anything be done about this feature of human nature?

- Would reducing the amount of goodwill produced in purchase method accounting by, in effect, transferring some of it to other intangible assets produce any real improvement in the way companies work out the value of other companies they acquire or merge with?

- What about the growing popularity of indicating cash flow per share? Does that indicate that accrual accounting, including and beyond accounting for corporate groups, is already in trouble?

U.S. firms have to adapt to big accounting change
PROFITABILITY MEASURE
In the short term, move will slow merger activity
BY KOPIN TAN

NEW YORK • With pooling-of-interests accounting poised to disappear from the world of mergers and acquisitions, investment bankers say consolidating companies will go through a period of adjustment before getting comfortable with the soon to be mandated purchase accounting methods.

In addition to the expected rash of mergers trying to beat the deadline, the demise of pooling of interests is expected to shift Wall Street's measure of a merged entity's profitability to cash flow-based earnings from net income.

The Financial Accounting Standards Board—the arbiter of U.S. accounting rules—has voted to end pooling-of-interests accounting.

The popular treatment allows merging companies to combine balance sheets and avoid future earnings charges from goodwill—the difference between the purchase price and fair market value of the acquired assets.

If the FASB adopts the proposed change after a three- to four-month comment period, deals completed after Jan. 1, 2001, will have to adopt purchase accounting, under which goodwill has to be written off over time and which has the unpopular effect of lowering earnings.

The immediate impact, bankers say, will be a temporary dampening of merger activity, particularly in industries such as banking and technology where stock mergers are common and where companies are followed on a price-earnings basis.

"The market is still very focused on earnings, and historically, companies have forgone transactions when they did not qualify for pooling-of-interest accounting," said Mark McDade, a partner at Pricewaterhouse Coopers. "Also, this could significantly affect pricing, exerting downward pressure on pricing of transactions."

In the long run, mergers driven by

strategic synergies will still get done; management can protect their profit and loss reports for only so long, industry observers say, before competition and market forces prompt the need to grow through acquisitions.

Bankers said the market will eventually adjust to using cash flow-based multiples and cash flow-based earnings per share to evaluate a merged company's performance.

"There is now a catalyst for focussing on cash earnings," says Robert Willens, a Lehman Brothers managing director and tax and accounting specialist. "How long the [dampening in M&A activity] lasts will depend on how quickly the concept of cash earnings gets accepted by the community."

Already, cash earnings—which do not include goodwill charges and hence can make financial performance look better—have been treated with prominence by a growing number of companies.

"In some ways, companies are adopting a two-tiered system, especially companies that have been moving toward purchase accounting," says Mark Alpert, an analyst at BT Alex. Brown.

So far this year, a growing list of companies have featured some form of cash-based earnings in reporting performance, including RJR Nabisco Holdings Corp., USA Networks Inc., Bank Rhode Island, SLM Holding Corp., Aurora Foods Inc., Household International Inc., Sovereign Bancorp. Inc., and Carolina First Corp. The practice is expected to continue to catch on.

"If companies inform the market of their cash EPS, and analysts and investors start to focus on that, and firms like First Call start to track that, it will become the important figure," says Rick Escherich, a J.P. Morgan managing director.

In fact, First Call has recently indicated it will begin tracking cash flow earnings per share figures for a group of Internet companies.

Industry observers say companies include cash-based earnings in their reports to give a better—or alternative—representation of their performance.

Also, in many cases, these companies feel that the positive value of their acquisitions may not be easily reflected and reduced to a write-off over a fixed period of time.

For these companies, what's really important is the ability to generate cash—a fact they want investors and market observers to pay at least equal attention to.

Also, as consolidating companies adjust to the elimination of pooling, the market may see some early movers seizing the opportunity to pursue coveted targets—at a time when there is less chance of a third party disrupting the deal.

"These early movers are taking on the risk of the market incorrectly valuing their merger to be able to align with the preferred partner," Mr. Escherich says.

Meanwhile, the FASB still has to sift through public comments over the next few months. The board is expected to announce next month whether it will preserve the current 40-year write-off period for goodwill or reduce that by half or more.

FASB could also spring a surprise by allowing a one-time write-off for a portion of the acquired goodwill.

"You may see FASB come up with an attractive proposal like that," Mr. Willens says, adding the board is unlikely unceremoniously to take away something like pooling-of-interests accounting without compensating for it.

Dow Jones

Reprinted from *National Post* (p. D4), 6 May 1999, by Kopin Tan.

New accounting rules would make mergers a little less attractive

OUTLAW "POOLING OF INTERESTS"

Firms would have to write off goodwill and other intangibles.

BY RICHARD WATERS

NEW YORK • U.S. accounting regulators are expected to release draft rules today that will outlaw a form of accounting that helped fuel the 1990s takeover boom.

The plan is likely to lead to a collision between the Financial Accounting Standards Board and acquisitive companies that have benefited from an accounting regime more lax than those in other major developed countries.

Under the proposal, "pooling of interests" accounting would be banned, ending a technique used in virtually all big business combinations in the United States during a record period of mergers and acquisitions.

The FASB floated its plan informally last December, drawing fire from companies and investment bankers. The formal proposal, contained in an exposure draft due to be released today, would be open to comment for three months, followed by public hearings.

The technique to be banned, called "merger accounting" in other countries, makes it possible for firms in takeovers to avoid reporting goodwill, the difference between the value of tangible assets they buy and the total price they pay on their balance sheets after a deal.

That benefits acquirers, since they would have had to write off goodwill against profits in future years, a move that depresses reported earnings and eats into the all-important earnings per share figure used on Wall Street as the yardstick for a company's performance.

The FASB plan would force all companies to treat business combinations as purchases rather than mergers. This would require them to account for the full value of their acquisitions on their balance sheets, either by showing goodwill or by putting a value on intangible assets such as brands or patents.

Investment bankers complain this would discourage some companies from undertaking acquisitions, since they would be at an accounting disadvantage to companies that do not have goodwill or other intangibles that have to be written off against profits.

Accounting rulemakers claim the new regulations should not hamper corporate activity.

"If a deal makes good economic sense, the accounting shouldn't make any difference," a FASB official said.

U.S. companies that do not qualify for "pooling of interests" accounting have to write off goodwill over a period of 40 years. This would be halved.

However, the plan would also encourage companies to show more intangible assets, a move that would reduce the amount of goodwill. The board will suggest up to 100 potential intangible assets, from airport landing slots to newspaper mastheads, said an official.

Financial Times

Reprinted from *Financial Post*, 8 September 1999.

NOTES

1. C. Byrd, I. Chen, and H. Chapman, *Financial Reporting in Canada 1999* (Toronto: Canadian Institute of Chartered Accountants, 1999), 388–91.
2. "Note M," IBM, 1999 Annual Report. On-line, World Wide Web, available from www.ibm.com.
3. C. Byrd, 391.
4. Ibid., 410.
5. Ibid., 330.
6. Ibid., 330.
7. Ibid., 349.
8. Suncor Energy Inc. 1999 Annual Report, 60.
9. C. Byrd, 508.
10. CAE, 2000 Annual Report, 32.
11. CAE, 2000 Annual Report, 36.
12. C. Byrd, 238.

Financial Accounting Analysis Wrap-Up

PART 4

CHAPTER

C 10   Financial Accounting Analysis

- Chapter 10 provides analysis relevant to preparing and using financial accounting information: financial statement analysis (focusing on the illustrative case of CAE Inc., made familiar by various examples in earlier chapters and so brought together in this chapter), "present value" analysis of the time value of money, and "what if" or "effects" analysis used to help managers understand the effects of accounting changes or various financial and other business deals.

10

CHAPTER

Financial Accounting Analysis

10.1   Chapter Overview

TO THE READER: This chapter is written to be used flexibly. Its three parts (sections 10.2–10.6, section 10.7, and sections 10.8–10.9) may be studied in any order, any time after Chapter 4 is covered.

This chapter is about various useful kinds of analysis.

This final chapter provides tools for analysis and evaluation of financial position and performance. The main focus (sections 10.2–10.6) is on ratio analysis, using ratios already illustrated and additional ones that expand and integrate the analysis, plus cash flow analysis, first encountered in Chapter 4. It is all based on the real CAE financial statements for March 31, 2000, used earlier in the book, so that this chapter can pull the ideas about financial statement analysis together. Section 10.7 covers basic present value analysis of cash flows. The chapter concludes (sections 10.8–10.9) by illustrating useful "what-if" (effects) analysis, including a framework for understanding how events and policies affect the financial statements.

Analysis is an essential skill for both accountants and nonaccountants.

For those of you who will not become accountants, this chapter will help you develop essential analytical skills. No matter where your career takes you, or what business-oriented courses you take from here, the ability to analyze a company's financial statements and determine how well the company is performing is highly valuable. If you *do* become an accountant, this chapter helps you develop the kind of analytical ability that the world expects accountants to have.

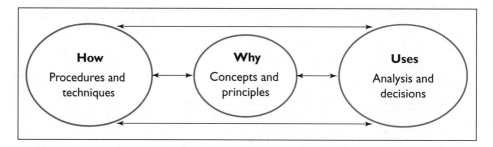

This chapter is about using financial information, so its emphasis is on the uses portion of the diagram. There are procedures and concepts behind using the information, so this is what you will learn in this chapter:

- *Procedures and techniques:* How to develop the information needed for analysis and the techniques involved in preparing good analyses.

- *Concepts and principles:* The conceptual basis of the three kinds of analysis in this chapter: ratios, present value, and effects analyses.

- *Analysis and decisions:* How to interpret the results of the ratio and other calculations and connect those to business decisions.

Accountant or not, you'll be pleased at how much you know about corporate performance by the time you have worked through the chapter's extensive examples and explanations.

10.2   INVESTMENT AND RELATIVE RETURN

Investment and Relative Return

An investment forgoes current consumption in order to provide future consumption.

A fundamental economic assumption is that wealth, or capital, has value because it can be used for consumption, to get "all the ... things your little heart pines for," as Fats Waller sang. If our wealth is used up on current consumption, there'll be no consumption next period, so generally we are willing to forgo some current consumption by investing some of our wealth in order to obtain consumption in the future. We hope that the investment will earn a return that we can consume in the future.

This takes us to the business concept that an investment is made to earn a return. How much of a return? Whether the return is satisfactory depends on the size of the investment required to earn it. For example, you might be pleased with a $1,000 annual return if you had invested $2,000, but horrified if you had invested $2,000,000. One way to relate the two components is via return on investment (ROI), in which the return is the numerator and the initial investment is the denominator:

$$\text{Relative return (return on investment)} = \frac{\text{Return}}{\text{Investment}}$$

The concept of ROI requires attention to both the return and the investment.

Later, we will examine relative returns, like return on investment, in more depth. For now, note that we have to have some way of measuring *both* return and investment if we are to be able to calculate (and evaluate) relative return.

Much of financial statement analysis is based on ratios like ROI. Here are some points you should remember about ratios:

- The purpose of a ratio is to produce a scale-free, *relative* measure of a company that can be used to compare to other companies, or to other years for the company. Such a measure is scale-free because both numerator and denominator are measured in the same units (dollars) and are both dependent on the size of the company. A large company will have a larger investment than a small one and should be expected to have a larger return as well, but a ratio like ROI cancels out some of the effects of size and so allows the large and small companies to be compared.

- The ratio will be unreliable as a comparison, or even misleading or useless, unless its numerator is appropriate. This means that the numerator must be properly calculated, as well as suitable for the comparison being made. The word "return" in ROI could be represented by several possible quantities, including net income, cash generated by operations, or interest. The appropriate quantity for the numerator depends on the context of the analysis, as we will see. Also, the role of GAAP and other rules in making figures such as net income meaningful is very important to the conclusions that may be drawn from ratio analysis.

- These same points apply equally to the denominator of the ratio. Additionally, sometimes a doubtful or ambiguous accounting method can create a problem in both the numerator and denominator, bringing the whole ratio into question. An example here is that if a company chooses a revenue recognition method that makes the validity of net income doubtful, that will also make the retained earnings figure doubtful, throwing into question one of the most widely used ROI-type ratios, called return on equity (ROE), which is calculated as net income divided by equity (including retained earnings).

"Net-of-tax" Analysis

Way back in section 1.9, net-of-tax analysis was introduced. Please take a moment and review the Kamble Manufacturing example in that section.

Net-of-tax analysis is a way of quickly estimating the effect on net income, and on ratios that use net income, of changes in revenues, expenses, gains, or losses. If you assume income tax is paid or refunded quickly, you can use it also to estimate effects on operating cash flows. The whole idea is to focus on income statement items that *change*, take out the income tax effect, and so get the effect on net income directly without having to include all the items that do not change. The analysis illustrated by the Kamble Manufacturing example follows this formula:

Net income = (1 − tax rate) × Income before income tax

Here's another example. Suppose Alcatraz Fencing Inc. has one revenue, one expense, and an income tax rate of 35%. You can look at net income as the residual after the income tax has been deducted. But this works just as well for the revenues and expenses. Suppose we recast the income statement as if the revenues and expenses were taxed directly, so that they are shown net of tax and the income tax effect is, therefore, included in them rather than being a separate expense:

	Statement	**Version**
Revenue (net = $1,000 × (1 − 0.35))	$1,000	$650
Expense (net = $700 × (1 − 0.35))	700	455
Income before income tax	$ 300	
Income tax expense (35%)	105	
Net income	$ 195	$195

The effect of a revenue or expense change on net income is the change × (1 − tax rate).

Suppose the president of Alcatraz has a plan to increase revenue by $200 without any increase in the $700 expense. What would that do to net income? Using the above formula, the new net income would be higher by $200 × (1 − 0.35) = $130, and so would be $325 ($195 + $130). There is no need to recalculate the whole income statement. (If you are doubtful, you can always do the analysis the longer way, by recalculating the income statement: The new revenue is $1,200, the expenses are still $700, so income before income tax is now $500. New income tax expense at 35% is $175, and so new net income is $325. Same answer, but longer, particularly for real companies that have many revenues and expenses.)

Interest and other expenses cost less than they seem because they reduce income tax.

Another net-of-tax example, which will be important for some of the ratio analyses in this chapter, concerns interest expense. Suppose $60 of Alcatraz's expense was interest and we wanted to know what the company's net income would be *prior* to considering the interest (as if it had no debt). The answer is that if the interest expense were not present, the net income would go up, but not by $60, because *deducting the interest expense saves income tax*. The net income would rise by $60 × (1 − 0.35) = $39. Interest really costs the company only $39, because it brings a tax saving, as does any tax deductible expense. (Again, we can calculate the net income effect the long way. Revenue is still $1,000, expense is now $640 ($700 − $60 interest), so new income before income tax is $360, new income tax expense is $126, and new net income is $234, which is $39 higher than the original $195.)

(H)OW'S YOUR UNDERSTANDING?

Here are two questions you should be able to answer, based on what you have just read:

1. The president of a company is thinking about changing the company's method of accounting for insurance expense, and wants to know what the effect of the policy will be on net income. Explain why all you need to know to estimate the effect is the amount of the expense under the present and proposed methods and the company's income tax rate.

2. A Canadian railway company had revenues of $10.5 billion in a recent year. Its income tax rate was 37%. If its revenues increased by 2%, with no effect on expenses other than income tax, what would be the effect on net income for that year? (Revenue effect = 2% × $10.5 billion = $210.0 million more revenue. Net income effect = $210 (1 − 0.37) = $132.3 million higher.)

10.3   INTRODUCTION TO FINANCIAL STATEMENT ANALYSIS

Financial Evaluation Is Not Just Calculation

Financial statement analysis is knowledge-based judgment, not just calculation.

The purpose of financial statement analysis is to use the statements to evaluate an enterprise's financial performance and position. Therefore, the value of the analysis depends on the contents of the financial statements. When you have completed sections 10.2–10.6, you will be able to take a set of financial statements of pretty well any company and make an evaluation of its performance and prospects. Such an evaluation *is not just a calculation*, it is a *judgment* based on the calculations that make sense for that company and based on substantial knowledge of the company. The more you know about a company, its business, its management, *and* its accounting, the more useful and credible your analysis will be.

There are many sources and kinds of financial statement analysis.

You may have noticed that the preceding paragraph used the word "company." Analytical techniques for governments and not-for-profit organizations are more specialized than those illustrated for this book's examples, though many of the ratios and other techniques are useful there too. Some companies, such as banks and insurance companies, also have sufficiently specialized financial statements and business operations that they require particular analytical techniques in addition to, or instead of, those illustrated in this book. Other methods of analysis can always be developed, in order to make the analysis fit the decision-making (use) objective of the user. Therefore, *this chapter is illustrative*: other techniques exist, and new ones are being invented all the time. Banks, on-line investment services, and various brokerages offer some analysis on their Web pages; the financial pages of newspapers like *The Globe and Mail, National Post,* and *The Wall Street Journal* contain analyses of companies pretty well daily; and magazines like *Canadian Business, Fortune,* and *Business Week* publish frequent comparisons of companies' performance, often of hundreds of companies at a time, using various financial statement numbers and ratios. When you use any of these, pay attention to how various numbers and ratios are defined, because these can vary significantly.

The financial statements should be analyzed given all the other available information.

Financial accounting information is not used in a vacuum, but is part of a vast array of information available to investors, creditors, managers, and others. The use of this information depends on its quality, such as whether the financial statements have been carefully prepared and are comparable to other companies' statements. Use is also affected by the availability of other sources of information that may contain all or part of what is in the financial statements. As is noted in the coverage of stock markets in Chapter 5, it is difficult to "beat the market" using financial statement information, because the statements reflect business events people already know something about and because there are many other people, all with their own sources of information, also trying to analyze what is going on and taking action on the basis of their analyses. Financial accounting information is part of a network of information; it doesn't stand alone. Consistent with this, various analytical techniques, though explained and illustrated separately in this chapter, work best together to tell an overall story. This is illustrated also.

Doing Intelligent Analysis

Ratios are indicators, given meaning by the analyst's understanding of the company.

Much of financial analysis involves ratios, which are *boiled-down summaries* of the financial statements. Ratios have little meaning on their own: they are merely *indicators*, which can be interpreted and used meaningfully only with a good understanding of the company and the accounting policies used in preparing the financial statements. The scale-free nature of a ratio means that it allows comparisons over certain periods of time, among companies of different sizes, and with other indicators such as interest rates or share prices. But it also can be tempting to think that when you have calculated a ratio, you have something meaningful in itself. While there is some fundamental meaning in each ratio, as we will see, what the comparisons mean to the analyst's decision must be added by the analyst, using knowledge and information beyond the ratios.

To do an intelligent and useful financial statement analysis, you should do the following:

The analysis depends on the decision or evaluation to be made from it.

a. Get a clear understanding of the decision or evaluation to which the analysis will contribute, who the decision maker is, and what assistance he or she requires. Helping an investor decide whether to make a long-term investment in shares requires a different set of evaluations than helping a bank manager decide whether to make a short-term secured loan. The two analyses share an interest in the enterprise's viability, economic prospects, and management quality, but the first implies an orientation to earnings performance, stock market behaviour, and investing activity by the enterprise, whereas the second is more concerned with ability to pay, quality of assets, and debt structure.

b. Learn about the enterprise, its circumstances, and its plans. This is essential in any real analysis: don't be misled by the more limited information given for the examples in this book. The annual report's Management Discussion and Analysis (MD&A) section and the notes to the financial statements will help you learn about the enterprise. Circumstances may make a big difference: for example, good performance for a new company in a troubled industry may be unsatisfactory for an established company in a prosperous industry

c. Calculate the ratios, trends, and other figures that apply to *your specific problem*. Don't calculate indiscriminately. The examples in this chapter show you how to calculate many ratios and other comparisons, but not all are relevant to every situation.

d. Find whatever comparative information you can to provide a frame of reference for your analysis. Industry data, reports by other analysts, results for similar companies or the same company in other years, and other such information is often plentiful.

e. Use the MD&A and other explanatory sections of the annual report to deepen the insight into performance and strategy that your analysis provides.

A useful analysis is focused, selective, informed, and organized.

f. Focus on the analytical results that are most significant to the decision maker's circumstances and integrate and organize the analysis so that it will be of most help to the decision maker.

There are many sources of information about companies to help you become knowledgeable about them and be able to place your analysis in context. As you might expect, there is more information about large companies than small ones and more about public companies (those whose shares and other securities are listed on stock exchanges) than about private ones (those that are closely held by a few owners). Companies will often send you their annual reports and other information about them, and many libraries have extensive sources of company, industry, and other economic information, much of it on computer-readable databases. Consult your university or public library, because new databases and other information products are coming out continuously.

The Web is increasingly important as a source of financial information: many companies have informative Web sites, as pointed out earlier, and there are numerous services that point you to financial information. Just one example is the U.S. Securities and Exchange Commission's site (www.sec.gov), which links to the SEC's EDGAR database that contains all of the thousands of information filings to the SEC, many by Canadian and other non-U.S. companies. The corresponding site in Canada, maintained by the Canadian Securities Administrators (the provincial securities commissions) in both English and French, is www.sedar.com. With SEDAR, you can select the name of any public company in Canada and get access to its publicly available information. Another example is the research and analysis service offered by on-line brokers—while some of this is offered only to the brokers' customers, much is available to anyone who accesses the brokers' sites. Similarly, business magazines such as *Canadian Business*, *Business Week*, *The Economist*, *Forbes*, and *Fortune* offer on-line information, sometimes for subscribers only. If you are analyzing a company, type the company's name into your Web search engine and you might be surprised at the variety of articles, news releases, analyses, and commentaries that is out there.

As you know, the preparer of financial statements has a choice from among a number of accounting policies on which to base the financial information. You, as the analyst of these statements, may wish to recast them using other policies that you prefer before computing any of the ratios. For example, some analysts deduct intangible assets, such as goodwill, from assets and owners' equity before computing ratios. They reason that because these assets are not physical in nature, some people may doubt their value; deleting them, therefore, may improve comparability with companies that don't have such assets. Sections 10.8–10.9 illustrate how to do "what if" analysis that considers possible changes, including changes to the way the company does its accounting.

The validity of financial analysis based on accounting ratios has been challenged. Among the criticisms are that (1) future plans and expected results, not historical numbers, should be used in computing ratios, especially liquidity ratios; (2) current market values, not historical numbers, should be used for assets, debts, and shareholders' equity in computing performance ratios; and (3) cash flow, not accounting income, should be used in computing performance ratios. Another objection is that because, at least for public companies, stock markets and other capital markets adjust prices of companies' securities as information comes out, ratios based on publicly available information cannot tell you anything the markets have not already incorporated into security prices. While these criticisms are controversial, they are reminders to use ratios with care and intelligence. Useful additional ideas on the issues raised in this section can be found in many accounting and finance texts. Be careful when reading such material: ratio analysis may be made to appear more cut-and-dried than it is, and some nonaccounting authors do not appear to know much about the nature of the accounting information used in the analysis.

Financial Statements and Managers' Performance

One of the main reasons top managers of public companies pay close attention to their companies' financial statements, earnings announcements, and other disclosures is that stock markets and other securities markets respond quickly to information and do so in accordance with the value of that information to the market traders. Markets impose a sort of "discipline" on such corporations and their management. Whatever the managers may hope, the market evaluates the information in accordance with its own views and quickly applies rewards, by bidding companies' stock or bond prices up, or penalties, by bidding them down, regardless of whether management thinks the reward or penalty is justified.

Managers are directly affected by the contents of the financial statements.

The less a company is in the public eye and/or the less it is involved in various securities markets, the less it is disciplined by such markets. However, even private companies are not immune to such discipline because they often compete or cooperate with, or are suppliers to, or customers of, more directly affected companies, and also because even private owners often wish to sell their companies, borrow heavily, or take other action that brings their performance information under scrutiny. (To calculate the value of a private business, it is common to make extensive use of financial statements and of the performance and trends they reveal, for example.) Managers also pay close attention to their companies' financial statement figures because important contracts are based on those, explicitly or indirectly. Many top managers are compensated based on the income shown in the financial statements, many own shares in their companies, and if the company is public, the top managers may be fired if stock market prices decline or fail to rise as the board of directors wishes. Managers' stewardship performance in running the company for the owners is scrutinized by the external auditors, so managers are also faced with justifying what the financial statements show. The MD&A section of the annual report is not covered by the auditors' report, but the auditors do review it to ensure that it is not inconsistent with the story told in the financial statements.

It is hard to determine how much a company's performance is really due to management and how much depends on other factors, such as economic trends, product price changes, union pressure, and even pure good or bad luck. Also, in most companies management is a group, so it is difficult to set one manager's performance apart from the group's. The result is that evaluating a manager's performance (even the president's) with financial statements requires great care and knowledge of the company and its industry—and is always somewhat arbitrary.

The ratios and other computations used in financial statement analysis can easily compound the problem of evaluating the manager. Let's take the example of return on assets. Consider the case of two companies, "A" and "B."

- Company A has assets of $100,000 and net income plus after-tax interest of $20,000, for a 20% return on assets (ROA is a ratio to be explained in section 10.4). Looks great. But the manager is not looking into the future much and so is not keeping the company's assets or maintenance up to date.

- Company B is exactly the same, except that the manager is very aware of the need to stay competitive and look after the assets, and so has spent $10,000 on new assets and $2,000 (after tax) on an improved maintenance program. B's assets are, therefore, $110,000 and its net income plus after-tax interest is $18,000, for a 16% ROA.

A ratio like ROA can make a good manager look worse than a poor manager.

Consequently, A looks better than B: ROA is reduced for B both by a smaller numerator and a larger denominator than A has. You can see that, unless the person doing the financial analysis really understands the situation, the prudent and responsible manager of B will look worse than the neglectful manager of A!

OW'S YOUR UNDERSTANDING?

Here are two questions you should be able to answer, based on what you have just read:

1. How should a person prepare before beginning to analyze a set of financial statements?

2. What are some limitations of financial statement analysis?

10.4   FINANCIAL STATEMENT RATIO ANALYSIS

CAE Inc.: An Example Company

The analyses in this and the next two sections use the March 31, 2000, financial information of CAE Inc., the company you will have become familiar with through use of its financial statements as illustrations in Chapters 2, 3, 4, and elsewhere. CAE is used in this chapter because it is familiar, so you will have some of the knowledge you need to interpret the ratios, and because this chapter's analysis will be able to pull together the various bits of knowledge scattered throughout the earlier chapters' examples. For more information about CAE, and to find out how it has been doing since the year 2000, consult its Web site, www.cae.com, which has lots of financial, strategic, managerial, product, and market information, or go to the SEDAR site www.sedar.com and select CAE. You can also use your search engine to find news reports and other information about the company. (One warning: the site www.caeinc.com is a different company!)

To save you having to dig around in earlier chapters, here are the year 2000 financial statements of CAE Inc. The four statements you used before are included, plus two notes (Notes 4 and 10) that provide supplementary information useful in the analysis to come. (Note 1, mentioned at the top of the Cash Flow Statement, points out that the statement was revised from 1999 to reflect a new *CICA Handbook* standard.) *Please review these statements before you go on.*

CAE Inc.
Consolidated Balance Sheets

As at March 31
(amounts in millions of dollars)

	2000	1999
Assets		
Current assets:		
Cash	$ 163.5	$ 25.6
Short-term investment	71.1	—
Accounts receivable	325.3	266.2
Inventories (note 3)	108.1	121.6
Prepaid expenses	14.5	14.9
Income taxes recoverable	28.6	26.8
	711.1	455.1
Net assets of discontinued operations (note 2)	105.2	147.6
Property, plant and equipment (note 4)	214.8	243.7
Goodwill	144.1	162.5
Other assets (note 5)	49.0	56.3
	$1,224.2	$1,065.2
Liabilities and Shareholders' Equity		
Current liabilities:		
Accounts payable and accrued liabilities	$ 306.7	$ 201.4
Deposits on contracts	219.2	141.1
Long-term debt within one year	0.9	0.9
	526.8	343.4
Long-term debt (note 6)	270.7	296.2
Deferred liabilities	40.6	75.5
Deferred income taxes	6.8	11.8
	844.9	726.9
Shareholders' equity:		
Capital stock (note 8):	122.1	154.2
Retained earnings	272.1	194.2
Currency translation adjustments	(14.9)	(10.1)
	379.3	338.3
	$1,224.2	$1,065.2

Approved by the Board:

D. H. Burney
Director

L. R. Wilson
Director

Exhibit 10-2

CAE Inc. Consolidated Statements of Earnings		
Years Ended March 31 (amounts in millions except per share amounts)	2000	1999
Revenue		
Commercial Simulation and Training	$ 480.2	$352.8
Military Simulation and Controls	384.9	355.7
Forestry Systems	299.2	197.4
	$1,164.3	$905.9
Operating earnings		
Commercial Simulation and Training	$ 82.3	$ 55.9
Military Simulation and Controls	15.4	25.2
Forestry systems	43.8	32.8
Earnings from continuing operations before interest and income taxes	141.5	113.9
Interest expense, net	10.0	9.6
Earnings from continuing operations before income taxes	131.5	104.3
Income taxes (note 9)	40.8	30.6
Earnings from continuing operations	90.7	73.7
Results of discontinued operations (note 2)	7.8	3.6
Net earnings	$ 98.5	$ 77.3
Earnings per share from continuing operations	$ 0.83	$ 0.66
Net earnings per share	$ 0.90	$ 0.70
Average number of shares outstanding	109.5	111.1

Exhibit 10-3

Consolidated Statements of Retained Earnings		
Years Ended March 31 (amounts in millions of dollars)	2000	1999
Retained earnings at beginning of year	$194.2	$134.7
Net earnings	98.5	77.3
Dividends	(20.6)	(17.8)
Retained earnings at end of year	$272.1	$194.2

Exhibit

CAE Inc.		
Consolidated Statements of Cash Flow		
Years ended March 31	**2000**	**1999**
(amounts in millions of dollars)		**(note 1)**
Operating activities		
Earnings from continuing operations	$ 90.7	$ 73.7
Adjustments to reconcile net earnings to cash flows from operating activities:		
Amortization	33.7	28.6
Deferred income taxes	(7.6)	(1.6)
Other	(0.3)	(2.0)
Decrease (increase) in non-cash working capital (note 10)	133.5	(70.3)
Cash provided by continuing operating activities	250.0	28.4
Investing activities		
Proceeds on disposition of business unit (note 2)	52.5	–
Acquisitions (note 15)	–	(111.5)
Short-term investments	(71.1)	–
Capital expenditures	(30.9)	(76.3)
Proceeds from sale and leaseback of assets	35.5	–
Other	(11.4)	(4.1)
Net cash used in continuing investing activities	(25.4)	(191.9)
Financing activities		
Proceeds from (repayments of) long-term debt borrowings	(5.5)	8.7
Dividends paid, net of stock dividends	(20.4)	(17.6)
Purchase of capital stock	(36.3)	–
Other	0.2	(3.5)
Net cash used in continuing financing activities	(62.0)	(12.4)
Net cash used in discontinued operations (note 2)	(21.6)	(8.9)
Effect of foreign exchange rate changes on cash	(3.1)	7.6
Net increase (decrease) in cash	137.9	(177.2)
Cash at beginning of year	25.6	202.8
Cash at end of year	$163.5	$ 25.6

10-5

Exhibit

Note 4 Property, Plant and Equipment

2000	Cost	Accumulated Amortization	Net Book Value
Land	$ 9.9	$ –	$ 9.9
Buildings and improvements	152.9	42.4	110.5
Machinery and equipment	203.2	114.7	88.5
Property under capital leases	10.6	4.7	5.9
	$376.6	$161.8	$214.8

1999	Cost	Accumulated Amortization	Net Book Value
Land	$ 9.9	$ –	$ 9.9
Buildings and improvements	173.6	33.7	139.9
Machinery and equipment	215.6	129.0	86.6
Property under capital leases	12.5	5.2	7.3
	$411.6	$167.9	$243.7

10-6

Exhibit

Note 10 Supplementary Cash Flow Information
Cash provided from (used for) non-cash working capital:

	2000	1999
Accounts receivable	$ (54.6)	$ 8.7
Inventories	9.3	(28.4)
Prepaid expenses	0.3	(9.4)
Income taxes recoverable	10.9	(10.6)
Accounts payable and accrued liabilities	88.4	(70.7)
Deposits on contracts	79.2	40.1
	$133.5	$(70.3)
Net cash paid during the year for		
Income taxes	$ 0.5	$ 16.8
Interest	$ 13.1	$ 12.7

Continue this section only after familiarizing yourself with the CAE financial statements.

To make sure you are familiar with the CAE financial statements and so are ready to start the analysis, answer the following questions:

• What were the company's total assets at March 31, 2000? Was that more or less than 1999?

• What was the total equity of the company at March 31, 2000? What were the specific causes of the change in that since March 31, 1999?

• What was the company's net income for the year ended March 31, 2000? What were the main revenues and expenses that led to this income?

- How much cash was generated by operations for the year ended March 31, 2000? Did the company end up with more or less cash at the end of the year than at the beginning?

- What was accumulated amortization at the end of 2000? At the end of 1999?

- How much did inventory changes contribute to the increases and decreases in noncash working capital used in calculating cash from operations in 2000?

This section focuses on extracting financial statement information and calculating ratios.

Twenty kinds of ratios that could be used to analyze a company's financial performance and position are outlined in the following pages. Each ratio is illustrated by showing how it is calculated from the CAE statements. Some interpretive and comparative comments are made as illustrations, but the main purpose of this section is to show you how to extract the needed information from the statements and figure out the ratios.

Most figures below are given in millions of dollars, as they are in CAE's statements. Ratios are calculated to three decimal places. They could be done to more decimals, but that would be false accuracy, because the ratios depend on all sorts of judgments and estimates made in assembling the financial statements and, therefore, should not be thought of as precise quantities, but rather as indicators.

This section's 20 ratios are summarized in Exhibit 10.7, near the end of the section. They all should be used in combination with each other, because each has only part of the story to tell, but to help you see their main uses, they are grouped into four categories:

- Performance ratios: ratios 1–11.

- Activity (turnover) ratios: ratios 12–14.

- Financing ratios: ratios 15–17.

- Liquidity and solvency warning ratios: ratios 18–20.

Performance Ratios

ROE = net income / owner's equity.

1. Return on equity (sometimes called return on shareholders' investment or return on net worth): calculated as net income / owners' equity. ROE, a very frequently used ratio, indicates how much return the company is generating on the historically accumulated owners' investment (contributed share capital and other capital items plus retained earnings). Owners' equity can be taken straight from the balance sheet or can be computed from the balance sheet equation as total assets minus total liabilities. The denominator can be year-end equity or average equity over the year; for a growing company, you'd expect a slightly larger ROE figure for the latter.

   For CAE, ROE (based on year-end equity) for the last two years was:

   - 2000: $98.5 / $379.3 = .260;
   - 1999: $77.3 / $338.3 = .228.

CAE's 2000 ROE is a healthy 26%, an increase over 1999's 23%.

The income return relative to equity is healthy. Many companies' ROE is much less than this. It is about 14% higher than 1999. This increase is due to a larger income, but the percentage increase has been both dampened by the increase in equity due to the large increase in retained earnings since 1999, and assisted by the company's decision to buy back some of its share capital during 2000. The analyses to come will tell us much more about why the ROE is relatively high and increasing, but for now, an investor in CAE should be pleased at the company's performance.

ROA = (income + interest expense) / total assets.

2. **Return on assets** (often also called return on investment or ROI): usually calculated as (net income + interest expense) / total assets. Income before income tax may be used instead of net income. As with the equity denominator in ROE, the total assets figure can be the year-end figure or the average over the year. **ROA** indicates the company's ability to generate a return on its assets *before considering the cost of financing those assets (interest)*. It helps in judging whether borrowing is worthwhile: presumably if it costs $x\%$ to borrow money, the company should expect to earn at least $x\%$ on the assets acquired with the money. (This relationship between ROA and borrowing cost is explored further in section 10.6.) Some financial databases calculate ROA just as income divided by total assets, but we will remove the financing cost because that provides more information.

We will use a slightly refined version of ROA: we'll calculate the interest expense *after income tax*, because if interest is just added back to income, the impact of the tax saving it brings is lost. Net income is after tax, so it makes sense to use an after-tax version of interest expense too.

Refined ROA(ATI) = (net income + after-tax interest expense) / total assets.

For our **refined ROA**, which will be designated **ROA(ATI)** as a reminder that it uses after-tax interest (ATI), we first have to calculate the after-tax interest cost. You will recall from section 10.2 that after-tax interest cost = interest expense × (1 – tax rate). CAE's effective income tax rate was 31.0% in 2000 ($40.8 income tax expense / $131.5 continuing earnings before tax) and 29.3% in 1999 ($30.6 / $104.3). (Note 9, not included in this text, shows why these rates are lower than the official statutory income tax rate that CAE says is 44.6%: lower tax rates in some jurisdictions, some tax credits CAE qualified for, and some tax losses carried forward from earlier years.) Total interest expense is shown on the income statement as $10.0 million for 2000 and $9.6 for 1999. These are described as "net," which means that CAE has deducted any interest revenues and any interest capitalized into assets—it would be better to use the interest expense before any deductions, because that expense would relate more closely to the company's borrowing, but CAE does not disclose what that is. We'll use the information we have.

With these figures, the refined ROA(ATI) on *year-end assets* was:

- 2000: ($98.5 + [$10.0 × (1 – .310)]) / $1,224.2
  = ($98.5 + $6.9) / $1,224.2
  = $105.4 / $1,224.2 = .086;

- 1999: ($77.3 + [$9.6 × (1 - .293)]) / $1,065.2
  = ($77.3 + 6.8) / $1,065.2
  = $84.1 / $1,065.2 = .079.

CAE's 2000 ROA(ATI) was moderate at 8.6% (7.9% in 1999).

Like ROE, ROA(ATI) was higher in 2000 than 1999. These ROAs were moderate: in 2000 and 1999, it was hard to get more than 6% or so on guaranteed investment certificates at the bank, Canada Savings Bonds, and similar investments. CAE has earned more than that on its assets, but CAE is taking more risk to earn its returns than you'd take on bank certificates or CSBs, so it should be able to do better. Many companies have ROAs in this range. The calculation above also shows some interesting results along the way. First, the interest really only cost the company $6.9 million in 2000 ($6.8 million in 1999) because it was a tax-deductible expense and so saved income tax. Second, if the company had not had any interest at all, its net income, after tax, would have been $105.4 million in 2000 and $84.1 million in 1999.

These two "relative return" ratios may be compared. In 2000, ROE was .260 while ROA(ATI) was .086. The return to owners was .174 higher than the company earned on its assets prior to the interest cost of financing the assets, almost three times as much. In 1999, ROE was .228 while ROA(ATI) was .079, so the difference was relatively similar. This difference, which was to the benefit of the shareholders (ROE greater than ROA(ATI)), is called leverage and is one of the subjects of section 10.6. Some other ratios that reflect leverage effects are shown later in this section.

3. **Sales return** (or **profit margin**): usually calculated as net income / revenue. Sales return indicates the percentage of sales revenue that ends up as income, so it is the average "bottom line" profit on each dollar of sales. For example, a .10 sales return would mean that 10 cents in net income are generated from each dollar of sales, on average. It is a useful measure of performance and gives some indication of pricing strategy or competition intensity. You might expect a discount retailer in a competitive market to have a low sales return, and an upscale jeweller to have a high return, for example.

In section 10.6, we will use an alternative version of the sales return ratio, calculated analogously to that of the refined ROA(ATI), by adding interest expense after tax back to net income in order to determine the operating return before the cost of financing that return. Here the usual simpler version will be illustrated.

For CAE, sales return for 2000 was .085 ($98.5 / $1,164.3) and for 1999 was the same .085 ($77.3 / $905.9). The company made about $8\frac{1}{2}$ cents in net income for every dollar of revenue. It is interesting that although both ROE and ROA(ATI) were higher in 2000 than in 1999, sales return was unchanged. The company's improvement in returns to shareholders and on assets came from somewhere else.

As we saw in section 3.4, CAE provides revenue and operating earnings information by line of business. We saw then that Military Simulation and Controls was the least profitable line, and Commercial Simulation and Training the most profitable. Let's calculate operating sales return for each line for each year. We'll define that return as earnings from continuing operations (before interest and income taxes) divided by revenue:

Business Line	Operating Sales Return	
	2000	1999
Commercial Simulation and Training	17.1%	15.8%
Military Simulation and Controls	4.0%	7.1%
Forestry Systems	14.6%	16.6%
Earnings from continuing operations	12.2%	12.6%

We can see that though the operating return has not changed much from 1999 (down a bit), which is consistent with the overall sales return above not changing, there have been noticeable changes within business lines.

CAE has positive leverage: ROE greater than ROA(ATI).

Sales return = net income / revenue.

Sales return was unchanged from 1999 to 2000, unlike the ROE and ROA(ATI) results.

Commercial Simulation has improved and the other two lines have declined in profitability, especially Military Simulation.

Common size analysis converts the statements to percentages of revenue or assets.

4. Common size financial statements: by calculating all balance sheet figures as percentages (ratios) of total assets and all income statement figures as percentages of total revenue, the size of the company can be approximately factored out. This procedure assists in comparing companies of different sizes and in spotting trends over time for a single company. You can think of it as turning the whole financial statement into ratios.

For CAE, using total revenue as 100%, the common size income statement for 2000 and 1999 would be (rounding to one decimal, with a few rounding errors in adding):

		2000	1999
Revenue:	Commercial Simulation and Training	41.2%	38.9%
	Military Simulation and Controls	33.1	39.3
	Forestry Systems	25.7	21.8
	Total revenue	100.0	100.0
Operating earnings	Commercial Simulation and Training	7.1	6.2
	Military Simulation and Controls	1.3	2.8
	Forestry Systems	3.7	3.6
	Total operating earnings	12.2	12.6
Interest expense, net		0.9	1.0
Earnings from continuing operations before income taxes		11.3	11.5
Income taxes		3.5	3.4
Earnings from continuing operations		7.8	8.1
Results of discontinued operations		0.7	0.4
Net earnings (net income)		8.5	8.5

The common size income statement shows the components of sales return.

Now we have the details of the sales returns calculated as Ratio 3. Although the overall sales return did not change from 1999 to 2000, various components of the return did change. The most profitable business line, Commercial Simulation, rose in percentage of revenue and contribution to operating earnings, as did Forestry Systems to a lesser extent. The least profitable line, Military Simulation, fell in percentage of revenue and contribution to operating earnings. Its fall dragged operating earnings down more than the other two lines' rise improved it, so that operating earnings declined slightly in relation to revenue, as we saw under Ratio 3. Going down the other items, we see that there was a general small decline in earnings relative to revenue in 2000, just offset by an increase in results of discontinued operations. This analysis also shows that there were no dramatic changes between the two years, though presumably there is pressure on the Military Simulations managers to improve performance.

A similar analysis may be done of the balance sheet, dividing all assets, liabilities, and equity items by total assets. You might try that yourself as an exercise and see what is revealed by it.

Gross margin = (revenue – COGS) / revenue.

5. Gross margin (or gross profit ratio): calculated as (revenue – cost of goods sold expense) / revenue. This provides a further indication of a company's product pricing and product mix beyond the business line analysis done

above. For example, a gross margin of 33% indicates that a company's average markup on cost is 50% (revenue equals 150% of cost, so cost is 67% of revenue and gross margin is 33%). This is a rough indicator only, especially for companies with a variety of products or unstable markets.

Gross margin cannot be calculated from CAE's financial statements.

This ratio cannot be calculated for CAE, because the income statement does not disclose cost of goods sold expense, or indeed any expenses other than interest and income taxes. In section 3.4, this lack of disclosure was discussed, so it will not be repeated now. However, it is a reminder that financial statement analysis is dependent on the contents of the financial statements! We cannot analyze information we do not have. If anyone was particularly interested in CAE's gross margin performance, she or he could ask CAE for the information, because the company's accounting system undoubtedly contains it. But we might guess from CAE's lack of disclosure that, unless the person was in some way entitled to the information (for example, the company's banker), it would not be forthcoming. As noted in Chapter 5, especially section 5.10, the company would have to be careful about disclosing information to only some users and therefore perhaps giving them an unfair advantage over others— lawsuits could result from an attempt to help one user but not all. Issues like these would probably have been considered when CAE decided not to disclose its cost of goods sold.

Average interest rate = interest expense / liabilities.

6. Average interest rate: calculated as interest expense / liabilities. This ratio shows what the company pays for interest relative to its borrowing. There are various versions of this ratio, depending on whether interest expense is calculated before or after income tax and on whether all liabilities are included or just the interest-bearing ones, such as bonds and mortgages. If the ratio is calculated on an after-tax basis and applied to all liabilities, it is likely to be quite low: interest is tax-deductible, so income tax savings amount to from a third to a half of it and many liabilities, such as future income tax, dividends payable, deposits on contracts (important for CAE), and most accounts payable, carry no interest. Interest rate calculations are discussed further in section 10.6, where the rate is calculated on an after-tax basis.

On a before-tax basis, we have interest expense of $10.0 million in 2000 and $9.6 million in 1999. Total liabilities were $844.9 million at the end of 2000 and $726.9 million at the end of 1999. Therefore, the average pre-tax interest rate on all year-end liabilities was .012 in 2000 and .013 in 1999. There is not much of a change, nor is interest very important to CAE. This ratio for CAE is only an approximation, because the income statement says that interest expense is net: but net of what? Presumably interest revenue from CAE's short-term investments has been deducted, and perhaps some interest has been capitalized (unlikely because CAE does not appear to have large long-term construction projects, the usual reason for capitalizing interest).

Average interest rate is very low and has not changed much in the two years.

If we dig around a bit, the very long Note 6 about the company's debt (not included in this text) mentions that interest expense on long-term debt was $14.5 million in 2000 and $15.6 million in 1999. Relating those to the long-term debt figures on the balance sheet ($0.9 + $270.7 million at the end of 2000 and $0.9 + $296.2 million at the end of 1999) gives average interest rates of 5.3% for 2000 and 1999. So we could refine the average interest rate calculation a little by using these expense numbers instead of the net numbers used above. If interest expense was a major item for CAE, it might be worthwhile to do that, but as it is not, we need not bother. It is useful to remember, though, that the average rate calculated above is a slight understatement of CAE's real borrowing cost.

Cash flow to total assets = cash from operations / total assets.

7. Cash flow to total assets: calculated as cash generated by operations / total assets. Cash generated by operations is found in the cash flow statement, and total assets may be taken from the year-end balance sheet figure or calculated as an average of the beginning and ending figures. This ratio relates the company's ability to generate cash resources to its size, which approximately factors out size. It provides an alternative return measure to ROA, focusing on cash return rather than on accrual income return as used in ROA.

Cash flow to total assets increased enormously in 2000 as compared to 1999.

For CAE, using year-end assets, the ratio was .204 in 2000 ($250.0 / $1,224.2 million) and .027 in 1999 ($28.4 / $1,065.2 million). This ratio increased almost eight-fold in 2000 because of the change in noncash working capital changes from negative $70.3 million in 1999 to positive $133.5 million in 2000 (see Note 10, which is included in the statements at the beginning of this section). There was an extensive discussion of the change in operating cash flows in section 4.7—a review of that might be useful. CAE's operating cash flows are certainly more variable than its earnings: we saw much less change in ROA(ATI), ROE, and sales return than in cash flow. (There will be more about cash flow in the next section of this chapter.)

EPS = (net income – preferred dividends) / average number of common shares outstanding.

8. Earnings per share: conceptually, this ratio is calculated as (net income – dividends on preferred shares) / average number of common shares outstanding. EPS relates earnings attributable to common shares (the numerator) to the number of common shares issued, thereby providing a sort of down-to-earth performance measure. It is also another way of factoring out the company's size. If you have only 100 shares of a large company, it is not easy to understand what the company's multi-million-dollar income means to you. But if you are told that the EPS = $2.10, you know that your 100 shares earned $210 for the year and can then relate the company's returns to your own circumstances.

EPS is provided in the audited financial statements of public companies.

Calculating EPS is a little complicated, so GAAP require that publicly traded companies provide it in their financial statements. This helps in evaluating the worth of the shares and in comparing various companies' returns to the prices of their shares on the stock market. (See price–earnings ratio below.) Because it is part of the financial statements, it is for public companies the only ratio routinely covered by the auditor's report. For small, closely held companies, EPS is not meaningful, and not required by GAAP, because the owners usually cannot trade their shares readily and are likely to be interested in the value of the overall company more than in that of individual shares.

There are different versions of EPS, depending on circumstances.

More than one version of EPS can appear in the same set of statements. If a company has extraordinary items, discontinued operations, or other anomalies, EPS is calculated both before and after such items, so that the effect of such items may readily be seen. Also, if the company has potential commitments to issue further shares, such as in stock-option plans to motivate senior management or preferred shares convertible to common shares at the option of the holder of the preferred shares, the potential effect of the exercise of such commitments is calculated by showing both ordinary EPS and "fully diluted" EPS. ("Dilution" refers to the potential lowering of return to present shareholders resulting from other people's exercising rights arising from commitments already made by the company.) Adding to the variety, EPS can be calculated a little differently in the U.S. than in Canada (though country differences like that are being reduced or eliminated, as noted in the discussion of international standards harmonization in section 5.5).

For CAE, the income statement does not mention fully diluted EPS, so that figure would not be materially different from the basic EPS. As there were discontinued operations, the income statement shows four EPS numbers: $0.90 in 2000 ($0.83 from continuing operations) and $0.70 in 1999 ($0.66 from continuing operations). EPS went up 28.6%, a much bigger increase than the increase in ROE or ROA(ATI). It was also a slightly bigger increase than that in net income (from $77.3 million to $98.5 million, a 27.4% increase). Elsewhere in the annual report five years' EPS figures are given, showing a steady increase from $0.54 in 1996.

EPS in 2000 rose nearly 29% over 1999, assisted a little by a share buy-back in 2000.

Part of the EPS increase was due to the net income increase, but it was also helped by the company's decision to buy back 4.3 million of the 111.5 million shares outstanding at the beginning of 2000. Those 4.3 million were only 3.9% of the 111.5 million, so the boost to EPS would not be large (the effect is also reduced, at least for 2000, because the number of shares is an average computed over the year, reducing the effects on the average of any changes in number of shares over the year unless those changes happened on the first day of the year. CAE's buy-backs were done at various times during 2000.) It's a reminder that ratio changes depend on the denominator as well as the numerator: for EPS we tend to think of the earnings numerator, but interpreting EPS requires noticing if there have been big changes in the share number denominator.

Book value per share = (shareholders' equity – preferred shares) / common shares issued.

9. Book value per share: calculated as (shareholders' equity – preferred shares) / number of common shares issued and outstanding. Similar to EPS, this ratio relates the portion of the shareholders' equity attributable to the residual common shareholders to the number of shares outstanding, and so brings the company balance sheet down to the level of the individual shareholder. It is not really a performance ratio, but shareholders' equity does include retained earnings, so it incorporates accumulated performance. Because the balance sheet's figures do not reflect the current market value of most assets or of the company as a whole, many people feel that book value per share is a largely meaningless ratio, but you will see it mentioned in many financial publications.

Book value per share rose from 1999 to 2000.

For CAE, Note 8 (not in this book) indicates that 111,466,032 common shares were issued and outstanding at the end of 1999, going down to 107,579,185 at the end of 2000 due to the buy-back noted above (a few shares were also issued in 2000, to managers exercising stock options and to any shareholders who preferred a stock dividend to a cash dividend). CAE is authorized to issue preferred shares too, but has not yet done so. Book value per share, therefore, equalled $3.53 at the end of 2000 ($379.3 million / 107,579,185) and $3.04 at the end of 1999 ($338.3 million / 111,466,032). The increase of $0.49 is a joint result of the EPS, the dividends declared out of those earnings, and the decrease in the number of shares outstanding.

CAE's market price per share was recently around $4^{1}/_{2}$ times its book value per share.

The book value per share and market price per share may be compared to indicate how similar the accounting figures are to the market's evaluation of the company. The two are determined by different processes (book value is measured by GAAP based largely on the historical cost basis, while market price is determined by the market's expectations of future performance as well as current value), so they would be the same only by coincidence. However, a comparison of the two for various companies may indicate companies that appear to be overvalued or undervalued by the market, according to accounting's measure of financial position. CAE's shares traded (on the Toronto Stock Exchange) at quite varying prices in the year ended March 31, 2000 (a volatile time in Canadian stock markets), from a low around $7.30 per share to a high around $17.00. By July 2000, the price was in the $16.00 range. If we take $16.00 as a rough price, applicable to CAE's more recent experience, that is $4\frac{1}{2}$ times the book value per share. CAE's balance sheet is no indication at all of the market worth of CAE's shares. Another way to look at this is to calculate CAE's market capitalization and compare that to the balance sheet equity. Using $16 per share times the 107.6 million shares outstanding at the end of 2000 gives a market capitalization of $1.7216 billion. That is what the market thought CAE was worth, based on regular share trading (we don't know what someone would pay for control of the whole company, but usually a premium would be paid, so the market capitalization is if anything a conservative estimate of the company's value). Comparing to the equity of $379.3 million indicates that the market capitalization is $4\frac{1}{2}$ times book value, the same comparison we got on a per-share basis.

PE ratio = current market price per share / EPS.	10. Price–earnings ratio: calculated as current market price per share / EPS. The PE ratio relates the accounting earnings and market price of the shares, but, since the relationship between such earnings and changes in stock market prices is not straightforward (as discussed in Chapter 5 especially), the interpretation of PE is controversial. Nevertheless, it is a widely used ratio, appearing in many publications and analyses of companies. Many newspapers include PE in their daily summaries of each company's stock market trades and prices.

The PE ratio varies because of general stock market changes unrelated to the company.

    The idea is that, because market price should reflect the market's expectation of future performance, PE compares the present performance with those expectations. A company with a high PE is expected to show greater future performance than its present level, while one with a low PE is not expected to do much better in the future. High-PE companies are those that are popular and have good share prices, while low-PE companies are not so popular, having low share prices relative to their present earnings. PE is highly subject to general increases and decreases in market prices, so it is difficult to interpret over time and is more useful when comparing similar companies listed in the same stock market at the same time. It is difficult to interpret when the stock market is going through a sudden change, as was happening in 1999 and 2000, when CAE's information was released during a period of highly fluctuating share prices.

CAE's PE ratio has increased in 2000, indicating more enthusiasm by the stock market.

    CAE's shares had a price on the TSE in the $7.30–$17.00 range in fiscal 2000 ($16.00 by July 2000) and the $13.50–$8.00 range (a decline) in fiscal 1999. It's hard to pick a representative share price given such variation. But using recent prices in each year, we'd get a PE of about 18 for 2000 (say $16.00 / $0.90) and about 14 for 1999 (say $10.00 / $70). These are approximate, and use full EPS rather than the smaller EPS from continuing operations only (using which would raise the PE a little), but they indicate that, as the general TSE prices improved in 2000, CAE was also seen more positively by investors. CAE does not have the very high PEs of many popular high-tech companies (which may have PEs over 100, or even uncalculable PEs because they are losing money but still are popular with investors), but neither is it viewed as a dull company without future prospects.

Dividend payout ratio = dividends declared / earnings (or dividends per share / EPS).

11. Dividend payout ratio: calculated as annual common dividends declared per share / EPS, or if dividends per share are not disclosed, just dividends declared / net income. This is a measure of the portion of earnings paid to shareholders. For example, if the dividend payout ratio is .40, 40% of income was distributed to shareholders and the remaining 60% was kept in the company (retained earnings) to finance assets or reduce debts. A stable ratio would suggest that the company has a policy of paying dividends based on earnings, and a variable ratio would suggest that other factors than earnings are important in the board of directors' decisions to declare dividends.

CAE's financial statements do not disclose the dividends per share. But elsewhere in the annual report, a mention is made that dividends per share were $0.19 in 2000 and $0.16 for 1999 and the previous three years. So the company does have a stable dividend policy, but that is not directly related to earnings. The dividend payout ratio was $0.19 / $0.90 EPS in 2000 (21.1%) and $0.16 / $0.70 in 1999 (22.9%). The company did not raise its dividend by quite as much as earnings increased in 2000.

CAE's dividend payout ratio was 21% in 2000, down slightly from 1999.

Let's see what we can derive for the payout ratio from the financial statements. According to the statement of retained earnings, dividends declared were $20.6 million in 2000 and $17.8 million in 1999. Corresponding net incomes were $98.5 million and $77.3 million. Thus CAE's dividend payout ratio was 20.9% in 2000 and 23.0% in 1999. These are very close to the per-share figures above, showing that the two alternative methods of calculating the dividend payout produce similar results (as they should). If we base the ratio on just continuing earnings ($90.7 million in 2000 and $73.7 million in 1999), we get a payout ratio of 22.7% in 2000 and 24.2% in 1999. The payout ratio has gone down a little in both cases, as well as in the per-share version calculated above, so CAE paid its shareholders a slightly smaller percentage of income in 2000. This is about what you would expect if the company's income grew substantially, as it did, because there tends to be a lag between knowing the income and declaring the dividends. By the time the board of directors knew the 2000 income for sure, it would be several weeks into the new fiscal year.

CAE's dividend payout and PE ratios indicate its board and its investors expect its growth to be moderate.

The dividend payout ratio is consistent with the company's PE ratio. Fast-growing companies are often strapped for cash and so pay little or no dividends, plowing earnings back into more growth. People hold the shares of such companies because they expect growth in share price, not dividends, and because of such expectations of future growth, the PE ratios of such companies are usually high. In contrast, people invest in some more dull, but safer, companies not because they expect high share price growth but because they expect regular dividends, almost like Canada Savings Bonds. CAE pays a lot more than zero dividends, but with its supply of cash could have paid a higher percentage of earnings than it did. It's neither a high-growth nor a low-growth company, but is in between, according to both the dividend payout ratio and the PE ratio.

Activity (Turnover) Ratios

Total asset turnover = revenue / total assets.

12. Total assets turnover: calculated as revenue / total assets. Total assets can be the year-end figure, which is used in this book, or an average of beginning and ending assets, which relates the revenue over a period to the average assets over the same period, and may be more relevant if a company is growing or shrinking rapidly in assets. This and similar turnover ratios relate the company's dollar sales volume to its size, thereby answering the question: How much revenue is associated with a dollar of assets? Turnover and profit-margin ratios are often useful together because they tend to move in opposite directions. Companies with high turnover tend to have low margins, and those with low turnover tend to have high margins. Those extremes represent contrary marketing strategies or competitive pressures: pricing low and trying for high volume versus pricing high and making more on each unit sold. (There is more about using profit margin and turnover together in section 10.6.)

Total asset turnover was up in 2000 as revenues grew faster than assets.

CAE's total assets turnover was 0.951 in 2000 ($1,164.3 million / $1,224.2 million) and 0.850 in 1999 ($905.9 / $1,065.2). Revenue is growing faster than assets, which is a good sign. The company is using its assets better in generating income: assets rose from 1999, but revenue rose faster. If we look into this ratio a little further, we see that most of CAE's assets are cash, receivables, and inventories, with property and plant actually smaller in 2000 than 1999. Taking the $163.5 million of cash and $71.1 million of short-term investments out of the assets would give an asset turnover of 1.176 ($1,164.3 / $989.6), while 1999's turnover would be only a little above 0.85 because then CAE had little cash and no short-term investments. CAE's business depends on high receivables from customers (and, as we saw in earlier chapters, on accounts payable), but even so, its turnover is improving markedly. It will be interesting to see what happens in 2001!

Inventory turnover = COGS / average inventories.

13. **Inventory turnover**: calculated as cost of goods sold expense / average inventory assets (or by year-end inventory, for convenience). If cost of goods sold is not disclosed, it is often replaced by sales revenue in calculating the ratio, which is all right for comparing one year to others for one company, as long as markups and product mixes do not change substantially. This ratio relates the level of inventories to the volume of activity: a company with low turnover may be risking obsolescence or deterioration in its inventory and/or may be incurring excessive storage and insurance costs. In recent years, many companies have attempted to pare inventories to the bone, keeping just enough on hand to meet customer demand or even ordering inventory as it is demanded by customers (as in the "just in time" method of minimizing inventories without running out of stock and irritating customers).

CAE's inventory turnover in 2000 appears to have increased since 1999.

For CAE, cost of goods sold is not disclosed, so the inventory turnover cannot be calculated. However, we can see that while revenues are *up* 28.5% in 2000 compared to 1999 ($1,164.3 million compared to $905.9), inventories are *down* 11.1% (from $121.6 to $108.1 million). Inventory turnover has almost certainly increased from 1999.

Collection ratio = accounts receivable / (revenue / 365).

14. Collection ratio (receivables turnover, often called days' sales in receivables): calculated as accounts receivable / (revenue / 365). As for the other turnover ratios, the balance sheet amount, accounts receivable, can be the year-end figure or an average over the year. This ratio indicates how many days it takes,

on average, to collect a day's sales revenue. It becomes large when accounts receivable become larger relative to sales, so its interpretation is the opposite of those of the previous two turnover ratios: a large collection ratio is a negative signal, raising questions about the company's policies of granting credit and the vigour of its collection attempts. The ratio is subject to significant seasonal changes for many companies, usually rising during heavy selling periods, such as just before Christmas for a retailer, and falling during slow times. (It would be preferable to use only revenue from credit sales in the denominator, since cash sales are collected immediately, but few companies break their revenue figures down to separate cash revenue.)

It takes CAE over three months, on average, to collect from its customers.

CAE's collection ratio was 102 days at the end of 2000 ($325.3 / ($1,164.3 / 365)) and 107 days at the end of 1999 ($266.2 / ($905.9 / 365)). It takes the company more than three months, on average, to collect from its customers. This is a long time, even though it is a slight improvement from 1999. Most businesses have credit terms of 30 or at most 60 days, so CAE is giving its customers a rather long time to pay. The high accounts receivable are related to the kind of business CAE does, building and helping customers run complicated aircraft simulators that probably take a while for customers to test and get working properly, and to the company's also-high customer deposits and accounts payable liabilities, noted in earlier chapters. Many of CAE's customers are governments and government agencies, which frequently are slow to pay but seldom fail to pay. As a byproduct of the collection ratio calculation, the average daily revenue (the denominator above) can be scrutinized. CAE's daily revenue rose from $2.48 million in 1999 to $3.19 million in 2000. If the collection ratio had risen even higher in 2000, we might have been concerned that CAE was trying to push sales that it might not be able to collect, but the slight decline in the collection ratio reassures that revenues and collections are under control. It's a situation to watch, however.

Financing Ratios

Debt–equity ratio = total liabilities / total equity.

15. Debt–equity ratio: calculated as total liabilities / total equity, or sometimes as total external debt / total equity, to exclude deferred revenue, deferred income tax, and other liabilities that are consequences of accrual accounting's revenue and expense matching more than they are real debt. This ratio, which we saw back in Chapter 2, measures the proportion of borrowing to owners' investment (including retained earnings) and thus indicates the company's policy of financing its assets. A ratio greater than one indicates the assets are financed mostly with debt, while a ratio less than one indicates the assets are financed mostly with equity. A high ratio, well above one, is a warning about risk: the company is heavily in debt relative to its equity and may be vulnerable to interest rate increases, general tightening of credit, or creditor nervousness. (A high ratio also indicates that the company is *leveraged*, which means it has borrowed to increase its assets over the amount that could be acquired with owners' funds only, and it hopes thereby to increase returns and benefit the owners. See the comments on leverage at the end of the discussion of ROA earlier in this section and in section 10.6.)

The debt–equity ratio increased slightly from 1999 to 2000, now well over 2:1.

CAE's balance sheet makes this calculation straightforward, by totalling both liabilities and equity. The ratio for 2000 is 2.23 ($844.9 / $379.3 million) and for 1999 is 2.15 ($726.9 / $338.3 million). This ratio indicates more risk in 2000 than in 1999: as we have seen before, it is a result of more reliance on accounts payable and a buy-back of some shares. But the increase in risk is perhaps more apparent than real. Accounts payable are not usually a very risky debt (suppliers have less power than secured lenders like banks and mortgage-holders), and we know that CAE has a good supply of cash and substantial accounts receivable to use to pay the accounts payable. However, the debt–equity ratio certainly shows that CAE is leveraged, relying on debt more than on equity, and that its relative reliance on debt increased slightly during 2000.

Long term debt–equity ratio = long-term debts / equity.

16. **Long-term debt–equity ratio:** calculated as (long-term loans + mortgages + bonds + similar long-term debts) / total equity. This ratio has many versions, depending on which specific items the analyst decides to include as debt. It is frequently referred to as the debt/equity ratio, under the apparent assumption that longer-term debt is more relevant to evaluating risk and financing strategy than are the components of ratio #15. (That ratio includes all liabilities, therefore including both the shorter-term debts, such as accounts payable, and the accrual accounting residuals, such as future income taxes and customer deposits liability.)

CAE is relying less on long-term debt and more on short-term accounts payable.

For CAE, this ratio involves just the one long-term debt figure on the balance sheet. Not including the debt's tiny current portion, the resulting ratio was .714 for 2000 ($270.7 / $379.3) and .876 for 1999 ($296.2 / $338.3). This is a relatively low reliance and has decreased since 1999. It is another way of saying that the high and increased debt–equity ratio (#15) is a function of more reliance on current (and largely non-interest-bearing) debt. There do not seem to be any long-term debt problems—indeed, the cash flow statement shows that there were no additional long-term borrowings in 2000; instead there was a small repayment.

Debt to assets ratio = total liabilities / total assets.

17. **Debt to assets ratio:** if calculated as total liabilities / total assets, this ratio is the complement of the debt–equity ratio discussed above (ratio #15) and indicates the proportion of assets financed by borrowing. It may also be calculated by just comparing long-term debt or external debt to assets.

About 70% of CAE's assets are financed by liabilities.

Using total liabilities, the ratio for CAE was 0.690 at the end of 2000 ($844.9 / $1,224.2) and 0.682 at the end of 1999 ($726.9 / $1,065.2). The company finances its assets over two-thirds by liabilities, which is what we also learned from the debt–equity ratio being over 2, since liabilities + equity = assets. As we also saw with the debt–equity ratio, the company relied a little more on liabilities for financing in 2000 than it did in 1999.

Liquidity and Solvency Warning Ratios

Working capital ratio = current assets / current liabilities.

18. **Working capital (current) ratio:** calculated as current assets / current liabilities. This ratio has already been scrutinized (section 2.9). It indicates whether the company has enough short-term assets to cover its short-term debts. A ratio above 1 indicates that **working capital** is positive (current assets exceed current liabilities), and a ratio below 1 indicates that working capital is negative. Generally, the higher the ratio, the greater is the financial stability and the lower is the risk for both creditors and owners. However, the ratio should not be too high because that may indicate the company is not reinvesting in long-term assets to maintain future productivity. Also, a high working capital ratio can actually indicate problems if inventories are getting larger than they should or collections of receivables are slowing down.

The working capital
ratio's meaning
depends on the
company's specific
circumstances.

The working capital ratio is a very commonly used indicator. Some analysts use a rough rule that says the working capital ratio should be around 2 (twice as much in current assets as current liabilities), but this is simplistic. Many large companies regularly operate with a working capital ratio closer to 1 than 2. The ratio's interpretation depends on the specific circumstances of each company, as does the interpretation of any ratio. Interpretation of it is also complex because it is a static ratio, measuring financial position at a point in time and not considering any future cash flows the company may be able to generate to pay its debts. This ratio is most useful for companies having cash flows that are relatively smooth during the year and hardest to interpret for those that have unusual assets or liabilities or that depend on future cash flows to pay current debts. An example of the latter would be a company that owns a rented building: there may be few current assets and large current liabilities for mortgage payments, but, as long as the building is mostly rented and rental income is steady, the company is not in difficulty even though its working capital ratio is low. However, it is more at risk than a similar company with a higher working capital ratio, because that company could more easily weather a loss of tenants due to recession or the opening of a competing building.

CAE's working capital ratio was 1.350 at the end of 2000 ($711.1 / $526.8) and 1.325 at the end of 1999 ($455.1 / $343.4). This is consistently in moderate territory: positive without indicating poor use of cash or inventory or collection problems. We know that CAE has a very long collection period, and that the company relied much more on accounts payable in 2000 than 1999 (so its cash was much higher), but all this is being managed adequately.

CAE's working capital
ratio is consistently in
the moderate range of
just over 1.3.

Acid test ratio = (cash
+ temporary
investments +
accounts receivable) /
current liabilities.

19. **Acid test (quick) ratio:** calculated as (cash + temporary investments + accounts receivable) / current liabilities. This is a more demanding version of the working capital ratio and indicates whether current liabilities could be paid without having to sell the inventory (in other words, without having to convince more customers to buy what the company has for sale). There is an even harsher version of this ratio, called the "extreme acid test," which uses only cash and equivalents in the numerator. A complementary ratio, inventory / working capital, is often used to indicate what percentage of working capital is tied up in inventory. These ratios are all used to signal lower levels of liquidity, and so greater degrees of risk, than may be revealed by the working capital ratio alone, and so tend to be used when that ratio is deteriorating or is worrisome for some other reason. We saw that the working capital ratio for CAE was not worrisome, but the acid test ratio will still tell us something about the company's liquidity.

CAE's acid test ratio
is over 1, indicating
good liquidity.

For CAE, the acid test ratio was 1.06 at the end of 2000 (($163.5 + $71.2 + $325.3) / $526.8) and 0.85 at the end of 1999 (($25.6 + $266.2) / $343.4). The company had enough near-cash resources to pay its current liabilities at the end 2000, an improvement over 1999 when it did not have enough. It could not pay the current liabilities immediately, given its long collection period, but on the other hand its liquidity is probably even better than this ratio shows because very large customer (contract) deposits are included in the current liabilities figure and these would not normally have to be repaid at all.

Interest coverage ratio = income before interest expense and income tax / interest expense.

20. **Interest coverage ratio:** usually calculated as (income before interest expense + income tax) / interest expense. This and similar coverage ratios that are based on cash flow figures from the cash flow statement indicate the degree to which financial commitments (in this case, those to pay interest on debts) are covered by the company's ability to generate income or cash flow. A low coverage ratio (especially below 1) indicates that the company is not operating at a sufficiently profitable level to cover the interest obligation comfortably and may also be a warning of solvency problems (difficulty in meeting obligations over the long haul).

CAE's interest coverage is very comfortable and improving.

We know that CAE's interest expense is minor. Its interest coverage ratio will therefore be high—it is hardly worth calculating. But just to demonstrate the calculation, it would be 14.9 times in 2000 (($98.5 + $40.8 + $10.0) / $10.0) and 12.2 times in 1999 (($77.3 + $30.6 + $9.6) / $9.6). CAE's income statement makes it easy to calculate a version based on continuing earnings: just the income right above the interest line divided by interest (14.2 times in 2000 ($141.5 / $10.0) and 11.9 times in 1999 ($113.9 / $9.6)). Clearly no problems here: the ratio was high in 1999 and got higher in 2000!

Concluding Comments about the Twenty Ratios

The twenty ratios are summarized in Exhibit 10.7. Each one focuses on a different aspect of performance, and the comparison of each with the previous or other years tells us something and also invites us to learn more about the company so we can understand what each ratio is indicating. Comments integrating the story told by all the ratios will be made in section 10.6 below.

10-7

Exhibit

Summary of the Twenty Ratios for CAE Inc.		
Ratio	2000	1999
1. ROE	.260	.228
2. ROA(ATI)	.086	.079
3. Sales return (based on net income)	.085	.085
4. Common size	see details	see details
5. Gross margin	not available	not available
6. Average interest rate (no tax correction)	.012	.013
7. Cash flow to total assets	.204	.027
8. EPS (reported audited figure)	$0.90	$0.70
9. Book value per share	$3.53	$3.04
10. PE (approximate)	18	14
11. Dividend payout	.211	.229
12. Total assets turnover	.951	.850
13. Inventory turnover	not available	not available
14. Collection	102 days	107 days
15. Debt–equity	2.23	2.15
16. Long-term debt–equity	.714	.876
17. Debt to assets	.690	.682
18. Working capital	1.350	1.325
19. Acid test	1.063	.850
20. Interest coverage	14.9	12.2

By the time you read this, CAE will have gone through at least one more fiscal year. To improve your understanding of the company and the ratios above, visit the company Web site www.cae.com and look for the year 2000 or subsequent annual reports. The company's explanations of performance in the letter to shareholders, the Management Discussion and Analysis (MD&A), the notes to the financial statements, and elsewhere in the annual report, plus other items such as press releases, and speeches contained in CAE's Web site, or elsewhere such as the SEDAR site (www.sedar.com) are likely to be informative.

FOR YOUR INTEREST

Here are some accounting research results relevant to the value of the kind of financial analysis included in this chapter:

1. Ratios computed from financial statements have some value in predicting bankruptcy or other financial problems. For some companies, but not all, financial problems can be predicted several years in advance using accounting ratios.

2. Even though annual reports come out rather a long time after the fiscal year-end, there is enough reaction by stock markets to them to indicate that analysis of the reports still has something to say to market traders.

3. People cannot cope with masses of disaggregated data: it takes too long and requires too much special expertise. So, summarizing techniques, such as financial analysis, play a major role in users' decision-making.

4. Analysts' forecasts of earnings, based partly on financial statement data, do help to predict companies' future earnings performance. The analysts often can anticipate significant changes in earnings because they are following companies closely, so market prices regularly change before the new financial statements are released. Sometimes financial statement analysis does turn up new information, allowing people to fine-tune their expectations about future performance.

5. Financial statement analysis helps to assess risk, and thus helps investors choose the shares that seem appropriate for their risk preferences.

6. Financial statement analysis is useful to corroborate what people already believe about a company's performance, position, or risk. Even if such analysis turns up little that is "new," it acts as a check on the other flows of information about companies, because the validity of that information can be verified later when the financial statements come out.

HOW'S YOUR UNDERSTANDING?

Here are two questions you should be able to answer, based on what you've just read:

1. How well did CAE perform in 2000 as compared to 1999?

2. How was CAE's liquidity at the end of 2000? Is that an improvement over 1999?

10.5   INTERPRETATION OF CASH FLOW INFORMATION

The cash flow
statement
supplements the
analysis of the other
statements.

Both in the theory of economics and finance and in the practical relationships between businesses and their owners and creditors, cash flow is an important measure of return. Income for the company is all very well, but owners sooner or later want to receive some of it in cash dividends, lenders want cash payments to cover interest and principal due, and so on. Income is revenue minus expenses, but the revenue may be tied up in uncollected receivables and the expenses may either not have been paid yet or have been paid in advance. In financial statement analysis, the cash flow statement's focus on cash provides important supplementary information about how the company was managed and how it performed.

To refresh your memory of the cash flow statement and help you think about using it for analysis, here is a summary of the kinds of effects on cash that the statement can indicate.

Exhibit

	Increase Cash	Decrease Cash
Net income:		
Positive net incomes	X	
Negative net incomes (net losses)		X
Noncash expenses (such as amortization of long-term assets and the deferred portion of income tax expense) are added back to net income and so *appear to*	X	
Noncash revenues (such as a gain on sale of a noncurrent asset) are deducted from net income and so *appear to*		X
Changes in noncash working capital accounts:		
Increases in noncash current assets		X
Decreases in such assets	X	
Increases in noncash current liabilities	X	
Decreases in such liabilities		X
Changes in noncurrent assets:		
Increases in cost of (investment in) such assets		X
Proceeds from disposal of such assets	X	
Changes in noncurrent debts and capital:		
Financing obtained from owners and creditors	X	
Repayments, redemptions, dividend payments		X

Here are some points about the cash flow statement, based on the above summary.

- The Operations section of the statement converts income from the complex accrual basis used in preparing the income statement to a simpler cash flow basis.

- Cash from operations thus is an alternative measure of return. We saw this in ratio #7, cash flow to total assets, in section 10.4.

- The conversion from accrual to cash basis reveals something about how the company has managed its current assets and liabilities over the period: for example, have receivables gone up, delaying the inflow of cash from revenue?

- The Investing and Financing sections of the statement show what the company did with the cash it generated from day-to-day operations, and how much nonoperating cash it raised during the period.

The cash flow statement helps to evaluate earnings quality, investment and financing policies, and risks.

The cash flow statement, *in combination with the income statement and balance sheet*, can be used in at least the following ways.[1] Each point is illustrated by reference to CAE's cash flow statement, given at the beginning of section 9.4 and in section 4.6.

a. Evaluate the relative significance of the cash flow figures by relating them to the size of the company's assets, liabilities, equity, and income. For CAE, we saw in section 10.4 that the ratio of operating cash flow to total assets was more than double the return on assets in 2000 but less than half that return in 1999. The ratio was in the same range as return on equity in 2000, but much less in 1999. So operating cash flows are as important to CAE as net income is, relative to assets and equity. As the cash flow statement shows relatively small investing and financing cash flows in 2000, though more investing activities in 1999, these other sources of cash are not currently important to the company.

b. Evaluate the company's relative dependence on internally generated cash (from operations) versus cash generated from external financing activities. In 2000, CAE's operating cash flow was almost ten times that in 1999: $250.0 million in 2000 compared to $28.4 million in 1999. In 2000 there was no reliance on external financing activities, as financing caused a cash outflow rather than inflow. The operating cash flow was used to pay back a small amount of long-term debt and to buy back some shares in 2000. Even in 1999, when operating cash flows were relatively small, they were still larger than the $8.7 million cash brought in by financing. Operating cash flow was CAE's main source of cash in 2000, but, based on those two years, was quite variable.

c. Evaluate solvency (ability to pay debts when due) and liquidity (having adequate reserves of cash and near-cash assets). We saw from section 10.4 that solvency and liquidity are no problem for CAE. The cash flow statement confirms this: in 1999, the company used its substantial supply of cash to make its investments, so it did not need external financing, and in 2000, cash built up to a large amount again. It would have been even larger, but some of it was put into short-term investments in 2000. Those investments, the cash on hand, and the good acid test ratio indicate short-term financial strength.

d. Evaluate the level of spending on long-term asset acquisitions in relation to the size of the company's assets and the amount of annual amortization, in order to help judge whether the company appears to be keeping its plant and equipment up to date. CAE stayed about even in 2000, spending $30.9 million on new plant and equipment and recording $33.7 million in amortization. In 1999, there was relatively more spending on new assets ($76.3 million) than amortization ($28.6 million). As we can see from the discontinued operations lines on the income statement and the cash flow statement, and the lack of acquisitions in 2000 (compared to spending of $111.5 million in 1999), the year 2000 involved some retrenchment, getting out of less attractive lines of business. It was not a year of expansion in property and plant either, but they were kept roughly up to date.

e. Evaluate the company's debt versus equity financing strategy. We saw in section 10.4 that CAE is leveraged, having more than twice as much in liabilities as equity. However, much of the debt is accounts payable, some (customer deposits) is not likely to have to be paid, and its long-term debt to equity ratio is well less than one. Looking at the cash flow statement, the financing strategy is revealed by absences. There was no new equity financing in either year (even some buying back of shares in 2000), and little action on long-term debt (a small repayment in 2000 and a small borrowing in 1999). The action was in current debts: the noncash working capital changes section of Operating activities, supported by Note 10, shows that the company's major sources of financing in 2000 were an $88.4 million increase in accounts payable and a $79.2 million increase in customer (contract) deposits. As noted earlier, such financing is attractive (as long as customers and suppliers go along) because it usually bears no interest and is less confining than secured bank debt, mortgages, etc.

f. Evaluate the company's dividend policy by comparing dividends with both income and cash flow, and reviewing the pattern over time. We saw in section 10.4 that CAE's dividend payout was over 20% of net income in both 2000 and 1999. Relative to operating cash flows, this payout varied because those cash flows varied: in 1999 the dividends were 62% of cash from operations ($17.6 / $28.4), but only 8% in 2000 ($20.4 / $250.0). CAE's dividend policy is related to earnings and number of shares outstanding, not to ability to pay cash as measured by operating cash flows.

g. Determine the relationship between income and cash flow to evaluate the "quality" of earnings (income): income should be reasonably consistent with cash flow, after adjusting for normal corrections such as amortization, and should not be so far out of line with cash flow that there's some question about its validity. Here the high variability of CAE's operating cash flows makes comparisons awkward. In 2000, the operating cash flow was nearly three times earnings, so there is no indication there of recognizing (recording) more income than is reasonable. But Note 10 indicates that accounts receivable went up $54.6 million in 2000—was CAE recognizing more revenue than it should have, than customers wanted to pay for? The collection ratio in section 10.4 is very high, supporting some concern on these grounds, but since it went down in 2000 compared to 1999, any concern has eased a little. In 1999, operating cash flows were much less than accrual earnings, which would be the circumstance people worry about (reporting more income than is being collected), but this does not seem to be a continuing problem given 2000's very high operating cash flows.

h. Identify possible manipulation of the cash flow figures, such as failing to replace inventories or delaying payment of current or noncurrent debts, by comparisons to the way cash flows were generated in past years. Well, that possibility seems to exist for CAE. The company's inventories have gone down a little, and accounts payable have gone way up. Note 10 shows that there was a swing of $159.1 million in accounts payable, from paying them down by $70.7 million in 1999 to letting them rise $88.4 million in 2000. (Earlier years' cash flow statements, available at www.cae.com, indicate that CAE has a history of large changes in accounts payable and accounts receivable.) These variations might be considered manipulation of cash flows if the company were in difficulty, but as there is no sign of that, the conclusion seems to be that they are just functions of CAE's business practices with its customers and suppliers.

i. Identify either the hazards of success, such as drains on cash flow due to the buildup of inventories or accounts receivable, or the benefits of decline, such as cash increases due to shrinking inventories or receivables. There don't seem to be hazards in CAE's cash flow information. We can see that the company is changing direction, divesting itself of some lines of business (which cost it $21.6 million cash in 2000) and stopping its previous policy of acquiring other companies ($111.5 million spent in 1999, zero in 2000). The company may be building up a "war chest" of cash and temporary investments for future acquisitions ($234.6 million at the end of 2000), but given that its accounts payable were higher than that at the end of 2000 ($306.7 million), it is more probable that we will see the same sort of cycle as in the past, with much of the cash used to pay down the accounts payable and so operating cash flows falling in the year 2001 as this is done.

 OW'S YOUR UNDERSTANDING?

Here are two questions you should be able to answer, based on what you have just read:

1. What were the main components of CAE's 2000 cash flow?

2. How does cash flow information contribute to financial statement analysis?

10.6   INTEGRATIVE RATIO ANALYSIS

The previous two sections contained a lot of ratios and comments. To pull all the details together to form some conclusions about performance, risk, earnings quality, and other factors is more an art than a science, because the conclusions depend on the decisions made or information used to craft the analysis, as well as on the degree of knowledge or detail the analyst brings to bear. It also depends on what is found among the various ratios and cash flow data. If the analysis reveals a serious liquidity problem, for example, that may well colour all the conclusions. Similarly, if the company's accounting methods were suspect for some reason, the conclusions would likely be particularly cautious or skeptical.

To help you think about how to pull your analysis together, this section contains two illustrations. The first is an overall summary of what the previous two sections' analyses have shown about CAE, and the second is an example of an integrated numerical analysis: leverage analysis.

Overall Conclusions from the CAE Analysis in Sections 10.4 and 10.5

Here are some conclusions to connect the various analyses in the preceding sections together into an overall portrayal of CAE's financial performance and position. The categories of section 10.4 plus section 10.5 are used to make some integrative comments; then a summary follows.

Performance

CAE has a strong and increasing return on equity, and earnings per share continue to grow, both before and after the effects of discontinued operations. Sales return has not changed from 1999 to 2000, even as the company divests itself of some unattractive lines of business, because it has kept one line of business (Military Simulations and Controls) that has a much lower return than the other two remaining business lines. Return on assets is only moderate, with some improvement over 1999. Investors see the company as moderately attractive and its moderate dividend policy is consistent with that. CAE's market capitalization is $4\frac{1}{2}$ times book value, indicating that future earnings and dividend prospects are more important to the company's share price than the accounting book values.

Activity (Turnover)

The company's asset turnover is relatively slow, largely because of its large level and slow collection of accounts receivable (though that has improved a little since 1999). The bulk of the company's assets are current, with accounts receivable alone having a considerably higher book value than property and plant.

Financing

CAE is leveraged, with more than twice as much debt as equity, and this ratio increased slightly in 2000 compared to 1999. This means that less than one-third of its assets are financed by equity. Relatively little of its financing is long-term: the company relies on accounts payable and customer deposits for much of the financing of its large current assets. This parallels the company's asset structure, which is also heavily weighted to current assets over long-term assets.

Liquidity/Solvency/Warning

The story here is short. There are no apparent problems. Working capital is being managed by a complex balance among accounts receivable, accounts payable, and customer deposits, so that the working capital ratio is, as with much of the rest of CAE's measures, in the moderate range. The acid test indicates considerable short-term liquidity, and there are no difficulties paying the small interest expense.

Cash Flow

Operating cash flows are highly variable, reflecting the company's balancing of current asset and current liability accounts. Though operating cash flows were low in 1999, they were high in 2000 as accounts payable in particular rose, having fallen in 1999. The variability makes evaluation of the quality of CAE's earnings difficult, but there is no real evidence of poor-quality earnings (such as from recognizing revenues that are not collectible). Some strategies are revealed in the cash flow statement: the halt to the company's acquisitions of other companies, moderate levels of property and plant replacement, buying back of some shares, and building up cash and temporary investments rather than paying off accounts payable (which likely carry little or no interest and so are cheap financing). No external financing was obtained in 2000 and very little in 1999.

Overall Summary

CAE in 2000 was a growing, profitable, low-risk company. It had good earnings performance, an improved share price, strong cash flows, no increase in debt, and no financial difficulties (other than continued slowness in collecting accounts receivable). The various ratios and stock market price performance agreed in portraying the company as not extreme on any dimension, positively or negatively, and so being an attractive investment though not a high-flyer. Its market capitalization and price–earnings ratio indicated that investors expect similar performance and continued growth in the future. Have a look at www.cae.com and www.sedar.com and see how CAE has performed since this evaluation!

Leverage Analysis

Leverage, also called "trading on the equity," "financial leverage," and, in Britain and some other countries, "gearing," is an important objective and consequence of borrowing money and then using it to generate returns. It works like this:

- Professor Grunion wants to invest $15,000 in a real estate project.
- Grunion has $5,000 available in personal funds.
- So, Grunion borrows $10,000 from the bank at 11% interest.
- Grunion invests the total $15,000 in the project and receives an annual return of $2,100.
- The project's return is 14% before tax ($2,100 / $15,000).
- Out of that, Grunion pays the bank interest (11% of $10,000 = $1,100).
- Grunion keeps the rest ($2,100 – $1,100 = $1,000).
- Grunion's before-tax return on the equity invested is 20% ($1,000 / $5,000).

Grunion has made extra money by borrowing at a rate less than the project earns.

Not bad! The project returns 14%, but Grunion gets 20% on the equity invested. The reason is that Grunion borrowed at 11% but used the borrowed funds to earn 14%. The extra 3% return on the borrowed funds is Grunion's to keep in return for taking the risk of investing in the project:

- Overall return = 14% on $15,000 = $2,100.
- Paid to the bank = 11% on $10,000 = $1,100 (3% less than the return).
- Kept by Grunion: 14% on $5,000 own funds + 3% on $10,000 borrowed funds.
- Grunion's return = the 14% ($700) + the 3% ($300) = $1,000, which is 20% of the $5,000, so Grunion has benefited from leverage: borrowing money to earn money.

Leverage is a good way to increase your return, as long as you can ensure that the project's total rate of return is greater than your borrowing cost. It's a double-edged sword, though, because leverage can hit you hard if returns are low or negative. Suppose Grunion's real estate project returns only 7%. Then look what happens:

- Overall return = 7% on $15,000 = $1,050.
- Paid to the bank = 11% on $10,000 = $1,100.

- Kept by Grunion: 7% on own funds minus 4% on $10,000 borrowed funds.

- Grunion's return = the 7% ($350) – the 4% ($400) = –$50, which is –1% of $5,000. Grunion has been hurt by leverage. The project earned a return, but not enough of a return to cover the cost of borrowing money to invest in the project.

Borrowing hurts if its interest rate is higher than the rate the project earns.

So, Grunion in this case loses on every dollar borrowed, because the project returns less than the cost of borrowing. It's not such a great deal any more! Grunion is losing 1% on the equity invested, but if just that equity had been invested, with no borrowing, Grunion would have made 7%, the project's return. Leverage is now hurting, not helping.

Leverage is therefore the difference between what the project earns before any return to the lenders and the investor and what the investor earns, after paying the lenders the cost of the borrowing. Keeping the Grunion example in mind, we have the following:

- The investor's return is after all costs of borrowing, so it is the project income minus interest that is the project net income. That is related to the amount of investment the investor made, the investor's equity. Net income divided by equity is return on equity. ROE is ratio #1, section 10.4.

- The project return before interest is what ratio #2, section 10.4, was getting at: return on assets, the refined ROA(ATI) version that is calculated prior to the after-tax cost of interest.

ROE – ROA = leverage, either positive or negative.

- Any difference between ROE and ROA(ATI) is leverage. In the two Grunion examples above:

  a. ROE = .20; ROA(ATI) = .14; leverage therefore = .06, so Grunion has benefited by 6% from favourable borrowing;

  b. ROE = –.01; ROA(ATI) = .07; leverage therefore = –.08; so Grunion has suffered by 8% from unfavourable borrowing.

Based on the above discussion, leverage can be defined by the following equation, in which any of the terms can be positive or negative:

$$\textbf{ROE = ROA + Leverage}$$

After-Tax Leverage

Before we can apply the leverage idea to CAE or any company, it is useful to consider the effects of income tax. They were included in the ROE and ROA(ATI) calculated in section 10.4, but were not included in the Grunion example above. It's easy to do. Let's assume Grunion's income tax rate is 40%.

- In the first example, the project net income would now be $1,000 × (1 – .4) = $600. This is 12% of Grunion's $5,000 investment, so ROE = 12%. (We could calculate the after-tax ROE directly as the before-tax 20% × (1 – .4) = 12%.)

- In that example, the project's return before interest would be $600 + ($1,100 × (1 – .4)) = $1,260, calculated the way the numerator in ROA(ATI) ratio #2 does it. This is also the $2,100 before-interest return × (1 – .4). So

ROA(ATI) = $1,260 / $15,000 = 8.4%. (As for ROE, we could calculate the after-tax ROA directly, as the before-tax 14% × (1 − .4) = 8.4%.)

- Following the same reasoning, the second project's ROE would be −1 × (1 − .4) = −0.6%, and its ROA(ATI) would be 7% × (1 − .4) = 4.2%. (The latter, calculated as ratio #2 does it, is also [(−$50 × (1 − .4)) + ($1,100 × (1 − .4))] / $15,000 = $630 / $15,000 = 4.2%.)

- Any difference between ROE and ROA(ATI) is leverage. In the two after-tax examples:

  a. ROE = .12; ROA(ATI) = .084; leverage therefore = .036, so Grunion has benefited by 3.6% from favourable borrowing (this is 60% of the before-tax leverage, which is what we would expect: original 6% × (1 − .4));

  b. ROE = −.006; ROA(ATI) = .042; leverage therefore = −.048; so Grunion has suffered by 4.8% from unfavourable borrowing (which is 1 − .4) × the original negative 8%.

Income tax reduces the impact of positive or negative leverage.	So after-tax leverage is just like after-tax anything else: take the before-tax calculation and multiply it by (1 − tax rate). Because of income tax, positive leverage is smaller as some of the gain is paid in income tax, and negative leverage is also smaller as some of the loss reduces income tax (assuming that the tax rate also applies to negative income, which is that there is other income against which the loss can be deducted). Leverage can be analyzed using either before or after-tax figures. The earlier equation defining leverage can be rewritten this way, in which all terms are after-tax:

ROE = ROA(ATI) + Leverage

What is CAE's leverage? According to section 10.4, its ROE in 2000 was .260, and its ROA(ATI) was .086. Therefore, its leverage was .174 in 2000 (.260 − .086). It was .228 − .079 = .149 in 1999. This is substantial: leverage made two-thirds of the contribution to ROE in 2000 and nearly that in 1999. If CAE had not borrowed, its ROE would have been two-thirds less. How did this happen?

Expanded Leverage Analysis: The Scott Formula

The Scott formula is an example of integrative use of ratio analysis.	To incorporate more of the ratios in section 10.4, and thus both integrate the ratio analyses and expand the story about leverage, Professor W. R. Scott, most recently at the University of Waterloo, developed the "Scott formula." This formula is a version of a group of integrative analyses (another, the "DuPont formula," has been used for nearly a century). It is based on combining ratios into a larger story. There are other approaches to numerical integrative analysis, such as using various ratios together in a "multiple regression" statistical analysis to try to predict bankruptcy or other problems, and you will probably see other ways of combining ratios because many analysts seek ways to combine them. The Scott formula is used to illustrate such expanded analysis, because it is an example of taking advantage of the double-entry nature of financial statements to increase analytical power.

This expanded analysis uses the after-tax version of leverage above, plus relying on the basic cause of leverage illustrated in the Grunion examples: leverage happens when there is borrowing and the rate of return earned on the project is different from the cost of borrowing. The impact of leverage depends on the extent of borrowing: if Grunion had positive leverage, the more borrowed, the better

ROE resulted, and if leverage was negative, the more borrowed, the worse the ROE. Using these ideas, four definitions are important:

1. Overall return ROE is the same as ratio #1 in section 10.4;
2. Project return is ROA(ATI), which was ratio #2;
3. Borrowing cost (interest rate after tax) is IN(ATI), the after-tax version of average interest rate ratio #6, calculated as (interest expense × (1 − tax rate)) / borrowing;
4. Extent of borrowing is L/E, the debt–equity ratio (ratio #15).

Leverage equals the difference between project return and borrowing cost, times the extent of borrowing:

$$\text{Leverage} = (\text{ROA(ATI)} - \text{IN(ATI)}) \times \text{L/E}$$

The two terms inside the brackets on the right show the *potential* for leverage, and determine whether the leverage is positive or negative. Let's call the part inside the brackets leverage potential. Therefore, we can write the leverage formula as:

$$\text{Leverage} = \text{Leverage potential} \times \text{Extent of borrowing}$$

Grunion borrowed $10,000 and the after-tax interest cost was $1,100 × (1 − .4) = $660, so IN(ATI) was 6.6% ($660 / $10,000). Grunion invested $5,000, so the debt–equity ratio was 2 ($10,000 / $5,000). In the first example, positive leverage, ROE(ATI) was 8.4%; in the second, negative leverage, ROA(ATI) was 4.2%. With these figures, we have the following results for the two examples:

a. Positive case: Leverage potential = (.084 − .066) = .018
                      Leverage = .018 × 2 = .036, which agrees with the earlier calculation;

b. Negative case: Leverage potential = (.042 − .066) × 2 = −.024
                       Leverage = −.024 × 2 = −.048, which agrees with the earlier calculation.

The expanded analysis shows *why* the leverage is as it was. In the first case, project return was greater than borrowing cost, so borrowing helped. In the second case, project return was less than borrowing cost, so borrowing hurt.

So we have the following expanded analysis:

$$\text{ROE} = \text{ROA(ATI)} + (\text{ROA(ATI)} - \text{IN(ATI)}) \times \text{L/E}$$

The Scott formula incorporates two more ratios by breaking the first term on the right, ROA(ATI) into two ratios: SR(ATI), an after-tax version of sales return (ratio #3), which uses the ROA(ATI) numerator and revenue as the denominator, and AT, the total assets turnover (ratio #12), which uses revenue as the numerator and has the same denominator as ROA(ATI). Thus the full Scott formula analysis is:

$$\text{ROE} = \text{ROA(ATI)} + (\text{ROA(ATI)} - \text{IN(ATI)}) \times \text{L/E}$$
$$\text{ROE} = \text{SR(ATI)} \times \text{AT} + (\text{ROA(ATI)} - \text{IN(ATI)}) \times \text{L/E}$$

The analysis integrates six different ratios and also shows leverage potential:

- ROE is the same return on equity you saw in the ratio list (ratio #1).

- SR(ATI) is a version of the sales return calculated by adding interest expense after tax back to net income (an after-tax-interest version of ratio #3).

The Scott formula integrates six ratios into its analysis of leverage.

- AT is the total assets turnover ratio (ratio #12).

- ROA(ATI) is the return on assets you saw previously, the "refined" version of ratio #2, computed by adding interest expense after tax back to net income.

- IN(ATI) is the average after-tax interest rate, calculated as after-tax interest expense divided by total liabilities (the after-tax version of ratio #6).

- ROA(ATI) – IN(ATI) is the leverage potential.

- L/E, the extent of borrowing, is the debt–equity ratio (ratio #15).

The Scott formula uses after-tax interest to bring in the effects of income tax systematically, but it can be done without the tax adjustment as long as it is left out of *all three* of the ratios mentioning ATI above. Let's see how this formula is calculated from the financial statements and then, how to use it. A brief arithmetic proof of the formula is included in the endnotes, if you're interested.[2]

Scott Formula for CAE

To illustrate how to apply the Scott formula to a real company, let's use CAE's figures. The formula can be applied to any set of balanced financial statement figures: it works because the balance sheet balances, as long as SR, ROA, and IN are either all before tax or after tax. (We'll do them all after tax.) To test your knowledge of the financial statements, put a piece of paper over the 2000 figures below and find them yourself in the financial statements at the beginning of section 10.4. (You should recognize the ratios as the same ones calculated in section 10.4, including ROA(ATI), but with SR(ATI) and IN(ATI) now adjusted for after-tax interest.)

10-9

Exhibit

	2000 Figures	Symbols
Total assets, end of 2000	$1,224.2	A
Total liabilities, end of 2000	844.9	L
Total equity, end of 2000	379.3	E
Total revenue for 2000	1,164.3	REV
Net income for 2000	98.5	NI
Interest expense for 2000	10.0	INT
Income tax rate for 2000 ($40.8 / $131.5)	.310	TR
After-tax 2000 interest expense (Expense × (1 – tax rate))	6.9	ATI = INT (1 – TR)
ROE (return on equity)	.260	NI / E
SR(ATI) (sales return before interest)	.091	(NI + ATI) / REV
AT (assets turnover)	.951	REV / A
ROA(ATI) (return on assets)	.086	(NI + ATI) / A
IN(ATI) (average interest rate after tax)	.008	ATI / L
L/E (debt–equity ratio)	2.23	L / E

Result:

$$ROE = SR(ATI) \times AT + (ROA(ATI) - IN(ATI)) \times L/E$$
$$.260 = .091 \times .951 \quad + (.086 - .008) \times 2.23$$
$$.260 = .086 \quad\quad\quad + (.078) \times 2.23$$
$$.260 = .086 \quad\quad\quad + .174$$

For comparison, here is the result for CAE for 1999. If you are not sure how it all works, check the amounts below by calculating them from the 1999 figures.

$$.228 = .093 \times .850 + (.079 - .009) \times 2.15$$
$$.228 = .079 \qquad + (.070) \times 2.15$$
$$.228 = .079 \qquad + .151$$

(Note a slight rounding error. The right term should equal .149.)

Summary Comments on Integrative and Leverage Analyses for CAE

ROE is explained exactly by the five other ratios.

The Scott formula result for CAE shows that the company's 26% return on equity in 2000 and 22.8% in 1999 were made up of:

2000	1999
• A 9.1% return on sales (adding back after-tax interest)	9.3%
• An asset turnover of 0.95	0.85
• Return on assets of 8.6% (adding back after-tax interest)	7.8%
• Average interest rate of 0.8% (after tax)	0.9%
• Leverage potential of 7.8% (8.6% − 0.8%) after tax	7.0%
• A debt–equity ratio of 2.23	2.15

This provides several points of comparison with other companies or other years. Those comparisons could have been made using the individual ratios listed earlier, but now the ratios are tied to one another so that you can see how each affects return on equity. The terms on the right of the equal sign can be collected together to summarize the two basic components of the return on equity:

- The first is the **operating return**, which indicates the company's ability to make a return on its assets before interest costs (2000: $0.91 \times 9.51 = 8.6\%$, the **return on assets**).

- The second is the **leverage return** (2000: $(.086 - .008) \times 2.23 = .078 \times 2.23 = .174$), which starts with the return on assets (.086) and then subtracts the interest cost to get the **leverage potential** and adjusts for the degree of borrowing. Leverage return is ROE − ROA(ATI), but the Scott formula's second term tells us more about how it arose.

ROE = operating return + leverage return.

So, we have for CAE:

Return on equity = Operating return	+ Leverage return
2000: 26.0% = 8.6%	+ 17.4%
1999: 22.8% = 7.9%	+ 14.9% (or 15.1% with rounding errors)

CAE's return on equity, therefore, is generated a third from operations and two-thirds from using borrowed funds to increase the return to owners. This is striking. From the Scott formula, we can see that this great increase over operating return is due to very low borrowing cost, only 0.8% after tax, plus substantial borrowing. CAE has a very large leverage potential due to its low borrowing costs. For CAE the leverage potential and the borrowing go together, as we saw earlier: it relies very much on accounts payable and customer deposits for financing its assets, and increased its reliance in 2000. So its average interest rate went down a bit, its debt–equity ratio went up a bit, and the result was even greater leverage than the 14.9% in 1999. The Scott formula also tells us a little more about operating return: the return on sales went down a tiny amount from 1999, but asset turnover improved markedly. So the improved return on assets was due to better use of assets in generating revenue rather than better returns on the revenue generated.

 OW'S YOUR UNDERSTANDING?

Here are two questions you should be able to answer, based on what you have just read:

1. You have prepared a leverage analysis for Pembina Manufacturing Ltd. for 2000 and determined that the return on equity was 12%, the return on assets was 7%, and the leverage return was 5%. Explain this result to the company's president.

2. Write a paragraph summarizing CAE's financial performance for 2000 compared with 1999.

10.7   FUTURE CASH FLOWS: PRESENT VALUE ANALYSIS

Cash flow is important to a company, and assessing cash flow is a significant part of the analysis of a company's financial performance and position. Sorting out the impact of interest rates on the company's returns is important to understanding how it has performed. Stock markets and other capital markets are concerned with the company's expected ability to generate returns in the future, especially cash returns that can be used to pay dividends or reinvest in the company. Many financial contracts, such as those for management compensation and supply or service arrangements, focus on future financial performance. Generally, management should be looking forward to the future and trying to combine its asset acquisition, borrowing, and income-generation strategies to produce a good future return for the owners.

Management decision-making must look to the future.

An important way of thinking about future performance, especially future cash flows, is present value (PV) or discounted cash flow (DCF) analysis. Future cash flows are not the same as present ones, because you have to wait for them. Because you have to wait, you lose interest or other returns you could have earned if you had had the cash sooner.

Detailed PV or DCF techniques are examined in management accounting and finance courses, and you may well have seen them already in economics or business mathematics courses. In this section, basic ideas will be outlined to help you think about how managers can assess projects that promise future cash flows and how traders in capital markets may use expectations of future cash flows and future interest rates when deciding on prices of securities. (Such traders would rarely do explicit PV or DCF calculations, but research shows that capital market prices behave as if they are doing something like that.)

Interest and the Time Value of Money

The existence of interest gives money (cash flow) a time value.

In Western society, it is permissible—even expected—that the owner of capital should charge a person who wants to use that capital a fee for that use. That fee is called interest and is computed by applying a specified percentage rate to the amount lent, which can be referred to as either the *investment* or the principal. For example, an 8% interest rate on a $200 loan would produce annual interest of $16 ($200 × 0.08). The existence of interest, which builds up as time passes, gives money a *time value*. The **time value of money** is the principle behind all the calculations in this section.

Here are some simple formulas you probably already know (P = principal or investment, i = interest rate):

Annual interest = $P \times i$

Amount due at the end of one year = $P \times (1 + i)$

Amount due after n years, with annual compounding, if no payments are made = $P \times (1 + i)^n$

Interest is added to the principal to compute the total future cash flow.

The amount due is the total future cash flow, consisting of repaying the principal plus paying the accumulated interest.

Suppose a loan provides for repayment of the principal plus interest after several years, with no payments in the meantime. Two examples of this are Canada Savings Bonds (when you buy them you are lending the government your money) and whole life insurance (some of the premiums you pay are invested on your behalf and you are entitled to the accumulated value if you don't die first). If the interest is **compounded**, which is normally the case, that means *interest builds up on the unpaid interest as well as on the unpaid principal*. In order to know how this works, you need to know how frequently interest compounds. Do you get interest on the interest:

Interest's impact depends on how frequently it is compounded.

- as soon as any interest arises ("continuous **compounding**")? or
- after a day's interest has been added ("daily compounding")? or
- after a month's interest has been added ("monthly compounding")? or
- only after a year's interest has been added ("annual compounding")?

Here's an example of annual compounding. We have the same $200, 8% loan as above, which is to be repaid in five years with annual compounding. We can then calculate the amount that the loan has built up to at the end of each year (its "**future value**," FV below) as follows:

10-10

Exhibit

Year	FV at Beginning of Year	Annual Interest at 8%	FV at End of Year
1	$200.00	$16.00	$216.00
2	216.00	17.28	233.28
3	233.28	18.66	251.94
4	251.94	20.16	272.10
5	272.10	21.77	293.87

You can see that the FV increases every year. Using the third formula above, we can calculate the FV at the end of any year:

- End of year 3: FV = $P \times (1 + i)^n$
  $$= \$200 \times (1 + 0.08)^3$$
  $$= \$251.94$$

- End of year 5: FV = $200 × (1 + 0.08)^5$

  = \$293.87 (just a rounding difference with above)

Interest and Present Value

The concept of interest can be "turned on its head" by considering what you *lose* by waiting some period of time for your money, or, putting it another way, what a future payment is worth in present terms if you assume your money should earn interest between now and when you get it back.

Suppose someone promises to give you \$100 a year from now. If you had the money now, instead, you'd be earning 9% interest on it. If you'd had some amount P now and earned 9% on it, you'd be in the same position as you will be after waiting the year for \$100. Using the second formula above, $100 = P × (1 + 0.09)$, where P is the amount on which you could have earned interest. Solving for P, we get P = \$100/(1.09) = \$91.74. If you had \$91.74, you could have invested it at 9% and ended up with \$100 at the end of the year (\$91.74 + [0.09 × \$91.74] = \$100).

The \$91.74 is the present value of \$100 received after waiting one year, "discounted at 9%." Present value is another way of thinking of the time value of money: it reminds us that as long as we wait for cash that could have earned interest starting now, we lose that interest. As long as the interest rate is greater than zero, present value is *less than* the actual future amount of cash that will be received because the interest included in that future cash flow has been deducted.

The following present value formulas are analogous to the above interest formulas (here C = future cash flow and i = interest rate):

Present value waiting one year	$= \dfrac{C}{1+i}$
Present value waiting n years with no payments in the meantime, interest compounded annually	$= \dfrac{C}{(1+i)^n}$
Combining these two, present value of a constant cash payment over n years, interest compounded annually	$= \dfrac{C}{i}\left[1 - \dfrac{1}{(1+1)^n}\right]$

(A comment on the derivation of the third formula is at the end of this chapter.[3])

Therefore the present value of \$1,000 received three years from now, discounted at an opportunity cost interest rate of 12%, would be \$711.78 (this is \$1,000 divided by $(1.12)^3$). The phrase "opportunity cost" is often used, because by waiting three years for the \$1,000, the opportunity is lost to invest at 12% in the meantime. The concepts of future value and present value are illustrated in Figure 10.1. The charts in the figure illustrate the difference between the future values of an investment made now and the present values of future cash flows. *Interest gets larger each period.* In the future values case, it becomes a larger component of the total value; in the present values case, it becomes a larger component of the cash flow.

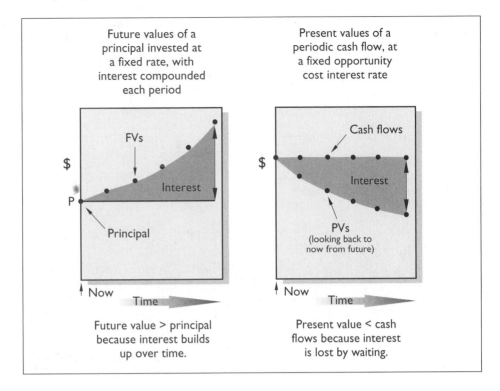

Future values of a
principal invested at
a fixed rate, with
interest compounded
each period

Present values of a
periodic cash flow, at
a fixed opportunity
cost interest rate

Future value > principal
because interest builds
up over time.

Present value < cash
flows because interest
is lost by waiting.

FIGURE 10.1

Here's a present value example. A company is considering an investment that will cost $10,000 now and will return $2,400 at the end of each year for five years. This looks good: 24% of the investment cost received each year, a total of $12,000 back on the $10,000 invested. To make the investment, the company will have to borrow at an interest rate of 7%. Should it go ahead?

Before we do the calculations, note three things about problems like this:

A project should earn a return that is at least equal to the rate paid to finance the project.

1. What we are trying to determine is if the money coming in is *equivalent* to a **cost of capital** of 7%. If the company has to raise its money at 7%, it will want the investments it makes to return at least that. A greater rate of return would be desirable, otherwise there would be little point in investing, but 7% is the *minimum* acceptable return.

Present value has future interest removed and so can be compared to the project's cost.

2. The idea of present value analysis is to take the future returns and subtract the 7% that the company has to pay on its borrowing, to determine if, after considering the borrowing cost, the returns equal the $10,000 that has to be invested. *Is the present value of the future cash flows equal to the present cost outlay that has to be made in order to get those flows?*

3. The 24% quoted above is *irrelevant* to the analysis. It compares the annual return to the investment cost, all right, but it does not consider the interest cost of waiting several years for some of that return. The whole idea of present value analysis is to build that interest cost, the time value of money, into the analysis.

Here's the present value analysis:

- Using the second present value formula above:

PV of first year's return is $\$2,400/(1.07)^1$	$2,242.99
PV of second year's return is $\$2,400/(1.07)^2$	2,096.25
PV of third year's return is $\$2,400/(1.07)^3$	1,959.11
PV of fourth year's return is $\$2,400/(1.07)^4$	1,830.95
PV of fifth year's return is $\$2,400/(1.07)^5$	1,711.17
Total PV	$9,840.47

- Since the annual flows are constant, the third present value formula above could have been used instead:

$$PV = (\$2,400/0.07)(1 - [1/1.07]^5) \qquad = \underline{\$9,840.48}$$

This is the same answer except for a minor rounding difference.

We can draw the needed conclusion from this and also see the effects of waiting for returns:

Present value is less than cost, which means the return is less than the financing rate.

- The conclusion is that the investment is not a good idea. It will cost $10,000, but after calculating the interest cost of waiting for the money to be returned, the present value of the $12,000 returned is only $9,840. Therefore, the investment is returning *less* than the 7% rate the company has to pay to finance it. It's close, but still not attractive.

- You can estimate the "internal rate of return" (IRR) of the project by equating the cost of $10,000 to the third formula above and solving for i:

$$\$10,000 = (\$2,400 / i)[1 - (1 / (1 + i)^5)] \text{ produces an i of } 6.4\%.$$

A higher interest rate means more interest is lost by waiting, so the present value is lower.

So the return of the project is less than 7%. The lower interest rate of 6.4% produced a higher PV ($10,000) than the higher required interest rate of 7% ($9,840). (Don't worry about having to solve for the nth root of a denominator as above: there are theoretical problems with calculating the IRR, mainly that it assumes the returns are reinvested at the IRR rate, 6.4% above, so we will not use it further. But you can see the idea that if the IRR is not at least equal to the borrowing cost, the project is not attractive.)

The farther into the future the cash flow is, the lower the present value is.

- From the annual calculations above, you can see that the present value of the $2,400 is smaller the longer we wait for it. The $2,400 received after one year has a PV of $2,243, but the $2,400 received after four years has a PV of $1,831. This is a necessary result: the longer the wait, the lower the PV because the greater is the amount of interest assumed included in the cash flow and, therefore, the lower is the residual PV. In the right-hand chart of Figure 10.1, you can see the PVs getting smaller as they go out farther into the future.

Some Present Value Examples

As we have seen with the example above, the concept of present value is very useful in evaluating investment possibilities ahead of time. Here are some more examples.

Present value at 11% exceeds cost, so the project is attractive (it earns more than 11%).

1. Suppose you are offered the chance to invest $2,000 in a project that will pay you back $4,500 after six years. Is it a good deal? Suppose, alternatively, you could invest your $2,000 at 11%. The present value of the $4,500 is $4,500/$(1 + 0.11)^6$, or $2,406. Therefore, the present value of what you'll get ($2,406) exceeds your cost ($2,000), and it does seem to be a good deal.

2. Gazplatz Ltd. issues bonds at 7% having a total face value of $100,000 that will pay interest every year in cash plus pay the principal back in 10 years. What would you pay for such a set of bonds if you could get 9% on your money elsewhere?

a. Present value of annual interest
$$= (\$7,000 / 0.09) (1 - 1 / [1 + 0.09]^{10}) = \$44,924$$

b. Present value of principal payment
$$= \$100,000 / (1 + 0.09)^{10} \qquad = \underline{42,241}$$

Total present value $= \underline{\underline{\$87,165}}$

(Note that the interest rate in the formula is the opportunity rate or required rate of 9%. The company's 7% rate just determines how much interest is paid each year—it does not represent the investor's interest expectations.)

As a rational investor, you'd be willing to pay $87,165 for the bonds. If the bonds sold for $87,165, they'd be "priced to yield" 9%. They'd sell at a discount below $100,000 to make them sufficiently attractive to investors who want a better return than the stated 7% rate. By paying $87,165, you'd actually earn the 9% you want, as we can show by constructing a table of each year's return:

If the bonds were priced to yield 9%, they'd sell for $87,165.

10-11
Exhibit

Date	Cash Paid Each Year	Return on Investment Demanded (9%)	Residual (Growth in Debt)	Effective Principal Balance
Purchase date				$87,165
1 year later	$ 7,000	$ 7,845*	$ (845)	88,010
2 years later	7,000	7,921	(921)	88,931
3 years later	7,000	8,004	(1,004)	89,935
4 years later	7,000	8,094	(1,094)	91,029
5 years later	7,000	8,193	(1,193)	92,222
6 years later	7,000	8,299	(1,299)	93,521
7 years later	7,000	8,417	(1,417)	94,938
8 years later	7,000	8,544	(1,544)	96,482
9 years later	7,000	8,683	(1,683)	98,165
10 years later	107,000	8,835	98,165	0
	$170,000	$82,835	$87,165	

* $7,845 = $87,165 × 0.09; $7,921 = $88,010 × 0.09; and so on.

3. Usually, in modern financial arrangements, "blended" payments are made to cover the specified interest plus some payment on the principal. House mortgages and car loans are two common examples. In such cases, to understand what is going on, we have to separate the return *on* investment (the interest) from the return *of* investment (repayment of the principal). Here is an example: a loan of $7,998 carrying an interest rate of 10% is being repaid by a blended annual payment of $2,110, made at the end of each year, which will cover all interest and pay off the principal as well in five years. In such a case, the interest amount gets smaller every year because the principal balance is falling, but the rate of return on investment is a constant 10%.

Exhibit 10-12

Date	Total Blended Payment	Return on Investment (Interest)	Residual Paid on Principal	Principal Balance
Loan date				$ 7,998
1 year later	$ 2,110	$ 800*	$1,310	6,688
2 years later	2,110	669	1,441	5,247
3 years later	2,110	525	1,585	3,662
4 years later	2,110	366	1,744	1,918
5 years later	2,110	192	1,918	0
	$10,550	$2,552	$7,998	

* $800 = $7,998 × 0.10; $669 = $6,688 × 0.10; and so on.

The present value of the blended payments equals the principal amount of the loan.

Using this example, the present value of $2,110 paid every year for five years, discounted at 10%, compounded annually, is $7,998. This is ($2,110/0.10) $(1 - 1/[1.10]^5)$: check it and see.

HOW'S YOUR UNDERSTANDING?

Here are two questions you should be able to answer, based on what you have just read:

1. What is the present value of $300 you will receive after two years if your opportunity cost of waiting is 11%? ($243.49, which is $300/$[1 + 0.11]^2$)

2. Wildwood Inc. issued a set of $1,000 face-value bonds carrying an interest rate of 10% and payable in eight years. The bonds were priced to yield 12%, which is what the capital market demanded for bonds of that risk and life. Did the bonds sell for more, or less, than $1,000 each? (Less)

10.8 "WHAT IF" (EFFECTS) ANALYSIS

You may want to see what difference an accounting method you prefer would make.

Suppose you are a financial analyst trying to determine what a recently released set of financial statements tells you about the company's performance. You can do various standard analyses, but before you do that you find that the company's accounting isn't quite comparable to that of another company you want to compare it to, or that the company has used an accounting method you don't agree with. You therefore want to alter the numbers to show "what if" the company used the other company's accounting method, or a method you do agree with.

Analysis of the effects of a method choice helps in making the choice.

Or perhaps you are the president of a company, and are assessing some alternative accounting methods to determine which would be the most appropriate for the company. You know that there are restrictions on the company's debt–equity ratio imposed by a major lender and that there are expectations of the year's net income resulting from a forecast you made earlier in the year. You also know that various financial analysts examine your company's performance quite closely and that, if that performance declines, your bonus and even your job could be in jeopardy. You therefore want to know what the effects on the company's financial statements would be if the company adopted each alternative accounting method.

Such questions are very common in business. Answering them requires analysis of the accounting information: we'll call this "what if" (effects) analysis. The ability to analyze accounting information to tell managers, bankers, and others what difference various changes in accounting policy choices or detailed methods, correction of errors in the financial statements, or business events in general would make to the financial statements is very important to accountants. If you are going to be an accountant, you have to develop this skill. If you are not going to be an accountant, you should have some idea of what the accountants are doing in such analyses, so that you can evaluate the results they give you. You may even want to do some basic analysis yourself. Computer spreadsheets are particularly good for this sort of analysis, but you have to know what to tell the spreadsheet to do.

Examples of "What If" Effects Analysis

Effects analysis can often be done using shortcuts, once you understand the idea.

A good way to think about what would result if one method was used instead of another, or one event happened instead of another, is to figure out the accounting numbers both ways and compare them. There are shortcuts to this, and if you see one, go ahead and use it! But for now, let's take the longer, and hopefully clearer, way.

a. Cash versus Accrual

Here's an example we've seen since Chapter 1. Suppose a company's president said, "I know we use accrual accounting, but what difference would it make to this year's income if we used the cash basis instead?"

We find that this year's accrual income is $11,800 (income statement), and this year's cash from operations is $13,400 (cash flow statement). Therefore, the answer to the president's question is that income would be $1,600 higher this year on a cash basis. No analysis is needed, because the financial statements provide the answer, if you know how to read them.

b. Revenue Recognition: During or after Production

Effects analysis can often be done from overall effects without knowing details.

Section 6.7 gives the example of Greenway Construction, which uses percentage of completion to recognize its construction revenues and expenses. Suppose the company's banker, more used to revenue recognition at completion of production (completion of the contract), wanted to know what difference there would be to income if the completion of production method were used instead. You can answer this without knowing the details of the accounting methods, as long as you know what the methods do to income. (If you have not yet studied section 6.7, the necessary data are given below.)

The percentage of completion project income (totalling $600,000 over three years) was:

- $120,000 for Year 1;
- $270,000 for Year 2; and
- $210,000 for Year 3.

If revenue and expenses were recognized only at completion of the project, the project income would be:

- $0 in Year 1;

- $0 in Year 2; and

- $600,000 in Year 3.

So the answer to the banker's question would be that income would be:

- $120,000 lower in Year 1;

- $270,000 lower in Year 2; and

- $390,000 higher in Year 3.

There has been no change in the three-year total, but the yearly figures are rearranged if the completion of production method is used.

c. Franchise Revenue Recognition

Similarly, section 6.8 compares the accrual and cash basis ways of recognizing income from WonderBurgers Ltd.'s franchising operations. Again, all we need to know is the effect of each method on income. If you have not yet studied section 6.8, here are that section's results for the accrual versus the cash basis of recognizing income.

10-13

Exhibit

	Accrual Basis Income			Cash Basis Income		
	(a)	(b)	(c)	(d)	(e)	(f)
Year	Revenue	Expense	Income	Received	Spent	Income
1	$10,000	$3,200	$ 6,800	$15,000	$4,000	$11,000
2	7,500	2,400	5,100	5,000	3,000	2,000
3	7,500	2,400	5,100	5,000	1,000	4,000
	$25,000	$8,000	$17,000	$25,000	$8,000	$17,000

	Difference		
Year	(a)–(d)	(b)–(e)	(c)–(f)
1	$(5,000)	$ (800)	$(4,200)
2	2,500	(600)	3,100
3	2,500	1,400	1,100
	0	0	0

If the cash basis were used instead of the accrual basis, the following income effects would result over the three years of the WonderBurgers example:

- Year 1 income would be $4,200 higher;

- Year 2 income would be $3,100 lower; and

- Year 3 income would be $1,100 lower.

Examples of Income Tax Effects in This Analysis

d. Income Tax Effects on Examples (b) and (c)

Suppose Greenway Construction pays income tax at a rate of 35% and WonderBurgers pays at a rate of 30%. What effect would that have on the figures above? Income tax reduces all the effects by the tax rate, because that proportion goes to the government. As shown elsewhere in this book (and below), a useful rule is to just multiply the before-tax effect by $(1 - \text{tax rate})$, in this case $(1 - 0.35)$ = 0.65 for Greenway and $(1 - 0.30)$ = 0.70 for WonderBurgers.

Here is a table of the effects, before and after income tax (for presentation purposes, Greenway's figures are in thousands of dollars):

Exhibit

	Greenway			WonderBurgers		
Year	Gross Effect 100%	Tax Effect 35%	After-tax Effect 65%	Gross Effect 100%	Tax Effect 30%	After-tax Effect 70%
1	$(120)	$(42)	$ (78)	$4,200	$1,260	$2,940
2	(270)	(94.5)	(175.5)	(3,100)	(930)	(2,170)
3	390	136.5	253.5	(1,100)	(330)	(770)
Total	0	0	0	0	0	0

Income tax reduces both positive and negative differences. The assumption here is that an increased income is taxed, and a decreased income produces tax savings (by reducing tax payable on other income or creating tax credits that can be used to get refunds on past years' taxes or reduce future taxes). Without knowing the details of the income tax law (which are beyond the scope of this book), we cannot say for sure how much of the income tax effect is current and how much is future. We know the effect on *total* income tax expense, as indicated above, but not how to allocate that effect between the current and future portions of the expense. We know the other side of the overall effect, the increase or decrease in *total* income tax liability, but not how to allocate that effect between the income tax payable liability and the deferred income tax liability.

e. "Net-of-Tax" Analysis and Interest Expense Net of Tax

Income tax tends to reduce both positive and negative effects on income.

If you have not studied section 10.2 yet, please read the latter part of it now. It reviews the idea of net-of-tax analysis, introduced way back in section 1.9, and continues it into the example of calculating the after-tax cost of interest. These analyses are examples of "what if" analysis, and net-of-tax analysis can be used to build tax effects into many evaluations.

H OW'S YOUR UNDERSTANDING?

Here are two questions you should be able to answer, based on what you have just read:

1. A company is thinking of changing its accounting policies in a way that will increase revenue by $500,000 this year, with $300,000 of that coming from a reduction in last year's revenue and $200,000 coming from a reduction in next year's revenue. Expenses would change too, with last year's expenses going down $215,000, this year's expenses going up $320,000, and next year's expenses going down $105,000. Ignoring income tax, what would this change do to net income this year, retained earnings at the beginning of this year, retained earnings at the end of this year, and retained earnings at the end of next year? (Up $180,000; down $85,000; up $95,000; no change. Calculations: $500,000 − $320,000 = $180,000; $(300,000) − $(215,000) = $(85,000); $(85,000) + $180,000 = $95,000; by that point, sum of revenue changes = 0, sum of expense changes = 0, so effect on retained earnings also = 0.)

2. Answer part 1 assuming the company's income tax rate is 40%. (Just multiply each answer above by (1 − 0.40), with the results: up $108,000; down $51,000; up $57,000; no effect.)

10.9   MULTI-YEAR "WHAT IF" (EFFECTS) ANALYSIS

The analysis approach outlined in section 10.8 can be extended to as many years as you need. Some of this was illustrated above in the Greenway and WonderBurgers examples, but now let's develop a framework for a complete multi-year analysis.

An Example

Earth Fabrics Inc. manufactures several lines of environmentally friendly dress fabrics, hiking clothes, and other cloth goods. It has been in business three years. There have been more returns of fabrics by retail stores in the current year than in the first two, and because of this, the president is considering a suggestion by the external auditor to recognize revenue from shipments to retailers a little more conservatively. The company's income tax rate is 34%, and revenue and accounts receivable data for the company's first three years, presented in the usual financial statement presentation order of having the most recent year to the left, are:

	Year 3	Year 2	Year 1
Revenue for the year	$1,432,312	$943,678	$575,904
Year-end accounts receivable	194,587	148,429	98,346

The auditor suggests that a more appropriate revenue recognition policy would reduce revenues by reducing year-end accounts receivable by 10% at the end of Year 1, 15% at the end of Year 2, and 25% at the end of Year 3. (Recognizing revenue includes a debit to accounts receivable and a credit to revenue, so reducing receivables implies reducing revenue, and vice versa.)

What effect would this have on:

1. Accounts receivable at the end of each year?
2. Revenue in each year?
3. Net income for the year?
4. Income tax liability at the end of each year?
5. Shareholders' equity at the end of each year?

1. Effects on accounts receivable:

Year 1	Receivables down 10% = $ 9,835	New balance = $ 88,511
Year 2	Receivables down 15% = $22,264	New balance = $126,165
Year 3	Receivables down 25% = $48,647	New balance = $145,940

It's important to realize what these receivables changes do. By reducing the receivables at the end of any year, all revenue recognized up to that point is reduced—you might say that the recognition of some of it is being postponed to the next year. So, for example, the Year 1 revenue is reduced $9,835, but because that revenue is postponed to Year 2, that year's revenue is increased by $9,835. By the end of Year 3, all the prior revenues are reduced by $48,647. Let's see how that divides up into the three years.

2. Effects on revenue:

Year 1	Revenue down	$ 9,835
Year 2	Revenue down $22,264 and up $9,835, net down	12,429
Year 3	Revenue down $48,647 and up $22,264, net down	26,383
	Total decrease in revenue over the three years	$48,647

3. Effects on net income:

Year 1	Net income down $9,835 (1 – 0.34)	$ 6,491
Year 2	Net income down $12,429 (1 – 0.34)	8,203
Year 3	Net income down $26,383 (1 – 0.34)	17,413
	Total decrease in net income over the three years	$32,107

We can check this. If accounts receivable are reduced by an accumulated amount of $48,647, then the accumulated net income must have gone down by this amount × (1 – 0.34). So, $48,647 (1 – 0.34) = $32,107. The rest is the income tax effect.

4. Effects on income tax liability:

Income tax is saved on the lower incomes. The amount of the accumulated saving is just the tax rate (0.34) times the accumulated change in accounts receivable at the same time:

Year 1	Year-end liability down $9,835 (0.34)	$ 3,344
Year 2	Year-end liability down $22,264 (0.34)	$ 7,570

(Check: this should equal the tax saved on the reduced revenue in the first two years: ($9,835 + $12,429) (0.34) = $3,344 + $4,226 = $7,570.)

Year 3	Year-end liability down $48,647 (0.34)	$16,540

(Check: ($9,835 + $12,429 + $26,383) (0.34) = $3,344 + $4,226 + $8,970 = $16,540.)

5. Effects on shareholders' equity:

Shareholders' equity is reduced by the reductions in net income, which reduce retained earnings. Therefore, the effects on shareholders' equity are the accumulations of those listed for income in part 3:

Year 1	Ending equity down	$ 6,491
Year 2	Ending equity down ($6,491 + $8,203)	$14,694
Year 3	Ending equity down ($6,491 + $8,203 + $17,413)	$32,107

An Analytical Framework

It may help you to keep multiple-year analyses straight if you use the analytical framework below. The framework relies on two important things:

- Because accounting is a double-entry system, all the effects at any point in time must balance out, so that the balance sheet stays in balance. This might help if, for example, you can't remember which way one effect goes; you know that it has to work so that everything stays in balance.

- Because each balance sheet is the accumulation of everything that has gone before, each balance sheet's effects are the sum of whatever the effects were on the previous balance sheet plus the effects on the income statement between the two balance sheets.

Figure 10.2 provides the framework, in blank. We'll fill it in shortly.

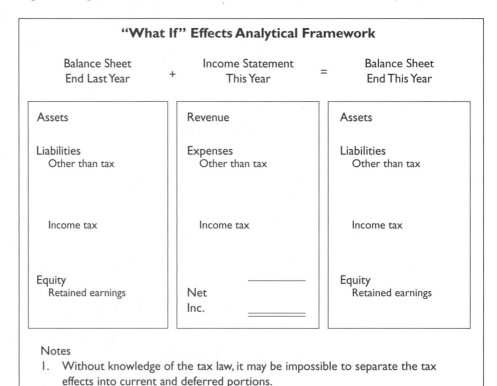

"What If" Effects Analytical Framework

| Balance Sheet End Last Year | + | Income Statement This Year | = | Balance Sheet End This Year |

Assets

Liabilities
  Other than tax

Income tax

Equity
  Retained earnings

Revenue

Expenses
  Other than tax

Income tax

Net
Inc.

Assets

Liabilities
  Other than tax

Income tax

Equity
  Retained earnings

Notes
1. Without knowledge of the tax law, it may be impossible to separate the tax effects into current and deferred portions.

2. For there to be a cash effect, some cash or cash equivalent account must be affected. For accounting policy changes, error corrections, and most other effects analyses, this will not happen.

FIGURE 10.2

Now let's fill the framework in three times, once for each of the three years of the Earth Fabrics example. Remember that the company has only existed for three years, so the "end of last year" figures for Year 1 are all zero.

Exhibit

	Balance Sheet End Last Year	+	Income Statement This Year	=	Balance Sheet End This Year
Year 1					
Assets			*Revenue*		*Assets*
Rec. down	$ 0		Down	$ 9,835	Rec. down	$ 9,835
Liabilities			*Expenses*		*Liabilities*
Other than tax			Other than tax		Other than tax
No effect			No effect		No effect
Income tax			*Income tax*		*Income tax*
Down	$ 0		Down	$ 3,344	Down	$ 3,344
Equity					*Equity*
Retained earn.			*Net income*		Retained earn.
Down	$ 0		Down	$ 6,491	Down	$ 6,491
Year 2					
Assets			*Revenue*		*Assets*
Rec. down	$ 9,835		Down	$12,429	Rec. down	$22,264
Liabilities			*Expenses*		*Liabilities*
Other than tax			Other than tax		Other than tax
No effect			No effect		No effect
Income tax			*Income tax*		*Income tax*
Down	$ 3,344		Down	$ 4,226	Down	$ 7,570
Equity					*Equity*
Retained earn.			*Net income*		Retained earn.
Down	$ 6,491		Down	$ 8,203	Down	$14,694
Year 3					
Assets			*Revenue*		*Assets*
Rec. down	$22,264		Down	$26,383	Rec. down	$48,647
Liabilities			*Expenses*		*Liabilities*
Other than tax			Other than tax		Other than tax
No effect			No effect		No effect
Income tax			*Income tax*		*Income tax*
Down	$ 7,570		Down	$ 8,970	Down	$16,540
Equity					*Equity*
Retained earn.			*Net income*		Retained earn.
Down	$14,694		Down	$17,413	Down	$32,107

The analysis can start from any point but has to add and cross-add in all directions.

You should note the following two points about the analytical framework:

- Each year's effects add vertically and horizontally. That is, vertically, the beginning and ending balance sheet effects and income statement effects work out exactly, and horizontally, the ending balance sheet effects are the sum of the beginning ones and the income statement ones.

- You can do the analysis at any point, working forward or backward from there. Probably, the most important analysis would be Year 3, because it accumulates everything from the beginning to now.

The analytical framework will help you think about effects analysis, but you have to consider the specific circumstances of each situation rather than hope for a general solution you can memorize. You have to exercise the knowledge and judgment you've acquired in your studies and experience! We'll do a further effects analysis example below to help you develop your analytical ability.

Journal Entry

You may be interested to know how the revenue recognition change would be entered in the accounts. It is quite straightforward, and uses the figures for the Year 3 analysis, because the company is just finishing Year 3 (let's assume the accounts for Year 3 have not yet been closed). Here is the entry, in the order of the accounts in the analytical framework:

CR Accounts receivable		48,647
DR Income tax liability (we don't know if this is current or deferred)	16,540	
DR Retained earnings (prior years' effects, aggregated)	14,694	
DR Revenue (Year 3)	26,383	
CR Income tax expense (Year 3)		8,970

Cash Effects

Cash is unlikely to be affected by accounting method changes.

You'll note that the analysis above and the journal entry to implement the change said nothing about cash. An important point to remember is that *analysis of accounting method changes almost never involves cash.* Accrual accounting, after all, is intended to go beyond cash flow, so accrual figures don't affect cash, before or after the change. If we are changing revenue, receivables, inventories, depreciation, etc., we will change net income, working capital, income tax liability, and/or owners' equity (retained earnings), but unless cash is being spent or received as part of the change, there is no cash effect. There will *eventually* be a cash effect through increased income tax or a tax refund, but at the time the accounting change is implemented, there is no tax effect.

It's pretty easy to see that if no cash (or cash equivalent) account is affected in the change, there is no cash effect. Remembering that may be enough for you! But you can also show, via examining effects on the cash flow statement's Operations section, that even if there appears to be a cash effect because net income is affected, that effect is cancelled out by effects on other account changes used to determine cash from operations. Let's use the Earth Fabrics example to show you how this works.

Exhibit

	Year 1	Year 2	Year 3
Accounts receivable:			
Total reduction at the end of the year	$9,835	$22,264	$48,647
Total reduction at the beginning of the year	0	9,835	22,264
Asset reduction over the year	$9,835	$12,429	$26,383
Income tax liability:			
Total reduction at the end of the year	$3,344	$ 7,570	$16,540
Total reduction at the beginning of the year	0	3,344	7,570
Liability reduction over the year	$3,344	$ 4,226	$ 8,970
Retained earnings:			
Total reduction at the end of the year	$6,491	$14,694	$32,107
Total reduction at the beginning of the year	0	6,491	14,694
Income reduction over the year	$6,491	$ 8,203	$17,413
Cash flow statement's Operations section changes:			
Income reduction appears to hurt cash	−$6,491	−$ 8,203	−$17,413
Receivables reduction appears to help cash	9,835	12,429	26,383
Liability reduction appears to hurt cash	−3,344	−4,226	−8,970
Net effect on cash from operations	$ 0	$ 0	$ 0

A Further Example

Rexdon Interiors Ltd. sells decorating supplies and does contract home and office decorating work. The company accounts for revenue at the point of delivery for ordinary sales and on the completed contract basis for contract work. Resulting accounts for 2002 and 2001 are:

	2002	2001
Revenue for 2002	$1,234,530	
Accounts receivable at the end of the year	114,593	$93,438
Bad debts expense for 2002	11,240	
Allowance for doubtful accounts at the end of the year	13,925	6,560

The president, Rex, is thinking of changing the revenue recognition method for contract work to the percentage of completion method. (You don't have to know the details of the method to do this analysis.) If this were done, accounts receivable would rise to $190,540 at the end of 2001 and $132,768 at the end of 2002. The controller advises that if this were done, revenue/expense matching would also require raising the allowance for doubtful accounts to $14,260 at the end of 2001 and to $16,450 at the end of 2002. No other expense recognition changes would be anticipated. Rexdon's income tax rate is 32%.

Using the analytical framework described above, here is a summary of the effects of the policy change. Explanations for the figures follow.

Exhibit

Balance Sheet End Last Year		+	Income Statement This Year		=	Balance Sheet End This Year	
Assets			*Revenue*			*Assets*	
Rec. up	$97,102		Down	$78,927		Rec. up	$18,175
ADA up	($7,700)					ADA up	($2,525)
Liabilities			*Expenses*			*Liabilities*	
Other than tax			Other than tax			Other than tax	
	No effect		BDs down	$ 5,175			No effect
Income tax			*Income tax*			*Income tax*	
Up	$28,609		Down	$23,601		Up	$ 5,008
Equity						*Equity*	
Retained earn.			*Net income*			Retained earn.	
Up	$60,793		Down	$50,151		Up	$10,642

You can see that the effects are much larger at the end of 2001 than at the end of 2002, resulting in effects on the 2002 income statement that might be opposite to what you expected. If a company does try to manipulate its net income through accounting policy changes, it can easily have such unexpected results. Financial statement manipulation is not for the faint of heart: unexpected effects are just one reason such manipulation is not a good idea. Rex should only change revenue recognition policies if he believes the new policy is really better, more appropriate, and fairer, and if he is therefore willing to stick with the new policy even when it produces awkward results, as it does in 2002.

Here are details behind the above framework summary:

a. Retained earnings at the end of 2001 would rise by the increase in receivables minus the increase in income tax expense:

$$([\$190,540 - \$93,438] - [\$14,260 - \$6,560]) \times (1 - 0.32)$$
$$= \$89,402 \times (1 - 0.32)$$
$$= \$60,793 \text{ increase.}$$

b. The 2001 income tax liability would increase by $89,402 \times 0.32 = \$28,609$.

c. Revenue for 2002 would decrease because more revenue that is now in 2002 would be pushed back to 2001 than would revenue now in 2003 be pushed back to 2002. The increase in 2001 accounts receivable ($190,540 − $93,438 = $97,102) would be transferred out of 2002 revenue and the increase in 2002 accounts receivable ($132,768 − $114,593 = $18,175) would be transferred into 2003 revenue, for a net decrease in 2002 revenue of $78,927 ($97,102 − $18,175).

d. Bad debts expense for 2002 would also decrease because of the corresponding revision in the timing of recognition of the expense. The increase in 2001 allowance ($14,260 − $6,560 = $7,700) would be transferred out of 2002 expense and the increase in 2002 allowance ($16,450 − $13,925 = $2,525) would be transferred into 2002 expense, for a net decrease in 2002 expense of $5,175.

e. Net income for 2002 would decrease due to the combined effect of the revenue decrease and the bad debts expense decrease, minus the tax effect:

$$(\$78,927 − \$5,175) \times (1 − 0.32) = \$73,752 \times (1 − 0.32) = \$50,151 \text{ decrease.}$$

f. The 2002 income tax expense would decrease by $73,752 × 0.32 = $23,601.

g. Income tax liability at the end of 2002 would increase $5,008 ($28,609 increase from 2001, minus $23,601 decrease from 2002).

h. There would be no immediate effect on cash or on 2002 cash flow, but eventually the $5,008 increased income tax liability would have to be paid.

Following the above framework summary, the journal entry to record the policy change as at the end of 2002 would be:

DR Accounts receivable	18,175	
CR Allowance for doubtful accounts		2,525
CR Income tax liability (payable or future)		5,008
CR Retained earnings (prior period policy change effect)		60,793
DR Revenue for 2002	78,927	
CR Bad debts expense for 2002		5,175
CR Income tax expense for 2002		23,601

Note that these examples assume policy changes and error corrections affecting prior years are entered directly into retained earnings and would be shown on the statement of retained earnings. That is consistent with present Canadian GAAP, as explained in section 3.5. However, GAAP in the U.S. would require that most of these be adjusted to the current year's income statement instead. This means that in the U.S., the current year's income would include the prior years' effects also. The net effect on the balance sheet at the end of the current year would be the same under either country's GAAP.

OW'S YOUR UNDERSTANDING?

Here are two questions you should be able to answer, based on what you have just read:

1. Hinton Inc. has found an error in its revenue account: an invoice for $1,400 was recorded as revenue in 2000 when it should have been recorded in 2001. The company's income tax rate is 35% and there was no corresponding error in cost of goods sold. What is the effect of the error on: 2000 net income; 2000 cash from operations; 2001 net income; retained earnings at the end of 2000; retained earnings at the end of 2001? ($1,400 (1 − 0.35) = $910 too high; no cash effect; $910 too low; $910 too high; no effect as the sum of 2000's and 2001's incomes is unaffected)

2. Granby Industrial Inc. decided to change its accounting for warranties, to accrue warranty expense sooner than had been done. The effect on warranty liability as at the end of 2000 was to increase it by $121,000. By the end of 2001, the liability would go up $134,000. The company's income tax rate is 30%. What would be the effect of the change on: 2001 net income; 2001 cash from operations; retained earnings at the end of 2001; income tax liability at the end of 2001?

   (($134,000 − $121,000) (1 − 0.30) = $9,100 lower; no cash effect;

   $134,000 (1 − 0.30) = $93,800 lower; $134,000 (0.30) = $40,200 lower)

10.10 TERMS TO BE SURE YOU UNDERSTAND

Here is this chapter's list of terms introduced or emphasized. Make sure you know what they mean *in accounting*, and if any are unclear to you, check the chapter again or refer to the Glossary of Terms at the back of the book.

Accounting policy choices
Acid test ratio
AT
Average interest rate
Book value per share
Cash flow analysis
Cash flow to total assets
Collection ratio
Common size financial statements
Compounded(ing)
Cost of capital
Current ratio
Days' sales in receivables
DCF
Debt to assets ratio
Debt–equity ratio
Discounted cash flow
Dividend payout ratio
Earnings per share
EPS

Financial statement analysis
Future value
FV
Gross margin
Gross profit ratio
IN(ATI)
Interest
Interest coverage ratio
Inventory turnover
L/E
Leverage
Leverage analysis
Leverage potential
Leverage return
Long-term debt–equity ratio
Management discussion and analysis
Market capitalization
MD&A
Net-of-tax analysis
Notes to the financial statements

Operating return	Return on investment
Opportunity cost	ROA
PE	ROA(ATI)
Present value	ROE
Present value analysis	ROI
Price–earnings ratio	Sales return
Principal	Scott formula
Profit margin	SR(ATI)
PV	Time value of money
Quick ratio	Total assets turnover
Ratio analysis	"What if" (effects) analysis
Ratios	Working capital
Refined ROA	Working capital ratio
Return on assets	Yield
Return on equity	

10.11 CONTINUING DEMONSTRATION CASE

INSTALLMENT 10

Data for Installment 10

In Installment 9, three financial statements for Mato Inc. were prepared: a Statement of Income and Deficit for the year ended February 28, 2001 (which might have been called the Statement of Loss and Deficit, because the company had a $54,066 loss); Balance Sheets at February 28, 2001, and March 1, 2000; and Cash Flow Statement for the year ended February 28, 2001.

These statements are the data for this Installment, which will illustrate the calculation of various financial ratios and the Scott formula. The illustration will not always be straightforward, because the company lost money and is not in a strong financial position. Unfortunately, you may well encounter such less-than-successful companies. So, seeing how to apply the analyses to them should increase your understanding of the analyses.

Results for Installment 10

To begin with, here are the ratios set out in section 10.4, in the order given there. Refer to the statements in Installment 9 (section 9.9), and make sure you know where the figures for the ratios below came from. Note that the company has made no provision for an income tax recovery on its first-year loss—such a recovery would depend on having future taxable income to deduct the loss against, and that is not likely enough to warrant creating an income tax recovery asset in the present circumstances.

Other versions of some of the ratios calculated below are quite possible. Dollar signs have been omitted and most ratios are rounded to three decimals.

Performance ratios:

1. Return on year-end equity: (54,066) / 70,934 = (.762), negative.
   Return on beginning equity: (54,066) / 125,000 = (.433), negative.
2. Return on ending assets: ((54,066) + 6,469) / 160,742 = (.296), negative.
3. Sales return before interest: [(54,066) + 6,469] / 229,387 = (.207), negative.
   Sales return after interest: (54,066) / 229,387 = (.236), negative.

4. Common size financial statements: not illustrated here.
5. Gross margin: 90,620 / 229,387 = .395. Cost of goods sold is .605 of sales revenue, so the average markup is .395 / .605 = 65% of cost.
6. Average interest rate: 6,469 / 89,808 = .072.
7. Cash flow to total ending assets: (55,028) / 160,742 = (.342), negative.
8. Earnings per share: number of shares not known, and EPS is not as meaningful for a private company as for a publicly traded one.
9. Book value per share: number of shares not known; however, the owners' original equity of $125,000 is now down to $70,934, which means the book value of the shares is only 56.7% of the amounts the owners contributed.
10. Price–earnings ratio: not determinable because the shares of a private company like this are not traded and their price, therefore, is not known.
11. Dividend payout ratio: no dividends declared since there was a loss.

Activity (turnover) ratios:

12. Total asset turnover: 229,387 / 160,742 = 1.427 times.
13. Inventory turnover: 138,767 / 33,612 = 4.128 times.
14. Collection ratio: 14,129 / (229,387/365) = 22.5 days.

Financing ratios:

15. Debt–equity ratio: 89,808 / 70,934 = 1.266.
    Beginning debt–equity ratio was: 16,100 / 125,000 = .129.
16. Long-term debt–equity ratio: zero (no long-term debt).
17. Debt to assets ratio: 89,808 / 160,742 = .559.

Liquidity and solvency warning ratios:

18. Working capital ratio: 54,684 / 89,808 = .609.
    Beginning working capital ratio was: 130,000 / 16,100 = 8.075.
19. Acid test ratio: (6,418 + 14,129) / 89,808 = .229.
20. Interest coverage ratio: not calculated because with this large a loss there is no coverage!

The ratios tell a grim story:

- The company has lost 43.3% of its beginning equity;

- Its working capital ratio is considerably less than 1 (its working capital is negative);

- Its acid test ratio is less than 25%; and

- Its cash and receivables would carry its operations for less than a month.

But, there are some positive signs:

- The collection ratio is low (only 22.5 days);

- The debt–equity ratio is not high, even though equity has been reduced by losses; and

- With a fairly low debt to assets ratio and no long-term debt, there may be room for some long-term borrowing, should that be necessary to improve the current position.

What does the Scott formula tell us? Using the year-end figures from the above ratios, we have (no tax adjustments to any ratios are necessary):

$$ROE = SR \times AT \quad + (ROA - IN) \times L/E$$
$$(.762) = (.207) \times 1.427 + ((.296) - .072) \times 1.266$$
$$(.762) = (.295) \quad\quad\quad + (.368) \times 1.266$$
$$(.762) = (.295) \quad\quad\quad + (.466)$$

The formula works out to within a .001 rounding error. It indicates that the company's woeful ROE is due to the negative effects of leverage compounding poor operating performance: the company was already losing money, and by borrowing, made things worse. Normally, a high asset turnover indicates good performance. But here, as the company was losing on every sale, getting more sales also made things worse. Perhaps Mavis and Tomas tried to do too much in their first year.

This example illustrates that most ratios and such aggregations as the Scott formula can be calculated for losing companies. Financial statement analysis is not limited to profitable, financially solid companies. However, the interpretation of the statements must be made carefully, because negative relationships may exist where they're not expected, as we saw with the effects of asset turnover above.

We should wish Mavis and Tomas well in their second year. If they don't do better, there won't be a third year!

10.12 HOMEWORK AND DISCUSSION TO DEVELOP UNDERSTANDING

PROBLEM 10.1*
List advantages and disadvantages of ratio analysis

List the advantages and disadvantages you see of using ratio analysis of financial statements (including leverage analysis) as a way of evaluating management's performance. For the disadvantages, try to think of a way around each problem you identify.

PROBLEM 10.2*
Ratios to measure different kinds of performance

1. Many financial performance measures are ratios of some return over some investment base. Why is such a concept of performance important in business?
2. With your answer to part 1 in mind, how might you measure the performance of each of the following investments owned by Professor Ann Mandel?

   a. Her $1,200 in a savings account at Solid Bank.
   b. Her investment of $15,000 in a little consulting business she runs off campus.
   c. Her Slapdash 210 sports car.

PROBLEM 10.3*
Comments on leverage, risk, and Scott formula's analysis

Use nontechnical language to answer the following:

1. What is financial leverage?
2. Why is such leverage risky?
3. How does the Scott formula incorporate leverage?
4. Which is more risky, a company whose Scott formula leverage component is $(.10 - .08) \times 2$, or one whose component is $(.09 - .08) \times 1$? Explain.

PROBLEM 10.4*
Answer various questions using ratio analysis

Company A is owned 100% by Mr. A. A summary of Company A's financial statement information is as follows:

Balance Sheet as at September 30, 2001:

Total assets	$80,000
Total liabilities	$35,000
Total shareholder's equity	45,000
Total liabilities and shareholder's equity	$80,000

Income Statement for the year ending September 30, 2001:

Revenue		$30,000
Expenses		
Interest	$ 2,000	
General and operating expenses	19,000	
Income tax ($33\frac{1}{3}\%$)	3,000	24,000
Net income for the year		$ 6,000

Statement of Retained Earnings for the year ending September 30, 2001:

Balance at beginning of year	$17,000
Net income for year	6,000
Balance at end of year	$23,000

1. Calculate Company A's return on equity for 2001.
2. What contributes more to return on equity: managerial performance (operating return) or leverage return (financial leverage)? Show all calculations.
3. Company A is considering borrowing $50,000 for additional assets that would earn the company the same return on assets it has historically earned, according to the financial statement information above. The cost of borrowing this money is 8%. Should the company borrow the money? (Assume there are no alternative sources of funding.) Show all calculations. Hint: this is not a present value question.
4. Place yourself in the role of the local bank manager. Mr. A has approached you to lend the company the required $50,000 mentioned above. Detailed financial statement information has already been presented to you.
   a. What additional information would you require, if any?
   b. What financial statement ratios, in addition to those calculated in previous parts of this problem, would be useful in aiding your decision? Do not calculate the ratios, just mention or describe them.

PROBLEM 10.5*
Identify ratios by function

Match the two columns below. The left column lists the names of ratios and analysis components, and the right column describes the functions of those ratios and analysis components.

1. ROE	a. Shows if the company makes enough income to pay its interest
2. Sales return	b. Measures return on investment before financing that investment
3. PE ratio	c. Shows the leverage potential
4. ROA(ATI) − IN(ATI)	d. Measures return on historical amount invested by owners
5. ROA(ATI)	e. Shows the components of operating return
6. SR(ATI) × AT	f. Indicates ability to pay short-term debts without selling inventory
7. Interest coverage	g. Relates share price to EPS
8. Debt–equity	h. Shows how much the company earns on a dollar of revenue
9. Quick ratio	i. Indicates the average markup on purchase price to get selling price
10. Gross margin	j. Shows the relative amount of investment by creditors vs. owners

INFORMATION FOR PROBLEMS 10.6*, 10.7*, AND 10.8*: PETRO-CANADA

Petro-Canada, headquartered in Calgary, is a national oil company with operations across Canada, including oil from the Grand Banks of Atlantic Canada and from the Syncrude project in Alberta, natural gas in various parts of Western Canada, and gas stations in most parts of the country. Below are its 1999 financial statements (without notes or accounting policies). Use those statements to answer the following three problems.

PETRO-CANADA
Consolidated Statement of Earnings
(stated in millions of Canadian dollars)

For the years ended Decembet 31,	1999	1998	1997
Revenue			
Operating	$6 095	$4 951	$6 017
Investment and other income	52	65	79
	6 147	5 016	6 096
Expenses			
Crude oil and product purchases	3 436	2 413	3 183
Producing, refining and marketing	1 236	1 309	1 352
General and administrative (Note 4)	221	265	194
Exploration	78	95	75
Depreciation, depletion and amortization	558	530	482
Taxes other than income taxes	55	63	68
Interest	141	122	106
	5 725	4 797	5 460
Earnings Before Income Taxes	422	219	636
Provision for Income Taxes (Note 5)			
Current	147	166	(41)
Deferred	42	(42)	371
	$ 189	$ 124	$ 330
Net Earnings	$ 233	$ 95	$ 306
Earnings per Share (dollars) (Note 6)	$ 0.86	$ 0.35	$ 1.13

(The indicated notes are not included in this book.)

Consolidated Statement of Retained Earnings
(stated in millions of Canadian dollars)

For the years ended Decembet 31,	1999	1998	1997
Retained Earnings (Deficit) at Beginning of Year	$147	$139	$(88)
Net earnings	233	95	306
Dividends on common and variable voting shares	(92)	(87)	(79)
Retained Earnings at End of Year	$288	$147	$139

PETRO-CANADA
Consolidated Statement of Cash Flows
(stated in millions of Canadian dollars)

For the years ended Decembet 31,	1999	1998	1997
Operating Activities			
Net earnings	$ 233	$ 95	$ 306
Items not affecting cash flow (Note 7)	653	640	882
Exploration expenses (Note 12)	78	95	75
Cash flow	964	830	1 263
(Increase) decrease in operating working capital and other (Note 8)	(155)	238	(167)
Cash flow from operating activities	809	1 068	1 096
Investing Activities			
Expenditures on property, plant and equipment and exploration	(1 021)	(1 116)	(1 049)
Proceeds from sales of assets (Note 9)	81	505	201
Increase in deferred charges and other assets, net	(5)	(17)	(15)
	(945)	(628)	(863)
Financing Activities and Dividends			
Dividends on common and variable voting shares	(92)	(87)	(79)
Reduction of long-term debt	(3)	(140)	(114)
Proceeds from issue of common and variable voting shares	6	6	3
Proceeds from issue of long-term debt	—	387	—
Reduction of notes payable – Hibernia	—	(250)	—
	(89)	(84)	(190)
(Decrease) Increase in Cash and Short-Term Investments	(225)	356	43
Cash and Short-Term investments at Beginning of Year	431	75	32
Cash and Short-Term Investments at End of Year	$ 206	$ 431	$ 75

(The indicated notes are not included in this book.)

PETRO-CANADA
Consolidated Balance Sheet
(stated in millions of Canadian dollars)

As at December 31,	1999	1998
ASSETS		
Current Assets		
Cash and short-term investments (Note 10)	$ 206	$ 431
Accounts receivable	941	683
Inventories (Note 11)	501	455
Prepaid expenses	25	15
	1 673	1 584
Property, Plant and Equipment, NET (Note 12)	6 719	6 433
Deferred Charges and Other Assets (Note 13)	269	381
	$8 661	$8 398
LIABILITIES AND SHAREHOLDERS' EQUITY		
Current Liabilities		
Accounts payable and accrued liabilities	$1 307	$1 063
Income taxes payable	72	94
Current portion of long-term debt	4	3
	1 383	1 161
Long-Term Debt (Note 14)	1 707	1 826
Deferred Credits and Other Liabilities (Note 15)	355	362
Deferred Income Taxes	1 133	1 113
Commitments and Contingent Liabilities (Note 21)		
SHAREHOLDERS' EQUITY (Note 16)	4 083	3 936
	$8 661	$8 398

(The indicated notes are not included in this book.)

Approved on behalf of the Board

Ronald A. Brenneman
Director

Claude Fontaine
Director

PROBLEM 10.6*
Interpret Petro-Canada's Cash Flow Statement

Use the above Petro-Canada cash flow statement, and other statements where relevant, to answer the following questions:

1. Why is the company's cash from operating activities ($809 million in 1999, for example) so much greater than its earnings ($233 million in 1999, for example)?
2. The notes to the financial statements are not included above. What kinds of accounts are likely to be mentioned in Notes 7 and 8?
3. Write a paragraph identifying the major components of the company's cash flows over the three years.
4. Interpret the company's cash flow and financial strategy, particularly for 1999, using for reference the points a–i set out in section 10.5 and used there to comment on CAE.

PROBLEM 10.7*
Analyze Petro-Canada's financial position

Prepare an analysis of and commentary on Petro-Canada's financial position at the end of 1999, as compared to 1998, using the balance sheet above and any relevant information from the other financial statements above.

PROBLEM 10.8*
Do a performance analysis of Petro-Canada

1. Using the Petro-Canada financial statements above, prepare a few ratios relevant to analyzing the company's financial performance for 1999 as compared to 1998 and 1997, and comment on what those ratios show.
2. Did Petro-Canada benefit from financial leverage in 1999? How did that compare to 1998? Answer these questions simply, without use of the Scott formula.
3. Answer the questions in part 2 using the Scott formula, and comment on the relative sizes of operating and leverage returns in 1999 and 1998.

PROBLEM 10.9*
Basis present value analysis

You have an opportunity to invest $200,000. You will be paid a single interest payment of $100,000 (and get your investment back) at the end of five years.

1. If 8% is the return you require, should you invest? Show all calculations.
2. Describe one other factor you should consider before you invest.

PROBLEM 10.10*
Bond pricing

Wescania Inc. plans to issue 100,000 $100 bonds, intending to use the bonds to invest in various business opportunities that are expected to earn an overall 10% return over the 10 years the bonds are outstanding. Bond markets are rather volatile right now, so the company is trying to set the interest rate on the bonds so that they will bring in the needed $10,000,000 without costing more interest than necessary. Right now, the bond market seems to price $100 bonds for companies like Wescania at $100 if they carry interest of 8%, so the company plans to pay 8% interest on the bonds.

1. What would the 8% bonds sell for if Wescania priced them to yield:
   a. 8%?
   b. 7%?
   c. 9%?

2. If the company could sell the bonds priced to yield 7%, it would obtain about $700,000 more than the $10,000,000 needed. Does that mean the company would make a greater net income on the projects than it planned, or would it make less?

PROBLEM 10.11*
Evaluate a possible investment

Hedda has been saving money for years and has it invested in bank investment certificates that earn 5%. She feels that is a little low and has been looking around for other investment opportunities. She has been considering investing in Placentia Lobster Pots Inc., which has been doing very well in recent years. Placentia's shares are selling for $35 right now on the Toronto Stock Exchange. Her investigation indicates that a share of Placentia may be expected to pay a dividend of $1.50 per year and should sell for somewhere between $30 and $50 in 5 years' time, at which Hedda plans to cash all her investments in and buy a condo in a warm place.

What advice would you give Hedda about investing in Placentia?

PROBLEM 10.12*
Explain effects of some changes on present values

You are working on some project evaluations for your company's president, and have just completed present value calculations. The president asks you to consider some possible changes in the project plans. Explain the effect of each on the present values you have just calculated.

a. One project's time line is extended for a further three years into the future, with the total cash flow from the project being the same as originally predicted.

b. The required rate of return on another project is reduced from 9% to 7%.

c. Some cash inflows on a third project are expected to be postponed so that they come in during the 5th to 8th years instead of the 3rd to 6th years, though the total cash inflow will remain the same and will still take place over the originally planned 15 years.

d. The company's cost of capital increases by 0.5% as a result of increases in market interest rates.

PROBLEM 10.13*
Effects of changing doubtful accounts allowance, with tax

"Karl, we have a problem in our accounts receivable. We've provided an allowance for doubtful accounts of 2% of the gross receivables, but during this recession more customers are running into trouble. The allowance should be raised to 5%."

"Tanya, we can't do that. It would wipe out our profitability and ruin our cash flow."

Given the data below, prepare an analysis for Karl and Tanya. (If you have not yet studied the allowance for doubtful accounts, Tanya's proposal would reduce income by the indicated increase in the allowance.)

Data:		
	Gross accounts receivable at year-end	$8,649,000
	Net income for the year at present	$223,650
	Income tax rate	30%

PROBLEM 10.14*
Effects of ending a policy of capitalizing advertising costs, with income tax

Checkup Auto Services Inc., which has been in business one year, has a chain of heavily advertised automobile service centres. The company's income tax rate is 30%. The company makes it a practice to capitalize a portion of its advertising costs as a "deferred asset." The amount of advertising cost capitalized this year was $75,000 and the new company's policy is to amortize the capitalized amount to expense at 20% per year. An accountant suggested to the company's vice-president of finance that the policy of capitalizing advertising should be ended because the future economic benefit from the expenditures is not clearly determinable. The vice-president wants to know what effect such policy changes would have.

PROBLEM 10.15*
Effects of proposed policy of capitalizing improvement costs, with income tax

Senior management of Telemark Skiing Ltd. wishes to capitalize $2,350,000 in ski hill improvement costs expended this year and amortize the capitalized costs over 10 years, rather than just expensing them all as is now done. The company's income tax rate is 25%, and the company would plan to continue deducting the costs as expenses in computing income tax payable for this year, assuming the tax authorities would permit that. What would be the effect on this year's net income and cash flow from operations if the company capitalized those costs?

PROBLEM 10.16*
Basic multi-year effects analysis, with income tax

Mistaya Ltd. has decided to change its revenue recognition policy to increase revenue $10,000 in the current year and by a total of $8,000 in prior years (accounts receivable are increased correspondingly). Matched expenses increase $4,000 in the current year and $3,000 in prior years (so accounts payable go up as well). The company's income tax rate is 35%.

Determine all effects of the change on the company's income statement and cash flow statement for the current year and balance sheet as at the end of the current year. Show your calculations and demonstrate that all the effects balance.

PROBLEM 10.17
How does financial statement analysis help users?

Many external parties rely on statements such as the balance sheet, the income statement, and the cash flow statement produced by a company. Identify two different types of major users of financial information and briefly explain how analysis of the three financial statements will help them. (This is a similar question to some asked about the value of financial statements in earlier chapters, but now you should be able to relate financial statement analysis to user value.)

PROBLEM 10.18
Draft a speech on analysis and the use of financial statements

Write the rough notes for a speech you have been asked to give to a local investment club. The members of the club are all experienced stock market investors and want a better understanding of companies' accounting information. The topic of your speech is "Analysis and Use of Financial Accounting Information."

PROBLEM 10.19
Comment on a complaint about financial statement analysis

A senior member of a large public company's management complained:

Accountants' financial analyses don't seem very useful to me. The analyses don't reveal the business management factors that are important to my company's success. They are biased toward the past rather than the future. And, anyway, the stock market is way ahead of the accountants in judging the company's performance.

Comment on the manager's complaint.

PROBLEM 10.20
Calculate and explain return on equity and effect of debt

A neighbour of yours finds out that you are taking business courses and engages you in a conversation to get some cheap investment advice. She was raised during the Depression and is very averse to debt, believing that solid companies should be debt-free and raise all their capital by issuing shares or by retaining earnings. You have handy a set of financial statements for a company she knows about, which you use to discuss the matter with her.

Use the financial information below, extracted from those financial statements, to calculate the company's return on equity. Explain to your neighbour the effect debt has on the company's return on equity, and, specifically, whether this return is helped or hindered by the company's debt.

Total assets	$251,600
Total liabilities	98,980
Interest-bearing long-term debt	42,580
Share capital	87,150
Income tax rate	43%
Retained earnings	$ 65,470
Total revenues	313,450
Interest expense	5,070
Income before-tax and unusual item	36,100
Net income	28,060

PROBLEM 10.21
Analysis of effects of events on Scott formula leverage analysis

You are the chief accountant for Yummy Cookies Inc. and have just calculated the following Scott-formula leverage analysis for the company:

$$\text{ROE} = \text{SR(ATI)} \times \text{AT} + (\text{ROA(ATI)} - \text{IN(ATI)}) \times \text{L/E}$$
$$.095 = .04 \times 2.00 + (.08 - .07) \times 1.5$$

The president is not happy with a return on equity of 9.5% and has asked you to estimate the effects of each of the following changes and events separately:

1. Raising selling prices to increase after-tax sales return by half and asset turnover by 5%.
2. Refinancing the company's debt to reduce the after-tax cost of borrowing to 6%.
3. Reducing operating costs to increase after-tax sales return to 5%.
4. Increasing long-term borrowing and reducing equity to increase the debt–equity ratio to 1.8.

INFORMATION FOR PROBLEMS 10.22, 10.23, AND 10.24: TYSON FOODS

Tyson Foods, Inc., headquartered in Arkansas, is the largest producer of poultry in the world. Below are its 1999 financial statements (without notes or accounting policies). Use those statements to answer the following three problems.

Consolidated statements of income **Tyson Foods, Inc. 1999 Annual Report** (in millions, except per share data)			
three years ended Oct. 2, 1999	1999	1998	1997
Sales	$7,362.9	$7,414.1	$6,355.7
Cost of Sales	6,054.1	6,260.1	5,318.0
	1,308.8	1,154.0	1,037.7
Operating Expenses:			
Selling	574.6	642.2	513.3
General and administrative	134.5	132.7	96.9
Amortization	35.9	33.3	27.6
Asset impairment and other charges	76.9	142.2	—
	821.9	950.4	637.8
Operating Income	486.9	203.6	399.9
Other expense (income):			
Interest	124.0	139.1	110.4
Foreign currency exchange	(2.7)	—	—
Other	(5.4)	(6.5)	(40.2)
	115.9	132.6	70.2
Income Before Taxes on Income and			
Minority Interest	371.0	71.0	329.7
Provision for Income Taxes	129.4	45.9	143.9
Minority Interest in Net Income of			
Consolidated Subsidiary	11.5	—	—
Net Income	$ 230.1	$ 25.1	$ 185.8
Basic Earnings Per Share	$ 1.00	$ 0.11	$ 0.86
Diluted Earnings Per Share	$ 1.00	$ 0.11	$ 0.85

See accompanying notes. (not included in this book)

Consolidated balance sheets
Tyson Foods, Inc. 1999 Annual Report
(in millions, except per share data)

Oct. 2, 1999 and Oct. 3, 1998	1999	1998
Assets		
Current Assets:		
Cash and cash equivalents	$ 30.3	$ 46.5
Accounts receivable	602.5	631.0
Inventories	989.4	984.1
Assets held for sale	74.5	65.2
Other current assets	30.2	38.3
Total Current Assets	1,726.9	1,765.1
Net Property, Plant and Equipment	2,184.5	2,256.5
Excess of Investments Over Net Assets Acquired	962.5	1,035.8
Other Assets	208.8	185.1
Total Assets	$5,082.7	$5,242.5
Liabilities and Shareholders' Equity		
Current Liabilities:		
Notes payable	$ 65.9	$ 84.7
Current portion of long-term debt	222.7	77.6
Trade accounts payable	351.9	330.6
Accrued salaries and wages	102.0	98.4
Federal and state income taxes payable	13.0	0.9
Accrued interest payable	22.9	22.3
Other current liabilities	208.6	216.5
Total Current Liabilities	987.0	831.0
Long-Term Debt	1,515.2	1,966.6
Deferred Income Taxes	398.0	434.4
Other Liabilities	54.5	40.1
Shareholders' Equity:		
Common stock ($.10 per value):		
Class A-authorized 900 million shares:		
Issued 137.9 million shares in 1999 and 1998	13.8	13.8
Class B-authorized 900 million shares:		
Issued 102.7 million shares in 1999 and 1998	10.3	10.3
Capital in excess of par value	740.0	740.5
Retained earnings	1,599.0	1,394.2
Other accumulated comprehensive income	(1.5)	(1.0)
	2,361.6	2,157.8
Less treasury stock, at cost—12 million shares in 1999 and 9.7 million shares in 1998	232.0	185.1
Less unamortized deferred compensation	1.6	2.3
Total Shareholders' Equity	2,128.0	1,970.4
Total Liabilities and Shareholders' Equity	$5,082.7	$5,242.5

See accompanying notes. (not included in this book)

Consolidated statements of shareholders' equity
Tyson Foods, Inc. 1999 Annual Report
(Retained earnings portion only)
(in millions, except per share data)

	1999	1998	1997
Retained Earnings			
Beginning balance	1,394.2	1,390.8	1,232.4
Net income	230.1	25.1	185.8
Three-for-two stock split			(7.4)
Dividends	(25.3)	(21.7)	(20.0)
Ending balance	1,599.0	1,394.2	1,390.8

Consolidated statements of cash flows
Tyson Foods, Inc. 1999 Annual Report
(in millions)

three years ended Oct. 2, 1999	1999	1998	1997
Cash Flows From Operating Activities:			
Net Income	$ 230.1	$ 25.1	$ 185.8
Adjustments to reconcile net income to cash provided by operating activities:			
Depreciation	255.2	243.1	202.8
Amortization	35.9	33.3	27.6
Asset impairment and other charges	76.9	214.6	—
Deferred income taxes	(13.5)	(144.5)	10.5
Minority interest	11.5	—	—
Foreign currency exchange loss	(2.7)	—	—
Gain on dispositions of property, plant and equipment	(0.5)	(2.3)	(34.8)
Decrease (increase) in accounts receivable	24.8	32.8	(68.4)
(Increase) decreases in inventories	(98.8)	79.8	143.6
Increase (decrease) in trade accounts payable	20.4	(6.6)	19.2
Net change in other current assets and liabilities	7.4	21.1	54.7
Cash Provided by Operating Activities	546.7	496.4	541.0
Cash Flows From Investing Activities:			
Net cash paid for acquisitions	—	(258.5)	(4.3)
Additions to property, plant and equipment	(363.3)	(310.4)	(291.2)
Proceeds from sale of assets	233.8	136.0	223.4
Net change in other assets and liabilities	(36.4)	(13.3)	(63.8)
Cash Used for Investing Activities	(165.9)	(446.2)	(135.9)

(continued)

three years ended Oct. 2, 1999	1999	1998	1997
Cash Flows From Financing Activities:			
Decrease in notes payable	(18.8)	(74.4)	(2.2)
Proceeds from long-term debt	76.1	1,027.1	131.4
Repayments of long-term debt	(382.4)	(954.7)	(420.8)
Purchase of treasury shares	(52.1)	(22.3)	(109.6)
Other	(17.6)	(2.9)	(17.2)
Cash Used for Financing Activities	(394.8)	(27.2)	(418.4)
Effect of Exchange Rate Change on Cash	(2.2)	(0.1)	0.3
(Decrease) Increase in Cash	(16.2)	22.9	(13.0)
Cash and Cash Equivalents at Beginning of Year	46.5	23.6	36.6
Cash and Cash Equivalents at End of Year	$ 30.3	$ 46.5	$ 23.6

See accompanying notes. (not included in this book)

PROBLEM 10.22
Analyze Tyson Foods' financial performance

Using the above financial statements, prepare an analysis and interpretation of Tyson Foods' 1999 financial performance in comparison to 1998. Use relevant performance-related ratios from section 10.4 plus the company's cash flow information.

PROBLEM 10.23
Analyze Tyson Foods' financial position

Using the above financial statements, prepare an analysis and interpretation of Tyson Foods' financial position as at October 2, 1999, in comparison to 1998. Use any relevant ratios and cash flow information.

PROBLEM 10.24
Analyze Tyson Foods' leverage

Using the above financial statements, prepare an analysis, using the Scott formula, of whether, and to what extent, Tyson Foods benefited from leverage in 1999 as compared to 1998.

PROBLEM 10.25
Use Scott formula to explain change in performance

The president of General Products Ltd. is curious about why—in spite of growth in revenue, assets, and net income since last year—the company's return on equity has gone down. Last year's ROE was 9.3%, but this year it is 9.0%.

This year's financial statement information shows:

- As at September 30, 2001: total assets, $5,000,000; total liabilities, $2,000,000; total owners' equity, $3,000,000.

- For the year ended September 30, 2001: revenue, $1,800,000; interest expense, $200,000; other expenses except income tax, $1,150,000; income tax expense (40%), $180,000; net income, $270,000; dividends declared, $50,000.

1. Prepare a Scott-formula analysis for the year ended September 30, 2001.

2. Explain to the president what the results you derived in part 1 indicate about the company's 2001 performance.

3. The president wants to know what the limitations of the Scott formula for assessing managerial performance are. Remembering that the formula is based on accounting figures, answer the president.

4. Last year's Scott formula for General Products Ltd. (rounded to three decimals) was: .093 = (.164) (.491) + (.080 − .025) (.240). Use this and your answer to part 1 to explain to the president why return on equity changed from last year to this year.

PROBLEM 10.26
Use statement analysis to evaluate president's claims

The president of a medium-sized manufacturing company wants to renew the company's operating loan. In discussions with the bank's lending officer, the president says, "As the accompanying financial statements show, our working capital position has increased during the past year, and we have managed to reduce operating expenses significantly."

The partial financial statements showed the following:

Titan Manufacturing Ltd.
Partial Balance Sheet
as at December 31, 2001 and 2000

	2001	2000
Current Assets		
Cash	$ 50,000	$200,000
Accounts receivable	250,000	100,000
Inventories	500,000	400,000
Total current assets	$800,000	$700,000
Current Liabilities		
Accounts payable	$250,000	$200,000
Operating loan	100,000	100,000
Total current liabilities	$350,000	$300,000

Titan Manufacturing Ltd.
Income Statement
for the Years Ended December 31, 2001 and 2000

	2001	2000
Sales	$1,200,000	$1,500,000
Less cost of goods sold	780,000	900,000
Gross profit	$ 420,000	$ 600,000
Operating expenses	350,000	400,000
Income before taxes	$ 70,000	$ 200,000
Income taxes	14,000	40,000
Net income	$ 56,000	$ 160,000

1. Evaluate the president's comments. Incorporate appropriate ratio analysis into your discussion.
2. What additional financial information (if any) would you request of the president? Why?

PROBLEM 10.27
Basic ideas of present value analysis

1. Explain what the "time value of money" or "present value" concept is all about. Why would business people be sensitive to it?
2. Calculate the present value of each of the following:
   a. $1,000 to be received a year from now. If it were on hand now, it would be invested at 10% interest.
   b. $1,000 to be received at the end of each of the next three years. The opportunity cost of interest or cost of capital in this case is 12%.
   c. Answer (b) again but assume a rate of 10%. Why is the present value higher when the rate is lower?

PROBLEM 10.28
Present value analysis—wrestle or play hockey?

Elbows Murphy, a feared hockey player, has come to you for financial advice. The Burlington Stars, in a bid to strengthen their team, have made him a contract offer that would pay a signing bonus now of $90,000, plus a salary of $85,000 for each of the next three years. Elbows is considering turning down the offer, because he thinks he can earn $120,000 per year for the next three years as a professional wrestler.

1. If Elbows could invest his hockey earnings (including signing bonus) at 11%, should he wrestle or play hockey?
2. If Elbows could invest at only 7%, what should he do?
3. At what interest rate would it make no difference to Elbows whether he wrestled or played hockey?

PROBLEM 10.29
Present value analysis—proposed investment in shares

Surprising Sleepwear Ltd. is considering making an investment in shares of a company that makes fibreglass underwear. The investment will cost $110,000 and will return $8,000 cash per year for four years. At the end of four years, Surprising expects to be able to sell the shares for $125,000. Surprising pays 11% to raise financing for such ventures. Based just on this data, should Surprising buy the shares?

PROBLEM 10.30
Present value analysis—buy or lease a truck?

Speedy Trucking is trying to decide whether it should buy a new truck for its business or lease the truck from another company. If Speedy decides to buy the truck, it must pay $140,000 cash immediately, and the truck is expected to last for five years. At the end of the five years, the truck will have no remaining value and will be disposed of. If Speedy decides to lease the truck, it must pay $30,000 at the end of each year for five years, at which point the truck must be returned to the leasing company.

1. If the current market interest rate (which Speedy has to pay to borrow) is 10%, should Speedy lease or buy the truck?
2. Suppose Speedy discovers that if the truck were bought, it could be sold at the end of the five years for $35,000. Would your answer to part 1 change?

3. Identify one or two important assumptions made in your analyses and explain why those assumptions are important.

PROBLEM 10.31
Buy a cappuccino machine or not?

Harriett is thinking of buying a kitchenette unit for her "handmade goods" store, so that she may sell coffee, cappuccino, cookies, and other such things to browsing customers. She thinks the unit would be a great success, bringing in net cash of $1,000 per year (sales from the unit, less expenses, plus increased sales of handcrafts, less expenses). The unit would cost $4,000 and Harriett would plan to sell it in four years for about $1,500 and buy a bigger one if the idea is a success. Harriett's company would pay about 12% interest on a bank loan to cover the cost of the unit.

Should Harriett's company buy the kitchenette unit? Support your answer with relevant calculations.

PROBLEM 10.32
Answer questions about a blended payments mortgage

You are the accountant for Red River Jeans, which has just obtained a mortgage on its factory. The mortgage carries interest at 7% and requires 10 annual payments of $15,000 beginning a year from when the cash was provided. Answer the following questions:

1. How much cash did Red River receive for the mortgage?
2. What will be the interest expense on the mortgage for the first year?
3. What will be owing on the mortgage at the end of the sixth year?
4. You have to do a balance sheet on the day the mortgage was obtained. In that balance sheet, what will be the current portion of the mortgage, and what will be the noncurrent portion?

PROBLEM 10.33
General effects analysis

Suppose that on December 31, the last day of its fiscal year, a large company sold bonds by which it borrowed $150,000,000 cash, to be paid back in six years. The money was used on the same day to reduce the company's short-term bank loans by $50,000,000 and buy additional equipment for $100,000,000.

Calculate the changes to the following that would result from the above:

a. Total current assets.
b. Total assets.
c. Total current liabilities.
d. Working capital ratio.
e. Total shareholders' equity.
f. Net earnings for the year ended on the day of the borrowing.
g. Cash and cash equivalents.
h. Cash used for investments.
i. Cash provided from financing.

Describe how predictions of the effects on the following could be made:

j. Return on equity for the period after the loan.
k. Leverage return.

PROBLEM 10.34
Some effects
analysis concepts

1. Why do changes in accounting methods usually have no effect on cash or cash flow?
2. Since the cash flow statement begins with net income, any method change that changes net income will appear to change cash flow. How can this happen when the cash flow statement's total cash flow is unaffected by the change?
3. Can you suggest a situation where an accounting method change *would* affect cash flow as reported on the cash flow statement?
4. Why is it important to take income tax into account when doing "what if" effects analysis?
5. If a company decides to recognize revenue earlier than had been its practice, its accounts receivable will increase. Does this mean that revenue and net income will increase for every year affected by the policy change?

PROBLEM 10.35
Multi-year effects
analysis without
considering income
tax

Fringle Sales Inc. has the following history for its first three years of existence:

	2002	2001	2000
Revenue:			
Credit sales	$900,000	$600,000	$500,000
Cash sales	80,000	75,000	40,000
Cash collected from customers*	910,000	640,000	420,000
Accounts receivable that became:			
Doubtful during the year	40,000	15,000	10,000
Worthless during the year	10,000	30,000	5,000

* Including cash sales

The president, Fringle, is wondering what difference to the company's working capital and income before income tax it would make if the company used one of the following accounts receivable valuation methods:

a. Make no allowance for doubtful or bad debts and just keep trying to collect.
b. Write off worthless accounts, but make no allowance for doubtful ones.
c. Allow for doubtful and worthless accounts when they become known.

Provide an analysis for the president.

PROBLEM 10.36
Effects of recogniz-
ing supplies inven-
tory, with tax

Magnic Manufacturing Co. has large amounts of manufacturing supplies that have been recorded as an expense when purchased. Now the company is considering recognizing the supplies on hand as an asset. If this were done, a new supplies inventory account would appear in the current assets. Its balance would be $148,650 at the end of last year and $123,860 at the end of this year. The company's income tax rate is 30%.

Calculate the effect on each of the following that would result if the company changed its accounting to recognize the supplies inventory:

1. Retained earnings at the end of last year.

2. Income tax liability at the end of last year.
3. Supplies expense for this year.
4. Net income for this year.
5. Current assets at the end of this year.
6. Income tax liability at the end of this year.
7. Retained earnings at the end of this year.
8. Cash flow for this year.
9. Cash flow for next year.

PROBLEM 10.37
Loan and policy change effects analyses

1. Strapped Ltd., which has $190,000 in current assets and $170,000 in current liabilities, borrows $40,000 from the bank as a long-term loan, repayable in four years. What is the effect of this loan on working capital? On the working capital ratio? On current net income?

2. Slipshod Inc. has discovered that it has not estimated enough warranty expenses because more customers are returning products for repair than had been expected. The company decides to recognize an additional $130,000 in noncurrent warranty liability, and therefore in corresponding expenses: $90,000 in respect to sales recognized in the current year and $40,000 in respect to prior years' sales. The company's income tax rate is 35%. What will this do to the current year's net income? To retained earnings? To cash from operations? To the working capital ratio?

PROBLEM 10.38
Effects analysis of truck fleet purchase and financing

Suppose that on May 1, 2002, Large Corporation decides to purchase a new fleet of delivery trucks at a total cost of $5,800,000. The trucks will be paid for in cash, which Large Corporation will raise by using $2,200,000 cash on hand, issuing shares for $2,000,000, and borrowing $1,600,000 over 20 years from the bank.

1. Using the preceding information, fill in the blanks below, indicating the magnitude and direction of the change in each category the truck purchase will cause.

Large Corporation
***Changes in* Balance Sheet at May 1, 2002**

Cash equivalent assets	$_____	Cash equivalent liabilities	$_____
Other current assets	$_____	Other current liabilities	$_____
Noncurrent assets	$_____	Noncurrent liabilities	$_____
		Share capital	$_____
		Retained earnings	$_____
Total assets	$_____	Total liabilities & owners' equity	$_____

2. What effect (if any) will this event have on the Financing Activities section of the cash flow statement for the year?

3. What effect (if any) will this event have on the income statement for the year?
4. Which important financial statement ratios would you expect this event to affect?
5. Record the above event as a journal entry.

PROBLEM 10.39 (CHALLENGING)
Use ratios to evaluate relative performance

A friend has asked you to evaluate information about two companies in the same industry. Your friend wants to invest in one or the other, but not both. Both companies are publicly traded, started with $10,000 of cash, have been in operation exactly one year, have paid the interest owing on their long-term debts to date, and have declared dividends of $1 per share.

The *beginning* balance sheets for the two companies at January 1, 2001, were as follows:

Alpha Company		Omega Company	
Total assets	$10,000	Total assets	$10,000
Long-term debt	$ 1,000	Long-term debt	$ 9,000
Shareholders' equity (900 common shares issued)	9,000	Shareholders' equity (100 common shares issued)	1,000
Total	$10,000	Total	$10,000

In 2001, Alpha Company had a net income of $2,400, while Omega Company's net income was $1,600. Your friend says, "Alpha Company seems the better investment. Its return on investment is 24%, and Omega's is only 16%."

Comment on your friend's observation and on the relative performance of the companies, and give your friend some investment advice.

PROBLEM 10.40 (CHALLENGING)
Performance evaluation using ratios

International Business Computers (IBC) has enjoyed modest success in penetrating the personal computer market since it began operations a few years ago. A new computer line introduced recently has been received well by the general public. However, the president, who is well versed in electronics but not in accounting, is worried about the future of the company.

The company's operating loan is at its limit and more cash is needed to continue operations. The bank wants more information before it extends the company's credit limit.

The president has asked you, as vice-president of finance, to do a preliminary evaluation of the company's performance, using appropriate financial statement analysis, and to recommend possible courses of action for the company. The president particularly wants to know how the company can obtain additional cash. Use the following summary financial information to do your evaluation and make your recommendations.

International Business Computers
Balance Sheets as at December 31 (in 000s)

	2001	2000	1999
Current assets:			
Cash	$ 19	$ 24	$ 50
Marketable securities	37	37	37
Accounts receivable — trade	544	420	257
Inventory	833	503	361
Total current assets	$1,433	$ 984	$ 705
Fixed assets:			
Land	$ 200	$ 200	$ 100
Buildings	350	350	200
Equipment	950	950	700
	$1,500	$1,500	$1,000
Less: Accumulated amortization, buildings and equipment	(447)	(372)	(288)
Net fixed assets	1,053	1,128	712
Total assets	$2,486	$2,112	$1,417
Current liabilities:			
Bank loan	$ 825	$ 570	—
Accounts payable — trade	300	215	$ 144
Other liabilities	82	80	75
Income tax payable	48	52	50
Total current liabilities	$1,255	$ 917	$ 269
Shareholders' equity:			
Common stock	$1,000	$1,000	$1,000
Retained earnings	231	195	148
Total shareholders' equity	$1,231	$1,195	$1,148
Total liabilities and shareholders' equity	$2,486	$2,112	$1,417

International Business Computers Combined Statements of Income and Retained Earnings for the Years Ended December 31			
	2001	2000	1999
Sales	$3,200	$2,800	$2,340
Cost of goods sold	2,500	2,150	1,800
Gross profit	$ 700	$ 650	$ 540
Expenses	584	533	428
Net income	$ 116	$ 117	$ 112
Opening retained earnings	195	148	96
	$ 311	$ 265	$ 208
Less: Dividends	80	70	60
Closing retained earnings	$ 231	$ 195	$ 148
Other related information included in total expenses:			
Interest expense	$ 89	$ 61	—
Income tax expense	$ 95	$ 102	$ 97

PROBLEM 10.41 (CHALLENGING) Present value analysis—investment choices

You are a rational investor facing a choice of two investment opportunities on December 31, 2001. Your required rate of return is 9%, the current market yield.

1. The first investment is in corporate bonds issued by Big Conglomerate, Inc. (an old and established firm), which have a face value of $100 and pay 8% annual interest on December 31 of each of the next four years, and repay the $100 principal on December 31 of the fourth year.

   What is the value of the $100 Big Conglomerate bond to you?

2. The second alternative is an investment in shares of a small gold mining company recently formed by your uncle. He is quite confident that the company will be able to pay cash dividends according to the following schedule:

Dec. 31/2002	Dec. 31/2003	Dec. 31/2004	Dec. 31/2005
$32 per share	$32 per share	$32 per share	$32 per share

   Based on this schedule, at what price per share would it not matter to you whether you invested some of your money in Big Conglomerate bonds or bought shares in your uncle's mining company?

3. What other factors might you want to consider before you make a decision?

PROBLEM 10.42 (CHALLENGING) Evaluate business disposition alternatives

A company has decided to discontinue one of its lines of business. It has put the business up for sale and has received three offers. The first is for $525,000 cash. The second is for $100,000 cash now and $60,000 for each of the next 10 years. The third is for a 10-year schedule of payments equalling $50,000 for each of the next 5 years and $90,000 for each of the remaining 5 years. The company has studied interest rates and believes it could earn 5% on the money for the next 5 years and 6% for the 5 years after that. Which offer is the best one?

**PROBLEM 10.43
(CHALLENGING)
Provide retirement
advice**

Your aunt has asked you how to decide about a possible retirement plan she is considering. The plan would have her save a fixed amount each year for 10 years and then would pay a different fixed annual retirement amount for 10 more years. She would like to have the annual retirement amount from this plan equal about $30,000 and is wondering how much she needs to save each year for the next 10 years to provide that retirement income. Explain to her how that annual saving would be calculated and what would have to be assumed to do the calculation.

**PROBLEM 10.44
(CHALLENGING)
Effects of an inven-
tory error, with tax**

On December 20, 2001, Profit Company Ltd. received merchandise amounting to $1,000, half of which was counted in its December 31 listing of all inventory items on hand. The invoice was not received until January 4, 2002, at which time the acquisition was recorded as of that date. The acquisition should have been recorded in 2001. Assume that the periodic inventory method is used (that is, the inventory asset is based on what was counted as being on hand, and the cost of goods sold expense is deduced as "beginning inventory + purchases – ending inventory) and that the company's income tax rate is 40%. Indicate the effect (overstatement, understatement, none) and the amount of the effect, if any, on each of the following:

1. Inventory as at December 31, 2001.
2. Inventory as at December 31, 2002.
3. Cost of goods sold expense, 2001.
4. Cost of goods sold expense, 2002.
5. Net income for 2001.
6. Net income for 2002.
7. Accounts payable as at December 31, 2001.
8. Accounts payable as at December 31, 2002.
9. Retained earnings as at December 31, 2001.
10. Retained earnings as at December 31, 2002.

**PROBLEM 10.45
(CHALLENGING)
Multiple-issue effects
analysis, with tax**

Cranberry Costumes Ltd. has been operating for several years now. So far the income for the current year is $75,000, before income tax at 30%. (The preceding year's income before tax was $62,000, and the tax rate then was also 30%.) Owner Jan Berry is considering a few changes and has asked your advice. The possible changes are:

- Change the revenue recognition policy to recognize revenue earlier in the process. This would increase accounts receivable by $26,000 immediately and $28,000 at the end of the previous year.

- Make a monthly accrual of the bonuses paid to employees at the end of each fiscal year. This would increase accounts payable by $11,000 immediately and $7,000 at the end of the preceding year.

- Postpone for five years repayment of a $19,000 loan (by Jan to the company), which has up to now been classified as a current liability.

- Capitalize as a trademark asset $14,000 of advertising supplies and wages expense recorded in the preceding year.

1. Calculate the net income after income tax for the current year that will result if all of the changes are adopted, and discuss the economic reasons for considering each change.
2. Calculate the effect on the amount of cash in the bank account of Cranberry Costumes Ltd. that these changes will have.
3. Explain any difference between results calculated for part 1 and part 2 above.

PROBLEM 10.46
(CHALLENGING)
Multi-year effects analysis, with tax

Kennedy Controls Inc. is considering a change in its accounting for maintenance costs. The chief financial officer proposes that the company capitalize 20% of its maintenance expenses, on the grounds that some of that expenditure has created additional plant assets. The company, the income tax rate for which is 40%, has existed for four years and depreciates its plant assets at 10% of year-end cost.

Here are some relevant account balances for the last four years, before considering the above proposal:

	Year 1	Year 2	Year 3	Year 4
Expenditures on plant assets	$1,243,610	$114,950	$34,770	$111,240
Balance in the plant assets account	1,243,610	1,358,560	1,393,330	1,504,570
Amortization expense	124,361	135,856	139,333	150,457
Accumulated amortization	124,361	260,217	399,550	550,007
Maintenance expense	43,860	64,940	73,355	95,440

Determine the effects of the proposed change on the *Year 4* income statement, cash flow statement, and balance sheet at the *end of Year 4*.

PROBLEM 10.47
(CHALLENGING)
Effects analysis, with ratios

Funtime Toys Inc. invents, manufactures, and sells toys and children's board games. In 2001, financial executives at Funtime decided to change two accounting methods.

- First, they decided to capitalize certain costs related to the development of new educational games, which had previously been expensed as incurred. It was thought that market demand for the games had been strong for several years, and that development costs were sure to provide future benefits.

- The second change was to the amortization method used on one class of equipment, to produce an annual amortization expense that was thought to better match the company's revenue generation process.

The effects of these changes on development and amortization expenses for the fiscal years 2000 and 2001 are shown below. The company's income tax rate is 30% and the method changes would affect future, not current, income tax.

Development Expense	2000	2001
Old method	$ 75,000	$ 85,000
New method	70,000	78,000

Amortization Expense	2000	2001
Old method	$150,000	$175,000
New method	160,000	170,000

Determine the combined impact the two method changes have on each of the following items for 2000 and 2001. Decide whether each item increases, decreases, or is not affected. (Check each ratio carefully to determine the impact on both the numerator and the denominator.)

a. Net income.
b. Working capital at the end of the year.
c. Total assets at the end of the year.
d. Debt–equity ratio at the end of the year.
e. Return on year-end equity.
f. Total asset turnover.

CASE 10A
Discuss further ideas about analyzing corporate performance

Below is a *Globe and Mail* article, "How to Profit from Annual Reports," that suggests ways of analyzing annual reports. Discuss the ideas and identify the ones that go beyond the techniques described in this chapter.

HOW TO PROFIT FROM ANNUAL REPORTS

Here are ways to assess the health of your investments

Reading annual reports can be a gruelling chore. Most investors can handle looking at the pictures, but find reading the fine print too much to endure.

Here are some ways to assess the health of your investments.

On the balance sheet, debt is the important issue to consider. On the income statement, operating margins take precedence, while on the statement of changes in financial condition, positive, or free cash flow, is the key to good cash management.

It's commendable when a company lists a mission statement in its annual report. That's because you get a chance to keep score to see if management accomplishes its goals. You should also read the comments by the chief executive officer. You can then decide if his or her vision is

realistic enough to be successful. Once you've read management's discussion, you should turn to the numbers.

For example, part of the mission of **Gennum Corp.** (GND — TSE, high $31, low $14.50, yesterday's close $25) was to achieve a 20-per-cent rate of return. The company succeeded in accomplishing that goal.

The Balance Sheet
On the balance sheet, the greatest concern is long-term debt — details are found in the annual report's footnotes. The best companies are those that spread out their debt maturities. It's easier for them to pay down or refinance debt with existing cash if only a small portion comes due in a year.

Canadian Airlines Corp. had most of its debt mature within a short period and therefore has had to spend a lot of time dealing with its bankers. Meantime, its performance has been affected by inadequate cash flow and the inevitable losses. As a result, shareholders have suffered as Canadian's share price these past few years has dropped precipitously.

You should also look at the interest rates charged on each debt instrument and whether the rates are fixed or variable. Many companies took advantage of low fixed rates between 1993 and 1996 and switched from variable to fixed interest.

One company that did so successfully was **Unican Security Systems Ltd.** (UCS.B — TSE, high $36, low $18.50, close $30.50). In 1992, variable debt made up 50 per cent of its total debt and it was exposed to any changes in interest rates. By the end of 1995, variable debt was only 25 per cent of outstanding debt.

Finally, you can assess a company's investment quality with a quick calculation of its debt-to-cash flow. This ratio is a standard used by the investment community. It's determined by dividing a firm's total debt by its cash flow. A number below two is preferred (all five companies profiled below meet that target). If higher, the company is spending too much of its cash on debt and, therefore, may have to postpone improvements to plant or equipment.

The Income Statement

On the income statement, look at the company's operating margins. It's calculated by dividing earnings before interest, taxes, depreciation and amortization (EBITDA) by revenue. By comparing the firm's operating costs to its sales, you're given a good impression of how efficiently management has run the organization.

Next, compare operating margins over a number of years. Margins of 15 per cent or more, achieved by the companies listed below, leave room for a company to cover its current expenses and still have room for profits.

Cash Flow Statement

On the statement of changes in financial position, often referred to as the cash flow statement,

it's vital that a company's cash flow (net income plus depreciation plus deferred taxes) covers its dividend payments and plant and equipment costs. This is known as "free cash flow" and is vital for a business to expand profitably.

If not, it means the company must find alternative sources of capital such as bank borrowing, equity issues or asset sales, actions that may have detrimental effects on the firm.

One company that turned a bad situation into a good one was **SNC-Lavalin Group Inc.** In 1991, the company was in the unenviable position of having negative cash flow, which caused higher borrowing. SNC's acquisition of **Lavalin Inc.** that year turned around the company's fortunes. Higher revenue from the acquisition created positive cash flows, which allowed the company to pay down its debt. As a result, earning and share prices rose.

The Leverage Factor

When a company carries debt on its books, the important thing to note is whether the business can earn a better rate of return with the use of leverage than if it were debt free. This works if the firm can keep its cost of debt below its internal rate of return.

One company that has used this strategy is Unican, a maker of keys and electronic locks. It's in the enviable position of generating surplus cash to expand its market share worldwide.

It has been acquiring similar European companies with little risk to shareholders. That's because its 9.3-per-cent cost of debt in fiscal 1996 ($2.5 million in interest expense divided by $27-million in outstanding debt) remains well below what it earned from the use of leverage. Last year, Unican's return on equity was 14 per cent ($17.8-million in net income divided by $126.9-million in equity).

Unican's acquisitions, therefore, have been profitable to shareholders because its spread — the difference between what it made (14 per cent) and what it paid (9 per cent) — was positive. As earnings rose during 1996, therefore, so did its share price — an admirable 88 per cent to $30.

If you pay attention to these calculations, you're apt to find solid companies worthy of your investment dollars. Below are five companies with strong financial statements that are perfect for self-directed registered retirement savings plans because you can buy them today and watch them appreciate over the next 20 years or so. They have little or no debt, positive free cash flow and operating margins and returns on equity above 15 per cent. It's been no surprise, therefore, why their stock prices have surged over the past five years.

- **Sceptre Investments Ltd.** (SZ.A — TSE, 52-week high $145, low $83.50, yesterday's close $125) is one of Canada's largest institutional money managers with interests in mutual funds, pension funds and personal portfolio management.
- **Gennum Corp.** makes silicon integrated circuits and thick-film hybrid circuits for specialized applications such as hearing aids and video broadcast control booths. The company has maintained high research and development spending (20 per cent of sales) and developed a microchip so that hearing aids can be placed out of view in the inner ear canal. Despite such high development spending, Gennum still ended the year with free cash flow of about $6.5-million. As the world's population ages, Gennum's hearing products should be in high demand.

- **Linamar Corp.** (LNR — TSE, high $50, low $21.50, close $47) makes automotive and agricultural components for the North American and European markets and is one of the most efficient engineering companies in Canada. The company operates through facilities that function as autonomous operating units.

  Its operating margins and return on equity are among the best in the automotive industry.
- **Samuel Manu-Tech Inc.** (SMT — TSE, high $23, low $11.25, close $21.25) makes steel products such as steel and plastic strapping, wire rope and chain and stainless steel pipe and tube. It had only served North American markets until it used its free cash flow to acquire a plastic strapping business in Britain. The purchase has doubled the company's size. As its market share rises, so too should its profits and share price.
- **Unican Security Systems Ltd.** As the world's largest company in its sector, Unican's current 20-per-cent growth rate should be maintained.

Bottom Line

It's more important to review a company's financial statement than listen to your neighbour's latest hot tip. If you take a moment to review a company's annual report, you'll know whether or not to invest. And when you find companies such as the five featured above, you should satisfy yourself with above-average investment returns.

Financial Performance in 1996

Company	Operating margin	Debt to cash flow	Return on equity	5-year return
Sceptre Investments	51	0.0%	87.8%	32.8%
Gennum Corp.	29	0.0	35.1	60.7
Linamar Corp.	16	0.2	26.3	75.7
Samuel Manu-Tech	15	1.1	19.6	25.4
Unican Security	17	1.0	15.0	48.1

Source: David Driscoll, "How to Profit from Annual Reports," *The Globe and Mail*, March 22, 1997, B24. © 1997 by M.P.L. Communications Inc., reproduced by permission of the *Investment Reporter*, 133 Richmond St. W., Toronto, ON, M5H 3M8.

CASE 10B
Analysis of a company's failure

This case is about a company that went under almost 30 years ago. The insight it provides into using financial information to spot trouble is still valuable!

W.T. Grant Company was a large U.S. retailer that enjoyed considerable success but then went bankrupt in the mid-1970s. The company had grown rapidly in the ten years up to 1973, establishing over 600 new stores in that period. A Canadian subsidiary was Zellers, now owned by the Hudson's Bay Company. It made some strategy changes during this time; for example, moving "upscale" from low-priced soft goods to higher-priced goods in competition with several department store chains. Its strategy was also to lease store space rather than to buy the property.

The company's share price fell dramatically between January 31, 1973, and January 31, 1974. In 1974, the company lost its credit rating, and after rescue attempts by 143 banks, the company was declared bankrupt shortly after the end of its 1975 fiscal year. Within another year, all the company's assets had been liquidated and the company ceased to exist.

Summary financial statements, several ratios, and the Scott formula calculations for W.T. Grant over the period 1970–75 are shown below.[4] Use those to identify some reasons for the company's share price crash in 1973–74 and its ultimate failure.

W.T. GRANT COMPANY
Some Balance Sheet Items as of January 31 (in millions $)

	1970	1971	1972	1973	1974	1975
Cash and marketable securities	33	34	50	31	46	80
Accounts receivable	368	420	477	543	599	431
Inventory	222	260	299	400	451	407
Total current assets	628	720	831	980	1103	925
Total assets	707	808	945	1111	1253	1082
Total current liabilities	367	459	476	633	690	750
Total liabilities	416	506	619	776	929	968
Equity	291	302	326	335	324	114

Some Income, SCFP, and Dividend Numbers (in millions $)
Year Ended January 31

	1970	1971	1972	1973	1974	1975
Revenue	1220	1265	1384	1655	1861	1772
Cost of goods sold	818	843	931	1125	1283	1303
Income before interest and tax	85	92	76	85	60	(87)
Interest expense	15	19	16	21	51	199
Tax expense	28	33	26	26	1	(119)
Net income	42	40	35	38	8	(177)
Tax rate	.40	.45	.43	.41	.11	.40
Dividends declared	20	21	21	21	21	5
Cash flow from operations	(3)	(15)	(27)	(114)	(93)	(85)
Financing activities	25	33	76	121	138	140
Investment activities	(14)	(17)	(32)	(28)	(29)	(21)

W.T. GRANT COMPANY
Some Summary Numbers (Year Ended January 31)

	1970	1971	1972	1973	1974	1975
Return on equity	0.144	0.132	0.107	0.113	0.025	−1.553
Return on assets	0.072	0.062	0.047	0.045	0.042	−0.057
Sales return	0.042	0.040	0.032	0.030	0.028	−0.035
Total asset turnover	1.73	1.57	1.46	1.49	1.49	1.64
Cash flow to total assets	−0.004	−0.019	−0.029	−0.103	−0.074	−0.079
Average interest rate	0.022	0.038	0.026	0.027	0.055	0.205
Debt/equity ratio	1.43	1.68	1.90	2.32	2.87	8.49
Inventory turnover	3.68	3.24	3.21	2.81	2.84	3.20
Collection ratio	110.1	121.2	125.8	119.8	117.5	88.8
Working capital ratio	1.71	1.57	1.75	1.55	1.60	1.23
Acid test ratio	1.09	0.99	1.11	0.91	0.93	0.67
Gross margin	0.32	0.33	0.33	0.32	0.31	0.26
Interest coverage ratio	5.67	4.84	4.75	4.05	1.33	negative
Earnings per share in $	2.94	2.67	2.50	2.71	0.57	negative
Dividends per share in $	1.40	1.40	1.50	1.50	1.50	zero
January 31 closing share price in $	47.0	47.1	47.8	43.9	10.9	1.1

Scott Formula Components*

	ROE	=	SR	×	AT	+	(ROA	−	IN)	×	(D/E)
1970	0.144	=	0.042	×	1.73	+	(0.072	−	0.022)	×	1.43
1971	0.132	=	0.040	×	1.57	+	(0.062	−	0.021)	×	1.68
1972	0.107	=	0.030	×	1.46	+	(0.047	−	0.015)	×	1.90
1973	0.113	=	0.030	×	1.49	+	(0.045	−	0.016)	×	2.32
1974	0.025	=	0.028	×	1.49	+	(0.042	−	0.049)	×	2.87
1975	−1.553	=	−0.035	×	1.64	+	(−0.057	−	0.119)	×	8.49

*Because of rounding, the numbers don't all satisfy the relationship precisely.

NOTES

1. The booklet *Reporting Cash Flows: A Guide to the Revised Statement of Changes in Financial Position* (Toronto: Deloitte, Haskins & Sells [now Deloitte & Touche], 1986) was helpful in developing points about interpreting cash flow information.

2. Proof of the Scott formula (A = Assets, L = Liabilities, E = Equity, and the "ATI" notation for ROA, SR, and IN is left out to avoid clutter):
   a. Define ROE = Net income / E
   b. Define ROA = (Net income + After-tax interest expense) / A
   c. Define IN = After-tax interest expense / L
   d. By double-entry accounting, A = L + E
   e. From (a), Net income = ROE × E
   f. From (b), Net income = (ROA × A) − After-tax interest expense
   g. Equate right sides of (e) and (f):
      ROE × E = (ROA × A) − After-tax interest expense
   h. From (d) and (c):
      ROE × E = (ROA × [L + E]) − (IN × L)
      ROE × E = ROA × L + ROA × E − IN × L
      ROE × E = ROA × E + (ROA − IN) × L
   i. Dividing the last through by E produces:
      ROE = ROA + (ROA − IN) × L / E
   j. Break up the first term to the right of the equal sign into two terms by multiplying it by REV / REV:
      ROA = (Net income + After-tax interest expense) / A
      ROA = (Net income + After-tax interest expense) / REV × REV / A
   k. Define the first new term as sales return SR and the second as asset turnover AT
   l. This produces the final version of the formula:
      ROE = SR × AT + (ROA − IN) × L / E
      Putting in the ATI notation produces:
      ROE = SR(ATI) × AT + (ROA(ATI) − IN(ATI)) × L / E

3. The formula for the present value of a constant cash payment comes from the sum of the following geometric series:

$$\frac{C}{(1+i)^1} + \frac{C}{(1+i)^2} + \frac{C}{(1+i)^3} + \ldots + \frac{C}{(1+i)^n}$$

See an algebra textbook for proof of how this series sums to the formula given.

4. For more information on this case and some interesting charts of various ratios' performance over time, see J.A. Largey, III, and C.P. Stickney, "Cash Flows, Ratio Analysis and the W.T. Grant Company Bankruptcy," *Financial Analysts Journal* (July–August 1980): 51–54.

Solution Outlines to Asterisked Homework and Discussion Problems

The first few homework and discussion problems in each chapter are marked with asterisks. For your use in self-study, outlines of solutions to these problems have been prepared. The outlines are informal and often chatty, and you should take them as suggestions of valid approaches, *not* as the *only* valid approaches. Students and instructors have various views of the world, and such views colour the way answers to accounting problems, as with other important problems, are developed. Coming up with a coherent personal view of accounting is the responsibility of each student, and the solutions provided here should be fitted to that view, and not override it. The solution outlines are intended to help you, so they are written to be clear, not vague or evasive. But they can never be complete, nor can they anticipate the intelligence and creativity that you will bring to the problems.

Sometimes, the solution to a problem will require some assumptions or data not explicitly given in the problem. That is the way real world problems tend to be formed: not necessarily completely laid out or unambiguously phrased. Become comfortable with stating your assumptions and knowing where they make a difference, because in dealing with the real problems you will face in your career, such assumptions can be replaced by evidence to produce high-quality solutions, but only if you know what the assumptions are and when they matter.

Always try each problem on your own, or with friends, and make rough notes of your solution, *before* you look at the outline below. If you look at the solution outline before you think about the problem, you will rob the solution of its main value to you, which is feedback on your own learning. Problems always look easier if you look at the solutions prematurely, so if you do that, you can fool yourself about what your ability is.

Solution Outline for PROBLEM 1.1*

1. An accountant is a person who prepares an enterprise's financial statements, whereas the auditor verifies the propriety of the statements, once they have been prepared. These roles can be a bit mixed together, because often auditors give advice about the preparation of the statements. Management is responsible for the financial statements, so accountants in effect work for management when doing the statements.

2. Accrual income is a measure of the enterprise's performance in gaining increased resources through sales or services. Accrual procedures are designed to make income a complete measure of this performance, whether or not all cash has yet been received or paid. Cash income is a less complete measure, incorporating only the cash receipts and payments made in connection with operations.

3. Users of financial statements are not all the same in their information needs. They are all different people, with differing objectives, preferences, and capabilities, so they are likely to need different information to meet these differences in decision-making. Probably most users share an interest in fair, timely information, but the details of that information depend on the decision(s) each user is making.

Solution Outline for PROBLEM 1.2*

Without knowing much specifically about managers and owners, some thought about them might lead to the following conclusions:

1. The owners will want to measure managers' performance to suit their (the owners') purposes, which will include motivating good managers to agree to work for the owners and do what the owners wish.

2. Managers are people, not machines: they will have their own wishes about such a measurement system and we might predict that managers, especially good managers, will not like a measurement system that is biased in favour of the owners.

3. Only some compromises in the measurement system would likely be acceptable to both owners and managers. Whether the compromises tend to favour the owners or the managers, or are completely neutral, will depend on whether it is easy for the owners to replace the managers, or for the managers to find other jobs, and on personal and ethical considerations. But the compromises might be along the following lines:

   a. The performance measurement should be done carefully and competently: significant errors should be avoided.

   b. The measures should be fair: significant biases in favour of one side or the other should be avoided, or at least clearly identified, so that both the owners and the managers will feel that their interests are being protected.

   c. To enhance fairness and reduce error, the owners and the managers might agree that someone independent of both should prepare the measures, or at least that the calculations should be checked by someone not biased toward either side.

   d. The system should not be too costly. A high-cost system would reduce the business's income and, therefore, result in a smaller "pie" for the owners and managers to share as dividends, bonuses, and so on.

   e. The measures should be verifiable, based on evidence rather than impression or opinion, so that both managers and owners could, if they wanted to, see for themselves that the results are proper.

   f. The system should be stable and the measures themselves "final" at some point, so that neither owners nor managers can go back and try to change the rules or the results afterwards.

   g. It would be helpful if the system were similar to those used by other businesses, so that the owners and the managers could compare the managers' performance to that of the managers of other businesses.

4. More principles could be listed: you may have thought of several. As your accounting knowledge develops, you'll see that the above principles (competence, fairness, verifiability, consistency, comparability, and so on) and others are everyday factors in the way financial accounting works. In its reliance on such principles, accounting isn't too different from other systems of measurement, such as statistics, medical recordkeeping, student course grades, and criminal court records.

5. Which principles would be easy to agree on and which would be more controversial? There is no general answer to this—a lot depends on the particular business and on its particular owners and managers. But we might expect that stability and accuracy would be easier to agree on than fairness and comparability, because the latter depend more on the different viewpoints, and possibly competing interests, of the owners and managers. Similarly, the cost-effectiveness principle depends on who bears the cost—if the owners pay all the costs, the managers would not care much what the costs are, and vice versa.

Solution Outline for PROBLEM 1.3*

These are definitely transactions: (a),(b), (f), (g). Item (d) is also, assuming there is documentation with the shipment to show the cost (otherwise recording the transaction may have to await an invoice). Therefore item (i) would be a transaction unless already recorded in item (d). Item (h) is a transaction, even if not a nice one, assuming that the amount stolen can be determined. (Probably it would be recorded as a reduction in cash as best could be determined, and whether recorded as an expense or loss, or instead as an amount due from the employee or Gould Inc.'s insurance company, would depend on whether a recovery was expected. Items(c), (e), and (j) are not transactions, not yet anyway.

Solution Outline for PROBLEM 1.4*

a. Cash in the bank as at the end of 2001:
$12,430 + $1,000 + $68,990 − $1,480 − $36,910 − $28,000 = $16,030.
b. Accrual accounting income for 2001:
$68,990 + $850 − $36,910 − $2,650 − $3,740 = $26,540.

Solution Outline for PROBLEM 1.5*

Assuming that the outstanding deposit and cheques do eventually reach Wayne's bank account, his "real" bank balance is:

Balance according to the bank	$365
Add outstanding deposit	73
	$438
Deduct outstanding cheques ($145 + $37 + $86 + $92)	360
Balance according to Wayne's records	$ 78

So, if Wayne's records are accurate and there is no holdup with the bank's crediting the $73 deposit to his account, he can repay the friend's $70.

Solution Outline for PROBLEM 1.6*

Cash income	$ 67,450
Uncollected revenue	18,730
Unpaid bills	(24,880)
Unsold supplies (inventory)	3,410
Prepaid expenses for next year	2,300
Amortization	(13,740)
Accrual income	$ 53,270

Solution Outline for PROBLEM 1.7*

1. Net income effect = ($645,000 − $342,500) × (1 − 0.30) = $211,750.

2. Longer version:

	Present	*Expected*
Revenue	$5,645,231	$6,290,231
Expenses	4,889,811	5,232,311
Income before income tax	755,420	1,057,920
Income tax at 30%	226,626	317,376
Net income	$ 528,794	$ 740,544
Difference in net income	$211,750	

Solution Outline for PROBLEM 1.8*

	Cash income	Accrual income
a.	• no effect — the $100 was spent previously	• up $100 — expenses decreased by $100 since $100 moved to the balance sheet as inventory
b.	• down $45 — the disbursement was omitted	• down $45 — an additional expense has occurred
c.	• no effect — amortization is a noncash entry	• down $15 ($35 − $120) — amortization expense increased
d.	• no effect — the cash owing has not been received	• down $30 — bad debt expense increased
e.	• no effect — the $75 is already included in cash income	• down $75 — revenue decreased by $75 since $75 moved to the balance sheet as customer deposit

Solution Outline for PROBLEM 1.9*

a. No transaction since no exchange yet.
b. Yes, an exchange of money for advice.
c. No transaction for Bartlett as the exchanges that changed share price were between investors, not involving Bartlett.
d. Yes, an exchange of advertising received for a promise to pay, so a credit transaction.
e. Yes, for same reason as (d)—work received in exchange for a promise to pay for it.
f. Yes, an exchange of a sort. The teenager got the repair and the company perhaps earned some goodwill, or avoided a later lawsuit or other problem.
g. Yes, goods received in exchange for a combination of cash and promise to pay.
h. Yes, an exchange of cash for a removal of the promise to pay.
i. Yes, an exchange of cash for political benefit. The illegality doesn't change the fact that a transaction happened.
j. Yes, an exchange of cash for a promise to repay it.

Solution Outline for PROBLEM 1.10*

	Vista	Dave
Apparent amount owing	$1,125	$ 904
Unbilled yet, as far as Dave can tell	112	
Cash advance Dave had forgotten about		200
Doubtful charge Vista had made	(148)	
Revised amount owing	$1,089	$1,104

The two columns still differ by $15. So Dave is close but has not sorted it out yet! He could just pay the Vista bill as is, expecting that Vista would sort the doubtful amount out next month, or he could deduct the $148 he doubts and pay only $1,125 – $148 = $977 until the amount is sorted out.

Solution Outline for PROBLEM 2.1*

Bluebird Bakery (A Partnership)
Balance Sheet as at July 31, 2001

Assets			Liabilities and Equity		
Current assets:			Current liabilities:		
Cash on hand	$	895	Demand bank loan		$ 14,500
Cash in bank		4,992	Accounts payable		11,240
Accounts receivable		3,823	Wages payable		2,246
Inventory of baked goods		245			$ 27,986
Inventory of supplies		13,220			
		$ 23,175	Partners' equity:		
Noncurrent assets:			Partners' capital — J. Bird		$ 52,921
Equipment (cost)	$129,153		Partners' capital — B. Blue		27,425
Accum. Amortization	(43,996)				$ 80,346
		$ 85,157			
TOTAL		$108,332	TOTAL		$108,332

Working capital = $23,175 − $27,986 = −$4,811
Working capital ratio = $23,175 / $27,986 = .83

Solution Outline for PROBLEM 2.2*

This problem illustrates the entity principle. In parts 1, 2, and 3 you are asked to develop a balance sheet for three entities: Janet, Sam, and both Janet and Sam together.

1.
Janet
Statement of Financial Position (Balance Sheet)
as of June 15, 2001

Assets		Liabilities and Equity	
Cash	$ 500	Liabilities	$ 0
Stereo	2,000	Janet's equity	2,800
Damage deposit	300		
	$2,800		$2,800

2.
Sam
Statement of Financial Position (Balance Sheet)
as of June 15, 2001

Assets		Liabilities and Equity	
Cash	$1,000	Liabilities	
Prepaid rent	400	Loan	$2,100
Furniture	500	Sam's equity (deficit)	(200)
	$1,900		$1,900

3.

Janet and Sam
Statement of Financial Position (Balance Sheet)
as of June 20, 2001

Assets		Liabilities and Equity	
Cash	$2,500	Liabilities	
Damage deposit	300	American Express	$ 600
Stereo	2,000	Equity	
Furniture	500	Janet and Sam	6,200
Gifts	1,500		
	$6,800		$6,800

We can reconcile their individual equities to their joint equity as follows:

Individually:		
Janet's equity	$2,800	
Sam's equity	(200)	$2,600
Changes due to marriage:		
Wedding presents	$5,600	
Hall rent	(400)	
Band	(1,000)	
Honeymoon	(600)	3,600
Joint equity after honeymoon		$6,200

Solution Outline for PROBLEM 2.3*

1. Here are the definitions, in enough detail so you can see if you've chosen the appropriate items from the balance sheet.

   a. A current asset is an item carrying future benefit that will be realized in cash or consumed within a year. This includes cash, which includes assets that are cash or can be converted to cash at any moment, and other current assets, which can be converted within the year, but not immediately. Examples: short-term investments, accounts receivable, prepaid expenses, and inventories. CAE also is waiting for some tax refunds: see its "income taxes recoverable" asset.

   b. A noncurrent asset is an asset that will be converted to cash or consumed in more than one year. Examples: land, buildings, equipment, long-term investments, and other assets such as development costs. CAE has goodwill (which arises when one company buys all or part of another or another's business) and some miscellaneous "other assets" in its noncurrent section.

   c. A current liability is any obligation that must be paid in cash within one year, or an estimated payment incorporated as part of accrual accounting. Examples: accounts payable, dividends payable, accrued (estimated) income taxes, and portion of long-term debt due within a year. CAE also has a large "deposits on contracts" current liability, which represents deposits on future deliveries made by CAE's customers, not earned by CAE yet.

   d. A noncurrent liability is an obligation or accrual that is due to be paid more than one year in the future (minus any part included in current liabilities). Examples: mortgages, long-term bank loans, bonds, pension liabilities, and future (or deferred) income taxes.

e. Equity represents the residual ownership interest in a company. It is one of the ways assets such as cash and long-term investments are financed (liabilities are the other way). It is composed of direct investments by owners (such as share capital) and the indirect investment represented by retained earnings, which is accumulated income the owners have chosen to leave in the company rather than withdrawing them as dividends. CAE has share capital ("capital stock"), retained earnings, and accumulated foreign currency translation adjustments.

2. Assets, liabilities, and equity have general definitions such as those above, but each company's particular circumstances may produce variations in how some items are classified. For a manufacturing company, the land its factory is on is a noncurrent asset, but for a real estate company that buys and sells land, land may be a current asset (inventory for sale). For you and CAE, a bank loan is a liability, but, for a bank, which is a lender rather than a borrower, a bank loan is an asset (an amount receivable from the borrower). See the TD Bank balance sheet in Section 2.10. Some kinds of debt are so much like shares that they may be classified as equity, while some shares are so much like debt that they may be classified as liabilities. Every company's balance sheet must fit its circumstances so that it will be a valid measure of the company's financial position. And for some companies such as banks, there may not only be rather different balance sheet accounts from commercial companies like CAE, but some categories such as current/noncurrent assets and liabilities may not be used.

Solution Outline for PROBLEM 2.4*

1. List your assets and any amounts due to others at one point in time. Anything left over is "owner's equity" or net worth. (Those with negative equity, which is not unusual for students, need a sense of humour!) Just list the assets; don't attempt to match liabilities and assets one for one. For instance, there must once have been $2,000 in cash for a $2,000 loan, but all the cash may have been spent by now. So there may be a liability, but no remaining asset. Are tuition payments assets? Is an anticipated student loan remission an asset? Are loans from parents liabilities (or are they partners with you and so contributing equity)? Try to decide on which items to include so that you get a meaningful measure of your financial position. Such a balance sheet could be used for loan or credit applications. It could also be used to help decide whether to make a major purchase (such as a car).

As an example, imagine a student with the following items:

a. $10—bank account
b. $500—clothing (purchase price)
c. $1,400—mountain bike with fancy parts and trim (purchase price)
d. $1,500—student loan
e. $300—books (purchase price)

Here is the balance sheet, which will be explained. Pay attention to the title and date of the balance sheet. Identify the *entity*—your name, or that of a married couple, if you can't really separate your assets from those of your spouse:

**Balance Sheet for Student X
as at a Specified Date**

Assets			Liabilities and Equity	
Current assets			Current liability	
Bank account	$	10	Student loan	
Clothing		0	(current portion)	$ 500
Books		130		
			Noncurrent liability	
Noncurrent asset			Student loan (rest)	1,000
Bike (with parts)		1,400		
			Equity (deduced)	40
Total assets		$1,540	Total liabilities & equity	$1,540

Some explanations:

a. The bank account is definitely a current asset, more specifically, a cash equivalent asset, because Student X can take out the cash at any time.

b. Clothing was left out of the balance sheet because upon looking it over, it was well-worn and a bit out of style, so there was no remaining future value in it and so it did not qualify as an asset.

c. Student X plans to sell the books at the beginning of the next term and expects to get $130 for them. So, that is the value used for them on the balance sheet. (Current assets are usually shown at the lower of cost or current market value, as this book explains.)

d. A new mountain bike with such fancy parts would cost about $2,000, but accounting uses the historical cost on the balance sheet ($1,400).

e. A portion of the student loan must be paid within the year ($500). Therefore this portion was taken out of the long-term area and placed in the current liabilities.

f. Equity here is a calculated (deduced) number (assets minus liabilities).

2. Some decision-making information:

a. There is some threat of immediate cash problems, since cash is only $10 and the balance sheet doesn't show any obvious sources of more cash other than the books.

b. The current portion of the student loan will have to be paid in a year, and Student X only has enough in current assets to cover $140 of the $500 to be paid, resulting in a $360 shortfall. The need to go out and earn money, or borrow from parents, is clear.

c. Equity is small but positive—not unusual since Student X has been in school for life! However, the alarm lights would be flashing if this equity position existed after the student had worked for a few years. Therefore, interpreting the financial information depends on other environmental circumstances.

3. Student X's debt–equity ratio is horrible: $1,500 / $40 or nearly 40 to 1! That student is not soundly financed, depending on future prospects rather than

present financial strength. With luck, your debt–equity ratio is better, but it is common that people just starting out in their financial lives, just like companies in the early developmental stage, have weak balance sheets. This doesn't mean bankruptcy is just around the corner (though it might!), but rather illustrates that financial accounting's historical, transaction-based information does not tell the whole story about a person, or a company.

Solution Outline for PROBLEM 2.5*

a. No transaction so no entry.

b. DR Prepaid expenses asset   200
        CR Accounts payable liability   200

There may not be an entry until December 31, because there is no economic exchange until the advertisement is run, so saying "no transaction" here is OK for that reason.

c. DR Bond asset   2,000
        CR Cash   2,000

The interest will be recorded periodically during the three years. In addition to cash interest, entries debiting bond asset and crediting interest revenue will eventually raise the asset value to the $2,500 to be received in three years. (Such entries are described much later in this book.)

d. No transaction yet so no entry.

e. DR Cash   300
        CR Customer deposits liability   300

No entry for the order itself as that is not a transaction yet.

f. DR Prepaid expenses asset   600
        CR Cash   600

None of the insurance coverage has yet been consumed, so it is all an asset now.

Solution Outline for PROBLEM 2.6*

Journal entry (start with the easy accounts first):

CR Cash		1,000,000
CR Long-term debt (price minus down payment)		3,200,000
DR Inventory	280,000	
DR Land	1,500,000	
DR Building	1,800,000	
DR Equipment	470,000	
DR Dealership rights asset	40,000	
CR Bank loan		130,000
DR Goodwill asset or Loss on overpayment*	240,000	

* Some accountants would call this residual (needed to balance the entry) a goodwill asset, having value because it represents worthwhile features like customer loyalty or reduced competition. Others would prefer to put it all into a loss or expense account (deducted from income), since Big Ideas has only purchased parts of the competitor and not the entire company.

Solution Outline for PROBLEM 2.7*

1. Balance sheet:

Clambake Kate's Inc.
Balance Sheet as at May 31, 2001

Assets		Liabilities and Equity	
Current assets:		Current liabilities:	
Cash in bank	$ 2,200	Payable to suppliers	$ 5,300
Food supplies cost	2,100	Wages payable	900
Other supplies cost	4,500		$ 6,200
	$ 8,800		
Noncurrent assets:		Noncurrent liabilities:	
Equip. and furniture cost	$64,900	Long-term loan	$25,000
Less accum. amort.	(27,400)		
	$37,500	Shareholders' equity:	
		Share capital issued	$10,000
		Retained earnings	5,100
			$15,100
	$46,300		$46,300

Possible notes (others may be suggested too):
- more information about the various supplies inventories
- more information about the equipment and furniture, including the amortization calculation
- more information about the long-term loan (such as repayment terms, interest rate)
- more information about the company's share capital (such as kinds of shares that could be issued and any shares issued recently)

2. Here are some comments, starting with two ratios. The company has a debt–equity ratio of 2.07 ($31,200 / $15,100), so it is relying on liabilities twice as much as on equity to finance its assets. Its working capital is $2,600 ($8,800 – $6,200) and its working capital ratio is 1.4 ($8,800 / $6,200) so its current assets are somewhat greater than its current debt. Most of its liabilities are noncurrent. All in all, there do not appear to be any pressing financial problems. The company appears reasonably well financed, but eventually that large long-term loan will have to be repaid. (You may think of more.)

3. This means that the "payable to suppliers" amount should be $2,900 lower, or $2,400. Cash in bank is also $2,900 lower, or negative $700. The bank account is therefore overdrawn, which banks frequently allow if arrangements have been made in advance to approve what is, in effect, a loan from the bank. This loan would be shown as a liability to the bank rather than a negative asset, so the balance sheet now becomes:

Current assets:		Current liabilities:	
$2,100 + $4,500	$ 6,600	$700 + $2,400 + $900	$ 4,000
Noncurrent assets:		Noncurrent liabilities:	
Unchanged	37,500	Unchanged	25,000
			$29,000
		Shareholders' equity:	
		Unchanged	15,100
	$44,100		$44,100

Solution Outline for PROBLEM 2.8*

Total assets and total liabilities and shareholders' equity are different; the debt–equity ratio is a little lower at 1.92 ($29,000 / $15,100); working capital is unchanged ($6,600 – $4,000 = $2,600); and the working capital ratio is now better at 1.65 ($6,600 / $4,000). So although the company has no cash, instead owing the bank $700, its financial position is a little better. There is no effect on the long-term loan, which still has to be repaid some time.

	DR (CR)	Transactions (DR are +, CR are −)	DR (CR)
Cash	24,388	− 10,000 + 11,240 + 22,000 − 22,000 − 12,000	13,628
Accts. receivable	89,267	− 11,240	78,027
Inventories	111,436	+ 5,320	116,756
Prepaid expenses	7,321	no transactions	7,321
Land	78,200	+ 52,000	130,200
Factory	584,211	+ 31,900	616,111
Accum. amort.	(198,368)	no transactions	(198,368)
Bank loan	(53,000)	+ 22,000	(31,000)
Accts. payable	(78,442)	− 5,320 − 13,900	(97,662)
Taxes payable	(12,665)	no transactions	(12,665)
Current mortgage	(18,322)	no transactions	(18,322)
Equipment loan	0	− 18,000	(18,000)
Mortgage payable	(213,734)	− 40,000	(253,734)
Pension liability	(67,674)	no transactions	(67,674)
Shareholder loan	(100,000)	+ 10,000	(90,000)
Share capital	(55,000)	− 22,000	(77,000)
Retained earnings	(97,618)	no transactions	(97,618)
	0		0

Journal entries for August 1, 2001 (supporting the transactions shown above):

1. DR Shareholder loan   10,000
        CR Cash   10,000
2. DR Cash   11,240
        CR Accounts receivable   11,240
3. DR Inventories   5,320
        Accounts payable   5,320
4. Cash   22,000
        Share capital   22,000
5. DR Bank loan   22,000
        CR Cash   22,000
6. Land   52,000
        Cash   12,000
        Mortgage payable   40,000
7. Factory   31,900
        Accounts payable   13,900
        Equipment loan (noncurrent)   18,000

South Shore Manufacturing Ltd.
Balance Sheet as at August 1, 2001

Assets		Liabilities and Equity	
Current assets		*Current liabilities*	
Cash	$ 13,628	Bank loan	$ 31,000
Accounts receivable	78,027	Accounts payable	97,662
Inventories	116,756	Taxes payable	12,665
Prepaid expenses	7,321	Current part of mortgage	18,322
	$215,732		$159,649
Noncurrent assets		*Noncurrent liabilities*	
Land (cost)	$130,200	Equipment loan,	
Factory (cost)	616,111	less current	$ 18,000
	$746,311	Mortgage, less current	$253,734
		Pension liability	67,674
		Loan from shareholder	90,000
			$429,408
Accumulated			
amortization	(198,368)		
	$547,943	*Shareholders' equity*	
		Share capital	$ 77,000
		Retained earnings	97,618
			$174,618
TOTAL	$763,675	TOTAL	$763,675

Solution Outline for PROBLEM 2.9*

1. An economic exchange between the organization and another party, therefore recorded as an event in the organization's accounting system.
2. Accountants use this word in two main ways. One is to refer to the number of dollars included in an account, such as "the balance of accounts receivable is $5,000." The other is to refer to the fact that on the balance sheet the sum of the assets equals the sum of the liabilities plus the equity: "the balance sheet balances."
3. The left-side of accounting's double-entry system: an increase in resources or a decrease in obligations or equity.
4. To increase an asset, decrease a liability, or decrease equity via a journal entry. If you debit something, you must also credit something by the same amount.
5. A record that summarizes similar transactions as well as adjustments for a type of asset, liability, equity, revenue, or expense.
6. A collection of all the enterprise's individual accounts.
7. A list of all of the enterprise's individual accounts and their account balances at a certain date.

Solution Outline for PROBLEM 2.10*

1. Journal entries (use other titles and/or group the equipment items if that is more descriptive for you):

DR Cash	15,000	
DR Sound system	1,500	
CR Proprietor's capital		16,500
DR Tanning equipment	21,200	
CR Cash		9,200
CR Equipment loan		12,000
DR Leasehold improvements	1,600	
CR Cash		1,600
DR Inventory	17,100	
CR Cash		2,300
CR Accounts payable		14,800

2. Ledger and accounts (T-account versions)

Cash		Inventory		Sound system		Tanning equipment	
15,000	9,200	17,100		1,500		21,200	
	1,600						
	2,300						
1,900		17,100		1,500		21,200	

Leasehold improvements		Accounts payable		Equipment loan		Capital	
1,600			14,800		12,000		16,500
1,600			14,800		12,000		16,500

3. Trial balance, start of business

	DR	CR
Cash	1,900	
Inventory	17,100	
Sound system	1,500	
Tanning equipment	21,200	
Leasehold improvements	1,600	
Accounts payable		14,800
Equipment loan		12,000
Capital		16,500
	43,300	43,300

4. Balance sheet

Beach Ready
(A Proprietorship Operated by Cynthia)
Balance Sheet at the Commencement of the Business

Assets		Liabilities and Proprietor's Capital	
Current assets		**Current liabilities**	
Cash	$ 1,900	Accounts payable	$14,800
Inventory	17,100	Equipment loan	
	$19,000	(current)*	6,000
			$20,800
Noncurrent assets		**Noncurrent liabilities**	
Sound system	$ 1,500	Equipment loan	
Tanning equipment	21,200	(less current)	6,000
Leasehold improvements	1,600		$26,800
	$24,300	**Proprietor's capital**	
		Capital	16,500
TOTAL	$43,300	TOTAL	$43,300

* The current–noncurrent split of the equipment loan was not shown in the accounts, but could have been.

5. Calculations

Working capital ratio = $19,000 / $20,800 = 0.913
Debt–equity ratio = $26,800 / $16,500 = 1.624

Solution Outline for PROBLEM 2.11*

Some problems with the given balance sheet: not categorized as to current and noncurrent assets and liabilities, equity not separated from liabilities, some accounts are on the wrong side, not titled properly, accounts in haphazard order.

Corporation X
Balance Sheet as at (Date)

Assets			Liabilities and Shareholders' Equity		
Current assets			**Current liabilities**		
Cash		$ 6,000	Bank overdraft		$ 7,100
Accounts receivable		31,200	Bank loan**		20,000
Other receivables*		2,000	Accounts payable		20,900
Inventory		17,100	Accrued interest		1,100
		$ 67,200			$ 49,100
Noncurrent assets			**Noncurrent liabilities**		
Property and plant		$ 83,000	Mortgage		$ 41,500
Accum. amortization		(36,400)	Minority interest		2,200
Goodwill (net)		14,000			$ 43,700
		$ 60,600			$ 92,800
			Shareholders' equity		
			Share capital		$ 40,000
			Deficit		(4,100)
			Currency translation adjust.		600
					$ 36,500
			Treasury shares		(1,500)
					$ 35,000
TOTAL		$127,800	TOTAL		$127,800

* $2,000 = $1,800 income tax refund + $200 overpaid account payable (could also put with accounts receivable).

** Bank loan is assumed current (prudent to assume it is due sooner rather than later).

Solution Outline for PROBLEM 2.12*

a:6; b:9; c:5; d:8; e:1; f:2; g:4; h:7; i:10; j:3.

Solution Outline for PROBLEM 3.1*

If you had trouble with any of the terms, the Glossary will help you.

Solution Outline for PROBLEM 3.2*

1. Land is on the balance sheet because it is an asset, that is, a resource owned or controlled and having economic value. Land carries the potential to produce revenues for the company in the future, as do other assets.
2. Assets = $5,222 + $2,410 = $7,632.
3. Share capital is one of the sources of funds used to acquire the assets on the left side of the balance sheet. Therefore, it is not an asset that can be used to purchase more land, but a co-creator of the assets that now exist. Assets can only be used to buy other assets. Therefore, you must use $3,000 cash or another asset to buy a new asset. The company did not have enough cash, since some had already been used to buy inventory and land, so more cash had to be borrowed.

4. Retained earnings is the accumulation of net income minus dividends for each year of the company's history. It is the accumulated residual undistributed earnings of the company and is on the balance sheet because it is a source of present assets (because assets created in the process of earning income were not all distributed to owners).

5. Net income = $10,116 – $9,881 = $235.

6. Ending retained earnings were $1,222. Subtracting income that had been added ($235) and adding back dividends that had been deducted ($120) gives beginning retained earnings of $1,107. Proof, going the other way: $1,107 + $235 – $120 = $1,222.

7. Ending retained earnings would be $1,107 + $10,116 – $11,600 = –$377. There would have been a net loss for the year of $1,484, and that would have turned the retained earnings at the beginning into a deficit at the end of $377.

8. If the debit for the deficit were shown among the assets, that would indicate that the company had something of value for the future, a resource that could be used to generate income in the future. This is not at all the case: instead, the company has incurred more expenses than revenue and has, therefore, diminished some of the equity (share capital) put into it by the owners. Its resources were decreased by this, not increased as would be indicated by showing it as an asset. That's why a deficit is deducted from other equity (such as share capital) and shown as a negative item on the right-hand side of the balance sheet.

Solution Outline for PROBLEM 3.3*

Assumptions (all affect the balance sheet only):

- Receivable amount due from Lucky Eddie appears to have been current because he paid it within a year.

- Loan also appears to have been current.

- Wages are payable over a short term; a reasonable assumption is that employees would not allow their wages to remain unpaid for long.

- Noncurrent liabilities have no current portion payable within the next year.

Arctic Limo Services Ltd.
Balance Sheet as at September 30, 2001
(with 2000 figures for comparison)

	2001	2000
Assets		
Current assets		
Cash	$ 2,000	$ 4,000
Accounts receivable	0	1,000
	$ 2,000	$ 5,000
Noncurrent assets		
Equipment (limos)	$90,000	$60,000
Less accumulated amortization	(30,000)	(20,000)
	$60,000	$40,000
Total assets	$62,000	$45,000
Liabilities and Equity		
Current liabilities		
Loan	$ 0	$10,000
Wages payable	2,000	0
	$ 2,000	$10,000
Noncurrent liabilities		
Long-term limo financing	$50,000	$30,000
Shareholders' equity		
Share capital	$ 1,000	$ 1,000
Retained earnings	9,000	4,000
	$10,000	$ 5,000
Total liabilities and equity	$62,000	$45,000

Arctic Limo Services Ltd.
Income Statement
for the Year Ended September 30, 2001

Revenue		$300,000
Less expenses:		
Wages	$100,000	
Other expenses	70,000	
Amortization	10,000	$180,000
Income before income tax		$120,000
Income tax expense		35,000
Net income		$ 85,000

Arctic Limo Services Ltd.
Statement of Retained Earnings
for the Year Ended September 30, 2001

Beginning balance (September 30, 2000)	$ 4,000
Net income for the year	85,000
Dividends declared	(80,000)
Ending balance (September 30, 2001)	$ 9,000

Solution Outline for PROBLEM 3.4*

Your explanations will have been in your own words, perhaps something like the following.

1. Net income is an increase in cash and other resources produced during a period of time by an enterprise's operating activities, that is, by selling goods and services to customers and incurring the costs of serving the customers.
2. Net income is part of owners' equity because the increase in resources earned as mentioned above belongs to the owners, who may withdraw it as dividends. Until they do withdraw it, it is part of their ownership interest.
3. Net income could be reported on the balance sheet by just showing that owners' equity has increased since the prior period. The income statement was developed to provide an explanation of the details of the change in owners' equity and to separate that from any dividends withdrawn by the owners during the period.
4. Including the dividends in the income calculation would confuse the enterprise's relationships with customers and owners, and would make it less clear whether the enterprise was successful in increasing resources (making income) before making a distribution to owners.

Solution Outline for PROBLEM 3.5*

1. Apparent income statement accounts:

Salaries expense	Office expenses
Employee benefits expense	Income tax expense
Cash sales revenue	Credit sales revenue
Amortization expense	Interest income
Cost of goods sold	Miscellaneous expenses
Insurance expense	Interest expense

2. Net income, based on part 1, and using the same account order as no income statement is asked for, just a calculation, is:

$$- 71{,}000 - 13{,}100 + 21{,}600 - 26{,}700 - 161{,}600 - 11{,}200 - 31{,}100 - 6{,}900 + 346{,}200 + 1{,}700 - 8{,}200 - 16{,}800 = 22{,}900$$

3. Ending retained earnings = 92,800 + 22,900 − 11,000 = 104,700

4. a.   **Geewhiz Productions**
Income Statement for the Year Ended November 30, 2001

Revenue	$367,800
Operating expenses*	322,900
Operating income	$ 44,900
Interest expense, net of interest income	15,100
Income before income tax	$ 29,800
Income tax expense	6,900
Net income for the year	$ 22,900

* All expenses are aggregated here. It would be quite acceptable to list them all, though most companies do not because such a list clutters the statement and gives information to competitors. The amount of amortization expense is normally disclosed by a footnote or by listing that account separately.

b.   **Geewhiz Productions**
Statement of Retained Earnings for the Year Ended November 30, 2001

Retained earnings, beginning of year	$ 92,800
Add net income for the year	22,900
	$115,700
Deduct dividends declared	11,000
Retained earnings, end of year	$104,700

c.   **Geewhiz Productions**
Balance Sheet as at November 30, 2001

Assets			Liabilities and Equity		
Current assets:			Current liabilities:		
Cash	$ 18,000		Bank Loan*	$ 21,800	
Accounts receivable	16,400		Accounts payable	41,000	
Inventory	68,000		Other payables**	17,800	
Prepaid insurance	2,400			$ 80,600	
	$104,800		Noncurrent liabilities:		
Noncurrent assets:			Mortgage payable*	114,000	
Land	$ 63,000			$194,600	
Building	243,000		Shareholders' equity:		
Trucks and equipment	182,500		Share capital	$200,000	
	$488,500		Retained earnings	104,700	
Less accum. amort.	94,000			$304,700	
	$394,500				
	$499,300			$499,300	

* Bank loan assumed all current; mortgage assumed all noncurrent.
** $2,800 + $5,400 + $4,100 + $5,500 = $17,800.

5. Brief points:

- The company had a positive income, equalling 6.2% of revenue and 7.5% of year-end equity.

- Dividends declared equalled half of the net income, which the board of directors determined was better in the shareholders' hands than in the company's.

- The company had positive year-end working capital ($104,800 – $80,600 = $24,200; ratio 1.300), so it was likely able to pay its bills on time (as long as it could sell its inventory).

- The year-end debt–equity ratio was 0.639 ($194,600 / $304,700) so the company was mostly financed by equity and was not particularly risky.

Solution Outline for PROBLEM 3.6*

	1998	1999	2000	2001
Revenue for the year	38,000	49,000	61,000	65,000
Expenses for the year (except income tax)	29,000	42,000	50,000	61,000
Income before income tax for the year	9,000	7,000	11,000	4,000
Income tax expense for the year	2,000	1,500	3,000	1,000
Net income for the year	7,000	5,500	8,000	3,000
Retained earnings, beg. of the year	21,000	25,000	29,500	33,000
Dividends declared during the year	3,000	1,000	4,500	0
Retained earnings, end of the year	25,000	29,500	33,000	36,000
Other owners' equity, end of the year	35,000	38,000	38,000	48,000
Liabilities, end of the year	80,000	85,000	111,000	105,000
Assets, end of the year	140,000	152,500	182,000	189,000

Solution Outline for PROBLEM 3.7*

1. Journal entries for the year ended December 31, 2001.

a. DR Cash   5,100
    CR Loan from Cline Senior   5,000
    CR Share capital   100

b. DR Prepaid expense   120
    CR Cash   120

   DR Storage expense   120
    CR Prepaid expense   120
Done as two entries, one at the beginning of the year, one at the end. No entry for the $130 until 2002.

c. DR Buns inventory   500
   DR Wieners inventory   1,500
    CR Cash   2,000
Purchase of inventory.

d. DR Hot dog stands expense   600
    CR Cash   100
    CR Accounts payable   500
Since the stands were expected only to last this summer, their cost is expensed.

DR Hot dog stands expense   60
    CR Cash   60
The cost of fixing up the stands.

DR Accounts payable   500
DR Interest expense   29
    CR Cash   529

Payment on December 31, 2001, of the payable and the interest (which = $500 \times 0.10 \times 7/12 = \$29$).

e. DR Cash   7,000
    CR Revenue   7,000

This assumes that hot dog sales were for cash only, none on credit.

f. DR Wages expense   2,400
    CR Cash   2,400
Student employee's wages.

g. DR Cost of goods sold expense   1,960
DR Leftover products expense   40
    CR Buns inventory   500
    CR Wieners inventory   1,500

Ten dozen buns and wieners remain in inventory. Therefore, 490 dozen were sold during the summer. This entry assumes that the remaining inventory will not last until next summer and sets the inventory on hand to 0.

h. DR Income tax expense   358
    CR Cash   358
Income before tax = 7,000 – 120 – 29 – 600 – 60 – 2,400 – 1,960 – 40 = 1,791.

Tax = $0.20 \times \$1,791 = \$358$.

i. DR Loan from Cline Senior   5,000
    CR Cash   5,000

Repayment to Graham's father. It is assumed here that the father would be repaid before a dividend would be paid to Graham, but the problem does not actually say that, so omitting this entry would not be wrong.

j. DR Dividends declared (Retained earnings)   500
    CR Cash   500
Dividend: $5 per share × 100 shares

2. Graham Cline Inc.
Balance Sheet as at December 31, 2001

Assets		Liabilities and Equity	
Cash	$1,033	Common shares	$ 100
		Retained earnings	933
Total Assets	$1,033		$1,033

Graham Cline Inc.
Statement of Income and Retained Earnings
for the Year Ended December 31, 2001

Sales revenue		$7,000
Cost of goods sold		1,960
Gross margin		$5,040
Operating expenses		
Leftover products	$ 40	
Storage	120	
Wages	2,400	
Interest	29	
Hot dog stands	660	
Total operating expenses		$3,249
Income before income tax		$1,791
Income tax expense		358
Net income for the year		$1,433
Beginning retained earnings		0
Less dividend declared		(500)
Ending retained earnings		$ 933

3. Graham did make some money. His company earned $1,791 ($1,433 after tax) over the summer and repaid his father, but his employee earned more than that for doing less work (one of the two stands, no management). All that Graham actually received was the $500 dividend. Therefore, Graham should consider whether the venture could be made more viable next year. He may have enjoyed being his own boss, but so far the hot dog stand business seems to have been a marginal one.

Solution Outline for PROBLEM 3.8*

1.

Fergama Productions Inc.
Balance Sheet as at the End of Last Year

Assets			Liabilities and Equity			
Current assets			*Current liabilities*			
Cash	$ 23,415		Accounts			
Accounts			payable	$37,778		
receivable	89,455		Taxes payable	12,250	$ 50,028	
Supplies inventory	10,240	$123,110	Long-term loan		15,000	
Noncurrent assets			*Shareholders'*			
Office equip.			*equity*			
cost	$ 24,486		Share capital	$20,000		
Accum. amort.	(11,134)	13,352	Retained earn.	51,434	71,434	
TOTAL		$136,462	TOTAL		$136,462	

2. Entries to record the activities:

a.	DR Accounts receivable	216,459	CR Revenue	216,459
b.	DR Production expenses	156,320	CR Cash	11,287
			CR Accounts payable	145,033
c.	DR Amortization expense	2,680	CR Accum. amortization	2,680
d.	DR Supplies inventory	8,657	CR Accounts payable	8,657
	DR Cost of supplies used			
	expense	12,984	CR Supplies inventory	12,984
e.	DR Income tax expense	12,319	CR Income tax payable	12,319
f.	DR Retained earnings	25,000	CR Dividend payable	25,000
g.	DR Cash	235,260	CR Accounts receivable	235,260
h.	DR Accounts payable	172,276	CR Cash	172,276
i.	DR Income tax payable	18,400	CR Cash	18,400
j.	DR Long-term loan	5,000	CR Cash	5,000
k.	DR Dividend payable	25,000	CR Cash	25,000

3. Ending trial balance:

	DR	CR
Cash	26,712	
Accounts receivable	70,654	
Supplies inventory	5,913	
Office equipment	24,486	
Accumulated amortization		13,814
Accounts payable		19,192
Income tax payable		6,169
Dividend payable		0
Long-term loan		10,000
Share capital		20,000
Retained earnings — beginning		51,434
Dividend	25,000	
Revenue		216,459
Production expenses	156,320	
Amortization expense	2,680	
Cost of supplies used expense	12,984	
Income tax expense	12,319	
	337,068	337,068

Fergama Productions Inc.
Balance Sheet as at the End of This Year

Assets			Liabilities and Equity		
Current assets			*Current liabilities*		
Cash	$26,712		Accounts		
Accounts			payable	$19,192	
receivable	70,654		Taxes payable	6,169	$ 25,361
Supplies inventory	5,913	$103,279	Long-term loan		10,000
Noncurrent assets			*Shareholders'*		
Office equip.			*equity*		
cost	$24,486		Share capital	$20,000	
Accum. amort.	(13,814)	10,672	Retained earn.	58,590	78,590
TOTAL		$113,951	TOTAL		$113,951

4. Income statement has revenue of $216,459, income before income tax of $44,475, and net income of $32,156. Retained earnings adds that to the beginning retained earnings of $51,434, subtract dividends and show ending retained earnings of $58,590. Balance sheet (end of this year) has current assets (cash, accounts receivable, and supplies) $103,279, noncurrent assets (office equipment minus accumulated amortization) net $10,672, total assets $113,951, current liabilities (accounts payable and taxes payable) $25,361, the long-term loan of $10,000, equity (share capital and retained earnings) $78,590, and total liabilities and shareholders' equity $113,951.

5. Is the company better off than last year? Well, first, substantial net income was earned this year, around 15% of revenue. By the definition of net income, the company has increased its net resources (assets minus liabilities). While most of this income was paid as a dividend to the owners, not all of it was, so the retained earnings are higher than last year. Regarding current position, the working capital was $73,082 last year and is higher, $77,918, this year. The working capital ratio was 2.46 last year and is 4.07 this year. So it appears that the company is better off this year than last. (More ways of answering this question are developed in later chapters.)

Solution Outline for PROBLEM 3.9*

1. Repairs of $573 obtained on credit	DR Repairs expense CR Accounts payable	573	573
2. Revenue of $1,520 mostly on credit	DR Cash DR Accounts receivable CR Revenue	200 1,320	1,520
3. New shares issued for $2,000	DR Cash CR Share capital	2,000	2,000
4. Dividend of $500 declared and paid	DR Retained earnings CR Cash	500	500
5. Accounts receivable of $244 collected	DR Cash CR Accounts receivable	244	244
6. $1,000 payment made on mortgage	DR Mortgage payable CR Cash	1,000	1,000
7. Inventory purchased on credit	DR Inventory CR Accounts payable	2,320	2,320
8. Inventory costing $400 was sold	DR Cost of goods sold expense CR Inventory	400	400
9. Building purchased for $25,000, $5,000 down	DR Building CR Cash CR Mortgage payable	25,000	5,000 20,000
10. Revenue closed off to retained earnings	DR Revenue CR Retained earnings	249,320	249,320

Solution Outline for PROBLEM 3.10*

Revenue		$4,200,650
COGS expense	$2,345,670	
Operating expenses	1,123,580	3,469,250
		$ 731,400
Interest expense	$ (139,200)	
Interest income	14,030	
Gain on sale of building	25,000	(100,170)
		$ 631,230
Income tax expense		213,420
		$ 417,810
Loss on discontinued operations	$ (200,000)	
Extraordinary gain	40,000	160,000
Net income		$ 257,810
Retained earnings, beginning		$1,693,740
Error correction		3,300
		$1,697,040
Cost of redeeming shares		(18,200)
Net income		257,810
Dividends declared		(85,000)
Retained earnings, ending		$1,851,650

Solution Outline for PROBLEM 3.11*

Comments and necessary adjustments for SOS:

a. DR Inventory 11,240 CR Accounts payable 11,240

b. DR Interest expense 330 CR Accrued interest liability 330

c. Not an event to be adjusted for—external to the company.

d. DR Amortization expense 14,500 CR Accumulated
amortization 14,500

e. DR Bad debts expense or CR Accounts receivable 2,100
loss 2,100

f. DR Warranty expense 780 CR Warranty liability 780

g. Not an event to be adjusted for—not effective until next year.

h. DR Prepaid expenses 2,000 CR Insurance expense
(10/12 × $2,400) 2,000

i. DR Sales revenue 400 CR Customer deposits
liability 400

j. DR Accounts receivable 7,200 CR Sales revenue 7,200
DR COGS expense 3,300 CR Inventory 3,300

Solution Outline for PROBLEM 3.12*   a:8; b:3; c:9; d:7; e:1; f:2; g:4; h:6; i:5; j:10.

Solution Outline for PROBLEM 3.13*

a.	Recording amortization	DR Amortization expense
b.	Recognizing interest cost that is building up	DR Interest expense
c.	Capitalizing expense(s)	CR Relevant expense(s)
d.	Recognizing unexpired insurance coverage	CR Insurance expense
e.	Recognizing estimated warranty costs on this year's revenue	DR Warranty expense
f.	Recording dividends declared	DR Retained earnings
g.	Estimating current income tax liability	DR Income tax expense
h.	Removing customer deposits from revenue	DR Revenue
i.	Unused supplies on hand	CR Relevant expense (supplies?)
j.	Recognizing year-end bonus	DR Bonuses expense

Solution Outline for PROBLEM 3.14*

1.
   a. DR Bad debts expense   2,400   CR Accounts receivable   2,400
   b. DR Amortization expense   13,000   CR Accum. amortization   13,000
   c. DR Accounts receivable   11,200   CR Revenue   11,200
   d. DR COGS expense   4,600   CR Inventory   4,600
   e. DR Operating expense   900   CR Accrued interest liability   900
   f. DR Operating expense   5,000   CR Bonus payable   5,000
   g. DR Income tax expense   2,700   CR Income tax payable   2,700

2. and 3.

	Unadjusted DR	Unadjusted CR	Adjustments DR	Adjustments CR	Adjusted DR	Adjusted CR
Cash	25,600				25,600	
Accounts receivable	88,200		(c) 11,200	(a) 2,400	97,000	
Inventory	116,900			(d) 4,600·	112,300	
Land	100,000				100,000	
Buildings & equip.	236,100				236,100	
Accum. amortization				(b)13,000		13,000
Accounts payable		74,900				74,900
Employee deductions due		2,500				2,500
Sales taxes due		3,220				3,220
Accrued interest				(e) 900		900
Bonus payable				(f) 5,000		5,000
Income tax payable				(g) 2,700		2,700
Mortgage		185,780				185,780
Share capital		275,000				275,000
Retained earnings		0				0
Revenue		349,600		(c) 11,200		360,800
COGS expense	142,500		(d) 4,600		147,100	
Operating expenses	181,700		(a) 2,400		203,000	
			(b) 13,000			
			(e) 900			
			(f) 5,000			
Income tax expense			(g) 2,700		2,700	
	891,000	891,000	39,800	39,800	923,800	923,800

4. DR Revenue   360,800   CR COGS expense   147,100
                                            CR Operating expenses   203,000
                                            CR Income tax expense   2,700
                                            CR Retained earnings   8,000

5. Net income = $8,000 (see part 4)
   Current assets = $25,600 + $97,000 + $112,300 = $234,900
   Current liabilities = $74,900 + $2,500 + $3,220 + $900 + $5,000 + $2,700 = $89,220
   Working capital = $234,900 – $89,220 = $145,680
   Shareholders' equity = $275,000 + $8,000 = $283,000

Solution Outline for PROBLEM 4.1*

1. Managing cash flow is important because in our economy cash is the medium of exchange by which business is done. An enterprise must have sufficient cash inflow to cover its need for cash outflow to pay bills, buy new assets, pay dividends, etc. In the short run, or at difficult times of the year, managing cash flow may be more important than managing overall performance as measured by the accrual basis income statement.

2. Yes. A company can show a good net income, but if it does not collect its accounts receivable, or if it buys too much inventory, so cash is either not coming in from customers or is "tied up" in inventory, the cash from operations can be smaller than the net income.

3. Because net income includes substantial noncash expenses (amortization, especially) that depress income but do not affect cash from operations, for most companies net income will be lower than cash income (cash from operations).

4. Cash and equivalents are cash on hand and in banks plus short-term certificates (maturity of three months or less is the usual rule) in financial institutions. Such very short-term investments are just places to put temporarily unneeded cash. In some cases, temporary bank overdrafts may be included in cash and equivalents by being deducted from the rest of the cash.

Solution Outline for PROBLEM 4.2*

1. The cash flow information covers at least the following:
   a. It tells you what the cash income (cash from operations) is.
   b. It tells you why the cash income differs from the accrual net income.
   c. If done by the traditional indirect method, it reports whether the company's noncash working capital is rising or falling (supplementing the working capital and working capital ratio: if working capital is growing, that may not be good because receivables are not being collected or inventories are increasing, and if such is going on, the indirect method cash flow statement will point out the negative effect of this on cash).
   d. It reports several cash activities that the income statement does not include and that can be determined from the balance sheet only if you know how to do it, such as expenditures on additional noncurrent assets, proceeds from the sale of such assets, and the raising and repayment of noncurrent liabilities and share capital.
   e. It reports how much cash was used to pay dividends.

2. Net change in cash = $127,976 − $238,040 + $107,000 = −$3,064.

3. Effects if the event had occurred during the year:
   a. Investing would show an expenditure of $38,950. The net change in cash would be $38,950 lower.
   b. Financing would show a cash inflow of $20,000. The net change in cash would be $20,000 higher.
   c. The change in accounts receivable would have been $6,000 higher in the direction of reducing cash in the Operations section of the statement, because this revenue is reflected in income but hasn't yet been collected. Cash from operations and the net change in cash would be $6,000 lower.
   d. Dividends would show a cash outflow of $15,000, which would reduce the cash inflow from Financing activities. The net change in cash would be $15,000 lower.
   e. The demand loan would increase the cash inflow from Financing by $25,000, and the change in cash would also be $25,000 more positive.
   f. No change. In Operations, net income would be $5,000 lower but then the amortization added back in the Operations section would be $5,000 higher, cancelling out the effect. Therefore, there is no effect on the net total change in cash. Amortization has no effect on cash or on total cash from operations.

Solution Outline for PROBLEM 4.3*

- Cash began and ended negative in spite of much activity, but the change in cash was positive so the situation improved.
- Cash from operations was more than twice net income so that is good, but increased accounts receivable (possible collection problems) and inventories (possible selling problems), combined with increased payables (possible problems keeping up with bills), suggest difficulty with managing the day-to-day cash and with working capital management.
- Investing activities were almost twice the cash from operations, and given the lack of cash on hand, the company had to get substantial financing to support the asset acquisitions. Not much cash was obtained by selling noncurrent assets, so management seems to be building up the company's plant and equipment.
- Amortization expense was twice the income and almost equal cash from operations, but only half the new long-term investment. This supports the idea that the company's productive capacity is growing and being kept up to date.
- Financing activities seemed to be complicated by substantial debt repayments—another demand on cash (we don't know if the debts had come due or if the company chose to repay them, perhaps to refinance and get lower interest rates); therefore, almost $550,000 of new financing was required. This was raised mostly through debt, but also additional shares were issued (perhaps to keep the debt–equity mix from becoming too much weighted to debt).
- The company chose to pay out almost 40% of net income as dividends. If that had not been done, there would have been almost no cash deficit at the end of the year.

Solution Outline for PROBLEM 4.4*

Cash Flow Statement for the Year X (Direct Method)	
Operating Activities	
Cash receipts ($31,610 + $797,640)	$ 829,250
Cash disbursements ($8,920 + $513,600 + $14,920 + $223,610)	761,050
Cash generated by operations	$ 68,200
Investing Activities	
Noncurrent assets acquired ($81,000 + $49,000)	$(130,000)
Proceeds from disposal of noncurrent assets	7,000
Cash used in investing activities	$(123,000)
Financing Activities	
Bank loan obtained	$ 60,000
Repayments on mortgage	(80,500)
Common shares issued	140,000
Paid to redeem preferred shares	(25,000)
Dividends paid	(15,000)
Cash obtained from financing activities	$ 79,500
Increase in cash for the year	$ 24,700
Cash on hand at the beginning of the year	68,920
Cash on hand at the end of the year	$ 93,620

**Solution Outline for
PROBLEM 4.5***

Aragon Ltd.
Cash Flow Statement for the Year X

Operations		
Net income for the year		$216,350
Add back: Amortization	$ 218,890	
Deferred income tax expense	21,210	240,100
Noncash working capital changes		
Increase in accounts receivable	(223,120)	
Decrease in inventory	80,200	
Decrease in accounts payable	(91,970)	
Increase in current income tax payable	6,530	(228,360)
Cash from operations		$228,090
Investing		
Additions to noncurrent assets	$(393,980)	
Proceeds from sales of noncurrent assets	11,260	(382,720)
Financing		
New noncurrent debt	$ 250,500	
Repayments of noncurrent debt	(78,000)	
Share capital issued	120,000	
Dividends paid	(75,000)	216,700
Change in cash for the year		$ 62,070
Beginning cash		(13,730)[1]
Ending cash		$ 48,340

[1] The beginning cash figure is deduced from the change in cash for the year and the ending cash
balance, both of which are known from Fred's draft statement.

Solution Outline for
PROBLEM 4.6*

Lambic Beverages Inc. Cash Flow Statement for This Year		
Operations		
Net loss		$ (210)
Add back: Amortization expense	$ 2,630	
Future income tax expense	250	2,880
Noncash working capital changes:		
Accounts receivable	$(1,150)	
Inventory	470	
Accounts payable	1,020	
Income tax payable	(330)	10
Cash from operations		$2,680
Investing		
Increase in noncurrent assets		(1,850)
Financing		
Repayment of bank loan	$(1,100)	
Repayment of debt	(540)	
Share capital issued	300	
Dividends paid	(50)	(1,390)
Change in cash and equivalents		(560)
Cash, beginning		1,120
Cash, ending		$ 560

Comments on the statement:

- Cash flow is quite positive in spite of negative income.

- The increase in accounts receivable suggests that there may be a problem with collections.

- The increase in accounts payable is inconsistent with the reduction in inventory.

- Less has been spent on new assets than amortization, so the book value of noncurrent assets is lower (are they being kept up to date?).

- Financing had a negative net effect because debt repayments and the large repayment on the bank loan exceeded new share capital.

- Overall, the company's entire financing came from operations because all other cash flows were negative. Cash remained positive, however, so reductions in the company's bank loan and debt were probably sensible, saving interest and reducing risk.

	This Year	Last Year
Working capital ratio	8,210 / 7,640 = 1.075	8,090 / 8,050 = 1.005
Debt–equity ratio	7,640 + 14,060 / 5,420 = 4.00	8,050, + 14,350 / 5,380 = 4.16

Comments on ratios:

- The decline in cash is countered by a slight improvement in the working capital ratio, but the current position is not strong because the working capital remains only slightly positive.

- The debt–equity ratio has also improved: the company paid off debt and raised share capital greater than the sum of the loss and dividend.

Solution Outline for PROBLEM 4.7*

Operations: $100,000 + $200,000 – $150,000 – $25,000
= $125,000 cash generated.

Investing: $600,000 – $30,000 proceeds = $570,000 cash used

Financing: $90,000 + $250,000 + $100,000 – $40,000 = $400,000 cash obtained

Change in cash overall = $125,000 – $570,000 + $400,000 = negative $45,000

Comments:

- Yes, the comfortable $50,000 cash on hand has been reduced to a marginal $5,000.

- Collection problems and increased inventory took a very large bite out of cash from operations. The receivables increase alone is three times the year's cash decline.

- Cash from operations would have been nearly enough to complete the company's financing needs, if dividends had not been paid.

- It can be argued that dividends are the least necessary payment to make if cash is short: if they had not been paid, there would have been only a small decline in cash, or else much less need for the bank loan.

- The company did not provide enough financing to pay for the new assets (given the collection problems): investing activities cost $570,000 but financing amounted to a net of only $400,000, and that included the $90,000 bank loan.

- The company spent three times as much on new assets as amortization expense, suggesting that the company is keeping assets up to date; indeed, the spending on new assets is so much above the cash from operations that the company appears to be growing rapidly. Cash strains often accompany growth.

Solution Outline for PROBLEM 4.8*

> ### Northern Star Theatre Company
> ### Cash Flow Statement for the Period
> ### November 5, 2000, to August 26, 2001
>
> | | |
> |---|---:|
> | Operations: | |
> | Partnership income for the period | $3,420 |
> | Add back amortization expense | 132 |
> | Increase in interest receivable and inventory | (100) |
> | Increase in accounts payable | 940 |
> | Cash from operations | $4,392 |
> | Investing activities: | |
> | Costumes and props | (660) |
> | Financing activities: | |
> | Contributions by partners | 1,450 |
> | Cash provided during the period and on hand at its end | $5,182 |

Solution Outline for PROBLEM 4.9*

1. Three figures in the cash flow statement are incorrect. The change in accounts payable (in Operations) includes the dividend payable, so the increase in that payable has the effect of increasing cash from operations, via an incorrect change in noncash working capital accounts. The dividend figure in the Financing section is also wrong, by the same amount, because so far, it will have been assumed that the whole dividend declared had been paid. The declared amount should have been reduced by the payable (unpaid) amount so that the Financing section showed only the cash paid for dividends. So cash from Financing is too low, and cash from Operations is too high, by the same amount. The two cancel out in their effect on the total change in cash.

2. a. Let x be the acquisitions during the year. Then x – $236,100 amortization expense – $840,000 cost removed when building was sold + $650,000 accumulated amortization removed when building was sold = $459,200 net change. Solving, x = $885,300. Going the other way, $885,300 – $840,000 – $236,100 + $650,000 = $459,200.

   b. The book value of the building was $840,000 – $650,000 = $190,000. The $200,000 proceeds – $190,000 book value = $10,000 gain on sale.

   c. Add back amortization of $236,100; subtract gain on sale of $10,000.

   d. Investing would show $885,300 acquisitions minus $200,000 proceeds, for a net expenditure of $685,300.

Solution Outline for PROBLEM 4.10*

a. Cash from operations = $11,000 income + $5,000 amortization – $4,000 gain + $3,000 future tax expense + $13,000 loss – $1,000 change in OCA + $2,000 change in OCL = $29,000.

b. Cash from financing = $2,000 shares + $4,000 debt* – $6,000 dividend = $0 (*Debt change: NCL begin = $18,000 + $3,000 regular future tax – $8,000 future tax reduction on special item = $13,000. Present NCL = $17,000, so it seems $4,000 more debt was incurred.)

c. Cash for investing = $34,000 new spending** – $7,000 proceeds = $27,000 net outflow
   (** New spending: NCA begin = $32,000 – $21,000 write-off – $3,000 book value of item sold – $5,000 amortization = $3,000. Present NCA = $37,000, so it appears that $34,000 of new spending happened.)

d. From above, $29,000 + $0 – $27,000 = $2,000. Looking at the CEA and CEL categories, the net cash (CEA – CEL) was $(2,000) at the beginning and $0 at the end, an improvement of $2,000.

Solution Outline for PROBLEM 4.11*

Tamarack Systems Inc.
Cash Flow Statement for the Year 2001

Operating Activities

Net income	$ 56,292
Noncash expenses ($139,904 amortization* + $5,000 garage loss + $35,000 land write-off + $4,075 warranty provision** + $4,516 future tax expense)	188,495
Noncash working capital changes ($65,000 temporary investments – $76,706 accounts receivable + $10,815 inventories + $5,317 prepaids + $35,987 accounts payable + $1,138 taxes payable)	41,551
Cash generated by operations	$ 286,338

Investing Activities

Additions ($37,500 land*** + $279,914 building****)	$(317,414)
Proceeds from disposal (garage)	25,000
Cash used in investing activities	$(292,414)

Financing Activities

Bank loan obtained	$ 21,700
Repayment of bonds ($22,000 – $2,000 current)	(20,000)
Warranty payments**	(7,000)
Shares issued ($50,000 – $5,000 non-cash exchange for land***)	45,000
Dividends paid ($24,000 declared + $6,000 from year before)	(30,000)
Cash obtained from financing activities	$ 9,700

Increase in cash for the year	$ 3,624
Cash on hand at the beginning of the year	12,440
Cash on hand at the end of the year	$ 16,064

* Change in accumulated amortization = $69,904, but the garage's $70,000 amortization would have been removed when it was sold, so there must have been an addition, due to expense, of $139,904.

** Warranty change = $2,925 down, but that was after paying out $7,000, so a further noncash expense provision of $4,075 must have been made.

*** Land change = $7,500. This was after a $35,000 write-off, so there must have been additions to land of $42,500. But $5,000 of that was a noncash exchange for shares, so the cash spent on land was $37,500.

**** Building cost change = $179,914, but the garage's $100,000 cost would have been removed when it was sold, so the additions to building must have cost $279,914.

Comments:

- Tamarack generated about all the cash it needed to finance its investing from operations, so it needed little noncurrent financing and still managed a small increase in cash.

- Cash from operations was five times net income. This demonstrates that accrual income can be a poor guide to cash flow.

- Cash was maintained partly by cashing in the temporary investments on hand last year. So you could say that near-cash resources actually went down this year: there are no temporary investments left to use if there are cash needs next year.

- The rise in accounts receivable was the only negative in the otherwise cash-increasing management of noncash working capital accounts. If the receivables had not risen so much, the company would not have had to cash in its temporary investments.

Solution Outline for PROBLEM 4.12*

1. If the garage had brought $40,000 instead of $25,000, cash used in investing activities would have gone down $15,000 for the proceeds, to $277,414. In Operations, income would have been $15,000 higher because the garage disposal would have produced a $10,000 gain instead of the $5,000 loss shown in the Problem 4.11* solution. But this would cancel out in calculating cash from operations, because instead of a $5,000 loss being added back to income of $56,292, there would have been a $10,000 gain deducted from an income of $71,292. So no effect on cash from operations, and the lower Investing net outflow would carry down to the bottom cash change, which would be $15,000 higher, and ending cash would therefore be $15,000 higher at $31,064. This makes sense, as the company would have $15,000 more cash from the garage disposal.

2. Ignoring part 1, this would have changed the $5,000 loss on sale to a $7,000 gain ($25,000 proceeds minus $18,000 book value). But that change would mean that the amortization expense deduced in Problem 4.11* would have been $12,000 higher. So in Operations, the amortization add-back would be $12,000 higher and instead of a $5,000 loss add-back there would be a $7,000 gain deducted, for a change of $12,000 in the opposite direction. So no net effect on cash from operations or cash on hand. This makes sense, because a change in the garage's accumulated amortization doesn't involve cash at all, so cannot have any effect on the cash flow statement.

Solution Outline for PROBLEM 5.1*

The financial statements are a set and should be interpreted as such because all the statements are prepared, directly or (for the cash flow statement) indirectly, from the set of balanced accounts. Therefore, they are all portions of the whole set of accounts and the meaning of each is inextricably linked to the others. Some examples:

- Income on the income statement is produced by increasing net resources, so the revenues and expenses are linked to balance sheet accounts such as accounts receivable (uncollected revenue), accounts payable (unpaid expenses), and accumulated amortization (the sum of amortization expenses over time).

- Income is carried from the income statement to the retained earnings statement.

- Dividends on the retained earnings statement are reflected in the balance sheet as either a decrease in cash or an increase in the dividends payable liability.

- Net income from the income statement is used as the beginning figure on the cash flow statement, which itself is an analysis of changes in balance sheet accounts.

Solution Outline for PROBLEM 5.2*

1. Independence is considered necessary so that it will not matter to the auditors what the financial statements say. Independence helps to ensure that the auditors will bring a detached, professional view to their task. If the auditors were not independent, they might "want" the results to turn out a certain way so that they were better off (for example, if the audit fee was a percentage of net income, then the auditors might go along with methods that make income higher because they would benefit).
2. Independence is difficult to maintain for several reasons. First, the auditors would not have the audit job the next year if the company were to fail, so they are likely to prefer that the company continue to exist, and might be tempted to agree to accounting methods that hide problems. Second, the auditors have to work closely with management, and may depend on management for other business (e.g., tax or accounting advice) that is nice to have. Third, though the auditors are officially appointed by the shareholders, a recommendation by management that the auditors be reappointed (or not) is likely to be accepted by the shareholders, who are not usually very close to the company or to the auditors. Fourth, the auditors are human and get to know and like the people they work with, such as the company management and employees, and usually would like such people to succeed—it's hard to be detached all the time.

Solution Outline for PROBLEM 5.3*

The annual report's financial information includes four statements: the balance sheet, the income statement, the statement of retained earnings, and the cash flow statement. They are important as a summary of a company's business transactions for the year, supplemented by adjustments for incomplete transactions and estimates about future effects. Financial performance, both in an economic ("accrual") sense and according to cash flows, is reported and can be analyzed and to some extent projected into the future. The balance sheet takes this performance information and adds it to the company's financial position at the end of last year, producing a summary of the company's financial position as accumulated over the company's whole life. Without these statements, investors would be unable to evaluate the performance of companies they invest in.

If an investor doesn't have the time to study all these statements, the annual report usually contains ratios, trends, charts, and other information to help digest the financial data. To help with this, the notes to the financial statements contain supplementary information to support the figures in the financial statements and to explain information that may not be contained in the financial statements, such as unsettled lawsuits. If there is an item on the financial statements that you would like to know more about, the notes may help you.

Summary comparative data going back five or ten years usually supplements the traditional financial statements. This information is useful if you want to know more about the company's past, since the financial statements themselves typically provide two-year comparative information. The additional comparative data may or may not give insights into where the company is headed in the future, but you can examine past trends.

The management discussion and analysis section of the annual report is useful in trying to understand the company's current position and what its plans are for the future. However, this section, being prepared by management, tends to focus on the image that management wants to present, so it should be read in conjunction with the more objective financial statements.

The auditor's report is important in determining how much reliance you can place on the fairness of the information contained in the financial statements. You should examine the wording of the auditor's report to ensure that the auditors did not have a concern about their fairness. The wording of the auditor's report will also indicate whether or not an audit was actually performed. It may actually be a "review engagement report," whereby less detailed verification procedures were performed and which is less reliable than an auditor's report.

Solution Outline for PROBLEM 5.4*

1. Simone's jewellery business, although not incorporated, can be separated from her personal affairs.
2. A bank is a legal and economic entity, just as any other corporation.
3. This is a large economic unit, which can be considered to include all the individual corporations contributing to Exxon's financial performance and position.
4. A university is not a "business" but is still an economic unit, quite aside from its nature as an educational and research institution.
5. Mato is a corporation and is therefore a legal entity for which financial statements can be prepared.
6. Ernst & Young is a partnership and is therefore a somewhat separate legal entity from its partners, being able to transact business, hire employees, etc., and generally operates as an economic entity separate from its partners' personal affairs.
7. As in part 4, the city is not a "business" but is still an economic unit.
8. McDonald's may be spread out all over the world, but its parts can be assembled into an accounting entity on similar arguments to those made for Exxon.

Solution Outline for PROBLEM 5.5*

1. • fund balance replaces owners' equity section
   • statement of revenues and expenditures instead of income statement
   • little or no amortization, lack of provision for long-term obligations, and lack of consolidation

2. • not really a business any more, as its assets are being sold off rather than being used to earn income
   • the use of historical financial statements to evaluate its performance while in bankruptcy may not make sense

- accrual accounting is probably less useful than just cash accounting

3. • no owners; therefore, like governments, fund balance replaces owners' equity section
   - lack of profit motive, so "net income" might not be meaningful to club members
   - probably lack of continuing management, as students come and go, so evaluation of any one year's management's performance using accounting information may be difficult
   - probably a focus on cash inflows and outflows rather than historical costs and accrual accounting estimates

4. • no owners
   - lack of profit motive and therefore no income statement
   - receives significant donations and grants and therefore needs an accounting system that will help it demonstrate its accountability for use of such money separately from operating cash inflows and outflows

5. • owned by the government, see part 1 above
   - given its broad ecological and preservation mandate, and varied sources of income and needs for expenditures, it combines some of the features of the student club and Sick Children's Hospital and so has more complex accounting needs than many ordinary businesses

Solution Outline for PROBLEM 5.6*

Here are some ideas in response to the sentences. You may well think of several other concepts/principles and probably will make additional points about some of them.

1. Three concepts/principles related to this are fairness, reliability, and verifiability. Some effects on financial statements of these are: accountants are careful that all cash transactions and day-to-day events such as credit sales and purchases are reflected in the financial statements; considerable care is taken to minimize errors and omissions in the accounting system that underlies the financial statements; and auditors ensure that important financial statement data can be traced back to underlying events and evidence.

2. Three concepts/principles related to this are conservatism, fairness, and matching. Conservatism results (or should result) in financial statements that contain prudent, not overly optimistic, estimates of future cash inflows and outflows regarding present assets and liabilities. Fairness has the effect of keeping conservatism in bounds so that the financial statements are not pessimistic (which would be unfair to present owners and managers). Matching says that estimates affecting revenues should be done on comparable bases to those affecting expenses, so that the net income makes sense, so it puts some bounds on conservatism too.

3. Three concepts/principles related to this are conformance with GAAP, consistency, and comparability. Conformance with GAAP ensures that the company's information is prepared in ways the user might expect, to permit meaningful analyses of its performance. The objective of consistency over time results in highlighting inconsistencies so that the user can consider their effects on the information. The goal of comparability refers directly to the idea of "relative performance" because if the previous two principles are met,

the company can be evaluated by comparison to others like it, or to others the user might consider investing in or lending to.

4. Two concepts/principles related to this are disclosure and decision relevance. Disclosure has the effect of helping users understand how the accounting numbers were computed and thus helping them to make estimates of future effects. Decision relevance is a reminder that the financial statements should be useful both in past-oriented decisions (such as evaluating management's performance or calculating bonuses) and in future-oriented decisions (such as whether to invest in or lend to the company).

5. Three concepts/principles related to this are fairness, reliability, and verifiability. The goal of all three is partly to minimize the effects of human error, biases, and wishes on the information by promoting objective, careful methods of preparing it and making it possible (in principle) for anyone else who prepares it to come up with, and agree with, the same information.

Solution Outline for PROBLEM 5.7*

Some of the many points that might be made:

1. a. If the market responds quickly and efficiently to information, it indicates the efficient allocation of capital resources. Money flows toward viable companies and away from less viable ones. So, accounting information assists in this allocation process.

   b. There are systematic and unsystematic (company-specific) risks in a stock market. Accounting information can help in assessing the latter.

2. a. Information is helpful to monitoring managers' "stewardship" role in their companies, and in maintaining contractual arrangements. Accounting therefore assists in the effective administration of contracts in the economy.

   b. Changes in the contractual arrangements will cause changes in the accounting information that is required. Accounting's use responds to the nature of the control/administration role assigned it.

Solution Outline for PROBLEM 5.8*

This question can be answered in many ways. You may be cynical and state that accounting is not appropriate for either purpose. Or you may say that external reporting is the most important, or that monitoring and control is. Whatever your position, make sure you can support it with cogent arguments.

One position is to say that financial accounting exists for both purposes, as outlined below.

1. Information for outsiders:

   • It allows comparisons by investors because each firm is reporting using the same guidelines (GAAP).

   • An independent auditor reviews the information to ensure that it fairly presents the financial position of the company.

   • The information is for everyone, because supposedly it is to be largely comprehended by general users who put some diligence into analyzing and understanding the statements.

2. Internal:

- It assists in such areas as control over accounts receivable, inventory, and accounts payable, which are important for the successful conduct of business and management of the company.

- Incentive plans can be based on the accounting information, which provides some control over managerial behaviour.

- Since the information is prepared for the owners (shareholders), it may eliminate some management bias and promote clearer evaluation of management performance.

Solution Outline for PROBLEM 5.9*

Some very sketchy comments, intended to generate ideas, are:

1. a. The economic entity that capital markets are presumably interested in does not necessarily coincide with the legal entity. For example, a set of consolidated statements is based on the presumed economic entity.

   b. The historical cost basis increases reliability of information but may reduce relevance to current decisions by market participants.

   c. Fairness aims to increase confidence in objectivity or impartiality of information. But is this term too vague? Is fairness open to too wide an interpretation by preparers of information and thus not really useful to markets and other agents?

   d. Although choice is permitted in the presentation of accounting information, GAAP form standards and guidelines that set boundaries. Therefore, markets can have some confidence that the information being presented has been prepared within some acceptable range of methods.

   e. There is potential for management and/or preparers to have undue influence over accountants and auditors. Users rely on the audit report since the auditors are independent. Professional ethics help ensure this independence and the care and expertise required to do a technically competent job of preparing the accounting information.

2. a. The financial statements are consolidated. The preparers have used a method of consolidation to create financial statements that represent the commonly controlled entity.

   b. Historical cost is the basic measure for most account balances in the large public company's financial statements, including the property, equipment, new debt issued, and so on. Since every company uses the original price under historical cost, the statements satisfy one of the main elements of information: objectivity.

   c. The main piece of evidence relating to fairness is in the auditor's report. This report gives the external auditor's opinion that the statements are fair.

   d. The auditor's report also says that the statements have been prepared following GAAP.

   e. Professional ethics is implied in the presumably expert, unbiased, independent status of the external auditor. That auditor is expected to act professionally, and not to follow anyone else's dictates in judging the fairness of the financial statements.

3. These concepts are still relevant to a small, private company. While the larger company's information is of interest to market traders and the private

company's is not, they otherwise have many similar users: banks, taxation authorities, managers, and perhaps potential owners. Though the use context may differ somewhat, these underlying concepts are still valuable.

Solution Outline for PROBLEM 5.10*

Again a discussion problem, which can be used to bring out some of the practicalities of preparing financial statements and help bring the "GAAP" topic to life. Some ideas follow.

1. How should you decide what to do to meet requirements?

   - What exactly are the facts of the situation?

   - What objectives is the information to meet (e.g., what use is likely)?

   - What was done last year?

   - What do other similar companies do?

   - What do other parts of the *Handbook* require for specific assets, liabilities, revenues, expenses, notes, etc.?

   - Ask experts about difficult issues.

   - Consult texts, legal cases, and other such reasonably authoritative sources.

   - What does it cost to produce the "best" information? Is the benefit worth the cost?

   - Do accounting professional organizations or firms offer any guidance?

2. Is the company free to do what it likes as long as it explains?

   - The standards can't cover everything, so such an "out" makes sense to allow variations as long as they are clearly explained.

   - But the result still has to meet the auditor's "fairness" test, so companies are not unconstrained.

   - Self-serving or over-optimistic presentations would be suspect.

   - The company's management is responsible for the contents of the financial statements and can be held accountable in a court of law, so gross violations of GAAP, even if explained, would be difficult to get away with.

   - It can be observed that many companies depart here and there from GAAP in order to present their information in a believed better way, so paragraph .06 (and other such provisions) do permit some variety.

   - Stock market oriented accounting research indicates that as long as the users can understand what is going on and have necessary background data, they can "adjust" for accounting variations and still make appropriate decisions, so the question given in this problem may well be answered affirmatively.

Solution Outline for PROBLEM 5.11*

1. "Stewards" managed the properties of the English aristocracy. Stewardship is important today in companies in which the owners are separate from the managers of the organization; in this sense, the managers are "stewards" for

the owners and are responsible for running the company on the owners' behalves.

2. Securities regulation arose over the last several hundred years because governments and the people they represented felt that too much fraudulent, incompetent, and otherwise unacceptable behaviour was going on in public companies and with their shares and other securities. It seems that such regulation continues to be important, and the regular, nearly daily, reporting of problems in the media indicate that regulation might need further tightening.

3. Authoritative accounting standards have developed largely over the last century. They are important in providing rules and guidelines that prevent each accountant from reinventing the wheel each time financial statements are prepared. The overall objective is to result in financial statements that are "fair" and therefore useful to the intended decision maker who is relying on the financial statements.

4. The harmonization of international standards is becoming increasingly important as the world becomes a global market place. The users of the financial statements need to be able to understand the content no matter which country the statements originated from.

5. Independence became more and more important in the last hundred years, especially after the Great Depression of the 1930s, because auditors had to be relied upon to form an objective part of the securities and financial reporting regulatory systems, and because investors and other users of financial information became both more competent in using the information and more skeptical about possible management-induced biases in it, and about possibly cozy relationships between auditors and client management.

6. Disclosure has increased in importance and volume with the increase in financial regulation and in business complexity. There is more to tell people about all the time, and less ability to fit it neatly into the double-entry accounting statements.

Solution Outline for PROBLEM 5.12*

The tradeoff between relevance and reliability arises because of the demand for timely information. Since users are not willing to wait years for financial statements, during which time uncertainties about the collection of receivable and pension liabilities would be resolved, they must accept estimates made for some accounts, based on the information that is available now. Therefore, the estimate is unlikely to be completely accurate (i.e., reliable), but it reflects a more complete picture of the company's current position and performance than if the estimate were not made at all (i.e., it is relevant).

Solution Outline for PROBLEM 5.13*

- Objectivity and neutrality—users need to be able to rely on the financial statements; their confidence is enhanced if the accountant/auditor has no interest in the results disclosed.

- Governed by professional standards and code of ethics—there are consequences if members of the profession do not follow the standards and codes of ethics; in extreme cases, the professional status of an individual can be revoked.

- Entrance is limited to competent members who can pass the examination process; again, the users' confidence is enhanced knowing that the auditor/accountant is an expert in his/her field. Most accounting associations require some demonstration of continued competence, especially among members who offer their services to the public.

- Legally protected status and related responsibilities—being a professional provides some status and income, but there are repercussions if the concomitant responsibilities are not met, including fines, dismissal from the professional association, even jail.

Solution Outline for PROBLEM 6.1*

1. Revenue is economic value created through a transaction with a customer, whether or not the customer pays the cash at the time. A cash receipt is the payment by the customer.
2. Revenue but not receipt: credit sales. Receipt but not revenue: a deferred revenue, such as down payments or cash advances for work yet to be performed. Both revenue and receipt: cash sales.
3. Expense: cost of assets used or commitments incurred to pay assets (usually cash) in producing revenue. Matched with revenue, not necessarily with outflow of cash. Recognition of expense may precede, accompany, or follow payment of cash (cash disbursement). Expenses are found on the income statement, their cash components are determined in preparing the cash flow statement.
4. Expense but not disbursement: depreciation, accrued interest, COGS (contrast with cash purchases, added to inventories). Disbursement but not expense: purchase asset, reduce a payable, pay dividends. Both expense and disbursement: small bills, utilities, donations.

Solution Outline for PROBLEM 6.2*

1:e; 2:d; 3:f; 4:g; 5:b; 6:i; 7:h; 8:j; 9:c; 10:a.

Solution Outline for PROBLEM 6.3*

Revenue (174,320 – 11,380 + 520 + 9,440)		$172,900
Bad debts expense	$ 520	
COGS, wages, etc. (145,690 – 12,770 + 15,510 + 21,340 – 24,650)	145,120	
Interest (12,000 × 8% × 1/12)	80	
Income tax (2,340 + 3,400 + 1,230)	6,970	152,690
Accrual net income		$ 20,210

Solution Outline for PROBLEM 6.4*

1. The critical event, i.e., the point where the revenue is actually earned, may or may not correspond with the point of sale. Revenue on long-term contracts, for example, may be earned at various stages of completion. The point of sale may not be far enough along for other reasons, such as substantial after-sale service or uncertainty of collection.
2. 2001 contract expense: $11,210 (38% of $29,500); 2001 contract income: $5,130 (38% of ($43,000 – $29,500)).

Solution Outline for PROBLEM 6.5*

Some points you might consider:

- The clash between the two objectives is real and yet unavoidable in all measurement systems intended for general use (for example, university grading systems).

- Somehow both objectives must be met (at least to some significant degree) or the financial statements will not be useful to anyone outside the company.

- One solution proposed (and used) is to rely on the expert judgment of accounting professionals to find solutions applicable to each company that are still sufficiently comparable to other companies.

- The conflict is important: it occupies much of the time and effort of accountants, auditors, and managers, and court cases have been fought over it. (It was determined in one important U.S. case that it was possible to follow GAAP and still provide financial statements that are unfair in representing the particular company.)

- The large structure of authoritative accounting standards and other development of GAAP began after the 1929 stock market crash and subsequent depression. Has all this helped to prevent repetitions of those problems?

- Perhaps a measurement system that does not adjust for individual circumstances (your height measure is not affected by your management objectives) provides a more credible, useful measure than our approach of fitting the measure to the company. Some countries have quite inflexible rules for financial statements—why not Canada?

Solution Outline for PROBLEM 6.6*

All parts in 000's of Dollars	Revenue	Expense	Income
a. Completed contract basis:			
Year 1	0	0	0
Year 2	0	0	0
Year 3	5,200	4,300	900
Total	5,200	4,300	900

b. Percentage completion basis:

	Revenue	Expense	Income
Year 1 ($900,000 / 4,300,000 = 21\%$)	1,092 (21%)	900 (21%)	192 (21%)
Year 2 ($1,990,000 / 4,300,000 = 46\%$)	2,392 (46%)	1,990 (46%)	402 (46%)
Year 3 ($1,410,000 / 4,300,000 = 33\%$)	1,716 (33%)	1,410 (33%)	306 (33%)
Total	5,200	4,300	900

All parts in 000's of Dollars	Revenue	Expense	Income
c. Cash received basis:			
Year 1			
(1,000,000 / 5,200,000 = 19%)	1,000 (19%)	817 (19%)	183 (19%)
Year 2			
(2,030,000 / 5,200,000 = 39%)	2,030 (39%)	1,677 (39%)	353 (39%)
Year 3			
(2,170,000 / 5,200,000 = 42%)	2,170 (42%)	1,806 (42%)	364 (42%)
Total	5,200	4,300	900

Solution Outline for PROBLEM 6.7*

1. $123,775 + $714,555 − $840,370 = $(2,040) so an accrued liability. Expense = $840,370. Injuries are irrelevant to the question as stated.
2. $(57,890) + $717,430 − $658,280 = $1,260 so prepaid expense. Expense = $658,280.

Solution Outline for PROBLEM 6.8*

a. Your answer should fit the circumstances. Some comments:

- Point of delivery is probably too soon, because there are substantial after-sale adjustments.

- However, point of delivery could be used as long as the revenue recognition was accompanied by an estimated reduction for later returns and allowances, if such an estimate is reliable.

- Or a reasonable time after point of delivery, to allow for time for returns and adjustments, could be selected.

- Point of cash collection subsequent to delivery could be considered, because some customers are very slow and there is some risk of noncollection.

- Explanation of why appropriate should refer to the four revenue recognition criteria at the end of section 6.6, and no criterion should be inconsistent with the policy recommended.

b. (i) An unfilled order is not normally considered to affect the accounting, by the transaction rule of section 1.6. However, in this case, an unfilled order does have some impact. First is the inventory (asset) obtained, special to each order as each is a one-time-only design. Second is the cash received for the deposit on the order. Third is the customer deposits liability representing the obligation to the customer.

(ii) Probably the best fiscal year-end would be in late fall to mid-winter, between the fall and spring busy seasons. There would be few deliveries then, and accounts receivable and inventories of specially ordered fabrics would likely be relatively small.

Solution Outline for PROBLEM 6.9*

a. Aggressive accounting can involve selecting accounting policies that recognize revenue sooner rather than later, thereby increasing current net income. It can also involve selecting accounting policies that support capitalizing rather than expensing items, thereby increasing income and also the balance sheet value of assets.

b. Articulation refers to the double-entry reality that recognizing a revenue or expense for the income statement affects a corresponding asset or liability (cash, accounts receivable, inventory, accounts payable, customer deposits, etc.). Therefore, income measurement and balance sheet valuation are directly related.

c. A deferred revenue represents revenue not used yet for income measurement because it has not yet been earned, and therefore kept on the balance sheet as a (usually) current liability. The existence of such an account means that revenue and income are lower than they would be otherwise, and that the balance sheet is weaker (higher current liabilities and lower working capital).

d. Matching is a process whereby expenses are recognized at the same time as the related revenue. An expense that does not yet match with current revenue is deferred on the balance sheet as a prepaid expense or other asset. Matching thus affects both income and balance sheet values.

e. Period expenses are those, like interest, that do not relate much to the revenue of a period but rather to the passage of time. Balance sheet values (like accrued or prepaid interest) thus relate also to the passage of time rather than revenue. So period expenses represent one of the weaker connections between income measurement and balance sheet valuation: they affect both, but do not tie them as the usual matching of revenues and expenses does.

f. Conservatism results in the recognition of anticipated losses but not anticipated gains. The effect is not to be overly optimistic in the reflection of net income and net assets. Thus income measurement is somewhat depressed, as are balance sheet values for such assets as accounts receivable and inventories, and balance sheet values for liabilities are raised.

Solution Outline for PROBLEM 6.10*

Monthly expenses:
Months in 1999: $375 ($4,500 / 12)
Months in 2000: $400 ($4,800 / 12)
Months in 2001: $425 ($5,100 / 12)

a. April 30, 2000
Accrued: 4 months × $400 = $1,600
Expense: 8 × $375 + 4 × $400 = $4,600

April 30, 2001
Accrued: 4 months × $425 = $1,700
Expense: 8 × $400 + 4 × $425 = $4,900

b. June 30, 2000
Accrued: 6 months × $400 = $2,400
Expense: 6 × $375 + 6 × $400 = $4,650

June 30, 2001
Accrued: 6 months × $425 = $2,550
Expense: 6 × $400 + 6 × $425 = $4,950

c. Sept. 30, 2000
Accrued: 9 months × $400 = $3,600
Expense: 3 × $375 + 9 × $400 = $4,725

Sept. 30, 2001
Prepaid: 3 months × $425 = $1,275
Expense: 3 × $400 + 9 × $425 = $5,025

d. Dec. 31, 2000　　Accrued or prepaid = 0
　　　　　　　　　　　Expense: 12 × $400 = $4,800
　　Dec. 31, 2001　　Accrued or prepaid = 0
　　　　　　　　　　　Expense: 12 × $425 = $5,100

Solution Outline for PROBLEM 6.11*

a. Cash, which is the same as point of sale for this fast-food business.
b. On delivery, or perhaps even later to ensure the customer is satisfied. Selling such software often involves substantial effort later to help the customer use it.
c. When production completed, but not necessarily when a specific customer has been found, might be considered, since selling gold is not a problem. But given the currently variable gold market prices, recognizing revenue on delivery might be most sensible.
d. Cash basis—these are installment sales for which the collection is uncertain.
e. Percentage of completion—these are long-term construction contracts with customers from which collection is reasonably assured, but may be slow and is unlikely to be earlier than the completion rate for the projects.
f. Delivery basis (i.e., on title transfer)—until this point, no customer or price is assured.

Solution Outline for PROBLEM 6.12*

Adjust?		Journal Entry		
a.	Y	DR Accounts receivable	3,200	
		CR Revenue		3,200
b.	Y	DR Cost of goods sold expense	1,900	
		CR Inventory		1,900
c.	Y	DR Customer deposits liability	3,900	
		CR Revenue		3,900
d.	Y	DR Store building (asset)	62,320	
		CR Maintenance expense		62,320
e.	Y	DR Warranty expense	4,300	
		CR Warranty liability		4,300
	N	No adjustment seems required for the pain and suffering claim.		
f.	Y	DR Audit expense	2,350	
		CR Accounts payable		2,350
g.	Y	DR Automobile (asset)	17,220	
		CR Accounts payable		17,220
h.	Y	DR Distribution rights amortization expense	500	
		CR Distribution rights (asset)		500

Solution Outline for PROBLEM 6.13*

a. Recognizing revenue when it has been earned means that accrual accounting records revenue when criteria have been met that provide reasonable assurance that the revenue is real. Thus, overly optimistic recording of revenue early on, such as when the customer makes an order, is unlikely, but so is overly pessimistic recording, waiting for all the cash to be collected. This procedure results in an asset called accounts receivable and means that the revenue on the income statement is different than the cash collected from customers. Reconciling the revenue with the cash collection is a major reason for having the cash flow statement to supplement the income statement.

b. Balance sheet assets and liabilities include real physical assets and financial assets and liabilities, such as land, investments, loans, and debts. But the balance sheet also includes accounts that result from the attempt to measure income on a sensible economic basis, in accordance with the company's way of doing business. These include such "residuals" as accounts receivable (revenue recorded in the income statement but not yet collected), accounts payable (expenses deducted from income but not yet paid), accumulated amortization (the sum of amounts deducted from income to represent the economic use of noncurrent assets), and long-term liability provisions such as for warranties, pensions, and income taxes, which all represent expenses deducted from income but not yet due to be paid.

c. Matching expense recognition to the period in which it was incurred means that expenses that arise due to the passage of time, or at least arise from other sources than the direct attempt to earn revenue, are deducted from income in the period in which they arose, not necessarily the period in which they were paid or had their greatest effect on income. Examples are interest expense, donations (whose effects on income may be much in the future due to increased reputation in the community), property taxes, and most research and development costs.

**Solution Outline for
PROBLEM 7.1***

a. This is an example of segregation of duties. The person who handles the cash is not the same person who records the receipts in the receivables records, thereby identifying differences between the two records and lessening the possibility for the cash handler to pocket the cash without recording it.

b. In the petty cash fund, the cash on hand plus the receipts of cash paid expenses should equal the total petty cash fund. This reconciliation reveals any cash shortages.

c. The retail inventory method combines inventory control with cash control. Inventory at the beginning of the period plus purchases less sales should equal inventory at the end of the period, with all inventory calculated at the retail price of the goods. Differences between actual ending inventory and the calculated amount could be the result of unrecorded cash sales or missing inventory.

d. Since inventory is usually susceptible to theft, keeping it in a locked warehouse is an important way to physically safeguard it.

e. The employee deductions liabilities are control accounts. Reconciling the control accounts to the payroll register and to actual payments is important since employee benefits are often a complicated area. The reconciliation ensures that payroll has been recorded correctly in the accounts and that the proper payments have been made.

Solution Outline for PROBLEM 7.2*

1. $1,693,784
2. $1,599,055
3. $8,293
4. $9,117
5. $9,117 / $1,693,784 = half a cent per dollar
6. $331,106 – $12,738 = $318,368
7. Accounts receivable = $244,620 + $1,693,784 – $1,599,005 = $339,399
   Allowance = $11,914 + $9,117 = $21,031
   Collectible value = $339,399 – $21,031 = $318,368 (same as part 6)

Solution Outline for PROBLEM 7.3*

a. The bookkeeping process recognizes only routine transactions; therefore, adjustments are required to record nonroutine economic events or to correct errors.

b. Contra accounts are used when an account needs to be adjusted to recognize an expense or loss but the original balance of the account needs to be preserved for informational or control purposes. The most common contra accounts are allowance for doubtful accounts and accumulated depreciation.

c. Internal control comprises the methods that a company uses to provide physical security and management control over its assets.

d. Control accounts are those supported by lists or "subsidiary ledgers" that contain details, thus the control account and the detailed lists provide a check on each other. Examples are accounts receivable (which should agree with the list of amounts due from individual customers), cash (which should agree with cash counts and bank records), and sales taxes due (which should agree with amounts determined from sales records and reported on government forms).

e. Books of original entry are the journals in which transactions are first recorded.

f. Writing off uncollectible accounts is the process of removing from accounts receivable and the allowance for doubtful accounts those receivables that will not be collected, on which the company is giving up and therefore are not worth keeping track of.

g. Accounting control means using accounting records to provide checks and documentation for physical assets such as inventories and plant assets, financial assets such as cash and accounts receivable, and various liabilities. Such records provide something for other records to be compared to (see control accounts above).

Solution Outline for PROBLEM 7.4*

1. $793,220
2. $1,032,568
3. Book value = $843,992 – $411,883 = $432,109
   Book value minus proceeds = $432,109 – $350,000 = $82,109 loss on disposal

DR Cash	350,000	
CR Factory assets		843,992
DR Accumulated amortization	411,883	
DR Loss on disposal	82,109	

4.   CR Factory assets   89,245
       DR Accumulated amortization   59,200
       DR Write-off loss (expense)   30,045
5. NBV = $5,597,219 – $2,299,458 = $3,297,761

Solution Outline for PROBLEM 7.5*				
a. DR Accounts receivable	81,360	CR Revenue	72,000
		CR PST due	4,320
		CR GST due	5,040
DR Cash	69,030	CR Accounts receivable	69,030
DR PST due	3,900	CR Cash	3,900
DR GST due	3,100	CR Cash	3,100
DR Inventories	26,286	CR Accounts payable	28,126
DR GST due	1,840		
b. DR Wages expense	39,250	CR Employee tax deductions due	11,180
		CR Fringes and other deductions due	4,990
		CR Wages payable	23,080
DR Fringes or wage expense	6,315	CR Fringes and other deductions due	6,315
DR Employee tax deductions due	12,668	CR Cash	12,668
DR Fringes or other ded. due	11,894	CR Cash	11,894

Solution Outline for PROBLEM 7.6*

- Packing slips and/or supplier invoices: received with inventory orders, matched with related purchase orders, and recorded in a purchases register.

- Cheques: issued to pay accounts payable, payroll, etc., and recorded in a cheque register or cash disbursements journal.

- Sales invoice: created upon completion of a sale and recorded in a sales journal.

- Payments received from customers: received upon collection of receivables and recorded in a cash receipts journal.

- Journal entries: created for nonroutine events and recorded in a general journal.

- Specialized or subsidiary ledgers: detailed backup, for example, by supplier (accounts payable subledger) or customer (accounts receivable subledger).

Solution Outline for PROBLEM 7.7*

1. Cost of goods sold   = Beginning inventory $ 246,720
                          + Purchases   1,690,000
                          – Ending inventory   (324,800)
                                                           $1,611,920

2. If the correct COGS is $1,548,325, this means that some of what appeared to have been sold was not. It was lost, or stolen, or it strayed! The amount lost

is $63,595, which could be left in the COGS expense or could be shown sep-arately, so that the COGS expense would be the accurate, smaller amount. Total expense would not be different; the perpetual method just allows it to be split into $1,548,325 COGS and $63,595 loss, which were lumped together under the periodic method. The need for the $63,595 adjustment indicates that the company has what seems a serious problem somewhere: there are errors in the records, inventories are being lost somehow, or there are more sinister things going on, like employee theft.

3. Companies may choose not to use the perpetual method because of its cost to operate. It may be felt that the improved recordkeeping is not worth its cost. Here, the losses are large enough that a reasonable perpetual control system would probably be affordable.

Solution Outline for PROBLEM 7.8*	1:d; 2:h; 3:g; 4:b; 5:f; 6:j; 7:c; 8:i; 9:a; 10:e.

Solution Outline for PROBLEM 7.9*	Numbering the components of internal control as in section 7.3 (a) violates #5; (b) violates #4; (c) violates #3; (d) violates #2; (e) violates #7; and (f) violates #1.

Solution Outline for PROBLEM 7.10*	Income tax effects are ignored in each answer below.

    a. Income decreased by $18,000 gain on sale ($28,000 – $10,000 book value).

    b. Income decreased by the direct write-off of $2,800.

    c. Income decreased by the $350,000 book value written off.

    d. Income decreased by $152,000 shortage expense ($2,850,000 – $2,698,000).

    e. Income decreased by $8,000 book value written off ($37,000 – $29,000).

    f. No effect on income.

    g. Income decreased by $4,000 loss on sale ($6,000 – $10,000 book value).

    h. Income increased by $350,000 capitalized.

    i. Income decreased by $129,000 ($110,000 + $19,000). Deductions are irrelevant.

    j. No effect on income.

Solution Outline for PROBLEM 7.11*	

a. DR Bad debts expense   2,800   CR Allowance for d.a.   2,800

b. DR Amortization expense   7,200   CR Accumulated amort. 7,200

c. DR GST due   420   CR Inventory   420

d. DR Employee tax ded. due   39,650   CR Wages expense   39,650

e. *If an allowance for doubtful accounts (d.a.) exists:*
    DR Allowance for d.a.   235   CR Accounts receivable   235

    Direct write-off if there is no allowance:
    DR Bad debts expense   235   CR Accounts receivable   235

f. DR Cash   14,200   CR Machine cost   72,600
    DR Accumulated amortization 52,900
    DR Loss on disposal   5,500

g. DR Inventory shortage expense 4,620   CR Inventory asset   4,620

h. DR Insurance claim receivable 10,000   CR Accounts receivable 35,000
    DR Loss from employee theft 25,000

i. DR Accumulated amortization 63,000   CR Storage shed cost   89,000
    DR Loss from storm   26,000

j. No adjustment is needed.

Solution Outline for PROBLEM 7.12*

Some examples:

- Sales records are also records of the additions to cash for cash sales and to accounts receivable for credit sales, as well as to sales taxes due for all sales.

- If a retail inventory control method is used, sales records also connect to inventory records directly. If not, sales records still provide evidence about reductions in inventory quantities that can be combined with cost information to determine reductions in the inventory asset.

- Employment records provide control information for wages expense and employee deductions due, plus the employer's share of any amounts due (for fringe benefits).

- Cash collection records provide control information for additions to cash on hand and reductions in accounts receivable.

- Accounts payable records provide control information for additions to inventories (among other accounts).

- Cash payment records provide control information for deductions from cash on hand, accounts payable, employee deductions and fringe benefits due, and sales taxes due.

Solution Outline for PROBLEM 8.1*

a. (1) A foreign bank account is included in cash as long as the currency can be readily converted or accessed for use.

b. (2) Not strictly cash since not available for immediate use (90 days is considered short term), but under GAAP for the cash flow statement, this is less than three months so it may be included with the cash for purposes of cash flow analysis, and therefore likely lumped with cash on the balance sheet too.

c. (1) Considered to be undeposited cash receipts in foreign banks—unlikely any problem accessing German or Spanish funds due to currency restrictions.

d. (1) Petty cash is considered cash on hand.

e. Neither—the customer needs to issue another cheque; meanwhile the amount remains receivable from the customer.

f. Neither—this would be classified as a long-term investment.

g. (1) This would show up as an "outstanding deposit" on the reconciliation of the bank statement balance to the general ledger's bank balance.

h. Neither—it would be grouped with prepaids or deposits.

i. (2) Probably considered a temporary investment, since shares of a public company can be readily traded, and the percentage of share owned is too low to be able to influence the operations of the company.

j.   Neither—bank overdrafts are included in bank indebtedness and are a current liability.

Solution Outline for PROBLEM 8.2*

a. Loss of $11,000 ($16,000 – book value of ($45,000 – $18,000))
b. Loss of $85,000 ($100,000 – $15,000: a write-down)
c. No gain or loss (book value $0, proceeds $0)
d. Gain of $23,000 (present value of ($100,000 – $27,000) – $50,000)
e. No gain or loss (no amortization given, so probably the cost minus proceeds would just be debited to accumulated amortization)
f. Gain on $30,000 ($340,000 proceeds – book value of ($670,000 – $240,000) – $120,000: discontinued operations, ignoring tax effect)

Solution Outline for PROBLEM 8.3*

Price-level adjusted historical cost

For:

* cost is still verifiable since based on historical cost
* useful in periods of high inflation

Against:

* just confuses an already meaningless historical cost figure
* more complex than the historical cost method

Current or market value

For:

* the balance sheet would better reflect the company's assets and liabilities in terms of what they are actually worth on the market
* represents relevant values if a sale of the business is contemplated

Against:

* market values are subject to much judgment and are therefore difficult to verify
* more complex than the historical cost method
* hypothetical in the absence of a purchase or sale

Value in use

For:

* useful in manager's decision-making
* represents presumed value that caused company to acquire asset

Against:

* difficult to determine values since many assumptions about the future are required
* difficult to determine values of individual assets that all contribute jointly to the company

Solution Outline for PROBLEM 8.4*

Item	Total cost	Total market	Lower of cost or market
Bombies	$ 81,000	$150,000	$ 81,000
Rockies	23,800	14,000	14,000
Yallies	130,000	150,000	130,000
Tackies	96,000	20,000	20,000
Glammies	32,500	41,000	32,500
	$363,300	$375,000	$277,500

1. Most conservative = $277,500
2. Less conservative = $363,300

Solution Outline for PROBLEM 8.5*

a: increase; b: increase; c: increase; d: increase, assuming purchase prices are increasing; e: increase net assets; f: decrease; g: decrease.

Solution Outline for PROBLEM 8.6*

a. Include $(10 \times \$50,000) - \$150,000 = \$350,000$. The interest is recorded in the future as it comes due.
b. Include $20,000.
c. Include $9,500.
d. Don't include this—it seems to be advertising expense, not land.
e. Include $35,200 - \$1,500 = \$33,700$.
f. Probably include the $25,000, although it could be just written off as a loss. Don't include the $110,000 since it relates to different land.
g. Don't include this—it seems to be for the building, not the land. However, if any of the drawings, etc., were used to guide the bulldozing, etc., some of the cost could be included.
h. Don't include the salary allocation, but probably include the $7,200 travel costs.

This gives a minimum cost of $413,200 ($350,000 + $20,000 + $9,500 + $33,700) with more probable and possible.

Solution Outline for PROBLEM 8.7*

In order to answer this, let's assume that, at least for some inventories, market is lower than cost. Otherwise, the accountant probably would not have been too concerned. The effects would be:

Balance sheet: the inventory, current assets, and working capital would all be reduced by the difference between cost and market for those inventories whose market is less than cost.

Income statement: that difference would be deducted as an expense on the income statement and therefore would result in a lower net income. (Income tax expense would be smaller on the lower income, which would reduce the negative effect on income somewhat.)

Cash flow statement: the net income figure would be smaller, but that change would be cancelled by a smaller change in the inventories from one year to the next (and in income tax payable, if there is a change in the income tax expense). These effects would all cancel each other out, so that there would be no net effect on cash from operations or on any other figure.

Solution Outline for PROBLEM 8.8*

1.

	2002	2001	2000
Highest income	LIFO	FIFO	FIFO
Lowest income	FIFO	AVGE	LIFO
Difference	$22,000	$13,000	$23,000

2. The company should choose an inventory cost policy that is fair and appropriate for its circumstances and stick with it. The fact that various methods might produce higher or lower incomes in various years is not a proper criterion for choice of a method. It smacks of manipulation.

Solution Outline for PROBLEM 8.9*

1. A salvage value has to be assumed to answer this. Assuming it is zero, the amortization would be 10% of cost per year, $10,000 in 2000 and 2001. The entry would debit amortization expense and credit accumulated amortization with the $10,000.
2. Here the declining balance rate must be known. Let's assume it is "double declining balance" so that the rate is double the straight-line rate of 10%.
   Amortization for 2000 would be 20% of $100,000 = $20,000.
   Amortization for 2001 would be 20% of ($100,000 – $20,000) = $16,000.
3. Effects analysis, ignoring income tax effects:
   a. End of 2000, net book value and retained earnings both down $10,000.
   b. For 2001, amortization expense would go up by $6,000 ($16,000 – $10,000 originally recorded), so income would go down by $6,000.
   c. End of 2001, net book value and retained earnings both down $16,000 ($10,000 from 2000 plus $6,000 from 2001).
   d. No effect on cash from operations or change in cash for the year, because cash is not affected. But the operations section will have some internal change: net income will go down $6,000 and the amortization add-back will go up $6,000.

Solution Outline for PROBLEM 8.10*

a. Net income would go down $46,900 (that is, $67,000 × [1 – 0.30]).
b. No immediate cash flow effect, but a cash savings within a year due to lower income tax.
c. Current tax liability is the only working capital account affected at present. It goes down $20,100 (that is, $67,000 × 0.30), so working capital is improved by that amount.

Solution Outline for PROBLEM 8.11*

Total available cost = 200 × $4.20 + 340 × $5.10 + 250 × $4.00 + 130 × $4.50
= $840 + $1,734 + $1,000 + $585
= $4,159 (for 920 units)

Quantities	Beginning =		200	Beginning	200
	Minus sales	−120	80	Purchases	720
	Plus purchase	+340	420	Sales	(650)
	Minus sales	−400	20	Ending	270
	Plus purchase	250	270		
	Minus sales	130	290		
	Minus sales	−20	270		

FIFO   End inv $= 130 \times \$4.50 + 140 \times \$4.00$ $= \$1,145$

COGS $= 120 \times \$4.20 + (80 \times \$4.20 + 320 \times \$5.10)$
$+ (20 \times \$5.10 + 90 \times \$4.00) + 20 \times \$4.00$
$= \$504 + \$1,968 + \$462 + \$80$ $= 3,014$

$\$4,159$

Annual avge   Overall avge $= \$4,159 / 920 = \$4.52$

End inv $= 270 \times \$4.52$ $= \$1,220$

COGS $= 650 \times \$4.52$ $= 2,938$

(out $1 because of rounding) $\$4,158$

Periodic LIFO   End inv $= 200 \times \$4.20 + 70 \times \$5.10$ $= \$1,197$
COGS $= 130 \times \$4.50 + 250 \times \$4.00$
$+ 270 \times \$5.10$ $= 2,962$

$\$4,159$

Moving avge   Avge #1 $= \dfrac{80 \times \$4.20 + 340 \times \$5.10}{80 + 340}$ $= 4.93$

Avge #2 $= \dfrac{20 \times \$4.93 + 250 \times \$4.00}{20 + 250}$ $= 4.07$

Avge #3 $= \dfrac{160 \times \$4.07 + 130 \times \$4.50}{160 + 130}$ $= 4.26$

End inv $= 270 \times \$4.26$ $= \$1,150$

COGS $= 120 \times \$4.20 + 400 \times \$4.93$
$+ 110 \times \$4.07 + 20 \times \$4.26$ $= 3,009$

$\$4,159$

Perpetual LIFO   End inv $= 20 \times \$4.20 + 140 \times \$4.00$
$+ 110 \times \$4.50$ $= \$1,139$

COGS $= 120 \times \$4.20 + (60 \times \$4.20$
$+ 340 \times \$5.10)$
$+ 110 \times \$4.00 + 20 \times \$4.50$ $= 3,020$

$\$4,159$

Solution Outline for PROBLEM 8.12*

Refer to section 8.11 for more about these outlined ideas:

a. Such "goodwill" is not objectively measurable, has not been subject to the market test that a transaction would be, and would increase assets and income and might therefore imply manipulation of the accounting information. If the company has been doing well, its good performance will have shown up in income and therefore it will be more attractive to investors, so the accounting information as it is still allows some awareness of such accumulating goodwill.

b. By double entry, showing more assets by reducing expenses would increase income and retained earnings. The income and equity effects are a principal reason for resistance to such capitalization.

c. Well, yes, it would violate the idea that assets are things owned. But accrual accounting goes beyond the idea of ownership to include economic use and control. If you are really treating these assets as yours for the purpose of earning income, it is thought fairer to include them in the assets (and liabilities) than to leave them out.

d. Here, you presumably paid for the right to be the unique supplier. If so, the cost is an asset in an economic sense: it has value to your future ability to earn income. So it is an asset just as much as land or buildings are. (If you got the rights for free, then there is no asset cost to record.)

Solution Outline for PROBLEM 8.13*

1. DR Sales revenue $115,000, CR Building cost $820,000, DR Accumulated amortization $762,000, CR Gain on sale $57,000.

2. AVGE would give lower income than FIFO, which in a period of rising prices has the lowest COGS (and highest asset values) of any assumed cost method, and therefore the highest income.

3. This is probably not appropriate. Lower of cost or market is used for reasons of conservatism, and since the goods are for resale net realizable value would be a more appropriate version of market, especially in this case where net realizable value is lower than cost (but replacement cost, used in the present policy, is higher than cost and so would not produce a downward adjustment).

4. The difference is $46,000: a $231,000 hit on income (president's suggestion) versus a $185,000 hit (vice-president's suggestion). Assuming that this customer formed no part of the current allowance, that allowance will still be needed for other customer accounts, so the president's more conservative suggestion probably makes the most sense.

5. DR Revenue $14,350, CR Accounts receivable $14,350, DR Inventory $9,120, CR COGS $9,120.

6. No question is stated here. Is there a problem? Yes, GAAP would require lower of cost or market accounting here. So the temporary investments account would be reduced by $10,000 (or a contra allowance for market value decline could be created) and a loss on market value decline would be included in the expenses.

7. Actual cost requires identifiable inventory items, such as serial numbers. This may be impossible. Or at least it may be impractical: operating an actual cost system may require a more careful and costly inventory system than the inventory warrants (cost greater than benefit).

Solution Outline for PROBLEM 8.14*

The same valuation basis is not used for all assets because the valuation basis is tailored to the kind of asset and is intended to be informative about the asset's usefulness in earning future income. Current assets are valued at lower of cost or market because they are expected to be available for use (or for paying liabilities) in the next year, whereas noncurrent assets are valued just at cost because there is no intention to use them up in the next year. For them, market value is not thought relevant. As in other areas of accounting, asset valuation is a judgment about which people may reasonably disagree: though GAAP have been designed to make the financial statements useful, if the analyst finds them not so useful because of the differences in asset accounting, then for that analyst, the usefulness of the statements has indeed been harmed.

Solution Outline for PROBLEM 8.15*

1. If you consider the accounts receivables' "cost" to be the amount determined in the original sale transaction, then providing an allowance for doubtful collection acts to reduce the receivables down to their estimated market value (collectible amount).
2. Banks disclose these amounts because they are likely to be material for them—banks suffer loans losses all the time, and as their main assets are loans receivable, such losses are a significant part of measuring the banks' performance. For most other companies, collection losses are less material, and so for competitive reasons are less likely to be disclosed. Also, banks are highly regulated in most countries, so requirements from regulators may prompt the bad loans disclosure, even if the banks did not like to do that.
3. These are not current assets and so should be included with noncurrent assets, perhaps described separately if material, or else included with "other" assets. Following this would not change total assets or income, but would reduce the working capital and working capital ratio.
4. The interest has not yet been earned, and so should not be included in revenue. The credit to revenue should be just $15,000. That records the contract at its "present value." The interest would be accounted for by adding it to revenue, and to the contract receivable, as it builds up over time (that is, as it is earned).
5. It would make sense to have separate disclosure if the nontrade receivables are material in comparison to the regular receivables, because the nontrade ones have no (direct) relationship to revenue and are subject to different collection expectations. Someone analyzing working capital or collection success may want to exclude the nontrade items.

Solution Outline for PROBLEM 9.1*

1. Liabilities are obligations and estimates of obligations to people outside the enterprise, whereas equity is the residual ownership interest in the enterprise after considering such obligations to have the first claim on the resources (assets). Equity is what would be left after all the bills were paid, assuming that the assets were disposed of at book value and the liabilities were paid off, also at book value. Owners can be creditors too, for example, for dividends or management fees, but such obligations will have been deducted from equity (as dividends or expenses) and so, to the extent owners are also creditors, they have less equity.

2. Liabilities include more than just debts. Debts are legally enforceable obligations, based on existing agreements regarding purchases, bank borrowings, and other borrowings. Liabilities also include estimates of future cash expenditures stemming from present activities, especially from present expense incurrence. Such estimates are not yet legal debts, but they are included as part of the expense recognition process in accrual accounting. They include deferred income tax, warranty liability, and short-term accruals for things like interest building up or power being used.

3. Examples of accruals that require difficult estimates:

   Short-term: (1) estimated income tax payable — the actual income tax payable is often not known until months or years have passed and may depend on the resolution of ambiguities in the tax law and even an audit by the tax authorities; (2) deferred revenue on the collection of container deposits by drink manufacturers — it is difficult to know how many containers will be returned for refund because many are lost or broken.

   Long-term: (1) estimated pension liability — the actual payment, many years in the future, depends on employees' income levels, their health, future interest rates, and whether they stay employed long enough to qualify for various benefits; (2) estimated warranty liability — this depends on the quality of products sold, changes in laws giving consumers various rights, customers' satisfaction, media coverage, and many other uncertainties.

4. The objective of accrual accounting is to augment accounting's transactional base. The augmentation process often involves making estimates of liabilities that aren't completely reliable; however, the information is still relevant if it presents a better economic reality of the organization. Estimates of liabilities like warranties and pensions are more likely to be recorded than estimates of assets due to the concept of conservatism — taking anticipated losses into account before the transaction happens but not taking anticipated gains into account until the transaction happens.

Solution Outline for PROBLEM 9.2*

1. There is only one overall equity account for a proprietorship because there is no legal distinction between the proprietor's original capital contribution and retained earnings.

2. The conversion privilege makes it a bit judgmental as to whether the security should be called a bond, a preferred share, or a sort of common share in waiting. Legal details are consulted in deciding where to put such securities, but the fuzzy distinction at least makes disclosure of the privilege a good idea so the reader of the financial statements can decide how important it is. Also, in calculating earnings per share, the possibility of such a conversion happening and changing the number of common shares outstanding is one of the things taken into account when calculating the "fully diluted" versions of EPS so people can judge the potential effect on earnings that common shareholders may expect to be attributed to their shares.

3. A split is ignored because it is thought to be just a recalculation of the number of shares, without much effect on the market price of the shares. A stock dividend, though, is thought to be an actual distribution of some retained earnings and is more likely to have an effect on the market price and to reflect

a real increase in the company's share capital. (These different expectations are traditional but have been questioned by some accounting research.)

4. The balance sheet is a sort of statement of record, in which each owner (and creditor) should be able to see his or her position accurately set out. The equity section is therefore driven by legal details and by a perceived demand that these details be described.

5. It doesn't matter much, given the protection to shareholders provided in most legal jurisdictions nowadays. The main effect on the balance sheet is that if a no-par share is issued for say $10, that whole amount is added to share capital, whereas if a par value share (say $3 par) is issued for $10, only $3 is added to share capital and the other $7 must be put into a special equity account called contributed surplus or capital in excess of par value. There may be legal rules about whether that extra over par may be used to pay dividends or used in other ways.

Solution Outline for PROBLEM 9.3*

a. (1) Discount = $2.50 × 10,000 = $25,000. (2) DR Cash 975,000, CR Bonded debt liability 1,000,000, DR Bond discount (contra liability) 25,000. (3) Higher, as the discount is amortized.

b. (1) Discount = $85,000. (2) DR Cash 915,000, CR Bonded debt liability 1,000,000, DR Bond discount (contra liability) 85,000. (3) Higher, as the discount is amortized.

c. (1) Premium = $50,000 (5% of $1 million). (2) DR Cash 1,050,000, CR Bonded debt liability 1,000,000, CR Bond premium "liability." (3) Lower, as the premium is amortized.

Solution Outline for PROBLEM 9.4*

1. Expense = $114,600. Liability = $32,000 + $114,600 − $123,000 = $23,600.
2. Expense = $78,500 + $62,000 = $140,500. Liability = $50,000 + $140,500 − ($84,000 + $78,000) = $28,500.
3. DR Warranty expense $140,500, CR Warranty liability $140,500. Then DR Warranty liability $162,000, CR Inventory $78,000, CR Cash (or Wages payable) $84,000.
4. The expense would be $162,000. No liability at the beginning or the end of the year.
5. It might be appropriate to handle this disaster on a cash basis, without disturbing the accounting for general warranty service dealt with above. It might be hard to estimate the future costs, but if those were thought significant, they should be accrued separately from the other warranty liability. It might be that the disaster would damage the company's reputation and prompt more returns and warranty problems on other products, so Balmer may need to revise the way it estimates other warranty costs as well.

Solution Outline for PROBLEM 9.5*

a. (1) (12 × $11,200) − $61,232 = $73,168.
(2) $842,500 − $73,168 = $769,332. (3) $61,232.

b. (1) $232,200 − $189,400 = $42,800. (2) $189,400.
(3) $60,000 − $42,800 = $17,200.

c. (1) 12 × $1,500 = $18,000. (2) $87,436 − ($25,674 − $18,000) = $79,762. (3) $25,674 − $18,000 = $7,674.

Solution Outline for PROBLEM 9.6*   1:d; 2:g; 3:f; 4:h; 5:i; 6:e; 7:a; 8:j; 9:b; 10:c.

Solution Outline for PROBLEM 9.7*   There might be a material effect. According to CAE's note, there would be an immediate gain of $2.5 million if the forward currency contracts were marked to market, offset by losses on those contracts in the future. In addition, marking the interest rate swap contracts to market would produce a gain of $5.8 million now. The two together would make a gain of $8.3 million, which is probably significant compared to the company's $98.5 million net income (ignoring any income tax consequences). As these effects would be gains, it would be consistent with accounting conservatism ("anticipate no gains") to leave them off the statements and not mark to market. However, they could be losses instead (as they were in 1999), so the policy should depend on conceptual appropriateness, not on the happenstance of each year's effects. The fact that the effects are disclosed, and not included in the financial statements' numbers, indicates that CAE management (and auditors) agree with the general presumption in present GAAP that note disclosure is sufficient.

Solution Outline for PROBLEM 9.8*

1. Future income tax expense and the related liability arise from a joint desire to represent the estimated liability for tax consequences of present accounting results and to match the income tax expense to the recognition of revenue and other expenses. Without this procedure, it is thought, both income statement and balance sheet would be deficient.
2. Income tax allocation allocates the income tax expense to different financial statement periods than the periods in which the tax is paid, in same way that accrual accounting allocates revenues and expenses potentially to different periods than the associated cash receipts and disbursements.
3. Using the now-GAAP liability method, the future portion of income tax expense is determined by adjusting the balance sheet estimated liability. This gets the balance sheet "right," but means that adjustments to that liability (e.g., for changes in tax rates or laws) are made against this year's income even though they may have little or nothing to do with the revenue earned and the other expenses matched to it.

Solution Outline for PROBLEM 9.9*

1. a. Current portion of tax expense:

Income before tax	$ 648,960
Minus nontaxable revenue	(29,650)
Add back amortization	1,149,612
Deduct capital cost allowance	(1,493,114)
Taxable income	$ 275,808

   Current tax = $275,808 × 0.32 = $88,259

   b. Future portion of tax expense:
   CCA-amortization difference $343,502 × 0.32 = $109,921 future portion.

   c. Net income = $648,960 − $198,180 total tax expense = $450,780

   d. Future income tax liability = $329,612 + $109,921 = $439,533

e. Retained earnings = $3,949,286 + $450,780 = $4,400,066

2. a. No change from part 1 ($88,259)
   b. Future portion = $420,500 – $329,612 = $90,888
   c. Net income = $648,960 – ($88,259 + $90,888) = $469,813
   d. Future income tax liability is the new estimate, $420,500
   e. Retained earnings = $3,949,286 + $469,813 = $4,419,099

Solution Outline for PROBLEM 9.10*

1. The noncontrolling interest is the part of equity of the subsidiary that the parent does not own. It is not a debt that has to be paid, but rather an acknowledgment of an obligation to meet the interests of the minority shareholders of the subsidiary who did not sell their shares to the parent.
2. Consolidated financial statements combine the financial statements of two or more companies in order to present them as one economic entity.
3. Goodwill on a consolidated balance sheet includes the difference between what the parent paid for the shares and its share of the fair market value of the assets and liabilities at the acquisition date.
4. There are various adjustments to consolidate net income, including the removal of the noncontrolling interest's share of net income, the removal of profit on intercompany sales, and amortization of additional goodwill.
5. The deciding factor is whether or not the "parent" has the ability to control the operations of the "subsidiary." Control is normally defined as ownership of greater than 50% of the voting shares, although there are other factors that are beyond the scope of this book.

Solution Outline for PROBLEM 9.11*

Income from Brassy on cost basis	(0.40 × 250,000)	$100,000
Income from Brassy on equity basis	(0.40 × 600,000)	240,000
Extra income if equity basis were used		$140,000
Present income of China Sports		800,000
Revised income		$940,000

Solution Outline for PROBLEM 9.12*

1. Goodwill on consolidation:

   a. Net fair value of Piddling's equity
       ($16,100,000 – $8,300,000) $7,800,000

   b. Portion acquired (80% of $7,800,000) $ 6,240,000

   c. Purchase price for that portion   10,800,000

   d. Goodwill (c) minus (b) $ 4,560,000

2. Minority is credited with no goodwill and so is assigned 20% of the book value of Piddling's equity. 20% of $6,400,000 = $1,280,000.

3. Consolidated balance sheet figures are below.

		Consolidated
General assets		
Big	$105,000,000	
Piddling	14,600,000	
Portion of fair value changes		
$(0.80 \times [\$16,100,000 - \$14,600,000])$	1,200,000	$120,800,000
Investment in Piddling		
Does not appear on consolidated balance		
sheet because it is an intercompany item		0
Goodwill		
From part 1		4,560,000
Total consolidated assets		$125,360,000
General liabilities		
Big	$ 83,700,000	
Piddling	8,200,000	
Portion of fair value changes		
$(0.80 \times [\$8,300,000 - \$8,200,000])$	80,000	$ 91,980,000
Minority interest		
From part 2 above		1,280,000
Equity		
Parent's equity only appears on the		
consolidated balance sheet; subsidiary's		
equity does not appear because it is		
an intercompany item		32,100,000
Total consolidated liabilities and equity		$125,360,000

Solution Outline for PROBLEM 9.13*

a:2 (or 5); b:3; c:5 (or 2); d:6; e:10; f:7; g:9; h:4; i:1; j:8.

Solution Outline for PROBLEM 10.1*

Some advantages and disadvantages of ratio analysis are below. You probably will think of others!

Advantages:

- Ratios summarize the financial statements and so provide information in a more concise way, more accessible to decision makers than wading through all the detailed numbers.

- Ratios are scale-free measures so they can be used to compare enterprises of different sizes, or the same enterprise over periods of time in which its size changes.

- Ratios can be aggregated into industry and other groupings, facilitating comparisons of the enterprise to others.

- Because they have both numerators and denominators, ratios can be usefully sensitive to changes in the underlying figures.

- As summarized information, ratios may be easier for nonaccountants in general to understand than are the detailed financial statements.

- Because they are ratios, the ratios can be related to the "relative return" goal that is presumed to lie behind investors' and creditors' decision-making.

Disadvantages and ways around them:

- Because they are summarizations, ratios are only as good as the underlying data (way around: establish that the financial statements are audited, with a "presents fairly" unqualified opinion by the auditors).

- If managers or others know that people will rely on certain ratios, they may strive to produce satisfactory ratios, such as by reducing maintenance expenses or not acquiring new assets, rather than focusing on the fundamental underlying business issues (way around: use ratios with care and find out what managerial actions lie behind them).

- Ratios are just numbers and have no meaning in themselves apart from the phenomena they summarize; for example, there is nothing magic about a working capital ratio of 2 (way around: become very knowledgeable about the enterprise and its competitors so that meaningful comparisons may be made).

- There are many different ratios and alternative ways of calculating most of them, so that comparing ratios as calculated by others can be frustrating and not very informative (way around: know how to calculate the ratios that are important to you and use those calculations instead of others' versions if there are problems with those versions).

Solution Outline for PROBLEM 10.2*

1. Such a concept of performance relates the return to the investment required to earn it, so enabling the relative return to be calculated. This is important because returns do require investment, people usually don't make investments without expecting a return, and the sizes of each have to be related to each other in order to evaluate the quality of the result. A $1,000 return would be great if the investment required was $2,000 (a ratio of 50%) but not so great if the investment were $200,000 (only 0.5%).

2. a. The interest earned could be compared to the $1,200 required to earn it.
   b. The consulting earnings could be compared to the $15,000 invested to earn them.
   c. This is harder because the returns are probably nonfinancial, such as the fun of driving a sports car, and so are not readily comparable to the car's cost—however, this sort of ratio is implicit in many buying decisions, in which we ask ourselves if the benefits we will obtain are worth the cost and we may well choose a cheaper car if the feeling of wind in our hair isn't all that important relative to what we have to pay for a convertible.

Solution Outline for PROBLEM 10.3*

1. Financial leverage is the use of borrowed money to earn money. The leverage is positive if the money earned is greater than the cost of borrowing (e.g., if $10,000 borrowed at 8% is used to earn a 12% return), and it is negative if the money costs more to borrow than the borrower can earn using it.

2. Such leverage is risky for two main reasons. First, the return earned might not be what is hoped, and, if it is less than the cost of borrowing, then the borrowing ends up making the borrower worse off than without borrowing at all. Second, the money obtained must be repaid, and the lender may take strong action, such as going to court or taking over management or taking assets, if the loan gets into difficulty. So borrowing may result in the loss of more than the money borrowed.

3. The Scott formula incorporates leverage by separating its effect on return on equity from the effect of the operating return (the day-to-day relative return without borrowing: return on assets). Leverage is computed by first of all calculating the difference between the return on assets and the cost of borrowing (in the example above, 12% minus 8%) and then multiplying that by the degree of borrowing relative to equity. If leverage is positive, the more borrowed, the better the effect on return on equity; if it is negative, the more borrowed, the worse the effect on return on equity.

4. The first company's leverage return is 4%; the second's is 1%. The two aspects of risk noted above are present in this comparison. The second company is more in danger of having leverage go negative, but the first company has borrowed relatively more. So the second company is at greater risk of leverage hurting, but the hurt will not be great because not as much is borrowed, whereas the first company has more to repay and so could get into more difficulty if problems do arise.

Solution Outline for PROBLEM 10.4*

1. Return on equity = $6,000 / $45,000 = .133

2. Calculations (using Scott formula terms):
   ROE = .133 as above
   ATI = $2,000 × (1 − .333) = $1,333
   ROA(ATI) = ($6,000 + $1,333) / $80,000 = .092
   Interest rate = $1,333 / $35,000 = .038 (IN(ATI))
   L/E = $35,000 / $45,000 = .778
   (ROA(ATI) − IN(ATI)) = .092 − .038 = .054 = leverage potential
   Leverage = (.054) (.778) = .042

So, managerial performance (ROA(ATI)) shows a 9.2% return and leverage shows a 4.2% return, only one-half of the ROA. Two-thirds of ROE are operating return and one-third is leverage return.

3. The assets financed would earn 9.2%, according to the above calculations. The cost of the money borrowed is 8%. Therefore, leverage is positive (1.2%) and the company should go ahead. This will, however, increase the company's risk because the interest has to be paid and return on assets could decline below that rate.

4. (a. and b.) Some possible additional information and ratios (more can be imagined, so this is an outline only):

- Terms and security of present debts

- Quality of management (especially Mr. A)

- Industry and competition prospects

- Personal guarantees Mr. A might offer

- Interest coverage ratio

- Receivables collection and inventory turnover

- Sales return

- Income tax information

Solution Outline for PROBLEM 10.5*

a:7; b:5; c:4; d:1; e:6; f:9; g:3; h:2; i:10; j:8.

Solution Outline for PROBLEM 10.6*

1. Cash from operations is much greater than earnings because earnings included net noncash expenses of $731 million, more than three times the earnings. This was offset only a little by $155 million net increases in noncash working capital accounts.

2. Note 7 would include things like amortization, losses on disposal, write-offs, and, as the cash flow statement line indicates, noncash exploration expenses (separately identified versions of amortization, etc.). With help from the working capital accounts in Petro-Canada's balance sheet, we can see that Note 8 would include a large increase in accounts receivable, small increases in inventories and prepaid expenses and decreases in income tax payable, and a large increase in accounts payable partly offsetting the rest.

3. Major cash flow components over the three years:

   - Earnings are always positive and significant.

   - Noncash expenses added back are always very large, and changes in noncash working capital are significant but vary in direction.

   - The result of the above is that cash from operations is a very large source of cash each year.

   - Cash from operations is also the only regular source of cash: each year, there are some proceeds from disposal, and in one year long-term debt was issued, but otherwise, financing (and investing) were cash *outflows* every year.

   - Expenditures on property, plant, and exploration were significant each year and were paid for largely through operations.

   - Total change in cash has bounced around, but only in 1999 did it become negative.

4. The details of the points in section 10.5 are left for you to refer to. Some remarks:

   - Financing strategy is to use operating cash flows, not borrow very often.

- Other than major rearrangements of debt and assets in 1998, the company had little activity in financing or investing beyond a constant high expenditure on property, plant, and exploration.

- The add-backs for noncash expenses are large each year, but are exceeded by the investments in property, plant, and exploration, so the company's assets are growing and there is no indication any are getting out of date.

- The company pays a regular and increasing amount in dividends each year, even in 1998 when the income was low.

Solution Outline for PROBLEM 10.7*

To start with, here are some financial position data for Petro-Canada (dollars are in millions):

	1999	1998	Change
Total assets	$8,661	$8,398	up 3%
Working capital	$290	$423	down 31%
Working capital ratio	1.21	1.36	down 11%
Quick (acid test) ratio	0.83	0.96	down 14%
Collection ratio (based on operating revenue only)	56 days	50 days	up 12%
Debt–equity ratio	1.12	1.13	no change
Long-term debt–equity ratio	0.42	0.46	down a bit
Cash flow to total assets ratio	0.09	0.13	down 31%
Net income	$233	$95	up 145%

Some comments on the company's position (you may think of more):

- The company's assets and net income grew from 1998, but they were about the only positive changes.

- The company's current position is weaker than in 1998, with working capital (and ratio) down, collection ratio up, and the quick ratio further below one.

- Petro-Canada did not rely much on leverage in either year, with only slightly more debt than equity, and relatively little long-term debt compared to equity. This is consistent with the finding in Problem 10.6* that the company has had little financing for the last three years, relying on operating cash flows (the net income part of which is in retained earnings, in equity).

- The company has relatively little cash, and had negative cash flow in 1999, so if it is to continue growing, it may have to go to debt or equity markets in the future.

Solution Outline for PROBLEM 10.8*

1. Some ratios (any dollars are in millions except per-share amounts):

	1999	1998	1997
ROE (1997 equity not known)	0.057	0.024	n.a.
Effective tax rate	0.448	0.566	0.519
After-tax interest	$78	$53	$51
ROA(ATI) (1997 assets not known)	0.036	0.018	n.a.
Sales return (net income / operating revenue)	0.038	0.019	0.051
Gross margin ("Purchases" treated as COGS)	0.436	0.513	0.471
EPS	$0.86	$0.35	$1.13
Dividend payout (dividends / earnings)	0.395	0.916	0.258
Total asset turnover (1997 assets not known)	0.704	0.590	n.a.

These data show that Petro-Canada does not have a high profitability relative to its size. ROE, ROA(ATI), and sales return are much lower than CAE's, for example. The year 1998 was an unusual year, both as shown by the low income and annual returns (sales return down but gross margin up), and other parts of the statements (see cash flow comments in the Problem 10.6* solution) indicate that much rearranging of assets and financing was going on. We see again by the variable dividend payout ratio that Petro-Canada sets its dividends other than in accordance with income, maintaining the dividends in the poor 1998 year, further evidence that 1998's results were an aberration (or at least that management viewed them as an aberration).

2. Financial leverage effects can be seen by comparing ROE and ROA(ATI). In 1999, ROE was 0.021 higher than ROA(ATI) and in 1998 it was .006 higher. Therefore, Petro-Canada benefited from leverage in both years, though barely in 1998.

3. Scott formula (using ratios from part 1 where possible):

	1999	1998
ROE (above)	0.057	0.024
After-tax interest (above)	$78	$53
IN(ATI) (not calculated above)	0.017	0.012
ROA(ATI) (above)	0.036	0.018
SR(ATI) (not calculated above)	0.051	0.030
AT (above)	0.704	0.590
L/E (see solution to Pr. 10.7*)	1.12	1.13

Scott formula (rounding errors adjusted):
$$1999: \quad 0.057 = (0.051 \times 0.704) + ((0.036 - 0.017) \times 1.12)$$
$$0.057 = 0.036 + 0.019 \times 1.12$$
$$0.057 = 0.036 + 0.021$$
$$1998: \quad 0.024 = (0.030 \times 0.590) + ((0.018 - 0.012) \times 1.13)$$
$$0.024 = 0.018 + 0.006 \times 1.13$$
$$0.024 = 0.018 + 0.006$$

Operating return was the larger part of ROE in both years, and was a greater part in 1998 than 1999. Operating return and ROE did not improve as much as might have been expected in 1999 because the average interest rate, though still low, rose in 1999 and reduced the improvement in leverage potential.

Solution Outline for PROBLEM 10.9*

1. Present value = ($100,000 + $200,000) / (1 + 0.08)^5
   = $204,175

   Therefore, the PV exceeds the investment cost of $200,000, which means the investment returns more than the 8% required. So you should invest. An investment of $204,175 would return 8%, but you only have to pay $200,000.

2. Other factors:

   • Risk (will the investee pay back what has been promised, on time?);

   • Stability (8% may seem enough today but if interest rates rise, locking up the $200,000 for five years may seem to have been a mistake);

   • Alternative sources of returns (this is barely above 8%; perhaps there are better places to invest the $200,000).

Solution Outline for PROBLEM 10.10*

1. a. If 8% bonds were priced to yield 8%, they'd sell for $100.

   b. If 8% bonds were priced to yield 7%:

   $$PV = \frac{\$8}{.07}\left(1 - \frac{1}{(1.07)^{10}}\right) + \frac{\$100}{(1.07)^{10}}$$

   $[(1.07)^{10} = 1.9671511]$

   $$PV = \frac{\$8}{.07}\left(1 - \frac{1}{1.9671511}\right) + \frac{\$100}{1.9671511}$$

   $\quad = \$56.19 \qquad\qquad + \$50.83 = \$107.02$

   c. If 8% bonds were priced to yield 9%:

   $$PV = \frac{\$8}{.09}\left(1 - \frac{1}{(1.09)^{10}}\right) + \frac{\$100}{(1.09)^{10}}$$

   $[(1.09)^{10} = 2.3673634]$

   $PV = \$51.34 \qquad\qquad + \$42.24 = \$ 93.58$

2. It would make more because the funding would cost only 7%, leaving a greater spread between cost and the 10% return anticipated. (This would be modified by whatever return the company earned on the extra $700,000 raised.)

Solution Outline for PROBLEM 10.11*

Share price of $30 after 5 years:

$$PV = \frac{\$1.50}{.05}\left(1 - \frac{1}{(1.05)^5}\right) + \frac{\$30}{(1.05)^5}$$

$[(1.05)^5 = 1.2762815]$

$$PV = \$6.49 \qquad\qquad + \$23.51 = \underline{\underline{\$30.00}}$$

Share price of $50 after 5 years:

$$PV = \$6.49 + \frac{\$50}{(1.05)^5}$$

$$= \$6.49 \qquad\qquad + \$39.18 = \underline{\underline{\$45.67}}$$

So, it makes a big difference whether the price will be $30 or $50. At $30, the present value is less than the investment cost of $35, so it is not an attractive investment. However at $50, present value exceeds cost and it is attractive.

Solution Outline for PROBLEM 10.12*

a. Present value will go down — the more into the future the cash flows are, the lower the present value.
b. Present value will go up — the lower the interest rate used to discount future flows, the higher the present value.
c. Present value will go down — delaying any cash flows reduces the present value.
d. Present value will go down because the required rates on all or some projects will increase (so, opposite of b).

Solution Outline for PROBLEM 10.13*

- Effect on net income $= \$8,649,000\ (0.05 - 0.02) \times (1 - 0.30)$
  $= \$181,629$ reduction

- Revised net income $= \$223,650 - \$181,629$
  $= \$42,021$

- So the change would reduce net income by over 80% but would not reduce it to zero.

- There would be no effect on cash flow (this is an accrual accounting change: cash flow effects come from the company's actual success in collections).

- Appropriate accounting should be chosen even if the managers are not pleased with the result.

Solution Outline for PROBLEM 10.14*

Data:

- The amount of advertising capitalized was $75,000 this year.
- The capitalized amount is being amortized at 20% per year.

Present method:

- Amortization expense is $15,000 this year (20% of $75,000);
- Balance sheet asset is $75,000 − $15,000 = $60,000 at end of this year.

Proposed method: Expenses this year would be $75,000.

Effects:

If advertising were *not* capitalized:

- This year's income would be lower by 70% of ($75,000 − $15,000) = $42,000;
- Income tax liability would go down by $18,000 (the other 30%);
- Retained earnings this year would be lower by $42,000;
- Assets would be lower by the removal of $60,000 net capitalized advertising asset;
- Balance sheet proof: $(60,000) = $(18,000) + $(42,000);
- No effect on cash flow, cash balance, or working capital.

Solution Outline for PROBLEM 10.15*

Effect on net income: (2,350,000 − 235,000) × 0.75 = 1,586,250 higher.
Effect on cash flow: none.

Solution Outline for PROBLEM 10.16*

Balance Sheet End Last Year	+	Income Statement This Year	=	Balance Sheet End This Year	
Assets		*Revenue*		*Assets*	
Rec. up	$8,000	Up	$10,000	Rec. up	$18,000
Liabilities		*Expenses*		*Liabilities*	
Other than tax		Other than tax		Other than tax	
Pay. up	$3,000	Exp. up	$ 4,000	Pay. up	$ 7,000
Income tax		*Income tax*		*Income tax*	
Up	$1,750	Up	$ 2,100	Up	$ 3,850
Equity				*Equity*	
Retained earn.		*Net income*		Retained earn.	
Up	$3,250	Up	$ 3,900	Up	$ 7,150

Note that this question could alternatively have been phrased something like this: "Receivables will increase $18,000 at the end of the current year and $8,000 at the end of the previous year; payables will increase $7,000 at the end of the current year and $3,000 at the end of the previous year." In that case, the current year's net income figures would be deduced from the balance sheet effects, whereas above, the current year's balance sheet effects were deduced from the income figures and the previous balance sheet. In this alternative wording, sometimes people think that the current balance sheet effects will be added to the prior ones (for example, the receivables increase would be calculated as $26,000). This would be incorrect, because the current balance sheet effects already include all prior effects: each balance sheet is the aggregation of everything recorded prior to that.

There is no effect on cash, but the cash flow statement's internal numbers will change:

Net income will go up	(positive apparent effect)	$ 3,900
Change in accts. rec'ble will go up	(negative apparent effect)	(10,000)
Change in accts. payable will go up	(positive apparent effect)	4,000
Change in tax payable will go up	(positive apparent effect)	2,100
Net effect on cash from operations		$ 0

Glossary of Terms

This glossary provides definitions for many terms in financial accounting[1] and refers readers back to those chapter sections in which the terms are discussed. If a good definition or discussion appears in a chapter section, the reference to that section may be provided without repeating the definition. Terms are crossreferenced to other terms where helpful. For additional help in finding things, consult the index at the end of the book. Technical terms used in any definition are themselves defined in their alphabetical location in the glossary.

A

Accelerated amortization (depreciation)   An amortization method, such as declining balance, that records more amortization in the earlier years of an asset's life, and less in later years, than does the straight-line method. See **Straight-line amortization, Declining balance amortization**, and section 8.10.

Account   A summary record of an asset, liability, owners' equity, revenue, or expense, in which the effects of transactions, accruals, and adjustments are indicated in dollars (where dollars are the currency of the country). See **General journal, General ledger, Transaction**, and sections 2.4 and 2.5.

Accountant   A person who performs accounting functions. Professional accountants are those who are granted designations by self-regulating bodies on the basis of special training and successful examination. For example: CA, or Chartered Accountant (Canada, the United Kingdom); CGA, or Certified General Accountant (Canada); CMA, or Certified Management Accountant (Canada, the United States); and CPA, or Certified Public Accountant (the United States). See sections 1.4 and 5.9.

Accounting   "To account" is to provide a record, such as of funds paid or received for something. Being "accountable" is to be responsible for, as in to account for one's actions. These two ideas together describe the practice of accounting as the recordkeeping and reporting of an enterprise's performance and position in monetary terms. Management is responsible for the decisions made in an enterprise. Accounting provides the reports that summarize the economic results of these decisions for inside use and transmits them to outside, interested parties (such as investors, creditors, and regulatory agencies). See **Financial accounting, Management accounting**, and section 1.2.

Accounting control   The practice of creating accounting records that provide expected quantities of important assets and liabilities and so improve the internal control over those assets. Used by most companies for cash, accounts receivable, sales taxes collected on behalf of governments and employee deductions, and by many companies for investments, inventories, property and equipment, and accounts payable. See **Internal control** and sections 7.3–7.8 for various examples of accounting control.

Accounting entity   The enterprise for which the accounting is being done. The entity may be a single legal corporation or other organization, an economic unit without legal standing (such as a proprietorship), or a group of corporations with connected ownership for which consolidated financial statements are prepared. See sections 2.8, 5.2, and 9.7.

Accounting policies   The chosen accounting methods used by a company to recognize economic events on an accrual basis, and to report the financial position and results of operations. For examples, see the notes immediately following the financial statements of any company. The first such note is usually a summary of significant accounting policies. See sections 5.7 and 6.4.

Accounting policy choice   A decision among acceptable accounting policies is often needed because more than one acceptable policy exists in many areas. See section 6.4.

Accounting principles   See **Generally accepted accounting principles** and section 5.2.

Accounting research   The practice of studying accounting phenomena to determine their effects on other phenomena, such as share prices, and effects of those on accounting. Introduced in section 1.4 and mentioned frequently throughout the book.

Accounting standards   The recommending of particular accounting methods or policies by an authoritative body. In Canada this is done by the Accounting Standards Board of the Canadian Institute of Chartered Accountants, in the United States, by the Financial Accounting Standards Board. See **Authoritative standards, Accounting policies, Generally accepted accounting principles,** and sections 5.4 and 5.5.

Accounting Standards Board   The committee of the Canadian Institute of Chartered Accountants that is responsible for setting financial accounting standards in Canada. See section 5.4.

Accounts payable   Liabilities representing amounts owed to short-term trade creditors. (An account payable for the debtor is an account receivable for the creditor.) See sections 2.2 and 9.2.

Accounts receivable   Amounts owing by debtors (customers), usually arising from sales of goods or services. See sections 2.2, 6.6, and 8.5.

Accrual accounting   The method of making an economically meaningful and comprehensive measurement of performance and position by recognizing economic events regardless of when cash transactions happen; as opposed to the simpler cash basis of accounting. Under this method, revenues and expenses (and related assets and liabilities) are reflected in the accounts in the period to which they relate. See sections 1.7, 3.8, 6.2, and 6.3.

Accrual basis   The use of accrual accounting in preparing financial statements.

Accrual income   The result of subtracting expenses from revenue(s), when both kinds of accounts are calculated by accrual accounting. See **Accrual accounting, Net income,** and sections 1.7, 3.2, 6.3, and 6.8.

Accrue   To enter amounts in the accounts to reflect events or estimates that are economically meaningful but that do not (at present) involve the exchange of cash. Examples would be recording interest that is building up on a debt prior to paying it or recording revenue from credit sales prior to receipt of cash from customers. See sections 3.8, 6.2, and 6.3, and **Accrual accounting**, **Revenue recognition**, and **Matching**; see also **Deferral**.

Accrued expense   An expense recognized in the accounts prior to paying for it. See sections 6.2, 6.3, 6.8, 6.9, and 9.2.

Accumulated amortization (depreciation)   A balance sheet account that accumulates total amortization (depreciation) expense over a number of years. The account balance is a credit and so is opposite to the debit-balance asset cost account. The difference between cost and accumulated amortization is the "book value" of the asset. See **Book value**, **Contra accounts**, **Fixed assets**, **Amortization and Amortization expense**, and sections 2.7, 7.7, 8.8, 8.9, and 8.10.

Accumulated foreign currency translation adjustment   An account arising as a consequence of the method used to convert foreign operations' accounting figures into Canadian dollars for the purpose of combining them with the figures for Canadian operations. Because income statement accounts are generally converted at average foreign exchange rates and balance sheet accounts are generally converted at year-end or historical rates, converted accounts do not quite balance. The difference is put into equity as a separate item because it does not seem to fit anywhere else and it is part of the (converted) residual equity of the owners. See sections 2.9 and 9.4.

Acid test ratio   Cash, temporary investments, and accounts receivable divided by current liabilities. Also called the quick ratio. See **Ratios** and section 10.4, ratio #19, where the ratio is explained.

Adjusted trial balance   The list of accounts prepared after all the accrual accounting adjustments and corrections have been made and so representing the final account balances used in preparing the financial statements. See **Trial balance**, **Adjusting (journal) entry**, and sections 3.8 and 3.9.

Adjusting (journal) entry   A journal entry to implement accrual accounting by recognizing in the accounts economic events not yet adequately accounted for by the routine transactional accounting system. (For example, if there is no transaction to reveal the gradual wear and tear of a fixed asset, an adjusting entry must be made to recognize this depreciation.) See sections 3.8 and 3.9.

Adjustment(s)   See **Adjusting (journal) entry**.

Agent   A person who is party to a contract between that person and another, called the principal. The agent's role is to carry out the wishes of the principal as specified in the contract. Some examples of agents are managers, auditors, lawyers, and physicians, who are entrusted with acting on behalf of one or more others (the principals, such as owners, creditors, defendants, and patients). Agents have a stewardship responsibility to the principal. See **Contract**, **Principal**, **Stewardship**, and section 5.11.

Aggressive accounting   Seeking out accounting methods and policy choices to meet management objectives for growth, financing, bonuses, or other purposes that seem to violate principles such as fairness and conservatism. See section 7.4.

Aging of accounts receivable   The process of classifying accounts receivable by the time that has passed since the account came into existence. This classification is used as an aid to estimating the required allowance for doubtful accounts for the estimated amount of uncollectible accounts receivable. See section 6.4.

Allocating, allocation Spreading the impact of an event out over time, as in amortization of an asset's cost over its useful life or recognition of revenue for a long-term contract over several periods. See **Amortization** and sections 6.2, 6.3, and 6.8. See also **Interperiod tax allocation** and section 9.3, and **Intraperiod tax allocation** and section 3.5. (Allocation is also used, especially in management accounting, to refer to spreading the impact of an event across activities, such as in allocating the cost of repairs to different departments.)

Allowance for doubtful accounts The estimated amount of accounts receivable that will not be collected (which are "doubtful"). The allowance, which is a contra account to accounts receivable, is used in order to recognize the bad debts expense related to such doubtful accounts but without removing those accounts from the books because the firm will still try to collect the amounts owing. See section 7.7.

American Institute of Certified Public Accountants (AICPA) The national self-regulating body in the United States that sets and monitors the auditing and professional standards by which CPAs practise.

Amortization Allocation of the cost of a noncurrent asset to expense over several accounting periods to recognize the "consumption" of the asset's economic value as it helps to earn revenue over those periods. Amortization expense for a period thus is deducted from revenue in that period, recognizing it as a cost of earning the revenue. The term amortization, and especially the common term depreciation, is used for the allocation of the cost of tangible assets over time; amortization is also used for the allocation of the cost of intangible assets such as patents, franchise rights, and goodwill. See **Accumulated amortization, Intangible assets,** and sections 1.7, 7.7, 8.8, 8.10, and 8.11.

Amortization expense The expense recorded to recognize asset amortization. See **Amortization, Accumulated amortization,** and section 8.8.

Amortize To allocate the cost of noncurrent assets (and sometimes liabilities) to expense over several accounting periods. See **Amortization, Allocating,** and section 8.8.

Analysis, analyze The technique, common in accounting, of comparing information derived from different sources or methods in order to understand what has happened, identify errors, and answer questions about the effects of possible actions or events. See **Reconciliation** and **"What-if" (effects) analysis.** Also used to refer to the detailed study of accounting information, such as by using **Ratios.** See sections 1.9, 10.1, 10.4, 10.7, and 10.8.

Annual report The document provided annually to the shareholders by the officers of a company. It includes the financial statements, the notes to the financial statements, the auditor's report, supplementary financial information such as multi-year summaries, and reports from the company's board of directors and management. See section 5.6.

Articulate, Articulation Of the income statement, retained earnings statement, and balance sheet; refers to the fact that because these three statements are prepared from one set of balanced accounts, changes in any one of the three normally affect the others. In particular, recognition of revenue and expense relies on the fact that a revenue causes a change in the balance sheet, as does an expense. See **Recognition, Revenue recognition,** and section 3.2.

Asset(s)   An asset is a resource available to do business in the future, represented by an ownership of or right to expected future economic benefits. Assets have value because they are expected to bring benefits as they are used or sold. See section 2.2 and 8.1, and **Cash equivalent assets, Inventory, Accounts receivable, Current assets, Fixed assets,** and **Intangible assets.**

Asset valuation   Determination of the amounts to be used for assets on the balance sheet. See **Balance sheet valuation** and section 8.2.

Assumed cost flow   The practice in inventory accounting of determining the cost of inventories purchased at varying unit costs by assuming a specific order in which the inventory will be taken to have flowed into and out of the country. See **Cost flow assumption** and section 8.6.

Assurance   A broader word than "audit," encompassing auditing and similar procedures to confirm or verify reports or events as fair and proper and assure users of such reports that they may be relied upon. See **Audit, Auditor's report,** and **Fairness.**

AT   The total assets turnover ratio, defined and explained in section 10.4, ratio #12. Used in the Scott formula in section 10.6.

Audit   The examination of accounting records and their supporting documentation with the objective of determining the fairness with which the financial statements present the financial position and performance of the company. See **Auditor, Auditor's report,** and section 5.8.

Audit committee   A committee of a corporation's **Board of directors,** usually composed largely or entirely of directors not also having management positions, which reviews the company's accounting statements and communicates directly with the **External auditor.** See section 5.9.

Auditor   The person or firm who performs an audit for the purpose of preparing a report on the credibility of the financial statements; also called the **External auditor.** See sections 1.4 and 5.8. Compare **Internal auditor.**

Auditor's report (or auditors' report)   The document accompanying the financial statements that expresses the auditor's opinion on the fairness of the financial statements. The auditor's report explains what the auditor did and states the auditor's opinion. See section 5.8.

Authoritative standards   Written rules and guidance established by official accounting standard-setters such as the CICA in Canada and the FASB in the United States. See *CICA Handbook* and section 5.4.

Available cost   The total dollar amount represented by the sum of beginning inventory and purchases during the period, and thus representing the total dollar cost of inventory available for sale or use during the period. See section 8.6.

Average cost (AVGE)   An inventory cost-flow assumption where the cost of an individual unit of inventory is the weighted average cost of the beginning inventory and subsequent purchases. See **Weighted average** and section 8.6.

Average interest rate   An average calculated by dividing interest expense by total liabilities. Defined and explained in section 10.4 (ratio #6). An after-tax version of this is used in the Scott formula in section 10.6 (see **IN(ATI)**).

AVGE   See **Average cost** and **Weighted average**.

B

Bad debts expense   An expense account that results from the reduction in carrying value of those accounts receivable that have been projected to be uncollectible or doubtful. See **Allowance for doubtful accounts** and section 7.7.

Balance (an account total)   The net sum of the amounts added to and subtracted from an account since the account began. In financial accounting's double-entry system, the balance is expressed as a net debit (DR) or net credit (CR). See **Account, Double-entry accounting**, and section 2.5.

Balance (in the balance sheet or the trial balance)   Refers to the double-entry accounting requirement that the sum of the accounts with debit balances and the sum of those with credit balances be equal. In the balance sheet, this means that the sum of the assets equals the sum of the liabilities and equity. See **Balance sheet, Balance sheet equation, Trial balance**, and sections 2.2, 2.7, and 3.9.

Balance sheet   The "balanced" list of assets, liabilities, and owners' equity constituting the formal statement of a company's financial position at a specified date, summarizing by category the assets, liabilities, and owners' equity. See **Balance, Balance sheet equation, Balance sheet valuation, Statement of financial position**, and sections 2.2, 2.7, and 2.9.

Balance sheet equation   The double-entry arithmetic by which Assets = Liabilities + Owners' Equity. See sections 2.2, 2.3, and 2.4.

Balance sheet valuation   Assigning numerical values to the balance sheet's assets, liabilities, and owners' equity accounts. See section 8.2.

Bankruptcy   The usually involuntary termination of an enterprise due to its inability to pay its debts and continue in operation. Bankruptcy usually involves significant losses to both creditors and owners. See **Going concern**.

Bank overdraft   A negative bank account balance (withdrawals exceeding deposits), which banks may allow as a de-facto loan as long as it is temporary. See **Line of credit** and sections 2.7 and 4.3.

Bank reconciliation   The practice of comparing the accounting records of the bank account with the information provided by the bank (such as in a monthly bank statement), to identify any errors in either record. See **Analysis** and sections 1.9 and 7.5.

Betterment   An expenditure to improve an asset's value to the business, more than just repairs and maintenance. See section 8.3.

Big Bath   A way of manipulating reported income to show even poorer results in a poor year in order to enhance later years' results. See section 3.10.

Board of directors   The senior level of management, representing and directly responsible to the owners (shareholders). Normally elected annually by the shareholders, the board is responsible for hiring and supervising the operating management (president, chief executive officer, etc.).

Bond, bonded debt   A certificate of debt issued by an enterprise in return for cash, in which a promise is made to repay the debt (usually at a particular date or on a specified schedule) plus interest. Many bonds may be sold to other people by those who received them in return for the original cash provided to the enterprise. See section 9.3.

Bond markets   Capital markets in which debt instruments (bonds and similar items), rather than shares, are traded. See **Capital markets**.

Bookkeeping   The process of recording, classifying, and summarizing transactions in the books of account. See sections 2.4 and 7.2.

Books   Colloquial term for the accounting records, including computerized records, left over from the time when the records were written in bound books. See section 7.2.

Books of original entry   The journals in which transactions are first recorded. See section 7.2.

Book value   The amount shown in the accounts for any individual asset, liability, or owners' equity item, after deducting any related contra account (for example, the book value of a truck is the recorded cost minus accumulated amortization). The term is also commonly used for the whole enterprise, to refer to the net amount of total assets less total liabilities (the recorded value of the owners' residual interest, which equals total equity: Assets = Liabilities + Equity). See sections 7.7 and 8.9 for the book value of individual assets and sections 9.4 and 9.7 for the book value of the whole enterprise. See also **Book value per share**.

Book value per share   Total shareholders' equity divided by the number of shares issued. It is defined and explained in section 10.4, ratio #9.

Bottom line   A colloquialism referring to the net income (the "bottom line" on the income statement). See **Net income**.

Business combination   A merger of separate corporations or an acquisition of control of one corporation by another, in which the corporations become a single economic entity. See **Accounting entity**, **Consolidation**, and section 9.7.

C

CA   Chartered accountant. See **Canadian Institute of Chartered Accountants**.

Canada Business Corporations Act (CBCA)   The federal corporations act that provides the authority for the incorporation of federally incorporated companies in Canada and generally sets the requirements for their activities. It requires any such company to prepare annual financial statements.

Canadian Certified General Accountants Association (CGA-Canada)   An association whose members (CGAs) have had training in accounting, taxation, auditing, and other areas of business and have passed qualifying exams. CGA-Canada and provincial associations of CGAs set and monitor standards by which CGAs practise. CGA-Canada is one of the three national professional accounting bodies. See **Accountant** and sections 1.4 and 5.9.

Canadian Institute of Chartered Accountants (CICA)   A national, self-regulating association of chartered accountants who have met education and examination standards in Canada. The CICA and provincial institutes of CAs set and monitor the standards by which CAs practise. One of the three national professional accounting bodies. See **Accountant** and sections 1.4 and 5.9.

Capital   The owner's contribution to or interest in a business (the equity). Often used specifically to refer to the equity of unincorporated businesses (proprietorships and partnerships). See **Equity** and sections 2.8 and 9.4.

Capital cost allowance   The Canadian Income Tax Act's version of amortization (depreciation), used in calculating taxable income for assessment of income tax. See section 9.3.

Capitalization, capitalize   The recognition of an expenditure that may benefit a future period as an asset rather than as an expense of the period of its occurrence. Expenditures are capitalized if they are likely to lead to future benefits, and, thus, meet the criterion to be an asset. See sections 8.3 and 8.11.

Capitalized costs   Costs that have been included with an asset on the balance sheet instead of being deducted as expenses on the income statement. See sections 8.3 and 8.11.

Capital lease   A lease having the economic character of asset ownership. See section 8.11.

Capital markets   Markets in which financial instruments such as shares and bonds are traded. See section 5.10, **Financial instruments**, and **Stock exchange**.

Cash   Currency and coin on hand, balances in bank accounts, and other highly liquid assets. See **Cash and equivalents** and sections 4.3, 7.5, and 8.4.

Cash and equivalents   Cash and near-cash assets minus near-cash liabilities: cash equivalent assets minus cash equivalent liabilities. Changes in cash and equivalents are explained by the cash flow statement (SCFP). See **Cash flow statement**, **Cash,** and section 4.3.

Cash disbursements   Cash payouts, by cheque, currency, or direct deductions from the bank account. See **Cash payments, Cash disbursements journal, Cash receipts, Cash income,** and section 4.4.

Cash disbursements journal   The record of cheques and other cash payments made. See **Books of original entry** and section 7.2.

Cash equivalent assets   A term used to describe cash plus very liquid bank deposits and similar assets that can be converted into cash on demand. See section 4.3.

Cash equivalent liabilities   Liabilities that are payable on demand and so represent a reduction in the liquidity otherwise apparent from the amount of cash. Under current accounting standards, temporary bank overdrafts are the only common cash equivalent liabilities. See **Bank overdraft** and section 4.3.

Cash flow   The inflows of cash (cash receipts) and outflows of cash (cash disbursements) over a period. Information about cash flow is presented in the **Cash flow statement**. See also sections 4.2 and 4.3.

Cash flow analysis A method of accounting **analysis** directed at understanding the enterprise's cash inflows, outflows, and resulting balances. This analysis lies behind the **cash flow statement**. See section 4.2.

Cash flow statement A statement that explains the changes in cash (and equivalent) balances during a fiscal period. Also referred to as "Statement of changes in financial position (SCFP)," "Funds statement," or "Statement of cash flows." See **Direct method of cash flow analysis, Indirect method of cash flow analysis,** and sections 4.2, 4.3, and 10.5.

Cash flow to total assets The ratio of cash from operations divided by total assets. It is defined and explained in section 10.4, ratio #7. See **Cash from operations.**

Cash from operations Cash generated by day-to-day business activities and highlighted as the first section in the **Cash flow statement.** See sections 4.3, 4.7, and 10.5.

Cash income Cash receipts minus cash disbursements, or that subset of both that relates to day-to-day operations. The operating subset is roughly equivalent to the Cash flow statement's **Cash from operations** figure. See **Cash receipts, Cash disbursements, Direct method of cash flow analysis,** and sections 1.8 and 4.4.

Cash payments Payments by currency, cheque, or other bank withdrawal. See **Cash transaction, Cash disbursements journal,** and section 4.4.

Cash receipts Cash inflows, by currency, others' cheques, or direct bank deposits. See **Cash transaction, Cash receipts journal,** and section 4.4.

Cash receipts journal The record of customers' cheques and other cash received. See **Books of original entry** and section 7.2.

Cash received basis Recognition of revenue only when the cash comes in. See **Revenue recognition, Conservatism,** and section 6.7.

Cash transaction The simplest kind of economic exchange routinely recorded by financial accounting, and an important starting point for the financial statements. See sections 1.6 and 4.4.

CCA See **Capital cost allowance.**

CGA Certified general accountant. See **Canadian Certified General Accountants Association (CGA-Canada).**

Change effects analysis Analysis of the effects on financial statements of economic or accounting policy changes. See sections 1.9 and 10.8 and **"What-if" (effects) analysis.**

Change in cash Demonstrating why cash changed as it did is the objective of the **Cash flow statement's** analysis. **Cash income** is part of this change. See sections 1.8, 4.3, and 4.4.

Chart of accounts An organized list of the accounts used in the accounting system. This can be contrasted with the "trial balance," which displays all the accounts and their debit or credit balances. See section 7.2.

Cheque A request by one party that the party's bank pay a specified amount to another party. See section 7.2.

CICA Handbook   The authoritative source of financial accounting standards in Canada. See section 5.4.

Classification   Choice of where in the financial statements to place an account, such as whether an investment asset should be shown as a current asset or a non-current asset. See sections 2.7 and 3.5.

Classification policies   Accounting policies covering where within a financial statement an account or description is to appear. See sections 2.7, 3.5, and 6.4 and **Accounting policies.**

Classified financial statements   Financial statement with accounts organized under headings that clarify the accounts' meaning, done to increase the information value of the statements. See sections 2.2, 2.7, 3.5, and 4.3.

Clean opinion   An external auditor's report which states the auditor's opinion that the financial statements are fairly presented. This is the kind of auditor's report that most companies receive because it indicates the auditor found no problems. See **Auditor's report, Qualified opinion**, and section 5.8.

Close, closing   Transfer(ring) the temporary accounts (revenues, expenses, and dividends declared) to retained earnings at the end of the fiscal period. See **Closing entry** and sections 3.6 and 3.7.

Closing entry or entries   Journal entries recorded at year-end to transfer the balances in temporary accounts (revenues, expenses, and dividends) to the balance sheet account retained earnings and set those balances to zero in preparation for entering the next year's transactions. See sections 3.6 and 3.7.

CMA   Certified management accountant. See **Society of Management Accountants of Canada.**

COGS   See **Cost of goods sold.**

COGS expense   See **Cost of goods sold expense.**

Collection ratio   The ratio of accounts receivable to the daily sales, expressed in number of days' sales represented by accounts receivable. Also called **Days' sales in receivables.** It is defined and explained in section 10.4, ratio #14.

Common shares   The basic voting ownership interests in a corporation. See **Corporation** and sections 2.8 and 9.4.

Common size financial statements   A technique of analyzing financial statements in which income statement figures are expressed in percentages of revenue and balance sheet accounts are expressed in percentages of total asset. It is defined and explained in section 10.4, ratio #4.

Company   See **Corporation.**

Comparability   Information that enables users to identify similarities in and differences between two sets of economic phenomena, such as two different years of a company's financial statements. Comparability between companies and consistency of one company over time are major objectives of financial accounting. See **Fairness, Consistency**, and sections 5.2 and 5.3.

Compilation   A service performed by accountants practising **Public accounting,** whereby they prepare financial statements for enterprises without taking responsibility for the quality of the accounting information used to prepare them, and without auditing them. See section 5.8.

Completed contract   A method of revenue recognition for long-term contracts in which the revenue is not reported on the income statement until the contract has been completed. See **Revenue recognition, Conservatism,** and section 6.7.

Compound, compounded, compounding   These refer to the frequency in which interest calculated on a loan or other debt is periodically added to the principal and so attracts future interest itself. Annual compounding, for example, means that interest built up on a loan starts to bear interest itself on each annual anniversary of the loan. See **Present value** and section 10.7.

Conditional sale contract   A form of borrowing whereby the title to an asset purchased on credit does not pass to the buyer until all the payments, usually plus interest, are made. See section 9.3.

Conservatism, conservative   A prudent reaction to uncertainty to ensure that risks inherent in business situations are adequately considered—often phrased as "anticipate possible losses but not possible gains." In situations where the accountant cannot decide on the superiority of one of two accounting treatments on the basis of accounting principles alone, being conservative means choosing the treatment that has the least favourable impact on the income of the current period. See **Historical cost, Cash received basis, Completed contract** method, and **Lower of cost or market** for examples of conservatism, and see also sections 5.2 and 5.3.

Consistency   Treatment of like transactions in the same way in consecutive periods so that financial statements will be comparable. The reporting policy implying that procedures, once adopted, should be followed from period to period by a company. See **Accounting policies** and sections 5.2 and 5.3.

Consolidated financial statements, consolidation   Consolidation is a method of preparing financial statements for a group of corporations linked by ownership as if they were a single corporation. Consolidated financial statements recognize that the separate legal entities are components of one economic unit. They are distinguishable from the separate parent and subsidiary corporations' statements, and from combined statements of affiliated corporations. See **Pooling of interests method, Purchase method,** and section 9.7.

Consolidated goodwill   A form of **Goodwill** arising only when companies' financial statements are combined in **Purchase method** consolidation. See section 9.7.

Contingency   An economic event (especially a negative one) that is in the process of occurring and so is not yet resolved. Contingencies would include, but are not limited to, pending or threatened litigation, threat of expropriation of assets, guarantees of the indebtedness of others, and possible liabilities arising from discounted bills of exchange or promissory notes. See **Conservatism.**

Contra accounts   Accounts established to accumulate certain deductions from an asset, liability, or owners' equity item. See **Book value, Amortization, Depreciation, Allowance for doubtful accounts,** and section 7.7.

Contract   A contract is an oral or written agreement between or among parties, setting out each party's responsibilities and specifying actions agreed to and resulting payments or other settlements. See **Agent** and **Principal** regarding one type of contract important in accounting, and section 5.11.

Contributed surplus   The difference between the legal **Par value** (or **Stated value**) of a share and the cash or other consideration received by the company when the share was issued. Also referred to with terms like "capital in excess of par value." Does not apply to **No-par shares**, which are the usual kind in Canada. See sections 2.8 and 9.4.

Control account   An account used to contain the aggregate amounts of many detailed transactions and so help to prevent or detect errors in the detailed records. The accounts receivable control account, for example, should have the same total as the sum of all the individual customers' accounts receivable. Control accounts with detailed backup include cash, accounts receivable, inventory, accumulated amortization, accounts payable, sales tax due, employee deductions due, and share capital. See **Internal control**, **Accounting control**, and sections 7.6–7.8.

Convertible   A bond or share that can be changed into another kind of **security**, usually a **preferred share** that can be converted into a **common share**. See section 9.5.

Corporate group   A group of corporations linked by common or mutual ownership. See **Consolidation** and sections 2.8, 9.6, and 9.7.

Corporation   A legal entity with or without share capital, legally separate from those who own it or work as a part of it. It enjoys most of the rights and responsibilities of a person except for those that only an actual person can enjoy. Its main feature is limited liability; in other words, only the assets of the company can be claimed by creditors, not the assets of owners. See **Partnership**, **Proprietorship**, and sections 2.8 and 9.4.

Cost   The value of an asset when it is acquired by the business. See **Historical cost** and sections 1.6, 8.2, and 8.3.

Cost allocation   Spreading the cost of an asset out over the periods in which it is useful. See **Allocating**, **Amortization**, and section 8.8. (Cost allocation is also used in managerial accounting to refer to spreading the cost of an activity out across various products or services affected by that activity.)

Cost basis   Usually used to account for a noncurrent intercorporate investment when a corporation owns less than 20% of another corporation. The investment is carried at cost, and any receipt of dividends or interest is recorded as "other income." See **Equity basis**, **Intercorporate investments**, and section 9.6.

Cost–benefit   The idea of comparing the benefits of a particular action with its costs, and taking action only if the benefits exceed the costs. See section 5.2.

Cost flow assumption   An assumption made about the order in which units of inventory move into and out of an enterprise, used to compute inventory asset value and cost of goods sold expense in cases where the order of flow is not or cannot be identified. Possible assumptions include FIFO, LIFO, and weighted average. See **Cost of goods sold**, **FIFO**, **AVGE**, **Weighted average**, and **LIFO** for specific examples. See also section 8.6.

Cost of capital   The cost of raising debt or equity funds (e.g., the cost of borrowed funds is mostly the interest to be paid to the lender). See section 10.7.

Cost of goods sold (COGS) expense   An expense account that reflects the cost of goods that generated the revenue (also called cost of sales). The method of calculating COGS depends on the method of inventory costing. See **Cost flow assumption, Inventory costing,** and sections 3.4, 7.8, and 8.6.

Cost principle   The use of the historical cost of assets to value them on the balance sheet. See **Historical cost, Balance sheet valuation,** and sections 5.2 and 8.2.

CPA   Certified public accountant (a designation used especially in the United States). See **American Institute of Certified Public Accountants.**

Credit (CR or Cr)   The right hand of double-entry accounting. The term credit can be used as a noun to refer to the right-hand side of a journal entry or account, or as a verb referring to the action of making an entry to the right-hand side of an account. Most accounts on the right-hand side of the balance sheets have credit balances (in other words, the credits to them exceed the debits to them). The term credit also refers to the right to buy or borrow on the promise of future payment. A credit journal entry to the liabilities and equity side of the balance sheet causes an increase in the account, while a credit to the assets side of the balance sheet causes a decrease. See **Double-entry accounting, Debit,** and sections 2.4–2.6.

Credit transaction   An economic exchange in which at least one party makes a promise to pay cash or other consideration later. This kind of transaction is recognized by most financial accounting systems, especially if it is a routine way of doing business. See **Accounts receivable, Accounts payable,** and section 1.6.

Creditor   One who extends credit (that is, gives someone the right to buy or borrow now in consideration of a promise to pay at a later date). See section 1.4.

Critical event   A point in the revenue generation and collection process chosen to represent the earning of the revenue, and so the point at which the revenue is recognized in the accounts. This is a simplification: a common critical event is the point at which the customer takes delivery of the goods sold. Not all revenue is accounted for this way: some is allocated over more than one point in the process: long-term construction projects and franchise revenue are examples where the critical event simplification is generally not used. See **Revenue recognition** and section 6.6.

Current assets   Cash and other assets such as temporary investments, inventory, receivables, and current prepayments that are realizable or will be consumed within the normal operating cycle of an enterprise (usually one year). See such current asset categories as **Cash equivalent assets, Inventory,** and **Accounts receivable.** See also sections 2.2, 2.9, and 2.10.

Current liabilities   Debts or estimated claims on the resources of a firm that are expected to be paid within the normal operating cycle of an enterprise (usually one year). See **Cash equivalent liabilities, Accounts payable,** and sections 2.2, 2.9, and 9.2.

Current or market value   The estimated sale value of an asset, settlement value of a debt, or trading value of an equity share. See sections 8.2, 8.4, and 8.7.

Current ratio   Also called **Working capital ratio,** equalling current assets divided by current liabilities. It is defined and explained in section 10.4, ratio #18.

Current value accounting   A proposed accounting method that would use current or market values to value assets and liabilities and to calculate income. See sections 2.8 and 8.2.

Cutoff   The end of a fiscal period and the procedures used to ensure accuracy in measuring phenomena up to that date. See section 6.5.

D

Days' sales in receivables   The ratio of accounts receivable to the daily sales, expressed in number of days' sales represented by accounts receivable. Also called **Collection ratio**. Defined and explained in section 10.4, ratio #14.

DCF   See **Discounted cash flows**, another phrase for "present value" analysis of future cash flows. See **Present value** and section 10.7.

Debenture   A form of **Security** taken by a creditor on a loan or bond, in which the creditor has a general ability to influence or direct management decisions if the debt payments are not made on schedule; not a claim on a specific asset as a **Mortgage** has. See sections 2.8 and 9.3.

Debit (DR or Dr)   The left-hand side of double-entry accounting. The term debit can be used as a noun to refer to the left-hand side of a journal entry or account or as a verb referring to the action of making an entry on the left-hand side of an account. Most accounts (except contra accounts) on the left-hand side of the balance sheet have debit balances, which means the debits to them exceed the credits to them. A debit will increase the amounts on the asset side of the balance sheet, but decrease the amounts on the liabilities and equity side. See **Double-entry accounting, Credit,** and sections 2.4–2.6.

Debt   An obligation to make a future payment in return for a benefit already received. See sections 9.2 and 9.3.

Debt–equity ratio   Total liabilities divided by total equity. It is defined and explained in section 10.4, ratio #15. See also section 2.2, and used in the Scott formula in section 10.6.

Debt to assets ratio   Total liabilities divided by total assets. It is defined and explained in section 10.4, ratio #17.

Decelerated amortization   The opposite of accelerated amortization or depreciation. Not acceptable for most enterprises. See **Accelerated amortization** and section 8.10.

Decision relevance   An accounting objective: information should be available to the user at a time and in a form that is useful to the user's decision-making. See **Relevance** and sections 5.2, 5.3, and 6.6.

Declining balance amortization   An accelerated amortization (depreciation) method in which the annual amortization (depreciation) expense is calculated as a fixed percentage of the book value of the asset, which declines over time as amortization is deducted. See **Accelerated amortization, Amortization,** and section 8.10.

Deferral   Part of accrual accounting but often used as the opposite to an accrual. A deferral involves keeping a past cash receipt or payment on the balance sheet, in other words, putting it on the income statement as revenue or expense at a later time. An example is recognizing a deferred revenue liability resulting from a recent cash receipt, such as for a magazine subscription to be delivered later. (In contrast, accruals involve recording a revenue or expense before the cash receipt or payment occurs.) See sections 6.2 and 6.3.

Deferral method   A way of accounting for future income tax expenses incurred by present activities, now largely replaced by future income tax liability estimates. See **Deferred income tax.**

Deferred charge   A noncurrent **Prepaid expense**, in which the costs of issuing bonds, incorporation costs, or other expenditures benefiting several future periods are shown as noncurrent assets and usually amortized to expense over several periods or otherwise charged to expenses in some future period. See section 8.11.

Deferred income tax (expense and liability)   An expense account and corresponding liability intended to recognize the future tax consequences of income reported on the current income statement but not to be reported on the tax return until a future period. Now largely replaced by future income tax liability estimates. See **Future income tax** and section 9.3.

Deferred revenue   A liability account used for customer deposits or other cash receipts prior to the completion of the sale (for example, before delivery). See section 9.3.

Deficit   Negative retained earnings and sometimes also used to refer to negative earnings. See **Retained earnings, Net loss,** and section 3.2.

Delivery   The most common basis of recognizing revenue. Revenue is said to be earned when the product or service has been delivered to the customer. See **Revenue recognition** and sections 6.6 and 6.7.

Depletion   An amortization (depreciation) method used for physically wasting assets such as natural resources. See section 8.10.

Depreciation   The recognition of the expense due to use of the economic value of fixed tangible assets (for example, trucks, building, or plant). Usage, at least in Canada, appears to be changing to replace the term depreciation with the more general term amortization. See **Amortization, Declining balance amortization, Straight-line amortization, Book value,** and **Accumulated amortization (depreciation).** See also sections 1.8, 7.7, 8.8, and 8.10.

Diminishing balance   Another name for **Declining balance amortization.**

Direct method of cash flow analysis   A method of preparing the **Cash flow statement,** especially the **Cash from operations** section, using records of cash receipts and disbursements instead of the adjustments to net income used in the more traditional **Indirect method of cash flow analysis.** See sections 4.2 and 4.3.

Direct write-off   Transferring the cost of an asset to an expense or **Loss** account by removing the amount entirely from the asset account. Used in cases where there is no prior allowance for the expense or loss, so used when there is no **Contra account** such as **Accumulated amortization** or **Allowance for doubtful accounts.** See section 7.7.

Disbursements   See **Cash disbursements** and section 4.4.

Disclosure Provision of information about economic events beyond that included in the financial statement figures. Usually given in the notes to the financial statements, but also provided outside the financial statements in press releases, speeches, and other announcements. See **Notes to the financial statements, Management of corporate financial disclosure**, and section 5.10.

Discontinued operations Portions of the business that the enterprise has decided not to keep going and/or to sell to others. It is good practice to separate the effects of discontinued operations from continuing operations when measuring income and cash flow. See sections 3.4 and 3.5.

Discount on bonds Arises when bonds are issued at a price below their legal face value, such as a $100 bond being issued for $95 cash, indicating a $5 discount. See section 9.3.

Discounted cash flows "Present value" analysis of future cash flows by removing their presumed interest components. See **Present value** and section 10.7.

Discretionary expenses Expenses that depend on management's discretion rather than on the necessities of producing, selling, or shipping goods and services. Examples might be donations, political contributions, some maintenance and warranty costs, and bonuses not specifically called for in employment contracts. See section 6.6.

DIT See **Deferred income tax.**

Dividend payout ratio The ratio of dividends declared to net income. It is defined and explained in section 10.4, ratio #11.

Dividends Distributions of a portion of net income to shareholders in the company. Since this type of payment does not relate to the operating performance of the company, it is placed on the statement of retained earnings and not the income statement. See **Statement of retained earnings, Stock dividend,** and sections 3.2, 3.4, and 9.4.

Double-entry accounting The practice of recording two aspects of each transaction or event: the resource effect and the source or story of that effect. Though much expanded since its invention several hundred years ago, it is still the basis of bookkeeping and financial accounting. See sections 2.3 and 2.4.

Double-entry bookkeeping See **Double-entry accounting.**

E

Earnings A common synonym for net income. See **Net income** and section 3.2.

Earnings management Choosing accounting methods and/or making business deals with the specific objective of altering the size, trend, or interpretation of the company's earnings (net income). Usually frowned on as a form of **Manipulation** of accounting information. See section 3.10.

Earnings per share (EPS) The ratio of net income to the average number of common (voting) shares outstanding, used to allow the owner of the shares to relate the corporation's earning power to the size of his or her investment. The calculation of EPS can be quite complex, so most public companies calculate it for the users (as required by generally accepted accounting principles for such corporations) and report it on their income statements. See **Ratios**, section 3.4, and section 10.4, ratio #8, where EPS is defined and explained.

E-commerce See **Electronic commerce** and section 7.2.

Economic entity The financial accounting definition of an enterprise, used to determine what is to be included in transactions and in the financial statements. Also used to refer to a group of companies considered to be under the same control and, so, constituting a larger economic group. See **Accounting entity**, **Transaction**, **Consolidation**, and sections 2.8, 5.2, and 9.7.

Effective income tax rate The income tax rate the company appears to incur, as deduced from the financial statements. Differs from the statutory or legal rate because of many possible tax incentives, varying rates across jurisdictions, etc. Can be estimated as the company's income tax expense divided by income before income tax, both from the income statement. See section 9.3.

Effects analysis See **"What if" (effects) analysis** and sections 1.9 and 10.8.

Efficiency (of information use, or informational efficiency) Refers to a market's prices quickly and appropriately changing to reflect new information. See section 5.10.

Efficient capital market A theoretical description of a capital market whose prices respond quickly and appropriately to information. See section 5.10.

Efficient market hypothesis The proposal that capital markets actually are "efficient," responding quickly, smoothly, and appropriately to information. Some seem to be efficient, and some do not. See **Efficient capital market** and section 5.10.

Electronic commerce Also called **e-commerce**, this is the conduct of financial transactions, and much of the business transactions behind them, over electronic media such as telecommunication lines or the Web. See section 7.2.

Electronic funds transfer (EFT) Transfer of money between a buyer's bank account and the seller's bank account without need to write cheques or make deposits. EFT is what is happening if a customer uses a bank card to pay for groceries in the supermarket and the amount is automatically deducted from the customer's bank account. See section 7.2.

Employee deductions Amounts an employer is required to deduct from an employee's pay and remit to someone else on behalf of the employee. Such deductions include income tax, pension contributions, union dues, and many other amounts the employee wants to or has to pay before receiving the net pay that is left over. See section 7.6.

Entity See **Accounting entity** and **Economic entity**.

Entry See **Journal entry** and sections 2.4, 2.6, and 3.6.

EPS See **Earnings per share**.

Equities A term sometimes used to refer to the right-hand side of the balance sheet (Equities = Liabilities + Owners' equity).

Equity   The net assets or residual interest of an owner or shareholder (Assets = Liabilities + Equity, or restated as Equity = Assets – Liabilities). See **Balance sheet equation** and the components of equity under **Shareholders' equity, Retained earnings,** and sections 2.2, 2.8, and 9.4.

Equity basis   A method of accounting for intercorporate investments usually used when a company owns between 20% and 50% of another company. The investment is carried at cost, and any profit or loss, multiplied by the percentage ownership of the owned company, is added to or deducted from the investment. Any dividends received are deducted from the investment. See **Cost basis** and section 9.6.

Exchange   A transfer of goods, services, or money between two parties. In financial accounting, the most significant kind of exchange is external, that is, between the enterprise and parties it deals with, such as customers, suppliers, owners, employees, and creditors. See **Transaction** and section 1.6.

Expenditure   The term can mean any **Cash payment,** but usually spending on noncurrent assets or debts is meant. Also used instead of the word **Expense** for governments and other nonbusiness organizations that may not use full accrual accounting and therefore do not have expenses as accountants usually mean them. See sections 3.2 and 5.5.

Expense   The cost of assets used and/or obligations created in generating revenue, whether or not paid for in cash in the period they appear on the Income statement. See **Revenue, Matching, Expense recognition, Accrual accounting,** and sections 3.2, 3.4, 6.3, and 6.8.

Expense recognition   Incorporating measures of expenses incurred into the measurement of income by entering into the accounts the amount of expense determined, according to the firm's accounting policies, to be attributable to the current period. See **Matching, Revenue recognition,** and sections 6.3 and 6.8.

Expensing   Classifying an expenditure or promised expenditure (accrual) as an expense rather than an asset. Opposite of **Capitalization.** See section 8.3.

External audit   The audit conducted by an **External auditor.**

External auditor   An independent outside auditor appointed to review the financial statements. See **Auditor** and sections 1.4 and 5.8.

Extraordinary items   Gains and losses that arise out of situations that are not normal to the operations of a firm, not under the control of management, and not expected to recur regularly in the future. See section 3.5.

F

Fair market value   A value or price determined by an unrelated buyer and seller who are separate and acting rationally in his or her own self-interest. The value is considered more meaningful if established in an actual transaction than if estimated hypothetically. **Historical cost** is assumed to have been the fair market value of an asset when it was acquired. See two forms of estimated fair market value under **Net realizable value** and **Replacement cost,** and section 8.2.

Fair value   An estimate of the fair market values of assets and liabilities of an acquired company used in the purchase method of consolidation accounting. See section 9.7.

Fairness   Because of all the estimations, judgments, and policy choices that go into preparing financial statements, there is no one correct set of figures or disclosures. Instead, there is the idea of fairness, which means playing by the rules and preparing statements honestly, without any intent to deceive or to present any particular view. The opinion paragraph of the auditor's report states that the financial statements "present fairly ... in accordance with generally accepted accounting principles." Attention to fairness in the application of accounting principles requires care and judgment in distinguishing the substance from the form of a transaction and identifying the accepted principles and practices. See **Generally accepted accounting principles**, **Accounting standards**, and sections 5.2, 5.3, and 6.4.

FASB   See **Financial Accounting Standards Board**.

FIFO   An inventory cost flow assumption by which cost of goods sold is determined from the cost of the beginning inventory and the cost of the oldest purchases since; thus the acronym FIFO, which stands for "first in, first out." It follows therefore that under FIFO, ending inventory cost is determined from the cost of the most recent purchases. Since the older inventory is assumed to be sold first, FIFO in a period of inflation usually creates a smaller cost of goods sold and higher income and ending inventory asset value than **LIFO** or **Weighted average**. See **Cost flow assumption**, **Cost of goods sold**, and section 8.6.

Financial accounting   The reporting in **Financial statements** of the financial position and performance of a firm to users external to the firm on a regular, periodic basis. See **Management accounting** and section 1.2.

Financial Accounting Standards Board (FASB)   A U.S. body responsible for setting the standards that financial reporting must follow. The Canadian counterpart is the Canadian Institute of Chartered Accountants. See *CICA Handbook*.

Financial assets   Near-cash assets such as traded shares, bonds, some kinds of loans, and accounts receivable, especially as would be held by financial institutions such as banks. Part of the general category of **Financial instruments**. See section 8.2.

Financial instruments   Debts, shares, foreign exchange contracts, and other financial obligations and assets, many of which are traded on **Stock markets** and other **Capital markets**. See sections 2.8, 5.10, and 9.5.

Financial leverage   See **Leverage** and section 10.6.

Financial performance   The enterprise's ability to generate new resources from day-to-day operations over a period of time, via dealing with customers, employees, and suppliers. Measured by the **Net income** figure in the **Income statement** and the **Cash from operations** figure in the **Cash flow statement**, as well as by the details of both statements. See section 3.1.

Financial position   The enterprise's set of assets, liabilities, and owners' equity at a point in time. Measured by the **Balance sheet**, also called the Statement of financial position. See section 2.1.

Financial reporting   Use of **Financial statements** and **Disclosure** to report to people outside the enterprise on its **Financial performance** and **Financial position**.

Financial statements   The reports, for people external to the enterprise but also of interest to management, referred to in the definition of **Accounting**, which generally comprise a **Balance sheet, Income statement, Statement of retained earnings, Cash flow statement,** and the **Notes** to these statements. See each of these statements in this glossary and section 5.6.

Financial statements analysis   Use of the financial statements to develop summary measures (ratios) and interpretive comments about an enterprise's financial performance and position. See **Ratios** and sections 10.3 and 10.4.

Financing activities   The category of the **Cash flow statement** that describes the cash obtained or used in connection with noncurrent debt and equity. See section 4.3.

First-in, first-out   See **FIFO**.

Fiscal period   The period (usually a year, a quarter, or a month) over which performance (net income) is measured and at the end of which position (balance sheet) is determined. See section 6.5.

Fixed assets   Tangible, noncurrent, physical assets that are not expected to be used up in one operating cycle, but are expected to be used in generating revenue for many periods (for example, machines, buildings, land). See **Noncurrent assets**.

Foreign currency translation, foreign currency translation adjustment   The conversion of foreign monies into domestic monies at a specific date—either a transaction date, if translating a single transaction, or a financial statement date, if translating a foreign operation for consolidation purposes. This process normally produces an adjustment to make the accounts balance, shown in the Equity section of the balance sheet. See **Accumulated foreign currency translation adjustment**.

Franchising   A franchisor sells the right to use the franchisor's name, products, or other economic goods to a franchisee. See section 6.8.

Fund accounting   A kind of accounting used by governments and other non-business organizations to segregate groups of assets, liabilities, some forms of equity, revenues, and expenditures, in accordance with the purpose for which the funds were obtained. For example, donations received might be segregated from research grants received so that each kind of money is put to the use intended when it was obtained. See comments at the end of section 9.4.

Funds statement   See **Cash flow statement**.

Future income tax   Income tax expected to be paid in future years based on business events and income tax calculations done up to the present. The liability and associated expense are calculated by the **Liability method**, which estimates the likely future tax payments directly, and which has recently replaced the **Deferral method** and its **Deferred income tax**. See section 9.3.

Future value (FV)   The amount to which presently held financial assets or liabilities will build up to as interest is added to the principal amount invested or borrowed. Often contrasted with **Present value**, which is the future cash flows minus interest included in them. See section 10.7.

G

GAAP   See **Generally accepted accounting principles**.

GAAS   See **Generally accepted auditing standards**.

Gain, gains   Usually refers to the profit (proceeds minus book value) obtained from the disposition of assets (or liabilities) not normally disposed of in the daily course of business, such as from selling land, buildings, or other noncurrent assets, or from refinancing debt. These are considered nonoperating items and so if material are segregated from normal revenues and expenses on the income statement and the cash flows involved are included in the investing or financing sections of the cash flow statement. See sections 7.7 and 8.9.

Gain (loss) on sale   A **gain** on sale occurs when a company receives a larger amount of proceeds for an asset than its book value. An income statement account is then credited with the difference. A **loss** on sale occurs when the asset's book value is more than the proceeds received from the sale. An income statement account is then debited with the difference. See **Book value** and sections 7.7 and 8.9.

General journal   An accounting record used mainly to record accrual adjustments (journal entries) not provided for in separate specialized journals. See section 7.2.

General ledger   A collection of individual accounts that summarizes the entire financial accounting system of an enterprise. See section 7.2.

Generally accepted accounting principles (GAAP)   Principles and methods of accounting that have the general support of standard-setting bodies, general practice, texts, and other sources. See **Accounting standards** and sections 5.2 and 5.3.

Generally accepted auditing standards (GAAS)   The professional standards of care and evidence compilation that external auditors are expected to follow when preparing their reports on financial statements. See **Auditor's report** and section 5.8.

Going concern   A fundamental assumption in financial accounting that a firm will be financially viable and remain in business long enough to see all of its current plans carried out. If a firm is not a going concern, normal accounting principles do not apply. See **Liquidation value** and sections 5.2 and 8.2.

Goods and services tax   See **GST**.

Goodwill   The difference between the price paid for a group of assets and the sum of their apparent fair (market) values. Arises when a bundle of assets or a whole company is acquired and when the difference is positive. ("Badwill," a negative difference, is not recognized.) See sections 8.11 and 9.7.

Goodwill arising on consolidation   Goodwill existing only in **Consolidated financial statements** accounted for using the **Purchase method**, indicating that the "parent" corporation paid more for its investment in a "subsidiary" corporation included in the consolidated statements than the fair values of the subsidiary's assets. See **Goodwill** and sections 2.8 and 9.7.

Governmental accounting Accounting procedures, usually different from **GAAP** for businesses but in recent years becoming more like GAAP, used to account for governments and their agencies. See section 5.5.

Gross margin or gross profit Revenue minus cost of goods sold expense.

Gross margin ratio or gross profit ratio Equals (revenue – cost of goods sold expense) / revenue. See **Ratios** and section 10.4, ratio #5, where the gross margin (or gross profit) ratio is defined and explained. See also section 3.4.

GST (Goods and services tax) The Canadian federal goods and services tax, a kind of sales tax which businesses must collect on most of their revenue and remit to the government after deducting any GST the businesses paid on their own purchases. See **HST, PST**, and section 7.6.

H

Harmonization The movement toward making countries' accounting standards the same as those of other countries, and that would strengthen the internationalization of accounting standards. See section 5.5.

Historical cost The dollar value of a transaction on the date it happens, normally maintained in the accounting records from then on because of accounting's reliance on transactions as the basis for recording events. The cost, or historical cost, of an asset is therefore the dollar amount paid for it or promised to be paid as of the date the asset was acquired. See **Cost, Lower of cost or market, Conservatism**, and sections 8.2 and 8.3; also section 1.6.

HST Harmonized sales tax. See **GST** and section 7.6.

I

IASC See **International Accounting Standards Committee**.

IN(ATI) The after-tax overall interest rate paid by an enterprise on its liabilities. Used in the **Scott formula**. See section 10.6.

Income The (net) income of a business is the residual after deducting expenses from revenues. Also referred to as profit or earnings. See **Accrual income, Cash income, Net income**, and sections 1.7, 3.2, and 3.4.

Income before (income) tax An amount equal to revenue plus other income minus all other ordinary expenses except income tax. Appears quite low down on the income statement. Some nontaxed or special items, such as **Extraordinary items**, are placed after income tax has been deducted, and are therefore not part of income before income tax. See section 3.5.

Income from continuing operations Income after deducting income tax but before adding gains or deducting losses from **Discontinued operations**. See section 3.5.

Income measurement A phrase used to describe financial accounting's way of calculating (net) income as shown on the income statement. The phrase is also used to describe the general problem of determining what income is and considering alternatives to the usual **Accrual accounting** basis. See sections 3.2 and 8.2.

Income smoothing The "manipulation" of net income so that the year-to-year variations in reported income are reduced. See section 3.10.

Income statement A financial statement that summarizes revenues and expenses of a business for a stated period of time and computes the residual net income (revenues minus expenses). Sometimes referred to as "Statement of Earnings," "Statement of Operations," or "Statement of Income." See components of the income statement such as **Revenue, Expense,** and **Net income;** also **Financial performance** and sections 3.2 and 3.5.

Income tax Tax assessed on income, according to laws about the computation of income for income tax purposes. See sections 3.5 and 9.3.

Income tax allocation The attempt to allocate income tax expense to the appropriate year or activity to which it applies even if it is paid in another year or in aggregate across activities. See **Income tax expense, Deferred income tax, Future income tax, Intraperiod tax allocation,** and sections 3.5 and 9.3.

Income tax expense An estimate of the current and future income tax arising from the income as computed on the income statement and matched to the revenues and expenses shown on the statement. See **Income tax allocation** and sections 3.5 and 9.3.

Income tax payable The liability for the amount of income tax due on the year's income, calculated according to the income tax law whether or not that matches the **Income tax expense.** See section 9.3.

Indenture A contract signed by a borrower and lender under which the borrower undertakes to meet certain conditions, such as keeping the working capital ratio above a specified amount, violation of which would give the lender the right to ask for immediate repayment of the loan or to take other action. See section 9.3.

Independence Having no financial or other interest that would influence one's decisions. **External auditors** are expected to be independent of the enterprises they audit, and so can hold no shares, nor management positions, etc. See sections 5.8 and 5.9.

Indirect method of cash flow analysis The traditional method of deriving the **Cash flow statement,** especially the **Cash from operations** section, by adjusting net income for noncash items. See sections 4.3 and 4.5.

Information system An organized and systematic way of providing information to decision makers. Accounting is an information system. See also **Management information system.**

Input market value The market value of an asset calculated as the amount it would cost to replace or reproduce it. See **Replacement cost** and section 8.2.

Intangible assets Nonphysical, noncurrent assets such as copyrights, patents, trademarks, import and export licences, other rights that give a firm an exclusive or preferred position in the market place, and goodwill. See **Assets, Amortization, Goodwill,** and section 8.11.

Intercorporate investments   Investments by one corporation in other corporations. See **Consolidation, Equity basis, Cost basis,** and section 9.6.

Interest   The amount charged by a lender for the use of borrowed money. See sections 3.5, 10.2, and 10.7.

Interest coverage ratio   Usually calculated as (income before interest expense + income tax) / interest expense. See **Ratios** and section 10.4, ratio #20, where the interest coverage ratio is defined and explained.

Internal auditor   An auditor who works for the enterprise and thus verifies information for management's use and to help the enterprise perform better. See section 1.4 and contrast with **External auditor.**

Internal control   Methods of providing physical security and management control over an enterprise's cash, inventories, and other assets. See sections 7.3–7.8.

International Accounting Standards Committee (IASC)   A committee made up of representatives of more than 50 countries that sets international accounting standards. See section 5.5.

Interperiod tax allocation   Allocating the enterprise's income tax expenses over several years to match the expenses to the incomes shown in the income statement. Necessitated by timing differences between GAAP and the income tax law in the recognition of various revenues and expenses. See sections 3.5 and 9.3. Contrast **Intraperiod tax allocation.**

Intraperiod tax allocation   The attempt to match income tax expense to the various items in the income statement, especially separating general income tax expense from that due to special items below that expense on the income statement, such as **Extraordinary items** and **Discontinued operations.** See section 3.5.

Inventory(ies)   The goods purchased or manufactured by a company for sale, resale, or further use in operations, including finished goods, goods in process, raw materials, and supplies. See **Current assets, Inventory costing,** and sections 2.2, 7.8, 8.3, and 8.6.

Inventory costing   Comprises various methods of determining the cost of inventory for balance sheet valuation purposes and of valuing cost of goods sold. The more common methods are **FIFO, LIFO,** and **Weighted average.** See also sections 8.3 and 8.6.

Inventory turnover   Cost of goods sold expense / average inventory assets. See **Ratios** and section 10.4, ratio #13, where inventory turnover is defined and explained.

Inventory valuation   The process of determining the amount at which inventory is shown on the balance sheet, normally the **Lower of cost or market.** See **Inventory costing** and section 8.6.

Investing activities   The category of the **Cash flow statement** that describes the cash used to acquire, or obtained by disposing of, noncurrent assets. See section 4.3.

Investments   Usually refers to such assets as shares or bonds held for their financial return (interest or dividends), rather than for their use in the enterprise's operations. See sections 8.4, 9.6, and 10.2.

Investors People who own **Investments** and who, because of their interest in the value of those shares or bonds, are interested in information about the enterprises issuing such shares and bonds. See sections 1.4 and 5.10.

J

Joint venture A business arrangement between corporations that is like a corporate partnership. See section 9.6.

Journal entry A record of a transaction or accrual adjustment that lists the accounts affected and in which the total of the debits equals the total of the credits. See **Account** and sections 2.4, 2.6, and 3.8.

Journals Records in which accounting transactions of a similar nature are permanently recorded. See **Books of original entry**, **General journal**, and section 7.2.

L

L/E Total liabilities / total equity, the **Debt–equity ratio** used in the **Scott formula**. See section 10.6.

Last-in, first-out See **LIFO**.

Lease A contract requiring the user of an asset to pay the owner of the asset a predetermined fee for the use of the asset. See section 8.11.

Leasehold improvements Assets such as fixtures, decorating, and alterations installed into rented (leased) premises and so being economic assets for the enterprise even though not strictly owned because they form part of the leased property. Such improvements are usually amortized over the period of the lease, as a reasonable estimate of their useful life. See sections 3.11 and 8.3.

Ledger Any book or electronic record that summarizes the transactions from the "books of original entry" in the form of accounts. See **Accounts**, **General ledger**, **Journals**, **Trial balance**, and section 7.2.

Letter to the shareholders Part of the **Annual report**, it is a letter from senior management to the shareholders, summarizing major decisions and strategies, commenting on the company's performance for the year and usually looking ahead to future performance. See section 5.6.

Leverage Leverage, or financial leverage, refers to the increased rate of return on owners' equity when assets earn a return larger than the interest rate paid for debt financing them. The **Scott formula** indicates how part of the **Return on equity** is made up of **Operating return** and **Leverage return**. See **Scott formula** and section 10.6.

Leverage analysis Study of the financial statements and corporate financial structure in order to determine how, and how well, the company is making use of **Leverage**. See section 10.6.

Leverage potential The difference between operating return (return on assets) and borrowing cost, which produces **Leverage** when multiplied by the degree of borrowing in the Scott formula. See section 10.6.

Leverage return   The portion of the **Return on equity** that is due to earning more return on borrowed funds than it costs in interest to borrow them. See **Scott formula**, **Operating return**, and section 10.6.

Liability   A debt or obligation, legally existing or estimated via accrual accounting techniques, of the enterprise to another party (creditor) arising from a past transaction (for example, a bank loan, a shareholder loan, an account payable, a mortgage, an accrued expense, or deferred revenue). See **Creditor** and sections 2.2, 2.8, 2.9, 9.2, and 9.3.

Liability method   A method of **Income tax allocation** in which the impact of **Future income tax** is estimated according to what is expected to be paid rather than according to past timing differences as done in the former **Deferred income tax** accounting. The liability method is common in other countries, and Canada has recently adopted it too. See section 9.3.

LIFO   A cost flow assumption that is the opposite of FIFO. "Last in, first out" assumes that the units sold are from the most recent purchases and thus bases cost of goods sold on the most recent purchases and ending inventory on the oldest purchases. Because of this, in a period of inflation the LIFO cost of goods sold figure is usually the highest of the inventory costing methods, and the inventory value on the balance sheet is usually the lowest. See **Cost flow assumption**, **FIFO**, **Weighted average**, **Inventory costing**, and section 8.6.

Line of credit   Advance approval from a bank to borrow money under agreed conditions. A line of credit usually means that the borrower can get the money as needed (for example, when the bank account is overdrawn), without further approval.

Liquidation value   The value of a firm's assets if they are all to be sold off when it is no longer a going concern. See section 8.2.

Liquidity   The excess of very short-term assets over short-term debts, and so the measure of a company's ability to pay its immediate obligations in cash at the present moment. See **Solvency** and sections 4.2 and 10.4 (ratios #18–#20).

Listed (shares)   A listed company (corporation) is one whose shares are available for trading on a **Stock exchange**. See **Public company** and section 5.10.

Loans from shareholder(s)   Informal loans to the corporation by shareholders(s), who therefore act as creditors as well as owners. It is most common in private company corporations. See section 9.3.

Long-term debt–equity ratio   Calculated as (long-term loans + mortgages + bonds + similar long-term debts) / total equity. See **Ratios** and section 10.4, ratio #16, where the ratio is defined and explained.

Loss, losses   Usually refers to the case of a negative return (proceeds being less than book value) obtained from the disposition of assets (or liabilities) not normally disposed of in the daily course of business, such as from selling land, buildings or other noncurrent assets, or from refinancing debt. These are considered nonoperating items and so if material are segregated from normal revenues and expenses on the income statement and the cash flows involved are included in the investing or financing sections of the cash flow statement. See sections 3.2, 7.7, and 8.9.

Loss on sale   Selling a noncurrent asset for less than its book value. See **Gain (loss) on sale**, **Book value**, **Loss**, and sections 7.7 and 8.9.

Lower of cost or market   A method of valuing items of inventory, temporary investments, or other current assets, under which losses inherent in declines of the market prices of items held below their costs are recognized in the period in which such declines become apparent. Gains from market increases above cost are not recognized until the items are sold. Lower of cost or market is a conservative procedure. See **Conservatism** and sections 8.2, 8.4, and 8.7.

M

Management   The people (managers) who run the day-to-day operations of an enterprise or other organization, in contrast to the shareholders (investors), members, and voters who own or legally control the enterprise.

Management accounting   Accounting information designed to aid management in its operation and control of the firm, and in its general decision-making. It is different from **Financial accounting**, which is aimed primarily at users external to the firm.

Management discussion and analysis (MD&A)   A section of a company's annual report in which management reviews the results for the year and explains what happened in some detail. The MD&A is used by many analysts to supplement ratios and other forms of analysis. See **Annual report** and sections 5.6 and 10.3.

Management information system   The accounting, marketing, production, employee, and other recordkeeping and reporting systems within the enterprise used by management in its internal decision-making. Often abbreviated as MIS and often associated with computer systems. See **Management accounting** and **Electronic commerce**.

Management of corporate financial disclosure   Steps taken by management to manage the outward flow of information about an enterprise, much as other aspects of the enterprise are managed. See section 3.10.

Managers   See **Management**.

Manipulation   The accusation that management, in choosing its accounting and disclosure policies, attempts to make the performance and position measures suit its wishes. See sections 3.10 and 6.4.

Marginal analysis   Focusing on revenues or expenses that change between two alternatives, rather than including all revenues and expenses, so as to highlight effects. See **"What-if (effects) analysis** and section 1.9.

Market capitalization   An estimate of the value of a listed public company made by multiplying the current share price times the number of shares issued and outstanding. See section 2.2 and comments under ratio #9 in section 10.4.

Marketable securities   Investments having a ready market for resale and held as a way of earning a return from temporarily unneeded cash. See **Temporary investments** and section 8.4.

Market value   See **Fair market value**.

Markup   The difference between the enterprise's selling prices for its products and the unit costs it incurs for those products, often a function of a specific decision to add a profit margin to the cost incurred. See comments about markup in section 3.4 regarding **Gross margin** and sections 7.8 and 8.7 regarding the **Retail inventory control method.**

Matching, matching principle   The concept of recognizing expenses in the same accounting period in which the related revenues are recognized. See **Accrual accounting, Expense recognition, Revenue recognition,** and sections 5.2, 5.3, 6.2, 6.3, and 6.8.

Material, materiality   In accounting, material means that the magnitude of an omission or misstatement of accounting information makes it probable that, in the in the light of surrounding circumstances, the judgment of a reasonable person relying on the information would have been changed or influenced by the omission or misstatement. Materiality and **Decision relevance** are both defined in terms of what influences, or what makes a difference to, a decision maker. A decision not to disclose certain information may be made because it is believed that investors or other users have no need for that kind of information (it is not relevant) or that the amounts involved are too small to make a difference (it is not material). See **Relevance** and sections 5.2 and 5.3.

MD&A   See **Management discussion and analysis.**

Measurement, measuring   The attachment of dollar figures to assets, liabilities, revenues, and expenses in order to produce the figures (values) on the balance sheet and to enable the computation of income (revenues minus expenses) and equity (assets minus liabilities). See **Asset valuation, Balance sheet valuation, Income measurement, Recognition, Income,** and section 8.2.

Merger   The joining together of two corporations such that the owners of both become the owners of the combined corporation and both corporations are approximately equal contributors to the combination. See section 9.7.

Minority interest, noncontrolling interest   An account in the liabilities part of the consolidated balance sheet. The percentage of the subsidiary's equity not owned by the parent company is designated as minority (noncontrolling) interest liability. A minority (noncontrolling) interest expense calculated in a similar way is also deducted in computing consolidated net income. See **Consolidation** and sections 2.8 and 9.7.

Mortgage   A form of **Security** on a loan in which the lender has a direct claim on title to property specified in the mortgage. Usually used to finance the acquisition of that property. See sections 2.8 and 9.3.

Moving average cost, moving weighted average   See **AVGE, Average cost,** and section 8.6.

N

Net   In accounting, net means the residual after one quantity is subtracted from another. Examples are **Net book value, Net income, Net-of-tax analysis,** and **Net realizable value.**

Net book value   The cost of an asset minus any accumulated depreciation, amortization, allowance for doubtful accounts, and so on. See **Book value** and sections 7.7 and 8.9.

Net income   Equals income minus income tax expense, plus or minus extraordinary and special items (each **Net** of any income tax). See **Income, Retained earnings, Matching,** and sections 3.2, 3.4, 3.5, and 6.2.

Net loss   Negative **Net income**.

Net-of-tax analysis   A method of determining the impact of management decisions or accounting changes in which the effects of income tax are included to produce the net after-tax effect of the decision or change. See sections 1.9, 10.2, and 10.8.

Net realizable value   The fair market value that an asset will bring if it is sold through the usual product market minus any completion or disposal costs. See **Fair market value, Lower of cost or market,** and sections 8.2 and 8.7.

Neutrality   An objective of preparing financial accounting information in which the information should represent phenomena neutrally, without attention to the particular interests of any party or parties. See **Objectivity, Independence,** and section 5.2.

Noncontrolling interest   The portion of a subsidiary corporation included in consolidated financial statements that is not owned by the controlling (majority) owners of the parent corporation. See **Minority interest, Consolidation,** and section 2.8.

Noncurrent assets   Assets expected to bring benefit for more than one fiscal year. See **Fixed assets, Current assets,** and section 2.2.

Noncurrent liabilities   Liabilities expected to be repaid or otherwise removed more than one year in the future. See **Liability** and sections 2.2 and 9.3.

Nonoperating cash flows   Cash inflows and outflows related to noncurrent investments, financing, and usually dividends, and so separate from the cash flows resulting from day-to-day operations. See **Cash flow statement** and sections 4.2 and 4.3.

No-par (shares)   Shares having no legal minimum issue price (**Par value**) and so the proceeds of which are simply added to share capital at whatever price is obtained in each issue. See section 2.8.

Notes payable   Accounts payable that are supported by signed contracts or other agreements and usually carrying interest. Often used to describe financing obtained from banks and other financial institutions used to provide operating funds or funds for construction prior to completion of projects and obtaining of more secured financing like a **Mortgage**.

Notes receivable   Accounts receivable supported by signed contracts or other agreements specifying repayment terms, interest rate, and other conditions. See section 8.5.

Notes, Notes to the financial statements   Notes appended to the statements, providing information about the accounting policies chosen and other supplementary information helpful to interpreting the figures. See sections 5.6, 5.7, and 6.4.

Not-for-profit accounting   Procedures used to account for nonbusiness, non-government entities. These procedures increasingly follow **GAAP**. See section 5.5.

O

Objectivity   The notion that the information in financial statements must be as free from bias as possible, in order that all user groups can have confidence in it. An accountant attempts to record and report data that are based on objective sources to make the data more acceptable to outside parties. Because completed arm's-length transactions are supported by documents that can be verified by any interested observer, these constitute the preferred basis of measurement. See **Fairness, Neutrality, Relevance, Reliability,** and sections 5.2 and 5.3.

Off-balance-sheet financing   Methods of obtaining financing that avoid having to record the sources as liabilities or equity. See sections 2.8 and 9.5.

Ontario Securities Commission (OSC)   The securities-trading regulator for Ontario and the leading such regulator in Canada. See section 5.4.

Operating activities   See **Cash from operations.**

Operating lease   A contract to rent or use an asset that does not convey rights similar to ownership of the asset and that therefore is accounted for simply as rental expense. See **Capital lease** and section 8.11.

Operating return   The return earned by an enterprise before considering the cost of financing and usually also before considering nonrecurring items. See **Leverage return, Scott formula,** and section 10.6.

Opportunity cost   The return that could have been earned if funds were used in another way than the way they are being used or are proposed to be used. It is called a cost because it is the return given up by not adopting that other use. See section 10.7.

OSC   See **Ontario Securities Commission.**

Other assets   A catch-all category used for noncurrent (and occasionally current) assets that do not fit into other categories, are not material individually but aggregate to a material total. See section 8.11.

Output market value   The market value of an asset if sold. See **Net realizable value** and section 8.2.

Overdraft   See **Bank overdraft.**

Overhead costs   Costs of manufacturing inventories or constructing other assets that are incurred indirectly, such as heat, power, and supervisors' salaries.

Owners   Parties who have contributed resources in return for the right to dividends and any residual value (equity) of the enterprise. See sections 2.8 and 9.4.

Owner's capital   The owner's equity of the proprietor of an unincorporated business. See **Capital, Equity,** and sections 2.8 and 9.4.

Owners' equity   See **Equity, Shareholders' equity,** and sections 2.2, 2.8, and 9.4.

P

Pacioli Luca Pacioli's *Suma* is the first known book describing double-entry bookkeeping. It was published in 1494 and quickly became influential in the development of accounting and business in Europe. See section 2.3.

Packing slip A document accompanying a shipment that describes the shipment's contents and can be used to verify the supplier's invoice for the cost of the shipment. See section 7.2.

Par value A value set as the legal minimum amount for which a corporations's shares may be issued. Used in earlier years to prevent "watering the stock" and other frauds in which managers sold shares cheaply to themselves or their friends and then outvoted more legitimate shareholders. With the protection to shareholders provided by greater regulation and scrutiny of companies' affairs in the present time, Canadian companies typically have **No-par** shares instead, but par value is still used in many other jurisdictions, including some in the United States. See **Contributed surplus** and sections 2.8 and 9.4.

Parent The dominant corporation in a corporate group linked by ownership, the name of which is usually used in the consolidated financial statements. See sections 2.8 and 9.7.

Partners' capital The owners' equity section of a partnership's balance sheet. See **Partnership** and sections 2.8 and 9.4, and the example in section 3.8.

Partnership A contractual agreement among individuals to share resources and operations in a jointly run business. This form of business does not have the privilege of limited liability. See **Corporation, Proprietorship**, and section 2.8.

PE ratio The price–earnings ratio is calculated as the current price of a share in the corporation divided by its earnings per share. See **Price–earnings ratio, Ratios**, and section 10.4, ratio #10, where the ratio is defined and explained.

Percentage of completion A method of allocating revenue (and associated expenses) over several fiscal periods during which the revenue is earned. Used for long-term construction contracts, franchise revenue, and similar multi-period revenues. See sections 6.7 and 6.8.

Period expenses Expenses that are related to the passage of time rather than to the level of sales volume or other activities. Examples are interest, many salaries, and portions of some **Overhead costs** such as heat, light, and property taxes. See section 6.6.

Periodic inventory control method A method of calculating inventory that uses data on beginning inventory, additions to inventory, and an end-of-period count to deduce the cost of goods sold. See **Perpetual inventory control method, Retail inventory control method**, and section 7.8.

Periodic reporting A basic convention of financial accounting that holds that accounting information must be assembled and presented to users at regular intervals (at least yearly and often quarterly or monthly). See section 6.5.

Perpetual inventory control method A method of controlling inventory that maintains continuous records on the flow of units of inventory. Thus, there are figures on record for beginning inventory, each unit added to inventory, and each unit removed from inventory for sale. From this, an ending inventory figure can be determined and checked against the figure from a physical count. This method provides better internal control than the periodic inventory method, but it is also more costly to maintain the extra records. See **Periodic inventory control method** and section 7.8.

Personal guarantees Additional **Security** on loans, often taken by banks lending to private corporations, in which some or all shareholders sign agreements to contribute personal assets if the corporation does not repay the loans or pay interest on schedule.

Petty cash A small fund of cash kept on hand by an employee for paying small expenses such as postage, minor supplies, and courier charges. See section 7.5.

Plug The double-entry system requires that debits equal credits. If adding up all the debits and the credits does not produce two equal figures, the statements must be adjusted so that a balance occurs. The amount of adjustment needed is often called a "plug." This would only be needed if there had been an error somewhere, though sometimes the word plug is used in criticism of accrual, consolidation, or other adjustments that produce amounts the critic does not like.

Point of sale Often used to refer to the point in time when a sale has been completed and the product or service has been delivered to the customer, which is the most common point of recognizing revenue. See **Revenue recognition** and sections 6.6 and 6.7.

Pooling of interests method A type of business combination (compare with **Purchase method**). In pooling of interests, the assets, liabilities, equities, revenues, and expenses of the firms are added together using their book values. See **Consolidation** and section 9.7.

Post-closing accounts The accounts as they exist after the revenues, expenses, and dividends accounts have been transferred to retained earnings ("closed"). See sections 3.6 and 3.7.

Post-closing trial balance A **Trial balance** of the **Post-closing accounts**. See section 3.7.

Post, posting, posted Transfer, transferring, or having transferred, journal entries to ledger accounts and thereby making them permanent. The only way to fix a mistake is to use an adjusting or correcting entry and post that. See sections 2.5, 2.6, and 7.2.

Preferred shares Ownership shares having special rights in addition to (or instead of) those going with common shares. See sections 2.8 and 9.4.

Premium on bonds Arises when bonds are issued at a price above their legal face value, such as a $100 bond being issued for $105 cash, indicating a $5 premium. See section 9.3

Prepaid expense An expenditure recorded as a current asset because the benefit will be obtained in the near future (for example, insurance coverage good for the next year). See section 6.9.

Preparers Managers and accountants who produce financial statements. See section 1.4.

Present value   Future cash inflows or outflows reduced to their "present" amount by removing from them the interest that could have been earned or paid had the money been on hand for investment today. See section 10.7.

Present value analysis   Analysis of future cash flows done by removing the presumed interest components of those flows. See **Discounted cash flows** and section 10.7.

Price–earnings ratio   Market price of one share of a corporation divided by earnings per share. See **PE ratio, Ratios,** and section 10.4, ratio #10, where the ratio is defined and explained.

Price-level-adjusted historical cost   A rarely used asset valuation method in which the historical cost of each asset is revalued for inflation. See **Historical cost, Fair market value,** and section 8.2.

Principal   (1) In interest calculations, the principal is the amount of money initially borrowed, lent, or invested and on which interest is calculated. See section 10.7. (2) In some kinds of **Contracts,** the principal is the person to whom the **Agent** is responsible. See section 5.11.

Prior-period adjustment   A method formerly used in Canada but not recommended any more by **Accounting standards,** in which accounting is done separately for a gain or loss specifically identified with and directly related to the activities of particular prior periods, but not attributable to economic events occurring subsequent to those periods (so net income of those later periods is not increased or decreased because doing so could cause a distortion in the later results).

Professional ethics   Codes of conduct to guide professionals in applying their professional judgment and that are conducive to their professional activities. See section 5.9.

Professionalism   Acting according to the levels of competence, ethics, independence, etc., expected of professionals. See section 5.9.

Professional judgment   The judgment of professionals about problems in their domain, for example, that of accountants or auditors about financial accounting matters. See section 5.9.

Profit   See **Net income.**

Profit margin   See **Sales return** ratio, **Ratios,** and section 10.4, ratio #3, where the sales return or profit margin ratio is defined and explained.

Proprietorship   A firm that is neither a corporation nor a partnership but is under the sole control of one individual. Such a firm is not legally separate from that individual. See **Partnership, Corporation,** and sections 2.8 and 9.4.

Prospectus   A formal document that includes detailed financial information, which is required by law when a company invites the public to subscribe to its securities.

Provision   Another phrase for a usually noncurrent accrual such as for future pension costs or warranties (see section 9.3). Particularly common when the liability is created to anticipate losses or major expenses involved in discontinuing a business line, refinancing debts, or disposing of major assets.

PST   Provincial sales tax. See section 7.6.

Public accounting, Public accounting firms   Offering auditing, accounting, tax, consulting, and related services to the public on a professional basis. Some of these firms are very large, with thousands of professionals and staff, while others are very small one-person offices. See sections 1.4 and 5.8.

Public company   A **Corporation** whose shares and related securities are sold widely, to members of the public and other investors, and whose securities are traded on **Stock exchanges** and other capital markets. See sections 2.8 and 5.10.

Purchase method   A type of accounting for business combinations (compare with the **Pooling of interests method**). Under this method, which is the overwhelmingly dominant method of determining consolidated financial statement figures, the assets and liabilities of the acquired company are added to those of the parent at fair values and any difference between the portion of the sum of fair values acquired by the parent and the total price paid is accounted for as goodwill. See **Consolidation** and section 9.7.

Purchase order   A document used when a formal request to buy products or services is made. See section 7.2.

PV   See **Present value**.

Q

Qualified opinion   A report by the external auditors that indicates there is a deficiency in the financial statements. See section 5.8.

Quick ratio   Cash, temporary investments, and accounts receivable divided by current liabilities. Also called the acid test ratio. See **Ratios** and section 10.4, ratio #19, where the ratio is defined and explained.

R

R&D   Research and development activities, a controversial accounting problem because the activities are intended to lead to future benefits and thus their costs may be considered to be assets, yet GAAP require that generally such costs be charged to expense as incurred. See section 8.11.

Ratios, ratio analysis   Numbers produced by dividing one financial statement figure by another figure; for example, the working capital ratio is the total current assets figure divided by the total current liabilities figure. Standard ratios are used to assess aspects of a firm, particularly profitability, solvency, and liquidity. See sections 10.2, 10.4, and 10.6. Section 10.4 describes 20 common ratios.

Realized   Used in this book as a synonym of received, or collected. Revenue is recognized when earned, but that is usually before it is collected, or realized. See **Revenue recognition** and sections 6.3 and 6.6.

Receivable   Funds expected to be collected by the enterprise. The usual kind is trade **Accounts receivable** but other kinds include taxes receivable, employee expense advances receivable, and **Notes receivable**.

Reclassification (entry) A journal entry or repositioning of an account that changes the location of the account within the balance sheet or within the income statement but does not affect income. See **Classification policies** and section 2.7.

Reclassified account An account moved to a different place within a financial statement without changing income or equity. See section 2.7.

Recognition Giving effect in the accounts to revenue believed to be earned, or expenses believed to be incurred, before (or after) the cash is collected or paid. See **Revenue recognition, Expense recognition**, and sections 6.3, 6.6, 6.7, and 6.8.

Recognized Revenues or expenses (usually), entered into the accounts or given effect in the accounts. See **Recognition.**

Reconcile, Reconciliation The **Analysis** technique of comparing two sets of information that relate to the same account or activity and identifying differences that indicate errors in either or both records. See **Bank reconciliation** and section 1.9.

Recordkeeping The bookkeeping and other methods used to create the underlying records on which accounting information is based. See sections 5.2, 5.3, 6.2, and 6.3.

Redeemable Shares or bonds that have the right to be sold back to the company. See section 9.5.

Refined ROA A version of the **Return on assets** ratio. See **ROA(ATI), Ratios,** and section 10.4, ratio #2, where the ratio is defined and explained.

Relevance The capacity of information to make a difference in a decision by helping users to form predictions about the outcomes of past, present, and future events, or to confirm or correct prior expectations. See **Decision relevance** and sections 5.2 and 5.3.

Reliability A characteristic of information that is represented faithfully and is free from bias and verifiable. See **Timeliness, Objectivity**, and sections 5.2 and 5.3.

Replacement cost The price that will have to be paid in order to replace an existing asset with a similar asset. This is likely to be a different amount than that of **Fair market value** or **Net realizable value**. See also **Lower of cost or market** and sections 8.2 and 8.7.

Resources In financial accounting, the recognized assets of the enterprise as shown on the balance sheet. See section 2.2.

Retail inventory control method Providing internal control and deducing inventory amounts for financial statements by using ratios of cost to selling price; for example, deducing cost of goods sold from sales revenue minus the markup on cost. Ending inventory cost can be determined by measuring inventory at retail prices minus markup. See **Perpetual inventory method, Periodic inventory method, Inventory costing,** and section 7.8.

Retained earnings Earnings not yet distributed to owners; the sum of net incomes earned over the life of a company, less distributions (dividends declared) to owners. See **Equity** and sections 2.2, 3.2, 3.5, and 9.4.

Retained earnings statement   See **Statement of retained earnings** and sections 3.2, 3.4, 3.5, and 5.5.

Return   Some amount of gain (income or performance) usually measured in relation to the amount invested to get the return. See **Risk**, sections 5.10 and 10.2, and such ratios as **Return on equity** and **Return on assets** in sections 10.4 and 10.6.

Return on assets (ROA or ROA(ATI))   Net income, before considering interest expense or the tax saving provided by interest expense, divided by total assets. This measures the **Operating return** before the cost of financing. See **Ratios** and section 10.4, ratio #2, where the ratio is defined and explained, and section 10.6, where it is used in the **Scott formula**.

Return on equity (ROE)   Net income divided by owners' equity. The most frequently used ratio for measuring the business's return to owners. See **Ratios** and section 10.4, ratio #1, where the ratio is defined and explained, and section 10.6, where it is used in the **Scott formula**.

Return on investment (ROI)   A general term for measures of return related to the investment needed to earn the return. See **Return on assets**, **Return on equity**, and section 10.2.

Review   A report prepared on an enterprise's financial statements by a **Public accounting** firm that is less than an **Audit** but more than a **Compilation**: the accounting firm studies the statements' contents and compliance with GAAP to determine if there are any apparent problems but does not verify individual accounts or the underlying records. See section 5.8.

Revenue   The amount of benefit received or promised from the sale of goods or services, before any deductions for the cost of providing the goods or services. See **Income statement**, **Revenue recognition**, and sections 3.2, 3.5, 6.3, and 6.6.

Revenue recognition   The entering into the accounts of the amount of revenue determined, according to the firm's accounting policies, to be attributable to the current period. See **Accrual accounting**, **Accounts receivable**, **Revenue**, and sections 6.3, 6.6, and 6.7.

Risk   The probable variability in possible future outcomes above and below the expected level of outcomes (for example, returns), but especially below. Risk and return go hand in hand, because a high risk should mean a higher potential return and vice versa. See section 5.10 and **Return**, and section 10.4, ratios #14–#20.

ROA   See **Return on assets**.

ROA(ATI)   See **Refined ROA** and **Return on assets**.

ROE   See **Return on equity**.

ROI   See **Return on investment**.

S

Sales invoice   A document containing the details of a sale. See section 7.2.

Sales journal   A record of sales made, used to produce the **Revenue** data in the accounts. See **Books of original entry** and section 7.2.

Sales return   The ratio of net income to revenue. See **Ratios** and section 10.4, ratio #3, where the ratio is defined and explained, and section 10.6, where a refined version (**SR(ATI)**) is used in the **Scott formula**.

Sales taxes   Taxes the enterprise must charge its customers and remit to the government. See section 7.6.

SCFP (Statement of changes in financial position)   See **Cash flow statement**.

Scott formula   A financial analysis technique for studying leverage effects by combining a group of ratios into a more comprehensive explanation of performance. The formula separates **Return on equity** into **Operating return** and **Leverage return**. See **Leverage, Ratios**, and section 10.6.

SEC   See **Securities and Exchange Commission**.

Securities   Shares, bonds, and other financial instruments issued by corporations and governments and usually traded on **Capital markets**. See section 5.10.

Securities and Exchange Commission (SEC)   An agency of the U.S. government that supervises the registration of security issues, prosecutes fraudulent stock manipulations, and regulates securities transactions in the United States. See section 5.4.

Security   (1) Singular of **Securities**. (2) Protection to a lender or other creditor in which the lender is given rights to specific assets (as in a **Mortgage**), more general rights to monitor the borrower (**Debenture** or **Indenture**), or other promises (such as **Personal guarantees**).

Segmented information   Financial statement information desegregated by geographical or economic area of activity in order to provide greater insight into financial performance and position. Segmented information is usually placed at the end of the notes to the financial statements.

Segregation of duties   An internal control technique whereby tasks involved in sensitive assets such as cash, accounts receivable, or inventories are divided up so that no one both handles the asset and keeps the records of the asset. See sections 7.3 and 7.5.

Share capital   The portion of a corporation's equity obtained by issuing shares in return for cash or other considerations. See sections 2.8 and 9.4.

Share split   Reissuing shares in which the number of new shares is some multiple of the previous number. For example, a two for one split results in a shareholder owning twice as many shares as before. Because there has been only a change in the number of shares but not in the underlying value of the corporation, the share price should fall in accordance with the split (e.g., the new shares above should have a share price about half the previous price). See section 9.4.

Shareholders   The holders of a corporation's **Share capital**, and so the owners of the corporation. See section 1.4.

Shareholders' equity   The sum of shareholders' direct investment (share capital) and indirect investment (retained earnings). See **Share capital, Equity, Retained earnings**, and sections 2.2, 2.8, and 9.4.

Shares (stock)   Units of **Share capital**, evidenced by certificates and, for **Public companies**, traded on **Capital markets** with other **Securities**. See section 2.8.

Significant accounting policies   The main choices among possible accounting methods made by the enterprise in preparing its financial statements. These policies are usually summarized in the first note to the financial statements. See **Accounting policies, Notes to the financial statements**, and sections 5.6, 5.7, and 6.4.

Significant influence   An investment in another corporation that is not large enough for voting control but is large enough to influence how that corporation does business. See **Equity basis** and section 9.6.

Society of Management Accountants of Canada (SMA-Canada)   A society whose members have had training in tax, accounting, internal audit, and other related areas, with a particular focus on internal management accounting, and have passed qualifying exams. It is one of the three national, professional accounting bodies. See **Accountant**.

Solvency   The condition of being able to meet all debts and obligations. See **Statement of changes in financial position, Liquidity**, section 3.4, and section 10.4, ratios #18–#20.

Source documents   The evidence required to record a **Transaction**. See section 7.2.

Sources   The right-hand side of the balance sheet (liabilities and equity) are the sources of the enterprise's assets. See section 2.2.

Specialized ledgers   Ledgers used to keep track of particular assets, liabilities, or equities, such as accounts receivable, fixed assets, or share capital. See section 7.2.

Specific identification   Accounting for inventories according to the specific cost of the items, which therefore requires some sort of identification of the items, such as by serial number. Contrast **Assumed cost flow** and see section 8.6.

SR(ATI)   See **Sales return**.

Standard cost   A method of determining manufactured inventory costs that uses expected normal production costs rather than actual costs. See section 8.7.

Stated value   A value provided to shares that is similar to **Par value** but less legally binding.

Statement of cash flows   See **cash flow statement**.

Statement of changes in financial position (SCFP)   See **cash flow statement**.

Statement of financial position   A synonym for **Balance sheet**.

Statement of retained earnings   A financial statement that summarizes the changes in retained earnings for the year. Change in retained earnings equals **Net income** minus **Dividends** plus or minus any retained earnings adjustments. See sections 3.2, 3.4, and 5.5.

Statement of source and application of cash   See **cash flow statement**.

Stewardship   The concept that some persons (for example, management) are responsible for looking after the assets and interests of other persons (for example, shareholders), and that reports should be prepared that will be suitable to allow the "stewards" to be held accountable for the actions taken on behalf of the other persons. See section 2.3 and **Agent**.

Stock dividend   A **Dividend** paid by issuing more shares to present shareholders rather than paying them cash. See section 9.4.

Stock exchange   A place where **Shares** and other **Securities** are traded. See section 5.10.

Stockholder   An alternative term for **Shareholder**, particularly used in the United States.

Stock market   A **Capital market** in which equity shares are traded. Often used as a generic term for stock exchanges and capital markets. See section 5.10.

Stocks   Usually used to mean **Shares**, but also used to mean **Inventories**, as in "stocktaking" for counting inventories.

Stock option(s)   Promises, usually made to senior managers, to issue shares to them at specified prices. The prices are usually set to be higher than present prices but lower than expected future prices, to provide an incentive to work to increase those future prices. See section 9.5.

Straight-line amortization (depreciation)   A method of computing amortization (depreciation) simply by dividing the difference between the asset's cost and its expected salvage value by the number of years the asset is expected to be used. It is the most common amortization method used in Canada. See **Amortization** and section 8.10.

Subsidiary   A company a majority of whose voting shares are owned by another company (the **Parent**). See **Consolidation** and section 9.7.

Subsidiary ledgers   See **Specialized ledgers**.

Sum-of-years'-digits   An accelerated method of computing amortization (depreciation) that produces a declining annual expense, which is used in the United States but rare in Canada. See **Accelerated amortization** and Note 19 to Chapter 8.

Synoptic   A bookkeeping record listing cash transactions of the business.

T

T-account   A T-shaped representation of a ledger account used in analysis or demonstration. See section 2.5.

Tangible assets   See **Fixed assets**.

Taxable income   Income calculated according to income tax law and used as the basis for computing income tax payable. See section 9.3.

Temporary differences   Differences between accounting calculations of income and calculations required for income tax purposes that will eventually net out to zero. These affect income tax expense calculations. See section 9.3.

Temporary investments   Investments made for a short term, often used as a place to put temporarily excess cash to work. See section 8.4.

Term preferred shares   Preferred shares issued with a fixed term and dividend rate, and therefore having some of the characteristics of debt. See section 9.5.

Timeliness   Timely information is usable because it relates to present decision needs. Information received late may be too late to be usable, since decisions pass it by. See **Relevance, Reliability,** and section 5.2.

Time value of money   Money can earn interest, so money received in the future is worth less in "present value" terms because the lower amount can be invested to grow to the future amount. Money has a time value because interest accrues over time. See **Present value** and section 10.7.

Toronto Stock Exchange   The leading **Stock exchange** in Canada.

Total assets turnover   The ratio of revenue to total assets. See **Ratios** and section 10.4, ratio #12, where the ratio is defined and explained. See also section 10.6, where the ratio is used in the **Scott formula**.

Trade receivables   These are **Accounts receivable** arising in the normal course of business with customers. See section 8.5.

Transaction   An accounting transaction is the basis of bookkeeping and is defined by four criteria described and explained in section 1.6.

Transaction base   The idea that financial accounting is substantially defined by the use of the **Transaction** as the fundamental recordkeeping basis underlying the accounting data. See section 1.6.

Treasury shares (stock)   Share capital issued and then reacquired by the firm that issued the shares. The result is a reduction of shareholders' equity because resources have been used to reduce the actual amount of outstanding equity. See sections 2.8 and 9.4.

Trial balance   A list of all the general ledger accounts and their balances. The sum of the accounts with debit balances should equal the sum of those with credit balances. This is contrasted with the **Chart of accounts**, which lists only the account names. See **Account** and sections 2.5, 3.7, and 3.8.

TSE   The **Toronto Stock Exchange**.

U

Unadjusted trial balance   The **Trial balance** of the accounts prior to making various accrual adjustments in preparation for the financial statements. See sections 3.8 and 3.9.

Units-of-production amortization   An amortization (depreciation) method in which the annual amortization expense varies directly with the year's production volume. See section 8.10.

Unusual items   Unusual revenues or expenses that are large enough to be worth identifying separately in the income statement. See section 3.5.

Users   People who use financial statements to assist them in deciding whether to invest in the enterprise, lend it money, or take other action involving financial information. See section 1.4.

V

Valuation Determining the amounts at which assets, liabilities, and equity should be shown in the balance sheet. See section 8.2.

Value in use The value of an asset determined by the future cash flows it brings in, or the future expenses that will be avoided by owning the asset. See section 8.2.

Verifiability Ability to trace an accounting entry or figure back to the underlying evidence of its occurrence and validity. See **Source documents** and sections 1.6, 5.2, and 5.8.

W

Warrants Attachments to shares or bonds giving rights to acquire further shares or bonds on specified terms. See section 9.5.

Weighted average An inventory cost flow assumption that determines cost of goods sold and ending inventory cost by averaging the cost of all of the inventory available during the period. See **AVGE, Average cost, LIFO, FIFO, Inventory costing**, and section 8.6.

"What if" (effects) analysis Analyzing potential business decisions or accounting policies by determining their effects on income, cash flow, or other important items. See sections 1.9, 10.8, and 10.9.

Work order A document specifying the components and assembly or other work to be done to provide a product ordered by a customer. See section 7.2.

Working capital The difference between current assets and current liabilities. See **Current assets, Current liabilities**, and section 2.2.

Working capital ratio Current assets divided by current liabilities. See **Ratios** and sections 2.2 and 10.4, ratio #18, where the ratio is defined and explained.

Write-off Refers to the elimination of an asset from the balance sheet. If there is a **Contra account** against the asset already, the write-off is made against the contra, so expense and income are not affected. If there is no contra account, the write-off (a **Direct write-off**, section 7.7) is made to expense or a loss account and income is reduced. See sections 7.7 and 8.9.

Y

Yield The effective interest rate a financial instrument such as a **Bond** earns, given the amount of money received when it was issued. See **Present value** and section 10.7.

OTES

1. Some supplementary help in developing this glossary originally came from the *CICA Handbook* (Toronto: Canadian Institute of Chartered Accountants, various versions); S. Davidson, C.L. Mitchell, C.P. Stickney, and R.L. Weil, *Financial Accounting: An Introduction to Concepts, Methods and Uses* (Toronto: Holt, Rinehart & Winston, 1986); *Funk & Wagnalls Canadian College Dictionary* (Markham: Fitzhenry & Whiteside, 1986); and Ross M. Skinner, *Accounting Standards in Evolution* (Toronto: Holt, Rinehart & Winston, 1987).

Index

To the owner of this book

We hope that you have enjoyed Gibbins' *Financial Accounting: An Integrated Approach,* Fourth Edition (ISBN 0-17-616845-1), and we would like to know as much about your experiences with this text as you would care to offer. Only through your comments and those of others can we learn how to make this a better text for future readers.

School _____ Your instructor's name _____

Course _____ Was the text required? _____ Recommended? _____

1. What did you like the most about *Financial Accounting*?

_____
_____
_____

2. How useful was this text for your course?

_____
_____
_____

3. Do you have any recommendations for ways to improve the next edition of this text?

_____
_____
_____

4. In the space below or in a separate letter, please write any other comments you have about the book. (For example, please feel free to comment on reading level, writing style, terminology, design features, and learning aids.)

_____
_____
_____
_____
_____

Optional

Your name _____ Date _____

May Nelson Thomson Learning quote you, either in promotion for *Financial Accounting,* or in future publishing ventures?

Yes _____ No _____
Thanks!

You can also send your comments to us via e-mail at
college@nelson.com

PLEASE TAPE SHUT. DO NOT STAPLE.

TAPE SHUT

TAPE SHUT

- - - FOLD HERE - - -

MAIL > POSTE

Canada Post Corporation
Société canadienne des postes

Postage paid   Port payé
if mailed in Canada si posté au Canada
Business Reply   Réponse d'affaires

0066102399   01

NELSON
THOMSON LEARNING

0066102399-M1K5G4-BR01

NELSON THOMSON LEARNING
HIGHER EDUCATION
PO BOX 60225 STN BRM B
TORONTO ON M7Y 2H1

TAPE SHUT

TAPE SHUT